HUMAN RESOURCE
MANAGEMENT

About the Companion Website

Visit the HUMAN RESOURCE MANAGEMENT Companion Website at
www.booksites.net/beardwell to access a rich, free resource of valuable teaching and
learning material, including the following content:

General

▶ How to use this book, which outlines suggested routes through the book for MBA, MA/MSc and
  CIPD students
▶ About the authors section, with brief descriptions of the author team's academic credentials
▶ A full table of contents
▶ Book features, explaining what's new and what's changed in this new edition

For the Lecturer

▶ A secure, password-protected site offering downloadable teaching support
▶ Customisable PowerPoint slides, including key figures and tables from the main text
▶ A fully updated Lecturer's Guide to using the book as a supplement to your own resources
▶ Extra case studies
▶ Learning objectives from each chapter

For the Student

▶ Internet exercises for self study, complete with suggested answers
▶ Extra self-check questions
▶ Searchable online glossary
▶ Multiple choice questions for every chapter, with instant feedback
▶ Annotated weblinks, both to relevant professional bodies and to specific, useful Internet
  resources to facilitate in-depth independent research

Online Course

Also available with this text is access to integrated, easy-to-use Online Course content for use with
Course Compass, Blackboard or Web CT. It contains 40 hours of interactive material. For further
information visit www.booksites.net and search under the subject or author's name.

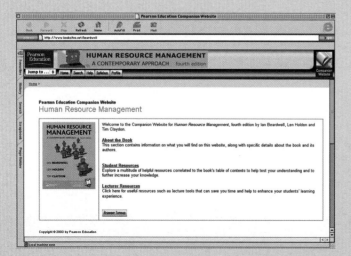

HUMAN RESOURCE
MANAGEMENT

A CONTEMPORARY APPROACH

Fourth Edition

Edited by

**Ian Beardwell, Len Holden
and Tim Claydon**

De Montfort University, Leicester

FT Prentice Hall

FINANCIAL TIMES

An imprint of **Pearson Education**

Harlow, England • London • New York • Boston • San Francisco • Toronto
Sydney • Tokyo • Singapore • Hong Kong • Seoul • Taipei • New Delhi
Cape Town • Madrid • Mexico City • Amsterdam • Munich • Paris • Milan

Pearson Education Limited
Edinburgh Gate
Harlow
Essex CM20 2JE
England

and Associated Companies throughout the world

Visit us on the World Wide Web at:
www.pearsoned.co.uk

First published in Great Britain in 1994
Second edition published in 1997
Third edition published in 2001
Fourth edition published in 2004

© Longman Group Limited 1994
© Financial Times Professional Limited 1997
© Pearson Education Limited 2001, 2004

ISBN 0 273 67911 2

British Library Cataloguing-in-Publication Data
A catalogue record for this book is available from the British Library

10 9 8 7 6 5 4 3 2 1
08 07 06 05 04

Typeset in 10pt Sabon by 30
Printed and bound by Scotprint, Haddington
The publisher's policy is to use paper manufactured from sustainable forests.

Professor Ian Beardwell 1946–2002
In memoriam

Sadly, Ian Beardwell died suddenly just after work had begun on this edition. Ian made a great contribution to the study and practice of HRM through his research and writing, his teaching, and his close engagement with the Chartered Institute of Personnel and Development, where he was Vice-President for Membership and Education from 1997 to 2001. Part of that contribution was his role in developing an HRM textbook that was scholarly and critical in its approach, yet accessible to students. This edition of that book is dedicated to his memory.

CONTENTS

5 Human resource planning
Julie Beardwell 157

6 Recruitment and selection
Julie Beardwell and Mary Wright 189

7 Managing equality and diversity
Mike Noon 230

Part 2 Case study
Employers exploit agency work boom 258

Part 3

DEVELOPING THE HUMAN RESOURCE

8 Learning and development
Audrey Collin 266

9 Human resource development: the organisation and the national framework
Len Holden 313

PREFACE

I know that Ian Beardwell was as surprised as the rest of the writing team by the fact that this book reached four editions. In doing so it has reflected developments in the field of Human Resource Management over a decade. It will also serve as a monument to Ian in that the book played a modest role in shaping conceptions and understanding in the thoughts of a large number of students and lecturers. A textbook, while reflecting on and critiquing the leading edge in HRM research, also acts as an interpreter of often complex trends. We hope that this edition maintains the analytical and critical standard of previous ones.

Since the first edition of this book the role and function of human resource management within organisations have become more complex and the issues and policies which have become associated with it have multiplied considerably. The continuing devolvement of HRM functions to line managers has had some commentators predicting the death of the personnel/HRM department and in the second edition there was consideration of the important questions about the role of the HRM professional in changing organisations. The second and third editions raised concerns about strategic policy-making and the strategic nature of not only HRM, but those areas and disciplines associated with it, such as human resource development (HRD), management development and performance management. It also examined the role and nature of HRM in relation to culture change schemes such as total quality management (TQM), customer service programmes, business process re-engineering (BPR), investors in people (IIP) and performance-related pay (PRP). These add to the role confusion and uncertainty for HRM practitioners, as well as for middle and line managers and supervisors with expanded HRM functions. The third edition also reflected on the rise in popularity of the learning organisation and its sister concept the knowledge-based organisation as well as empowerment initiatives, all of which constitute types of organisational style and culture and exist as entities within themselves resting on HRM and related practices.

HRM has also become more ambiguous in relation to other managerial initiatives which place emphasis on employee flexibility and teamwork aimed at enhancing commitment through empowerment policies. The contradictions inherent in its role and function remain, not least in the conflicting ethical positions which are often posed by changing economic circumstances. A decade of growth in HRM popularity has also revealed its changing nature. There is less interest in finding a universal paradigm or model of HRM than in understanding how it operates in diverse situations and what contribution it can make to the effectiveness and the profitability of the organisation.

In addition, the growing uncertainties of work in the flexibilised world of portfolio and vendor workers aligned with the decreasing core of permanent employees has also directly and indirectly impacted on HRM policy, posing new forms of employee relations associated with short-term contracts, part-time working, agency and outsource working. The inconstancy of the organisational form is continually reshaping HRM role and policy, and HRM models rooted in the certainties of previous decades no longer apply.

The history of the employment relationship over the past decade and a half indicates some kind of 'managerial revolution' and within this movement the influence of HRM has not been small. The role and function of HRM beyond the millennium have continued to evolve, fuelling debate amongst practitioners and academics. What is and will remain certain is the working out of its role and function against a backdrop of contra-dictory and in some cases conflicting change, which is part of the inherent dynamics of global capitalism.

We have sought to add new areas to the book. Most notably, a chapter on the developments in strategic HRM critically examines concepts such as high-performance work systems, the resource-based view of HRM, the balanced scorecard concept and 'bundles' of HR policies. In this edition these concepts are explored much more fully. While equal opportunities has always been part of previous editions we offer a new chapter that devotes itself entirely to this in the context of what is now increasingly being retitled 'managing diversity'. There is also a new chapter on international HRM which examines it from an institutional and business systems perspective, and reshapes and updates the international organisational context of HRM. There is a new chapter on human resource planning and, while the chapter on job design has been dropped, this has been briefly tackled in the chapter on employee involvement. There is a totally new chapter on the important area of reward and performance. All of the remaining chapters have been updated but it is inevitable that one single volume cannot encompass the huge area in and around the HRM sphere, and we apologise for any omissions. Nevertheless, we have covered the broad sweep of the HRM field and some aspects in considerable detail.

We hope that our readers like the new design and layout of the book which we believe enhances user friendliness without compromising academic standards.

We would once again like to thank our group of trusty and willing authors who worked valiantly to get this edition to press under the difficult circumstances that the present world of higher education continues to impose. We would also like to thank our partners and families as well as our colleagues whose patience and perseverance enabled the production of this book.

Finally, we dedicate this volume to Ian's memory.

GUIDED TOUR OF THE BOOK

CHAPTER 3

Human resource management in context

Audrey Collin

OBJECTIVES

▶ To indicate the significance of context for the understanding of human resource management.

▶ To discuss ways of conceptualising and representing the nature of context generally and this context in particular.

▶ To analyse the nature of the immediate context of HRM: the nature of organisations and the need for management.

▶ To indicate the significance of context for the understanding of HRM.

▶ To discuss ways of conceptualising and representing the nature of context generally and this context in particular.

▶ To analyse the nature of the immediate context of HRM: the nature of organisations and the need for management.

▶ To indicate the significance of context for the understanding of human resource management.

Introduction

The marketing intelligence system – which provides data on developments in the external marketing environment (which you will remember from Chapter 2). This system includes the scrutiny of newspapers and trade publications, reports from sales representatives and distributors, the purchase of information from specialist organisations and the establishment of a bureau within the organisation to collect and disseminate such marketing intelligence.

In many respects this agenda has posed the most fundamental threat to established patterns of Personnel Management and Industrial Relations in the post-1945 era. Any assessment of the emergence of Human Resource Management has, at least, to take account of this changing context of employment and provide some explanations as to the relationships that exist between the contribution HRM has made to some of these changes on the one hand and, on the other hand Any assessment of the emergence of Human Resource Management has, at least, to take account of this changing context of employment and provide some explanations as to the relationships that exist between the contribution HRM has made to some of these changes on the one hand and, on the other hand sent luptatum zzril delenit augue duis dolore te feugait nulla facilisi. Nam liber tem-

New, vibrant text design, colourfully highlighting key pedagogical features

Objectives provide an overview of the topics to be covered in each chapter, giving a clear indication of what you should expect to learn

Activities appear throughout the text to reinforce learning with problems and practical exercises

Figures are used to illustrate key points, models, theories and processes

---

The immediate context of HRM **81**

The scope and variety of marketing research operations as an aid to management in this way can best be illustrated by one or two examples. As this edition was being prepared, the author was notified that RSL (Research Services Ltd), a British marketing research organisation of the type described in Chapter 3, had recently completed the following research projects.

Or again, imagine that a business organisation approaches a marketing research agency with the question: 'Is it better to advertise our products on television or local radio?' The agency's answer could be defined as 'information' and after carrying out the necessary investigation the agency might well reply as follows.

ACTIVITY

● Read the case study, Jet Airlines, at the end of the chapter. Which of the approaches identified by Whittington best describes Jet Airline's approach to strategy formulation?

● Why do you think it is important to concider the nature of strategy to aid our understanding of strategic human resoure management?

In many respects this agenda has posed the most fundamental threat to established patterns of Personnel Management and Industrial Relations in the post-1945 era. Any assessment of the emergence of Human Resource Management has, at least, to take account of this changing context of employment and provide some explanations as to the relationships that exist between the contribution HRM has made to some of these changes on the one hand and, on the other hand, the impact that such changes have had on the theory and practice of HRM itself.

If you are reading this book in preparation for an examination it might be helpful to memorise the AMA definition, or the stages of the research process set out below it. This should help you to deal with a question on research in a comprehensive way. Professor Philip Kotler,1 the international authority on marketing, regards marketing research as

Figure 3.1 Model of strategic change and human resource management

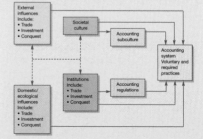

Source: Storey (1992: 38). Reproduced by kind permission of Chapman & Hall, a division of International Thomson Publishing Services.

Summary

The **Summary** allows you to recap and review your understanding of the main points of the chapter

- The immediate significance of the emergence of HRM, certainly in the British context, is to have opened up a vigorous debate about just what constitutes the change from traditionally conceived employee management policies to those which are claimed to be derived from a different mix of managerial concerns.

- Among the more prominent aspects which have been claimed for HRM are that it is derived from a more focused managerial perspective which is often strategically driven, and that it represents a more unified and holistic approach than the 'technical-piecemeal' approach of Personnel Management.

- In this manner HRM is depicted as having an agenda which addresses 'business-related' issues, and thereby contributes to the overall success of the organisation in a proactive manner, while Personnel Management is depicted as having an agenda set for it by the more mundane requirements of the day in a more reactive manner. Neither of these type-cast approaches are wholly correct, of course, but they do indicate the arena within which debate has occurred.

- Managing human resources is one of the key elements in the coordination and management of work organisations. Whatever means are used to ensure the creation and delivery of services and goods in modern economies, the role of individuals and groups as employees and the ability of management to effectively deploy such a resource is vital to the interests of both employee and organisation alike.

Questions

Questions can be used for self-testing, class exercises or debates

1 Why do the 'segments' (i.e. sections) of the market that look most promising to target?

2 What product ideas that appear to be the most promising; the ideas that warrant further investment of time and money?

3 How many 'segments' (i.e. sections) of the market that look most promising to target?

4 Why do the product ideas that appear to be the most promising; the ideas that warrant further investment of time and money?

Exercises

Exercises can be used to test your learning of theory and concepts

1 ABC & Sons is one of the key elements in the coordination and management of work organisations. Whatever means are used to ensure the creation and delivery of services and goods in modern economies, the role of individuals and groups as employees and the ability deal of the analysis of how organisations are run.

2 Consider one of the key elements in the coordination and management of work organisations. Whatever means are used to ensure the creation and delivery of services and goods in modern economies, the role of individuals and groups as employees.

3 Outline which is one of the key elements in the coordination and management of work organisations. Whatever means are used to ensure the creation and delivery of services and goods.

4 Decide which product ideas that appear to be the most promising; the ideas that warrant further investment of time and money.

Case studies at the end of each chapter help consolidate your learning of major themes by applying them to real-life examples

Case study

ASDA and staff retention

Asda, the supermarket chain, uses a variety of methods to gather information on employee attitudes, including attitude surveys, ad hoc focus groups and questionnaires to staff who have left the organisation. These various sources of information indicated that lack of career progression was seen as a problem: for example, in the attitude survey conducted in 1997, fewer than half of hourly-paid staff (the vast majority of Asda employees) agreed with the statement 'there is ample opportunity for promotion at Asda'.

In response, Asda developed a new programme to train hourly-paid staff to become managers. Staff nominate themselves for the programme but must meet stiff entry criteria in terms of skill and training levels before being accepted; for example, they must have reached the final stage of the job ladder for their current role. The programme consists of three stages:

Stage 1 – staff attend an open day that explains the good and bad aspects of being a manager. Staff also complete four off-the-job courses in communication skills, coaching, training and organising work. At the end of each course participants complete a small project. Once they have been satisfactorily completed, staff attend a one-day development centre where they are assessed against the competencies required for managers. Once they have reached a certain level of competence they progress to stage 2.

Stage 2 – staff undertake four weeks of full-time training in store. This includes both on- and off-the-job training and focuses on people management skills, including how to give feedback and conduct appraisal interviews. Once this training is successfully completed, they spend the next four weeks undergoing in-depth management training in one of eight 'stores of learning', chosen for being well run by highly experienced managers. A self-learning package is included here as well as more on and off-the-job training. On successful completion, participants move directly to stage 3.

Stage 3 – appointment to a departmental manager post. Asda believes that the new programme has contributed to reduced turnover rates amongst hourly-paid staff and managers. In addition, the proportion of hourly paid staff who agreed that Asda offers ample opportunity for promotion had increased to 64% in 2000.

Source: IDS (2000).

Questions

1 To what extent is this programme likely to reduce turnover?

2 In what circumstances might Asda find it difficult to retain staff and what could they do about it?

References and further reading support the chapter by giving printed and electronic sources for additional study

References and further reading

Armstrong, M. (2001) *A Handbook of Human Resource Management Practice*, 8th edn. London: Kogan Page.

Arthur, J. (1992) 'The link between business strategy and industrial relations systems in American steel minimills', *Industrial and Labor Relations Review*, Vol. 45, No. 3, pp. 488–506.

Bartholomew, D. (ed.) (1976) *Manpower Planning*. Harmondsworth: Penguin.

Beaumont, P. (1992) 'The US human resource management literature', in Salaman, G. *et al.* (eds) *Human Resource Strategies*. London: Sage.

Bennet, A. (1991) 'Downsizing doesn't necessarily bring an upswing in corporate profitability', *The Wall Street Journal*, 6 June, p. 1.

Bevan, S. (1997) 'Quit stalling', *People Management*, 20 Nov.

Bevan, S., Barber, L. and Robinson, D. (1997) *Keeping the Best: A Practical Guide to Retaining Key Employees*. London: Institute for Employment Studies.

Boxall, P. and Purcell, J. (2003) *Strategy and Human Resource Management*. London: Palgrave.

Bramham, J. (1988) *Practical Manpower Planning*, 4th edn. London: IPM.

Bramham, J. (1989) *Human Resource Planning*. London: IPM.

Bramham, J. (1994) *Human Resource Planning*. London: IPD.

Brews, P. and Hunt, M. (1999) 'Learning to plan and planning to learn: resolving the planning school/learning school debate', *Strategic Management Journal*, Vol. 20, pp. 889–913.

Buckingham, G. (2000) 'Same indifference', *People Management*, 17 Feb, pp. 44–46.

Cascio, W. (1993) 'Downsizing: what do we know, what have we learned?', *Academy of Management Executive*, Vol. 7, No. 1, pp. 95–104.

PLAN OF THE BOOK

Part 1		
HUMAN RESOURCE MANAGEMENT AND ITS ORGANISATIONAL CONTEXT		
Chapter 1 An introduction to human resource management: strategy, style or outcome	Chapter 2 Strategic human resource management	Chapter 3 Human resource management in context

Part 2			
RESOURCING THE ORGANISATION			
Chapter 4 Human resource management and the labour market	Chapter 5 Human resource planning	Chapter 6 Recruitment and selection	Chapter 7 Managing equality and diversity

Part 3		
DEVELOPING THE HUMAN RESOURCE		
Chapter 8 Learning and development	Chapter 9 Human resource development: the organisation and the national framework	Chapter 10 Management development

Part 4			
THE EMPLOYMENT RELATIONSHIP			
Chapter 11 The employment relationship and employee rights at work	Chapter 12 Establishing the terms and conditions of employment	Chapter 13 Reward and performance management	Chapter 14 Employee involvement and empowerment

Part 5		
INTERNATIONAL HUMAN RESOURCE MANAGEMENT		
Chapter 15 HRM in multinationals: a comparative international pespective	Chapter 16 Human resource management and Europe	Chapter 17 Human resource management in Asia

HOW TO USE THIS BOOK

This text is designed to meet the needs of a range of students who are studying HRM either as a core or option subject on undergraduate degrees in Business and Social Science, MBAs, specialised Masters programmes, or for the CIPD professional qualification scheme.

All the chapters are designed to take a critically evaluative approach to their subject material. This means that this is not written in a prescriptive or descriptive style as are some other HRM textbooks, though there will be sections that must necessarily incorporate aspects of that approach. Some chapters will be more easily absorbable by the novice student than others. For example, Chapters 1 (Introduction to HRM) and 2 (Strategic HRM) are good introductions to the subject, while Chapter 3 takes a more unusual perspective on HRM in an organisational context and for the able student will prove both rewarding and stimulating. This is similarly the case for Chapter 4 on HRM in the labour market. Likewise, Chapter 8 is a demanding and stimulating introduction to the processes of learning and development, while Chapter 9 contains more elements of what the student might expect in a chapter on HRD.

In this edition there are also activities and 'Stop and think' exercises peppering the text. These are to give students pause for thought and enable them to reflect on the ideas and knowledge to help them absorb and understand the concepts and ideas in both a practical and theoretical context. As in the first edition, there are case studies, exercises, activities and questions at the end of most chapters and a longer case study at the end of each Part. These can be given by lecturers as course work exercises and the Lecturers Guide that accompanies this volume gives detailed suggested answers. Additional material is also available on the companion website (www.booksites.net/beardwell).

The outlines which follow are intended to indicate how the material in this book can be used to cover the requirements of these varying programmes; the one exception to this scheme is an outline for undergraduates, because of the multiplicity of courses at this level which individual tutors will have devised. Nevertheless, it is hoped that these suggested 'routes' through the book will be helpful guidelines for tutors who have responsibility for some or all of these courses.

MBA Route

Introduction: Chapters 1, 2, 3
Core: Chapters 4, 5, 6, 9, 11, 12, 13, 14, 15
Options: Chapters 7, 8, 10, 16, 17

MA/MSc Route

Introduction: Chapters 1, 2, 3, 4
Core: Chapters 5, 6, 9, 11, 12, 13, 14, 15
Options: Chapters 7, 8, 10, 16, 17

CIPD Professional Development Scheme (PDS)

Introduction: Chapters 1, 2, 3
People Management and Development: Chapters 4, 5, 6, 7, 8, 9, 12, 13
People Resourcing: Chapters 1, 2, 3, 4, 5, 6, 7, 13
Employee Relations: Chapters 1, 2, 3, 4, 7, 11, 12, 14
Learning and Development: Chapters 8, 9, 10
Employee Reward: Chapter 13
Advanced Practitioner Standard: Chapters 1, 2, 15, 16, 17

The available range of CIPD specialist modules may be supported by the use of the relevant chapter or part, thus Management Development and Vocational Education and Training can be supported by the whole of Part 3.

CONTRIBUTORS

Editors

Ian Beardwell, BSc, MSc, PhD, CCIPD. For the first three editions of this book Ian was Professor of Industrial Relations and Head of the Department of Human Resource Management at Leicester Business School. In 2002 he took up the post of Professor of Human Resources and Co-ordinator of Institutional HR Strategy at North East Wales Institute of Higher Education. Experienced in industrial relations and manpower policy with the CBI, CIR and NEDO, he researched and published in the areas of low pay, public recognition, public sector labour relations and the management of industrial relations. He gave formal evidence to both the Megaw Committee of Inquiry into Civil Service pay (1981) and the Review Body for Nursing Pay (1987). His more recent work included an ESRC-supported study of non-union firms in the UK and contemporary developments in 'new' industrial relations. Ian died on 25 June 2002.

Len Holden, BSc, MPhil, CIPD, CertEd, PhD, is Principal Lecturer in Human Resource Management at Leicester Business School, De Montfort University. He has lived and worked in Eastern Europe and has written on the changes which have taken place there since 1989. He has also researched, lectured and written on Western Europe, specialising in aspects of Swedish human resource management. He has recently returned to writing about the car industry but is also a member of a research project based at Leicester Business School examining mechanisms for transfer of HRM in US MNCs to a European context.

Tim Claydon, BSc, MSc(econ), PhD, is Principal Lecturer in Industrial Relations in the Department of HRM at De Montfort University. He has written on trade union history, union derecognition, union–management partnership, and ethics and human resource management. His current teaching and research interests include contemporary changes in work and employment, international and comparative human resource management and current developments in trade unionism in the UK, Europe and the USA.

Contributors

Phil Almond, BSc, MA, PhD, is a lecturer in Human Resource Management at De Montfort University. His main research interests are in comparative and international HRM, and comparative industrial relations. He is currently a member of the team on an ESRC-funded project investigating HRM in US multinational corporations in the UK. He also has an active research interest in industrial relations in France.

Julie Beardwell, BA, MA, is Principal Lecturer in Human Resource Management at Leicester Business School, De Montfort University. She joined the university after ten years' experience in the retail sector. She currently contributes to a range of professional and postgraduate courses, teaching employee resourcing and interpersonal skills. She is also course director of the MA in Personnel and Development and an FCIPD. Her research interests include HRM in non-union firms and personnel careers.

Ian Clark, BA, MA, PGCE, PhD, is Principal Lecturer in Industrial Relations in the Department of HRM, De Montfort University. Ian is currently a member of the department's team of ESRC-funded researchers examining employment relations in subsidiaries of US multinationals in Europe. Ian has published widely on the issues of economic performance and industrial relations, the effects of sector on management techniques and the management of human resources in engineering services.

Audrey Collin, BA, DipAn, PhD, is Emeritus Professor of Career Studies, De Montfort University. Her early career was in personnel management, and she is now MCIPD. She was awarded a PhD for her study of mid-career change; she has researched and published on career and lifespan studies, mentoring, and the employment of older people. She has co-edited (with Richard A. Young) two books on career which reflect her questioning of traditional understandings of career and commitment to interpretative research approaches. Now formally retired, she continues her writing on career for the international academic readership, while also addressing the relationship between theory and practice.

Trevor Colling, BA, MA, is Senior Research Fellow in the Department of Human Resource Management, De Montfort University, Leicester. He has written and published widely on public sector industrial relations, particularly the implications of privatisation and contracting out. His current research interests include employment practice in US multinational companies and trade union roles in the enforcement of individual employment rights.

Mike Doyle, BA, MA, is Principal Lecturer in Human Resource Management, De Montfort University. He teaches on a range of postgraduate management programmes in the area of management development and organisational change. His current research interests include the exploration of major change initiatives in public and private sector organisations and the selection and development of middle managers as 'change agents'.

Linda Glover, BA, MBA, is Principal Lecturer in Human Resource Management, De Montfort University. She teaches undergraduate and postgraduate programmes and is involved in a number of research projects. Linda has managed industry-funded research projects that have been investigating employee responses to quality management and HRM. She is working with Olga Tregaskis and Anthony Ferner on a CIPD-sponsored research project that is examining the role of international HRM committees in transferring HR knowledge across borders within multinational companies. She has collaborated with Noel Sui of Hong Kong Baptist University on a project examining the human resource issues associated with the management of quality in the People's Republic of China. She has written on the human resource problems associated with managing the subsidiaries of multinational companies.

Nicky Golding, BA, MSc, is a Senior Lecturer in Human Resource Management, De Montfort University. She teaches on a range of postgraduate and post-experience programmes in the area of Strategic Human Resource Management and Learning and Development. She is involved in a range of consultancy projects and her current research interests are in the relationship between strategic management and human resource management.

Sue Marlow, BA, MA, PhD, is Reader in HRM at De Montfort University, Leicester; she teaches gender studies, industrial relations, and entrepreneurship and innovation on both undergraduate and postgraduate programmes in Leicester, the Far East and France. Susan Marlow has researched and published extensively in the area of small firms, with a particular interest in women in self-employment, labour management, employment regulation, and training and development issues. Along with two colleagues, she is currently editing a book for Routledge on employment relations in smaller firms and has recently been invited to the USA as a Visiting Professor to lecture on entrepreneurship and gender issues.

Mike Noon, BA, MSc, PhD, is Professor and Head of the Department of Human Resource Management at Leicester Business School, De Montfort University. He has previously researched and taught at Imperial College (University of London), Cardiff Business School and Lancaster University. He has published widely in academic journals, and his recent books are: *The Realities of Work* (second edition, 2002, co-authored with Paul Blyton, published by Palgrave); *Equality, Diversity and Disadvantage in Employment* (2001, co-edited with Emmanuel Ogbonna, published by Palgrave); *A Dictionary of Human Resource Management* (2001, co-authored with Ed Heery, published by Oxford University Press).

Julia Pointon, BA, MA, PGCE, CIPD, is a senior lecturer in Organisational Behaviour at De Montfort University teaching on a range of undergraduate and professional courses. Julia has particular research interests in professional roles and responsibilities in multidisciplinary health-care teams. She is a committee member of the local CIPD branch, a member of the CIPD National Upgrading Panel and serves on the CIPD Membership and Education Committee.

Alan J. Ryan, BA, is a Senior Lecturer in the Department of HRM at De Montfort University. His teaching is focused on the implications of legal change for the management of people at work and the development of managerial responses to legislative activity. He teaches courses at undergraduate and post-graduate level as well as being actively involved in courses and programmes delivered to HMP service, Ford, and UK Interpreters' Service as well as other local businesses. His research interest lies in the development of soft systems analysis as a way of understanding changes in managerial behaviour following the introduction of legislation. He has undertaken some consultancy work in both the private and the voluntary sector. He has written on reward management, participation regimes in SMEs and the legal implications of flexibility.

Olga Tregaskis, BSc, MSc, PhD, is Senior Research Fellow in International Management at De Montfort University's Leicester Business School. A University of

Ulster Psychology graduate, Olga gained her masters in Applied Psychology from Cranfield University. After spending some time working within the Industry Training Organisation (ITO) network in the UK, Olga returned to Cranfield where she worked in the research Centre for European HRM and was awarded her PhD in International HRM from Cranfield School of Management. Olga teaches HRM on a range of postgraduate courses and has undertaken research projects sponsored by the European Commission, national funding bodies, private organisations and the CIPD. She is a frequent contributor to international conferences as speaker, referee and/or session chair and publishes academic and practitioner pieces in the areas of International HRM, Comparative HRM, Employee Development and Flexible Working.

Mary Wright, BA, MBA, FIPD, is Principal Lecturer in Human Resource Management at De Montfort University. She has wide experience of teaching on under-graduate and professional courses and is actively involved with the CIPD at local level. She has researched and written on international executive search and selection.

ACKNOWLEDGEMENTS

The editors would like to thank the contributors to this volume who have valiantly met deadlines despite a demanding year within the HRM department at De Montfort University. We would also like to thank their partners and families for their forbearance. In addition we convey a special thank you to Margaret Spence (the De Montfort University HRM departmental secretary) who has put in considerable time and effort in creating earlier editions and has been of great service to many of us on this one.

Thanks also go to our commissioning editors and other staff at Pearson Education for their patient support in helping this edition towards the printing press and website. The support, help and advice of Louise Lakey and David Cox, who took over from Louise, and did an excellent job in picking up the threads is greatly appreciated. Thanks also go to Amanda Thompson, Nicola Chilvers, Jacqueline Senior and Alison Kirk who were ever helpful and diplomatic in dealing with our gripes and moans.

Publisher's acknowledgements

Table 1.1 from *New Perspectives on Human Resource Management*, Routledge (Storey, J. 1989), Table 2.1 and Figure 2.3 from *What is Strategy and Does it Matter?* 2nd Edition (Whittington, R. 2001), Figure 5.4 from *Human Resource Management: A Critical Text*, Routledge (Rothwell, S. 1995), Figure 14.1 from *Towards A New Industrial Democracy: Worker's Participation in Industry*, Routledge & Kegan Paul (Poole, M. 1986), with permission of Thomson Publishing Services; Table 1.2 and Figure 1.5 from *Developments in the Management of Human Resources: An Analytical Review*, Blackwell (Storey, J. 1999), Table 2.8 and Figure 2.1 from *Contemporary Strategy Analysis: Concepts, Techniques, Applications*, 4th Edition, Blackwell (Grant, R. M. 2002), Table 17.4 and Table 17.5 from 'Re-inventing China's industrial relations at enterprise level: an empirical field-study in four major cities', *Industrial Relations Journal*, Vol. 30, No. 3, pp. 243–260 (Ding, Z & Warner M. 1999), Figure 6.3 *Successful Selection of Interviewing*, Blackwell (Anderson, N. & Shackleton, V. 1993), with permission of Blackwell Publishing Limited; Table 2.2 from Academy of Management Executive by Schuler & Jackson, Table 2.3 from Academy of Management Journal by Delery & Doty, Table 2.6 Academy of Management Journal by Becker & Gerhart, copyright 1987, 1996 and 1996, respectively, by Acad of Mgmt, reproduced with permission of Acad of Mgmt in the format Textbook via Copyright Clearance Center; Table 2.4 from *Competing for the Future* (Hamel, G. and Prahalad, C. 1994), reprinted by permission of Harvard Business Review, © 1994 by the Harvard School of Publishing Corporation, all rights reserved, Figure 2.2 from 'Crafting strategy', *Harvard Business Review*, July–August, pp. 65–75 (Mitzberg, H. 1987), copyright © 1987 by the Harvard Business School Publishing Corporation, all rights reserved; Table 2.5, this material is taken from *People Management and Development*, 2nd Edition (Marchington, M. & Wilkinson, A. 2002), Table 6.6 from 'Recruitment and retention', *Survey Report*, p. 12 (CIPD, 2002a), Table 6.7 from 'Recruitment on the internet', *Quick Facts* (CIPD, 2002c), with the permission of the Chartered Institute of Personnel and Development, London; Table 2.7 from *Strategic Human Resource Management Practice, A Guide to Action*, 2nd Edition, Kogan Page (Armstrong, M. and Baron, A. 2002), Figure 5.5 from *A Handbook of Human Resource Management*, 8th Edition, Kogan Page, p. 363 (Armstrong, A. 2001); Table 6.3 from 'Human resource issues of the European Union', *Financial Times*, p. 247 (Leat, M. 1998), Chapter 13. p. 510 from *Organizational Behaviour: An Introductory Text*, 4th Edition, Financial Times, Prentice Hall (Huczynski, A. A. and Buchanan, D. A. 2001), Figure 2.4 from *Human Resource Management*, 4th Edition (Torrington, D. and Hall, L. 1998), Figure 5.1 from *People Resourcing: Human Resource Management in Practise* (Pilbeam, S. and Corbridge, M. 2002), with permission of Pearson Education Limited; Table 6.4 from *Social Trends 2002*, Table 9.3 from Department of Education and Science 'International statistics comparisons of the education and training of 16 and 18 year olds' *Statistical Bulletin 1/90, January: DES* and Table 13.1 from New

Earnings Surveys 1993–1997, reproduced with permission of the Controller of HMSO; Table 6.5 from *Recruitment and Selection*, Advisory Booklet No. 6. (ACAS 1983), with the permission of Advisory, Conciliation & Advisory Service, London; Table 9.5 from 'Does strategic training policy exist? Some evidence from ten European countries', *Personnel Review*, Vol. 21, No. 1, pp. 12–23 (Holden, L. and Livian, Y. 1992), Table 17.6 from 'Globalisation and a new human resource policy in Korea: transformation to a performance based HRM', *Employee Relations*, Vol. 19, No. 4, pp. 298–308 (Kim, S. and Briscoe, D. R. 1997), Figure 8.1 from 'Design for learning in management training and development: a view', *Journal of European Industrial Training*, Vol. 4, No. 8, whole issue (Binsted, D. S. 1980), with permission of MCB UP Limited; Table 10.1 from 'Management development for the individual and the organisation', *Personnel Management*, June, pp. 40–44 (Burgoyne, J. 1988), Figure 5.2 from 'Quit stalling', *People Management*, November, p. 34 (Bevan, S. 1997), with the permission of People Management Magazine (formerly Personnel Management) Limited; Table 14.3 from 'Total quality management and employee', from *Human Resource Management Journal* Vol. 2, No. 4, pp. 1–20 (Wilkinson, A. *et al.* 1992) and Table 17.3 from 'Human resources in the People's Republic of China: the "three systems reforms"', *Human Resource Management Journal*, Vol. 6, No. 2, pp. 32–43 (Warner, M. 1996), reproduced by permission of Reed Elsevier (UK) Limited, trading as Lexis Nexis UK; Table 15.1 adapted from *OECD Employment Outlook 2002*, Organisation for Economic Co-operation and Development, Paris; Table 15.3 from 'Strategic human resource management: a global perspective', in R. Piper (ed.) *Human Resource Management: An International Comparison* (Adler, N. and Ghadar, F. 1990), permission granted, Walter de Gruyter GMBH & Co. KG; Table 17.1 from 'Changes in labour supply and their impacts on human resource management: the case in Japan', *International Journal of Human Resource Management*, Vol. 4, No. 1, pp. 29–44 (Sasajima, Y. 1993) and Figure 1.4 'Human resource management: an agenda for the 1990s', *International Journal of Human Resource Management*, Vol. 1, No. 1, pp. 17–43 (Hendry, C. and Pettigrew, A. 1990), reproduced with permission of Taylor & Francis Ltd, http://www.tanf.co.uk/journals/routledge/09585192.html; Figure 1.2 from 'A framework for a strategic human resource management', in M. A. Devanna, C. J. Forburn and N. M. Tichy, (eds) *Strategic Human Resource Management*, copyright © 1984 John Wiley, this material is used by permission of John Wiley & Sons, Inc. (Devanna, M. A. *et al.* 1984); Figure 1.3 from *Managing Human Assets*, Free Press, reproduced with permission of B. Spector (Beer, M. *et al.* 1984); Figure 4.3 from *The 'Flexible' Firm* (Institute of Employment Studies, 1985); Figure 6.2 from *Human Resource Management: Rhetoric and Realities* (Legge K. 1995) and Figure 7.2 *The Realities of Work*, 2nd edition (Noon, M. and Blyton, P. 2002), with permission of Palgrave Macmillan; Figure 9.2 from *Training Without Trainers? How Germany Avoids Britain's Supply-side Bottleneck* with permission of Anglo-German Foundation for the Study of Industrial Society (Rose, R. and Wignanek, G. 1990); Figure 14.2 from *Developments in the Swedish Labour Law*, The Swedish Institute, © Anders Suneson, www.technadebilder.se. (Edlund, S. and Nystrom, B. 1988); Figure 15.2 from 'An integrative framework of strategic international human resource management', *Journal of Management*, Vol. 19, No. 2, with permission of Elsevier (Schuler, R. *et al.* 1993).

Investors in People for extracts from case studies on The Cumberland Hotel and Wealden District Council; Labour Research Department for an extract from 'Employers exploit agency work boom' published in *Labour Research* 1st August 2002; *The Sentinel*, Stoke-on-Trent, for an extract from 'Fears for the thread of industry' by Stephen Houghton published in *The Sentinel* 4th May 2003; and Jane Bird for the case study Inside Track Enterprise: Appoint in haste, repent at leisure, from *Financial Times*, 9 January 2003, © Jane Bird. Extract on p. 75 from John Webster's 1985 advertisement for the *Guardian*, reproduced with kind permission of The Guardian/BMP DDB. Extracts on pp. 271 and 272 taken from *Effective Mentoring and Teaching* by L. A. Daloz, copyright © 1986 John Wiley & Sons Inc. This material is used by permission of John Wiley & Sons Inc.

We are grateful to the Financial Times Limited for permission to reprint the following material:

Box 2.5, How BMW put the Mini back on track, © *Financial Times*, 19 March 2003; Chapter 3 Case study, Awkward squad promises a rough ride at Blackpool, © *Financial Times*, 9 September 2002; Part 1 Case study, Retailer derided for 'moving the deckchairs' at a crucial time – fears of double-digit fall in sales, © *Financial Times*, 22 December 1999; Chapter 12 Case study, Business views two-tier workforce agreement as dynamite, © *Financial Times*, 14 February 2003; Box 16.1, Hire and fire, is no recipe for Europe, © *Financial Times*, 12 November 2002.

In some instances we have been unable to trace the owners of copyright material and we would appreciate any information that would enable us to do so.

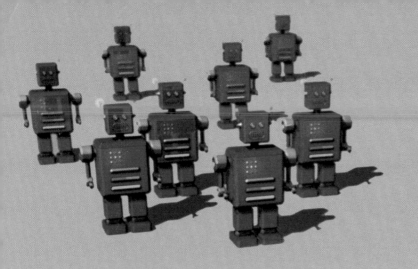

Part 1

HUMAN RESOURCE MANAGEMENT AND ITS ORGANISATIONAL CONTEXT

Introduction to Part 1

Human resource management has become a pervasive and influential approach to the management of employment in a wide range of market economies. The original US prescriptions of the early 1980s have become popularised and absorbed in a wide variety of economic settings: there are very few major economies where the nature of human resource management, to include its sources, operation and philosophy, is not actively discussed. As a result, the analysis and evaluation of HRM have become major themes in academic, policy and practitioner literatures.

These first three chapters are strongly related in that they consider the nature of HRM from a number of perspectives. The first chapter looks at the antecedents of HRM in the USA and its translation to other economies, with particular emphasis on Britain – where the HRM debate has been among the most active and has involved practitioner and academic alike. There are many unresolved questions in HRM: What sort of example is it? Can it be transposed from one economy to another? Does it have qualities that make it truly international? Is it a major contribution to strategic management?

The second chapter continues this last theme in examining the strategic nature of HRM in depth: how it is aligned to and configured with organisational strategy and how the debate has moved through a number of incarnations, from the 'best-fit approach' to the 'configurational approach' to the 'resource-based view' and 'best practice approach'. In making claims for the importance of the strategic nature of HRM it raises questions as to its efficacy in helping meet organisational objectives, creating competitive advantage and 'adding value' through what has now become known as 'high-performance' or 'high-commitment work practices'. Whether or not the claims for these approaches are supportable, it is becoming clear that no one system or approach can be applied to all organisations owing to the increasing complexity of organisational forms and organisational contexts.

The third chapter continues this contextual theme and examines the context in which human resource management has emerged and in which it operates. This is important in understanding some of the assumptions and philosophical stances that lie behind it. The purpose of the discussion is to create a critical awareness of the broader context in which HRM operates, not simply as a set of operational matters that describe the functional role of personnel management, but as part of a complex and sophisticated process that helps us to understand the nature of organisational life.

The type of questions raised by HRM indicates the extent to which it has disturbed many formerly accepted concepts in the employment relationship. For some it has become a model for action and application; for others it is no more than a map that indicates how the management of employees might be worked out in more specific ways than HRM can adequately deal with.

CHAPTER 1

An introduction to human resource management: strategy, style or outcome

Ian Beardwell (revised by Julie Beardwell and Ian Clark)

OBJECTIVES

▶ To outline the development of HRM as an area of practice and analysis in terms of:
   – strategy
   – style
   – outcomes.
▶ To debate the nature of the HRM phenomenon and the different perspectives from which it is viewed:
   – as a restatement of existing personnel practice
   – as a new managerial discipline
   – as a resource-based model
   – as a strategic and international function.
▶ To review and evaluate the main models of HRM, and to assess current developments.

Introduction

The fourth edition of this book provides an opportunity to reflect on the extent of the debate about human resource management, the changing nature of the employment relationship, and the consequences for how organisations and individuals are managed. It is now over a decade since the idea for a comprehensive treatment of HRM was conceived by the authors, and a great deal of the prevailing analysis and data that was available at that time was derived from such sources as the 1984 WIRS 2, the 1988 Company Level Survey and MacInnes' *Thatcherism at Work* (MacInnes, 1987). The story was broadly one of change, but not so much that a radical reshaping of the employment relationship had occurred. Rather, the effects of deflation and recession in the early and late 1980s had wrought greater damage to the infrastructure of employment than any legally enforced reform, while the move to privatisation, and a stronger role for market-based models of economic activity, had shifted the primary scope of industrial relations away from job regulation and collective bargaining towards coping with outsourcing and downsizing.

Despite all these shifts, however, a large part of the analysis and discussion that constitutes the HRM debate today had yet to reveal itself. Some initial studies of non-unionism were only just beginning to see the light of day (McLoughlin and Gourlay,

1994), while the role of HRM in transforming and adding value to organisational performance (Pfeffer, 1994, 1998), the relationship between HRM 'bundles' and business performance (McDuffie, 1995; Huselid, 1995), the role of the psychological contract in gaining employee assent (Guest and Conway, 1997) and wider changes in the infrastructure of the employment relationship (Cully *et al.*, 1999) would come later in the decade. The situation is now one of a rich and complex diversity of analyses, in which UK-based research and analysis is playing as significant a contribution as that of the USA – even if some of the policy and research initiatives still derive, *prima facie*, from a US agenda.

What is striking about the HRM debate of the past decade is that two common themes have persisted, and yet neither has turned out to be the determining feature of the way the employment relationship is managed. The first theme is that of HRM's replacement of the older traditions of personnel management and industrial relations. The approach of what might be termed the 'Desperately Seeking HRM' school of analysis seeks to explore the incidence, volume and influence of HRM-based approaches and practices, and to assess whether they are supplanting the historical patterns of UK employee management (Sisson, 1993). The second theme is concerned to examine the specific impact of focused types of HRM – such as high-commitment management – in order to assess their superiority over both more generalised HRM interventions and traditional methods. While there are obvious limitations in seeking to assess the total impact of HRM, whether by large-scale survey material or by case analysis, there are similar limitations to measuring discrete choices of 'tools' with the aim of achieving 'best practice', as Purcell (1999) has noted. Thus we have entered the new millennium without a universal model of HRM on the one hand, but, on the other, with a range of HRM activities that are under sustained examination in order to assess their efficacy in achieving superior organisational performance. What is clear is that the HRM agenda still continues to develop and provide opportunities for analysis and prescription. For some commentators HRM seems to have hit its high water mark and is now on the ebb (Bach and Sisson, 2000), while for others (such as Guest, 1997) there is fragmentary but clear evidence that 'HRM works', but we need to put flesh on the bones to consolidate that assertion.

■ A framework for HRM analysis: strategy, style and outcome

How can we attempt to construct a framework to encompass these divergent views about the relative strength and vitality of HRM? As the subtitle of this chapter suggests, there are at least three approaches to looking at the phenomenon that might help to explain different groups of arguments, based on whether the analysis focuses on the role of strategy, style or outcomes in the conduct of HRM.

● HRM as strategy

The strategic emphasis has by far the longest pedigree in the HRM debate; indeed, it is probably the strategic aspirations of the US models that were the defining feature of HRM as it emerged in the 1980s (see also Chapter 2). As we shall see later in the chapter, strategy has been seen as one of the touchstones of HRM's viability. The extent to which HRM has come to play a role in the direction and planning of organisations has been a persistent theme not simply in the academic literature but in practitioner activity too. For example, the HRM Initiative in the UK National Health Service stresses the key role that HR practitioners will play at both national and regional levels in achieving nationally determined and nationally assessed goals for health care delivery. A key part of this initiative is the integration of HRM with the strategic goals of the NHS.

Within strategic approaches two further strands might be noted. The first remains centred around macro-strategic issues and the general location of HRM within organisational structures overall – perhaps best summed up by the debate over whether HRM has a seat on the Board. The second strand has been more concerned with the formal inputs that HRM can provide – such as better recruitment and selection procedures or better alignment of reward systems with activity – as a way of providing linkages that are demonstrable and robust. In the NHS, for example, a major factor in stimulating these closer linkages is the realisation that variability of treatment rates between different hospitals may be as much to do with the management of the clinical personnel as with their access to medical technology. Thus the health service provides an excellent example of the strategic positioning of HRM and the linkage of its inputs. This brings together their respective relationships in the debate over the role of HRM in the health service overall.

A contemporary explanation for HRM's strategic positioning has emerged in the use of the term *business focus*. This has become a popular and widely used phrase to describe a wide range of organisational activity into which HRM is expected to link. However, it has an ambiguity and a potential for use across not only strategy, but also style and outcomes. If it has a meaning, it is probably best viewed as a general description of the territory that HRM now inhabits, rather than the technically defined and narrower role of personnel management of a quarter of a century ago.

● HRM as style

The second approach, based around styles of HRM, has also had an active life, and one that has attracted much discussion within the UK. Some of the antecedents to this can be traced back through the analysis of personnel as a function and personnel managers as actors within organisational settings. Thus Watson's (1977) analysis of the professional role of personnel managers and Legge's (1978) analysis of their political location within organisational roles can be seen as important precursors of this approach, while Tyson and Fell (1986) further refined the styles of personnel managers within their tasks. Other antecedents can be traced back to the industrial relations tradition, with the 'unitarist–pluralist' analysis of Fox (1966) and the 'traditionalist/sophisticated paternalist/sophisticated modern/standard modern' formulation of Purcell and Sisson (1983). The idea that style of personnel management or industrial relations can materially affect the operation of the function is deeply rooted in UK analysis, and suggests too that it has proved difficult to change over time, except through profound disturbance or acute threat. In these contexts the reason why UK management has not demonstrated a greater interest in, or success with, strategic approaches to HRM (in contrast to the USA) is largely attachment to a style that is the product of history and institutions over time, each of which is now an embedded feature of the British business system.

The analysis of HRM in terms of style has also revolved around whether it can be regarded as hard or soft (Legge, 1995) in its intent. *Hard HRM* is sometimes defined in terms of the particular policies that stress a cost-minimisation strategy with an emphasis on leanness in production, the use of labour as a resource, and what Legge calls a 'utilitarian instrumentalism' in the employment relationship; at other times hard HRM is defined in terms of the tightness of fit between organisational goals and strategic objectives on the one hand and HRM policies on the other. *Soft HRM*, by contrast, is sometimes viewed as 'developmental humanism' (Legge, 1995) in which the individual is integrated into a work process that values trust, commitment and communication. What is probably more at issue than either of these two characterisations is the question of whether they are equally routes to work intensification and greater demands on the employment relationship by the organisation at the expense of the employee. As Legge points out, it is quite feasible that hard HRM variants can contain elements of soft practice, while the criticism that can be made of soft variants is that they can be held to deliver hard outcomes in terms of the tightness of the fit with business strategy that is sought. Indeed, just as with the broad definition and usage of the term 'business focus', noted earlier, so with the meaning and use of the term 'fit'. Each of the three descriptions of HRM discussed here – strategy, style and outcome – is concerned with fit and the extent to which each achieves it, with the result that 'fit' has itself become an infinitely flexible term, and one that becomes increasingly difficult to apply to HRM as a single concept.

A more recent approach to the question of style can be found in the work of Ulrich (1998). The tradition that sought to present practitioner roles in terms of the organisational location of their work provides a good background to Ulrich's model of the HRM profession and its contribution to the business. For Ulrich, there are four possible styles or routes that HRM can take. The first is in what he terms *work organisation*, which involves the practitioner servicing the needs of the organisation in as efficient a manner as possible, but no more than that. In this mode, the style of HRM is as a support function 'doing the job right' but with little opportunity to add value or contribute to organisational performance. It might be that minimal HRM mistakes will be made, but conducting HRM in this manner will not provide any particular competitive advantage for any one organisation. The second style is to become the *employee champion*. In this mode the HR practitioner takes on the role of 'voice' for employees, seeking to reduce the frictional differences between the organisation and its staff and ensuring that senior management are aware of the concerns of employees. While this might be a different role from the maintenance function of work organisation, it still places the practitioner in a servicing role and does not necessarily create a role with added value; the emphasis is still on reducing dysfunctions. In the third mode, that of *agent for change*, the practitioner becomes the protagonist in active change management that has the capacity for added value, while in the fourth mode of *business partner* the practitioner becomes a fully contributing member of the management team, who is able to participate in the corporate planning process and bring the expertise of HRM into the equation with the responsibility to demonstrate how HRM can add value and give competitive advantage. For Ulrich the danger for HRM lies in its inability to move on from work organisation and seize the developmental opportunity of becoming the business partner. The attractions of this approach to style for practitioners are obvious, with its message of hope and a promise of a substantial role at the heart of organisational structures, and Ulrich's work has become particularly popular in the professional associations for HR managers in both the USA and the UK.

Stop and think	Consider the role of HR in an organisation known to you. How closely does it fit with Ulrich's model of the profession and its contribution to the business?

● HRM as outcomes

Over the second half of the 1990s, a further turn in the HRM debate saw a move away from attempts to define what its 'input' characteristics might be in favour of examining what consequences flowed from applying HRM in fairly tightly defined circumstances. Whereas both strategic and style approaches to HRM analysis had been concerned with its architecture, an 'output'-based model concerned itself with examining those organisations that not only constructed their HRM in particular configurations but also found that resultant outcomes could give them a competitive advantage. The impetus for this approach was predominantly American, in particular the work of Arthur (1992, 1994), McDuffie (1995) and Huselid (1995), although UK work has also developed in this area, West and Patterson (1997) in particular.

The unifying theme of these studies is that particular combinations of HRM practices, especially where they are refined and modified, can give quantifiable improvements in organisational performance. Arthur's work studied 54 mini-mills (new technology steel mills using smaller workforces and new working practices) and demonstrated that firms using a 'commitment' model of HRM saw higher productivity, lower labour turnover, and lower rates of rejected production. In other words, it took the HRM style element a stage further in order to establish whether there was an output effect that could benefit the firm. McDuffie's work examined 70 plants in the world car industry, and the use of HR techniques that were regarded as innovative. His analysis argued that it is when practices are used together, rather than simply in isolation or only for the specific effect of some more than others, that superior performance can be achieved. An important part of this analysis is the extent to which employees gave 'extra' in the form of discretionary effort that would otherwise have not been forthcoming without the effect of the chosen practices. Three factors were noted in particular: *buffers* (the extent to which plants adopted flexibility), *work system* (the work arrangements that complemented flexibility), and *HRM policies* (the HRM practices that complemented flexibility). The marked effect on performance was in the combined impact of all three factors working together. This approach moves the impact of HRM from being concerned with strategic choice or style *per se* to following the output consequences of constructing what have come to be known as 'bundles' of HR practice.

Huselid's study examined the relationships between the HR system (the groups of practices rather than individual practices), outcome measures (such as financial performance as well as HR data on turnover and absence), and the fit between HR and competitive strategy in 986 US-owned firms employing more than 100 employees. Huselid's results indicated a lowering of labour turnover, higher sales performance, improved profitability and higher share valuations for those firms that performed well on his indices. In the UK the study by West and Patterson (1997) indicated that HR practices could account for 19 per cent of the variation between firms in changes in profitability and 18 per cent of the variation in changes in productivity. Once again, the complementarity of HR practices was held to be significant.

As a result of these types of analysis a great deal of attention is now being paid to what constitutes a 'bundle' of HR practices that will afford firms superior performance. But this is no easy matter to settle conclusively. What is obvious about each of these studies is that they were examining patterns of HR strategies, choices, applications and refinements after their introduction. We have little information about how all these factors came to be in place in some firms and not in others. For practitioners there is no easy or readily available checklist that can be applied. For each firm contemplating an output model of HRM there has to be a difficult internal process of selecting and testing the bundle that will work in their own circumstances. The mere application of a group of practices, without some assessment of their interconnectedness, is unlikely to have discernible beneficial outcomes.

Claims for the contribution of HRM to enhanced organisational performance have been criticised on a number of grounds. Richardson and Thompson (1999) raise several concerns about the research studies. They question the lack of consensus in the measures used to define HRM; the apparent arbitrary selection of items included in HRM 'bundles'; and the assumption that all HR practices are equally important. Furthermore, they suggest that many of the studies ignore other measures of managerial effectiveness and thus risk overstating the impact of HRM. Whitfield and Poole (1997) express doubts over attributions of causality; i.e. is it that HRM leads to better organisational performance or is it that better performing organisations are able to invest more time and effort into the management of human resources?

Thus the debate over HRM, whether it is pursued by analysts, academics or practitioners, continues to expand and develop. So far from reaching the high-water mark and ebbing, HRM as a phenomenon continues to thrive. Indeed, the fusion of HRM with business focus, noted above, has ensured that many major organisational changes now intimately involve HRM as part of the equation. These changes provide the background against which human resource management has emerged as the predominant contemporary influence on managing employment relationships. It is now commonplace to describe HRM as a managerially derived and driven set of precepts with both line and HR managers actively involved in its operation. What is distinctive about the debate, and perhaps explains its capacity to renew itself after each wave of analysis has been assessed and absorbed, is the shift from the broad question of whether HRM exists at all to more focused analyses – for example, whether particular combinations of HRM policies produce better results in output or services so that competitive advantage might accrue to those organisations that adopt them. Thus HRM continues to provide agendas and prescriptions for debate amongst both practitioners and analysts that are contentious and compelling, and have no settled orthodoxy.

Why should this be so? Part of the answer lies in the perspective brought to bear upon HRM: there is a diversity in the HRM debate, derived from the manner in which particular participants view the essential elements of HRM and what they believe it is representing, that colours the discussion. For the purposes of this analysis four broad perspectives are set out here:

- that HRM is no more than a renaming of basic personnel functions, which does little that is different from the traditional practice of personnel management;
- that HRM represents a fusion of personnel management and industrial relations that is managerially focused and derives from a managerial agenda;
- that HRM represents a resource-based conception of the employment relationship, incorporating a developmental role for the individual employee and some elements of cost minimisation;
- that HRM can be viewed as part of the strategic managerial function in the development of business policy, in which it plays both a determining and a contributory role and is particularly so for multinational firms.

HRM as a restatement of existing personnel practice

It is possible to view this first standpoint as a basic but natural reaction to a new and somewhat threatening reformulation of traditional functions. There is, perhaps, an understandable scepticism that HRM can, or ever could, live up to the wider claims of its ability to transform the employment relationship so totally that some of the inherent problems of managing a volatile set of employee issues can be resolved more satisfactorily than by approaches that have grown out of the historical development of personnel management. Throughout the past 15 years this view has remained as a strong reaction to what is seen as the renaming pretensions of HRM. In large part such a reaction can be explained in terms of the gulf that appears to exist between personnel management 'on the ground' and the rather more theoretical and 'strategic' nature of a great deal of the discussion surrounding human resource management. For many practitioners the notion that their roles and functions can be seen in anything other than a highly pragmatic light is no more than wishful thinking: there is an important, if straightforward, task of recruiting, selecting, rewarding, managing and developing employees that must be carried out as 'efficiently' as possible. In this sense, HRM might be viewed as no more than another trend in the long line of management prescriptions that have each enjoyed a vogue and then lost favour, while the pragmatic nature of established personnel management has ensured that the operational tasks have been accomplished.

◾ HRM as a new managerial discipline

The second perspective contains more diversity and complexity, and incorporates such issues as the philosophies of personnel and industrial relations, the professional desire to present the management of employees as a holistic discipline (akin to the inclusive approaches of accounting and marketing, for example), and the belief that an integrated management approach can be provided by HRM. This would not only unite the differing perspectives of PM and IR but also create a new and broader discipline as a result of the fusion of these traditional elements. An important outcome of this approach is to view some of these traditional components as now irrelevant or outdated and as dealing with problems that typify past, as opposed to current, practice: this is perhaps most noticeable in the renaming of functional activities so that industrial relations becomes 'employee relations', and training becomes 'employee development'. This retitling is not designed solely to update an image, although that is important in itself, but is more specifically aimed at expressing the nature of the employment relationship in what are seen as changed circumstances. Thus industrial relations is seen as expressing a relationship based upon a manual, manufacturing (and, often by implication, male) unionised workforce – rather than the supposedly wider concept of 'employee relations', which involves a total workforce that includes white-collar and technical staff, of whom many will be female and some or all non-union.

A further significant shift in thinking connected with this second approach is that of the desire by management to extend control over aspects of the collective relationship that were once customarily regarded as jointly agreed between employees (usually via their unions) and management. Treating employees as a primary responsibility of management, as opposed to the jointly negotiated responsibility of both unions and management, suggests an approach that is concerned to stress the primacy of the managerial agenda in the employment relationship, and marks a shift away from one of the fundamental assumptions of the approach (after the Second World War) to managing collective workforces. This shift was underlined in the 1993 employment legislation, which removed from ACAS the duty, originally given to it on its inception in 1974, to promote collective bargaining. In reality, this duty was a reflection of a deeply rooted presumption stretching back throughout most of the twentieth century and, in the UK at least, largely shared by employers, unions and the state, that collective bargaining represented a 'politically' acceptable compromise between management and labour; for more discussion of this see Clark (2000).

Over recent years, the UK professional body for practitioners, the Chartered Institute of Personnel and Development, has sought to establish an agenda that is concerned to show this integration into a business-led managerial discipline and the added value that can accrue from effective people management. The annual autumn conference is now the largest management conference held in Europe, and it attracts the most well-known 'guru' speakers; its annual HRD spring conference is as influential, and presents as extensive a range of speakers within the learning and development domain, while setting the programme in a business context. With membership now well over 110 000 the Institute was successfully granted a Royal Charter in 2000, in recognition of its role as a major professional management association. Within this framework HRM is one factor in transforming personnel management into a powerful managerial role in its own right. To that extent it is part of a 'transformation' within the profession, which sees a move away from technical specificity towards a more rounded and sophisticated contribution to wider organisational objectives. The extent to which such transformations can be achieved is also connected to the third HRM perspective, which is discussed next.

■ HRM as a resource-based model

A further perspective has been brought to bear on HRM from those approaches that stress the role of the individual in organisations, rather than the collective employment models outlined so far. Personnel management, to a large degree at least, has always been concerned with the interface between the organisation and the individual, and with the necessity of achieving a trade-off between the requirements of the organisation and the needs of individual employees. Traditional personnel management policies that have been developed to cope with this trade-off have often taken a piecemeal approach to certain aspects of this issue: historically, the early twentieth-century personnel function stressed the 'welfare' role that could be afforded employees so that basic working conditions (both physically and contractually) could be established.

Subsequently, other styles of personnel management sought to introduce, administer or rectify particular aspects of jobs and roles that individuals carried out. This tradition fostered a belief in equitable selection and reward systems, efficient procedures for discipline, dismissal and redundancy, and clear and operable rules for administering large numbers of employees to avoid arbitrary judgements over individual cases. The prevailing rationale behind all these activities could be seen as a desire to manage the difficulties of the organisation/individual relationship in as technically neutral a manner as possible. This emphasis has fostered a culture within personnel management that is characterised as *cost minimisation*, often identified with some forms of hard HRM, with the individual as the cost that has to be controlled and contained. In these circumstances employees become one of the aggregate commodities within the organisation that have to be managed within the organisation's resources, in the same way that, for example, the finance available to the organisation has to be managed within a framework and according to accounting conventions. The logical extent of this model is reached in human resources planning, with precise numerical assessments of internal and external demand for and supply of labour (see Chapter 5).

Any alternative to this formalised approach, which treats the individual as a resource rather than an expense and views expenditure on training as an investment rather than a cost, associated with some aspects of soft HRM, can be seen to pose a profound threat to the conventional wisdom of personnel management.

The conception of personnel as having an enabling capacity for employees has a long tradition, not least in the United States, where organisational analysis has often provided prescriptions concerning the role of supervisors, work groups and work organisation. The advent of Japanese management systems has, however, highlighted the impact of this approach on the employment relationship. Whether sustainable or not in the West, the Japanese large-firm emphasis on developing individual employees along particular job paths while undertaking to provide continuous employment throughout the normal working life of the individual has at least provided a model in which the employer seeks to maximise employment opportunities. This approach goes further, however: it regards all employees as potentially able to benefit from further training and development, from which the organisation itself then benefits. So, far from viewing the employee as a cost, which has to be borne by the employer, this philosophy sees the employee as an actual and potential return on investment, which ultimately strengthens the company. The responsibility of the employer for investment and employment has, at least in the post-war period to date, encouraged large corporate Japanese employers to develop products and markets that have used the invested skills of their workforces.

There has been strong interest in what is termed 'resource-based' HRM, in which human resources are viewed as the basis of competitive advantage (see also Chapter 2). This means that advantage is not only derived from the formal reorganisation and reshaping of work, but is also powerfully derived from within the workforce in terms of the training and expertise available to the organisation, the adaptability of employees which permits the organisation strategic flexibility, and the commitment of employees to the organisation's business plans and goals.

■ HRM as a strategic and international function

The advent of human resource management has also brought forward the issue of the linkages between the employment relationship and wider organisational strategies and corporate policies. Historically, the management of industrial relations and personnel has been concerned either to cope with the 'downstream' consequences of earlier strategic decisions or to 'firefight' short-term problems that threaten the long-run success of a particular strategy. In these instances the role has been at best reactive and supportive to other managerial functions, at worst a hindrance until particular operational problems were overcome.

In the private sector the well-known case of British Leyland in the 1970s demonstrated a situation where considerable amounts of managerial effort (up to 60 per cent of operational managers' time by some estimates) were devoted to 'fixing' shopfloor problems. In order to re-establish managerial control the company effectively turned the reshaping of industrial relations into its strategy so that it could refashion its product range and market position. In the public sector throughout the 1980s a series of major disputes affected the operations of schools, hospitals and local authorities (among many such examples); in each of these cases changes to the nature of the employment relationship were the root causes of the dislocation. The Leyland case and the public sector experiences are extreme examples, but each demonstrates the impact that the employment relationship can have on total operations.

Human resource management lays claim to a fundamentally different relationship between the organisation's employment function and its strategic role. The assumption behind HRM is that it is essentially a strategically driven activity, which is not only a major contributor to that process but also a determining part of it. From this standpoint the contribution that the management of the employment relationship makes to the overall managerial process is as vital and formative as that of finance or marketing, for example. Indeed, the notion that HRM is central to such managerial decision-making indicates the extent to which its proponents feel that it has come out of the shadows to claim a rightful place alongside other core management roles. In this respect one of the traditional stances of the personnel practitioner – that of the 'liberal' conception of personnel management as standing between employer and employee, moderating and smoothing the interchange between them – is viewed as untenable: HRM is about shaping and delivering corporate strategies with commitment and results.

One further component in this construction of HRM points towards its international potentialities. While the employment relationship is materially affected and defined by national and related institutional contexts, these variations in labour markets and national business systems give rise to a wide variety of employment policies and strategies for the management of labour within broadly defined capitalist economies. To the extent that an employer operates within the confines of a national business system, characteristics therein do not impinge upon neighbouring business systems. For example, the Americanness of US firms does not impinge on Canadian firms and their employment systems; similarly, the Britishness of UK firms does not impinge on the Irish business system. In contrast to this, in circumstances where employers operate across national borders, these different institutional characteristics may become factors that an employer wishes to change or override. Thus multinational corporations (MNCs) may seek to deploy centralised – more homogenous – employment strategies, regardless of the institutional character of national business systems where they locate subsidiary operations.

Multinational corporations are significant international actors in the world economy and play a key role in the trend towards 'globalisation', contributing to industrial development and restructuring within and across the borders of national business systems. But MNCs are not itinerant or transnational as is often suggested. Management style, strategies and policies are shaped by home business systems – the financial, institutional, legal and political frameworks in which they developed as domestic firms. Thus there is a persistent 'country of origin' effect in the behaviour of MNCs whereby the country from where an MNC originates exerts a distinctive effect on management style, particularly the management of human resources. Hirst and Thompson (1999: 84) demonstrate that the majority of MNCs are disproportionately concentrated in their country of origin, sell the majority of their goods and services there and hold the majority of their assets there. In addition to this home country or country of origin effect, government regulation in countries where subsidiary operations of MNCs are located may also have an effect on shaping company practices for the management of human resources. In some respects the impact of a 'host country' business system may constrain the preferred practices that reflect embedded patterns of regulation in an MNC's country of origin.

This interplay between home and host country influences raises important questions (for HR academics and practitioners employed in national and multinational firms) about the nature of international competitiveness and associated questions about how MNCs draw on and seek to diffuse competitive advantage from the business system in which they originate. *International* human resource management for global workforces is central to this question; policies to attract, retain, remunerate, develop and motivate staff are increasingly vital for the development of international competitive advantage. Thus the significance of these issues is not confined to theoretical debates on the nature and scope of globalisation; they are of considerable significance in respect of what becomes 'best practice' in and between different business systems. For example, in the UK, US MNCs are widely diffused and account for approximately 50 per cent of foreign direct investment (Ferner, 2003), and there is considerable evidence to suggest that subsidiaries of US MNCs diffuse *international* HRM, that is, within individual MNCs. But in addition to this there is evidence that US MNCs act as innovators in business systems where they operate. In the British context, productivity bargaining, performance-related pay, job evaluation, employee share option schemes, appraisal, single-status employment and direct employee involvement are now widely diffused in indigenous firms but were pioneered in subsidiaries of US MNCs; see Edwards and Ferner (2002) for a review of empirical material on US MNCs.

In summary, MNCs may seek to deploy centralised employment policies to subsidiary operations, a tendency that is more pronounced in US and Japanese subsidiaries but less so in the case of German MNCs. Some MNCs, notably US ones, have powerful corporate HR functions which 'roll out' programmatic approaches to HRM that monitor subsidiaries against an array of detailed performance targets. So within MNCs *international* HRM may create broad-based HR systems that minimise or override differences between national business systems and, by contrast, emphasise the importance of organisational cultures that are drawn from the strategic goals of the firm. Management style and practices for HRM in MNCs are shaped by the interplay between home and host country and, as Chapter 15 demonstrates, this interplay focuses ongoing debates about the institutional embeddedness of national business systems and the cultural impact of MNCs in overseas economies.

| **Stop and think** | This section has proposed four broad perspectives of HRM. Which most closely corresponds to your interpretations of HRM and why? |

Some assumptions about human resource management

Figure 1.1 sets out the four perspectives on HRM discussed above, and locates key aspects of the HRM focus within its framework. Such a schematic presentation not only demonstrates the breadth of these operational assumptions, but also underlines their ambiguity. Within many organisations the circumstances in which human resource management is pursued will be critically determined by the state of the labour market at any particular time: it is thus perfectly understandable for an organisation to be moving towards a strategic dimension of HRM in its own terms, but to find it necessary to revert or regroup to a modified version of its original policy. A case in point here might be that of British Airways, which deployed both the developmental and strategic/international models of HRM throughout the 1980s in order to support its 'Customer Care' business plan, but found itself increasingly relying on the restatement and fusion models as it sought to reorganise its Gatwick operations (including Dan-Air) in the 1990s. This gave rise to industrial relations difficulties, with strong residual problems over wage levels for cabin staff leading to strike threats in 1996, which were realised in 1997. At a cost of some £125 million BA sustained strike action by cabin crews, worldwide, over pay and conditions. One outcome of the dispute was that BA hired new staff for a start-up company *Go* on contracts that were 20 per cent cheaper than those for BA staff, thus further emphasising the cost-minimisation model of hard HRM and linking this with the fusion model. By 2002 BA's corporate and HR strategies were in disarray. In the wake of 11 September and the collapse of transatlantic travel BA announced its 'future shape and size' strategy which involved two aspects: firstly, a concentration on first and business class travellers, an aspiration that renewed its customer care plan pioneered in the

| Figure 1.1 | Four perspectives on human resource management |

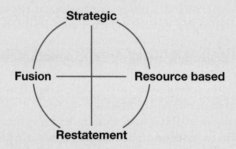

Strategic	**Fusion**
Employment policy derived from business objectives; HRM major contributor to business policy; translation of HRM policy across cultures	PM and IR no longer seen as operationally distinct; managerially derived agenda; replacement of collectivism with stronger role for individualism

Restatement	**Resource based**
PM and IR as prevailing model; HRM style outcomes sought within a pluralist framework	Individualistically derived; stress on input provided by organisation on behalf of employee

1980s, and secondly, rationalisation of services at, or withdrawal from, some regional airports, an announcement that in effect conceded BA's inability to compete with low-cost carriers on some routes. This admission appears all the more painful owing to BA's recent sell-off of *Go* to a management buy-out. In effect, BA's lack of competitiveness in a period of global downturn in international travel, combined with the emergence of low-cost airlines which have outperformed the market (increased market share), forced the company to revert to harder HRM, further emphasising the cost reduction model; see Clark *et al.* (2002).

If further evidence were needed of the shifts in HRM that can occur when businesses come under pressure, then BMW's handling of the Rover group sale and Barclays' branch closure programme, both in the spring of 2000, provide ample evidence that approaches to HRM are prone to severe buffeting, whatever the original intent of the business. In BMW's case it sought to fuse a European style of communication and involvement with the Japanese style already existing within Rover as a result of the latter's Honda collaboration over the previous decade; in Barclays' case it saw the need to maintain its role as a 'big bank in a big world' by cutting 10 per cent of its branch network in one operation. Competitive product and service market pressures can quickly overwhelm the best of HRM intentions.

More recently, closure announcements by Corus (formerly British Steel), motor manu-facturers Ford and General Motors and relocation decisions made by the Prudential, British Telecom and Massey Ferguson demonstrate the UK's exposure to MNCs. Here an emergent pattern of strategic decision-making, sometimes made on a pan-European basis, illustrates some embedded characteristics of the British business system, such as compara-tively loose redundancy laws, to demonstrate that host country characteristics need not constrain MNCs (see Almond *et al.*, 2003). In each case the competitive pressures associ-ated with the value of sterling, comparative labour costs, skill levels and unit labour costs, or delayed investment decisions overrode softer developmental aspects of HRM. This pattern illustrates how European consolidation in MNCs and the more general pur-suit of 'shareholder value' further consolidate the cost-minimisation model of hard HRM.

Although these four interpretations of HRM each contain strong distinguishing char-acteristics, they are by no means mutually exclusive: indeed, it would be surprising if that were so. In this sense they constitute not a model of HRM but a set of perspectives on HRM that organisations bring to bear on the employment relationship. A more useful approach to interpreting these perspectives might be to recognise that many organisations may display at least one of these principal perspectives but will also rely on several characteristics drawn from at least one and probably more of the other three constructs. In this sense HRM, as a set of issues as well as a set of practices, contains ambivalence and contradiction quite as much as clarity and affirmation. In many organ-isations the tension that arises from this outcome is part of the internal process of the management of uncertainty. With the privatisation of British Rail and the multiplicity of operating companies, there has been a distinct move away from the business-led strate-gies of the former BR operating divisions to a more traditional pattern of collective agreements involving negotiations between the unions and the individual owners of the new companies. A further discussion of some of these aspects of HRM can be found in Guest (1989a).

The search for the defining characteristics of HRM

An important part of the debate, both in the USA and in the UK, has been the search for the defining characteristics that will describe, analyse and explain the HRM phenome-non. To a considerable extent this quest has proved largely unresolved because of the wide range of prescriptions and expectations placed upon the term, and the relative lack of available evidence to determine systematically whether or not HRM has taken root as a sustainable model of employee management. This difficulty is further compounded if one considers a series of critical questions about human resource management:

- Is HRM a practitioner-driven process that has attracted a wider audience and prompted subsequent analytical attention?
- Is HRM an academically derived description of the employment relationship, to which practitioners have subsequently become drawn?
- Is HRM essentially a prescriptive model of how such a relationship 'ought' to be?
- Is it a 'leading edge' approach as to how such a relationship actually 'is' within certain types of organisation?

Each of these questions leads the search for the innate qualities of HRM along different routes and towards different conclusions. If the first approach is adopted, then evidence is required that would identify the location, incidence and adoption of defined HRM practices and suggest factors that caused organisations to develop those approaches. The second approach would have to locate the HRM debate in the academic discussion of the employment relationship and demonstrate why this particular variant of analysis emerged. The third approach would have to explain why, among so many other prescriptions concerning management, the HRM prescription emerged and quite what the distinctive elements were that permitted its prescriptive influence to gain acceptance. The final approach would have to provide satisfactory evidence that, where HRM had developed within certain organisational contexts, the evidence of the particular setting could be applied to the generality of the employment relationship.

However, when these questions have all been taken into account there still remains the residual problem that none of them can conclusively define the nature of HRM in its own terms to the exclusion of each of the others. What are seen as practitioner-derived examples of HRM can be matched by similar policies in non-HRM-espousing organisations; what are seen as academically derived models of HRM are each open to large areas of contention and disagreement between analysts; what are seen as prescriptive models of 'what ought to be' might well be just that and no more; and what could be held up as 'leading edge' examples could be wholly determined by the particular circumstances of organisations that are either incapable of translation into other contexts, or may indeed be unsustainable within the original organisations as circumstances change. Storey (1992: 30) outlines this competing set of considerations within the debate very clearly.

These considerations have not prevented the active debate about the nature of HRM proceeding with increasing velocity and breadth. A significant division can be noted between those analyses that seek to stress the innovative element of HRM, which is claimed to address the fundamental question of managing employees in new ways and with new perspectives, and those that stress its derivative elements, which are claimed to be no more than a reworking of the traditional themes of personnel management. Thus Walton (1985: 77–84), in attempting definitions of HRM, stresses mutuality between employers and employees:

> Mutual goals, mutual influence, mutual respect, mutual rewards, mutual responsibility. The theory is that policies of mutuality will elicit commitment which in turn will yield both better economic performance and greater human development.

Beer and Spector (1985) emphasised a different set of assumptions in shaping their meaning of HRM:

- proactive system-wide interventions, with emphasis on 'fit', linking HRM with strategic planning and cultural change;
- people as social capital capable of development;
- the potential for developing coincidence of interest between stakeholders;

- the search for power equalisation for trust and collaboration;
- open channels of communication to build trust and commitment;
- goal orientation;
- participation and informed choice.

Conversely, some writers, most notably Legge (1989) and Fowler (1987), have commented that personnel management was beginning to emerge as a more strategic function in the late 1970s and early 1980s before the concept was subsumed under the title of HRM, and that in this sense there is little new in HRM practice.

However, allowing for problems of definitions and demarcation lines between various conceptions of human resource management, there is little doubt that HRM became a fashionable concept and a controversial subject in the 1980s, with its boundaries very much overlapping the traditional areas of personnel management, industrial relations, organisational behaviour and strategic and operational management. Its emergence created a controversy, which extends through most of the issues that touch on the employment relationship. Many proponents of HRM argue that it addresses the centrality of employees in the organisation, and that their motivation and commitment to the organisational goals need to be nurtured. While this is by no means a new concept, the HRM perspective would claim at least to present a different perspective on this issue, namely that a range of organisational objectives have been arranged in a strategic way to enhance the performance of employees in achieving these goals. Before examining these arguments in more detail, a brief account of the origins and recent historical development of HRM would be appropriate in order to understand why it emerged when and as it did.

The origins of human resource management

As we saw earlier in this chapter, HRM can be seen as part of the wider and longer debate about the nature of management in general and the management of employees in particular. This means that tracing the antecedents of HRM is as elusive an exercise as arriving at its defining characteristics. Certainly there are antecedents in organisational theory, and particularly that of the human relations school, but the nature of HRM has involved important elements of strategic management and business policy, coupled with operations management, which make a simple 'family tree' explanation of HRM's derivation highly improbable.

What can be said is that the origins of HRM lie within employment practices associated with welfare capitalist employers in the United States during the 1930s. Both Jacoby (1997) and Foulkes (1980) argue that this type of employer exhibited an ideological opposition to unionisation and collective relations. As an alternative, welfare capitalists believed the firm, rather than third-party institutions such as the state or trade unions, should provide for the security and welfare of workers. To deter any propensity to unionise, especially once President Roosevelt's New Deal programme commenced after 1933, welfare capitalists often paid efficiency wages, introduced health care coverage, pension plans and provided lay-off pay. Equally, they conducted regular surveys of employee opinion and sought to secure employee commitment via the promotion of strong centralised corporate cultures and long-term cum permanent employment. Welfare capitalists pioneered individual performance-related pay, profit-sharing schemes and what is now termed teamworking. This model of employment regulation had a pioneering role in the development in what is now termed HRM but rested on structural features such as stable product markets and the absence of marked business cycles. While the presence of HRM was well established in the American business system before the 1980s, it was only after that period that HRM gained external recognition by academics and practitioners.

There are a number of reasons for its emergence since then, among the most important of which are the major pressures experienced in product markets during the recession of 1980–82, combined with a growing recognition in the USA that trade union influence in collective employment was reaching fewer employees. By the 1980s the US economy was being challenged by overseas competitors, most particularly Japan. Discussion tended to focus on two issues: 'the productivity of the American worker', particularly compared with the Japanese worker, 'and the declining rate of innovation in American industries' (Devanna *et al.*, 1984: 33). From this sprang a desire to create a work situation free from conflict, in which both employers and employees worked in unity towards the same goal – the success of the organisation (Fombrun, 1984: 17). Beyond these prescriptive arguments and as a wide-ranging critique of institutional approaches to industrial relations analysis, Kaufman (1993) suggests that a preoccupation with pluralist industrial relations within and beyond the period of the New Deal excluded the non-union sector of the US economy for many years. In summary, welfare capitalist employers (soft HRM) and anti-union employers (hard HRM) are embedded features within the US business system, whereas the New Deal Model was a contingent response to economic crisis in the 1930s.

In the UK in the 1980s the business climate also became conducive to changes in the employment relationship. As in the USA, this was partly driven by economic pressure in the form of increased product market competition, the recession in the early part of the decade and the introduction of new technology. However, a very significant factor in the UK, generally absent from the USA, was the desire of the government to reform and reshape the conventional model of industrial relations, which provided a rationale for the development of more employer-oriented employment policies on the part of management (Beardwell, 1992, 1996). The restructuring of the economy saw a rapid decline in the old industries and a relative rise in the service sector and in new industries based on 'high-tech' products and services, many of which were comparatively free from the established patterns of what was sometimes termed the 'old' industrial relations. These changes were overseen by a muscular entrepreneurialism promoted by the Thatcher Conservative government in the form of privatisation and anti-union legislation 'which encouraged firms to introduce new labour practices and to re-order their collective bargaining arrangements' (Hendry and Pettigrew, 1990: 19).

The influence of the US 'excellence' literature (e.g. Peters and Waterman, 1982; Kanter, 1984) also associated the success of 'leading edge' companies with the motivation of employees by involved management styles that also responded to market changes. As a consequence, the concepts of employee commitment and 'empowerment' became another strand in the ongoing debate about management practice and HRM.

A review of these issues suggests that any discussion of HRM has to come to terms with at least three fundamental problems:

● that HRM is derived from a range of antecedents, the ultimate mix of which is wholly dependent upon the stance of the analyst, and which may be drawn from an eclectic range of sources;
● that HRM is itself a contributory factor in the analysis of the employment relationship, and sets part of the context in which that debate takes place;
● that it is difficult to distinguish where the significance of HRM lies – whether it is in its supposed transformation of styles of employee management in a specific sense, or whether in a broader sense it is in its capacity to sponsor a wholly redefined relationship between management and employees that overcomes the traditional issues of control and consent at work.

This ambivalence over the definition, components and scope of HRM can be seen when examining some of the main UK and US analyses. An early model of HRM, developed by Fombrun *et al.* (1984), introduced the concept of strategic human resource management by which HRM policies are inextricably linked to the 'formulation and implementation of strategic corporate and/or business objectives' (Devanna *et al.*, 1984: 34). The model is illustrated in Figure 1.2.

Figure 1.2	The matching model of HRM

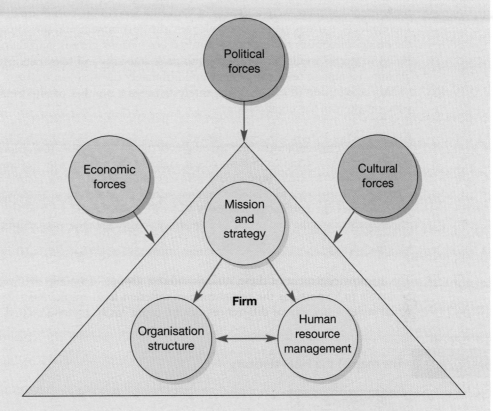

Source: Devanna *et al.* (1984) in Fombrun *et al.*, *Strategic Human Resource Management*. © 1984 John Wiley & Sons, Inc. Reproduced with permission of John Wiley & Sons, Inc.

The matching model emphasises the necessity of 'tight fit' between HR strategy and business strategy. This in turn has led to a plethora of interpretations by practitioners of how these two strategies are linked. Some offer synergies between human resource planning (manpower planning) and business strategies, with the driving force rooted in the 'product market logic' (Evans and Lorange, 1989). Whatever the process, the result is very much an emphasis on the *unitarist* view of HRM: unitarism assumes that conflict or at least differing views cannot exist within the organisation because the actors – management and employees – are working to the same goal of the organisation's success. What makes the model particularly attractive for many personnel practitioners is the fact that HRM assumes a more important position in the formulation of organisational policies.

The personnel department has often been perceived as an administrative support function with a lowly status. Personnel was now to become very much part of the human resource management of the organisation, and HRM was conceived to be more than personnel and to have peripheries wider than the normal personnel function. In order for HRM to be strategic it had to encompass all the human resource areas of the organisation and be practised by all employees. In addition, decentralisation and devolvement of responsibility are also seen as very much part of the HRM strategy as it facilitates communication, involvement and commitment of middle management and other employees deeper within the organisation. The effectiveness of organisations thus rested on how the strategy and the structure of the organisation interrelated, a concept rooted in the view of the organisation developed by Chandler (1962) and evolved in the matching model.

A more flexible model, illustrated in Figure 1.3, was developed by Beer *et al.* (1984) at Harvard University. 'The map of HRM territory', as the authors titled their model, recognised that there were a variety of 'stakeholders' in the corporation, which included shareholders, various groups of employees, the government and the community. At once the model recognises the legitimate interests of various groups, and that the creation of HRM strategies would have to recognise these interests and fuse them as much as possible into the human resource strategy and ultimately the business strategy.

This recognition of stakeholders' interests raises a number of important questions for policy-makers in the organisation:

> How much responsibility, authority and power should the organisation voluntarily delegate and to whom? If required by government legislation to bargain with the unions or consult with workers' councils, how should management enter into these institutional arrangements? Will they seek to minimize the power and influence of these legislated mechanisms? Or will they share influence and work to create greater congruence of interests between management and the employee groups represented through these mechanisms?
>
> (Beer *et al.*, 1984: 8)

The acknowledgement of these various interest groups has made the model much more amenable to 'export', as the recognition of different legal employment structures, managerial styles and cultural differences can be more easily accommodated within it. This

---

Figure 1.3   The map of the HRM territory

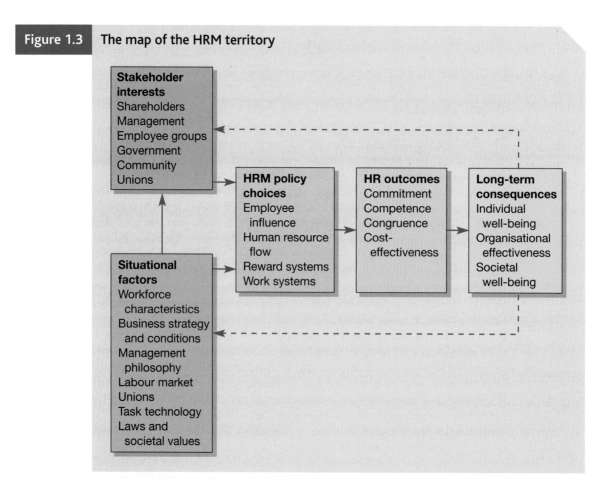

Source: Beer *et al.* (1984: 16). Reprinted with permission of The Free Press, a division of Simon & Schuster, from *Managing Human Assets* by Michael Beer, Bert Spector, Paul R. Lawrence, D. Quinn Mills and Richard E. Walton. Copyright © 1984 by The Free Press.

neopluralist model has also been recognised as being useful in the study of comparative HRM (Poole, 1990: 3–5). It is not surprising, therefore, that the Harvard model has found greater favour among academics and commentators in the UK, which has relatively strong union structures and different labour traditions from those in the United States. Nevertheless, some academics have still criticised the model as being too unitarist, while accepting its basic premise (Hendry and Pettigrew, 1990).

The first two main approaches to HRM that emerged in the UK are based on the Harvard model, which is made up of both prescriptive and analytical elements. Among the most perceptive analysts of HRM, Guest has tended to concentrate on the prescriptive components, while Pettigrew and Hendry rest on the analytical aspect (Boxall, 1992). Although using the Harvard model as a basis, both Guest and Pettigrew and Hendry have some criticisms of the model, and derive from it only that which they consider useful (Guest, 1987, 1989a, 1989b, 1990; Hendry and Pettigrew, 1986, 1990).

As we have seen, there are difficulties of definition and model-building in HRM, and this has led British interpreters to take alternative elements in building their own models. Guest is conscious that if a model is to be useful to researchers it must be useful 'in the field' of research, and this means that elements of HRM have to be pinned down for comparative measurement. He has therefore developed a set of propositions that he believes are amenable to testing. He also asserts that the combination of these propositions, which include strategic integration, high commitment, high quality and flexibility, creates more effective organisations (Guest, 1987).

- *Strategic integration* is defined as 'the ability of organisations to integrate HRM issues into their strategic plans, to ensure that the various aspects of HRM cohere and for line managers to incorporate an HRM perspective into their decision making'.
- *High commitment* is defined as being 'concerned with both behavioural commitment to pursue agreed goals and attitudinal commitment reflected in a strong identification with the enterprise'.
- *High quality* 'refers to all aspects of managerial behaviour, including management of employees and investment in high-quality employees, which in turn will bear directly on the quality of the goods and services provided'.
- Finally, *flexibility* is seen as being 'primarily concerned with what is sometimes called functional flexibility but also with an adaptable organisational structure with the capacity to manage innovation' (Guest, 1989b: 42).

The combination of these propositions leads to a linkage between HRM aims, policies and outcomes as shown in Table 1.1. Whether there is enough evidence to assess the relevance and efficacy of these HRM relationships will be examined later.

Hendry and Pettigrew (1990) have adapted the Harvard model by drawing on its analytical aspects. They see HRM 'as a perspective on employment systems, characterised by their closer alignment with business strategy'. This model, illustrated in Figure 1.4, attempts a theoretically integrative framework encompassing all styles and modes of HRM and making allowances for the economic, technical and socio-political influences in society on the organisational strategy. 'It also enables one to describe the "preconditions" governing a firm's employment system, along with the consequences of the latter'

Table 1.1 **A human resource management framework**

HRM aims	HRM policies	HRM outcomes
For example: • high commitment • quality • flexible working	For example: • selection based on specific criteria using sophisticated tests	For example: • low labour turnover • allegiance to company

Source: Storey (1989: 11)

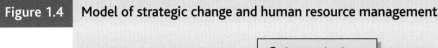

Figure 1.4   Model of strategic change and human resource management

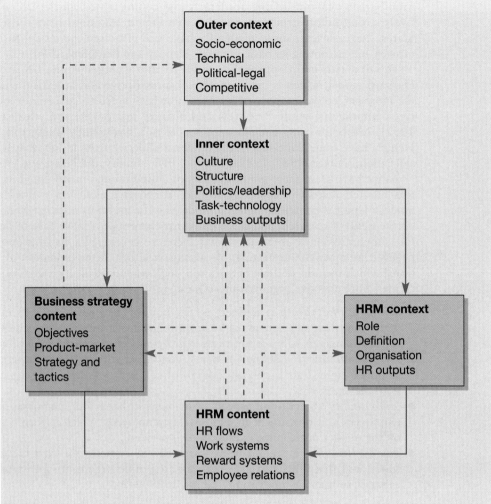

Source: Hendry and Pettigrew (1990: 6). Reproduced by kind permission of Chapman & Hall, a division of International Thomson Publishing Services.

(Hendry and Pettigrew, 1990: 25). It thus explores 'more fully the implications for employee relations of a variety of approaches to strategic management' (Boxall, 1992).

Storey studied a number of UK organisations in a series of case studies, and as a result modified still further the approaches of previous writers on HRM (Storey, 1992). Storey had previously identified two types of HRM – 'hard' and 'soft' (Storey, 1989) – the one rooted in the manpower planning approach and the other in the human relations school. He begins his approach by defining four elements that distinguish HRM:

1   It is 'human capability and commitment which, in the final analysis, distinguishes successful organisations from the rest'.
2   Because HRM is of strategic importance, it needs to be considered by top management in the formulation of the corporate plan.
3   'HRM is, therefore, seen to have long-term implications and to be integral to the core performance of the business or public sector organisation. In other words it must be the intimate concern of line managers.'
4   The key levers (the deployment of human resources, evaluation of performance and the rewarding of it, etc.) 'are to be used to seek not merely compliance but commitment'.

Storey (1992) approaches an analysis of HRM by creating an 'ideal type', the purpose of which 'is to simplify by highlighting the essential features in an exaggerated way' (p. 34). This he does by making a classificatory matrix of 27 points of difference between personnel and IR practices and HRM practices (see Table 1.2). The elements are categorised in a four-part basic outline:

- beliefs and assumptions;
- strategic concepts;

Table 1.2 Twenty-seven points of difference

Dimension	Personnel and IR	HRM
Beliefs and assumptions		
1 Contract	Careful delineation of written contracts	Aim to go 'beyond contract'
2 Rules	Importance of devising clear rules/mutuality	'Can-do' outlook; impatience with 'rule'
3 Guide to management action	Procedures	'Business need'
4 Behaviour referent	Norms/custom and practice	Values/mission
5 Managerial task vis-à-vis labour	Monitoring	Nurturing
6 Nature of relations	Pluralist	Unitarist
7 Conflict	Institutionalised	De-emphasised
Strategic aspects		
8 Key relations	Labour management	Customer
9 Initiatives	Piecemeal	Integrated
10 Corporate plan	Marginal to	Central to
11 Speed of decision	Slow	Fast
Line management		
12 Management role	Transactional	Transformational leadership
13 Key managers	Personnel/IR specialists	General/business/line managers
14 Communication	Indirect	Direct
15 Standardisation	High (e.g. 'parity' an issue)	Low (e.g. 'parity' not seen as relevant)
16 Prized management skills	Negotiation	Facilitation
Key levers		
17 Selection	Separate, marginal task	Integrated, key task
18 Pay	Job evaluation (fixed grades)	Performance-related
19 Conditions	Separately negotiated	Harmonisation
20 Labour management	Collective bargaining contracts	Towards individual contracts
21 Thrust of relations with stewards	Regularised through facilities and training	Marginalised (with exception of some bargaining for change models)
22 Job categories and grades	Many	Few
23 Communication	Restricted flow	Increased flow
24 Job design	Division of labour	Teamwork
25 Conflict handling	Reach temporary truces	Manage climate and culture
26 Training and development	Controlled access to courses	Learning companies
27 Foci of attention for interventions	Personnel procedures	Wide-ranging cultural, structural and personnel strategies

Source: Storey (1992: 38). Reproduced by kind permission of Blackwell Publishers.

Figure 1.5	A model of the shift to human resource management

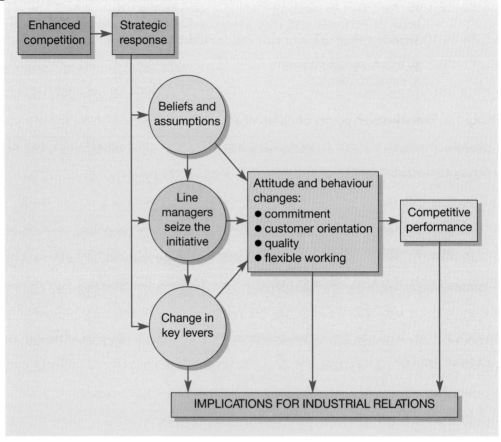

Source: Storey (1992: 38). Reproduced by kind permission of Blackwell Publishers.

- line management;
- key levers.

This 'ideal type' of HRM model is not essentially an aim in itself but more a tool in enabling sets of approaches to be pinpointed in organisations for research and analytical purposes.

Storey's theoretical model is thus based on conceptions of how organisations have been transformed from predominantly personnel/IR practices to HRM practices. As it is based on the ideal type, there are no organisations that conform to this picture in reality. It is in essence a tool for enabling comparative analysis. He illustrates this by proposing 'a model of the shift to human resource management', shown in Figure 1.5.

Human resource management: the state of the debate

The question of whether human resource management has the capacity to transform or replace deeply rooted models of personnel management and industrial relations, or could become a fully worked-through theory of management, is one that cannot be answered in a simple manner. Human resource management has many cogent critics and many sceptical supporters. Initial criticism which claimed that it was 'old wine in new bottles', the restatement perspective outlined earlier in this chapter, still has strong adherents (Keenoy and Anthony, 1992). Others see it as a version of 'the emperor's new clothes' (Legge, 1989) or a 'wolf in sheep's clothing' (Armstrong, 1987; Fowler, 1987; Keenoy, 1990a).

Tom Keenoy is one of the most eloquent and persuasive of critics, and his examination of HRM has exposed many of the *a priori* assumptions and non-sequiturs that abound in the reasoning of its supporters. He claims that HRM is more rhetoric than reality and has been 'talked up' by its advocates. It has little support in terms of evidence, and has been a convenient dustbin of rationalisation to support ideological shifts in the employment relationship brought about by market pressures. It is also full of contradictions, not only in its meanings but also in its practice.

In examining the meanings of HRM Keenoy notes that a 'remarkable feature of the HRM phenomenon is the brilliant ambiguity of the term itself'. He later continues: 'On the "Alice principle" that a term means whatever one chooses it to mean, each of these interpretations may be valid but, in Britain, the absence of any intellectual touchstones has resulted in the term being subject to the process of almost continuous and contested conceptual elision' (Keenoy, 1990b: 363–384).

Legge (1989) has shown that a close examination of the normative models of HRM and personnel management reveals little difference between the two, and that HRM contains a number of internal contradictions. Legge points out that there is a problem with integration in the sense that HRM policies have to integrate with business policy. She asks: 'Is it possible to have a corporation-wide mutually reinforcing set of HRM policies, if the organisation operates in highly diverse product markets, and, if not, does it matter, in terms of organisational effectiveness?' (p. 30). She also asks: 'If the business strategy should dictate the choice of HRM policies, will some strategies dictate policies that . . . fail to emphasise commitment, flexibility and quality?' (p. 30). Legge also comments on the probable incompatibility of creating an organisational culture that attempts to pursue both individualistic and teamwork policies at the same time.

Other critics have indicated that many organisations are driven by stronger objectives than HRM. Armstrong (1989) has pointed to the financial orientations of most companies, which are incompatible with those prescriptions described as imperative in the practice of HRM. Furthermore, the belief that human resource management can transcend national cultures has attracted considerable critical comment (Pieper, 1990).

The 1990s saw a growing sophistication in the nature of the debate involving HRM. The nature of the debate at the conclusion of that decade was much more extensive than that which ushered it in. One signal factor was the reconstruction and expansion of the most important research 'engine' in the UK, the Workplace Employee Relations Survey of 1998 (Cully *et al.*, 1999), which has specifically addressed HRM-based issues of techniques and performance. Part of this development has been promoted by the realisation that traditional sources of competitive advantage, such as technological supremacy, patents and capital, are much less important than they were, in a world in which many countries can display equal advantage in at least some of these critical aspects (Pfeffer, 1994, 1998). Thus the extent to which an organisation can mobilise its internal human resources may hold the key to achievable advantage in the future (Prahalad and Hamel, 1990).

Wood (1995) has examined high-commitment management in terms of what he calls the 'four pillars of HRM' and their ability to deliver significant HRM performance; Guest and Hoque (1996) have examined the concept of 'fit' in the specific circumstances of HRM techniques in greenfield sites and the 'bundles' of practice that might affect performance; Purcell (1996, 1999) has critically examined the notion of 'bundles' but has provided a thoughtful analysis of resource-based HRM in the context of corporate strategy (1995); while Boxall has sought to relate resource-based analysis to the strategic HRM debate (1996).

A number of commentators (e.g. Storey, 1992; Guest, 1997; Gratton *et al.*, 1999) have noted that there appears to be fairly extensive use of individual HR practices in UK organisations. However, the extent to which these are linked together into a meaningful strategic whole is more contentious (Storey, 2001). WERS (Cully *et al.*, 1999) found evidence of each of the 15 practices identified by the survey as indicative of HRM but only three of them (formal grievance and disciplinary procedures, team-briefing and regular appraisals) appear in more than half of workplaces. The practices are more likely to occur in workplaces with an employment relations specialist and an integrated employee development plan, suggesting some level of strategic integration. However, only 14 per cent of workplaces have eight or more of the practices while 29 per cent have fewer then three. The WERS team argue that 'there is evidence that a number of practices consistent with a human resource management approach are well entrenched in many British workplaces' (Cully *et al.*, 1999:82) but the practices are often adopted in a pragmatic and piecemeal way.

Stop and think   Why hasn't the adoption of HRM practices been more widespread in the UK?

Sisson (2001: 80–81) identifies two main explanations to account for the low take-up of some HR practices. The first is that the time, resources and costs associated with change may tempt managers to adopt an incremental approach, i.e. 'to try one or two elements and assess their impact before going further, even though this means forgoing the benefits of the integration associated with bundles of complementary practices'. The second (and in Sisson's words, 'less comfortable') explanation is that HRM is only one means of achieving competitive advantage and other methods adopted by organisations, e.g. mergers, joint ventures, cost-cutting and new forms of Taylorism, do not involve a change in the way people are managed.

A further element in the contemporary discussion is the question of whether HRM affords line management more control of the HR function than HR specialists themselves have. If one of the attributes of HRM is its devolution to the line, then perhaps a logical consequence is the relative loss of influence and control by the erstwhile keepers of the corporate personnel conscience. Does this matter? In the words of Fernie *et al.* (1994), is HRM all 'Big Hat, No Cattle'? The extent to which HRM activity has shifted to the line, and the associated question of whether personnel managers are any more strategic in their role than in the past, is difficult to determine conclusively. The Second Company Level Industrial Relations Survey (Marginson *et al.*, 1993) found no evidence to support general strategic involvement, and some evidence that, without a personnel director on the board, involvement in the formulation of human resource policy was weakened – findings largely supported by Purcell and Ahlstrand's (1994) study of multi-divisional organisations. Perhaps the clearest evidence to suggest that personnel management was losing out to the line is provided by Storey's (1992) study of 'mainstream' companies and the introduction of HRM, although a study of 28 organisations by Kelly and Gennard (1994) presented a different picture based on interviews with personnel directors.

In an important sense, therefore, one answer to Storey's (1995) rhetorical question 'HRM: still marching on or marching out?' is that 'the domain is still lively, vibrant and contested' (Storey, 2001: 16). And a reaction to Bach and Sisson's (2000) view that the flood-tide of HRM is waning is to note that the tide appears still to be flooding strongly, with new aspects appearing on the agenda or existing issues further strengthening their position. What are the agenda items that are currently concerning academics and practitioners? Perhaps three particular aspects can serve from the strategy, style and outcome debate explored at the outset.

From a strategic perspective, one can explore the tendency of organisations to adopt similar approaches. Purcell (2001: 75) outlines three factors that might account for this:

firstly, the tendency to copy 'best practice' because it appears to work but without understanding why this might be the case. Secondly, organisations might be pressured by the short-termism in the capital market or by major customers to do – or not do – certain things, e.g. training. Thirdly, the rise of HR consultancies has led to a spread of ideas that encourage conformity.

An approach to the style perspective might be seen in the role of the psychological contract and employee motivation. Guest and Conway (1997) point to evidence that suggests that employees report positive responses to issues such as fairness, trust and delivery on promises. The Fourth WERS survey of 1998 noted that 68 per cent of workplaces with over 500 employees report participation in problem-solving groups. There is a large agenda item that is concerned with examining and assessing the scope and significance of managerial styles in terms of involvement, commitment and delivery on the part of the employer, and the resultant response from employees to give assent and commitment to management systems that stress these aspects of the employment relationship. What is unclear is how these factors hold over time, and whether component elements within this agenda will remain significant or important and thus weaken or strengthen the concept.

The third area for further work lies in the area of outcomes. At the present time there is much work exploring the nature of HRM 'bundles', and one might expect more as the data from WERS 98 are analysed further. Perhaps one strand of this debate is worth emphasis – high-commitment management and the emphasis on work management systems that achieve specific outcomes (Wood and De Menezes, 1998). This approach seems to have found good evidence that a particular managerial style, allied to a particular combination of practices, will lead to beneficial business outcomes. Again, whether this is sustainable over time remains a key question and, as we have already discussed, a number of doubts have been raised over the validity of the claims. Nevertheless, it represents a significant addition to the literature and practice of HRM.

If these three approaches to research, analysis and practice in HRM are indicative of its breadth and strength at the beginning of the twenty-first century, is there a way in which one can summarise these initiatives? Given that emphasis has been placed in the past on strategy, fit and integration, perhaps one final element ought to be noted as a key ingredient – that of *mix*. Whatever the strategic intent, managerial style, outcomes sought or tight–loose 'fit' adopted by organisations, it will be in the mix of these components that we will find not only some answers to questions but also the further development of HRM as a significant approach to managing employees.

Summary

- Human resource management presents significant issues for the analysis and operation of employment relationships. The management of employees is one of the key elements in the coordination and general management of work organisations. Considerable controversy exists as to the origins, characteristics and philosophy of HRM, and its capacity to influence the nature of that relationship. The debate surrounding HRM can be characterised by these four predominant approaches:
  - HRM as a contemporary 'restatement' of industrial relations and personnel management policies;
  - HRM as a 'fusion' of industrial relations and personnel management to create a 'new' management discipline and function;
  - HRM as a 'resource-based' approach, stressing the potential of the individual employee in terms of an investment rather than a cost;
  - HRM as a 'strategic/international' phenomenon, making a determining contribution to corporate strategy and capable of being translated across cultures.

● The origins of HRM may be traced back to the 1930s in the United States. By the early 1980s a number of US analysts were writing about HRM and devising models and explanations for its emergence. Among the most significant of these commentators are Devanna (the matching model), Beer (the Harvard model), and Walton. In the UK, significant commentary on HRM has been provided by Guest, Pettigrew and Hendry, Storey, and Poole. More recently, Huselid, McDuffie and Arthur have extended the analysis to HRM 'bundles'.

● For Guest the test of HRM is its applicability 'in the field' and its capacity to satisfy some key propositions such as 'strategic integration', 'high commitment', 'high quality' and 'flexibility'. Pettigrew and Hendry stress the analytical elements of the Harvard model, and argue that HRM is characterised by its close alignment with business strategy. Storey defines the 'schools' of HRM – 'hard' (rooted in the manpower planning tradition) and 'soft' (rooted in the human relations approach to organisational analysis), and has developed a model that sets out four areas for analysis: beliefs and assumptions; strategic aspects; line management; key levers as major determinants of HRM practice. Poole has suggested that the Harvard model of HRM is useful in the study of comparative HRM.

● Particularly critical perspectives on HRM in the UK have been provided by Legge, Armstrong and Keenoy. Legge argues that the underlying values of personnel management and HRM differ little, and that organisational constraints may well make a truly integrated HRM approach highly impractical, while Armstrong has noted that financial orientations may well clash with HRM prescriptions. Keenoy sees HRM as being constructed around the highly ambiguous nature of the term, which can come to mean anything to anyone.

● Whatever the perspective taken on HRM, two important points cannot be overlooked: first, it has raised questions about the nature of the employment relationship that have stimulated one of the most intense and active debates to have occurred in the subject over the past 40 years; and second, the management of employment relations and the question of employee commitment to the employment relationship remain at the heart of the debate.

ACTIVITY

VP – Human Resources

Headquartered in the USA, our client is a Fortune 500 company with sales offices in 59 countries and a turnover exceeding $9 billion. This is an electronics distribution business, which markets, inventories and adds value to the products of the most prestigious manufacturers worldwide.

The European operation, employing over 2000 people with sales of $2 billion, has grown dramatically through recent and extensive acquisitions. The challenge facing the new Vice President of Human Resources is to lead the integration of this newly amalgamated group of companies into a single dynamic entity with high productivity, commitment and morale. He or she must also organise a new Pan European HR team and move it quickly to best practice.

Electronics distribution is an extremely fast-moving and complex business. While previous experience in this industry is not essential, you will definitely need a breadth of European HR experience in a fast-moving and tough business environment, and have high levels of mental agility, flexibility and perseverance.

You will probably have a degree, speak more than one European language, and have excellent interpersonal skills, although ability to deliver is what really counts.

Director of Human Resources

We are one of Britain's leading broadband communications companies, providing residential cable, business communication and network services. Our aim is to create an integrated communications and media group delivering a range of voice, video and interactive services across multiple platforms underpinned by branded digital media content.

We are restructuring our organisational capabilities following rapid year-on-year growth, and are now seeking an exceptional and dynamic individual to join our human resources team. Reporting to the Corporate Human Resources Director, the successful applicant will:

- operate as a key member of the senior executive team for the Business, Network and Commercial Services groups, supporting 2500 employees nationwide;
- develop and deliver a human resources strategy that meets current and future business needs;
- manage a diverse brief including resourcing and retention, change management, organisational design, succession planning and performance management.

Candidates will currently be operating at senior human resources management level in a fast-paced consumer goods or service environment, and may now be seeking their first directorship. Qualified to graduate level, with a highly commercial approach and the ability to contribute to strategic decision-making, candidates must be customer focused and results driven, with a strong operational edge. Outstanding drive and leadership skills will be vital in ensuring rapid and professional organisational transition.

This is a high-profile role with one of the UK's most dynamic and fast-growing companies, providing exceptional career development opportunities. The remuneration package will be commensurate with the profile of the role, including an excellent range of benefits.

Examine these two advertisements, which are seeking senior strategic-level HRM positions. Consider the following two points:

1 Assess whether there are any significant differences in either the strategy, style or outcome of the HRM processes described in these advertisements. What factors would you consider to be significant in the organisational profile of each company?

2 In reviewing the person requirements for these two posts, which kinds of personnel experience and development would you consider suitable for this level of appointment?

References and further reading

Those texts marked with an asterisk are recommended for further reading.

Almond, P., Edwards, T. and Clark, I. (2003 forthcoming) 'Multinationals and changing national business systems in Europe: towards the "shareholder value" model'? *Industrial Relations Journal*, Vol. 34, No. 5.

Armstrong, M. (1987) 'Human resource management: a case of the emperor's new clothes?', *Personnel Management*, Vol. 19, No. 8, pp. 30–35.

Armstrong, P. (1989) 'Limits and possibilities for HRM in an age of management accountancy', in Storey, J. (ed.) *New Perspectives on Human Resource Management*. London: Routledge, pp. 154–166.

Arthur, J.B. (1992) 'The link between business strategy and industrial relations systems in American steel mini-mills', *Industrial and Labour Relations Review*, Vol. 45, No. 3, pp. 488–506.

Arthur, J.B. (1994) 'Effects of human resource systems on manufacturing performance and turnover', *Academy of Management Journal*, Vol. 37, No. 3. pp. 670–687.

Bach, S. and Sisson, K. (eds) (2000) *Personnel Management*. Oxford: Blackwell.

Beardwell, I.J. (1992) 'The new industrial relations: a review of the debate', *Human Resource Management Journal*, Vol. 2, No. 2, pp. 1–8.

Beardwell, I.J. (1996) 'How do we know how it really is?', in Beardwell, I.J. (ed.) *Contemporary Industrial Relations*. Oxford: Oxford University Press, pp. 1–10.

Beer, M. and Spector, B. (1985) 'Corporate wide transformations in human resource management', in Walton, R.E. and Lawrence, E.R. (eds) *Human Resource Management Trends and Challenges*. Boston, Mass.: Harvard Business School Press.

*Beer, M., Spector, B., Lawrence P.R., Quinn Mills, D. and Walton, R.E. (1984) *Managing Human Assets*. New York: Free Press.

Boxall, P.F. (1992) 'Strategic human resource management: beginnings of a new theoretical sophistication?', *Human Resource Management Journal*, Vol. 2, No. 3, pp. 60–79.

*Boxall, P. (1996) 'The strategic HRM debate and the resource-based view of the firm', *Human Resource Management Journal*, Vol. 6, No. 3, pp. 59–75.

Chandler, A. (1962) *Strategy and Structure*. Cambridge, Mass.: Harvard University Press.

Clark, I. (2000) *Governance, The State, Regulation and Industrial Relations*. London: Routledge.

Clark, I., Colling, T., Almond, P., Gunnigle, P., Morley, M., Peters, R. and Portillo, M. (2002) 'Multinationals in Europe 2001–2002: home country, host country and sector effects in the context of crisis', *Industrial Relations Journal*, Vol. 33, No. 5, pp. 446–464.

Cully, M., Woodland, S., O'Reilly, A. and Dix, G. (1999) *Britain at Work: As Depicted by the 1998 Workplace Employee Relations Survey*. London: Routledge.

*Devanna, M.A., Fombrun, C.J. and Tichy, N.M. (1984) 'A framework for strategic human resource management', in Fombrun, C.J., Tichy, M.M. and Devanna, M.A. (eds) *Strategic Human Resource Management*. New York: John Wiley.

Edwards, T. and Ferner, A. (2002) 'The renewed American challenge', *Industrial Relations Journal*, Vol. 33, No 2, pp. 94–111.

Evans, P.A.L. and Lorange, P. (1989) 'Two logics behind human resource management', in Evans, P., Doz, Y. and Laurent, A. (eds) *Human Resource Management in International Firms*. Basingstoke: Macmillan.

Ferner, A. (2003) 'Foreign multinationals and industrial relations innovation in Britain', in Edwards, P. (ed.) *Industrial Relations in Britain*, 2nd edn. Oxford: Blackwell.

Fernie, S., Metcalf, D. and Woodland, S. (1994) *Does HRM Boost Employee Management Relations?* LSE CEP Working Paper No. 546. London: London School of Economics.

Fombrun, C.J. (1984) 'The external context of human resource management', in Fombrun, C.J., Tichy, N.M. and Devanna, M.A. (eds) *Strategic Human Resource Management*. New York: John Wiley, p. 41.

*Fombrun, C.J., Tichy, N.M. and Devanna, M.A. (1984) *Strategic Human Resource Management*. New York: John Wiley.

Foulkes, F. (1980) *Personnel Policies in Large Non-Union Companies*. New Jersey: Prentice Hall.

Fowler, A. (1987) 'When chief executives discover HRM', *Personnel Management*, January, p. 3.

Fox, A. (1966) *Industrial Sociology and Industrial Relations*, Royal Commission on Trade Unions and Employers' Associations, Research Paper No. 3. London: HMSO.

Gratton, L., Hope-Hailey, V., Stiles, P. and Truss, C. (1999) *Strategic Human Resource Management*. Oxford: OUP.

Guest, D. (1987) 'Human resource management and industrial relations', *Journal of Management Studies*, Vol. 24, No. 5, pp. 503–521.

Guest, D. (1989a) 'Personnel and human resource management: can you tell the difference?', *Personnel Management*, January, pp. 48–51.

Guest, D. (1989b) 'Human resource management: its implications for industrial relations and trade unions', in Storey, J. (ed.) *New Perspectives on Human Resource Management*. London: Routledge, pp. 41–55.

*Guest, D. (1990) 'Human resource management and the American dream', *Journal of Management Studies*, Vol. 27, No. 4, pp. 377–397.

Guest, D. (1997) 'Human resource management and performance: a review and research agenda', *International Journal of Human Resource Management*, Vol. 8, No. 3, pp. 263–276.

Guest, D. and Conway, N. (1997) *Employee Motivation and the Psychological Contract*, Issues in Personnel Management 21. London: IPD.

*Guest, D. and Hoque, K. (1996) 'Human resource management and the new industrial relations', in Beardwell, I.J. (ed.) *Contemporary Industrial Relations*. Oxford: Oxford University Press, pp. 11–36.

Hendry, C. and Pettigrew, A. (1986) 'The practice of strategic human resource management', *Personnel Review*, Vol. 15, No. 5, pp. 3–8.

Hendry, C. and Pettigrew, A. (1990) 'Human resource management: an agenda for the 1990s', *International Journal of Human Resource Management*, Vol. 1, No. 1, pp. 17–43.

Hirst, P. and Thompson, G. (1999) *Globalization in Question*, 2nd edn. London: Polity.

*Huselid, M. (1995) 'The impact of HRM practices on turnover, productivity and corporate financial performance', *Academy of Management Journal*, Vol. 38, No. 3, pp. 635–672.

Jacoby, S. (1997) *Modern Manors: Welfare Capitalism Since the New Deal*. New Jersey: Princeton University Press.

Kanter, R. (1984) *The Change Masters*. London: Allen & Unwin.

Kaufman, B. (1993) *The Origins and Evolution of the Field of Industrial Relations*. New York: ILR Press.

Keenoy, T. (1990a) 'HRM: a case of the wolf in sheep's clothing?', *Personnel Review*, Vol. 19, No. 2, pp. 3–9.

*Keenoy, T. (1990b) 'Human resource management: rhetoric, reality and contradiction', *International Journal of Human Resource Management*, Vol. 1, No. 3, pp. 363–384.

Keenoy, T. and Anthony P. (1992) 'Human resource management: metaphor, meaning and morality', in Blyton, P. and Turnbull, P. (eds) *Reassessing Human Resource Management*. London: Sage, pp. 233–255.

Kelly, J. and Gennard, J. (1994) 'HRM: the views of personnel directors', *Human Resource Management Journal*, Vol. 5, No. 1, pp. 15–30.

Legge, K. (1978) *Power, Innovation and Problem Solving in Personnel Management*. London: McGraw-Hill.

*Legge, K. (1989) 'Human resource management: a critical analysis', in Storey, J. (ed.) *New Perspectives on Human Resource Management*. London: Routledge, pp. 19–40.

*Legge, K. (1995) *HRM: Rhetorics and Realities*. Basingstoke: Macmillan Business.

MacInnes, J. (1987) *Thatcherism at Work*. Milton Keynes: Open University Press.

Marginson, P., Armstrong, P., Edwards, P., Purcell, J. and Hubbard, N. (1993) *The Control of Industrial Relations in Large Companies*, Warwick Papers in Industrial Relations No. 45. IRRV School of Industrial and Business Studies, University of Warwick.

McDuffie, J.P. (1995) 'Human resource bundles and manufacturing performance', *Industrial and Labour Relations Review*, Vol. 48, No. 2, pp. 197–221.

McLoughlin, I. and Gourlay, S. (1994) *Enterprise without Unions*. Milton Keynes: Open University Press.

Peters, T.J. and Waterman, R.H. (1982) *In Search of Excellence: Lessons from America's Best Run Companies*. New York: Harper & Row.

Pfeffer, J. (1994) *Competitive Advantage Through People*. Boston, Mass.: Harvard Business School Press.

Pfeffer, J. (1998) *The Human Equation*. Boston, Mass: Harvard Business School Press.

Pieper, R. (ed.) (1990) *Human Resource Management: An International Comparison*. New York: Walter de Gruyter.

Poole, M. (1990) 'Editorial: human resource management in an international perspective', *International Journal of Human Resource Management*, Vol. 1, No. 1, pp. 1–15.

*Prahalad, G. and Hamel, C.K. (1990) 'The core competencies of the corporation', *Harvard Business Review*, May–June, pp. 79–91.

*Purcell, J. (1995) 'Corporate strategy and its link with human resource management strategy', in Storey, J. (ed.) *Human Resource Management: A Critical Text*. London: Routledge, pp. 63–86.

Purcell, J. (1996) 'Human resource bundles of best practice: a utopian cul-de-sac?' Department of Management, University of Bath.

Purcell, J. (1999) 'Best practice and best fit: chimera or cul-de-sac?', *Human Resource Management Journal*, Vol. 9, No. 3, pp. 26–41.

Purcell, J. (2001) 'The meaning of strategy in human resource management', in Storey, J. (ed.) *Human Resource Management: A Critical Text*, 2nd edn. London: Thomson Learning.

Purcell, J. and Ahlstrand, B. (1994) *Human Resource Management in the Multi-Divisional Company*. Oxford: Oxford University Press.

Purcell, J. and Sisson, K. (1983) 'Strategies and practice in the management of industrial relations', in Bain, G. (ed.) *Industrial Relations in Britain*. Oxford: Blackwell, pp. 95–120.

Richardson, R. and Thompson, P. (1999) 'The impact of people management practices on business performance: a literature review' in *Issues in People Management*. London: IPD.

Sisson, K. (1993) 'In search of HRM', *British Journal of Industrial Relations*, Vol. 31, No. 2, pp. 201–210.

*Sisson, K (2001) 'Human resource management and the personnel function: a case of partial impact?' in Storey, J. (ed.) *Human Resource Management: A Critical Text*, 2nd edn. London: Thomson Learning.

Storey, J. (1992) *Developments in the Management of Human Resources: An Analytical Review*. London: Blackwell.

Storey, J. (1995) *Human Resource Management: A Critical Text*. London: Routledge.

*Storey, J. (2001) 'Human resource management today: an assessment', in Storey, J. (ed.) *Human Resource Management: A Critical Text*, 2nd edn. London: Thomson Learning.

Storey, J. (ed.) (1989) *New Perspectives on Human Resource Management*. London: Routledge.

Tyson, S. and Fell, A. (1986) *Evaluating the Personnel Function*. London: Hutchinson.

Ulrich, D. (1998) *Human Resource Champions*. Boston: Harvard Business School Press.

Walton, R.E. (1985) 'From control to commitment in the workplace', *Harvard Business Review*, Vol. 63, No. 2, March–April, pp. 76–84.

Watson, T. (1997) *The Personnel Managers*. London: Routledge.

West, M. and Patterson, M. (1997) *The Impact of People Management Practices on Business Performance*. IPD Research paper No. 22. London: IPD.

Whitfield, K. and Poole, M. (1997) 'Organising employment for high performance', *Organisation Studies*, Vol. 18, No. 5, pp. 745–764.

Wood, S. (1995) 'The four pillars of HRM: are they connected?', *Human Resource Management Journal*, Vol. 5, No. 5, pp. 49–59.

Wood, S. and De Menezes, L. (1998) 'High commitment management in the UK', *Human Relations*, Vol. 51, No. 4, pp. 485–515.

For multiple choice questions, exercises and annotated weblinks specific to this chapter visit this book's website at www.booksites.net/beardwell

CHAPTER 2

Strategic human resource management

Nicky Golding

OBJECTIVES

▶ To indicate the significance of the business context in developing an understanding of the meaning and application of SHRM.

▶ To analyse the relationship between strategic management and SHRM.

▶ To examine the different approaches to SHRM, including:
  – The best-fit approach to SHRM
  – The configurational approach to SHRM
  – The resource-based view of SHRM
  – The best-practice approach to SHRM.

▶ To evaluate the relationship between SHRM and organisational performance.

▶ To present a number of activities and case studies that will facilitate readers' understanding of the nature and complexity of the SHRM debate, and enable them to apply their knowledge and understanding.

 ## Introduction to strategic human resource management

This chapter charts the development of strategic human resource management. It assumes a certain familiarity with the evolution of HRM, early HRM models and frameworks and their theoretical underpinning as discussed in Chapter 1. The aim of this chapter is to provide a challenging and critical analysis of the strategic human resource management literature, so that you will be able to understand the synthesis both within and between strategic human resource management and strategic management in its various forms.

Since the early 1980s when human resource management arrived on the managerial agenda, there has been considerable debate concerning its nature and its value to organisations. From the seminal works emerging from the Chicago school and the matching model of HRM (Fombrun *et al.*, 1984), the emphasis has very much concerned its *strategic* role in the organisation. Indeed, the now large literature rarely differentiates between human resource management (HRM) and strategic human resource management (SHRM). Some writers have associated HRM with the strategic aspects and concerns of 'best-fit', in vertically aligning an organisation's human resources to the needs of the organisation as expressed in the organisational strategy (Fombrun *et al.*, 1984) or by creating 'congruence' or 'horizontal alignment' between various managerial and HRM policies (Beer *et al.*, 1984; Walton, 1985). Others have focused on HRM as a means of gaining commitment and linked this to outcomes of enhanced organisational performance (Beer *et al.*, 1984; Guest, 1987; Guest *et al.*, 2000a); through best-practice models (Pfeffer, 1994, 1998; MacDuffie, 1995; Arthur, 1994) or high-performance work practices (Huselid, 1995; Guest, 1987). Others have recognised the 'harder' nature of strategic HRM (Storey, 1992), emphasising its contribution to business efficiency. Interlaced with this debate has been the wider controversy concerning the nature of business strategy itself, from which strategic HRM takes its theoretical constructs.

Add to this, transformations in organisational forms, which have impacted simultaneously on both structures and relationships in organisations. Bahrami (1992) describes tensions in the US high-technology sector that should be familiar to the UK audience. The need for increased flexibility (Atkinson, 1984) or 'agility' (Bahrami, 1992) in organisational structures and relationships has led to 'delayering, team-based networks, alliances and partnerships and a new employer–employee covenant' or psychological contract. These changes in organisational structuring and employer–employee relationships have led to difficulties in finding new organisational forms that both foster creativity and avoid chaos. Thus tensions can arise between 'innovation and maintaining focus, between rapid response and avoiding duplication, between a focus on future products and meeting time to market criteria, between long-term vision and ensuring performance today'. These tensions need to be considered within business and human resource strategies, as organisations grapple with remaining lean and focused, yet maintain a loose hands-off management style to encourage creativity and rapid response. These dilemmas are not new to the strategic HRM literature; Kanter in 1989 noted contradictions between remaining 'lean, mean and fit' on the one hand, yet being seen as a great company to work for on the other.

Development in SHRM thinking, charted in this chapter through the development of the best-fit approach, the configurational approach, the resource-based view approach and the best-practice approach, have a profound impact on our understanding of the contribution SHRM can make to organisational performance, through increased competitive advantage and added value. Indeed, it becomes clear that whether the focus of SHR practices is on alignment with the external context or on the internal context of the firm, the meaning of SHRM can only really be understood in the context of something else, namely organisational performance, whether that be in terms of economic value added and increased shareholder value, customer value added and increased market share, or people added value through increased employee commitment and *reservoirs* of employee skills and knowledge.

The debate therefore becomes extremely complex in its ramifications for analysing processes, evaluating performance and assessing outcomes. The observer therefore must come to the view, in the best postmodern tradition, that the profusion and confusion of policy make straightforward analysis of SHRM in empirical and analytical terms extremely difficult and contingent on positional stances of the actors and observers involved in the research process. However, some kind of analytical context is useful in beginning our evaluations.

In order to understand the development of strategic human resource management, and recognise that SHRM is more than traditional human resource management 'tagged' with the word 'strategic', it is necessary to consider the nature of strategic management. This will provide an understanding of the 'strategic' context within which strategic human resource management has developed, and enable us to understand the increasingly complex relationship between strategic management and strategic human resource management.

Understanding the business context

The nature of business strategy

Boxall (1996) has commented that 'any credible attempt at model-building in Strategic HRM involves taking a position on the difficult questions: What is Strategy? (content) & How is strategy formed? (process)'. It is the intention of this section to explore these questions, and identify the difficulties and complexities involved in the 'strategy-making' process. This section provides an overview of some of the issues and debates, and sets the context for the SHRM debate discussed later in the chapter. It is not within the remit of this chapter, however, to provide a comprehensive review of strategic management theory. Readers are encouraged to seek further reading on strategic management, particularly if the material is completely new to them.

The roots of business strategy stretch far back into history (Alexander the Great 356–323 BC, Julius Caesar 100–44 BC), and early writers linked the term 'strategy' to the ancient Greek word 'strategos', which means 'general' and has connotations of 'to lead' and 'army'. Thus it is not surprising that many dictionary definitions convey a military perspective:

> Strategy. The art of war, especially the planning of movements of troops and ships etc. into favourable positions; plan of action or policy in business or politics etc.'
>
> (*Oxford Pocket Dictionary*)

Early writings on business strategy adopted a military model combined with economics, particularly the notion of rational-economic man (Chandler, 1962; Sloan, 1963; Ansoff, 1965). This is known as the classical or rational-planning approach, and has influenced business thinking for many decades. The meaning of strategy has changed, however, and become more complex over the past 20 years or so, where the literature has moved from emphasising a long-term planning perspective (Chandler, 1962) to a more organic evolutionary process occupying a shorter time frame (Ansoff and McDonnell, 1990). Thus strategic management in the late 1990s, early 2000s is seen to be as much about vision and direction as about planning, mechanisms and structure.

> Throughout the first half of our century and even into the early eighties, planning with its inevitable companion, strategy – has always been a key word, the core, the near ultimate weapon of 'good' and 'true' management. Yet many firms including Sony, Xerox, Texas Instruments ... have been remarkably successful ... with minimal official, rational and systematic planning.
>
> (*Aktouf, 1996*)

ACTIVITY

How would you define the word 'strategy'? Note down five words you associate with strategy.

Consider your organisation's strategy, and identify the vision statement, mission statement, corporate objectives and values.

What do you know about the 'strategy-making' process in your organisation? Try to map out the process, identifying the key influences, stakeholders and processes.

If you feel unable to use your current organisation, use an organisation you are familiar with or where you have access to company information. If this is not possible, you can use the case study, Jet Airlines, at the end of this chapter.

Approaches to the strategy-making process

This chapter uses the four distinctive approaches to strategy-making identified by Whittington (1993, 2001) as a model of analysis. These are the *classical* or *rational-planning approach, the evolutionary approach, the processual approach* and the *systemic approach*. As you will see, an organisation's approach to its 'strategy-making' process has implications for our understanding and application of strategic human resource management.

■ The classical or rational-planning approach

This view suggests that strategy is formed through a formal and rational decision-making process. The key stages of the strategy-making process emphasise: firstly, a comprehensive analysis of the external and internal environment, which then enables an organisation to evaluate and choose from a range of strategic choices, which in turn allows for plans to be made to implement the strategy. With this approach, profitability is assumed to be the only goal of business, and the rational-planning approach the means to achieve it. Alfred Chandler (1962), a business historian, Igor Ansoff (1965), a theorist, and Alfred Sloan (1963), President of General Motors, identified these key characteristics of the classical approach in their work and writings. Chandler defined strategy as:

> the determination of the basic, long-term goals and objectives of an enterprise, and the adoption of courses of action and the allocation of resources necessary for those goals.

Grant (2002) highlighted the classical approach in his model of common elements in successful strategies (Figure 2.1): where clear goals, understanding the competitive environment, resource appraisal and effective implementation form the basis of his analysis.

Within the classical perspective, strategy can be and often is viewed at three levels: firstly, at the *'corporate' level*, which relates to the overall scope of the organisation, its

---

Figure 2.1   **Common elements in successful strategies**

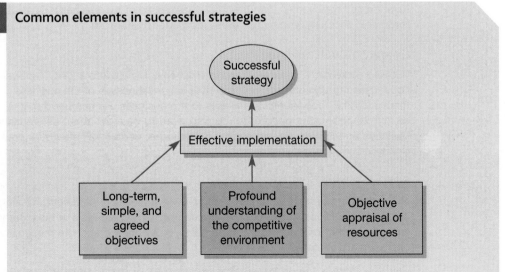

Source: Grant (2002: 11)

structures, financing and distribution of key resources; secondly, at a *'business' level*, which relates to its competitive positioning in markets/products/services; thirdly, at an *'operational' level*, which relates to the methods used by the various functions: marketing, finance, production and of course human resources to meet the objectives of the higher-level strategies. This approach tends to separate out operational practices from higher-level strategic planning; this is not always helpful in reality, as it is often operational practices and effective systems that are 'strategic' to success in organisations (Boxall and Purcell, 2003). This prompted Whittington (2001: 107) to comment that 'the rigid separation of strategy from operations is no longer valid in a knowledge-based age'. This is not to suggest that external analysis and planning should be ignored, but proposes a recognition that operational practices or 'tactical excellence' may provide sustainable competitive advantage by ensuring that an organisation is adaptable and can flex with the environment. This becomes significant in contributing to our understanding of SHRM later in the chapter.

The classical approach, however, forms the basis of much of our early understanding of how organisations 'make strategy' and define competitive advantage. It is worth spending time on the activity below, which will enable you to understand and apply the strategic management process from a classical rational-planning perspective. Drawing on Johnson and Scholes (2002), it focuses on *strategic analysis*, which requires you to analyse the external and internal environment of an organisation and identify its key source of competitive advantage, which will then enable you to identify and evaluate the range of *strategic choices* open to the organisation. This in turn will enable you to consider the *implementation* stage of the strategy-making process in the organisation.

In this activity, you have probably raised more questions than answers, and you have probably identified some of the shortcomings of the classical approach. Mintzberg (1990)

ACTIVITY | ## Analysing an organisation

Analyse the external environment

Analyse the external environment your business operates in. Consider the political, legal, technological, economic influences on your business. Now categorise these into opportunities and threats.

Analyse the internal environment

Now identify the internal strengths and weaknesses of the business. Consider the internal resources, structure, leadership, skills, knowledge, culture etc.

Conduct a SWOT analysis

Put your analysis of the external and internal environment into a SWOT analysis. You might find it useful to prioritise the key strengths and weaknesses of the business, and the main threats and key opportunities available to the business. Remember that it is important to be able to justify your decisions. You also need to be clear about differentiating between business and HR issues, although it is likely that certain HR strengths could be a core business competence/weakness.

Strategic choice

Now consider the organisation's strategy, review its vision statement, mission statement, corporate objectives and values. Does a comprehensive analysis of the external and internal environment of your organisation help you to understand the reasoning behind the organisation's strategy?

Can you identify the organisation's key sources of competitive advantage? Does this analysis help you to understand why the organisation has made certain strategic choices?

What other information do you think you would need to fully understand the strategy-making process in the organisation?

Do you think the organisation adopts a classical approach to 'strategy-making'?

Implementation

What changes has the organisation made in terms of culture, structures, leadership and HR practices to deliver its strategy? Have these changes been effective? Why? Why not?

You can either use the case study 'Jet Airlines' at the end of this chapter to complete this exercise, or you can use the organisation you work for or one you are familiar with and where you have access to company information.

clearly identified the 'basic premises' of the classical approach as being the disciplined 'readiness and capacity of managers to adopt profit-maximising strategies through rational long-term planning' (Whittington, 2001: 15). He questioned the feasibility of adopting this approach as either a model for prescription of best practice or as a model of analysis, as he considered it to be an inflexible and oversimplified view of the 'strategy-making' process, relying too heavily on military models and their assumed culture of discipline. Mintzberg (1987) argued that making strategy in practice tends to be complex and messy, and he preferred to think about strategy as 'crafting' rather than 'planning'.

The classical approach is, however, the basis for much strategy discussion and analysis, and, as we will see later, underpins much strategic HRM thinking, particularly the 'best-fit' school of thought and the notion of vertical integration. If, however, we accept that devising and implementing strategies in organisations is a complex and organic process, it highlights the complexity of both defining and applying strategic human resource management.

The evolutionary approach

An alternative view of the strategy-making process is the evolutionary approach. This suggests that strategy is made through an informal evolutionary process in which managers rely less upon top managers to plan and act rationally and more upon the markets to secure profit maximisation. Whittington (2001) highlights the links between the evolutionary approach and the 'natural law of the jungle'. Henderson (1989: 143) argued that 'Darwin is probably a better guide to business competition than economists are', as he recognised that markets are rarely static and indeed likened competition to a process of natural selection, where only the fittest survive. Darwin noted that more individuals of each species are born than can survive, thus there is a frequently recurring struggle for existence. Evolutionarists, therefore, argue that markets, not managers, choose the prevailing strategies. Thus in this approach, the rational-planning models that analyse the external and internal environment, in order to select the most appropriate strategic choices and then to identify and plan structural, product and service changes to meet market need, become irrelevant. The evolutionary approach suggests that markets are too competitive for 'expensive strategizing and too unpredictable to outguess' (Whittington, 2001: 19). They believe that sophisticated strategies can deliver only a temporary advantage, and some suggest focusing instead on efficiency and managing the 'transaction costs'.

BOX 2.1

Bishop bemoans slump at Bmi

Bmi, the airline formerly known as British Midland slumped £19.6m into the red last year in what it described as an 'exceptionally tough trading environment for the airline industry'.

Sir Michael Bishop, Bmi's chairman and controlling shareholder, said he was 'disappointed to report the airline's first pre-tax losses for 10 years', but stressed operating losses had been cut by £7.3m to £21.7m.

The previous year's £12.4m profits before tax were flattered by a £58m exceptional gain from its ground-handling sale to public transport group Go-Ahead, while last year Bmi took an £8.5m hit for grounding four planes after September 11 and a raft of restructuring charges. These were to reorganise the business into four distinct segments, including the launch of Bmibaby, the no frills airline which carried more than 700,000 passengers last year and is on course for 3m in 2003.

Sir Michael said the results 'reflected the mayhem in the first quarter of 2002 after September 11', though Bmi still managed to increase passengers by 11.9pc to 7.5m.

He cautioned that 2003 'promises to be another tough year' following the Iraq war and the outbreak of Sars – Severe Acute Respiratory Syndrome.

He noted that as hostilities reduced in Iraq, trading had improved. 'In the last 10 days we have seen quite an encouraging tick up in confidence and bookings', he said, but cautioned against over optimism.

He added: 'I think that Sars is going to have more impact on the airline industry than the war.'

Source: Daily Telegraph, 18 April 2003 by Alistair Osbourne

Question

To what extent do you think the evolutionary approach to the strategic management process contributes to your understanding of the problems at Bmi?

The processual approach

Quinn (1978) recognised that in practice strategy formation tends to be fragmented, evolutionary and largely intuitive. His 'logical incrementalist' view, therefore, while acknowledging the value of the rational-analytical approach, identified the need to take account of the psychological, political and behavioural relationships which influence and contribute to strategy. Quinn's view fits well within Whittington's processual approach which recognises 'organisations and markets' as 'sticky, messy phenomena, from which strategies emerge with much confusion and in small steps' (2001: 21).

The foundations of the processual school can be traced back to the work of the American Carnegie School, according to Whittington (2001) and the work of Cyert and March (1956) and Simon (1947). They uncovered two key themes: first, the cognitive limitations of human action, and secondly, that human beings are influenced by 'bounded rationality' (Simon, 1947). Thus no single human being, whether the chief executive or a production worker, is likely to have all the answers to complex and difficult problems, and we all often have to act without knowing everything we would like to know. Thus complexity and uncertainty become facts of life in strategic management and consequently in SHRM (Boxall and Purcell, 2003). It is important for organisations to recognise this to avoid falling into a fog of complacency or the 'success trap' (Barr *et al.*, 1992), and it also highlights the limitations of some of the prescriptions for success advocated in both the strategic management and SHRM literature. In practice, an organisation's approach to SHRM has considerable influence here on the strategic management process, as to effectively manage the environment better than their competitors, some writers would suggest that the organisation needs to adopt a learning and open

Figure 2.2   Emergent strategy

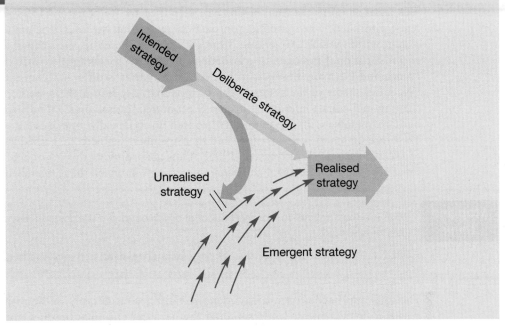

Source: Mintzberg (1987)

systems perspective. Mintzberg (1987) recognised this in his ideas on 'crafting strategy', and the fluid and organic nature of the strategy-making process. He compared the skills required of those involved in the process to those of a traditional craftsperson – traditional skill, dedication, perfection, mastery of detail, sense of involvement and intimacy through experience and commitment. Thus he recognised that planned strategies are not always realised strategies, and that strategies can often emerge and evolve (Figure 2.2). Thus the classic sequence of plan first, implementation second can become blurred, as 'strategy is discovered in action' (March, 1976). Secondly, the processualists noted the significance of the micro-politics within organisations, a theme since developed by Pettigrew (1973, 1985) and Wilson (1992). This approach recognises the inherent rivalries and conflicting goals present within organisations, and the impact this can have on strategy implementation. As we will see later in the chapter, it is these pluralist tensions that are sometimes ignored in certain branches of the SHRM literature, most notably the best-practice approach.

Stop and think

Can you think of reasons why an intended strategy might not be realised? Why do strategies sometimes emerge?

Illustrate your answers with examples from your own experience. If you do not have organisational examples, reflect upon your personal development so far.

What factors have influenced your choice of university? degree subject? career?, etc. Have you followed your original plans? What changes have you made? Have new strategies emerged? Using Mintzberg's model, you could plot your development so far on a time-line, identifying where and why planned strategies have failed to be realised and new ones have emerged.

■ The systemic approach

This leads us on to the final perspective identified by Whittington (1993, 2001), the systemic approach. The systemic approach suggests that strategy is shaped by the social system within which it operates. Strategic choices, therefore, are shaped by the cultural and institutional interests of a broader society. So, for example, state intervention in France and Germany has shaped HRM in a way that is different from the USA and the UK. A key theme of the systemic approach is that 'decision-makers are not detached, calculating individuals interacting in purely economic transactions' (Whittington, 2001: 26) but are members of a community 'rooted in a densely interwoven social system'. Therefore, in reality, organisations and their members' choices are embedded in a network of social relations (Whittington, 1993). Thus according to this approach, organisations differ according to the social and economic systems in which they are embedded.

Stop and think

What are the implications for multinational organisations if we assume a systemic view of strategy?

What are the implications for the HR professional involved in mergers and acquisitions?

The four approaches to strategy identified differ considerably in their implications for advice to management. Understanding that strategy formulation does not always occur in a rational-planned manner, owing to complexities in both the external and internal environment, is significant for our understanding of strategic human resource management. Whittington (1993) summarised his four generic approaches of *classical, evolutionary, systemic and processual*, discussed above, in Figure 2.3.

By plotting his model on two continua of outcomes (profit maximisation–pluralistic) and processes (deliberate–emergent), Whittington (1993, 2001) recognises that the strategy process changes depending upon the context and outcomes. In terms of strategic

Figure 2.3 **Whittington's model**

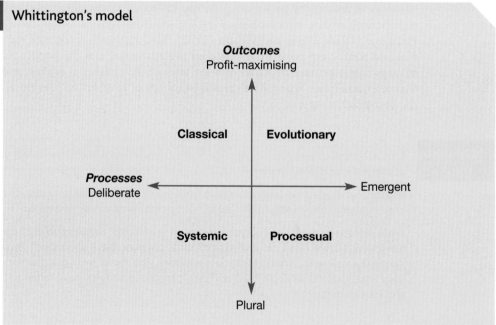

Source: Whittington (2001: 3)

human resource management, therefore, the term 'strategic' has broader and more complex connotations than those advocated in the prescriptive 'classical' strategy literature. As turbulence in the environment increases, organisations are recognising the importance of human resources to the competitive performance of the organisation, and therefore its role at a strategic level rather than an operational one.

ACTIVITY

● Read the case study, Jet Airlines, at the end of this chapter. Which of the approaches identified by Whittington (2001) best describes Jet Airline's approach to strategy formulation?

● Why do you think it is important to consider the nature of strategy to aid our understanding of strategic human resource management?

By now you should be familiar with different approaches to understanding the nature of strategy, and have gained an appreciation of the complexities involved in the strategic management process. You may have realised that our understanding and interpretation of SHRM will, to a certain extent, be influenced by our interpretation of the context of strategic management. It is to the definition and the various interpretations of strategic human resource management that we turn next.

The rise of strategic human resource management

In the past 20 years or so, the management of people within organisations has moved from the sidelines to centre stage. The contribution that human resources may make to an organisation's performance and effectiveness has become the subject of much scrutiny. Much of this change has been linked to changes in the business environment, with the impact of globalisation leading to the need for increased competitiveness, flexibility, responsiveness, quality and the need for all functions of the business to demonstrate their contribution to the bottom line. As we have already recognised, it is against this backdrop that the traditional separation between strategy and operational activities, such as personnel and then HRM, has become blurred, particularly in a knowledge-based age.

There is confusion over the differentiation between human resource management and strategic human resource management. Part of the reason for this confusion will be familiar to you, as it arises from the varying stances of the literature, those of prescription, description or critical evaluation. Some writers see the two terms as synonymous (Mabey *et al.*, 1998), while others consider there to be differences. A wealth of literature has appeared to prescribe, describe and critically evaluate the way organisations manage their human resources. It has evolved from being highly critical of the personnel function's contribution to the organisation as being weak, non-strategic and lacking a theoretical base (Drucker, 1968; Watson, 1977; Legge, 1978; Purcell, 1985), through the development of human resource management models and frameworks (Beer *et al.*, 1984; Fombrun *et al.*, 1984; Schuler and Jackson, 1987; Guest, 1987), to critics of the HRM concept who question the empirical, ethical, theoretical and practical base of the subject (Legge, 1995; Keenoy, 1990; Blyton and Turnbull, 1992; Keenoy and Anthony, 1992), to a wave of strategic human resource management literature focusing on the link or *vertical integration* between human resource practices and an organisation's business strategy, in order to enhance performance (Schuler and Jackson, 1987; Kochan and Barocci, 1985; Miles and Snow, 1984), and on the relationship between best-practice or high-commitment HR practices and organisational performance (Pfeffer, 1994, 1998; Huselid, 1995; MacDuffie, 1995; Guest, 2001).

Confusion arises because embedded in much of the HRM literature is the notion of strategic integration (Guest, 1987; Beer *et al.*, 1984; Fombrun *et al.*, 1984), but critics have been quick to note the difference between the rhetoric of policy statements and the reality of action (Legge, 1995) and the somewhat piecemeal adoption of HRM practices (Storey, 1992, 1995) and the ingrained ambiguity of a number of these models (Keenoy, 1990; Blyton and Turnbull, 1992). Thus, while the early HRM literature appeared to emphasise a strategic theme, there was much critical evaluation that demonstrated its lack of strategic integration. Thus terms such as 'old wine in new bottles' became a familiar explanation for the development of personnel to HRM and then to SHRM.

ACTIVITY Consider the reading you have done in Chapter 1 and draw your own model of HRM, demonstrating its theoretical and applied origins.

- In what ways do you believe strategic HRM to be different from your model of HRM?

- Would you make any alterations to your model to ensure its strategic nature?

Exploring the relationship between strategic management and SHRM: the best-fit school of SHRM

The best-fit (or contingency) school of SHRM explores the close link between strategic management and HRM, by assessing the extent to which there is *vertical integration* between an organisation's business strategy and its HRM policies and practices. This is where an understanding of the strategic management process and context can enhance our understanding of the development of SHRM, both as an academic field of study and in its application in organisations.

The notion of a link between business strategy and the performance of every individual in the organisation is central to 'fit' or vertical integration. Vertical integration can be explicitly demonstrated through the linking of a business goal to individual objective-setting, to the measurement and rewarding of that business goal. Vertical integration between business strategy or the objectives of the business and individual behaviour and ultimately individual, team and organisational performance is at the core of many models of SHRM. This vertical integration, where 'leverage' is gained through procedures, policies and processes, is widely acknowledged to be a crucial part of any strategic approach to the management of people (Dyer, 1984; Mahoney and Deckop, 1986; Schuler and Jackson, 1987; Fombrun *et al.*, 1984; Gratton *et al.*, 1999). Vertical integration therefore ensures an explicit link or relationship between internal people processes and policies and the external market or business strategy, and thereby ensures that competences are created which have a potential to be a key source of competitive advantage (Wright *et al.*, 1994).

Tyson (1997) identifies the move towards greater vertical integration (between human resource management and business strategy) and horizontal integration (between HR policies themselves and with line managers) as a sign of 'HRM's coming of age'. In recognising certain shifts in the HRM paradigm, Tyson identified 'vertical integration' as the essential ingredient that enables the HR paradigm to become strategic. This requires, in practice, not only a statement of strategic intent, but planning to ensure that an integrated HR system can support the policies and processes in line with the business strategy. It is worth while considering the earlier discussions on the nature of strategic management here, as a number of critics, notably Legge (1995), have questioned the applicability of the classical-rational models on the grounds that there is a dearth of empirical evidence to support their credibility. Legge (1995: 135) tends to prefer the

Table 2.1 Whittington's typology of strategy

	Classical	Processual	Evolutionary	Systemic
Strategy	Formal and planned	Crafted and emergent	Efficient	Embedded
Rationale	Profit maximisation	Vague	Survival of the fittest	Local
Focus	Fitting internal plans to external context	Internal (politics)	External (markets)	External (societies)
Processes	Analytical	Bargaining/Learning	Darwinian	Social/Cultural
Key influences	Economics/Military	Psychology	Economics/Biology	Sociology
Emergence	1960s	1970s	1980s	1990s

Source: Adapted from Whittington (2001: 39)

processual framework (Whittington, 1993), which is grounded in empirical work and recognises that 'integrating HRM and business strategy is a highly complex and iterative process, much dependent on the interplay and resources of different stakeholders'.

Stop and think

In what way does Whittington's typology (1993, 2001) of strategy impact on your understanding of 'vertical integration'? You may find it useful to use Table 2.1 to guide your thinking.

There have been a number of SHRM models that have attempted to explore the link between business strategy and HR policies and practices, and develop categories of integration or 'fit'. These include the life-cycle models (Kochan and Barocci, 1985) and the competitive advantage models of Miles and Snow (1978) and Schuler and Jackson (1987) based on the influential work of Porter (1985).

◼ Life-cycle models

A number of researchers have attempted to apply business and product life-cycle thinking or 'models' to the selection and management of appropriate HR policies and practices that fit the relevant stage of an organisation's development or life cycle (Baird and Meshoulam, 1988; Kochan and Barocci, 1985). So, for example, according to this approach, during the start-up phase of the business there is an emphasis on 'flexibility' in HR, to enable the business to grow and foster entrepreneurialism. In the growth stage, once a business grows beyond a certain size, the emphasis would move to the development of more formal HR policies and procedures. In the maturity stage, as markets mature and margins decrease, and the performance of certain products or the organisation plateaus, the focus of the HR strategy may move to cost control. Finally, in the decline stage of a product or business, the emphasis shifts to rationalisation, with downsizing and redundancy implications for the HR function (Kochan and Barocci, 1985). The question for HR strategists here is, firstly, how can HR strategy secure and retain the type of human resources that are necessary for the organisation's continued viability, as industries and sectors develop? Secondly, which HR policies and practices are more likely to contribute to sustainable competitive advantage as organisations go through their life cycle? (Boxall and Purcell, 2003). Retaining viability and sustaining competitive advantage in the 'mature' stage of an organisation's development is at the heart of much SHRM literature. Baden-Fuller (1995) noted that there are two kinds of mature organisations that manage to survive industry development: 'one is the firm that succeeds in dominating the direction of industry change and the other, is the firm that manages to adapt to the direction of change' (Boxall and Purcell, 2003: 198). Abell (1993), Boxall (1996) and Dyer and Shafer (1999) identify that the route to achieving human resource advantage as organisations develop and renew lies in the preparation for retaining viability and competitive advantage in the mature phase. The need for organisations to pursue 'dual' HR strategies, which enable them to master the present while preparing for and pre-empting the future, and avoiding becoming trapped in a single strategy, is identified by Abell (1993), while Dyer and Shafer (1999) developed an approach that demonstrates how an organisation's HR strategy could contribute to what they termed 'organisational agility'. This implies an inbuilt capacity to flex and adapt to changes in the external context, which enables the business to change as a matter of course. Interestingly, this work appears to draw on the resource-based view and best-practice view of SHRM discussed later in the chapter, as well as the best-fit approach, reflecting the difficulty of viewing the various approaches to SHRM as distinct entities.

Stop and think	How does the life-cycle approach contribute to your understanding of SHRM? How could Jet Airlines have prepared better for organisational renewal and industry changes?

■ Competitive advantage models

Competitive advantage models tend to apply Porter's (1985) ideas on strategic choice. Porter identified three key bases of competitive advantage: cost leadership, differentiation through quality and service, and focus or 'niche' market. Schuler and Jackson (1987) used these as a basis for their model of strategic human resource management, where they defined the appropriate HR policies and practices to 'fit' the generic strategies of cost reduction, quality enhancement and innovation. They argued that business performance will improve when HR practices mutually reinforce the organisation's choice of competitive strategy. Thus in Schuler and Jackson's model (Table 2.2), the organisation's mission and values are expressed through their desired competitive strategy. This in turn leads to a set of required employee behaviours, which would be reinforced by an appropriate set of HR practices. The outcome of this would be desired employee behaviours, which are aligned with the corporate goals, thus demonstrating the achievement of vertical integration.

As you can see, the 'cost-reduction'-led HR strategy is likely to focus on the delivery of *efficiency* through mainly 'hard' HR techniques, whereas the 'quality enhancement' and 'innovation'-led HR strategies focus on the delivery of *added value* through 'softer' HR techniques and policies. Thus all three of these strategies can be deemed 'strategic' in linking HR policies and practices to the goals of the business and the external context of the firm, and therefore in contributing in different ways to 'bottom-line' performance. Another commonly cited competitive advantage framework is that of Miles and Snow (1978), who defined generic types of business strategy as *defenders, prospectors* and

Stop and think	What are the advantages and disadvantages inherent in the competitive advantage models?
	Can you see any difficulties in applying them to organisations?

Table 2.2 Business strategies and associated HR policies

Strategy	Employee role behaviour	HRM policies
Innovation	A high degree of creative behaviour	Jobs that require close interaction and coordination among groups of individuals
	Longer-term focus	Performance appraisals that are more likely to reflect long-term and group-based achievement
	A relatively high level of cooperative interdependent behaviour	Jobs that allow employees to develop skills that can be used in other positions in the firm
	A moderate degree of concern for quality	Pay rates that tend to be low, but allow employees to be stockholders and have more freedom to choose the mix of components that make up their pay package
	A moderate concern for quantity; an equal degree of concern for process and results	Broad career paths to reinforce the development of a broad range of skills
	A greater degree of risk-taking; a higher tolerance of ambiguity and unpredictability	
Quality enhancement	Relatively repetitive/predictable behaviours	Relatively fixed and explicit job descriptions
	A more long-term or immediate focus	High levels of employee participation in decisions relevant to immediate work conditions and job itself
	A moderate amount of cooperative interdependent behaviour	A mix of individual and group criteria for performance appraisal that is mostly short term and results oriented
	A high concern for quality	Relatively egalitarian treatment of employees and some guarantees of job security
	A modest concern for quantity of output	Extensive and continuous training and development of employees
	High concern for process; low risk-taking activity; commitment to the goals of the organisation	
Cost reduction	Relatively repetitive and predictable behaviour	Relatively fixed and explicit job descriptions that allow little room for ambiguity
	A rather short-term focus	Narrowly designed jobs and narrowly defined career paths that encourage specialisation, expertise and efficiency
activity	Primarily autonomous or individual appraisals	Short-term results-oriented performance
	Moderate concern for quality	Close monitoring of market pay levels for use in making compensation decisions
	High concern for quantity of output	Minimal levels of employee training and development
	Primary concern for results; low risk-taking activity; relatively high degree of comfort with stability	

Source: Schuler and Jackson (1987)

analysers and matched the generic strategies to appropriate HR strategies, policies and practices, the rationale being that if appropriate alignment is achieved between the organisation's business strategy and its HR policies and practices, a higher level of organisational performance will result.

■ Configurational models

One criticism often levelled at the contingency or best-fit school is that they tend to over-simplify organisational reality. In attempting to relate *one dominant variable* external to the organisation (for example, compete on innovation, quality or cost) to another internal variable (for example, human resource management), they tend to assume a *linear, non-problematic relationship*. It is unlikely, however, that an organisation is following one strategy alone, as organisations have to compete in an ever-changing external environment where new strategies are constantly evolving and emerging. How often in organisational change programmes have organisations issued new mission and value statements, proclaiming new organisational values of employee involvement etc. on the one hand, with announcements of compulsory redundancies on the other? Thus cost-reduction reality and high-commitment rhetoric often go hand in hand, particularly in a short-termist-driven UK economy. Delery and Doty (1996) noted the limitation of the contingency school, and proposed the notion of the configurational perspective. This approach focuses on how *unique patterns or configurations of multiple independent variables* are related to the dependent variable, by aiming to identify 'ideal type' categories of not only the organisation strategy but also the HR strategy. The significant difference here between the contingency approach and the configurational approach is that these configurations represent '*non-linear synergistic effects and higher-order interactions*' that can result in maximum performance (Delery and Doty, 1996: 808). As Marchington and Wilkinson (2002: 222) note, the key point about the configurational perspective is that it 'seeks to derive an internally consistent set of HR practices that maximise horizontal integration and then link these to alternative strategic configurations in order to maximise vertical integration'. Thus, put simply, strategic human resource management, according to configurational theorists, requires an organisation to develop an HR system that achieves both horizontal and vertical integration. Delery and Doty use Miles and Snow's (1978) categories of 'defender' and 'prospector' to theoretically derive 'internal systems' or configurations of HR practices that maximise horizontal fit, and then link these to strategic configurations of, for example, 'defender' or 'prospector' to maximise vertical fit (Table 2.3).

The configurational approach provides an interesting variation on the contingency approach, and contributes to the strategic human resource management debate in recognising the need for organisations to achieve both vertical and horizontal fit through their HR practices, so as to contribute to an organisation's competitive advantage and therefore be deemed strategic. While Table 2.3 provides only for the two polar opposites of 'defender' and 'prospector' type strategies, the approach does allow for deviation from these ideal-type strategies and recognises the need for proportionate deviation from the ideal-type HR systems.

ACTIVITY   Chart the differences between the two theoretical perspectives identified in the discussion so far (contingency and configurational approaches). In what ways have these approaches contributed to your understanding of *strategic* HRM?

Table 2.3 Gaining maximum vertical and horizontal fit through strategic configurations

HR practices	Internal career opportunities	Training and development	Performance management	Employment security	Participation	Role of HR
Defenders Low-risk strategies Secure markets Concentration on narrow segments Focus on efficiency of systems	Sophisticated recruitment and selection systems Build talent and skills Career development opportunities Retention of key skills valued	Focus longer-term development for the future and emphasis on learning	Appraisals development oriented Clear grading structure and transparency valued Employee share schemes	Job security highly valued	Employee voice valued, through established systems of employee involvement, grievance, trade unions where recognised Commitment to the organisation emphasised	Potential for strategic role Well-established department, with established HR systems
Prospectors Innovative High-risk strategies Change and uncertainty Focus on entering new markets	Buy-in talent and skills Limited internal career paths	Focus short-term skill needs Onus on individual to take responsibility for personal learning and development	Appraisals results-oriented Reward short-term, and incentive-based Performance-related pay based on bottom-line measures	Employability valued	Participation and employee voice limited	Administrative role Support role

Source: Adapted from Delery J. and Doty H. (1996) 'Modes of theorising in strategic human resource management: tests of universalistic, contingency and configurational performance predictions', *Academy of Management Journal*, Vol. 39, No. 4, pp. 802–835.

In analysing the level of vertical integration evident in organisational practice, it soon becomes clear that organisations pursue and interpret vertical integration in different ways. Some organisations tend to adopt a top-down approach to HR 'strategy-making', with senior management cascading defined strategic objectives to functional departments, who in turn cascade and roll out policies to employees, while other organisations recognise HRM as a business partner. Torrington and Hall (1998) have explored the varying interpretations of 'fit' or 'integration' by attempting to qualify the degree or levels of integration between an organisation's business strategy and its human resources strategy. They identified five different relationships or levels of 'vertical integration' (Figure 2.4).

In the separation model, there is clearly no vertical integration or relationship between those responsible for business strategy and those responsible for HR, thus there is unlikely to be any formal responsibility for human resources in the organisation. The 'fit' model, according to Torrington and Hall, recognises that employees are key to achieving the business strategy, therefore the human resources strategy is designed to fit the requirements of the organisation's business strategy. This 'top-down' version of 'fit' can be seen in the matching model (Fombrun *et al.*, 1984) and in the best-fit models of Schuler and Jackson (1987) and Kochan and Barocci (1985). As you have probably already identified, these models assume a classical approach to strategy. Thus they assume that business objectives are cascaded down from senior management through departments to individuals.

The 'dialogue' model recognises the need for a two-way relationship between those responsible for making business strategy decisions and those responsible for making HR decisions. In reality, however, in this model the HR role may be limited to passing on essential information to the Board, to enable them to make strategic decisions. The

| Figure 2.4 | Torrington and Hall's five levels of 'vertical integration' |

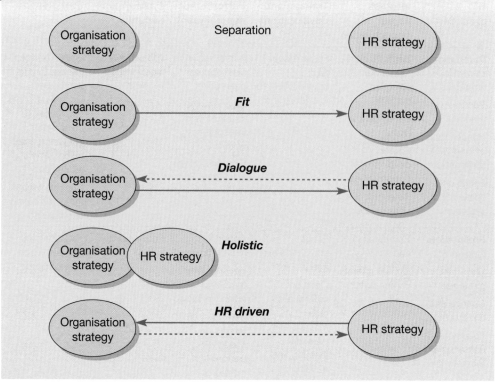

Source: Torrington and Hall (1998: 27)

'holistic' model, on the other hand, recognises employees as a key source of competitive advantage, rather than just a mechanism for implementing an organisation's strategy. Human resource strategy in this model becomes critical, as people competences become key business competences. This is the underpinning assumption behind the resource-based view of the firm (Barney, 1991; Barney and Wright, 1998), discussed later in this chapter. The final degree of integration identified by Torrington and Hall is the HR-driven model, which places HR as a key strategic partner.

| Stop and think | Having considered Torrington and Hall's (1998) levels of vertical integration, which of these approaches to HR strategy represents your organisation's approach to human resources? Alternatively, you can use the case study, Jet Airlines, at the end of the chapter. |

■ Limitations of the best-fit models of SHRM

Criticisms of the best-fit approach have identified a number of problems, both in their underlying theoretical assumptions and in their application to organisations. One of these key themes is the reliance on the classical rational-planning approach to strategy-making, its reliance on determinism and the resulting lack of sophistication in their description of generic competitive strategies (Miller, 1992; Ritson, 1999; Boxall and Purcell, 2003). This criticism is partly answered by the configurational school, which recognises the prevalence of hybrid strategies and the need for HR to respond accordingly (Delery and Doty, 1996). A further criticism is that best-fit models tend to ignore employee interests in the pursuit of enhanced economic performance. Thus, in reality, alignment tends to focus on 'fit' as defined by Torrington and Hall (1998), and relies on assumptions of unitarism rather than the alignment of mutual interests. It has been argued that 'multiple fits' are needed, to take account of pluralist interests and conventions within an organisation, by ensuring that an organisation's HR strategy meets the mutual interests of both shareholders and employees. A third criticism could be levelled at the lack of emphasis on the internal context of individual businesses within the same sector, and the unique characteristics and practices that might provide its main source of sustainable competitive advantage. Marchington and Wilkinson (2002: 225) ask, for example: Why did Tesco choose to work closely with trade unions while Sainsbury's preferred to minimise union involvement?

 ACTIVITY   Make a list of the advantages and disadvantages of the best-fit approach to SHRM.

We have explored the best-fit school of SHRM and its relationship to strategic management through the contingency and configurational approaches. The contingency approach recommends a strong relationship to strategic management, whether it be to an organisation's life cycle or competitive forces; this obviously assumes a classical rational-planning model of strategic management. We have considered this relationship or *vertical integration* between an organisation's business strategy and its human resource strategy in some detail, defining the varying degrees of 'fit'. The configurational approach attempts to answer some of the limitations of the contingency approach, by identifying 'ideal type' categories of both the organisation strategy and the HR strategy. It 'seeks to derive an internally consistent set of HR practices that maximise horizontal integration and then link these to alternative strategic configurations in order to maximise vertical integration' and therefore organisational performance. An alternative approach to understanding the relationship between an organisation's approach to SHRM and its business performance is the resource-based view of SHRM, with its focus on the internal context of the business and its recognition of human resources as 'strategic assets'.

The resource-based view of SHRM

The resource-based view of the firm (RBV) represents a paradigm shift in SHRM thinking by focusing on the internal resources of the organisation, rather than analysing performance in terms of the external context. Advocates of the resource-based view of SHRM help us to understand the conditions under which human resources become a scarce, valuable, organisation-specific, difficult-to-imitate resource, in other words key 'strategic assets' (Barney and Wright, 1998; Mueller, 1998; Amit and Shoemaker, 1993; Winter, 1987). Proponents of the resource-based view of the firm (Penrose, 1959; Wernerfelt, 1984; Amit and Shoemaker, 1993) argue that it is the range and manipulation of an organisation's resources, including human resources, that give an organisation its 'uniqueness' and source of sustainable competitive advantage. Their work has resulted in an 'explosion of interest in the Resource-Based perspective' (Boxall and Purcell, 2003: 72), particularly in seeking ways to build and develop 'unique bundles' of human and technical resources that will lead to enhanced organisational performance and sustainable competitive advantage.

Barney (1991, 1995) and Barney and Wright (1998) contribute to the debate on strategic HRM in two important ways. Firstly, by adopting a resource-based view (Barney, 1991; Wernerfelt, 1984), they provide an economic foundation for examining the role of human resource management in gaining sustainable competitive advantage. Secondly, in providing a tool of analysis in the VRIO framework, and by considering the implications for operationalising human resource strategy, they emphasise the role of the HR executive as a strategic partner in developing and sustaining an organisation's competitive advantage. The resource-based view therefore recognises the HR function (department) as a key 'strategic' player in developing sustainable competitive advantage and an organisation's human resources (employees) as key assets in developing and maintaining sustainable competitive advantage.

■ The VRIO framework

The resource-based view of SHRM explores the ways in which an organisation's human resources can provide sustainable competitive advantage. This is best explained by the VRIO framework:

● Value
● Rarity
● Inimitability
● Organisation

● Value

Organisations need to consider how the human resources function can create value; it is quite common in organisations to reduce costs through HR such as the reduction in headcount and the introduction of flexible working practices etc., but it is also important to consider how they might increase revenue. Reicheld (1996) has identified human resources' contribution to the business as *efficiency*, but also as customer selection, customer retention and customer referral, thus highlighting the impact of HR's contribution through enhanced customer service and *customer added value*. This view is reflected by Thompson (2001), in recognising the paradigm shift from traditional added value through economy and efficiency to ensuring that the potential value of outputs is maximised by ensuring that they fully meet the needs of the customers for whom the product or service is intended. The suggestion of the resource-based view is that if Human Resources wishes to be a 'strategic partner', they need to know which human resources contribute the most to *sustainable competitive advantage* in the business, as some human resources may provide greater leverage for competitive advantage than others. Hamel and Prahalad (1993) therefore identify that productivity and performance can be improved by gaining the same output from fewer resources (*rightsizing*) and by achieving more output from given resources (*leveraging*). In order to achieve this, Human Resources may ask themselves the following questions:

● On what basis is the firm seeking to distinguish itself from its competitors? Production efficiency? Innovation? Customer service?
● Where in the value chain is the greatest leverage for achieving differentiation?
● Which employees provide the greatest potential to differentiate a firm from its competitors?

ACTIVITY Try to answer these questions on your organisation or one with which you are familiar. Alternatively, you could use the case study 'Jet Airlines' at the end of this chapter.

This approach has further implications for the role of human resource managers in a firm, as they need to understand the economic consequences of human resource practices and understand where they fit in the value chain. Barney and Wright (1998: 42) suggest that the Human Resources function needs to be able to explore the following questions:

- Who are your internal customers and how well do you know their part of the business?
- Are there organisational policies and practices that make it difficult for your internal clients to be successful?
- What services do you provide? What services should you provide? What services should you not provide?
- How do these services reduce internal customers' costs/increase their revenues?
- Can these services be provided more efficiently by outside vendors?
- Can you provide these services more efficiently?
- Do managers in the HR function understand the economic consequence of their jobs?

The *value* of an organisation's resources is not sufficient alone, however, for *sustainable* competitive advantage, because if other organisations possess the same value, then it will only provide *competitive parity*. Therefore an organisation needs to consider the next stage of the framework: rarity.

● Rarity

The HR Executive needs to consider how to develop and exploit rare characteristics of a firm's human resources to gain competitive advantage.

BOX 2.2

Nordstrom exists in the highly competitive retailing industry. This industry is usually characterised as having relatively low skill requirements and high turnover for sales clerks. Nordstrom, however, has attempted to focus on individual salespersons as the key to its competitive advantage. It invests in attracting and retaining young, college-educated sales clerks who desire a career in retailing. It provides a highly incentive-based compensation system that allows Nordstrom's salespersons to make as much as twice the industry average in pay. The Nordstrom culture encourages sales clerks to make heroic efforts to attend to customers' needs, even to the point of changing a customer's tyre in the parking lot. The recruiting process, compensation practices, and culture at Nordstrom have helped the organisation to maintain the highest sales per square foot of any retailer in the nation.

Source: Barney J. B. and Wright P.M. (1998) 'On becoming a strategic partner: the role of human resources in gaining competitive advantage', *Human Resource Management*, Spring, Vol. 37, No. 1, p. 34.

Question

How did Nordstrom exploit the rare characteristics of their employees?

Nordstrom is an interesting case, because it operates in a highly competitive retail industry where you would usually expect a lower level of skill and subsequently high labour turnover. Nordstrom, however, focused on individual salespeople as a key source of its competitive advantage. It therefore invested in attracting and retaining young college-educated people who desired a career in retailing. To ensure horizontal integration, it also provided a highly incentive-based compensation system (up to twice the industry average), and it encouraged employees to make a 'heroic effort' to attend to customers' needs. Thus, by investing in its human resources, and ensuring an integrated approach to development and reward, Nordstrom has taken a 'relatively homogeneous labour pool, and exploited the *rare* characteristics to gain a competitive advantage' (Barney and Wright, 1998: 34).

Consider current advertising campaigns, either on television, radio or in the media. Can you identify any organisations that are attempting to exploit the rare characteristics of their employees as a key source of their competitive advantage? Once you have identified an organisation, try to find more out about that organisation, their business strategy and their organisational performance in relation to their competitors.

● Inimitability

If an organisation's human resources add value and are rare, they can provide competitive advantage in the short term, but if other firms can imitate these characteristics, then over time competitive advantage may be lost and replaced with *competitive parity*.

The third element of the VRIO framework requires Human Resources to develop and nurture characteristics that cannot be easily imitated by the organisation's competitors. Barney and Wright (1998) recognise the significance of 'socially complex phenomena' here, such as an organisation's unique history and culture, which can be used to identify unique practices and behaviours which enable organisations to 'leapfrog' their competitors. Alchian and Demsetz (1972) also identified the contribution of *social complexity* in providing competitive advantage, in their work on the potential *synergy* that results from effective teamwork. They found that this ensured a rare and difficult-to-copy commodity for two reasons: firstly, it provided competitive advantage through its *causal ambiguity*, as the specific source of the competitive advantage was difficult to identify;

BOX 2.3

Southwest Airlines exemplifies the role that socially complex phenomena such as culture play in competitive advantage. According to the company's top management, the firm's success can be attributed to the 'personality' of the company; a culture of fun and trust that provides employees with both the desire and the discretion to do whatever it takes to meet the customers' needs. The 'fun' airline uses an extensive selection process for hiring flight attendants who will project the fun image of the airline. Applicants must go through a casting call type exercise where they are interviewed by a panel that includes current flight attendants, managers and customers ... Those who make it through the panel interview are then examined against a psychological profile that distinguished outstanding past flight attendants from those who were mediocre or worse.

In addition to the extensive selection process, employees are empowered to create an entertaining travelling environment by a strong organisational culture that values customer satisfaction. Says Herb Kelleher, CEO:

> We tell our people that we value inconsistency. By that I mean that we're going to carry 20 million passengers this year and that I can't foresee all of the situations that will arise at the stations across our system. So what we tell our people is, 'Hey, we can't anticipate all of these things, you handle them the best way possible. You make a judgement and use your discretion; we trust you'll do the right thing. If we think you've done something erroneous, we'll let you know – without criticism, without backbiting'.   (Quick, 1992)

The extensive selection process and the strong organisational culture contribute to the differentiated service that has made Southwest Airlines the most financially successful airline over the past 20 years ... with the fewest customer complaints.

Source: Barney J.B. and Wright P.M. (1998) 'On becoming a strategic partner: the role of human resources in gaining competitive advantage', *Human Resource Management*, Spring, Vol. 37, No. 1, p. 35.

Questions

How did SW Airlines create a culture that was difficult to copy?

secondly, through its *social complexity*, as synergy resulted as team members were involved in socially complex relationships that are not transferable across organisations. So characteristics such as trust and good relationships become firm-specific assets that provide value, are rare and are difficult for competitors to copy.

The extract above (Box 2.3) demonstrates the strength of *inimitability*: SW Airlines exemplifies the role that socially complex phenomena, such as culture, can play in gaining competitive advantage. Top management attribute the company's success to its 'personality', a culture of 'fun' and 'trust', that empowers employees to do what it takes to meet the customers' needs. This is reinforced through an extensive selection process, and a culture of trust and empowerment reinforced by the CEO. SW Airlines attributes its strong financial success to its 'personality', which CEO Kelleher believes cannot be imitated by its competitors. So the human resources of SW Airlines serve as a source of sustainable competitive advantage, because they create value, are rare and are virtually impossible to imitate.

● Organisation

Finally, to ensure that the HR function can provide *sustainable* competitive advantage, the VRIO framework suggests that organisations need to ensure that they are *organised* so that they can capitalise on the above, adding value, rarity and inimitability. This implies a focus on horizontal integration, or *integrated, coherent systems of HR practices* rather than individual practices, that enable employees to reach their potential (Guest, 1987; Gratton *et al.*, 1999; Wright and Snell, 1991; Wright *et al.*, 1996). This requires organisations to ensure that their policies and practices in the HR functional areas are coordinated and coherent, and not contradictory. Adopting such a macro-view, however, is relatively new to the field of SHRM, as 'each of the various HRM functions have evolved in isolation, with little coordination across the disciplines' (Wright and McMahan, 1992). Thus there is much best-practice literature focusing on the micro-perspective, for example on identifying appropriate training systems, or conducting performance appraisals, or designing selection systems. Although this literature has now evolved and recognised the 'strategic' nature of the functional areas, it has tended to focus on vertical integration at the expense of horizontal integration, thus there is still limited development in the interplay between employee resourcing, employee development, performance, reward and employee relations strategies. This discussion is explored in more detail in the next section: best-practice SHRM.

So, to conclude on the VRIO framework, if there are aspects of human resources that do not provide value, they can only be a source of competitive disadvantage and should be discarded; aspects of the organisation's human resources that provide value and are rare provide competitive parity only; aspects that provide value, are rare but are easily copied provide temporary competitive advantage, but in time are likely to be imitated and then only provide parity. So to achieve competitive advantage that is sustainable over time, the HR function needs to ensure the organisation's human resources provide value, are rare, are difficult to copy and that there are appropriate HR systems and practices in place to capitalise on this.

Stop and think

Which approach to strategic management identified by Whittington (1993) could be used to explain the resource-based view of SHRM?

How does the resource-based view contribute to your understanding of strategic HRM?

What implications does the resource-based view have for operationalising human resource strategy?

Mueller (1998), in advocating the resource-based view of SHRM, argues that 'the existing theorising in strategic HRM needs to be complemented by an evolutionary perspective on the creation of human resource competencies'. He echoes Mintzberg's concerns (1987) that an overly-rationalistic approach to strategy-making tends to focus too much attention on past successes and failures, when what is really needed is a level of strategic thinking that is radically different from the past. He identifies a lack of theoretical and empirical evidence to justify the emphasis on rational, codified policies of HRM, and reflects Bamberger and Phillips (1991) in describing human resource strategy as an 'emergent pattern in a stream of human-resource related decisions occurring over time'. Thus the strategic planning approach may be viewed by some as a 'metaphor employed by senior management to "legitimise emergent decisions and actions"' (Gioia and Chittipeddi, 1991). Unlike contingency and universalist theorists (Schuler and Jackson, 1987; Miles and Snow, 1978; Kochan and Barocci, 1985; Pfeffer, 1994, 1998; Huselid, 1995), Mueller is more wary of the claimed relationship between strategic HRM and the overall financial performance of an organisation. He recognises that enlightened best-practice HR activities do not automatically translate into competitive superiority but rather require more complex and subtle conditions for human resources to become 'strategic assets'. He defines these as 'the social architecture' or 'social patterns' within an organisation which build up incrementally over time and are therefore difficult to copy. The focus on 'social architecture' rather than culture is deliberate as it provides an emphasis on developing and changing behaviours rather than values, which are notoriously difficult to change (Ogbonna, 1992). Mueller identifies an organisation's 'social architecture' as a key element in the resource-based view of SHRM, together with an embedded 'persistent strategic intent' on the part of senior management and embedded learning in daily work routines, which enable the development of 'hidden reservoirs' of skills and knowledge, which in turn can be exploited by the organisation as 'strategic assets'. The role of Human Resources is then to channel these behaviours and skills so that the organisation can tap into these hidden reservoirs. This thinking is reflected in the work of Hamel and Prahalad (1993, 1994), discussed below.

Stop and think	How does Mueller's view on the rational-planning approach to strategic management aid your understanding of HR strategy in practice? Compare Mueller's approach to Barney and Wright's VRIO framework.

■ Applying the resource-based view of SHRM

In adopting a focus on the internal context of the business, HR issues and practices are core to providing sustainable competitive advantage, as they focus on how organisations can define and build core competencies or capabilities which are superior to those of their competitors. One key framework here is the work of Hamel and Prahalad (1993, 1994) and their notion of 'core competencies' (Table 2.4) in their 'new strategy paradigm'. They argue that 'for most companies, the emphasis on competing in the present, means that too much management energy is devoted to preserving the past and not enough to creating the future'. Thus it is organisations that focus on identifying and developing their core competencies that are more likely to be able to stay ahead of their competitors. The key point here is not to anticipate the future, but *create* it, by not only focusing on organisational transformation and competing for market share, but also *regenerating strategies* and competing for *opportunity share*. Thus in creating the future, strategy is not only seen as learning, positioning and planning but also forgetting, foresight and strategic architecture, where strategy goes beyond achieving 'fit' and resource allocation to achieving 'stretch' and resource 'leverage'. The level of both tacit and explicit knowledge within the firm, coupled with the ability of employees to learn, becomes crucial. Indeed, Boxall and Purcell (2003) argue that there is little point in making a distinction between the resource-based view and the knowledge-based view of the firm, as both approaches advocate that it is a firm's ability to learn faster than its competitors that leads to sustainable competitive advantage.

Table 2.4 Hamel and Prahalad's notion of 'core competency'

A core competency:

- is a bundle of skills and technologies that enable a company to provide particular benefits to customers
- is not product specific
- represents ... the sum of learning across individual skill sets and individual organisational-units
- must be competitively unique
- is not an 'asset' in the accounting sense of the word
- represents a 'broad opportunity arena' or 'gateway' to the future

Source: Hamel and Prahalad (1994: 217–218)

Alternatively, Boxall and Purcell present Leonard's (1998) similar analysis based on 'capabilities'. These are 'knowledge sets' consisting of four dimensions: employee skills and knowledge, technical systems, managerial systems, and values and norms. In this model, employee development and incentive systems become a key driving force in achieving sustainable competitive advantage through core capability. Interestingly, Leonard emphasises the interlocking, systemic nature of these dimensions and warns organisations of the need to build in opportunities for renewal, to avoid stagnation.

When organisations grow through mergers or acquisitions, as they appear increasingly to do (Hubbard, 1999), it has been argued that the resource-based view takes on further significance. When mergers and acquisitions fail, it is often not at the planning stage but at the implementation stage (Hunt *et al.*, 1987) and people and employee issues have been noted as the cause of one-third of such failures in one survey (Marks and Mirvis, 1982). Thus 'human factors' have been identified as crucial to successful mergers and acquisitions. The work of Hamel and Prahalad (1994) indicated that CEOs and directors of multidivisional firms should be encouraged to identify clusters of 'know-how' in their organisations which 'transcend the artificial divisions of Strategic Business Units' or at least have the potential to do so. Thus the role of Human Resources shifts to a 'strategic' focus on 'managing capability' and 'know-how', and ensuring that organisations retain both tacit and explicit knowledge (Nonaka and Takeuchi, 1995) in order to become more innovative, as organisations move to knowledge-based strategies as opposed to product-based ones.

Stop and think   How does the work of Hamel and Prahalad (1993, 1994) contribute to the RBV debate? Do you think the RBV model is appropriate for all organisational contexts?

The resource-based view of SHRM has recognised that both human capital and organisational processes can add value to an organisation; however, they are likely to be more powerful when they mutually reinforce and support one another. The role of Human Resources in ensuring that exceptional value is achieved and in assisting organisations to build competitive advantage lies in their ability to implement an integrated and mutually reinforcing HR system which ensures that talent, once recruited, is developed, rewarded and managed in order to reach their full potential. This theme of *horizontal integration* or achieving congruence between HR policies and practices is developed further in the next section, best-practice approach to SHRM.

■ Limitations of the resource-based view

The resource-based view is not without its critics, however, particularly in relation to its strong focus on the internal context of the business. Some writers have suggested that the effectiveness of the resource-based view approach is inextricably linked to the external context of the firm (Miller and Shamsie, 1996; Porter, 1991). They have recognised that the resource-based view approach provides more added value when the external environment is less predictable. Other writers have noted the tendency for advocates of the resource-based view to focus on differences between firms in the same sector, as sources of sustainable competitive advantage. This sometimes ignores the value and significance of common 'base-line' or 'table stake' (Hamel and Prahalad, 1994) characteristics across industries, which account for their legitimacy in that particular industry. Thus in the retail sector, there are strong similarities in how the industry employs a mix of core and peripheral labour, with the periphery tending to be made up of relatively low-skilled employees, who traditionally demonstrate higher rates of employee turnover. Thus in reality, economic performance and efficiency tend to be delivered through rightsizing, by gaining the same output from fewer and cheaper resources, rather than through leverage, by achieving more output from given resources. The example of B&Q in the UK, employing more mature people as both their core and particularly their peripheral workforce, is a good example of how an organisation can partially differentiate themselves from their competitors, by focusing on adding value through the knowledge and skills of their human resources. Thus leverage is gained, as the knowledge of B&Q's human resources add value to the level of customer service provided, which theoretically in turn will enhance customer retention and therefore shareholder value. An exploration of the empirical evidence to support this relationship between SHRM and organisational performance is discussed in more detail in the next section: the best-practice approach to strategic human resource management.

Best-practice SHRM: high-commitment models

The notion of best-practice or 'high-commitment' HRM was identified initially in the early US models of HRM, many of which mooted the idea that the adoption of certain 'best' human resource practices would result in enhanced organisational performance, manifested in improved employee attitudes and behaviours, lower levels of absenteeism and turnover, higher levels of skills and therefore higher productivity, enhanced quality and efficiency. This can be identified as a key theme in the development of the SHRM debate, that of *best-practice SHRM* or *universalism*. Here, it is argued that all organisations will benefit and see improvements in organisational performance if they identify, gain commitment to and implement a set of best-HRM practices. Since the early work of Beer *et al.* (1984) and Guest (1987), there has been much work done on defining sets of HR practices that enhance organisational performance. These models of best practice can take many forms; while some have advocated a *universal* set of HR practices that would enhance the performance of all organisations to which they were applied (Pfeffer, 1994, 1998), others have focused on high-commitment models (Walton, 1985; Guest 2001) and high-involvement practices (Wood, 1999) which reflect an underlying assumption that a strong commitment to the organisational goals and values will provide competitive advantage. Others have focused on 'high-performance work systems/practices (Berg, 1999; Applebaum *et al.*, 2000). This work has been accompanied by a growing body of research exploring the relationship between these 'sets of HR practices' and organisational performance (Pfeffer, 1994; Huselid, 1995; Huselid and Becker, 1996; Patterson *et al.*, 1997; Guest, 2001). Although there is a wealth of literature advocating the best-practice approach, with supporting empirical evidence, it is still difficult to reach generalised conclusions from these studies. This is mainly as a result of conflicting views about what constitutes an ideal set of HR best practices, whether or not they should be horizontally integrated into 'bundles' that fit the organisational context and the contribution that these sets of HR practices can make to organisational performance.

Universalism and high commitment

One of the models most commonly cited is Pfeffer's (1994) 16 HR practices for 'competitive advantage through people' which he revised to seven practices for 'building profits by putting people first' in 1998. These have been adapted for the UK audience by Marchington and Wilkinson (2002) (Table 2.5).

Table 2.5 HR practices for 'competitive advantage through people'

Building profits by putting people first	'High-commitment' HRM
Employment security	and internal promotion
Selective hiring	and sophisticated selection
Extensive training	and learning and development
Sharing information	Extensive involvement and voice
Self-managed teams/teamworking	Self-managed teams/teamworking and harmonisation
High pay contingent on company performance	High compensation contingent on organisational performance
Reduction of status differentials	

Source: Pfeffer (1998), adapted by Marchington and Wilkinson (2002)

Pfeffer (1994) explains how changes in the external environment have reduced the impact of traditional sources of competitive advantage, and increased the significance of new sources of competitive advantage, namely human resources that enable an organisation to adapt and innovate. Pfeffer's relevance in a European context has been questioned owing to his lack of commitment to independent worker representation and joint regulation (Boxall and Purcell, 2003), hence Marchington and Wilkinson's adaptation, highlighted in Table 2.5. With the universalist approach or 'ideal set of practices' (Guest, 1997), the concern is with how close organisations can get to the ideal set of practices, the hypothesis being that the closer an organisation gets, the better the organisation will perform, in terms of higher productivity, service levels and profitability. The role of Human Resources, therefore, becomes one of identifying and gaining senior management commitment to a set of HR best practices, and ensuring that they are implemented and that reward is distributed accordingly. The first difficulty with the best-practice approach is the variation in what constitutes best practice. Agreement on the underlying principles of the best-practice approach is reflected in Youndt *et al.*'s (1996: 839) summary below:

> At the root, most (models) ... focus on enhancing the skill base of employees through HR activities such as selective staffing, comprehensive training and broad developmental efforts like job rotation and cross-utilisation. Further (they) tend to promote empowerment, participative problem-solving and teamwork with job redesign, group based incentives and a transition from hourly to salaried compensation for production workers.

Lists of best practices, however, vary intensely in their constitution and in their relationship to organisational performance. A sample of these variations is provided in Table 2.6. This results in confusion about which particular HR practices constitute high commitment, and a lack of empirical evidence and 'theoretical rigour' (Guest 1987: 267) to support their universal application. Capelli and Crocker-Hefter (1996: 7) note:

> We believe that a single set of 'best' practices may, indeed, be overstated ... We argue that (it is) **distinctive** human resource practices that help to create unique competencies that differentiate products and, in turn drive competitiveness.

Table 2.6 **Comparative lists of best practices**

Pfeffer (1998)	Kochan and Osterman (1994)	MacDuffie (1995)	Huselid (1995)	Arthur (1994)	Delery and Doty (1996)
Employment security	Self-directed work teams	Self-directed work teams	Contingent pay	Self-directed work teams	Internal career opportunities
Selective hiring	Job rotation	Job rotation	Hours per year training	Problem-solving groups	Training
Extensive training	Problem-solving groups	Problem-solving groups	Information sharing	Contingent pay	Results-oriented appraisals
Sharing information	TQM	TQM	Job analysis	Hours per year training	Profit-sharing
Self-managed teams		Suggestions forum	Selective hiring	Conflict resolution	Employment security
High pay contingent on company performance		Hiring criteria, current job versus learning	Attitude surveys	Job design	Participation
Reduction of status differentials		Contingent pay	Grievance procedure	Percentage of skilled workers	Job descriptions
		Induction and initial training provision	Employment tests	Supervisor span of control	
		Hours per year training	Formal performance appraisal	Social events	
			Promotion criteria	Average total labour costs	
			Selection ratio	Benefits/total labour costs	

Source: Adapted from Becker and Gerhart (1996: 785), *Academy of Management Journal*, Vol. 39, No. 4, pp. 779–801.

◼ Integrated bundles of HRM: horizontal integration

A key theme that emerges in relation to best-practice HRM is that individual practices cannot be implemented effectively in isolation (Storey, 1992) but rather combining them into integrated and complementary bundles is crucial (MacDuffie, 1995). Thus the notion of achieving horizontal integration within and between HR practices gains significance in the best-practice debate.

The need for *horizontal integration* in the application of SHRM principles is one element that is found in the configurational school of thought, the resource-based view approach and in certain best-practice models. It emphasises the coordination and congruence between HR practices, through 'a pattern of planned action' (Wright and McMahan, 1999). In the configurational school, cohesion is thought likely to create synergistic benefits, which in turn enable the organisation's strategic goals to be met. Roche (1999: 669), in his study on Irish organisations, noted that 'organisations with a relatively high degree of integration of human resource strategy into business strategy are much more likely to adopt commitment-oriented bundles of HRM practices'. Where some of the best-practice models differ is in those that advocate the '*universal*' application of SHRM, notably Pfeffer (1994, 1998). Pfeffer's argument is that best practice may be used in any organisation, irrespective of product life cycle, market situation or workforce characteristics, and improved performance will ensue. This approach ignores potentially significant differences between organisations, industries, sectors and countries however. The work of Delery and Doty (1996) has highlighted the complex relationship between the management of human resources and organisational performance, and their research supports the contingency approach (Schuler and Jackson, 1987) in indicating that there are some key HR practices, specifically internal career opportunities, results-oriented appraisals and participation/voice, that must be aligned with the business strategy or, in other words, be context-specific. The 'bundles' approach, however, is additive, and accepts that as long as there is a core of integrated high-commitment practices, other practices can be added or ignored, and still produce enhanced performance. Guest *et al.*'s analysis of the WERS data (2000a: 15), however, found that the 'only combination of practices that made any sense was a straightforward count of all the practices'. As with many high-commitment-based models, there is an underlying assumption of unitarism, which ignores the inherent pluralist values and tensions present in many organisations. Coupled with further criticisms of context avoidance and assumed rationality between implementation and performance, the best-practice advocates, particularly the universalists, are not without their critics.

High-performance work practices

In recognising HRM systems as 'strategic assets' and in identifying the strategic value of a skilled, motivated and adaptable workforce, the relationship between strategic human resource management and organisational performance moves to centre stage. The traditional HR function, when viewed as a cost centre, focuses on transactions, practices and compliance; when this is replaced by a strategic HRM system it is viewed as an investment and focuses on developing and maintaining a firm's strategic infrastructure (Becker *et al.*, 1997). This systems approach and concentration on 'bundles' of integrated HR practices is at the centre of thinking on *high-performance work practices*. The work of Huselid (1995) and Huselid and Becker (1996) identified integrated systems of high-performance work practices as significant economic assets for organisations, concluding that 'the magnitude of the return on investment in High Performance Work Practices is substantial' (Huselid, 1995: 667) and that plausible changes in the quality of a firm's high-performance work practices are associated with changes in market value of between $15 000 and $60 000 per employee. This differs from the universal approach, in that high-performance work practices are recognised as being highly idiosyncratic and in need of being tailored to meet an individual organisation's specific context in order to provide maximum performance. These high-performance work practices will only have a strategic impact, therefore, if they are aligned and integrated with each other, and if the total HRM system supports key business priorities. This requires a 'systems' thinking approach on the part of HR managers, which enables them to avoid 'deadly combinations' of HR practices which work against each other, for example team-based culture and individual performance-related pay, and to seek out 'powerful connections' or synergies between practices, for example building up new employees' expectations through sophisticated selection and meeting them through appropriate induction, personal development plans and reward strategies.

The impact of human resource management practices on organisational performance has been recognised as a key element of differentiation between HRM and strategic human resource management. Much research interest has been generated in exploring the influence of 'high-performance work practices' on shareholder value (Huselid, 1995) and in human capital management (Ulrich, 1997; Ulrich et al., 1995). A survey by Patterson et al. (1997), published for the CIPD, cited evidence for human resource management as a key contributor to improved performance. Patterson argued that 17 per cent of the variation in company profitability could be explained by HRM practices and job design, as opposed to just 8 per cent from research and development, 2 per cent from strategy and 1 per cent from both quality and technology! Other studies have reviewed the links between high-commitment HRM and performance, and two recent studies by Guest et al. (2000a, b) have argued the economic and business case for recognising people as a key source of competitive advantage in organisations and therefore a key contributor to enhanced organisational performance. In terms of HR managers, research has highlighted the need for the development of business-related capabilities (an understanding of the business context and the implementation of competitive strategies) alongside professional HRM capabilities. Huselid et al. (1997) concluded that while professional HRM capabilities are necessary, but not sufficient alone for better firm performance, business-related capabilities are not only underdeveloped within most firms but represent the area of greatest economic opportunity. The important message for HR managers is not only to understand and implement a systems perspective, but to understand how HR can add value to their particular business, so that they can become key 'strategic assets'.

Stop and think	How can HR professionals demonstrate their business capability? What systems and measurement processes do they need to put in place in order to demonstrate the contribution of HR practices to bottom-line performance?

SHRM and performance: the critique

Criticisms aimed at advocates of the high-commitment/performance link are mainly centred on the validity of the research methods employed and problems associated with inconsistencies in the best-practice models used (Marchington and Wilkinson, 2002). In terms of evidence it is difficult to pinpoint whether it is the HR practices that in turn lead to enhanced organisational performance or whether financial success has enabled the implementation of appropriate HR practices. It is difficult to see how organisations operating in highly competitive markets, with tight financial control and margins, would be able to invest in some of the HR practices advocated in the best-practice models. This is not to say that HR could not make a contribution in this type of business environment, but rather that the contribution would not be that espoused by the best-practice models. Here, the enhanced performance could be delivered through the efficiency and tight cost control more associated with 'hard' HR practices (Storey, 1995) and the contingency school. A further difficulty is the underlying theme of 'unitarism' pervading many of the best-practice approaches. As Boxall and Purcell (2003) note, many advocates of best-practice, high-commitment models tend to 'fudge' the question of pluralist goals and interests. If the introduction of best-practice HR could meet the goals of all stakeholders within the business equally, the implementation of such practices would not be problematic. However, it is unlikely that this would be the case, particularly within a short-termist-driven economy, where the majority of organisations are looking primarily to increase return on shareholder value. Thus if this return can best be met through cost reduction strategies or increasing leverage in a way that does not fit employees' goals or interests, how can these practices engender high commitment and therefore be labelled 'best practice'? It is not surprising, therefore, that ethical differences between the *rhetoric* of human resource best practice and the *reality* of human resource real practices are highlighted (Legge, 1998). High-commitment models, therefore, which at first appear to satisfy ethical principles of deontology in treating employees with respect and as ends in their own right, rather than as means to other

BOX 2.4 — Shareholders fight back!!

Defence giant BAE Systems yesterday faced a massive shareholder revolt at a heated annual meeting in London, where almost half the voters called for a rethink over its pay policies. Investors heckled directors over 'rewards for failure' and last year's £616 million loss … Discontent with the performance of BAE was palpable. Over the last year, its shares slumped from 384p to as low as 104p as it revealed £1.8 billion cost overruns yet ex-boss John Weston had received a £1.5 million pay-off.

The row over executive pay generated fresh controversy at steel firm Corus yesterday, where shareholders slammed directors for accepting pay rises and ex-boss Tony Pedder's £720,000 pay-off, while British Corus workers suffer pay freezes and compulsory redundancies.

Source: Adapted from *Daily Mail*, City & Finance, April 2003

For years, it seems, shareholders have bought the argument that top-quartile performance meant top-quartile pay for the Chief Executive. Now, plenty of bottom-quartile American companies still seem to be richly rewarding the boss, and shareholders have been protesting … American Airlines made a $41 million pre-tax payment to a trust fund to protect the pensions of 45 executives if the company went bust and Delta Airlines, another floundering airline, put $25.5 million in a protected pension trust for the Chief Executive and 32 other executives … Again the aim was clearly to make sure that the chaps at the top have lifebelts if the ship sinks. Increasingly, bosses' pay is structured to protect them from risk.

Source: Adapted from *The Economist*, 3–9 May 2003: 72

Questions

1 How do you think this tension between shareholders' interests and senior management goals should be managed?

2 What recommendations on senior management reward strategies would you make?

ends (Legge, 1998), in reality can assume a utilitarian perspective, where it is deemed ethical to use employees as a means to an end, if it is for the greater good of the organisation. This might justify *downsizing* and *rightsizing* strategies, but it is difficult to see how this might justify recent tensions between shareholder interests and senior management goals. A common theme of the best-practice models is *contingent pay*; thus, when an organisation is performing well, employees will be rewarded accordingly. There have been many recent cases, however, where senior managers of poor performing organisations have been rewarded with large pay-offs.

Becker and Gerhart (1996) discuss and debate the impact of HRM on organisational performance further. They compare the views of those writers that advocate synergistic systems, holistic approaches, internal–external fit and contingency factors (Amit and Shoemaker, 1993; Delery and Doty, 1996; Dyer and Reeves, 1995; Huselid, 1995; Milgrom and Roberts, 1995) with those that suggest that there is an identifiable set of best practices for managing employees which have universal, additive, positive effects on organisation performance (Applebaum and Batt, 1994; Kochan and Osterman, 1994; Pfeffer, 1994). They provide a useful critique of the Best-Practice School as they identify difficulties of generalisability in best-practice research and the inconsistencies in the best-practice models, such as Arthur's (1994) low emphasis on variable pay, whereas Huselid (1995) and MacDuffie (1995) have a high emphasis on variable pay.

BOX 2.5   How BMW put the Mini back on track

A pioneering bonus scheme has given fresh impetus to workers at a once run-down car factory, writes James Mackintosh

Engineers and production line workers from the body shop at BMW's Mini factory in Oxford face a difficult choice in the next few weeks. Should they spend the company's money on an evening's go-karting or a trip to a comedy club?

The group, who work mainly on roofs for the new version of the iconic car, are being rewarded for coming up with the month's best money-saving idea. They realised that the number of soundproofing foam blocks could be halved without any adverse effect. Annual saving: £115 000.

Their evening's entertainment appears a long way removed from the negotiations last year, when the plant's German managers and union officials hammered out a pay deal. But the two have a common purpose. Both are designed to harness staff creativity to cut costs.

Under a ground-breaking deal with the union, workers must come up with an average of three ideas and save £800 each to qualify for the full £260 annual bonus – in addition to meeting standard quality and productivity targets. The agreement, thought to be the first of its kind in the UK, is designed to save £3.6m this year. 'It

certainly focuses the employees on these targets,' says Werner Rothfuss, director of corporate communications at the plant. 'Employees can make a difference; this is to encourage their engagement.'

BMW is delighted with the arrangement. But it did not come cheaply. Union acquiescence was bought by promising a minimum bonus of £130, even if targets are missed, and one of the largest wage rises in the industry. The plant has also increased the number of workers dramatically, from 2,500 to 4,500, to allow a seven-day operation, although many are employed on a temporary basis.

The deal is the latest attempt by the company to change the culture at the factory – the only part of the old Rover Group that BMW retained when it broke up the once-nationalised company in 2000.

When BMW took on the plant it was half-empty and surrounded by crumbling buildings. Restrictive contracts meant the workers were paid when the plant was shut and earned overtime when extra production was needed. And the machinery for making the Mini was installed in Birmingham, at MG Rover's Longbridge factory.

So far, BMW has been remarkably successful in turning the plant round. Investment of £230m was needed to swap the equipment for making Rover 75s in Cowley with the Mini machinery from Birmingham. The new assembly line is quiet and clean. It even has a sprung floor, as in a dance hall, to make it more comfortable for workers forced to stand all day.

The disused buildings have been ripped down and replaced by lawns and car parks in a £50m clean-up.

'We had an open day for old workers and they just couldn't believe the transformation of the plant,' says Bernard Moss, convener of the Transport and General Workers' Union in Cowley.

Most importantly, though, working practices have been revamped. 'I think the workforce has been exceptional,' says Mr Moss. 'We have had to do a lot of things that maybe a few years ago we wouldn't have done.'

The biggest change has been the scrapping of the traditional contract and introduction of a working time account similar to those now operating in Germany. When the plant shuts for retooling or to reduce production, workers continue to be paid; but up to 200 missed hours are 'banked' to be made up later. This also works the other way. If workers put in overtime, they can later take the time off as extended holidays.

This initially caused some resentment, not least because the long break to install the Mini machinery meant every worker started with 200 hours of unpaid overtime to make up. 'They [workers] are starting to see the advantages now of taking long holidays,' Mr Moss said.

But the less generous contract clearly increased the hurdles to the acceptance of BMW. Staff were already sceptical of the German company's intentions, after it bought Rover only to break it up.

The level of investment, particularly in improving the site, has convinced most that the turmoil of the past few years is over and that BMW is committed to Oxford.

'There is a general acceptance that BMW has demonstrated its commitment to the Oxford plant with the money it's put in,' says Mr Moss. 'People are generally happy.'

There are some issues that irk workers, especially those who have been there a long time. One of BMW's first acts was to introduce draconian rules on smoking, now allowed only in certain areas, even outdoors, and eating, which is forbidden by the side of the production line.

However, the overall success is shown by last year's phenomenal output. The factory made more than 160,000 Minis, 40,000 more than planned, as British and US drivers raced to buy the stylish new car – and chose the more expensive, and more profitable, Cooper and Cooper-S models.

This success has helped boost morale, workers say. They can be proud of what they are producing – a powerful little car that has cachet, rather than the dowdy old Rover 800 they built until 1998.

Certainly staff have proved willing to help. Under a voluntary suggestion scheme last year more than £6m was saved from 10,339 ideas – more than two per worker. The detailed knowledge of the working environment required for many of these proposals makes it difficult for anyone but the staff on the line to come up with the ideas.

For example, 4p per car was saved by changing the fixings on the cross-braces below the windscreen, for total savings of £6,400. Another £4,500 was saved by changing the paper used for the body shop's report cards from A3 to A4.

But their co-operation may be tested as the factory refocuses on cost-cutting and productivity improvement. After the hectic growth last year, BMW wants to stabilise production.

'We are in a consolidation phase,' says Anton Heiss, who has just taken over as plant manager. 'We have to get cost down; we have to improve quality.' He would like to eliminate the expensive Sunday shift, making up the missed cars by increased productivity during the week.

There is no sign of staff unrest. But as one of his three ideas for the year Mr Moss, the union representative, proposes working on morale. 'I would like to see the camaraderie back and the characters that used to be here,' he says. 'If people are happy, they are more efficient. If they are unhappy they are not going to bother looking at suggestions. When they are happy they are more involved.'

Source: Financial Times, 19 March 2003

▶

Questions

1 How has BMW enhanced organisational performance through the implementation of Human Resource systems and practices?

2 Which approach to SHRM discussed in this chapter best explains BMW's approach to strategic human resource management?

3 What human resources advice would you give to BMW, so that they can manage the consolidation stage of their strategy effectively? Which approach to SHRM has influenced your thinking and why?

Measuring the impact of SHRM on performance and the balanced scorecard

We have so far considered the complexity of the strategic human resource management debate, and recognised that our understanding and application of strategic HRM principles is contingent upon the particular body of literature in which we site our analysis. What then are the implications for the HR practitioner, and particularly the HR strategist? We started to consider the role of the HR practitioner at the end of our consideration of the best-fit school. It is now appropriate to consider in more detail how strategic management processes in firms can be improved to deal more effectively with key HR issues and take advantage of HR opportunities. A study by Ernst & Young in 1997, cited in Armstrong and Baron (2002), found that more than a third of the data used to justify business analysts' decisions were non-financial, and that when non-financial factors, notably 'human resources', were taken into account better investment decisions were made. The non-financial metrics most valued by investors are identified in Table 2.7.

Table 2.7 **Non-financial metrics most valued by investors**

Metric	Question to which measurable answers are required
1 Strategy	How well does management leverage its skills and experience? Gain employee commitment? Stay aligned with shareholder interests?
2 Management credibility	What is management's behaviour? And forthrightness in dealing with issues?
3 Quality of strategy	Does management have a vision for the future? Can it make tough decisions and quickly seize opportunities? How well does it allocate resources?
4 Innovativeness	Is the company a trendsetter or a follower? What's in the R&D pipeline? How readily does the company adapt to changing technology and markets?
5 Ability to attract talented people?	Is the company able to hire and retain the very best people? Does it reward them? Is it training the talent it will need for tomorrow?
6 Management experience	What is the management's history and background? How well have they performed?
7 Quality of executive compensation	Is executive pay tied to strategic goals? How well is it linked to the creation of shareholder value?
8 Research leadership	How well does management understand the link between creating knowledge and using it?

Source: Adapted by Armstrong and Baron (2002): Ernst & Young: Measures that Matter, 1997

This presents an opportunity for HR managers to develop business capability and demonstrate the contribution of SHRM to organisational performance. One method that is worthy of further consideration is the balanced scorecard (Kaplan and Norton, 1996, 2001). This is also concerned with relating critical non-financial factors to financial outcomes, by assisting firms to map the key cause–effect linkages in their desired strategies. Interestingly, Kaplan and Norton challenge the short-termism found in many Western traditional budgeting processes and, as with the Ernst & Young study, they imply a central role for HRM in the strategic management of the firm and, importantly, suggest practical ways for bringing it about (Boxall and Purcell, 2003).

Kaplan and Norton identify the significance of executed strategy and the implementation stage of the strategic management process as key drivers in enhancing organisational performance. They recognise, along with Mintzberg (1987), that 'business failure is seen to stem mostly from failing to implement and not from failing to have wonderful visions' (Kaplan and Norton, 2001: 1). Therefore, as with the resource-based view, implementation is identified as a key process which is often poorly executed.

Kaplan and Norton adopt a stakeholder perspective, based on the premise that for an organisation to be considered successful, it must satisfy the requirements of key stakeholders; namely investors, customers and employees. They suggest identifying objectives, measures, targets and initiatives on four key perspectives of business performance:

- *Financial*: 'to succeed financially how should we appear to our shareholders?'
- *Customer*: 'to achieve our vision how should we appear to our customers?'
- *Internal business processes*: 'to satisfy our shareholders and customers what business processes must we excel at?'
- *Learning and growth*: 'to achieve our vision, how will we sustain our ability to change and improve?'

They recognise that investors require financial performance, measured through profitability, market value and cash flow or EVA (economic value added); customers require quality products and services, which can be measured by market share, customer service, customer retention and loyalty or CVA (customer value added); and employees require a healthy place to work, which recognises opportunities for personal development and growth, and these can be measured by attitude surveys, skill audits and performance appraisal criteria, which recognise not only what they do, but what they know and how they feel or PVA (people value added). These can be delivered through appropriate and integrated systems, including HR systems. The balanced scorecard approach therefore provides an integrated framework for balancing shareholder and strategic goals, and extending those balanced performance measures down through the organisation, from corporate to divisional to functional departments and then on to individuals (Grant, 2002). By balancing a set of strategic and financial goals, the scorecard can be used to reward current practice, but also offer incentives to invest in long-term effectiveness, by integrating financial measures of current performance with measures of 'future performance'. Thus it provides a template that can be adapted to provide the information that organisations require now and in the future, for the creation of shareholder value. The balanced scorecard at Sears, for example (Yeung and Berman, 1997: 324), focused on the creation of a vision that the company was 'a compelling place to invest', 'a compelling place to shop', and 'a compelling place to work', whereas the balanced scorecard at Mobil North American Marketing and Refining (Kaplan and Norton, 2001) focused on cascading down financial performance goals into specific operating goals, through which performance-related pay bonuses were determined. An abridged version of this, including some of the strategic objectives and measures in Mobil's Balanced Scorecard, is included in Table 2.8.

Kaplan and Norton (2001) recognise the impact that key human resource activities can have on business performance in the learning and growth element of the balanced

Table 2.8 Abridged balanced scorecard for Mobil North American Marketing and Refining

Values	Strategic objectives	Strategic measures
FINANCE *To be financially strong*	ROCE Cash flow Profitability Lowest cost Profitable Growth	ROCE Cash flow Net margins Cost per gallon delivered to customer Comparative volume growth rate
CUSTOMER *To delight the customer*	Continually delight targeted customer	Market share Mystery shopper rating
ORGANISATION *To be a competitive supplier* *To be safe and reliable*	Reduce delivered costs Inventory management Improve health and safety and environment	Delivered cost per gallon vs. customer's inventory level Number of incidents Days away from work
LEARNING AND GROWTH *To be motivated and prepared*	Organisation involvement Core competencies and skills Access to strategic information	Employee survey Strategic competitive availability Availability of strategic information

Source: Adapted from Grant, R.M. (2002: 58) based on Kaplan and Norton (2001)

scorecard, where employee skills, knowledge and satisfaction are identified as improving internal processes, and therefore contributing to customer added value and economic added value. Thus, the scorecard provides a mechanism for integrating key HR performance drivers into the strategic management process. Boxall and Purcell (2003) highlight the similarities between Kaplan and Norton's (2001: 93) Learning and Growth categories of *strategic competencies*, skills and knowledge required by employees to support the strategy, *strategic technologies*, information support systems required to support the strategy and *climate for action*, the cultural shifts needed to motivate, empower and align the workforce behind the strategy, and the *AMO theory of performance*, where performance is seen as a function of employee *ability, motivation and opportunity*. Thus the balanced scorecard contributes to the development of SHRM, not only in establishing goals and measures to demonstrate cause–effect linkages, but also in encouraging a process that stimulates debate and shared understanding between the different areas of the business. However, the balanced scorecard approach does not escape criticism, particularly in relation to the measurement of some HR activities which are not directly linked to productivity, thus requiring an acknowledgement of the multidimensional nature of organisational performance and a recognition of multiple 'bottom lines' in SHRM. Boxall and Purcell (2003) suggest the use of two others besides *labour productivity*, these being *organisational flexibility and social legitimacy*. So, although the balanced scorecard has taken account of the impact and influence of an organisation's human resources in achieving competitive advantage, there is still room for the process to become more HR driven.

ACTIVITY

Either

Draw up a strategy map for your organisation or Jet Airlines and identify appropriate balanced scorecard measures. Share your ideas with your colleagues and consider how you would audit HR.

Or

Evaluate your organisation's strategy map and balanced scorecard measures. How effective has this approach been in your organisation? Has it focused all stakeholders' attention on strategy implementation? Consult your colleagues, and prepare an audit of your HR provision.

Conclusion

Given the increasing profile of strategic human resource management in creating organisational competitive advantage, and the subsequent complexity in interpreting and applying strategic human resource management principles, there appears to be agreement on the need for more theoretical development in the field, particularly on the relationship between strategic management and human resource management, and the relationship between strategic human resource management and performance (Guest, 1997; Wright and McMahan, 1992; Wright and McMahan, 1999; Boxall and Purcell, 2003). This chapter has reviewed key developments and alternative frameworks in the field of strategic human resource management in an attempt to clarify its meaning so that the reader is able to make an informed judgement as to the meaning and intended outcomes of strategic human resource management. Thus strategic human resource management is differentiated from human resource management in a number of ways, particularly in its movement away from a micro-perspective on individual HR functional areas to the adoption of a macro-perspective (Butler *et al.*, 1991; Wright and McMahon, 1992), with its subsequent emphasis on vertical integration (Guest, 1989; Tyson, 1997; Schuler and Jackson, 1987) and horizontal integration (Baird and Meshoulam 1988; MacDuffie, 1995). It therefore becomes apparent that the meaning of strategic human resource management tends to lie in the context of organisational performance, although organisational performance can be interpreted and measured in a variety of ways. These may range from delivering efficiency and flexibility through cost-reduction-driven strategies, through the implementation of what may be termed 'hard HR techniques' (Schuler and Jackson, 1987), to delivering employee commitment to organisational goals through 'universal sets' of HR practices (Pfeffer, 1994, 1998) or 'bundles' of integrated HR practices (Huselid, 1995; Delery and Doty, 1996), to viewing human resources as a source of human capital and sustainable competitive advantage (Barney, 1991; Barney and Wright, 1998) and a core business competence and a key strategic asset (Hamel and Prahalad, 1993, 1994). There are therefore conflicting views as to the meaning of SHRM and the contribution strategic human resource management can make to an organisation. The implications of this are twofold: firstly, for academics and researchers there is a need for further theory development to define the relationship between strategic management and strategic human resource management, and subsequently organisational performance; and secondly, for HR practitioners, there is a need to develop business capabilities (Boxall and Purcell, 2003) and become 'thinking performers' (CIPD, 2001) so that they are credible strategic partners in the business.

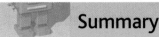

Summary

● This chapter has charted the development of strategic human resource management, exploring the links between the strategic management literature and strategic human resource management. It has examined the different approaches to strategic human resource management identified in the literature, including the best-fit approach, the best-practice approach, the configurational approach and the resource-based view, in order to understand what makes human resource management strategic.

● A key claim of much strategic human resource management literature is a significant contribution to a firm's *competitive advantage*, whether it is through cost reduction methods or more often *added value* through best-practice HR policies and practices. An understanding of the business context and particularly of the 'strategy-making' process is therefore considered significant to developing an understanding of strategic human resource management.

● Whittington's typology (1993, 2001) was used to analyse the different approaches to 'strategy-making' experienced by organisations, and to consider the impact this would have on our understanding of the development of strategic human resource management. The influence of the classical rational-planning approach on the strategic management literature and therefore strategic HRM literature was noted, with its inherent assumption that strategy-making was a rational, planned activity. This ignores some of the complexities and 'messiness' of the strategy-making process, identified by Mintzberg and others. Other approaches, which recognised the constituents of this 'messiness', namely the processual approach, the evolutionary approach and the systemic approach, were identified. These took account of changes and competing interests in both the external and internal business environment. Significantly, for human resource management, there is a recognition that it is not always appropriate to separate operational policies from higher-level strategic planning, as it is often operational policies and systems that may provide the source of 'tactical excellence', and thus the traditional distinction between strategy and operations can become blurred.

● The best-fit approach to strategic HRM explored the close relationship between strategic management and human resource management, by considering the influence and nature of vertical integration. Vertical integration, where leverage is gained through the close link of HR policies and practices to the business objectives and therefore the external context of the firm, is considered to be a key theme of *strategic* HRM. Best-fit was therefore explored in relation to life-cycle models and competitive advantage models, and the associated difficulties of matching generic business-type strategies to generic human resource management strategies were considered, particularly in their inherent assumptions of a classical approach to the strategy-making process.

● The configurational approach identifies the value of having a set of HR practices that are both vertically integrated to the business strategy and horizontally integrated with each other, in order to gain maximum performance or synergistic benefits. This approach recognises the complexities of hybrid business strategies and the need for HRM to respond accordingly. In advocating unique patterns or configurations of multiple independent variables, they provide an answer to the linear, deterministic relationship advocated by the best-fit approach.

● The resource-based view represents a paradigm shift in strategic HRM thinking by focusing on the internal resources of the firm as a key source of sustainable competitive advantage, rather than focusing on the relationship between the firm and the external business context. Human resources, as scarce, valuable, organisation-specific and difficult to imitate resources, therefore become key *strategic assets*. The work of Hamel and Prahalad (1994) and the development of core competencies is considered significant here.

● The best-practice approach highlights the relationship between 'sets' of good HR practices and organisational performance, mostly defined in terms of employee commitment and satisfaction. These sets of best practice can take many forms: some have advocated a universal set of practices that would enhance the performance of all organisations to which they were applied (Pfeffer, 1994, 1998); others have focused on integrating the practices to the specific business context (high-performance work practices). A key element of best practice is horizontal integration and congruence between policies. Difficulties arise here, as best-practice models vary significantly in their constitution and in their relationship to organisational performance, which makes generalisations from research and empirical data difficult.

● In endeavouring to gain an understanding of the meaning of strategic human resource management, it soon becomes apparent that a common theme of all approaches is enhanced organisational performance and viability, whether this be in a 'hard' sense, through cost reduction and efficiency-driven practices, or through high-commitment and involvement-driven value-added. This relationship is considered significant to understanding the context and meaning of strategic human resource management.

● Finally, the need for further theory development in the field of strategic human resource management and for human resource practitioners to develop business capability was noted.

ACTIVITY | **Defining the effective human resource manager**

What does an effective HR manager look like? What skills, competencies and knowledge does he or she require to become a business partner?

Try to collect information from a range of sources, for example:

● corporate websites,

● HR practitioner journals (*Personnel Today*, *People Management*),

● other journals (*Human Resource Management Journal*, *Management Learning*),

● the CIPD website and HRM textbooks, to develop a profile of an **effective HR manager in the 21st century**. Which skills, competencies and knowledge would you identify as *strategic* HR competencies?

Questions

1 In what way does an understanding of *strategic management* contribute to your understanding of strategic human resource management?

2 How would you differentiate human resource management from strategic human resource management?

3 Compare and contrast the best-fit and best-practice approach to strategic human resource management.

4 Evaluate the relationship between strategic human resource management and organisational performance.

5 Why do human resources practitioners need to develop business capabilities?

Case study

Jet Airlines

Jet Airlines is a successful 'no frills' airline operating from a regional airport in the UK on short-haul routes to European destinations. Its founder, Ben Mahon, recognised a shift in airline operations in the 1990s. Since the launch of Jet in 1996, it has continued to grow and return a profit when the rest of the airline industry has been forced to downsize and diversify.

Ben Mahon recognised the advantage of operating at the lowest cost, with the highest load factor. He achieved this by flying intensively between major European cities, but avoiding major airports with imposed high landing fees. This also involved cutting out expensive hub operations (timetabling aircraft to connect at a chosen city base) and it therefore avoided the delays incurred when planes ran late. A schedule of regular flights would ensure transfer passengers could catch a convenient later flight. Without a hub, it had no need to transfer luggage between flights.

The customer service approach adopted by Jet Airlines was radically different from traditional airlines. Ben Mahon recognised that many passengers wanted nothing more than to fly cheaply, quickly and with the minimum of hassle. Thus Jet dispensed with lengthy check-ins and seat allocations and introduced a swipe-card ticketing system at the gate, which allowed 'walk-on', 'walk-off' operations. He also recognised that many passengers did not like or require airline food, so dispensed with a non-essential service and eliminated one of the key elements that lengthen turn-round time at airports. These initiatives allowed Jet to offer the lowest prices for high load factors.

Jet Airlines increased its routes and enhanced its scheduling, thereby increasing its profit year on year. Recognising this, a number of other 'no frills' airlines have been launched in the UK, and a number of major airlines have recognised the advantages of the 'no frills' market, and diversified. Jet Airlines is concerned about this increase in competition, as it has led to reduced passenger levels on certain routes. It has been forced to reduce the number of flights to Frankfurt, Zurich and Munich. Jet has also experienced increasing employee turnover owing to poaching by a local competitor. This, together with an increase in customer complaints about unfriendly and inefficient staff, and a number of unfavourable newspaper reports about the lengthy distance between destination airports and destination cities, has led Ben Mahon to reassess his strategy. He recognises that Jet can no longer compete on price alone, and he believes that it is Jet's human resources that can add extra value to the customer experience, and therefore retain Jet's position as the number one 'no frills' airline in the UK.

Ben Mahon has reintroduced Jet's mission to all employees, with a new corporate value programme that emphasises quick, efficient and friendly service at the lowest price. He organised a series of away-days where he explained Jet's new mission statement.

Jet Airlines the first choice for efficient, affordable travel provided by helpful, friendly staff.

He introduced the new strategy with a personal presentation and issued all employees with a card with the new company objectives, detailed below:

Business
- To be the number one 'no frills' airline
- Attract new customers through reputation for efficiency
- Retain existing customers through Loyalty Service
- Discounts for Internet booking

Customer Service
- Provide excellent service at all times
- Commit to continuous improvement
- Internal and external customers valued

Case study continued

People

- Diversity valued
- Openness and trust
- Pride and enthusiasm in your work

Systems

- Performance management
- Involvement in decision-making
- Teamwork throughout the organisation

He recognises that Jet's human resources are crucial to the success of his strategy to sustain increased competitive advantage. He also recognises that he has to keep costs down, and therefore utilises a high proportion of flexible labour. He has also recently commissioned an attitude survey, which highlighted a number of issues:

- Perception of senior managers as autocratic
- Lack of training and development
- Lack of career opportunities
- Frustration among new managers
- Increased feeling of stress-related symptoms
- Perception that customer service not important as offering cheap product
- Poor recognition of new customer ethos

- Lack of skills/product knowledge in new part-time staff
- Lack of motivation among full-and part-time staff

Ben Mahon is concerned, as he feels that a motivated and committed workforce is essential to the success of his strategy.

Questions

1 Reflecting on the approaches to strategic human resource management discussed in this chapter:

  - the best-fit approach
  - the configurational approach
  - the resource-based view
  - the best-practice approach

  analyse the extent to which Ben Mahon has adopted a strategic approach to human resource management.

2 Drawing on your answer to question 1, Ben Mahon would like your recommendations for a human resources strategy that will enable Jet Airlines to meet its business priorities and retain its position as the number one no frills airline. He would like you to present your ideas in a presentation to the senior management team.

Useful websites

Confederation of British Industry	www.cbi.org.uk
Chartered Institute of Personnel & Development	www.cipd.co.uk
Department of Trade and Industry	www.dti.gov.uk
Detailed information about EVA	www.evanomics.com
Chartered Institute of Management	www.managers.org.uk
Strategic Management Society	www.csmintl.premierdomain.com/menu.htm

References and further reading

Those texts marked with an asterisk are recommended for further reading.

Abell, D.F. (1993) *Managing with Dual Strategies: Mastering the Present, Pre-empting the Future.* New York: Free Press.

Alchian, A. and Demsetz, H. (1972) 'Production information costs and economic organisation', *American Economic Review*, Vol. 62, pp. 777–795.

Amit, R. and Shoemaker, P. (1993) 'Strategic assets and organisational rent', *Strategic Management Journal*, Vol. 14, pp. 33–46.

Ansoff, H. I. (1965) *Corporate Strategy.* Harmondsworth: Penguin.

Ansoff, H. I. and McDonnell, E. (1990) *Implanting Strategic Management*, 2nd edn. Englewood Cliffs, NJ: Prentice Hall.

Applebaum, E., Bailey, T., Berg, P and Kalleberg, A. (2000) *Manufacturing Competitive Advantage: Why High-Performance Systems Pay Off.* Ithaca, NY: ILR Press.

Applebaum, E. and Batt, R. (1994) *The New American Workplace.* Ithaca, NY: ILR Press.

Armstrong, M. and Baron, A. (2002) *Strategic Human Resource Management: A Guide to Action*, 2nd edn. London: Kogan Page.

Arthur, J. (1994) 'Effects of human resource systems on manufacturing performance and turnover', *Academy of Management Journal*, Vol. 37, No. 3, pp. 670–687.

Atkinson, J. (1984) 'Manpower strategies for the flexible organisation', *Personnel Management*, August, pp. 28–31.

Baden-Fuller, C. (1995) 'Strategic innovation, corporate entrepreneurship and matching outside-in to inside-out approaches to strategy research', *British Journal of Management*, Vol. 6 (Special Issue), pp. 3–16.

Bahrami, H. (1992) 'The emerging flexible organisation: perspectives from Silicon Valley', *California Management Review*, Vol. 34, No. 4, pp. 33–48.

Baird, L. and Meshoulam, I. (1988) Managing two fits of strategic human resource management', *Academy of Management Review*, Vol. 13, No. 1, pp. 116–28.

Bamberger, P. and Phillips, B. (1991) 'Organisational environment and business strategy: parallel versus conflicting influences on human resource strategy in the pharmaceutical industry', *Human Resource Management*, Vol. 30, No. 2, pp. 153–82.

Barney, J.B. (1991) 'Firm resources and sustained competitive advantage', *Journal of Management*, Vol. 17, No. 1, pp. 99–120.

Barney, J. (1995) 'Looking inside for competitive advantage', *Academy of Management Executive*, Vol. 9, No. 4, pp. 49–61.

Barney, J.B. and Wright, P.M. (1998) 'On becoming a strategic partner: the role of human resources in gaining competitive advantage', *Human Resource Management*, Vol. 37, No. 1, pp. 31–46.

Barr, P., Stimpert, J. and Huff, A. (1992) 'Cognitive change, strategic action, and organisational renewal', *Strategic Management Journal*, Vol. 13, pp. 15–36.

Becker, B. and Gerhart, B. (1996) 'The impact of human resource management on organisational performance: progress and prospects', *Academy of Management Journal*, Vol. 39, No. 4, pp. 779–801.

Becker, B.E., Huselid, M.A., Pickus, P.S. and Spratt, M.F. (1997) 'HR as a source of shareholder value: research and recommendations', *Human Resource Management*, Vol. 36, No. 1, pp. 39–47.

Beer, M., Spector, B., Lawrence, P.R., Quinn Mills, D. and Walton, R.E. (1984) *Managing Human Assets*. New York: Free Press.

Berg, P. (1999) 'The effects of high performance work practices on job satisfaction in the US steel industry', *Industrial Relations*, Vol. 54, pp. 111–35.

Blyton, P. and Turnbull, P. (eds) (1992) *Reassessing HRM*. London: Sage.

Boxall, P. (1996) 'The strategic HRM debate and the resource-based view of the firm', *Human Resource Management Journal*, Vol. 6, No. 3, pp. 59–75.

*Boxall, P. and Purcell, J. (2003) *Strategy and Human Resource Management*. New York: Palgrave MacMillan.

Butler, J.E., Ferris, G.R. and Napier, N.K. (1991) *Strategy and Human Resource Management*. Cincinnati, OH: Southwestern Publishing Co.

Capelli, P. and Crocker-Hefter, A. (1996) 'Distinctive human resources are firms' core competencies', *Organisational Dynamics*, Vol. 24, No. 3, pp. 7–22.

Chandler, A. D. (1962) *Strategy and Structure: Chapters in the History of the American Industrial Enterprise*. Cambridge, MA: MIT Press.

CIPD (2001) *Professional Standards for the Professional Development Scheme*. London: Chartered Institute of Personnel and Development.

Cyert, R.M. and March, J.G. (1956) 'Organisational factors in the theory of monopoly', *Quarterly Journal of Economics*, Vol. 70, No. 1, pp. 44–64.

Delery, J. and Doty, H. (1996) 'Modes of theorizing in strategic human resource management', *The Academy of Management Journal*, Vol. 39, No. 4, pp. 802–835.

Drucker, P. (1968) *The Practice of Management*. London: Pan.

Dyer, L. (1984) 'Studying human resource strategy', *Industrial Relations*, Vol. 23, No. 2, pp. 156–69.

Dyer, L. and Reeves, T. (1995) 'Human resource strategies and firm performance: what do we know and where do we need to go?', *International Journal of Human Resource Management*, Vol. 6, No. 3, pp. 656–670.

Dyer, L. and Shafer, R. (1999) 'Creating organisational agility: implications for strategic human resource management', in Wright, P., Dyer, L., Boudreau, J. and Milkovich, G. (eds) *Research in Personnel and HRM*. Stamford, CT and London: JAI Press.

Fombrun, C., Tichy, N. and Devanna, M. (eds) (1984) *Strategic Human Resource Management*. New York: Wiley.

Gioia, D.A. and Chittipeddi, K. (1991) 'Sensemaking and sensegiving in strategic change initiation', *Strategic Management Journal*, Vol. 12, No. 6, pp. 433–48.

*Grant, R.M. (2002) *Contemporary Strategy Analysis: Concepts, Techniques, Applications*, 4th edn. Oxford: Blackwell.

Gratton, L., Hope-Hailey, V., Stiles, P. and Truss, C. (1999) 'Linking individual performance to business strategy: the people process model', in Schuler, R.S. and Jackson, S.E. (eds) *Strategic Human Resource Management*. Oxford: Blackwell Business, pp. 142–158.

Guest, D. (1987) 'Human resource management and industrial relations', *Journal of Management Studies*, Vol. 24, No. 5, pp. 503–521.

Guest, D. (1989) 'Personnel and HRM: can you tell the difference?', *Personnel Management*. Vol. 21, pp. 48–51.

Guest, D. (1997) 'Human resource management and performance: a review and research agenda', *International Journal of Human Resource Management*, Vol. 8. No. 3, pp. 263–276.

Guest, D. (2001) 'Human resource management: when research confronts theory', *International Journal of Human Resource Management*, Vol. 12, No. 7, pp. 1092–1106.

Guest, D., Michie, J., Sheehan, M. and Conway, N. (2000a) *Employment Relations, HRM and Business Performance: An Analysis of the 1998 Workplace Employee Relations Survey*. London: CIPD.

Guest, D., Michie, J., Sheehan, M., Conway, N. and Metochi, M. (2000b) *Effective People Management: Initial Findings of the Future of Work Study*. London: CIPD.

Hamel, G. and Prahalad, C. (1993) 'Strategy as stretch and leverage', *Harvard Business Review*. Vol. 71, No. 2, pp. 75–84.

Hamel, G. and Prahalad, C. (1994) *Competing for the Future*. Boston, MA: Harvard Business School Press.

Henderson, B.D. (1989) 'The origin of strategy', *Harvard Business Review*, November–December, pp. 139–143.

Hubbard, N. (1999) *Acquisition Strategy and Implementation*. Basingstoke: Macmillan.

Hunt, J., Lees, S., Grumber, J. and Vivian, P. (1987) *Acquisitions: The Human Factor*. London: London Business School and Egon Zehender International.

Huselid, M.A. (1995) 'The impact of human resource management on turnover, productivity, and corporate financial performance', *Academy of Management Journal*, Vol. 38, pp. 635–672.

Huselid, M. and Becker, B. (1996) 'Methodological issues in cross-sectional and panel estimates of the HR–firm performance link', *Industrial Relations*, Vol. 35, pp. 400–422.

Huselid, M.A., Jackson, S.E. and Schuler, R.S. (1997) 'The significance of human resource management effectiveness for corporate financial performance', *Academy of Management Journal*, Vol. 40, pp. 171–88.

Johnson, G. and Scholes, K. (2002) *Exploring Corporate Strategy*. Harlow: Prentice Hall.

Kanter, R. (1989) 'The new managerial work', *Harvard Business Review*, Nov/Dec, pp. 85–92.

Kaplan, R. and Norton, D. (1996) *The Balanced Scorecard: Translating Strategy into Action*. Boston, MA: Harvard Business School Press.

Kaplan, R. and Norton, D. (2001) *The Strategy-Focussed Organization*. Boston, MA: Harvard Business School Press.

Keenoy, T. (1990) 'HRM: a case of the wolf in sheep's clothing', *Personnel Review*, Vol. 19, No. 2, pp. 3–9.

Keenoy, T. and Anthony, P. (1992) 'HRM: metaphor, meaning and morality', in Blyton, P. and Turnbull, P. (eds) *Reassessing Human Resource Management*. London: Sage.

Kochan T. and Barocci, T. (1985) *Human Resource Management and Industrial Relations*. Boston, MA: Little Brown.

Kochan, T.A. and Osterman, P. (1994) *The Mutual Gains Enterprise*. Boston, MA: Harvard Business School Press.

Legge, K. (1978) *Power, Innovation and Problem-Solving in Personnel Management*. London: McGraw-Hill.

Legge, K. (1995) *Human Resource Management: Rhetoric and Realities*. London: Macmillan.

Legge, K. (1998) 'The morality of HRM', in Mabey, C., Salaman, G. and Storey, J. (eds) *Strategic Human Resource Management: A Reader*. London: Open University/Sage, pp 18–29.

Leonard, D. (1998) *Wellsprings of Knowledge: Building and Sustaining the Sources of Innovation*. Boston, MA: Harvard Business School Press.

Mabey, C., Salaman, G. and Storey, J. (1998) *Strategic Human Resource Management: A Reader*. London: Open University/Sage.

MacDuffie, J.P. (1995) 'Human resource bundles and manufacturing performance', *Industrial Relations Review*, Vol. 48, No. 2, pp. 199–221.

Mahoney, T. and Deckop, J. (1986) 'Evolution of concept and practice in personnel administration/human resource management', *Journal of Management*, Vol. 12, pp. 223–241.

March, J.G. (1976) 'The technology of foolishness', in Marsh, J. and Olsen, J. (eds) *Ambiguity and Choice in Organisations*. Bergen: Universitetsforlaget.

Marchington, M. and Wilkinson, A. (2002) *People Management and Development*, 2nd edn. London: CIPD.

Marks, M. and Mirvis, P. (1982) 'Merging human resources: a review of current research', *Merger and Acquisitions*, Vol. 17, No. 2, pp. 38–44.

Miles, R. and Snow, C. (1978) *Organisational Strategy, Structure and Process*. New York: McGraw-Hill.

Miles, R.E and Snow, C.C. (1984) 'Designing strategic human resource systems', *Organisational Dynamics*, Summer, pp. 36–52.

Milgrom, P. and Roberts, J. (1995) 'Complementarities and fit: strategy, structure and organisational change in manufacturing', *Journal of Accounting and Economics*, Vol. 19, No. 2, pp. 170–208.

Miller, D. (1992) 'Generic strategies: classification, combination and context', *Advances in Strategic Management*, Vol. 8, pp. 391–408.

Miller, D. and Shamsie, J. (1996) 'The resource based view of the firm in two environments: the Hollywood Film Studios from 1936–1965', *Academy of Management Journal*, Vol. 39, No. 3, pp. 519–543.

Mintzberg, H. (1987) 'Crafting strategy', *Harvard Business Review*, July–August, pp. 65–75.

Mintzberg, H. (1990) 'The Design School: Reconsidering the basic premise of strategic management', *Strategic Management Journal*, Vol. 11, pp. 171–195.

Mueller, F. (1998) 'Human resources as strategic assets: an evolutionary resource-based theory', in Mabey, C., Salaman, G. and Storey, J. (eds) *Strategic Human Resource Management: A Reader*. London: OU Press/Sage, pp. 152–169.

Nonaka, I. and Takeuchi, H. (1995) *The Knowledge-Creating Company*. New York: Oxford University Press.

Ogbonna, E. (1992) 'Organisational culture and human resource management: dilemmas and contradictions', in Blyton, P. and Turnbull, P. (eds) *Reassessing Human Resource Management*. London: Sage, pp. 74–96.

Patterson, M.G., West, M.A., Lawthom, R. and Nickell, S. (1997) *The Impact of People Management Practices on Business Performance*. London: IPD.

Penrose, E. (1959) *The Theory of the Growth of the Firm*. Oxford: Blackwell.

Pettigrew, A.M. (1973) *The Politics of Organisational Decision-Making*. London: Tavistock.

Pettigrew, A.M. (1985) *The Awakening Giant: Continuity and Change in ICI*. Oxford: Blackwell.

Pfeffer, J. (1994) *Competitive Advantage through People*. Boston, MA: Harvard Business School Press.

Pfeffer, J. (1998) *The Human Equation: Building Profits by Putting People First*. Boston, MA: Harvard Business School Press.

Porter, M. (1985) *Competitive Advantage: Creating and Sustaining Superior Performance*. New York: Free Press.

Porter, M. (1991) 'Towards a dynamic theory of strategy', *Strategic Management Journal*, Vol. 12 (s), pp. 95–117.

Purcell, J. (1985) 'Is anybody listening to the corporate personnel department?', *Personnel Management*, Sept, pp. 28–31.

Quick, J. (1992) 'Crafting an organizational culture: Herb's Land at Southwest', *Organizational Dynamics*, Vol. 21, pp. 45–56.

Quinn J.B. (1978) 'Strategic change: logical incrementalism', *Sloan Management Review*, Vol. 1, No. 20. pp. 7–21.

Reicheld, F. (1996) *The Loyalty Effect: The Hidden Force behind Growth, Profits and Lasting Value*. Boston, MA: Harvard Business School Press.

Ritson, N. (1999) 'Corporate strategy and the role of HRM: critical cases in oil and chemicals', *Employee Relations*, Vol. 21, No. 2, pp. 159–175.

Roche, W. (1999) 'In search of commitment-oriented HRM practices and the conditions that sustain them', *Journal of Management Studies*, Vol. 36, No. 5, pp. 653–678.

Schuler, R.S. and Jackson, S.E. (2000) *Managing Human Resources, A Partner Perspective* 7th edn. London: Thomson Learning.

*Schuler, R.S. and Jackson, S.E. (eds) (1999) *Strategic Human Resource Management*. Oxford: Blackwell Business.

Simon, H.A. (1947) *Administrative Behavior*. New York: Free Press.

Sloan, A.P. (1963) *My Years with General Motors*. London: Sedgewick & Jackson.

Storey, J. (1992) *Developments in the Management of Human Resources*. Oxford: Blackwell.

Storey, J. (1995) *Human Resource Management: A Critical Text*. London: Routledge.

Thompson, J. (2001) *Understanding Corporate Strategy*. London: Thomson Learning.

Torrington, D. and Hall, L. (1998) *Human Resource Management*, 4th edn. Hemel Hempstead: Prentice Hall, Europe.

Tyson, S. (1997) 'Human resource strategy: a process for managing the contribution of HRM to organisational performance', *International Journal of Human Resource Management*, Vol. 8, No. 3, pp. 277–290.

Ulrich, D. (1997) 'Measuring human resources: an overview of practice and a prescription for results', *Human Resource Management*, Vol. 36, No. 3 (Fall), pp. 303–320.

Ulrich, D., Brockbank, W., Yeung, A. and Lake, D. (1995) 'Human resource competencies: an empirical assessment', *Human Resource Management*, Vol. 34, pp. 473–495.

Walton, R. (1985) 'From control to commitment in the workplace', *Harvard Business Review*, Vol. 63, March–April, pp. 76–84.

Watson, J. (1977) *The Personnel Managers: A Study in the Sociology of Work and Employment*. London: Routledge & Kegan Paul.

Wernerfelt, B. (1984) 'A resource based view of the firm', *Strategic Management Journal*, Vol. 5, No. 2, pp. 171–180.

Whittington, R. (1993) *What is Strategy and Does it Matter?*, London: Routledge.

*Whittington, R. (2001) *What is Strategy and Does it Matter?*, 2nd edn. London: Thomson Learning.

Wilson, D. (1992) *A Strategy of Change*. London: Routledge.

Winter, S. (1987) 'Knowledge and competence as strategic assets', in Teece, D.J. (ed.) *The Competitive Challenge: Strategies for Industrial Innovation and Renewal*. Cambridge, MA: Ballinger, pp. 159–184.

Wood, S. (1999) 'Human resource management and performance', *International Journal of Management Reviews*, Vol. 1, No. 4, pp. 367–413.

Wright, P. and Snell, S. (1991) 'Towards an integrative view of strategic human resource management', *Human Resource Management Review*, Vol. 1, pp. 203–225.

Wright, P.M. and McMahan, G.C. (1992) 'Alternative theoretical perspectives for strategic human resource management, *Journal of Management*, Vol. 18, pp. 295–320.

Wright, P.M. and McMahan, G.C. (1999) 'Theoretical perspectives for strategic human resource management', in Schuler, R.S. and Jackson, S.E (eds) *Strategic Human Resource Management*, pp. 49–72.

Wright, P., McCormick, B., Sherman, S. and McMahan, G. (1996) The Role of Human Resource Practices in Petro-chemical Refinery Performance. Paper presented at the 1996 Academy of Management, Cincinnati, OH.

Wright, P., McMahan, G. and McWilliams A. (1994) 'Human resources and sustained competitive advantage: a resource-based perspective', *International Journal of Human Resource Management*, Vol. 5, No. 2, pp. 301–326.

Yeung, A. and Berman, B. (1997) 'Adding value through human resources: reorienting human resource management to drive business performance', *Human Resource Management*, Vol. 36, No. 3, pp. 321–335.

Youndt, M., Snell, S., Dean, J., and Lepak, D. (1996) 'Human resource management, manufacturing strategy and firm performance', *Academy of Management Journal*, Vol. 39, pp. 836–866.

For multiple choice questions, exercises and annotated weblinks specific to this chapter visit this book's website at www.booksites.net/beardwell

CHAPTER 3

Human resource management in context

Audrey Collin

OBJECTIVES

▶ To indicate the significance of context for the understanding of HRM.

▶ To discuss ways of conceptualising and representing the nature of context generally and this context in particular.

▶ To analyse the nature of the immediate context of HRM: the problematical nature of organisations and the need for management.

▶ To indicate the nature of the wider context of HRM and illustrate this through selected examples.

▶ To examine how our ways of interpreting and defining reality for ourselves and for others construct and influence the way we understand and practise HRM.

▶ To suggest the implications for the readers of this book.

▶ To present a number of activities and a case study that will facilitate readers' understanding of the context of HRM.

Introduction

The significance and nature of context

An event seen from one point-of-view gives one impression. Seen from another point-of-view it gives quite a different impression. But it's only when you get the whole picture you fully understand what's going on.

(Reproduced with kind permission of the *Guardian*/BMP DDB.)

The need to be aware of the context of human affairs was demonstrated dramatically in this prize-winning advertisement for the *Guardian* newspaper that is still remembered today. We can easily misinterpret facts, events and people when we examine them out of context, for it is their context that provides us with the clues necessary to enable us to understand them. Context locates them in space and time and gives them a past and a future, as well as the present that we see. It gives us the language to understand them, the codes to decode them, the keys to their meaning.

   This chapter will carry forward your thinking about the issues raised in Chapter 1 by exploring the various strands within the context of HRM that are woven together to form the pattern of meanings that constitute it. As that chapter explained, and the rest of the book will amplify, HRM is far more than a portfolio of policies, practices, procedures and prescriptions concerned with the management of the employment relationship. It is this, but more. And because it is more, it is loosely defined and difficult to pin down precisely, a basket of multiple, overlapping and shifting meanings, which users of the term do not always specify. Its 'brilliant ambiguity' (Keenoy, 1990) derives from the context in which it is embedded, a context within which there are multiple and often competing perspectives upon the employment relationship, some ideological, others theoretical, some conceptual. HRM is inevitably a contested terrain, and the various definitions of it reflect this.

From the various models of HRM in Chapter 1, you will recognise that the context of HRM is a highly complex one, not just because of its increasing diversity and dynamism, but also because it is multi-layered. The organisation constitutes the immediate context of the employment relationship, and it is here that the debate over how this relationship should be managed begins. The nature of organisation and the tensions between the stakeholders in it give rise to issues that have to be addressed by managers: for example, choices about how to orchestrate the activities of organisational members and whose interests to serve.

Beyond the organisation itself lie the economic, social, political and cultural layers, and beyond them again the historical, national and global layers of context. Considerable change is taking place within those layers, making the whole field dynamic. It is not the purpose of this chapter to register these many changes; you will become aware of some of them as you read the remainder of this book. However, we need to note here that the events and changes in the wider context have repercussions for organisations, and present further issues to be managed and choices to be made.

The various layers and the elements within them, however, exist in more than one conceptual plane. One has a concrete nature, like a local pool of labour, and the other is abstract, like the values and stereotypes that prejudice employers for or against a particular class of person in the labour market. The abstract world of ideas and values overlays the various layers of the context of HRM: the ways of organising society, of acquiring and using power, and of distributing resources; the ways of relating to, understanding and valuing human beings and their activities; the ways of studying and understanding reality and of acquiring knowledge; the stocks of accumulated knowledge in theories and concepts.

It is the argument of this chapter that to understand HRM we need to be aware not just of the multiple layers of its context – rather like the skins of an onion – but also of these conceptual planes and the way they intersect. Hence, 'context' is being used here to mean more than the surrounding circumstances that exert 'external influences' on a given topic: context gives them a third dimension. The chapter is arguing, further, that events and experiences, ideas and ideologies are not discrete and isolatable, but are interwoven and interconnected, and that HRM itself is embedded in that context: it is part of that web and cannot, therefore, be meaningfully examined separately from it. Context is highly significant yet, as we shall see, very difficult to study.

■ Conceptualising and representing context

How can we begin to understand anything that is embedded in a complex context? We seem to have awareness at an intuitive level, perceiving and acting upon the clues that context gives to arrive at the 'tacit knowledge' discussed later in Chapter 8. However, context challenges our formal thinking. First, we cannot stand back to take in the complete picture, which has traditionally been one way to gain objective knowledge of a situation. Because we are ourselves part of our context, as defined in this chapter, it is not possible for us to obtain a detached perspective upon it. In that respect we are like the fish in water that 'can have no understanding of the concept of "wetness" since it has no idea of what it means to be dry' (Southgate and Randall, 1981: 54). However, humans are very different from the 'fish in water'. We can be *reflexive*, recognising what our perspective is and what its implications are; *open*, seeking out and recognising other people's perspectives; and *critical*, entering into a dialogue with others' views and interrogating our own in the light of others', and vice versa. The 'stop and think' boxes, activities and exercises throughout the chapter are there to encourage you in this direction.

Second, we need the conceptual tools to grasp the wholeness (and dynamic nature) of the picture. To understand a social phenomenon such as HRM, we cannot just wrench it from its context and examine it microscopically in isolation. To do this is to be like the child who digs up the newly planted and now germinating seed to see 'whether it is growing'. In the same way, if we analyse context into its various elements and layers, then we are already distorting our understanding of it, because it is an indivisible whole. Rather, we have to find ways to examine HRM's interconnectedness and interdependence with other phenomena.

The study of context, therefore, is no easy task, and poses a major challenge to our established formal, detached, and analytical ways of thinking. Nevertheless, as we shall discuss later in this chapter, there are ways forward that enable us to conceptualise the many loops and circularities of these complex interrelationships in an often dynamic context.

Stop and think

Before you continue, spend a few minutes reflecting upon this way of understanding context. How different is it from the way in which you would have defined context? Does this have any implications for you as you read this chapter?

Meanwhile, we shall try to conceptualise context through metaphor: that is, envisage it in terms of something concrete that we already understand. We have already used the metaphor of the many-skinned onion to depict the multiple layers of context, but we need another metaphor to suggest its interconnectedness and texture. We could, therefore, think of it as a tapestry. This is a 'thick hand-woven textile fabric in which design is formed by weft stitches across parts of warp' (*Concise OED*, 1982). The warp threads run the length of the tapestry, the weft are the lateral threads that weave through the warp to give colour, pattern and texture. This metaphor helps us to visualise how interwoven and interrelated are the various elements of the context of HRM, both the concrete and the abstract; and how the pattern of HRM itself is woven into them. In terms of this metaphor, our ways of seeing and thinking about our world – the assumptions we make about our reality – could be said to be the warp, the threads which run the length of the tapestry contributing to its basic form and texture. Ideologies and the rhetoric through which they are expressed – ways of defining reality for other people – are the weft threads that weave through the warp threads, and give the tapestry pattern and texture. Events, people, ephemeral issues are the stitches that form the surface patterns and texture of HRM. We see this in Figure 3.1. In the case of the context of HRM, this tapestry is being woven continuously from threads of different colours and textures. At times one colour predominates, but then peters out. In parts of the tapestry patterns may be intentionally fashioned, while observers (such as the authors of this book) believe they can discern a recognisable pattern in other parts.

This metaphor again reminds us that an analytical approach to the study of context, which would take it apart to examine it closely, would be like taking a tapestry to bits: we would be left with threads. The tapestry itself inheres in the whole, not its parts. How, then, can the chapter begin to communicate the nature of this tapestry without destroying its very essence through analysis? The very representation of our thinking in written language is linear, and this undermines our ability to communicate a dynamic, interrelated

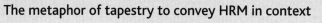

Figure 3.1	The metaphor of tapestry to convey HRM in context

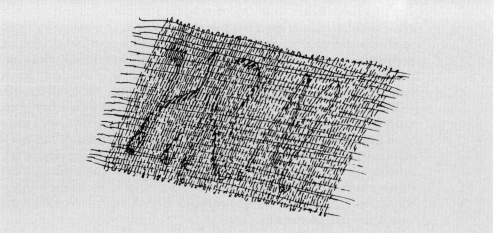

complexity clearly and succinctly. We need to think in terms of 'rich pictures', 'mind-maps', or 'systems diagrams' (Checkland, 1981; Senge, 1990; Cameron, 1997).

It is not feasible nor, indeed, necessary to attempt to portray the whole tapestry in detail; the chapter will focus instead upon a number of strands that run through it. You will be able to identify and follow them through the remainder of the book, and observe how their interweaving gives us changes in pattern and colour, some distinct, others subtle. Before beginning to read the exposition of the context of HRM, you will find it helpful to carry out the following activity.

ACTIVITY

Look at the various models that were presented in Chapter 1 and identify some of the elements of context and the relationships between them that are explicit or implied there. This will help you develop your own view of the context of HRM before you read further, and give you some mental 'hooks' upon which to hang your new understanding.

■ The concepts and language needed to understand context

To understand context, it has been suggested so far, we need to recognise its wholeness. We therefore need to incorporate both the concrete world and the world of abstract ideas. Although the appropriate language to enable us to do this may be largely unfamiliar to you, you will find that you already have considerable understanding of the concepts it expresses. Your own experience of thinking about and responding to one aspect of context – the natural, physical environment – will have given you the basic concepts that we are using and a useful set of 'hooks' upon which to hang the ideas that this chapter will introduce to you. It would be helpful to your understanding of this chapter, therefore, if you examined some of the 'hooks' you are already using, and perhaps clarify and refine them. (In this way, as Chapter 8 explains, the new material can be more effectively transferred now into, and later retrieved from, your long-term memory.)

Carry out the exercise at the end of the chapter. This will focus your thinking and enable you to recognise that you already have the 'hooks' you will need to classify the material of this chapter in a meaningful way and increase your understanding of the nature of the context of HRM. It will show you that, although you may not necessarily use the terminology below, from your present knowledge of the environment you already recognise that:

- Context is *multi-layered, multidimensional, and interwoven.* In it, concrete events and abstract ideas intertwine to create issues; thinking, feeling, interpreting and behaving are all involved. It is like the tapestry described above.
- Our understanding depends upon our *perspective.*
- It also depends upon our *ideology.*
- Different groups in society have their own interpretations of events, stemming from their ideology. There are therefore *competing* or *contested interpretations* of events.
- These groups use *rhetoric* to express their own, and account for competing, interpretations, thus distorting, or even suppressing, the authentic expression of competing views.
- Powerful others often try to impose their interpretations of events, their version of reality, upon the less powerful majority: this is *hegemony.*

This subsection has perhaps given you a new language to describe what you already understand well. You will find some of these terms in the Glossary at the end of this book, and their definitions will be amplified in later sections of this chapter as it continues its exploration of the context of HRM.

The immediate context of HRM

Human resource management, however defined, concerns the management of the employment relationship: it is practised in organisations by managers. The nature of the organisation and the way it is managed therefore form the immediate context within which HRM is embedded, and generate the tensions that HRM policies and practices attempt to resolve.

The nature of organisations and the role of management

At its simplest, an organisation comes into existence when the efforts of two or more people are pooled to achieve an objective that one would be unable to complete alone. The achievement of this objective calls for the completion of a number of tasks. Depending upon their complexity, the availability of appropriate technology and the skills of the people involved, these tasks may be subdivided into a number of subtasks and more people employed to help carry them out. This division of labour constitutes the lateral dimension of the structure of the organisation. Its vertical dimension is constructed from the generally hierarchical relationships of power and authority between the owner or owners, the staff employed to complete these tasks, and the managers employed to coordinate and control the staff and their working activities. Working on behalf of the organisation's owners or shareholders and with the authority derived from them, managers draw upon a number of resources to enable them to complete their task: raw materials; finance; technology; appropriately skilled people; legitimacy, support and goodwill from the organisation's environment. They manage the organisation by ensuring that there are sufficient people with appropriate skills; that they work to the same ends and timetable; that they have the authority, information and other resources needed to complete their tasks; and that their tasks dovetail and are performed to an acceptable standard and at the required pace.

The very nature of organisation therefore generates a number of significant tensions: between people with different stakes in the organisation, and therefore different perspectives upon and interests in it; between what owners and other members of the organisation might desire and what they can feasibly achieve; between the needs, capabilities and potentials of organisational members and what the environment demands of and permits them. Management (see Watson, 2000) is the process that keeps the organisation from flying apart because of these tensions, that makes it work, secures its survival and, according to the type of organisation, its profitability or effectiveness. Inevitably, however, as Chapter 11 discusses, managerial control is a significant and often contentious issue.

The need to manage people and relationships is inherent in the managing of an organisation, but the very nature of people and the way they constitute an organisation make management complex. Although the organisation of tasks packages people into organisational roles, individuals are larger and more organic than those roles have traditionally tended to be. The organisation, writes Barnard (1938, in Schein, 1978) 'pays people only for certain of their activities . . . but it is whole persons who come to work' (p. 17). Unlike other resources, people interact with those who manage them and among themselves; they have needs for autonomy and agency; they think and are creative; they have feelings; they need consideration for their emotional and their physical needs and protection. The management of people is therefore not only a more diffuse and complex activity than the management of other resources, but also an essentially moral one (again, see Watson, 2000). This greatly complicates the tasks of managers, who can only work with and through people to ensure that the organisation survives and thrives in the face of increasing pressures from the environment.

Owners and managers are confronted with choices about how to manage people and resolve organisational tensions. The next subsection examines some of these choices and the strategies adopted to handle them. Before then, however, it must be noted that as organisations become larger and more complex, the division of managerial labour often leads to a specialist 'people' function to advise and support line managers in the complex and demanding tasks of managing their staff. This is the personnel function (sometimes now called 'HRM'), which has developed a professional and highly skilled expertise in certain aspects of managing people, such as selection, training and industrial relations, which it offers in an advisory capacity to line managers, who nevertheless remain the prime managers of people. However, this division of managerial labour has fragmented the management of people: the development of human resource management beyond the traditional personnel approach can be seen as a strategy to reintegrate the management of people into the management of the organisation as a whole.

The approaches adopted by managers to resolve the tensions in organisations

The previous subsection suggested that there are inherent tensions in organisations. In brief, these are generated by:

● the existence of several stakeholders in the employment relationship;
● their differing perspectives upon events, experiences and relationships;
● their differing aims, interests and needs;
● the interplay between formal organisation and individual potential.

Stop and think In your own experience of being employed, however limited that might be so far, have you been aware of some of these tensions? What were their effects upon you and your colleagues? How did the management of the organisation appear to respond to these tensions? Has this coloured how you look at management and HRM?

These tensions have to be resolved through the process of management or, rather, continuously resolved, for these tensions are inherent in organisations. Thus Weick (1979) writes that organising is a continuous process of meaning-making: 'organizations keep falling apart . . . require chronic rebuilding.' (p. 44). A continuing issue, therefore, is that of managerial control: how to orchestrate organisational activities in a way that meets the needs of the various stakeholders. The owners of organisations, or those who manage them on their behalf, have explored many ways to resolve these tensions: the emergence of HRM to develop alongside, subsume or replace personnel management is witness to this. The strategies they adopt are embodied in their employment policies and practices and the organisational systems they put in place (see also Chapter 11). They are also manifested in the psychological contract they have with their employees, the often unstated set of expectations between organisation and individual that embroiders the legal employment contract. (The notion of the psychological contract now in current use goes back to a much earlier literature – for example, Schein (1970) – and it is some of the earlier terminology that is used here.) This subsection will briefly outline some of the strategies that managers have adopted, while the next will discuss the interpretations by theorists and other commentators of those strategies. However, it must be kept in mind that managers are to some extent influenced by the concepts and language, if not the arguments, of these theorists.

In very crude terms, we can identify four strategies that managers have adopted to deal with these tensions. The first is represented by what is called scientific management, or the classical school of management theory. The second is the human relations approach, and the third is the human resource management approach. The fourth approach is perhaps more an ideal than a common reality. It must be emphasised that we cannot do justice here to the rich variety of approaches that can be found in organisations. You can elaborate upon the material here by reading about these differing views in an organisational behaviour textbook, such as Huczynski and Buchanan (2002) or Clark *et al.* (1994).

The first approach addressed the tensions in the organisation by striving to control people and keep down their costs: the *scientific management* approach. It emphasised the need for rationality, clear objectives, the managerial prerogative – the right of managers to manage – and adopted work study and similar methods. These led to the reduction of tasks to their basic elements and the grouping of similar elements together to produce low-skilled, low-paid jobs, epitomised by assembly-line working, with a large measure of interchangeability between workers. Workers tended to be treated relatively impersonally and collectively ('management and labour'), and the nature of the psychological contract with them was calculative (Schein, 1970), with a focus on extrinsic rewards and incentives. Such a strategy encouraged a collective response from workers, and hence the development of trade unions.

These views of management evolved in North America, and provided a firm foundation for modern bureaucracies (Clegg, 1990). In Britain they overlaid the norms of a complex, though changing, social class system that framed the relationships between managers and other employees (Child, 1969; Mant, 1979). This facilitated the acceptance of what Argyris (1960) saw were the negative outcomes of McGregor's (1960) X-theory of management which were hierarchy; paternalism; the attribution to workers of childlike qualities, laziness, limited aspirations and time horizons. While this strategy epitomised particularly the management approach of the first half of the twentieth century, it has left its legacy in many management practices, such as organisation and method study, job analysis and description, selection methods, an overriding concern for efficiency and the 'bottom line', appraisal and performance management. Moreover, it has not been completely abandoned (see Clegg, 1990; Ritzer, 1996 on 'McDonaldization'; and ongoing debates about employment in call centres, for example Callaghan and Thompson, 2002; Hatchett, 2000; Taylor *et al.*, 2002).

The *human relations* approach to the tensions in organisations emerged during the middle years of the twentieth century, and developed in parallel with an increasingly prosperous society in which there were strong trade unions and (later) a growing acceptance of the right of individuals to self-fulfilment. Child (1969) identifies its emergence in

British management thinking as a response to growing labour tensions. It tempered scientific management by its recognition that people differed from other resources, that if they were treated as clock numbers rather than as human beings they would not be fully effective at work and could even fight back to the point of subverting management intentions. It also recognised the significance of social relationships at work – the informal organisation (Argyris, 1960). Managers therefore had to pay attention to the nature of supervision and the working of groups and teams, and to find ways of involving employees through job design (see Chapter 14), motivation, and a democratic, consultative or participative style of management. The nature of the psychological contract was cooperative (Schein, 1970).

The third and most recent major approach adopted by managers to address the tensions within the organisation has developed as major changes and threats have been experienced in the context of organisations (recession, international competition, and globalisation). It is a response to the need to achieve flexibility in the organisation and workforce (see Chapters 4 and 5) and improved performance through devolving decision-making and empowerment (see Chapter 14). As Chapter 8 notes, employees have had to become multi-skilled and to work across traditional boundaries. Unlike the other two strategies, the third approaches the organisation holistically and often with greater attention to its culture, leadership and 'vision', the 'soft' Ss of McKinsey's 'Seven S' framework (Pascale and Athos, 1982: 202–206). It attempts to integrate the needs of employees with those of the organisation in an explicit manner: the psychological contract embodies mutuality (Schein, 1970). It recognises that people should be invested in as assets so that they achieve their potential for the benefit of the organisation. It also pays greater attention to the individual rather than the collective, so that these notions of developing the individual's potential have been accompanied by individual contracts of employment (see Chapter 11), performance appraisal, and performance-related pay (see also Chapter 13).

The very title of *human resource management* suggests that this third approach to the management of organisational tensions is also an instrumental one. Although it differs greatly from the approaches that see labour as a 'cost', to be reduced or kept in check, it nevertheless construes the human being as a resource for the organisation to use. The fourth, idealistic, *humanistic* approach aims to construct the organisation as an appropriate environment for autonomous individuals to work together collaboratively for their common good. This is the approach of many cooperatives. It informed the early philosophy of organisation development (see Huse, 1980), although the practice of that is now largely instrumental. It also underpins the notion of the learning organisation (see Senge, 1990, and Chapter 9).

Although we have identified here four different strategies for managing the inherent tensions in organisations, they might be less easy to distinguish in practice. Some managers adopt a hybrid version more appropriate to their particular organisation. They will always be seeking new approaches to deal more effectively with those tensions, or to deal with variations in them as circumstances change (for example, with globalisation).

ACTIVITY | **Comparing these managerial strategies**

Many of you have worked in a call centre, or know someone who does. Working on your own or in a group, examine your experiences of working there. Could you identify one or more of these managerial strategies in your workplace? What might have been your experiences had the management adopted a different strategy?

When we look more deeply into these four managerial strategies, we can recognise that they implicate some much deeper questions. Underlying the management of people in organisations are some fundamental assumptions about the nature of people and reality itself, and hence about organising and managing. For example, managers make assumptions about the nature of the organisation, many interpreting it as having an objective reality that exists separately from themselves and other organisational members – they reify it (see Glossary). They make assumptions about the nature of their own and the organisation's goals, which they interpret as rational and objective. They make assumptions about the appropriate distribution of limited power throughout the organisation.

However, these assumptions are rarely made explicit, and are therefore rarely challenged. Moreover, many other members of the organisation appear to accept these premises on which they are managed, even though such assumptions might conflict with their own experiences, or virtually disempower or disenfranchise them. For example, many might assert the need for equal opportunities to jobs, training and promotion, but do not necessarily challenge the process of managing itself despite its often gender-blind nature (Hearn et al., 1989; Hopfl and Atkinson, 2000). Nevertheless, these assumptions inform the practices and policies of management, and hence define the organisational and conceptual space that HRM fills, and generate the multiple meanings of which HRM is constructed. In terms of the metaphor used by this chapter, they constitute some of the warp and weft threads in the tapestry/context of HRM. They will be examined in greater detail in a later section.

◼ Competing interpretations of organisations and management

When we turn from the concrete world of managing to the theories about organisations and management, we find that not only have very different interpretations been made over time, but that several strongly competing interpretations coexist. Again, this chapter can only skim over this material, but you can pursue the issues by reading, for example, Child (1969), who traces the development of management thought in Britain, or Morgan (1997), who sets out eight different metaphors for organisations through which he examines in a very accessible way the various ways in which theorists and others have construed organisations. Reed and Hughes (1992: 10–11) identify the changing focus of organisation theory over the past 30 years, from a concern with organisational stability, order and disorder, and then with organisational power and politics, to the present concern with the construction of organisational reality.

The reification (see Glossary) of the organisation by managers and others, and the general acceptance of the need for it to have rational goals to drive it forward in an effective manner, have long been challenged. Simon (see Pugh et al., 1983) recognised that rationality is 'bounded' – that managers make decisions on the basis of limited and imperfect knowledge. Cyert and March adopt a similar viewpoint: the many stakeholders in an organisation make it a 'shifting multigoal coalition' (see Pugh et al., 1983: 108) that has to be managed in a pragmatic manner. Others (see Pfeffer, 1981; Morgan, 1997) recognise the essentially conflictual and political nature of organisations: goals, structures and processes are defined, manipulated and managed in the interests of those holding the power in the organisation. A range of different understandings of organisations has developed over time: the systems approach (Checkland, 1981), the learning organisation (Senge, 1990), transformational leadership and 'excellence' (Peters and Waterman, 1982; Kanter, 1983), the significance of rhetoric (Eccles and Nohria, 1992). This range is widening to include even more holistic approaches, with recent interest in the roles in the workplace of emotional intelligence (Cherniss and Goleman, 2001; Pickard, 1999), spirituality and love (Welch, 1998; Zohar and Marshall, 2001). The influence of many of these new ideas can be seen in the recently developed concern for work–life balance (for example, People Management, 2002).

The established views of managers are subject to further interpretations. Weick (1979) argues the need to focus upon the process of organising rather than its reified outcome, an organisation. As we noted earlier, he regards organising as a continuous process of meaning-making: '[p]rocesses continually need to be re-accomplished' (p. 44). Cooper and Fox (1990) and Hosking and Fineman (1990) adopt a similar interpretation in their discussion of the 'texture of organizing'.

Brunsson (1989) throws a different light on the nature and goals of organising, based on his research in Scandinavian municipal administrations. He suggests that the outputs of these kinds of organisations are 'talk, decisions and physical products'. He proposes two 'ideal types' of organisation: the *action* organisation, which depends on action for its legitimacy (and hence essential resources) in the eyes of its environment, and the *political* organisation, which depends on its reflection of environmental inconsistencies for its legitimacy. Talk and decisions in the action organisation (or an organisation in its action phase) lead to actions, whereas the outputs of the political organisation (or the organisation in its political phase) are talk and decisions that may or may not lead to action.

> . . . hypocrisy is a fundamental type of behaviour in the political organization: to talk in a way that satisfies one demand, to decide in a way that satisfies another, and to supply products in a way that satisfies a third.
>
> (p. 27)

There are similarly competing views upon organisational culture, as we see in Aldrich (1992) and Frost *et al.* (1991). The established view interprets it as a subsystem of the organisation that managers need to create and maintain through the promulgation and manipulation of values, norms, rites and symbols. The alternative view argues that culture is not something that an organisation has, but that it is.

Just as many managers leave their assumptions unaddressed and unstated, taken for granted, so that their actions appear to themselves and others based upon reason and organisational necessity, so also do many theorists. Many traditional theorists leave unstated that the organisations of which they write exist within a capitalist economic system and have to meet the needs of capital. They ignore the material and status needs of owners and managers, and their emotional (Fineman, 1993) and moral selves (Watson, 2000). Many also are gender-blind and take for granted a male world-view of organisations. These issues tend to be identified and discussed only by those writers who wish to persuade their readers to a different interpretation of organisations (for example, Braverman, 1974; Hearn *et al.*, 1989; Calas and Smircich, 1992).

Stop and think   At the close of the Introduction some of the concepts and terminology relevant to the understanding of context were noted. Have you been aware of any of these concepts in this discussion of the immediate context of HRM?

The wider context of HRM

Defining the wider context

The definition of the wider context of HRM could embrace innumerable topics (from, for example, the Industrial Revolution to globalisation) and a long time perspective (from the organisation of labour in prehistoric constructions, such as Stonehenge, onwards). Such a vast range, however, could only have been covered in a perfunctory manner here, which would have rendered the exercise relatively valueless. It is more appropriate to give examples of some of the influential elements and how they affect HRM, and to encourage you to identify others for yourself.

Go back to the models of HRM presented in Chapter 1 and, working either individually or in a group, start to elaborate upon the various contextual elements that they include. Look, for example, at the 'outer context' of Hendry and Pettigrew's (1990) model illustrated in Chapter 1, Figure 1.4.

1 What in detail constituted the elements of the socio-economic, technical, political-legal and competitive context at the time Hendry and Pettigrew were writing? What would they be now?

2 What other elements would you add to these, both then and now?

3 What are the relationships between them, both then and now?

4 And what, in your view, has been their influence upon HRM, both then and now?

Echoes from the wider context

Here the focus will be on distant events from the socio-political sphere that have nevertheless influenced the management of the employment relationship and still do so indirectly. Although what follows is not a complete analysis of these influences, it illustrates how the field of HRM resonates with events and ideas from its wider context.

The First and Second World Wars

The two world wars, though distant in time and removed from the area of activity of HRM, have nevertheless influenced it in clearly identifiable and very important ways, some direct and some indirect. These effects can be classified in terms of changed attitudes of managers to labour, changed labour management practices, the development of personnel techniques, and the development of the personnel profession. We shall now examine these, and then note how some outcomes of the Second World War continue, indirectly, to influence HRM.

Changed attitudes of managers to labour

According to Child (1969: 44), the impact of the First World War upon industry hastened changes in attitudes to the control of the workplace that had begun before 1914. The development of the shop stewards' movement during the war increased demand for workers' control; there was growing 'censure of older and harsher methods of managing labour'. The recognition of the need for improved working conditions in munitions factories was continued in the postwar reconstruction debates: Child (1969) quotes a Ministry of Reconstruction pamphlet that advised that 'the good employer profits by his "goodness"' (p. 49). The outcome of these various changes was a greater democratisation of the workplace (seen, for example, in works councils) and, for 'a number of prominent employers', a willingness 'to renounce autocratic methods of managing employees' and 'to treat labour on the basis of human rather than commodity market criteria' (pp. 45–46). These new values became incorporated in what was emerging as a distinctive body of management thought, practice and ideology (see Glossary and later section on 'Ways of seeing and thinking'), upon which later theory and practice are founded.

Changed labour management practices

The need to employ and deploy labour effectively led to increased attention to working conditions and practices during both wars; the changes that were introduced then continued, and interacted with other social changes that ensued after the wars (Child, 1969). For example, the Health of Munitions Workers Committee, which encouraged the systematic study of human factors in stress and fatigue in the munitions factories during the First World War, was succeeded in 1918 by the Industrial Fatigue Research Board (DSIR, 1961; Child, 1969; Rose, 1978). During the postwar reconstruction period progressive employers advocated minimum wage levels, shorter working hours and improved security of tenure (Child, 1969).

'The proper use of manpower whether in mobilizing the nation or sustaining the war economy once reserves of strength were fully deployed' was national policy during the Second World War (Moxon, 1951). As examples of this policy, Moxon cites the part-time employment of married women, the growth of factory medical services, canteens, day nurseries and special leave of absence.

The development of personnel techniques

Both wars encouraged the application of psychological techniques to selection and training, and stimulated the development of new approaches. Rose (1978: 92) suggests that, in 1917, the American army tested two million men to identify 'subnormals and officer material'. Seymour (1959) writes of the Second World War:

> the need to train millions of men and women for the fighting services led to a more detailed study of the skills required for handling modern weapons, and our understanding of human skill benefited greatly . . . Likewise, the shortage of labour in industry led . . . to experiments aimed at training munition workers to higher levels of output more quickly.
>
> (pp. 7–8)

The wars further influenced the development of the ergonomic design of equipment, and encouraged the collaboration of engineers, psychologists and other social scientists (DSIR, 1961).

The exigencies of war ensured that attention and resources were focused upon activities that are of enormous significance to the field of employment, while the scale of operations guaranteed the availability for testing of numbers of candidates far in excess of those usually available to psychologists undertaking research.

The development of the personnel profession

Very significantly, the Second World War had a major influence on the development of the personnel profession. According to Moxon (1951), the aims of national wartime policy were:

> (i) to see that the maximum use was made of each citizen, (ii) to see that working and living conditions were as satisfactory as possible, (iii) to see that individual rights were reasonably safeguarded and the democratic spirit preserved. The growth of personnel management was the direct result of the translation of this national policy by each industry and by each factory within an industry.
>
> (p. 7)

Child (1969) reports how government concern in 1940 about appropriate working practices and conditions

> led to direct governmental action enforcing the appointment of personnel officers in all but small factories and the compulsory provision of minimum welfare amenities. (p. 111)

Moxon (1951) comments on the 'four-fold increase in the number of practising personnel managers' at this time (p. 7). Child (1969) records the membership of what was to become the Institute of Personnel Management as 760 in 1939, and 2993 in 1960

(p. 113). He also notes a similar increase in other management bodies. (The Institute has now become the Chartered Institute of Personnel and Development, with a membership of 120 000 in 2002.)

The postwar reconstruction of Japan

This subsection has so far noted some of the direct influences that the two world wars had upon the field of HRM. It now points to an indirect and still continuing influence. The foundation of the philosophy and practice of total quality management, which has been of considerable recent significance in HRM, was laid during the Second World War. Edward Deming and Joseph Juran were consultants to the US Defense Department and during the Second World War ran courses on their new approaches to quality control for firms supplying army ordnance (Pickard, 1992). Hodgson (1987) reports that:

> Vast quantities of innovative and effective armaments were produced by a labour force starved of skill or manufacturing experience in the depression.   (p. 40)

After the war, America 'could sell everything it could produce' and, because it was believed that 'improving quality adds to costs', the work of Deming and Juran was ignored in the West. However, Deming became an adviser to the Allied Powers Supreme Command and a member of the team advising the Japanese upon postwar reconstruction (Hodgson, 1987: 40–41). He told them that 'their war-ravaged country would become a major force in international trade' if they followed his approach to quality. They did.

Western organisations have since come to emulate the philosophy and practices of quality that proved so successful in Japan and that now feature among the preoccupations of human resource managers (see, for example, Chapter 14).

Stop and think   What other distant socio-political events have influenced HRM?

■ Contemporary influences on HRM

The two topics to be examined now also come from fields distant from that of HRM but nevertheless influence it. However, they differ from those examined above. First, they belong primarily to the world of ideas, rather than action. Secondly, whereas the influences discussed above contributed to the incremental development of HRM thinking and practice, those discussed below have the potential to unsettle and possibly disrupt established thinking, and hence practice. Thirdly, the two world wars are, for us, history: interpretations of them have by now become established and, to a large degree, generally accepted (though always open to question: see the later subsection 'Defining reality for others'). However, what are discussed below are ideas of our own time, not yet fully formed or understood. They both originated in fields outside social science, but have been introduced into it because of their potential significance for the understanding of social phenomena.

Postmodernism

It was in the fields of art and architecture, in which there had been early twentieth-century schools of thought and expression regarded as 'modernism', that certain new approaches came to be labelled 'postmodern'. In due course, the concepts of modernism and postmodernism spread throughout the fields of culture (Harvey, 1990) and the social sciences. They are now used to express a critical perspective in organisation studies (for example, Gergen, 1992; Hassard and Parker, 1993; Hatch, 1997; Morgan, 1997) and in the HRM field (Legge, 1995; Townley, 1993). Connock (1992) includes postmodern thinking among the contemporary 'big ideas' of significance to human resource managers, while Fox (1990) interprets strategic HRM as a self-reflective cultural intervention responding to postmodern conditions. Although questions about postmodernism merge with others on post-industrialism, post-Fordism, and the present stage of capitalism (see Legge, 1995; Reed and Hughes, 1992 and Chapter 14), here we focus only on postmodernism.

Postmodernism is proving to be a challenging and unsettling concept for those socialised into what would now be called a 'modern' understanding of the world. There is considerable debate about it. Does it refer to an epoch (Hassard, 1993), a period of historical time, namely the 'post-modern' present which has succeeded 'modern times'? If so, does it represent a continuation of or a disjunction with the past? Or does it refer to a particular, and critical, perspective, which Hassard (1993) calls an 'epistemological position' (see Glossary)? Many, such as Legge (1995), distinguish this from the epochal 'post-modern' by omitting the hyphen ('postmodern').

An example of the epochal interpretation is Clegg's (1990: 180–181) discussion of post-modern organisations, the characteristics of which he identifies by contrasting them with modern organisations. For example, he suggests that the latter (that is, the organisations that we had been familiar with until the last decade or so of the twentieth century) were rigid, addressed mass markets and were premised on technological determinism; their jobs were 'highly differentiated, demarcated and de-skilled'. Post-modern organisations, however, are flexible, address niche markets, and are premised on technological choices; their jobs are 'highly de-differentiated, de-demarcated and multiskilled'.

It is less easy to pin down postmodernism as an epistemological position but, in brief, it is somewhat like the little boy's response to the 'emperor's new clothes'. Whereas modernism was based on the belief that there existed a universal objective truth which we could come to know by means of rational, scientific approaches (though often only with the help of experts), postmodernism denies that. It assumes that truth is local and socially constructed (see Glossary and later section) from a particular perspective. It asks: 'What truth?', 'Whose truth?', 'Who says so?' Hence it challenges the authority of the established view, for example, of the 'meta-narratives' of 'progress', 'the value of science' or 'Marxism vs. capitalism' which had become the accepted framework of twentieth-century understanding. Instead it recognises the claims of diverse and competing interpretations, and accepts that everything is open to question, that there are always alternative interpretations. Hence postmodernism has considerable significance for HRM. It recognises that multiple and competing views of organisations and HRM are legitimate; that the significance of theory lies not in its 'truth' but in its usefulness for practice. (This, perhaps, is a significant issue for the learning organisation, which is discussed in Chapter 8.) Moreover, it throws into question (Hassard and Parker, 1993; Kvale, 1992) the traditional (Western) understanding of the individual as a '"natural entity", independent of society, with "attributes" which can be studied empirically' (Collin, 1996: 9). That modern interpretation has underpinned the understanding and practices of HRM, such as psychometric testing: the postmodern view challenges the accepted way of dealing with, for example, competencies and assessment (Brittain and Ryder, 1999).

Moreover, postmodernism recognises that, far from being objective and universal as modernism assumed, knowledge is constructed through the interplay of power relationships and often the dominance of the most powerful. This makes a critical interpretation of established bodies of thought such as psychology (Kvale, 1992), which could be seen as a Western cultural product (Stead and Watson, 1999). Thus, whereas modernism often ignored or, indeed, disguised ideologies (see Glossary and the section later on

'Ways of seeing and thinking'), postmodernism seeks to uncover them. It also encourages self-reflexivity and, therefore, a critical suspicion towards one's own interpretations, and an ironic and playful treatment of one's subject.

Another important difference between modernism and postmodernism lies in the way they regard **language**. Modernism assumes that language is neutral, 'the vehicle for communicating independent "facts"' (Legge, 1995: 306). The postmodern argument, however, is that this is not the case (see Reed and Hughes, 1992; Hassard and Parker, 1993). Language 'itself constitutes or produces the "real"' (Legge, 1995: 306). Moreover, it is 'ideological' (Gowler and Legge, 1989: 438): both the means through which ideologies are expressed and the embodiment of ideology (see Glossary and later subsection). This can be seen in sexist and racist language, and in 'management-speak'.

Postmodernism highlights the significance of **discourse**. 'Why do we find it so congenial to speak of organizations as structures but not as clouds, systems but not songs, weak or strong but not tender or passionate?' (Gergen, 1992: 207). The reason, Gergen goes on to say, is that we achieve understanding within a 'discursive context'. A discourse is a 'set of meanings, metaphors, representations, images, stories, statements and so on that in some way together produce a particular version of events' (Burr, 1995: 48), a version belonging to a particular group of people. It provides the language and meanings whereby members of that group can interpret and construct reality, and gives them an identifiable position to adopt upon a given subject, thereby constituting their own identity, behaviour and reality (Gavey, 1989). By interpreting competing positions in its own terms, the group's discourse shuts down all other possible interpretations but its own.

For example, in order to engage in academic discourse, academics have to learn

> a vocabulary and a set of analytic procedures for 'seeing' what is going on . . . in the appropriate professional terms. For we must see only the partially ordered affairs of everyday life, which are open to many interpretations . . . as if they are events of a certain well-defined kind.
> (Parker and Shotter, 1990: 9)

Parker and Shotter (1990), using the contrast between 'everyday talk' and academic writing, explain how academic text standardises its interpretations:

> The strange and special thing about an academic text . . . is that by the use of certain strategies and devices, as well as already predetermined meanings, one is able to construct a text which can be understood (by those who are a party to such 'moves') in a way divorced from any reference to any local or immediate contexts. Textual communication can be (relatively) decontextualised. Everyday talk, on the other hand, is marked by its vagueness and openness, by the fact that only those taking part in it can understand its drift; the meanings concerned are not wholly predetermined, they are negotiated by those involved, on the spot, in relation to the circumstances in which they are involved . . . Everyday talk is situated or contextualised, and relies upon its situation (its circumstances) for its sense.
> (pp. 2–3)

There are many discourses identifiable in the field of organisation and management studies – managerial, humanist, critical, industrial relations – that offer their own explanations and rhetoric. You can explore them further in, for example, the chapters that follow, and Clark *et al.* (1994), but you should remain aware that academic discourse itself enables writers to exercise power over the production of knowledge and to influence their readers. Awareness of discourse is also important for the understanding of organisations:

organisational life is made up of many 'discourses' – that is, flows of beliefs, experiences, meanings and actions. Each of these discourses shapes the behaviour of the organisation and of teams and individuals within it. These discourses are in turn created and reworked by individuals' actions and their expressed beliefs. This may not sound much, but it shifts the management of change, for example, from a simplistic view of changing culture, processes and structures to one of altering these aspects of organisational life by building on and reshaping the various discourses flowing around a company.

(Baxter, 1999: 49).

The notion of discourse is relevant to our understanding of HRM. From today's vantage point we can now perhaps recognise that the way in which we once conceptualised and managed the employment relationship was influenced by modernism. However, Legge (1995: 324–325) considers HRM to be both post-modern and postmodern. 'From a managerialist view' it is post-modern in terms of epoch and its basic assumptions (p. 324), whereas 'from a critical perspective' it is a 'postmodernist discourse' (p. 312). HRM, with its ambiguous, or contested, nature, discussed in Chapter 1, emerged alongside the spread of post-modern organisations and postmodern epistemology. The recognition of multiple, coexisting yet competing realities and interpretations, the constant reinterpretation, the eclecticism, the concern for presentation and re-presentation – all of which you will recognise in this book – can be interpreted as a postmodern rendering of the debate about the nature of the employment relationship. We must therefore expect that there will be even more, perhaps very different, interpretations of HRM to be made.

Stop and think	The way David Brent, in Ricky Gervais's *The Office*, communicates with his staff is a caricature of managerial discourse. Can you identify from that what kind of managerial strategy (see earlier), he appears to have adopted?

The 'new science'

We shall now turn briefly to another possible source of influence upon the HRM field. The so-called 'new science' derives from new developments in the natural sciences that challenge some of the key assumptions of Newton's mechanistic notion of the universe (see Wheatley, 1992, for a simplified explanation). Traditionally, science has been 'reductionist' in its analysis into parts and search for 'the basic building blocks of matter' (Wheatley, 1992: 32). It has assumed that 'certainty, linearity, and predictability' (Elliott and Kiel, 1997: 1) are essential elements of the universe. However, new discoveries have questioned those assumptions, generating the theories of complexity and chaos. Complexity refers to a system's 'interrelatedness and interdependence of components as well as their freedom to interact, align, and organize into related configurations' (Lee, 1997: 20). 'Because of this internal complexity, random disturbances can produce unpredictable events and relationships that reverberate throughout a system, creating novel patterns of change ... however, ... despite all the unpredictability, coherent order *always* [emphasis in original] emerges out of the randomness and surface chaos' (Morgan, 1997: 262). To understand complexity, new approaches that recognise the whole rather than just its parts – a holistic approach – and attention to relationships between the parts are needed, and these are being developed.

Although theories of complexity and chaos are sometimes referred to as a 'postmodern science', this is a 'common misconception', for 'while recognizing the need for a modification of the reductionist classical model of science, [these theories] remain grounded within the "scientific" tradition' (Price, 1997: 3). They are, nevertheless, recognised as relevant to the understanding of complex social systems. For example, 'chaos theory appears to provide a means for understanding and examining many of the uncertainties, nonlinearities, and unpredictable aspects of social systems behavior' (Elliott and Kiel, 1997: 1). The literature on the application of these theories to social phenomena tends to be very demanding (for example, Eve *et al.*, 1997; Kiel and Elliott, 1997). However, Morgan's (1997) and Wheatley's (1992) applications to organisations are more accessible. There has been some application in the HRM field. For example, Cooksey and Gates (1995) use non-linear dynamics and chaos theory as a way of conceptualising how common HRM practices translate into observable outcomes. Brittain and Ryder (1999: 51) draw on complexity theory in their attempt to improve the assessment of competencies, and conclude that 'HR professionals and psychologists need to challenge widely held beliefs about assessment processes, move away from simplistic assumptions about cause and effect and take a more complex view of the world'.

Ways of seeing and thinking

The chapter will now turn its attention to our ways of seeing and thinking about our world: ways that generate the language, the code, the keys we use in conceptualising and practising HRM. It is at this point that we become fully aware of the value of representing context as a tapestry rather than as a many-skinned onion, for we find here various strands of meaning that managers and academics are drawing upon to construct – that is, both to create and to make sense of – HRM. These ways of seeing are the warp, the threads running the length of the tapestry that give it its basic form and texture, but are generally not visible on its surface. They are more apparent, however, when we turn the tapestry over, as we shall do now, and examine how we perceive reality, make assumptions about it, and define it for ourselves. We shall then look at the weft threads of the tapestry as we examine how we define reality for others through ideology and rhetoric.

Perceiving reality

Perception

Human beings cannot approach reality directly, or in a completely detached and clinical manner. The barriers between ourselves and the world outside us operate at very basic levels:

> Despite the impression that we are in direct and immediate contact with the world, our perception is, in fact, separated from reality by a long chain of processing.
>
> (Medcof and Roth, 1979: 4)

Psychologists indicate that perception is a complex process involving the selection of stimuli to which to respond and the organisation and interpretation of them according to patterns we already recognise. (You can read more about this in Huczynski and Buchanan, 2002.) In other words, we develop a set of filters through which we make sense of our world. Kelly (1955) calls them our 'personal constructs', and they channel the ways we conceptualise and anticipate events (see Bannister and Fransella, 1971).

Defence mechanisms

Our approach to reality, however, is not just through cognitive processes. There is too much at stake for us, for our definition of reality has implications for our definitions of ourselves and for how we would wish others to see us. We therefore defend our sense of self – from what we interpret as threats from our environment or from our own inner urges – by means of what Freud called our 'ego defence mechanisms'. In his study of how such behaviour changes over time, Vaillant (1977) wrote:

> Often such mechanisms are analogous to the means by which an oyster, confronted with a grain of sand, creates a pearl. Humans, too, when confronted with conflict, engage in unconscious but often creative behaviour.   (p. 7)

Freudians and non-Freudians (see Peck and Whitlow, 1975: 39–40) have identified many forms of such unconscious adaptive behaviour, some regarded as healthy, others as unhealthy and distorting. We may not go to the lengths of the 'neurotic' defences which Vaillant (1977: 384–385) describes, but a very common approach to the threats of the complexity of intimacy or the responsibility for others is to separate our feelings from our thinking, to treat people and indeed parts of ourselves as objects rather than subjects. The scene is set for a detached, objective and scientific approach to reality in general, to organisations in particular, and to the possibility of treating human beings as 'resources' to be managed.

Making assumptions about reality

We noted earlier that the very term 'human resource management' confronts us with an assumption. This should cause us to recognise that the theory and practice of the employment relationship rest upon assumptions. The assumptions to be examined here are even more fundamental ones for they shape the very way we think. Some are so deeply engrained that they are difficult to identify and express, but they are nevertheless embodied in the way we approach life. They include the way we conceptualise, theorise about and manage the employment relationship, so our assumptions have important implications for our interpretation of HRM.

Writing about Kelly's (1955) personal construct theory, Bannister and Fransella (1971) argue:

> we cannot contact an interpretation-free reality directly. We can only make assumptions about what reality is and then proceed to find out how useful or useless those assumptions are.   (p. 18)

However, we have developed our assumptions from birth, and they have been refined and reinforced by socialisation and experience so that, generally, we are not even aware of them. We do not, therefore, generally concern ourselves with epistemology, the theory of knowledge, and we find the discussion of philosophical issues difficult to follow. Nevertheless, we are undoubtedly making significant assumptions about 'what it is possible to know, how may we be certain that we know something' (Heather, 1976: 12–13). These assumptions underpin thinking and contribute to the filters of perception: they therefore frame any understanding of the world, including the ways in which researchers, theorists and practitioners construe HRM. To understand something of HRM we need at least to recognise some of the implications of these epistemological and philosophical issues.

Pepper's (1942) 'world hypotheses' help us distinguish some fundamentally different assumptions that can be made about the world. He classifies them as two pairs of polarised assumptions. The first pair is about the universe. At one pole is the assumption that there is an ordered and systematic universe, 'where facts occur in a determinate order, and where, if enough were known, they could be predicted, or at least described' (Pepper, 1942: 143). At the other pole, the universe is understood as a 'flowing and unbroken wholeness' (Morgan, 1997: 251), with 'real indeterminateness in the world' (Harré, 1981: 3), in which there are 'multitudes of facts rather loosely scattered and not necessarily determining one another to any considerable degree' (Pepper, 1942: 142–143). Pepper's second polarity is about how we approach the universe: through analysis, fragmenting a whole into its parts in order to examine it more closely, or through synthesis, examining it as a whole within its context.

Western thinking stands at the first pole in both pairs of assumptions: it takes an analytical approach to what is assumed to be an ordered universe. Hence 'we are taught to break apart problems, to fragment the world' (Senge, 1990: 3); we examine the parts separately from their context and from one another, 'wrenching units of behaviour, action or experience from one another' (Parker, 1990: 100). These approaches, which underpin the positivism discussed in the next subsection, lead us in our research to examine a world that we interpret as

abstract, fragmented, precategorized, standardized, divorced from personal and local contexts or relevance, and with its meanings defined and controlled by researchers.

(Mishler, 1986: 120)

By contrast, and of particular relevance to this chapter, is 'contextualism', Pepper's world hypothesis that espouses the assumptions at the second pole of both pairs above. This regards events and actions as processes that are woven into their wider context, and so have to be understood in terms of the multiplicity of interconnections and interrelationships within that context. This is what our tapestry metaphor has attempted to convey. We can use further metaphors to glimpse just how different this view is from our orthodox understanding of the world: from the user's perspective, the latter is like using a library, while the former is more like using the Internet (Collin, 1997). The information in a library is structured and classified by experts in a hierarchical system according to agreed conventions; users have to follow that system, translating their needs for information into a form recognised by that system. The Internet, however, is an open-ended network of providers of information, non-linear, constantly changing and expanding. It presents users with a multitude of potential connections to be followed at will and, moreover, the opportunity to participate through dialogue with existing websites or through establishing their own Web page.

Differences as basic as those between Pepper's world hypotheses inevitably lead to very different ways of seeing and thinking about reality and, indeed, of understanding our own role in the universe. However, we are rarely aware of or have reason to question our deepest assumptions. Not only does our orthodox approach itself impede our recognition of these epistemological issues, but the processes of socialisation and education in any given society nudge its members in a particular direction (although some may wander off the highway into the byways or, like the author of *Zen and the Art of Motorcycle Maintenance* (Pirsig, 1976), into what are assumed to be badlands). It can be easier to discern these issues in the contrast offered by the epistemological positions adopted in other societies. We can, for example, recognise more of our own deeply embedded assumptions when we encounter a very different world view in an anthropologist's account (Castaneda, 1970) of his apprenticeship to a Yaqui sorceror. Of this, Goldschmidt (1970) writes:

> Anthropology has taught us that the world is differently defined in different places. It is not only that people have different customs; it is not only that people believe in different gods and expect different post-mortem fates. It is, rather, that the worlds of different peoples have different shapes. The very metaphysical presuppositions differ: space does not conform to Euclidean geometry, time does not form a continuous unidirectional flow, causation does not conform to Aristotelian logic, man [sic] is not differentiated from non-man or life from death, as in our world . . . The central importance of entering worlds other than our own – and hence of anthropology itself – lies in the fact that the experience leads us to understand that our own world is also a cultural construct. By experiencing other worlds, then, we see our own for what it is . . .   (pp. 9–10)

Most of the epistemological threads in the tapestry examined in this chapter reflect Western orthodoxy. (Note how Western orthodoxy has exerted hegemony (see Glossary and below) over non-Western thinking (Stead and Watson, 1999).) And this orthodoxy itself might be gradually changing; some commentators have argued that it has reached a 'turning point' (Capra, 1983), that they can detect signs of a 'paradigm shift' (see Glossary). Indeed, over the last decade or so there have emerged new developments in the natural sciences (see the 'new science' above), and elsewhere (see feminist thinking: below) that challenge orthodoxy.

Stop and think	How could you use Pepper's ideas to explain the challenges of postmodernism and the 'new science' to conventional thinking?

This chapter will now turn to a more accessible level of our thinking, easier to identify and understand, although again we do not customarily pay it much attention.

■ Defining reality for ourselves

The distinctions between the epistemological positions above and the philosophical stances examined here appear very blurred (Heather, 1976; Checkland, 1981). There is certainly considerable affinity between some of Pepper's (1942) 'world hypotheses' and the approaches noted below. The discussion here will be restricted to aspects of those approaches relevant to our understanding of concepts and practices like HRM.

● Orthodox thinking

By orthodoxy we mean 'correct' or currently accepted opinions inculcated in the majority of members in any given society through the processes of socialisation and education and sustained through sanctions against deviation. In our society, for example, most people trust in rationality and 'orthodox medicine' and have doubts about the paranormal and 'alternative medicine'. We do not generally question our orthodox beliefs: they 'stand to reason', they work, everyone else thinks in the same way. By definition, therefore, we do not pay much attention to them, nor consider how they frame the interpretations we make of our world, nor what other alternatives there could be. We shall therefore now first examine this orthodoxy and then some alternatives to it.

ACTIVITY	Either on your own or in a group, make a list of the characteristics of Western orthodoxy that have already been mentioned in this chapter.

The orthodox approach in Western thinking is based on positivism. Positivism forms the basis of scientific method, and applies the rational and ordered principles of the natural sciences to human affairs generally. It manifests itself (see Heather, 1976; Rose, 1978: 26) in a concern for objectivity, in the construction of testable hypotheses, in the collection of empirical data, in the search for causal relationships and in quantification. It is, therefore, uneasy with subjective experience, and attempts to maintain distance between the researcher and those studied (called 'subjects', though regarded more as objects). For example, the Western view is that the individual has (rather than is) a self, which is a natural object, bounded, reified, highly individualised, and autonomous (see Collin, 1996).

We can perceive the role of positivism in orthodoxy in the contrast Kelly draws between the assumptions underpinning his personal construct theory (see previous subsection) and those of orthodox science:

> A scientist . . . depends upon his [sic] facts to furnish the ultimate proof of his propositions . . . these shining nuggets of truth . . . To suggest [as Kelly does] . . . that further human reconstruction can completely alter the appearance of the precious fragments he has accumulated, as well as the direction of their arguments, is to threaten his scientific conclusions, his philosophical position, and even his moral security . . . our assumption that all facts are subject . . . to alternative constructions looms up as culpably subjective and dangerously subversive to the scientific establishment.
>
> (quoted in Bannister and Fransella, 1971: 17–18)

Positivism has informed most social science research, which in turn has reproduced, through the kind of new knowledge generated, Western orthodoxy. Hence, it 'reigns' in much HRM research (Legge, 1995: 308). It will be clear from the discussion of the immediate context of HRM that many managers and theorists of management espouse it. It underpins many organisational activities such as psychometric testing for selection and human resource planning models.

● Challenging alternatives

There are several alternative ways of thinking that challenge orthodoxy, and you could read more about them in Denzin and Lincoln (1994). The approaches outlined here differ from one another, having different origins and, to some extent, values and constituencies, though they are largely similar in their express opposition to positivism. However, it is important to note that it is only the non-positivist forms of feminist and systems thinking that are covered here: in other words, there are also positivist versions.

ACTIVITY   Either on your own or in a group, make a list of the characteristics of alternatives to Western orthodoxy that have already been mentioned in this chapter.

Phenomenology, constructivism and social constructionism

These three approaches stand in marked contrast to positivism, being concerned not with objective reality, but with our lived, subjective, experience of it.

Phenomenology is concerned with understanding the individual's conscious experience. Rather than analysing this into fragments, it takes a holistic approach. It acknowledges the significance of subjectivity, which positivism subordinates to objectivity. Phenomenological researchers try to make explicit the conscious phenomena of experience of those they study, seeking access to these empathically, through shared meanings and inter-subjectivity. This is not a commonplace approach in the field of HRM and management (Sanders, 1982), although it is sometimes discussed in qualitative research studies.

Constructivism is also concerned with individual experience, but with emphasis upon the individual's cognitive processes: 'each individual mentally constructs the world of experience … the mind is not a mirror of the world as it is, but functions to create the world as we know it' (Gergen, 1999, p. 236). (Note that some constructivists appear to retain something of the positivist approach.)

Social constructionism holds that an objective reality is not directly knowable (and hence we cannot know whether it exists). The reality we do know is socially constructed: we construct it through language and social interaction.

> Human beings in the social process are constantly creating the social world in interaction with others. They are negotiating their interpretations of reality, those multiple interpretations at the same time constituting the reality itself.   (Checkland, 1981: 277)

To make sense of our experiences, we have to interpret and negotiate meaning with others. There can be no single objective meaning but, Hoffman (1990) suggests,

> an evolving set of meanings that emerge unendingly from the interactions between people. These meanings are not skull-bound and may not exist inside what we think of as an individual 'mind'. They are part of a general flow of constantly changing narratives.   (p. 3)

Knowledge is thus a social phenomenon (Hoffman, 1990), and language, rather than depicting objective reality, itself constructs meaning. Weick (1979) quotes a baseball story that illustrates this nicely:

> Three umpires disagreed about the task of calling balls and strikes. The first one said, 'I calls them as they is.' The second one said, 'I calls them as I sees them.' The third and cleverest umpire said, 'They ain't nothin' till I calls them.'   (p. 1)

As also suggested by Pepper's (1942) contextualism, discussed earlier, this view of the social construction of meaning implies that we cannot separate ourselves from our created reality: 'man [sic] is an animal suspended in webs of significance he himself has spun' (Geertz, 1973: 5). Again as with contextualism, this approach emphasises the significance of perspective, the position from which an interpretation is made (remember the *Guardian* advertisement at the start of this chapter?). Further, it also draws attention to the way in which some people contrive to impose their interpretations upon, and so define the reality of, others, with the result that less powerful people are disempowered, overlooked, remain silent, are left without a 'voice' (Mishler, 1986; Bhavnani, 1990). This is a point to which the chapter returns later.

Stop and think   Can you identify social constructionist perspectives among the competing interpretations of organisations and management discussed earlier in the chapter?

Feminist thinking

Feminist thinking, which recognises differences between the world-views of women and men, challenges what is increasingly regarded as the male world-view of the positivist approach (Gilligan, 1982; Spender, 1985). Gilligan's (1982) landmark study concluded that women value relationship and connection, whereas men value independence, autonomy and control. Bakan (1966) made a distinction between 'agency' and 'communion', associating the former with maleness and the latter with femaleness. Agency is 'an expression of independence through self-protection, self-assertion and control of the environment' (Marshall, 1989: 279), whereas the basis of communion is integration with others.

> The agentic strategy reduces tension by changing the world about it; communion seeks union and cooperation as its way of coming to terms with uncertainty. While agency manifests itself in focus, closedness and separation, communion is characterized by contact, openness and fusion.
> (Marshall, 1989: 289)

Therefore, Marshall (1989) argues, feminist thinking 'represents a fundamental critique of knowledge as it is traditionally constructed . . . largely . . . by and about men' and either ignores or devalues the experience of women:

> its preoccupation with seeking universal, immutable truth, failing to accept diversity and change; its categorization of the world into opposites, valuing one pole and devaluing the other; its claims of detachment and objectivity; and the predominance of linear cause-and-effect thinking. These forms reflect male, agentic experiences and strategies for coping with uncertainty. By shaping academic theorizing and research activities, they build male power and domination into the structures of knowledge . . .
> (p. 281)

Calas and Smircich (1992: 227) discuss how gender has been 'mis- or under-represented' in organisation theory, and explore the effects of rewriting it in. These would include the correction or completion of the organisational record from which women have been absent or excluded, the assessment of gender bias in current knowledge, and the making of a new, more diverse organisation theory that covers topics of concern to women. Hearn *et al.* (1989) identify similar shortcomings in organisation theory in their discussion of the sexuality of organisations, while Hopfl and Hornby Atkinson (2000) point to the gendered assumptions made in organisations.

Systems and ecological thinking

Systems thinking offers particularly useful insights into the understanding of context. As with feminist thinking, there are both positivist and alternative views of systems, but here we are concerned with the latter. Checkland (1981), for example, adopts a phenomenological approach in his 'soft systems methodology', employing systems not as 'descriptions of actual real-world activity' (p. 314), but as 'tools of an epistemological kind which can be used in a process of exploration within social reality' (p. 249). (Note that his later book – Checkland and Scholes, 1990 – updates the methodology but does not repeat the discussion of its philosophical underpinnings.) As with feminist thinking, systems thinking gives us a different perspective from that of orthodox thinking. It allows us to see the whole rather than just its parts and to recognise that we are a part of that whole. It registers patterns of change, relationships rather than just individual elements, a web of interrelationships and reciprocal flows of influence rather than linear chains of cause and effect.

The concept of system denotes a whole, complex and coherent entity, comprising a hierarchy of subsystems, where the whole is greater than the sum of its parts. Much of what has been written about systems draws upon General Systems Theory, a meta-theory that offered a way to conceptualise phenomena in any disciplinary area. Very importantly, the systems approach does not argue that social phenomena are systems, but rather that they can be modelled (conceptualised, thought about) as though they had systemic properties. The concept of system used in the social sciences is therefore a very abstract kind of metaphor. However, we can give only a brief outline of systems concepts here: you will find further detail in Checkland (1981), Checkland and Scholes (1990), Senge (1990) and Morgan (1997).

Systems may be 'open' (like biological or social systems) or 'closed' to their environment (like many physical and mechanical systems). As shown in Figure 3.2, the open system imports from, exchanges with, its environment what it needs to meet its goals and to survive. It converts or transforms these inputs into a form that sustains its existence and generates outputs that are returned to the environment either in exchange for further inputs or as waste products. The environment itself comprises other systems that are also drawing in inputs and discharging outputs. Changes in remote parts of any given system's environment can therefore ripple through that environment to affect it eventually. There is a feedback loop that enables the system to make appropriate modifications to its subsystems in the light of the changing environment. Thus the system constantly adjusts to achieve equilibrium internally and with its environment.

Figure 3.2   Model of an open system

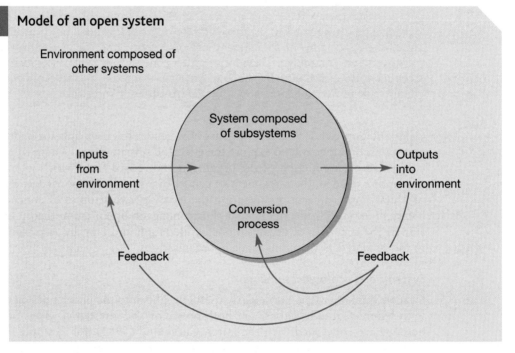

Reflecting upon the management approaches identified earlier, we can now recognise that the scientific management, human relations and perhaps also the humanistic approaches treated the organisation as a closed system, whereas the human resource approach recognises it as open to its environment. Brunsson's (1989) identification of the 'action' and 'political' organisations could also be seen as an open system approach.

The significance of systems thinking, then, lies in its ability to conceptualise complex, dynamic realities – the system and its internal and external relationships – and model them in a simple, coherent way that is yet pregnant with meaning and capable of further elaboration when necessary. This means that we can use it to hold in our minds such complex ideas as those discussed in this chapter, without diminishing our awareness of their complexity and interrelationships.

According to Senge (1990), systems thinking – his 'fifth discipline' – is essential for the development of the effective organisation – the learning organisation (Chapter 8):

> At the heart of a learning organization is a shift of mind – from seeing ourselves as separate from the world to connected to the world, from seeing problems as caused by someone or something 'out there' to seeing how our own actions create the problems we experience. A learning organization is a place where people are continually discovering how they create their reality. And how they can change it.   (pp. 12–13)

Stop and think   What similarities do you see between systems thinking and the 'new science'?

Systems thinking therefore enables us to contextualise organisations and HRM. It conceptualises an organisation in an increasingly complex and dynamic relationship with its complex and dynamic global environment. Changes in one part of the environment – global warming, poor harvests, international and civil wars – can change the nature of the inputs into an organisation – raw materials and other resources. This can lead to the need for adjustments in and between the subsystems – new marketing strategies, technologies, working practices – either to ensure the same output or to modify the output. The environment consists of other organisations, the outputs of which – whether intentionally or as by-products – constitute the inputs of others. A change in output, such as a new or improved product or service, however, will constitute a change in another organisation's input, leading to a further ripple of adjustments. Consider, for example, how flexible working practices and call centres have been developed.

ACTIVITY
HRM as an open system

How would you represent the HRM activities of an organisation in a changing world in terms of the open systems model? Working individually or in groups, identify its inputs (where they come from, and how they could be changing), how it converts these, and what its (changing?) outputs might be. What are its feedback mechanisms?

■ Defining reality for others

This chapter has defined the warp of the tapestry of context as our ways of seeing and thinking. It will now examine some of the weft threads – the ways in which others define our reality (or we define reality for others): ideology, hegemony, and rhetoric. These interweave through the warp to produce the basic pattern of the tapestry, but with differing colours and textures, and also differing lengths (durations), so that they do not necessarily appear throughout the tapestry. They constitute important contextual influences upon HRM, and in part account for the competing definitions of it.

● Ideology

Gowler and Legge (1989) define ideology as 'sets of ideas involved in the framing of our experience, of making sense of the world, expressed through language' (p. 438). It has a narrower focus than the 'ways of thinking' we have been discussing above, and could be seen as a localised orthodoxy, a reasonably coherent set of ideas and beliefs that often goes unchallenged:

> Ideology operates as a reifying, congealing mechanism that imposes pseudoresolutions and compromises in the space where fluid, contradictory, and multivalent subjectivity could gain ground.   (Sloan, 1992: 174)

Ideology purports to explain reality objectively, but within a pluralist society it actually represents and legitimates the interests of members of a subgroup. It is a 'subtle combination of facts and values' (Child, 1969: 224), and achieves its ends through language and rhetoric (see below). What we hear and what we read is conveying someone else's interpretations. The way those are expressed may obscure the ideology and vested interest in those interpretations. For example, in contrast to the orthodox view of culture, Jermier argues that culture is:

> the objectified product of the labor of human subjects . . . there is a profound forgetting of the fact that the world is socially constructed and can be remade . . . Exploitative practices are mystified and concealed.
>
> (Frost *et al.*, 1991: 231)

As you will recognise from earlier in the chapter, the organisation is an arena in which ideologies of many kinds are in contest: capitalism and Marxism, humanism and scientific approaches to the individual, feminism and a gender-biased view.

Child (1969) discusses the ideology embodied in the development of management thinking, identifying how the human relations approach chose to ignore the difference of interests between managers and employees and how this dismissal of potential conflict influenced theory and practice. Commentators such as Braverman (1974), Frost *et al.* (1991) and Rose (1978), and many of the readings in Clark *et al.* (1994), will help you to recognise some of the ideologies at work in this field.

● Hegemony

Hegemony is the imposition of the reality favoured by a powerful subgroup in society upon less powerful others. Such a group exerts its authority over subordinate groups by imposing its definition of reality over other possible definitions. This does not have to be achieved through direct coercion, but by 'winning the consent of the dominated majority so that the power of the dominant classes appears both legitimate and natural'. In this way, subordinate groups are 'contained within an ideological space which does not seem at all "ideological": which appears instead to be permanent and "natural", to lie outside history, to be beyond particular interests' (Hebdige, 1979: 15–16).

It is argued that gender issues are generally completely submerged in organisations and theories of them (Hearn *et al.*, 1989; Calas and Smircich, 1992; Hopfl and Atkinson, 2000) so that male-defined realities of organisations appear natural, and feminist views unnatural and shrill. You could use the readings in Clark *et al.* (1994) to identify instances of hegemony and the outcomes of power relations, such as the 'management prerogative'; Watson (2000) throws light on the manager's experience of these.

● Rhetoric

Rhetoric is 'the art of using language to persuade, influence or manipulate' (Gowler and Legge, 1989: 438). Its 'high symbolic content' *'allows it to reveal and conceal but above all develop and transform meaning'* (Gowler and Legge, 1989: 439, their italics). It *'heightens and transforms meaning by processes of association, involving both evocation and juxtaposition'.* In other words, its artfulness lies in playing with meanings. It is something with which we are familiar, whether as political 'spin' or as the terminology used in effecting organisational change (Atkinson and Butcher, 1999). In the 'eco-climate' of an organisation, where meanings are shared and negotiated, power and knowledge relations are expressed rhetorically. For example, changes to structure and jobs might be described as 'flexibility' rather than as the casualisation of work (see, for example, Chapter 4), and increased pressures upon employees as 'empowerment' (see

Chapter 14). Moreover, Legge (1995) proposes, one way of interpreting HRM is to recognise it as 'a rhetoric about how employees should be managed to achieve competitive advantage' that both 'celebrates' the values of its stakeholders while 'at the same time mediating the contradictions of capitalism' (p. xiv). In other words, it allows those stakeholders to 'have their cake and eat it'.

Conclusion . . . and a new beginning?

This chapter has examined something of the warp and weft that give the tapestry its basic form, pattern, colour and texture. To complete our understanding of the context of HRM we need to recognise that issues and people constitute the surface stitching that is drawn through the warp and weft to add further pattern and colour. You will be aware of examples from your own experience and the reading of this and other books, but we can instance the influences of recession, equal opportunities legislation, European directives, management gurus, Margaret Thatcher, 'New Labour', the euro debate, 11 September, that resonate with the warp and weft to produce the pattern that has come to be known as 'HRM'.

The tapestry of which HRM forms a part is continuously being woven, but we can now become aware of the sources of the differing approaches to organisation and management and of the contesting voices about the management of people. We can now recognise that their contest weaves multiple meanings into the organisational and conceptual pattern which is HRM. However, this awareness also allows us to recognise that yet other meanings, and hence potentials for the management of the employment relationship, remain to be constructed.

By pointing to the need to recognise the significance of the context of HRM, this chapter is also acknowledging that you will find therein more interpretations than this book of 'academic text' (Parker and Shotter, 1990: see 'Discourse' earlier), shaped by its writers' own agendas and values and the practicalities of commercial publication, can offer you. The process both of writing and of publication is that of decontextualisation, fragmentation, standardisation, and presentation of knowledge as 'entertaining education', in bite-sized chunks of knowledge or sound bites. But by urging you to become aware of the context of HRM, this chapter is at the same time inviting you to look beyond what it has to say, to recognise the nature of its discourse or, rather, discourses, to challenge its assumptions (and, indeed, your own) and to use your own critical judgements informed by your wider reading and personal experience.

This, then, is why this book has begun its exploration of HRM by examining context. This chapter had a further aim (and this betrays this writer's 'agenda and values'). This is to orientate your thinking generally towards an awareness of context, to think contextually, for ultimately awareness of context is empowering. One of the outcomes could well be greater knowledge but less certainty, the recognition that there could be competing interpretations of the topic you are considering, that the several perspectives upon the area could all yield different conclusions. Attention to context, therefore, encourages us not to be taken in by our initial interpretations, nor to accept unquestioningly the definitions of reality that others would have us adopt (the 'hegemony' of the previous section). There are, however, no easy answers, and we have to make the choice between alternatives. Reality is much messier and more tentative than theory and, like 'everyday talk', it is 'marked by its vagueness and openness', its meaning open to interpretation through negotiation with others. The acceptance of this, however, as we shall later see in Chapter 8, is one of the marks of the mature learner: the ability to recognise alternative viewpoints but, nevertheless, to take responsibility for committing oneself to one of them.

By definition, one chapter cannot begin to portray the details of the context of HRM. Those, after all, are constantly changing with time. It will have achieved its purpose if it causes you to recognise the significance of context and the need to adopt ways of thinking that enable you to conceptualise it. It can point you in some directions, and you will find many others in the chapters that follow, but there are no logical starting points, because context is indivisible; and you will never reach the end of the story for, from the perspective of context, the story is never-ending.

Summary

- The chapter argues that the keys to the understanding of human affairs, such as HRM, lie within their context. Although context is difficult to conceptualise and represent, readers can draw on their existing understanding of environmental issues to help them comprehend it. Awareness and comprehension of context are ultimately empowering because they sharpen critical thinking by challenging our own and others' assumptions.

- Multiple interests, conflict, and stressful and moral issues are inherent in the immediate context of HRM, which comprises the organisation (the nature of which generates a number of lateral and vertical tensions) and management (defined as the continuous process of resolving those tensions). Over time, managers have adopted a range of approaches to their task, including scientific management; the human relations school; humanistic organisation development; and now HRM. To understand this layer of HRM's context calls for the recognition of the existence of some significant assumptions that inform managers' differing practices and the competing interpretations that theorists make of them.

- The wider social, economic, political and cultural context of HRM is diverse, complex and dynamic, but three very different and unconnected strands of it are pulled out for examination. The two world wars left legacies for the management of the employment relationship, while emerging 'postmodern' experiences and critiques and the 'new science' locate HRM within a contemporary framework of ideas that could eventually challenge some assumptions about the management of the employment relationship.

- The chapter, however, finds it insufficient to conceptualise context as layered, like an onion. Rather, HRM is embedded in its context. The metaphor of a tapestry is therefore used to express the way in which its meaning is constructed from the interweaving and mutual influences of the assumptions deriving from basic perceptual, epistemological, philosophical and ideological positions. The notions of 'warp' and 'weft' are used to discuss such key contextual elements as positivism, phenomenology, constructivism, social constructionism, feminist thinking, systems thinking, ideology, hegemony, and rhetoric. People, events and issues are the surface stitching.

- The nature of this tapestry, with its multiple and often competing perspectives, ensures that HRM, as a concept, theory and practice, is a contested terrain. However, the chapter leaves readers to identify the implications of this through their critical reading of the book.

ACTIVITY	**Drawing on your understanding of the environment**

The nature of our environment concerns us all. As 'environment' and 'green issues' have crossed the threshold of public awareness to become big business, we have become concerned about our natural environment as no previous generations have been. We are now aware of the increasing complexity in the web of human affairs. We recognise the interrelationships within our 'global village', between the world's 'rich' North and the 'poor' South, and between politics, economics and the environment, and at home between, for example, health, unemployment, deprivation and crime. Another feature of our environment that we cannot ignore is its increasingly dynamic nature. Our world is changing before our very eyes. Comparing it with the world we knew even ten years ago, and certainly with that known by our parents when they were the age we are now, it has changed dramatically and in ways that could never have been anticipated.

1 You will have considerable knowledge, and perhaps personal experience, of many environmental issues. These might be the problems of waste disposal and pollution, BSE and genetically modified food, the impact on the countryside of the construction of new roads, or the threats to the survival of many species of animals and plants.

   As a step towards helping you understand better the nature of context as defined in this chapter, and working individually or in groups, choose two or three such issues for discussion, and consider the following points.

(a) Identify those who are playing a part in them (the actors) and those directly or indirectly affected by them (the stakeholders). How did the event or situation that has become an issue come about? Who started it? How do they explain it? Who benefits in this situation? How do they justify this? Who loses in it? What can they do about it? Why? Who is paying the cost? How and why?

(b) Look for concrete examples of the following statements.

   – 'We have an impact upon the environment and cause it to change, both positively and negatively.'

   – 'The environment and changes within it have an impact upon us and affect the quality of human life, both positively and negatively.'

   – 'The interrelationships between events and elements in the environment are so complex that they are often difficult to untangle.'

   – 'It may not be possible or even meaningful to identify the cause of events and their effects; the cause or causes may have to be inferred, the effects projected.'

   – 'Sometimes these effects are manifested far into the future, and so are not easily identifiable now, though they may affect future generations.'

   – 'Our relationship with our environment therefore has a moral dimension to it.'

   – 'To deal with some of the negative causes may be gravely damaging to some other groups of people.'

   – 'The understanding of these events will differ according to the particular perspective – whether of observer, actor, or stakeholder – and will arise from interpretation rather than ultimately verifiable "facts".'

   – 'These issues often involve powerful power bases in society, each of which has its own interpretation of events, and wishes others to accept its definition of them.'

   – 'The nature of our relationship with our environment challenges our traditional scientific ways of thinking, in which we value objectivity, analyse by breaking down a whole into its parts, and seek to identify cause and effect in a linear model.'

   – 'It also therefore challenges our traditional methods of research and investigation, deduction and inference.'

▶

2 The opening section of the chapter suggested that your examination of environmental issues would allow you to recognise that:

- Context is multilayered, multidimensional and interwoven, like a *tapestry*. Concrete events and abstract ideas intertwine to create issues, and thinking, feeling, interpreting and behaving are all involved.

- Our understanding of people and events depends upon our *perspective*.

- It also depends upon our *ideology*.

- There are therefore *competing or contested interpretations* of events.

- Different groups in society have their own interpretations of events, stemming from their *ideology*. Their *discourse* incorporates an explanation for competing interpretations. They use *rhetoric* to express their own interpretations and to explain those of other people, thus distorting, or even suppressing, the authentic expression of competing views.

- Powerful others often try to impose their interpretation of events, their version of reality, upon the less powerful majority: this is *hegemony*.

  From your knowledge of the environmental issues you have just discussed, can you give concrete examples of these points?

Questions

1 In what ways does the conceptualisation of context adopted by this chapter differ from more commonly used approaches (for example, in the models of HRM in Chapter 1)? Does it add to the understanding they give of HRM and, if so, in what way?

2 What assumptions and 'world hypotheses' underpin those models, and what are the implications for your use of them?

3 What assumptions and 'world hypotheses' appear to underpin this chapter, and what are the implications for your use of the chapter?

4 Identify some recent events that are likely to play a significant part in the context of HRM.

5 This chapter has been written from a British perspective. If you were working from a different perspective – South African, perhaps, or Scandinavian – what elements of the context of HRM would you include?

6 The chapter has been written for students of HRM. Is it also relevant to practitioners of HRM and, if so, in what way?

Exercise

Having started to think in terms of context and to recognise the significance of our ways of thinking, you should be reading the rest of this book in this same critical manner. As you go through it, try to identify the following:

- the assumptions (at various levels) underlying the research and theory reported in the chapters that follow;

- the implications of these assumptions for the interpretations that the researchers and theorists are placing upon their material;

- the possibility of other interpretations deriving from other assumptions;

- the assumptions (at various levels) that the writers of the following chapters appear to hold;

- the implications of these assumptions for the interpretations that these writers are placing upon their material;

- the possibility of other interpretations deriving from other assumptions;

- the implications of the various alternatives for the practice of HRM.

Case study

Awkward squad promises a rough ride at Blackpool

Blair faces bruising from less compliant union leaders, say David Turner and Christopher Adams

The awkward squad is up and running at this year's Trades Union Congress, and they have a ring-leader with attitude and power promising a rough ride for Tony Blair. Yesterday, the eve of conference was the first big opportunity for this expanding group of left-wingers to grab attention – and they revelled in it.

None more so than Derek Simpson, who seized joint control of Britain's biggest private sector union two months ago and is now threatening a series of high-profile industrial disputes with a promise to tear up long-standing 'sweetheart' deals with employers. Many of the agreements bar strikes.

The left-winger and former communist, propelled to power at the Amicus union by grassroots discontent with the direction taken by Mr Blair's government, chose robust terms to signal that the days of compliant trade unionism were over.

Ramming home his campaign on workers' rights, Mr Simpson predicted the prime minister would leave Blackpool after his address to the TUC in Blackpool tomorrow with a 'fucking migraine'.

Bob Crow, leader of the RMT rail union, picked up the theme. Mr Blair, he quipped, would be needing Anadin to treat his headache and he would be happy to supply it.

Mr Blair's first address to the TUC for two years, having been called away from last year's conference by the September 11 attacks, is keenly awaited in Blackpool. Union leaders, moderate and militant, yesterday vented their dissatisfaction on a range of issues: Iraq, the demise of final salary pensions, privatisation of public services and the plight of manufacturing.

Discontent has boiled over in a series of hostile motions agreed for debate this week. The government is criticised for neglecting workers' rights and doing too little for public sector employees. Unions have united in support of the firefighters who, on Thursday, are expected to vote for strike action over a pay claim for the first time in 25 years.

But underlying all this venom directed at the government is a recognition by moderate union leaders that their members are being swayed by the arguments of the left and that they themselves need to toughen their rhetoric.

In truth, the TUC is more divided than at any time since Mr Blair became leader. Evidence of this is an angry split on the euro, reflecting the 'anti' views of several new generation leaders. Bill Morris, TGWU leader and a close ally of chancellor Gordon Brown,

is to defy a motion advocating euro membership.

The TUC line chiming with the government's 'in principle' policy on joining faces challenge at the hands of the anti-euro union leaders who include Dave Prentis of Unison, Mr Simpson and Mr Crow.

The split extends to Iraq, where union leaders have struggled for days to come up with a carefully constructed compromise opposing unilateral US action but leaving open the option of a military strike with United Nations support.

Already facing backbench unrest and public scepticism about the need for war against Iraq, the prime minister has the additional problem of a long battle over public sector reforms, peppered with disputes over pay.

Now Mr Simpson, who came from nowhere to unseat Sir Ken Jackson, is set on unpicking his Blairite predecessor's employer-friendly regime.

Amicus is to ask its million members whether they want to renegotiate agreements with employers that set out the terms for collective bargaining.

Mr Simpson said many deals negotiated in the 1980s and 1990s contained compulsory arbitration, no time off for union work and no right to negotiate pay and conditions.

The recognition process had become an unseemly 'beauty parade', he said. To secure sole recognition, unions were falling over themselves to offer favourable terms to employers rather than their members. 'We will tear up the form book on industrial relations and seek agreements that achieve real benefits for our members.'

The number of deals could run into several hundred, but union officials say they have already identified at least 30.

The move is a significant break with policy for a union that, under Sir Ken, pioneered the kind of 'partnership' agreements that have become commonplace throughout industry.

Mr Simpson said partnership had become a 'euphemism for exploitation'. Other unions like the sound of that – Ucatt, the construction workers' union, said it would 'bring to an end the practice of employers choosing a union for their workers'.

Mr Simpson, who has declined a meeting with the prime minister, personified the reception Mr Blair will face. There will be little escape from union leaders, awkward squad and moderates alike.

All this makes for a week of hard-talking and drawn-out debate that will define relations with the government up until the next election.

At the end of it, the unions may have found more common ground than they share now. On the other hand, and this is by far the more likely outcome, the true extent of the differences with the more vocal left will be clear. And the headache for Mr Blair is that the broad base of union support that underpinned him during his first term will be that little bit narrower.

Source: Turner, D. and Adams, C., *Financial Times*, 9 September 2002.

Questions

1 This article about the 2002 Trades Union Congress points to a number of elements within the context of HRM that threaten ultimately to affect HRM policies and practices within many organisations. Identify them, and develop a systems map to help you examine their likely influences upon the HRM of an organisation. (If you are working in a group, split in two, one half looking at this from the perspective of an HR director of a large private sector organisation, and the other from that of an HR director of a public sector organisation. Compare the two models. Are there differences between them? Why?)

2 What are the implications of changes in the wider context for the planning and development of an organisation's HRM policies and practices? What are the implications for HRM strategy?

3 How many different perspectives are evident in this article?

4 Identify the several instances of 'ideology', 'rhetoric', and 'discourse' recognisable in this article.

5 (You can carry out the following individually or in two groups.) First, as a member of Mr Blair's government, write a report on these TUC preoccupations for your colleagues. Next, as an HR director of a private sector organisation, write a report on them to your board. Now compare the two reports. How do they differ in rhetoric and discourse, and what do these differences suggest about their underlying ideology?

6 What are the implications of the significance of rhetoric and discourse for managing people in organisations?

References and further reading

Those texts marked with an asterisk are particularly recommended for further reading.

Aldrich, H.E. (1992) 'Incommensurable paradigms? Vital signs from three perspectives', in Reed, M. and Hughes, M. (eds) *Rethinking Organization: New Directions in Organization Theory and Analysis*. London: Sage, pp. 17–45.

Argyris, C. (1960) *Understanding Organisational Behaviour*. London: Tavistock Dorsey.

Atkinson, S. and Butcher, D. (1999) 'The power of Babel: lingua franker', *People Management*, Vol. 5, No. 20, 14 October, pp. 50–52.

Bakan, D. (1966) *The Duality of Human Existence*. Boston, Mass.: Beacon.

Bannister, D. and Fransella, F. (1971) *Inquiring Man: The Theory of Personal Constructs*. Harmondsworth: Penguin.

Baxter, B. (1999) 'What do postmodernism and complexity science mean?', *People Management*, Vol. 5, No. 23, 25 November, p. 49.

Bhavnani, K.-K. (1990) 'What's power got to do with it? Empowerment and social research', in Parker, I. and

Shotter, J. (eds) *Deconstructing Social Psychology*. London: Routledge, pp. 141–152.

Braverman, H. (1974) *Labor and Monopoly Capital: The Degradation of Work in the Twentieth Century*. New York: Monthly Review Press.

Brittain, S. and Ryder, P. (1999) 'Get complex', *People Management*, Vol. 5, No. 23, 25 November, pp. 48–51.

Brunsson, N. (1989) *The Organization of Hypocrisy: Talk, Decisions and Actions in Organizations*. Chichester: Wiley.

Burr, V. (1995) *An Introduction to Social Constructionism*, London: Routledge.

Calas, M.B. and Smircich, L. (1992) 'Re-writing gender into organizational theorizing: directions from feminist perspectives', in Reed, M. and Hughes, M. (eds) *Rethinking Organization: New Directions in Organization Theory and Analysis*. London: Sage, pp. 227–253.

Callaghan, G. and Thompson, P. (2002) 'We recruit attitude: the selection and shaping of routine call centre labour', *Journal of Management Studies*, Vol. 39, No. 2, pp. 233–254.

Cameron, S. (1997) *The MBA Handbook: Study Skills for Managers*, 3rd edn. London: Pitman.

Capra, F. (1983) *The Turning Point: Science, Society and the Rising Cultures*. London: Fontana.

Castaneda, C. (1970) *The Teachings of Don Juan: A Yaqui Way of Knowledge*. Harmondsworth: Penguin.

Checkland, P. (1981) *Systems Thinking, Systems Practice*. Chichester: Wiley.

Checkland, P. and Scholes, J. (1990) *Soft Systems Methodology in Action*. Chichester: Wiley.

Cherniss, C. and Goleman, D. (eds.) (2001) *The Emotionally Intelligent Workplace: How to Select for, Measure, and Improve Emotional Intelligence in Individuals, Groups, and Organizations*. San Francisco, Calif.: Jossey-Bass.

Child, J. (1969) *British Management Thought: A Critical Analysis*. London: George Allen & Unwin.

*Clark, H., Chandler, J. and Barry, J. (1994) *Organisation and Identities: Text and Readings in Organisational Behaviour*. London: Chapman & Hall.

Clegg, S.R. (1990) *Modern Organizations: Organization Studies in the Postmodern World*. London: Sage.

Collin, A. (1996) 'Organizations and the end of the individual?', *Journal of Managerial Psychology*, Vol. 11, No. 7, pp. 9–17.

Collin, A. (1997) 'Career in context', *British Journal of Guidance and Counselling*, Vol. 25, No. 4, pp. 435–446.

Concise Oxford Dictionary (1982) 7th edn. Oxford: Clarendon Press.

Connock, S. (1992) 'The importance of "big ideas" to HR managers', *Personnel Management*, June, pp. 24–27.

Cooksey, R.W. and Gates, G.R. (1995) 'HRM: A management science in need of discipline', *Asia Pacific Journal of Human Resources*, Vol. 33, No. 3, pp. 15–38.

Cooper, R. and Fox, S. (1990) 'The "texture" of organizing', *Journal of Management Studies*, Vol. 27, No. 6, pp. 575–582.

Denzin, N.K. and Lincoln, Y.S. (eds) (1994) *Handbook of Qualitative Research*. Thousand Oaks, Calif.: Sage.

Department of Scientific and Industrial Research (1961) *Human Sciences: Aid to Industry*. London: HMSO.

*Eccles, R.G. and Nohria, N. (1992) *Beyond the Hype: Rediscovering the Essence of Management*. Boston, Mass.: Harvard Business School Press.

Elliott, E. and Kiel, L.D. (1997) 'Introduction', in Kiel, L.D. and Elliott, E. (eds) *Chaos Theory in the Social Sciences: Foundations and Applications*. Ann Arbor, Mich.: The University of Michigan Press, pp. 1–15.

Eve, R.A., Horsfall, S. and Lee, M.E. (eds) (1997) *Chaos, Complexity, and Sociology: Myths, Models, and Theories*. Thousand Oaks, Calif.: Sage.

Fineman, S. (ed.) (1993) *Emotion in Organizations*. London: Sage.

Fox, S. (1990) 'Strategic HRM: postmodern conditioning for the corporate culture', in Fox, S. and Moult, G. (eds) *Postmodern Culture and Management Development*, Special Edition: *Management Education and Development*, Vol. 21, Pt 3, pp. 192–206.

*Frost, P.J., Moore, L.F., Louis, M.R., Lundberg, C.C. and Martin, J. (1991) *Reframing Organizational Culture*. Newbury Park, Calif.: Sage.

Gavey, N. (1989) 'Feminist poststructuralism and discourse analysis: contributions to feminist psychology', *Psychology of Women Quarterly*, Vol. 13, pp. 459–475.

Geertz, C. (1973) *The Interpretation of Cultures*. New York: Basic Books.

Gergen, K.J. (1992) 'Organization theory in the postmodern era', in Reed, M. and Hughes, M. (eds) *Rethinking Organization: New Directions in Organization Theory and Analysis*. London: Sage, pp. 207–226.

Gergen, K.J. (1999) *An Invitation to Social Construction*. London: Sage.

Gilligan, C. (1982) *In a Different Voice: Psychological Theory and Women's Development*. Cambridge, Mass.: Harvard University Press.

Goldschmidt, W. (1970) 'Foreword', in Castaneda, C., *The Teachings of Don Juan: A Yaqui Way of Knowledge*. Harmondsworth: Penguin, pp. 9–10.

Gowler, D. and Legge, K. (1989) 'Rhetoric in bureaucratic careers: managing the meaning of management success', in Arthur, M.B., Hall, D.T. and Lawrence, B.S. (eds) *Handbook of Career Theory*. Cambridge: Cambridge University Press, pp. 437–453.

Harré, R. (1981) 'The positivist-empiricist approach and its alternative', in Reason, P. and Rowan, J. (eds) *Human Inquiry: A Sourcebook of New Paradigm Research*. Chichester: Wiley, pp. 3–17.

Harvey, D. (1990) *The Condition of Postmodernity*. Oxford: Blackwell.

Hassard, J. (1993) 'Postmodernism and organizational analysis: An overview', in Hassard, J. and Parker, M. (eds) (1993) *Postmodernism and Organizations*. London: Sage, pp. 1 – 23.

Hassard, J. and Parker, M. (eds) (1993) *Postmodernism and Organizations*. London: Sage.

Hatch, M.J. (1997) *Organization Theory: Modern, Symbolic and Postmodern Perspectives*. Oxford: Oxford University Press.

Hatchett, A. (2000) 'Call collective: ringing true', *People Management*, Vol. 6, No. 2, January, pp. 40–42.

*Hearn, J., Sheppard, D.L., Tancred-Sheriff, P. and Burrell, G. (1989) *The Sexuality of Organization*. London: Sage.

Heather, N. (1976) *Radical Perspectives in Psychology*. London: Methuen.

Hebdige, D. (1979) *Subculture: The Meaning of Style*. London: Methuen.

Hendry, C. and Pettigrew, A. (1990) 'Human resource management: an agenda for the 1990s', *International Journal of Human Resource Management*, Vol. 1, No. 1, pp. 17–43.

Hodgson, A. (1987) 'Deming's never-ending road to quality', *Personnel Management*, July, pp. 40–44.

Hoffman, L. (1990) 'Constructing realities: an art of lenses', *Family Process*, Vol. 29, No. 1, pp. 1–12.

Hopfl, H. and Hornby Atkinson, P. (2000) 'The future of women's career', in Collin, A. and Young, R.A. (eds) *The Future of Career*, Cambridge: Cambridge University Press, pp. 130–143.

Hosking, D. and Fineman, S. (1990) 'Organizing processes', *Journal of Management Studies*, Vol. 27, No. 6, pp. 583–604.

Huczynski, A. and Buchanan, D. (2002) *Organizational Behaviour: An Introductory Text*, 4th edn. Harlow: FT/Prentice Hall.

Huse, E.F. (1980) *Organization Development and Change*. 2nd edn. St. Paul, Minn.: West Publishing.

Kanter, R.M. (1983) *The Change Masters*. New York: Simon & Schuster.

Keenoy, T. (1990) 'Human resource management: rhetoric, reality and contradiction', *International Journal of Human Resource Management*, Vol. 1, No. 3, pp. 363–384.

Kelly, G.A. (1955) *The Psychology of Personal Constructs*, Vols 1 and 2. New York: W.W. Norton.

Kiel, L.D. and Elliott, E. (eds) (1997) *Chaos Theory in the Social Sciences: Foundations and Applications*. Ann Arbor, Mich.: The University of Michigan Press.

Kvale, S. (ed.) (1992) *Psychology and Postmodernism*. London: Sage.

Lee, M.E. (1997) 'From enlightenment to chaos: toward nonmodern social theory', in Eve, R.A., Horsfall, S. and Lee, M.E. (eds) *Chaos, Complexity, and Sociology: Myths, Models, and Theories*. Thousand Oaks, Calif.: Sage, pp. 15–29.

Legge, K. (1995) *Human Resource Management: Rhetorics and Realities*. Basingstoke: Macmillan Business.

Mant, A. (1979) *The Rise and Fall of the British Manager*. London: Pan.

Marshall, J. (1989) 'Re-visioning career concepts: a feminist invitation', in Arthur, M.B., Hall, D.T. and Lawrence, B.S. (eds) *Handbook of Career Theory*. Cambridge: Cambridge University Press, pp. 275–291.

McGregor, D. (1960) *The Human Side of Enterprise*. New York: McGraw-Hill.

Medcof, J. and Roth, J. (eds) (1979) *Approaches to Psychology*. Milton Keynes: Open University Press.

Mishler, E.G. (1986) *Research Interviewing: Context and Narrative*. Cambridge, Mass.: Harvard University Press.

*Morgan, G. (new edn) (1997) *Images of Organization*. Thousand Oaks, Calif.: Sage.

Moxon, G.R. (1951) *Functions of a Personnel Department*. London: Institute of Personnel Management.

Parker, I. (1990) 'The abstraction and representation of social psychology', in Parker, I. and Shotter, J. (eds) *Deconstructing Social Psychology*. London: Routledge, pp. 91–102.

Parker, I. and Shotter, J. (eds) (1990) 'Introduction', in *Deconstructing Social Psychology*. London: Routledge, pp. 1–14.

*Pascale, R.T. and Athos, A.G. (1982) *The Art of Japanese Management*. Harmondsworth: Penguin.

Peck, D. and Whitlow, D. (1975) *Approaches to Personality Theory*. London: Methuen.

People Management (2002) *The Guide to Work–Life Balance*. London: *People Management* (www.peoplemanagement.co.uk/work-life).

Pepper, S.C. (1942) *World Hypotheses*. Berkeley, Calif.: University of California Press.

Peters, T.J. and Waterman, R.H. Jr (1982) *In Search of Excellence: Lessons from America's Best Run Companies*. New York: Harper & Row.

Pfeffer, J. (1981) *Power in Organizations*. London: Pitman.

Pickard, J. (1992) 'Profile: W. Edward Deming', *Personnel Management*, June, p. 23.

Pickard, J. (1999) 'Emote possibilities: sense and sensitivity', *People Management*, Vol. 5, No. 21, 28 October, pp. 48–56.

Pirsig, R.M. (1976) *Zen and the Art of Motorcycle Maintenance*. London: Corgi.

Price, B. (1997) 'The myth of postmodern science', in Eve, R.A., Horsfall, S. and Lee, M.E. (eds) *Chaos, Complexity, and Sociology: Myths, Models, and Theories*. Thousand Oaks, Calif: Sage, pp. 3–14.

Pugh, D.S., Hickson, D.J. and Hinings, C.R. (1983) *Writers on Organizations*. 3rd edn. Harmondsworth: Penguin.

*Reed, M. and Hughes, M. (eds) (1992) *Rethinking Organization: New Directions in Organization Theory and Analysis*. London: Sage.

Ritzer, G. (1996) *The McDonaldization of Society: An Investigation into the Changing Character of Contemporary Social Life*. Thousand Oaks, Calif.: Pine Forge Press.

Rose, M. (1978) *Industrial Behaviour: Theoretical Development since Taylor*. Harmondsworth: Penguin.

Sanders, P. (1982) 'Phenomenology: a new way of viewing organizational research', *Academy of Management Review*, Vol. 7, No. 3, pp. 353–360.

Schein, E.H. (1970) *Organizational Psychology*. 2nd edn. Englewood Cliffs, New Jersey: Prentice Hall.

Schein, E.H. (1978) *Career Dynamics: Matching Individual and Organizational Needs*. Reading, Mass.: Addison-Wesley.

*Senge, P. (1990) *The Fifth Discipline: The Art and Practice of the Learning Organization*. London: Century.

Seymour, W.D. (1959) *Operator Training in Industry*. London: Institute of Personnel Management.

Sloan, T. (1992) 'Career decisions: a critical psychology', in Young, R.A. and Collin, A. (eds) *Interpreting Career: Hermeneutical Studies of Lives in Context*. Westport, Conn.: Praeger, pp. 168–176.

Southgate, J. and Randall, R. (1981) 'The troubled fish: barriers to dialogue', in Reason, P. and Rowan, J. (eds)

Human Inquiry: A Sourcebook of New Paradigm Research. Chichester: Wiley, pp. 53–61.

Spender, D. (1985) *For the Record: The Making and Meaning of Feminist Knowledge*. London: Women's Press.

Stead, G.B., and Watson, M.B. (1999) 'Indigenisation of psychology in South Africa', in Stead, G.B. and Watson, M.B. (eds.) *Career Psychology in the South African Context*. Pretoria, South Africa: Van Schaik, pp. 214–225.

Taylor, P., Mulvey, G., Hyman, J. and Bain, P. (2002) 'Work organisation, control and the experience of work in call centres', *Work, Employment and Society*, Vol. 16, No. 1, pp. 133–150.

Townley, B. (1993) 'Foucault power/knowledge, and its relevance for human resource management', *Academy of Management Review*, Vol. 18, No. 3, pp. 518–545.

Vaillant, G.E. (1977) *Adaptation to Life: How the Brightest and Best Came of Age*. Boston, Mass.: Little, Brown.

*Watson, T.J. (2000) *In Search of Management: Culture, Chaos and Control in Managerial Work*. London: Thomson Learning.

*Weick, K.E. (1979) *The Social Psychology of Organizing*. New York: Random House.

Welch, J. (1998) 'The new seekers: creed is good', *People Management*, Vol. 4, No. 25, 24 December, pp. 28–33.

Wheatley, M.J. (1992) *Leadership and the New Science: Learning about Organization from an Orderly Universe*. San Francisco, Calif.: Berrett-Koehler.

Zohar, D. and Marshall, I. (2001) *Spiritual Intelligence: The Ultimate Intelligence*. London: Bloomsbury.

For multiple choice questions, exercises and annotated weblinks specific to this chapter visit this book's website at www.booksites.net/beardwell

Retailer derided for 'moving the deckchairs' at a crucial time – fears of double-digit fall in sales

M&S to split into seven business units. By Susanne Voyle

Marks and Spencer yesterday re-shuffled its management and split the group into seven business units to improve its focus on customers.

M&S, which has suffered a dramatic fall from grace in the fiercely competitive UK retail environment, has changed the job description of three board members and appointed seven executives just below board level to head the new units.

The news came at the start of the crucial pre-Christmas trading week.

M&S is believed to be suffering a steep fall-off in sales as rivals slash prices. The group has refused to comment ahead of a trading statement due in January. But people close to the company believe the fall in like-for-like sales has hit double digits.

The group has yet to make its most eagerly awaited appointment – that of a chairman to replace Sir Richard Greenbury, who took early retirement in the summer.

Shares in M&S, currently the centre of bid speculation, rose 3¼p to 277¾. Last week, Philip Green, the retail entrepreneur, admitted he was considering a bid after the group's shares jumped on repeated rumours.

M&S yesterday stressed that the management changes were not a reaction to the possibility of a take-over. 'The changes are a continuation of the move to more customer focused, flatter structures which were announced with the interim results in November,' it said.

M&S said the new business units would each be fully profit-accountable. 'This means no one under-performing part of the business will be able to hide behind results of the group as a whole,' said one insider.

The biggest change comes for Barry Morris, formerly head of the food division, who has been put in charge of womenswear retail. Guy McCracken and Joe Rowe saw their roles changed slightly to reflect the devolution to buying power to the new business units.

The group has been split with immediate effect into retail units for womenswear, menswear, lingerie, children's wear, home, beauty and food. The heads of each unit will report directly to Peter Salsbury, chief executive.

Most of the unit heads are long-serving M&S employees, in line with the group's tradition of promoting from within. But there are two exceptions. Rory Scott, who heads lingerie, joined the group less than two years ago from logistics group TNT, while Jacqueline Paterson, at beauty, joined from Boots just four months ago.

The changes left some analysts unimpressed. 'In the middle of one of the most important trading weeks in the calendar they have decided to reshuffle the deckchairs,' said one. Another said: 'Most people don't know the insiders at M&S well enough to know whether changes like these will make any difference.'

Some institutional shareholders said the changes were unimportant while the chairmanship remains vacant. 'The only interesting news will be when they appoint a chairman, and we don't know when that will be,' said one.

M&S yesterday repeated that it had a preferred candidate and hoped to announce an appointment in the New Year.

Source: Financial Times, 22 December 1999.

Questions

This case describes the complex organisational issues facing Marks and Spencer. Assess the following HRM issues for the company.

1 What might be the strategic HRM issues facing the company in deciding to create business units?

2 To what extent does the company need to overhaul the relationship between HRM and its core businesses?

3 Using the styles and approaches to HRM outlined in this part, suggest a suitable HRM approach that Marks and Spencer might adopt for the medium term.

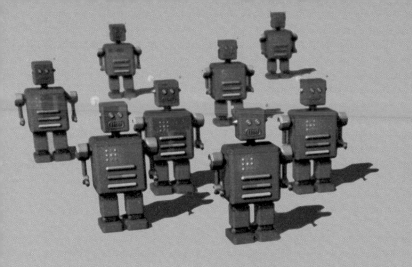

Part 2

RESOURCING THE ORGANISATION

Introduction to Part 2

This part deals with how organisations define and meet their needs for labour and how the ways in which they do this are influenced by factors internal and external to the organisation.

For students and practitioners of management the main theme of the past decade has been change, uncertainty and risk. Technological change has transformed the nature of products and production systems, services and their delivery. Markets have become more unpredictable and competition more intense. Organisations have responded to this turbulence in a variety of ways, but the dominant trend has been towards smaller, 'leaner' organisations in which operational responsibilities are devolved and decentralised. These changes have called into question established approaches to management, not least the management of labour. Here the response to uncertainty and the competitive pressure to cut costs has been large-scale workforce reductions and an insistence on the need for greater 'flexibility' in the use of labour. This has had implications for employee recruitment as organisations consider the wider use of non-standard workers such as temporary, fixed-term and subcontracted labour. In many cases it has led to the erosion of employment systems based on offers of long-term employment security and internal promotion and has transferred risk from the employer to the employee, creating new patterns of advantage and disadvantage in the labour market. It has also called into question the usefulness of traditional approaches to planning as future labour requirements have come to be less predictable.

These issues are explored in the chapters that make up this part of the book. Chapter 4 examines the factors that shape organisations' employment systems – that is, their structured arrangements for acquiring, deploying, rewarding and controlling labour. It also explains why employment systems vary between organisations; why it is that some firms offer long-term employment security and career prospects and above-average pay, while others offer no such benefits. It analyses how recent changes in organisations and their environment influenced employment systems and examines recent debates concerning the future of employment; for example, are we seeing the end of long-term employment and is the traditional concept of employment itself becoming obsolete?

Chapter 5 examines the specific issue of human resource planning. Traditionally, 'manpower' planning was seen as a set of objective techniques to enable managers to predict their future labour requirements and assess future labour supply. The emphasis was on quantitative measurement and predictions based on the extrapolation of trends derived from past data. The chapter explains this approach and the problems involved in attempting to plan in this way, particularly in the current organisational context as outlined above. It goes on to provide a critical explanation of how, in the light of these difficulties, the manpower planning concept has given way to more tentative, flexible and focused approaches embodied in human resource planning.

Chapter 6 explains how contemporary developments are increasing the potential importance of having effective methods of recruiting and selecting employees. These developments include the growing need to ensure that diverse groups are treated fairly in terms of employment opportunity and the growing emphasis on the need for flexible, adaptable and cooperative (some might say compliant) workers. It goes on to explore the principles of employee recruitment and selection, how to judge the effectiveness of different methods of recruitment and selection, and the nature of recent developments in this area of HRM.

Chapter 7 takes up the theme of advantage and, more specifically, disadvantage in employment in depth by examining the nature and effects of unfair discrimination in employment, why managers should act to promote fairness in employment, and different, sometimes conflicting ideas on how they should do so. It highlights the complex nature of the issues raised by attempts to tackle disadvantage due to unfair discrimination. For example, should managers seek to treat all employees equally irrespective of ethnicity or gender, or should they take these differences into account when framing their employment policies? Should policies for combating disadvantage aim at equality of opportunity or equality of outcome? How useful is the concept of institutional discrimination? It also discusses the significance of the recent tendency to shift the focus of discussion away from the traditional idea of 'equal opportunities' to the concept of 'managing diversity'.

CHAPTER 4

Human resource management and the labour market

Tim Claydon

OBJECTIVES

▶ Explain the concept of employment systems and the ways in which different employment systems can be defined.

▶ Present an analysis of the factors that determine the type of employment system that an organisation operates.

▶ Show how changes in these factors have influenced trends in employment systems in the late twentieth and early twenty-first century.

▶ Present a critical appraisal of current ideas concerning the future of employment systems and their implications for HRM.

Introduction

This chapter is concerned with how we think about the labour market and the place of employing organisations within it. Traditionally, those within the dominant paradigm in economics – known as *neoclassical economics* – have argued that competition means that market forces leave individual firms little scope for choice. High-cost firms eventually go out of business and the competitive search for lower costs means that firms tend to converge on the most efficient methods of production. This suggests that firms operating in the same industry or product market will employ the same technologies and types of labour, operate the same rates of pay and have pretty much the same employment/HRM policies. However, in recent years the growth of corporate strategy and HRM as bodies of ideas has encouraged scholars to focus on the ability of managers of organisations to exercise 'strategic choice' over a range of decisions, including employment matters. The implication of this is that employers' decisions are not just determined by external market forces. Instead, employers have a certain amount of freedom to interpret their external environment and choose from a range of possible responses in a search for competitive advantage.

This is an important issue for students of HRM in the light of its claim to be a strategic approach to the management of labour and thus superior to 'traditional' personnel and industrial relations management. One problem with the literature is that it often appears to be inconsistent. On the one hand it argues for the ability of managers to make strategic choices while on the other it tells us that contemporary developments such as the increased use of 'flexible' forms of employment are the inevitable result of changes in technology and markets. In order to avoid this inconsistency we need to ask how market environments might simultaneously create and constrain the scope for strategic choice in HRM. The specific focus of this chapter is the labour market.

The chapter is divided into four main sections. In the first we consider various ideas about the nature of the labour market and employment systems. In the second we explore the factors that influence the type of employment system that an organisation operates. The third section discusses how and why employment has changed over the past 20 years and the final part of the chapter discusses some ideas about the future of employment systems and their implications for HRM.

The nature of labour markets and employment systems

The most general definition of the labour market is that it consists of workers who are looking for paid employment and employers who are seeking to fill vacancies. The amount of labour that is available to firms – *labour supply* – is determined by the number of people of working age who are in employment or seeking employment and the number of hours that they are willing to work. This number will be determined by the size and age structure of the population and by the decisions made by individuals and households about the relative costs and benefits of taking paid employment. These decisions are influenced by various factors, one of which is the level of wages on offer. Generally speaking, a higher wage will attract more people into the labour market and a lower wage will attract fewer as long as other factors, such the level of welfare benefits and people's attitudes towards work, remain constant.

The number of jobs on offer to workers – *labour demand* – is the sum of people in employment plus the number of vacancies waiting to be filled. The demand for labour is determined by the level of demand for the goods and services produced by firms in the market. When sales and production are rising, firms' demand for labour rises. When sales fall and production is cut back, firms' demand for labour falls.

ACTIVITY

Currently the UK and many other member states within the European Union face possible future problems of labour supply. The population of Europe is ageing as the birth rate has fallen and life expectancies have risen. More people than ever before are leaving the labour pool for retirement. At the same time there are fewer young people entering the labour market. Because of this, there is concern that the supply of labour will be inadequate to support desired rates of economic growth and to provide for the growing proportion of the population that is dependent on pensions and state benefits. Therefore policy initiatives are being put in place to develop new sources of labour supply to contribute to the available pool of labour. For example, more women are being encouraged to enter the labour market and governments are considering ways of encouraging immigrant workers to augment the domestic supply of labour. There is also widespread discussion of the possibility of reducing the rate at which people leave the labour market by increasing the age of retirement.

Identify some of the implications of these developments for HR managers.

The simplest view of the labour market is that it is an arena of competition. Workers enter the arena in search of jobs and employers enter it in search of workers. Competition between employers for workers and between workers for jobs results in a 'market wage' that adjusts to relative changes in labour demand and supply. Thus, when labour demand rises relative to labour supply, the market wage rises as firms try to outbid each other for scarce labour. When labour demand falls relative to labour supply, the market wage falls as workers compete with each other for the smaller number of available jobs.

Competition means that no individual firm can set a wage that is out of line with the competitive market wage. Neither can workers demand such a wage. Should a firm try to offer a wage that is below the market rate, it will be unable to hire workers. Should a firm set a wage above the market rate, it will go out of business because its costs of production will be above those of its competitors. For the same reason, workers who demand a wage higher than the market rate will price themselves out of jobs. No firm will hire them because to do so would increase their costs of production relative to those of their competitors.

While it is undeniable that competitive forces operate in the labour market to a degree, few would seriously pretend that this is a wholly accurate description of the real world. There are limits to competition between firms and among workers. Empirical research has shown that rates of pay vary between firms in the same industry operating in the same local labour market (Nolan and Brown, 1983). Wages do not respond instantly to changes in labour demand. Employment policies vary considerably among firms. For example, some employ labour on a casual hire and fire basis while others offer long-term employment security and career development. This has led labour economists to recognise that firms are not all equally influenced by the external labour market. Instead they develop a variety of employment systems which can be differentiated from each other in terms of the extent to which competitive labour market forces influence terms and conditions of employment.

■ Employment systems

Some of the most important contributors to the discussion of employment systems are Kerr (1954), Doeringer and Piore (1971) and Osterman (1984, 1987). Their classifications of employment systems vary in terms of the number of different systems they identify and the labels that they attach to them. For clarity and brevity a threefold classification is developed here.

Employment systems can be seen to vary in terms of the extent to which they are based on three different types of labour market. These are:

- the open or unstructured external labour market;
- the occupational labour market;
- the internal labour market.

These types can be differentiated from each other in terms of how close they are to the basic competitive model of the labour market. This in turn can be examined in terms of where they lie along three conceptual axes:

- *External–Internal.* The extent to which firms rely on external or internal sources of labour to fill vacancies.
- *Unstructured–Structured.* The extent to which there are clear boundaries to the labour market in which the firm operates.
- *Competitively–Institutionally regulated.* The extent to which entry to jobs, progression within and between jobs, and terms and conditions of employment are determined by market competition or by formal rules administered through internal institutions (i.e. institutions developed by workers and employers) in addition to statutory protections afforded by the law (see Chapters 11 and 12).

Employment systems that are closest to the basic competitive model will be external, unstructured and competitively regulated. Those furthest from it will be internal, structured and institutionally regulated.

● The open external labour market

This corresponds most closely to the simple model of the labour market as an arena of competition. It is *external* in the sense that employers draw their labour from an external pool and do not seek to foster long-term employment relationships. Workers are hired and fired as needed. It is also *unstructured* because there are no clear occupational boundaries within it and it is easy for workers to enter the market and move from job to job because no prior training or qualifications are necessary. Furthermore, there is little *institutional regulation* in the open external labour market. Workers have few legal rights or protections and trade unions are weak or non-existent. Therefore workers compete with each other for employment and employers determine the level of wages in the light of how abundant or scarce labour is in the market. This means that employees are continually exposed to external market forces.

ACTIVITY

In researching her recently published book *Hard Work*, extracts from which were published in the *Guardian* newspaper in January 2003, the journalist Polly Toynbee reported how she had seen a temporary nursery assistant's job advertised in a London job centre. The job was advertised as paying £5 an hour. However, when Toynbee applied she found that in this case 'temporary' meant a zero hours contract. In other words, she would be 'on call' and only paid for the hours she actually worked. As she put it, 'It would be one shift this week, and three next, on call whenever necessary, never knowing what the hours or the pay would be from week to week.'

(P. Toynbee, *Guardian* G2, 14 January 2003, p. 9)

Why do some workers accept jobs on these terms? What are the advantages and disadvantages for employers of this type of employment?

● The occupational labour market

Occupational labour markets arise where workers have skills that can be transferred from one firm to another. Labour markets for professional workers are often of this type; for example, doctors can work in different hospitals, teachers can move from one school to another and lawyers from one law firm to another without having to retrain. Occupational labour markets are *external* in the sense that, because workers' skills are transferable across firms, employers can fill vacancies by drawing on the pool of qualified workers that exists outside the firm. Workers can also look to further their careers by moving from one firm to another in search of promotion and better opportunities. Clearly there is potentially an element of competition in the occupational labour market.

However, unlike workers in the open external labour market, those in structured occupational labour markets are able to insulate themselves from pressures of labour market competition to a considerable extent. Many analysts, following Kerr (1954), have argued that this means that the structured occupational labour market has been internalised to a degree, since it operates on the basis of rules generated internally within the occupation rather than being ruled by open competition. The reasons for this are as follows.

Occupational labour markets are *structured* on an occupational basis, with occupational boundaries being defined in terms of the tools or materials used, or skills and qualifications. Movement between occupations is therefore difficult because of the time and expense involved in retraining to obtain a new set of occupational qualifications.

This limits the extent to which workers in an occupation are exposed to competition from workers outside it. This in turn enables workers to act collectively to influence their terms and conditions of employment through *institutional regulation* rather than leaving them to be determined by competitive market forces. Professional associations or trade unions control entry to the occupation, for example by making the right to work in it conditional on having certain minimum qualifications. Control of entry means that the number of workers can be restricted. This limits competition further and means that those in the occupation are ensured of employment. It also gives trade unions and professional associations a measure of bargaining power, which they can use through negotiation with employers to regulate pay and conditions.

Stop and think	What do structured occupational labour markets and open external labour markets have in common? Now recall the two main ways in which structured occupational labour markets *differ* from open external labour markets.

● The internal labour market

Internal labour markets are essentially enterprise-based employment systems. In other words, terms and conditions of employment are determined by rules that are internal to the organisation rather than by competitive forces in the wider labour market. They are *internal* in the sense that external recruitment is limited to junior and trainee positions within the organisation. Other vacancies are filled through internal transfers and promotion. Skills are learned on the job and are specific to the organisation in which they are acquired, rather than being transferable across firms. This restricts the mobility of workers between firms, since the skills learned in one organisation are not equally useful in another. Workforce reductions are achieved through 'natural wastage', that is by non-replacement of workers who leave, rather than by dismissals. Therefore there is a high degree of long-term employment security for workers.

Internal labour markets are also highly *structured* in that they consist of hierarchies of jobs that are graded in relation to each other in terms of skill, responsibility and pay. Job hierarchies are also designed to provide career progression paths or 'job ladders' that provide opportunities for internal transfer and promotion and so retain and motivate trained workers. Workers can climb job ladders by acquiring training and experience in lower-level jobs that prepare them for the next rung on the ladder. In practice, promotion is often based on length of service in a lower-level job.

Internal labour markets are subject to a high degree of internal *institutional regulation*. This takes the form of bureaucratic, administrative rules that define the content of jobs, order the place of jobs in the job hierarchy, establish rules for promotion and set rates of pay for jobs (see Marsden, 1999). This results in a pay structure that reflects the different levels of skill and responsibility that attach to jobs as workers move up the job ladder. Such pay structures are unresponsive to pressures from the external labour market. Firms are reluctant to alter wage rates for particular jobs even when their demand for labour in these jobs falls or when they face labour shortages, because to do so would risk upsetting the entire pay structure. There may also be rules that regulate management's ability to dismiss workers should this become unavoidable. A common example is the 'last in, first out' or seniority rule whereby it is those with the shortest length of service who are first selected for dismissal.

In practice, internal labour markets vary in terms of the opportunities for internal promotion that they offer and the strength of their guarantee of long-term employment security. Empirical research has found that internal labour markets are more highly developed for technical and administrative workers in these respects than for manual workers (George and Shorey, 1985; Osterman, 1987). Therefore we can identify two variants of internal labour market: *the salaried internal labour market* (technical and administrative workers) and the *industrial internal labour market* (manual workers) (Osterman, 1987). Long-term employment security, structured career paths and opportunities for internal promotion are more highly developed in the salaried internal labour market than in the industrial internal labour market. This has led some to argue that the industrial internal labour market should be seen as a fourth type of employment system rather than as a variant of the internal labour market (Hendry, 1995).

In reality, firms' employment practices do not fit neatly into these categories. Firms that wish to keep employment costs low frequently draw back from casualised employment and the extremes of the open external labour market because they fear that it will demoralise workers and undermine the quality of production or service delivery. Firms that operate in occupational labour markets often seek to retain existing employees as they value their experience and it is not always easy to replace workers when they leave. This leads them to move, to some degree at least, in the direction of the internal labour market. Furthermore, the example of the industrial internal labour market above also shows that many organisations tend towards an employment system without conforming to it completely. It is clear that the employment policies of particular organisations cannot always be fitted exactly into one of the three employment system 'boxes' outlined above. It has also been argued that more than one employment system may exist within the same firm: a salaried internal labour market for managerial, administrative and technical staff, occupational labour markets for skilled production workers and open external labour markets for unskilled workers (Adnett, 1989).

Therefore the categories of open external labour markets, structured occupational labour markets and internal labour markets are probably best seen as *ideal types*, that is, as conceptual categories that help to organise our thinking, rather than as completely accurate empirical categories into which organisations can be slotted neatly and unambiguously. The next section of this chapter looks at the factors that encourage employing organisations to internalise or externalise their employment systems.

Stop and think   What features distinguish internal labour markets from external labour markets?

Externalisation or internalisation of employment?

In the competitive model of the labour market, employment is externalised. There is no commitment to providing long-term employment. Wage rates are set in line with what appears to be the 'going rate' in the local labour market. In other words, labour is a variable factor of production. The advantage to employers of employment systems based on open external labour markets and occupational labour markets is that they can minimise labour costs by quickly adjusting the size of their workforce in response to changes in their production requirements. In the case of open external labour markets, where wage rates are set in line with the 'going rate' in the market, employers can be sure that they are paying the minimum that is necessary to attract a supply of workers.

However, there are powerful reasons for internalising employment within the firm, at least to some extent. Internalisation includes a variety of measures that create, to varying degrees, a long-term employment relationship that is, also to varying degrees, insulated from external labour market pressures. Efforts are made to retain existing workers. Wages are set according to internal criteria, such as job evaluation or the need to motivate and reward performance, rather than by reference to an external 'going rate'. Rather than being a variable cost, labour becomes a quasi-fixed cost. In such cases firms tend towards an employment system based on an internal labour market.

Employment systems are shaped by a wide variety of factors that can be grouped into the following categories:

- the nature of employers' labour requirements;
- organisational constraints;
- workers' pressure and influence;
- features of the wider labour market context;
- the influence of non-labour market institutions.

Employers' labour requirements

One view of employment systems is that they represent different ways in which management addresses three fundamental issues with respect to labour:

- how to obtain and retain an appropriately skilled workforce;
- how to ensure that workers deliver the levels of effort and the quality of performance that management requires for profitable or cost-effective production;
- how to achieve the first two objectives in such a way as to minimise employment costs relative to output.

How they do this – the employment strategy that they follow and the employment system that develops from it – will depend on the specific nature of their labour requirements, i.e.:

- the extent of their need for a stable workforce;
- the relative importance of transferable and firm-specific skills;
- the extent of their need for workers' active consent and cooperation in production.*

The need for a stable workforce

The influence of labour turnover costs

The basic competitive model of the labour market assumes that the only cost to the employer of hiring workers is the wage that has to be paid. Consequently, replacing workers who leave does not add to costs. This means that the workforce at any point in time is disposable and the employer has no particular interest in retaining current workers in preference to hiring new ones from outside the firm. In practice, however, it is costly to replace workers who leave. The main costs are:

- Disruption of production owing to the unplanned reductions in the workforce that result from workers leaving. There is usually a delay in replacing workers who leave because of the time it takes to advertise the vacancies and recruit a pool of job applicants and select from among the applicants. Once selected, new workers may also have to work out a notice period with their previous employer. During this time there may be a loss of production, causing revenues to fall.
- The costs of recruitment and selection, such as the financial costs of advertising for recruits and the cost in terms of management time spent in recruiting and selecting replacements.

---

* How these requirements are defined is bound up with consideration of a range of factors that include the nature of the product or service being provided, the technology of production and the extent and nature of product or service market competition. The extent to which labour requirements and employment strategies are derived from these factors or alternatively, how far they help to define them, depends on whether the firm takes a strategic approach to HRM and if so, whether it is 'best fit', 'configurational', 'resource-based' or 'best practice'. See Chapter 2.

- The costs of training new recruits. These include more than just the direct costs of providing training, such as materials and equipment, paying trainers, etc. It also includes the costs in terms of reduced output while the new recruits are being trained. While undergoing training, new recruits are less productive because they are not fully occupied in production and neither are they fully competent. Where training includes a significant element of on-the-job training by experienced workers, the time spent training new recruits will also reduce the experienced workers' productivity. Even after completing their training, new recruits may not be fully competent until they have gained some further experience in the job.

This means that employers may have a strong interest in limiting the extent of labour turnover. They will prefer to retain 'insiders' – those currently employed – to having to replace them with 'outsiders' drawn from the external labour market. In order to retain workers and reduce labour turnover, employers can adopt a variety of policies:

- Deferred benefits. These are benefits that are contingent on workers remaining with the organisation. Examples are company pensions and holiday entitlements that become available only after a minimum period of service.
- Seniority wages, whereby pay increases with length of service. Where the cost of replacing workers is high, the addition to wage costs by 'paying for seniority' may be less than the costs saved by reducing labour turnover.
- Avoidance of redundancy dismissals during temporary downturns in production. Employers will try to avoid laying off workers by not replacing those who leave, cutting overtime and introducing 'short time' working. This is because, should the employer dismiss workers, there is no guarantee that they will be available when production recovers. The employer would then have to incur the costs of recruitment, selection and training. If these costs are perceived to be high it may be worth the employer's while to retain workers even if they are temporarily under-employed.
- During upturns in production, employers may initially prefer to achieve higher output by increasing the output of the current workforce, for example through overtime working, before hiring additional workers. This is because the costs of overtime working may be lower than the costs of recruiting, selecting and training new recruits. Only if employers become confident that the increase in demand is going to be sustained will they add to the size of the workforce.

Policies such as these internalise employment by fostering long-term employment relationships and giving workers a degree of protection from external labour market pressures. Employers prefer to retain their current workforce to incurring the costs of replacing them with outsiders. However, measures to create stable workforces, such as pension schemes and other incentives to remain with the organisation, are themselves costly. Therefore the extent to which employers seek to internalise employment depends on the cost of labour turnover. The lower the costs of labour turnover, the less the incentive for employers to internalise employment.

The need to protect investments in training

When firms invest significantly in training their employees they will want to keep them once they are trained. This creates pressures for internalisation of employment and can be seen as an extension of the costly labour turnover argument above.

The basic competitive model of the labour market assumes for simplicity of analysis that workers come to firms with the skills that are needed for their jobs. In reality this is often not the case, particularly for new entrants to the labour market. This is because many skills can only be learned through practical experience on the job in addition to off-job training. Training is usually seen as an investment in human capital, i.e. there is an initial cost of training (the investment) that increases skills (the addition to human capital) that produces a return on the investment in the form of higher productivity and higher wages.

One of the main costs of investing in training from the employer's point of view is that workers are not very productive while they are being trained, so during the training period the value of what they produce is less than the cost of their employment to the employer. Once trained, however, the value of their output starts to exceed the costs of employment and the firm begins to get a return on its investment. However, the employer will only get a positive return on that investment if the employee, once trained, stays with the firm for a sufficient length of time. The greater the training investment by the employer, the longer the period that workers have to stay with the firm before it can get a return on its investment and the greater the loss should they leave during that time. The need to retain trained workers will reinforce pressure on employers to offer deferred benefits, long-term employment security and the possibility of further training, internal promotion and career progression.

Stop and think	What types of workforce will have low turnover costs and why? What types of workforce will have high turnover costs?

● Transferable versus firm-specific training and skills

As shown above, occupational labour markets arise when workers have skills that are transferable from one firm to another. These skills are often acquired through formal training that leads to a certified qualification that serves as proof of ability. Occupational labour markets are efficient institutions for matching workers with defined occupational skills to jobs that have been designed to use them. In this respect they are in line with the competitive model of the labour market, which assumes that workers already possess the skills needed for their jobs when they are hired, as skills are acquired through training outside the firm. Also, the skills that are acquired are assumed to be transferable, that is, equally useful in all firms. However, employers frequently require *firm-specific* skills. Firm-specific skills are needed when a firm designs jobs in such a way that they do not match existing occupational skills. In such cases, firms will have to provide their own customised training for workers. Because the training is specific to a particular firm the skills it imparts are not transferable to other firms. Therefore firm-specific training and skills only increase the value of the worker (and hence their wage) in the firm where the training is provided. This provides an incentive for the worker to remain with the firm in which he or she was trained.

How does a need for firm-specific skills arise? It may be that the firm in question operates an *idiosyncratic* technology. In other words, the firm's technology is dissimilar to that of other firms. This means that workers who are not already employed in the firm will not be trained in the use of the technology. The training that workers are given will of necessity be specific to the firm. Because the technology is not widely used, this training will be of little use to workers should they leave the firm. Technological idiosyncrasy is less unusual than might be imagined. Not only does equipment vary significantly between firms, even in the same industry or sector; even where it is similar it may be configured differently, leading to differences in work organisation and to jobs being designed differently across firms. Workers trained in the operation of one firm's system will be less competent in the operation of another and may well require further training.

Designing jobs so that they require firm-specific skills creates a strong basis for internalising employment. It becomes easier to develop and promote an existing employee into a vacancy than hire someone from outside. This is because the insider's familiarity with the internal systems and routines of the firm and its technology means that they require less formal training before they become competent in their new role than an outsider does. It also increases the mutual dependence of the employer and the employee. Management's dependence on the existing workforce is increased because they alone possess firm-specific skills. This protects them from competition from outsiders. At the same time the workers are more dependent on their current employer because their skills are not marketable in other firms and loss of their current job would mean a reduction in pay. Moves from transferable to firm-specific skills are, therefore, strong forces promoting internalisation of employment and the development of internal labour markets.

ACTIVITY

A paper manufacturing company reported that it used temporary workers for low-skilled labouring occupations only and not for skilled work. In contrast, a National Health Service hospital trust reported increased use of temporary workers because of a shortage of nurses and other skilled workers.

Explain why one organisation can employ temporary workers in skilled jobs while the other cannot. What can you infer about the types of employment system in these two organisations?

● The need to gain workers' cooperation in production

A further assumption behind the basic model of the labour market is that workers exert full effort in their work and that issues of motivation do not arise. In reality, workers can and do control and limit their effort levels. What employers want from workers is actual productive effort. What they get when they hire workers is their productive *potential*. The extent to which productive potential is utilised, that is, the actual level of effort provided by the worker, cannot be determined at the time the worker is hired and is dependent on a number of factors, one of which is the worker's own motivation. One of the functions of management is to ensure that workers' productive potential is converted into desired levels of actual productive effort because if this does not happen, firms will be paying for effort that is not being supplied and their costs will be increased. Of course, this begs the question of what is a reasonable level of effort relative to the wage and this is one of the most frequently contested issues between workers and management (see Chapter 12).

One way of trying to ensure that workers supply the required level of effort is by subjecting them to *direct control* (Friedman, 1977). Traditionally, this took the form of direct personal supervision by a superior and externally imposed discipline. Today, direct supervision is supplemented with electronic surveillance, 'mystery customers' and customer questionnaire surveys in a managerial effort to make workers' effort levels increasingly visible. Supervision is, however, costly and in certain circumstances the costs of implementing effective supervision may be so high that it is impractical as a means of ensuring workers' compliance.

These circumstances arise when the nature of the product or the production process makes it difficult to define what the appropriate effort levels are for each worker and to measure how hard they are actually working. Normally effort is defined and measured in terms of outputs achieved during a defined time-span, such as a working shift. However, this is not always straightforward. Some 'outputs', such as many services, are intangible and hard to quantify. Even when the product is tangible, the production process may involve complex links between operations that make it difficult to measure individual workers' contributions to output. These problems become more intractable for managers when workers have detailed knowledge of the production process that managers do not. This makes it very difficult for managers to define appropriate effort levels without the agreement of workers. It also raises the possibility that workers might mislead managers about the level of effort needed to achieve a given level of output in an attempt to slow down the pace of work and/or increase their earnings.

Heavy reliance on supervision and surveillance may also be counterproductive because of the resistance that it can generate among workers. Workers often perceive supervisors to be using their authority in arbitrary ways that fail to appreciate workers' knowledge of production and disregard their concerns. Workers also often feel that close supervision means that management does not trust them. In such situations workers may resist managerial authority by restricting their effort levels and using what collective power they have to challenge management authority directly, for example by support for trade unions and possibly some form of industrial action. Alternatively, they may quit the organisation in search of more attractive working conditions.

The costs of direct supervision mean that it is not always the best way for managers to obtain the levels of effort that they want from workers. The alternative is to encourage workers to exercise *responsible autonomy* at work (Friedman, 1977). In other words, it may be more cost-effective for managers to offer positive incentives to ensure that workers cooperate with management and use their job knowledge and their initiative to maintain and improve efficiency. These incentives are generally taken to include guarantees of long-term employment security, opportunities for training and internal promotion, fringe benefits and pay that is higher than the market rate. In other words, employment is internalised. The intention behind this is to generate a climate of trust between workers and management that provides a basis for cooperation and an incentive to high effort. It also raises the cost to the employee of losing their job should they fall short of the standards demanded by management.

Stop and think

How does management control your performance in your own job? How do you feel about it? Does your management provide positive incentives to encourage effort and initiative? Do you sometimes try to resist management control in order to make your work easier or more enjoyable?

As shown above, the extent of employers' reliance on positive incentives to effort is related to the complexities of the production process and workers' tasks. This suggests that positive incentives to effort will figure more highly in the management of highly skilled workers than low-skilled workers. From this it is tempting to argue that incentives to internalise employment will be greater where skilled workers are employed rather than unskilled workers. However, while this may be largely true, it is important to recognise that employers often rely on workers' willingness to exercise a degree of responsible autonomy even when little skill is required, and that even low-skilled jobs require some training. Managers in service sector organisations often regard workers' attitudes and behaviour towards customers as being important to the organisation's success. This is particularly important for organisations that compete on the quality of their service and whose workers can control the way in which they interact with customers. Because of this, employers often provide training to enhance workers' interpersonal skills and rely on a significant degree of voluntary cooperation from even relatively unskilled workers. This limits the scope for developing casualised employment systems. This is illustrated in the activity box overleaf.

This example shows that although supermarket employees do not possess significant firm-specific skills, the two companies in question depended on them to develop attitudes and behaviours that create a favourable impression among customers. Therefore they had to offer terms and conditions that enabled them to achieve this and this meant offering permanent jobs to the majority of their employees. This differentiated them as employers from other supermarket chains that compete mainly on price rather than on quality of service and therefore seek to keep labour costs as low as possible. Here we can see that the need for cooperation limits the extent to which these employers felt able to operate extreme versions of the open external labour market.

During 1998 two leading supermarket chains converted two-thirds of their temporary staff onto permanent contracts. Temporary workers had been hired to cope with seasonal peaks in demand or to enable stores to adjust more easily under uncertain trading conditions. However, workers who remained on temporary contracts for too long lost motivation and this had a damaging effect on the quality of customer service. Other problems that managers associated with employing workers on temporary and zero hours contracts were lack of training and difficulty of communication.

Source: People Management, June 1998

Why is it likely that workers on temporary contracts are less motivated than permanent employees? Identify other lines of employment that do not require high levels of skill but do rely on workers to provide a high level of customer service.

● Labour requirements and employment systems – summary

Different employment systems can be seen as ways in which firms seek to minimise the total costs of employment, including costs of turnover and the costs of gaining workers' cooperation in production. These costs vary according to the technology of production and the levels and types of skill that employers require.

Incentives to internalise employment will be greater where:

● Costs of labour turnover are high. Costs of turnover will be higher the more the employer has to invest in training workers.
● There is a need for firm-specific training and skills.
● Costs of direct supervision are high and there is a need for workers to use their initiative and judgement to ensure the efficiency of the production process.

Conversely, there will be little incentive to internalise employment where turnover costs are low, employers invest little in training, firm-specific training and skills are unimportant, and desired effort levels can be achieved through various forms of direct supervision.

It is possible to use this analysis to generate some hypotheses concerning the type of employment system that firms will develop as a result of their labour requirements. These are illustrated in Figure 4.1.

The idea that an organisation's employment system should provide the most efficient way of meeting its labour requirements is central to the concept of strategic human resource management. As shown in Chapter 1, there is an emphasis within HRM literature on the need for 'fit' between HRM policies and wider business strategy. Labour requirements are derived from competitive strategy in the product market. The analysis above indicates specific ways in which the employment systems of organisations reflect their strategic labour requirements from this point of view.

This is a useful approach, since it focuses attention on how firms can act rationally to minimise labour costs, including those of labour turnover and supervision. However, it would be misleading to argue that there is a simple, direct link between firms' labour requirements and the degree to which they internalise their employment systems. It is not just employers' labour requirements that determine employment systems, but a broader range of factors that includes organisational constraints, workers' pressure, the labour market environment and the wider institutional environment in which organisations operate.

■ Organisational constraints

Managers are constrained in their choice of employment system by features of their organisation such as size, financial and managerial resources. These constraints mean that what management may desire in principle cannot always be achieved in practice.

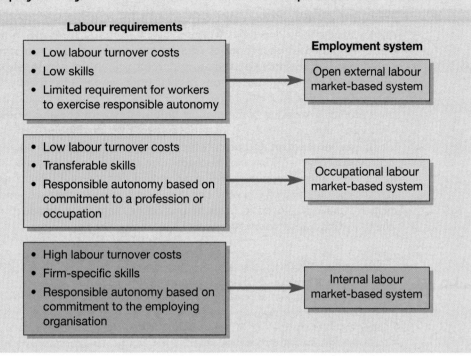

| Figure 4.1 | Employment system chosen as a result of labour requirements |

The size of an organisation has considerable effect on the financial and managerial resources that it possesses and hence on its ability to develop particular types of employment system. Large organisations have greater financial resources than small ones and can support a wider range of specialist management functions, such as a human resource management function. Their financial resources also make them better able to provide favourable terms and conditions of employment and finance long-term investments in training. Opportunities for promotion are also greater in large organisations than in small ones. An organisation's size therefore has a significant influence on the likelihood that it will develop an employment system based on an internal labour market. For the reasons just given, internal labour markets will be more likely in large organisations, less so in small ones. Small firms are more likely to have to rely on systems based on occupational or open external labour markets. This may create dilemmas for managers of small firms who wish to have long-term, stable and committed workforces.

ACTIVITY   Identify examples of the dilemmas faced by owner/managers of small businesses when trying to retain valued workers.

It is evident at this point that employers' labour requirements are often complicated and that management's choice of strategy is constrained by features of the organisation itself. Nevertheless, it is still possible to argue that employment systems embody management strategies. But this proposition becomes open to question once the influence of workers is taken into account.

■ Employee pressure and influence

Pressure from employees can exert a powerful influence on how an organisation's employment system develops. Workers have an interest in trying to protect themselves from the risks and uncertainties of a labour market that is otherwise controlled by employers. Workers have played an important role in the development of occupational labour markets through the actions of their trade unions. Historically, trade unions have imposed or negotiated rules that restrict entry to occupations and prevent employers from replacing workers being paid at union rates with cheaper, unqualified labour. In some cases unions gained considerable control over the labour market and were able to use this to boost wages and protect the employment of their members.

Pressure from workers can also generate internal labour markets. Writers such as Kerr (1954) and Osterman (1984) have argued that internal labour markets are, in part at least, the outcome of workers' and unions' attempts to improve conditions of employment for those employed in firms by protecting them from competition from outsiders. The following quote from Osterman (1984) makes the point clear.

> If a group of workers remains in the same firm for some time, then a set of expectations, or customs, will develop. These expectations, which can be enforced through non-cooperation or even sabotage on the job, tend over time to become codified into a set of rules. The process of unionisation speeds this up and formalizes it, and hence many internal labor markets emerge out of unionisation drives. However, even in non-union situations customary rules and procedures and the force of group expectations can lead to internal labor markets.
>
> (p. 12)

What Osterman is saying is that where workers stay with the same employer for a long time they develop a sense of group identity. This forms the basis for group norms concerning what is a reasonable level of effort in relation to pay and other rewards. It also provides a basis for collective organisation and action by workers to establish rules that shelter them from competition from outsiders and limit management's freedom to hire, fire and redeploy labour and alter the pay structure. These rules can be established formally by trade unions negotiating agreements with employers, or informally by groups of workers on the shopfloor putting pressure on managers to accept them as 'custom and practice'. Once these rules have been established they are difficult to remove because of workers' ability to act collectively to maintain and even extend them.

The influence of workers means that employment systems are not necessarily determined simply by management's labour requirements. Where workers are able to develop significant bargaining power, employment systems represent a compromise between the conflicting goals and priorities of workers and their employers.

■ The labour market environment

All organisations operate within a wider external context that comprises their product markets, the markets for their inputs, i.e. labour, capital and raw materials, and political, economic and legal environments. The labour market environment provides employers with various ways of defining their labour requirements and meeting them. At the same time it constrains their choice by making some routes harder to follow than others. The relevant features of the labour market environment are as follows:

● *the overall state of the labour market* as measured by the unemployment rate and the number of unfilled vacancies;

- *the operation of labour market institutions* such as the system of vocational education and training, the industrial relations system and the framework of employment law;
- *the pattern of labour market segmentation*, in other words the extent to which the labour market is divided into advantaged and disadvantaged groups of workers and how.

The overall state of the labour market

Low unemployment means that employers have to compete more actively for workers and it also means that workers have a wider choice of employment opportunities. This will lead to higher rates of labour turnover as workers leave organisations for better jobs elsewhere. In response, firms may adopt policies aimed at retaining employees, since vacancies arising from labour turnover will be hard to fill. The difficulty of filling vacancies through external recruitment will mean that there will be more internal promotion and redeployment and this may necessitate increased investments in firm-specific training. While these responses might be seen as moves towards an internal labour market system, they are not driven by the technical and skill requirements of production or a long-term employment strategy but by immediate pressures from the labour market environment. These pressures may be reinforced by the increase in trade union bargaining power that results from low unemployment and unfilled vacancies. Once established, these practices may become embedded, although employers may seek to reverse them should labour demand slacken and unemployment rise.

The operation of labour market institutions

Two major institutional influences on employment systems are how well the vocational education and training system ensures an adequate supply of skilled workers, and how the industrial relations system shapes relations between capital and labour. The system of vocational education and training at industry and national level plays a crucial role in influencing the extent to which employment systems are based on occupational labour markets. It was argued earlier in this chapter that for occupational labour markets to operate effectively there has to be a training system that ensures a plentiful supply of workers with transferable skills. This means a system that provides broad, all-round training for the occupation so that, once trained, workers possess skills that are transferable from one firm to another. It is also necessary that there is clear regulation of training and qualification standards so that employers and workers have confidence in them. Otherwise workers will see little point in undertaking training, as the qualification will have low status. Finally it is essential that there is an institutional mechanism for preventing 'free riding', that is preventing some firms from obtaining the benefits of trained labour without contributing to the costs of training. Without such a mechanism, firms that provide training for the occupation risk having their trained workers 'poached' by competitors who do not train. This makes firms less willing to bear the costs of training workers in transferable skills. Therefore firms will invest less in training workers to develop transferable skills and this will reduce the supply of labour with these skills further.

Stop and think	Why does the risk of having trained workers 'poached' by rivals deter firms from training workers in transferable skills?

In the absence of institutions that support training in transferable skills firms will, over time, act in one of two ways. One way is to redesign jobs on the basis of firm-specific skills to ensure that, once trained, workers stay with the firm. The other is to deskill jobs, i.e. redesign them so that they become simpler, thus removing the need for significant training.

The first response encourages a move towards internal labour market structures. The second enables employers to externalise employment more completely because unskilled labour is relatively plentiful and so costs of turnover are low (Marsden, 1986).

The system of industrial relations, including labour legislation, influences the development of employment systems through its effects on the balance of power between employers and workers. Strong trade unions and legal rights for workers raise pay, restrict employers' freedom to hire and fire, and may put pressure on employers to provide training opportunities and promotion paths for workers. This has the effect of protecting employed workers from unilateral management action and from being exposed to competition from the external labour market. It can encourage occupational or internal labour markets, depending on the nature of the training system and the way in which collective bargaining between unions and employers is organised. Where unions negotiate detailed agreements with employers that cover all or most firms in an industry, the effect will be to provide a framework of regulation that supports occupational labour markets. Where unions negotiate with employers on a company-by-company basis there may be more of a tendency for firms to move towards internal labour markets. Conversely, if trade unions are weak and workers are granted few legal rights, employers have a freer hand to hire and fire and determine terms and conditions of employment unilaterally. Therefore they will be freer to determine their employment systems in the light of their labour requirements and the constraints imposed by their size and financial and managerial resources.

● The pattern of labour market segmentation

Some theorists have argued that the existence of different types of labour market reflects the division of the labour market as a whole into privileged and underprivileged, advantaged and disadvantaged segments. The advantaged segment, often referred to as the primary sector, is characterised by internal labour markets and institutionally regulated occupational labour markets. Workers enjoy high earnings, good working conditions, opportunities for training and promotion, and considerable employment security. These are the 'good jobs'. The disadvantaged segment or secondary sector is characterised by open external labour markets. Workers in this sector have low status and pay, poor working conditions, no significant access to training or promotion (they are in 'dead end' jobs), and experience considerable employment insecurity. These are the 'bad jobs'.

How good and bad jobs get created has been a matter of ongoing debate surrounding the theory of labour market segmentation. One line of explanation, advanced by two economists, Doeringer and Piore (1971), is based on the analysis of employers' labour requirements outlined above. Some firms face strong pressures to develop internal labour markets in order to train, develop and retain suitably skilled workers and gain their voluntary cooperation in production. Others do not and are able to meet their labour requirements by drawing on open external labour markets.

Another explanation (Gordon *et al.*, 1982) is that some firms enjoy monopoly power in their product markets and are able to use this power to increase the selling price of the product, thereby increasing profits. Some of these companies will be faced by workers who have developed strong trade unions that can use their bargaining power to gain a share of these profits in the form of high wages and other benefits, including job security provisions. Management seeks to limit union solidarity and bargaining power by dividing the workforce into horizontal segments and offering the prospect of promotion to those who are cooperative and trustworthy. Meanwhile, firms that are unable to use monopoly power to raise their prices do not have surplus profits to share with trade unions, so terms and conditions of employment will be less favourable. Since it is more likely that large, rather than small firms are able to exercise monopoly power, primary sector employment will be concentrated in large rather than small firms.

One of the central predictions of the labour segmentation thesis is that there will be little movement of workers between the primary and secondary sectors of the labour market. Workers in the primary sector are unwilling to move to the secondary sector and the high level of employment security that they enjoy means that they are unlikely to be forced to do so through job loss. Workers who make up the disadvantaged segments of the labour market are unable to move up into the primary sector because employers see them as undesirable candidates for jobs. Primary sector employers want disciplined, cooperative workers with good work habits. Thus when selecting from applicants for jobs, primary sector employers will tend to reject those with unstable employment histories that involve frequent unemployment and job changes because they will assume that this indicates a poor-quality worker. This will automatically rule out secondary sector workers, regardless of their personal qualities, since by definition secondary workers are in unstable, insecure jobs. It is also the case, however, that because of their experience of poor work, some secondary sector workers will tend to develop negative attitudes to work and poor patterns of work behaviour that reinforce employers' prejudices against secondary sector workers as a whole.

These explanations for labour market segmentation emphasise the way in which firms' employment decisions influence the wider labour market by dividing it into advantaged and disadvantaged groups. The question of whether the labour market is divided into primary and secondary sectors as a result of employers' labour policies has generated considerable debate. Numerous empirical studies to test the theory have been carried out in Britain and the United States, with mixed results (see Joll *et al.*, 1983; King, 1990 for a discussion of these).

However, these are not the only explanations for the presence of disadvantaged groups in the labour market. Labour market segmentation can and does occur as a result of 'broader social forces leading to discrimination within the labour market' (Rubery, 1994: 53). Discrimination in the labour market means that workers' chances of gaining access to 'good' or 'bad' jobs are heavily and unfairly influenced by non-work characteristics such as gender, race, class, work-unrelated disability and age. Thus two equally skilled workers will find themselves in different sectors of the labour market because one is a white male from a middle-class social background and the other is a working-class black woman. This reflects deep-seated patterns of discrimination within society in general as well as in the labour market.

To take ethnic minorities as one example, the return to investments in education, that is, the amount that each extra year of education beyond minimum school-leaving age adds to lifetime earnings, is lower for most ethnic minority groups than for comparable white workers. This may be due to any or all of the following reasons that reflect patterns of racial discrimination:

● Ethnic minority workers suffer unfair discrimination when they apply to enter higher-paying occupations and/or when employers are considering candidates for promotion. Therefore they get crowded into low-paid jobs.
● Ethnic minority workers are paid less than whites for doing the same jobs or jobs that are of equal value.
● Unfair discrimination means that ethnic minority workers are disproportionately likely to experience unemployment, so they spend less time in work and their lifetime earnings are reduced.

Women also occupy a disadvantaged place in the labour market, although their position relative to men does seem to be improving in some respects. Women's employment disadvantage reflects deep-seated societal norms concerning the family and the respective roles of women and men in domestic roles and paid work. Women take a disproportionate share of domestic labour and still tend to be regarded as secondary income earners. The domestic roles played by many women mean that their employment opportunities are restricted geographically and contractually. This is particularly true of women with children. In the absence of highly developed systems of childcare, childcare responsibilities mean that many women cannot travel long distances to work and also that they cannot work 'standard' hours. Therefore they are restricted to part-time work in the immediate locality. This means that they have limited choice of employment and therefore little bargaining power and may have to accept secondary sector terms and conditions of employment.

The effect of such institutionalised patterns of discrimination is to increase the range of options open to employers. The presence of disadvantaged groups in the labour market means that some employers can fulfil their requirements for a stable, cooperative workforce without having to offer the positive incentives associated with internal labour markets or regulated occupational labour markets (Rubery, 1994). This is because, as indicated above, disadvantaged groups have few employment alternatives so they have to take what they can get. The absence of better alternatives makes these jobs more attractive than they would otherwise be and therefore more highly valued by workers. This is reflected in the willingness of many disadvantaged workers to remain with their employer and cooperate with management in order to keep their jobs.

ACTIVITY

Recently a do-it-yourself supermarket chain announced that it was hiring older people to work part-time in its stores because they had better interpersonal skills than young workers did and they were more loyal and committed.

Explain why older people with these positive attributes would be prepared to work in low-paying, part-time jobs with few, if any, prospects.

Non-labour market institutions

Finally, employment systems are influenced by institutional arrangements that lie outside the labour market. As shown above, the family as a social institution is one of the main bases for defining gendered roles in employment and as such contributes to women's disadvantage in the labour market. Another example of wider institutional influence on employment systems is the system of company finance. In the United Kingdom and the United States, financial systems are based on active stock markets, with investors buying and selling shares in order to maximise the value of their holdings on a yearly, monthly or even daily basis. This puts great pressure on managers to maximise the short-term financial performance of their companies. In order to do this, they minimise their expenditure on long-term investment because the amount invested counts immediately as a negative item on the balance sheet while the returns, which count on the positive side, do not start to accrue for some time. Therefore large long-term investments make short-term financial performance look poor. This leads to a fall in the share price and to threats of hostile takeovers, which threaten managers' jobs. The pressure to minimise long-term investment means that firms will invest relatively little in training and developing employees. Pressure to maximise short-term performance also puts pressure on firms to avoid committing themselves to long-term employment security for workers because if demand falls they need to be able to reduce costs quickly by cutting the workforce.

Where financial systems are based more on bank credit, as in Germany, there is less pressure to maximise short-term profits and more scope for managers of firms to take a long-term view of how to grow the company. This means that they will be readier to make long-term investments in training and equipment and will be more prepared to commit themselves to providing long-term employment security for workers.

What other non-labour market institutions might influence the nature of employment systems and how?

● Summary

In order to explain how employment systems develop it is necessary to take a wide range of influences into account. These are summarised in Figure 4.2.

From the diagram it is possible to see how the various factors discussed above interact with each other to influence employment systems in complex ways. For example, an organisation might require a stable, cooperative workforce. This might suggest that the employment system should be internalised to a significant extent, e.g. above-average pay and benefits, long-term job security and career prospects. This could pose difficulties for organisations that are constrained by small size and limited financial resources or by pressures from financial institutions that judge firms on their short-term financial performance. However, as long as there is no need for a significant level of organisation-specific skill, it might be possible to attract such a workforce without having to internalise employment if the firm can draw from disadvantaged labour market groups. Yet again, the extent to which this is possible will be influenced by the power of workers to influence terms and conditions of employment through trade unions and collective bargaining as well as the extent to which employment practices such as fixed-term and temporary employment are restricted by legislation.

Therefore we can say that:

- An organisation's employment system is the outcome of the combined effects of firms' labour requirements, organisational constraints, pressure from workers, the labour market environment and the wider institutional environment.
- The wider institutional environment interacts with the labour market environment. Social institutions such as the family and institutionalised patterns of behaviour such as racism contribute to the presence of disadvantaged groups in the labour market. At the same time, labour market pressures may generate pressures for change in wider social institutions; for example, the growing participation of women in the labour market is beginning to challenge the traditional gendered division of family roles.
- The labour market environment affects how employers define their labour requirements. For example, the nature of the vocational training system will influence the

Figure 4.2   Influences on the development of employment systems

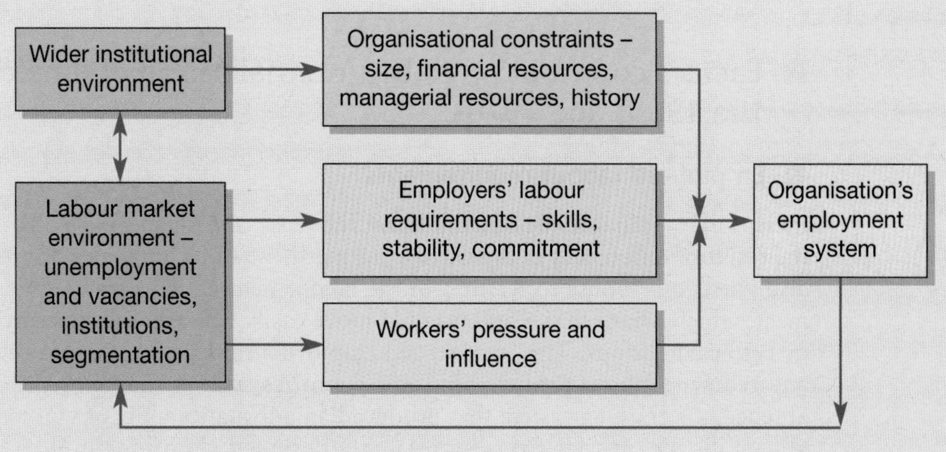

extent to which firms organise production on the basis of low skills, firm-specific skills or transferable skills.

- The labour market environment influences the nature and extent of workers' ability to influence employment systems. For example, where trade unions and collective bargaining are highly developed, workers can exert more pressure on employers than where unions are weak and collective bargaining is uncommon. The presence of disadvantaged groups enables some firms to meet their requirements for stable, committed workers without having to offer primary sector employment conditions.
- Organisational constraints reflect features of the wider institutional environment, for example how the financial system influences the financial resources available for long-term investment in the workforce.
- The ways in which organisations develop their employment systems feed back into the wider labour market environment. For example, organisational responses to skill shortages such as poaching undermine occupationally based training systems and contribute to the decline of occupational labour markets. How organisations select their workforces can reinforce or modify patterns of labour market segmentation.

The rise and fall of internalised employment systems?

Internalised labour market systems became more widespread during the 1960s and 1970s. In the United States, salaried and industrial internal labour markets, first developed during the 1920s and 1930s, became increasingly widespread in large corporations during the 1960s and 1970s. Internal labour markets also began to develop more widely in the UK, despite the continued importance of occupational labour markets. Long-term employment and opportunities for internal promotion had been characteristic of the civil service, local government, banking and certain sections of retailing for many years. However, a number of studies also found evidence of salaried internal labour markets for professional engineers and professional chemists (Mace, 1979; Creedy and Whitfield, 1986) and more restricted versions of industrial internal labour markets for skilled and semi-skilled workers in engineering (George and Shorey, 1985). Moreover, even though fully developed internal labour markets were far from universal in the UK, the salaried internal labour market was an important influence on the development of ideas concerning personnel management and human resource management during the 1970s and 1980s. Increasingly, internalisation of employment came to be seen as best practice (Boxall and Purcell, 2003; Nolan and Slater, 2003). Corporations such as IBM, with highly developed salaried internal labour markets, were held up as examples of sophisticated personnel management and pioneers of human resource management.

Factors contributing to the internalisation of employment in the 1960s and 1970s

● Employers' labour requirements

Increasingly, managers designed jobs on the basis of firm-specific skills. This was partly the result of differences in the ways firms made use of technologies of production. It was also partly a response to features of the labour market. This was a time of full employment, which meant that workers could move easily between jobs in search of higher pay or better conditions. This encouraged employers to develop ways of retaining workers and reducing labour turnover. In some countries such as the USA, UK and France, the absence of a training system that produced an adequate supply of workers with transferable skills meant that firms increasingly designed shopfloor jobs to require limited firm-specific skills and trained their workers internally. In some other countries, notably Germany, the presence of highly effective apprentice training maintained a stronger basis for skilled occupational labour markets.

Organisational constraints

Steady economic growth during the 1950s and 1960s provided a foundation for increasingly large-scale enterprises geared to producing for stable mass markets. As firms grew in size and complexity they needed more supervisory and administrative staff. This in turn created more layers of hierarchy, which extended job ladders and opened up career paths. At the same time, stable long-term growth made it rational for firms to commit themselves to developing long-term career paths for more of their employees. Large enterprises also had the financial and managerial resources to develop internal systems of training and promotion and set up formal internal pay structures.

Employee pressure and influence

Trade union membership and influence rose during the 1960s and 1970s. In Britain, unions extended their membership and representation among white-collar workers during the 1970s, contributing to the development of salaried internal labour markets. In representing their more traditional constituency among manual workers they were also able to establish 'seniority' rules with respect to redundancy dismissals and restrict management's freedom to hire and fire.

In a number of European countries, workers' ability to influence employment systems was encouraged to varying degrees by legally supported structures of collective bargaining and co-determination, as in West Germany and Sweden, or the ability of unions to influence government legislation, as in France. In West Germany an elaborate system of collective bargaining and employee co-determination was established after the Second World War, supported and regulated by law. German workers, through their representatives, were empowered to influence not only wages and hours but also procedures for 'layoffs, promotion criteria, changes in working conditions, the use of overtime and of "short time", and the introduction of new technologies' (Osterman, 1988: 119). This resulted in management providing a high degree of employment security for incumbent workers in return for their acceptance of flexible working practices, i.e. broadly defined job roles and 'willingness to learn new skills' (Osterman, 1988: 123). In France, new developments in collective bargaining after the political unrest among workers and students in 1968 led to enhanced 'job security, vocational training, [and] salaried status for manual workers' (Goetschy and Rozenblatt, 1992).

In the United States, even though trade union membership peaked in the mid-1950s and declined thereafter, unions were increasingly successful in pushing up wages in unionised firms. This gave firms an increasing incentive to avoid unionisation. Therefore, during the 1960s and 1970s, more employers began to introduce personnel policies that combined long-term employment security, training linked to internal promotion, high wages and employee involvement in an attempt to buy workers' loyalty and avoid or weaken unionisation (Kochan et al., 1986).

The labour market environment

The growth in trade union influence in most countries was supported by developments in the labour market. Unemployment was low throughout the 1950s and 1960s. This enhanced unions' bargaining power and influence. However, the labour market retained long-established structural features. One of the most important of these was the gendered division of labour, leading to gendered patterns of labour market segmentation.

Women continued to be regarded as secondary income earners. The concept of the man as the main 'breadwinner' remained dominant. Consequently, long-term jobs and careers were developed for men rather than women. The fact that household income depended on male earnings shaped trade union demands, which were for better pay, greater job security and better prospects for wage progression for men. During the 1960s and 1970s there was also a growth of legislative protection for workers in many countries, e.g. restricting employers' freedom to make workers redundant, and laws protecting workers from unfair dismissal.

● The wider institutional environment

Developments in the wider institutional environment affected labour market policy and trade union influence. The development of social democracy in Europe after the Second World War involved the fuller recognition of the place of workers and their organisations within the nation-state. This was reflected in a commitment by governments to maintain full employment and create and support welfare states. These commitments reduced, although by no means eliminated, the inequality of power in the employment relationship and thus gave workers greater power to influence their terms and conditions of employment. The social democratic spirit also led to a greater degree of political legitimacy and support for trade unions, reflected in the development of 'tripartite' institutions of economic management. These involved trade unions, together with government and employer representatives, in decisions concerning economic and social policy. In addition, as shown above, the 1970s saw legal extensions of workers' rights to participate in decision-making at workplace level in countries such as West Germany, Sweden and France.

■ Restructuring employment since the 1980s: the externalisation of employment?

Since the 1980s, large corporations, particularly in Britain and the United States but also in Europe, have undertaken processes of 'restructuring', aimed at reducing costs and improving responsiveness to more rapidly changing, intensely competitive and less predictable markets. Job cuts on a large scale have been a central feature of the process, as have new patterns of work organisation and changes to employment structures. The effect has been to weaken internal labour market structures (Cappelli et al., 1997; Boxall and Purcell, 2003: 121):

● First, employers in Britain, the USA and a number of European countries have made greater use of part-time and temporary labour and in a minority of cases, highly casualised forms of employment such as zero hours contracts (Cappelli et al., 1997; Cully et al., 1999; Millward et al., 2000). During the 1990s, although the total number of jobs grew, there was a net reduction in the number of *full-time* jobs in Britain. All of the growth in employment was accounted for by a growth of part-time employment. This trend was replicated across the European Union, where the share of part-time jobs in total employment rose from 12.7 per cent to 17.9 per cent and that of fixed-term-contract jobs from 8.4 per cent to 13.4 per cent between 1985 and 2001 (European Commission, 2002: 173).
● Second, a number of companies have transferred some of their workers from employed to self-employed status by dismissing them and then offering them a contract to perform their job as self-employed workers.
● Third, employers have reduced their commitment to providing long-term employment security for 'permanent' employees. Increasingly, employers and employers' organisa-

tions in Britain and the USA have claimed that workers should take greater responsibility for their own careers and 'employability' and be less reliant on employers to provide long-term employment security and career paths. The risk of job loss increased significantly for managers during the late 1980s and 1990s as restructuring usually involved changes in management organisation. It also increased for workers in occupations previously regarded as offering jobs for life, such as public administration, banking and education (Cappelli *et al.*, 1997; Heery and Salmon, 2000).

- Fourth, senior managers have 'downsized' and 'delayered' their organisations. This has not only resulted in job cuts. It has also reduced the number of job levels. The result is that workers have fewer opportunities to gain access to internal promotion ladders. This has been noticeable in the banking and finance sector and in supermarkets, where jobs that used to provide stepping stones from junior to more senior grades have largely been eliminated (Cappelli *et al.*, 1997; Grimshaw *et al.* 2001; Hudson, 2002).

- Fifth, a growing number of organisations no longer employ their own staff to perform jobs that are not 'core' functions of the business, e.g. cleaning, catering, security, payroll administration, but buy these services in from outside companies instead. In the UK this has been widespread in public administration, the public utilities sector, i.e. electricity, gas and water, and the financial services sector (Cappelli *et al.*, 1997; Cully *et al.*, 1999).

- Finally, employers have increased the variability of pay by linking elements of pay to measures of individual, team or organisational performance. This has undermined the principle of the 'rate for the job' which has been an important feature of internal labour markets. It has meant that in some organisations there is no longer a clear pay structure that links to different job levels so as to provide a path to promotion and higher pay (Cappelli *et al.*, 1997; Grimshaw *et al.*, 2001).

ACTIVITY   Consider the organisation that you or a friend or a family member works for. Which of the changes listed above has it introduced and for what reasons?

We can use the analytical framework developed in the previous section of this chapter to explain these developments.

● Changes in employers' labour requirements

The effects of sectoral change – the shift from manufacturing to services

The proportion of workers employed in manufacturing has declined in the USA and all the major European Union economies since the 1970s. At the same time there has been absolute and relative growth in the number of people employed in the service sector. The decline of employment in manufacturing and the growth of the service sector have altered the nature of skills required by employers. Manufacturing is more likely to make use of idiosyncratic technologies and to require firm-specific skills. The growth of service sector employment has been concentrated at two poles – high-level professional and managerial skills at one pole, and low-skilled jobs at the other. High-level professional skills are largely acquired through formal training leading to nationally or internationally recognised qualifications. These skills are predominantly transferable, so there is no strong incentive for employers to develop internal labour markets for these workers, as they can easily move between firms in search of higher rewards. Under-performers can be dismissed and replaced with new hires from the external (occupational) labour market.

At the low-skilled end of the labour market there are even fewer incentives for employers to develop internal labour markets. Even where certain behaviours are needed in order to ensure satisfactory levels of customer service, these are usually fairly rudimentary, easily learnt and transferable. Therefore there is only limited training investment and consequently little need to retain workers in order to protect long-term investments in training. Consequently, it can be argued that the shift away from manufacturing to service employment means that fewer employers have strong incentives to develop internal labour markets.

The effects of increased competition – cost reduction and labour flexibility

Since the 1970s, organisations have been subject to increasingly intense pressure from three main sources. First, markets have become increasingly competitive as a result of the emergence of new low-cost areas of production in China, South-East Asia and the Pacific Rim and, recently, Central and Eastern Europe. International competition has been encouraged by tariff reductions and freer trade between countries as a result of long-term projects such as the European Union and the World Trade Organisation. Within individual countries, government policies of privatisation and deregulation have encouraged domestic competition by enabling more firms to enter certain areas of economic activity, such as mail services, gas, electricity and water supply, telecommunications and transport. Competition has put pressure on producers to reduce costs as well as improve the quality of their products.

Secondly, markets for goods and services have become more volatile. Customers are more demanding than they used to be and products become obsolete much more quickly. As a result of these changes, organisations have to be more innovative and responsive to change. Furthermore, the level of market demand is subject to sharper and more frequent variations than used to be the case, which means that organisations also have to be able to adjust the level of their labour inputs in line with changes in demand for their output.

Organisational restructuring has been the widespread response to these pressures. Efforts at organisational restructuring have focused on decentralisation of hitherto large, centralised corporations and reductions in headcount in an attempt to eliminate unnecessary labour costs. Increasingly, organisations have sought to cut costs by reducing the number of employees who are not contributing directly to production or service delivery. This restructuring of organisations consists of four main elements:

- *Downsizing*, i.e. reducing the size of the workforce while reorganising the production process and intensifying work so that production can be achieved with fewer workers.
- *Externalisation* of those activities that are required by the organisation but are not central to the production process by 'contracting out' or 'outsourcing'. Outsourcing enables firms to reduce the number of workers they employ directly, together with the associated costs, by transferring responsibility for provision to specialist external organisations. Examples of such activities include cleaning and catering, security and maintenance, and some administrative services such as payroll administration.
- *Delayering*, i.e. stripping out layers of supervision and management. This cuts employment costs and also, in theory, increases the speed of communication and decision-making by 'flattening' the organisation, i.e. reducing the number of levels in the hierarchy.
- *Devolution* of responsibility for decision-making and problem-solving to more junior managers and production workers. This is a necessary consequence of delayering.

The result of restructuring is a 'lean' organisation that uses fewer employees to produce the same or a higher level of output.

As part of organisational restructuring, employers and governments have come to insist on the need for greater **labour flexibility** in order to reduce costs and improve quality and competitiveness. From the employer's standpoint labour flexibility refers to the ability of managers to:

● Vary the size of the workforce in line with demand for output. This aspect of flexible labour utilisation is known as *numerical flexibility*. This is partly in response to the increased volatility of markets and the consequent unpredictability of demand. Firms cannot afford to carry workers who are surplus to requirements. At the same time they need to be able to respond rapidly to rising demand if they are to retain their shares of the market. Therefore they need to be able to reduce or increase labour inputs in line with changes in demand. Numerical flexibility can be achieved in various ways, i.e. by employing more workers on part-time, temporary, or fixed-term contracts of employment and by substituting outside contractors and self-employed workers for direct employees.

● Move away from fixed hours of work, such as the 9 to 5 working day. This means making more use of shift-working and part-time working to maximise the utilisation of plant and equipment or ensure that customer expectations are met while matching labour inputs to peaks and troughs in demand. This aspect of labour flexibility is known as *temporal flexibility*.

● Redeploy workers across tasks and jobs. Employers need to be able to ask workers to perform a wider range of tasks than before. There are various reasons for this. One is that organisational downsizing means smaller workforces. These have to be more productive. This has led managers to reorganise and intensify work in order to raise labour productivity by introducing multi-tasking and multi-skilling to ensure that when workers are not occupied with one task they transfer to another. Another reason is to enable organisations to make effective use of new technology. This creates a need for highly trained workers with a broad range of skills. This aspect of labour flexibility is known as *functional flexibility*.

● Control wage and salary costs by linking pay to various measures of performance such as individual performance, team performance or organisational performance, and to local labour market conditions. This is referred to as *financial flexibility*.

Stop and think	To what extent do you think these forms of labour flexibility operate in the organisations where you have worked?

Employers' search for labour flexibility has led to an attack on 'rigidities' associated with internal labour markets and structured occupational labour markets. Both the narrowly defined jobs of the industrial internal labour market and the demarcation lines between jobs in structured occupational labour markets are claimed to be incompatible with the need for functional flexibility of labour. Narrowly designed jobs that are separated from each other by clear boundaries do not allow management to make full use of new technology and new methods of work organisation, which require broader skills and more versatile, adaptable workers. Pay scales that set a uniform rate of pay for the job, as in both variants of internal labour markets and in structured occupational labour markets, are seen by managers to be incompatible with their desire to link pay to team or individual performance. Finally, the guarantees of long-term employment and career progression associated with salaried internal labour markets restrict management's ability to adjust the size of the workforce in response to changes in market demand.

● Organisational constraints

Increased international competition, combined with financial deregulation and the mobility of capital, has reinforced pressures on British and US firms to maximise short-term profits to meet the demands of shareholders and introduced them to countries where they used to be relatively absent, such as Sweden and Germany. These pressures make it harder for senior managers to commit themselves to long-term investment in workers' training and provisions for long-term employment security and career progression. Furthermore, the successive rounds of job cuts that were made during the 1980s and 1990s as corporate restructuring aimed to create 'lean organisations' meant that many firms reduced or ended their commitment to long-term job security for employees. In addition, externalisation, decentralisation and delayering have also meant that organisations are smaller and more fragmented and have fewer hierarchical levels. This has broken up the internal promotion ladders that underpinned salaried internal labour markets in previously large, centralised corporations (Hudson, 2002).

● Employee pressure and influence

Changes in the labour market environment and the wider institutional environment have weakened workers' bargaining power and their ability to influence employment systems. High unemployment in the main European economies during the 1980s and 1990s weakened trade union membership and bargaining power. The impact of unemployment was reinforced by government policies that were aimed at reinvigorating European capitalism by encouraging competition and restricting the power of organised labour. In Britain the decline in trade union membership and power was dramatic, leading to the erosion of the trade union-based industrial relations system that had developed after the Second World War. This reflected the collapse of employment in manufacturing during the 1980s together with anti-union policies and legislation that were implemented by Conservative governments under Margaret Thatcher and John Major during the 1980s and 1990s and have largely continued under Tony Blair's Labour government since 1997. In other countries such as Sweden, France and Germany, although unemployment rose significantly, public policy did not shift powerfully against the unions as it did in Britain. Thus while union membership has declined in relation to the employed workforce and unions have been forced to make concessions to employers in order to reduce costs, maintain competitiveness and save jobs, unions have not lost their influence in employment matters to the same extent they have in Britain. Thus it is to varying extents that employers have a freer hand to restructure employment systems in line with their own needs and constraints and with less regard to pressure from employees.

● The labour market environment

The 1970s in Europe saw a slowing down in the rate of economic growth, increasing inflationary pressures and rising unemployment. Unemployment increased more rapidly during the 1980s and 1990s. For example, unemployment across the 12 member states of the European Union (excluding East Germany) rose from 3.7 per cent in 1975 to 9.9 per cent in 1985 and was still 8.1 per cent in 1991. In 2001 the unemployment rate across the 15 member states was 7.4 per cent (European Commission, 1996, 2002).

On the supply side of the labour market there has been a significant increase in the proportion of women in employment. Across the European Union the proportion of women aged 15–64 in employment rose from 45.1 per cent in 1985 to 54.9 per cent in 2001 (European Commission, 1996, 2002). In the UK and the USA there has also been a significant increase in the number of young people in part-time employment. This reflects the growth in the number of young people in further and higher education, for whom part-time or temporary work is a convenient way of supplementing their income. In terms of Rubery's analysis outlined earlier, these groups have swollen the secondary segment of the labour market, providing a pool of cheap yet compliant labour from which employers can draw and so avoid having to invest in positive incentives to obtain desired levels of behaviour at work. Policies that are currently aimed at increasing labour market participation among ethnic minorities, women and older people may add to the disadvantaged segments of the labour market unless they are linked to improve-ments in educational and training opportunities and forms of regulation that deter employers from adopting 'cheap labour' policies.

However, high unemployment and low rates of job creation have led to growing criticism of labour market regulation in many EU member states. It has been argued increasingly that high levels of protection against dismissal and restrictions on employers' freedom to employ people on part-time and temporary contracts deter employers from creating new jobs. The proposed remedy has been to increase labour market flexibility by reducing these protections and restrictions and in some cases by legislating to reduce the bargain-ing power of trade unions.

Nevertheless, the European Union has not followed a simple course of labour market deregulation. Instead it has tried to encourage increased labour market flexibility within a reformed framework of regulation. While this has meant relaxing a number of regula-tions limiting, for example, the employment of workers on temporary and fixed-term contracts, there is a commitment to ensuring that such 'non-standard' workers enjoy the same employment rights as full-time, permanent workers (European Commission, 1999). The European Commission has also espoused the principle that in a more flexible, decen-tralised labour market, workers should have enhanced rights of representation and participation in decision-making (Gill *et al.*, 1999). This is linked to the Commission's con-tinued emphasis on the importance of Europe competing internationally on the basis of highly skilled, adaptable workforces (see Chapter 16 for further discussion).

The most radical policy shift in the direction of labour market flexibility has occurred in the UK, where trade unions and collective bargaining, rather than government legisla-tion, were traditionally the main curbs on unilateral management action. The decline of trade union membership and collective bargaining coverage that resulted from economic policy and anti-union legislation during the 1980s and 1990s, together with the determi-nation to minimise statutory protection for workers as far as possible, means that the British labour market is now the least regulated in Europe. Originally a Conservative government project, labour market flexibility has continued to be a priority for the Labour government since 1997. The introduction of a national minimum wage, the strengthening of workers' protection against unfair dismissal and legislation providing trade unions with a legal right to claim recognition from employers can be seen as a par-tial reversal of some aspects of Conservative policy. However, the level of the minimum wage is low, workers in Britain continue to have weaker employment rights than their counterparts in Europe and British trade unions continue to be subject to the most restrictive laws in the European Union. The current government claims that labour market flexibility has enabled Britain to reduce unemployment far more successfully than the more highly regulated economies in Europe such as Germany and France. However, Britain has a higher incidence of low-paid employment than other major European economies and the most unequal earnings distribution (Rubery and Edwards, 2003).

To varying degrees therefore, changes in the labour market emvironment have given employers greater freedom to restructure employment systems in line with their changing labour requirements and organisational constraints.

● The wider institutional environment

These policy shifts have been closely linked to radical changes in economic institutions. Financial markets have been deregulated, allowing capital to flow freely from one financial centre to another in search of the best possible short-term profits. This, together with advances in information and communications technology, has helped stimulate the growth of multinational corporations, which began during the 1970s. Furthermore, increasing pressures for free trade in goods and services, embodied in the formation of the Single European Market, the North American Free Trade Agreement and the World

Trade Organisation, have given further stimulus to international competition and the internationalisation of production. This has in turn intensified the pressures on governments to pursue economic policies that are acceptable to international investors, such as promoting labour market flexibility, and on firms to offer consumers better value for money by reducing costs and prices while improving the quality of products and services.

These pressures have also been transmitted to workers and their unions. They are increasingly aware that the continuation of jobs depends on maintaining the competitiveness of their workplaces. This competition is not confined to competition between companies. Multinational companies scrutinise the performance of their plants in different countries, comparing cost and productivity levels and concentrating investment in those that are deemed to be most efficient. This means that workers employed in different plants of the same company are in increasingly direct competition with each other. The consequence is that workers and their unions are less able to influence terms and conditions of employment or resist managerial initiatives aimed at weakening internal labour markets. This is true even in economies such as Germany, where public policy has not shifted as radically in favour of labour market flexibility as in the UK (Katz and Darbishire, 2000; Whittall, 2001).

ACTIVITY   Refer back to Figure 4.2. Construct your own version of the diagram, showing how specific influences have affected specific features of employment systems since the 1980s.

The future of employment systems: theory and evidence

The changes outlined above suggest that there is a move away from internalised employment systems and that organisations are having increased recourse to occupational and open external labour markets (Guest and Hoque, 1994; Katz and Darbishire, 2000). However, the question of how far organisations will go down the externalisation road is open to discussion. In moving away from long-term commitments to employment security, transparent pay structures and opportunities for internal training and promotion, organisations run the risk of undermining employees' morale and commitment and possibly losing valued employees as a consequence.

Organisations are subject to contradictory pressures with respect to the management of labour. On the one hand employers need to be able to treat labour as a commodity to be hired and fired as production requirements dictate (recall that the demand for labour is derived from the demand for goods and services). At the same time, employers need workers to cooperate actively in the production process. This means more than following management instructions. It also means using their creativity and judgement and taking some responsibility for the quality of their own performance.

The contradiction exists because each of these requirements undermines the other. Workers' awareness that they will be dismissed when the market dips reduces their trust in the employer and therefore their willingness to cooperate with management. After all, why cooperate in improving efficiency if it means that the job that is lost is your own? At the same time, managers' need for workers' cooperation limits the extent to which they can treat workers as a disposable commodity. Therefore there is never complete trust and cooperation between management and workers but at the same time management has to give some consideration to workers' interests and concerns. This contradiction can never be ultimately resolved, but it can be managed; how to do this is one of the central concerns of personnel management and HRM.

The drive to restructure organisations and employment since the 1980s has intensified these contradictory pressures on workers and managers and the personnel/HRM function. On the one hand, management claims to need more highly skilled, functionally flexible workers who can be trusted to exercise responsible autonomy. This means that organisations have an interest in developing and retaining skilled employees and establishing a climate of trust and cooperation in employee relations. As we have seen, such outcomes are associated with long-term, stable employment relationships. On the other hand, pressures to reduce costs and achieve numerical flexibility of labour imply personnel policies that run counter to this by weakening employers' commitments to long-term employment security and reducing opportunities for career development within the organisation. This raises the questions of how employers are attempting to manage this contradiction and what the implications are for HRM.

ACTIVITY Review the activity relating to the two supermarkets on page 126. Explain to yourself how it illustrates the contradictory nature of management's labour requirements.

■ The 'flexible firm' model

One model of how organisations could respond to the problem of managing these contradictions is for organisations to operate different employment systems for different sections of their workforce (Atkinson, 1984, 1985). This model, known as the 'flexible firm', became very influential in HRM thinking during the late 1980s and early 1990s. The model purported to show how firms could minimise employment costs and become more responsive to changes in markets and technology by reorganising their employment systems to achieve a combination of functional, numerical and financial flexibility. The model is illustrated in Figure 4.3.

The model assumes that various labour requirements can be separated from each other so that they can be satisfied by different sections of the workforce. This enables different employment systems to be applied to the different segments.

The main division of the workforce is into 'core' and 'peripheral' segments. 'Core workers' are trained in a range of firm-specific skills that make them *functionally flexible*, that is, competent to perform a range of different tasks and able to undertake further training as new technologies are adopted. These workers are the source of creativity, problem-solving capacity and adaptability within the organisation. They may include workers at most levels within the firm, from managerial and professional to skilled production workers. The employer has a strong interest in retaining these workers, so depending on the degree of responsible autonomy and discretion that they are required to exercise in their roles, they will be subject to salaried or industrial internal labour market systems of employment, i.e. favourable pay and benefits, long-term employment security and, to varying degrees, opportunities for internal training and promotion.

'Peripheral workers' are workers whose contribution to production, while significant, is not central and whose skills are transferable rather than firm-specific. The size of the peripheral workforce can be expanded or contracted as demand for the firm's output rises or falls, so it is a source of *numerical flexibility* for the firm. This group is itself split into further segments that are subject to occupational labour market-based and open external labour market-based employment systems. Peripheral group I is made up of employees on full-time contracts but with no guarantee of long-term employment, i.e. an occupational labour market. Peripheral group II consists of various 'non-standard' forms of employment contract such as short-term contracts, temporary workers, job shares and part-time workers drawn from the open external labour market.

A further characteristic of the 'flexible firm' model is that it envisages that organisations will cease to use their own employees to carry out some 'non-core' functions.

Figure 4.3	The 'flexible firm'

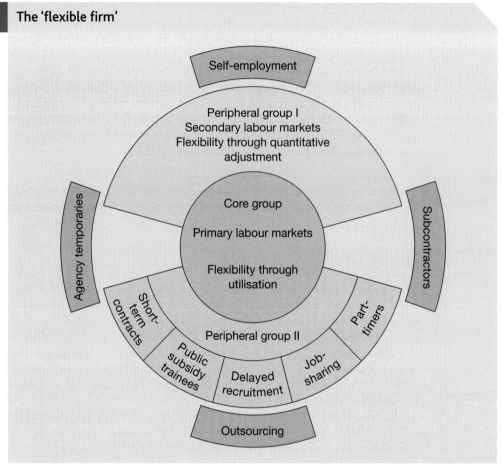

Source: Institute for Employment Studies (1995)

Instead they will contract these activities out to 'distanced workers', i.e. self-employed workers, temporary help agency workers and specialist contracting companies that operate their own employment systems.

A key feature of the model is that the peripheral workers provide a 'buffer' that protects core workers from external market pressures. When faced with a dip in demand for its product, the firm will cut peripheral jobs while retaining core workers. It can also offset the costs of maintaining high rates of pay and benefits for core workers by ensuring that the pay of peripheral workers is adjusted in line with market rates.

● The flexible firm: model and reality

It is clear that this model focuses almost entirely on organisations' labour requirements and neglects the other influences on employment systems that have been identified in this chapter. This is a weakness, since it assumes that managers are free to organise their employment systems in this way. Empirical research in the UK has found very little evidence for the emergence of the flexible firm, largely because of some of these other influences.

Organisations have been constrained in their ability to take such a sophisticated approach to their employment systems because of the inability or unwillingness of managers to take a strategic, long-term approach to business decisions (Hunter and MacInnes, 1992; Sisson and Marginson, 1995). This may have reflected pressure from financial institutions in the City to concentrate on short-term financial performance rather than long-term planned development. Research has also found little evidence of multi-skilling and a functionally flexible core workforce. This reflects the low priority and limited investment that most British firms give to training, something that has been aggravated by the relatively heavy emphasis on short-term profits in British business that discourages long-term investment in training.

Rather than developing internally differentiated employment systems along the lines of the flexible firm, British management has been found to have taken one of three approaches to labour flexibility, each of which is biased towards numerical rather than functional flexibility. These are:

- To seek cost minimisation through the employment of so-called 'flexible' labour, i.e. low-paid, part-time, female workers. This approach takes advantage of the relatively high degree of 'labour market flexibility' in the UK. Put simply, this means the relative absence of constraints on hiring and dismissal and until recently, the absence of a minimum wage and the ability to pay part-time and temporary workers less *pro rata* than permanent full-time workers. However, recent changes in British and European Union legislation may make this cost-cutting route more difficult to pursue in future.
- To minimise costs by achieving numerical flexibility in 'core' as well as 'peripheral' functions. Extensive use is made of temporary workers and subcontracting.
- To combine functional flexibility in core functions with numerical flexibility in peripheral functions by contracting peripheral functions out to external agencies. However, functional flexibility is not developed to a high degree and consists more in the multi-tasking of semi-skilled labour than in the multi-skilling of highly trained workers (Cully *et al.*, 1999).

Evidence from the USA suggests that employers have tended to divide their workforces into primary and secondary segments. The employment system for primary workers continues to be internalised, i.e. based on long-term commitments from the employer and the employee, while that for the secondary segment is externalised, i.e. organised on a short-term hire and fire basis. There is also some evidence that 'firms which provide better benefit packages to their full-time, more permanent workers are more likely to rely on flexible staffing arrangements' (Rosenberg and Lapidus, 1999: 77). This is in line with the idea that numerical flexibility in the periphery protects the employment conditions of core workers.

However, this does not mean that US firms have made a strategic HRM choice to adopt the model of the flexible firm in order to combine functional and numerical flexibility. As in Britain, there is little evidence of widespread multi-skilling of 'core' workers. As in Britain, the main motive for hiring non-standard workers, particularly self-employed and temporary agency workers, is to reduce costs. US employment law forbids employers from offering benefits to one group of full-time employees and withholding them from another, but employers are allowed to withhold such benefits from non-standard workers, i.e. self-employed workers and workers hired through temporary agencies (Rosenberg and Lapiches, 1999: 77; Heckscher, 2000). This has encouraged the wider use of these workers.

Overall therefore, while there is evidence of increased differentiation and segmentation of employment systems in Britain and the USA, there is little evidence that the flexible firm model has been adopted as an employment strategy. Specifically, there is little evidence that employers have reorganised their employment systems to combine numerical and functional flexibility. Instead, numerical flexibility appears to have been extended to the majority of functions within enterprises as employers have taken advantage of weakened employee pressure and influence to reduce costs.

■ An alternative model? 'Flexible specialisation'

Critics of developments in Britain and the USA argue that they amount to a 'low road' path of economic development based on cheap labour. Low wages reflect low skills and low productivity, which are in turn the product of management's pursuit of short-term profits and its neglect of long-term investment in training. These biases have been reinforced over the years by the operation of the British and American financial systems and their governments' unwillingness to provide workers with strong, legally enforced employment rights. By making it easy for employers to make use of 'cheap labour' it has reduced incentives for employers to invest in highly skilled, functionally flexible workforces (Nolan, 1989; Cappelli *et al.*, 1997; Dex and McCulloch, 1997). These critics argue that the long-run consequences of this are increasing technological backwardness, inability to compete in the markets for high-value, sophisticated goods and services, and an increase in low-paid, insecure employment.

The alternative to the 'low road' is the 'high road' path of development that is based on high skills, high productivity and high wages. The 'high road' strategy is one of 'flexible specialisation'. This seeks to develop new areas of competitive advantage by exploiting new technologies and new market opportunities rather than defending old ones against low-cost competition. The emphasis is on internal, functional flexibility of labour to support adaptation to new technologies and innovations in product design and production methods. Advocates of the 'high road' strategy argue that countries that develop a highly educated and trained workforce and foster labour–management cooperation are better placed to compete in the markets for high-quality goods and services. This is because highly skilled workforces are crucial to high levels of research and development, sophisticated design of goods and services and high quality in their manufacture or delivery. The benefit of this strategy is that premium goods and services sell at premium prices, with higher mark-ups and hence profits. This supports high wages, good working conditions and comprehensive, generous levels of social welfare provision. The 'high road' position on labour market policy is that it should aim to increase the capacity of workers to acquire new, high-level skills, broaden their range of skills and adapt to changes in technology, rather than pursuing wage and numerical flexibility.

The viability of this alternative has come to be questioned in recent years. The main reason for this is that competition on the basis of quality is no longer a straight alternative to competition on the basis of price. High-quality goods can be produced using low-cost methods of production and high-cost producers are less able to rely on product quality to protect them from lower-cost competition. During the 1970s and 1980s, West Germany was seen as the best example of a country that was attempting to take the 'high road'. Although sometimes exaggerated, the strengths of the German system included a strong legal framework of rights for workers, including co-determination rights, that limited management's freedom to hire and fire workers at will and provided a basis for worker–management cooperation in the workplace. They also included a strongly developed system of initial vocational training that ensured a relatively large supply of skilled labour. However, in recent years German producers have come under increased competition and a growing number have located more of their production capacity outside Germany in order to avoid high labour costs. This has also created pressures for greater labour market flexibility in Germany. Trade unions in private and public sector organisations have agreed to various concessions in order to protect job security for incumbent workers, including the systematic use of part-time and fixed-term contracts to fill new vacancies. This creates a growing division between 'insiders', who retain job and income security and access to promotion and career progression, and the 'outsiders' on part-time, temporary and fixed-term contracts who increasingly occupy the periphery of the employment system (Jacobi *et al.*, 1998; Katz and Darbishire, 2000).

The virtual organisation, networks and the end of long-term employment?

Some analysts have interpreted recent developments as indicating a transformation in work patterns as greater flexibility is demanded of firms and workers. In their view, traditional careers are a thing of the past. As traditional internal labour markets decline, rather than progressing careers through vertical job mobility based on internal promotion within one organisation, workers now have to make sideways moves across organisations as they search for better pay and opportunities. It has been claimed that, in future, workers will have to change their careers several times in their working lives, acquiring new sets of skills and changing occupations as old skills and occupations become obsolete (Bayliss, 1998).

For some of these observers, the whole concept of employment is becoming outmoded as a result of the emergence of the 'virtual organisation'. The virtual organisation is presented as the antithesis of bureaucracy and hierarchy. There is minimal formal, permanent organisation and there are almost no direct employees. The virtual organisation is based on networks that bring individuals and groups of workers together for specific projects. Once the projects are complete, the assemblages of workers break up and new assemblages are created for the next set of projects. Some commentators have claimed that this is the future of work and that eventually most workers will no longer be employees of a single employer. Instead they will be 'portfolio workers' doing a range of jobs for different employers, as a 'freelance' worker or a self-employed producer of services. The most frequently cited examples of this emergent breed are the self-employed business consultant, the freelance journalist and television producer (Bridges, 1995; Handy, 1995; Leadbeater, 2000). Therefore the picture being painted is one in which not only are long-term employment relationships giving way to more contingent forms of employment, such as temporary and fixed-term contracts; the employment relationship in general is giving way to commercial transactions between self-employed workers and organisations buying in their services.

Stop and think

What do you think are the main advantages and disadvantages of being a 'portfolio worker'? Is this a pattern of work that appeals to you? Why or why not?

This picture, most frequently painted in popular management literature and press comment, is greatly exaggerated. It is true that there has been an increase in the number of temporary and fixed-term contracts of employment in various countries such as the UK, the USA and Spain. It is also true that prospects of long-term, stable jobs have declined for some labour market groups. In Britain and the USA in particular, men are facing increased competition for long-term jobs. Young men and older workers have been particularly affected in both countries and, in the USA, black workers have suffered the greatest drop in job stability (Gregg and Wadsworth, 1999; Bernhardt and Marcotte, 2000). Despite this, however, long-term employment relationships remain the norm. In 1985, 31.1 per cent of the UK working population were in jobs that had lasted more than ten years. In 1998, the proportion was 28.6 per cent. In 1998, 48.8 per cent of workers were in jobs that had lasted more than five years (Gregg and Wadsworth, 1999). Clearly the employment relationship is still a long-term one. Neither is there much evidence that the self-employed worker is replacing the employee. Freelance workers and self-employed teleworkers operating from home via computer modems remain a small minority of the British workforce. The proportion of workers who are self-employed in Britain fell continuously as a proportion of total employment between 1994 and 2001, from 13.5 per cent to 11.7 per cent, and in the European Union from

16.2 per cent to 14.8 per cent (Millward *et al.*, 2000: 48; European Commission 2002: 173, 188).

One reason for this is that most workers value the security and stability of long-term employment relationships. While there is evidence from the USA that most self-employed workers and independent contractors are happy with their status and do not want standard jobs, most temporary workers would rather be in permanent employment (Polivka *et al.*, 2000; Heckscher, 2000). Dissatisfaction is also widespread among temporary workers in Britain. Moreover, even among self-employed freelancers, there is evidence that insecurity is perceived as a problem (Gallie *et al.*, 1998; Baines, 1999).

A second reason is that the network form of organisation can carry significant disadvantages from a managerial point of view, so managers continue to have an interest in maintaining long-term employment relationships. The widespread use of temporary workers generates friction between temporary and permanent staff, leading to reduced commitment from permanent workers, especially where temporary workers are employed on inferior terms and conditions (Geary, 1992; Heckscher, 2000). Moving from conventional employment to 'networks' has been shown to carry the potential for considerable disruption. A study of a major shift from long-term employment to freelance and contract labour in the British television and broadcasting industry in the 1990s (Saundry and Nolan, 1998) found that it led to an increase in administrative costs, skill shortages and lower morale among workers. Eventually companies began to return to more traditional employment patterns through efforts to 'improve job security for existing staff and persuade freelancers to return to permanent contracts' (Nolan and Slater, 2003). Case study research in the USA has produced similar results. After an initial phase of radical organisational restructuring that broke up internal labour markets, problems of declining product quality, skill shortages and lower morale and employee commitment have led organisations to reintroduce elements of internal labour markets (Moss *et al.*, 2000).

The US economist Charles Heckscher gives a vivid summary of these issues from a US perspective:

> For the vast majority of employees, the open labor market *is* a fearful place. It is hard to get training, it is hard to get placement, it is hard to get health care, and it is hard to explain to your family and friends – and to yourself – why you are not working. For managers the turbulence caused by employee turnover is far more dangerous than the possible gain from getting better people. Managers are better off working with what they have, which is at least predictable, than taking a wildly uncertain bet on the labor market.
>
> (Heckscher 2000: 277).

For workers, long-term employment provides security of income and is also frequently valued as a source of psychological stability and personal identity (Sennett, 1998). For employers, the costs of labour turnover, the need for firm-specific skills and the need to gain workers' cooperation in production will continue to provide a basis for long-term employment, even in the face of weakened trade unions, changes in the labour market and the wider institutional environment. However, this does not mean that internalised employment systems have remained unchanged. As shown above, although they have not collapsed, they have been weakened and modified as a result of organisational restructuring and the search for labour flexibility.

■ Implications for HRM: strategic HRM and the new psychological contract

HRM has been distinguished from so-called 'traditional personnel management' on the grounds that:

- HRM fulfils a strategic business function, i.e. is integrated closely with broader business strategy, i.e. it is vertically integrated.
- HRM policies are designed to support each other to generate strategic HRM outcomes, i.e. employee commitment, high-quality performance and flexibility in the use of labour. In other words, it is horizontally integrated.

In the context of this chapter, strategic integration of HRM with broader business strategy means defining what an organisation's labour requirements are given its chosen competitive strategy, e.g. price or quality. The internal coherence or horizontal integration of HRM policies means operating an employment system that satisfies these requirements at least cost. In reality, as we have seen, things are not so simple. For one thing, employment systems are not the simple embodiment of employers' strategies for meeting their labour requirements. They are also the outcome of organisational constraints, pressure from workers and external influences from the labour market and wider institutions. The force of these constraints varies across space and time. In Britain and the USA since the 1980s, the decline of trade union influence and connected changes in government policy towards the labour market have provided employers with relative freedom to develop employment systems unimpeded by externally imposed restrictions. One probable effect of this has been to limit the take-up of HRM by organisations and to bias it in particular directions. Minimal legal regulation of the labour market and weak trade union organisation and influence mean that employers and managers are under little pressure to develop long-term employment relationships, embark on long-term processes of training to develop high-level skills, or involve workers in decision-making. This means that they are less likely to take a strategic, forward-looking approach to the management of labour.

A second and more fundamental factor that undermines the coherence of HRM as strategy is the fact that management's labour requirements are not straightforward but contradictory. Management requires disposability on the one hand, commitment and cooperation on the other. This means that HRM policies can never be entirely coherent, even in the relative absence of external constraints on managerial action. For example, as we have seen, commitment and flexibility are contradictory goals; policies that aim to achieve one threaten to undermine the other. Consequently HRM strategies can never be wholly successful. This is illustrated by the way strategies aimed at reducing labour costs by downsizing and delayering organisations and increasing labour flexibility have generated significant costs in terms of skill shortages, lower morale and declining organisational commitment which threaten organisational performance.

Within HRM one of the major themes in recent discussion has been how organisational restructuring has undermined employees' trust in the organisations that employ them and what can be done to build a new basis for employee commitment and cooperation with management. As shown in Chapter 13, discussion of this issue has revolved around the concept of a 'new psychological contract' between the organisation and the individual employee to replace the 'old' (Bendall *et al.*, 1998; Sparrow, 1998). Significantly, in most accounts, the 'new' psychological contract being 'offered' by organisations seeks to replace commitments to providing long-term employment security with commitments to providing workers with educational and training opportunities to enable them to acquire transferable skills to enhance their employability. This indicates that management is persuaded, for the time being at least, that commitment to long-term employment security and planned career progression within the firm are no longer practical propositions and is trying to get workers to accept this proposition also.

What are the prospects for negotiating a new basis for the employment relationship on these lines? How can employers expect to get high commitment and effort while offering less security and fewer prospects for career advancement? One possible answer is that workers who are still in jobs are too afraid to resist, since to do so would be to invite dismissal. Slower economic growth, the decline of manufacturing and, of course, organisational restructuring itself have led to widespread job losses, historically high levels of unemployment and a heightened sense of insecurity among workers. The extent to which employment has become less secure has been debated widely in Britain and the USA. There is no strong evidence for a major increase in employment insecurity in general but there is evidence that for certain groups such as younger men, the risk of job loss has increased and the probability of getting a long-term job declined (Gregg and Wadsworth, 1999; Heckscher, 2000). Such workers may well be willing to submit to management's demands in the hope of avoiding job loss or being taken on as a permanent employee. On this view the 'new psychological contract' is nothing more than an expression of the increased inequality of power between employer and employee. A more optimistic and sympathetic judgement would be that the success of the 'new psychological contract' depends on the ability of employers to provide workers with opportunities to develop their skills and experience in ways that enable them to improve their external job prospects. But how likely is it that employers will do this? It seems probable that those best able to take advantage of such opportunities will be the most able employees, yet these will be the ones that employers want to retain.

Conclusion

The simple economic model of the labour market and the employment relationship is that labour is a commodity like any other and its price is determined by competition in the labour market; between employers competing for the available supply of labour and between workers competing for job vacancies. The outcome is a uniform set of terms and conditions of employment across firms employing the same type of labour. The reality of labour markets is somewhat different. It is clear that firms adopt a variety of employment systems, i.e. open external labour markets, structured occupational labour markets or internal labour markets. These differ from each other in:

● the degree to which they rely on external or internal sources of labour to fill vacancies;
● the extent to which they operate within occupational boundaries;
● the extent to which terms and conditions are regulated by market competition or by formal rules administered through internal institutions.

The extent to which employment systems are externalised or internalised depends on the interaction of the following influences:

● employers' labour requirements;
● organisational constraints;
● the ability of workers to influence terms and conditions;
● the labour market environment;
● the wider institutional context.

Using this framework of analysis we can explain recent changes in employment patterns and policies in the UK and elsewhere.

Since the 1980s employers have responded to competitive pressures to reduce costs by restructuring organisations and their employment systems. Restructuring has involved downsizing, delayering, devolution of responsibilities, and the reorganisation of work. Work reorganisation has involved externalisation of non-core functions and greater use of part-time, temporary and fixed-contract workers. These efforts by employers have received growing support in government policies that are aimed at increasing labour market flexibility. These developments have challenged the internalised employment systems that became widespread in large organisations during the 1960s and 1970s. This has given rise to speculation that not only are internal labour markets in decline but the concept of long-term employment is no longer relevant. Some have argued the concept of employment itself will soon become obsolete as the employment relationship is replaced by commercial contracts between freelance workers and 'virtual' or 'network' organisations.

Empirical evidence shows that these speculations are exaggerated and that employment and indeed, long-term employment, continue to be valued by employers as well as workers. This is because long-term employment and internalised employment systems frequently provide employers with efficient ways of developing and retaining skilled labour and motivating workers to exercise responsible autonomy in their jobs. Such systems do, however, carry costs. Commitments to employment security make it difficult for employers to vary headcount at short notice. Clearly defined job demarcations get in the way of functional flexibility. Formal pay structures that link pay to jobs prevent employers from rewarding individual performance. These so-called 'rigidities' have come to be seen as increasingly unacceptable as managers have looked for ways to reduce labour costs. Therefore, while long-term employment is far from dead, internalised employment systems have been reformed and in many cases weakened and eroded.

Attempts by managers to curtail internalised employment systems and move towards greater externalisation have, however, created problems in the form of skill shortages and declining morale and commitment. These problems stem from the contradictions between a search for flexibility and cost reduction on the one hand and commitment and cooperation on the other. In recent years managers have increasingly demanded more of both from their workforces. This has heightened the contradiction in the employment relationship and influenced the way mainstream HRM thinking has developed. There has been a retreat from the idea that employment security is an essential condition for employee commitment. This has been replaced with the following argument. The need for greater numerical flexibility of labour makes it impossible for employers to commit themselves to providing long-term employment security. At the same time, organisational performance depends on the committed efforts of workers. HRM has so far offered two ways of squaring this particular circle. The first is to develop internally differentiated employment systems, i.e. internalised systems for employees who are highly valued and externalised systems for the rest. There is evidence that while some organisations may operate in this way, it is often problematic, particularly where organisations have devolved responsibilities to more junior employees after downsizing and delayering. The second route to regaining commitment is the new psychological contract. The problem here is that it is doubtful whether employers will be willing to set up opportunities for workers to improve their employability if it increases the risk that they will lose their best employees.

Summary

- There are different types of labour market – open external, structured occupational and internal labour markets. They are the basis for different organisational employment systems.

- Labour market types can be differentiated from each other in terms of how close they are to the basic competitive model of the labour market. This in turn can be examined in terms of where they lie along three axes: *external–internal; unstructured–structured: competitively–institutionally regulated.*

● Open external labour markets are closest to the competitive model of the labour market; internal labour markets are least like the basic competitive model.

● Organisations' employment systems may range from externalised systems that draw on open external labour markets to highly internalised systems based on salaried internal labour markets.

● The extent of externalisation/internalisation is influenced by a variety of factors. These include employers' labour requirements, organisational constraints, workers' pressure and influence, the labour market environment, and the wider institutional environment.

● These factors interact in complex ways, sometimes reinforcing, sometimes counter-acting each other in the way they shape an organisation's employment system.

● There was a tendency to internalise employment systems during the 1960s and 1970s. This reflected the need to retain scarce skills at a time of full employment, increased reliance on firm-specific skills, increase in the size of organisations, rising trade union power and influence, government employment and industrial relations policies and the spread of social democracy in Europe.

● Internalised employment systems have been weakened during the past 20 years by organisational restructuring and government policies aimed at increasing labour market flexibility.

● Organisational restructuring has aimed at increasing flexibility in the use of labour – functional, numerical and financial flexibility.

● The flexible firm is a model for achieving a strategic combination of these different types of flexibility but there is little evidence that it has been adopted in practice. The emphasis of most organisations, especially in the UK and the USA, is on increasing numerical flexibility.

● The weakening of internalised employment systems has heightened the contradiction between the commodity status of labour (labour flexibility) and management's need for workers' commitment and cooperation. This has limited the extent to which many organisations have felt able to externalise employment. Even so, the decline of employee commitment is seen as a major issue for organisations.

● The concept of the new psychological contract has been offered as a way of rebuild-ing commitment in the absence of employment security but the practicability of such a contract is questionable.

ACTIVITY Discuss critically the following quote from the management 'guru' Charles Handy:

> Frankly I now believe that life-time employment is bad economics and bad morals. It is bad economics because it puts the organisation into a straitjacket and limits its flexibility. It is bad morals because it promises, or appears to promise, what it cannot deliver to more than a few...
>
> It would, I think, be more honest and more sensible to think in terms of specific jobs with fixed-term contracts of varying lengths, of money purchase pension schemes for all instead of retirement pensions, of 'opportunities' rather than 'planned careers', with people bidding for jobs but sometimes in competition with outsiders. It would be more sensible for individu-als to think of 'moving on' rather than always 'moving up', as professionals move from one partnership to another to gain experience or look for richer pickings. Tenure, after all, is something that the good don't need and the bad don't deserve. (Handy, 1995a: 89–90)

Questions

1 What are the advantages to employers and employees of structured occupational labour markets? In what circumstances would employers prefer them to open external labour markets?

2 What are the possible reasons why internal labour markets are more highly developed for technical and administrative workers than for manual production workers?

3 What factors might be encouraging the re-emergence of open external labour markets in some areas of employment?

4 How do firms' labour requirements influence the nature of their employment systems?

5 Identify the forces that encouraged the internalisation of employment systems during the 1960s and 1970s.

6 Explain why internal labour market-based employment systems have been weakened since the early 1980s.

7 How concerned should we be about any tendency to restrict or dismantle employment systems based on internal labour markets?

Case study

'Fears for the thread of industry'

Stephen Houghton

North Staffordshire's manufacturing base could lose hard-earned skills forever amid fears of a further slowdown in the sector. That was the view today of Allan Bourne, joint managing director of Trentham-based Biltmore Garments, after he closed the factory last week due to increased red tape and foreign competition.

The move, which claimed the jobs of 125 people, came as warnings grew of a fresh crisis in the manufacturing sector.

Mr Bourne, aged 66, explained many people no longer valued manufacturing as a credible or worthwhile career.

He said: 'For the last few years we haven't been able to attract young people into the industry. For some reason they don't want to come into manufacturing.

'They are quietly told that if they don't get on with their studies, this is where they will end up.

'Everybody has this attitude now. When I was taught at school, I was taught the country had to be self-reliant in manufacturing.

'We had girls at the factory with 20 or 30 years' experience, who were always retraining because of changing styles.

'That is now lost. They will never come back, and will be too old to train others in a few years.' Mr Bourne added it was 'sad' that North Staffordshire and the rest of the country appeared to be depending on the service sector for wealth.

His own company at Newstead Industrial Estate, which mainly supplied the retail chain Next, had suffered from price competition from overseas.

North Staffordshire's economy is predicted to lose a quarter of its 68,000-strong industrial workforce in the decade to 2010, partly due to cheap labour in the Far East and Eastern Europe.

These would be on top of thousands of jobs already lost from coal mining, steel-making, textiles, ceramics and engineering.

The Confederation of British Industry (CBI) is this week set to add to the gloom surrounding the sector by revealing more firms than expected will cut jobs in the first half of the year as foreign competitors make further in-roads into the British market.

Its quarterly regional health check of UK manufacturing, due to be published tomorrow, will point to a sharp downturn in confidence and orders.

Case study continued

CBI West Midlands assistant regional director Gil Murray told Sentinel Sunday that the situation was caused by 'underlying factors' rather than the Iraq war.

Mr Murray pointed to poor trading conditions, as well as a lack of labour market 'flexibility' caused by legislation from the European Union.

He said: 'We have not detected any of the optimism that the Chancellor has been talking about recently.'

Source: *The Sentinel* (Stoke) 5 May 2003.

Questions

1 What type of labour market/employment system do you think used to be dominant in the North Staffordshire region?

2 The CBI regional director claims that European legislation is causing a lack of labour flexibility.

Discuss what kind of flexibility he has in mind and how far it would help Biltmore Garments.

3 Debate whether it would be possible for firms such as Biltmore Garments to adopt a 'high road' approach to competing in world markets.

References and further reading

Those texts marked with an asterisk are particularly recommended for further reading.

Adnett, N. (1989) *Labour Market Policy*. London: Longman.

Atkinson, J. (1984) 'Manpower strategies for flexible organisations', *Personnel Management*, August, pp. 28–31.

Atkinson, J. (1985) *Flexibility, Uncertainty and Manpower Management*. Brighton: Institute of Manpower Studies.

Baines, S. (1999) 'Servicing the media: freelancing, teleworking and "enterprising" careers', *New Technology, Work and Employment*, Vol. 14, No. 1, pp. 18–31.

Bayliss, V. (1998) *Redefining Work: An RSA Initiative*. London: Royal Society for the Encouragement of Arts, Manufactures and Commerce.

Bendall, S.E., Bottomley, C.R. and Cleverly, P.M. (1998) 'Building a new proposition for staff at NatWest UK', in Sparrow, P. and Marchington, M. (eds) *Human Resource Management: The New Agenda*. London: Financial Times-Pitman, pp. 90–105.

Bernhardt, A. and Marcotte, D.E. (2000) 'Is "standard employment" still what it used to be?', in Carre, F., Ferber, M.A., Golden, L. and Herzenberg, S. (eds) *Nonstandard Work: The Nature and Challenges of Changing Employment Arrangements*. Urbana-Champaign, Ill.: Industrial Relations Research Association, pp. 21–40.

*Beynon, H., Grimshaw, D., Rubery, J. and Ward, K. (2003) *Managing Employment Change: The New Realities of Work*. Oxford: Oxford University Press.

*Boxall, P. and Purcell, J. (2003) *Strategy and Human Resource Management*. Basingstoke: Palgrave Macmillan.

Bridges, M. (1995) *Job Shift: How to Prosper in a Workplace Without Jobs*. London: Nicolas Brealey.

*Cappelli, P., Bassi, L., Katz, H., Knoke, D., Osterman, P. and Useem, M. (1997) *Change at Work*. New York: Oxford University Press.

Creedy, J. and Whitfield, K. (1986) 'Earnings and job mobility. Professional chemists in Britain', *Journal of Economic Studies*, Vol. 13, pp. 23–37.

Cully, M., Woodland, S., O'Reilly, A. and Dix, G. (1999) *Britain at Work. As Depicted by the 1998 Workplace Industrial Relations Survey*. London: Routledge.

Dex, S. and McCulloch, A. (1997) *Flexible Employment: The Future of Britain's Jobs*. Basingstoke: Macmillan.

Doeringer, P.B. and Piore, M.J. (1971) *Internal Labor Markets and Manpower Analysis*. Lexington, Mass.: Heath.

European Commission (1996) *Employment in Europe 1996*. Luxembourg: Office for Official Publications of the European Communities.

European Commission (1999) *Employment in Europe 1999*. Luxembourg: Office for Official Publications of the European Communities.

European Commission (2002) *Employment in Europe 2002*. Luxembourg: Office for Official Publications of the European Communities.

Friedman, A. (1977) *Industry and Labour*. London: Macmillan.

Gallie, D., White, M., Chang, Y. and Tomlinson, M. (1998) *Restructuring the Employment Relationship*. Oxford: Oxford University Press.

Geary, J.F. (1992) 'Employment flexibility and human resource management: the case of three American electronics plants', *Work, Employment and Society*, Vol. 6, pp. 251–270.

George, K. and Shorey, J. (1985) 'Manual workers, good jobs and structured internal labour markets', *British Journal of Industrial Relations*, Vol. 23, No. 4, pp. 424–447.

Gill, C., Gold, M. and Cressey, P. (1999) 'Social Europe: national initiatives and responses', *Industrial Relations Journal*, Vol. 30, No. 4, pp. 313–329.

Goetschy, J. and Rozenblatt, P. (1992) 'France: the industrial relations system at a turning point?', in Ferner, A. and Hyman, R. (eds.) *Industrial Relations in the New Europe*. Oxford: Blackwell, pp. 404–444.

Gordon, D.M., Edwards, R. and Reich, M. (1982) *Segmented Work, Divided Workers: The Historical Transformation of Labor in the United States*. Cambridge: Cambridge University Press.

Gregg, P. and Wadsworth, J. (1999) 'Job tenure, 1975–98', in Gregg, P. and Wadsworth, J. (eds) *The State of Working Britain*. Manchester: Manchester University Press, pp. 109–126.

*Grimshaw, D., Ward, K.G., Rubery, J. and Beynon, H. (2001) 'Organisations and the transformation of the internal labour market', *Work, Employment and Society*, Vol. 15, No. 1, pp. 25–54.

Guest, D.E. and Hoque, K. (1994) 'The good, the bad and the ugly: employment relations in new non-union work-places', *Human Resource Management Journal*, Vol. 5, No. 1, pp. 1–14.

Handy, C. (1995) *The Empty Raincoat: Making Sense of the Future*. London: Arrow.

Handy, C. (1995a) *Beyond Certainty: The Changing Worlds of Organisations*. London: Hutchinson.

Heckscher, C. (2000) 'HR strategy and nonstandard work: dualism versus true mobility', in Carre, F., Ferber, M.A., Golden, L. and Herzenberg, S. (eds) *Nonstandard Work: The Nature and Challenges of Changing Employment Arrangements*. Urbana-Champaign, Ill.: Industrial Relations Research Association, pp. 267–290.

Heery, E. and Salmon, J. (2000) 'The insecurity thesis', in Heery, E. and Salmon, J. (eds) *The Insecure Workforce*. London: Routledge, pp. 1–24.

*Hendry, C. (1995) *Human Resource Management: A Strategic Approach to Employment*. Oxford: Butterworth-Heinemann.

Hudson, M. (2002) 'Disappearing pathways and the struggle for a fair day's pay', in Burchell, B., Day, D., Hudson, M., Ladipo, D., Mankelow, R., Nolan, J., Reed, H., Wichert, I. and Wilkinson, F. *Job Insecurity and Work Intensification: Flexibility and the Changing Boundaries of Work*. York: Joseph Rowntree Foundation, pp. 77–93.

Hunter, L.C. and MacInnes, J. (1992) 'Employers and labour flexibility: the evidence from case studies', *Labour Gazette*, June, pp. 307–315.

Jacobi, O., Keller, B. and Muller-Jentsch, W. (1998) 'Germany: facing new challenges', in Ferner, A. and Hyman, R. (eds) *Changing Industrial Relations in Europe*. Oxford: Blackwell, pp. 190–238.

Joll, C., McKenna, C., McNab, R. and Shorey, J. (1983) *Developments in Labour Market Analysis*. London: George Allen & Unwin.

Katz, H.C. and Darbishire, O. (2000) *Converging Divergences: Worldwide Changes in Employment Systems*. Ithaca, NY: ILR Press.

Kerr, C. (1954) 'The balkanisation of labor markets', in Bakke, F.W. (ed.) *Labor Mobility and Economic Opportunity*. Cambridge, Mass.: MIT Press, pp. 92–110.

King, J.E. (1990) *Labour Economics*, 2nd edn. London: Macmillan.

Kochan, T.A., Katz, H.C. and McKersie, R.B. (1986) *The Transformation of American Industrial Relations*. New York: Basic Books.

Leadbeater, C. (2000) *Living on Thin Air: The New Economy*. London: Viking.

Mace, J. (1979) 'Internal labour markets for engineers in British industry', *British Journal of Industrial Relations*, Vol. 17, pp. 50–63.

Marsden, D. (1986) *The End of Economic Man?* Brighton: Wheatsheaf.

Marsden, D. (1999) *A Theory of Employment Systems: Micro Foundations of Societal Diversity*. Oxford: Oxford University Press.

Millward, N., Bryson, A. and Forth, J. (2000) *All Change at Work? British Employment Relations as Portrayed by the Workplace Industrial Relations Survey Series*. London: Routledge.

*Moss, P., Salzman, H. and Tilly, C. (2000) 'Limits to market-mediated employment: from deconstruction to reconstruction of internal labour markets', in Carre, F., Ferber, M.A., Golden, L. and Herzenberg, S. (eds) *Nonstandard Work: The Nature and Challenges of Changing Employment Arrangements*. Urbana-Champaign, Ill.: Industrial Relations Research Association, pp. 95–122.

Nolan, P. (1989) 'Walking on water? Performance and industrial relations under Thatcher', *Industrial Relations Journal*, Vol. 20, No. 1, pp. 81–92.

Nolan, P. and Brown, W. (1983) 'Competition and workplace wage determination', *Oxford Bulletin of Economics and Statistics*, Vol. 45, pp. 269–287.

Nolan, P. and Slater, G. (2003) 'The labour market: history, structure and prospects', in Edwards, P. (ed.) *Industrial Relations: Theory and Practice*, 2nd edn. Oxford: Blackwell, pp. 58–80.

Osterman, P. (1984) 'The nature and importance of internal labor markets', in Osterman, P. (ed.) *Internal Labor Markets*. Cambridge, Mass.: MIT Press, pp. 1–22.

Osterman, P. (1987) 'Choice of employment systems in internal labour markets', *Industrial Relations*, Vol. 26, No. 1, pp. 46–67.

Osterman, P. (1988) *Employment Futures: Reorganisation, Dislocation, and Public Policy*. New York: Oxford University Press.

Polivka, A.E., Cohany, S.R. and Hipple, S. (2000) 'Definition, composition, and economic consequences of the nonstandard workforce', in Carre, F., Ferber, M.A., Golden, L. and Herzenberg, S. (eds) *Nonstandard Work: The Nature and Challenges of Changing Employment Arrangements*. Urbana-Champaign, Ill.: Industrial Relations Research Association, pp. 41–94.

Rosenberg, S. and Lapidus, J. (1999) 'Contingent and non-standard work in the United States: towards a more poorly compensated, insecure workforce', in Felstead, A. (ed.) *Global Trends in Flexible Labour*. Basingstoke, Macmillan, pp. 62–79.

Rubery, J. (1994) 'Internal and external labour markets: towards an integrated analysis', in Rubery, J. and Wilkinson, F. (eds) *Employer Strategy and the Labour Market*. Oxford: Oxford University Press, pp. 37–68.

Rubery, J. and Edwards, P. (2003) 'Low pay and the minimum wage', in Edwards, P. (ed) *Industrial Relations: Theory and Practice*, 2nd edn. Oxford: Blackwell, pp. 447–469.

Saundry, R. and Nolan, P. (1998) 'Regulatory change and performance in TV production', *Media, Culture and Society*, Vol. 20, No. 3, pp. 409–426.

Sennett, R. (1998) *The Corrosion of Character: The Personal Consequences of Work in the New Capitalism.* London: Norton.

Sisson, K. and Marginson, P. (1995) 'Management: systems, structures and strategy', in Edwards, P. (ed.) *Industrial Relations: Theory and Practice in Britain.* Oxford: Blackwell, pp. 89–122.

Sparrow, P. (1998) 'New organisational forms, processes, jobs and psychological contracts: resolving the HRM issues', in Sparrow, P. and Marchington, M. (eds) *Human Resource Management: The New Agenda.* London: Financial Times-Pitman, pp. 117–141.

Whittall, M. (2001) '*Modell Deutschland*: regulating the future?', in Jefferys, S., Beyer, F.M. and Thornqvist, C. (eds) *European Working Lives: Continuities and Change in Management and Industrial Relations in France, Scandinavia and the UK.* Cheltenham: Edward Elgar, pp. 115–129.

For multiple choice questions, exercises and annotated weblinks specific to this chapter visit this book's website at www.booksites.net/beardwell

CHAPTER 5

Human resource planning

Julie Beardwell

OBJECTIVES

▶ To identify multiple interpretations of human resource planning and define the concept.

▶ To discuss key stages in the traditional human resource planning process.

▶ To analyse and evaluate quantitative and qualitative methods of demand and supply forecasting.

▶ To identify and discuss contemporary approaches to human resource planning.

▶ To discuss the advantages and disadvantages of human resource planning.

▶ To investigate the application of human resource planning in practice.

▶ To explore the link between human resource planning and strategic HRM.

Introduction

Planning for human resources has had a fairly chequered history (Torrington *et al.*, 2002). The subject, initially termed 'manpower planning', first rose to prominence in the 1960s when the emphasis was on the means of achieving growth in production against a backdrop of skills shortages and relatively stable, predictable world markets. At this time, much of the emphasis was on the application of statistical and mathematical techniques (see, for example, Bartholemew, 1976). However, by the early 1980s manpower planning was seen by many as largely irrelevant as it had become associated with growth, five-year plans and bureaucracy at a time when many organisations were preoccupied with having to contract and become more flexible (Cowling and Walters, 1990: 3). Since then, human resource planning has often been denigrated, with the result that it has received relatively little attention in the literature and has become less widely used in organisations (Taylor, 2002). The demise of HRP can seem rather ironic as it appears to have occurred at the same time as there have been increasing calls for people management to become a more strategic activity. After defining the terminology, the chapter outlines the traditional approach to HRP; it then considers more contemporary variants; explores the application of HRP in practice; and finally explores the link between HRP and strategic HRM.

Defining human resource planning

In *Through the Looking Glass* Humpty Dumpty tells Alice, 'When I use a word it means exactly what I choose it to mean, neither more nor less.' The same might be said of 'human resource planning' (HRP) as the phrase can be used in a number of different ways. The main distinction is between those who view the term as synonymous with 'manpower planning' and those who believe that 'human resource planning' represents something rather different (Taylor, 2002).

Manpower planning has been defined as 'a strategy for the acquisition, utilisation, improvement and retention of an enterprise's human resources' (Department of Employment, 1974). The prime concern is generally with enabling organisations to maintain the status quo; 'the purpose of manpower planning is to provide continuity of efficient manning for the total business and optimum use of manpower resources' (McBeath, 1992: 26), usually via the application of statistical techniques. The term 'human resource planning' emerged at about the same time as 'human resource management' started to replace 'personnel management', and for some (e.g. McBeath, 1992; Thomason, 1988) the terminology is just a more up-to-date, gender-neutral way of describing the techniques associated with manpower planning.

For others, human resource planning represents something different but the extent of this difference can vary. In some instances, human resource planning is seen as a variant of manpower planning more concerned with qualitative issues and cultural change, than with hierarchical structures, succession plans and mathematical modelling (e.g. Cowling and Walters, 1990). In other instances, the term can be used to signal a significant difference in both thinking and practice (Liff, 2000). For example, Bramham (1989) argues that there are fundamental differences between the two approaches:

> There are particularly important differences in terms of process and purpose. In human resource planning the manager is concerned with motivating people – a process in which costs, numbers, control and systems interact to play a part. In manpower planning the manager is concerned with the numerical elements of forecasting, supply-demand matching and control, in which people are a part. There are therefore important areas of overlap and interconnection but there is a fundamental difference in underlying approach.
>
> (Bramham, 1989: 147)

This broad interpretation of HRP can be seen as rather vague and lacking explicit practical application or specification. For example, Marchington and Wilkinson (1996) argue that Bramham's conception of HRP is synonymous with HRM in its entirety and, as such, loses any distinctive sense. Indeed, in his book *Human Resource Planning*, Bramham (1989) discusses a very wide range of people management issues, including employee development, reward management and employee relations, and only focuses on specific planning issues in one chapter.

A third approach is to define HRP as a distinct process aimed at predicting an organisation's future requirements for human resources that incorporates both the qualitative elements of human resource planning and the quantitative elements of manpower planning. These two elements are often labelled as 'soft' and 'hard' human resource planning respectively. Tansley (1999: 41) summarises the general conceptions of **'hard' HRP** in the literature as follows:

● emphasis on 'direct' control of employees – employees are viewed like any other resource with the need for efficient and tight management;

● akin to the notion of manpower planning – with emphasis on demand–supply matching;

- undertaken by HR specialists;
- related HR strategies are concerned with improving the utilisation of human resources.

In contrast, she summarises the general characteristics of **'soft' HRP** as:

- emphasis on 'indirect control of employees – with increasing emphasis on employee involvement and teamwork;
- a wider focus to include an emphasis on organisational culture and the clearer integration between corporate goals and employee values and behaviour;
- involves HR specialists, line managers and possibly other employees;
- greater emphasis on strategies and plans for gaining employee commitment.

Like the broader interpretations of HRP, definitions of 'soft' HRP tend to assume a 'best practice', high-commitment approach to people management. Although there is emphasis on the need to integrate human resource planning activity with corporate goals, the implicit assumption is that this will be achieved via the design and application of plans aimed at developing employee skills and securing their commitment to organisational goals. However, as we shall discuss later in the chapter, there may be some business strategies, e.g. cost minimisation, that require different approaches to people management.

Stop and think	Which definition of human resource planning do you prefer and why?

In order to convey the meaning of HRP as a set of activities that represent a key element of HRM but are distinct from it, and to include both the soft and hard aspects of the planning process, the definition used in this chapter is as follows:

> *HRP is the process for identifying an organisation's current and future human resource requirements, developing and implementing plans to meet these requirements and monitoring their overall effectiveness.*

There are a number of ways in which this process can be undertaken. The chapter begins with an exploration of the key stages in the traditional approach to HRP (incorporating many of the 'hard' elements) and then considers more contemporary variants.

The traditional approach to HRP

The prime concern within traditional or 'hard' HRP relates to balancing the demand for and the supply of human resources. **Demand** reflects an organisation's requirements for human resources while **supply** refers to the availability of these resources, both within the organisation and externally. Key stages within the traditional HRP process are largely derived from the techniques associated with manpower planning. The approach can be depicted in a number of different ways (see, for example, Armstrong, 2001; Bramham, 1988; Torrington *et al.*, 2002) but the models have a number of key features in common. All are essentially concerned with forecasting demand and supply and developing plans to meet any identified imbalance resulting from the forecasts.

The Bramham model has proved to be one of the most influential. It was initially devised in 1975 and the basic structure is still relevant, albeit with minor modifications, for example by Pilbeam and Corbridge (2002). This is the model used in this chapter as a framework for the key stages of traditional HRP; see Figure 5.1.

Figure 5.1   The process of human resource planning

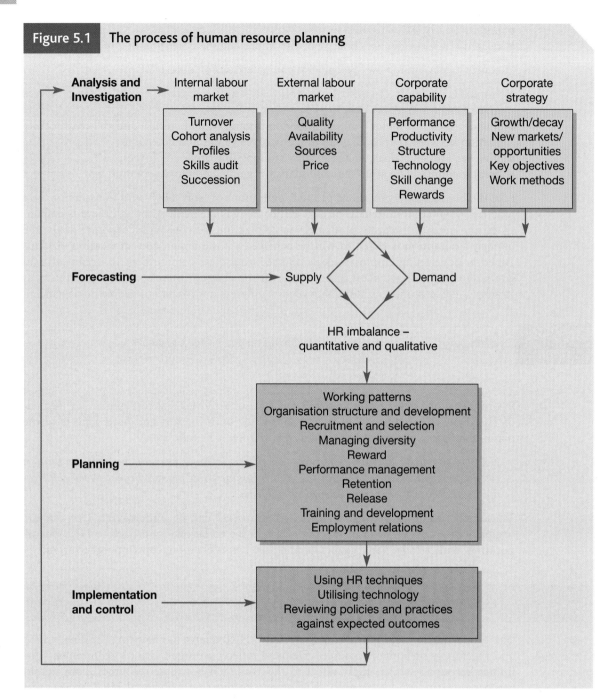

Source: Adapted from Pilbeam & Corbridge (2002), adapted from Bramham (1994)

■ Investigation and analysis

This stage is not explicit in all models but, arguably, those responsible for human resource planning need to know something about the current situation in order to assess the extent to which it is likely to alter or be affected by future developments.

● Internal labour market

A combination of quantitative and qualitative data can provide a 'snapshot' of the existing workforce. This can include analysis of the workforce on a variety of levels such as skills, qualifications, length of experience and job type as well as on factors relating to equal opportunities, i.e. gender, ethnic origin, disability and age. This can help to ensure that the organisation is making most effective use of existing resources and can identify any potential problem areas; for example, if the composition of the workforce does not reflect the local community or if the organisation is not fully utilising the skills it has available. Movement through the organisation can also be investigated by tracking promotions, transfers and the paths of those in more senior positions.

● External labour market

Investigation and analysis are primarily concerned with the availability of the type of labour the organisation requires at the price it can afford. It is likely that those responsible for human resource planning will need to collect data from local, national and international labour markets depending on the nature of jobs and the skills required. Data can be collected by formal and informal means, including local and national surveys, benchmarking and information provided by applicants on application forms and CVs. Analysis and investigation can potentially cover a broad range of issues as the external supply of labour can be affected by a number of factors.

Stop and think	What factors are likely to affect the external supply of human resources?

A number of factors can influence the availability of people and skills at both local and national level, for example:

- *competitor behaviour* – the activity of other firms operating in the same labour markets, i.e. expansion or contraction; whether organisations secure the necessary skills through training or poaching from other firms; comparative pay and conditions;
- *location* – whether or not the organisation is based in a location that is attractive and affordable for potential recruits; factors to be considered here might include the availability and cost of housing and the reputation of local schools;
- *transport links* – the availability and cost of public transport and accessibility of the organisation;
- *economic cycle* – can affect people's willingness to move jobs, e.g. people may be more concerned with job security in times of high unemployment;
- *unemployment levels* – nationally and regionally;
- *education output* – numbers and qualifications of school and college leavers, numbers going on to higher education;
- *legislation* – e.g. working hours, minimum wage, employment protection, flexible working.

● Corporate capability

Data can be gathered to provide a snapshot of the current situation within the organisation in order to identify current strengths and weaknesses. Information on organisational performance can include productivity and service levels, turnover and profitability and these may be measured at organisational, unit or department level. Analysis may also relate to ways in which human resources are currently managed, e.g. the extent to which the current workforce structure, job design and reward systems enhance or restrict productivity and performance levels.

● Corporate strategy

Whereas corporate capability is primarily concerned with the current situation in the organisation, corporate strategy focuses on future direction. Factors to be considered here might include the organisation's stage in its life cycle (see, for example, Kochan and Barocci, 1985); plans for consolidation or diversification; mergers, acquisitions and key organisational objectives. Each of these factors is likely to have some impact on the numbers and types of human resources required in the future. For example, a common consequence of mergers is for the rationalisation of merged activities to lead to a significant number of redundancies (CIPD, 2000).

■ Forecasting

The next stage in the process involves predicting how the need for and availability of human resources is likely to change in the future. Demand and supply forecasting can involve quantitative and qualitative techniques and the most popular approaches are outlined below.

ACTIVITY

This is an example of demand forecasting in a tyre and exhaust centre using the work study method. The main tasks have been classified as follows:

Key tasks	Hours per task
Exhausts	0.6
Tyres	0.3
Brakes	1.1

Forecasts jobs in 000s

	Year 1	Year 2	Year 3
Exhausts	30	31	32
Tyres	100	115	130
Brakes	25	29	34

Convert into total work hours

	Year 1	Year 2	Year 3
Exhausts	18	18.6	19.2
Tyres	30	34.5	39
Brakes	27.5	31.9	37.4
TOTAL	75.5	85	95.6

Convert into employees required (assuming 1800 hours/employee)

	Year 1	Year 2	Year 3
Employees (full-time equivalents)	41.9	47.2	53.1

What key external and internal factors are likely to affect the accuracy of these forecasts?

● Forecasting the demand for human resources

Demand forecasting is concerned with estimating the numbers of people and the types of skills the organisation will need in the future. There are three main approaches to demand forecasting: objective methods, subjective methods and budgets.

Objective methods

Objective methods identify past trends, using statistical and mathematical techniques, and project these into the future to determine requirements. Three methods frequently referred to in the literature are time trends, ratio analysis and work study. **Time trends** consider patterns of employment levels over the past few years in order to predict the numbers required in the future. This can be undertaken either for the organisation as a whole or for sub-groups of employees. It can also be used to identify cyclical or seasonal variations in staffing levels. **Ratio analysis** bases forecasts on the ratio between some causal factor, e.g. sales volume, and the number of employees required, e.g. sales people (Dessler, 2003). **Work study** methods break jobs down into discrete tasks, measure the time taken to complete each component and then calculate the number of people-hours required. The effectiveness of this approach is largely determined by the ease with which the individual components of jobs can be measured. For many jobs, e.g. knowledge workers, this is extremely difficult and therefore work study will only be appropriate in certain circumstances. Even when it is appropriate, care has to be taken to avoid manipulation of timings by either employee or employer.

One of the major criticisms levelled at objective methods is that they are based on assumptions of continuity between past, present and future and are therefore only appropriate if the environment is relatively stable and productivity remains the same. In less stable environments, supplementary data on the causes of particular trends are necessary to distinguish between changes that are likely to recur and those that are not. Alternatively, past data can be used as a starting point and then amended to reflect potential or real productivity improvements.

ACTIVITY   Return to the forecasting exercise in the tyre and exhaust centre. This time management estimate that productivity improvements can be made each year as follows:

	Time per job:		
	Year 1	**Year 2**	**Year 3**
Exhausts	0.6	0.55	0.5
Tyres	0.3	0.25	0.2
Brakes	1.2	1.1	1.0

Calculate the full-time equivalent employees required for each year, incorporating these improvements.

How does this affect employee demand?

Subjective methods

The most common approach used in demand forecasting is **managerial judgement**, i.e. managers estimate the human resources necessary for the achievement of corporate goals. Estimates are likely to be based on a combination of past experience, knowledge of changing circumstances and gut instinct. The approach is more flexible and adaptable than objective methods but is inevitably less precise. There is also a danger that forecasts will be manipulated due to organisational politics and 'empire building'. For example, managers may inflate estimates of future requirements because they want to increase the size of their department (and thus possibly protect or improve their own position) or because they expect that estimates will be cut and want to secure at least some improvements in staffing levels.

A more systematic use of the subjective approach is via the **Delphi technique**. A group of managers make independent forecasts of future requirements. The forecasts are then amalgamated, recirculated and managers then modify their estimates until some sort of consensus is reached. The process can help to minimise problems of manipulation in forecasts produced on an individual basis but, although the literature frequently refers to the technique as a common approach, empirical data suggest that it is rarely used in practice (Torrington *et al.*, 2002).

Budgets

In this method the starting point is not past data but future budgets, i.e. what the organisation can spend if profit and market targets are met. According to Bramham (1988: 59), this is an extremely attractive approach: 'it has the supreme advantage that, in working from the future to the present, the manager is not necessarily constrained by past practices'. However, future budgets are likely to be determined, at least in part, by assumptions about changes to past and current performance and are still reliant on the accuracy of predictions.

These different approaches to demand forecasting can be combined to provide more comprehensive forecasts. So, for example, objective methods may be used to give an indication of future requirements but projections can then be modified by managerial judgement or to take account of budgetary constraints. Similarly, estimates based on ratio data may be adjusted to take account of productivity improvements resulting from new working methods or the introduction of new technology.

● Forecasting the supply of human resources

Forecasts of internal supply are based primarily on labour turnover and the movement of people within the organisation. As with demand, the process for forecasting supply uses a combination of quantitative and qualitative techniques.

Measuring labour turnover – quantitative methods

The most common method of measuring labour turnover is to express leavers as a percentage of the average number of employees. The **labour turnover index** is usually calculated using the following formula:

$$\frac{\text{Number of leavers in a specified period}}{\text{Average number employed in the same period}} \times 100\%$$

This measure is used most effectively on a comparative basis and frequently provides the basis for external and internal benchmarking. Labour turnover can vary significantly between different sectors and industries; for example, a recent survey into labour turnover (CIPD, 2002a) reports that the average turnover rate in the UK is 26.6 per cent but this varies from 56 per cent in wholesale and retail to 11 per cent in transport and storage. There is no single best level of labour turnover so external comparisons are essential to gauge whether rates in an organisation are out of line with others in the same industry or sector (IRS, 2001a). However, even organisations with lower than average turnover rates can experience problems if people have left from critical jobs or from posts that are difficult to fill. Conversely, high turnover is not necessarily problematic. In circumstances where an organisation is seeking to reduce costs or reduce the numbers employed a high turnover rate might prove very useful (Sadhev *et al.*, 1999). The main limitation of the labour turnover index is that it is a relatively crude measure that provides no data on the characteristics of leavers, their reasons for leaving, their length of service or the jobs they have left from. So, while it may indicate that an organisation has a problem, it gives no indication about what might be done to address it.

> *Example*:
>
> Company A has 200 employees. During the year 40 employees have left from different jobs and been replaced. The turnover rate is 20%.
>
> Company B also has an average of 200 employees. Over the year 40 people have left the same 20 jobs (i.e. each has been replaced twice). The turnover rate is also 20%.

Limitations about the location of leavers within an organisation can be addressed to some extent by analysing labour turnover at department or business unit level or by job category. For example, managers generally have lower levels of resignation than other groups of employees (IRS, 2001a). Any areas with turnover levels significantly above or below organisational or job category averages can then be subject to further investigation. Most attention is levelled at the cost and potential disruption associated with high labour turnover. CIPD survey data (2002a) estimates the average cost per leaver to be £3933 a year, increasing to £6086 for managers. However, low levels of labour turnover should not be ignored as they may be equally problematic.

Stop and think   What are the key problems associated with low labour turnover?

Low labour turnover can cause difficulties as a lack of people with new ideas, fresh ways of looking at things and different skills and experiences can cause organisations to become stale and rather complacent. It can also be difficult to create promotion and development opportunities for existing employees.

Nevertheless, many organisations are keen for some levels of stability. While the labour turnover index focuses on leavers, the **stability index** focuses on the percentage of employees who have stayed throughout a particular period, often one year. This therefore allows organisations to assess the extent to which labour turnover permeates the workforce. The formula used to calculate stability is:

$$\frac{\text{Number of employees with 1 year's service at a given date}}{\text{Number employed 1 year ago}} \times 100\%$$

This can be a useful indicator of organisational stability but does require a pre-set decision about a relevant period for which it is important to retain staff. To return to our earlier example:

> Company A has 160 employees with more than one year's service and has a stability rate of 80%.
>
> Company B has 180 employees with more than one year's service and has a stability rate of 90%.

As with demand forecasting, labour turnover and stability indices are frequently used to project historical data into the future. So, for example, if an organisation identifies an annual turnover rate of 8 per cent it may build this into future projections of available supply. Alternatively, managerial judgement may predict a reduction or an increase in turnover rates in the light of current circumstances and forecasts can be adjusted accordingly.

More data on the length of service of leavers can be provided through the **census** method. This is essentially a 'snapshot' of leavers by length of service over a set period, often one year. Length of service has long been recognised as an influential factor in labour turnover. Hill and Trist (1955) identified three phases in labour turnover, the 'induction crisis', 'differential transit' and 'settled connection'. People are more likely to leave during the first few months, as the relationship between the individual and the organisation is unsettled and insecure, and less likely to leave the longer they are in the organisation. The census method can help to identify patterns of leavers and any key risk periods.

Another way of investigating the relationship between labour turnover and length of service is to consider the **survival rate**, i.e. the proportion of employees recruited in a specific year who are still with the organisation at a certain later date. So, for example, plotting the survival rate of a cohort of 30 graduate trainees might show that 12 remain with the organisation after five years, giving a survival rate of 40 per cent. It is also common to measure the half-life of a cohort, i.e. the time taken for the cohort to reduce to half its original size. Both survival rates and half-life measures can be useful for identifying problem periods and for succession planning purposes.

The major drawback with all quantitative methods of turnover analysis is that they provide no information on the reasons why people are leaving. So, for example, the census method may show that the highest proportion of people leave in the first six months but the information on its own does not show whether this is due to poor recruitment or induction practices, the nature of the job, management style or other factors. Thus, quantitative analyses can help to highlight problems but they give those responsible for planning no indication about how these problems might be addressed.

Measuring labour turnover – qualitative methods

Investigations into reasons for turnover are usually undertaken via qualitative analysis. Popular methods include **exit interviews** and **leaver questionnaires**. Exit interviews are normally conducted soon after an employee has resigned. The benefits of exit interviews are that they can investigate reasons for leaving, identify factors that could improve the situation in the future and gather information on the terms and conditions offered by other organisations. Generally, exit interviews collect information on the following (IRS, 2002a):

- reasons for leaving;
- conditions under which the exiting employee would have stayed;
- improvements the organisation can make for the future;
- the pay and benefits package in the new organisation.

There can also be a number of problems. The interview may not discover the real reason for leaving, either because the interviewer fails to ask the right questions or probe sufficiently or because some employees may be reluctant to state the real reason in case this affects any future references or causes problems for colleagues who remain with the organisation, for example in instances of bullying or harassment. Conversely, some employees may choose this meeting to air any general grievances and exaggerate their complaints. Some organisations collect exit information via questionnaires. These can be completed during the exit interview or sent to people once they have left the organisation. They are often a series of tick boxes with some room for qualitative answers. The questionnaire format has the advantage of gathering data in a more systematic way which can make subsequent analysis easier. However, the standardisation of questions may reduce the amount of probing and self-completed questionnaires can suffer from a low response rate.

Reasons for leaving can be divided into four main categories:

- voluntary, controllable – people leaving the organisation due to factors within the organisation's control, e.g. dissatisfaction with pay, prospects, colleagues;
- voluntary, uncontrollable – people leaving the organisation due to factors beyond the organisation's control, e.g. relocation, ill-health;

- involuntary – determined by the organisation, e.g. dismissal, redundancy, retirement;
- other/unknown.

Attention is usually concentrated on leavers in the voluntary, controllable category as organisations can do something to address the factors causing concern. However, distinctions between controllable and uncontrollable factors can become blurred. For example, in some instances, advances in technology and greater flexibility can facilitate the adoption of working methods and patterns to accommodate employees' domestic circumstances, while the 'reasonable adjustments' required under the Disability Discrimination Act can reduce the numbers of people forced to leave work on health grounds. The involuntary category is also worthy of attention as high numbers of controlled leavers can be indicative of organisational problems, e.g. a high dismissal rate might be due to poor recruitment or lack of effective performance management, while a high redundancy rate might reflect inadequate planning in the past.

While exit interviews or leaver questionnaires can provide some information about why people are leaving, they do not necessarily get to the root of the problem. For example, someone might say that they are leaving to go to a job with better pay but this does not show what led the person to start looking for another job in the first place. In order to produce human resource plans that address labour turnover problems, organisations need to differentiate between 'push' and 'pull' factors. The former relate to factors within the organisation (e.g. poor line management, inadequate career opportunities, job insecurity, dissatisfaction with pay or hours of work) that weaken the psychological link between an individual and their employer (IRS, 2001a). Once an individual has decided to look for another job they are likely to base their decision on 'pull' factors, i.e. the attractions of the new job or organisation in relation to their existing circumstances. A report from the HR benchmark group (cited in IRS, 2002a) listed the top five factors affecting an employee's decision to stay or leave an organisation as:

- the quality of the relationship with their supervisor or manager;
- an ability to balance work and home life;
- the amount of meaningful work they do – giving a feeling of making a difference;
- the level of cooperation with co-workers;
- the level of trust in the workplace.

One way to identify the key 'push' factors is to conduct **attitude surveys** within the organisation. Over half of respondents to a recent survey (IRS, 2002a) use surveys to gather data that can be used to address labour turnover. Attitude surveys have an advantage over exit interviews and leaver questionnaires in that they can identify potential problems experienced by existing employees rather than those that have already decided to leave. This means that any response can be proactive rather than reactive. However, it also means that organisations can make problems worse if they do not act on the findings. 'Telling employees that an organisation cares enough to get their opinion and then doing nothing can exacerbate the negative feelings that already existed, or generate feelings that were not present beforehand' (IRS, 2002a: 40).

The final method to investigate labour turnover to be discussed here is **risk analysis**. This involves identifying two factors: the likelihood that an individual will leave and the consequences of the resignation (Bevan *et al.*, 1997). Statistically, people who are younger, better qualified and who have shorter service, few domestic responsibilities, marketable skills and relatively low morale are most likely to leave (IRS, 2001b). The consequences of any resignations are likely to be determined by their position in the organisation, performance levels and the ease with which they can be replaced. The risk analysis grid (Bevan, 1997) shows how the two factors can be combined (Figure 5.2). This then enables the organisation to target resources or action at the people it would be most costly to lose.

Figure 5.2	Risk analysis grid

		Likelihood of leaving	
		High	*Low*
Impact on organisation	*High*	Danger zone	Watching brief
	Low	'Thanks for all you've done'	No immediate danger

Source: Bevan (1997) p. 34

Within human resource planning literature most attention is concentrated on forecasts of people joining and leaving the organisation but internal movement is also a key factor in internal supply. Techniques to analyse movement of employees within an organisation are potentially more sophisticated than the techniques for analysing wastage rates but the most sophisticated tools, e.g. Markov chains and renewal models, are rarely used (Torrington *et al*, 2002). A simpler approach is to track employee movement to identify patterns of promotion and/or lateral mobility between positions as well as movement in and out of the organisation or function, see Figure 5.3.

In many respects forecasting is *the* key stage of traditional human resource planning. A combination of quantitative and qualitative methods can be used to determine the organisation's future requirements and the availability of human resources. Therefore much hinges on the accuracy of forecasting but there are a number of potential problems that can affect the reliability of any predictions. The first issue here is the difficulty of relying on past data to cope with a volatile and uncertain environment. Recent examples of significant discontinuities include the foot and mouth epidemic in the UK and the terrorist attacks in New York on 11 September 2001. Both events were largely unforeseen and both had significant impact on certain industries, e.g. foot and mouth affected farming and tourism in the UK and the terrorist attacks severely affected the airline industry. Other problems can include the lack of reliable data, the manipulation of data for political ends and the low priority given to forecasting in many organisations.

◼ Human resource plans

The likely results of forecasting activity are the identification of a potential mismatch between future demand and supply. If future demand is likely to exceed supply, then plans need to be developed to match the shortfall but if future supply is likely to exceed demand, then plans need to be developed to reduce the surplus. A number of options are illustrated in Figure 5.4.

While the detailed content of action plans will be determined by the nature of the imbalance between demand and supply and HR and corporate objectives, they are likely to cover at least some of the following areas:

- *working patterns* – e.g. balance of full-time and part-time workers, overtime, short-term contracts, annualised hours, job sharing, remote working;
- *organisation structure and development* – e.g. workforce size and structure, degree of centralisation, use of subcontracting;

Figure 5.3   Employee 'movements' in an organisation

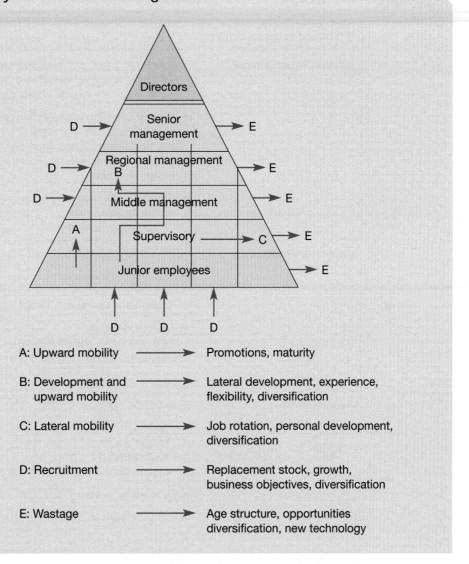

A: Upward mobility   ⟶   Promotions, maturity

B: Development and   ⟶   Lateral development, experience,
    upward mobility   flexibility, diversification

C: Lateral mobility   ⟶   Job rotation, personal development,
                                      diversification

D: Recruitment   ⟶   Replacement stock, growth,
                                      business objectives, diversification

E: Wastage   ⟶   Age structure, opportunities
                                      diversification, new technology

- *recruitment and selection* – e.g. skills and experience required, main sources of applicants, methods to attract suitable candidates, recruitment freezes;
- *workforce diversity* – e.g. monitoring of current and prospective employees, equal opportunities/diversity policies, awareness training;
- *pay and reward* – e.g. mix of financial and non-financial rewards, use of contingent pay, market position;
- *performance management* – e.g. type of performance appraisal, links to reward, attendance management;
- *retention* – e.g. family friendly policies, terms and conditions, employee development;
- *training and development* – induction, training programmes, development reviews, education;
- *employment relations* – e.g. union recognition, communication, grievance and disciplinary policies;
- *release* – e.g. natural wastage, redundancy programmes, outplacement support.

Figure 5.4   Reconciling demand and supply

If demand exceeds supply:	

Increase external supply	• Alter recruitment and selection criteria
	  – different ages, gender, ethnic origin
	  – different skills, qualifications and experience
	
	• Alter recruitment and selection practices
	  – advertise in different ways
	  – target different labour markets
	  – introduce new selection techniques
	  – offer relocation
	
	• Change terms and conditions
	  – more flexible working
	  – improve pay and benefits

Increase internal supply	• Train & develop existing staff
	
	• Alter internal movement patterns
	  – promote differently
	  – encourage lateral movement
	
	• Improve retention
	  – change terms and conditions
	  – more flexible working patterns
	
	• Reduce absenteeism

Reduce demand	• Redesign work
	
	• Use existing staff differently
	  – overtime
	  – multi-skilling
	  – high performance work teams
	
	• Subcontract work
	
	• Relocate work
	
	• Automate

If supply exceeds demand:	
Decrease supply	• Early retirements • Compulsory/voluntary redundancy • Assisted career change and alternative employment • Secondments, sabbaticals, career breaks
Discourage retention	• Short-term contracts • Part-time contracts
Increase demand	• Increase markets for products and services • Diversification

Source: Adapted from Rothwell (1995)

| BOX 5.1 | Shortage of nurses in the UK |

The Labour government has put in place targets to cut hospital waiting lists, increase the numbers of patients treated and improve the quality of health care in the UK. One of the key problems in achieving these targets is a shortage of nurses and many hospitals are now recruiting from overseas.

For example, Manchester Royal Infirmary has recruited more than 250 nurses from India over the last two years – placing advertisements in local newspapers, hiring recruitment agencies and holding interviews by video link. Staff are also recruited from a number of other countries, including the Philippines, Australia, Spain, Ghana, Germany, Iceland and the Yemen. The head of nursing stated that 'we anticipate there will be 4000 vacancies across Greater Manchester by 2005 unless we do something to boost recruitment ... services are expanding but the available workforce has shrunk. There is huge competition for staff.'

In total, over 15000 nurses from countries outside the European Union arrived in Britain in 2001, four times as many as the number entering in 1998–99. The recruitment of overseas nurses has meant that the government target of an additional 20000 nurses by 2005 has already been achieved. A new target of 35000 nurses by 2008 has now been set.

Source: Laurance (2002)

Questions

1 What are the main short- and long-term implications for the NHS of a focus on the recruitment of nurses from overseas?

2 What other options could be considered to address skills shortages?

The scope and content of plans are also influenced by the time-scales involved. Schuler (1998) suggests that the main phases of HRP should be undertaken for three different time horizons – short term (1 year), medium term (2–3 years) and long term (3 years+).

Advocates of human resource planning argue that the process helps to ensure vertical and horizontal integration, i.e. the alignment of human resource policies and practices with corporate goals and with each other. So, for example, plans to address supply shortages by altering selection criteria can influence the type of training required, the level of pay and reward offered to existing and prospective employees and the way the employment relationship is managed. However, in practice the situation is likely to be complicated by the fact that the balance between demand and supply may vary in different parts of the organisation; for example, supply shortages may be identified in some areas while surpluses are predicted in others. The development of action plans can potentially help to ensure that managers are aware of significant inconsistencies. The adoption of a more holistic approach can therefore reduce some of the problems associated with these complexities; for example, an organisation may need to recruit some staff at the same time as it is making others redundant but knowledge of this can help to ensure that both activities are handled sensitively.

■ Implementation and control

The final stage of the traditional HRP process is concerned with implementation of HR plans and evaluation of their overall effectiveness. This stage of the model tends to be rather neglected in the literature but there is little point in developing comprehensive plans if they are not put into practice. Implementation of plans is likely to involve a number of different players, including line managers, employee representatives and employees, but the extent of involvement can vary considerably. The shift towards 'softer', more qualitative aspects of human resource planning places far more emphasis on the need to involve employees throughout the process (e.g. through the use of enhanced communication and tools such as attitude surveys) than is apparent in a 'harder' focus on headcount. Control relates to the extent to which the planning process has contributed to the effective and efficient utilisation of human resources and ultimately to the achievement of corporate objectives. The IPM (now CIPD) suggests three criteria for evaluating the effectiveness of the HRP process (IPM, 1992):

- the extent to which the outputs of HR planning programmes continue to meet changing circumstances;
- the extent to which HRP programmes achieve their cost and productivity objectives;
- the extent to which strategies and programmes are replanned to meet changing circumstances.

This latter point emphasises the need for the constant review and modification of human resource plans in the light of changing circumstances. One of the main criticisms levelled at traditional approaches to HRP has been the inflexibility of plans resulting from the extrapolation of past data and assumptions about the future. The emphasis on flexibility is much more explicit in later models of HRP as the purpose of HRP has become less concerned with ensuring continuity and more on enabling organisations to adapt within unpredictable environments.

Human resource planning – a contemporary approach

Armstrong (2001) has modified the phases of traditional human resource planning to reflect aims more appropriate for contemporary circumstances. He outlines these aims as:

- to attract and retain the number of people required with the appropriate skills, expertise and competences;
- to anticipate problems of potential surpluses or deficits of people;
- to develop a well-trained and flexible workforce, thus contributing to the organisation's ability to adapt to an uncertain and changing environment;
- to reduce dependence on external recruitment when key skills are in short supply by formulating retention and development strategies;
- to improve the utilisation of people by introducing more flexible systems of work.

This approach differs from traditional HRP in that it puts greater emphasis on the 'soft' side of HRP but there are still elements of the 'hard' approach, e.g. in the balance between demand and supply forecasting. It also differs from the traditional approach in its emphasis on the internal labour supply. The key stages of the model are shown in Figure 5.5.

A fundamental difference between this model and the traditional HRP model is the underlying assumption that much of the process might be rather vague:

> It cannot be assumed that there will be a well-articulated business plan as a basis for the HR plans. The business strategy may be evolutionary rather than deliberate; it may be fragmented, intuitive and incremental. Resourcing decisions may be based on scenarios that are riddled with assumptions that may or may not be correct and cannot be tested. Resourcing strategy may be equally vague or based on unproven beliefs about the future. It may contain statements about, for example, building the skills base, which are little more than rhetoric.
>
> (Armstrong, 2001: 362)

| Figure 5.5 | HRP – A contemporary approach |

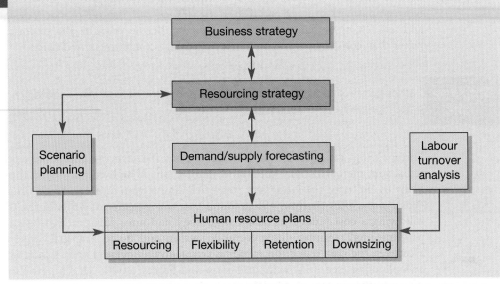

Source: Adapted from Armstrong (2001) *A Handbook of Human Resource Management Practice*, p. 363. Reprinted with permission of Kogan Page.

Such statements could lead one to question whether there is any point to the process at all! Armstrong (2001) goes on to argue that even if all that is achieved is a broad statement of intent, 'this could be sufficient to guide resourcing practice generally and would be better than nothing at all'. However, this does suggest that any plans inevitably have to be tentative, flexible and reviewed and modified on a regular basis.

Business strategy

The first key element of this model is business strategy. Strategy has been defined as:

> the direction and scope of an organisation over the long-term, which achieves competitive advantage for the organisation through its configuration of resources within a changing environment and to fulfil stakeholder expectations.
>
> (Johnson and Scholes, 2002: 10)

Business strategy can be either deliberate or emergent (Whittington, 1993). Deliberate strategies assume a rational evaluation of external and internal circumstances and an identification of the best way to ensure competitive advantage. Emergent strategies, on the other hand, are the product of market forces: 'the most appropriate strategies … emerge as competitive processes that allow the relatively better performers to survive while the weaker performers are squeezed out' (Legge, 1995: 99).

Resourcing strategy

In this model the resourcing strategy derives from the business strategy and also feeds into it. For example, the identification of particular strengths and capabilities might lead to new business goals, especially if strategy formation is emergent rather than deliberate. The rationale underpinning Armstrong's perception of this strategy is related to the resource-based view of the firm (see Chapter 2): 'the aim of this strategy is therefore to ensure that a firm achieves competitive advantage by employing more capable people than its rivals' (Armstrong, 2001: 364). Thus, the implicit assumption is that the vertical integration between business strategy and resourcing strategy will include practices designed to attract and retain a high-quality workforce, such as offering rewards and opportunities that are better than competitors and seeking to maximise commitment and trust.

Stop and think	Under what circumstances might a high-commitment resourcing strategy not be appropriate for an organisation?

Porter (1985) proposes three strategic options for securing competitive advantage: cost reduction, quality enhancement and innovation. A high-commitment approach is more likely to 'fit' with the latter two strategies than with a strategy based on cost reduction. Work in the USA (Arthur, 1992) found that the majority of firms in the study that were following a cost reduction business strategy had poor HR practices (e.g. relatively low pay, minimal training, little communication and no formal grievance mechanisms). However, the cost reduction model is frequently associated with a lack of formalisation and planning (see, for example, Sisson and Storey, 2000; Marchington and Wilkinson, 2002) so the process of developing a resourcing strategy may be more likely to include a high-commitment approach.

■ Scenario planning

This element is not explicit in traditional HRP models and reflects a development in planning models designed to cope with increased uncertainty and unpredictability in the environment. Scenario planning can be used to supplement or replace more traditional demand and supply forecasting. This approach is 'predicated on the assumption that if you cannot predict *the* future, then by speculating on a variety of them, you might just hit upon the right one' (Mintzberg, 1994: 248). Mintzberg (1994) argues that it is difficult to determine the required number of scenarios, i.e. enough to have a good chance of getting it right but not so many as to be unmanageable. The ease with which scenario planning can be undertaken has been greatly improved by the use of computer modelling, in which figures and formulae can be altered to calculate the implications of different predictions. However, this can in itself lead to problems of information overload and difficulties in how to respond to the results. Porter (1985) suggests five key options:

- Bet on the most probable one.
- Bet on the best one for the organisation.
- Hedge bets so as to get satisfactory results no matter which one results.
- Preserve flexibility.
- Exert influence to make the most desirable scenario a reality.

This approach can help to broaden perspectives and consider a number of future options but each decision has its own costs and these also need to be considered. For example, opting to preserve flexibility might be at the expense of following a clear-cut business strategy to secure competitive advantage. Similarly, devoting resources to the best scenario for the organisation might be little more than wishful thinking.

Scenario planning has been described here as a fairly formal process but it can also be regarded as an informal approach to thinking about the future in broad terms, based upon an analysis of likely changes in the internal and external environment (Armstrong, 2001).

■ Forecasting and labour turnover

Demand and supply forecasting in the model includes all the objective and subjective techniques described in the traditional model. The key difference lies in the emphasis given to labour turnover analysis; in the traditional model this is seen as an element of supply forecasting but here it is deemed worthy of its own category. Nevertheless, the techniques used to measure it are the same as discussed earlier in the chapter.

■ Human resource plans

Human resource plans are derived from the resourcing strategy and take into account data from a combination of scenario planning, demand and supply forecasting and labour turnover analysis. The model again reflects the lack of certainty and predictability: 'the plans often have to be short term and flexible because of the difficulty of making firm predictions about human resource requirements in times of rapid change' (Armstrong, 2001: 375). The plans are divided into four broad areas: resourcing, flexibility, retention and downsizing.

● Resourcing plan

This is primarily concerned with effective use of the internal labour market as well as attracting high-quality external applicants. Armstrong (2001) identifies two main components to the resourcing plan: **the recruitment plan** (e.g. numbers and types of people required, sources of candidates, recruitment techniques, etc.) and **the 'employer of choice' plan**. Steps that organisations have taken to find additional sources of applicants to address skills shortages and improve the diversity of the workforce are discussed in Chapter 6, so here we highlight some of the initiatives used to make employers more attractive to high-quality applicants. The CIPD Recruitment and Retention Survey (2002b) found that nearly two-thirds of employers have increased starting salaries or benefits for recruits and 70 per cent have either introduced or improved the flexibility of working hours. Some organisations also offer 'golden hellos' (financial inducements to new recruits), particularly to graduates. The CIPD survey found little evidence of this but other studies (e.g. IRS, 2001c) list a number of organisations that offer signing-on bonuses, e.g. Boots, Barclays, HSBC and PriceWaterhouseCoopers. The practice is mainly restricted to larger, private sector organisations but has recently spread to the public sector, e.g. teaching and some areas of local government. The main reasons for introducing a golden hello (IRS, 2001c) are:

- to ease recruitment difficulties;
- as a response to competition;
- to help graduates settle in a new job;
- to help retain staff.

Stop and think	To what extent would you be more attracted to an employer that offered a 'golden hello' than one that did not?

In addition to being able to attract high-quality applicants, organisations also have to be able to keep them. Other initiatives to become an 'employer of choice' might include providing opportunities for development and career progression and addressing work–life balance issues. Williams (2000) takes this a step further by arguing that organisations need to create the right environment in order to win 'the war for talent':

> In essence, creating a winning environment consists of developing a high-achieving company with values and brand images of which employees can be proud. At the same time, their jobs should permit a high degree of freedom, give them a chance to leave a personal mark and inject a constant flow of adrenalin. Leadership, of course, should be used to enhance, enable and empower, rather than to inhibit, constrain or diminish.
>
> (Williams, 2000: 31)

● Flexibility plan

The flexibility plan is likely to involve the use of functional and numerical flexibility (discussed more fully in Chapter 4). Armstrong (2001: 376) suggests that the aim of the flexibility plan should be to:

- provide for greater operational flexibility;
- improve the utilisation of employees' skills and capabilities;
- reduce employment costs;
- help to achieve downsizing smoothly and avoid the need for compulsory redundancies;
- increase productivity.

From this perspective, flexibility appears to be mainly employer-driven rather than a means to help employees achieve work–life balance and therefore there may be some potential contradictions between this and the 'employer of choice' plan described above. Alternatively, it may be that different plans can be applied to different sections of the workforce. Purcell (1999) suggests that distinctions are growing in the treatment of core workers, who may be nurtured owing to their contribution to competitive advantage, and non-core peripheral or subcontracted workers.

● The retention plan

Manfred Kets de Vries (cited in Williams, 2000: 28) stated that 'today's high performers are like frogs in a wheelbarrow: they can jump out at any time'. It seems that increasing numbers of organisations recognise this and are turning their attention to the retention of key staff. The exact components of the retention plan will be largely determined by the outcomes of labour turnover analysis and risk analysis and initiatives are likely to focus on 'pull' factors. Retention measures can include some or all of the following (Bevan, 1997; IDS, 2000):

- *Pay and benefits* – competitive rates of pay, deferred compensation (e.g. share options, generous pension scheme), retention bonuses, flexible benefits, benefits package that improves with service.
- *Recruitment and selection* – set appropriate standards, match people to posts, provide an accurate picture of the job.
- *Training and development* – good induction processes, provision of development opportunities to meet the needs of the individual and the organisation, structured career paths.
- *Job design* – provision of interesting work, as much autonomy and teamworking as possible, opportunities for flexible working to meet the needs of the individual.
- *Management* – ensure managers and supervisors have the skills to manage effectively.

Attention to the skills and abilities of managers is perceived by some as a key element of retention: 'put simply, employees leave managers not companies' (Buckingham, 2000: 45). Buckingham (2000) argues that employees are more likely to remain with an organisation if they believe that their manager shows interest and concern for them; if they know what is expected of them; if they are given a role that fits their capabilities; and if they receive regular positive feedback and recognition. However, he also suggests that 'most organisations currently devote far fewer resources to this level of management than they do to high-fliers' (p. 46).

● Downsizing plan

The fourth element of the human resource plan is the downsizing plan. This is concerned with the numbers to be 'downsized', the timing of any reductions and the process itself. Methods of reducing the size of the workforce include natural wastage, redeployment, early retirement, voluntary and compulsory redundancy. Armstrong (2001: 382) implies that this plan is implemented as a last resort: 'if all else fails, it may be necessary to deal with unacceptable employment costs or surplus numbers of employees by what

---

BOX 5.2 | **Improving retention at Makita Manufacturing Europe (MME)**

The UK site of MME is based in Telford. It is owned by the Japanese Makita Corporation and was set up as a greenfield site in July 1991. MME manufactures power tools for the professional end of the market. It promotes and sells its products to the various Makita sales subsidiaries around the world, competing with other Makita manufacturing sites on its range and prices.

The Telford site currently has 460 permanent employees, of whom 444 are full time. About 300 employees are 'direct workers' employed on the production side; the remainder fulfil service functions. Two-thirds of the production workforce are semi-skilled assembly operators who manufacture tools from ready-made components. The other third – who are mostly machine operators and setter operators – manufacture electric motors. Their role requires slightly higher skill levels than assembly line work. About 40% of the total workforce are women.

High labour turnover has been a problem since the site opened. Having a constantly changing team on the assembly line causes problems because new recruits are inevitably slower, increasing pressure on the other workers to meet production schedules. High staff turnover can also affect the quality of products, leading to delivery problems and complaints from customers.

MME is not alone in experiencing high turnover in Telford; many businesses suffer from shortages of unskilled and semi-skilled workers, particularly assembly operators. Low unemployment in the area has encouraged job-hopping. Operators can leave a company one day and get another job the next – even if they have been dismissed. Some employees do not even give formal notice – they just disappear and never return. Another characteristic of the Telford labour force is the large number of temporary workers. MME has found that many people do not want to work permanently for one employer, preferring to try out a few working environments before they commit themselves.

While MME realises that these external factors contribute to its turnover problem, it has also recognised that there is scope for improvement in the way people are managed. Questionnaires sent out to people who have recently left the company indicate a variety of reasons for leaving, including transport difficulties, the way employees had been managed and problems during induction.

Source: IDS (2000) Study 692, July

Questions

1 What steps would you recommend to improve retention?
2 How might your recommendations be best implemented?
3 How would you monitor the effectiveness of action taken?

has euphemistically come to be known as downsizing'. However, other commentators suggest that downsizing is fairly endemic in the UK:

> The lack of labour market protection, the weakness of unions and the intense pressure on private and public sector companies alike to improve their profitability and efficiency have meant that the fashionable doctrine of downsizing has spread like contagion.
>
> (Hutton, 1997: 40)

Hutton was writing in the late 90s but it is still relatively easy to find examples of organisations radically reducing the size of the workforce. For example, Shell plans to lay off 4000 staff (Griffiths, 2003) and Corus plans to lose a further 3000 (Harrison, 2003). Several studies (e.g. Bennet, 1991; Cascio, 1993) suggest that downsizing frequently fails to bring the anticipated cost savings for organisations, leading Redman and Wilkinson (2001: 319) to state that ' despite the real sufferings of many workers in an era of redundancy there have been few long-term benefits to justify its level of severity, nor an overwhelming economic justification for its continuing blanket use'.

■ 'It's human resource planning, Jim, but not as we know it'

Changes in organisational structures and the uncertainty of the environment have led to the development of more flexible and focused approaches to planning. Taylor (2002: 78–85) suggests a number of variants on the traditional planning process that may be more appropriate to organisations with unpredictable markets and structures.

Micro-planning uses similar techniques to more traditional HRP but concentrates on key problem areas rather than the organisation as a whole. The more limited scope, both in terms of coverage and time, makes the process more manageable and the results more immediately visible. Micro-planning is likely to be a one-off activity rather than an ongoing process. It can be used to address a variety of issues such as skills shortages, new legislation, competitor activity or a new business opportunity.

Contingency planning is based on scenario planning and enables organisations to draw up a number of different plans to deal with different scenarios. This can enable HRP to switch from being a reactive process undertaken in order to assist the organisation achieve its aims, to become a proactive process undertaken prior to the formulation of wider organisational objectives and strategies (Taylor, 2002: 79). On the other hand, Mintzberg (1994: 252) argues that, in practice, contingency planning presents several problems. Firstly, the contingency that does occur may not be one that was thought of; and secondly, the presentation of a number of different options may lead to no action at all – 'paralysis by analysis'.

In **succession planning** the focus is primarily on recruitment and retention and the ability of the organisation to fill key posts. It is likely that this will relate to a relatively narrow group of people. There is nothing new about organisations identifying and grooming people to fill key posts; in fact, succession planning has always been an element of traditional HRP. The traditional approach relied on identifying a few key individuals who would be ready to take on senior roles at certain points in time. However, to be effective, this requires a stable environment and long-term career plans. In response to a rapidly changing environment where the future is uncertain, the focus has moved away from identifying an individual to fill a specific job towards developing talent for groups of jobs and planning for jobs that do not yet exist. In addition, the emphasis is on balancing the needs of the organisation with the aspirations of employees and on increasing the diversity of the senior management group in terms of competencies and qualities (IRS, 2002b).

BOX 5.3   Succession planning at Astra Zeneca

Astra Zeneca is a pharmaceutical company, formed from the merger of the Swedish-based Astra and the UK-based Zeneca in 1999. The organisation employs 50 000 staff worldwide. Its main products are prescription-only medicines, including cardiovascular, oncological, gastrointestinal and respiratory.

The key drivers of the succession planning process are to:

- ensure a leadership capability that can drive a larger, more global business;
- integrate the business culturally;
- ensure a diverse cross-functional talent base to take this new business forward;
- develop the ability to lead teams across functional and national boundaries.

Succession planning is not a stand-alone activity but is incorporated into a wider framework of employee development in a number of ways:

- informing staff about internal job opportunities and encouraging cross-functional mobility;
- ensuring individual and team development targets are set in line with business goals;
- ensuring developmental feedback is future-focused and encourages open discussion about needs and aspirations;
- offering global leadership programmes, local and functional development programmes (both internal and external), mentoring and coaching;
- building the internal talent pool.

Source: IRS (2002b)

Succession planning is often linked to competency frameworks and the key challenge is to identify the competencies that will contribute to future organisational performance rather than those that have been valued in the past. Astra Zeneca identifies seven leadership competencies: provides clarity about strategic direction, builds relationships, ensures commitment, develops people, focuses on delivery, builds self-awareness and demonstrates personal conviction (IRS, 2002b: 42). Holbeche (2000) cites the five key types of skills, knowledge and aptitude critical to future success identified by Brent Allred *et al.*:

- *technical specialisms, including computer literacy* – the ability to make practical use of information is more likely to lead to career advancement than the management of people;
- *cross-functional and international experience* – the ability to create and manage multidisciplinary teams and projects;
- *collaborative leadership* – the ability to integrate quickly into new or existing teams;
- *self-managing skills* – with an emphasis on continuous development and the ability to manage work–life balance;
- *flexibility* – including the ability to take the lead on one project and be a team-member on another.

Another key issue in contemporary succession planning concerns the balance between internal and external labour markets. Succession planning can be used as a means to retain and motivate key members of the existing workforce but there is a danger that the organisation can become stale in the absence of 'new blood'. Some senior external appointments are therefore necessary to improve diversity and to bring on board people with different skills and experience but too many can result in frustration and the loss of some key talent.

Skills planning, an adaptation of traditional HRP, moves away from a focus on planning for people to one that looks primarily at the skills required (Taylor, 2002).

Forecasting concentrates on the identification of competencies necessary for future organisational performance rather than on the numbers and types of people required. Skills planning builds on the ideas inherent in Armstrong's (2001) flexibility plan in its assumption that the required skills might be secured by a variety of means, including short-term contracts, agency workers, subcontracting, outsourcing, etc.

Various meanings of **soft human resource planning** were discussed earlier in the chapter. Taylor (2002: 84) interprets this in its relatively narrow sense, i.e. as a distinct range of activities focusing on forecasting the supply and demand for particular attitudes and behaviours rather than attitudes and skills. Part of this process involves gathering data on employee attitudes in a number of areas, e.g. motivation, job satisfaction, management effectiveness and commitment to the organisation. This can be done in a variety of ways, such as employee interviews, attitude surveys and focus groups. Attitude surveys appear to be growing in popularity: a recent survey (IRS, 2001d) found that 66 per cent of respondents are currently using them and a further 21 per cent are either planning to use them in the next year or are seriously considering their use in the future. The same study (IRS, 2001c: 8) found the main topics covered in attitude surveys to be:

- management style and performance;
- internal communication;
- personal morale;
- job satisfaction;
- organisation's values;
- career development opportunities;
- personal motivation;
- working environment;
- working conditions;
- teamwork;
- training opportunities;
- assessment of senior management;
- training needs;
- relations with immediate colleagues;
- pay and benefits.

As in traditional HRP, forecasting is also concerned with external supply issues. The main difference is that soft HRP is less concerned with the availability of people and skills than with the attitudes and expectations of potential employees. Schuler (1998: 79) highlights the different expectations and values of three distinct age groups in today's workforce:

- *Traditionalists* (born between 1925 and 1945) value job security, employment security and income security.
- *Baby Boomers* (born between 1946 and 1964) tend to value trust and authority; see work as a duty and a means to financial wealth; and expect that performance will be rewarded more than years of experience.
- *Generation X* (born between 1965 and 1985) value recognition and praise; time with their managers; opportunities to learn new things; fun at work; unstructured, flexible time; and small, unexpected rewards for jobs well done.

Stop and think	What are the main implications of these different expectations and values for effective people management?

Acting on the results of attitude surveys and assessments of broader societal expectations can help organisations attract and retain the attitudes believed necessary for future success. Retention can be viewed as one of the key aims of soft HRP, but again the concern is less with keeping specific people and more to do with securing commitment and loyalty to the organisation. One way to achieve this is through **career management,** i.e. processes to encourage the progression of individuals in line with personal preferences and capabilities and organisational requirements. Like succession planning, this can provide a potential win–win situation in that employees gain opportunities for development and feel valued while the organisation is able to fill posts internally. However, it can be difficult to sustain in times of uncertainty when job security is threatened.

The advantages and disadvantages of human resource planning

HRP, in both its traditional and more contemporary forms, can be perceived to have a number of distinct advantages. Firstly, it is argued that planning can help to reduce uncertainty as long as plans are adaptable. Although unpredictable events do occur, the majority of organisational change does not happen overnight so the planning process can provide an element of control, even if it is relatively short term. Taylor (2002: 73–74) suggests that in the HR field there is potentially more scope for change and adaptation in six months than there is in relation to capital investment in new plant and machinery. Thus he argues that many of the assumptions about the difficulties of planning generally are less relevant to HR.

Other advantages relate to the contribution of planning to organisational performance. For example, the planning process can make a significant contribution to the integration of HR policies and practices with each other and with the business strategy, i.e. horizontal and vertical integration. Marchington and Wilkinson (2002: 280) suggest that HR plans can be developed to 'fit' with strategic goals or they can contribute to the development of the business strategy, but conclude that 'either way, HRP is perceived as a major facilitator of competitive advantage'. Another way that HRP can contribute is by helping to build flexibility into the organisation, either through the use of more flexible forms of work or through identification of the skills and qualities required in employees. IRS (2002c) report that a number of organisations have predicted that jobs are likely to change radically over the next few years and so are using selection techniques to assess core values rather than job-specific skills.

One of the key problems with planning relates to the difficulties of developing accurate forecasts in a turbulent environment but this does not reduce the need for it. Rothwell (1995: 178) suggests that 'the need for planning may be in inverse proportion to its feasibility', while Liff (2000: 96) argues that 'the more rapidly changing environment ... makes the planning process more complex and less certain, but does not make it less important or significant'. Bramham (1988, 1989) states that the process is more important in a complex environment and uses a navigation metaphor to emphasise the point:

> The good navigator uses scientific methods in applying his [sic] knowledge and skills, within the limits of the equipment available, in order to establish first his position and then his best possible course and speed, with a view to arriving at the chosen destination by the most suitable route. From time to time during the voyage he will take fresh readings; calculate what action is necessary to compensate for hitherto unforeseen changes in wind, current and weather; and adjust his course accordingly. If the wind changes dramatically the navigator is not likely to abandon compass and sextant, go below and pray to God to get him to port. He is more likely to apply his knowledge and skills to a reassessment of his position and course as soon as it is practicable.
>
> (Smith, 1976 cited in Bramham, 1988: 6)

This metaphor suggests that HRP can make a significant contribution to the achievement of strategic goals but does imply that the destination remains constant even if other factors change. It also suggests that the person responsible for planning has sufficient information on which to make accurate judgements. Sisson and Storey (2000) argue that the planning process is based on two, highly questionable assumptions: firstly, that the organisation has the necessary personnel information to engage in meaningful HR and succession planning; and secondly, that there are clear operational plans flowing from the business strategy. Furthermore, they suggest that business planning is incremental rather than linear and therefore 'the implication is that the would-be planner will never have the neat and tidy business plan that much of the prescriptive literature takes for granted' (p. 55).

Other key criticisms of the process relate particularly to the difficulties of forecasting accurately. Mintzberg (1994) highlights problems in predicting not only the changes to come but also the type of changes, i.e. whether they are likely to be repeated or are a one-off event. Incorrect forecasts can be expensive but accurate forecasts might provide only limited competitive advantage if other organisations also adopt them:

> The ability to forecast accurately is central to effective planning strategies. If the forecasts turn out to be wrong, the real costs and opportunity costs ... can be considerable. On the other hand, if they are correct they can provide a great deal of benefit – if the competitors have not followed similar planning strategies.
>
> (Makridakis, 1990 cited in Mintzberg, 1994: 229)

Furthermore, Mintzberg (1994) argues that the reliability of forecasts diminishes as the time-scale of projections increases: two or three months may be 'reasonable' but three or four years is 'hazardous'. This is because predictions are frequently based on extrapolations from the past, adjusted by assumptions about the future so there is considerable room for error in both.

The relevance of HRP to contemporary organisations can also be questioned. Taylor (2002) argues that the traditional systematic approach is still appropriate for large organisations operating in relatively stable product and labour markets but other conditions might be less compatible. For example, moves towards decentralisation and the devolution of HR matters to managers at business unit level can make detailed planning impractical. At the same time, the increased fluidity in some organisational structures (e.g. the emphasis on flatter structures, the absence of clearly delineated jobs and the variety of contractual arrangements) can be incompatible with some objective methods of forecasting. Finally, the short-term focus evident in many UK organisations means that long-term planning is just not given high priority.

Human resource planning in practice

While much is written about HRP in theory, evidence about its application in practice is harder to obtain. The Workplace Employee Relations Survey (Cully *et al.*, 1999) reports that 91 per cent of managers with senior responsibility for employment relations include 'staffing or manpower planning' in their list of tasks. Analysis of data from the three most recent workplace surveys (Millward *et al.*, 2000) shows a shift in responsibility for HRP. The proportion of HR specialists with responsibility for HRP declined from 87 per cent in 1984 to 80 per cent in 1990 and remained stable at 80 per cent in 1998, while the proportion of non-specialists with responsibility for HRP has increased from 85 per cent in 1984 to 90 per cent in 1998. This could be seen as indicative of a general trend in the devolution of people management matters to line and general managers. However, HRP seems to be a unique case as, of the six HR functions covered in the surveys, reduced responsibility for HRP is 'the only enduring change' (Millward *et al.*, 2000: 62). There are significant sectoral variations in this shift: the proportion of HR specialists with responsibility for 'staffing or manpower planning' declined in the private sector but increased substantially in the public sector. However, the scope for different interpretations inherent in the term 'staffing or manpower planning' means that we know little about the type of HRP activity actually carried out and so are unable to draw firm conclusions about the reasons for shifts in responsibility.

There is also the potential danger that the high proportion of respondents reporting HRP activity could be indicative of intent rather than actual practice. A number of authors (see, for example, Liff, 2000; Rothwell, 1995) have noted the gap between widespread claims and relatively limited activity. Storey (1992) observed that the majority of companies in his sample would have 'ticked' survey questions about HRP, but a substantial number were not doing it. In the past, studies investigating HRP in practice (e.g. Mackay and Torrington, 1986; Cowling and Walters, 1990) have tended to find evidence of only partial activity and limited implementation of any plans. Rothwell (1995: 178–179) suggests four principal reasons for the lack of empirical proof of HRP activity:

- The extent of change impacting on organisations makes planning too problematic, even though there is a growing need for it. This might also explain why plans, even if developed, are rarely implemented.
- The need to account for the 'shifting kaleidoscope of policy priorities' (p. 178) and the relatively weak power-base of the HR function meaning that either inadequate resources are devoted to planning activities or there is a lack of ability to ensure implementation of plans.
- The preference for pragmatism and the distrust of theory and planning prevalent amongst UK management and the potential inconsistencies in organisational goals, e.g. need for consistency and flexibility, for prediction and planning and speed of response, etc.
- Research into HRP is often over-theoretical and fails to take sufficient account of organisational reality. A lot of HRP activity is undertaken but because it is on an ad hoc rather than a systematic basis it is frequently discounted by researchers.

This last reason could help to account for the potential discrepancy between the proportion of managers reporting involvement in 'staffing or manpower planning' in WERS and the limited evidence of systematic planning activity in more detailed studies. In his study into people management practices in SMEs, Hendry (1995) found some evidence of HRP-related activities (e.g. managers considered recruitment and selection, training and pay in relation to issues identified in labour and product markets) but approaches tended to be tentative and incremental rather than classical and rational.

HRP and strategic HRM

The concept of strategic human resource management (SHRM) has many different interpretations (as discussed in Chapter 2) and 'different definitions carry different assumptions, assert different causal relationships, even seek different goals' (Mabey *et al.*, 1998: 58). Nevertheless, there are two key assumptions that are particularly relevant to the role of HRP: firstly, human resources are the key source of competitive advantage; and secondly, the importance of vertical and horizontal integration. The need for planning is therefore a key component of SHRM in that it can help organisations determine the best use of human resources to meet organisational goals and can facilitate the integration of HR policies and practices with each other and with the business strategy.

Planning is such a key component of SHRM that the terms planning and strategy are sometimes used interchangeably, for example: 'the key message of the HRM literature is the need to establish a close, two-way relationship between business strategy or planning and strategic HRM strategy or planning' (Beaumont, 1992: 40). However, it is useful to differentiate between the HRP process and the long-term HR strategy of the organisation. Brews and Hunt (1999) highlight the difference between ends and means; ends relate to what an organisation desires to achieve while means relate to how it intends to achieve them. Thus, the HRP process produces action plans (means) to help the organisation achieve its key objectives or strategy (ends).

Many of the SHRM models are particularly concerned with the notion of 'fit', i.e. the matching of HR policies and practices with the business or product strategy (see, for example, Kochan and Barrocci, 1985: Fombrun *et al.*, 1984; Schuler and Jackson, 1987). The models have been subject to criticism on a number of grounds (see Chapter 2 for a more detailed discussion of the key criticisms). Criticisms relate principally to the over-simplification of the concepts of strategy and 'fit'; for example, 'both these elements are much more complex and uncertain in reality than they are in many SHRM models' (Mabey *et al.*, 1998: 81). This complexity and ambiguity challenges a number of assumptions underpinning SHRM models, for example: the assumption that a preferred business strategy can be identified; that consistency in HR practices can be achieved; and that these practices can be implemented with no resistance from the human resources involved. While these logistical problems are recognised, the process of HRP can help to identify the preferred approach (or approaches, if scenario planning is used) and attempt to predict any potential barriers to implementation.

At the very least, HRP 'allows managers to consider a range of solutions rather than feeling pressurised into adopting the only realistic option which remains open to them as a last-ditch attempt to avoid a crisis' (Marchington and Wilkinson, 1996: 105). Lam and Schaubroeck (1998: 5) go further and argue that:

> Planning is critical to strategy because it identifies gaps in capabilities which would prevent successful implementation; surpluses in capabilities that suggest opportunities for enhancing efficiencies and responsiveness; and poor utilisation of highly valued organisational resources because of inappropriate HR practices.

This emphasises the need for a two-way relationship between business strategy and HR strategy. However, in the UK it appears that 'the dominant model of the link between business plans and HR plans sees HR as the "dependent variable" – fleshing out the personnel implications of pre-determined business plans, implementing appropriate policies to fulfil the requirements identified' (Liff, 2000: 98). Lam and Schaubroeck (1998) found that, in the majority of firms in their study, the approach to planning was operational rather than strategic. This reflects findings from another study into HRP in large UK organisations (Hercus, 1992) which noted that the priority given to HRP was largely determined by a mismatch between demand and supply. Four of the eight firms had made significant staff reductions in response to difficult economic conditions and 'as they emerged from this period, HR planning has been given priority . . . because of the shortages of professionals and skilled employees, and corporate goals emphasising productivity improvement and quality' (Hercus, 1992: 422). Thus, even if HR is the 'dependent variable', HRP can contribute to the achievement of organisational goals.

HRP has a role to play even in the absence of a clear-cut strategy. Sisson and Storey (2000) suggest that:

> The would-be HR planner will never have the neat and tidy business plans that so much of the prescriptive literature takes for granted. Even so, pressure has to be applied to secure operational plans, however rudimentary, if there is to be any sensible attempt to forecast the number of employees and their skills.   (Sisson and Storey, 2000: 59)

However, Boxall and Purcell (2003: 235) argue that 'it is not a question of choosing between short-term or long-run planning systems. Both forms of planning are important and HR planning needs to play an appropriate role in both.' They also cite research (Koch and McGrath, 1996) that shows that labour productivity is better in firms that formally plan for their future human resource needs. The study by Brews and Hunt (1999) also identifies a link between improvements in organisational performance and the HRP process but the findings indicate that this only becomes apparent after at least four years of formal planning. Thus, firms who prioritise HRP only on a 'needs-must' basis may miss out on the potential advantages.

Hercus (1992: 425) found that 'the role of senior management and the board, and that of the HR director, appears to be particularly important to the success of the HR planning process'. Findings from the Workplace Industrial Relations Survey series show an overall decline in HR representation at board level, thus suggesting that HR issues are not given priority by senior management in many UK workplaces, particularly smaller, non-union workplaces (Millward *et al.*, 2000). The most recent survey, WERS (Cully *et al.*, 1999) found that over two-thirds (68 per cent) of workplaces had a strategic plan which included employee development issues and in more than half of workplaces (57 per cent) the strategic plan was drawn up with some input from the person with responsibility for employment relations. This strategic approach was most likely to be found in larger workplaces and in the public sector.

Stop and think

What factors might account for the discrepancy between the proportion of workplaces with strategic plans that include employee development issues and the proportion of workplaces that involve HR in the development of these plans?

Future directions

Much of the criticism levelled at traditional HRP concerned its inflexibility and inability to cope with changing circumstances. Many of the more contemporary variants attempt to address these problems in some way. For example, contingency planning provides greater flexibility by considering the implications of a number of different scenarios while other approaches (e.g. succession planning) focus on specific issues rather than attempting to tackle everything at once. It seems likely that this drive for greater flexibility will continue and HRP will become increasingly dynamic. Boxall and Purcell (2003) argue that 'it is vital to accept that change is inevitable and that some preparation for the future is therefore crucial' (p. 232). They further suggest that short-term planning is necessary for survival but long-term planning is a good thing providing it does not make the organisation inflexible. Schuler (1998: 176) makes a similar point, suggesting that planning will become more tentative and short-term to deal with the rapidly changing environment but long-term needs are still important because some changes take time. These arguments can be seen to underpin the need for both traditional HRP techniques for short-term forecasting and for more contemporary variants such as scenario planning for longer-term plans.

HRP appears to have moved a long way from the mechanistic approach associated with traditional manpower planning. Contemporary approaches are less concerned with maintaining stability and more with shaping and managing change. Brews and Hunt (1999) argue that unstable environments make HRP more, rather than less, necessary but the key focus needs to be on adapting to change:

When the going gets tough, the tough go planning: formally, specifically, yet with flexibility and with persistence. And once they have learned to plan, they plan to learn.

(Brews and Hunt, 1999: 906)

Summary

The chapter began by outlining seven key objectives and these are revisited here.

● Human resource planning can be interpreted in a number of different ways. For some it means the same as manpower planning, for others it is significantly different and has many similarities to HRM. The definition used in this chapter relates to HRP as a set of distinct activities that incorporates both the hard elements associated with manpower planning and some of the softer elements associated with HRM.

● The key stages in the traditional human resource planning process are investigation and analysis, forecasting demand and supply, developing action plans to address any imbalance, implementing the plans and evaluating their effectiveness.

● Methods of demand forecasting discussed are time series, ratio analysis, work study, managerial judgement, the Delphi technique and working back from budgets. Quantitative methods can be problematic as the extrapolation of past data might be inappropriate in a changing environment but they can provide a reasonable starting point for forecasts. Qualitative methods are more flexible but can be manipulated for political ends. Supply forecasting tends to focus mainly on various analyses of labour turnover and stability and movement through an organisation. Quantitative analysis can help to highlight problem areas but gives little indication about how problems might be addressed. Qualitative data can help to address this gap but can sometimes be difficult to obtain. Organisations can exacerbate problems if they are not seen to act on the information they receive.

● A more contemporary approach to HRP aims to enable the organisation to adapt to an uncertain and changing environment and emphasises the need to develop a well-trained and flexible workforce. Variants to HRP include micro-planning, contingency planning, succession planning, skills planning and soft human resource planning.

● The main advantages of HRP are that plans can help reduce uncertainty, can build flexibility and can contribute to vertical and horizontal integration. The key disadvantages relate to difficulties of predicting an uncertain future, the lack of necessary data to make accurate predictions and the absence of clear business plans.

● Evidence of HRP in practice is varied but the dominant approach seems to view HR as the 'dependent variable' and tends to be tentative and incremental rather than systematic.

● HRP's main role in SHRM is as a means to facilitate the integration of HR strategy with business strategy and to ensure that HR policies and practice are compatible with each other. In addition, some studies associate formal planning activity with improved organisational performance, particularly if planning is sustained over a number of years. The key emphasis, however, needs to be on building adaptability and managing change.

Questions

1 Explain the importance and limitations of demand and supply forecasting to the human resource planning process.

2 To what extent is it worth undertaking HRP activity in the face of economic and business uncertainty?

3 How successfully have contemporary approaches to HRP addressed the criticisms levelled at traditional HRP?

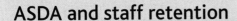

Case study

ASDA and staff retention

Asda, the supermarket chain, uses a variety of methods to gather information on employee attitudes, including attitude surveys, ad hoc focus groups and questionnaires to staff who have left the organisation. These various sources of information indicated that lack of career progression was seen as a problem: for example, in the attitude survey conducted in 1997, fewer than half of hourly-paid staff (the vast majority of Asda employees) agreed with the statement 'there is ample opportunity for promotion at Asda'.

In response, Asda developed a new programme to train hourly-paid staff to become managers. Staff nominate themselves for the programme but must meet stiff entry criteria in terms of skill and training levels before being accepted; for example, they must have reached the final stage of the job ladder for their current role. The programme consists of three stages:

Stage 1 – staff attend an open day that explains the good and bad aspects of being a manager. Staff also complete four off-the-job courses in communication skills, coaching, training and organising work. At the end of each course participants complete a small project. Once they have been satisfactorily completed, staff attend a one-day development centre where they are assessed against the competencies required for managers. Once they have reached a certain level of competence they progress to stage 2.

Stage 2 – staff undertake four weeks of full-time training in store. This includes both on- and off-the-job training and focuses on people management skills, including how to give feedback and conduct appraisal interviews. Once this training is successfully completed, they spend the next four weeks undergoing in-depth management training in one of eight 'stores of learning', chosen for being well run by highly experienced managers. A self-learning package is included here as well as more on and off-the-job training. On successful completion, participants move directly to stage 3.

Stage 3 – appointment to a departmental manager post. Asda believes that the new programme has contributed to reduced turnover rates amongst hourly-paid staff and managers. In addition, the proportion of hourly paid staff who agreed that Asda offers ample opportunity for promotion had increased to 64% in 2000.

Source: IDS (2000).

Questions

1 To what extent is this programme likely to reduce turnover?

2 In what circumstances might Asda find it difficult to retain staff and what could they do about it?

References and further reading

Armstrong, M. (2001) *A Handbook of Human Resource Management Practice*, 8th edn. London: Kogan Page.

Arthur, J. (1992) 'The link between business strategy and industrial relations systems in American steel mini-mills', *Industrial and Labor Relations Review*, Vol. 45, No. 3, pp. 488–506.

Bartholemew, D. (ed.) (1976) *Manpower Planning*. Harmondsworth: Penguin.

Beaumont, P. (1992) 'The US human resource management literature', in Salaman, G. *et al.* (eds) *Human Resource Strategies*. London: Sage.

Bennet, A. (1991) 'Downsizing doesn't necessarily bring an upswing in corporate profitability', *The Wall Street Journal*, 6 June, p. 1.

Bevan, S. (1997) 'Quit stalling', *People Management*, 20 Nov.

Bevan, S., Barber, L. and Robinson, D. (1997) *Keeping the Best: A Practical Guide to Retaining Key Employees*. London: Institute for Employment Studies.

Boxall, P. and Purcell, J. (2003) *Strategy and Human Resource Management*. London: Palgrave.

Bramham, J. (1988) *Practical Manpower Planning*, 4th edn. London: IPM.

Bramham, J. (1989) *Human Resource Planning*. London: IPM.

Bramham, J. (1994) *Human Resource Planning*. London: IPD.

Brews, P. and Hunt, M. (1999) 'Learning to plan and planning to learn: resolving the planning school/learning school debate', *Strategic Management Journal*, Vol. 20, pp. 889–913.

Buckingham, G. (2000) 'Same indifference', *People Management*, 17 Feb, pp. 44–46.

Cascio, W. (1993) 'Downsizing: what do we know, what have we learned?', *Academy of Management Executive*, Vol. 7, No. 1, pp. 95–104.

Chartered Institute of Personnel and Development (2000) *The People Management Implications of Mergers and Acquisitions, Joint Ventures and Divestments*. CIPD Research Report, September.

Chartered Institute of Personnel and Development (2002a) *Labour Turnover*. CIPD Survey Report.

Chartered Institute of Personnel and Development (2002b) *Recruitment and Retention*. CIPD Survey Report.

Cowling, A. and Walters, M. (1990) 'Manpower planning – where are we today?', *Personnel Review*, Vol. 19, No. 3, pp. 3–8.

Cully, M., Woodland, S., O'Reilly, A. and Dix, G. (1999) *Britain at Work*. London: Routledge.

Department of Employment (1974) *Company Manpower Planning*. London: HMSO.

Dessler, G. (2003) *Human Resource Management*, 9th edn. Englewood Cliffs, New Jersey, Prentice Hall.

Fombrun, C., Tichy, N. and Devanna, M. (1984) *Strategic Human Resource Management*. New York: John Wiley.

Griffiths, K. (2003) 'The face of corporate Britain', *The Independent*, 24 April, p. 1.

Harrison, M. (2003) 'Sir Brian Moffat forced out at Corus', *The Independent*, 24 April, p. 21.

Hendry, C. (1995) *Human Resource Management: A Strategic Approach to Employment*. Oxford: Butterworth-Heinemann.

Hercus, T. (1992) 'Human resource planning in eight British organisations: a Canadian perspective' in Towers, B. (ed.) *The Handbook of Human Resource Management*. Oxford: Blackwell.

Hill, J. and Trist, E. (1955) 'Changes in accidents and other absences with length of service', *Human Relations*, Vol. 8, May.

Holbeche, L. (2000) 'Work in progression', *People Management*, 8 June.

Hutton, W. (1997) *The State to Come*. London: Vintage.

IDS (2000) 'Improving staff retention', *IDS Study 692*, July.

IPM (1992) *Statement on Human Resource Planning*. London: IPD.

IRS (2001a) 'Benchmarking labour turnover 2001/02, part 1', *IRS Employment Review 741*, 3 Dec.

IRS (2001b) 'Risk analysis and job retention', *IRS Employee Development Bulletin 141*, Sept.

IRS (2001c) 'Hanging up the welcome sign', *IRS Employee Development Bulletin 135*, March.

IRS (2001d) 'Reality check: using attitude surveys to manage retention', *IRS Employee Development Bulletin 137*, May.

IRS (2002a) 'Facing the retention challenge', *IRS Employment Review 750*, 29 April.

IRS (2002b) 'The changing face of succession planning', *IRS Employment Review 756*, 22 July: 37–42.

IRS (2002c) 'Focus of attention,' *IRS Employment Review 749*, 15 April, pp. 36–42.

Johnson, G. and Scholes, K. (2002) *Exploring Corporate Strategy*. Harlow: Prentice Hall.

Koch, M. and McGrath, R. (1996) 'Improving labor productivity: human resource management policies do matter', *Strategic Management Journal*, Vol. 17, pp. 335–354.

Kochan, T.A. and Barocci, T. (1985) *Human Resource Management Industrial Relations: Text, Readings and Cases*. Boston, Mass.: Little, Brown.

Lam, S. and Schaubroeck, J. (1998) 'Integrating HR planning and organisational strategy', *Human Resource Journal*, Vol. 8, No. 3, pp. 5–19.

Laurance, J. (2002) 'Why foreign nurses hold the nation's health in their hands', *The Independent*, 26 Nov. p. 18.

Legge, K. (1995) *Human Resource Management: Rhetorics and Realities*. Basingstoke: Macmillan.

Liff, S. (2000) 'Manpower or human resource planning – what's in a name?', in Bach, S. and Sisson, K. (eds) *Personnel Management: A Comprehensive Guide to Theory and Practice*, 3rd edn. Oxford: Blackwell.

Mabey, C., Salaman, G. and Storey, J. (1998) *Human Resource Management: A Strategic Introduction*, 2nd edn. Oxford: Blackwell.

Mackay, L. and Torrington, D. (1986) *The Changing Nature of Personnel Management*. London: IPM.

Marchington, M. and Wilkinson, A. (1996) *Core Personnel and Development*. London: IPD.

Marchington, M. and Wilkinson, A. (2002) *People Management and Development*. London: CIPD.

McBeath, G. (1992) *The Handbook of Human Resource Planning*. Oxford: Blackwell.

Millward, N., Bryson, A. and Forth, J. (2000) *All Change at Work?* London: Routledge.

Mintzberg, H (1994) *The Rise and Fall of Strategic Planning*. Hemel Hempstead: Prentice Hall.

Pilbeam, S. and Corbridge, M. (2002) *People Resourcing: HRM in Practice*. Harlow: FT/Prentice Hall.

Porter, M. (1985) *Competitive Advantage: Creating and Sustaining Superior Performance*. New York: Free Press.

Purcell, J. (1999) 'The search for best practice and best fit in human resource management: chimera or cul-de-sac?', *Human Resource Management Journal*, Vol. 9, No. 3, pp. 26–41.

Redman, T. and Wilkinson, A. (2001) *Contemporary HRM*. Harlow: FT/Prentice Hall.

Rothwell, S. (1995) 'Human resource planning', in Storey, J. (ed.) *Human Resource Management: A Critical Text*. London: Routledge.

Sadhev, K., Vinnicombe, S. and Tyson, S. (1999) 'Downsizing and the changing role of HR', *International Journal of HRM*, Vol. 10, No. 5, pp. 906–923.

Schuler, R.S. (1998) *Managing Human Resources*, 6th edn. Cincinnati, Ohio: South-Western College Publishing.

Schuler, R. and Jackson, S. (1987) 'Linking competitive strategies with human resource management', *Academy of Management Executive*, Vol. 1, No. 3, pp. 207–219.

Sisson, K. and Storey, J. (2000) *The Realities of Human Resource Management*. Buckingham: Open University Press.

Storey, J. (1992) *Developments in the Management of Human Resources*. Oxford: Blackwell.

Tansley, C. (1999) 'Human resource planning: Strategies, systems and processes', in Leopold, J., Harris, L. and Watson, T. (eds) *Strategic Human Resourcing: Principle, Perspectives and Practice*. Harlow: FT/Pitman.

Taylor, S. (2002) *People Resourcing*. London: CIPD.

Thomason, G. (1988) *A Textbook of Human Resource Management*. London: IPM.

Torrington, D., Hall, L. and Taylor, S. (2002) *Human Resource Management*. Harlow: FT/Prentice Hall.

Whittington, R. (1993) *What is Strategy and Does It Matter?*, London: Routledge.

Williams, M (2000) 'Transfixed assets', *People Management*, 3 August, pp. 28–33.

CHAPTER 6

Recruitment and selection

Julie Beardwell and Mary Wright

OBJECTIVES

▶ To explore the external and internal context in which recruitment and selection occur.

▶ To examine recent developments in the systematic approach to recruitment and selection.

▶ To consider the effectiveness of recruitment and selection practices.

Introduction

The importance of ensuring the selection of the right people to join the workforce has become increasingly apparent as the emphasis on people as the prime source of competitive advantage has grown. Beaumont (1993) identifies three key issues that have increased the potential importance of the selection decision to organisations. First, demographic trends and changes in the labour market have led to a more diverse workforce, which has placed increasing pressure on the notion of fairness in selection. Second, the desire for a multi-skilled, flexible workforce and an increased emphasis on teamworking has meant that selection decisions are concerned more with behaviour and attitudes than with matching individuals to immediate job requirements. And third, the emphasis between corporate strategy and people management has led to the notion of strategic selection: that is, a system that links selection processes and outcomes to organisational goals and aims to match the flow of people to emerging business strategies.

Selective hiring (i.e. the use of sophisticated techniques to ensure selection of the 'right' people) is frequently included in the 'bundles' of best HR practice (see, for example, Pfeffer, 1998). The contribution of effective recruitment and selection to enhanced business performance is also illustrated by the findings of empirical studies. For example, a study into small and medium-sized manufacturing establishments (Patterson *et al.*, 1997) found the acquisition and development of employee skills through the use of sophisticated selection, induction, training and appraisals to have a positive impact on company productivity and profitability. Thus the practice of recruitment and selection is increasingly important from an HRM perspective.

At the same time, however, many of the traditional methods of recruitment and selection are being challenged by the need for organisations to address the increased complexity, greater ambiguity and rapid pace of change in the contemporary environment. This chapter, therefore, discusses key contemporary approaches to recruitment and selection, and examines the influence of external and internal factors on the process. After clarifying what we mean by recruitment and selection, we begin by describing the external context in which recruitment and selection occur, including government policy and legislation. Next, we turn our attention to the internal organisational context in order to examine factors that might account for variations in recruitment and selection practice. We then explore the systematic approach to recruitment and selection, and discuss recent developments at each stage of the process. In the final section we emphasise the two-way nature of recruitment and selection, and consider ethical issues in the treatment of individuals. The chapter concludes with a summary and a number of self-test exercises.

■ Definitions

Stop and think	What do you see as the key differences between recruitment and selection?

The recruitment and selection process is concerned with identifying, attracting and choosing suitable people to meet an organisation's human resource requirements. They are integrated activities, and 'where recruitment stops and selection begins is a moot point' (Anderson, 1994). Nevertheless, it is useful to try to differentiate between the two areas: Whitehill (1991) describes the recruitment process as a positive one, 'building a roster of potentially qualified applicants', as opposed to the 'negative' process of selection. So a useful definition of recruitment is 'searching for and obtaining potential job candidates in sufficient numbers and quality so that the organisation can select the most appropriate people to fill its job needs' (Dowling and Schuler, 1990); whereas selection is concerned more with 'predicting which candidates will make the most appropriate contribution to the organisation – now and in the future' (Hackett, 1991).

The external context

The processes of recruitment and selection take place within a framework of external and internal influences. External direction, through legislation and published codes of practice, suggests that approaches will be standardised, in the UK at least. However, other factors in both external and internal contexts result in variations in both philosophy and practice.

The overall context in which human resources are managed is well illustrated in Figure 6.1 (Schuler and Jackson, 1996). This section concentrates on the potential impact of factors in the external environment on recruitment and selection activities. A later section considers the impact of internal organisational factors.

■ External labour market factors

When organisations choose to recruit externally (as opposed to in-house), the search takes place in local, regional, national and/or international labour markets, depending on numbers, skills, competences and experiences required, the potential financial costs involved and the perceived benefits involved to the organisation concerned.

External labour markets vary considerably in size, as Table 6.1 demonstrates. Some, like China, Brazil and Mexico, are growing rapidly, others such as Germany, Japan and Great Britain are static or falling.

Within a given external labour market, the recruiter requires knowledge on the make-up of that population. Age profiles give a potential indication of 'trainees' as opposed to

Figure 6.1   The contexts of managing human resources

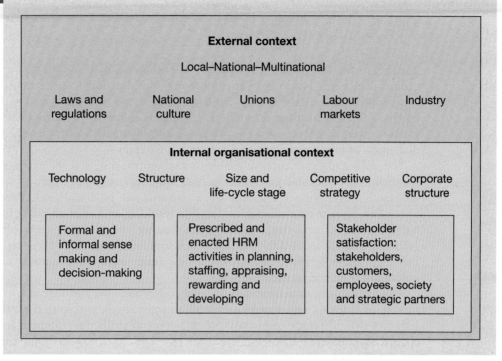

Source: Adapted from Schuler and Jackson (1996).

Table 6.1 National comparisons of economically active populations 2001

Country	Million	Country	Million
China	728	Germany	40
India	346	Great Britain	28
United States	139	France	27
Indonesia	95	South Korea	22
Brazil	83	Egypt	19
Japan	67	Canada	16
Russia	65	Australia	9
Mexico	41	Sweden	4

Source: Euromonitor plc (2002a, 2002b)

'experienced' people available, as well as the proportion of those close to retirement age. Knowledge of gender breakdown is important. While some southern European countries have only half or less of women active in the labour market, nearly three-quarters of women in Scandinavian countries are deemed 'economically active' (Social Trends, 2002). In 2001, UK census figures suggest that 13.2 million women and 16.3 million men make up the UK labour force, with nearly 5 million of the women working part-time. A high proportion of women in the labour market may suggest a higher proportion of people seeking part-time or 'family friendly' contracts as opposed to inflexible and/or full-time hours.

Unemployment rates affect the number of people potentially available and in the UK unemployment levels were running at a national average of 4.9 per cent in spring 2001. However,

> unemployment is not equally distributed across the UK labour force. Age, qualifications, gender, ethnicity and location all have an impact on whether or not people become unemployed and on the length of time people spend out of work.   (Social Trends, 2002)

Younger rather than older people, men rather than women, people from minority ethnic groups (especially black and Pakistani/Bangladeshi groups) rather than white groups, and people with a disability have a greater tendency to be unemployed. Difficulties overcoming ill health (men) and family commitments (women) were the two most common reasons given by those not actively seeking employment (Social Trends, 2002). Further discussion of labour market issues is found in Chapter 4.

The skills and experiences available in a labour market, and the extent of competition for them, are critical factors for recruiters. Where shortages of appropriate recruits have occurred, moves towards flexible work patterns can be considered. The 2002 Labour Force Survey reports statistics on flexible working and annualised hours, four and a half-day weeks, term-time working, job sharing and nine-day fortnights (Office for National Statistics, 2002a). While it is not suggested that all of these have been established to alleviate recruitment difficulties, some have the potential to increase the number of potential recruits available.

The availability of required skills and competences is influenced by the range and quality of learning experiences available to individuals within that market. Table 6.2 suggests that illiteracy levels still block potential skills development in a number of countries and affect the potential use of these labour forces by firms looking to recruit in the global labour market

Table 6.2 **Adult literacy rates as percentage of population**

Country	Literacy rate (2000)
Egypt	52.7
India	53.5
Nigeria	57*
Brazil	80*
China	83

*figures only available for 1997

NB figures disguise considerable differences in some countries between male and female illiteracy rates.

Source: Euromonitor (2002b)

However, Crabb (2003: 30) reports a rapidly growing pattern of UK organisations shifting their operations to the Indian sub-continent (especially where these operations involve information technology and/or financial services), taking advantage of significantly lower wage rates available in the 'huge, well-educated, English speaking labour force'.

The number of young people remaining in full-time compulsory education in European countries varies considerably, as Table 6.3 demonstrates. Take-up of higher education influences both the extent of higher-level skills available within the economy and conversely the numbers of young people available to undertake focused work-based learning.

Labour markets, education and learning activities are considerably influenced by government policy. For example, within the UK there has been a long-standing debate about the relative roles and responsibilities of central and local government, employers and individuals in respect to skills training and qualifications. Historically, reliance has been placed on voluntarist approaches, with employers expected to achieve an adequate level of skill for the nation as a whole, the market supposedly ensuring that such provision is made.

Table 6.3 Education and training rates 1995 (%)

	Aged 15–19	Aged 20–24
France	93.2	42.5
Germany	93.0	39.1
Ireland	83.7	30.1
Greece	80.0	29.2
Spain	79.1	41.8
UK	71.2[a]	23.6
Luxembourg	38.8	36.5

[a] By 1998 this had risen to 74% (Social Trends, 2000)

Source: Adapted from Leat (1998: 247)

More recently, the issue of preparing current and future workforces through lifetime learning has resulted in national learning targets being set by the UK government for young people and adults (see also Chapter 9).

Table 6.4 UK national learning targets 2002

Selection of national learning targets for 2002: (NB all at stated level or equivalent)

50% of 16-year-olds to achieve 5 GCSEs grades A*–C
85% of 19-year-olds qualified to at least NVQ level 2
60% of 21-year-olds qualified to at least NVQ level 3

Economically active adults to be qualified:
28% to at least NVQ level 4
50% to at least NVQ level 3

Source: Social Trends (2002)

By autumn 2002 it was reported that nearly 52 per cent of 19-year-olds, 54 per cent of 21-year-olds and 49 per cent of adults had qualifications at NVQ level 3 or equivalent, with 28 per cent of adults possessing NVQ level 4 or equivalent qualifications (Department for Education and Skills, 2003).

The highest qualification held appears to be related to a number of factors, such as ethnic group (the highest percentage of people of working age with qualifications at levels 4 and 5 being of Chinese origin), gender (with males far more likely to hold qualifications at GCE A level or equivalent) and age (with older people of both genders, but especially women, more likely to hold no qualifications at all) (Social Trends, 2002).

Other government initiatives to influence the number of people and levels of skill available in the labour market include the New Deal (for young people age 18–24, 25+, 50+ and New Deal jobseekers with disabilities) and Modern Apprenticeship schemes (foundation and advanced). Current proposals in the government White Paper on higher education may affect the demand for traditional and foundation higher education places. Through the growth of technological applications, alternative 'university' provision becomes possible, some via government initiatives (e.g. University for Industry under its brand name Learn Direct, and the National Health Service University) or private initiatives such as Barclays University or Unisys University.

Despite these initiatives to increase the quality and quantity of skills and competencies available in the UK, difficulties remain when recruiting externally. The sixth CIPD annual report on recruitment and selection practices, issues and trends reports widespread and increased recruitment difficulties in 2001. Major causes cited are:

- candidates' lack of relevant experience (54.8%);
- candidates' lack of relevant technical skills (53.5%);
- recruiters' inability to meet salary expectations, (48.8%);
- a shortage of high-quality applicants (48.8%). (CIPD, 2002a)

Organisations experiencing severe problems included those in the public sector (where over a quarter of employers reported receiving no applications for some posts) and those in the South East and South West, irrespective of organisational size. These difficulties exist despite 'harsher economic conditions for manufacturers and some services firms in the private sector'. (CIPD, 2002a: 6)

● Technological developments

Advances in technology, particularly the growth and use of both the Internet as a whole and organisation-specific intranets, are affecting the type of labour demanded, with more requirements for those with expert systems and knowledge management experiences and knowledge. By the end of 2004, it is estimated that the number of jobs in call centres world-wide will have doubled since 1999 to 10.5 million from 1999. 'Call centres are getting ready to become overall customer contact centres, working with the opportunities afforded by the Web to offer a full range of services at a cost effective price' (Bradshaw, 1999).

Within existing organisations the potential for a growth in employment based away from the traditional office environment grows as technology allows individuals to communicate with others and be supervised at a distance. Homeworking and teleworking become possible through the use of e-mail and videoconferencing. The potential exists for wide-scale change from traditional classroom-based group learning to individual and ongoing computer-based training and development. Technological developments permit the constant (and sometimes covert) monitoring of employee behaviour.

As jobs are lost in manufacturing (with technological advances replacing shopfloor employees with robots), traditional retailing (a wide range of goods and services are available via the Internet), and the financial sector (where Internet and internal computer systems are introduced to enhance profitability and retain competitiveness), new employment opportunities are found in organisations supporting and using this technological growth. Further discussion of the impact of job redesign is found in Chapter 14.

These changes impact on the skills required by both existing jobholders and potential applicants. The recruiter has to be able to locate those possessing these skills (or the potential to learn and apply them effectively).

■ Government policy and legislation

While organisations have considerable freedom of choice in the type of people they want to recruit, legislation plays a significant role in the recruitment and selection process, particularly in attempts to prevent discrimination on the grounds of sex, race or disability (see also Chapter 7).

● Sex and race discrimination

Two Acts are specifically designed to prevent discrimination in employment on the basis of sex or race. The Sex Discrimination Act 1975 makes it unlawful to discriminate against a person directly or indirectly in the field of employment on the grounds of their sex or marital status. The Race Relations Act 1976 makes it unlawful to discriminate against a person in the field of employment on the grounds of their race, colour and nationality, including ethnic or national origin.

Both Acts prohibit direct and indirect discrimination. Direct discrimination occurs when an individual is treated less favourably than another because of their sex, marital status or race. Indirect discrimination occurs when requirements are imposed that are not necessary for the job, and that may disadvantage a significantly larger proportion of one sex or racial group than another.

Both Acts make it lawful for employers to take positive action to encourage applications from members of one sex or of racial groups who have been under-represented in particular work over the previous 12 months. However, positive discrimination is unlawful, which means that, although advertisements can explicitly encourage applications from one sex or particular racial group, no applicant can be denied information or be discriminated against in selection because they do not fit the 'preferred' category. Sex or race discrimination is permitted only where sex or race is a defined 'genuine occupational qualification' (GOQ). Examples of GOQs include those for models, actors and some personal welfare counsellors.

These Acts have had only limited success in achieving sexual and racial equality: there has been a significant reduction in overt discrimination, particularly in recruitment advertising, but there is less evidence of eradication of discrimination in employment practices generally. National statistics indicate that, at a macro level, little has changed in the distribution of employment on the grounds of gender and race.

Gender

- 44% of all those of working age in employment are women.
- 43% of women are in part-time employment, compared with 8% of men.
- Women account for 69% or more of administrative and secretarial, personal service, sales and customer service occupations, while men make up 69% or more of managers and senior officials, skilled trades, and process, plant and machine operatives (ONS, 2002a).
- Female employees working full-time earn on average 82% of the average pay of men in full-time employment (ONS, 2002b).

Ethnic minorities (ONS, 2002a)

- 58% of the working age population of ethnic minority groups are in employment compared with 76% of white people.
- Unemployment statistics vary widely for different ethnic communities: for example, unemployment rates are highest for Bangladeshi men at 21%, compared with 7% for Indian men and 6% for Chinese men.
- Cultural diversity is also reflected in varying rates of labour market participation for women. Bangladeshi and Pakistani women have the lowest employment rates at 17% and 24%, compared with 69% for Black Caribbean women and 71% for white women.

Continued indications of inequality in the labour market may be partly due to the fact that, until fairly recently, legislation has been aimed at ending discrimination rather than requiring organisations to promote equality. The situation has now changed, at least with regard to race in the public sector. The Race Relations (Amendment) Act 2001 imposes a positive duty on public authorities to promote racial equality. In relation to recruitment and selection this includes:

- ensuring that employment practices attract good candidates from all ethnic groups;
- setting targets and taking action to encourage applicants from ethnic groups currently under-represented in particular areas of work;
- monitoring employees and applicants for employment, training and promotion by ethnic group.

Findings of the fourth Workplace Employee Relations Survey, WERS 4 (Cully *et al.*, 1999), suggest that monitoring does not occur as much as one might expect. Fewer than half of organisations with a formal equal opportunities policy collect statistics on posts held by men and women, or keep employee records with ethnic origin attached, and only a third review selection procedures to identify indirect discrimination. The new requirements should increase the incidence of monitoring in the public sector but whether or not the private sector will follow suit is open to debate. In the private sector, equalising opportunity is still largely dependent on initiatives undertaken voluntarily by organisations such as targeted recruitment, pre-recruitment training or participation in national initiatives such as the CRE's Leadership Challenge for ethnic minorities.

In order to encourage diversity, some organisations are adopting a more flexible approach to recruitment and selection. The CIPD Recruitment and Retention Survey (CIPD, 2002a) highlights a number of measures, including:

● Advertise vacancies in media targeted towards under-represented groups.
● Ensure that images or words in advertisements do not discourage any groups from applying.
● Take account of a broader range of qualities when selecting (e.g. personal skills rather than formal qualifications).
● Appoint people who have the potential to grow but don't currently have all that is required.

Other initiatives to increase the diversity of the workforce include building up relationships with community groups. The retailer Littlewoods did this and reported some positive results, including more applicants, lower recruitment costs and the generation of extra sales (Pickard, 1999: 42). Pre-employment training can also help to increase the number of employees from previously under-represented groups, but is used by only a small number of organisations (Dickens, 2000). These forms of positive action may be aimed at improving opportunities for previously disadvantaged groups by creating a 'level playing field'. However, these types of initiatives can be seen as counter-productive because people who are perceived to have gained advantage through positive action may be viewed negatively by others. In addition, offering extra training and help to under-represented groups implies 'that they are deficient in some way and that consequently they are the problem . . . [when] invariably the problem lies not with the targeted group itself but elsewhere in an organisation's own processes or culture' (Kandola, 1995: 20).

● Disability discrimination

The Disability Discrimination Act (1995) came into force at the end of 1996. The Act defines disability as a physical or mental impairment that has a substantial and long-term adverse effect on a person's ability to carry out normal day-to-day duties, and includes progressive conditions such as cancer and multiple sclerosis. The legislation makes it unlawful for companies with 15 or more employees to treat people with disabilities less favourably than they do others unless they can justify their actions. In addition, employers are required to make 'reasonable adjustment' to the workplace or to working arrangements where this would help to overcome the practical effects of a disability. The requirement for reasonable adjustment includes modifying the recruitment and selection procedure if required: for example, providing application forms in large print or accepting applications by audio tape. The use of testing during the selection process may present a potential problem for people with disabilities, and reasonable adjustments might include modifying test materials, allowing a disabled candidate assistance during a test, or flexibility in the scoring and interpretation of test results (IRS, 1999a).

Discrimination against disabled people has been unlawful only since 1996. Before then, legislation relating to the treatment of disabled people at work was primarily to 'secure for the disabled their full share, within their capacity, of such employment as is ordinarily available' rather than preventing discrimination. It is therefore not surprising that disabled people still appear to be disadvantaged in the labour market. *Labour Force Survey* (ONS, 2002a) statistics show that:

- 1 in 5 people of working age in the UK has a long-term disability.
- 52% of disabled people are economically active compared with 79% for the whole working age population.
- Disabled people are more likely than non-disabled people to be unemployed (9% and 5% respectively) and are also more likely to have been unemployed for at least a year.

Despite these rather depressing statistics, it is possible to find examples of companies that have gone beyond compliance with the Disability Discrimination Act. In 2002 Lloyds TSB won a Business in the Community Award for its work on eliminating barriers for disabled employees and customers. The company is investing £26.2 million over six years and initiatives include targeted recruitment programmes; a thorough programme of 'reasonable adjustments' for employees; a career progression scheme for disabled employees; and the establishment of a national network of disabled employees, managers and advisers (IRS, 2002a).

Age discrimination

There is no current legislation prohibiting discrimination on grounds of age, although this is likely to change in 2006 in order to comply with the EU Equal Treatment Directive. In 1999 the UK government introduced a code of practice designed to promote age diversity in employment, arguing that 'to base employment decisions on preconceived ideas about age, rather than on skills and abilities, is to waste the talents of a large part of the population' (DfEE, 1999). The code covers six aspects of the employment cycle: recruitment, selection, promotion, training, redundancy and retirement. Specifically in terms of recruitment the code recommends employers to recruit on the basis of skills and abilities necessary to do the job rather than imposing age requirements or making stereotypical judgements based on the age of the applicants. Similarly, for selection the code recommends that employers select on merit by focusing on application form information relating to skills and abilities and on interview performance. The government claims that the elimination of unfair age discrimination will enable businesses to reap a number of benefits, including a greater ability to create a more flexible, multi-skilled workforce.

Employment of people with criminal records

People who have a criminal record are also likely to be disadvantaged in the workplace: current estimates suggest that it is at least eight times harder for a person with a criminal record to obtain employment than someone without (CIPD, 2002b). The Rehabilitation of Offenders Act (ROA) 1974 provides some protection for certain categories of ex-offenders, as it enables offenders who have received sentences of 30 months or less to have their convictions 'spent'. This means that, after a specified period, they can reply 'no' when asked if they have a criminal record. Although it is unlawful for an employer to discriminate on the grounds of a 'spent' conviction, the candidate who is discriminated against has no individual remedy (IDS, 1992). In addition, a wide range of jobs and professions are exempt from the provisions of this Act, including teachers, social workers, doctors, lawyers and accountants.

The potential for discriminating against people with a criminal record has increased with the establishment of the Criminal Records Bureau, set up as part of the 1997 Police Act. Once fully operational, the bureau will undertake three different levels of criminal record checks (CIPD, 2002b):

- *Basic disclosure*: shows current, unspent convictions.
- *Standard disclosure*: contains details of spent and unspent convictions and is available for posts exempt from the ROA, e.g. those involved with children or vulnerable adults and for certain professions such as law and accountancy.
- *Enhanced disclosure*: standard disclosure plus relevant, non-conviction information held on police records. This level of disclosure is only for posts involving regular care for, training, supervising or being in sole charge of children or vulnerable adults.

Government research (cited in IRS, 2002b) concludes that the availability of these checks will make it more difficult for people with criminal records to get a job, or may increase their chances of dismissal through the discovery of previously undisclosed convictions. In the light of this, a number of public bodies, including the CIPD, CBI and TUC, are trying to raise awareness of the business case for recruiting ex-offenders. One of the main supporting arguments is that in the continuing battle to recruit the best talent, employers simply cannot afford to exclude such a large group of people. It is estimated that more than 5 million people in the UK have convictions for crimes that could have involved imprisonment (CIPD, 2002b). At the same time, a number of government initiatives have been introduced to develop the skills of ex-offenders to increase their chances of employment. For example, the New Deal for Unemployed People targets ex-offenders and a partnership between the Department for Education and Skills and the Prison Service aims to raise prisoners' qualifications (Manocha, 2002).

● Professional codes of practice

The Chartered Institute of Personnel and Development has over 110 000 members, and is perceived as the body representing a large number of those involved in the recruitment and selection activities carried out in the UK. Members are expected to follow Institute policy and can in fact lose their membership for major breaches. Guidelines on various aspects of recruitment and selection are available, thus demonstrating that 'best practice' is both prescribed and expected. Other bodies, including the Equal Opportunities Commission and the Commission for Racial Equality, also produce codes of practice relating to recruitment and selection.

The internal context

The discussions above relate to external factors influencing recruitment and selection activities and go some way to explaining why we see both similarities and differences in recruitment activity. While legislation and codes of conduct would suggest a certain approach in the UK, differences in job/occupation being recruited, labour markets and skills availability might cause this approach to be modified. However, factors within organisations also affect the way recruitment and selection is handled. In this section we explore the extent to which recruitment and selection activities are aligned with overall business strategy; the impact of an organisation's approach to HRM, its financial position, the size of the organisation, its industrial sector, and its culture. This section also considers the approaches adopted by multinational corporations.

■ A strategic HRM approach?

The reasons for preferring certain approaches to the management of people received considerable attention in the 1980s as the influence of HRM grew. Within academic literature, normative models, based on a classical view of strategic decision-making, suggest that recruitment and selection policies should be aligned to a variety of organisa-

Figure 6.2 **Kochan and Barocci's model of recruitment, selection and staffing functions at different organisational stages**

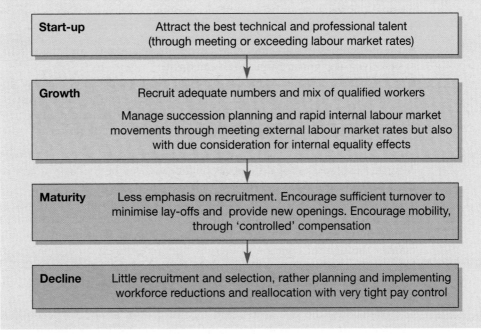

Start-up	Attract the best technical and professional talent (through meeting or exceeding labour market rates)
Growth	Recruit adequate numbers and mix of qualified workers. Manage succession planning and rapid internal labour market movements through meeting external labour market rates but also with due consideration for internal equality effects
Maturity	Less emphasis on recruitment. Encourage sufficient turnover to minimise lay-offs and provide new openings. Encourage mobility, through 'controlled' compensation
Decline	Little recruitment and selection, rather planning and implementing workforce reductions and reallocation with very tight pay control

Source: Adapted from Legge (1995: 105)

tional factors. Most illustrate the view that HR strategies and activities, including recruitment and selection, should be both vertically integrated with the organisation's position or preferred business strategy and horizontally integrated with each other. Parallel strategies in recruitment, selection, pay and development, in particular, are suggested. For more detailed discussions of strategic HRM see Chapter 2.

A discussion of the following models can be found in Legge (1995). The Kochan and Barocci model, outlined in Figure 6.2, argues that organisations have life cycles, and that recruitment, selection and staffing policies vary according to an organisation's perceived stage in the cycle. Other models attempt to link recruitment and selection to product strategies (e.g. Fombrun *et al.*, 1984) or overall business strategy (e.g. Miles and Snow, 1984).

Goold and Campbell (1987) consider that human resource strategies, including recruitment and selection, depend on whether an organisation's strategic management style can be classified as one of strategic planning (maximum competitive advantage through the pursuit of ambitious long-term goals, with subsequent investment in the long-term development of employees), financial control (with an emphasis on short-term utilisation of, and minimal investment in, employees), or strategic control (a balance of the two).

The US writers Schuler and Jackson (1996) argue that the organisation's competitive strategy (cost reduction, quality improvement and customer focus, innovation or speed of response) is crucial:

These different ways of competing are significant for managing human resources because they help determine needed employee behaviors. That is, for competitive strategies to be successfully implemented, employees have to behave in certain ways. And for employees to behave in certain ways, human resource practices need to be put in place that help ensure that those behaviors are explained, are possible, and are rewarded.   (p. 64)

The models serve to highlight possible reasons for variations in approach to recruitment and selection.

However, there is considerable debate about the extent to which a classical and rational approach to decision-making in organisations is either sensible or even exists. The problems include:

- the difficulties in agreeing what corporate strategy is, and the extent to which it is perceived as planned rather than emergent;
- a perception of critical time lag between 'strategic decision-making' and implementation of the policies deemed necessary to achieve corporate objectives;
- pressures to recruit and select in the short term via the external labour market to meet urgent needs, which may conflict with the chosen longer-term strategy of internal labour market development.

A further explanation of differences might therefore be the lack of adopting and pursuing a strategic approach to HRM within an organisation.

Schuler and Jackson (1996) highlighted an international insurance company where successful development had been through key competences in marketing, rapid response to new business areas, and creation of new products. Working in a 'highly decentralised manner through the creation of literally hundreds of new companies to attack new markets', it poached experts with the skills needed in the industry, through offering much higher pay. When the market dried up or tough competition arrived, these employees were 'let go' to return to the labour market.

Littlewoods, the UK stores and leisure group, aimed to become 'the UK's most admired consumer business' with equal opportunities in recruitment and selection necessary for the aim to be achieved. By reaching out to minority groups, they appear to have recruited a more effective workforce through 'fishing in the biggest possible pool', and to have increased profitability through widening the customer base (Pickard, 1999).

In an attempt to increase profitability and finance anticipated growth, the strategic objectives of many growing call centres in the UK at the turn of the century included reducing labour turnover (running at around 30 per cent per annum) and waste in recruitment and training costs (estimated at over £100 million) (Davis, 1999). Of several suggestions made, one approach that appeared to have considerable success was the introduction of more rigorous selection techniques (such as competence-based interviews, psychometric tests, work sample tests and simulations) to identify the 'ideal person' for call centre work (which industry research suggests is 'rule conscious, dutiful, conscientious, perfectionist and introverted') (Whitehead, 1999).

■ A soft or hard approach to HRM?

Whether or not an organisation is pursuing a strategic HRM approach to the management of people, organisations still have to choose whether to fill a vacancy through internal or external labour markets, or both.

Some organisations prefer to fill as many vacancies as possible with existing employees. The opportunities for promotion and transfer can be perceived to be highly motivational and attractive in terms of personal development, with critical skills retained in-house. Such an approach is consistent with 'soft' HRM, and has implications for human resource activities:

> Soft contracting implies an elaborate internal labour market, managed by a sophisticated HR function, with strong HR policies to govern relationships, pay, promotions, appraisal and development.
> (Storey and Sisson, 1993)

This 'soft' approach implies long-term commitment to investment in training and development and probably a rigorous appraisal scheme with an emphasis on identifying potential and on engendering commitment from employees. The organisation's expectations are of loyalty and retention from staff in return.

Alternatively, organisations pursuing a 'hard' HRM approach search for new employees in external labour markets. This may suggest a short-term focus, or an unwillingess or inability to invest in the human resource (see also Chapter 1). Within the UK the unwillingness may be a fear of engaging in costly development activities with staff, which could make them attractive to competitors. Alternatively, the organisation may be aware that the future may pose problems in offering long-term employability or promotion and not wish to raise unrealistic expectations.

Hard HRM may also be seen as an approach that brings new skills, ideas and experiences into an organisation as they are needed, rather than in expectation of need. In addition, rapidly changing competences may mean there is no time to develop the *required* competences in-house, which must be bought in from outside (Schuler and Jackson, 1996).

Financial position of organisation

The financial position of an organisation can impact significantly on recruitment and selection practices. 'Cash rich' organisations may find it easy to find agreement for the budgets required for a soft approach to recruitment and selection but a constrained financial situation can forestall the investment in training and development necessary to tap the potential of the internal labour market, with decision makers seeing training budgets as costly 'extras'. Financial constraints can push an organisation towards a 'hard' approach to HRM, but can limit the number and quality of recruitment and selection methods available for use. Assessment centres may be deemed appropriate in terms of their purpose and suitability, but remain unused because cheaper selection tools exist. In addition, tight budgets may limit the amount of cash available to fund higher reward packages expected by highest-quality applicants.

Size of organisation

While large organisations with over 500 employees comprise only 3 per cent of total workplaces, they account for nearly a third of all employees in the UK (Cully *et al.*, 1999) and 'size matters, all other things being equal, because larger units increase the complexity of the management task ... and the greater the need for rules and procedures to achieve consistency of behaviour on the part of individual managers' (Sisson and Marginson, 1995).

Within the largest organisations HR policy may be decided by a powerful central function, developed over time, with individual business or service units expected to maintain strict adherence to written policy and procedure. Small organisations (25–49 employees), on the other hand, account for over half of UK workplaces. Within them, well-developed personnel functions or recruitment and selection systems may not exist. Recruitment may be irregular, with a heavy reliance on informal methods of recruitment, especially if these have worked well previously. Responsibility for the recruitment activity, in particular, may be passed to enthusiastic 'amateurs' within the organisation, or outsourced to a third party. However 'best practice' models in recruitment and selection are available for small organisations via government agencies and publications (e.g. Jobcentre Plus and local Chambers of Commerce), for those that know of, and wish to use them.

> Small organisations are less likely to use certain recruitment methods (e.g. radio and tele-vision, national newspaper advertising, educational links or promotional events) because of the resources required ... tend to favour informal and less structured selection prac-tices, are less likely to get involved in assessment centres, check references, or carry out selection testing but are more likely to use CVs and letters of application.
>
> (CIPD, 2002a)

■ Industrial sector

'The output of a workplace, and the type of environment in which it operates, are likely to be significant determinants of how work is organised' (Cully *et al.*, 1999) and marked differences between public and private sector recruitment and selection practice is reported (CIPD, 2002a). WERS 4 data suggest that 72 per cent of all workplaces in the UK are in the private sector, with financial services, manufacturing, wholesale/retail, hotels and restaurants almost totally within private ownership (Cully *et al.*, 1999). The probable usage of third parties in recruitment appears high within this group, and the financial services and manufacturing industries are key users of executive search and selection. Financial services, information technology, customer care, engineering and design organisations are also predicted to grow the extent to which they outsource their processes, including HR, in the next five years (Crabb, 2003).

Conversely, public administration and education are firmly located in the public sector, where third-party recruitment has traditionally been very limited, with both recruitment and selection being maintained in-house by teams of professionals and spe-cialists. The use of application forms is more prevalent, as is the checking of references and skills, literacy and numeracy tests. Similarly, assessment centres and competency-based selection are more common in this sector (CIPD, 2002a). The public sector organisations tend to have policies which require all posts to be advertised externally (as well as internally) in the pursuit of equal opportunities.

■ Cultural differences between organisations

Differences exist even within similar industries, sectors and sized organisations. Several factors need to be considered: perhaps those who hold power in organisations have a strong preference for one particular recruitment method or have a dislike of any selec-tion method except one-to-one interviewing? Perhaps expectations of the processes are based on custom and practice built over many years, which may or may not include a well-established routine, backed by written policies, procedures and monitoring systems, and an insistence on formal training for individuals in recruitment and selection? Perhaps recruitment is seen as a marginal activity, undertaken as required in an ad hoc manner by some delegated employee or outsourced to a third party as and when need arises? The roles (and training) of those engaged in recruitment and selection may vary from one business unit to another, as may the extent to which divergence from organisa-tional policy is permitted (Cully *et al.*, 1999).

Regional differences influence methodology. Head offices tend to be in London and the South East, and here the use of headhunters is far greater (with more than 50 per cent using them), the use of job centres is lower, as is the use of local press in advertis-ing. In Northern Ireland strong anti-discrimination legislation leads to less use of informal recruitment methods or headhunters.

Multinational perspectives on recruitment and selection

Earlier in the chapter we discussed differences that may occur in national labour markets because of levels of education and government support for training. Other international differences can include attitudes regarding the sourcing of recruits (see also Chapter 15). In many areas of the world the main sources of recruits are relatives, friends or acquaintances of existing employees:

> in certain parts of Africa, where you studied is not as important as who you know, and the people you know may be more important than what you know.   (Langtry, 1994)

This nepotistic approach may challenge our Western view of employee relations and equal opportunities, although even within the UK it is possible to find examples of organisations that recruit predominantly via word of mouth:

> Much of the world still runs its organisations on a model of human relationships that is more akin to the traditional family than the functionally organised, formal, vision led type of organisation prevalent in the US and North West Europe.   (Hall, 1995: 22)

In some countries (such as Australia and Spain) a large proportion of organisations are in foreign ownership. In these companies recruitment and selection practices often reflect organisational rather than national values, especially where organisation culture is strong and recruitment and selection activity is carried out by those who are not host country nationals (Hollingshead and Leat, 1995). An examination of the WERS 4 data (Cully *et al.*, 1999) suggests that the growth of wholly foreign or partly foreign ownership in the UK is also on the increase. Private sector figures indicate that 6 per cent of workplaces were partly foreign owned and 13 per cent predominantly (that is, 51 per cent or more) or wholly foreign owned. The larger the workplace, the more likely it is to be foreign owned. The result of a growth in multinational presence may include different approaches to recruitment and selection, different competences required in the workforce, and alternative recruitment methods and selection techniques.

> Variations in employment relations policies and practices within foreign-owned workplaces may reflect the cultures and management styles imported into, or adapted to fit in with, British industrial relations.   (Cully *et al.*, 1999: 19)

Four distinct approaches have been identified for recruitment in multinational companies. They imply different patterns of control over the 'overseas' activities', and have varying impacts on career development for the employees concerned:

- *Ethnocentric*, where all key positions are filled by nationals of the parent company. This is a typical strategy employed in the early days of the new subsidiary, and suggests that power, decision-making and control are maintained at parent headquarters.
- *Polycentric*, where host country nationals fill all key positions in the subsidiary. Each subsidiary is treated as a distinct national entity, though key financial targets and investment decisions are controlled by parent headquarters, where key positions remain with parent country nationals.
- *Regiocentric*, where decisions will be made on a regional basis (the new subsidiary will be based in one country of the region), with due regard to the key factor for suc-

cess of the product or service. For example, if local knowledge is paramount, host country nationals will be recruited; if knowledge of established product is the key factor, parent country nationals are likely to be targets, though anyone from the geographical region would be considered.

● *Geocentric*, where the 'best people' are recruited regardless of nationality for all parent and subsidiary positions: for example, a national of a country in which neither the parent nor subsidiary is based could be considered. This results in a thoroughly international board and senior management, and is still relatively uncommon.

Increased internationalisation of business generates other issues of relevance when considering recruitment and selection. Hendry (1995) identifies an increasing number of managers and professionals affected by international assignments, leading to increased importance of managing international careers. PriceWaterhouseCoopers report growth of over 40 per cent in expatriate, especially short-term, assignments throughout the world between 1997 and 1999 (PriceWaterhouseCoopers, 1999). Competence in language and technical skills are deemed to be key requirements, and many organisations provide language training for potential recruits. International awareness has been found useful in successful placements, as has an individual's ability to change his or her personal behaviour to fit with cultural requirements. Without international experience, opportunities for individuals to develop career paths appear increasingly limited in multinational organisations.

Sparrow (1999) concludes, however, that there are 'no simple recipes that can be followed when selecting for international assignments. Rather there are choices to be made and opportunities to be pursued' (p. 40). He identifies three main resourcing philosophies. The first is a traditional, predictive approach, using psychometrics and competence frameworks to assess a person's suitability; the second is a risk assessment approach, which concentrates on cultural adaptability. His third philosophy involves reversing the process, and designing the assignment to match the skills of the manager. Specific training and preparation become vitally important to ensure that such relocation is effective, and that high levels of expatriate failure are avoided. Likely interventions include pre-move visits to the proposed host country (often with family members), language and cross-cultural training for managers and families, and briefing by both host country and in-house representatives.

Developments in the systematic approach to recruitment and selection

The key stages of a systematic approach can be summarised as: defining the vacancy, attracting applicants, assessing candidates, and making the final decision. Another way of expressing this is as a series of questions:

● Who do we want?
● How can we attract them?
● How can we identify them?
● How do we know we have got it right?

In addition, a supplementary question that is increasingly asked is:

● Who should be involved in the process?

Here we describe the main components of each stage, and indicate ways in which recruitment and selection activities are changing to meet current and future demands.

Who do we want?

● Authorisation

Securing authorisation ensures that the need to start the recruitment process is agreed by management as being compatible with the organisational/departmental objectives: that is, necessary, timely and cost-effective. At the same time, it provides an opportunity to consider options other than recruitment and selection, for example:

- to debate the potential for restructuring workloads/departments and redeploying existing staff;
- to delay or eliminate expenditure on staffing and recruitment budgets.

Neither of these opportunities is risk-free: redeployment of surplus staff may mean that the incoming jobholder is not necessarily the 'best person for the job' and result in management resentment against the system; inadequately thought-through restructuring or short-term cost-saving measures may damage the department and organisation in the long term, as opportunities fail to be exploited for lack of suitable human resources.

These decisions may be made on an operational or strategic basis. The latter emphasises the contribution of effective staffing levels to the achievement of organisational goals and may include long-term human resource development (HRD) objectives and succession planning alongside the immediate requirement to fill a post.

● Defining the job and the person

The traditional approach involves writing a comprehensive job description of the job to be filled. This enables the recruiter to know exactly what the purpose, duties and responsibilities of the vacant position will be and its location within the organisation structure. The next step involves drawing up a person specification that is based on the job description, and which identifies the personal characteristics required to perform the job adequately. Characteristics are usually described within a framework consisting of a number of broad headings. Two frequently cited frameworks are the seven-point plan (Rodger, 1952) and the five-fold grading system (Munro Fraser, 1954), illustrated in Table 6.5. Both frameworks are somewhat dated now, and some headings can appear to be potentially discriminatory (e.g. physical make-up and circumstances), but nevertheless they continue to form the basis of many person specifications in current use. It is

Table 6.5 **Person specification frameworks**

Rodger (1952)	**Munro Fraser (1954)**
Physical make-up: health, appearance, bearing and speech	*Impact on others*: physical make-up, appearance, speech and manner
Attainments: education, qualifications, experience	*Acquired qualifications*: education, vocational training, work experience
General intelligence: intellectual capacity	*Innate abilities*: quickness of comprehension and aptitude for learning
Special aptitudes: mechanical, manual dexterity, facility in use of words and figures	*Motivation*: individual goals, consistency and determination in following them up, success rate
Interests: intellectual, practical, constructional, physically active, social, artistic	*Adjustment*: emotional stability, ability to stand up to stress and ability to get on with people
Disposition: acceptability, influence over others, steadiness, dependability, self-reliance	
Circumstances: any special demands of the job, such as ability to work unsocial hours, travel abroad	

Source: ACAS (1983)

common to differentiate between requirements that are essential to the job and those that are merely desirable.

The person specification is a vital part of the recruitment and selection process as it can form the basis of the recruitment advertisement, it can help determine the most effective selection methods and, if applied correctly, can ensure that selection decisions are based on sound, justifiable criteria. However, the compilation of a person specification needs to be handled with care. Predetermined criteria can contribute to effective recruitment and selection only if full consideration has been given to the necessity and fairness of all the requirements. Preconceived or entrenched attitudes, prejudices and assumptions can lead, consciously or unconsciously, to requirements that are less job-related than aimed at meeting the assumed needs of customers, colleagues or the established culture of the organisation. Examples of this might include insistence on a British education, unnecessary age restrictions, or sex role stereotyping.

The job-based approach to recruitment and selection can be inflexible in a number of ways. For example, the job description may fail to reflect potential changes in the key tasks or the list of duties and responsibilities may be too constraining, especially where teamworking is introduced. This concentration on a specific job and its place in a bureaucratic structure may be detrimental to the development of the skills and aptitudes needed for the long-term benefit of the organisation. In order to accommodate the need for greater flexibility and the desire to encourage working 'beyond contract', some organisations have replaced traditional job descriptions with more generic and concise job profiles, consisting of a list of 'bullet points' or accountability statements.

The recognition that jobs can be subject to frequent change can also reduce the importance of the job description and increase the relative importance of getting the 'right' person. This approach has the potential for greater flexibility as it enables organisations to focus 'more on the qualities of the jobholder and the person's potential suitability for other duties as jobs change' than on the job itself (IRS, 1999b). Findings from the Workplace Employee Relations Survey (Cully *et al.*, 1999: 60–61) show that skills, experience and motivation were the most common selection criteria used by employers. Recent research into call centre recruitment and selection found that a positive attitude was more important in candidates than their ability to use a keyboard (Callaghan and Thompson, 2002).

In many instances, a combination of the job-oriented and person-oriented approaches may be adopted, in order to recruit people who can not only do the job but also contribute to the wider business goals of the organisation. One way to achieve this is via the use of competencies. The term has many definitions but most refer to 'the work-related personal attributes, knowledge, experience, skills and values that a person draws on to perform their work well' (Roberts, 1997: 6). Competency-based recruitment and selection involves the identification of a set of competencies that are seen as important across the organisation, such as planning and organising, managing relationships, gathering and analysing information, and decision-making. Each competency can then be divided into a number of different levels, and these can be matched to the requirements of a particular job.

Feltham (in Boam and Sparrow 1992) argues that a competency-based approach can contribute to the effectiveness of recruitment and selection in three main ways:

● the process of competency analysis helps an organisation to identify what it needs from its human resources and to specify the part that selection and recruitment can play;
● the implementation of competency-based recruitment and selection systems results in a number of direct practical benefits; and
● where systems are linked to competencies, aspects of fairness, effectiveness and validity become amenable to evaluation. These competence frameworks can be used for more than just recruitment and selection.

The application of the same competencey framework to all areas of HRM can ensure consistency and aid vertical and horizontal integration (for further details on competencies and competency frameworks, see Whiddett and Hollyforde, 1999).

Occasionally competencies can be identified at national levels. For example, in answer to calls for increased effectiveness of non-executive directors in the wake of corporate scandals in the USA and UK, Derek Higgs, appointed to lead an independent review of the role and effectiveness of non-executive directors in the UK, identified a set of competencies to be assessed via assessment centres, psychological testing and competency-based interviews, to ensure that appropriate non-executive directors make up at least half of organisations' boards (Dulewicz, 2003).

What a competency-based approach may discover is that recruitment is not always the answer. There is usually a variety of strategies for achieving a particular competency mix and no 'right' solutions. For example, if specialist skills are scarce, an organisation may choose to replace the skills with new technology, train existing staff, or hire specialist consultants when needed in preference to employment of permanent staff (Feltham, 1992).

Where recruitment and selection is deemed appropriate, a competency-based approach achieves a visible set of agreed standards which can form the basis of systematic, fair and consistent decision-making.

● Agree terms and conditions

Decisions on terms and conditions are made at various points in the process. Some of these are often not negotiated (e.g. hours, reward) until the final selection stages. There is a case for deciding the salary band (if not the specific amount) and other elements of the reward package before attracting candidates. This can take time (for example, if the position has to be processed through a job evaluation exercise), but potential candidates may fail to apply without some indication of the reward offered, as this often gives an indication of the level and status of the position.

The alternative is to wait and see who applies and then negotiate terms and conditions with the favoured candidate. This is a less restrictive approach, and may provide a better chance of employing high-calibre people who match the long-term aims of the organisation. However, it can be problematic on a number of grounds: the organisation may project a poor image if it appears to be unsure of what is on offer or may damage its reputation by being perceived to pay only what it can get away with. Furthermore, this reactive approach could lead to breaches of equal pay legislation. In practice, the approach adopted is likely to be determined by the organisation's reward strategy, including the relative importance of internal pay equity and external competitiveness and the emphasis on individual and collective pay-setting.

Stop and think

What experiences and skills do you possess? What are your expectations of salary? To what extent are you confident that there is harmony between your two answers when considered against factors currently influencing your labour market?

■ How do we attract them?

the actual channels or vehicles used to attract candidates . . . seem to influence whether the right kinds of applicants are encouraged to apply, and to persist in their application.

(Iles and Salaman, 1995: 211)

● Recruitment methods

Organisations can choose from a wide variety of methods, including the use of:

● informal personal contacts, such as existing employees, informal grapevine (word of mouth) and speculative applications;
● formal personal contacts, such as careers fairs, open days and leaflet drops;
● notice boards, accessible by current staff or the general public;
● advertising, including local and national press, specialist publications, radio and TV, and the Internet;
● external assistance, including job centres, careers service, employment agencies and 'head-hunters'.

The relative popularity of these different methods are shown in Table 6.6.

Table 6.6 **Percentage of organisations using particular recruitment methods**

Local newspaper advertisements	87	National newspaper advertisements	53
Electronic methods (any)	75	Corporate website	52
Specialist journals/trade press	66	Links with education	44
Commercial employment agencies	64	Headhunters	30
Job centres	62	Promotional events/fairs	30
Word of mouth	62	Job board	29
Speculative applications	55	Radio/TV	10

Number of employers in survey = 747.
Source: CIPD (2002a : 12)

Decisions about the most appropriate method (or methods, as many organisations will use more than one) are likely to be influenced by the level of the vacancy and its importance within the organisation. The CIPD survey (2002a) found that recruitment for managerial and professional posts was most likely to be via advertisements in specialist journals and the national press, whereas the local press was more popular for clerical and manual vacancies. Other factors to be taken into account when choosing the most appropriate method include the resources available within the organisation (in terms of personnel and finance), the perceived target groups, and the organisation's stance on internal versus external recruitment. Human resource management literature emphasises the need to have well-developed internal labour market arrangements for promotion, training and career development, which would suggest that many openings can and should be filled internally (Beaumont, 1993). However, a number of organisations, particularly those in the public sector, have policies that require the majority of posts to be advertised externally.

● Design of advertisements

The most popular formal recruitment method continues to be press advertising. Good communication from the employer to potential applicants requires thought and skill, and many organisations use the services of a recruitment agency for the design of the advertisement and advice on the most effective media. The aim of the advertisement is to attract only suitable applicants, and therefore it should discourage those who do not possess the necessary attributes while, at the same time, retaining and encouraging the interest of those with potential to be suitable. Taylor (2002) suggests a number of key decisions faced by recruiters in the style and wording of advertisements:

● Wide trawls or wide nets – i.e. whether the advert aims to attract a wide range of candidates or only those with very specific qualities. For example, an advertisement for the Royal Marines currently showing in UK cinemas claims that 99 per cent of candidates won't make it.

- Realistic or positive – in terms of the language used and information provided on the job and the organisation.
- Corporate image or specific job – the emphasis most likely to appeal to the target audience can depend on a number of factors, e.g. whether the organisation is a household name or has a good reputation in the area, or whether the type of job is well known or highly sought-after.
- Precise vs. vague information – variations are especially apparent in relation to salary information: some organisations (particularly in the public sector) provide very precise information, e.g. 'salary up to £23 889 dependent on qualifications and experience (pay award pending)', whereas others include little more than 'competitive salary'.

● Electronic recruitment

Over recent years there has been a growth in the use of electronic methods by both recruiters and job hunters. Overall, 75 per cent of employers now use some form of electronic recruitment, especially e-mail response to enquiries and the acceptance of CVs sent by e-mail. Around half of employers post vacancies on their corporate website and about a third use the Internet to provide background information for candidates. A fifth of organisations accept completed application forms by e-mail (CIPD, 2002c).

The impact of the growth of electronic recruitment methods is very variable depending on whether they are used to supplement or replace more traditional approaches. Corporate and external websites can be used to advertise vacancies in addition to press adverts, while the handling of enquiries and applications via e-mail can lead to a duplication of activity (electronic as well as paper-based systems) rather than a replacement of one system with another. Alternatively, the impact may be more substantial and can alter the process up to and including the shortlisting stage, as illustrated in Table 6.7.

Table 6.7 Traditional versus Internet-based recruitment

Step	Traditional	Internet
1	A job vacancy is advertised in the press	A job vacancy is advertised on the Internet
2	A job seeker writes or telephones for more details and/or an application form	All the company and job details are on the website together with an online application form
3	A job seeker returns the application form and/or CV by post	A job seeker returns the completed application form electronically
4	Personnel review the written application forms or CVs	Specialised computer software reviews the application forms for an initial match with the organisation's requirements

Source: CIPD (2002c)

Neither approach is exclusive and activities can be combined at almost any stage. For example, a press advertisement may direct readers to a website providing further information or a corporate website may require applicants to request an application form via e-mail or telephone that will then be processed manually (CIPD, 2002c).

> **Stop and think**
>
> What are the key advantages and disadvantages of using the Internet for recruitment?

The key advantages of Internet-based recruitment (CIPD, 2002c) include:

- a shorter recruitment cycle time;
- it can reduce costs if used instead of more expensive methods;
- it can reach a wider range of applicants;
- organisations can display a more up-to-date image;
- it provides global coverage 24/7.

The key disadvantages (CIPD, 2002c) are:

- It is most effective when used as part of an integrated recruitment process and many organisations currently lack the resources and expertise to achieve this.
- It is not yet the first choice for most job seekers.
- Not all potential applicants have access to the Internet, so using it alongside press advertising might increase costs.
- It can lead to more unsuitable applications being received which have to be screened out, thus increasing costs.

● Recruitment documentation

The response to applicants should indicate the overall image that the organisation wishes to project. Some organisations prepare a package of documents, which may include the job description, the person specification, information about the organisation, the equal opportunities policy, the rewards package available, and possible future prospects. Some give candidates the opportunity to discuss the position with an organisational representative on an informal basis. This allows the candidate to withdraw from the process with the minimum activity and cost to the organisation. Much relevant information can now be supplied via the Internet: for example, BT uses a question and answer approach to supply information on a wide rage of issues, including salary and benefits, development opportunities and career prospects (IRS, 2002c).

The design of application forms can vary considerably, but the traditional approach tends to concentrate on finding out about qualifications and work history, and usually includes a section in which candidates are encouraged to 'sell' their potential contribution to the organisation. A more recent development is the adoption of a competency-based focus, requiring candidates to answer a series of questions in which they describe how they have dealt with specific incidents such as solving a difficult problem, or demonstrating leadership skills. Some organisations, particularly in the retail sector, include a short questionnaire in which applicants are asked to indicate their preferred way of working.

A variant on the traditional application form, 'biodata' (short for biographical data), may also be used. Forms usually consist of a series of multiple-choice questions that are partly factual (e.g. number of brothers and sisters, position in the family) and partly about attitudes, values and preferences (Sadler and Milmer, 1993). The results are then compared against an 'ideal' profile, which has been compiled by identifying the competencies that differentiate between effective and non-effective job performance in existing employees. Biodata questionnaires are costly to develop and need to be designed separately for each job (Taylor, 2002). There are also problems with potential discrimination and intrusion into privacy, depending on the information that is sought. For these reasons, biodata is used by only a small number of employers.

Stop and think

How much time does it take an individual to obtain details about a post, consider the details received and complete an application which attempts to match the requirements of the post against that individual's experiences and qualifications?

Why is it important for an organisation to be aware of the answers to the above question?

How do we identify them?

The stages described above constitute recruitment, and are primarily concerned with generating a sufficient pool of applicants. The focus now shifts to selection, and the next stages concentrate on assessing the suitability of candidates.

Shortlisting

It is extremely unlikely that all job applicants will meet the necessary criteria, and so the initial step in selection is categorising candidates as probable, possible or unsuitable. This should be done by comparing the information provided on the application form or CV with the predetermined selection criteria. The criteria may either be explicit (detailed on the person specification) or implicit (only in the mind of the person doing the shortlisting). However, this latter approach is potentially discriminatory, and would provide no defence if an organisation was challenged on the grounds of unlawful discrimination (see discussion on legislative requirements earlier in this chapter). Potentially suitable candidates will continue to the next stage of the selection process. CIPD guidelines state that unsuccessful candidates should be informed as soon as possible. In practice, written notification of rejection is increasingly less common, and many application forms warn candidates that if they have not had a response by a set date they can assume they have been unsuccessful.

The increased emphasis on personal characteristics rather than job demands may result in some changes to the way shortlisting is undertaken. For example, the use of biodata can provide a clearer focus than more traditional methods, as 'selectors can concentrate solely on those areas of the form found in the biodata validation exercise to be particularly relevant to the prediction of effective performance in the job concerned' (IRS, 1994). Other developments chiefly reflect a desire to reduce the time and effort involved in shortlisting from large numbers of applicants. One option is to encourage unsuitable candidates to self-select themselves out of the process. Advances in technology allow for the provision of self-selection questionnaires and feedback on the answers on corporate websites. A variant on this is to use 'killer' questions; these are asked at certain stages of an online application process and the wrong answer will terminate the application at that point (IRS, 2003). Another option is to use a software package that compares CVs with the selection criteria and separates the applications that match the criteria from those that do not. This has the advantage of removing some of the subjectivity inherent in human shortlisting, but does rely on the selection criteria being correctly identified in the first instance. It can also reject good candidates who have not used the right keywords so needs to be handled with caution. A third option is to reduce large numbers of applicants via random selection. Although there is concern that this may operate against equal opportunities, it is also claimed that 'randomised selection may produce a better shortlist than one based on human intervention where the wrong selection criteria are used consistently or where the correct selection criteria are applied inconsistently' (IRS, 1994: 6).

Selection techniques

Various selection techniques are available, and a selection procedure will frequently involve the use of more than one. The most popular techniques are outlined here, and their validity and effectiveness are discussed later in the chapter.

Interviews

Interviewing is universally popular as a selection tool. Torrington *et al.* (2002: 242) describe an interview as 'a controlled conversation with a purpose', but this broad definition encompasses a wide diversity of practice. Differences can include both the number of interviewers and the number of interview stages. Over the years interviews have received a relatively bad press as being overly subjective, prone to interviewer bias, and therefore unreliable predictors of future performance. Such criticisms are levelled particularly at unstructured interviews, and in response to this, developments have focused on more formally structuring the interview or supplementing the interview with less subjective selection tools such as psychometric tests and work sampling.

There are different types of structured interview, but they have a number of common features (Anderson and Shackleton, 1993: 72):

- The interaction is standardised as much as possible.
- All candidates are asked the same series of questions.
- Replies are rated by the interviewer on preformatted rating scales.
- Dimensions for rating are derived from critical aspects of on-the-job behaviour.

The two most popular structured interview techniques are behavioural and situational interviews. Both use critical incident job analysis to determine aspects of job behaviour that distinguish between effective and ineffective performance (Anderson and Shackleton, 1993). The difference between them is that in behavioural interviews the questions focus on past behaviour (for example, 'Can you give an example of when you have had to deal with a difficult person? What did you do?'), whereas situational interviews use hypothetical questions ('What would you do if you had to deal with a team member who was uncooperative?').

Decisions about the number of interviewers, the type of interview and the number of interview stages are likely to take account of the seniority and nature of the post and the organisation's attitude towards equal opportunities.

ACTIVITY

Imagine you are responsible for selecting operators to work in a call centre. Prepare a set of behavioural questions suitable for the interview. You are looking for evidence of strong social skills, e.g. good verbal communication, positive attitude, good sense of humour, energy and enthusiasm; and good technical skills, e.g. numeracy and keyboard skills.

Test out these questions on friends and colleagues to assess their effectiveness. What do you see as the key strengths and weaknesses of this approach?

Telephone interviewing

Some organisations are now using telephone interviews as part of their selection procedure, particularly for jobs that involve a lot of telephone work, such as call centre operators. Telephone interviews are usually used as part of the shortlisting process rather than to replace the face-to-face selection interview. For example, a short, highly structured telephone interview can be used to identify and discount unsuitable applicants or a longer more in-depth approach can be used to shortlist candidates for a face-to-face interview, particularly for more senior posts (CIPD, 2001a). Advances in technology continue to facilitate other forms of 'remote' interviewing, for example by video link or via the Internet, but take-up is still relatively low.

Stop and think

What are the main benefits and drawbacks of telephone interviews?

CIPD (2001a) and IRS (2002d) report a number of benefits and drawbacks to telephone interviewing, including:

- They can be quicker to arrange and conduct than more conventional methods.
- They can be cost-effective as an initial screen.

- They can maintain a degree of confidentiality about the post as these details will only be provided once initial screening is complete (particularly useful for senior posts).
- They provide an ideal way to assess a candidate's telephone manner.
- There are fewer interpersonal distractions.
- They provide less opportunity to discriminate on grounds of race, disability, age or other non-job-related factors.
- The lack of non-verbal communication (which accounts for 60 per cent of total interpersonal communication).
- Interviewers may be biased against people with a particular accent or manner.

Tests

'Testing is essentially an attempt to achieve objectivity, or, to put it more accurately, to reduce subjectivity in selection decision-making' (Lewis, 1985: 157). The types of test used for selection are ability and aptitude tests, intelligence tests and personality questionnaires. Ability tests (such as typing tests) are concerned with skills and abilities already acquired by an individual, whereas aptitude tests (such as verbal reasoning tests or numerical aptitude) focus on an individual's potential to undertake specific tasks. Intelligence tests can give an indication of overall mental capacity, and have been used for selection purposes for some considerable time. Personality questionnaires allow quantification of characteristics that are important to job performance and difficult to measure by other methods (Lewis, 1985). The debate about the value of personality tests is ongoing, and centres around lack of agreement on four key issues (Taylor, 2002):

- the extent to which personality is measurable;
- the extent to which personality remains stable over time and across different situations;
- the extent to which certain personality characteristics can be identified as being necessary or desirable for a particular job;
- the extent to which completion of a questionnaire can provide sufficient information about an individual's personality to make meaningful inferences about their suitability for a job.

The CIPD survey (2002a: 15) reports widespread use of psychometric testing: 54 per cent of employers use tests of specific skills and 37 per cent use tests of literacy and/or numeracy. More than a third use personality questionnaires. Tests have the benefit of providing objective measurement of individual characteristics, but they must be chosen with care. Armstrong (2001) lists four characteristics of a good test:

- It is a *sensitive* measuring instrument which discriminates well between subjects.
- It has been *standardised* on a representative and sizeable sample of the population for which it is intended so that any individual's score can be interpreted in relation to others.
- It is *reliable* in the sense that it always measures the same thing. A test aimed at measuring a particular characteristic should measure the same characteristic when applied to different people at the same time, or to the same person at different times.
- It is *valid* in the sense that it measures the characteristic which the test is intended to measure. Thus, an intelligence test should measure intelligence and not simply verbal facility. (Armstrong, 2001: 473)

One recent development has been the growth of interest in online testing. Currently, fewer than 2 per cent of organisations administer selection tests online (CIPD, 2002a) but an IRS survey (IRS, 2002e) reports that 8 per cent are planning to introduce online testing in the future. Online testing has the potential to reduce delivery costs, thus making testing more affordable for lower-paid jobs. However, there are also some potential disadvantages, including lack of control of the environment in which the test takes place, problems verifying candidates' identity and the need for candidates (under data protection legislation) to have access to any personal information stored about them (IRS, 2002e).

Assessment centres

An assessment centre is not a place but rather a process that 'consists of a small group of participants who undertake a series of tests and exercises under observation, with a view to the assessment of their skills and competencies, their suitability for particular roles and their potential for development' (Fowler, 1992). There are a number of defining characteristics of an assessment centre:

- A variety of individual and group assessment techniques are used, at least one of which is a work simulation.
- Multiple assessors are used (frequently the ratio is one assessor per two candidates). These assessors should have received training prior to participating in the centre.
- Selection decisions are based on pooled information from assessors and techniques.
- Job analysis is used to identify the behaviours and characteristics to be measured by the assessment centre.

Assessment centres are used by just over a quarter of organisations (CIPD, 2002a). The assessment centre process allows organisations to observe candidate behaviour in a work-related setting; and the combination of techniques used helps to improve the consistency and objectivity of the selection process. The use of such a sophisticated technique, if handled well, can also help the organisation to display a positive image to potential candidates. The drawbacks primarily relate to the costs and resources required. For this reason, assessment centres are most likely to be used in public sector organisations and by larger private sector employers. A number of recent trends have been identified in the design and delivery of assessment centres (IRS, 2002f), including: more emphasis on the integration of exercises (i.e. using the same business context and same characters in different exercises); a clearer link between exercises and work content; more candidate friendly (i.e. better briefing on how people will be assessed, more comprehensive feedback); and a focus on core values to identify candidates who will contribute most in rapidly changing circumstances.

Job simulation/work sampling

A key component of an assessment centre is the job simulation exercise, which is designed to be an accurate representation of performance in the job itself. Candidates are placed in situations that they are likely to face if selected: examples include in-tray exercises and role-play interviews.

An extension of job simulation is work sampling: that is, giving the candidate the opportunity to perform in the role for a specified length of time. An example of this is given in the Pret à Manger box on page 220.

References

These are used to obtain additional information about candidates from third parties such as previous employers, academic tutors, colleagues or acquaintances. The accuracy of the information is variable; Armstrong (2001) suggests that factual information (e.g. nature of previous job, time in employment, reason for leaving, salary, academic achievement) is essential, but opinions about character and suitability are less reliable. He goes on to say that 'personal referees are, of course, entirely useless. All they prove is that the applicant has at least one or two friends' (p. 408).

References can be used at different stages in the selection process: some organisations use them only to confirm details of the chosen candidate after the position has been offered, whereas others will request references for all shortlisted candidates prior to interview. The format may also vary, with some organisations requesting verbal references by telephone and others requiring written references. In either case, organisations may require referees to answer specific structured questions or provide some general comments on the candidate's performance and suitability. The most popular types of information requested by employers include absence record, opinion of candidate's personality and suitability for the vacancy, work history, punctuality and disciplinary record (IRS, 2002a: 752). Many employers consider references to be 'only marginally effective' (Industrial Society, 1994), yet there is little doubt that they remain a popular component of the selection process, with approximately three-quarters of respondents to the CIPD (2002a) survey using them.

Other methods

Two of the more unconventional and controversial selection tools include graphology and astrology. Graphology is based on the idea that handwriting analysis can reveal personal traits and characteristics. Although it is not widely used in the UK, its effectiveness as a selection tool continues to be the subject of considerable debate. Having reviewed the available data on graphology, the CIPD concludes that 'the evidence in favour is inconclusive, anecdotal and therefore prone to bias and misinterpretation' (CIPD, 2001b). If anything, astrology is even more controversial, and few organisations appear to use it in selection decisions.

● Factors influencing choice of selection techniques

What determines the choice of different techniques? One could reasonably assume that a key factor in determining the type of method would be its ability to predict who is suitable and unsuitable for the position. In other words, whatever technique is used, people who do well should be capable of doing the job and people who do badly should not.

Accuracy

'None of the techniques, irrespective of how well they are designed and administered, is capable of producing perfect selection decisions that predict with certainty who is or who is not bound to be a good performer in a particular role' (Marchington and Wilkinson, 1996: 119). Figure 6.3 shows the accuracy of selection methods measured on the correlation coefficient between predicted and actual job performance, with zero for chance prediction and 1.0 for perfect prediction.

The increased use of more accurate methods such as assessment centres and selection testing can help to improve the effectiveness of the selection process. However, findings from the CIPD survey (2002a) show that assessment centres are considered to be the most influential selection method in fewer than 5 per cent of organisations. In contrast, 33 per cent of organisations consider interviews to be the most important selection method. Nevertheless, doubts about accuracy appear to have encouraged employers to adopt more structured interview formats or supplement the interview with other selection methods such as tests or work simulation.

Statistics on the accuracy of different types of selection techniques mask wide variations within each technique. Two key criteria to be considered are reliability and validity. Reliability generally relates to the ability of a selection technique to produce consistent results over time or among different people, whereas validity relates to the extent to which the technique is able to measure what it is intended to measure. These have already been discussed in relation to selection testing, but can be applied to other techniques too. For example, the reliability of interviews can vary if interviewers have differing levels of interviewing skills or different perceptions of the selection criteria. Reliability can also vary when just one person is involved in interviewing, as the conduct

| Figure 6.3 | The predictive accuracy of selection methods |

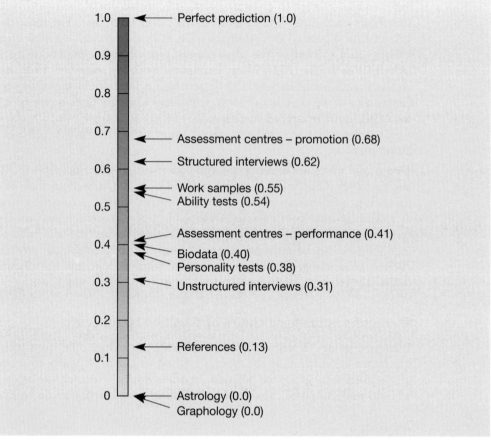

Source: Adapted from Anderson and Shackleton (1993)

of the interview can be affected by the timing of the interview and by how many interviews have been conducted already.

In assessment centres, the effectiveness of the exercises in predicting job performance is dependent on the extent to which they represent the performance content and competency requirements of the job they are designed to sample. In practice, the standard of assessment centres can vary from organisation to organisation:

> Because properly designed and applied ACs work well, it does not mean that anything set up and run with the same name is equally good. A lot of so-called ACs in the UK use badly thought-out exercises and inadequately trained assessors; they probably achieve little other than to alienate candidates, who are usually quick to spot their shortcomings.
>
> (Fletcher, 1993: 46)

The same can be said of tests that are relevant only if the behaviours and attitudes they measure are those necessary for effective job performance. Additional problems are also associated with the use of tests. Both the British Psychological Society (BPS) and the CIPD have issued codes of practice on the use of tests, which stress that everyone responsible for the application of tests, which includes evaluation, interpretation and feedback, should be trained to at least the level of competence recommended by the BPS (CIPD, 2001c). The guidelines also make it clear that 'the results of a single test should not be used as the sole basis for decision-making' (IPD, 1997). However, a survey conducted by Newell and Shackleton (1993) found that, although companies used trained personnel to administer tests, the majority did not always give feedback of results to candidates, and some were using the tests to make definitive judgements about people.

Level of vacancy

IRS (1997: 16) argues that the type of job is 'the most significant influence on the choice of selection methods for any one vacancy'. Assessment centres, in particular, are more likely to be used for managerial and graduate posts. This may indicate an organisation's willingness to invest more heavily in future managers than in other parts of the workforce, but may also be due to candidate expectations and the organisation's need to attract the highest-quality applicants. A growing number of organisations have started to use assessment centre techniques for non-managerial appointments but the process tends to be shorter and therefore cheaper. For example, easyJet holds half-day assessment centres for cabin crew (IDS, 2002).

Cost of selection techniques

There is no doubt that recruitment and selection can be costly activities, and the costs incurred by some selection techniques can make them prohibitive for all but a few 'key' vacancies in an organisation. For example, assessment centres require considerable investment of resources and are particularly demanding in terms of the time commitment required from assessors (IDS, 2002). However, in deciding on the most cost-effective methods, the 'up-front' costs need to be balanced against the costs of wrong decisions, which may include costs associated with labour turnover owing to lack of ability. Jaffee and Cohen (cited in Appelbaum et al., 1989: 60) suggest that consideration should include some or all of the following:

● the start-up time required by a replacement for the jobholder;
● the downtime associated with the jobholder changing jobs internally or externally;
● training and/or retraining for the replacement and the jobholder;
● relocation expenses;
● the shortfall in productivity between an effective and ineffective jobholder;
● the psychological impact on the 'failed' jobholder and the morale of others in the department.

Custom and practice

A possible explanation for the continued use of interviews is the simple fact that people are familiar with them. Although, at an academic level, the general consensus is that interviews are unreliable, invalid and provide ample opportunity for personal prejudice (Herriot, 1989), at a practical level many interviewers feel that they are good judges of people and can make effective selection decisions, and most of us would probably feel unhappy in starting a job without undergoing some form of face-to-face meeting with our prospective employer.

ACTIVITY The CIPD (2003) suggests that key aims of assessment centres are to select, recruit and impress candidates. Evaluate the impact of the following 'real' experiences during the recruitment and selection process for **impression**:

● Professionally handled recruitment and selection process for specialist position. Feedback after unsuccessful interview was in relation to lack of experience which hadn't been explicit on the person specification.

● Applicant received notification that application form was not being considered for short listing ... it had taken nine days from posting to reach the administrator concerned.

- Applicant participates in full day of assessment testing for one of ten national irregular and part-time posts.

- Applicant travels 100+ miles for half-hour-long interview. No expenses or refreshments are offered.

- Applicant unable to establish whether e-mail application to national organisation has actually been received. Closing date passes and no communication several months later.

- Applicant informed of safe receipt of application and subsequently informed in writing that 'had not been successful'.

- Applicant offered two, 2-day familiarisation visits, a 2-day pre-selection visit, a 3-day assessment centre and a 2-day pre-employment induction (expenses are paid throughout).

- Applicant (making initial enquiry as to whether any positions for which he might be considered) offered specialist work abroad, followed up by e-mail confirmation and a 2-day induction, which included completing application form.

- Applicant has initial discussion followed by formal application, interview, offer and acceptance. Subsequent role fails to meet applicant's expectations because of economic slowdown.

Making the decision

The aim of the overall recruitment and selection process is to provide enough information to enable recruiters to differentiate between those who can do the job and those who can't. The prescriptive approach stresses that the final decision should involve measuring each candidate against the selection criteria defined in the person specification and not against each other (Torrington *et al.*, 2002). The combination of a number of different selection methods can enhance the quantity and quality of information about each candidate, although Anderson and Shackleton (1993) warn of the dangers of information overload in selection.

Even the decision-making process might be affected by the contemporary situation and employers' increased desire for flexibility. Sparrow and Hiltrop (1994) suggest that the combination of technological change, low economic growth, low voluntary turnover rates and an increasingly legislated environment may lead to new employees having to perform a series of jobs over time with changes not necessarily linked to promotion, which may lead to a different approach to selection:

> Traditional 'go/no go' decisions, based on information and data relating to a specific job, will be replaced by decisions to manage a gradual entry of people into the organisation (via probationary periods, fixed term contracts, part time work and so forth).   (p. 316)

How do we know if we've got it right?

The final stage of the recruitment and selection process concerns measurement of its success, both qualitatively and quantitatively. ACAS guidelines suggest that any recruitment and selection system should be based on three fundamental principles: effectiveness, efficiency and fairness (ACAS, 1983). Effectiveness is concerned with distinguishing accurately between suitable and unsuitable candidates: Mayo (1995) suggests a number of ways in which this can be measured for recruits, including retention rates, promotion rates, and percentage of recruits perceived as having high potential after three to five years. However, these factors can also be influenced by working conditions and the emphasis on employee development within the organisation. Efficiency is concerned more with the costs of the exercise, and measures here may include average cost per recruit, average time lapsed between various stages, percentage of offers made, and offer-acceptance rate (Mayo, 1995). Fairness is concerned with dealing with all applicants fairly and honestly, but has often been taken to refer to equal opportunity monitoring, and has been limited to record keeping on the gender, ethnic origin and disability of successful and unsuccessful candidates.

In theory, the integration of recruitment and selection activity with other HR initiatives and business objectives should lead to more extensive evaluation. In practice there is little to indicate that this is happening:

> The ripple effects of recruitment practices on other HRM areas, such as . . . the effects of salary incentives offered to one group of recruits having a knock-on effect on salary claims of existing staff, or the effects of going outside to recruit staff on the aspirations and commitment of existing staff, are . . . often not considered.
>
> (Iles and Salaman, 1995: 214)

BOX 6.1   Monitoring the effectiveness of recruitment

Between 2000 and 2002 the Government spent £50 million on recruitment advertising for essential services such as the police, the NHS and teachers.

The police recruitment campaign, which featured celebrities such as Lennox Lewis, Bob Geldorf and Patsy Palmer saying that they could not cope with everyday situations faced by the police, cost £12 million.

A BBC survey found that only 13 forces could verify the number of officers attracted by the campaign – a paltry 120. Extrapolating this figure across all of the UK's 43 regional forces would mean that the campaign led to the recruitment of only 400 officers, i.e. £30 000 per recruit.

The advertising agency, M & C Saatchi, argued against these findings, stating that the number of recruits between September 2000 and 2001 was 70% up on the previous year, thus making it one of the most successful police recruitment campaigns ever. However, the Home Office admits that it is unable to find out whether or not recruits were inspired by the adverts or were joining for other reasons. Recruitment is conducted regionally and it is up to regional forces to check why recruits have joined. There are some suggestions that regional forces are reluctant to acknowledge the success of the campaign, since this would detract from their role in recruitment and could jeopardise the jobs of local recruitment officers

Source: Benady, 2002: 24–27

Questions

1 What methods could have been used to monitor the effectiveness of the recruitment campaign?

2 What could be done to integrate national and regional recruitment?

◼ Who is involved in the process?

Recruitment and selection have long been seen as two of the key activities of the HR function. However, increasingly organisations are choosing to involve other parties such as line managers or specialist agencies, or to outsource the activity altogether.

● Line managers

A key feature of HRM is the extent to which activities once seen as the remit of HR specialists are devolved to others, particularly line managers and supervisors. Findings from WERS (Cully *et al.*, 1999) show that around 80 per cent of managers considered they had responsibility for employment relations matters, with 94 per cent of these including 'recruitment and selection of employees'. In workplaces (with supervisors and over 25 employees), 30 per cent of private sector and 17 per cent of public sector supervisors had the final say in decisions about taking on the people who worked for them, though relevant training was not given in the majority of cases. It appears therefore that devolved responsibility for recruitment and selection to managers and supervisors is a reality in many UK organisations.

● Peers

Employees can be involved at various stages in the recruitment and selection process. The most popular level of involvement is to encourage existing employees to introduce candidates to the organisation; almost half of respondents to the CIPD (2002a) survey have either introduced or improved bounty payments to staff for introducing successful candidates. A less common approach is to involve peers or team members in the selection of candidates, as illustrated in the example below.

BOX 6.2 | **Selection at Pret à Manger**

Pret à Manger, the sandwich chain, employs 2400 staff in its 118 shops. In 2001 the company received 55 000 applications for fewer than 1500 vacancies. The first stage of selection consists of a competency-based interview. To be successful at this stage candidates have to demonstrate an outgoing personality, a positive attitude to life, some knowledge of the company and enthusiasm to work there. Those who successfully complete this interview are then invited to undertake a day's on-the-job experience at the shop with the vacancy. Candidates are required to start at 6.30 a.m., the same time as their future colleagues. An existing team member will be assigned to act as a guide and mentor for the day but candidates will work with as many other team members and do as many different jobs as possible. Team members will assess each candidate on a number of competencies, including enthusiasm and ability to follow instructions, and then vote on whether or not they want to offer them a job. Candidates will also be interviewed by the shop manager who doesn't get a vote but can lobby for or against someone. Towards the end of the day, the manager gathers team members' votes and lets the candidate know the outcome. Feedback is provided for both successful and unsuccessful candidates.

Source: Carrington, 2002

Questions

1 What are the benefits and drawbacks of including peer assessment as part of the selection process?

2 What factors need to be considered before introducing peer assessment?

● Specialist employment agencies

The specialist skills of the external recruitment advertiser have been used for many years by HR departments looking outside the organisation for design skills and a contemporary knowledge of successful media. Employment agencies have also traditionally been used for the temporary recruitment of staff cover for periods when permanent staff have been absent on holiday or through unexpected illness.

Recently the reasons for using third parties in recruitment have intensified. The increasing use of non-permanent contracts increases the need for recruitment to temporary or fixed-term contracts. Cully *et al.* (1999) indicate that temporary workers are used in 28 per cent of workplaces and that fixed-term contracts are now found in 44 per cent of workplaces sampled.

'Executive search and selection' are two different methods used for the recruitment of executives. Search (or head-hunting) refers to the recruitment of executives through direct or personal contact by a specialist consultancy acting as an intermediary between the employer and prospective candidate(s). Selection is the identification and shortlisting of a small number of potential candidates, by an intermediary, via recruitment advertising. The individuals targeted by executive search consultants work at senior levels, and have responsibility at regional, national or international level. Income generated from executive search in 2000 was estimated to exceed $10 billion, of which a third is generated in Europe. The top 15 multinational consultancies are judged to have at least 25 per cent of the market between them (Garrison-Jenn, 1998). Key reasons for using executive search and selection consultants include the need for confidentiality, a lack of in-house recruitment knowledge and skills at this level, and simply a lack of senior management time to devote to the activity.

● Outsourcing

'Outsourcing' is the term used to describe the transfer of a distinct business function from inside the business to an external third party. Outsourcing of parts of the HR function has become more common. Lonsdale and Cox (1998) argue that outsourcing decisions can be classified under the following three headings:

- outsourcing for short-term cost and headcount reductions;
- core-competence-based outsourcing, where peripheral activities are passed to third parties and core activities are retained in-house;
- iterative and entrepreneurial outsourcing, where periodic reviews of critical market activities are undertaken, with subsequent decisions to retain or outsource.

A recent CIPD report shows significant growth in this area, with 15 per cent of organisations outsourcing HR activities for the first time and a further 14 per cent improving their outsourcing activities (CIPD, 2002a). Examples include Cable and Wireless, who transferred 93 people to the outsorucing company, e-peopleserve, in 2001 (IRS, 2002h), BPAmoco (Pickard, 2000) and local authorities in Lincolnshire and Westminster (McLuhan, 2000). If one considers that much initial recruitment is routinely administrative, outsourcing this activity becomes attractive because it can release time for the HR function to spend on more 'strategic' matters. In addition, the anticipated switch of operations to the developing world, discussed earlier in this chapter, has potential implications for HR as well as for general operations. HR 'offshoring' activity is estimated to grow at an annual compound rate of 77 per cent over the next five years, with recruitment seen as one of the most promising areas, along with pensions and payroll (Crabb, 2003).

■ Ethical issues in recruitment and selection

Up to now we have focused on recruitment and selection from an organisational perspective. We should not forget that recruitment and selection is a two-way process, and so our final topic for discussion concerns the extent to which any approach respects the rights of individuals participating in the process. Ethical issues arise concerning the treatment of people during recruitment and selection. To a large extent, whether certain activities are perceived as ethical or unethical reflects the prevailing attitudes within the society or societies in which an organisation operates. However, differences in attitudes also reflect the judgement and positioning chosen by major stakeholders, and can be determined by traditional values inherent within the organisation itself.

● Recruitment

Providing equality of opportunity for a diverse number of groups is considered important by certain organisations. However, opportunity to apply for positions can be restricted through the (sometimes unnecessary) insistence on previous experience, or prior development of skills and competences. 'Glass ceilings' exist in internal labour markets for women and minority groups. In the case of third-party recruitment, particularly executive search, opportunities to widen the net can be forestalled, with organisations frequently relying on the knowledge and networking of one consultant to deliver the chosen recruit, often to a specification that ensures that the status quo is maintained. The continued existence of such practices suggests a society in which those in power tolerate them as rational and sound, and where there is insufficient groundswell of opinion from society at large to insist on change. As Goss (1994) remarks:

> If HRM is to be serious in its commitment to the development of all human resources, it may need to face the challenge of wider patterns of social inequality. This means looking not only at disadvantage, but also addressing the issue of who benefits from the status quo.
>
> (p. 173)

In a similar vein, multinational and other organisations that have overseas supplier links have to consider their ethical position in relation to both employment conditions and more particularly targeted recruits. To some extent a similar discussion can be held concerning UK organisations where work is subcontracted to UK agencies and suppliers, on relatively poor conditions of employment, or where schoolchildren (already 'fully employed') are recruited in lieu of those already available in the external labour market.

The business decision may be difficult and involve weighing up important economic, financial, marketing and public relations considerations. While component costs may fall dramatically through the use of overseas subsidiaries and suppliers, bad publicity and loss of sales can ensue through dealing with an organisation where, for example, child labour is found to be extensively used, employment conditions are unsafe, or recruits are paid less than a living wage. Model codes of practice have been drawn up, but for many organisations the ethical issues in 'make or buy' decisions will continue to be debated.

● Selection

Issues in selection revolve around areas of individual rights, the potential for abuse of power, issues of control and social engineering, use of certain assessment techniques, and the issues of equality of opportunity implied in the above.

The ownership of information about an individual passes in the recruitment and selection process from the individual to the organisation. While some protection is afforded by data protection legislation, the organisation is perceived to increase its power over the individual by holding such information and by accumulating more through the use of various selection techniques, the findings of which are not always made known to the candidate.

An individual's right to privacy is further challenged by the impact of scientific developments assisting the prediction of future employment scenarios. For example, tests now exist to enable organisations to conduct pre-employment medicals that predict the future health of candidates. In the USA, where most health costs are met by the employer, discrimination against apparently healthy people who have, or may have, a genetic defect is common, and health insurance has been found to be refused to one in five of this group (Thatcher, 1996). With genetic tests becoming increasingly available, will UK employers use them to screen out anyone whom they see as potentially expensive to employ? As certain genes occur more frequently in particular ethnic groups, the issues become even more complex.

Apart from questions about the technical effectiveness of various selection techniques, ethical questions remain about their use at all:

> There are questions of a more ethical nature surrounding personality tests. It has been suggested that organisations have no right to seek to control access to jobs on the grounds of individual personality.
>
> (Goss, 1994: 47)

Professional guidance in the area of occupation testing exists, both in specific codes of practice (CIPD and BPS) and as part of ethical codes of practice within large organisations in particular. However, research has shown that, while selectors claim to recognise the rights of those being tested (for example, to be fairly treated, to expect counselling where needed, to confidentiality of data, to know the tests used are valid), these rights are not always upheld in practice (Baker and Cooper, 2002). In addition, questions remain to be asked as to whether:

- the selection of one personality type leads to a weakened 'inbred' profile of employees in organisations, incapable of thinking or acting in original ways when the situation demands;
- an organisation has the right to enforce a unitarist perspective on employees – some selection tests, for example, are designed to filter out those who are 'prone to unionise' (Flood *et al.*, 1996), others to ensure that potential employees' values are in line with the organisation's thinking:

> At the heart of these concerns seems to be a fear about the totalitarian possibilities of work organisations and the role of personality profiling as a form of 'social engineering' for corporate conformity.
>
> (Goss, 1994: 47)

The use of interviews as a selection method has long been open to criticism on the grounds of subjectivity and stereotyping. Using biodata as a basis of selection has potential for misuse, discriminating against individuals and groups on factors that are beyond their control (education, social class and gender, for example). Graphology attracts criticism for similar reasons of social stereotyping and superficial judgements.

In conclusion, the use of both external and internal labour markets and associated selection techniques can raise ethical issues. Poaching experienced people from the external labour market implies an approach that only 'takes' from society, in terms of the costs of education and previous training and development, and the higher wages needed to attract applicants can be perceived as inflationary. Alternatively, one can view the use of the internal labour market through in-house development around organisation-based objectives as somewhat menacing, tying the individual closely to the organisation from which escape is perceived as increasingly difficult and from which the measurement of individual freedom, and the quality of the conditions of employment enjoyed, become more difficult to judge.

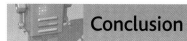

Conclusion

The focus of this chapter has been to outline contemporary approaches to recruitment and selection, and to consider the influence of external and internal factors on the process. We conclude that the systematic approach to recruitment and selection still provides a useful framework for analysing activity. The key stages – defining the vacancy, attracting applicants, assessing candidates, and making the final decision – are applicable most of the time, but the way in which each stage is tackled can vary considerably. Key developments within the process itself include the increased use of technology. The Internet has emerged as a new recruitment medium, and its use is likely to continue to grow. At the same time, the availability of software to aid the selection process is increasing. Developments in selection techniques appear to reflect growing awareness of the limitations of interviews, and so there is evidence of a growth in the use of more structured formats as well as greater use of supplementary tools such as tests and job simulations. For some organisations, however, it is business as usual and little has changed.

The current state of recruitment and selection is complex because a variety of internal and external factors continue to influence the process. The underlying philosophy regarding the management of human resources and the degree of adoption of technological advances affects the way work is organised and the resultant skills needed by employees. Externally, labour market conditions, legislation and government policy in training and education dictate who is available to fill contemporary jobs. Further complexity is added by the growth of multinational enterprises. These factors are constantly changing, and the environment in which the recruitment and selection process operates is uncertain and increasingly ambiguous. What is certain, however, is that there is no universal solution to this complexity – no 'one size that fits all' – and this is how one can account for the coexistence of both new and traditional approaches to the recruitment and selection of employees. Organisations tend to adopt a pragmatic approach to the attraction and selection of employees based on their assessment of current and future conditions and their response to the critical questions outlined in this chapter. Thus, one will find differences in approaches not only between organisations but also within organisations, depending on the level of vacancies and organisational requirements.

Although this chapter has concentrated on recruitment and selection from an organisational perspective, readers should not forget that recruitment and selection is a two-way process. Not all the developments can be endorsed wholeheartedly. On the positive side, the use of more sophisticated techniques can be seen as an attempt to improve the quality of the selection decision, through increasing objectivity and reducing the scope for bias and prejudice. On the negative side, the emphasis on personality and behavioural characteristics can be used to create and manipulate a workforce that is more amenable to management initiatives. Ethical considerations continue to be important, and care must be taken in the use of these techniques, particularly in handling the increasingly large amount of information that can be gained about prospective workers.

The most appropriate recruitment and selection techniques will continue to be those that balance the requirements of organisations with those of current and prospective employees, and the approach adopted is likely to be determined, at least in part, by external circumstances. If predictions about the demise of 'jobs for life' and the growth of 'portfolio careers' are true, then the experience of recruitment and selection may become an increasing feature in all our lives, regardless of the techniques involved.

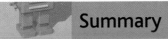

Summary

The chapter began with three key objectives. Here we revisit those objectives and outline our key responses:

- The external factors most likely to affect recruitment and selection practices are conditions in external labour markets, national approaches to education and training, technological developments, and legislation and professional codes of practice. The combination of these factors can be contradictory: on the one hand, legislative requirements can suggest a common 'best' practice, whereas on the other hand variations in labour supply and market conditions can indicate the need for a more diverse, pragmatic approach.

- A range of internal organisational factors can influence approaches to recruitment and selection. We have identified the key influences as the way in which the employment relationship is managed (soft or hard HRM) and the extent to which recruitment and selection are perceived as strategic activities. Additional factors include industrial, sectoral and size variation and the growth in multinational corporations. The combination of organisational diversity and pressures from the external environment can account for variations in recruitment and selection practice.

- The key stages of a systematic approach to recruitment and selection can be summarised as defining the vacancy, attracting applicants, assessing candidates, making appropriate decisions, and evaluating the effectiveness of the process. Recent developments within this framework include greater use of the Internet for recruitment, greater emphasis on competencies and the increased use of more sophisticated selection techniques such as psychometric tests and assessment centres. At the same time, more traditional methods such as press advertising, interviews and references continue to be very popular. In addition, recruitment and selection activities are increasingly devolved to other parties both inside and outside the organisation.

- There is considerable variation in the effectiveness of recruitment and selection techniques. Although the use of selection methods with higher predictive validity is increasing, the most widely used methods are not necessarily the most accurate at differentiating between people who can and cannot do the job. Effectiveness can also be considered in relation to equal opportunity and ethical issues, such as the extent to which employment of people from previously under-represented groups is encouraged, and the existence of checks that selection methods are 'fair' – that is, discriminate only on job ability. In measuring effectiveness, organisations need to balance the costs involved in the actual process against the costs of selecting the wrong person.

ACTIVITY ## Competency-based recruitment and selection at DHL Aviation

DHL is the world's largest international air express company, delivering packages, documents and parcels worldwide and employing over 63 500 staff in total and more than 5000 in the UK.

DHL Aviation was founded in 1988 to deal with import and export consignments generated in Europe. DHL Aviation (UK) reports to the European Air and Hub operations in Brussels and its primary responsibility is to provide a fast distribution base for the delivery of products and packages by air to UK and other European airports and by road to customers in the UK. DHL Aviation (UK) employs over 800 staff at two main bases – East Midlands Airport and London Heathrow. There are also small numbers of staff at other UK airports.

Until recently, recruitment and selection was conducted on a fairly traditional basis. Shortlisting was based on selection criteria detailed on a person specification and successful applicants were invited for interview. The interview was conducted by two interviewers using a semi-structured format. Questions were not standardised. An investigation into the selection process found that, although the format provided flexibility and the ability to probe candidates' answers, the interviews were inconsistent, largely subjective and heavily dependent on the interviewer's personal style.

DHL Aviation (UK) therefore decided to improve consistency by adopting a competency-based interview, using a selection of predetermined, behavioural questions and a more systematic approach to scoring the answers. The organisation identified four core competencies, which all potential and existing staff are expected to display, and role-specific competencies, which apply only to certain jobs. The competencies are as follows:

Core competencies
- Passion for customer service
- Teamwork
- Achievement drive
- Initiative

Role-specific competencies
- Influencing business
  - Impact and influence
  - Planning and organising
  - Communication

- Interpersonal communication
  - Interpersonal understanding
  - Building and leading teams
  - Developing people
  - Holding people accountable

- Personal
  - Adaptability and change
  - Attention to detail
  - Self-belief

- Problem-solving
  - Analytical thinking
  - Decision-making
  - Information seeking
  - Understanding the key issues

- Technical and professional
  - Job knowledge and skills

Interviewers are provided with a selection of questions for each competency, dependent on the level of the job. Each set of questions also has different indicators divided into three sections: negative, expected and outstanding. The marking criteria for each answer is as follows:

1 an answer displaying mostly negative indicators;
2 an answer displaying equal negative and positive indicators;
3 an answer displaying mostly positive indicators;
4 an answer displaying equal expected and outstanding indicators;
5 an answer displaying mainly outstanding indicators.

After the interview, each interviewer must add up the candidate's scores to give a total rating. The candidate with the highest score has displayed the most examples of the desired competencies for the position.

Questions:

1 What are the key advantages and disadvantages to DHL Aviation (UK) of adopting this competency-based approach?

2 What other issues need attention to ensure that the competency-based approach is effective?

Questions

1 To what extent is the use of the Internet challenging more traditional methods of recruitment and selection?

2 Why have interviews remained so popular and what steps can be taken to improve their effectiveness?

3 What can an organisation do to minimise potential indirect discrimination during the recruitment and selection process?

References and further reading

Those texts marked with an asterisk are particularly recommended for further reading.

ACAS (1983) *Recruitment and Selection*, Advisory Booklet No. 6. London: Advisory, Conciliation & Arbitration Service.

Anderson, A.H. (1994) *Effective Personnel Management: A Skills and Activity-Based Approach*. Oxford: Blackwell Business.

*Anderson, N. and Shackleton, V. (1993) *Successful Selection Interviewing*. Oxford: Blackwell.

Appelbaum, S., Kay, F. and Shapiro, B. (1989) 'The assessment centre is not dead! How to keep it alive and well', *Journal of Management Development*, Vol. 8, No. 5, pp. 51–65.

Armstrong, M. (2001) *A Handbook of Human Resource Management Practice*, 8th edn. London: Kogan Page.

Baker, B. and Cooper, J.N. (2002) 'Occupational testing and psychometric instruments: an ethical perspective', in Winstanley, D. and Woodall, J. (eds) *Ethical Issues in Contemporary Human Resource Management*. Houndmills: Palgrave.

Beaumont, P. (1993) *Human Resource Management: Key Concepts and Skills*. London: Sage.

Benady, D. (2002) 'Money for nothing?', *Marketing Week*, 22 August, pp. 24–27.

Boam, R. and Sparrow, P. (eds) (1992) *Designing and Achieving Competency: A Competency-based Approach to Developing People and Organisations*. Maidenhead: McGraw-Hill.

Bradshaw, D (1999) *Next Generation Call Centres: CTI, Voice and the Web*. Step-London ovum.

Callaghan, G. and Thompson, P. (2002) 'We recruit attitude: the selection and shaping of routine call centre labour', *Journal of Management Studies*, Vol. 39, No. 2, pp. 233–254.

Carrington, L. (2002) 'At the cutting edge', *People Management*, Vol. 8, No. 10, pp. 30–31.

CIPD (2001a) Telephone interviewing, *Quick Facts*. London: CIPD.

CIPD (2001b) Graphology, *Quick Facts*. London: CIPD.

CIPD (2001c) Psychological testing, *Quick Facts*. London: CIPD.

CIPD (2002a) Recruitment and Retention, *Survey Report*. London: CIPD.

CIPD (2002b) Employment of people with criminal records, *Quick Facts*. London: CIPD.

CIPD (2002c) Recruitment on the Internet, *Quick Facts*. London: CIPD.

CIPD (2003) Assessment Centres for recruitment and selection, *Quick Facts*. London: CIPD.

Crabb, S. (2003) 'East India companies', *People Management*, Vol. 8, No. 4, pp. 28–32.

*Cully, M., Woodland, S., O'Reilly, A. and Dix, G. (1999) *Britain at Work: As Depicted by the 1998 Workplace Employee Relations Survey*. London: Routledge.

Davis, R. (1999) 'Smoother operators', *People Management*, 6 May, pp 56–57.

Department for Education and Employment (1999) *Age Diversity in Employment*. Nottingham: DfEE Publications.

Department for Education and Skills (2003) National Statistics First release: the level of highest qualification held by young people and adults: England 2002. www.dfes.gov.uk/statistics/DB/SFR

Dickens, L. (2000) 'Still wasting resources? Equality in employment', in Bach, S. and Sisson, K. (eds) *Personnel Management: A Comprehensive Guide to Theory and Practice*, 3rd edn. Oxford: Blackwell, pp. 137–169.

Dowling, P.J. and Schuler, R.S. (1990) *International Dimensions of HRM*. Boston, Mass: PWS-Kent.

Dulewicz, V. (2003) 'How to prepare for the board', *People Management*, 6 March, p. 54.

Euromonitor (2002a) *European Marketing Data and Statistics 2002*. London: Euromonitor.

Euromonitor (2002b) *International Marketing Data and Statistics 2002*, Marketing Handbooks Series. London: Euromonitor.

Feltham, R. (1992) 'Using competencies in selection and recruitment', in Boam, R. and Sparrow, P. (eds) *Designing and Achieving Competency: a Competency-based Approach to Developing People and Organisations*. Maidenhead: McGraw-Hill.

Fletcher, C. (1993) 'Testing times for the world of psychometrics', *People Management*, December, pp. 46–50.

Flood, P.C., Gannon, M.J. and Paauwe, J. (1996) *Managing Without Traditional Methods: International Innovations in Human Resource Management*. Wokingham: Addison-Wesley.

Fombrun, C., Tichy, N. and Devanna, M. (1984) *Strategic Human Resource Management*. New York: Wiley.

Fowler, A. (1992) 'How to plan an assessment centre', *PM Plus*, December, pp. 21–23.

Garrison-Jenn, N. (1998) *The Global 200 Executive Recruiters*. San Francisco, Calif.: Jossey-Bass.

Goold, M. and Campbell, A. (1987) *Strategies and Styles: The Role of the Centre in Managing Diversified Organisations*. Oxford: Blackwell.

Goss, D. (1994) *Principles of Human Resource Management*. London: Routledge.

Hackett, P. (1991) *Personnel: The Department at Work*. London: IPM.

Hall, K. (1995) 'Worldwide vision in the workplace', *People Management*, May, pp. 20–25.

Hendry, C. (1995) *Human Resource Management: A Strategic Approach to Employment*. Oxford: Butterworth-Heinemann.

Herriot, P. (1989) *Recruitment in the 1990s*. London: IPM.

Hollingshead, G. and Leat, M. (1995) *Human Resource Management: An International and Comparative Perspective on the Employment Relationship*. London: Pitman Publishing.

IDS (1992) Employment Law Supplement: Recruitment, *IDS Brief 64*, April.

IDS (2002) Assessment Centres, *Study 569*, January.

Iles, P. and Salaman, G. (1995) 'Recruitment, selection and assessment', in Storey, J. (ed.) *Human Resource Management: A Critical Text*. London: Routledge, pp. 203–233.

Industrial Society (1994) *Recruitment and Selection*, Managing Best Practice No. 4. London: The Industrial Society.

IPD (1997) *Psychological Testing, key facts*. London: IPD, August.

IRS (1994) 'Ensuring effective recruitment' and 'Random selection', *Employee Development Bulletin 51*, March, pp. 2–8.

IRS (1997) 'The state of selection: an IRS survey', *Employee Development Bulletin 85*, January, pp. 8–18.

IRS (1999a) 'Testing time for people with disabilities', *Employee Development Bulletin 113*, May, pp. 5–9.

IRS (1999b) 'The business of selection: an IRS survey', *Employee Development Bulletin 117*, September, pp. 5–16.

IRS (2002a) 'Going beyond the DDA', *IRS Employment Review 758*, 19 August.

IRS (2002b) 'The uses and abuses of the new Criminal Records Bureau', *IRS Employment Review 753*, 10 June, pp. 37–40.

IRS (2002c) 'Internet recruiting the FTSE-100 way', *IRS Employment Review 746*, 25 February, pp. 35–40.

IRS (2002d) 'I've got your number: telephone interviewing', *IRS Employment Review 756*, 22 July, pp. 34–36.

IRS (2002e) 'Psychometrics: the next generation', *IRS Employment Review 744*, 28 January, pp. 36–40.

IRS (2002f) 'Focus of attention', *IRS Employment Review 749*, 15 April, pp. 36–42.

IRS (2002g) 'The check's in the post', *IRS Employment Review 752*, May, pp. 34–42.

IRS (2002h) 'A pay-as-you-go personnel function', *IRS Employment Review 748*, 25 March, pp. 39–40.

IRS (2003) 'Spinning the recruitment web', *IRS Employment Review 767*, 10 January, pp. 34–40.

Kandola, B. (1995) 'Firms must rework race bias policies', *Personnel Today*, 25 October, p. 20.

Langtry, R. (1994) 'Selection', in Beardwell, I. and Holden, L. (eds) *Human Resource Management: A Contemporary Perspective*. London: Pitman Publishing, pp. 230–263.

Leat, M., (1998) *Human Resource Issues of the European Union*. London: Financial Times Management.

*Legge, K. (1995) *Human Resource Management: Rhetorics and Realities*. Basingstoke: Macmillan Business.

Lewis, C. (1985) *Employee Selection*. London: Hutchinson.

Lonsdale, C. and Cox, A. (1998) 'Falling in with the out crowd', *People Management*, 15 October, pp. 52–55.

McLuhan, R. (2000) 'Change management', *Personnel Today* 18 April, pp. 25–26.

Manocha, R (2002) 'Unlocking potential', *People Management*, Vol. 8, No. 19, pp. 28–34.

Marchington, M. and Wilkinson, A. (1996) *Core Personnel and Development*. London: IPD.

Mayo, A. (1995) 'Economic indicators of HRM', in Tyson, S. (ed.) *Strategic Prospects for HRM*. London: IPD, p. 34.

Miles, R.E and Snow, C.C. (1984) 'Designing strategic human resource systems', *Organisational Dynamics*, Summer, pp. 36–52.

Munro Fraser, J. (1954) *A Handbook of Employment Interviewing*. London: Macdonald & Evans.

Newell, S. and Shackleton, V. (1993) 'The use and abuse of psychometric tests in British industry and commerce', *Human Resource Management Journal*, Vol. 4, No. 1, pp. 14–23.

Office for National Statistics (2002a) *Labour Force Survey*, London.

Office for National Statistics (2002b) *New Earnings Survey*, London.

Patterson, M., West, M., Lawthorn, R. and Nickell, S. (1997) *Impact of People Management Practices on Business Performance*, Issues in People Management No. 22. London: IPD.

Pfeffer, J (1998) *The Human Equation: Building Profits by Putting People First*. Boston, Mass: Harvard Business School Press.

Pickard, J. (1999) 'Equality counts', *People Management*, 11 November, pp. 38–43.

Pickard, J. (2000) 'A sell-out strategy', *People Management*, 23 November, pp. 32–36.

PriceWaterhourseCoopers (1999) *International Assignments: European Policy and Practice 1999/2000*. London: PriceWaterhouseCoopers.

*Roberts, G. (1997) *Recruitment and Selection: A Competency Approach*. London: IPD.

Rodger, A. (1952) *The Seven Point Plan*. London: National Institute of Industrial Psychology.

Sadler, P. and Milmer, K. (1993) *The Talent-Intensive Organisation: Optimising your Company's Human Resource Strategies*, Special Report No. P659. London: The Economist Intelligence Unit.

Schuler, R.S. and Jackson, S.E. (1996) *Human Resource Management: Positioning for the 21st Century*, 6th edn. St Paul, Minn.: West Publishing Company.

Sisson, K. and Marginson, P. (1995) 'Management: systems, structures and strategy' in Edwards, P. (ed) *Industrial Relations: Theory and Practice in Britain*. Oxford: Blackwell.

Social Trends (2000) London: HMSO.

Social Trends (2002) London: HMSO.

Sparrow, P. (1999) 'Abroad minded', *People Management*, 20 May, pp. 40–44.

Sparrow, P. and Hiltrop, J.–M. (1994) *European Human Resource Management in Transition*. Englewood Cliffs, New Jersey: Prentice Hall.

Storey, J. and Sisson, K. (1993) *Managing Human Resources and Industrial Relations*. Buckingham: Open University Press.

*Taylor, S. (2002) *People Resourcing*. London: CIPD.

Thatcher, M. (1996) 'Contending with a genetic time bomb', *People Management*, 7 March, pp. 30–33.

Torrington, D., Hall, L. and Taylor, S (2002) *Human Resource Management*, 5th edn. Harlow: Prentice Hall.

Whiddett, S. and Hollyforde, S. (1999) *The Competencies Handbook*. London: IPD.

Whitehead, M. (1999) 'Churning questions', *People Management*, 30 September, pp. 46–48.

Whitehill, A.M. (1991) *Japanese Management: Tradition and Transition*. London: Routledge.

For multiple choice questions, exercises and annotated weblinks specific to this chapter visit this book's website at www.booksites.net/beardwell

CHAPTER 7

Managing equality and diversity

Mike Noon

OBJECTIVES

▶ Define discrimination and describe its potential impact on different groups.

▶ Describe and compare the social justice and business case arguments for pursuing policies of equality and diversity.

▶ Explain the purpose of equal opportunity policies and assess their limitations.

▶ Explain the concepts of 'sameness' and 'difference', and evaluate their importance in guiding policy within organisations.

▶ Describe and critically evaluate the concept of institutional discrimination.

▶ Assess the process of discrimination in an organisation and outline its possible consequences.

Introduction

There is a short story by H.G. Wells called 'The Country of the Blind' in which a mountaineer falls into a hidden valley in South America where all the inhabitants have been blind for fifteen generations. His initial reaction is that among such a disadvantaged group of people he can easily establish himself as superior because of his sight; indeed, as the saying expresses it, 'in the country of the blind the one-eyed man is king'. However, he soon learns that the whole of this society is constructed around the norm of blindness, so his sightedness provides no advantages and in many ways disadvantages him from becoming integrated and accepted into the community. For instance, all work is undertaken in the dark at night (when it is cool); there are no lights and the buildings have no windows; his descriptions and explanations based on sight, colour and so forth have no meaning to the inhabitants; and his under-developed alternative senses mean he cannot participate fully in the culture of the community. In the end, in order to fit in, he has to choose either to conform to the dominate norms and have his eyes removed or else leave the community.

The relevance of this story is that it illustrates how being different to the dominant social group can produce disadvantages for an individual irrespective of his or her qualities and abilities. In this example the disadvantage suffered by the main character is due to his sight in a society in which sight is undervalued. In the real world, of course, key characteristics such as gender, race/ethnicity, disability, age, religion and sexuality are typically the bases for disadvantage. People can suffer rejection, non-acceptance and unfair treatment within a particular setting (especially the workplace) because they differ from the dominant social group across one of more of these characteristics. They can feel excluded and marginalised, or in extreme cases become the victims of abuse and harassment. This disadvantage can manifest itself in many of the key processes within organisations that are explained in other chapters: recruitment and selection, training and development; appraisals; promotion; career development; remuneration; and work organisation.

The purpose of this chapter is to explore how managers can take action to minimise the disadvantages and provide a working environment that supports equality and diversity. To investigate these issues the chapter is divided into six main sections. First, there is an examination of the meaning of discrimination; section two addresses the question of why managers should be concerned about equality and diversity; section three explains the role of equal opportunity policies; section four analyses the different approaches to devising such policies; section five evaluates the concept of institutional discrimination; and section six explains the process of discrimination within organisations.

The nature of discrimination

One of the assumptions sometimes made is that discrimination is experienced in the same way by different groups of people. In other words, discrimination based on sex, race/ethnicity, disability and age is often assumed to be the same. While it is certainly the case that the effects of discrimination (the disadvantage suffered) are the same or very similar for the victims, the nature of the discrimination often differs and the response and attitudes of the social groups can also differ. It is important to elaborate these statements to show how there might be differences between social groups and within social groups.

One starting point for this is to consider the characteristics that identify a person as different: sex, age, ethnicity, etc. In particular, these characteristics differ in terms of whether they can be considered *stable* and *visible*:

- *Stable* characteristics are features such as race and sex – with the exception of the tiny minority of people that undergo gender reassignment. In contrast, a person's age differs throughout their life, thus everyone is susceptible to being a victim of ageism, and the type of ageism will change at different life stages.
- *Visible* characteristics are features that a person cannot hide – such as sex, race/ethnicity and some forms of disability. Others, such as sexual orientation, can be hidden and so although discrimination occurs, some potential victims can dodge it through behaviour that disguises their true identities.

A further consideration concerns the differences between the perpetrators and the victims. Whereas discrimination is perpetrated typically by one group against a different group (men over women, able-bodied over less able, ethnic majority over minority), this is not true of age discrimination. For instance, research by Oswick and Rosenthal (2001) reveals that older workers are frequently discriminated against by managers of similar ages; it is not simply the case that the 'old' are discriminated against by the 'young' (or vice versa). As the authors vividly express it, 'the purveyors of ageism are also in other circumstances its recipients'. Thus there is 'same-group' discrimination, rather than 'different-group' discrimination.

Turning to the victims of discrimination, it is important to recognise differences within social groups, rather than consider each group to be homogeneous. For instance, Reynolds *et al.* (2001) point out how disability can be a diverse and wide-ranging categorisation. People may move into a state of disability from ill-health, work accidents or ageing, and so while some people are 'born disabled', there is an increasing proportion of employees who 'become disabled'. Moreover, the needs of those with different 'disabilities' are so wide-ranging that it might be suggested there is very little meaning in such a broad category as 'disability'. The same conclusion might be reached for race/ethnicity. Increasingly, commentators (for example, Modood *et al.*, 1997; Pilkington, 2001) are arguing that research evidence suggests there is so much ethnic diversity that to describe discrimination as being the same across different ethnic groups fails to take into account its differential impact. This means it is essential to recognise the differences between ethnic groups not only in terms of their experiences of discrimination, but also in their varied requirements for redressing the discrimination. Furthermore, it is possible to challenge the assumptions that a person's ethnic group can be clearly defined and remains stable (note the discussion above). First, there are increasingly people with multiple cultural identities who simply do not 'fit' the ethnic categories, and second, exposure to varied cultural influences means that ethnic identity might change across one's lifetime.

It is equally important to recognise differences between social groups. Indeed, if people within the same social group experience discrimination in different ways and in different circumstances, there is little reason to suppose that people from different social groups will have similar experiences. They may be victims of discrimination but there is little reason to suppose that the experience of being discriminated against because you are a woman is the same as that of being discriminated against on the grounds of sexual orientation; or that the discrimination experienced by disabled employees is the same as that endured by ethnic minority employees. Box 7.1, 'The Royal Mail', illustrates these sometimes competing interests, see also Liff, 2002.

BOX 7.1 The Royal Mail

The UK's postal service, The Royal Mail, has traditionally operated a system of seniority for employees who sort and deliver the mail. This means that the greater the length of service the postal workers have behind them, then the more privileges they get. In particular, this means that they get first choice of holidays, overtime and shifts. The system was designed to reward loyalty and experience, but as demands on the form of postal work changed, in particular with the introduction of new technology and different ways of working, the managers required far greater flexibility from employees and so they proposed changes to working practices that would lead to the abolition of the seniority system. Interestingly, this led both sides (the trade unions and the management) to claim that they were working in the interest of equal opportunities.

The trade unions argued that seniority protected equal opportunities because it produced a rational, transparent and equitable means of allocating duties. In particular, they said that it protected employees against favouritism and prejudice by managers in the allocation of duties – an issue of importance to ethnic minority members of the trade unions.

The management argued that it was not fair on part-time employees who were at the back of the queue because their length of service was less and who nevertheless made an important contribution to the business. In particular, they suggested that it had a discriminatory effect on women because the majority of part-timers were women.

These two viewpoints illustrate how both parties were able to make a claim that their position was in defence of equal opportunities. Indeed, the logic of both cases can be seen. It provides a vivid illustration of how different groups might require different (and in this case competing) policies and action in order to ensure fairness. Part-time employees, particularly those who were women, might have felt betrayed by the trade unions. Similarly, ethnic minority employees might have felt that management were attempting to remove a system that had protected against discrimination.

A final issue that further underlines the diversity of the nature of discrimination is that some people experience multi-discrimination. For example, an employee may be discriminated against because she is both a woman and Asian, and might therefore not identify with or share the same concerns as her white women colleagues or black male colleagues. Similarly, consider the following comment:

I'm a 54-year-old fitter who'd been made redundant, and I've been trying for months to get back into work. I've even done all these special courses at the Job Centre to make myself more employable and to practise interviews and things. The problem is that when an employer sees 54 on the application form the majority of them don't want to know – but of course I can't prove that. Then, after weeks of trying I got an interview, and I was really excited because it was a chance to get back to doing something useful and earning again. I can remember I was full of enthusiasm and hope when I walked into the interview room, but then I saw the look on the faces of the panel as I walked through the door and they realised I'm black.

The picture is of diversity in the nature of discrimination and difference in the needs of the various groups and individuals that experience discrimination. These are important issues because it means:

- Managers should not assume that discrimination means the same thing irrespective of group concerned.
- Managers should not assume that a policy solution for one social group (for example, women) will be appropriate or welcomed by a different social group (for example, disabled people).
- Managers should expect that attitudes will differ within social groups (for example, Asian employees and black employees).

The recognition of this diversity has led some commentators to argue that rather than defining people by their similarities to others, managers should see all employees as individuals with unique skills and needs. This is an issue that we will return to later in the chapter.

Stop and think
On the basis of the preceding discussion, summarise for yourself the diverse patterns of discrimination and disadvantage that can exist.

Why be concerned with equality and diversity?

A key question that needs to be addressed is why managers should care whether some people are disadvantaged and suffer unfair treatment. In answering this question, it is useful to distinguish between two different sets of arguments, which can be labelled 'the social justice case' and 'the business case'.

■ The social justice case

The social justice case is that managers have a moral obligation to treat employees with fairness and dignity. Part of this involves ensuring that decisions are made without resorting to prejudice and stereotypes. You may already be familiar with these concepts, but in case not, they can be defined as follows.

Prejudice
In the context of discrimination at work, prejudice means holding negative attitudes towards a particular group, and viewing all members of that group in a negative light, irrespective of their individual qualities and attributes. Typically we think of prejudice as being against a particular group based on gender, race/ethnicity, religion, disability, age and sexual orientation. However, prejudice extends much further and is frequently directed at other groups based on features such as accent, height, weight, hair colour, beards, body piercings, tattoos and clothes. It is extremely rare to find a person who is not prejudiced against any group – although most of us are reluctant to admit to our prejudices.

(Heery and Noon, 2001: 279)

Stereotyping

Stereotyping is the act of judging people according to our assumptions about the group to which they belong. It is based on the belief that people from a specific group share similar traits and behave in a similar manner. Rather than looking at a person's individual qualities, stereotyping leads us to jump to conclusions about what someone is like. This might act against the person concerned (negative stereotype) or in their favour (positive stereotype). For example, the negative stereotype of an accountant is someone who is dull, uninteresting and shy – which, of course, is a slur on all the exciting, adventurous accountants in the world. A positive stereotype is that accountants are intelligent, conscientious and trustworthy – which is an equally inaccurate description of some of the accountants you are likely to encounter. The problem with stereotypes is that they are generalisations (so there are always exceptions) and can be based on ignorance and prejudice (so are often inaccurate). It is vital for managers to resist resorting to stereotyping when managing people, otherwise they run the risk of treating employees unfairly and making poor-quality decisions that are detrimental to the organisation.

(Heery and Noon, 2001: 347)

If decisions are made free from prejudice and stereotyping then there is a lower risk of any particular group being disadvantaged and therefore less chance of an individual feeling that he or she has been discriminated against.

Discrimination is very much a core concept for the social justice case so its meaning needs to be considered. 'Discrimination' is the process of judging people according to particular criteria. For example, in the selection process for a teaching post, the appointment panel might discriminate in favour of a candidate who answers their questions clearly and concisely, and discriminate against a candidate who mutters and digresses from the point. However, when most people use the term discrimination they tend to mean *unfair* discrimination. The word is mainly used to denote that the criteria on which the discrimination has occurred are unjust. It is likely that most people would not describe the example above as 'discrimination' because they would not consider the criteria the panel used (clarity, conciseness) as unfair. However, if the criterion the appointment panel used to choose between candidates was gender or race, then most people would recognise it as discrimination. Essentially it is the problem of deciding upon the 'fairness' of the process which makes it a concern for social justice.

There is a further complication to the social justice case. This concerns the question of whether the focus should be on justice in terms of procedures ('a level playing field') or outcomes ('a fair share of the cake').

For example, in a recruitment process, this would mean either a person is selected according to merit (procedural justice) or he or she is selected in order to fill a quota (to ensure representativeness of different social groups). Selection on merit alone will not produce representativeness unless such merit is evenly distributed throughout all groups. Of course, such even distribution is highly unlikely due to structural disadvantages and inequalities (schooling, economic support, connections, social stereotypes, and so forth) which limit a person's potential to acquire meritorious characteristics (Noon and Ogbonna, 2001: 4).

As shall be seen later in the chapter, this dilemma leads to different policy suggestions as to how organisations should address the problem of ensuring fairness. Those who favour procedural intervention tend to advocate a 'light touch' in terms of legal regulation and best practice guidelines, while those who focus on outcomes advocate stronger legislation and/or more radical changes to organisational processes and practices.

● Limitations of the social justice argument

Critics of the social justice case tend to argue that while the pursuit of fairness is laudable, it is not the prime concern of organisations. The goals of managers in organisations are profit and efficiency, rather than morality. If social justice were to guide their decision-making it might have a detrimental effect on the operation of the business and ultimately the bottom line. This line of argument has led to an additional rationale for equality and diversity: the business case.

■ The business case

The second set of arguments that can be used to justify why managers should be concerned with eliminating disadvantage is based on making a business case. The point is that, aside from any concerns with social justice, fair treatment simply makes good business sense for four main reasons:

1 *It is a better use of human resources.* By discriminating on the basis of sex, race/ethnicity, disability, and so on, managers run the risk of neglecting or overlooking talented employees. The consequence is that the organisation fails to maximise its full human resource potential and valuable resources are wasted through under-utilising the competences of existing employees or losing disgruntled, talented staff to other organisations.
2 *It leads to a wider customer base.* By broadening the diversity of the workforce, managers might help the organisation to appeal to a greater range of customers. This might be particularly important where face-to-face service delivery is a central part of the business and requires an understanding of the diverse needs of customers.
3 *It creates a wider pool of labour for recruitment.* By being more open-minded about the people they could employ for various jobs, managers will have a wider pool of talent from which to recruit. This is particularly important when an organisation is attempting to secure scarce resources, such as employees with specific skills or experience.
4 *It leads to a positive company image.* By having a clear statement of the organisation's commitment to equal opportunities, backed by meaningful practices that result in a diverse workforce, managers will be able to project a positive image of the organisation to customers, suppliers and potential employees. In terms of employees, the organisation will be perceived as good to work for because it values ability and talent, and so is more likely to attract and retain high-calibre people.

● Limitations of the business case argument

Although these arguments are quite persuasive, there might be some circumstances when 'good business sense' provides the justification for not acting in the interest of particular groups. For example, Cunningham and James (2001) find that line managers often justify the decision not to employ disabled people on the grounds that the necessary workplace adjustments would eat into their operating budgets. Indeed, equality and diversity initiatives often have a cost associated with them, the recovery of which cannot always be easily measured and might only be realised in the long term. The danger (highlighted by commentators such as Dickens, 1994, 2000 and Webb, 1997) is that such initiatives can only be justified as long as they contribute to profit. For example, in Webb's (1997) case study of an international computing systems manufacturer, the corporate philosophy was to encourage employee diversity to bring in new ideas, meet customer needs and achieve success in the global marketplace. However, at divisional level in the UK, the requests from women for childcare provision and flexible hours were rejected on the basis that these would adversely affect profitability. Furthermore, although managerial opportunities were open to women, this was clearly on men's terms, as Webb (1997: 165) explains.

> Women graduate engineers are aware that they have to fit in as 'one of the boys' and however supportive the line manager, these are all men: 'I think the difficulty is still being able to sit down, map out your career and possibly say that at a certain time you many well wish to have a family ... (graduate sales rep.). ... Even for those willing to adopt male work norms, the corporate orientation to innovation and change mean that the uncertainties experienced by managers are likely to result in the continuing exclusion of women, who continue to be regarded as a riskier bet than men.

This type of problem is common and is expressed vividly by Liff and Wajcman (1996: 89) in the following quote.

> Managers' perceptions of job requirements and procedures for assessing merit have been shown to be saturated with gendered assumptions ... Feminists can argue (as they have for years) that not all women get pregnant, but it seems unlikely that this will stop managers thinking 'yes, but no men will'.

For an alternative example of how the business case argument can work against a particular group of employees, see the activity below.

ACTIVITY   The department store

The following quote is from a research interview with a personnel manager of a large departmental store in a city in the UK. She had been asked why there were no ethnic minority employees on the sales floor, even though the city had an ethnic minority population of over 5 per cent.

'Our customers are mainly white, middle-class women. They would be uncomfortable being served by ethnic minorities and they would probably shop elsewhere. That is why we don't have black sales assistants and only have men in certain areas such as the electrical department. We have some Asian employees in the stockroom and doing other vital jobs behind the scenes.'

What are the potential problems for the organisation in taking this approach?

A further problem is the issue of measuring the effects of extending opportunities. The underlying assumption is that any initiatives will have a positive effect on business (hence they make good business sense). But this logic requires that they are subsequently measured and evaluated to assess their effects. This poses two difficulties:

1 *Finding a meaningful measure.* In some instances this is feasible. For example, it would be possible to recruit more Asian salespeople in order to increase sales to Asian customers, and in this case appropriate measures would be the number and value of sales and the number of Asian customers (identified by their family name). However, in other instances measurement is very difficult. For example, how would you measure the impact of ethnic-awareness training? Or the effects of flexible working arrangements? In both these cases it might be possible to measure the effects in terms of attitudes or changes in performance, but it would be more difficult to attribute these solely to the specific initiatives.

2 *Measuring in the short term.* In many instances the full effects of an equality or diversity initiative would only be realised in the long term. For many managers within organisations this would be a disincentive to invest in such initiatives, particularly if the performance of their department was measured in the short term. Moreover, it would be an even greater disincentive to invest if the manager's salary or bonus was affected by the short-term performance of his or her department.

Overall, the business case argument can make an impact – for example in circumstances of skills shortages, needs for particular types of employees, or local labour market conditions – but this is likely to be variable and patchy. As Dickens (1999: 10) states:

> The contingent and variable nature of the business case can be seen in the fact that business case arguments have greater salience for some organisations than others. ... The appeal of a particular business case argument can also vary over time as labour or product markets change, giving rise to 'fair weather' equality action.

Stop and think

Should the absence or weakness of a 'business case' for eliminating unfair discrimination and disadvantage absolve managers from trying to do so?

■ Justice and business sense

As you might have noticed, the two sets of arguments are not necessarily mutually exclusive. Indeed, it is feasible and practical for managers to use both sets to justify equality or diversity initiatives in their organisations. Increasingly, groups such as the UK's Commission for Racial Equality (www.cre.gov.uk) and Equal Opportunity Commission (www.eoc.org.uk) are stressing both sides. It is, in part, a pragmatic realisation that by stressing both arguments there is more chance of gaining commitment to equality and diversity from a wider group of people. Whether a manager is committed to equality because of justice or business sense reasons does not really matter – it is the fact he or she is committed that counts. Of course, this is not quite as simple in practice because once commitment has been gained, there is then the question of what to do about it – and that is when equal opportunities policies have a role to play.

Before proceeding with a discussion of policy choices, there is an important point to note that underpins much of the following discussion. Efforts to tackle unfair discrimination have not been able to develop through a simple reliance on voluntary commitment to social justice by managers or their rational acceptance of the business case. In most countries legislation has been introduced which sets limits to lawful managerial action and places obligations on managers to act in accordance with principles of fairness. Bearing this general point in mind, you should also note the following:

● The type and extent of this legislation varies from country to country, so it is important to read about the specific legislation in your own national context.
● Opinion varies as to whether state regulation is necessary or the extent to which it is legitimate or practical to legislate to prevent discrimination and promote equality of opportunity.
● Even when legislation is in place there is no guarantee that this will ensure that equality of opportunity prevails. This might be because the legislation is flouted (unlawfully) or because it is ineffective (too weak, too many loopholes, easily ignored, difficult to enforce, and so on).

In summary, as has been noted in other chapters (and which is specifically addressed in terms of the UK in Chapter 10), the external context is an important feature in guiding all managerial action and policy.

Equal opportunity policies

In order for an organisation to address the issue of disadvantage in a systemic and consistent way, it needs to be guided by a policy. Increasingly, organisations are creating equal opportunity policies in order to guide managers in decision-making. The rationale for such policies can be based on a mix of justice and business sense arguments, as was noted above. The form of these policies varies from organisation to organisation, and the next section will explain why this is the case. Before this, it is necessary to make some general points about the purpose and forms of equal opportunity policies and to note some of the criticisms made of them.

The ten points that follow are from the website of the UK's Commission for Racial Equality (www.cre.gov.uk) and are typical of the recommended good practice that employers are encouraged to adopt. The initiatives from 3 to 10 are often described as 'positive action' and organisations are encouraged to adopt some, if not all, of these.

1 Develop an equal opportunities policy, covering recruitment, promotion and training.
2 Set an action plan, with targets, so that you and your staff have a clear idea of what can be achieved and by when.
3 Provide training for all people, including managers, throughout your organisation, to ensure they understand the importance of equal opportunities. Provide additional training for staff who recruit, select and train your employees.
4 Assess the present position to establish your starting point, and monitor progress in achieving your objectives.
5 Review recruitment, selection, promotion and training procedures regularly, to ensure that you are delivering on your policy.
6 Draw up clear and justifiable job criteria, which are demonstrably objective and job-related.
7 Offer pre-employment training, where appropriate, to prepare potential job applicants for selection tests and interviews; consider positive action training to help ethnic minority employees to apply for jobs in areas where they are under-represented.
8 Consider your organisation's image: do you encourage applications from under-represented groups and feature women, ethnic minority staff and people with disabilities in recruitment literature, or could you be seen as an employer who is indifferent to these groups?
9 Consider flexible working, career breaks, providing childcare facilities, and so on, to help women in particular meet domestic responsibilities and pursue their occupations; and consider providing special equipment and assistance to help people with disabilities.
10 Develop links with local community groups, organisations and schools, in order to reach a wider pool of potential applicants.

The willingness of organisations to adopt such guidelines varies considerably. Moreover, there is also considerable variation in the extent to which all the points are adopted. You might think of this as a sliding scale: at one extreme are those organisations that adopt a policy that meets very few of the points, and at the other extreme those organisations that have addressed all ten points. Another way of looking at this is to think of different categories into which an organisation might be placed according to its approach to equal opportunities. Table 7.1 is an example of this type of categorisation.

Table 7.1 **Types of equal opportunity organisation**

The negative organisation	Has no equal opportunity policy
	Makes no claims of being an equal opportunity employer
	Might not be complying with the law
The minimalist organisation	Claims to be an equal opportunity employer
	Has no written equal opportunity policy
	Has no procedure or initiatives, but will react to claims of discrimination as they arise
The compliant organisation	Has a written equal opportunity policy
	Has procedures and initiatives in place to comply with some aspects of good practice recommendations
The proactive organisation	Has a written policy backed up with procedures and initiatives
	Monitors the outcomes of initiatives to assess their impact
	Promotes equality using full set of good practice guidelines, and might even go beyond these

Source: based on Healy (1993) and Kirton and Greene (2000)

ACTIVITY **Good practice guidelines**

1 For each of the ten points, assess whether your own organisation (or an organisation you are familiar with) has adopted these good practice guidelines.

2 Where would you place your organisation on the sliding scales described above?

3 In which category in Table 7.1 would you place your organisation?

■ Two key components: positive action and monitoring

To ensure the effectiveness of equal opportunity policies, the organisation needs to adopt positive action initiatives and ensure that equal opportunity monitoring takes place. These two components are a feature of those organisations categorised as 'proactive', so they need some elaboration.

● Positive action

Equal opportunity policies are based on the notion of positive action (sometimes called affirmative action). These are specific initiatives designed to encourage under-represented groups to apply for jobs or promotion within the organisation. They also might be concerned with making changes to working arrangements to encourage the retention of employees by making the environment more suited to the needs they have that differ from the majority of employees. There are examples of such initiatives throughout this chapter, but to show the variety of positive action initiatives that might occur within a single organisation, consider the UK police force. There had been a government report on the police force, branding it as racist and criticising it for failing to have enough ethnic minority police officers. As a consequence, a range of initiatives was launched in various police forces throughout the UK, which included the following specific actions designed to improve the recruitment and retention of ethnic minorities:

- running pre-joining courses for ethnic minority groups, giving prospective candidates a chance to experience the reality of life in the force, and dispelling any myths;
- introducing a national recruitment campaign featuring black role models;
- placing advertisements in Bollywood cinemas, ethnic minority press and radio stations that carried the message, 'It's not where you're from, it's where we're going';
- creating Positive Action Teams to run roadshows;
- setting up recruitment stalls at high-profile minority events and in locations where there is a large ethnic minority population;
- encouraging senior officers to visit religious venues;
- allowing Muslim female officers to wear the hijab (a scarf that covers the head and shoulders worn by some Muslim women) on duty;
- allowing officers wishing to observe Ramadan (when it is forbidden to drink or consume food from sunrise to dusk) to take later breaks rather than the set one;
- introducing prayer rooms to allow Muslim officers to pray during working hours;
- providing halal food in staff canteens;
- introducing mentors to provide career guidance;
- introducing a High Potential Development Scheme (HPDS) to seek out those with the potential to be future leaders.

Initiatives such as these are considered a central component in encouraging a more diverse workforce. However, it is not sufficient simply to put such actions into place; they have to be regularly audited to ensure they are working. In addition, it is often necessary for the organisation to collect data on the problem prior to the introduction of a particular initiative in order to be able to establish a benchmark and then assess the effect it is having. This is why equal opportunities monitoring is the second key component.

● Monitoring

One of the key ways of helping to ensure the effectiveness of policies is through the use of equality monitoring. This is a process of systematically collecting and analysing data on the composition of the workforce, particularly with regard to recruitment and promotion. The rationale behind monitoring is that it is impossible for managers to make an assessment of what action to take (if any) unless they are aware of the current situation. Of course, the supposition behind this is that managers want to take action – but if this is not the case then logically managers might not see the value in collecting the data in the first place. Therefore, equal opportunity monitoring has both advocates and detractors who will marshal different arguments to justify their position. These are summarised in Table 7.2.

Stop and think Does monitoring take place in the university or college where you are studying? If so, how is the data collected and what happens to it?

■ Criticism of equal opportunity policies

Naturally, there are some criticisms of equal opportunity policies. The first of these is that they are not worth the paper they are written on. Just because an organisation has a policy, it does not mean that the policy is effective. Indeed, it might be argued that in some organi-

Table 7.2 **The arguments for and against monitoring**

The case in favour of equal opportunities monitoring	The case against equal opportunities monitoring
• It allows an organisation to demonstrate what they are doing and identify particular problem areas so that they can take action.	• It stirs up trouble and discontent, and can create problems that would otherwise not arise.
• It encourages managers to think creatively about positive action initiatives. It removes the need for stronger legislation such as quotas (positive discrimination).	• It puts undue pressure on managers, and might encourage them to lower standards or appoint for the wrong reasons. It is positive discrimination by the back door.
• The data can be kept confidential, just like any other information.	• It is an invasion of privacy and open to abuse.
• It provides useful information to help management decision-making.	• It creates the requirement to collect information that is unnecessary.
• Organisations conducting their activities in line with the legal requirements have nothing to fear.	• Organisations with no problems regarding equal opportunities do not need this burdensome bureaucratic mechanism.
• The costs are modest.	• It is an unnecessary expenditure.
• It is good business practice.	• The business needs to focus on its commercial activities.

sations managers want to present the positive image of being aware of equal opportunities, but do not wish to introduce procedures or initiatives that might (in their opinion) constrain or limit their decisions about who to appoint, train, promote and so on.

A second criticism is that although equal opportunity policies result in formalised procedures with some organisations, this is no guarantee of fairness. Studies have shown that managers can find ways of evading or distorting the procedures. For example, in their case study of a local government authority in the UK, Liff and Dale (1994) interviewed a black woman on a clerical grade who had been told that she needed to get a professional qualification if she wanted promotion. 'After obtaining the qualification she was turned down again, this time in favour of a white woman without qualification: a decision justified [by the managers] on the grounds of "positive action"' (Liff and Dale, 1994: 187). In another study (Collinson *et al.*, 1990), even the personnel/HR managers, who are supposedly the guardians and promoters of good practice, were colluding with line managers to avoid equal opportunity guidelines.

A third criticism is that even where managers are working within the procedures, there is a huge amount of informal practice and discretion that means unfair treatment can persist. In the quote below, Liff (2002: 434) gives examples from two studies that show how this might occur during selection interviewing.

Collinson *et al.* (1990) during detailed observation of interviews, found that managers used different (gender-based) criteria to assess whether applicants were able to meet the job requirements. For example, a form of behaviour described as 'showing initiative' and assessed as desirable when demonstrated by a male applicant, in a woman applicant was seen as 'pushy' and undesirable. Similarly Curran (1988: 344) showed that managers often found it hard to separate the assessment of a characteristic such as leadership from the concept of masculinity, or a 'requirement for a pleasant personality and one for a pretty girl with a smile'. What is important about these findings is that they show that for some managers at least gender becomes part of their assessment of suitability criteria. ... Such findings also reduce the force of the prescriptive advice to excluded groups that they can succeed simply by gaining the necessary skills and demonstrating their ability at job-related tasks.

It will be noted that these three types of criticism are concerned with the ineffective-ness of equal opportunity policies. However, there are other critics who simply reject the whole idea of equal opportunities. They tend to suggest that policies are unnecessary and positive action initiatives are providing special privileges for particular groups. It is a viewpoint that is common among those of an extreme right-wing political persuasion and sometimes stems from a belief in the inferiority of some groups over others. Within organisations it can manifest itself in the form of verbal abuse and harassment – in these extreme circumstances the issue is not simply an organisational concern, but might also be a criminal matter. A dramatic example of the way that such extreme views can cause misery for employees is the case of a Ford UK employee:

> Mr Parma suffered years of routine abuse by his foreman and his team leader. Once, he opened his sealed pay packet to find the word 'Paki' scrawled inside. In another incident, he saw graffiti threatening to throw him to his death.[...]
>
> On one occasion he was ordered into the 'punishment cell', a small booth in which oil is sprayed over engines, but he was not allowed to wear protective clothing. He became ill and needed medical attention.
>
> On another occasion Mr Parma had his lunch kicked out of his hands and was told: 'We're not having any of that Indian shit in here.' He was also warned that he would have his legs broken if he ever named any of his tormentors. The police were called in at one stage, but the Crown Prosecution Service decided to drop charges.
>
> (*The Independent*, 24 September 1999)

Incidents such as this may be extreme but their existence makes the case for all organisa-tions both to have an equal opportunity policy and to ensure that it is enforced through positive action initiatives and monitoring.

Devising equality and diversity policies

It has been noted above that equal opportunity policies are seen as desirable and that recommendations are often made to organisations about how to frame such policies. Ultimately, however, it is up to the decision makers within organisations to choose the form and content of their policies – although there might be certain legal requirements within which they are expected to operate.

When formulating policy, managers are faced with addressing the key question of how to treat people at work in order to ensure fairness. To express this more specifically: to ensure fairness, should managers ignore the differences between people and treat them the same, or should managers acknowledge differences and treat people differently?

In many respects this is a key question that lies at the heart of any discussion about equality of opportunity. The reason why people often vehemently disagree about equal opportunities is because they are approaching the issue from very different perspectives. In other words, if you believe that, for example, men and women, or different ethnic groups, are fundamentally (as human beings) the same, then you are approaching the issues from an alternative perspective to someone who sees people as fundamentally different.

These differing perspectives also lead to different ways of dealing with the issue of ensuring fairness at work. It is therefore important to understand the two perspectives and look at the organisational initiatives that each might lead towards.

The sameness perspective

A word of warning is needed here. This concept of 'sameness' acknowledges genuine differences between people, but means that the variations of attributes such as intelligence, potential to develop skills, values, emotions, and so forth are distributed across different social groups. Consequently, it is argued that any differences between people on these attributes are not determined by their gender, ethnicity, age, sexual orientation and so forth, but arise from their upbringing, experiences, socialisation and other contextual factors. Therefore, the important guiding principle for managers is that people should be treated equally regardless of their sex, ethnic group, age and so forth.

Below are a few examples of the kinds of practices that this perspective might lead organisations to adopt:

- Ensure that age is not used as a criterion to decide whether an employee is suitable for retraining.
- Ensure that the same questions are asked of men and women during selection interviews.
- Ensure that gender-specific language does not appear in job adverts, job descriptions and other organisation documents.
- Ensure that part-time working opportunities are available to men and women.
- Ensure that any company benefits (for example, pensions, insurance rights, health scheme subsidies) are available to partners of non-married couples and same-sex partners.
- Ensure the same pay for the same job.

The guiding policy behind these types of initiative is *equal treatment*. Obviously, any such organisational initiatives are influenced by the legal context in which the organisation is based. There is likely to be legislation that requires organisations to undertake some actions. For instance, in the UK the legislation sets some of the parameters in the recruitment process (see Chapter 6) in terms and conditions of employment (Chapter 12) and in reward systems (Chapter 13).

ACTIVITY — Equal opportunities initiatives

1 Draw up a list of the equal opportunities initiatives in your organisation (if you work full-time or part-time) or an organisation with which you are familiar (if you are a full-time student). Your list does not need to be exhaustive, but try to include initiatives additional to the examples already given.

2 Which of the initiatives have arisen because of legal requirements and which have been introduced out of choice (i.e. voluntarily)?

3 Select one or two of those initiatives that have been introduced voluntarily and assess the influences that led to the initiatives being adopted. These could be internal or external pressures.

Limitation of the sameness approach

There is a substantial problem with this sameness approach. It assumes that disadvantage arises because people are not treated the same. While this is sometimes the case, disadvantage can also arise due to treating people the same when their differences ought to be considered. This is eloquently summed up by Liff and Wajcman (1996: 81) in relation to gender:

All policies based on same/equal treatment require women to deny, or attempt to mini-mize, differences between themselves and men as the price of equality. This, it is suggested, is neither feasible nor desirable. Such an approach can never adequately take account of problems arising from, say, women's domestic responsibilities or their educa-tional disadvantage. Nor does it take account of those who want to spend time with their children without this costing them advancement at work. Sameness is being judged against a norm of male characteristics and behaviour. ... [The sameness approach to equal opportunities takes] an over-simplistic view both of the problem of inequality (seeing it as a managerial failure to treat like as like) and its solution ('equality' can be achieved by treating women the same as men).

■ The difference perspective

The 'difference' perspective assumes that key differences exist between people and that these should be taken into account when managers are making decisions. In other words, it can be argued that ignoring differences can lead to disadvantage.

Again there is a word of warning. There tend to be two strands to this perspective and this must be taken into account: (1) the collectivist strand; (2) the individualist strand.

● 1. The collectivist strand

This approach argues that the differences are associated with the social groups to which a person belongs. For example, as the quote above from Liff and Wajcman (1996) underlines, women's domestic responsibilities are different in general from those of men – most notably in the time spent on childcare – so, to ignore this difference will disad-vantage women. For instance, imagine a job had the following statement as part of the essential requirements: 'Applicants must have at least five years' previous experience of international sales and be aged between 28 and 35.' These requirements would have a disadvantageous effect for women because (based on the uneven division of childcare responsibilities) a lower proportion of women would be able to meet the condition of being under 35 *and* having 5 years of relevant experience. This is due to the fact that more women than men would have taken career breaks to have children and rear chil-dren. Therefore, by ignoring the differences between men and women the requirements are disadvantaging women. In the UK this could be construed as 'indirect discrimina-tion', which means instances where there might be no intention to discriminate against a particular group but where the effect is discriminatory because certain conditions have been set down that advantage or disadvantage some groups over others (see Chapter 6).

The collectivist strand therefore argues that differences between social groups exist and should be considered in relation to ensuring fairness at work. This means that it might be relevant to introduce practices that are based on recognising differences between social groups, rather than ignoring differences. Below are some examples of the types of initiatives that might arise from taking this collectivist difference perspective:

- single-sex training schemes (developing skills to allow access to a wide range of jobs);
- payment for jobs based on principles of equal value (see also Chapter 13);
- job advertisements aimed at encouraging applications from under-represented groups;
- reassessment of job requirements to open opportunities up to a wider range of people;
- choice of food in the workplace cafeteria that reflects different cultural needs.

The guiding policy behind these types of initiative is *special treatment according to social group membership*. Such initiatives are usually described as 'positive action' or 'affirmative action'. There is a wide range of such initiatives, the most extreme sort being quotas that set a requirement for organisations to recruit and promote a specific percentage of people from disadvantaged groups. Setting quotas is the most extreme form of positive action initiative, and in the UK, as in other European countries, it is unlawful. The other forms of positive action – such as those listed above – are permissible in many countries. Again the legal context is important because some principles, such as equal value, might be a legal requirement for all organisations, while others are left entirely to the discretion of managers within organisations.

One of the notable problems with this perspective is that it leads some people to argue that special treatment constitutes an unfair advantage. There is a tendency among critics to emphasise the extreme examples, and there has been considerable backlash to some affirmative action programmes in the United States where quotas are set for organisations to recruit and promote ethnic minorities. Some of this criticism is politically driven, but it also comes from some of the supposed benefactors of positive discrimination, particular ethnic minorities. These critics argue that it demeans their achievements because it leads others to suspect that they only got the job or promotion to meet the required 'quota', rather than because they were the best candidate. Furthermore, some commentators argue that it is simply wrong in principle to redress the disadvantage suffered by one group of people because of favouritism and privilege with measures that are specifically designed to favour and privilege an alternative group of people. Indeed, this is the perspective of the UK's Chartered Institute of Personnel and Development, who use the term 'reverse discrimination' to describe extreme measures such as quota systems.

Although the policy of special treatment presents some problems, it also offers a persuasive approach for some people because it recognises that disadvantage is often an intrinsic part of existing organisational structures, practices and culture. Simply adopting a policy of equal treatment would not remove this existing disadvantage; instead, something more radical has to be done to get to the root of the problem and redress the existing imbalance. One of the best expressions of this comes from former US President Lyndon Johnson at the time of the introduction of race legislation in 1965:

> Imagine a hundred yard dash in which one of the two runners has his legs shackled together. He has progressed 10 yards, while the unshackled runner has gone 50 yards. At that point the judges decide that the race is unfair. How do they rectify the situation? Do they merely remove the shackles and allow the race to proceed? Then they could say that 'equal opportunity' now prevailed. But one of the runners would still be forty yards ahead of the other. Would it not be the better part of justice to allow the previously shackled runner to make up the forty yard gap; or to start the race all over again?
>
> (Quoted in Noon and Blyton, 2002: 278)

Stop and think

Look again at the questions raised in President Johnson's analogy. What would you do and how would you justify it?

Before reading about the second strand of this difference approach, you might want to see a further illustration of how sameness and difference can lead to alternative interpretations of workplace issues. If so, look at Box 7.2, 'Sameness and difference'.

BOX 7.2	Sameness and difference

Billing and Alvesson (1989) were interested in the question of why there are relatively few women at senior levels in organisations and they conclude that different explanations arise depending on whether men and women are judged to be fundamentally the same or fundamentally different from each other. The discussion below draws on their analysis and brings in some of the other issues explored so far in the chapter.

If you think men and women are basically the same, any dissimilarity in terms of getting into senior positions has to be explained in terms of discriminatory practices in organisations. And if you think something should be done about this it might be because you believe it is ethical to do so, or else because it is organisationally inefficient not to do anything (or perhaps both). These should be familiar arguments because they are reflective of the discussion of social justice and the business case earlier in the chapter.

If you believe men and women have different qualities, strengths and values, any dissimilarity might be explained by these differences. This could suggest that the appointment of women to senior posts would only be possible if the fundamental male-dominated values of the organisation changed. Simply changing policies and practices would not be adequate – a more radical overhaul would be necessary. Of course, you might think that such an overhaul would be unnecessary, in which case you are arguing for keeping the status quo. However, some observers suggest that changes in the business environment mean that contemporary businesses increasingly require more managers with skills traditionally associated with women: communication, teamworking, cooperation, nurturing, transforming and so forth. According to this line of argument, women are able to make a special contribution to the organisation and, based on business efficiency arguments, are more likely to be promoted to senior levels.

● 2. The individualist strand

The second way of looking from a difference perspective can be called the individualist strand because the main focus is the individual rather than the social group. This approach emphasises the individuality of all employees. People have unique strengths and weaknesses, abilities and needs. Therefore it is not important to focus on characteristics that associate people with a particular group – for instance, their sex or whether they have a disability – rather it is their individuality that becomes the central pertinent issue.

A label that is often associated with this approach is 'managing diversity'. It is increasingly being used by organisations as a term to describe their approach to ensure fairness and opportunities for all. However, a particular problem is that the term 'managing diversity' can have various meanings. It has become one of those widely used management phrases, so can mean different things in different organisations. At one extreme it is simply a synonym for 'equal opportunities' – used because the latter is seen as old-fashioned or backward looking – and therefore has no distinct or special meaning of its own. At the other extreme, managing diversity represents a new approach to dealing with disadvantage at work.

A notable example of the new approach based on recognising individual differences is Kandola and Fullerton (1994). They argue that managing diversity is superior to previous approaches to equality at work for five reasons:

1 It ensures that all employees maximise their potential and their contribution to the organisation.
2 It covers a broad range of people – no one is excluded.
3 It focuses on issues of movement within an organisation, the culture of the organisation, and the meeting of business objectives.

4 It becomes the concern of all employees and especially all managers.
5 It does not rely on positive action/affirmative action.

Below are some examples of the types of initiatives that might arise from taking this individualist difference perspective.

- Offer employees a choice of benefits from a 'menu' so they can tailor a package to suit their individual needs.
- Devise training and development plans for each employee.
- Provide training to ensure that managers are aware of, and can combat, their prejudices based on stereotypes.
- Explore and publicise ways that diversity within the organisation improves the organisation – for example, public perceptions, sensitivity to customer needs, wider range of views and ideas.
- Re-evaluate the criteria for promotion and development and widen them by recognising a greater range of competences, experiences and career paths.

The guiding policy behind these types of initiative is *special treatment according to individual needs*. Of course, this approach has its critics, and in particular three objections can by raised.

1 The approach tends to understate the extent to which people share common experiences. It has a tendency to reject the idea of social groups which is somewhat counter to people's everyday experiences. For example, while several disabled people might differ considerably across a whole range of attributes and attitudes, their common experience of disability (even different forms of disability) might be sufficient to create a feeling of cohesion and solidarity. In particular, some people might actively look for social group identity if they feel isolated or vulnerable.
2 The approach ignores material similarities between social groups. For example, Kirton and Greene (2000: 115) note that 'women of all ethnic groups typically take on the responsibility for children and are less able to compete for jobs with men, not withstanding qualitative ethnic differences in how women may "juggle" their multiple roles'.
3 The approach has a tendency to emphasise the value of diversity in terms of the business sense arguments outlined earlier in the chapter. As was noted, such arguments have their limitations because they focus only on those initiatives that can be shown to contribute to the profitability or other performance indicators of the organisation. In practice, this extends opportunities only to a selective number of individuals whose competencies are in short supply or have been identified as being of particular value.

So far, two perspectives (sameness and difference) have been identified and compared. To help you conceptualise this, Figure 7.1 puts it in diagrammatic form.

Sameness and difference

As has been shown in the discussion above, disadvantage can arise by treating people the same or by treating people differently, so any policy that emphasises one perspective more than the other runs the risk of leaving some disadvantages unchecked. What is called for is a mixed policy that recognises that to eliminate disadvantage it is necessary in some circumstances to treat people the same, and in other circumstances to treat people differently. Of course, this is a challenge in itself because in what circumstances do you apply one criterion and not the other? For example, imagine the following situation.

A woman applies for a job as an adviser selling financial products in a company that is dominated by men.

Scenario 1: she has the same qualifications and experience as male applicants, but the all-male selection panel might reject her because they consider that she would not 'fit in' with the competitive, aggressive culture of the organisation.

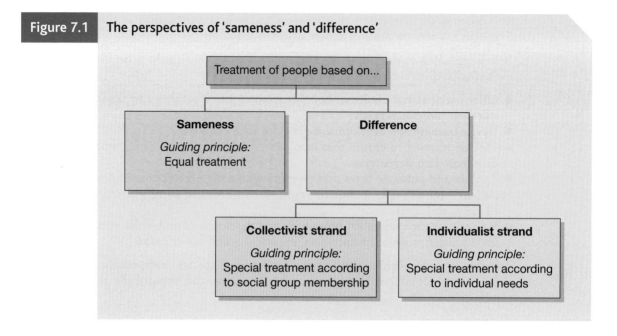

Figure 7.1   The perspectives of 'sameness' and 'difference'

Scenario 2: she has the same qualifications as male applicants but has taken a career break for childcare purposes. The selection panel reject her because compared with men of the same age she has less work experience.

In the first scenario the panel are rejecting her by using the criterion of difference (recognising gender); in the second by using the criterion of sameness (ignoring gender). But if the panel were to reverse their logic of difference and sameness, it might lead them to different conclusions. In the first scenario, if the panel ignored gender, they would arrive at the conclusion that she was appointable. In the second scenario, if they recognised that, because of her gender, she has had extra domestic commitments so cannot be compared with men of the same age, then again they might conclude she is appointable.

This illustrates that managers have a key role in dealing with disadvantage because they determine the criteria and define the circumstances in which sameness and difference are either recognised or ignored.

Institutional discrimination

One of the key issues that managers must face is whether their organisation operates in ways that are fundamentally discriminatory. This is sometimes referred to as institutional racism, institutional sexism, institutional homophobia and so on. The term means that rather than discrimination being seen simply as the actions of individuals, it is deep-rooted in the processes and culture of the organisation.

Examples of processes that are sometimes described as evidence of institutional discrimination are:

- word-of-mouth methods for recruitment;
- dress codes that prevent people practising their religious beliefs;
- promotions based on informal recommendations, rather than open competition;
- informal assessments rather than formal appraisals;
- assumptions about training capabilities;
- assumptions about language difficulties and attitudes.

Often these types of processes are not recognised as being discriminatory and have been in operation for many years. It is only when a company is faced with a legal challenge that such practices are seen to be having a discriminatory impact. Managers should regularly scrutinise organisational procedures, and the use of data collected through equal opportunity monitoring can be particularly effective in highlighting areas where the processes might be disadvantaging particular groups.

ACTIVITY

Recruitment at SewCo

Consider the following case:

SewCo is a family-run business that makes garments. Most of its employees are sewing machine operators (all women) who assemble the garments. It has a stable core workforce, but there is fluctuation in demand for its products, so extra employees are brought in when the order books are full and 'let go' at slack periods. When managers need to recruit extra employees, or when they need to replace someone, they rely on word-of-mouth methods. This means that the women on the shopfloor ask around their friends and family. When likely candidates are identified their names are given to the factory manager. He calls them in for a chat and assesses their suitability. If he approves them he asks the supervisor to check if the candidate has the required sewing skills.

1 Identify the problems with this approach to the recruitment process in terms of equal opportunities.

2 Suggest an alternative approach that might address the problems you have identified.

Just as pernicious are workplace cultures that have the effect of excluding people from particular social groups by making them feel unwelcome or uncomfortable. This is a key issue for managers because organisations might have cultures that are long established and deeply embedded. An interesting review of the way organisational cultures can marginalise social groups is provided by Kirton and Greene (2000: 76–93). Most notable among their conclusions are the following points:

- Organisational cultures are infused with gendered meanings, which are often unarticulated and thus rendered invisible. The gendered hierarchy is an example, as are various unwritten codes, rules, customs and habits which guide gendered behaviour and underpin expectations of organisational members.
- Sexual harassment and the use of sexual humour are pervasive and the outcome of workplace gendered social relations, which are powerful mechanisms for the control and subordination of women.
- Stereotypes (based on gender, race, disability, sexual orientation and age) are reinforced through jokes and humour, leading to negative organisational experiences for some people.
- Non-disabled people's lack of contact with disability reinforces their fear and ignorance surrounding the issue.

Stop and think

Consider whether your own employing organisation, university or college operates practices that might support institutionalised discrimination.

◼ Problems with institutional discrimination

The first problem is inertia. Even when institutional discrimination has been identified, there is no incentive to make changes because those people in positions of influence have benefited (and continue to benefit) from the system. Furthermore, those people most likely to change policies within the organisation (the 'victims' of discrimination) are denied access to decision-making processes.

The second problem is with the concept of institutional discrimination itself. Some critics argue that it can lead to a tendency to blame 'the system', rather than focusing on the people who shape and sustain the system. In some circumstances this can be helpful because by removing blame from individuals it might be easier to encourage action to address the problem. In other circumstances it can result in nothing being done because no one is deemed responsible or held accountable.

In defence of the concept of institutional discrimination, it can be argued that it alerts people to the way that the fundamental structures and processes can be detrimental to equality and diversity, and that unless action is taken to address these fundamentals, nothing will improve. This is an important point because it suggests that in many instances the drive to equality and diversity requires some radical changes, rather than just equal opportunity statements and positive action initiatives.

◼ The need for radical changes: the long agenda

The existence of institutional discrimination leads some commentators to argue that fundamental change is needed if the elimination of disadvantage is to be achieved. Foremost among these commentators is Cockburn (1989, 1991) who has pointed out that many of the equal opportunity initiatives adopted by managers in organisations are concerned only with the short term. Typically, these initiatives are fixing current problems, responding to outside pressures, or perhaps seeking to make a pre-emptive move to impress customers and clients. This ignores the possibilities of more radical, long-term initiatives that might fundamentally change the structures and processes that produce disadvantage.

The proposition forwarded by Cockburn is that as well as this short agenda (with its laudable aim of eliminating bias) there is the need to consider the long agenda. This would be a challenging project of organisational transformation, requiring fundamental changes to the processes, roles, norms, attitudes and relationships within organisations. Cockburn (1989: 218) explains:

> As such it brings into view the nature and purpose of institutions and the processes by which the power of some groups over others in institutions is built and renewed. It acknowledges the needs of disadvantaged groups for access to power. [...] But it also looks for change in the nature of power, in the control ordinary people of diverse kinds have over institutions, a melting away of the white male monoculture.

The obvious problem for enacting the long agenda is that those in positions of influence within organisations have little incentive to make changes that might challenge their own power and dominance. The long agenda therefore has to be led by activists and advocates. This might be through committed individuals within organisations, but it would also require collective voice and action. It might also require a political context that encourages a more active approach by organisations to ensuring equality of opportunity – through, for example, compulsory monitoring or employment quotas for disadvantaged groups.

The process of discrimination in an organisation

The discussion so far has explored many of the complex and sometimes contradictory issues surrounding equality and diversity. It makes sense to bring this together by considering the range of pressures and influences that are brought to bear when managing equality and diversity. Figure 7.2 is a flowchart that maps the relationship between the key components and thereby shows how the process of discrimination occurs in organisations (Noon and Blyton, 2002). Each of the components of this flowchart is discussed in this section, and is linked with many of the issues raised in the earlier part of the chapter.

At the centre of the process lie two vital questions: what should be the basis of any specific policy, and is the policy fair? Try to envisage this in terms of specific policies, such as promotion, awarding of merit pay, entitlement to career development opportunities, and so on. The first question is of vital concern to managers since their decisions are going to shape a particular policy. However, as the diagram shows, such decisions are not made in isolation but are subject to a range of influences: personal influences (beliefs, values and political agenda), external pressures and organisational pressures:

1 *Personal influences.* A manager will have his or her individual beliefs and values that fundamentally guide behaviour and influence decisions. So, for instance, a strong belief in social justice is going to affect the choices that a manager makes, as is a particular

Figure 7.2   **The process of discrimination in an organisation**

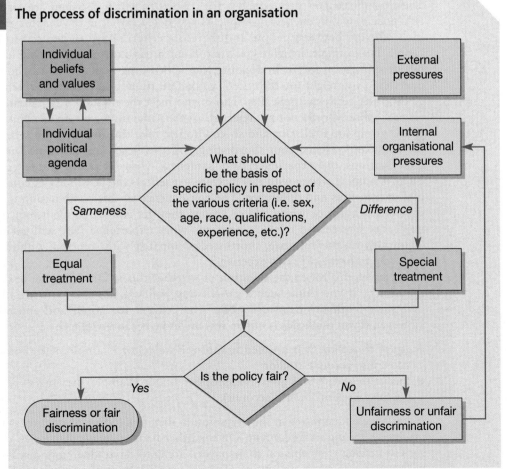

Source: Adapted from Noon and Blyton (2002)

prejudice or stereotype about a social group. Combined with this is the individual political agenda of the manager, which might moderate the values and beliefs in some way. For example, a male manager might believe that women do not make good leaders but knows that in order to get promotion he must suppress this view in order not to alienate his boss – who is a woman. This, of course, is the *realpolitik* of normal organisational life and will operate at all levels. This intermixing of beliefs, values and political manoeuvring is going to have an influence on the manager's decisions.

2 *External pressures.* In addition to these personal pressures, the manager is faced with external pressure. This could be legislation requiring (or prohibiting) certain action, public opinion, customer or client pressure, supplier influence, labour supply issues, and so forth. For instance, it was noted in the discussion about the business case how organisations might adopt equal opportunity initiatives in order to improve their public image, or access a wider customer base.

3 *Internal organisational pressures.* The final set of pressures comes from within the organisation. They might arise from other managers, employees (especially through satisfaction surveys and grievances), trade unions, works councils, and so forth. There might also be pressure as a result of data collected within the organisation. For example, high levels of employee turnover might encourage positive action initiatives that help to retain employees, develop and make better use of skills, and provide a more supportive and encouraging environment. In addition, there are likely to be pressures because of the workplace culture and traditions of the organisation – the sorts of issues that were discussed in the section on institutional discrimination.

These combined pressures establish the context in which decisions are made about specific policies within the organisation. As was noted earlier in the chapter, managers must make choices between people and therefore criteria have to be used to differentiate people. For example, imagine you are running a recruitment process and have received a pile of application forms. In deciding your shortlisting policy (that is, who to call for an interview), you might use the criteria of qualifications and previous experience as a way of choosing between applicants. Those who meet the minimum requirements are interviewed, those who do not are rejected. At the same time, you might think that age and ethnic group are irrelevant and so you do not take this into account when shortlisting the applicants. Hence your shortlisting policy is based on 'difference' with regard to qualifications and experience, and 'sameness' with regard to ethnic group and age. There is nothing wrong with this mixture – it reflects the possibility of combining principles of sameness and difference. The consequence of this combination is that whether someone is black or white, old or young, they get equal treatment, but if they have a university degree and relevant previous work experience they will get treated more favourably (in this instance, shortlisted) compared with someone without a degree or with inappropriate previous experience.

Logically, this raises the question of whether this is fair (note the next stage in the flowchart). If you think such a shortlisting policy is fair then you are likely to be in agreement with the decisions about the criteria for equal and special treatment. However, if you think this is unfair, this might be because you feel:

● equal treatment was applied inappropriately (for example, age should have been taken into account) and/or
● special treatment was given inappropriately (for example, previous experience should not have been taken into account).

If you were an employee in the organisation then this feeling of unfairness might simply produce a feeling of discontent. On the other hand, it might drive you to take action such as voicing your opinion to managers, going to the trade union, discussing the issue with other employees or leaving. This in turn might produce internal organisational pressures on future decisions (shown by the feedback loop in Figure 7.2).

Mapping out the process in this way reveals that every managerial decision over appointments, promotions, allocation of work, merit pay, training opportunities and so forth is likely to be met with a variety of responses: some individuals and groups will interpret the decision as fair and others as unfair, depending on whether they consider the equal or special treatment to be justifiable. The extent to which employees concern themselves with issues of fairness will vary according to the circumstances and is likely to reflect whether they are directly involved with, or affected by, the outcome.

Stop and think	Have you directly experienced treatment you considered unfair? If so, what did you do about it? What other options did you have?

Concluding comment

It can be seen from the preceding sections that managing equality and diversity is about making choices between various courses of action. It was also shown that there are competing viewpoints as to why particular approaches should be taken. In many instances there is no clear-cut right or wrong method – rather it is a matter of judgement and conscience. What is important, however, is that any action or policy is backed up by a clear rationale.

Obviously, this chapter cannot conclude by recommending a particular approach because it depends on whether you are persuaded by the rationale behind that approach. The chapter's purpose has been to show you the approaches and provide you with an understanding of the key concepts and dilemmas. These should allow you to make your own choices and equip you to predict and challenge opposing viewpoints. The summary provides you with a review of the key points to reflect upon in forming your opinions.

Summary

- The differences that define disadvantaged groups are far more imprecise than might at first appear. It is important to recognise the diversity between social groups and within the same social group. Such diversity means policies need to be sensitive to different experiences of discrimination and different needs of disadvantaged groups and individuals.

- The reason for managers to intervene in order to prevent discrimination can be based on arguments of social justice or business needs – or both. The social justice case stresses the moral case for fairness, but critics argue that managers should be concerned with profit and efficiency, not morality. The business case stresses ways that equality and diversity are good for business, but critics point to instances where it can make good business sense *not* to pursue equal opportunities.

- Equal opportunity policies vary between organisations; they range from those that are simply empty statements to others which are backed up by effective action programmes. For policies to be effective, they need to have positive action initiatives to ensure that policy is implemented, and monitoring to assess the effectiveness of the initiatives over time.

- When devising policies to ensure fairness managers can base them on assumptions of sameness or assumptions of difference. These two perspectives help to explain why there is often a lack of agreement about how to ensure fairness. The sameness perspective emphasises similarities between people and advocates equal treatment. The difference perspective emphasises diversity either between social groups or between individuals. These two variations of the difference perspective are similar in that they both advocate special treatment that takes the differences between people into account, but they differ in their suggestions about the types of initiatives that organisations should adopt.

● The term managing diversity is often used to describe the approach to fairness that emphasises the individual differences between people. In some instances it is an alternative approach advocated by commentators who think traditional equal opportunities policies have failed and are fundamentally flawed.

● It is important for managers to recognise that unfair treatment sometimes results from treating people differently when they ought to be treated the same, and sometimes from treating people the same when key differences ought to be recognised. Policies, procedures and attitudes within an organisation should therefore be based on recognising both the similarities and differences between people.

● Institutional discrimination is a term used to describe organisations that have processes and practices that are fundamentally discriminatory – sometimes without managers realising – and are reinforced through existing organisational structures and workplace cultures. Tackling such fundamental problems might require a more radical agenda than that being proposed by many advocates of equality and diversity.

● The process of discrimination can be seen in the combination of personal, external and internal pressures on managers to make choices in their decisions about appointments, promotions, allocation of work, training opportunities, and so forth, according to principles of sameness or difference. Perceptions of unfairness are the result of a mismatch between the expectations of employees and the manager's decisions. Seen in this way, all decisions are susceptible to claims of unfairness, depending on the perspective of the individuals concerned, the perceived appropriateness of the criterion for the decision and the individual and social acceptability of the type of treatment (special or equal).

Questions

1 'We don't employ people over 50 years old because they find it difficult to learn new skills.' This statement was made by a training manager in a call centre. Comment on the statement using the concepts of stereotyping, prejudice, social justice and the business case.

2 What is the purpose of equal opportunity policies? Why do they sometimes fail to live up to expectations?

3 Without looking back through the chapter, give at least one example of a workplace initiative from each of the following approaches:
   (a) the sameness perspective;
   (b) the collectivist strand of the difference perspective;
   (c) the individualist strand of the difference perspective.

4 'I treat everyone the same – so that's how I ensure fairness.' This quote is from a section manager in a supermarket. Explain why such an approach can sometimes lead to unfairness.

5 'Everyone is unique. Everyone is an individual. As a manager you should treat them as such.' If you were being critical of this opinion, what points would you make?

6 The Fire Service in the UK has been described as institutionally racist, sexist and homophobic. What does this mean? How would you evaluate whether such a description was legitimate?

Case study

Safe Future Finance

The following is a true story, although for legal reasons names have been changed.

Gordon Burrows graduated from university last year with a Business degree, took some time out to go travelling around the world and then returned to his university town. He was unsure about his career but he saw an advert pinned to the notice board in the university careers office that read as follows.

Are you qualified to degree level, highly self-motivated, diligent and keen to make a fortune? Then you could be the person for us! We are looking for confident, young graduates to join our financial advisory team. Excellent prospects and high earning potential. Call us to find out more.

With nothing to lose, Gordon made the phone call and within the week found himself outside the offices of Safe Future Finance, about to go for an interview with Mr Fletcher. The woman at reception escorted Gordon into a large open plan office, full of desks occupied by men in dark suits and brightly coloured ties. Mr Fletcher was among them and, it turned out, was not much older than Gordon.

'I have your interviewee, Mr Fletcher.'

'Thanks, Brenda. Could you fetch us a couple of coffees? Is coffee okay for you, Gordon? Sorry I can't offer you anything stronger! Call me Dave, by the way.'

Gordon soon learned that the job involved being part of Dave's team selling financial products – particularly investment plans with life cover. There was no fixed salary but he would be paid on a commission-only basis and would have 'self-employed' status. However, the bonuses were good; potentially they were very high if he reached Dave's level who, as a team leader, also received a percentage cut of all his sales team.

During the next half-hour Dave read through Gordon's application form and asked a series of questions. He enquired about Gordon's background and seemed particularly interested that Gordon had been to a private school. He also noted that Gordon was a keen golfer. The interview was not as Gordon had expected – it was more like a chat than the formal process he had learned about at Business School.

'Right,' said Dave. 'Let's give you a tour of the office then we'll finish this off in the bar across the road. That's where I can find out if you're the right man for the job – you know, find out if we'd be able to work together.'

As they wandered around the large air-conditioned office, Dave explained that the teams were in competition with each other so a good team spirit with everyone 'singing from the same hymn sheet' was essential. He added, 'There's no room for mavericks in my team. We work together and we play together – it's all part of building up good team spirit and getting sales. There's a lot of banter – you know, nicknames, piss-taking, that sort of thing – but it's all part of the culture of the place. They must have taught you all about organisational culture at Business School.'

Gordon nodded, although this was not quite what he remembered about organisational culture.

As they walked between the desks Dave exchanged a few pleasantries and a few light-hearted insults with the various sales advisers. He explained to Gordon, 'One of the most important things you need to know about this place is that you are very much seen as an individual. Okay, you'd be part of my team but you work on your own and you sink or swim according to your own abilities. You could come to me for advice but I'd be expecting you to work your balls off. I've got no room for passengers on my team.'

Gordon was unsure whether to respond but commented. 'I work well on my own and I'm not scared of hard work.'

Dave nodded approvingly. 'Good. This is a tough job. It is all about closing a deal. I can teach you the basics but the drive comes from within. Sometimes you've got to be ruthless for the sake of your own bonus and the team. You see the chart on the wall over there? You see the long line?'

Gordon stared at a multicoloured chart that had everyone's name listed down the side and a performance line alongside. One of the lines stretched noticeably further than the rest.

'The longest line is me,' said Dave loud enough for the men at the nearby desks to hear. 'I clean up on the amount of business I sign up.

Case study continued

None of these tossers can get anywhere near me!' There were a few smirks and some obscene gestures before Dave said in a mocking tone, 'Come on, let's leave these ladies to it.'

'Funny you should say that,' ventured Gordon. 'Aren't there any women working here?'

'Sure,' said Dave, 'All the girls are on the next floor. They handle the paperwork.'

'So don't they apply for sale adviser jobs?' asked Gordon.

'Yes, they apply, but they don't get them because they tend not to have the drive and hard-nosed attitude to sales. But we're not prejudiced here, it's just that skills are used where they are best suited. For instance, you'll see we've got some Asians in the office. They've got excellent contacts, particularly among their families, who have money and are willing to invest it in the financial products we sell. On the other hand, you won't see any black faces because they have a different attitude to investments and they aren't well connected. Being well connected to people with money to invest is one of the key factors for success in this job. In fact we've just recruited a couple of shirt-lifters because the company is hoping they'll bring in "pink cash" from their community.'

Dave checked his watch, and announced that it was time for them to finish off the interview in the bar across the road. He added, 'Besides, I'm desperate for a cigarette. That's one of the downsides of working here – it's a no-smoking office. Bloody discrimination if you ask me.'

Questions

1 Evaluate Dave's attitude using your knowledge of the social justice and business case arguments.

2 Evaluate the recruitment procedure used in this instance, drawing upon your knowledge of equal opportunity best-practice guidelines.

3 Does Dave treat people according to principles of sameness or difference?

4 Assess whether or not there is evidence of institutional discrimination at Safe Future Finance.

5 Using Figure 7.2 as a process map, identify the critical junctures where problems have or could occur and where change interventions could/should be made.

References and further reading

Billing, Y.D. and Alvesson, M. (1989) 'Four ways of looking at women and leadership', *Scandanavian Journal of Management*, Vol. 5, No. 1, pp. 63–80.

Cockburn, C. (1989) 'Equal opportunities: the short and long agenda', *Industrial Relations Journal*, Vol. 20, No. 3, pp. 213–25.

Cockburn, C. (1991) *In the Way of Women*. Basingstoke: Macmillan.

Collinson, D.L., Knights, D. and Collinson, M. (1990) *Managing to Discriminate*. London: Routledge.

Cunningham, I. and James, P. (2001) 'Managing diversity and disability legislation', in Noon, M. and Ogbonna, E. (eds) *Equality, Diversity and Disadvantage in Employment*. Basingstoke: Palgrave, pp.103–117.

Curran, M. (1988) 'Gender and recruitment: people and places in the labour market', *Work, Employment and Society*, Vol. 2, No. 3, pp. 335–351.

Dickens, L. (1994) 'The business case for women's equality', *Employee Relations*, Vol. 16, No. 8, pp. 5–18.

Dickens, L. (1999) 'Beyond the business case: a three-pronged approach to equality action', *Human Resource Management Journal*, Vol. 9, No. 1, pp. 9–19.

Dickens, L. (2000) 'Still wasting resources? Equality in employment', in Bach, S. and Sisson, K. (eds) *Personnel Management*, 3rd edn. Oxford: Blackwell, pp.137–69.

Healy, G. (1993) 'Business and discrimination', in Stacey, R. (ed.) *Strategic Thinking and the Management of Change*. London: Kogan Page.

Heery, E. and Noon, M. (2001) *A Dictionary of Human Resource Management*. Oxford: Oxford University Press.

Kandola, R. and Fullerton, J. (1994) *Managing the Mosaic*. London: IPD.

Kirton, G. and Greene, A.M. (2000) *The Dynamics of Managing Diversity*. Oxford: Butterworth-Heinemann.

Liff, S. (2002) 'The industrial relations of a diverse workforce', in Edwards, P. (ed.) *Industrial Relations*, 2nd edn. Oxford: Blackwell, pp. 420–446.

Liff, S. and Dale, K. (1994) 'Formal opportunity, informal barriers: black women managers within a local authority', *Work, Employment and Society*, Vol. 8 No. 2, pp. 177–198.

Liff, S. and Wajcman, J. (1996) '"Sameness" and "difference" revisited: which way forward for equal opportunity initiatives?', *Journal of Management Studies*, Vol. 33, No. 1, pp. 79–94.

Modood, T., Berthoud, R., Lakey, J., Nazroo, J., Smith, P., Virdee, S. and Beishon, S. (1997) *Ethnic Minorities in Britain: Diversity and Disadvantage*. London: Policy Studies Institute.

Noon, M. and Blyton, P. (2002) *The Realities of Work*, 2nd edn. Basingstoke: Palgrave.

Noon, M. and Ogbonna, E. (2001) 'Introduction: the key analytical themes', in Noon, M. and Ogbonna, E. (eds) *Equality, Diversity and Disadvantage in Employment*. Basingstoke: Palgrave, pp. 1–14.

Oswick, C. and Rosenthal, P. (2001) 'Towards a relevant theory of age discrimination in employment', in Noon, M. and Ogbonna, E. (eds) *Equality, Diversity and Disadvantage in Employment*. Basingstoke: Palgrave, pp. 156–171.

Pilkington, A. (2001) 'Beyond racial dualism: racial disadvantage and ethnic diversity in the labour market', in Noon, M. and Ogbonna, E. (eds) *Equality, Diversity and Disadvantage in Employment*. Basingstoke: Palgrave, pp. 171–189.

Reynolds, G., Nicholls, P. and Alferoff, C. (2001) 'Disabled people, (re)training and employment: a qualitative exploration of exclusion', in Noon, M. and Ogbonna, E. (eds) *Equality, Diversity and Disadvantage in Employment*. Basingstoke: Palgrave, pp. 172–189.

Webb, J. (1997) 'The politics of equal opportunity', *Gender, Work and Organization*, Vol. 4, No. 3, pp. 159–169.

For multiple choice questions, exercises and annotated weblinks specific to this chapter visit this book's website at www.booksites.net/beardwell

Employers exploit agency work boom

Agency work is soaring, thanks to the huge benefits it affords both agencies and the employers that use them. As ever, it is the workers who are losing out. The extent of temporary working through employment agencies has rocketed in recent years and shows no sign of stopping. According to market research company KeyNote, the requirement for temporary workers is 'insatiable'. It says the value of the market for temporary and contract recruitment rose by 74% between 1997 and 2000, and is set to almost double from GBP 17.14 billion in 2000 to more than GBP 32 billion in 2005. A survey commissioned by the Department of Trade and Industry (DTI) and carried out by the Bostock Marketing Group estimated that 529,000 people were employed by agencies in 1999.

While this is still a small proportion of the total workforce (around 24 million), it is increasing rapidly. A KeyNote report, Recruitment agencies (temporary and contract) 2000 market report, shows that the number of workers placed in temporary jobs or in contract positions increased by 46.8% between 1997 and 2000. According to TUC figures, 18% of temporary workers are now agency workers, compared to just 7% eight years ago.

And the Workplace Employee Relations Survey (WERS) 1998 reported that more than a quarter of workplaces (28%) now use agency temporary workers. The increase is good news for the temporary recruitment industry, as supplying agency workers can be a lucrative business, with agencies typically charging commissions of between 10% and 25% and many

making huge profits. But it can be bad news for unions and workers.

Although part of the increase reflects the difficulties experienced by particular sectors in recruiting and retaining groups of workers, in others, permanent workers are being replaced by temporary agency staff with fewer employment rights and worse pay and conditions. The image of the typical agency worker being an 'office temp' is also outdated. Secretarial and clerical workers accounted for only 13.5% of temporary and contract workers in 2000–2001, compared with 29% three years before, when they made up the largest group.

Although around 70% of agency workers are women, this percentage has been declining over several years as the clerical and secretarial sector declines in importance. A survey by the trade association for the private recruitment and staffing agency, Recruitment and Employers Confederation (REC), shows that industrial workers are now the largest group of temporary or contract workers, making up nearly 29% of the total. And there has been a large increase in the number of professional and managerial temporary and contract workers. These now make up nearly 9% of the total, compared to only 1.4% in 1997–98. There are a number of reasons for the increasing use of agency workers.

The TUC points out that they are no longer used mainly to cover holiday and sickness absences – with only a third of agency workers having worked for their current employer for less than three months. KeyNote reports: 'Outsourcing and downsizing have been responsible for

the growth in temporary workers, as has the fast pace of technological and customer change.

'Most companies now operate with the smallest complement of staff possible, which means that when their markets change suddenly, or when client demand shifts, they may be without the necessary staff. Recruiting temporary workers is a speedy means of filling gaps in staff requirements.' But the TUC detects a more sinister rationale. It has reported a worrying trend for employers in areas like call centres or further education colleges to terminate staff contracts and re-employ people as agency workers on less pay and with fewer rights. Its general secretary, John Monks, said: 'Too many businesses are using the lack of protection for agency workers to keep permanent parts of their business going with agency workers on worse terms and conditions.' This is precisely what has been happening in further education.

A few years ago a number of further education colleges sacked their part-time workers after a ruling which entitled them to the same rights as full timers. They then rehired the staff through agencies, without the employment rights enjoyed by their permanent colleagues. According to further and higher education union NATFHE, one in three colleges now employ staff via agencies such as Education Lecturing Services and Nord Anglia, and the sector is now the most casualised, after catering.

Last year, a TUC survey, Permanent rights for temporary workers, found that in nearly half of the 196 workplaces surveyed, temps were paid less than permanent workers. In nearly three-quarters they could not join pension schemes and in a quarter they did not get sick pay. Many did not receive maternity pay or leave, even though they may have worked as temporary staff for the same employer for many years. And as well as facing substantial job insecurity, they could not join their employer's pension scheme.

Agency working also has safety implications. The Simon Jones Memorial Campaign was set up by the friends and relatives of Simon, a 24-year-old student who was killed on his first day at work as an agency worker at Shoreham docks in 1998. He had been placed by the Personnel Selection agency in a job unloading cargo from a Euromin-owned ship – a dangerous job which he was not qualified to do. The campaign has been fighting under the slogan 'casualisation kills' against the replacement of skilled unionised workforces with cheaper, casual labour. It organised a day of action against casualisation in April this year, with demonstrations outside employment agencies profiting from casual labour, including Personnel Selection.

The European Commission has recently put forward proposals for a directive giving agency workers increased rights and outlawing dis-crimination in pay and conditions, although it does not contain any entitlement to join the employer's pension scheme. Under current plans the directive would come into effect after an agency worker has been continuously employed at a workplace for six weeks, and should provide some disincentive to casualisation. The CBI employers' organisation is lobbying for the proposals to be watered down, and wants temps to have to work for at least 18 months before being entitled to equal rights with their permanent colleagues.

And it appears that they are pushing against an open door. Patricia Hewitt, the trade and industry secretary, recently told the European Parliament that the government would oppose the new legislation, arguing that agency workers should only have equal rights after being placed at a firm for at least 12 months. Even if the legislation was to go through as currently proposed, it will not help the situation of the most vulnerable agency workers, like transport union RMT member Paula Mason and her colleagues.

Mason has been leading a campaign, with the help of Portsmouth MP, Syd Rapson, to highlight the plight of agency workers in the shipping industry. She works on a P&O Portsmouth ferry where the vast majority – around 80% of the 60 crew members – are now agency staff, employed by Sealife Crewing. This situation has arisen because P&O Ferries Portsmouth have only employed agency workers for the last 10 years or so. Although many of the agency workers have worked for the company for several years, they work a 90-hour week from Wednesday to Wednesday, and are then laid off for a week, so in legal terms they would not meet the six-week qualification period. Instead of being paid an annual wage of GBP 18,500 as the permanent P&O workers are, they are paid just GBP 9,500 for doing exactly the same job for exactly the same number of hours. They have no rights to sick pay, paid holidays, pensions or maternity pay. Paula Mason told Labour Research, 'We call ourselves the sea elves – we're just like the house elves in the Harry Potter stories who keep the school in order but don't exist. In terms of our rights at work, we don't exist either.'

She is concerned that any employer could do the same as P&O Portsmouth. 'They've seen a loophole in the law and they've exploited it to drive down pay and conditions,' she said.

Source: Labour Research, 1 August 2002. Copyright 2002 LRD Publications Ltd.

Questions

1 Discuss the following questions:

   a) In terms of the analysis developed in Chapter 4, what does this case study suggest is happening to employment in the UK?

   b) What are the reasons for the increased use of temporary workers and what does it indicate about the types of labour flexibility commonly sought by British employers?

   c) In terms of the analysis developed in Chapter 5, does the increased use of temporary workers indicate a planned approach to acquiring and utilising labour and if so, what type of planned approach?

2 Debate the advantages and disadvantages of an increased use of temporary workers from the point of view of employers, managers and workers.

3 The CBI has opposed the Temporary Workers' Directive proposals coming from the European Commission. Assuming the role of a CBI spokesperson, prepare a press statement that:

   a) outlines your arguments against the Directive;

   b) explains why the CBI believes that temporary workers should have 18 months' employment with an organisation before qualifying for the same employment benefits as comparable permanent workers in the organisation.

4 As a trade union official, prepare a statement that makes the case for ensuring that temporary workers are employed on the same terms and conditions as permanent staff.

Part 3

DEVELOPING THE HUMAN RESOURCE

Introduction to Part 3

One of the main outcomes of the spread of human resource management (HRM) over the past decade has been increasing attention to what has become labelled *human resource development* (HRD). However, like HRM, this is a term that is often used loosely, and indeed poses problems of definition. Stewart and McGoldrick (1996), who write authoritatively in the HRD area, suggest that the question of what it is 'is not yet amenable to a definitive answer', but offer the following 'tentative' definition:

> Human resource development encompasses activities and processes which are intended to have impact on organisational and individual learning. The term assumes that organisations can be constructively conceived of as learning entities, and that the learning processes of both organisations and individuals are capable of influence and direction through deliberate and planned interventions. Thus, HRD is constituted by planned interventions in organisational and individual processes. (p. 1)

This definition emphasises HRD of the individual and her or his relation to the organisation. HRD, however, can be viewed much more broadly than this. In Asian and African countries, for example, HRD encompasses government initiatives and policies to improve knowledge and skills to enhance economic growth. As Rao (1995) states:

> at the national level HRD aims at ensuring that people in the country live longer; live happily; free of disease and hunger; have sufficient skill base to earn their livelihood and well being; have a sense of belongingness and pride through participation in determining their own destinies. The promotion of the well-being of individuals, families and societies provides a human resource agenda for all countries the world over. (p. 15)

We therefore need to recognise the role that the HRD that takes place in organisations plays in the overall economy and hence in the well-being of society. This concept is represented by the three concentric circles in Figure 1. The more overlap (the shaded area) there is between these three elements, the more likely HRD is to be mutually beneficial for the individual, the organisation and the economy as a whole. For example, support from government initiatives, such as legislation on vocational training, enhances the skills and knowledge of those seeking work in the labour market, which enhances the efficiency of organisations, which in turn enhances the growth and development of the economy. It is therefore not surprising that training and development are important issues, to which governments give careful consideration. For these reasons Part 3 looks beyond and beneath organisational HRD and examines both its national context and the basic processes that constitute it; where appropriate, it invites readers to reflect on their own individual learning and development.

HRD is also seen as having a significant part to play in achieving and maintaining the survival and success of an organisation. Managers have not only to acquire appropriate people to resource it, as discussed in Part 2, they also need to train and develop them, for the following reasons:

- New employees are, in some respects, like the organisation's raw materials. They have to be 'processed' to enable them to perform the tasks of their job adequately, to fit into their work group and into the organisation as a whole, but in a manner that respects their human qualities.
- Jobs and tasks may change over time, both quantitatively and qualitatively, and employees have to be updated to maintain adequate performance.

- New jobs and tasks may be introduced into the organisation, and be filled by existing employees, who need redirection.
- People need training to perform better in their existing jobs.
- People themselves change their interests, their skills, their confidence and aspirations, their circumstances.
- Some employees may move jobs within the organisation, on promotion or to widen their experience, and so need further training.
- The organisation itself, or its context, may change or be changed over time, so that employees have to be updated in their ways of working together.
- The organisation may wish to be ready for some future change, and require (some) employees to develop transferable skills.
- The organisation may wish to respond flexibly to its environment and so require (some) employees to develop flexibility and transferable skills.
- Management requires training and development. This will involve training for new managers, further development and training for managers, management succession, and the development of potential managers.

As the chapters that follow show, changes in the context of the organisation increase the need to train and develop its members to ensure effectiveness, quality and responsiveness. Because these changes are not being made once and for all, employees are having to adjust to continuous change, and their managers are having to pay greater attention to HRD than ever before. However, HRD does not take place in an organisational vacuum. To be effective, it presupposes effective selection, effective supervision and an appropriate management style, the opportunity to transfer learning to the workplace, career paths and promotion possibilities, appropriate incentives and rewards. It also presupposes some degree of planning and linkage to the strategy of the organisation, and is therefore implicit within organisation development. Indeed, for the organisation that espouses 'human resource management' and addresses the human resource implications of its strategic positioning, training and development become investment decisions and operations that are as important as investments in new technology, relocation or entry into new markets.

Figure 1   HRD: the individual, the organisation and the economy

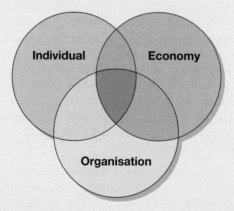

Chapter 8 identifies the need for HRD in the organisation, and considers the basic processes of learning and development involved and the ways in which they can be facilitated in the organisation. This chapter underpins the subsequent chapters of Part 3 and introduces some of the concepts they use. Chapter 9 examines the processes and activities intentionally undertaken within organisations to enable employees to acquire, improve or update their skills, and then explores the national framework for vocational education and training, with some international comparisons, which is the context within which organisational HRD operates. Chapter 10 examines the development of managers, noting both their formal and informal modes of development, and relates management to organisation development.

As these chapters show, HRD takes several forms: the development of the employee both as an individual and as an employee; development of the employee by the employer or by self; training; education; career development; group development; staff development; professional development, management development and, even more widely, organisation development. These differ not only in terms of the hierarchical levels of the organisation but also in purpose and form. While recognising these different kinds of training and development in organisations, we have to understand that they are not necessarily easily distinguishable in practice, and that some activities contribute to more than one form of development. There is necessarily some overlap between the chapters of Part 3. Thus specific training to enable an employee to perform more effectively can now also contribute to that person's overall career development. What is intended as instrumental by the employer may be construed as empowering by the individual. This raises the question about who owns the individual's development, one of the controversial issues addressed in Chapter 8.

References

Rao, T.V. (1995) *Human Resource Development*. New Delhi: Sage.

Stewart, J. and McGoldrick, J. (eds) (1996) *Human Resource Development: Perspectives, Strategies and Practice*. London: Pitman

CHAPTER 8

Learning and development

Audrey Collin

OBJECTIVES

▶ To highlight the learning and development demanded by the significant changes taking place in organisations.

▶ To note the characteristics of different types of learners.

▶ To indicate the outcomes of learning.

▶ To outline the process of learning.

▶ To discuss the concept of development.

▶ To note various kinds of development.

▶ To discuss the implications of learning and development for human resource managers.

▶ To consider the context of learning and development within and beyond the organisation.

▶ To examine how learning and development can be facilitated and designed within organisations.

▶ To pose some controversial issues for reflection and discussion.

▶ To offer some activities that encourage readers to review their own learning and development.

 ## Introduction

Learning is 'the central issue for the 21st century', asserts Honey (1998: 28–29) when setting out the Declaration of Learning drawn up by some of the 'leading thinkers on learning in organisations':

> Changes are bigger and are happening faster, and learning is the way to keep ahead . . . to maintain employability in an era when jobs for life have gone. It enables organisations to sustain their edge as global competition increases. Learning to learn . . . [is] the ultimate life skill.

This makes human resource development a key activity in today's organisations, and lifelong learning crucial for individuals. The purpose of this chapter, which forms a foundation for Chapters 9 and 10, is to explain what learning and development are.

The chapter starts by identifying some of the ways in which work and organisations are changing, and why these changes demand continuous learning in individuals and organisations. It then explains what learning and development are, identifies how their context influences them, and examines how they can be facilitated in work organisations.

The changing world of work and organisations

By the end of the twentieth century, the firmly established nature of work and organisations was changing so dramatically that some observers had foreseen the 'end of work' (Rifkin, 1995) and workplaces without jobs (Bridges, 1995). Changes are being brought about through the new information and communications technologies, and through the way in which organisations are responding to the need to achieve and maintain their competitive edge in increasingly global markets. Castells (1996) argues that a new 'network society' is emerging. The new technologies are making economies interdependent, organised around global networks of capital, management and information, and thereby are profoundly transforming capital and labour. While capital and information flow around the globe, unconfined in space and time, labour is local: individuals live and work in time and place. 'Labor is disaggregated in its performance, fragmented in its organization, diversified in its existence, divided in its collective action' (p. 475).

For the future, according to Bayliss (1998), many of the traditional boundaries and distinctions – between organisations, between jobs, between employment and self-employment – will shift or become eroded. The relationship that individuals will have with employing organisations will change: individuals will move more frequently, have projects rather than long-term jobs, work in different locations and at different times, make their own work, no longer have fixed working lives. Many careers will be 'boundaryless', transcending traditional boundaries between organisations (Arthur and Rousseau, 1996). To express these changes in metaphors: whereas during much of the twentieth century jobs were like pigeon-holes, or boxes piled up to form organisations, at the start of the twenty-first century they are more like nets and networks.

To be competitive, organisations have had to become more flexible, innovative, quality-conscious, customer-oriented, constantly improving their performance. During the past 20 years or so they have undertaken what amount to massive experiments with various ways of achieving these ends. During the 1980s the imperatives were excellence, world-class and 'lean' manufacturing (a collection of techniques contributing significantly to organisational performance), and total quality management (TQM), resulting in downsizing, delayering, and breaking bureaucracies down into business units. During the early 1990s the new soft approaches were multi-skilling and the learning organisation, while the hard approach was business process re-engineering (BPR). In the later 1990s, attention turned to knowledge management and innovation, with a further emphasis on teamworking. As the twenty-first century opened, the management and measurement of human capital, 'the contribution of human skills and knowledge to the production of goods and services' (Scarborough, 2003: 32), became recognised as key issues. Thus wave after wave of new approaches have brought about new tasks, new ways of working, new roles, relationships and skills, so that lifelong learning and human resource development have now become central to the effectiveness of organisations.

For example, TQM (see also Chapter 14) holds that quality is achieved through continuous improvement in the processes, products and services of the organisation: Deming's 'journey of never-ending improvement' (Hodgson, 1987: 41). It requires new relationships between organisations and their suppliers and customers, and calls for the transformation of the management of people 'so that employees become involved in quality as the central part of their job' (Sheard, 1992: 33). Business process re-engineering, which radically restructured bureaucratic organisations by focusing on their lateral processes rather than their vertical functions, not only 'downsized' organisations, but also redesigned the nature of jobs within them:

> For multi-dimensional and changing jobs, companies don't need people to fill a slot, because the slot will be only roughly defined. Companies need people who can figure out what the job takes and people to do it, people who can create the slot that fits them. Moreover, the slot will keep changing. (Hammer and Champy, 1994: 72)

Whereas work had previously been packaged into jobs, Martin (1995: 20) argues, it now had to be reconstructed into the 'competences' needed to achieve customer satisfaction. 'The future will see a world based more on skills than on organisations' (Tyson and Fell, 1995: 45).

If TQM and BPR can be seen as natural heirs – in spirit if not in practice – of scientific management and Taylorism (see Chapters 3 and 11), then knowledge management (see also Chapter 9) could be recognised as an echo of Trist and the Tavistock school (Pugh *et al.*, 1983). They saw the working group as a socio-technical system: to be effective, the introduction of new technology had to take that into account. Fifty years later, it is once more being recognised (Malhotra, 1998) that it is people who make the difference. The wealth of information generated by information technology becomes meaningful and of competitive advantage to the organisation only when knowledge workers share, interpret and elaborate it. This enables them to anticipate challenges to the organisation's goals and practices, and thus to adapt the organisation in appropriate and timely fashion. However, knowledge is now no longer regarded as 'abstract, objective' truth but a cultural construction within 'communities of practice', and hence 'essentially pragmatic, partial, tentative and always open to revision' (Blackler, 2000: 61). Organisations are beginning to understand that different kinds of knowledge have to be managed in different ways: some knowledge is explicit, and can easily be documented, whereas other knowledge is tacit. 'The knowledge needed to develop a new product is largely in people's heads . . . [it] cannot be written down, because an individual may not even know it is there until the situation demands a creative response' (Dixon, 2000: 37). Importantly, argues Scarborough (1999), HR managers need to have a direct involvement in this area.

It is now also recognised that, although the UK has shone in invention, it has lagged in innovation: '"the creation, successful exploitation and impact of new ideas at all levels – the economy, sector, enterprise, workplace and individual"' (Guest *et al.*, 1997: 1, quoting from the Economic and Social Research Council's Innovation Programme material). However, innovation is 'the source of sustained competitiveness in organisations':

> Creating, disseminating and embodying knowledge – tacit and explicit – becomes a key strategic resource to be leveraged. It holds the key to unlocking the organisation's ability to learn faster than its environment is changing. In summary, learning and development lie at the heart of innovation in organisations. (Guest *et al.*, 1997: 3)

Research suggests that financial results account for only 50 to 70 per cent of a firm's market value, the remainder being attributed to 'intangibles' (Ulrich and Smallwood, 2002), such as intellectual property and human capital. Scarborough (2003: 32–34) suggests that the human capital approach is 'more than a recycling of cliches about the importance of our employees. It also reflects a shift in thinking about ways to make the best use of the whole range of abilities that people bring to the workplace.' He cites the television programme *Jamie's Kitchen*, in which cook Jamie Oliver turned a team of inexperienced and unemployed young people into top-class chefs. 'This blending of new skills and attitudes into high-level performance sums up exactly what human capital can be and why it is so important to business' (Scarborough, 2003: 32).

Ulrich and Smallwood (2002: 43) include learning or knowledge management among the seven 'critical organisation capabilities that [create] intangible shareholder value': 'Learning capacity is an intangible value when organisations have the ability to move ideas across vertical, horizontal, external and global boundaries.' However, accountants have traditionally not found satisfactory ways of measuring human capital, and so have treated employees as costs to an organisation rather than assets. In the increasing effort to achieve competitive advantage this approach is now changing, and the Accounting Standards Board now recommends that human capital policies and practices should be included in company annual reports (Hammond, 2002). It is also becoming clear that employees are beginning to recognise the need to invest in their own learning and development – their human capital – and so employers have to take steps to retain talent, nurture it, and manage it effectively, which in turn calls for effective means of measuring human capital, which Mayo (2002) discusses.

All these changes are of considerable significance for individuals and organisations, as we shall shortly see.

ACTIVITY | **Identifying contextual changes leading to HRD**

Before proceeding further, on your own or in a small group identify some of the changes taking place in organisations in response to changes in its context. What are the implications for human resource development and for the learning and development of individuals?

■ The strategic importance of learning and development

'Change matters more than ever before', said the president of the Chartered Institute of Personnel and Development (CIPD, formerly IPD) in his message in the Annual Report for 2000 (Beattie, 2002: 2–3). 'People are our only source of differentiation and sustainable competitive advantage. Essential to that is learning.' Hence the director-general of the IPD claims that 'staff management and development will become the primary weapon available to managers to generate success' (Rana, 2000). The continuous learning and development of individuals are, therefore, of crucial and strategic importance to organisations, and thus also to the overall economy. This national significance is now fully recognised by the government which, for example, in 2001 set up the Learning and Skills Council (see Chapter 9), and human resource developers and trainers now have to address the new responsibilities of their increasingly strategic role (Chartered Institute of Personnel and Development, 2002a).

● The need for individuals to learn and develop

The new ways of working are demanding not just extensive training in new task skills, but completely new ways of thinking about work, doing work, and relating with one another. Individuals at all levels need to be able to challenge traditional ways of thinking and working; think and work 'outside the box' of traditional job descriptions; and work without prior experience, clear guidelines or close supervision; be flexible, prepared to change, undertake new tasks or move to a different organisation. In the struggle to 'think global and act local', organisations need people who have 'a "matrix of the mind"'; sharing learning and creating new knowledge are among the key capabilities that organisations must have (Ulrich and Stewart Black, 1999). Overall, this amounts to the need for using high levels of cognitive skills, which will be discussed below.

For much of the industrial age, such abilities, when sought, were expected mainly in the upper echelons of organisations. In the twenty-first century, competitive organisations need to find these abilities much more widely in their workforce, in what Castells (1998: 341) calls the 'self-programmable' labour in the global economy. This has 'the capability constantly to redefine the necessary skills for a given task, and to access the sources for learning these skills'. Nevertheless, there will still be work that does not require those particular abilities – for example, serving in fast food outlets – jobs that will be undertaken by what Castells calls 'generic' labour, which, lacking self-programmable skills, would be:

> 'human terminals' [which could] be replaced by machines, or by any other body around the city, the country, or the world, depending on business decisions. While they are collectively indispensable to the production process, they are individually expendable . . .
>
> (Castells, 1998: 341)

(It should not be assumed, however, that all jobs giving personal service demand low-level skills: they may require high levels of social, emotional and other non-cognitive intelligences (Gardner, 1985, 1999; Pickard, 1999b).)

Although many employers are now recognising the need to invest in their employees' learning, it is also held that individuals must take some responsibility for it; that they must invest in their own learning and development to ensure their own 'employability' (Arnold, 1997). This personal investment changes the balance of the 'psychological contract' (see Chapters 3 and 13), and raises the question of who owns the individual's learning (see Controversial Issues at the end of the chapter).

● The need for higher-order skills

According to Wisher (1994: 37), among the 'competencies that occur frequently in the most successful clusters of different organisations' are conceptual, 'helicopter' and analytical thinking. Organisations are thus demanding more of their employees than new or enhanced task skills. They are requiring higher-order thinking skills that are not easily picked up within the constraints of many existing jobs.

However, there is a long way to go for many organisations. According to Myers and Davids (1992):

> workers are a resource which has not been well understood by management in the past. Blue-collar workers in particular have been regarded as a static commodity incapable of innovation and self-development. Consequently reservoirs of skill and ability remain untapped.   (p. 47)

Cooley (1987) reports how the Lucas Aerospace Shop Stewards' Combine Committee, as long ago as 1975, recognised the value of human capital. It challenged the organisation not to lay its highly skilled workforce off when its market was failing, but to retain it by moving into new markets for 'socially useful' products:

> What the Lucas workers did was to embark on an exemplary project which would inflame the imagination of others. To do so, they realised that it was necessary to demonstrate in a very practical and direct way the creative power of 'ordinary people'. Further, their manner of doing it had to confirm for 'ordinary people' that they too had the capacity to change their situation, that they are not the objects of history but rather the subjects, capable of building their own futures.   (p. 139)

As this chapter will show, 'ordinary people' have the capacity to learn and develop.

● The need for organisations to invest in their employees' learning and development

As well as training and developing new employees, organisations have to invest in their human capital and, importantly, not just in their knowledge workers but in their lower-skilled employees as well (Chartered Institute of Personnel and Development, 2002a). This means that they have to train and develop their existing workforce, facilitate their learning within a learning culture, and with appropriate resources (see Chapters 9 and 10). Hence, human resource managers need to understand the processes and nature of the learning of the higher-order and other task skills in order to be able to facilitate that learning and development. It is the purpose of this chapter to explain these.

● The need for a learning society

The need for learning and development is not just an issue for individuals and their employers. It is now widely recognised that we need to become a learning society, in which there is a culture of, and opportunities for, lifelong learning. To this end, the government has introduced a number of initiatives (see Chapter 9).

> **Stop and think**
>
> What are the implications of the issues raised so far in this chapter for your own learning and development needs? How would you attempt to meet these needs? In the light of this, what would you seek from any prospective employer?

Learning and development

> Deep down, we are all learners. No one has to teach an infant to learn. In fact, no one has to teach infants anything. They are intrinsically inquisitive, masterful learners who learn to walk, speak . . . Learning organizations are possible because not only is it our nature to learn but we love to learn.
>
> (Senge, 1990: 4)

From birth, humans, like all animals, learn and develop: learning is a natural process in which we all engage. It is not just a cognitive activity, and it affects the person as a whole. This learning and development lead to skilful and effective adaptation to and manipulation of the environment, which is one element in a much-quoted definition of intelligence (Wechsler, 1958, in Ribeaux and Poppleton, 1978: 189). People continue learning throughout life, whether encouraged or not, whether formally taught or not, whether the outcomes are valued or not. Moreover, the process of their learning knows no boundaries: learning in one domain, such as employment, hobbies or maintenance of home and car, cross-fertilises that in another and thereby achieves a wider understanding and more finely honed skills.

> Most of us have learned a good deal more out of school than in it. We have learned from our families, our work, our friends. We have learned from problems resolved and tasks achieved but also from mistakes confronted and illusions unmasked. Intentionally or not, we have learned from the dilemmas our lives hand us daily.
>
> (Daloz, 1986: 1)

Society fosters and facilitates these activities of its members, but also channels and controls them through socialisation and education so that they yield outcomes that contribute to and are acceptable to it.

However, although individuals have a lifetime's experience of being learners, some of their experiences (especially those in formal educational settings) might not have been happy ones, as some of those who responded to the Declaration of Learning (Honey, 1998) illustrated (Honey, 1999). They might be experienced learners, but not necessarily competent or confident learners.

Lifelong learning means continuous adaptation. Increased knowledge and improved skills enlarge the individual's capacities to adapt to the environment and to change that environment. As the systems model in Chapter 3 implies, such external changes will lead on to further internal changes, allowing new possibilities for the individual to emerge. Moreover, these changes feed the individual's self-esteem and confidence, and enhance social status. Hence learning generates potentially far-reaching changes in the individual: learning promotes development. In his very warm-hearted and insightful book on 'the transformational power of adult learning experiences', Daloz (1986) draws on mythology to convey the nature of this development:

> The journey tale begins with an old world, generally simple and uncomplicated, more often than not, home . . . The middle portion, beginning with departure from home, is characterized by confusion, adventure, great highs and lows, struggle, uncertainty. The ways of the old world no longer hold, and the hero's task is to find a way through this strange middle land, generally in search of something lying at its heart. At the deepest point, the nadir of the descent, a transformation occurs, and the traveler moves out of the darkness toward a new world that often bears an ironic resemblance to the old.
>
> Nothing is different, yet all is transformed. It is seen differently . . . Our old life is still there, but its meaning has profoundly changed because we have left home, seen it from afar, and been transformed by that vision. You can't go home again.   (pp. 24–26)

The outcomes of a person's learning and development are the way they think, feel and interpret their world (their cognition, affect, attitudes, overall philosophy of life); the way they see themselves, their self-concept and self-esteem; and their ability to respond to and make their way in their particular environment (their perceptual-motor, intellectual, social, and interpersonal skills). Some of the transformational impact of learning can be seen in Daloz's description above of the journey of development. Learning and development are therefore significant experiences for individuals and for organisations. Following from this, it should also be noted, the facilitation of another's learning is a moral project: it has the potential to promote changes that may have a profound effect in the other's life. This, too, has implications for the debate about the ownership of learning, one of the controversial issues at the end of the chapter.

Learning and development are processes that we all experience, active processes in which we all engage: we do not have learning and development done to us. However, we rarely pay conscious attention to them and so might not fully understand them. This chapter therefore addresses you, the reader, directly, and here and throughout this chapter invites you to draw upon your own experience in order to understand and make use of the issues that are discussed.

Your very reading of this book might itself entail some of these issues. Before proceeding further, therefore, it makes sense to identify and reflect on them so that you will then have ready in your mind the 'hooks' on to which to hang the information this chapter will give you. In the language of a learning theory to be noted later, you will be ready to 'decode' these new 'signals'.

ACTIVITY **Your aims and motivation for learning**

List your reasons for reading this book, noting:

- both short-term and long-term aims;

- those aims that are ends in themselves and those that are means to an end;

- the most important and the least important;

- the aims that you can achieve by yourself;

- those that require others to facilitate them;

- what else you need to achieve these aims;

- what initiated your pursuit of these aims;

- who or what has influenced you during this pursuit.

This chapter will help you to understand the motivation for and influences on learning. It will also examine how people learn, and what helps or hinders them. By paying attention now to how you are reading this book, you can begin to understand your own processes of learning. Later you will have the opportunity to identify who benefits from and who pays for your learning. This will help you to understand something of the problematical issues inherent in employee development.

Defining learning and development

To understand the processes of learning and development and use this understanding to good effect in developing people and their organisations, you have to be able to think clearly about the concepts you are using. The concepts 'learning' and 'development' are frequently used loosely and even interchangeably, so it is important to define how they are being used here. The following definitions will enable you to distinguish them and understand the relationship between them.

Learning is

> a process within the organism which results in the capacity for changed performance which can be related to experience rather than maturation.
>
> (Ribeaux and Poppleton, 1978: 38)

It is now widely recognised that intelligence is not just a cognitive capacity – note the theory of multiple intelligences (Gardner, 1985, 1999), and the recent interest in emotional intelligence (Pickard, 1999b). Hence learning is not just a cognitive process that involves the assimilation of information in symbolic form (as in book learning), but also an affective and physical process (Binsted, 1980). Our emotions, nerves and muscles are involved in the process, too. Learning leads to change, whether positive or negative for the learner. It is an experience after which an individual 'qualitatively [changes] the way he or she conceived something' (Burgoyne and Hodgson, 1983: 393) or experiences 'personal transformation' (Mezirow, 1977). Learning can be more or less effectively undertaken, and it could be more effective when it is paid conscious attention.

Development, however, is the process of becoming increasingly complex, more elaborate and differentiated, by virtue of learning and maturation. (As will be noted later, it is sometimes assumed that development connotes progression and advancement.) In an organism, greater complexity, differentiation among the parts, leads to changes in the structure of the whole and to the way in which the whole functions (Reese and Overton, 1970: 126). In the individual, this greater complexity opens up the potential for new ways of acting and responding to the environment. This leads to the need and opportunity for even further learning, and so on.

Development, whether of an organism, individual or organisation, is a process of both continuity and discontinuity. Quantitative changes lead to qualitative changes or transformations; development is irreversible, although regression to earlier phases can occur.

> The disintegration of the old phase of functioning . . . creates the conditions for the discontinuous 'step-jump' to a new phase. This succeeding phase incorporates yet transforms the repertoire of principles, values, etc., of earlier phases and adds to them. The new phase is therefore not entirely new – it is a transformation. Each succeeding phase is more complex, integrating what has gone before.   (Pedler, 1988: 7–8)

Overall, then, learning contributes to development. It is not synonymous with it, but development cannot take place without learning of some kind.

■ Many types of learner

Much of what we know about learning and teaching derives from the study of children and young people (pedagogy). However, learners in organisations are not children, and have different needs and experiences.

Stop and think	From your own experience and observing others' behaviour, how do adult learners differ from young learners? What are likely to be the implications for human resource developers?

● Adult learners

Instead of a pedagogical model of learning, an androgogical model is needed to understand adult learning. According to Knowles and Associates (1984), this needs to take into account that adult learners are self-directing, and motivated by their need to be recognised, to prove something to themselves and others, to better themselves, and achieve their potential. Their learning does not take place in a vacuum. Not only are they ready to learn when they recognise their need to know or do something, but they have experience on which to draw and to hang their new learning, and to assess its utility. Earlier (especially formal) learning experiences might have been far from effective or comfortable, so that many adults have developed poor learning habits or are apprehensive about further learning.

Human resource development has to address these various needs appropriately, as will be suggested in the later section on the organisation as a context for learning.

● Learners in the organisation

Older workers

Older people have been widely discriminated against when seeking employment and when employed (Naylor, 1987; Dennis, 1988; Laslett, 1989; Waskel, 1991). They are commonly stereotyped as having failing cognitive and physical abilities, as being inflexible, unwilling and unable to learn new ways. However, the Carnegie Inquiry into the Third Age (Trinder et al.,1992) reports:

> There does seem to be a decline in performance with age . . . but such deterioration as there is, is less than the popular stereotype . . . Except where such abilities as muscular strength are of predominant importance, age is not a good discriminator of ability to work; nor of the ability to learn.   (p. 20)

Trinder *et al.* (1992) also note that performance is influenced as much by experience and skill as by age: skill development in earlier years will encourage adaptability in later life.

Although older people are 'at a disadvantage with speedy and novel (unexpected) forms of presentation', Coleman (1990: 70–71) reports little or no decline with age in memory and learning, particularly 'if the material is fully learned initially'. (The role of rehearsal and revision in memory will be examined later in this chapter.) Pickard (1999a: 30), discussing changing attitudes to the employment of older people, and the possibility of retirement age rising to the upper 70s, quotes a 72-year-old Nobel prize-winning scientist as saying: 'You may forget where you were last week, but not the things that matter.' Coleman (1990) goes on to cite a study in which the majority of the 80 volunteers aged 63 to 91 years learned German from scratch, and in six months reached the level of skill in reading German normally achieved by schoolchildren in five years.

Until recently, there were few examples to cite of organisations that employed older people. The do-it-yourself retail chain B&Q was a notable exception, staffing one store solely by people over the age of 50. It was 'an overwhelming success . . . In commercial terms the store has surpassed its trading targets' (Hogarth and Barth, 1991: 15). In this trial these older workers were found to be willing to train, although initially reluctant to use new technology, and did not require longer or different training from other workers. Since then, as Pickard (1999a) reports, B&Q has been joined by other employers in giving employment opportunities to older people. These older workers demonstrate the ability to continue to learn through life. Their learning will be facilitated if employers adopt appropriate approaches, which will be examined in the section on the organisation as a context for learning.

It seems likely that in the future there will be a greater need to understand the capacity of older workers. One response to the growing pressure on pensions provision because of the ageing population would be to scrap compulsory retirement ages so that more older people would continue in employment. Such ideas, and new appraisals of older workers, can be found on the www.agepositive.gov.uk website.

Other classes of employees

Three classes of people – women, disabled people, and individuals from cultural and ethnic minorities – are often socialised and educated in ways that do not advantage them in labour markets or organisations; they may develop correspondingly low expectations and aspirations. Negative stereotyping of them in employment is frequently discussed (Gallos, 1989; Thomas and Alderfer, 1989). This section will briefly note some aspects of their experience that will influence them as learners in the organisation: these need to be viewed in terms of the barriers to learning referred to later.

Until recently, little seemed to have been written about the training of disabled people in organisations. Moreton (1992) identified the role of the Training and Enterprise Councils in providing training programmes for them, and Arkin (1995) summarised the implications for employers of the 1995 Disability Discrimination Act. Clearly, there is a wide range of disability, but in 1999 Whitehead was able to report on the employment of disabled people at Centrica, and Littlefield (1999) reported how some residents with learning disabilities accompanied staff at their community care home on training days, some achieving NVQ (see Chapter 8) level 1 qualifications.

As was noted in Chapter 3, there is now a considerable body of theory, including feminist critiques, that addresses the nature of women and their experiences in their own right, rather than as a subset of a supposed 'universal' (but often Eurocentric, middle-class male) nature. For example, Gilligan (1977: see Daloz, 1986: 134–135) argues that unlike men, who see their world as 'a hierarchy of power', women see theirs as 'a web of relationships'. The connected self interprets the environment differently, and so responds to it differently, from the separate self. These and other ways in which women may differ from men (Bartol, 1978) will influence their approach to, experience of, and outcomes from, learning. They may, indeed, advantage women in the development of some of the higher-order skills needed in organisations.

Different cultures imbue their members with different basic assumptions about the nature of reality and the values and the roles in social life. Cultural experiences differ, and hence the accumulated experience of the members will also differ. The concept of intelligence is not culture-free. Gardner (1985), who expounds a theory of multiple intelligences that include interpersonal and intrapersonal intelligence, recognises that

> because each culture has its own symbol systems, its own means for interpreting experiences, the 'raw materials' of the personal intelligences quickly get marshaled by systems of meaning that may be quite distinct from one another ... the varieties of personal intelligence prove much more distinctive, less comparable, perhaps even unknowable to someone from an alien society.
>
> (p. 240)

Hence some members of cultural and ethnic minorities have many ways of learning that are dissimilar to those of the dominant culture, and also different outcomes from their learning. It is therefore important to assess such constructs as intelligence in as culture-fair a manner as possible (Sternberg, 1985: 77, 309), and to seek appropriate means to facilitate learning of the skills required in organisations. Clements and Jones (2002) point to the importance of self-learning when addressing diversity. Learning through action might also be particularly appropriate.

Understanding of and fluency with English are not the only language issues in organisations. As discussed in Chapter 3, language is ideological and can embody racism and sexism. Similarly, the construction of knowledge is a social and ideological process. Through the very nature of language and knowledge, these learners may be internalising constructions of themselves that ultimately undermine their self-esteem, alienate them from self-fulfilment, and erect barriers to their effective learning.

The outcomes and process of learning

Managers responsible for human resource development need to understand the nature of learning and development. This section will, therefore, first examine the outcomes of learning, such as skill, competence and tacit knowledge, and employability, an indirect outcome. It will then look at the process of learning, the various levels of cognitive and other skills, at models of learning, and finally at barriers to learning.

The outcomes of learning

● Skill

> . . . the performance of any task which, for its successful and rapid completion, requires an improved organisation of responses making use of only those aspects of the stimulus which are essential to satisfactory performance.   (Ribeaux and Poppleton, 1978: 53–54)

> . . . an appearance of ease, of smoothness of movement, of confidence and the comparative absence of hesitation; it frequently gives the impression of being unhurried, while the actual pace of activity may of course be quite high . . . increasing skill involves a widening of the range of possible disturbances that can be coped with without disrupting the performance.
>
> (Borger and Seaborne, 1966: 128–129)

These definitions are particularly appropriate to perceptual-motor skills, which involve physical, motor responses to perceived stimuli in the external world. Such skills are needed at every level of an organisation, from the senior manager's ability to operate a desktop computer to the cleaner's operation of a floor-scrubbing machine. High levels of such skills are particularly needed to operate complex and expensive technology. There are many other kinds of skills needed in organisations, such as cognitive, linguistic, social and interpersonal skills, that could also be defined in these terms. However, their complexity suggests that various levels of skill have to be recognised, which is what a later subsection will do in presenting some hierarchies of skills.

■ Competence

Competence – also referred to as competency in the literature – has been defined as

> an underlying characteristic of a person which results in effective and/or superior performance in a job.   (Boyatzis, 1982)

> the ability to perform the activities within an occupational area to the levels of performance expected in employment.   (Training Commission, 1988)

The core of the definition is an ability to apply knowledge and skills with understanding to a work activity.

Competences are now a major element in the design of training and development in Britain (Cannell *et al.*, 1999), and seem to fit well with what is happening in organisations. Martin (1995: 20) proposes that they are a means of 'aligning what people can offer – their competencies – against the demands of customers rather than against the ill-fitting and ill-designed demands of jobs'. Nevertheless, the notions of competence and competency are still matters of debate: from the confusion suggested by differences between the definitions above (Woodruffe, 1991) to the challenge of postmodern (see Chapter 3) thinking (Brittain and Ryder, 1999). Despite considerable variation in the number of competences being used in competence frameworks (one study suggested between 21 and 30 and 300–400), and often a lack of validation of such frameworks, there is claimed to be a 'dramatic increase' in the number of companies using them. 'Personnel professionals must stop dismissing competencies as fads' (Walsh, 1998: 15).

What needs to be noted at this point is that the concept of competence integrates knowledge and skill that are assessed via performance. This leads on to the distinction between formal knowledge and 'know-how', in which tacit knowledge has a significant part to play.

● 'Know-how' and tacit knowledge

'Knowing how to do something' is a very different matter from knowing about 'knowing how to do something'. This truism is captured in the everyday suspicion and disparagement of 'the ivory tower': 'those who can, do; those who can't, teach'. It is also apparent in the reluctance of British employers to value higher education, evidenced in the small proportion of managers with degrees, documented in the Handy (1987) and Constable and McCormick (1987) reports (see Chapters 9 and 10). By contrast, 'can do' became a buzzword for pragmatic effectiveness in the 1980s.

Gardner (1985) makes the distinction between 'know-how' and 'know-that'. For him, 'know-how' is the tacit knowledge of how to execute something, whereas 'know-that' is the statement of formal thinking (propositional knowledge) about the actual set of procedures involved in the execution:

> Thus, many of us know how to ride a bicycle but lack the propositional knowledge of how that behaviour is carried out. In contrast, many of us have propositional knowledge about how to make a soufflé without knowing how to carry this task through to successful completion. (p. 68)

Tacit knowledge is an essential ingredient of 'know-how'. Sternberg (1985) recognises this in his definition of practical intelligence:

> Underlying successful performance in many real-world tasks is tacit knowledge of a kind that is never explicitly taught and in many instances never even verbalized. (p. 169)

The example that he gives is of the tacit knowledge relevant to the management of one's career. The individual also draws upon tacit knowledge in the fluent performance of perceptual-motor skills, as seen in the definition of skill above; indeed, Myers and Davids (1992) write of 'tacit skills'. Moreover, as you will have seen earlier, one of the purposes of knowledge management is to capture the tacit knowledge that employees have.

This tacit knowledge would appear to be acquired through experience rather than through instruction, and is embedded in the context in which this experience is taking place. This can be seen in Stage 2 of the model of Dreyfus *et al.* (see below), in which the learner becomes independent of instruction through the recognition of the contextual elements of the task, and thereafter develops the ability to register and 'read' contextual cues. However, unlike the formal knowledge that it accompanies, this tacit knowledge never becomes explicit, although it remains very significant. Myers and Davids (1992: 47) question whether 'tacit skills' can be taught, and identify that they are often transmitted in 'an environment of intensive practical experience' and in task performance: 'We may yet be able to learn much from "sitting next to Nellie"!' They also note the need to take account of both formal and tacit knowledge in selection. A later section will examine the concept of action learning, which contextualises learning and hence draws upon tacit knowledge.

Traditionally, practical knowledge tends to feature at a lower level in any representation of the social hierarchy of skills, and is thereby institutionalised in lower-level occupations. In discussing the public's understanding of science, Collins (1993) writes about:

> the all too invisible laboratory technician . . . Look into a laboratory and you will see it filled with fallible machines and the manifest recalcitrance of nature . . . Technicians make things work in the face of this . . . Notoriously, techniques that can be made to work by one technician in one place will not work elsewhere. The technician has a practical understanding of aspects of the craft of science beyond that of many scientists. But does the technician 'understand science'? (p. 17)

Cooley (1987: 10–13) draws attention to the way in which practical knowledge, craft skill, is devalued in the face of technological progress. This is the starting point for his reflections upon the way 'ordinary people' could achieve something extraordinary. He believes that technological systems

> tend to absorb the knowledge from ['ordinary people'], deny them the right to use their skill and judgement, and render them abject appendages to the machines and systems being developed.

Myers and Davids (1992: 47) come to a similar conclusion after their discussion of the significance of 'tacit skills'. In contrast, it could be argued that knowledge management regards technology, rather than people, as the 'appendages'.

It is clear, however, that organisations need both 'know-how' and 'know-that': the concept of competence, therefore, as defined above is potentially a significant one for them. However, it can be argued that the institutionalised, transorganisational process of identifying and defining competences has wrenched them from their context and hence from the tacit knowledge that contributes so significantly to them.

● Employability

An indirect outcome of learning and development is 'employability', a notion that became current because of the proliferation of flexible contracts of employment and insecurity in employment during the 1990s. According to Kanter (1989a), employability is the 'new security': if individuals have acquired and maintained their employability then, should their job come to an end, they would be able to find employment elsewhere.

Employability results from investment in the human capital of skills and reputation. This means that individuals must engage in continuous learning and development, update their skills and acquire others that might be needed in the future by their current or future employer (Fonda and Guile, 1999). It is also argued that, as part of the 'new deal' in employment, good employers will ensure that their employees remain employable (Herriot and Pemberton, 1995) by keeping them up to date through training and development.

■ The process of learning

The chapter started by identifying the significance of learning for today's organisations. It will now first consider theories of the process of learning and of elements within it, and then examine that process in terms of various levels, stages, and cyclical models of learning. This is a very rich and complex field, to which justice cannot be done here, and you are recommended to read a text such as Atkinson *et al.* (1993) or Ribeaux and Poppleton (1978).

● Theories of the process of learning

Behaviourist approach to learning

The behaviourist approach has been one of the most influential in the field of psychology. It proposes that learning is the process by which a particular stimulus (S), repeatedly associated with, or conditioned by, desirable or undesirable experiences, comes to evoke a particular response (R). This conditioning can be of two kinds. Classical conditioning occurs when a stimulus leads automatically to a response. Dogs, for example, salivate at the presentation of food; Pavlov demonstrated that they could also be conditioned to salivate at the sound of a bell rung before food is presented.

Operant conditioning (Skinner) takes place after a desired response, which is then reinforced, or rewarded, to increase the probability of the repetition of the same response when the stimulus recurs.

There has been much experimental research (including many animal studies) into such issues as the nature of the reinforcement (negative reinforcement, or punishment, is not as effective for learning as positive reward); the schedule of reinforcement (whether at fixed or variable intervals: intermittent reinforcement is more effective than continuous reinforcement). This form of conditioning is also used to shape behaviour: that is, to continue to reinforce responses that approximate to the desired behaviour until that behaviour is finally achieved. We are familiar with this kind of approach to the encouragement of simple behaviours: we use it with small children, with animals, and in basic forms of training.

Cognitive learning theory

The S–R approach pays no attention to the cognitive processes whereby the stimulus comes to be associated with a particular response: it does not investigate what is in the 'black box'. Cognitive learning theory, however, offers a more complex understanding of learning, proposing, again originally on the basis of animal studies, that what is learned is not an association of stimulus with response (S–R), but of stimulus with stimulus (S–S). The learner develops expectations that stimuli are linked; the result is a cognitive 'map' or latent learning. Hence insightful behaviour appropriate to a situation takes place without the strengthening association of S–R bonds. Social learning theory also addresses what is in the 'black box'. It recognises the role in learning of the observation and imitation of the behaviour of others, but as seen in, say, the debates over the influence of the media upon young people's behaviour, there are clearly many moderating variables.

Information-processing approach to learning

This approach regards learning as an information-processing system in which a signal, containing information, is transmitted along a communication channel of limited capacity and subject to interference and 'noise' (Stammers and Patrick, 1975). The signal has to be decoded before it can be received, and then encoded to pass it on. In learning, data received through the senses are filtered, recognised and decoded through the interpretative process of perception; this information is then translated into action through the selection of appropriate responses. The effectiveness of learning depends on attention being paid only to the relevant parts of the stimuli, the rapid selection of appropriate responses, the efficient performance of them, and the feeding back of information about their effects into the system. Overload or breakdown of the system can occur at any of these stages.

Gagné (1974, in Fontana, 1981: 73) expresses this as a chain of events, some internal and others external to the learner. It begins with the learner's readiness to receive information (motivation or expectancy), and continues as the learner perceives it, distinguishes it from other stimuli, makes sense of it and relates it to what is already known. The information is then stored in short- or long-term memory. Thereafter it can be retrieved from memory, generalised to, and put into practice in, new situations. Its final phase is feedback from knowledge of the results obtained from this practice. Those concerned to facilitate learning in others can use their understanding of this chain to prevent failure to learn, which can take place at any one of these levels.

● Elements in the process of learning

This subsection will deal briefly with other important elements in the process of learning that need to be taken into account when designing or facilitating learning.

Feedback (or knowledge of results)

The feedback to learners of the results of their performance is recognised as essential to their effective learning. This is discussed in Ribeaux and Poppleton (1978) and Stammers and Patrick (1975). Feedback will be either intrinsic or extrinsic (or augmented). Learners receive visual or kinaesthetic feedback (intrinsic) from their responses to stimuli in the learning situation; they need to be encouraged to 'listen' to such bodily cues in order to improve performance. They may also receive feedback (extrinsic, augmented) from an external source while they are performing (concurrent feedback) or after it (terminal). Learners may also benefit from guidance given before their performance about what to look out for during it. The sources cited above set out the characteristics, advantages and disadvantages of these different kinds of feedback.

The notion of feedback is frequently discussed in terms of learning perceptual-motor or similar skills. It is also of considerable importance in the learning of the higher-order skills discussed in this chapter, but here it is very complex in nature, and difficult for the learner to be aware and make sense of it. However, by reflecting and engaging in the whole-loop learning discussed below, the learner will have opportunity to pay attention to both intrinsic and extrinsic feedback.

The choice of whole or part learning

Psychologists continue to debate the appropriateness of whole or part learning in learning to perform various tasks: that is, whether the task is learned as a whole, or in parts. Ribeaux and Poppleton (1978: 61) report on one approach that classifies tasks according to their 'complexity' (the difficulty of the component subtasks) and 'organisation' (the degree to which they are interrelated). Where complexity and organisation are both high, whole methods appear superior; where either is low, part methods are superior in most cases; when both are low, part and whole methods are equally successful. Stammers and Patrick (1975: 85–88), however, report on research that appears to draw opposite conclusions: where the elements of a task are highly independent the task is best learned as a whole, but where they are interdependent, they should be learned in parts.

It tends to be the whole method in operation when learning takes place during the performance of a job, through action learning, or through observing others.

The role of memory in learning

Memory plays a significant role in learning, and some understanding of it can therefore be used to make learning more effective. Once again, it is not possible to do more than present an outline here, but texts such as Stammers and Patrick (1975), Ribeaux and Poppleton (1978), Fontana (1981) and Atkinson et al. (1993) give further information.

Memory involves three kinds of information storage: the storage of sensory memories, short-term or primary memory, and long-term or secondary memory. Unless transferred to short-term memory, the sensory memory retains sense data for probably less than two seconds. Unless incoming information is paid particular attention or rehearsed, short-term memory holds it for up to 30 seconds and appears to have limited capacity, whereas long-term memory appears to have unlimited capacity and to hold information for years. What is therefore of concern for effective learning is the ability to transfer information to the long-term memory.

There are two aspects to such transfer. The first is 'rehearsal' – that is, paying attention to and repeating the information until it is coded and enters the long-term store; it is otherwise displaced by new incoming information. The second aspect of the transfer of information to long-term memory is coding: the translation of information into the codes that enable it to be 'filed' into the memory's 'filing system'. Information is largely coded according to meaning (a semantic code) or through visual images, but sometimes (where the meaning itself is unclear) according to sound.

The ability to retrieve information from long-term memory depends in part upon how effectively it has been organised ('filed') in storage (for example, words may be stored according to sound and meaning), but also upon having the most appropriate retrieval cue. We experience this when we are searching for something that we have lost: we think systematically through what we were doing when we believe we last used the lost object. Recognition is easier than recall from memory because it follows the presentation of clear retrieval cues.

Difficulty in retrieving information, or forgetting, occurs for several reasons apart from those concerning the degree of organisation in storage. Interference from other information can disrupt long-term as well as short-term memory (where new items displace existing items in the limited capacity). Interference may be retroactive, when new information interferes with the recall of older material, or proactive, when earlier learning seems to inhibit the recall of later information. Forgetting also takes place through anxiety or unhappy associations with the material to be learned, which might become repressed. Unhappy childhood experiences, for example, might be repressed for many years.

Finally, memory does not just operate as a camera recording what is experienced: it is an active and a constructive process. This is particularly so when learning the kind of complex material that constitutes the world of organisations and human resource management. As well as recording its data inputs, the process of memory draws inferences from the data and so elaborates upon them, filtering them through the individual's stereotypes, mindset and world-view. What is then stored is this enhanced and repackaged material.

An understanding of the nature of memory suggests various ways in which it might be improved to make learning more effective. The transfer of new information to long-term memory is clearly crucial: attention, recitation, repetition and constant revision (known as *overlearning*) are needed. The coding and organisation of material to be stored are also important: this is helped by associating the new information with what is already familiar, especially using visual imagery, by attending to the context giving rise to the information to be learned, and by making the effort to understand the information so that it can be stored in the appropriate 'files'. Facilitators of learning need to ensure that the learning context or event does not provoke anxiety.

● Levels of learning

An earlier section concluded that today's organisations need their employees generally, and their managers in particular, to practise higher-order thinking skills. This implies that there are several types and levels of skill. This subsection presents several classifications, some of different types of skill, others of different levels or stages. Some are couched in terms of stages rather than levels: the individual can progress from the lower to the higher stages, but does not necessarily do so. The lower levels are prerequisites for, and subsumed by, the higher. (See the section on development for a discussion of the concept of stages.)

Organisations require several types and levels of skills, not only the higher-level thinking skills. The human resource manager can therefore use these classifications, first to identify the prior learning that needs to take place before skills of various levels can be attained, and then to plan ways of facilitating the learning of such skills.

Fitts's stages of skills acquisition

Fitts (1962, in Stammers and Patrick, 1975) distinguished three stages of learning, in particular of perceptual-motor skills acquisition. It is recognised that they may overlap.

- *Cognitive stage.* The learner has to understand what is required, its rules and concepts, and how to achieve it.

- *Associative stage.* The learner has to establish through practice the stimulus–response links, the correct patterns of behaviour, gradually eliminating errors.
- *Autonomous stage.* The learner refines the motor patterns of behaviour until external sources of information become redundant and the capacity simultaneously to perform secondary tasks increases.

Dreyfus et al.'s stage model of skills acquisition

Dreyfus *et al.* (1986, in Cooley, 1987: 13–15, and Quinn *et al.*, 1990: 314–315) set out a more elaborate model of the acquisition of skills that is relevant to understanding the development of cognitive skills. Their five-stage model moves from the effective performance of lower- to higher-order skills.

- *Stage 1: the novice.* Novices follow context-free rules, with relevant components of the situation defined for them: hence they lack any coherent sense of the overall task.
- *Stage 2: the advanced beginner.* Through their practical experience in concrete situations learners begin to recognise the contextual elements of their task. They begin to perceive similarities between new and previous experiences.
- *Stage 3: competent.* They begin to recognise a wider range of cues, and become able to select and focus upon the most important of them. Their reliance upon rules lessens; they experiment and go beyond the rules, using trial and error.
- *Stage 4: proficient.* Those who arrive at this stage achieve the unconscious, fluid, effortless performance referred to in the definitions of skill given earlier. They still think analytically, but can now 'read' the evolving situation, picking up new cues and becoming aware of emerging patterns; they have an involved, intuitive and holistic grasp of the situation.
- *Stage 5: expert.* At this stage, according to Cooley (1987), 'Highly experienced people seem to be able to recognise whole scenarios without decomposing them into elements or separate features' (p. 15). They have 'multidimensional maps of the territory'; they 'frame and reframe strategies as they read changing cues' (Quinn *et al.*, 1990: 315). With this intuitive understanding of the implications of a situation, they can cope with uncertainty and unforeseen situations.

Managers' levels of learning (Burgoyne and Hodgson)

A similar hierarchy has been proposed specifically for the learning of managers. Burgoyne and Hodgson (1983) suggest that managers have a gradual build-up of experience created out of specific learning incidents, internalise this experience, and use it, both consciously and unconsciously, to guide their future action and decision-making. They identify three levels of this learning process:

- *Level 1 learning,* which occurs when managers simply take in some factual information or data that is immediately relevant but does not change their views of the world.
- *Level 2 learning,* which occurs at an unconscious or tacit level. Managers gradually build up a body of personal 'case law' that enables them to deal with future events.
- *Level 3 learning,* when managers consciously reflect on their conception of the world, how it is formed, and how they might change it.

Perry's continuum of intellectual and ethical development

Perry's (1968) schema (see Daloz, 1986) emerged from his research into his students' experiences. He interpreted their intellectual and ethical development as a continuum, and mapped out the way in which individuals develop multiple perspectives while at the same time becoming able to commit themselves to their own personal interpretation. At one extreme is basic dualism, where everything is seen as good or bad. This moves through the perception of the diversity of opinion; of extensive legitimate uncertainty;

through perception that all knowledge and values are contextual and relativistic; to the recognition of the need to make a commitment to a viewpoint; the making of the commitment; experiencing its implications; and, finally, to the affirmation of identity as this commitment is expressed through lifestyle.

Bloom et al.'s taxonomy of cognitive skills

Bloom *et al.* (1956) offer a classification, rather than a hierarchy, of skills:

- knowledge (simple knowledge of facts, of terms, of theories, etc.);
- comprehension (an understanding of the meaning of this knowledge);
- application (the ability to apply this knowledge and comprehension in new concrete situations);
- analysis (the ability to break the material down into its constituent parts and to see the relationship between them);
- synthesis (the ability to reassemble these parts into a new and meaningful relationship, thus forming a new whole);
- evaluation (the ability to judge the value of material using explicit and coherent criteria, either of one's own devising or derived from the work of others) (Fontana, 1981: 71).

Single- and double-loop learning

Another useful classification of learning is found in the concept of two different types of learning: single- and double-loop learning. Individuals do not necessarily progress from single- to double-loop learning, nor is the former an essential prerequisite for the latter.

Single-loop learning refers to the detection and correction of deviances in performance from established (organisational or other) norms, whereas double-loop learning (Argyris and Schön, 1978) refers to the questioning of those very norms that define effective performance. Learning how to learn calls for double-loop learning.

Gagné's classification of learning

Gagné (1970, in Stammers and Patrick, 1975) studied both the process of learning and the most effective modes of instruction, and has made several classifications of types of learning. For example, he identified the ability to make a general response to a signal; to develop a chain of two or more stimulus–response links, including verbal chains and associations; to make different responses to similar though different stimuli; to achieve concept learning and identify a class of objects or events; to learn rules through the acquisition of a chain of two or more concepts; and, finally, to combine rules and so achieve problem-solving.

Gagné's classification allows us to identify the processes whereby skills of all levels are acquired, and hence suggests how to facilitate learning and prevent failure to learn at the various levels.

ACTIVITY ## Higher-order thinking skills

On your own or in a small group, return to the section 'The changing world of work and organisations' and identify the higher-order thinking skills it suggests are now needed in organisations. Where would they be classified in the various classifications above? What does this tell you about these skills and how they could be developed?

● Cyclical models of learning and learning styles

Another, and more dynamic, way of conceptualising the learning process is to see it as cyclical. The process has different identifiable phases, and individual learners have preferred learning styles. If methods appropriate to the various phases and individual styles are used, more effective learning will result. (The assumptions about phases echo those underlying the concept of development, which is to be discussed in the next section.) The various models below offer a number of important insights to the human resource manager concerned to facilitate higher-order skills in the organisation. They draw attention to the significance of learning through action and reflection, as well as through the traditional channels of teaching/learning. They recognise that individuals might prefer different phases of the cycle and have different styles: they offer means to identify those preferences; to engage in dialogue with individuals about their preferences; and to identify means of helping individuals to complete the whole cycle.

Kolb's learning cycle

The best-known learning cycle in the field in which we are interested is that of Kolb. There are two dimensions to learning (Kolb *et al.*, 1984): concrete/abstract (involvement/detachment) and active/reflective (actor/observer). Learning is an integrated cognitive and affective process moving in a cyclical manner from concrete experience (CE) through reflective observation (RO) and abstract conceptualisation (AC) to active experimentation (AE) and so on (Kolb, 1983).

Effective learning calls for learners:

- to become fully involved in concrete, new experiences (CE);
- to observe and reflect on these experiences from many perspectives (RO);
- to use concepts and theories to integrate their observations (AC);
- to use those theories for decision-making and problem-solving (AE).

However, many people have a preference for a particular phase and so do not complete the cycle: thus they do not learn as effectively or as comprehensively as they could. Kolb's Learning Styles Inventory identifies these preferences (Mumford, 1988: 27). The 'converger' (AC and AE) prefers the practical and specific; the 'diverger' (CE and RO) looks from different points of view and observes rather than acts; the 'assimilator' (AC and RO) is comfortable with concepts and abstract ideas; and the 'accommodator' (CE and AE) prefers to learn primarily from doing.

Honey and Mumford's learning styles

Honey and Mumford (1992) also identify four learning styles, based on the individual's preference for one element in the learning cycle, and have developed norms based on the results of those who have completed their Learning Styles Questionnaire. Their **activists** learn best when they are actively involved in concrete tasks; **reflectors** learn best through reviewing and reflecting upon what has happened and what they have done; **theorists** learn best when they can relate new information to concepts or theory; **pragmatists** learn best when they see relevance between new information and real-life issues or problems (Mumford, 1988: 28). This information can be used to design effective learning events, including, Mumford (2002) reminds us, e-learning. Individuals, too, can use it to build on their strengths and reduce their weaknesses in learning.

The Lancaster cycle of learning

A cyclical model said to represent 'all forms of learning including cognitive, skill development and affective, by any process' (Binsted, 1980: 22) is the Lancaster model. This identifies three different forms of learning: receipt of input/generation of output, discovery and reflection. As Figure 8.1 shows, they take place in both the inner and outer world of the individual. The receipt of input results from being taught or told information, or reading it in books. Learners follow the discovery loop (action and feedback) through action and experimentation, opening themselves to the new experiences generated, and becoming aware of the consequences of their actions. They follow the reflection loop

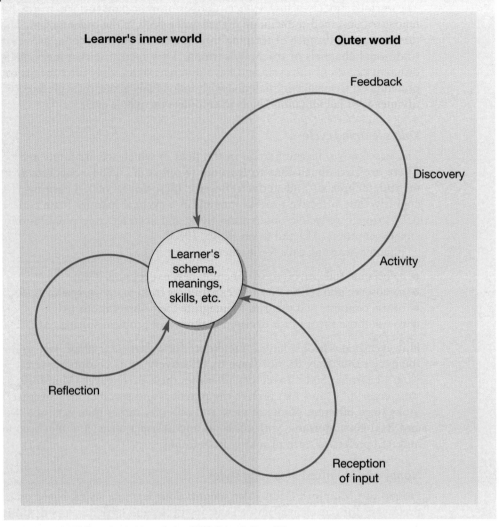

| Figure 8.1 | The Lancaster model of the learning cycle |

Source: Binsted (1980). Reproduced with permission of MCB University Press Ltd.

(conceptualising and hypothesising) when making sense of the information they receive and the actions they undertake, and when, on the basis of this, theorising about past or future situations.

Each form of learning is cyclical, and the cycles can be linked in various ways (for example, learning in formal classroom settings links the receipt of input with reflection), but in effective learning the learner will complete the overall cycle.

The learning curve

Though not a cyclical model, the learning curve is included here for convenience.

The notion of a curve is based on the recognition that there is a relationship between the rate of learning and the passage of time. Managers working on the introduction of a new system, for example, might say 'we are on a learning curve'. This curve is often represented as being S-shaped, that is, proficiency in a new skill begins slowly at first, increases steadily over time, and then remains on a plateau. However, since the shape of the curve must clearly depend on the nature and circumstances of the learning, this notion of a learning curve perhaps adds little of value to the understanding of learning.

Barriers to learning

Although learning is a natural process, people can experience significant barriers, particularly to their learning in formal settings such as school and work. Some of these barriers can be internal: the learner might have poor learning skills or limited learning styles; poor communications skills; unwillingness to take risks; fear or insecurity. Anxiety and lack of confidence are frequently emphasised as significant impediments to learning. Other barriers can be thrown up by the situation: lack of learning opportunities or of support, inappropriate time or place (see Mumford, 1988).

The process of development

The word 'development' is often used quite loosely, but here we use it to mean the process whereby, over time, the individual becomes more complex and differentiated through the interaction of internal and external factors. Learning plays a part in development. For example, the individual's innate tendencies towards growth and maturation are facilitated or constrained – shaped – by the influences in the individual's specific context, and by how the individual responds to them.

Development is difficult to conceptualise, though the systems thinking discussed in Chapter 3 is helpful. It is also difficult to study, embracing as it does both the individual's (or organisation's) inner life and the changing nature of a complex world, often with the lifespan as the time dimension. Researchers and theorists may therefore have focused upon segments of the lifespan and drawn implications for the remainder, or upon aspects, rather than the whole range, of development.

Some developmental theorists have devised models to represent universal, normative patterns of experience – all individuals follow similar patterns of experience – and these models suggest that some degree of prediction could be made about the basic outline of individual lives (for example, Levinson *et al.*, 1978). Further, as has already been noted, development – as in 'career development' – is sometimes used to connote progression or advancement. In other words, it is being assumed that there are accepted norms against which an individual's development can be calibrated, and that those norms and the individuals' experiences can be clearly identified. If you recall the nature of various assumptions about social and personal reality discussed in Chapter 3, you will recognise that these are positivist assumptions. Positivist assumptions about individuals and the social and economic environment within which their lives are led (construed as an objective, orderly, stable framework) give rise to the definition of development in terms of sequential phases or stages, often with their own developmental tasks. However, these models frequently interpret the experiences of women and black people in terms of those of white males. Those working with these assumptions might also recognise that individuals have subjective experiences that cannot be studied in this scientific manner. They might therefore disregard them, although individuals base decisions about their life on their subjective experiences.

However, as Chapter 3 outlined, there are alternative approaches. The phenomenological approach acknowledges the significance of a person's subjective experiences, and the social constructionist approach recognises that, because individual experiences are socially constructed, the context of the individual has to be taken into account. These alternative assumptions lead to a focus upon individual cases and the search for insights rather than generalisable conclusions. They also emphasise the significance of context, and the dynamic, intersubjective processes through which individuals interpret and make decisions about their lives and careers.

When trying to understand development, then, it is important to be aware of the kind of assumptions that are being made about it.

■ Lifespan development

Lifespan development embraces the total development of the individual over time, and results from the interweaving of the biological, social, economic and psychological strands of the individual's life. People develop through their lifespan, achieving greater degrees of complexity, even transformation. They are therefore continuously engaging in learning processes as they seek balance between changing self and changing environment. The theories and models of lifespan development have several implications for human resource development, for the organisation is one of the major arenas in which this adult development is taking place.

● The influence of the socio-cultural context

There are two perspectives in the literature upon the influence of the socio-cultural context on the individual's lifespan experiences. The first interprets that there are tendencies towards common patterns in individual experiences resulting from socialisation. In any given social setting, whether culture, class or organisation, the members of that social group experience pressures to conform to certain patterns of behaviour or norms. Sometimes these pressures are expressed as legal constraints: the age of consent, marriage, attaining one's majority (becoming an adult); or as quasi-legal constraints such as the age at which the state pension is paid and hence at which most people retire from the labour force; or as social and peer group expectations. For example, Neugarten (1968) recognises how family, work and social statuses provide the 'major punctuation marks in the adult life', and the

> way of structuring the passage of time in the life span of the individual, providing a time clock that can be superimposed over the biological clock . . .   (p. 146)

Organisations also have their own 'clocks'. Sofer (1970) writes of his respondents' 'sensitive awareness' of the relation between age and organisational grade, for they were:

> constantly mulling over this and asking themselves whether they were on schedule, in front of schedule or behind schedule, showing quite clearly that they had a set of norms in mind as to where one should be by a given age.   (p. 239)

The other perspective, however, emphasises that the environment offers different opportunities and threats for individual lives. The process of development or elaboration takes place as the individual's innate capacity to grow and mature unfolds within a particular context, which in turn facilitates or stunts growth, or prompts variations upon it. For example, it is argued that there are significant differences in physical, intellectual and socio-economic attainments between children from different social classes (Keil, 1981). The interaction and accommodation between individuals and their environment therefore cannot be meaningfully expressed in a model that is cross-cultural or universal. Hence Gallos (1989) questions the relevance of many of the accepted views of development to women's lives and careers, while Thomas and Alderfer (1989) note that 'the influence of race on the developmental process' is commonly ignored in the literature.

● Models of lifespan development

There are many different models of the lifespan: here you can see two that have been influential in lifespan psychology. It is important to be aware of the assumptions underlying these models, as discussed above. Their implications for human resource development will be noted below.

Erikson's psychosocial model

Erikson (1950) conceives of development in terms of stages of ego development and the effects of maturation, experience and socialisation (see Levinson *et al.*, 1978; Wrightsman, 1988). Each stage builds on the ones before, and presents the expanding ego with a choice or 'crisis'. The successful resolution of this 'crisis' achieves a higher level of elaboration in individuality and adaptation to the demands of both inner and outer world, and hence the capacity to deal with the next stage. An unsuccessful or inadequate resolution hinders or distorts this process of effective adaptation in the subsequent stages.

For example, the adolescent strives for a coherent sense of self, or identity, perhaps experimenting with several different identities and as yet uncommitted to one; entry to work and choice of work role play a part here. A choice, however, has to be made and responsibility assumed for its consequences: unless this occurs, there is identity confusion. Young adults have to resolve another choice. This is between achieving closeness and intimate relationships *or* being ready to isolate themselves from others.

Erikson paid less attention to the remainder of the lifespan, but indicated that the choice for those aged 25 to 65 is between the stagnation that would result from concern only for self, indulging themselves as though they were 'their own only child' (Wrightsman, 1988: 66), *or* 'generativity'. This is the reaching out beyond the need to satisfy self in order to take responsibility in the adult world, and show care for others, the next generation, or the planet itself. The choice of the final stage is between construing life as having been well *or* ill spent.

The model of Levinson et al.

Levinson *et al.* (1978) studied the experiences of men in mid-life, and from these constructed a model of the male lifespan in terms of alternating, age-related, periods of stability and instability. In the stable period, lasting six to eight years, a man builds and enriches the structure of his life: work, personal relationships and community involvement. That structure, however, cannot last, and so there follows a transitional period, of four to five years, when the individual reappraises that structure and explores new possibilities. These can be uncomfortable or painful experiences, but they are the essential prelude to adapting or changing the life structure, and so achieving a further stable period.

You can read more about this model in Daloz (1986) and Wrightsman (1988), but should be aware of the assumptions underpinning it. The definition of the periods within the lifespan in terms of chronological age – for example, between ages 22 and 28 a man embarks on a stable period and entry into the adult world, and between ages 33 and 40 enters another stable period in which he settles down – reflects an assumption about the universal, normative patterning of experiences.

Stop and think	What are the implications for your effectiveness, or potential effectiveness, as an employee, of your personal development so far?

▪ Career development

Individual development interacts with the organisation and its development through the individual's career. Career development therefore is of significance for both individual and organisation, and hence for human resource development.

● Defining career

Although the term 'career' is well understood in everyday language, the concept is a complex one with several levels of meaning. It is therefore open to several definitions (see Glossary, p. 714, and Collin and Young, 2000). The core of the concept suggests the experience of continuity and coherence while the individual moves through time and social space. As with development generally, an individual's career results from the interaction of internal and external factors. As individuals become more skilled and flexible through learning and development, they gain more opportunities for intra- or inter-organisational moves, including promotion. Their learning and development also influence the rewards they gain from their work, their relationship with their employer, the role of work in their lives, and the way they view themselves and are viewed by others. However, 'career' refers not only to their observable movement through and experiences in organisations and the social structure generally. That is their objective career, while the personal interpretation they make of those experiences, the private meaning and significance it has for them, is their subjective career.

Because career is such a broad, often ambiguous, yet widely used concept, there are several perspectives that can be taken upon it. For example, it can be considered as a concept in both social science and everyday speech. This is the focus adopted by Collin and Young (2000). *Inter alia*, they identify the various stakeholders in this concept, such as the individual, the employer, the career counsellor, the government, and society itself, and draw attention to how the power relationships are glossed over by the rhetorical use of this concept. (For a discussion of rhetoric see Chapter 3.) Collin and Young (2000) also suggest that career may be changing from being a linear, future-oriented trajectory to becoming more of a collage of experiences. Another viewpoint upon career, found within vocational psychology, and underpinning career guidance theories and practice, focuses upon career choice and the most effective ways of matching people to jobs (for example, Holland, 1997). Or the concern may be with career development through life (for example, Cytrynbaum and Crites, 1989; Dalton, 1989). A further perspective looks at the nature and management of careers in organisations (for example, Arnold, 1997; Arthur *et al.*, 1989; Arthur and Rousseau, 1996; Hall and Associates, 1996; Herriot, 1992; Jackson, 1999), while yet another adopts a self-help approach to careers (for example, Bolles, 1988).

● Traditional theories of career development

Because career is such a rich concept, there are many theories that have attempted to explain it. Although it is not possible to examine all these theories here (for further details see Watts *et al.*, 1996), by classifying them into families we can see something of their range and major concerns:

- Theories concerned with external influences upon the individual's career:
  - the economic system and labour markets;
  - social class, social structure and social mobility;
  - organisational and occupational structure and mobility.
- Theories concerned with factors internal to the individual:
  - factors such as age, gender;
  - psychoanalytical explanations;
  - personality traits;
  - lifespan development;
  - implementation of self-concept.
- Theories concerned with the interaction of internal and external factors:
  - decision-making;
  - social learning.

- Theories concerned with the interpretation of the individual's subjective experiences:
  - narrative approaches;
  - social constructionist approaches (see Chapter 3).

The theories of career development have similar characteristics to those of lifespan development. Because of the assumptions commonly made about objectivity and subjectivity (see Chapter 3, and the discussion about the concept of development above), they:

- are more frequently formulated from a positivist than from a phenomenological or constructionist stance (see Chapter 3);
- focus upon objective rather than subjective experience;
- emphasise intra-individual rather than contextual factors;
- make assumptions about the universality of career, disregarding the significance of diversity: gender, race and social class (see Hopfl and Hornby Atkinson, 2000; Leong and Hartung, 2000; Marshall, 1989; Thomas, 1989).

● Careers in the twenty-first century

The theories above reflect our traditional understandings of career. However, the flatter and more flexible forms of today's organisations, and the changing relationship between employees and employers ('the new deal', according to Herriot and Pemberton (1995)) could well change the nature of career dramatically. There are also some slow, deep-seated changes taking place in the context of career. Demographic changes and shifts in public and private values, for example, may over time have significant impacts upon individuals' opportunities, attitudes and aspirations. It is for this reason that questions are being asked not only about future careers (Chartered Institute of Personnel and Development, 2002b), but also about the future of the concept of career itself (Collin and Young, 2000).

The potentials and implications of some of these changes – for individuals, employers, educationalists, careers guidance practitioners and policy-makers of various kinds – are being discussed widely (see Jackson *et al.*, 1996). It has been suggested that it is the traditional 'onward and upward' form of career that is under threat. However, Guest and McKenzie Davey (1996: 22), who have found little evidence of major organisational transformations in their own research, caution 'don't write off the traditional career'.

Theorists are attempting to understand what career is likely to become in the twenty-first century: three examples of their views are given here.

Bureaucratic, professional and entrepreneurial forms of career

Kanter (1989b: 508) draws our attention to the way in which the 'bureaucratic' career, defined by a 'logic of advancement', although only one of three forms of career, has come to dominate our view of organisational careers generally. The 'professional' form of career (Kanter, 1989b: 516) is wider than that pursued by members of professional bodies. It is defined by craft or skill; occupational status is achieved through the 'monopolization of socially valued knowledge' and 'reputation' is a key resource for the individual. Career opportunities are not dependent in the same way as in the 'bureaucratic' career upon the development of the organisation, nor is satisfaction as dependent upon the availability of extrinsic rewards. Some professional careers may be only weakly connected to employing organisations. The 'entrepreneurial' career develops 'through the creation of new value or new organisational capacity' (Kanter, 1989b: 516). Its key resource is the capacity to create valued outputs, and it offers freedom, independence and control over tasks and surroundings. However, while those with a 'bureaucratic' career have (relative) security, and 'professionals' can command a price in the marketplace, 'entrepreneurs' 'have only what they grow'.

It is the 'bureaucratic' form of career that is now under threat, but attributes of the 'professional' and 'entrepreneurial' forms are likely to be found far more extensively in the twenty-first century (Collin and Watts, 1996; Chartered Institute of Personnel and Development, 2002b).

The subjective career

Weick and Berlinger (1989) argue that in 'self-designing organizations' (the learning organisation of a later section), the focus will be on the subjective career. In the absence of the typical attributes of career such as advancement and stable pathways, 'the objective career dissolves' and the subjective career 'becomes externalized and treated as a framework for career growth' (Weick and Berlinger, 1989: 321), and a resource for the further organisational self-design. They liken career development in such organisations to what Hall (1976) describes as the 'Protean career', in which people engage in 'interminable series of experiments and explorations'. Such a career calls for the acceptance of frequent substantial career moves in order to incorporate a changing, complex and multi-layered sense of self; the 'decoupling' of identity from jobs; the preservation of the ability to make choices within the organisation; the identification of distinctive competence; and the synthesis of complex information (Weick and Berlinger, 1989: 323–326).

The boundaryless career

Arthur and Rousseau (1996: 3) indicate that whereas careers traditionally took place 'through orderly employment arrangements' within organisations, many are now 'boundaryless', crossing traditional boundaries – between organisations, and home and work.

Stop and think

How do you envisage your future career? How will it be likely to differ from the career of your parents' and grandparents' generations?

What are the implications for your learning and development needs?

■ Implications of the changing nature of career

Many have regarded the traditional career as elitist, available to only a few, characterised largely by social background and education. The future career may also be elitist, available to a few, but perhaps a different few. At this point it is possible to identify some of the winners and losers from the changes that are taking place. So far the losers have included workers in manufacturing, unskilled workers of many kinds, clerical workers of many kinds, middle managers of many kinds, and full-time workers of many kinds; many of these have been men. The winners have been the knowledge workers, those with the skills required by the new technologies, those with the attitudes and skills needed in service jobs, those who are able (or want) to work only part-time. Women seem to be benefiting from some of the changes. To be employed and to have a career in the future – to be self-programmable (Castells, 1998, see earlier) – individuals will have to remain employable, as this chapter has reiterated, with the ability to learn new knowledge and skills, and above all to learn how to learn.

The changing nature of career is of considerable significance for society as a whole, as well as for individuals and for the economy. For example, the future orientation that a career gives an individual is essential when making decisions about such key issues as starting a family, taking out a mortgage, changing one's occupation, re-entering education, or retiring from employment. Uncertainty about career could therefore over time affect the structure of the population or the housing market, while the effects of unemployment could damage the social fabric severely.

Implications for human resource development

On your own or in a small group, identify and discuss the implications for the ways in which an organisation sets out to develop its employees of an individual's

- lifespan development;
- career development.

Development of the individual within organisations

We shall now note some ways in which individuals develop within organisations – or are developed by their organisations.

● Employee development

One definition of employee development is:

> . . . the skilful provision and organization of learning experiences in the workplace . . . [so that] performance can be improved . . . work goals can be achieved and that, through enhancing the skills, knowledge, learning ability and enthusiasm at every level, there can be continuous organizational as well as individual growth. Employee development must, therefore, be part of a wider strategy for the business, aligned with the organization's corporate mission and goals. (Harrison, 1992: 4; see also Harrison, 2002)

Although, as the chapter has already argued, it is important for the organisation to develop its employees generally, many British employers have traditionally neglected employee development. This is reflected in the quotations from Cooley (1987) used in this chapter. However, recent interest in knowledge management, human capital and the learning organisation, and the establishment of the Investors in People award (see Chapter 9), are raising employers' awareness of the need for employee development and the benefits that flow from it. Furthermore, those employers who have already recognised their own self-interest in their employees' continuous learning and employability often encourage their employees to engage in learning activities for self-development (see below).

In employee development schemes, of the kind established by a consortium of TECs (now Learning and Skills Councils; see also Chapter 9) and local employers, the employer provides for employees some degree of financial support for activities that are not necessarily related to their jobs. A much-quoted example of this is Ford Motor Company's Employee Development and Training Programme (Corney, 1995). Moreover, many organisations have now established learning centres that often support opportunities for learning beyond what those organisations specifically need. Others have set up corporate universities, such as Motorola and Unipart (Miller and Stewart, 1999; see also Coulson-Thomas, 2000). (See also the subsection on e-learning.)

Nevertheless, even though their employers may not formally 'develop' them or encourage them to develop themselves, people still continue to learn, as we shall note later in the chapter.

● Staff development

This is similar to employee and professional development, but generally refers to the development of administrative, technical and professional staff in organisations, such as local authorities, in which such staff form a large proportion of those employed. Its aim is to enable such employees to perform their current and future roles effectively, but does not generally include their systematic development as managers.

● Self-development

Self-development is the term used to denote both 'of self' and 'by self' types of learning (Pedler, 1988). People developing themselves take responsibility for their own learning, identify their own learning needs and how to meet them, often through the performance of everyday work, monitor their own progress, assess the outcomes, and reassess their goals. The role of others in self-development is not to teach or to train, but perhaps to counsel or act as a resource.

It is now becoming widely recognised that, with the increasing flexibility of organisations and their contracts of employment, individuals need to engage in lifelong learning. However, many (including managers) do not receive from their employers the training and continuous development they need, so their need for self-development, associated with their need for employability, is likely in the future to be greater than ever.

Although self-development is regarded positively as proactive and entrepreneurial, it can be difficult for the individual to provide evidence of it without some form of accreditation. This has often involved arduous part-time study, which can increase the pressures on, and conflict between, the individual's work and home roles. Such programmes of study have in the past been largely dictated by the traditions and values of the educational providers, rather than the specific needs of the learner. This has now changed with the establishment of the Credit Accumulation and Transfer Scheme, the Accreditation of Prior Learning and of Experiential Learning (see Chapter 9). Moreover, the approach and framework of S/NVQs (see Chapter 9) now allows individuals to gain recognition for aspects of their work performance. Employee development schemes (see above) should also help individuals in their self-development, whether systematic or sporadic.

● Management and organisational development

It is not within the remit of this chapter to examine management development – this forms the subject of Chapter 10 – or organisation development, but they are included here for completeness. However, it should be noted that organisations, like people, need to develop to become more flexible, differentiated and adaptable to their environment. Indeed, the very development of organisational members will contribute to the development of the organisation itself. For example, as Chapter 10 recognises, management development is both needed by the developing organisation and sets in train further organisation development.

● Continuing professional development

Many professional institutions (see Arkin, 1992) require their members to engage in continuing professional development (CPD) because the changing environment is rendering obsolete some of their original professional skills and knowledge, and demanding the development of others. However, CPD is more than updating: it calls for a continuous process of learning and of learning-to-learn, and so is likely to have considerable benefits for organisations employing professionals, especially when part of the overall corporate strategy (Young, 1996).

Likely to be of particular relevance to readers of this book is the requirement for CPD that the Chartered Institute of Personnel and Development (CIPD) places on its members. For the Institute, Whittaker (1992) states that CPD is needed to ensure that members remain up to date in a changing world and that the reputation of the profession is enhanced; and to encourage members to aspire to improved performance and become committed to learning as an integral part of their work. She identifies the following principles underlying CPD:

- Development should always be continuous, the professional always actively seeking improved performance.
- Development should be owned and managed by the learner.
- Development should begin from the learner's current learning state – learning needs are individual.
- Learning objectives should be clear, and where possible serve organisational as well as individual goals.
- Investment in the time required for CPD should be regarded as being as important as investment in other activities.

CIPD members ensure their continuing development by engaging in professional activities, formal learning, and self-directed and informal learning (see also Haistead, 1995).

The subsection on career development referred briefly to the 'professional' form of career, and suggested that it might be more widely adopted in future. Continuing development, even where not required or monitored by a professional body, would be an important element of this. It should also be noted that the framework of vocational qualifications outlined in Chapter 9 is expected to accommodate the work of professionals at its level 5 (see Welch (1996) and Whittaker (1995) on the routes to the personnel and development profession).

The organisation as context for learning and development

This chapter has already noted how the process of learning knows no boundaries. People bring the fruits of this naturally occurring and continuous process into their place of work and so, as Cooley (1987: 169) shows, 'ordinary people' have the potential to contribute the knowledge, skills, attitudes and creative thinking that organisations need for survival, flexibility and development. Moreover, individuals' learning and development continue within the organisation, so here we shall examine how human resource managers can provide an environment in which the capacity to learn and adapt can be harnessed to benefit the organisation.

Employers benefit from – indeed, depend on – their employees' naturally occurring learning. Some recognise this and encourage, facilitate and extend those aspects of their employees' learning that are essential for the organisation, and support them informally or undertake formal employee development activities (see earlier). However, organisations themselves can sometimes make inhospitable environments for the learning and development individuals bring to them (e.g. Honey, 2002). The section on different types of learners noted that learning involves the whole person, but organisations are systems of roles (see Chapter 3), and these roles can distort or straitjacket individuals, as Argyris (1960) and McGregor (1960) argue. While they were both writing in a very different organisational era, and much has already moved in the directions they were advocating, nevertheless, the urgent calls for human resource development and for the development of the learning organisation hint that there still remain vestiges of those traditional assumptions and practices.

Some employers ignore the significance for the organisation of this learning, and do little either to overcome the way in which their organisation may thwart the development of their employees, or to foster that learning and development. In these cases, employee development is not a planned or systematic process. It takes place nevertheless: employees learn for themselves how to carry out their jobs, or improve their performance; how to make job changes or achieve promotions; how to become managers and develop others.

It must therefore be recognised that much employee learning might not be intended, planned or systematic; Chapter 9 indicates that this may be the case in the majority of organisations. Nevertheless, individuals may:

- learn how to carry out their initial and subsequent jobs through doing and observing, through trial and error, through the influence of and feedback from their peers and supervisors, through modelling themselves on others, and through informal mentors;
- develop themselves through their own more or less systematic analysis of their learning needs;
- take the initiative to acquire additional knowledge or understanding by attending educational and other courses.

Because of this, employee learning is problematical. Employers will receive many of its benefits without effort on their part, while at the same time, unlike recruitment and selection, they cannot fully control or contain it. Some employers might feel threatened by the potential of their employees' learning and development, and not welcome significant changes in the people they had been at pains to select as employees. Through their work, employees might acquire knowledge and skills that make them marketable to other employers, and perhaps less than fully committed to their present employer. Equally, not exposed to best practice, they might learn poor lessons; they might also learn ineffectively and in an unnecessarily uncomfortable, effortful or wasteful manner. Thus they might not necessarily benefit from the learning and development they contribute to their organisation, although they would not be able to withhold some of its benefits from their employers.

To manage people effectively and fairly, and in a way that benefits the organisation, therefore, it is important, first, to be aware of these thorny and, at times, moral issues. (You will have the opportunity to consider them in greater depth in the section on controversial issues.) Then, it is necessary to understand how the processes of learning and development can be facilitated in the organisation and, indeed, how the organisation can itself learn. This is the subject of this section.

Influences upon learning and development outside the organisation

Many significant influences upon learning and development emanate from outside the organisation. Government-driven education and training initiatives and changes have contributed to the institutionalisation of competence-based education and training. The history, purpose and nature of these developments are discussed by Harrison (1992: 17–77; see also Harrison, 2002). Within a comprehensive and continually updating national framework agreed across all sectors and occupations (see Chapter 9), elements in an individual's learning and development, whether achieved through formal education, training or experiential learning across the lifespan, are identified and assessed against nationally agreed standards. The language, philosophy and procedures of this framework are likely to shape individuals' perceptions of their learning and learning needs, and to influence how employers articulate the learning needs of their employees. Moreover, the Investors in People initiative (see Chapter 9 and Arkin, 1999) also both prompts, shapes and supports human resource development practices.

Facilitating learning and development within the organisation

Employees learn and develop through carrying out their jobs: this chapter has already noted the significance of action for learning. For example, the design of those jobs and the organisation structure, the degree to which it is centralised and bureaucratised, all influence employees' learning opportunities. People need to be able to grow in their jobs, and might outgrow their jobs as they learn, or to move into new jobs that would allow them to continue the process of their development. An organisation that is growing or changing is more likely to offer these opportunities than one that is static or declining. However, a 'world-class manufacturing' organisation, such as Oral-B Ireland, is a challenge to manage:

> When everyone participates in creating a quality culture, functional boundaries become fuzzy, and the 'seamless' organisation emerges. This culture makes people easier to lead, but difficult to drive.
> (Ryan, 1995: 41)

Here, then, are some of the features of organisation and management that would facilitate learning and development within organisations.

● The style of management

Reporting on the results of research by the New Learning for New Work Consortium, Fonda and Guile (1999) set out the guiding principles for managing 'capable' organisations that seek to develop the learning of their employees. These are 'respect for the views of the workforce and clarity about the capabilities that the whole workforce will need; the creation of both challenge and support for developing and sustaining these capabilities; and an individualised approach to potential' (p. 41).Thus, as well as specific training, individuals need feedback on their performance, encouragement, support, and resources to give them self-confidence, to stimulate and sustain their learning and development. To develop the higher-order skills needed in organisations, employees need the opportunity to take risks and hence to make mistakes. This presupposes not only a risk-taking and confident approach on the part of employees, but also a risk-taking and supportive management. Effective learning and development in the organisation therefore call for a managerial style that is compatible with this need. The existence and nature of an appraisal scheme (see Chapter 13) could have positive or negative effects upon employees' learning (Thatcher, 1996). Essentially, organisations that want to develop these characteristics need also themselves to learn to learn, to become learning organisations, to have a learning culture and a learning centre (Coulson-Thomas, 2000).

● The learning organisation

The structure and operation of an organisation can influence the process of learning within it. It is evident that the human resource development argued for throughout this chapter would be achieved in a learning organisation.

As Chapter 9 discusses, the concept of the learning organisation is open to criticism, not least because it is often expressed in theoretical terms. This is recognised by Senge (Pickard, 2000: 39), one of its early and influential proponents (Senge, 1990), who has now elaborated his thinking in more concrete terms (Senge et al., 1998). Nevertheless, the learning organisation continues to be 'an aspirational concept' (Burgoyne, 1995: 24), a 'transitional myth' that makes sense both in the world that is passing and in the one that replaces it. Hence it enables people to bridge the gap – in this case as 'more emotionally involving, inclusive forms of organisation' emerge from the information-based organisation. However, Burgoyne (1999: 44), another early and key proponent, acknowledges that it has not 'delivered its full potential or lived up to all our expectations', and sets out what the characteristics of the second generation will have to be.

● The holographic organisation

In his metaphor of the organisation as a brain, Morgan (1997) offers us a new way of appreciating how the organisation itself can facilitate, constrain or repress the learning of its members. He suggests that both brain and organisation can be understood as holograms, 'where qualities of the whole are enfolded in all the parts so that the system has an ability to self-organize and regenerate itself on a continuous basis' (p. 100). The holographic nature of the learning organisation provides the stimulus, prompts and cues for individuals to learn and develop the higher-order skills they need to sustain and develop the organisation in a changing world, and 'to develop a discursive, networking culture in which everyone constantly questioned their own assumptions' (Pickard, 2000: 39).

Reminding us that the brains of employees and the brain-like capacities of computers and the Internet already have holographic features, Morgan considers how to design these features into organisations as well. He identifies five principles: the 'whole' built into the 'parts', redundant functions, requisite variety, minimum critical specification, and learning to learn.

Building the 'whole' into the 'parts'

One way of building the 'whole' into the parts of the organisation is through its culture. When this, Morgan suggests, embodies the organisation's 'vision, values, and sense of purpose', then it will act like a 'corporate "DNA"' (p. 102), which carries the holographic code of the human body in each of its parts. Another way is to network information throughout the organisation, so that it can be widely accessed, enabling organisational members 'to become full participants in an evolving system of organizational memory and intelligence' (p. 104). Further ways are to have the kind of structure that allows the organisation to 'grow large while remaining small' (p. 104), and to organise work tasks not into specialised jobs but into holistic teams of individuals having multiple skills.

Redundancy

In the traditional mechanistic design of organisations, each part has a specific function, with additional parts for backup or replacement. This allows a degree of passivity and neglect in the system ('"that's not my responsibility"', p. 111); with the capacity for redesigning the system delegated to specialised parts, the capacity to self-organise is not generalised throughout the system. Instead, Morgan suggests that the organisation needs an 'excess capacity that can create room for innovation and development to occur' (pp. 108–110). It needs redundancy of functions rather than redundancy of parts (pp. 111–112). Where each part has additional functions currently redundant but potentially available – through multi-skilling and teamworking, for example – the capacities for the functioning of the whole are built into the parts. Thus the system as a whole has flexibility, with the capacity to reflect on and question how it is operating and to change its mode of operating.

Requisite variety

The internal diversity of a self-regulating system must match the variety and complexity of its environment in order to deal with the challenges from that environment. All elements of the organisation should therefore 'embody critical dimensions' of the environment with which they have to deal; this variety can be achieved, where appropriate, through 'multifunctioned teams' (p. 112).

Minimum critical specification

Overdefinition and control, as in a bureaucracy, erode flexibility and stifle innovation. Hence the manager should define no more than is essential, but should instead have a role focusing on 'facilitation, orchestration and boundary management, creating "enabling conditions" that allow a system to find its own form' (p. 114). The challenge is to avoid the extremes of anarchy and overcentralisation.

Learning to learn

Finally, the organisation needs to engage in double-loop learning (see earlier), allowing its operating norms and rules to change as the wider environment changes.

Morgan concludes by noting that these five interconnected principles should not be regarded as 'a blueprint or recipe' (p. 115), but as a way of looking at how organisations could ensure that they remain adaptive.

● Mentoring

Mentor was the friend to whom Ulysses entrusted the care of his young son before embarking on his epic voyages. Although the notion of mentoring is, therefore, a very old one, its value in organisations started to be recognised 20 or so years ago. Since then many organisations have introduced mentoring programmes. You can read about this in Kram (1985), Collin (1988), Megginson (1988), Bennetts (1995), Fowler (1998), Brockbank and Beech (1999), Clutterbuck and Megginson (1999), Whittaker and Cartwright (1999), and Klasen and Clutterbuck (2001).

The nature and purpose of mentoring

In organisations, mentors are more experienced employees (and often managers) who guide, encourage and support younger or less experienced employees, or 'protégés'. Their relationship is a developmental one that serves career-enhancing and psychosocial functions for the protégé while also benefiting the mentor. Moreover, mentoring facilitates the learning-to-learn of the employees and contributes to the process of meaning-making in the organisation (see Chapter 3) and hence to its responsiveness to its environment, while meeting the developmental needs of employees.

Although being or having a mentor can occur naturally both outside and within organisations, this does not necessarily occur universally or systematically. To reap the benefits of mentoring, organisations set up formal programmes. Their purpose might be to support a graduate intake or other trainees and develop 'high fliers' or senior managers; encourage career advancement of women or those from minority groups (see Crofts, 1995); nurture employees with skills in short supply; stimulate and foster innovation in the organisation; and support managers in training, or other learners in the organisation. Examples are to be found in a wide range of private and public sector organisations in Britain, Europe and North America.

Protégés are not the only beneficiaries of mentoring: mentors also gain greatly from being challenged to understand their own jobs and the organisation, and to find ways of helping their protégés share this understanding and work effectively. Mentors might also find that they, too, need mentoring. Mentors draw upon their own networks to give experience and support to their protégés, and encourage them to develop networks of their own. In this way, the practice and benefits cascade through the organisation.

| Stop and think | Have you had, or been, a mentor? What does your experience suggest would be the benefits of a mentoring programme in an organisation? How could it be made to work effectively? |

The requirements for effective mentoring

This literature generally agrees on the following requirements for effective mentoring.

- *The status and characteristics of the mentor.* Mentors will generally be senior to protégés in status, experience and probably age. They should not have a line relationship with their protégé because the element of control inherent in it would conflict with the developmental nature of the mentoring relationship. It is highly desirable that senior managers act as mentors, and that top management be involved with the programme. Mentors should have the skills and qualities that protégés respect, good empathic and people-developing skills, good organisational knowledge and personal networks, and patience and humility to be able to learn from the protégé. Not all managers, therefore, would make appropriate mentors.

- *The protégé.* Protégés should have potential, and be hungry to learn and develop in order to realise it. There will be many more potential protégés in the organisation than can be effectively mentored; it is therefore commonly noted that mentoring is elitist.

- *The relationship.* The relationship should be one of mutual trust, and will develop over time. Unless limits are set by the programme, it might continue until the protégé no longer needs its support. Sometimes it develops into a full friendship.

- *The activities.* Mentors encourage their protégés to analyse their task performance and to identify weaknesses and strengths. They give feedback and guidance on how weaknesses can be eliminated or neutralised. They help them recognise the tacit dimensions of the task skills, an important element in the development of competence and 'know-how'. Mentors act as a sounding board for their protégés' ideas, and support them as they try out new behaviours and take risks. They give honest, realistic but supportive feedback, an important element in learning generally and learning-to-learn in particular. They encourage their protégés to observe and analyse the organisation at work through their own and others' actions. Through this process the protégé begins to identify and then practise tacit knowledge and political skills. Mentors help protégés to identify and develop potentials, question and reflect on experiences and prospects within the organisation, apply formal learning to practice, learn more widely about the organisation and develop networks. Overall, the mentor stimulates, encourages, guides, supports and cautions, acts as a role model, nurtures learning-to-learn, and encourages the adoption of a future orientation.

ACTIVITY   **Developing higher-order skills through mentoring**

On your own or in a small group, identify the higher-order skills that mentoring could develop, and discuss how it might do so.

■ Designing learning in the organisation

● Formal programmes

The messages about how to design effective learning are very consistent. For example, the advice that Sternberg (1985: 338–341), a theorist of intelligence, gives on how intelligent performance can be trained includes the following: make links with 'real-world' behaviour; deal explicitly with strategies and tactics for coping with novel tasks and situations; be sensitive to individual differences and help individuals capitalise on their strengths and compensate for their weaknesses; be concerned with motivation. The implications of the androgogical model of learning introduced in an earlier section (Knowles and Associates, 1984: 14–18) are that the facilitator of adult learning needs to:

- set a climate conducive to learning, both physical and psychological (one of mutual respect, collaborativeness, mutual trust, supportiveness, openness and authenticity, pleasure, 'humanness');
- involve learners in mutual planning of their learning;
- involve them in diagnosing their own learning needs;
- involve them in formulating their learning objectives;
- involve them in designing learning plans;
- help them carry out their learning plans – use learning contracts;
- involve them in evaluating their learning.

Belbin and Belbin (1972) draw upon their experience of studying training in industry for this advice on training 40- to 55-year-old adults:

1 Reduce anxiety and tension in the adult learner:
   - provide social support and allow social groups to form;
   - use acceptable instructors;
   - offer a secure future.
2 Create an adult atmosphere.
3 Arrange the schedule:
   - appropriate length of sessions;
   - preference for whole rather than part method;
   - start slowly.
4 Correct errors:
   - at the appropriate time.
5 Address individual differences:
   - different instructional approaches;
   - effects of previous education and work;
   - spare-time interests.
6 Follow up after training.

The value of these approaches is illustrated in the lessons drawn from the adoption in Britain of the Deming-inspired quality and continuous improvement programmes (Hodgson, 1987):

> Train with extreme sensitivity – pick trainers who have operators' confidence, are alert to remedial training needs and people's fears about going back to class; minimise the gap between awareness, training and use; gear course contents to people's learning needs – don't impose blanket programmes.
>
> (p. 43)

However, if those principles of design are ignored, barriers to effective learning, such as anxiety and lack of confidence, will be set up (see earlier). Barry (1988: 47), for example, notes that the considerable apprehension felt by the fitters and electricians who were returning to college after 20 years was an obstacle in the introduction of a multi-skilling programme. Their anxieties were dissipated once they learned that some of the tutors belonged to the same union and had the same craft background as themselves.

● E-learning

Information technology has provided the opportunity for e-learning, through which learning can be customised, and individuals can learn at their desks, rather than taking time out to study in a classroom (Sloman, 2001). For e-learning to be effective, it is not only the technology that has to be considered. The purpose of this form of learning has to be clear: it is more appropriate where knowledge is to be acquired than where inter-personal interactions are required.

Despite initial apparent enthusiasm for it, e-learning has not taken off as had been expected (Sloman, 2002). However, major lessons have been learned. An overall systematic approach, that includes e-learning, classroom and on-the-job learning, has to be developed, and it has to be recognised that e-learning is learner-centred, requiring new relationships between learners, trainers and line managers. Very importantly, it demands effective support provided for the learner (Sloman, 2002).

● Informal and tacit learning

Other people are major actors in the context of the individual's learning, and significant for an individual's learning and development, providing instruction and feedback (see earlier), support and encouragement, confidence-building, perhaps even inspiration. They might be, perhaps unknown to themselves, mentors, models or points of comparison for learners who learn not just from their formal instructors or supervisors, but also from peers and subordinates. This informal method of learning, including 'sitting next to Nellie', might have its weaknesses, but it also has strengths. It offers whole rather than part learning, and the opportunity to apprehend tacit knowledge (see earlier).

Some organisations attempt to capture and use formally some of these otherwise informal ways of learning through people. Knowledge management (see earlier) and mentoring (see earlier) are examples of this. Shadowing is a method that gives the opportunity for a learner to observe the actions of a senior manager systematically and over a period of time. From this observation the learner can infer certain general principles, grounded in everyday organisational realities. However, as the novel *Nice Work* (Lodge, 1988) suggests, without feedback from the manager, the 'shadow' can misinterpret some of the situations witnessed.

● Action learning

> There can be no action without learning, and no learning without action.
>
> (Revans, 1983: 16)

The role of action in learning, and the role of tacit knowledge in action, noted earlier, is now examined more closely here. The competence movement's focus upon outcomes rather than inputs into learning, and the integration of knowledge and skill assessed via performance, appears to offer a route towards the development of learning through action, but the reservations about competences expressed earlier should be noted. However, there is an established approach that has been shown (Pedler, 1983) to achieve the kind of learning that organisations, and particularly managers, are seeking. This is action learning, and is discussed more fully in Chapter 10.

Action learning offers a philosophy and a practice that human resource managers can adopt to help bring about the higher-order skills needed in an organisation. It is a greatly demanding process, one that will change the organisation and its members, but nevertheless one that could be carried out at all levels of the organisation, perhaps as a continuation of 'the restless searching for continuous improvement' and total quality management (see earlier). However, it demands commitment and support from the top, and would need to be cascaded down from higher learning sets.

● Reflective practice

Reflection, as well as action, we have already noted, plays a part in learning. Schön (1983) suggested that effective professionals engage in reflective practice: they build reflection into their actions. When faced with a unique and uncertain situation, they enter into a 'reflective conversation' with it, hypothesise on the basis of their existing knowledge and theories about how it could be changed, reframe it, experiment to identify the consequences and implications of this frame, listen to the situation's 'talk back' and, if necessary, 'reframe' again.

Other kinds of employee could also be encouraged to engage in Schön's (1983) reflective practice, thereby strengthening their learning to learn. See also Brockbank *et al.*, (2002).

Controversial issues

Although the argument for the need for learning and development within organisations is incontrovertible, it nevertheless raises some controversial issues, which you should consider. For example,

- Who owns the individual's learning and development?
- As generally presented, the value and purpose of human resource development is not questioned. Are there other ways of interpreting it?

ACTIVITY | *Who owns the individual's learning and development?*

Reflect on your own experience. Then, on your own or in a small group, identify the stakeholders in the individual's learning and development.

Reflect on your own experience

- What is it costing you to learn? For example, take your reading of this book: what does this cost you?
- How do you benefit from your learning and development?

Who are the stakeholders in the individual's learning and development?

- What other costs are incurred in your learning and development? Who pays them?
- Who else benefits from your learning and development?
- What benefits do they receive?

ACTIVITY | *As generally presented, the value and purpose of human resource development is not questioned. Are there other ways of interpreting it?*

The philosophy underpinning this chapter's presentation of its material is humanistic – learning and development have largely been interpreted as empowering of the individual. The chapter has not questioned whether the harnessing of individual learning and development by the organisation could be interpreted differently.

- Should the question that Legge (1995) asked of human resource management also be asked of human resource development – rhetoric or reality?

The awareness that the ownership of individual learning is a matter of debate, however, presents the opportunity to look for other interpretations. Consider this on your own or in a small group.

- What interpretations might the other chapters of this book make of human resource development?

- How idealistic or cynical are calls for activities such as mentoring and the learning organisation in today's flexible organisations?
- Is mentoring elitist or empowering?
- Is the learning organisation rhetoric or reality?
- Are there other possible interpretations?

(You may find it helpful to return to the section on ideology and rhetoric in Chapter 3.)

 ## Conclusions

This chapter has identified the significance of learning and development for individuals and organisations. Many organisations have recognised this, and have invested in their human resource development, as *People Management* reports in its regular company profiles (e.g. Birmingham City Council, Bradford & Bingley Building Society, the Post Office, SmithKline Beecham, Stagecoach Holdings) and annual features on the National Training Awards (e.g. Clamason Industries, Dupont, Lloyds TSB). It is assumed that both organisations and their employees have benefited.

However, by reflecting upon your own motivation and experiences, you will already have an insight into some of the thorny issues inherent in human resource development (others are discussed by Rainbird and Maguire, 1993). These issues can be summarised as follows:

- Learning and development take place throughout life, and in every aspect of life, as well as through performance of the job.
- Employer-initiated and sponsored and delivered learning can constitute only a small part of an individual's total learning.
- Some of such activities are undertaken as part of planned development; some are random or opportunistic.
- The employer cannot ring-fence such employer-provided learning.
- Employer-provided learning will be infiltrated by learning from other arenas – from home or social life, but also from undertaking the daily job, or observing boss or colleagues. Such learning may influence, strengthen, challenge or undermine employer-provided learning.
- The processes of learning and development might work counter to the processes of matching and control in which some employers invest heavily through the selection process.
- Learning and development are difficult to evaluate, because they often need an interval of time for their outcomes to be manifested.
- It is not easy to apportion their benefits to either employer or employee.
- It is not easy to calculate their costs, nor apportion them between employer and employee.
- Some of the costs are not borne by either of these; partners, families and the state through the educational and vocational training systems also pay some of the price of employee development.
- Individuals expect reward for their training or development – they have put effort in, become more skilled – expect greater reward. This reward might be either extrinsic (promotion, increase in pay) or intrinsic (greater fulfilment through a more demanding or higher-status job).
- As employees learn and develop, they might become less compliant to their employer and more demanding of changes at work and further development.

- This might result in the employee's dissatisfaction with his or her present job or employer.
- Because of all the above, employers might be reluctant to pay to develop their employees.
- It is difficult formally to provide effective learning – it often seems false in comparison with the ongoing spontaneous learning from life in general, and there are often difficulties in transferring from formal learning situations to everyday work.
- Some of the processes, activities and benefits depend upon the individual's context (including the presence of significant others), age and stage of development in life.

The issue of the ownership of the learning and development of individuals, as employees, reminds us that managing people has a moral dimension – human resource management juggles with empowering and controlling. This is the unanswered (and unanswerable?) question at the heart of human resource development, and poses dilemmas to both employer and employee.

Summary

- This chapter addressed the issue of why individuals generally and human resource managers in particular need to understand learning and development.

- It began with a series of definitions of learning that essentially rested on the view that the acquisition of knowledge and understanding facilitates change in perceptions and practice. These attributes are increasingly essential in the modern world of work, in which employees are expected to cope with change and new technology, take more responsibility, become more skilled and knowledgeable, and develop the ability for problem solving and creative thinking.

- The attributes that today's organisations need for their survival were examined – in particular, the need for quality and continuous improvement, flexibility, adaptability, and the exploitation of knowledge. Individual employees therefore must engage in a continuous process of learning how to learn, and managers must learn how to facilitate this.

- The nature of the learner was examined; but it was also emphasised that learning is a lifelong process that means making continuous adaptations. In many senses it is a journey. In the process of learning, many barriers are thrown up, including anxiety and lack of confidence on behalf of the learner. Discrimination also exists and often creates barriers for certain groups such as older workers, women, disabled people and cultural and ethnic minorities. This might impair their ability to learn by undermining their confidence and/or preventing them from taking courses and training programmes that will lead to greater opportunities. Many in these groups belong to the most disadvantaged in our society.

- The outcomes of learning – the acquisition of new skills, competence, 'know-how', tacit knowledge and employability – were highlighted. It is equally important for managers to have an awareness of the hierarchies of learning, the various levels of learning through which learners proceed in the pursuit of knowledge and understanding. Each level adds a further layer of sophistication to this process, from the simple acquisition of knowledge of facts through to the ability to understand complicated analyses involving complex abstract processes. Such understanding will take the learner through the various stages of learning: novice, advanced beginner, competent, proficient and, finally, expert. Various theories and models of learning and learning styles were also examined.

● The concept of development was explored. It is a process in which the learner 'becomes increasingly complex, more elaborate and differentiated, and thereby able to adapt to the changing environment'. A number of theories and models of lifespan, career and other forms of development were then examined and their implications for human resource development noted.

● Much learning and development takes place within the organisational context, itself influenced from outside by national training initiatives. Although learning knows no frontiers, organisations can often make inhospitable environments for the learning and development of individuals, and with this in mind it must be recognised that learning has to be supported by managers, mentors, and the overall learning climate of a learning organisation.

● The final part of the chapter examined two controversies for the reader to reflect on. These focused on who owns the individual's learning and development, and whether human resource development should be accepted at face value. Rather than giving 'answers' the author posed a number of probing questions for the reader to reflect upon – a form of self-development in itself.

Questions

1 What do human resource managers need to know about learning and development and how they take place? Draw up a list of questions that they could ask a learning specialist.

2 How can practical knowledge be developed in an organisation?

3 How might learning transform an individual? What are the implications of such transformation for an organisation?

4 What are the implications for an individual's career of new flexible forms of organisation?

5 The chapter has highlighted two controversial issues for discussion. What other thorny issues do learning and development in organisations raise?

Exercises

1 Keep a learning diary

Reflection is essential for effective learning. Systematically reflect upon what and how you learn by keeping a learning diary. It will also help you remember issues to discuss with your tutor, and might also contribute to your continuing professional development portfolio. Spend half an hour every week recording the following:

● the most meaningful or stressful events of the week;
● how they came about and who was involved;
● your interpretation of them;
● the emotions evoked by them;
● how you dealt with them;
● the outcomes of your actions;
● your evaluation of your actions;
● what you would do or avoid doing in future;
● what further skills, knowledge and understanding you need to perform more effectively;
● how you could acquire these;
● your action plan.

2 Find yourself a mentor

If you are not fortunate enough to have a mentor already, then find yourself one. Phillips-Jones (1982) suggests the following steps:

- Identify what (not who) you need.
- Evaluate yourself as a prospective protégé.
- Identify some mentor candidates.
- Prepare for the obstacles that they might raise.
- Approach your possible mentors.

3 How can you make and keep yourself employable?

- Assess your present employability.
- What do you need to do to achieve, maintain or improve this?
- What would be the implications for the nature and quality of your life overall if your career proved to be flexible and/or fragmented?

4 Review and make plans for your career development

To make effective plans for your future development, you need to be aware of how you have arrived at where you are and become who you are.

- Write a brief story of your life and career to date. Why and how have you become who you are today? What are your strengths and weaknesses?
- Now write your story again through the eyes of people who know you well: your parents or partner; your best friend or boss. Would they have a different interpretation of your life and career from you? Does this tell you anything about yourself that you might not have noticed before?
- Are you content with yourself and your present life? What would you like to be different? Why? What are the opportunities and threats to your life and career? What would you have to do (and forgo) to bring this change about? Would it be worth it? And what would the effect(s) be?
- Who else would such changes affect? Who could help or hinder you in these changes? What resources would you need to effect them? In what sequence would these changes have to come about, and how do they fit into the other timetables of your life?
- Now draw up an action plan, identifying the actions you will have to carry out over the short, medium and long term.
- Take the first step in implementing it today. Commit yourself to it by telling someone else about it and enlist their support to keep you motivated.
- At the end of the first month and every three months thereafter, review the progress of your plan and make any necessary adjustments.

Case study

Appoint in haste, repent at leisure

By Jane Bird

One general cannot win a battle single-handed, however skilled, and a small company will fail to grow unless it can find additional staff to take on important tasks. But skills are in short supply and small enterprises have little time or budget for recruitment and train-ing. Staffing mistakes are easy to make and expensive to put right.

Take Sally Thomas, managing director of Thomas Norton Consultants, a software company based in Guildford, Surrey, with annual turnover of around £500 000. Last year, Ms Thomas thought she had found the ideal project coordinator to handle long-term client relationships, releasing her to focus on new business development. The search had taken more than two years. 'We had already tried a couple of internal people but they were not

▶

suited to the role, which is a very important one because of the link with clients,' Ms Thomas says. 'The right person does not need a detailed knowledge of [information technology] but enough expertise to understand current and future projects and to talk about them meaningfully and sensitively to customers.'

Ms Thomas, who says she was cautious, and her technical director gave several short-listed candidates in-depth interviews and psychometric tests, which tend to look at personality and aptitude rather than straightforward ability. They then decided to follow their instinct and pick the individual who had performed least well in the tests but felt like the right person for the job.

The new project coordinator lasted just six weeks. 'It was very disappointing,' says Ms Thomas. 'We had looked carefully at who to have in that position but in the end the psychometric test proved to be more accurate than our own belief in who was best.' Luckily, the candidate who scored most highly in the tests was still available and is now doing well in the job.

Tony Jones, co-founder of Lektronix, an electronic repair services company, based near Walsall, West Midlands, agrees that recruitment is probably his biggest problem. Mr Jones used personal contacts when setting up the company, which began trading in August. He recruited four people he already knew for the top management team, which worked well, but on technical staff he has been less successful, with a 50 per cent drop-out rate.

'It's easy to make snap judgments because you're so busy running the business,' Mr Jones says. 'Instead of a thorough testing process you tend to do it too fast. Someone seems like a nice chap who knows what he is doing so you give him the job and repent at leisure.'

He has tried agencies but finds them expensive and lacking in knowledge of sectors such as electronics. Finding electronic engineers is not like looking for plumbers or bankers, he says. 'The right people for us tend to have been stuck in the bedroom with a soldering iron in their youth, rather than [having] done particularly well academically. We could be talking about the dark side of the moon as far as most agencies are concerned.'

Now new candidates for technical posts at Lektronix are put through an exhaustive interview and evaluation routine lasting four hours and including a practical test. 'It takes half a day but the result is that we select people who are much more likely to meet our requirements,' says Mr Jones. 'For senior appointments, we would ask candidates to give a presentation or lecture and impress the hell out of us.'

Recruitment is a huge problem for small companies – but essential if they are to get fresh ideas and make the transition to become bigger businesses, says Louise Punter, chief executive of the Surrey Chamber of Commerce. 'People who have jumped companies bring a fresh look and a big injection of new ideas.'

Those who have worked for medium or large companies are particularly valuable, Mrs Punter believes, because they are familiar with processes and systems that can be just as effective in a company of, say, 10 people as in a company of thousands. 'Small companies tend to be a bit tactical in problem-solving whereas a larger organisation would put in place a process that would prevent the same thing going wrong again. People who know how to do this can be very valuable.'

On the other hand, given the current skills shortage, low unemployment and the expense involved in recruitment, it makes sense to promote from within where possible. 'A classic mistake is that companies overlook the skills their existing staff have – for example, a marketing person might have good financial skills or vice versa,' says Mrs Punter. She recommends conducting a skills audit to identify staff expertise and what is transferable or not being used. In larger companies, these issues often come out in appraisals but in smaller ones they are easily missed.

Once you have the people, you must be prepared to let them fail and hope they learn from their mistakes, says Mr Jones, who now employs 25 people. Even so, he believes finding the right staff presents his biggest challenge. 'It's the one factor that would undermine our plans for expansion.'

Source: Financial Times, 9 January 2003.

Questions

Working on your own or in a small group, answer the following questions:

1 Will effective recruitment alone address the smaller organisation's need for effective and flexible employees?

2 What are the difficulties that face small businesses that want to develop their staff?

3 How might they address these difficulties?

4 What benefits would they gain if they were able to do so?

5 Bearing in mind the need to restrict costs, what steps would you suggest that Ms Thomas could take in the future to make her employees more flexible than they are at present?

6 What steps could she take to develop the new project coordinator further?

7 Mrs Punter recommends a skills audit of existing staff to enable a small organisation to promote

from within. What else would you suggest it could do?

8 Mr Jones recognises that employees have to learn from their mistakes. What would you suggest a small organisation could do to prevent that approach proving disastrous?

9 As an employee in a small organisation, what can you do to develop yourself further?

References and further reading

Those texts marked with an asterisk are particularly recommended for further reading.

Argyris, C. (1960) *Understanding Organizational Behaviour*. London: Tavistock Dorsey.

Argyris, C. and Schön, D.A. (1978) *Organisational Learning: A Theory of Action Perspective*. Reading, Mass.: Addison-Wesley.

Arkin, A. (1992) 'What other institutes are doing', *Personnel Management*, March, p. 29.

Arkin, A. (1995) 'How the act will affect you', *People Management*, Vol. 1, No. 23, 16 November, pp. 20, 23.

Arkin, A. (1999) 'Investors in future: above and beyond', *People Management*, Vol. 5, No. 3, pp. 40–41.

Arnold, J. (1997) *Managing Careers into the 21st Century*. London: Paul Chapman.

Arthur, M.B., Hall, D.T. and Lawrence, B.S. (eds) (1989) *Handbook of Career Theory*. Cambridge: Cambridge University Press.

Arthur, M.B. and Rousseau, D.M. (1996) (eds) *The Boundaryless Career: A New Employment Principle for a New Organizational Era*. Oxford: Oxford University Press.

*Atkinson, R.L., Atkinson, R.C., Smith, E.E. and Bem, D.J. (1993) *Introduction to Psychology*, 11th edn. New York: Harcourt Brace Jovanovich.

Barry, A. (1988) 'Twilight study sheds new light on craft development', *Personnel Management*, November, pp. 46–49.

Bartol, K.N. (1978) 'The sex structuring of organizations: a search for possible causes', *Academy of Management Review*, October, pp. 805–815.

Bayliss, V. (1998) *Redefining Work: An RSA Initiative*. London: The Royal Society for the Encouragement of the Arts, Manufactures and Commerce.

Beattie, D. (2002) President's Message, Annual Report 2002, London: Chartered Institute of Personnel and Development.

Belbin, E. and Belbin, R.M. (1972) *Problems in Adult Retraining*. London: Heinemann.

Bennetts, C. (1995) 'The secrets of a good relationship', *People Management*, Vol. 1, No. 13, 29 June, pp 38–39.

Binsted, D.S. (1980) 'Design for learning in management training and development: a view', *Journal of European Industrial Training*, Vol. 4, No. 8, whole issue.

Blackler, F. (2000) 'Collective wisdom', *People Management*, Vol. 6, No. 13, 22 June, p. 61.

Bloom, B.S., *et al*. (1956) *Taxonomy of Educational Objectives, Handbook 1: The Cognitive Domain*. London: Longmans Green.

Bolles, R.N. (1988) *What Color is Your Parachute?* Berkeley, Calif.: Ten Speed.

Borger, R. and Seaborne, A.E.M. (1966) *The Psychology of Learning*. Harmondsworth: Penguin.

Boyatzis, R.E. (1982) *The Competent Manager: A Model for Effective Performance*. New York: Wiley.

Bridges, W. (1995) *Job Shift: How to Prosper in a Workplace Without Jobs*. London: Nicholas Brealey.

Brittain, S. and Ryder, P. (1999) 'A certain *je ne sais quoi*: get complex', *People Management*, Vol. 5, No. 23, 25 November, pp. 48–51.

Brockbank, A. and Beech, N. (1999) 'Mentor blocks: guiding blight', *People Management*, Vol. 5, No. 9, 6 May, pp. 52–54.

Brockbank, A., McGill, I. and Beech, N. (2002) (eds) *Reflective Learning in Practice*. Aldershot: Gower.

Burgoyne, J. (1995) 'Feeding minds to grow the business', *People Management*, Vol. 1, No. 19, 21 September, pp. 22–25.

Burgoyne, J. (1999) 'Better by design: design of the times', *People Management*, Vol. 5, No. 11, 3 June, pp. 39–44.

Burgoyne, J.G. and Hodgson, V.E. (1983) 'Natural learning and managerial action: a phenomenological study in the field setting', *Journal of Management Studies*, Vol. 20, No. 3, pp. 387–399.

Cannell, M., Ashton, D., Powell, M. and Sung, J. (1999) 'Training: auditory perceptions: ahead of the field', *People Management*, Vol. 5, No. 8, 22 April, pp. 48–49.

Castells, M. (1996) *The Information Age: Economy, Society and Culture. Vol. I: The Rise of the Network Society*. Oxford: Blackwell.

Castells, M. (1998) *The Information Age: Economy, Society and Culture. Vol. III: End of Millennium*. Oxford: Blackwell.

Chartered Institute of Personnel and Development (2002a) *Training in the Knowledge Economy*. London: Chartered Institute of Personnel and Development.

Chartered Institute of Personnel and Development (2002b) *The Future of Careers*. London: Chartered Institute of Personnel and Development.

Clements, P. and Jones, J.J. (2002) *Diversity Training: A Practical Guide to Understanding and Changing Attitudes.* London: Kogan Page.

Clutterbuck, D. and Megginson, D. (1999) *Mentoring Executives and Directors.* London: Butterworth-Heinemann.

Coleman, P. (1990) 'Psychological ageing', in Bond, J. and Coleman, P. (eds) *Ageing and Society: An Introduction to Social Gerontology.* London: Sage, pp. 62–88.

Collin, A. (1988) 'Mentoring', *Industrial and Commercial Training*, Vol. 20, No. 2, pp. 23–27.

Collin, A. and Watts, A.G. (1996) 'The death and transfiguration of career – and of career guidance?', *British Journal of Guidance and Counselling*, Vol. 24, No. 3, pp. 385–398.

Collin, A. and Young, R. A. (eds) (2000) *The Future of Career.* Cambridge: Cambridge University Press.

Collins, H. (1993) 'Untidy minds in action', *The Times Higher Education Supplement*, No. 1066, 9 April, pp. 15, 17.

Constable, J. and McCormick, R. (1987) *The Making of British Managers.* London: British Institute of Management and Confederation of British Industry.

*Cooley, M. (1987) *Architect or Bee? The Human Price of Technology.* London: Hogarth Press.

Corney, M. (1995) 'Employee development schemes', *Employment Gazette*, Vol. 103, No. 10, pp. 385–390.

Coulson-Thomas, C. (2000) 'Carry on campus', *People Management*, Vol. 6, No. 4, 17 February, p. 33.

Crofts, P. (1995) 'A helping hand up the career ladder', *People Management*, Vol. 1, No. 18, 7 September, pp. 38–40.

Cytrynbaum, S. and Crites, J.O. (1989) 'The utility of adult development theory in understanding career adjustment process', in Arthur, M.B., Hall, D.T. and Lawrence, B.S. (eds) *Handbook of Career Theory.* Cambridge: Cambridge University Press, pp. 66–88.

*Daloz, L. A. (1986) *Effective Mentoring and Teaching.* San Francisco, Calif.: Jossey-Bass.

Dalton, G.W. (1989) 'Developmental views of careers in organizations', in Arthur, M.B., Hall, D.T. and Lawrence, B.S. (eds) *Handbook of Career Theory.* Cambridge: Cambridge University Press, pp. 89–109.

Dennis, H. (1988) *Fourteen Steps in Managing an Aging Work Force.* Lexington, Mass.: D.C. Heath.

Dixon, N. (2000) 'Common knowledge: the insight track', *People Management*, Vol. 6, No. 4, 17 February, pp. 34–39.

Dreyfus, H.L., Dreyfus, S.E. and Athanasion, T. (1986) *Mind Over Machine: The Power of Human Intuition and Expertise in the Era of the Computer.* New York: Free Press.

Erikson, E. (1950) *Childhood and Society.* New York: W.W. Norton.

Fitts, P.M. (1962) 'Factors in complex skills training', in Glaser, R. (ed.) *Training Research and Education.* New York: Wiley.

Fonda, N. and Guile, D. (1999) 'A real step change: joint learning adventures', *People Management*, Vol. 5, No. 6, 25 March, pp. 38–44.

Fontana, D. (1981) 'Learning and teaching', in Cooper, C.L. (ed.) *Psychology for Managers: A Text for Managers and Trade Unionists.* London: The British Psychological Society and Macmillan, pp. 64–78.

Fowler, A. (1998) 'How to run a mentoring scheme: guide lines', *People Management*, Vol. 4, No. 20, 15 October, pp. 48–50.

Gagné, R.M. (1970) *The Conditions of Learning*, 2nd edn. New York: Holt, Rinehart & Winston.

Gagné, R.M. (1974) *Essentials of Learning for Instruction.* Hinsdale, Ill.: Dryden Press.

Gallos, J.V. (1989) 'Exploring women's development: implications for career theory, practice, and research', in Arthur, M.B., Hall, D.T. and Lawrence, B.S. (eds) *Handbook of Career Theory.* Cambridge: Cambridge University Press, pp. 110–132.

Gardner, H. (1985) *Frames of Mind: The Theory of Multiple Intelligences.* London: Paladin.

Gardner, H. (1999) *Intelligence Reframed: Multiple Intelligences for the 21st Century.* New York: Basic Books.

Gilligan, C. (1977) 'In a different voice: women's conception of the self and of morality', *Harvard Educational Review*, Vol. 47, pp. 481–517.

Guest, D. and McKenzie Davey, K.M. (1996) 'Don't write off the traditional career', *People Management*, Vol. 2, No. 4, 22 February, pp. 22–25.

Guest, D., Storey, Y. and Tate, W. (1997) *Opportunity Through People.* IPD Consultative Document, June. London: IPD.

Haistead, N. (1995) 'A flexible route to life-long learning', *People Management*, Vol. 1, No. 19, 21 September, p. 40.

Hall, D.T. (1976) *Careers in Organizations.* Pacific Palisades, Calif.: Goodyear.

Hall, D.T. and Associates (1996) *The Career is Dead – Long Live Career: A Relational Approach to Careers,* San Francisco, Calif: Jossey-Bass.

Hammer, M. and Champy, J. (1994) *Reengineering the Corporation: A Manifesto for Business Revolution.* New York: Harper Business.

Hammond, D. (2002) 'Firms urged to report on HR', *People Management*, Vol. 8, No. 13, 27 June, p. 8.

Handy, C. (1987) *The Making of Managers: A Report on Management Education, Training and Development in the United States, West Germany, France, Japan and the UK.* London: Manpower Services Commission, National Economic Development Office and Institute of British Management.

Harrison, R. (1992) *Employee Development.* London: Institute of Personnel Management.

Harrison, R. (2002) *Learning and Development.* London: Chartered Institute of Personnel and Development.

Herriot, P. (1992) *The Career Management Challenge.* London: Sage.

Herriot, P. and Pemberton, C. (1995) *New Deals: The Revolution in Managerial Careers.* Chichester: John Wiley.

Hodgson, A. (1987) 'Deming's never-ending road to quality', *Personnel Management*, July, pp. 40–44.

Hogarth, T. and Barth, M.C. (1991) 'Costs and benefits of hiring older workers: a case study of B & Q', *International Journal of Manpower*, Vol. 12, No. 8, pp. 5–17.

Holland, J. L. (1997) *Making Vocational Choices: A Theory of Vocational Personalities and Work Environments*, 3rd edn. Odessa, Fl.: Psychological Assessment Resources.

Honey, P. (1998) 'The debate starts here', *People Management*, Vol. 4, No. 19, 1 October, pp. 28–29.

Honey, P. (1999) 'Not for the faint-hearted', *People Management*, Vol. 5, No. 21, 28 October, p. 39.

Honey, P. (2002) 'Tough love on learning', *People Management*, Vol. 8, No. 9, 2 May, p. 42.

Honey, P. and Mumford, A. (1992) *Manual of Learning Styles*, 3rd edn. London: Peter Honey.

Hopfl, H. and Hornby Atkinson, P. (2000) 'The future of women's career', in Collin, A. and Young, R.A. (eds.) *The Future of Career*, Cambridge: Cambridge University Press, pp. 130–143.

Jackson, C., Arnold, J., Nicholson, N. and Watts, A.G. (1996) *Managing Careers in 2000 and Beyond*. Brighton: Institute for Employment Studies.

Jackson, T. (1999) *Career Development*. London: IPD.

Kanter, R.M. (1989a) *When Giants Learn to Dance*. New York: Simon & Schuster.

Kanter, R.M. (1989b) 'Careers and the wealth of nations: a macro-perspective on the structure and implications of career forms', in Arthur, M.B., Hall, D.T. and Lawrence, B.S. (eds) *Handbook of Career Theory*. Cambridge: Cambridge University Press, pp. 506–521.

Keil, T. (1981) 'Social structure and status in career development', in Watts, A.G., Super, D.E. and Kidd, J. M. (eds) *Career Development in Britain: Some Contributions to Theory and Practice*. Cambridge: CRAC, Hobson's Press, pp. 155–192.

Klasen, N. and Clutterbuck, D. (2001) *Implementing Mentoring Schemes: A Practical Guide to Successful Programs*. London: Butterworth-Heinemann.

Knowles, M.S. and Associates (1984) *Androgogy in Action*. San Francisco, Calif: Jossey-Bass.

Kolb, D.A. (1983) *Experiential Learning*. New York: Prentice Hall.

Kolb, D.A., Rubin, I.M. and MacIntyre, J.M. (1984) *Organizational Psychology: An Experiential Approach*, 4th edn. New York: Prentice Hall.

Kram, K.E. (1985) *Mentoring At Work: Developmental Relationships in Organizational Life*. Glenview, Ill.: Scott, Foresman.

Laslett, P. (1989) *A Fresh Map of Life: The Emergence of the Third Age*. London: Weidenfeld & Nicolson.

Legge, K. (1995) *Human Resource Management: Rhetorics and Realities*. Basingstoke: Macmillan.

Leong, F.T.L and Hartung, P. J. (2000) 'Adapting to the changing multicultural context of career', in Collin, A. and Young, R.A. (eds) *The Future of Career*, Cambridge: Cambridge University Press, pp. 212–227.

Levinson, D.J., Darrow, C.M., Klein, E.B., Levinson, M.H. and McKee, B. (1978) *The Seasons of a Man's Life*. New York: Alfred A. Knopf.

Littlefield, D. (1999) 'Ormerod Home Trust: independence day', *People Management*, Vol. 5, No. 23, 11 November, pp. 52–54.

Lodge, D. (1988) *Nice Work: A Novel*. London: Secker & Warburg.

Malhotra, Y. (1998) *Knowledge Management for the New World of Business*, WWW Virtual Library on Knowledge Management, http://www.brint.com/km/

Marshall, J. (1989) 'Re-visioning career concepts: a feminist invitation', in Arthur, M.B., Hall, D.T. and Lawrence, B.S. (eds) *Handbook of Career Theory*. Cambridge: Cambridge University Press, pp. 275–291.

Martin, S. (1995) 'A futures market for competencies', *People Management*, Vol. 1, No. 6, 23 March, pp. 20–24.

Mayo, A. (2002) 'A thorough evaluation', *People Management*, Vol. 8, No. 7, 4 April, pp. 36–39.

McGregor, D. (1960) *The Human Side of Enterprise*. New York: McGraw-Hill.

Megginson, D. (1988) 'Instructor, coach, mentor: three ways of helping for managers', *Management Education and Development*, Vol. 19, Pt 1, pp. 33–46.

Mezirow, J. (1977) 'Personal transformation', *Studies in Adult Education* (Leicester: National Institute of Adult Education), Vol. 9, No. 2, pp. 153–64.

Miller, R. and Stewart, J. (1999) 'U and improved: opened university', *People Management*, Vol. 5, No. 12, 17 June, pp. 42–46.

Moreton, T. (ed.) (1992) 'The education, training and employment of disabled people', *Personnel Review*, Vol. 21, No. 6. pp. 2–87.

*Morgan, G. (1997) *Images of Organization*, 2nd edn. Thousand Oaks, Calif.: Sage.

Mumford, A. (1988) 'Learning to learn and management self-development', in Pedler, M., Burgoyne, J. and Boydell, T. (eds) *Applying Self-Development in Organizations*. New York: Prentice Hall, pp. 22–27.

Mumford, A. (2002) 'Horses for courses', *People Management*, Vol. 8, No. 13, 27 June, p. 51.

Myers, C. and Davids, K. (1992) 'Knowing and doing: tacit skills at work', *Personnel Management*, February, pp. 45–47.

Naylor, P. (1987) 'In praise of older workers', *Personnel Management*, November, pp. 44–48.

Neugarten, B.L. (1968) 'Adult personality: toward a psychology of the life cycle', in Neugarten, B.L. (ed.) *Middle Age and Aging: A Reader in Social Psychology*. Chicago, Ill.: University of Chicago Press, pp. 137–147.

Pedler, M. (1988) 'Self-development and work organizations', in Pedler, M., Burgoyne, J. and Boydell, T. (eds) *Applying Self-Development in Organizations*. New York: Prentice Hall, pp. 1–19.

Pedler, M. (ed.) (1983) *Action Learning in Practice*. Aldershot: Gower.

Pedler, M., Burgoyne, J. and Boydell, T. (eds) (1988) *Applying Self-Development in Organizations*. New York: Prentice Hall.

Perry, W.G. (1968) *Forms of Intellectual and Ethical Development in the College Years: A Scheme*. New York: Holt, Rinehart & Winston.

Phillips-Jones, L. (1982) *Mentors and Protégés: How to Establish, Strengthen and Get the Most from a Mentor/Protégé Relationship*. New York: Arbor House.

Pickard, J. (1999a) 'Lifelong earning: grey areas', *People Management*, Vol. 5, No. 15, 29 July, pp. 30–37.

Pickard, J. (1999b) 'Emote possibilities: sense and sensitivity', *People Management*, Vol. 5, No. 21, 28 October, pp. 48–56.

Pickard, J. (2000) 'Profile: high-mileage meditations', *People Management*, Vol. 6, No. 7, pp. 38–43.

Pugh, D.S., Hickson, D.J. and Hinings, C.R. (eds) (1983) *Writers on Organizations*. Harmondsworth: Penguin.

Quinn, R.E., Faerman, S.R., Thompson, M.P. and McGrath, M.R. (1990) *Becoming a Master Manager*. New York: Wiley.

Rainbird, H. and Maguire, M. (1993) 'When corporate need supersedes employee development', *Personnel Management*, February, pp. 34–37.

Rana, E. (2000) '2000 predictions: Enter the people dimension', *People Management*, Vol. 6, No. 1, 6 January, pp. 16–17.

Reese, H.W. and Overton, W.F. (1970) 'Models of development and theories of development', in Goulet, L.R. and Baltes, P.B. (eds) *Life-Span Developmental Psychology: Theory and Research*. New York: Academic Press, pp. 115–145.

*Revans, R. (1983) *ABC of Action Learning*. Bromley: Chartwell-Bratt (Publishing and Training).

Ribeaux, P. and Poppleton, S.E. (1978) *Psychology and Work: An Introduction*. London: Macmillan.

Rifkin, J. (1995) *The End of Work: The Decline of the Global Labor Force and the Dawn of the Post-Market Era*. New York: Putnam.

Ryan. J, (1995) 'Giving people the chance to sparkle', *People Management*, Vol. 1, No. 13, 29 June, pp. 40–42.

Scarborough, H. (1999) 'Science friction: system error', *People Management*, Vol. 5, No. 7, 8 April, pp. 68–74.

Scarborough, H. (2003) 'Recipe for success', *People Management*, Vol. 5, No. 2, 23 January, pp. 32–35.

Schön, D. A. (1983) *The Reflective Practitioner: How Professionals Think in Action*. New York: Basic Books.

*Senge, P. (1990) *The Fifth Discipline: The Art and Practice of the Learning Organization*. London: Century.

Senge, P., Kleiner, A., Roberts, C., Ross, R., Roth, G. and Smith, B. (1998) *The Dance of Change*. London: Nicholas Brealey.

Sheard, M. (1992) 'Two routes to quality: why Dow went for BS 5750', *Personnel Management*, November, pp. 33–34.

Sloman, M. (2001) *The E-Learning Revolution*. London: Chartered Institute of Personnel and Development.

Sloman, M. (2002) 'Don't believe the hype', *People Management*, Vol. 8, No. 6, 21 March, pp. 40–42.

Sofer, C. (1970) *Men in Mid-Career*. Cambridge: Cambridge University Press.

Stammers, R. and Patrick, J. (1975) *The Psychology of Training*. London: Methuen.

Sternberg, R.J. (1985) *Beyond IQ: A Triarchic Theory of Human Intelligence*. Cambridge: Cambridge University Press.

Thatcher, M. (1996) 'Allowing everyone to have their say', *People Management*, Vol. 2, No. 6, 21 March, pp. 28–30.

Thomas, D.A. and Alderfer, C.P. (1989) 'The influence of race on career dynamics: theory and research on minority career experiences', in Arthur, M.B., Hall, D.T. and Lawrence, B.S. (eds) *Handbook of Career Theory*. Cambridge: Cambridge University Press, pp. 133–158.

Thomas, R.J. (1989) 'Blue-collar careers: meaning and choice in a world of constraints', in Arthur, M.B., Hall, D.T. and Lawrence, B.S. (eds) *Handbook of Career Theory*. Cambridge: Cambridge University Press, pp. 354–379.

Training Commission (1988) *Classifying the Components of Management Competences*. Sheffield: Training Commission.

Trinder, C., Hulme, G. and McCarthy, U. (1992) *Employment: the Role of Work in the Third Age*, The Carnegie Inquiry into the Third Age, Research Paper Number 1. Dunfermline: The Carnegie United Kingdom Trust.

Tyson, S. and Fell, A. (1995) 'A focus on skills, not organisations', *People Management*, Vol. 1, No. 21, 19 October, pp. 42–45.

Ulrich, D. and Smallwood, N. (2002) 'Seven up', *People Management*, Vol. 8, No. 10, 16 May, pp. 42–44.

Ulrich, D. and Stewart Black, J. (1999) 'All around the world: worldly wise', *People Management*, Vol. 5, No. 21, 25 October, pp. 42–46.

Walsh, J. (1998) 'Competency frameworks give companies the edge', *People Management*, Vol. 4, No. 18, 17 September, p. 15.

Waskel, S. A. (1991) *Mid-Life Issues and the Workplace of the 90s: A Guide for Human Resource Specialists*. New York: Quorum.

Watts, A.G., Law, B., Killeen, J., Kidd, J. M. and Hawthorn, R. (1996) *Rethinking Careers Education and Guidance: Theory, Policy and Practice*. London: Routledge.

Wechsler, D. (1958) *The Measurement and Appraisal of Adult Intelligence*, 4th edn. London: Baillière, Tindall & Cox.

Weick, K.E. and Berlinger, L.R. (1989) 'Career improvisation in self-designing organizations', in Arthur, M.B., Hall, D.T. and Lawrence, B.S. (eds) *Handbook of Career Theory*. Cambridge: Cambridge University Press, pp. 313–328.

Welch, J. (1996) 'HR qualifications get the go-ahead at last', *People Management*, Vol. 2, No. 11, 30 May, p. 11.

Whitehead, M. (1999) 'Centrica: energy efficient', *People Management*, Vol. 5, No. 22, 11 November, pp. 60–62.

Whittaker, J. (1992) 'Making a policy of keeping up to date', *Personnel Management*, March, pp. 28–31.

Whittaker, J. (1995) 'Three challenges for IPD standards', *People Management*, Vol. 1, No. 23, 16 November, pp. 30–34.

Whittaker, M. and Cartwright, A. (1999) *The Mentoring Manual*. London: Gower.

Wisher, V. (1994) 'Competencies: the precious seeds of growth', *Personnel Management*, July, pp. 36–39.

Woodruffe, C. (1991) 'Competent by any other name', *Personnel Management*, September, pp. 30–33.

Wrightsman, L.S. (1988) *Personality Development in Adulthood*. Newbury Park, Calif.: Sage.

Young, C. (1996) 'How CPD can further organisational aims', *People Management*, Vol. 2, No. 11, 30 May, p. 67.

For multiple choice questions, exercises and annotated weblinks specific to this chapter visit this book's website at www.booksites.net/beardwell

CHAPTER 9

Human resource development: the organisation and the national framework

Len Holden

- ▶ To examine the strategic nature of HRD and its relationship to the individual and to organisational development.
- ▶ To outline and explain a human resource development plan, including the assessment of training needs, an outline of training methods, and the processes of monitoring and evaluating the plan.
- ▶ To examine the concepts of the learning organisation and knowledge management.
- ▶ To examine vocational education and training in the leading industrial nations, with an in-depth investigation of the training systems of Germany, Japan and France.
- ▶ To examine the implications of these international comparisons for the UK.
- ▶ To examine the national framework for vocational education and training in the UK.
- ▶ To outline possible future policy developments in vocational education and training.
- ▶ To identify some controversial issues in the field of vocational education and training.

Introduction

As we have seen from the previous chapter on employee development, it is difficult to arrive at a consensus definition of terms such as 'development', 'education' and 'training' because of the varied ways in which they are translated into work and life situations.

The Manpower Services Commission, set up by the 1973 Employment and Training Act but replaced in 1988, defined training as

> a planned process to modify attitude, knowledge or skill behaviour through learning experience to achieve effective performance in an activity or range of activities. Its purpose, in the work situation, is to develop the abilities of the individual and to satisfy the current and future needs of the organisation. (Manpower Services Commission, 1981a)

This definition is no longer adequate or wide enough in a world where organisations are in a constant state of transformation in a turbulent and rapidly changing economic environment. Training was seen as a series of mechanistic interventions through which trainers poured knowledge into an employee's head, with the expectation of automatic improvement in individual and organisational performance.

Such a concept is too narrow for the modern organisation. First, the skills and knowledge that employees need are rapidly changing, and what is relevant now may not be relevant in the future. Second, there is an increasing need for employees to 'own' their learning. This means being aware of their own needs for both the organisation's requirements and their own long-term development. In other words, individuals also need to be aware of their own learning strategies. Third, increasing competition is forcing organisations to improve the quality of the products and services they provide, and this requires a closer relationship with the customer, empowerment of employees, and improved communication for exchanging knowledge and skills. Some commentators have suggested that this need to constantly improve knowledge and skill must lead to an environment where learning and sharing knowledge are at the centre of the organisation's operation – what has come to be called the *learning organisation* or the *knowledge-based organisation* (Senge, 1990; Nonaka, 1991; Pedler *et al.*, 1997; Dixon, 2000).

However, even in a learning environment there may be a conflict between developing the skills of employees and the future needs of the organisation. For example, many organisations prefer to train employees in firm-specific skills rather than transferable skills, and thus these two objectives may prove mutually exclusive or, at best, only partly achievable. A survey in the early 1990s concluded:

> Much of the training reported was for organisational rather than individual development, suggesting that many employees would not regard the training they receive as training at all, since it neither imparts transferable skills nor contributes to personal and educational development.
>
> (Rainbird and Maguire, 1993)

There is little to suggest that this situation has changed radically at the start of the new millennium. The loss of employees in whom considerable sums have been invested in training and development influences some employers to concentrate on training in areas that are specific to their organisation, while the 'poacher' organisations use money as an attractor and invest little or nothing in training their employees.

Other commentators believe that the idea of transferable skills is used far too widely, and that many processes are particular to organisations and their products and services. Even in a country such as Japan, whose training systems are much admired, the programmes involve a considerable proportion of training for firm-specific skills (Dore and Sako, 1989).

The need for training

Until the 1980s, training and development in British organisations were inadequate compared with some other industrialised countries.

This negative attitude towards training was confirmed by a number of surveys at the time (Coopers & Lybrand, 1985; Industrial Society, 1985; Mangham and Silver, 1986; Constable and McCormick, 1987; Handy, 1987), which collectively had a considerable impact on the nation's consciousness. This added to an increasing awareness of the importance of change and the key role that training had played in helping that process.

Encouragingly, surveys in the early 1990s revealed that British companies seemed to be taking training more seriously (Saggers, 1994). The Price Waterhouse Cranfield Project Surveys indicate that training and staff development are the leading issues for most personnel departments across Europe, including the UK (Brewster and Hegewisch, 1993).

BOX 9.1	A 1980s training reminiscence from a large investment bank

'I remember my introductory meeting with one of the heads of business. No sooner had I stepped through the door than he told me that in his view the training function should be abolished. Put on the back foot, I informed him that a number of staff had expressed interest in the company MBA we were about to establish. His response was immediate: "Give me their names and I'll sack them."'

Source: Martyn Sloman (2002) 'Ground Force', *People Management*, 27 June, p. 42

Question

Have you had any similar experiences?

This growing awareness of the importance of training over the past decade was also supported by reports that employers were spending more in aggregate terms on training activities (Training Agency, 1989). However, the measurement of training expenditure is still controversial, and those figures that do exist are open to question, interpretation and political manipulation (Finegold, 1991; Ryan, 1991).

Thus there seems to be a gap between the perceived importance of training and the willingness to do something about it. The view strongly persists in the commercial and industrial culture of the UK that training is a 'cost' and not an 'investment.'

■ HRD and human resource management

Recognition of the importance of human resource development (HRD) in recent years has been heavily influenced by the intensification of overseas competition and the relative success of economies such as Japan, Germany and Sweden, where investment in employee development is emphasised. Technological developments and organisational change have gradually led some employers to realise that success relies on the skills and abilities of their employees, and this means considerable and continuous investment in training and development.

This has also been underscored by the rise in human resource management, with its emphasis on the importance of people and the skills they possess in enhancing organisational efficiency. Such HRM concepts as 'commitment' to the company and the growth in the 'quality' movement have led senior management teams to realise the increased importance of training, employee development and long-term education. There has also been more recognition of the need to complement the qualities of employees with the needs of the organisation. Such concepts require not only careful planning but also a greater emphasis on employee development. Indeed, some commentators have seen this aspect of HRM as so important that they see HRD as an equally important discipline in its own right (Hall, 1984; Nadler, 1984).

In HRM companies such as Hewlett-Packard, Xerox, IBM, Caterpillar and The Body Shop, HRD is seen as a major key to the success of the organisation, and is emphasised at all levels. HRD has also served as an agent for change or even survival in organisations such as Harley Davidson and Euro-Disney.

HRD programmes are continuous, and shaped to fit the culture changes in the organisation in relation to the needs of the individual. In this way training and HRD become tools for effecting change, and the policy ramifications can be wide-ranging and strategic. As a result, HRD takes on a variety of forms and covers a multitude of subjects.

HRD is just one of the instruments at the disposal of the HR department and the organisation in creating HR strategy.

ACTIVITY

Read the following statements and answer the question below.

Strategic purpose of HRD

- To help realise the business strategy.
- A means to assess and address skill deficiencies.
- To act as a catalyst for management initiatives: culture change, TQM, BPR, team building, customer service programmes, etc.
- To give the organisation competitive edge.
- To encourage a learning climate (learning organisation, knowledge-based organisation).

What other strategic HRD purposes could you add to this list?

Keep (1989) also reminds us:

> The interrelationship between training and recruitment strategies is usually a very close one, not the least because if an organisation wishes to improve the skills of its workforce, it has the choice of either training its existing employees or recruiting pre-skilled labour that has been trained elsewhere.

Employee development needs

As noted in the previous chapter, HRD has significance for employees in fulfilling their own needs. One problem is that individuals are often unaware of those needs. It is important to help them towards some awareness, especially in terms of the emphasis on self-development, another important issue raised in the previous chapter.

Stop and think

Consider your own development needs. What would you need to do to acquire skills and knowledge for your career development in five years' time?

Now consider what you think bar staff in a large hotel and a classroom assistant in a primary school might need to further their careers.

Sadly, the further down the organisational ladder one descends the less money is spent on training. Thus managers and professionals generally receive more financial support for training than clerical and manual workers do (Price Waterhouse Cranfield Project, 1990; Brewster, 1999: 16). Given the need to encourage individuals to recognise their training needs and, more importantly, to seek ways to improve their knowledge and skills to advance their career prospects, the advantage seems to lie with individuals further up the organisational hierarchy.

The divide between professional and non-professional workers is increasing with the growing use of flexible work patterns, which emphasise core and periphery workers engaged on part-time or restricted contracts (see Chapter 4 and elsewhere). As a result of these changes, management is less likely to be committed to training periphery workers, and this is reflected in the time and money devoted to training and developing these groups (Syrett and Lammiman, 1994).

Another issue that further emphasises the status divide is that non-professional and non-managerial employees are less aware of the need for training and, more importantly, less able to do something about it, which places considerable barriers in the way of improving their working life prospects. Professionals are imbued with the value of education and self-development, which is often acquired in the routes to, and in, higher education. This need for continual self-development is becoming increasingly important throughout the working life of most professionals, who continue to embark on courses of varying kinds into their 40s and 50s.

Importantly, this process also helps them to cope with change. Awareness of the power of education and training leads to self-activation in meeting career changes and organisational change. By contrast, non-professional workers often rely heavily on the services of external agencies to help them cope with redundancy resulting from skills obsolescence. In the UK in the past agencies such as Employment Training have been less than adequate in dealing with the needs of the long-term unemployed and those wishing to retrain for employment that needs new skills, such as a redundant coalminer seeking to learn computer skills. Most importantly, once new skills are acquired there must be opportunities to practise them. This is difficult in areas undergoing structural change or industrial decay, such as mining and shipbuilding areas. This subject will be explored more fully later in the chapter.

Creating a human resource development plan

There are no set procedures that organisations should follow in creating a human resource development plan, but the eight points listed in Table 9.1 should act as guidance. This can also be summed up diagrammatically as in Figure 9.1.

Table 9.1 A human resource development plan

- Discern the training and development requirements from the organisational strategy and business objectives
- Analyse the training requirements for effective work performance in organisational functions and jobs
- Analyse the existing qualities and training needs of current employees
- Devise an HRD plan that fills the gap between organisational requirements and the current skills and knowledge of employees
- Decide on the appropriate training and development methods to be used for individuals and groups
- Decide who is to have responsibility for the plan and its various parts
- Implement the plan, and monitor and evaluate its progress
- Amend the HRD plan in the light of monitoring/evaluation and changes in business strategy

ACTIVITY   Using the training cycle above, make an HRD plan for a department or organisation of which you have knowledge.

This has strong elements of the systems approach to training (SAT), but the mechanistic overtones of SAT should be moderated by recognising the human needs of employees and the changes (sometimes rapid) that can affect organisations. Therefore a more flexible or

| Figure 9.1 | A training cycle based on an HRD plan |

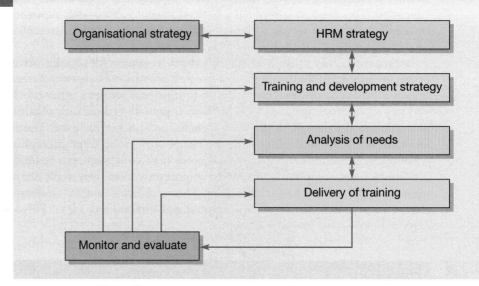

'organic' approach is recommended: training schemes that are patently not working, perhaps because of changes in personnel, occupations, job specifications, personal relationships, business plans or economic performance, should be abandoned, or adapted to accommodate the change.

| *Stop and think* | Which parts of the HRD training cycle are likely to be less effectively implemented and why? |

■ Analysing training needs

The first vital step in HRD is 'the identification of needed skills and active management of employees learning for their long-range future in relation to explicit corporate and business strategies' (Hall, 1984).

For training to be effective it is necessary to discern not only the training needs of the individual and the group, but also how their needs fit the overall organisational objectives. As we have already suggested, this may be more difficult to achieve than it appears.

Researchers and commentators doubt whether managerial hierarchies recognise the importance of these relationships in training initiatives or, if they do, doubt whether they have the will or the ability to carry them out. As Hall (1984) comments:

> Many organisations invest considerable resources in training and development but never really examine how training and development can most effectively promote organisational objectives, or how developmental activities should be altered in the light of business plans.

Bernhard and Ingolis (1988), in studying training and its strategic implementation in US companies, believe that a considerable amount of money is 'thrown away' mainly because fundamental issues such as analysis of training needs in relation to the short- and long-term business plans have not been addressed.

A prominent French bank witnessed less than beneficial results after a huge investment in an extensive training scheme. This was seen to be primarily a consequence of the failure to analyse training needs within the organisation (Holden and Livian, 1992). Investors in People (IIP) schemes have been set up by numerous organisations in the UK in an attempt to align training needs to organisational strategy. However, as we shall see on examining IIP in greater depth later in this chapter, the results have been variable.

An integral part of analysing training needs is recognising what will 'fit' the company culture, as well as the company strategy and objectives. The training scheme that fits one company may not fit another, and these company differences can only be ignored at great cost. This is part and parcel of the organic approach to HRD, and a view shared by those organisations that claim to be (or on their way to being) learning organisations.

The training and development needs of the individual must be reconciled with those of the organisation. Conflicts here need to be resolved, for the benefit of both. Unfortunately, this may be easier to achieve for professional and managerial employees than for the workforce lower down the organisation. For example, many companies recognise the advantages of having managers with an MBA degree or a Diploma in Management Studies, a situation mutually beneficial to the individual and the organisation. Professionals such as accountants and lawyers have the advantage of transferable knowledge and expertise. But a shopfloor worker in a production company is much more likely to be trained in firm-specific skills that cannot be easily transferred to other organisational contexts.

● For the job

Job description

Given the recent popularity of flexible work practices in many organisations, criticism has been levelled at job descriptions that are too highly structured. Critics claim that this narrows too strictly the perceived responsibilities of the employee, and can be counterproductive, by creating protectionist attitudes in employees towards their jobs, which could lead to demarcation disputes and other problems related to work roles.

Nevertheless, employees are usually hired to take a specific responsibility within the organisation (whether that be accountant, receptionist or cleaner), but they may have to take on other responsibilities in times of emergency, to enhance organisational efficiency. Therefore job descriptions are necessary in order to give employees a sense of purpose, and to enable their immediate superiors to appraise their performance, but a culture must prevail that enables employees to deal with problems that may be outside their immediate work domain.

Thus job descriptions are useful for the HRD strategy in that they help to identify the skills and knowledge needed for certain roles and functions in the organisation.

Stop and think	What difficulties could there be in analysing training needs?

Job analysis

Job analysis is a more sophisticated method of evaluating job functions, and is often used to discern the levels of skill necessary to do a job, primarily for the purpose of creating pay structures. Many modern organisations have rejected such techniques, as one executive of IKEA states: 'We reward individuals and not the job' (Pickard, 1992). However, the information gleaned from such procedures can be useful in analysing the skill needs and requirement of jobs.

Interview with jobholders

This is one of the most commonly used methods: a manager, supervisor or member of the personnel department interviews the current jobholder about the duties and functions of the job. The interview can be structured, in the sense of having a series of questions framed to cover all aspects of the job.

Interview with managers and supervisors

Alternatively, a personnel manager or senior manager can interview the immediate supervisors of the job. Often descriptions arising are compared with the interview responses of the jobholder to act as a double check for discrepancies or elements missed by either party.

Performance objectives

The aim of increased quality, for example, will require performance objectives to be laid down. In doing so, assessment must take place as to whether current employees need training to reach these objectives. This has become increasingly popular in organisations that have adopted performance management programmes or *high-performance work systems* as they are known in the USA.

Analysis of competences

An analysis of competence requirements could be useful to match 'NVQ (National Vocational Qualification) or MCI (Management Charter Initiative) standards which are considered relevant to the various jobs involved. These can be compared with assessments of the current general levels of employee skills and abilities' (Fowler, 1991).

● For the individual

Concomitant with an analysis of organisational needs is the analysis of the training needs of current employees. Much information about employees can be gleaned from organisational records, including original application forms and other databases.

Characteristics of people required (person specification)

In the effort to identify skills and competence requirements, the characteristics of the people required for the job are often forgotten. This will to some extent emerge in the competences analysis. For example, sales personnel would need an ability to deal with people, and this would undoubtedly be identified as an essential part of the job; but in other occupations and jobs, personal characteristics are often forgotten in the desire to isolate purely functional job requirements.

Personal profiles

Personal profile records are increasingly used in organisations, and useful for training needs analysis. They also include information on employees' career aspirations, which may well be of significance in creating training initiatives.

Appraisal

Appraisal has come in for much criticism recently, but a good appraisal can reveal much about the strengths and weaknesses of individuals in terms of their performance. Indications of areas where training and development programmes could improve performance are vital to both the individual and the organisation. Indeed the appraisal and variations of it are now used in many organisations as a central part of the learning organisation concept, whereby individuals can negotiate their training needs with their line manager. Some organisations have allocated training budgets for individuals to use for their own development in negotiation with their line managers. In this way an employee gains a sense of ownership of their development, with positive results for the organisation.

Assessment centre techniques

Though rather elaborate and expensive, assessment centres are the most thorough way of analysing individual strengths and weaknesses. Using a variety of methods, including in-depth interviews and re-interviews, psychometric tests, team performance simulation exercises and other techniques, a detailed profile of employees can be constructed, which is useful for analysing training needs. Caution must be counselled, however, in terms of cost-effectiveness and an unrealistic expectation that infallible results are produced (Dulewicz, 1991).

Global review and training audits

The most wide-ranging method of training needs analysis is a global review, or more modestly a training audit. These are usually undertaken when far-reaching changes are planned within an organisation. Survey questionnaires and in-depth interviews are often used, together with all, or combinations of, the approaches previously mentioned.

Relating resources to the training objective

An across-the-board use of all these methods could be too expensive in terms of both time and money. Reid *et al.* (1992) point out that the global review could end up producing large amounts of paperwork, unjustified by the returns gained. It is therefore essential to assess the cost-effectiveness of training needs analysis in relation to the outcomes and returns expected.

Hirsch and Reilly (1998) warn that 'organisational structures and employee attitudes have an impact. Simply having appropriately skilled individuals does not automatically yield high performance' (p. 40). They give the example of the UK Post Office, where managers have learned that thinking through the skill implications of organisational change early enough gives them time to change the composition of the workforce. Hirsch and Reilly also stress that it may 'be important to design jobs and technology around the skills of the workforce, rather than to assume that the workforce will adjust to the new situation'.

> **Stop and think**
>
> The most common way training needs are discovered in organisations is when a problem occurs or a key employee leaves. This is a very reactive approach and is not assessing, analysing or predicting training requirments. Unfortunately, this is all too common in many organisations.
>
> Can you think of an incident where this has occurred in an organisation that you have worked in?

Training methods

A careful use of training methods can be a very cost-effective investment in the sense of using the appropriate method for the needs of a person or group. However, many commentators have mentioned that organisations often use inappropriate methods, which can be both costly and time wasting and bring very little improvement in the performance of the employee. Storey (1991), in a comparative analysis of training in British and Japanese organisations, found that some British training is wasted as it is not embedded in the organisation as is the Japanese. British organisations also suffered from the 'bandwagon effect' and what he calls 'programmitis' – a constant series of newly launched programmes and initiatives which led to chopping and changing rather than consistently coherent long-term training initiatives.

In general, training can be divided into *on-the-job* and *off-the-job* methods. There is a place for both types, and each can be effective at meeting certain training requirements.

● On-the-job training

On-the-job training (OJT) is probably the most common approach to training. It can range from relatively unsophisticated 'observe and copy' methods to highly structured courses built into workshop or office practice. Cannell (1997) defines OJT as

> training that is planned and structured that takes place mainly at the normal workstation of the trainee – although some instruction may be provided in a special training area on site – and where a manager, supervisor, trainer or peer colleague spends significant time with a trainee to teach a set of skills that have been specified in advance. It also includes a period of instruction where there may be little or no useful output in terms of productivity.
>
> (p. 28)

'Sitting by Nellie' and learning by doing

These traditional methods are still very popular ways of teaching new skills and methods to employees, and they can be very effective. However, there are many acknowledged weaknesses that still persist in many organisational practices. Some people are better at it than others, and 'Nellie' may not be trained herself in the methods of transmitting knowledge and skills. There is often a lack of structure and design in the training given, which leads to the passing-on of bad or even dangerous working practices (Cannell, 1997).

Far more successful is to use a senior or experienced worker who has been trained in instruction or training methods and whose teaching skills are coordinated with a developed programme linked to off-the-job courses. Self-proclaimed learning organisations such as Analog Devices make very effective use of OJT, and claim that people learn and retain more of the training by performing the actual process at the place of work.

Mentoring

This is another version of the system, in which a senior or experienced employee takes charge of the training and development of a new employee. This suggests a much closer association than master–apprentice, and elements of a father–son or mother–daughter relationship can exist, whereby the mentor acts as an adviser and protector to the trainee. A study by Brockbank and Beech (1999) of mentors in the health sector reveals that overemphasis on the technical side of the mentoring process and an underestimation of the emotional side can have negative results. They recommend that appropriate support should be provided for mentors themselves. This dual role of providing professional and emotional support may clash, and it might be advisable for the two roles to be performed by different people.

Shadowing and job rotation

Shadowing is another oft-practised on-the-job training method. It usually aims to give trainee managers a 'feel' for the organisation by providing experience of working in different departments. It is an old technique, and has been criticised not so much for the concept itself as for the way it is often implemented. Trainees may feel it is time wasting, and people in the various departments in which they are temporarily working must also feel committed to and involved in the training if it is to work. Trainees are often not warmly welcomed, and are seen by supervisors and workers in the department as obstacles to the daily routines. However, if well structured, and planned with the cooperation of all departmental supervisors, this method can be a worthwhile learning experience.

Another version of training by switching roles is *job rotation*, which became popular in the 1970s to help relieve boredom and thereby raise the productivity of shopfloor workers. If appropriately implemented, it can be an excellent learning experience for workers, and it fits suitably with HRM concepts of teamworking and empowerment, whereby people are encouraged to take greater responsibility for their work and that of the team. On the negative side there have been criticisms that not enough structured training is given to enable workers to do these jobs well, and that it is also bound up with functional flexibility initiatives, often criticised for their deskilling and exploitative propensities.

E-learning

A more recent concept of the informational and learning exchange environment is *e-learning (electronic learning)*. This emphasises the use of new technology such as e-mail, Internet, intranet and computer software packages to facilitate learning for employees whenever they need it. As one of its advocates (Masie, 1999) states:

> I expect to see an increasing alignment between e-learning and e-commerce. Information collected on the World Wide Web about product knowledge, for example, can be accessed in the same way for someone else to learn from. Organisations are even focusing on delivering knowledge and competencies to their whole supply chain by this method.   (p. 32)

The adoption of online learning is attractive to organisations because the required data is available when learners want to learn. This will speed up the learning process and knowledge exchange. It also allows for 'granularisation' of learning. Until recently, a unit of learning was expressed in terms of a three-day course, a morning course or a two-hour course. Granularisation can deliver a course in bite-sized chunks when the learner needs it. The e-learning forms can be formal (an actual course delivered via soft-

---

BOX 9.2   Strategic HRD and e-learning at Nestlé

Dorothy Walker, learning and development specialist states that 'at Nestlé UK, learning and development have always been integrated with the business and HR; we have never stood alone,' she says. 'It's always been tied back to the business objectives.'

At the beginning of 2001, Nestlé began a worldwide roll out of e-learning courses for staff. Provided by e-learning companies NETg and Intellexis, the package contained 850 courses on subjects ranging from finance to management skills.

'We weren't happy just to make a whole load of courses available via the intranet without first understanding how they fitted with our culture and the rest of our support for the business.'

Nestlé UK launched the e-learning course in November last year, when the shared service structure went live. The structure has an '@hr' branding, which aims to emphasise an increased use of technology. It comprises Recruitment@hr, Payroll@hr, Policy@hr, Information & Advice@hr, Business Partners@hr and Learning and Development@hr, which includes e-learning. Learning and Development@hr offers its services to employees under 17 different topic headings, under which the relevant e-learning packages are integrated. Walker believes launching the HR shared service and e-learning projects at the same time was important as it created a fully coordinated approach.

Source: E. Rana (2002), *People Management*, 27 June, p. 42

ware or the Internet) or informal (exchange of information and knowledge via e-mail or an intranet). The recently established University for Industry (UfI) in the UK will base a great deal of its approach to learning and delivery of courses on the use of new technology, a trend that is increasing rapidly in universities and other educational institutions.

Problems with e-learning

E-learning has had many enthusiastic advocates in recent years. Tom Peters has argued that 90 per cent of training could be delivered in this way (Sloman, 2001: 57). Already, however, experience of it in practice and research is pinpointing a number of problems. These criticisms are less about e-learning itself than the techniques and methods of its application, and, indeed, its popularity. The annual training and development survey conducted by the CIPD clearly shows that less than a third of training managers said that they used e-learning and when they did the main recipients were IT staff. The report states:

> If, as some believe, e-learning heralds a revolution, it is clear that its main impact is still to be felt.
>
> (cited in Sloman, 2002: 41)

Those that have used e-learning have experienced a number of problems and complaints from the users. One such complaint is of the 'sheep dip approach' whereby the same process is applied to everyone. Mumford (2002: 51) claims that

> designers of e-learning and buyers should consider how the design embraces learning preferences. For example: Are the learning style preferences affecting the way they deliver the content of e-learning? How far does the programme design relate only to the provision of information, rather than taking action on it? How can the programme be designed or complemented by other programmes in a way that meets different needs of individuals?

Among other criticisms are that learners are often left without support for e-learning packages and in consequence they feel isolated and frustrated when they do not fully understand how to access the programme fully and what the content is actually about. Other criticisms are that e-learning packages available in the work situation are not accessed so much as busy employees simply do not feel that they have time to use them in the work situation.

It is clear that e-learning has to be used in conjunction with other training methods and not used solely in isolation and without support. A form of blended learning is the ideal way to use it. As Reynolds (2002: 42) states:

> E-learning will add to – rather than replace – existing channels (of learning). . . . So jumping on the e-learning bandwagon could result in expensive and ineffective training programmes. E-learning doesn't so much replace face-to-face learning as supplement and extend it.

● Off-the-job training

Courses and other types of 'off-the-job' training have come in for much criticism, and are often viewed by both recipients and fellow employees as a waste of time and money. Yet off-the-job training is sometimes necessary to get people away from the hustle and bustle of the work environment. This enables the trainee to study theoretical information or be exposed to new and innovative ideas. The problem arises when those ideas or learning experiences do not appear to relate to the work situation. As we have seen from the research of Storey (1991), the predilection for sending employees on courses that do not appear to have much relevance to the employee or the job ('programmitis') only enhances the negative view of this type of training.

Perceptions of courses

Being sent on a course can be interpreted by the trainee as a sign of official approval or disapproval. For example, an approval sign would be that you are considered suitable for promotion, and the course is part of the training required for that position. A negative perception could be that the employee feels that they are being sent on a course because they are not very efficient in their job. Sending the correct messages to the trainees is also an important aspect of training initiatives.

● A variety of methods

It is impossible to cover in depth in this book all the rich variety of approaches to training. Many of these the reader will have experienced before – sometimes with negative consequences. It is best to bear in mind that there may be nothing wrong with the methods, but that they may be utilised ineffectively by the trainer or the learner. In other words, the key is to make the appropriate match between the training requirements of the employee and the training methods available.

● Active and passive learning

Much traditional training is a one-way learning process, in which the student is a passive learner receiving information from a lecturer, tutor or instructor. This can be an efficient way of imparting information, but all education theorists agree that the best form of learning is one in which the student is actively involved in the learning process.

Interactive learning methods

There are a wide variety of interactive learning techniques, some of them adaptations of one-way approaches:

- workshops;
- case studies;
- role play;
- simulations;
- interactive computer learning packages;
- video and audio tapes (interactively used);
- the Internet (websites), intranet (organisational systems);
- problem-solving.

For a fuller explanation of these techniques and others, see Harrison (1997) and Barrington and Reid (1999).

■ Blended learning

There has been much criticism of approaches to human resource development that relies on systematic strategies and those that only cater for organisational needs and not those of the individual. One answer is a form of 'blended learning'. This attempts to cater for both the individual and the organisation – a tricky equation to balance.

This boils down to meeting the training needs of the organisation and the individual in a mix of approaches that suit the individual's learning style, work–life situation and short-term and long-term skill and knowledge requirements. As Chris Dennis (2002) states:

> The beauty of well blended learning is that people can learn through a medium, or media that suits them personally.

The following case study illustrates how this has worked at News International, which publishes *The Times* and *The Sun*.

BOX 9.3 | **Blended learning at News International**

In the past year News International examined how it could update and revitalise its certificate in management aimed at junior and middle managers. In the past the programme had followed a traditional 'workshop cookbook'. Worldwide Learning training consultants were brought in to address the problem of devising a new user-friendly programme.

They made two fundamental changes:

Firstly, they broke down the existing programme into its constituent parts, testing them with a cross-section of training professionals. Secondly, having identified the most appropriate delivery mechanism for each part, the team revised the underlying teaching theory to give learners much more responsibility for their own learning.

The revamped course comprises 12 modules each covering a core element of management, from building and leading teams to financial management. The number of workshops has been reduced from 36 half days to 12 full days – one for each module – which significantly reduced both cost and administration. The main change is the introduction of a companion website. This is not only a way for learners, tutors and course administrators to communicate between workshops; it also allows tutors to post articles, exercises and projects for delegates to complete online. Learners can carry out background research and access topical business information as well.

The first delegate to work through the remodelled programme appreciated its versatility. Mike McQueen, field sales manager from HarperCollins, one of News International's sister companies said:

'I've found previous courses to be incredibly intense and always felt under great pressure to apply the new knowledge and skills as soon as I got back to the office. Here the process of learning is ongoing and continues in the workplace.'

News International feels it has invested wisely and found a blend of learning that works well.

Source: Partially edited version of Chris Dennis article 'A special blend', *People Management*, 7 March, 2002, p. 51

Responsibility for and delivery of training

It is important to consider who is to be responsible for training, and who will deliver training.

● Training departments

From the 1950s and (particularly) the 1960s, the responsibility for and delivery of training in many large organisations rested very much with specialist departments. By the 1980s and 1990s, however, training departments had come in for considerable criticism. They were accused of:

- being too rigid to respond to the changing needs of the organisation;
- being too much of an administrative expense;
- having lost contact with the changing skills needed on the shopfloor or at the place of work;
- being self-serving and bureaucratic;
- providing off-the-job training at their various centres that did not match up to 'on-the-job' needs;
- providing training that was too theoretical and not sufficiently practically based;
- not providing training and development that met individual needs – courses were too class/group based.

Despite these criticisms, training departments remain important in many organisations because they have personnel who have specialised knowledge and skills in the provision of training. As HRD becomes more important in the organisation the role of providers is becoming increasingly pivotal as facilitators of learning and the exchange of information and knowledge. The concepts of the learning organisation and the knowledge-based organisation place learning and HRD at the very heart of the organisation. HRD departments also act as internal consultants giving support to line managers alongside the HR department.

● Training consultancies

Over the past decade the number of consultancies, many of them specialising in training, has burgeoned into an industry. While there are many excellent consultancies, there are also the inevitable 'cowboy' operations, which sometimes have unqualified, inexperienced and untrained staff, and at present there is no regulation to stop such operations from being set up. Some client companies and organisations have spent considerable sums on ineffective programmes, or to be told things they already knew. Of course, it is in the interest of the consultancy to push sometimes costly and unwarranted programmes on to unsuspecting clients, in order to drum up business.

It would be naïve to believe that consultants are brought into organisations only to provide training programmes. They are also used to resolve political conflicts, to add kudos and status, to justify having larger budgets, to support political manoeuvring, and for other questionable reasons.

However, used carefully, reputable consultancies can provide invaluable specialist services and expertise that are often not available within client organisations, particularly small and medium-sized ones.

● Training and the line manager

In order to counteract the perceived inflexibilities of training and personnel departments, there has been a notable trend to devolve many functions to line managers, including training policy. The justification is usually couched in terms of meeting the needs of people where it matters – at workplace level. Part of the line manager's brief is to discern the training needs of individuals in their department, and to suggest suitable training for them, usually in consultation with the personnel or training department. Training budgets have increasingly been devolved to line managers, in the belief that funding can be spent most effectively at the point where needs have been identified.

This can be very effective, because the assessment and delivery of training is more closely attuned to people in their working environment, but its efficacy depends very much on how it is carried out.

Research by the Price Waterhouse Cranfield Project team shows that there are many problems in splitting responsibilities between line managers and the personnel department:

> First there is often a dichotomy between the decentralised role and increasing responsibility of line managers, and the centralised role of the personnel/human resource function which must act as an interpreter of organisation-wide information and as a creator of human resource strategies. Secondly, the desire to empower the line manager may lead to sacrifices by the central personnel function in ensuring the relevant information is being relayed back.
>
> (Holden and Livian, 1992)

For example, 41 per cent of personnel departments in the UK survey did not know how much money was spent on training, and 38 per cent did not know the average number of training days allocated per person in the organisation (Holden, 1991; Holden and Livian, 1992).

■ Evaluation and monitoring of training

The penultimate stage in the training strategy is the evaluation and monitoring of training. It is one of the most important but often the most neglected parts of the training process.

This stage can be viewed as both simple and complicated. It is simple in that monitoring consists in gleaning information from the trainees and then amending the courses and programmes in the light of these comments. But it is also complex because there are other stakeholders in the process as well as the trainees: the designers of the courses, the trainers, and the sponsors. Each has their own purposes, aims and objectives, and these must be clearly identified before evaluation can proceed (Easterby-Smith and Mackness, 1992).

Another problem is that, while it is relatively easy to evaluate a formal off-the-job course, much on-the-job training often takes place in an informal way, which is usually subjective and open to interpretation (Holden, 1991).

Methods of evaluation include the following:

- *Questionnaires* (feedback forms) or 'happiness sheets' are a common way of eliciting trainees' responses to courses and programmes.
- *Tests or examinations* are common on formal courses that provide a certificate, such as a diploma in word-processing skills, and end-of-course tests can be provided after short courses to check the progress of trainees.
- *Projects* are initially seen as learning methods, but they can also provide valuable information for instructors.
- *Structured exercises and case studies* are opportunities to apply learned skills and techniques under the observation of tutors and evaluators.
- It is important to have the opinions of those who deliver the training. *Tutor reports* give a valuable assessment from a different perspective.
- *Interviews of trainees* after the course or instruction period can be informal or formal, individual or group, or by telephone.
- *Observation* of courses and training by those devising training strategies in the training department is very useful, and information from these observations can be compared with trainee responses.
- *Participation and discussion* during training must be facilitated by people who are adept at interpreting responses, as this can be highly subjective.
- Over the past decade *appraisal* has become an increasingly important method of evaluation. It has the advantage that the line manager and trainee can mutually assess the training undergone in terms of performance and employee development.

A combination of these approaches is advisable. It is also wise to receive feedback from the trainees and the tutors or trainers, and others involved in the assessment process.

■ Amending the HRD plan

While many organisations carry out excellent training programmes, the final and perhaps most vital stage is often ignored. As Easterby-Smith and Mackness (1992) wryly state:

> Training evaluation is commonly seen as a feedback loop, starting with course objectives and ending by collecting end-of-course reactions which are then generally filed away and not acted on.

Adjustments can be carried out after a small course to tighten up its effective operation, or when a training strategy cycle has been completed after six months or a year. At the end of such a phase it is essential to see whether training has effectively met the business objectives. Usually adaptations and changes are necessary, and the evaluation and monitoring process is invaluable in ensuring that these are appropriate.

Comment

In reading this section on training strategy, two points need to be borne in mind:

● These training prescriptions can appear too simplistic, particularly in a textbook that has limited space to give to this complicated subject. The reality of creating training strategies is much more complex, and frustration and failure to achieve objectives are common, even in organisations that take such approaches seriously.
● There is limited evidence of a positive link between training and organisational efficiency and profitability, although there is a widespread belief that this is the case.

The learning organisation

The approach described above in the HRD strategy has been rejected by a number of organisations as far too mechanistic, controlling and inefficient. Writers such as Senge (1990) and Pedler *et al.* (1997) have put forward the concept of the *learning organisation*, in which learning and HRD are central functions of the organisation. In such an organisation the learning process is so embedded that learning and development become subconscious acts through which the business of the organisation operates. In this way its adherents claim that HRD becomes automatically strategic.

■ What is a learning organisation?

A clear definition of the learning organisation is elusive. Pedler *et al.* (1997) suggest that it is a vision of what might be possible when organisations go beyond merely training individuals towards developing learning at the whole organisation level. Their definition states:

> A Learning Company is an organisation that facilitates the learning of all its members and consciously transforms itself and its context.   (p. 3)

Dixon (1994) added to the concept, suggesting that organisational learning, a key characteristic of a learning company, can be defined as

> the intentional use of learning processes at the individual, group and system level to continuously transform the organisation in a direction that is increasingly satisfying to its stakeholders.

Senge (1990) states that the basic meaning of the learning organisation is:

> an organisation that is continually expanding its capacity to create its future. For such an organisation it is not enough to merely survive . . . for a learning organisation 'adaptive learning' must be joined by 'generative learning', learning that enhances our capacity to create.
>
> (p. 14)

■ Why the need for the learning organisation?

The concept has gained popularity in recent years because of the turbulent and increasingly competitive business environment. The impact of new technology and changing organisational forms that cater for customer needs mean dealing with continual change. This has led to what learning organisation (LO) adherents feel is *not* an add-on HRD system that is a lowly function driven by corporate strategy, but one that is central to the strategy of the organisation. The ability to respond swiftly to product and market developments is crucial. There has also been an increasing recognition of the importance of utilising not just the physical abilities of employees but also their mental powers. Senior managers are becoming aware that if their people are their greatest resource, they are also the source of any longer-term competitive advantage. This realisation has led to increased competition for skilled, flexible, adaptable staff, and to the development of organisational programmes that attempt to fully utilise the talents and knowledge of the workforce. It is also being recognised that international competitiveness means raising the standards of training to world-class levels. Failure to meet these pressures leads to organisational stagnation and ultimately organisational death.

■ Pedler *et al.*'s view of the learning organisation

A learning company is one that looks beyond mere survival. By developing an ability to constantly adapt its operations it is able to sustain market leadership. Such companies not only change with differing contexts but learn from their people and their environments while 'contributing to the learning of the wider community or context of which they are part' (Pedler *et al.*, 1997: 4). As leading-edge organisations they move beyond the visions of their founders or the conservatism of many companies formed in the same era or culture, evolving through an allegiance between internal and external environments.

Thus for Pedler *et al.* (1988: 4) a learning organisation is one that:

● has a climate in which individual members are encouraged to learn and develop their full potential;
● extends the learning culture to include customers, suppliers and other significant stakeholders;
● makes human resource development strategy central to business policy;
● is in a continuous process of organisational transformation.

While it is not possible to construct a model of a learning company, principally because there is no predetermined structure, Pedler *et al.* (1997: 15–17) identify 11 key characteristics that a learning company must possess:

● a learning approach to strategy;
● participative policy-making;
● 'informating' (information technology is used to inform and empower people to ask questions and take decisions);
● formative accounting and control (control systems are structured to assist learning from decisions);

- internal exchange of ideas and knowledge;
- reward flexibility to promote performance and reward learning;
- enabling structures that remove barriers to communication and learning;
- boundary workers as environmental scanners benchmarking and using knowledge gained by sales staff and those who deal with the organisation's suppliers and customers; seeing what rival oganisations are doing;
- inter-company learning;
- a learning climate;
- self-development opportunities for all.

Knowledge-managing organisation

Another concept that emerged in the 1990s was the *knowledge-managing organisation*. It is also known as the *knowledge-based organisation* or the *knowledge-creating company* (Nonaka, 1991). The process by which it is carried out is often known as *knowledge management* (Mayo, 1998).

A definition of knowledge management offered by Mayo (1998: 36) states that the following processes are essential:

- managing the generation of new knowledge through learning;
- capturing knowledge and experience;
- sharing, collaborating and communicating;
- organising information for easy access;
- using and building on what is known.

This list contains elements not greatly different from the learning organisation concept, and some observers claim that in effect they are the same phenomenon. Both concepts rely heavily on the exchange of knowledge and the desire of employees to be receptive to knowledge and learning – employees are the repositories of the organisation's knowledge and wisdom. As Tom Watson, former president of IBM, states: 'If you burnt down all our plants and we just kept our people and our files, we would soon be as strong as ever.' This underscores and adds to the strength of HRM and HRD departments, many of which have been preaching for years that 'our people are our greatest assets', often with the reality not living up to the slogan.

While the visionary concepts of knowledge management and the LO are inspiring, the reality is that, like most large-scale initiatives, implementation of such systems requires a massive change of attitude in most organisations that is not always easy to achieve. Success rests in creating a high-trust organisation where knowledge is readily exchanged. In practice, there are many barriers. Knowledge is seen as power, and jealously guarded. Its possession and use can further ambitions. A culture of openness may be difficult to achieve, particularly in organisations where suspicion has been the norm. Knowledge management thus has serious implications for communication structures, employee involvement systems, reward systems and industrial relations.

There are many examples of companies that claim to be, or are on their way to being, learning organisations, including Anglia Water, Transco, IBM, Analog Devices, Nokia, GM, ICL, Xerox, and Hanover Insurance.

Criticisms of the learning organisation concept

Despite its relatively new entrance on the corporate scene, there have already been a number of critical studies that have highlighted the weaknesses of LO. Garvin (1993) partly blames academics such as Senge, whose writings are often 'reverential and utopian (and) filled with near mystical terminology. Paradise, they would have you believe, is just round the corner.' He continues:

> Nonaka suggested that companies use metaphors and organisational redundancy to focus thinking, encourage dialogue, and make tacit, instinctively understood ideas explicit. Sound idyllic? Absolutely. Desirable? Without question. But does it provide a framework for action? Hardly. These recommendations are far too abstract, and too many questions remain unanswered. How, for example, will managers know when their companies have become learning organisations? What concrete changes in behaviour are required? What policies and programmes must be in place? How do you get from here to there?
>
> (p. 49)

Sloman (1999) believes that 'the concept of the learning organisation should be redefined or declared redundant' (p. 31). The language and vocabulary of the learning organisation need to make sense to the hard-pressed line manager, and for these reasons alone the concept 'is in urgent need of review'.

An international study carried out by Chase (1997) for the *Journal of Knowledge Management* examined approaches to creating knowledge-based organisations. He found that while organisations acknowledge 'the importance of creating, managing and transferring knowledge, they have so far been unable to translate this need into organisational strategies. Mayo (1998: 38), cited in Chase's work, believes that 'most organisations are also struggling to use information technology to support implementation' and a learning organisation. Chase's survey also pointed out that the biggest obstacles to creating a knowledge-based organisation were the existing company culture, lack of ownership of a problem, lack of time, inappropriate organisational structure, lack of senior management commitment, inappropriate rewards and recognition, and an emphasis on individuals rather than team work.

Lähteenmäki *et al.* (1999) have pointed to a number of criticisms that can be levelled at the concept:

- lack of clarity and multiplicity of definitions;
- lack of explanation of the detailed implementation of LO systems;
- lack of explanation as to how these systems are integrated;

(all these factors point to the need for a holistic model of the learning organisation, which should convincingly link theory and practice, bringing together 'pieces of theory')

- too much stress on learning by individuals and not by the organisation;
- a dearth of research on measurement of the learning process in organisations;
- a need to recognise the historical antecedents of the learning organisation;
- a need to recognise the relationship of the LO with organisational change literature;
- the need for further investigation of the link between HR strategy and change;
- the need for more research on LO in the international context, particularly the transfer of learning between units within multinational organisations, and the cultural barriers that may exist in that process.

■ The failure of LOs

Lähteenmäki *et al.* (1999), in summing up a number of research projects, emphasised these reasons for failure:

- failure to deal with feelings of uncertainty and insecurity in employees during periods of intense competition and culture change;

- a work situation that lacks trust – this can only make failure more certain, because it inhibits the learning process, as employees recede into defensive coping styles;
- poor feedback, limited encouragement, insufficient discussion of mistakes and the lack of empowerment, which serve to further undermine the effectiveness of LO initiatives;
- failure to give all employees the responsibility for learning;
- failure to understand the linkages between the LO and HRM strategy.

They suggest some recommendations in moving towards a learning organisation:

- An environment of openness and trust must be created.
- An atmosphere of certainty and security must be generated.
- This can be achieved by developing strategy from the bottom up, through building a shared vision, team learning, and developing core competences that are recognised and valued by all.
- It is essential to have objectives that are clearly and positively linked to HRM strategy.
- It must be recognised that measurement of learning can feed more positively into an evaluation of the effectiveness of the learning process.
- Finally, it is of paramount importance to create a learning atmosphere that all members of the organisation share.

There are no easy prescriptions for creating a learning organisation; it takes a considerable time to engender the right attitudes and conditions in the change process. Those organisations that can learn these lessons not only are well on the way to becoming learning organisations, but also are more likely to have the skills, competences and, above all, the right attitudes for survival in our increasingly competitive globalised environment.

ACTIVITY   There is a case study of a learning organisation at the end of Part 3 on 'Transforming Anglian Water'. Read the case study and answer the two questions that follow.

HRD and the national framework for vocational education and training

● Introduction

Learning and development are not solely matters of concern for individuals and their employers. An educated and skilled workforce is essential for the effective functioning of the economy, for the competitiveness and wealth of the nation, and for the overall well-being of society. Indeed, Tyson and Fell (1995) suggest that 'the future will see a world of work based more on skills than organisations' (p. 45). To ensure that a nation achieves the level of skills it needs, its government therefore puts in place the vocational education and training (VET) policies and systems that will facilitate their development. Such national strategies therefore form an important part of the context (see Chapter 3) of individual learning and organisational human resource development.

As new technology progresses, replacing jobs and changing skill requirements, there is an increasing need for a skilled and highly trained workforce able to meet these changing situations. Traditional skills, for example in the engineering and construction industries, are rapidly changing, and the type of economy in which a young person can receive an apprenticeship that would stand them in good stead for a lifetime career is dwindling.

This trend is international, and poses problems for the USA, Japan, Germany, France, Sweden and other industrialised nations. However, comparisons with competitor nations indicate that Britain is suffering from a severe skills shortage. Its 'first ever national audit of job skills', which the government published in 1996 to accompany its third 'competitiveness' White Paper, compares Britain with France, Germany, Singapore and the USA:

> Its findings confirm fears that Britain's skills are lagging behind those of Germany, which has had a policy of investment in vocational training for years. More worrying is the rapidly shrinking gap between the UK and Singapore in the league tables.
>
> (Welch, 1996b: 11)

Britain's greatest deficiency is in basic and level 2 skills (low-level NVQ skills including numeracy and literacy), though 'Britain is ahead of its competitors both on quality and the quantity of its population' possessing degrees and vocational qualifications of a comparable level.

Many see the solution to be the investment of more capital in education and training, and the creation of an ever more skilled and knowledgeable workforce, partly because the industrialised countries can never compete with developing world economies in terms of cheap labour. The developments in VET in Britain, as elsewhere, have to be seen within this context. However, the efficacy of VET to achieve such national needs is not fully demonstrated. For example, the relative economic decline in Britain has led to much debate as to the adequacy of training in helping to arrest this trend. (This is a controversial issue that will be discussed in a later section.)

The purpose of this section is to outline some of the VET policies and systems currently in place in Britain, and to indicate possible future developments. However, it first recognises the key stakeholders in VET, and then sets British provision in the context of that of some of its major competitors.

■ Stakeholders in vocational education and training

Chapter 8 identified several stakeholders in the individual's learning and development, and it examined the needs and responses of the individual and the employer in particular. There are several stakeholders in VET too, and their values and actions constitute the framework within which individual learning and development and organisational HRD have to take place. The part the government plays in this field will be examined in some detail later in this chapter.

Employers are also significant stakeholders in VET. This is apparent in the international comparisons in the following section. During the 1990s, the British employers' body, the Confederation of British Industry (CBI), played an influential role. For example, recognising the need for a 'skills revolution' (Confederation of British Industry, 1989), it proposed training targets (later adopted by the government) for the minimum standards needed to increase Britain's competitiveness.

The trade unions are further stakeholders in VET. At present the role of British unions in this regard is somewhat limited compared with that of their counterparts in France and Germany:

> where unions are involved widely at national, regional, sectoral and company levels in promoting and regulating the training process. This role is supported in France by law. In Germany it constitutes one part of the corporatist system of compromise and consensus between the 'social partners'. (Claydon and Green, 1992)

Since 1997 and the election of a Labour government, unions have been welcomed into a partnership with employers and the government, and have collectively been a large contributor to the National Skills Task Force (NSTF), which has investigated national skills shortages and has produced several reports and recommendations. Regional TUC organisations are also involved in implementing and operating Learning and Skills Councils, which replaced Training and Enterprise Councils (TECs) in April 2001.

Unions such as the Communications Workers' Union (CWU) are set to become the number one providers of workplace training within five years, claims Dave Ward, national education officer at the CWU college.

> It is a way of showing our commitment to improving efficiency and productivity in the companies we are involved with. Changes in post-16 education funding over the past two years mean unions can now become education and training providers in their own right.
>
> (Roberts, 2002a, p. 7)

Stop and think   What difficulties and criticisms could be levelled at unions and private companies having sole charge of training initiatives?

VET in the leading industrialised nations

Comparisons have been made between leading industrial nations in an attempt to discover elements of education and training that create successful economies. Much attention has been focused on the German VET system, training in large Japanese corporations and human resource development in HRM-style US companies. Latterly, comparative studies have questioned how much of these nationally embedded training systems can be transposed to other institutional and cultural settings. (For a fuller discussion of the wider aspects of this, see Chapter 15). The dual system of training in Germany, for example, has a uniqueness forged out of the historical development of its institutions at a national and local level and these cannot be replicated in, for example, the UK, as these pre-conditions do not exist in the same way.

Another issue is how much can government policy consciously enhance training and education through public policy initiatives? Crouch *et al.* (2001) strongly doubt that government policy alone can achieve these ends and that a more realistic approach is to form strong partnerships between the state, employers and employee organisations such as trade unions. Their recommendations for the future of VET would lie in a form of neo-corporatism, whereby the state acts as a catalyst but in response to demands from companies for skills and knowledge. In other words, the state has to be responsive to changes in skill and knowledge demands in a rapidly changing world. The old model of monolithic state institutions laying down directives encasing training in specific and inflexible structures would be inappropriate in the rapidly changing world of work in the twenty-first century.

Neither can companies by themselves enhance national economic performance through their own initiatives. A good example is the USA, where excellent training is carried out in many companies yet there is still a skills shortage in the economy as a whole, combined with a widening gap between the highest- and lowest-paid workers. There are no easy solutions and the catalogue of failed VET initiatives in the UK is testament to this.

This section attempts to compare and contrast VET in six leading industrialised nations: Britain and five competitor countries. There are a number of similarities. All six countries have compulsory education of similar ages (Table 9.2) and therefore recognise the importance of at least a basic education in a modern industrialised society. All six countries experienced decline in the number of children of school-leaving age in the 1990s (Table 9.3); Germany experienced the most severe decline.

Table 9.2 **Compulsory school education ages**

Britain	5–16 yrs
Germany	6–15 yrs
France	6–16 yrs
Sweden	7–16 yrs
Japan	6–15 yrs
USA	6–16 yrs[a]

[a] Varies from state to state

Table 9.3 **Indices of the 16- to 18-year-old population and participation in education rates**

	16- to 18-year-old population indices (year)			16- to 18-year-old participation in education and training (%)		
	1980	1990	2000	Full	Part	All
Britain	121	106	94	33	31	64
Germany	125	83	72	47	43	90
France	100	103	90	66	8	74
Sweden	99	102	86	76	2	78
Japan	91	114	92[a]	77	3	79
USA	102	83	85[a]	79	1	80

100 = 1970

[a] 1996

Source: DES (1990). Reproduced by permission of the Controller of Her Majesty's Stationery Office.

An examination of the statistics for 16- to 18-year-olds shows that the majority continue with some form of education or training, either full- or part-time (Table 9.3). Britain, however, has the fewest involved, being 10 per cent below the comparable French figure, for example.

Germany has a thoroughgoing VET infrastructure, and Sweden has a well-established vocational system, which begins when children are 14 years old.

■ VET policies and practices

An examination of the VET systems beyond compulsory school age for the same six countries reveals a varying, and sometimes widely varying, set of practices (see Table 9.4). They can be roughly divided into *voluntarist* and *directed*. By voluntarist is meant a system that has little or no government interference, and effectively leaves training to the choice of the individual or the organisation. By directed is meant the existence of state legislation or regulation that has an element of compulsion for employers to train their staff.

Britain and the United States clearly have voluntarist systems and Germany, France and Sweden have directed systems, whereas Japan, while not having legislation that makes VET compulsory, has strong directives set by local and central government that enforce high-quality training standards (Dore and Sako, 1989). The Japanese also have a culture that values training and education highly, and such policies have a collectivist rather than an individualist imperative (Hofstede, 1984).

What can also be discerned is that in each country there are a considerable number of routes through vocational education and training, which vary from relatively low-grade schemes such as Training for Work in Britain to university graduate and postgraduate

Table 9.4 VET policies and practices

Britain
- New Deal – Training for 18–24-year-olds out of work longer than 6 months, and training for over-24-year-olds out of work for longer than 2 years
- National Training Organisations (NTOs) – sectoral bodies whose function is to analyse skills gaps using international benchmarking, scenario planning and local focus groups
- National Skills Task Force (NSTF) – body composed of government, employees and union representatives investigating skills shortages nationally and recommending proposals
- Learning and Skills Councils – regional bodies replaced Training and Enterprise Councils in April 2001. Have been expanded in 2002 to look at skills needs in specific sectors.
- National Vocational Qualifications (NVQ) levels 1 to 5
- Competence movement, e.g. Management Charter Initiative (MCI)
- Investors in People (IIP) – to encourage companies to attain a recognised level of strategic training
- New apprenticeships – set up in the early 1990s to encourage quality skilled training
- Colleges of higher and further education
- Universities (including the 'old polytechnics')
- Business schools, usually part of universities

Training culture – voluntarist: finance rather than industry oriented; class based; public/private education

Germany
- Dual system – in-company training (practical); vocational school (theoretical)
- Apprenticeships – 319 000 places, though demand is decreasing
- Technical colleges
- Universities

Training culture – directed: functionalist; industry oriented, particularly engineering

France
- Much VET in school system
- Apprenticeship places 300 000
- University institutes of technology
- Universities
- Grandes écoles
- Law requiring employers to spend 1.2% of total gross salaries on training employees

Training culture – directed: mathematical/engineering orientation; centralised; elitist, e.g. grandes écoles; the educational establishment attended often decides career prospects

Sweden
- Upper secondary school – large vocational content
- Technical and specialist universities
- Universities
- VET in most organisations is strong; heavy emphasis on HRD
- Retraining for unemployed
- Labour Market Training Board (AMU) is very influential
- Considerable free adult education
- Emphasis on 'self-development' and open learning systems

Training culture – directed: state will use training to affect labour market policy. Companies are strongly encouraged to train

Japan
- High schools take up to 90% of pupils up to 18 years
- Two-year college – vocationally specific training
- Four-year university courses
- Five-year college of technology courses
- Considerable continuous in-company training

Training culture – directed/voluntarist: central and local government set and enforce training standards; meritocratic – top companies will take from top universities etc.; lifetime employment and training in large companies; self-development emphasised

USA
- Junior or community college two-year associate degree course
- Technical institutes
- Vocational, trade and business schools
- 'GI Bill' federal loans/grants for four years' higher education after completion of four years' military service
- Private schools and colleges
- University courses
- Apprenticeships are increasingly less common and of low status
- Excellent training by leading companies but this is not universal

Training culture – voluntarist: anti-federalist in nature with wide variation; uncoordinated, with emphasis on individual effort and individual payment

Source: Dore and Sako (1989); Carnevale *et al*. (1990); Brewster *et al*. (1992), DfEE Web page.

degrees. However, it is apparent that the British system lacks homogeneity and consistency in courses and standards of occupational qualifications compared with those of Japan, Sweden and Germany.

In Europe there are two main types of vocational training: the sequential and the dual systems. The *sequential system* is practised in France, Italy, Belgium, the Netherlands and Sweden, and is conducted in specialist vocational training colleges, which school leavers attend full time. The German *Berufsbildungssystem* is the main exemplar of the *dual system*, and is described below.

● The German system of VET

The German 'directed' and dual system of vocational training has frequently been referred to as an example of excellent practice. A common misunderstanding is that the VET is funded and run by the state. In reality, employers fund two-thirds of VET, and employers and trade unions have a considerable influence on the control of the system, together with central and local government. Laws and guidelines of VET regulate the system so that employers are duty bound to provide funding and resources for training. The institutions and procedures that operate the system are, however, administered jointly by employers, unions and the state.

There are three stages in the dual system (see Figure 9.2). The first begins in the latter years of school, where emphasis is placed on a high level of education for all. A good general education, it is recognised, provides the solid basis for later learning. Nearly all young school leavers enter apprenticeships, as do a quarter of youths with qualifications similar to A levels; the rest enter the college and university system (Rose and Wignanek, 1990).

The dual system stresses the strong relationship between theoretical and practical training; part of the apprentice's time is taken up in attending vocational college, and part in receiving structured training from a *meisterwerker* (skilled craftsman) in the workplace. The *meisterwerker*, it must be stressed, is also trained in instruction techniques (Thorn, 1988). On- and off-the-job instruction is carefully coordinated to produce a vocational course that gives a thorough grounding in the skills of the apprentice's trade, and this, once acquired, is acceptable in all parts of the German labour market.

The costs of the dual system are shared by firms, government and youths. Firms pay for on-the-job training, youths accept relatively low wages, and the vocational colleges are paid for by public funds (Rose and Wignanek, 1990). There are approximately 319 000

| Figure 9.2 | Outline of the dual system of VET |

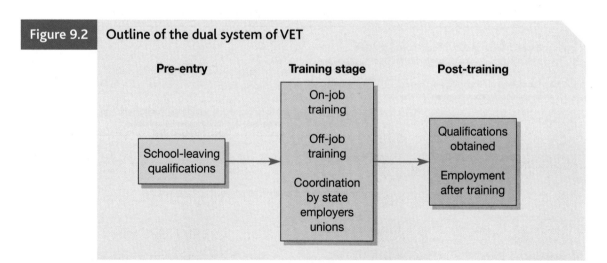

Source: Adapted from Rose and Wignanek (1990). Adapted with permission of the Anglo-German Foundation, publishers of Rose and Wignanek

apprenticeship places available in Germany compared with approximately 13 000 in Britain. However, since 1986 young people in Germany have taken up only about 172 000 apprentice places, but that number may have declined with the advent of more difficult times in the 1990s (Gaugler and Wiltz, 1992).

Germany has three times more skilled workers than Britain, even though the labour force of each country is of similar size (Rose and Wignanek, 1990). Nevertheless, as will be noted in the section on controversial issues, Germany's much admired VET policies and practices are apparently no longer effective in reducing the number of the unemployed.

● The Japanese system of VET

While the German system illustrates the comparative efficiency of its youth training programmes, an examination of the Japanese system of VET reveals the advantages of continuous development of employees throughout their careers. 'Lifetime employment' is a much-referred-to Japanese employment practice, although in reality '40% of new recruits leave within three years of entering their first job' (Dore and Sako, 1989). However, there is still a considerable proportion of lifetime employment in large-scale companies among the managerial and professional workforce in particular, who tend to form the core (those with relatively permanent positions and career structures) of company employees.

Lifetime employment allows for the long-term development of employees, and enables the creation of a structured succession programme that is mutually beneficial to the organisation and the individual employee. Decision-making is shared at all levels, there is a strong sense of collective responsibility for the success of the organisation, and cooperative rather than individual effort is emphasised, although achievement is encouraged. Training and development are an integral part of company policy in helping to reinforce these working practices, and in improving skills in technology and other related working practices. Training and development are thus 'embedded' in Japanese companies, rather than extraneous as in British organisations. A study of eight comparable British and Japanese companies revealed the inherent weaknesses of the British system (Storey, 1991). While the study concentrated on management development, the fact that the Japanese have no term for this was significant. They believe all workers should be developed, and this should be an ongoing part of systematic employee development. Line managers in Japanese organisations are expected to spend time developing their subordinates, and this is deeply imbued in their expectations:

> In the main, the Japanese treated training and development more seriously. In Britain, despite many good intentions and recent advances, there was a level of ambiguity about the real value of training and development that was not found in Japan.   (Storey, 1991)

● The French system of VET

In the 1970s training initiatives and expenditure were similar in Britain and France. In the 1970s and 1980s, however, successive French governments initiated a number of training laws that compelled organisations to train, making this a 'directed' system. The *taxe d'apprentissage* (apprenticeship tax) required employers engaged in commercial, industrial and handicraft activities to be subject to a tax of 0.6 per cent, which was to be used to finance technical and apprenticeship training. An employee training tax was also introduced, which compelled employers of nine people or more to allocate a minimum amount equal to 1.2 per cent of total annual wages and salaries to staff training (Price Waterhouse, 1989). The effects on training were dramatic. At first, a considerable number of training consultancies came into existence to cater for the expected demand

Table 9.5 **Proportion of salaries and wages spent on training 1991–92**

	Switzerland	Germany	Denmark	Spain	France	Italy	Norway	Netherlands	Sweden	UK
0.01–2.0%	64	61	66	76	25	76	63	65	57	62
4% and above	11	16	13	10	32	9	19	16	25	18
Don't know	25	42	33	18	2	24	30	23	44	38

Source: Price Waterhouse Cranfield Survey (Holden and Livian, 1992: 15). Reproduced with permission of MCB University Press

(Barsoux and Lawrence, 1990). Another longer-term factor was that, as companies were forced to train, many found that it brought benefits, and they began to spend above the 1.2 per cent requirement, as Table 9.5 indicates.

French organisations, in conforming to French law, have a much greater knowledge of their training expenditure compared with other European countries, as the Price Waterhouse data consistently show in both years of the survey, even when extended from five to ten countries (see Tables 9.4 and 9.5). Only 2 per cent of French organisations did not know how much they spent on training, but well over 40 per cent did not know this in the UK, Sweden and Germany. Similar figures can be found in the 1991–92 survey.

Overall, French organisations

have been forced to pay more attention to training since under law they also have to draw up a training plan to be submitted and discussed with the *comité d'entreprise* [works council] [and] . . . gradually firms have begun to look on it [training tax] as an investment that can be integrated into the firm's strategy. (Barsoux and Lawrence, 1990)

The implications of these international comparisons for Britain

Statistics reveal that Britain has one of the lowest percentages of young people between the ages of 16 and 18 years of age staying on at school or undertaking vocational education schemes (see Table 9.3), compared with other industrialised countries of the European Union and the world (DES, 1990). A more recent report published by the OECD stated that of 14 countries studied in depth only Hungary and Portugal had a record as poor as the UK for smoothing the transition from school to work. Of those students staying on in full-time education, 20 per cent dropped out within one year, and an astonishing 10 per cent could not be traced as in work or in education. It also stated that 40 per cent of British young people aged 19–24 had not reached what the OECD considered to be a minimum-level qualification (Atkinson and Elliott, 2000: 6).

Concerns have also been raised regarding the relative decline of literacy and numeracy among school leavers and the relevance of the school curriculum to the world of work, for example the narrow and restrictive role of A levels. Moreover, there is also considerable concern about long-term unemployed people condemned to a life of inactivity because they have not been able to receive adequate training to create a suitable career. There has been disquiet regarding the role of training and education policy in helping to halt or reverse that trend. Yet despite high unemployment in some areas, there are organisations experiencing difficulties in recruiting certain highly skilled positions. The comparisons made above between the British system of VET and those of some of its major competitors do little to allay such concerns. Recent nationwide skills audit reports show that Britain's workforce has slipped further behind its main economic rivals in training and education. In comparing Britain with France, Germany, Singapore and the United States, the report indicated that, while the number of young people staying on in full-time education in Britain had improved, it was still behind the other four nations. It was in VET, particularly in craft and technical skills, that the report stated that Britain still had much to do to equal its rivals (Targett, 1996: 3; Macleod and Beavis, 1996: 6).

Some critics claim that Britain is becoming a 'low-tech' (untrained and unskilled), cheap-labour economy, with an increasing proportion of the potential labour force condemned to a lifetime of economic inactivity. In the early 1990s Layard stated that 'two-thirds of British workers had no vocational or professional qualification, compared with only a quarter in Germany' (Anon, 1992).

These issues raise many questions as to the scope and type of training that is needed. The following subsections outline some of the recent VET initiatives designed to improve Britain's competitiveness. It is too soon to judge their effects, but the conclusion that Britain lags behind its competitors is now being questioned: 'the UK system may eventually be seen as an example of how to create a more flexible workforce' (Merrick, 1995: 8).

VET in Britain

■ The involvement of government in VET in the UK

With its voluntarist system of VET, Britain has traditionally left the provision of training and employee development to employers, and has largely had an educational system that was geared to preparing young people as members of society rather than as workers. However, the experience of relative economic decline in Britain has raised a number of questions regarding the role of education and training policy in helping to halt or reverse that trend. It has become clear that employers by themselves cannot achieve the major investment needed by the nation in training and development. This is not only because they serve their own self-interest rather than that of the economy at large, but also because they have had to operate within a patchwork of complex and poorly integrated VET courses, standards and qualifications. The only way to deal strategically with the nation's shortfall in skills has been for the government to modify its voluntarist approach and develop an overall framework for VET. However, whether voluntarism should be abandoned entirely is being currently debated, although in February 2000 the Labour government stated that it will not be adopting a training levy proposal at present, an indication that the voluntarist approach will remain predominant (see the subsection on Labour government policies later in this chapter).

● The recent history of government involvement

The history of government initiatives in training is a relatively short one. Not until 1964, when Industrial Training Boards (ITBs) were set up, was there an attempt by government to influence employer training behaviour. Subsidies were given to companies that were able to show that they were carrying out training programmes of a type approved by the Training Boards, and Boards were set up to oversee most sectors of the economy.

The ITBs did have some impact on popularising training by pointing to its benefits, which also helped to influence companies to set up training departments and improve their training methods (Manpower Services Commission, 1981b).

The neo-liberalist Conservative governments from 1979 were directly opposed to any form of compulsion, and thus the voluntarist tradition was re-emphasised and bolstered. It is surprising, therefore, that more government policies directed at improving training were initiated than before. The Employment and Training Act 1981 abolished most of the ITBs, and the government stressed that 'it is for employers to make the necessary investment in training for the work that they require' (IMS, 1984).

During this same period the government introduced initiatives in education that were intended to generate an enterprise culture. Moreover, the new national curriculum for schools was designed expressly to meet the needs of employers. The merging of the Department for Education and Department of Employment into one ministry expressed how close the relationship between education and employment was deemed to be.

● Government training initiatives

A further impetus for the government's increasing involvement in VET during the 1980s and 1990s was the dramatic rise in unemployment among young people and adults, with a high incidence of long-term unemployment. Consequently, a plethora of initiatives in the fields of education and training were introduced. These included schemes for training the unemployed, the establishment of bodies to initiate, foster and undertake training of direct relevance to employers (Training and Enterprise Councils now replaced by Learning and Skills Councils), the development of a comprehensive national framework of vocational qualifications, based partly on competencies, and national targets for training. The following subsections will outline recent major elements of this context.

■ The competency approach

Chapter 8 has identified competence as one of the outcomes of learning and development. Defined as the ability to apply knowledge and skills with understanding to a work activity and, importantly, assessed via performance, the notion has resonated with the values that have come to pervade the recent thinking of government policy-makers on VET, with their increasing emphasis upon outcomes rather than inputs into education and training. During the later 1980s, therefore, competence and competency were adopted as a major building block in the new thinking about VET, and have now achieved wide currency in this field.

However, these notions are not universally accepted, and there has been considerable debate about the way they have been conceptualised and used in practice (Kandola, 1996). A key issue for those critical of this approach is the status given to the knowledge underpinning the performance of skills. The issue rumbles on in the various debates (e.g. Armstrong, 1996).

Nevertheless, the competency approach has been a major innovation in the field of HRD, and has permeated it widely during the 1990s. Although it may be applied in different ways (Kandola, 1996), there is no sense yet that it is fragmenting or fading. Buttressed by its adoption in various government-led VET initiatives (see below), it is likely that it will withstand its critics for some time yet, and will therefore continue to influence the format of and philosophy underpinning much individual and organisational training and development activity.

■ A national framework of vocational qualifications

The establishment in 1986 of the National Council for Vocational Qualifications (NCVQ) and the Scottish Vocational Educational Council (SCOTVEC) institutionalised the competency approach. These bodies provided a framework of National Vocational Qualifications (S/NVQs, or VQs) that accredited competencies across organisations so that an individual's performance at work could be taken into account in an educational qualification. In addition, GNVQs are an alternative to academic A levels for those preparing for the world of work. These bodies have now merged with the school curriculum and assessment authority to form the Qualifications and Curriculum Authority (QCA).

In the S/NVQs are statements 'confirming that the individual can perform to a specified standard' and that he or she 'possesses the skills, knowledge and understanding which makes possible such performance in the workplace' (Harrison, 1992: 28). There are five levels of S/NVQ: from the most basic level through craft, technician and lower-level professional skills to the higher professional levels. The standards of competence for particular occupations and professions are, after a lengthy analytical and consultative process, set by industry lead bodies, which include representatives of employers and trade unions, as Townsend (1992) illustrates in the work of the Personnel Standards Lead Body, to ensure that the standards are relevant to work and are valued by employers.

There is a wide range of lead bodies, such as the Small Firms Lead Body and the Guidance and Counselling Lead Body. The comparable body in the field of management is the Management Charter Initiative (MCI), the work of which is described in Chapter 10. Many occupational areas are therefore embraced in the new qualifications framework: bouncers, caterers, translators, teachers etc. Awarding bodies such as City and Guilds, RSA and BTEC have changed their awards to meet S/NVQ criteria. The nature of the lead bodies has evolved, and some have formed themselves into occupational standards councils (OSCs) for particular sectors of employment. For example, the Personnel Standards Lead Body, the Training and Development Lead Body and the Trade Union Sector Development Body merged in 1994 to become the Employment OSC. This has not always been a smooth process, as Welch (1996a) indicates when reporting the eventual accreditation by NCVQ of the IPD's new qualifications in personnel, training and development.

The developments so far, however, have not been an unqualified success. There have been criticisms of definitions, purposes and methodology. There has been considerable frustration with their excessive bureaucracy and the 'jargon-ridden language' of the standards, and recognition of the need for the lead bodies or OSCs to provide external quality checks on the standard of assessment. The controversy and debate surrounding this issue will undoubtedly exercise the minds of the interested parties for some time to come.

Nevertheless, like the competency approach, the language and framework of VQs are influencing how individuals construct their own development, and how organisations approach and deliver HRD, and hence the nature of the learning environment they offer their employees.

Stop and think	What weaknesses and strengths can you identify in the competency-based approach?

■ Investors in People

Investors in People (IIP) was launched in 1991 and created out of the collaborative work of the National Skills Task Force (NSTF), CBI, Department of Employment, TUC and IPD (now CIPD). Since 1993 it has been a private company limited by guarantee – Investors in People UK (IIP UK, 1995; Taylor and Thackwray, 1995). Based on 'the practical experience of businesses that have improved their performance through investing in people' (Employment Department Group, 1990), IIP gives a national framework that specifies 'the principles which tie training and development activity directly to business objectives', ensures that the 'resources committed to training and development are put to the most effective use', and provides 'a clear benchmark of good practice . . . against which any organisation, large or small, can measure progress towards improved business performance' (IIP UK, 1995: 1). This can clearly be tied into the kind of HRD strategy outlined earlier in this chapter.

The Employment Department Group's (1990) brochure *What is an Investor in People?* states:

> An Investor in People makes a public commitment from the top to develop all employees to achieve its business objectives.
>
> - Every employer should have a written but flexible plan which sets out business goals and targets, considers how employees will contribute to achieving the plan and specifies how development needs in particular will be assessed and met.
> - Management should develop and communicate to all employees a vision of where the organisation is going and the contribution employees will make to its success, involving employee representatives as appropriate.
>
> An Investor in People regularly reviews the training and development needs of all employees.
>
> - The resources for training and developing employees should be clearly identified in the business plan.
> - Managers should be responsible for regularly agreeing training and development needs with each employee in the context of business objectives, setting targets and standards linked, where appropriate, to the achievement of National Vocational Qualifications (or relevant units) and, in Scotland, Scottish Vocational Qualifications.
>
> An Investor in People takes action to train and develop individuals on recruitment and throughout their employment.
>
> - Action should focus on the training needs of all new recruits and continually developing and improving the skills of existing employees.
> - All employees should be encouraged to contribute to identifying and meeting their own job-related development needs.
>
> An Investor in People evaluates the investment in training and development to assess achievement and improve future effectiveness.
>
> - The investment, the competence and commitment of employees, and the use made of skills learned should be reviewed at all levels against business goals and targets.
> - The effectiveness of training and development should be reviewed at the top level and lead to renewed commitment and target setting.

IIP has been in existence for over a decade and boasts that over 25 000 organisations (or units within them) have achieved the national award, which represents more than a third of the working population (Spellman, 2002). Taylor and Thackwray (1995) report that organisations find considerable benefit in working for and achieving the standard. They quote a survey and case studies that suggest that the benefits derive from ensuring that training is strategic and relates to the organisation's business needs. In particular, organisations cite that working towards IIP helps to clarify and communicate business objectives, stimulates continuous improvement initiatives (see Chapter 8), increases the involvement of managers in individuals' development, brings together some seemingly unrelated activities, and gives attention to administrative staff who are often otherwise overlooked. Taylor and Thackwray (1995: 30) also note that some organisations believe that through IIP they have increased profitability, efficiency, sales and income, and reduced costs.

Alberga (1997) in a survey in 1996 warns that there could be difficulties over re-recognition as organisations seek to retain the reward after three years: 'The problem is that it enables people to let things slide and then drag them up just in time for the re-

recognition process' (p. 32). The achievement of this standard calls for considerable effort, but it is becoming clear that its benefits lie in the diagnostic and reflective process that it sets in train.

BOX 9.4 The Cumberland Hotel

The organisation

The Cumberland Hotel, Harrow, Middlesex, grew from a small guest house established in 1956 to its present size of 84 bedrooms with a capacity for over 140 guests, an award-winning restaurant and the recent extension of its conference and leisure facilities. This privately owned hotel employs 100 people, and has progressed to four Crown Commended status from the English Tourist Board for its facilities and quality of service, together with three-star AA and RAC rating.

The hotel serves the international business market for Wembley and the north-west London area, providing a service for visitors to the capital and, increasingly, for overseas guests from France, Germany, Japan and the United States. Investors in People has been crucial to the success of the Cumberland Hotel in what is, after all, a people-led business.

The hotel is unique in having recently won the prestigious London Regional Training Award for the exceptionally high standard of staff training: in 1996 it also won the Rubicon Award for Employer of the Year.

The challenge and the strategy

The principal elements of the strategy needed to meet defined business priorities required the following:

- hotel management and staff to perform to their maximum potential;
- the business to develop the ability to change and become more efficient and profitable;
- systematic sales and marketing activity, particularly regarding competition and the identification of new markets;
- a culture change for the recognition of the importance of new skills;
- the increasing amounts of new legislation covering health and safety and food hygiene to be understood and applied;
- improvement of personnel practices encompassing employee induction, ongoing training provision and performance appraisal;
- elimination of wastage, reducing operating overheads and preserving margins;
- improvement in continuity of action between departments and functions through better communication and interpersonal skills;
- consistent standards that met or exceeded the expectations of customers.

The results

Implementation of this strategy has resulted in significant business performance, including:

- increase in revenue of 50% in the past three years;
- growth in gross operating profit of 200%;
- reduction in labour costs and staff recruitment;
- savings used to invest in a £500 000 conference and banqueting suite.

The Cumberland Hotel was formally recognised as an Investor in People in 1993 and successfully reassessed in 1996. The hotel's recognition sets it apart from all competition in the area, and will continue to ensure high standards of customer service.

Source: Printed with the kind permission of Investors in People

As we have already noted, despite effusive support for IIP from many quarters there have also been critics.

▇ National training targets

Various VET initiatives have been pulled together by the setting of national training targets, first proposed by the CBI in 1989 to benchmark the UK's skills base against that of other nations, and launched in 1991. The National Advisory Council for Education and Training Targets (NACETT) came into being in 1993 to monitor and report on progress towards achievement of the targets, and in 2000 it was incorporated into the Learning and Skill's Council's corporate plan. While targets were well received, Armstrong (1996) warned that the 'qualification cuckoo should not be allowed to push competence-based learning out of the nest' (p. 23). This is an issue for many commentators on the British VET policy. Welch (1996b) reports that 'a quarter of large British firms' do not see higher academic qualifications 'as reliable indicators of skills', and 40 per cent do not consider that they indicate 'basic skills'.

The targets were ambitious, and despite wide consultation and updating in 1995 the revised targets for the year 2000 were not met. New and revised targets were set for 2002 and again fell short of intentions, although improvements were made in most categories. Targets have been revised in 2002 with the continuing aim of raising the UK's international competitiveness by raising standards and attainment levels in education and training to world-class levels. This is to be achieved by the following training targets for 2006:

1 Targets for 11-year-olds – Increase the percentage of 11-year-olds who achieve level 4 in each key stage 2 English and maths tests beyond 2002 targets of 80% in English and 75% in maths. (The actual targets had not been announced at the time of writing.)
2 By 2007, 85% of 14-year-olds achieve level 5 in key stage 3 tests in English, maths and ICT and 80% in science. Increase the percentage of students gaining grades A–C in GCSEs.
3 Increase by 3 percentage points the number of 19-year-olds achieving a qualification equivalent to NVQ level 2, compared to 2002, by 2004. Increase the number of 19-year-olds achieving a level 3 qualification from 51% in 2000 to 55% in 2004. Ensure that there is an apprenticeship place for everyone who wants one and meets the required standard.
4 Increase participation towards 50% of those aged 18–30 by the end of the decade. Reduce the number of adults with numeracy and literacy problems by 750 000 by 2004.
5 Increase the percentage of adults attaining a level 3 qualification from 47% to 52% in 2004. Establish half of all colleges to be Centres of Vocational Excellence by 2003/4. (DfES, 2001)

(*Note*: restrictions of space have allowed only the main targets to be included here.)

Once again there is speculation whether the targets will be achieved. However, these targets also serve the important purpose of directing, motivating and reinforcing the various other VET initiatives already referred to in this chapter, so that what is emerging in the UK is a systematic, self-reinforcing framework for VET rather than, as hitherto, a patchwork of piecemeal initiatives. A common characteristic of the elements of this framework is the emphasis upon observable, tightly defined and often measurable outcomes. This, in some respects, contrasts with other contemporary developments. For example, as noted in Chapter 3, in the fields of philosophy and the social sciences those (positivist) approaches that favour measurement are being increasingly challenged by those favouring interpretation; in organisations, multi-skilling and flexible working are to some extent eroding the traditional boundaries and definitions of jobs; while notions of total quality management and of the learning organisation are breaking down traditional internal and external organisational boundaries. This contrast prompts the question whether the underpinning philosophy of today's VET will remain unchallenged for long, and what would become of the VET framework if its philosophy were undermined.

Labour government initiatives: building a VET framework

As we have already noted, the Labour government claims that one of its primary concerns has been education and training, and it visualises these as being fundamental tools to create a viable economic future for all in Britain in the twenty-first century. These are lofty but necessary ambitions, and – building on Conservative reforms – the Labour government has attempted to create a VET framework for all. We have already noted that training and education targets have been set for school pupils, students, young employed 16–21-year-olds, adults and organisations. Building on the Dearing Report's recommendations, attempts have been to harmonise diverse qualifications in the academic and technical worlds, with mixed results and some more development needed.

Since Labour has come to office VET initiatives have been abundant. The following subsections briefly describe the major initiatives that have been instituted to date.

The New Deal

This initiative is an attempt to provide training for 18–24-year-olds who have been out of work for more than six months, and 25-year-olds and over who have been unemployed for longer than two years. The idea behind the scheme is to make the unemployed more employable by providing them with skills. It offers four options (Pickard, 1997):

- a job subsidised for six months with an employer;
- six months' work with a governmental environment task force;
- six months' work with a voluntary sector employer;
- a year's full-time education and training for people who do not hold an NVQ level 2 or equivalent.

Scepticism has been expressed, partly because of the negative experiences of previous schemes such as YTS and ET, but also because of the failure of the Australian New Deal scheme, where employers were not enthusiastic about taking on the long-term unemployed because of 'low skills, poor attitudes to work and low levels of motivation' (Pickard, 1997: 34). These are concerns that remain in the minds of members of the CBI and other employer bodies, but nevertheless they are willing to cooperate with the TUC and other bodies. The government has made provisions to overcome these predicted difficulties by proposing the following:

- There will be a prolonged 'gateway' of up to four months' intensive counselling for the unemployed before being presented to an employer.
- Each individual will get an Employment Service case worker, who will stay with them throughout the programme.
- Each client will have a 'mentor' – someone from the community or local company but independent of the scheme's organisers – who can represent their interests.

The nationwide launch of the scheme took place in April 1998. Concerns have already been expressed about too much red tape, the low quality of the recruits, the lack of support from the Employment Service, and the fact that case workers have been overloaded with clients and do not have enough time to deal with individuals (Rana, 1999a: 14). Further criticisms are that the scheme has not met the needs of single parents, and has failed ethnic groups – claims rebutted by Andrew Smith, Minister of State for Employment in 1999 (Smith, 1999: 33). A study of employers found that one in three have failed to train their New Deal recruits, and that 21 per cent had no training planned for them. 'This is exactly what happened to YTS recruits and it discredited the scheme', claims Nick Isles, an IPD representative (Rana, 1999b: 18).

At present the jury is still out, with supporters claiming that the New Deal has achieved far more than any previous scheme. If cooperation between the partners does break down, then the government may have to resort to more compulsory measures.

● Learning and Skills Councils and the Small Business Service

From April 2001 TECs were replaced by Learning and Skills Councils (LSCs), and the Small Business Service replaced Business Links (bodies that promised training and development of local companies). LSCs also took over the role of National Training Organisations (NTOs). NTOs were launched in 1998 to deal with training in sectors but in March 2002 their role was taken over by newly formed Sector Skills Councils (SSCs) which have more employer input. The rationale being, according to then Minister of Education, Estelle Morris that

> Sector skills councils will be created by business for business. Governments across the UK recognise that employers are best placed to identify skills gaps and to create strategies close to them.
>
> (*People Management*, 9 August 2001, p. 9)

The role of LSCs is to

> build a new culture of learning which will underpin national competitiveness and personal prosperity, encourage creativity and innovation and help build a cohesive society.
>
> (DfEE, 1999)

The role of the Small Business Service will be

> to provide a single gateway for all government programmes directed primarily at mainly small business . . . and it will have the right to monitor all and existing proposals for business support.
>
> (DfEE, 1999)

There are 47 local LSCs and 45 Small Business franchises, their boundaries being co-terminous. They are overseen by a national LSC that, among other things:

- works to a three-year plan;
- assesses national skills and learning needs;
- allocates budgets to local LSCs;
- sets strategy on attainment of the National Learning Targets;
- secures information, advice and guidance for adults;
- develops national partnerships with local authorities and local education authorities, the Employment Service, the University for Industry, NTOs, trade unions, new support services for young people, major and multi-site employers, and education and training providers.

● Other VET measures

A number of other initiatives are worth mentioning, although space does not permit extensive information. They include the following.

Modern apprenticeships

These are mainly for 16- and 17-year-old school leavers and training includes at least an NVQ at level 3, showing that the apprentice can do the job to the standard that industry and commerce require. Over 82 frameworks have been approved so far, from accountancy to warehousing. The scheme aims to cater for more than a quarter of young people by 2004–5. The CIPD claims that this target can only be reached

> if employers realise the importance of this scheme to future skills needs. Modern apprenticeship is the only scheme for 14- to 19-year-olds that really integrates both on- and off-the-job learning. But research shows that the on-the-job element of the modern apprenticeship is often its Achilles heel. (Stevens, 2002, p. 47)

National traineeships

These are aimed at a lower level than modern apprenticeships, and are for school leavers from 16 upwards. They offer quality training to industry standards at NVQ level 2. They are designed by employers for employers. Trainees, like apprentices, can earn while they learn.

Learning Card

The Learning Card is issued to young people in their final year of compulsory education. It acts as a reminder to young leavers of their right to further learning and careers information and guidance. The card entitles holders to discounts from a number of organisations, such as BT, YHA, National Express, Letts and BSM. It also gives access to a Career Bank to help in the choice of careers.

Lifelong learning

Lifelong learning is an ill-defined concept, although its name suggests the encouragement of continuous learning for all throughout their lives. Various initiatives have been set up by the government in collaboration with universities, local authorities and employers to examine the possibilities of regional lifelong learning projects and support mechanisms. Local authorities have been cast in the leading role, but they have been sluggish in taking the initiative (Pollock, 1999). By implication they will have to turn themselves into learning organisations, and one – Norwich, a pioneer in the initiative – calls itself a 'Learning City'. One of the problems is that the lifelong learning brief maybe too wide and thus too amorphous to manage effectively. If the idea is to create a learning climate for citizens in general, then there needs to be a considerable degree of coordination of existing support mechanisms in cooperation with the various partners and local bodies.

Learning accounts

A cornerstone of the Labour government's skills revolution was the creation of learning accounts. This voluntarist measure was implemented in favour of training levies with their air of compulsion. By 2002 these were being withdrawn (temporarily, claims the government) as a howl of complaints (over 8500) revealed a series of frauds perpetrated by a number of providers (Roberts, 2002b). The aim had been to target people in most need of basic training. The programme had attracted two and half million learners who were given £150 each after contributing £25 from their own pocket. 'This would allow individuals to take the first step up the learning ladder by enrolling on, say, an IT course for beginners or taking basic literacy skills' (Littlefield and Welch, 1996: 5). This 'Learn as You Earn' proposal was 'designed to give people the freedom to choose the training courses and skills which fit with their aspirations' (Butters, 1996: 2). It also formed the basis for lifelong learning initiatives.

University for Industry

The University for Industry was proposed in 1996 by the Labour Party and came into being in November 1999. Its aim is to prepare individuals for the rapid economic and social changes in the modern, more flexible world of work, where there are 'weaker relationships between employers and employees' (Hillman, 1996: v). Among its aims are to:

- be the hub of a national learning network extending to workplaces, homes and local learning centres;
- provide access to user-friendly services on the Internet and create links with tutors, experts and other learners;
- commission new learning programmes in strategic areas;
- sustain an accessible system of support and guidance services;
- stimulate mass-marketing of learning opportunities.

An aim is to become a main support for lifelong learning. Another of its principal aims to this effect is to widen accessibility of learning opportunities, in terms of time, place and pace. This obviously suggests the use of individualised programmes on the Internet, CD-ROMs and distance learning initiatives, combined with local learning support mechanisms. Sixty eight Learndirect centres have been set up across England that will work with UfI to develop a new approach to the delivery of flexible learning.

● Conclusion

The Labour government hopes that these VET initiatives will provide a framework for the encouragement and development of a learning atmosphere in the nation as a whole. Whether this is the case or not depends on the enthusiasm, funding and continuing importance that the government places on the overall strategy and its individual programmes and institutions. It also remains to be seen whether these become a number of disparate schemes desperately operating to keep afloat despite lack of funding and support at national level. They will also be a test as to the success of the voluntarist system that the Labour government has continued from its Conservative forebears.

 # Controversial issues

▪ Training for an advanced industrial society: are skills enough?

We have been subjected to a barrage of comments by experts in the world of vocational and educational training that advanced economies need to expand the number of people with the requisite skills if they are to compete in the twenty-first century. The extract below gives a flavour of these warnings.

> Industry is no longer drawn to the comparative advantage of abundant natural resources, but instead to pools of human skills. American – and British – governments neither provide the education nor the training in depth, nor the infrastructural foundations necessary for the post-electro-mechanical society.   (Ford, 1993; in Thurow, 1992)

It is obvious that Britain and other advanced industrial economies can never compete with Third World countries in terms of cheapening the labour supply. If economies are to remain relatively prosperous, one of the policy imperatives for the future must be a considerable investment in education and training by both organisations (public and private sector) and governments, to increase skill levels for potential and actual employees.

In the past, governments in the UK have created an 'alphabet soup' of VET initiatives to engender a workforce with the right skills and knowledge for future economic and labour market requirements. But is this enough? By all accounts, past experience has shown that it is not! The continual chopping and changing of policies by various governments have not provided a training environment of continuity compared with Japan, Germany and France. This has had the effect of creating confusion and there has been a tendency to fill in tick-box report forms in order to please those in authority higher up the training and education ladder, rather than attend to the spirit of an HRD strategy in a national context.

Compulsory or voluntary VET?

One major concern to the fore in debates concerning the need for greater skills has been whether training should be voluntary or compulsory. If organisations and companies will not train their staff adequately, even with certain inducements, then should the state step in and force them by means of legal regulation? Observers and interested bodies are divided on the issue. The Liberal Democrats, the TUC, the Commission for Social Justice and, previously, the Labour Party have argued 'that the problem must be tackled with legislation. Employers should be compelled to provide training' (Harrison, 1995: 38). On the other hand, a strong case can be made for 'voluntarism' (Harrison, 1995). The Labour Party has now moved its position from one where organisations should be compelled to provide training (the levy system) to the most recent proposal of coordination of initiatives through the Learning and Skills Council, which backs away from elements of compulsion and retains the elements of persuasion. While welcoming the partnership approach, John Monks of the TUC expressed concerns about the emphasis on voluntarism (Rana, 2000:13).

The CBI, the Institute of Directors and the CIPD have argued for 'carrot' rather than 'stick' measures, as levies or compulsory learning accounts could act as a tax on jobs. In the face of the failure of the Australian levy system and the fact that proposals for levy systems in New Zealand, Ireland and Sweden have not been taken up, it would appear that the Labour Party has seen these as precautionary tales (Beresford and Gaite, 1994; Harrison, 1995).

A number of observers have welcomed the fact that British governments are coming to the realisation that

more skills supply initiatives on their own, would not be enough to solve our long standing skills 'problem.'

The Cabinet Office Performance and Innovation Unit also signalled a recognition that organisations' needs for skills are a derived demand – ie, driven by business requirements, not government schemes. This means workforce development needs to be addressed in the wider context of government and business strategies on products, innovation, market positioning, IT, HR and so on. Tackling low levels of employer demand for skill and ensuring that skills are deployed to maximum effect are key issues in solving the problem.   (Keep, 2002: 53)

The Learning and Skills Council will become a major hub in helping coordinate this activity where coordination and cooperation is the key to aiding effective skill provision. Thinking now believes that a series of disparate agencies acting on their own initiatives can no longer produce the requisite skills required by the economy; nor could a monolithic government training programme, forcing companies to follow the same blueprint regardless of sectoral requirements and individual company and organisational needs. Nevertheless, elements of control and strategic direction are elemental to success and the LSC already 'encourages sectors to adopt a "licence to practice" qualification requirements, which at one time would have been politically unacceptable' (Keep, 2002: 53).

There will have to be greater accessibility to universities for more of the population, a coherent system of VET in which harmonised qualifications are accredited and appreciated by all employees, and a commitment to lifelong learning. This implies an increase in funding for education. As noted in Chapter 8, the future organisation is a learning organisation, and future employees are those who are continually seeking to develop themselves.

Further developments in VET are therefore inevitable in the UK. The Labour governments elected in 1997 and 2001 have strongly recognised this in the flurry of VET initiatives put into practice. It is clear that further attention will be paid to education and VET in the UK for some time to come, although critics within the system at school, college and university levels claim that there is insufficient funding to meet all their needs.

◼ The contribution of training to national competitiveness

It has also been recognised that in a comparative context skill generation needs to meet national labour market requirements. Crouch *et al.* (2001) propose that coordination of private and government agencies in some neo-corporatist structure is the way forward. Alternative proposals do not work by themselves. For example, many private companies will engage in large amounts of training under their own volition

> But it will be targeted on selected groups of employees. There is no inherent tendencies for firms' market driven search for improved skills also to supply a strategy for skill maximization for a society as a whole.
> (p. viii)

They also argue that improved skill levels do not necessarily solve unemployment, and higher levels of education may produce more highly educated unemployed people or over qualified employees, such as graduates, filling McJobs.

If skill generation is left mainly to companies, this inevitably means that government agencies are left with the residual role of taking care of the unemployed, and training policy in this area cannot solve unemployment by itself nor stimulate economic growth. Alternatively, all-pervading government control of VET is not likely to be able to provide the skills and knowledge that companies need.

In the past, economic growth has been seen to have been bound up as much with the wealth of a nation's 'human capital' as with its material resources. Japan and Germany are two oft-cited cases. Both countries have relatively few natural resources, and have relied heavily on the development of the skills, aptitudes and efforts of their people. Both had suffered considerable wartime destruction by 1945, but had largely rebuilt their economies by the 1960s as a launch pad from which to challenge world markets.

The problem with training and education is that, although most observers acknowledge their importance, it is very difficult, if not impossible, to correlate directly their contribution to economic growth. Attempts have been made by some researchers to do this, albeit with questionable results (Prais and Steedman, 1986; Steedman, 1988; Prais and Wagner, 1988; Prais *et al.*, 1989). Comparative economic research by Freeman (BBC, 1996) finds that although the Philippines has increased and improved education, it is not doing as well economically as China, which has not significantly increased its education and training but is experiencing high economic growth. He warns that education and training alone are not a prescription for pulling a country out of low economic growth, and other writers from developing nations have also attested that the hopes invested in education in the 1960s and 1970s have not been realised in economic terms for many Asian and African countries (Halls, 1990).

However, Ashton and Sung (1994) cite the impressive economic growth of the Singaporean economy in the 1990s, and claim that much of this can be related to a comprehensive state-directed VET programme integrated into the Singaporean government's long-term economic aims. They claim that 'the relative autonomy of the state apparatus is the ability of the political elite to define long-term goals for political and economic action' (p. 5). From these examples we can at best conclude that the experience of developing economies is varied, and that the way VET policy is conceived and implemented is of utmost importance: this is an area of research that is receiving increasing attention.

In recent years the much-vaunted German VET system has come under criticism, in that training for the unemployed is not affecting the labour market in the way it had done previously, and levels of unemployment are now equivalent to, if not greater than, those in Britain. It would seem that in certain areas of the economy training and retraining in practical skills are proving less effective, largely because of the changing nature of the economy, which is requiring fewer and fewer engineering, construction and other manual skills. As world competition increases, and new technology replaces many occupations that would once have absorbed the unemployed, retraining schemes appear increasingly out of date and ill equipped to help the 'new' unemployed (BBC, 1996). Unification has also had a negative economic impact on the new German state. The changing labour requirements of the economy, in terms of numbers of employees and skills needed, will be an increasingly pressing problem for the major economies, with ramifications for social as well as economic policy-making.

Similarly, while in-firm training has increased considerably in France, there remains the problem of what to do with the unemployed, particularly youth and ethnic minorities – groups of unemployed that are disproportionately large. Long-term unemployment in France has also risen over the past decade, and labour-market policies have not been particularly effective in providing the skills-based training needed to help these people find jobs. France, like Britain, has not succeeded in bridging the skills gap, and this may be partly due to the low esteem in which vocational training initiatives are held (Bournois, 1992).

Training is also regarded as an instrument for solving specific economic problems such as unemployment, and for bridging the skills gap. Many advanced economies have pursued such training policies with, at best, mixed results and usually little long-term effect on the unemployment register. Social arguments seem to fare better, and according to Lord Young it is preferable to have unemployed youngsters on training schemes than out 'ram-raiding' (BBC, 1996). In addition, as we shall see in Chapter 15 on international HRM, factors such as the influence of national institutions, social attitudes and culture are also bound up with explanations of the economic success of these nations and their education and training systems. Nevertheless, comparative study can highlight weaknesses and strengths in national systems of training and education, from which we may learn some vital lessons.

Summary

- This chapter examined the practicalities of human resource development, offering a definition and highlighting the problem of transferable and non-transferable skills. Although there has been a growing recognition of the need for training in organisations, controversy still exists as to the extent and quality of training required.

- Training is seen as a key instrument in the implementation of HRM policies and practices, particularly those involving cultural change and the necessity of introducing new working practices. Of equal importance in the training process is the recognition of individual needs. These may, however, clash with organisational needs, and it is crucial to harmonise these demands, to the mutual benefit of both parties.

- The first part of the chapter dealt with the practicalities of creating a human resource development plan. The first and most vital step in an HRD plan is to analyse the training needs of the organisation in relation to its strategy, and equate these with the needs of the individuals within it. Proposals were then made as to how this might be effected, including the use of various forms of analysis of job requirements and personnel performance. A choice of methods was then outlined, which fell into the basic categories of on-the-job and off-the-job training, followed by the equally important consideration of who was to deliver the training. The last and perhaps least well-performed part of the HRD plan is evaluating and monitoring the training. This section reviewed various methods by which this can be carried out, the results of which should be fed back into the HRD process to improve the effectiveness and increase the relevance of future programmes.

● The notion of the learning organisation and the knowledge-based organisation, and the difficulties in defining, modelling and implementing these concepts, were examined.

● The second half of the chapter examined the stakeholders in the individual's learning and development, concentrating on the role of the employer, the state and the trade union movement.

● An examination was undertaken of training in a comparative international context, which made an in-depth exploration of vocational training policies and practices in Germany, Japan and France, and outlined some of the lessons they might afford for the British experience.

● This was followed by an in-depth critical examination of the recent history of training in the UK context. Recent and past public policy training initiatives were examined, such as the competency approach, vocational qualifications, Investors in People, national training targets, the New Deal, and more recently the Learning and Skills Councils and the University for Industry.

● The chapter also examined the debate concerning whether or not training policies should be compulsory or voluntary, and the contribution of training to national competitiveness.

ACTIVITY **A debate on national vocational education and training**

Divide the lecture group/class into groups.

● One group is to assume the position of Secretary of State for Education and Employment and his/her supporters.

● Another group is to assume the critical position of members of the parliamentary opposition.

● A third group is made up of critics of the voluntarist approach to vocational education and training (VET): the TUC, for example.

By referring to this chapter, its references and further reading and other sources, each group must state its position. This should include a critique of the other two groups' case, and the reasons why you support your present views.

Elect a chairperson to order the debate.

Questions

1 The learning organisation is purely an aspiration, and can never be achieved in reality. How far would you agree with this statement?

2 What are the advantages of organisations adopting a learning organisation or knowledge-based approach to HRD? What difficulties could possibly develop in the implementation and operation of these systems?

3 Examine the experience of those countries mentioned in the international section, and comment on whether Britain can learn from their policies and approaches.

4 What are the potential effects of government initiatives such as National Training Targets, Vocational Qualifications (S/NVQs) or the Investors in People award upon the human resource development of an organisation?

Exercises

1 Divide into three groups. One group should identify the particular strengths of the French VET as compared with the British; the second should do the same for the German; and the third for the Japanese. Report back to the whole class.

2 Outline the strengths and weaknesses of the Investors in People programme. How does it fit in with government overall VET strategy? You may wish to contact your local IIP office or the national office: Investors in People UK, 7–10 Chandos Street, London W1M 9DE. E-mail: information@iipuk.co.uk

3 What steps would you follow if you were charged with devising an IIP programme for your company or organisation?

Note: In the chapter and below are actual IIP case studies that may guide you. The one in the text shows how one organisation achieved IIP status and how it helped its performance. The second sets the problem, and the Lecturer's Guide that accompanies this textbook gives you the full report.

Case study 1

Wealden District Council

The organisation

Wealden District Council was established as a local authority in 1974. Embracing 320 miles of East Sussex, it stretches from the Kent borders to the sea, and is the largest district council in the South East. Its 135 000 population is scattered among rural villages and four substantial market towns.

It provides a range of services, including planning and development, refuse collection, environmental health, housing and leisure services. A staff of 560 is divided between two offices, four leisure centres, two depots and 19 sheltered dwellings. The Council, with no overall control, has 58 elected councillors, serving on ten committees and subcommittees.

The challenge

The Council aims to offer the highest possible standard of service within the constraints of its budget, customer care being of paramount importance.

Particular challenges have continued to include:

- the introduction of compulsory competitive tendering, with the cost of services being tested in the open market against commercial operators;
- new legislation affecting large areas of the Council's work;
- the consolidation of Audit Commission performance indicators against which service performance is stringently measured;
- the requirement to work to constrained budgets, while delivering consistently high levels of service;
- introducing and developing new indicators for the benefit of the customer.

The objective continues to be to deliver a consistently high standard of service across an organisation widespread in location and function, with all the elements working harmoniously together, against a background of change.

Source: Printed with the kind permission of Investors in People.

Question

What strategy would you recommend Wealden District Council to follow in order to achieve its aims?

Case study 2

Smart cookies

This case study is concerned with a training programme instituted in Fox's Biscuits that won a training award from the CIPD.

The Fox's Biscuits factory near Kirkham, near Preston, was the poorest performing site within Northern Foods five years ago. Today it is viewed as the jewel in the group's crown.

The plant, which produces 12 000 biscuits every minute for the likes of Marks and Spencer, Asda and Sainsbury's, has an impressive list of achievements since 1995. Of the 345 employees in manufacturing, 181 have achieved NVQ level 1 in food and drink, 128 have completed level 2 and 25 are about to finish level 3. Absence rates have decreased significantly, while staff turnover has dropped from 11 per cent to 9 per cent.

According to its managers, it is also now the most cost-effective biscuit manufacturer in the industry. It has even opened its doors to share best practice with household names such as Guinness, Eden Vale and Ross Young.

'We have used training to revolutionise both the manufacturing process and the company's culture,' says Charlotte Greenwood, senior personnel and training officer.

What's more, it has achieved all this without external help. 'It's unusual not to use consultants for this type of project,' says Linda Atkins, personnel manager. 'But we felt that we had enough skills and expertise on site and the right people to carry it through.'

Before 1995, millions of pounds had been invested in new technology for the site, but little had been spent on giving employees the skills to operate it. Several other key people management problems also needed tackling, so the senior management team had to act.

'We have a long-serving workforce with a low skills base and, in some cases, poor literacy. There were also communication problems,' Atkins says. 'Because of the way in which the work teams were structured, there was little accountability or ownership. We had a traditional, autocratic culture and there was a lack of trust in managers. There were also too many layers of management – about seven or eight – and a very complex shift system that created huge problems.'

The first stage of the turnaround saw the reorganisation and delayering of the management team. Areas of responsibility were defined more clearly and appraisals were introduced to identify skills gaps among managers.

The restructuring also applied to the factory floor. Previously, separate teams of mixers, bakers and packers had worked across all six production lines. The employees now work in multidisciplinary teams, which are responsible for all processes from mixing ingredients to packing the finished products on each line. 'Under the old system, the process could – and did – fall down quickly,' says Ian Jackson, factory manager. 'There were grey areas surrounding who was responsible for what stage of the process. Each of the teams operated as its own little unit. They didn't talk to each other. In fact there was very little communication along the manufacturing process.'

While members of each team are now able to do each other's work, the company has introduced the concept of 'principal job' to allow people to specialise. It has also established standard working practices for each job type and rationalised the shift system.

The company then turned its attention to developing the skills of the operating teams. Senior managers and factory staff worked with advisers from Blackpool and Fylde College to tailor an NVQ course in food and drink that would meet their specific requirements. The training was delivered through the time-honoured system of 'sitting by Nellie'.

'People have different speeds of learning, so we wanted to help them to get the most out of the training without feeling pressured to keep up – as they might have been on a structured programme,' Atkins says.

While the NVQ was developed, charge hands and managers on the production line received accreditation as internal D32 assessors. The college acted as an internal verifier. With all the employees working towards the same study goals, they were able to help each other improve – in effect becoming trainers themselves.

'It helps to know that there is someone you can go to if there are things you don't know,' says Trish Butcher, a hygiene operator with 18 years' experience. 'It also means that you're not afraid to admit that you don't know something. Before now we would have been too scared to show a lack of knowledge.'

The confidence that learning has given many employees has inspired a high proportion of them to carry on studying. They include Sean Mangan, who has been with the company 15 years. A charge hand and D32 assessor, he is working towards an NVQ level 3.

'When I started here, there was nothing in the way of training,' he says. 'You were shadowed for six weeks on the job and then simply told to get on with it. Training has come on in leaps and bounds. Having an NVQ qualification shows people that you know your job and it sets a good example to new starters. It's also a qualification that you have under your belt if you go anywhere else.'

The pride that many employees now take in their work is evident in the five core action teams (Cats) that have been established. Ideas for improvement are invited from all parts of the workforce and every week a Cat member logs all of these ideas and posts them on notice boards around the site. Voluntary action teams then get together and develop these ideas. Their proposals are submitted to Cats for scrutiny. Approved ideas are then developed further and, every five weeks, each Cat updates the senior management team on the progress it has made. It's at this point that the senior managers approve any expenditure required or ask for more work to be carried out on a proposal.

In the past year alone, ideas from employees have saved the site more than £350 000. One person submitted 40 ideas, most of which were implemented.

'We put about half the ideas into action, and there's more than 60 per cent participation in these projects, which is a tremendous figure,' Atkins says. 'There's a culture here now of everyone wanting to be involved and wanting to work towards improving the quality of everything we do.'

The company's £300 000 investment in its employees over the past five years has obviously paid off. As Dave Smith, the general manager, puts it: 'Improving capability through developing and involving our people has been the catalyst for our success.'

Source: Celia Poole *People Management*, 25 January 2002: 46, 47.

Questions

1 How do you think this training programme contributed to improving employee attitudes towards the company?

2 What aspects of a 'blended learning' approach can you identify at Fox's Biscuits?

3 In what ways has the HRD strategy of Fox's Biscuits paid off for all its stakeholders?

4 Could Fox's Biscuits be called a learning organisation?

(*A full answer to this question is given in the Lecturer's Guide that accompanies this textbook.*

References and further reading

Those texts marked with an asterisk are particularly recommended for further reading.

Alberga, T. (1997) 'Investors in People: time for a check up', *People Management*, 6 February, pp. 30–32.

Anon (1992) 'Call for training system reform', *Financial Times*, 11 December, p. 2.

Armstrong, G. (1996) 'A qualifications cuckoo in the competency nest?', *People Management*, 16 May, p. 23.

Ashton, D. and Sung, J. (1994) *The State, Economic Development and Skill Formation: A New Asian Model?*, Working Paper No. 3, Centre for Labour Market Studies. Leicester: University of Leicester.

Atkinson, M. and Elliott, L. (2000) 'UK fails to provide path from school to work', *Guardian*, 11 February, p. 6.

*Barrington, H. and Reid, M.A. (1999) *Training Interventions: Promoting Learning Opportunities*, 6th edn. London: Institute of Personnel and Development.

Barsoux, J.-L. and Lawrence, P. (1990) *Management in France*. London: Cassell.

BBC (1996) 'Train and prosper', *Analysis*, BBC Radio 4, broadcast 11 April.

Beresford, K. and Gaite, J. (1994) *Personnel Management*, April, pp. 38–41.

Bernhard, H.B. and Ingolis, C.A. (1988) 'Six lessons for the corporate classroom', *Harvard Business Review*, Vol. 66, No. 5, pp. 40–48.

Bournois, F. (1992) 'France', in Brewster, C., Hegewisch, A., Holden, L. and Lockhart, T. (eds) *The European Human Resource Management Guide*. London: Academic Press, pp. 113–162.

Brewster, C. (1999) 'Who is listening to HR?', *People Management*, 25 November, pp. 16–17.

Brewster, C., Hegewisch, A., Holden, L. and Lockhart, T. (eds) (1992) *The European Human Resource Management Guide*. London: Academic Press.

Brewster, C. and Hegewisch, A. (1993) 'A continent of diversity', *Personnel Management*, January, pp. 36–40.

Brockbank, A. and Beech, N. (1999) 'Guiding blight', *People Management*, 6 May, pp. 52–54.

Butters, T. (1996) 'Labour's plans for a skills revolution', *Guardian*, Careers Supplement, 27 April, pp. 2, 3.

Cannell, M. (1997) 'Practice makes perfect', *People Management*, 6 March, pp. 26–33.

Carnevale, A., Gainer, L. and Schulz, E. (1990) *Training the Technical Workforce*. San Francisco, Calif.: Jossey-Bass.

Chase, R. (1997) 'The knowledge based organisation: an international study', *Journal of Knowledge Management*, Vol. 1, No. 1, pp. 38–49.

Claydon, T. and Green, F. (1992) *The Effect of Unions on Training Provision*. Discussion Papers in Economics, No. 92/3, January. Leicester: University of Leicester.

Confederation of British Industry (1989) *Towards a Skills Revolution*. London: CBI.

Constable, J. and McCormick, R. (1987) *The Making of British Managers*. London: British Institute of Management.

Coopers & Lybrand Associates (1985) *A Challenge to Complacency: Changing Attitudes to Training*. London: MSC/National Economic Development Office.

Crouch, C., Finegold, D. and Sako, M. (2001) *Are Skills the Answer? The Political Economy of Skill Creation in Advanced Industrial Nations*, Oxford: Oxford University Press.

Dennis, C. (2002) 'A special blend', *People Management*, 7 March, p. 51

Department for Education and Employment (1999) *Learning to Succeed: A New Framework for Post 16 Learning*. Nottingham: DfEE Publications.

Department of Education and Science (1990) 'International statistical comparisons of the education and training of 16 to 18 year olds', *Statistical Bulletin*, 1/90, January. London: DES.

DfES (2001) *Education and Skills: Delivering Results*. A Strategy to 2006. London: Department for Education and Skills

Dixon, N. (1994) *The Organisational Learning Cycle*. London: McGraw-Hill.

*Dixon, N. (2000) *Common Knowledge*. Cambridge, Mass: Harvard Business School Press.

*Dore, R. and Sako, M. (1989) *How the Japanese Learn to Work*. London: Routledge.

Dulewicz, V. (1991) 'Improving assessment centres', *Personnel Management*, June, pp. 50–55.

Easterby-Smith, M. and Mackness, J. (1992) 'Completing the cycle of evaluation', *Personnel Management*, May, pp. 42–45.

Employment Department Group (1990) *What is an Investor in People?*, IIP 17, September. London: Employment Department Group.

Finegold, D. (1991) 'The implications of "Training in Britain" for the analysis of Britain's skills problem: a comment on Paul Ryan's "How much do employers spend on training?"', *Human Resource Management Journal*, Vol. 2, No. 1, pp. 110–115.

Ford, G. (1993) 'Losing ground', *New Statesman*, 19 March, p. 41.

Fowler, A. (1991) 'How to identify training needs', *Personnel Management Plus*, Vol. 2, No. 11, pp. 36–37.

Garvin, D. (1993) 'Building a learning organisation', in *Harvard Business Review on Knowledge Management*. Cambridge, Mass: Harvard Business School Press, pp. 47–80.

Gaugler, E. and Wiltz, S. (1992) 'Federal Republic of Germany', in Brewster, C., Hegewisch, A., Holden, L. and Lockhart, J. (eds) *The European Human Resource Management Guide*. London: Academic Press, pp. 163–228.

Hall, D.T. (1984) 'Human resource development and organisational effectiveness', in Fombrun, C., Tichy, N. and Devanna, M. (eds) *Strategic Human Resource Management*. New York: John Wiley.

Halls, W. D. (1990) *Comparative Education: Contemporary Issues and Trends*. London: Jessica Kingsley Publishers for UNESCO.

Handy, C. (1987) *The Making of Managers: A Report on Management Education, Training and Development in the United States, West Germany, France, Japan and the UK*. London: NEDO.

Harrison, R. (1992) *Training and Development*. London: Institute of Personnel Management.

Harrison, R. (1995) 'Carrots are better levers than sticks', *People Management*, 19 October, pp. 38–40.

Harrison, R. (1997) *Employee Development*. London: Institute of Personnel and Development.

Hillman, J. (1996) *University for Industry: Creating a National Learning Network*. London: Institute for Public Policy Research.

Hirsch, W. and Reilly, P. (1998) 'Cycling proficiency: how do large organisations identify their future skill needs among their thousands of employees?', *People Management*, 9 July, pp. 36–41.

Hofstede, G. (1984) *Culture's Consequences*. Newbury Park, Calif.: Sage.

Holden, L. (1991) 'European trends in training and development', *International Journal of Human Resource Management*, Vol. 2, No. 2, pp. 113–131.

Holden, L. and Livian, Y. (1992) 'Does strategic training policy exist? Some evidence from ten European countries', *Personnel Review*, Vol. 21, No. 1, pp. 12–23.

Industrial Society (1985) *Survey of Training Costs: New Series No. 1*. London: Industrial Society.

Institute of Manpower Studies (IMS) (1984) *Competence and Competition: Training and Education in the Federal Republic of Germany, the United States and Japan*. London: MSC/NEDO.

Investors in People (IIP) UK (1995) *The Investors in People Standard*. London: Investors in People UK.

Investors in People (IIP) UK (2000) *Management Report 1999, No. 10*. London: Investors in People UK.

Kandola, B. (1996) 'Are competencies too much of a good thing?', *People Management*, 2 May, p. 21.

Keep, E. (1989) 'Corporate training strategies: the vital component?', in Storey, J. (ed.) *New Perspectives on Human Resource Management*. London: Routledge.

Keep, E. (2002) 'Joined–up thinking', *People Management*, 12 September, p. 53.

Lähteenmäki, S., Holden, L. and Roberts, I. (eds) (1999) *HRM and the Learning Organisation*. Turku, Finland: Turku School of Economics and Business Administration, Series A-2.

Littlefield, D. and Welch, J. (1996) 'Training policy steals the political limelight', *People Management*, 4 April, pp. 5, 6.

Macleod, D. and Beavis, S. (1996) 'Britain trails rivals for want of skills', *Guardian*, 14 June, p. 6.

Mangham, I.L. and Silver, M.S. (1986) *Management Training: Context and Practice*, ESRC/DTI Report. Bath: University of Bath, School of Management.

Manpower Services Commission (1981a) *Glossary of Training Terms*. London: HMSO.

Manpower Services Commission (1981b) *A Framework for the Future: A Sector by Sector Review of Industrial and Commercial Training*. London: MSC.

Masie, E. (1999) 'E-learning: joined-up thinking', *People Management*, 25 November, pp. 32–36.

Mayo, A. (1998) Knowledge management: memory bankers', *People Management*, 22 January, pp. 34–38.

Merrick, N. (1995) 'Moving up the class?', *People Management*, 30 November, pp. 8–9.

Mumford, A. (2002) 'Horses for courses', *People Management*, 27 June, p. 51.

Nadler, L. (1984) *The Handbook of Human Resource Development*. New York: John Wiley.

National Advisory Council for Education and Training Targets (NACETT) (1996) *Skills for 2000: Report on Progress Towards the National Training Targets for Education and Training*. London: NACETT.

Nonaka, I. (1991) 'The knowledge creating company', in *Harvard Business Review on Knowledge Management*. Cambridge, Mass.: Harvard Business School Press, pp. 21–45.

Pedler, M., Burgoyne, J. and Boydell, T. (1988) *Learning Company Project Report*, Sheffield: Training Agency.

*Pedler, M., Burgoyne, J. and Boydell, T. (1997) *The Learning Company: A Strategy for Sustainable Development*. London: McGraw-Hill.

Pickard, J. (1992) 'Job evaluation and total management come under fire', *Personnel Management*, May, p. 17.

Pickard, J. (1997) 'The New Deal: just the job', *People Management*, 28 August, pp. 32–35.

Pollock, L. (1999) 'Upskill task', *People Management*, 14 October, pp. 58–60.

Prais, S., Jarvis, V. and Wagner, K. (1989) 'Productivity and vocational skills in services in Britain and Germany', *National Institute Economic Review*, No. 130, November, pp. 52–74.

Prais, S. and Steedman, H. (1986) 'Vocational training in France and Britain', *National Institute Economic Review*, No. 116, May, pp. 45–56.

Prais, S. and Wagner, K. (1988) 'Productivity and management: the training of foremen in Britain and Germany', *National Institute Economic Review*, No. 123, pp. 34–37.

Price Waterhouse (1989) *Doing Business in France*. Paris and London: Price Waterhouse.

Price Waterhouse Cranfield Project (1990) *Report on International Strategic Human Resource Management*. London: Price Waterhouse.

Rainbird, H. and Maguire, M. (1993) 'When corporate need supersedes employee development', *Personnel Management*, February, pp. 34–37.

Rana, E. (1999a) 'Dim view of New Deal', *People Management*, 3 June, p. 14.

Rana, E. (1999b) 'New Deal firms come under fire for training deficiencies', *People Management*, 19 August, p. 18.

Rana, E. (2000) 'National Skills Task Force rules out levy,' *People Management*, 20 January, p. 13.

Rana, E. (2002) 'Ground force', *People Management*, 27 June, pp. 42–46.

Reid, M.A., Barrington, H. and Kenney, J. (1992) *Training Interventions: Managing Employee Development*, 3rd edn. London: Institute of Personnel Management.

Reynolds, J. (2002) 'Method and madness: the real value of e-learning', *People Management*, 4 April, pp. 42, 43.

Roberts, Z. (2002a) 'Unions "to lead in training"', *People Management*, 29 August, p. 7.

Roberts, Z. (2002b) 'The blame game', *People Management*, 16 May, p. 15.

Rose, R. and Wignanek, G. (1990) *Training Without Trainers? How Germany Avoids Britain's Supply-side Bottleneck*. London: Anglo-German Foundation.

Ryan, P. (1991) 'How much do employers spend on training? An assessment of "Training in Britain" estimates', *Human Resource Management Journal*, Vol. 1, No. 4, pp. 55–57.

Saggers, R. (1994) 'Training climbs the corporate agenda', *Personnel Management*, July, pp. 40–45.

*Senge, P. (1990) *The Fifth Discipline: The Art and Practice of the Learning Organisation*. London: Century.

Sloman, M. (1999) 'Learning Centre: seize the day', *People Management*, 20 May, p. 31.

Sloman, M. (2001) 'Plug, but no play: the hype surrounding e-learning', *People Management*, 13 September, p. 57.

Sloman, M. (2002) 'Don't believe the hype', *People Management*, 21 March, p. 41.

Smith, A (1999) 'Get with the programme', *People Management*, 3 June, p. 33.

Spellman, R. (2002) 'Raising the standard', *People Management*, 18 April, p. 23.

Steedman, H. (1988) 'Vocational training in France and Britain: mechanical and electrical craftsmen', *National Institute Economic Review*, No. 126, November, pp. 57–71.

Stevens, J. (2002) 'A foundation for the future', *People Management*, 8 August, pp. 47–48.

Storey, J. (1991) 'Do the Japanese make better managers?' *Personnel Management*, August, pp. 24–28.

Syrett, M. and Lammiman, S. (1994) 'Developing the peripheral worker', *Personnel Management*, July, pp. 28–31.

Targett, S. (1996) 'Shepherd admits skills shortage', *Times Higher Education Supplement*, 14 June, p. 3.

Taylor, P. and Thackwray, B. (1995) *Investors in People Explained*. London: Kogan Page.

Thorn, J. (1988) 'Making of a Meister', *Industrial Society Magazine*, June, pp. 19–21.

Thurow, L. (1992) *Head to Head: The Coming Economic Battle Among Japan, Europe and America*. London: Nicholas Brealey.

Tobin, A. (2002) 'Investors in People: standard bearers or just a bad joke?' *Guardian*, Jobs and Money Section, 12 October, pp. 26-27.

Townsend, T. (1992) 'How the lead body sees it', *Personnel Management*, November, p. 39.

Training Agency (1989) *Training in Britain*. Norwich: HMSO.

Tyson, S. and Fell, A. (1995) 'A focus on skills, not organisations', *People Management*, pp. 42–45.

Welch, J. (1996a) 'HR qualifications get the go-ahead at last', *People Management*, 30 May, p. 11.

Welch, J. (1996b) 'Britain slipping behind in the race for skills', *People Management*, 27 June, p. 11.

 For multiple choice questions, exercises and annotated weblinks specific to this chapter visit this book's website at www.booksites.net/beardwell

Management development

Mike Doyle

► To explain the meaning and nature of management development in organisations.

► To acknowledge the significance of management development to organisational success.

► To contrast 'piecemeal' and open system approaches to management development.

► To examine the methods, techniques and processes used to develop managers.

► To draw attention to the way management development can be varied to meet special needs and different contexts.

► To speculate about the future direction of management development in the UK and beyond.

Introduction

The main aim of this chapter is to assist you in exploring contemporary management development from within increasingly complex and diverse organisational contexts. Our exploration begins with a discussion of management development: how it is defined, and how it might be differentiated from management training and education. Consideration is then given to the role and objectives of management development and its contribution to organisational strategies.

We then move to examine the more functional aspects of organising, implementing and evaluating management development programmes. Here, the analysis begins with an examination of those who have responsibility for development and how that responsibility is shared. We affirm the need for management development to be supported by a robust HR infrastructure. We then explore the range of formal and less formal methods and techniques employed in the development of managers – making the argument that the choice and implementation of methods must be contingent to meet diverse organisational or individual situations.

Picking up this theme of contingency and diversity, the chapter then explores how management development meets special needs in different contexts. Areas that are examined include management development in the public sector and small firms and the special needs of professionals, international and women managers.

Management development, like management itself, is now in a state of considerable flux. As you would expect, this is giving rise to considerable controversy and tension, and against that backdrop, the final section of the chapter examines some of the issues that face management development in the future.

The chapter concludes with questions, exercises and a case study. These will help you to review and consolidate what you have learned. There is also a list of recommended and further reading included for guidance and reference purposes.

 # Defining management development

■ What is management?

The nature of management and the work that managers do was explored in detail in Chapter 3. In that chapter, an argument was made that managers have to deal with the ambiguities and complexities that arise from tensions in the employment relationship, the different aims and interests that reside in organisations and the varying interpretations of managerial roles and what they represent. It would appear reasonable to contend, therefore, that management development approaches should seek to accommodate the functional complexities of the managerial role and the diverse needs of those individuals who occupy those roles. For instance, different people, at different times, have different conceptions of what 'management' is about. This will shape individual views about the development of managers and this, in turn, may give rise to a number of tensions and contradictions which themselves have to be managed (Watson, 1994, 2002). Logically, if development activity is to be effective, it has to be pragmatic in its approach and implemented within what managers consider is *their* unique organisational context. It has to help them adapt and cope with the diversity and complexity that resides therein and meet their specific needs (Hales, 1993). In other words, any investment in development has to be congruent with the 'reality' of what managers do, and not (however well intentioned) be rooted in abstract or increasingly redundant models of what others might think they should do or used to do (Salaman, 1995).

It therefore follows that during an era of rapid and far-reaching change, the use of rigid and inflexible approaches to management development can no longer be tolerated if they create frustration and disillusionment among managers. Such approaches will inevitably lead to lower levels of morale and motivation amongst managers and ultimately waste resources and threaten future organisational success (Doyle, 1995, 2000; Currie, 1999).

As you study the rest of this chapter you will become aware that there are in existence different interpretations of what we mean by the terms 'management', 'managing' and 'the manager'. You should also note that these differences will influence the way organisations, professional bodies, government agencies and academic institutions view and approach management development. This gives rise to a number of issues and debates and these will be identified and critically explored throughout the chapter.

■ What is management development?

There are many definitions of management development to select from, but most contemporary definitions share the characteristics contained in the view of development suggested by Thomson *et al.* (2001).

We have used the term in a comprehensive sense to encompass the different ways in which managers improve their capabilities. It includes management education, which is often taken to refer to formal, structured learning in an institutional context, and management training which is often used to mean acquiring knowledge and skills related to work requirements, also by formal means. But our use of the term 'development' goes beyond the sum of these to mean a wider process than the formal learning of knowledge and skills, which includes informal and experiential modes of human capital formation. Management development is thus a multi-faceted process in which some aspects are easier to identify and measure than others.   (Thomson *et al.*, 2001 p. 10)

A key point to note from Thomson *et al.*'s definition is the distinction they make between what constitutes management education, training and development. Unfortunately, these terms are often used in overlapping and interchangeable ways within organisations and as such they can generate confusion, leading to ineffective development. For example, management development is often seen as synonymous with 'sending people on training or education courses' – even when such courses may be the least appropriate way to develop individuals or groups of managers and may even generate resistance and frustration (Roberts and McDonald, 1995; Mole 1996, 2000; Currie, 1999).

 ## Management development as a strategic imperative

Major environmental shifts are now demanding a more strategic perspective from those who manage and lead in organisations. Many organisations are now 'globalising' in their quest for markets that will bring them new opportunities for growth and prosperity. Advances in technology, especially in the field of information technology and telecommunications, are leading to greater efficiencies, reduced costs and opportunities to launch new products and services. The nature of organisational life itself is changing.

BOX 10.1   A management development strategy for Unilever

Unilever is a huge international organisation with 1000 brands, employing some 255 000 people in 300 operating units across 88 countries. In recent years the business strategy has been refocused to achieve significant economies of scale, reduce the number of products offered and increase penetration in successful product markets.

This refocusing has had a major impact on HR strategies and policies. One area that the company has identified as a priority has been the development of its managers as 'global players' with the ability to implement the new business plan.

Success in developing managers is based on the following principles:

- Management development is a business responsibility.
- Responsibility for development is shared between Unilever and the manager.
- Individuals drive their own learning and development.
- Explicit responsibilities are placed on line and senior managers for developing their managers.

Unilever aims to create a 'seamless' system of management development – delivered in one language worldwide in a way that facilitates the transfer of people across different operating units. A framework of worldwide competences and skills is available on the Internet for managers to plan their personal development. An emphasis is placed on managers developing both professional and generalist skills that are transferable to different global contexts. Development activity is closely linked to performance management and measurable outcomes. Managers are required to produce an improvement development plan and advancement is tightly linked to meeting performance targets.

Source: Adapted from Reitsma, 2001

Organisations are becoming more complex and diverse. Change and its impact is now the dominant feature of organisational life. Employee adaptability and flexibility are the essential characteristics for organisational survival and success. As a consequence, organisations are now espousing values that regard people not as costs to be minimised but as assets to be maintained and developed.

Such changes are setting new challenges for managers and employees alike. Managers are being challenged to respond as strategic leaders and perform in the role of change agent (Salaman, 1995; Rosenfeld and Wilson, 1999). Their task is to establish a clear mission, linked to a set of strategic business objectives that enable organisations to acquire, control and allocate resources to maximise the opportunities available and to minimise any threats to their survival and success. But managers need the knowledge and skills to do this and in this sense, management development has now become a *strategic imperative* within many organisations (Woodall and Winstanley, 1998; Thomson *et al.*, 2001).

An illustration of how management development is being integrated with and used to support business strategy can be found in the major international company Unilever (see Box 10.1).

■ Devising a management development policy

> Management development will fail if there is no clear policy. (Margerison, 1991)

Policy statements are useful because they express an organisation's commitment to development, and set out clearly a framework within which it can take place. It makes it explicit who is responsible for development, the support that is available, methods used etc. Research has also suggested that those organisations having a formal policy for developing their managers 'undertook significantly more management training than did companies without such a policy' (Thomson *et al.*, 2001).

However, what is sometimes less clear is the extent to which organisations are committed to and prepared to implement their policies. Policies may be viewed with some scepticism – especially during times of radical downsizing involving the loss of managerial jobs (Thomson *et al.*, 2001). There are also difficulties evaluating the effectiveness of policies in achieving desired outcomes. The difficulties associated with evaluating management development outcomes will be explored later in the chapter.

● Extracts from a management development policy

- We accept that it is the Group's responsibility to provide every manager with the opportunity to develop his/her ability and potential so that he/she does their existing job effectively.
- We believe that people derive more satisfaction from working when they themselves have helped to establish and are committed to the objective of their job.
- The policy requires that through the Divisions we create an environment in which all managers contribute to the objectives of the business to their maximum ability.
- We have undertaken to support this policy by providing an organisational structure within which the responsibilities of each manager are clearly defined.
- We expect that increasing the influence and scope for initiative and self-motivation of managers and their subordinates will lead to increasing job satisfaction and to direct improvement in the Group's commercial performance.

Source: Mumford, 1997: 11. This extract is taken from *Management Development* (1997) by Alan Mumford and is reproduced by permission of the publishers, The Institute of Personnel and Development

Does your organisation have a management development policy? If it does, how far does it reflect the aims listed in the extract above?

If it doesn't have a policy, what has been the impact on management development outcomes?

Having determined its policy guidelines, the next step for the organisation is to consider how it should *approach* the development of its managers.

Organisational approaches to management development

■ Why develop this manager?

Having devised a clear and communicated policy for management development, those responsible for implementing development need to think through and be able to justify why they are developing an individual manager (or a group of managers). The reasons for developing managers are varied. For example:

- to introduce new attitudes and behaviours to promote culture change;
- to encourage more empowerment and innovation;
- to develop the knowledge and the skills to seek new market opportunities;
- to develop the knowledge to maximise the use of new technology;
- to facilitate the introduction of new systems, processes and working practices.

You will have noted that in addition to developing new knowledge and skills, management development is a way of shaping individual and collective attitudes and behaviours – an important consideration when implementing organisational change.

As well as organisations ensuring that development is linked to the philosophies and strategic objectives of the organisation, they must also take account of individual needs, expectations and aspirations. This can often be a difficult balance to achieve, and frequently becomes a source of tension (Hopfl and Dawes, 1995; Currie, 1999).

For instance, senior managers who are seeking a quick-fix solution to a deep-rooted managerial or organisational problem will often consult with development 'experts', who are only too pleased to solve the problem by introducing them to the latest development fad. When the 'quick-fix' solution fails to produce the anticipated results or (worse) exacerbates an existing problem, management development is at risk of being undermined and discredited (Roberts and McDonald, 1995; Currie, 1999). It is therefore vital that organisations view management development as a long-term investment and select an approach that is suited to their specific needs and requirements.

■ Selecting the right approach

Management development can be approached in a number of different ways. Mumford (1997) describes three different types of approach that are broadly representative of current UK management development (see the box on the next page).

Type 1: 'Informal managerial' – accidental processes

Characteristics:
- occurs within manager's activities
- explicit intention is task performance
- no clear development objectives
- unstructured in development terms
- not planned in advance
- owned by managers.

Development consequences:
- learning real, direct, unconscious, insufficient.

Type 2: 'Integrated managerial' – opportunistic processes

Characteristics:
- occurs within managerial activities
- explicit intention is both task performance and development
- clear development objectives
- structured for development by boss and subordinate
- planned beforehand and/or reviewed subsequently as learning experiences
- owned by managers.

Development consequences:
- learning is real, direct, conscious, more substantial.

Type 3: 'Formalised development' – planned processes

Characteristics:
- often away from normal managerial activities
- explicit intention is development
- clear development objectives
- structured for development by developers
- planned beforehand or reviewed subsequently as learning experiences
- owned more by developers than managers.

Development consequences:
- learning may be real (through a job) or detached (through a course)
- is more likely to be conscious, relatively infrequent.

(This article first appeared in *Management Education and Development*, Vol. 18, Part 3 (1987). We are grateful to the editor for permission to reproduce it here.)

Burgoyne (1988) argues that management development may be considered as progressing through different levels of maturity (see Table 10.1). At Level 1 there is no systematic approach to management development, and at Level 6 management development not only shapes and informs corporate strategy, it actually enhances the process of strategy formation. In practice, management development approaches for most organisations rarely extend beyond Levels 1 and 2. Those who reach Levels 5 and 6 find it is 'often precariously achieved and lost' (p. 44). Burgoyne argues that to progress through the levels of maturity to the point where management development is making the fullest contribution to organisation development demands a much more holistic approach to development. In this approach, both 'hard' (roles, duties, technical competence, etc.) and 'soft' (career, quality of life, ethos, values, etc.) managerial issues are considered when framing approaches to development.

Table 10.1 Levels of maturity or organisational management development

1	2	3	4	5	6
No systematic management development	Isolated tactical management development	Integrated and coordinated structural and development tactics	A management development strategy to implement corporate policy	Management development strategy input to corporate policy formation	Strategic development of the management of corporate policy
No systematic or deliberate management development in a structural or developmental sense; total reliance on laissez-faire, uncontrived processes of management development	There are isolated and ad hoc tactical management development activities, of either structural or developmental kinds, or both, in response to local problems, crises, or sporadically identified general problems	The specific management development tactics that impinge directly on the individual manager, of career structure management, and of assisting learning, are integrated and coordinated	A management development strategy plays its part in implementing corporate policies through managerial human resource planning, and providing a strategic framework and direction for the tactics of career structure management and of learning, education and training	Management development processes feed information into corporate policy decision-making processes on the organisation's managerial assets, strengths, weaknesses and potential, and contribute to the forecasting and analysis of the manageability of proposed projects, ventures, changes	Management development processes enhance the nature and quality of corporate policy-forming processes, which they also inform and help implement

Source: Burgoyne (1988)

ACTIVITY   Study Mumford and Burgoyne's models. Identify where you believe your organisation is positioned in relation to the different 'types' and 'levels of maturity'.

A 'piecemeal' approach

Many approaches to development have characteristics similar to Mumford's Type 1 and Type 3 development and Burgoyne's Levels 1 and 2 and accordingly may be labelled as *piecemeal*. Implementing piecemeal approaches will almost certainly lead to inefficient and ineffective development.

Piecemeal approaches to development are characterised by the following:

- There is no management development infrastructure. Development is not linked to business strategy. Activities are unrelated, and lack overall direction or philosophy. They fail to reinforce each other, and reduce the potential for organisational effectiveness.
- Development often focuses on the needs of the organisation, and fails to meet the learning needs and aspirations of individuals and groups.
- Development is largely defined in terms of a range of universal, off-the-shelf internal or external courses.
- There is tacit support for management education and training because it is seen as a 'good thing to be doing' irrespective of organisational needs.

- There is a lack of common vision among those responsible for management development. For instance, some managers see development as a central part of their job, others see it as peripheral and a nuisance.
- Management development effort can be wasted because it is used as a solution to the wrong problem. Rather than developing managers, the correct solution may be to change aspects of organisation structure or systems.
- It is difficult to evaluate the effectiveness of a piecemeal approach that lacks clear direction and established objectives.

Sadly, piecemeal and fragmented approaches to management development are all too commonplace (Roberts and McDonald, 1995; Mole, 2000). Such approaches are a significant contributor to the failure of management development to fulfil personal and organisational expectations (Temporal, 1990; Mumford, 1997; Mole, 2000). Not only do they waste investment, time and effort, there is also a risk of damage to existing levels of morale and commitment among managers as efforts to develop them founder on organisational barriers to change (Doyle, 1995, 2000a). As Molander and Winterton (1994) contend:

> Where such conditions exist, what is required is an organisation-wide assessment of the elements in the culture which require changing, followed by an effective change programme. Focusing attention on individual managers . . . will not bring about required change. In this case the organisation itself should be the focus of change. (p. 89)

■ An open systems view of management development

In Chapter 3, the *open systems model* was introduced as a way of conceptualising and making sense of the complexity of organisational life (Kast and Rosenweig, 1985; Morgan, 1997). In this section, it will be argued that if organisations can be persuaded to adopt an open systems perspective in relation to management development, then they are likely to overcome many of the problems created by a piecemeal approach to development. Instead of looking at management development in isolation (as a closed system) it is now being considered as an integral part of a wider organisational system, and, more importantly, is linked to the context and 'reality' of managerial work (see, for example, Mumford's Type 2 development).

Viewing management development from an open systems perspective recognises and focuses attention on the following factors:

- Management development is viewed as both a *system* and a *process* (see Figure 10.1). It is composed of identifiable parts or components that act together in an organised way. Inputs to the process of development are transformed into a range of outputs that affect both the individual and the organisation in some way.
- Figure 10.1 also demonstrates that in an open system the management development process *interacts with* and *is influenced by* variables from other environmental and organisational subsystems (structural, social, technological and cultural). For example, prevailing ideologies, values and beliefs within the organisation represent a *cultural subsystem*. Management development can be used as a way of reinforcing this cultural subsystem by shaping and moulding managers' attitudes and values and exerting pressure upon them to conform and display 'acceptable' behaviour patterns – an important consideration during times of radical change.
- Management development becomes *integrated* with, and *mutually dependent* upon, other organisational subsystems, activities and processes. For example, as we saw earlier in this chapter, the system for strategic planning and the setting of organisational

Figure 10.1 Management development as an open system

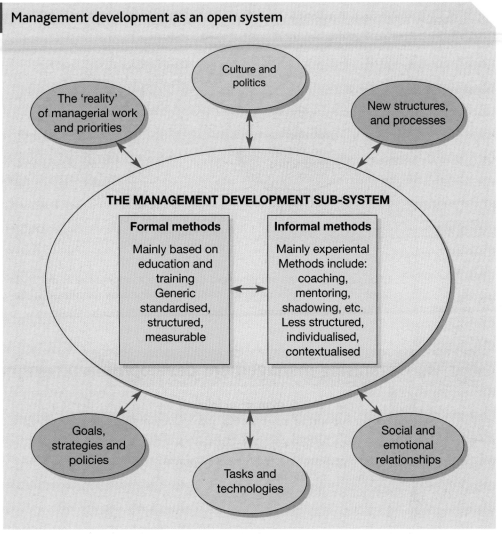

goals must interact with a management development system that seeks to develop the managerial skills and knowledge to organise and implement the business strategy (Ready *et al.*, 1994; Thomson *et al.*, 2001).

● Such an interaction means that *if you develop the manager, you develop the organisation*, and vice versa (see Figure 10.2). As the organisation changes and develops, so positive influencing 'loops' are created that lead to the further development of managers (Morgan, 1997). Similarly, as managers are developed, positive influencing 'loops' lead to changes in the organisation which produce greater effectiveness. It can, of course, work the other way. Poor or ineffective development can create negative influencing 'loops' that undermine organisational or managerial effectiveness. The need therefore is to focus on *managing* management development as well as *doing* management development.

● Viewing management development in open systems terms reveals the full extent of its influence on the organisation, and is likely to lead to more detailed and objective assessment of the performance and overall effectiveness of managers who are developed.

In the subsequent sections of this chapter, an open systems perspective of management development will become the basis for both theoretical and practical analysis and discussion.

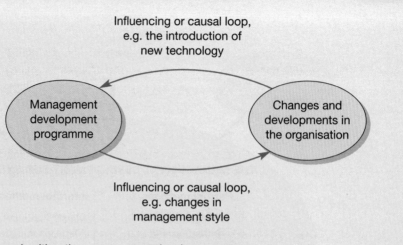

Figure 10.2   Develop the manager, develop the organisation

Organising management development programmes

Working from open system principles, if management development is to succeed it requires the support of a robust HR infrastructure that addresses issues such as:

- who is responsible for development;
- how managers are selected for development;
- performance management;
- career progression.

Determining who is responsible for management development

If a development programme is to be successfully planned and implemented, there has to be clear and unambiguous allocation of responsibility and a willingness to accept that responsibility by the parties involved.

Traditionally, responsibility for development has rested with the HR function, with some input from the manager's boss. The individual manager was often passive in the process: they were only required to 'turn up and be developed'.

To be effective, development demands the involvement of a range of stakeholders, or 'helpers', each of whom will have an impact on the development process and its outcomes (Mabey and Salaman, 1995; Mumford, 1997). Figure 10.3 identifies a number of key stakeholders who each share a measure of responsibility. At the core of the process, the main responsibilities are shared between the personnel specialist, the boss and the individual (Davis, 1990).

An active process of discussion and negotiation should ensure that they each accept and own a share of the responsibility for setting development objectives, planning and implementing the process. However, although these three parties are central to the development process, other stakeholders will have an input (Mabey and Salaman, 1995; Mumford, 1997). For example, the role of senior management is vital in terms of resourcing, commitment and establishing a supportive culture. Colleagues and mentors will advise and assist in overcoming particular problems and issues (Mumford, 1997).

Figure 10.3   Who is responsible for management development? A stakeholder model

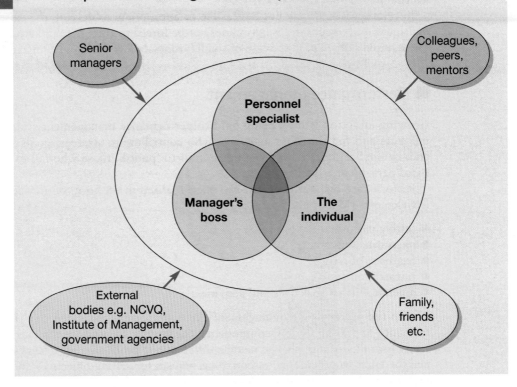

ACTIVITY   Prepare a list of those who are responsible for your development. How effective is the support you receive? Does it need to be improved in any way?

National bodies such as the Chartered Management Institute, NVQ lead bodies and Learning and Enterprise Councils are influential in shaping management development policies and direction through mechanisms such as funding, reports, lobbying, and contact with industry representatives. Similarly, academic and vocational institutions are able to influence development methods and agendas through their research, teaching, awards and other activities (see Chapter 9). And finally it must be remembered that the individual's friends and family have a crucial role to play in providing support and encouragement (Mumford, 1997). As Mabey and Salaman (1995) point out, the linkages between each stakeholder are complex and each will 'help shape the ethos and practice of training and development within organisations' (p. 176).

■ Ensuring the availability of suitable managers

To achieve their strategic objectives, organisations must ensure that they have the right numbers of managers, with the right skills and available at the right time. A core element of human resource planning (explored in more detail in Chapter 5) is the assessment of existing managerial stock and, where necessary, the replenishment of that stock through the recruitment of new managers. A *managerial audit* is normally carried out, utilising information from sources such as assessment centres, performance appraisals, personnel files and discussions with bosses, to reveal the skills available to meet forecast demand. These skills are then compared with the organisation's HRM plan, and development objectives are established (Vineall, 1994; Woodall and Winstanley, 1998; Prokopenko, 1998).

In certain cases, it may not be feasible or appropriate to develop the existing stock of managers, and organisations may choose or be forced to enter the marketplace to 'buy-in' the required skills, e.g. in the case of small businesses (Woodall and Winstanley, 1998).

■ Performance management

Growing attention is now being paid to performance management systems that both motivate and reward those managers who contribute to strategic goals and objectives and, by implication, to exert sanctions on or to 'punish' those who fail to deliver anticipated performance levels.

Performance management can be conceptualised in the form of a cycle consisting of five elements (Mabey and Salaman, 1995):

● setting performance objectives;
● measuring outcomes;
● feedback of results;
● rewards linked to outcomes;
● amendments to objectives and activities.

Within the performance management cycle, performance-related pay (PRP) and performance appraisal are key components: the former to produce the extrinsic financial rewards in the form of shares, income differentials, profit-sharing schemes and bonuses, and the latter to provide the essential mechanism for setting objectives and feeding back performance criteria (Hendry, 1995).

In terms of management development, there is a close interaction with performance management systems. First and foremost, performance management systems must be seen to reward personal development and achievement. This is leading a number of organisations to link their systems of reward more closely to the attainment of higher levels of competence, which is one way of overcoming 'the subjectivity and arbitrariness of assessment' (Hendry, 1995: 309). The achievement of objectives is also closely linked to management training and education, which act to provide the skills and knowledge required to meet objectives. Performance appraisal provides the forum for identifying development needs. It also serves as the mechanism for feeding back information to the manager about current levels of performance, enabling them to identify and negotiate adjustments or further development needs.

Although the focus of performance management is on extrinsic rewards, intrinsic rewards through praise, encouragement and reassurance are vital components in management development, particularly in the area of coaching and mentoring. For example, for younger managers who may be on fast-track graduate programmes (see section on graduate development later in this chapter), continuous positive feedback during the early stages of the programme is vital to sustain motivation and commitment. Older, more experienced managers also need regular praise, encouragement and, above all, reassurance that their skills and experience are still valued and appreciated, and that any investment in personal development is seen as being positive from the organisation's viewpoint (Mumford, 1997).

■ Career development

Management development can only be effective if careful consideration is given to career paths and opportunities for promotion and progression (Mumford, 1997; Margerison, 1994a). This requires a well-prepared human resource plan that is future oriented. In the past, career development very much reflected more traditional organisational structures and cultures. Hierarchical progression was seen to be upwards through clearly defined junior, middle and senior management roles based on tenure and the possession of specialist skills and the display of patterns of expected behaviours. However, in the face of radical organisational change such pathways are now giving way to a more uncertain and less clearly defined progression where 'automatic' promotion is no longer available to many. Citing research by Benbow, Thomson *et al.* (2001) capture the mood amongst UK and US managers about their future career development:

> A high proportion of respondents do not feel in control of their future career development. The pace of change over the last decade has shattered career and financial expectations, generating a need for individuals to re-examine many of the inherited wisdoms of the past. The demise of the job for life and the trend towards a wholly flexible employment market are clear examples of the extent to which new agendas are being set.
>
> (p. 181)

Such concerns reflect in part the emphasis now being placed on managers to ensure their employability and marketability. This in turn reflects a redefining of the psychological contract that exists between managers and their employing organisation (Herriot and Pemberton, 1995). In terms of career progression, the emphasis is shifting towards individuals who display greater flexibility, adaptability and personal characteristics such as emotional resilience (Watson, 2002). Some will find themselves facing a 'boundaryless' career in which there will be less job security and career progression opportunities will be limited. Instead, career progression is likely to involve a greater emphasis on horizontal or diagonal rather than vertical movement, e.g. projects, overseas secondments and postings, departmental and job shifts, internal consultancy roles, acting as mentors and coaches etc. (Arnold, 1997; Thomson *et al.*, 2001).

In terms of management development strategies, some significant rethinking of HR policies and approaches will be required at both an individual and an organisational level if they are to fit and support these significant shifts in management career prospects. Organisational policies in terms of career planning workshops, mentoring arrangements, performance management systems and processes etc. will all require reviewing. The new imperative for organisations will be to ensure that their managers are made fully aware of the realities of the changing nature of their careers, with concomitant efforts being made to reward, retain and motivate those who find themselves moving sideways, not upwards. The risk of not attending to these issues is that the relationship between managers and their employing organisation becomes one that is short termist and calculative, stifling innovation, creativity and a developmental outlook (Watson and Harris, 1999). Unfortunately, there is evidence to suggest that some organisations appear to be unaware or unwilling to communicate the harsh reality of the changing nature of managerial careers to their managers.

> The picture emerging then is one of traditional career management structures and approaches struggling to balance and reconcile organisational and individual goals which themselves are changing in response to an increasingly self-centred, instrumental climate.
>
> (Doyle, 2000b: 231)

In respect of management development approaches therefore, it is important that these reflect shifts in philosophy about managerial careers and that they encourage managers first and foremost to take a greater responsibility for their own development. In addition, managers will require the knowledge and skills to progress horizontally and diagonally, e.g. how to work in and lead a project team or how to make a success of an overseas posting. In this sense, management development approaches will have to reflect the required self-reliant, adaptive and intellectual capacities that such career moves suggest.

Implementing and evaluating management development programmes

Earlier in this chapter the question was posed: 'Why are we developing this manager?' In this section attention will turn to the techniques and choices available to organisations when they seek to implement their development programmes. Again, in keeping with our open systems principles and ideas, it is important that any implementation plan acknowledges the diversity of management roles and responsibilities and the contexts in which they operate.

Acknowledging the diversity of management

We saw earlier that development has to be linked to the reality of managerial work. When organising development programmes, it is important to cater for the diversity of management skills, attitudes and experience that reside within the organisation. One useful example is given by Odiorne (1984), who advocates a *portfolio* approach to development to improve the overall efficiency of the process and ensure the optimal allocation of resources. This requires organisations to make a range of decisions and develop a 'mix' of contingent objectives and techniques arranged to match the profile of the management team in the organisation.

A portfolio approach to development

'*Stars*': high-performing, high-potential managers

Aim:
- create challenge
- provide incentives and reward
- allocate adequate resources and effort.

'*Workhorses*': high-performing, limited-potential managers

Aim:
- emphasise value and worth of experience
- motivate and reassure
- utilise experience on assignments, projects, coaching.

'*Problem employees*': high-potential, underperforming managers

Aim:
- identify weaknesses
- channel resources to address weaknesses
- regular performance monitoring and feedback.

'*Deadwood*': low-performing, low-potential managers
Aim:
- identify weaknesses, resolvable?
- if not, consider release, early retirement, demotion.

(Adapted from Odiorne, 1984)

Shaping development activity in this way to accommodate the diverse needs of the managers and their employing organisations requires certain questions to be considered before development commences:

- *Who is being developed?*
  - Is it older managers seeking new challenges or younger 'high fliers' on a fast-track development programme?
  - Is it senior managers seeking to enhance their strategic skills, middle managers seeking to update and broaden existing skills, or junior-level managers looking to acquire additional managerial skills?
  - Is it technical specialists or professionals seeking to expand their cross-functional capabilities, or supervisors receiving training for the first time?
- *What is being developed?*
  - Does the programme seek to develop new attitudes and values, as in the case of a recently privatised public utility or a private sector company that has just undergone a takeover?
  - Does the programme aim to develop technical, financial, business or interpersonal skills? What are the priorities?
  - Does the programme seek to change existing managerial behaviours and styles to reflect an internal organisational restructuring, such as the introduction of new technology?
- *Where will the development take place?*
  - Should development be on-the-job in the office, factory or sales territory, or off-the-job in a residential hall, academic institution or individual's home, or a combination of all of these?
- *What are the most appropriate techniques to achieve the best fit between individual and organisational requirements?*
  - What are the most cost-effective/appropriate techniques available?
  - How much scope is there to accommodate individual learning needs and preferences?
  - How much choice is delegated to the individual over the choice of development techniques?
  - How is conflict resolved between individual and organisational needs?

(You should note that some of these questions are explored later in the chapter in the section that deals with special needs in different contexts.)

It is only when these questions have been considered that the organisation is in a position to construct a framework of development that best fits its needs and the needs of its managers. In practice, however, this can prove problematical. Organisations may be unclear about the aims and objectives of their development activities and how they meet their needs, e.g. longer-term supply of future managers or short-term expediency to meet sudden strategic changes in structure? There may be confusion about different learning methods and what they mean in different contexts, e.g. are special projects the same as in-company job rotation? There may be a failure to fully assess the implications of different methods when they are used in these different contexts, e.g. managers may prefer on-the-job, work-based development (Woodall, 2000). But without effective support from motivated and competent line managers and HRD professionals, such approaches may become piecemeal and ineffective or even lead to resentment and frustration (Doyle, 1995; Currie, 1999).

Development needs analysis

If managers are to be developed effectively, their individual development needs must be assessed in a careful and systematic fashion. There are several ways to do this. Traditionally, the diagnosis of development needs for managers has often relied upon an ad-hoc and piecemeal process of selective observation in the role joined with the 'constructive' but often subjective input from others in the organisation (usually senior managers or HR professionals).

To counter this, organisations are turning to performance appraisal as a structured way of identifying the skills and behaviours that are required to meet business objectives (Mumford, 1997; Woodall and Winstanley, 1998). During the appraisal process, both the individual and their boss review performance against departmental/organisational objectives and other performance criteria to determine development needs. Once analysed, the development needs form the basis of a negotiated and agreed *personal development plan*, which is regularly reviewed and modified in the light of changing organisational and individual circumstances.

> **ACTIVITY** Have you got a personal development plan? If you haven't, make a mental note to discuss this with your boss at your next appraisal interview. If you have got a plan, when was it last reviewed? Is it still valid and up to date?

In addition to performance appraisal, more and more organisations are turning to the use of assessment/development 'centres' to analyse development needs. These 'centres' are 'workshops which measure the abilities of participants against the agreed success criteria for a job or role' (Lee and Beard, 1994). It should also be borne in mind that the term 'development centre' relates to the process of identifying needs, not to a specific place (Munchus and McArthur, 1991).

The main aim of a development centre is to 'obtain the best possible indication of people's actual or potential competence to perform at the target job or job level' (Woodruffe, 1993: 2). Most development centres operate in the following way:

- There is careful selection of job-related criteria. These may be in the form of competences, dimensions, attributes, critical success factors, etc.
- A group of managers is identified and brought together in the form of a workshop normally lasting one or two days. In the workshops a series of diagnostic instruments and/or multiple assessment techniques are administered that aim to measure an individual's ability to perform against the job-related criteria. These can take the form of psychometric tests, planning exercises, in-tray exercises, interviews, games, or simulations.
- A team of trained assessors observe and measure performance, evaluate and provide structured feedback and guidance to individuals.
- After the workshop, line managers and/or trainers utilise the feedback to help the individual construct a personal development plan.

Although the use of development centres is growing, there have been a number of criticisms, which tend to revolve around: assessment techniques that do not relate to the task or job, poor organisation, poorly trained assessors, ineffective feedback and the lack of follow-up action (Dulewicz, 1991; Whiddett and Branch, 1993).

Whichever method or combination of methods is selected, it is vital that each manager's needs are carefully assessed before implementing a development programme, and that an effective system of providing feedback is established.

Formalised methods for developing managers

A great deal of management development is formalised, planned and structured. It can take place 'on-the-job' – within the workplace environment, for instance a training centre. Or it can take place 'off-the-job' – away from the workplace in a college, university or conference/seminar (Mumford, 1997; Prokopenko, 1998; Woodall and Winstanley, 1998; Woodall, 2000).

Research by Burgoyne and Stuart (1991) reveals that the following methods are likely to be used in more formalised and structured approaches (in order of predominance of use):

- lectures;
- games and simulations;
- projects;
- case studies;
- experiential (analysis of experience);
- guided reading;
- role playing;
- seminars;
- programmed instruction (computerised/packaged).

Although these methods are widely used in education and training, they can often appear to be abstract, detached and somewhat artificial in nature (Burgoyne and Stuart, 1991). Criticisms have been levelled at the relevance of much of the taught material and the problems of transferring knowledge and skills into the reality of the workplace (Roberts and McDonald, 1995; Mumford, 1997).

● Competency-based development programmes

Competency-based development is a good example of a formalised and structured method for developing managers. This approach to development was introduced with the aim of improving the overall effectiveness of UK managers following severe criticism of their performance and its impact on the national economy in the late 1980s.

National standards for management competency (competency here is defined as an ability to apply knowledge and skills to a required standard of performance) were devised in the early 1990s by the Lead Body for management standards – the Management Charter Initiative (MCI). The standards are part of the UK system of National Vocational Qualifications (see Chapters 8 and 9). There are now national standards of competence for supervisory, middle and senior managers that equate to NVQ levels 3, 4 and 5 respectively. Within each area of activity or role, there are associated *units of competence* derived from a functional analysis of what constitutes 'the manager's job'. For example, in the role of managing people, one unit of competence is to 'contribute to the recruitment and selection of personnel'. Having identified units of competence, there is a further subdivision into a series of elements against which there are established *performance criteria* and *range statements*. A standard is therefore established by which managerial performance can be assessed. Evidence can then be gathered and presented by the manager to a trained assessor, who will judge whether their performance is deemed to be 'competent' in their current position.

The management standards were revised in 1997 to take account of concerns and reservations expressed about the administration and implementation of the original standards. The aim has been to produce a more flexible framework of mandatory and optional units from which managers can select the pathway of competence that best suits their circumstances and the qualification they wish to pursue. The new standards relate to the following key management roles:

- manage activities;
- manage resources;
- manage people;
- manage information;
- manage energy;
- manage quality;
- manage projects.

Since their inception, competence-based development programmes based on the MCI national standards have attracted considerable criticism, in both philosophical and practical terms. Philosophically, there has been a long-standing, fundamental disagreement about the whole basis on which competences were conceived and the way in which they are being enacted. For instance, attention has been drawn to the behaviourist orthodoxy that underpins competence-based training and development, which, ideologically, grew from the 'social efficiency' movement in the USA, and which, some argue, represents a form of 'social engineering' in which habitual behaviour is a key principle (Hyland, 1994). In the case of management development, this objection is particularly relevant as such a philosophical stance seemingly precludes a consideration of the more complex, innovative, creative elements that underpin managerial work, especially in a time of radical change (Jacobs, 1989). As Jacobs observes, although competence-based forms of management training and development can introduce more structure and discipline, they can only ever be a partial solution because they fail to deal with the softer, qualitative aspects of managing.

Others have challenged the functional, reductionist, mechanistic approach and the extent to which it leads to an 'abstraction of reality', and have questioned how far competences can be generalised from a particular context (Antonacopoulou and Fitzgerald, 1996; Loan-Clarke, 1996). As Kilcourse (1994) remarks: 'competencies thought to have general application will fit where they touch when it comes to specific organisations' (p. 14). Managers, who may be viewed as competent in one contextual setting, may become 'incompetent' when faced with new challenges in another context. Indeed, as Kilcourse (1994) argues, during a time of radical change, when innovation and creativity are at a premium, competence-based forms of development may be the 'antithesis of what is required'. However, others would appear to disagree. Cockerill (1994) argues that, on the basis of work done at NatWest Bank, it is possible to identify 'high performance managerial competences, relevant to rapidly changing environments and flexible forms of organisation' (p. 74). Winterton and Winterton (1997), in a study of 16 UK organisations, found that a competency-based approach was a useful basis for needs analysis and gave coherence and structure to management development. However, (and somewhat controversially) they claim it appeared to 'prove' the causal link between management development and business performance (see the later section on evaluating management development).

Some have argued that there may be too much emphasis on assessment and not enough on learning (Loan-Clarke, 1996). This might be interpreted as a way of saying that the focus on practical, workplace outcomes is subordinating learning and understanding to the extent that the competence approach might be seen as almost anti-theory/anti-academic. There may therefore be a case for reasserting the role of established methodologies within the existing and expanding educational and vocational framework (Stewart and Hamlin, 1992a and 1992b). However, many managers might argue (and regularly do) that the gulf between learning and knowledge and its application in the workplace still remains. Theory, it would seem, does not travel easily into the workplace, and competence-based management development is presented as one attempt to overcome this problem.

At an operational, practical level, there are major concerns about the way competence-based approaches are seen to operate (cost, time, bureaucracy, inflexibility etc.), and many of these concerns carry over into the way management development strategies and approaches are being implemented to generate frustration and resentment in some contexts when this approach is seen not to be appropriate or relevant to the needs of managers (Stewart and Hamlin, 1992a; Currie and Darby, 1995; Antonacopoulou and Fitzgerald, 1996; Loan-Clarke, 1996).

What can we conclude in respect of competency-based approaches? Despite the criticisms, it would appear that the notion of competence-based development has now been established within the framework of UK management development. Evidence suggests that competency-based development is increasingly viewed as a way of strengthening the link between management development investment and business strategy (Winterton and Winterton, 1997; Thomson *et al.*, 2001).

However, since its inception there have also been some interesting changes and adaptations to the generic competency model. For example, in an MCI-sponsored survey, 20 per cent of those surveyed reported that they were using the MCI competency framework, but within that figure 45 per cent said they had customised the standards to suit their own purposes (Management Charter Initiative, 1993). More recent evidence supports this, and shows that many organisations are beginning to move away from the generic model originally developed by MCI to a more contextually based approach. Rather than adhere to what they judge to be a somewhat costly, bureaucratic, prescriptive and rigid framework of national standards, organisations appear to be 'doing their own thing'. They are retaining the competence philosophy and principle, but devising their own competence framework for managers within the unique context of their organisational situation. They feel this is necessary if they are to respond to the complexity induced by rapid environmental change (Cockerill, 1994; Roberts, 1995). Evidence would also suggest that competence frameworks for managers are now becoming more fragmented and differentiated as they adapt to suit changing circumstances, for example shortened organisational lifecycles (Sparrow and Bognanno, 1994; Roberts, 1995).

Other adaptations of the original model include the growing use of competences to assess management behaviour and performance: 'the majority of organisations favour frameworks based on the development of behaviour rather than prescribed national standards' (Mathewman, 1995: 1). But somewhat more controversially, there is now a growing quest to identify higher-order, supra- or meta-competences that can be used to inform personality testing for selection and other 'judgements' about managerial behaviour and performance (Sparrow and Bognanno, 1994).

What appears to be happening, therefore, is a process of adjustment whereby the original NVQ/MCI framework of management competences is being utilised for basic skills provision in a bottom-up approach, while new behavioural competences are being cascaded down to set behavioural patterns and cultural imperatives (Mathewman, 1995). This adjustment may be seen as an inevitable consequence of what some would judge to be inherent flaws in a nationally driven, generic framework. But although this more pragmatic, flexible response by organisations is likely to be welcomed by many, it does raise a number of issues, not least how to maintain and guarantee a system of assessment and national accreditation for management qualifications with any measure of confidence. Finally, it is important to remember that 'competence-based development is not seen to be a panacea for all management development ills but is one approach which may be taken with others' (Currie and Darby, 1995: 17).

ACTIVITY

- List what you see as the pros and cons of Competency Based Development (CBD).

- To what extent would CBD make a difference to the way managers in your organisation are currently being developed?

- If your organisation already operates CBD, how effective has it been?

Less formal methods for developing managers

There is a growing interest in less formalised methods for developing managers. As we saw earlier, this may in part reflect a general dissatisfaction with generic, formal off-the-shelf courses or education programmes that do not meet unique organisational or individual needs (Roberts and McDonald, 1995; Mole, 2000). It may also reflect the desire by individuals and organisations to take advantage of more flexible and cost-effective methods that fit with changing lifestyles and rapidly changing organisational situations.

Action learning

In Chapter 8, the significance of experiential learning processes to the development of managers was identified. Much of the theory relating to experiential learning is drawn from the theoretical work of Kolb (1984) and Honey and Mumford (1986), who introduced the concept of a learning cycle in which managers learn through a process of:

- implementation;
- reflection;
- making changes;
- initiating further action.

Burgoyne and Stuart (1991) point out that a greater focus on experiential learning in the workplace, coupled to a reaction against the 'remoteness', complication and institutionalisation of management development, has encouraged organisations to adopt new methods of learning. Many of these new approaches are built around the principles of action learning pioneered by writers such as Reg Revans.

Revans' key principles of action learning

1. Management development must be based on real work projects.
2. Those projects must be owned and defined by senior managers as having a significant impact on the future success of the enterprise.
3. Managers must aim to make a real return on the cost of the investment.
4. Managers must work together and learn from each other.
5. Managers must achieve real action and change.
6. Managers must study the content and process of change.
7. Managers must publicly commit themselves to action.

(Margerison, 1991: 38)

Revans saw learning (L) as a combination of what he terms 'programmed knowledge' (P) and 'questioning insight' (Q): thus $L = P + Q$. When facing unprecedented changes, managers cannot know what programmed knowledge they will need. Instead, they need to 'understand the subjective aspects of searching the unfamiliar, or learning to pose useful and discriminating questions'. Therefore action learning becomes a 'simple device of setting them to tackle real problems that have so far defied solution' (Revans, 1983: 11).

Revans argues that managerial learning has to embrace both 'know-how' and 'know-that', and be rooted in real problem-solving, where 'lasting behavioural change is more likely to follow the reinterpretation of past experiences than the acquisition of fresh knowledge' (p. 14). Managers will be more able to make their interpretations, which are 'necessarily subjective, complex and ill-structured' (p. 14), and reorder their perceptions by working with colleagues who are engaged in the same process, rather than with non-managers such as management teachers who are 'not exposed to real risk in responsible action'. In other words, managers form 'learning sets' (groups of four to six people) who, with the aid of a facilitator, work together and learn to give and accept criticism, advice and support. Margerison (1994b), citing Revans, likens this approach to 'comrades in adversity'. Managers will only 'learn effectively when they are confronted with difficulties and have the opportunity to share constructively their concerns and experiences with others' (p. 109).

Margerison (1991), drawing on case studies and personal experience of supervising action learning programmes, points out that managers learn a considerable amount:

- about themselves,
- about their job,
- about team members, and most of all
- about how to improve things and make changes.

Experiential learning methods such as action learning are gaining prominence in the field of management development. As organisations confront the growing uncertainty and instability brought about by far-reaching and radical change, they are discovering that management development is likely to be more effective when it is rooted in the reality of what managers actually do and how they actually behave.

However, some raise doubts about the efficacy of action learning. For example, will managers truly engage in double-loop learning if this challenges current management cultures and political structures with concomitant risks for the individual (Pedler, 1997)?

Coaching and mentoring

Coaching

To many managers, coaching and mentoring represent the most tangible, practical and, if carried out effectively, possibly most useful forms of relatively informal on-the-job development.

Coaching is defined by Torrington *et al.* (1994) as 'improving the performance of somebody who is already competent rather than establishing competence in the first place' (p. 432). It is analogous to the sports coach who is seeking to improve performance by continually analysing and offering constructive criticism and guidance to an athlete or player. The coach (boss) must be willing to share tasks and assignments with the individual. Each task must have scope, responsibility and authority to challenge and test the individual. Coaching usually begins with a period of instruction and 'shadowing' to grasp the essential aspects of the task. There is then a transfer of responsibility for the task to the individual. Throughout the process there is a dialogue, with regular feedback on performance in the form of constructive criticism and comments. The effectiveness of this feedback is dependent upon a sound working relationship.

In most organisations, coaching is done on an informal basis and is dependent on the boss having the inclination, time and motivation to do it, as well as possessing the necessary expertise and judgement for it to succeed.

ACTIVITY   Have you recently experienced coaching – either being coached or coaching one of your own staff? List the benefits you or your staff felt they gained from the experience.

Mentoring

Mentoring was described more fully in Chapter 8. It differs from coaching in two ways:

- The relationship is not usually between the individual and his or her immediate boss. An older, more experienced manager unconnected with the individual's immediate workplace is normally selected or agrees to act as mentor.

- Mentoring is about developing and sharing relationships rather than engaging in specific activities.

Mentoring represents a powerful form of management development for both the parties involved. For the individual, it allows them to discuss confusing, perplexing or ambiguous situations, and their innermost feelings and emotions, with somebody they can trust and respect. They gain the benefit of accumulated wisdom and experience from somebody who is knowledgeable and 'street-wise' in the ways of the organisation, especially its political workings. For older managers looking for new challenges and stimulation in their managerial role, mentoring represents an ideal development opportunity. It gives them an opportunity to achieve satisfaction and personal reward by sharing in the growth and maturity of another individual.

Stop and think If you haven't already done so, think seriously about finding yourself a mentor to provide you with support and guidance in your managerial role.

Projects and secondments

Project management is increasing in prominence as the role and function of a manager changes within an increasingly turbulent, uncertain and often ambiguous world (Watson and Harris, 1999). Managers are developing new skills and having to take on board new values (Rosenfeld and Wilson, 1999). Buchanan and Boddy (1992) highlight the need to develop the notion of the 'flexible manager' who has the ability to:

- understand and relate to the wider environment;
- manage in that environment;
- manage complex, changing structures;
- innovate and initiate change;
- manage and utilise sophisticated information systems;
- manage people with different values and expectations.

One way to develop these attitudes and competences is to delegate responsibility for managing a cross-functional team of people, tasked with achieving a specific organisational goal within a fixed time-scale and to a set budget. This cross-functional project management role not only improves core management skills such as communication and motivation but is also effective at developing 'higher order' diagnostic, judgemental, evaluative and political skills (Buchanan and Boddy, 1992).

Secondments are also increasingly being used for manager development. Multinational companies have highly sophisticated management exchange programmes that are used not only to develop important language and cultural skills in managers, but also to reinforce the organisation's central belief and value systems (see the example of Unilever earlier in this chapter and the later section that explores international management development).

Exchange programmes also exist between public and private sector organisations to transfer knowledge and broaden understanding. Some larger organisations are seconding their managers to various initiatives designed to assist small business ventures and community programmes.

ACTIVITY Projects and secondments offer many developmental benefits. Identify a possible project or secondment opportunity that you could take advantage of in your organisation.

● Outdoor management development

In a climate and environment of greater risk, challenge, change and ambiguity for managers, increasing attention is focusing on the benefits of outdoor management development (OMD) as a development tool. OMD has its roots in the Outward Bound movement founded by Kurt Hahn (Burnett and James, 1994). The aim is to provide opportunities for personal growth and for managers to realise the potential of their 'inner resources' (Irvine and Wilson, 1994). In OMD, managers are exposed to emotional, physical and mental risks and challenges in which skills such as leadership and teamwork become *real* to the individuals and groups concerned (Burnett and James, 1994) and where 'the penalties for wrong decisions are painful; the consequence of bad judgements can be as real as being lost in a cold rainstorm at the edge of a dark forest' (Banks, 1994: 11). Others have likened OMD to 'outdoor action learning' in which 'the physical tasks at the core of outdoor development courses, whether they be abseiling down a cliff, climbing a mountain peak or navigating rapids in canoes are real tasks which present real problems to real people in real time with real constraints' (Banks, 1994: 9).

However, OMD has received considerable criticism in the past. Perhaps the most controversial was the 1993 TV documentary from the Channel 4 *Cutting Edge* series, which featured a group of managers being 'damaged in body and mind' while on such a course (Banks, 1994). Others have been critical of the degree of risk and adventure that managers *actually* experience, and argue that many of the claimed 'benefits' of OMD can be attained within existing development frameworks (Irvine and Wilson, 1994). Jones and Oswick (1993) identify a plethora of claimed benefits for OMD, many of which they say are anecdotal and unsubstantiated. When they are evaluated, there is evidence of bias as much of the evaluation is carried out by those who provide the training.

● Self-development

Organisations that invest in effective management development programmes are encouraging their managers to take more responsibility and control of their own development. As Boydell and Pedler (1981) remark:

> Any effective system for management development must increase the manager's capacity and willingness to take control over and responsibility for events, and participating for themselves in their own learning.
> (p. 3)

If managers take responsibility for their own development they are likely to:

- improve career prospects;
- improve performance;
- develop certain skills;
- achieve full potential/self-actualisation.

Stop and think	What arrangements have you made for your self-development?

A range of techniques exist for managers to undertake self-development. Some involve managers helping each other by sharing experiences in self-managed learning groups (see previous section on action learning). Other approaches are more personally focused, using techniques such as distance learning materials, computer-based training and interactive videos. (For a fuller discussion of the methods used for self-development, see Pedler *et al.*, 1990.)

In summary, this section has outlined some of the formal and informal methods that are currently being used to develop managers. However, it must be borne in mind that a great deal of development takes place in ways that are not only less formal, they are incidental and opportunistic (Mumford, 1997). There may be times when the individual manager is unaware that development has even taken place, e.g. trial and error, learning from mistakes, playing political games etc. This suggests that development may have as much to do with the provision of organisational support and facilitation for the creation of a learning culture (Woodall 2000) and managing the influence of organisational context (social, political, cultural) in which managers operate (Doyle, 2000a) as it does with the selection and implementation of specific development methods.

■ Evaluating management development

If management development is to be effective in meeting individual needs and delivering organisation goals, the whole process must be effectively evaluated to make judgements about its cost-effectiveness and aid ongoing organisational learning and improvement (Easterby-Smith, 1994). Traditionally, the literature on evaluation has focused heavily on the training and education 'components' of development (Warr *et al.*, 1970; Rae, 1986). Evaluation is concerned with the immediate training or educational 'event': measuring the inputs to the event, the process itself and immediate outcomes (see Figure 10.4). Measurement is against identified development needs and training objectives within the framework of a systematic training cycle (Harrison, 1997). There is often less concern with the longer-term impact and effects of the event or activity (Rae, 1986).

● Approaching evaluation

There are different approaches to evaluation. Some are regarded as being objective, rigorous and scientific, while others are much more pragmatic, subjective and interpretative in orientation (Easterby-Smith, 1994). In collecting data, it is normal to employ a range of quantitative and qualitative methods (Smith and Porter, 1990).

Methods will include:

- in-course and post-course questionnaires;
- attitude surveys and psychological tests before and after the event;
- appraisal systems;
- observations by trainers and others;
- self-reports and critical incident analysis.

● Some issues in evaluation

In attempting evaluation, a number of issues emerge. Most evaluation is short termist in outlook – captured in the ubiquitous 'happy sheet' questionnaire where questions focus on the immediacy of development activity rather than its longer-term outcomes. But to

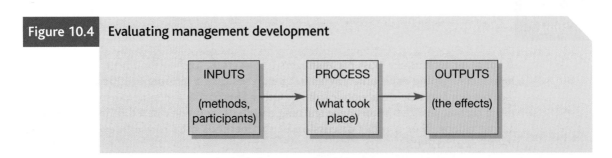

Figure 10.4 Evaluating management development

be effective, development must permit managers (a) the opportunity to transfer and apply new knowledge and skills and (b) a period of learning and adjustment in respect of newly acquired attitudes and behaviours. This implies that any evaluation of development outcomes has to have a longer-term orientation.

Figure 10.5 presents a more developed view of the evaluation process. It incorporates pre and post development evaluation but critically, it suggests that attention must be given to evaluating post development activity after a period of time has elapsed – ideally somewhere between 6 and 12 months. This permits those responsible for development to make informed judgements about knowledge and skills transfer to the management role and attitudinal and behavioural change. However, it should be borne in mind that, while the process shown in Figure 10.5 may be easier to apply to structured and formal development activity such as management training courses and education programmes, it can also be applied to less formal approaches such as coaching or mentoring.

In addition to assessing changes in the performance and behaviour of individual managers, evaluation must include some assessment of the impact of the organisational context in which managers are seeking to apply their new knowledge, e.g. the cultural and political environment that may promote or inhibit development. As Smith (1993) observes, 'management development programmes are not context free but dependent on the cultural baggage of the participants and the organisation' (p. 23). Therefore any judgment about the outcomes of management development programmes must be viewed within the context in which they are embedded. This raises further issues about the way management development outcomes themselves are interpreted and justified. For example, any claims about the efficacy of management development investment may fall prey to political games. As Fox (1989) explains, 'because a pseudo-scientific approach [to evaluation] does not deal with human issues and value judgements, it is not surprising that they fall into disuse or are simply done by token [then] politics takes over' (p. 192). Both Fox (1989) and Currie (1994), who have examined the evaluation of management development programmes in the National Health Service, conclude that political and cultural factors were heavily influential in shaping the evaluation process.

Another issue relates to the way development outcomes are measured. It is common to encounter evaluation methodologies that are left striving to display some form of pseudo-scientific objectivity to win or protect investment in development activity. For example, those responsible for development might be tempted to make unsubstantiated causal links between an investment in development and some aspect of organisational

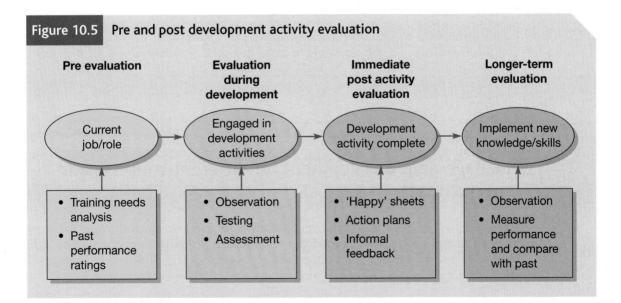

Figure 10.5 Pre and post development activity evaluation

performance, e.g. annual sales. Another problem is that the environment in which evaluation is taking place is often highly complex and subjective and evaluation methodologies may be judged simplistic and inadequate (Smith, 1993; Mole, 1996). For example, some of the criticisms levelled at competency-based development discussed earlier revolve around the doubts and reservations over supposedly objective and structured internal and external verification procedures as a means of determining the level of an individual's competency (Loan-Clarke, 1996). In other words, 'the complexity of management training and development demonstrates the point that measuring its effectiveness cannot be adequately accomplished by using a single, generic formula' (Endres and Kleiner, 1990).

Concerns surround the need to ensure that emotional, attitudinal and behavioural outcomes are measured and have an equal validity alongside harder aspects such as financial performance and technical competence. This necessitates the use of carefully constructed and focused methodologies incorporating ethnographic, interpretative techniques (Fox, 1989; Currie, 1994). But this presupposes that those tasked with evaluation have the time, commitment and skills to conduct research in these areas.

Looking at all these issues, it seems inevitable that the evaluation of management development will always be a somewhat difficult, complex and at times contentious process where it involves the measurement of changes in some aspect of human behaviour. One way to improve evaluation is for organisations to adopt a more systemic, holistic perspective of evaluation. This can be done by:

- Examining the extent to which development activity fits with individual needs and organisational context.
- Assessing how far new behaviours can be transferred and applied in the workplace, whether or not new behaviour corresponds with espoused organisational culture and values.
- Adopting methodologies that can measure both hard and soft aspects of performance (Easterby-Smith, 1994; Mole, 1996).
- From a more practical perspective, rather than focus on the benefits of development, consider the ramifications of not doing development.
- Rather than looking forward to eventual outcomes, it might be more prudent to look back at, for example, past mistakes, which can often be quantified. Improvements can be measured from that point, i.e. how mistakes and associated cost have been eliminated through development activity.

But are we asking too much? Is evaluation a chimera? As Easterby-Smith (1994) states:

> Thus attempts to evaluate development methods may fail to satisfy the purist, and much of this stems from the diffuseness of the target that is being examined and the difficulty of isolating procedures from the real constraints and politics of the organisations in which they are taking place.
>
> (p. 143)

Management development for different contexts and special needs

Up until now we have stressed an open systems perspective in which the need for management development to acknowledge contextual diversity and complexity is a significant consideration. This section will explore a variety of different contexts in which development takes place and looks at the needs of different managers.

▇ Senior manager development

Many of those involved in planning, organising and facilitating management development in organisations encounter a paradox when they seek to address senior management development. On the one hand, senior managers are viewed as a valuable and critical resource to the survival and success of the organisation (Woodall and Winstanley, 1998; Syrett and Lammiman, 1999). Logic therefore dictates that during periods of radical change their knowledge and skills must be maintained at levels consistent with meeting the challenges of change. And yet on the other hand, their development often appears to be inadequate or neglected. For instance, a survey of 295 HR specialists in the late 1990s revealed that 50 per cent of organisations surveyed did not have a strategy for developing their senior managers (Industrial Society, 1997).

● Barriers to senior manager development?

What might explain this apparent neglect of senior manager development activity? Explanations range from the pressure of work and a lack of time that prevent them from engaging in their personal development – individually and collectively – to deeper emotional and political attitudes about their perceived need for development. As Syrett and Lammiman (1999) identify:

> the distressing thing about boardroom education at the end of the 20th century is not the availability of suitable courses, which has improved immensely in the last decade, but the lack of take-up at a time when the need for properly educated directors has never been clearer
>
> (p. 148)

Stop and think	Reflecting on the earlier sections of this chapter, can you spot an important issue arising from this statement by Syrett and Lammiman?

In identifying the problem, Syrett and Lammiman may also have uncovered a contributory factor when they appear to suggest that development should revolve around the availability of *suitable courses*. However, as we have already seen in the preceding sections, management development should be viewed as being far broader than merely sending people on management training courses – important as they are.

But there may be a deeper reason inhibiting some senior managers from participating in development activity. Simply put, they do not believe they need it! Logically in their mind, the very fact they have attained senior level shows that they possess the skills and capabilities to perform at that level. There may also be political and credibility considerations which prevent them participating. Admitting you may need developing could offer your opponents a political advantage or undermine your credibility with senior management colleagues.

● How should senior managers be developed?

Individually, the role of a senior manager demands a considerable emphasis on strategic leadership coupled to legal and regulatory duties that are not found in other management roles. Collectively, senior managers have to be developed to work as an effective team while at the same time maintaining a required independence of thought and behaviour (Mumford, 1997).

BOX 10.2   The author was engaged by a company to act as a development mentor and adviser to a newly appointed operations director. The hidden agenda communicated to the author by the CEO was to 'persuade' him that he lacked the necessary skills to perform his increasingly strategic role and if he did not develop those skills, his position was under threat. Despite a number of meetings with the operations director in which issues such as career planning, development needs, etc. were discussed, it was clear that he was not prepared to admit he needed development and always found an excuse not to participate in framing a development plan. The author concluded from his observations that the operations director felt that any admission that he needed development would weaken his power and credibility in the boardroom. His lack of strategic skills was a major reason for him being asked to leave the company 18 months later.

Woodall and Winstanley (1998) identify four stages in the process of developing senior managers:

● *Grooming* – managers are prepared for the transition to the boardroom by giving them wider responsibilities and exposure to a range of managerial experiences.
● *Induction* – having entered the boardroom, senior managers are familarised with the cultures, processes and practices that prevail there – both formal and informal.
● *Competencies within the role* – an assessment of the individual's current level of skills and ability benchmarked against what is required to develop senior manager competence. Individual development plans are prepared through joint discussion and negotiation.
● *Team effectiveness* – the collective development needs of the senior manager team are assessed in areas such as group interaction, team roles etc. and a development plan for the top team is implemented.

Research suggests that senior managers prefer to learn through informal learning processes. They are 'less comfortable with formal settings where the agenda is written by someone else and they do not have control over whom they exchange views with' (Syrett and Lammiman, 1999). In many ways, development for senior managers mirrors the approaches that are used at lower levels. They will incorporate a blend of formal and informal methods, e.g. job rotation, secondments, mentoring, role shadowing, project working, special assignments, action learning combined with management education, conferences, seminars, forums etc. (Mumford, 1988, 1997; Industrial Society, 1997; Syrett and Lammiman, 1999). However, it is important to note that the content and emphasis given to aspects such as political, leadership and change skills are likely to differ markedly to reflect strategic, legal, regulatory and fiduciary roles as well as the added emotional and psychological burden that is inherent in such roles.

■ Developing professionals as managers

The development of professionals (scientists, doctors, engineers, accountants etc.) as managers presents those responsible for management development with a number of interesting challenges.

ACTIVITY   Think about the way that professionals are being developed in your organisation (this may include you). List what you see as the challenges facing developers in your organisation.

● The special characteristics of professionals

Woodall and Winstanley (1998) identify professionals as having the following characteristics:

- expertise based on a distinct body of knowledge;
- altruistic service orientation to work;
- autonomy and independence;
- restrictive entry;
- collective peer group collegiate relations;
- code of professional ethics;
- power through expertise;
- professional goals above the organisation.

Bittel (1998) argues that the main challenge for developers stems from the highly individualistic approach that professionals have towards their work. They view professional work as rewarding and intellectually challenging. They are generally loyal to their profession and the values it espouses. But when faced with the challenge of moving into management, they may display a number of what Bittel deems are 'counterproductive characteristics'. They:

- over-apply their analytical skills and can become paralysed by analysis;
- are insensitive to others and feel they are above organisational politics;
- expect their technical expertise to solve organisational problems;
- respect logic and intuition over emotion;
- lack feeling and empathy;
- lack awareness of common-sense solutions to problems.

There is of course a danger of generalising too far here and becoming a prey to stereotyping. Undoubtedly, some professionals make very good managers and are particularly good with people (Woodall and Winstanley, 1998). But others face conflict between their role as professional and their role as manager. For example, recent research in secondary education amongst heads of department and deputy heads highlights the clash between the professional role as teacher and the role of middle manager (Adey, 2000). In the NHS, similar clashes were identified. Some doctors who found themselves moving into management by default became more concerned with protecting their corner and loyalty to their professional colleagues. However, other doctors welcomed their move into management, were loyal and committed to the organisation and viewed themselves as a member of the management team (Woodall and Winstanley, 1998).

● How to approach the management development of professionals?

As we have seen, one area that demands close attention is the conflict between professional and managerial value systems. Clearly, approaches to development that challenge these values are likely to be resented and resisted. For example, in the NHS, competence-based approaches that were seen to be generic, highly prescriptive and structured did not go down well with professional groups (Currie and Darby, 1995). As Currie (1999) remarks

> Whilst recognising that every organisation is unique, the history and professional elaboration of groups in the public sector make a hospital particularly unique. The weakness of the competence approach and insensitivity of delivery to context reinforce the ideological gap between managerial and professional values. (p. 58)

Other research highlights the potential dangers of using what are perceived to be generic, simplistic, off-the-shelf training courses for developing professionals. For example, in education, the government has made the management development of head teachers a key priority. But amongst some head teachers management theory is seen as 'applied social science' offering simplistic recipes to complex problems. Research suggests that overall, professionals in education may prefer a more contingent, personalised approach to their development and the issues it raises (Bolam, 1997).

The spirit of this personalised approach is captured in the notion of continuous professional development (CPD).

> The essential principles of CPD are that development should be continuous; it should be owned and managed by the learner; learning objectives should be clear and wherever possible, serve both organisational needs as well as individual goals. And regular investment of an individual's time in learning should be seen as an essential part of professional life.
>
> (Little, 1997: 28)

| **Stop and think** | What arrangement have you made/are you making for your professional development? |

As most professions now incorporate elements of management into their requirement for CPD, the issue then becomes one of identifying what is the best approach for professionals to adopt and what, from the requisite professional body viewpoint, constitutes 'good' development.

In summary, it would seem that in terms of professional development, the issue is not so much one of access and the availability of management development but recognising that professionals have special needs and prefer to plan and organise their own development to meet those needs in a contingent manner. For developers the message is clear: resist the temptation to direct professionals into structured, mechanistic and simplistic approaches. Instead, offer advice and support within the framework and spirit of CPD where reflective and experiential on-the-job approaches such as multidiscipline projects and individual assignments linked to coaching and mentoring seem to work best.

■ Graduate management development

Recent research reveals that of those organisations surveyed, 68 per cent viewed graduate recruitment and development as a key feature of their business strategy (The Industrial Society, 1998). Graduates are recruited – usually directly from university or shortly after they graduate – for broadly two purposes. Firstly, they provide essential specialist knowledge and skills, e.g. scientific, engineering, computing etc. Secondly, they 'create a pool of intelligent people with high potential as a means of providing for management of the future' (Mumford, 1997: 222).

● Developing graduates as managers

Following a rigorous selection process – usually involving an assessment centre – successful graduates will work with their organisation to prepare a personal development plan. The plan will normally focus on the development of both hard and soft managerial skills – building on the information obtained at the assessment centre and other identified needs.

In respect of the way in which graduates are developed as managers, Mumford (1997) argues:

> There is no mystery about what to do with graduates. There needs to be a formal development programme for them which will include appropriate courses; they need to have assignments in particular units or departments long enough to establish that they have done a definable piece of work.
>
> (p. 223)

In most cases, management development will last between one and two years and involve joint and independent project working across a number of functional areas. Increasingly, there is the probability of being seconded to other divisions and undertaking overseas assignments (see the section on international management development later in this chapter). Development at all stages should be supported by a comprehensive system of mentoring and performance appraisal to provide essential feedback at critical stages in the development plan. Upon successful completion of the development plan, graduates will normally assume a junior management position and progress in their chosen career.

Management development in the small firm

The economic role of small firms (defined generically as less than 50 people) in creating wealth and employment is widely acknowledged in the UK and beyond. For example, small firms account for 90 per cent of employing companies in the EU and employ some 30 million people (Kerr and McDougall, 1999). In the UK, 75 per cent of employers are classified as small firms. However, while small firms employ the bulk of the workforce, they also display a high failure rate. In Australia, for example, some 30 000 small firms fail each year, 50 per cent fail in the first two years and only 20 per cent survive beyond ten years (Saee and Mouzytchenko, 1999). In the UK 65–75 per cent collapse or are sold during first-generation ownership tenure (Syert and Lammiman, 1999).

Management development as a strategic issue for the small firm

While there are many factors that may be cited as contributing to this high rate of failure, the lack of management knowledge and expertise is viewed as a major factor (Saee and Mouzytchenko, 1999). Certainly, there appears to be sound evidence to suggest that few managers in small firms receive formal management training. For instance, research indicates that one in four managers receives no training and only 15 per cent of managers had received a maximum of two weeks' training over two years – comparable to larger firms (IRS Employment review, 1997). A similar picture is revealed by Thomson *et al.* (2001), who found that while there had been improvements in the development of managers in small firms in recent years, one in five managers received no training at all.

Stop and think To what extent are the problems facing the development of managers in small firms similar or different to those in larger firms?

Why the apparent lack of management development in the small firm?

The quoted statistics above may be a cause for some pessimism but you should note that, in the main, they relate to formal modes of development such as training and management education rather than less formal, on-the-job development. Nevertheless, research suggests that the reasons why small firms appear to ignore or avoid investing in management development are fairly clear and consistent. The following reasons are identified as the main barriers to development (Saee and Mouzytchenko, 1999; Kerr and McDougall, 1999; Thomson *et al.*, 2001):

- lack of time;
- lack of resources to fund formal training;
- lack of previous formal education;
- concerns about realising returns on investment in management training;
- not knowing where or how to get advice and assistance;
- complicated procedures and bureaucracy when applying for assistance.

Another significant barrier arises from the peculiarities, idiosyncrasies and diversity of the small firm sector. This often makes the transfer and take-up of mainstream, large-organisation-focused methods problematical (Tolentino, 1998). Problems also emerge when management development is reduced to the provision of 'enterprise training' encompassing basic skills in operations, HRM marketing, finance etc.

> This view however, springs from an economic model of small businesses as large firms scaled down, a model which many consider to be deeply flawed. … Management development is seen as a subordinate priority to the need to improve the institutional and structural framework within which small firms operate.   (Thomson *et al.*, 2001: 205)

Other barriers may arise from the attitudes and values that are to be found in small firms. Kerr and McDougall (1999), researching 130 small firms in Scotland, found that a short-term outlook, pragmatism, a desire for informality and the need to survive were considerations that often took precedence over training or business planning. In another study of small firms in the hotel and leisure industry, Beaver and Lashley (1998) found that 'managers running small firms have a wider variety of roles and different priorities than those running larger enterprises' (p. 234); for instance, the assumption that all owner/managers are motivated solely by commercial objectives 'is naïve'. Many in fact attach more significance to personal lifestyle considerations. In the same vein, Tolentino (1998) makes the point that small firm managers have a different outlook to managers in larger firms in areas such as entrepreneurship, risk-taking, personal achievement and control. They have a much closer identification with the business and the family/community in which it is located.

● Promoting management development in the small firm

Considerations for a strategy for developing managers in the small firm would include the following:

- identifying the knowledge and skills required by small firm owner/managers;
- delivering development in a way that acknowledges the sector's diversity and uniqueness;
- finding ways to overcome the bureaucracy and provide accessible and affordable approaches to development.

● Managerial knowledge and skills for the small firm

In terms of the knowledge and skills required, these are seemingly well understood and documented. Thomson *et al.* (2001) cite Bolton's list of skills as typical of those that are felt to be required:

- raising and using finance;
- costing and control information;

- organising and delegating;
- marketing;
- using information;
- personnel management;
- dealing with technological change;
- production scheduling and purchase control.

Other studies have shown that while these areas were important, many small firm managers were lacking the required level of knowledge and skills in these key areas. For example, one survey found that small firm managers were particularly lacking in areas such as: the ability to appraise performance; strategic planning; teamworking and communication (IRS Employment Review, 1997).

So what might constitute a suitable framework of delivery methods and approaches? Tolentino (1998) suggests that the following points should constitute a framework for good management development practice:

- Identify training needs in conjunction with managers.
- Adopt a demand-led approach to learning.
- Ensure that training is close to the workplace and at suitable times.
- Provide support with costs but ensure that the firm makes some contribution.
- Use of consultancy-led approach.
- Work with managers from other small firms for advice and benchmarking.

In terms of support to facilitate development of managers, the role of the CEO/owner is seen as a crucial factor, as is the support given by experienced external consultants/advisers (Wong *et al.*, 1997; Kerr and McDougall, 1999). Other studies highlight the role of various government agencies, tax incentives and loans, and the impact of the Investors in People initiative in promoting and supporting management development in small firms (Beaver and Lashley, 1998).

In summary, it is clear that the needs of the small firm manager have similarities to those of managers in larger organisations but they also differ sharply in a number of important respects. Success in developing these managers has to begin with a careful and considered examination of the context in which they are managing, allied to an understanding of their individual and collective motives and needs; and ensuring that whatever methods or approaches that are adopted are relevant and affordable.

Management development in the public sector

Management in the UK public sector has often been the butt of criticism from politicians, journalists and other commentators about its seemingly bureaucratic, inefficient and unfocused approach to organisation and management. Cooper (2002) captures the mood in a recent newspaper article:

> many senior public sector managers thought that 'management' was about changing organisational systems, committee structures, and hierarchy charts rather than developing and investing in their vision/long term objectives and the people who achieve them. For them management meant bureaucratic action, fiddling with committees, setting up control systems and dealing with detail.

While some of this criticism may be justified, other criticisms of public sector management often come from those who are ill-informed about the many conflicting and competing pressures that face many public sector managers. According to Bicker and Cameron (1997), managers in public sector organisations face a number of conflicting demands stemming from:

- resource constraints;
- a hostile owner;
- pressure to emulate private sector practices;
- the need to maintain the public sector ethic;
- union pressures and demands.

It is not difficult to see how these demands may conflict when, for example, pressures to emulate profit-driven commercial organisations have to be reconciled with attitudes and behaviours that give primacy to values such as public service and patient care. Similarly, public sector managers increasingly have to motivate employees to attain higher standards of national or local government-imposed performance standards in situations where working conditions are often inferior to those in the private sector and where incentive opportunities are severely curtailed by public sector spending constraints.

With these pressures in mind, the choice of management development methods is important. The focus for management development in the public sector should, according to Bicker and Cameron, be on 'key enablers':

- *roles and responsibilities* – providing clarity and accountability;
- *leadership skills* – including influencing, decision-making and communication skills;
- *attitudes* – including risk-taking and openness.

For many public sector organisations, expensive management training courses are not an option – given the resource restrictions they face. As a recent study of a management training initiative in the NHS revealed, there may be resistance to externally driven courses that are premised on values that run counter to or deviate from those that predominate in the public sector (Currie, 1999).

Given these resource or value-driven constraints, managers in the public sector are more likely to be predisposed towards less formal, on-the-job methods that are rooted in their organisational context and meet the challenges they face (Currie, 1999). Methods such as project working, coaching, mentoring, action learning and, where appropriate, professional partnerships with colleges and universities are likely to receive greater support (Mavin and Bryans, 2000). There is more information on the public sector and HRM in Chapter 12.

◼ International management development

A growing number of organisations are now seeking to 'globalise' their organisations in their quest for greater market and product opportunities. A number of factors appear to have facilitated this trend:

- the fluidity of global capital;
- advances in technology and transport;
- greater cooperation between organisations in different countries;
- encouragement given to inward investment for job creation.

Globalisation raises a number of issues for managerial learning, work and managerial careers (Anderson *et al.*, 1998; Kumar and Usunier, 2001; Miroshnik, 2002). For example:

- To what extent does the concept of management move easily across international boundaries, e.g. what is the impact of national culture on management behaviour?
- Are we seeing the appearance of the 'truly' international manager?
- What skills and knowledge do managers need to develop to enable them to work and survive in a global marketplace?
- How do you develop international managers?

● Management as an international concept

You should read and study this section in conjunction with Chapter 15 which deals with the topic of international HRM.

You should note as you read these chapters that there are methodological and conceptual issues and controversies connected with studying HRM from an international perspective. Of particular relevance to this section are issues connected with the lack of accurate and longitudinally focused data; diversity in language and culture leading to variations in meaning and interpretation; and a tendency to generalise from specific data sources, which makes any comparison between countries difficult.

Noting these qualifiers, there is some evidence to suggest that certain aspects of HRM are starting to converge across the globe. For example, there is some evidence of a shared technical language and certain HR practices such as job evaluation, staff appraisal and teamworking share a common understanding (Brewster and Tyson, 1992; Phillips, 1992).

However, others argue that it is *divergence* not *convergence* that is taking place in terms of management thinking and practice. It is argued that national cultural diversity (residual effects of history, beliefs, values, attitudes, religion and language) has now become a key determinant in influencing management behaviour. Furthermore, 'these differences may become one of the most crucial problems for management – in particular, for the management of multinational, multicultural organisations whether public or private' (Hofstede, 1990: 392). This view is supported by others such as Hansen and Brooks (1994) who observe that, while structures and technologies may converge, divergent 'cultural factors influence management models, thinking styles, career expectations, organisational culture, change efforts and instructional needs and development' (p. 70).

Two examples illustrate the way cultural diversity can lead to a divergence in management thinking and behaviour:

> A French manager working in a subsidiary of an American corporation that insists upon an open-door policy may well leave his office door open – thus adjusting to the behavioural requirements of the corporate culture – without any modification whatsoever to his basic concept of managerial authority.
>
> (Laurent, cited in Hansen and Brooks, 1994)

> Chinese managers tend to view themselves as technical specialists and value a clear demarcation between what is right and wrong. They dislike softer, more abstract concepts such as empowerment and being given feedback on their performance that may cause them to lose face.
>
> (Syrett and Lammiman, 1999)

The issue of cultural diversity influencing the transplantation of management concepts across the globe is normally associated with the transfer of Western, Anglo-Saxon management concepts to other parts of the globe. But the influence of cultural diversity can be detected when efforts are made to transfer ideas to the West. For example, problems have been encountered in transferring Japanese management concepts such as quality circles to a Western cultural context (Miller and Cangemi, 1993; Redman *et al.*, 1995b).

● How are organisations approaching international management development?

For multinational organisations such as Philips and Unilever, development is focused on the creation of elite cadres of international managers tasked with building efficient networks of organisations operating across national boundaries (Bartlett and Ghoshal,

1989; Handy and Barham, 1990; Barham and Oates, 1991). We saw earlier in this chapter that Unilever's aim is to develop a common philosophy and system of management development that is 'seamless' and permits managers to move easily between different countries (Reitsma, 2001).

However, while organisations such as Unilever may adopt a strategic, integrated approach to development, others are adopting an approach to international management development that – like UK management development – is best described as 'piecemeal' in orientation (Woodall and Winstanley, 1998). In addition to piecemeal approaches, those who develop international managers are faced with the perception that many managers in the USA and UK are 'simply not global animals' (Ferner, 1994: 91). The problem is rooted in what might be termed a 'cultural blindness' which seemingly limits the ability of many Western managers to work in multicultural environments (Miroshnik, 2002). It is axiomatic therefore that an inability to address cultural diversity has the potential to undermine management development strategies in an international context (Liu and Vince, 1999). The primary focus for international management development therefore becomes the need to ensure that 'working effectively in multiple cross-cultural contexts is ... a vital competence' (Harris and Kumra, 2000).

It is crucial that managers who are going to undertake an international assignment are properly prepared for the experience of expatriation. Preparation may include company briefings, short visits to host countries, cultural awareness and a language skills course. If families are accompanying the manager, an increasing number of organisations will involve spouses and partners in such preparation activities to include relocation, housing and education considerations (Woodall and Winstanley, 1998). Alongside this, the development of social cultural, communication and empathetic knowledge and skills will be a priority. As Miroshnik (2002) points out, 'Different cultural environments require different managerial behaviours ... managing relations between multicultural organisations and cultural environments is thus a matter of accurate perception, diagnosis and appropriate adaptation' (p. 524). It is clear that to be effective, this process of cultural awareness must begin well before the manager arrives at their international destination (Harris and Kumra, 2000).

As well as effective pre-preparation, successful development of the international manager must also be predicated on the establishment of clear international management development policies supported by and integrated with an appropriate international manager selection, recruitment, appraisal, career and reward infrastructure (Harzing and Van Ruysseveldt, 1995). For instance, Unilever's strategic approach ensures that managers are fully supported to work overseas through the introduction of detailed HR policies aimed at a global alignment of management development. Policies must also support the reintegration of the managers following their overseas assignment where there are issues such as status, ongoing career development, adapting to a different lifestyle to consider.

● Who are these international managers?

Before we discuss the methods used to develop managers for international assignments, it is useful to reflect on what we mean by the term 'international manager'. Unpacking the concept, we find that there are different types of international manager:

- local nationals employed by multinational to manage locally (host);
- managers who live abroad and run overseas divisions or companies (expatriates);
- managers on short missions or projects (sales teams, plant installation);
- managers who work across national boundaries (Euro-manager, Middle East).

In the past, the emphasis has been on expatriate managers whose primary role was to protect the interests of the multinational organisation (Rosenfeld and Wilson, 1999).

They were generally male, married and working overseas was a permanent career for them. However, this type of international manager is giving way to a more 'flexible' type of international manager – one who may undertake 'one or two assignments in the course of their careers in order to gain international experience' (Harris and Kumra, 2000: 603). In addition, a small but growing number of these managers are women. But as we shall see shortly, this raises a further set of issues for developers to consider.

The knowledge and skills required for effective international management?

Phillips (1992) summarises the views of most commentators and practitioners in the following list:

- *technical skills and experience* often beyond those normally required at home, for example the engineer who needs sound financial management skills;
- *people skills* – cultural empathy, team-building and interpersonal skills;
- *intellectual skills* – seeing the big picture, and thinking in a macro not micro way;
- *emotional maturity* – being adaptable, independent, sensitive, self-aware;
- *motivation* – drive, enthusiasm, stamina, resilience and persistence.

But despite the recognition of the importance of softer skills, there is a risk that technical expertise may come to dominate and dictate the development agenda at the expense of softer skills development. Other risks include:

- the reliance on selection processes that rest heavily on personal recommendations;
- a successful track record in a national rather than an international context;
- selection criteria based on Western competences and personality traits which may not be suitable for an overseas appointment.

If such risks are not addressed, organisations may be in danger of setting their international managers up to fail, with serious consequences for the organisation and the individual.

Methods used to develop international management skills

Methods to develop international skills are eclectic and will vary according to the organisation, the type of international assignment that is planned, the nature of the host country etc. They will include formal programmes of management education to develop language skills and cultural awareness. They will also include on-the-job activities such as international exchanges, projects and action learning programmes to develop technical expertise, communication and interpersonal skills. But picking up the earlier point about cultural diversity, the emphasis will always be on cross-cultural training that is designed to 'get beyond the home country mentality' (Handy and Barham, 1990). Organisations must engender a new level of cultural awareness in their managers and 'management development must contribute to the creation of a new corporate culture and a new managerial mind-set' (Barham and Oates, 1991). GrandMet provides a useful example of how one organisation has implemented this approach:

GrandMet's approach to management development is founded on an active interventionist approach to careers in which the individual must agree to 'mortgage' any short-term career considerations. Started in 1988, the 'cadre' programme aims to send young managers of high potential on international assignments before ultimately placing them in senior management positions in their home countries. At any one time there are 12–15 managers of 25–30 years of age sent on a maximum of four assignments each lasting

18–24 months. Selection is via a rigorous assessment process designed to detect 'international traits'. The process is designed to flush out any prejudices that might hinder a manager from adjusting to an unfamiliar culture.   (Barham and Oates, 1991)

● Developing women as international managers

A recent KPMG survey of 164 Western companies found that 94 per cent said it was important to send people on international assignments; however, they also pointed out that finding the right people for international assignments was a major HR concern (Caligiuri and Cascio, 1998). This is leading some Western organisations to break with tradition and consider women managers as candidates for international assignments. In addition to women managers meeting a growing demand for international assignments, organisations are recognising that women managers may have personality and communication skills that are better suited to international assignments (Caligiuri and Cascio, 1998). Their non-aggressive and more subtle, process-oriented approach to business, it is argued, has a better fit with many non-Western cultures (Wah, 1998).

But a paradox emerges. If women managers possess the qualities that make them suited for international assignments, why is it that only 3 per cent of expatriate managers are women (Linehan and Walsh, 2000)? There are a number of possible reasons. The first possibility stems from a lack of organisational support and the continuing stereotyping and prejudice women may face from within their own organisation about their suitability for overseas responsibilities (Varma *et al.*, 2001). In addition, while organisations may be good at providing training in areas such as cultural sensitivity, they rarely address gender specific issues facing potential women expatriate managers (Wah, 1998).

The second possibility revolves around the threat of hostility from host country male managers. The role of women in the host society may be viewed differently to that of the home country, e.g. women do not have a role to play in business (Linehan and Walsh, 2000; Owen and Scherer, 2002).

In Brazil, male managers will automatically address their male counterparts assuming that any woman manager in the team is a subordinate. In the Middle East, male managers will only address women managers if they do not shake their hands or look into their face.   (Wah, 1998)

The third possible reason relates to the practical and emotional issues that seemingly face women expatriate managers, such as the 'trailing male spouse' who may have difficulty in adjusting to life overseas in his new role. In addition, there is the challenge of caring for and educating children in unfamiliar surroundings (Woodall and Winstanley, 1998). The final possible reason relates to the single woman manager. Here, the threat is of sexual harassment and possible exclusion from decision-making when business is done in male-dominated bars and clubs (Wah, 1998).

So what can be done to assist women managers faced with international assignments? In terms of development needs, the focus needs to be on helping women to cope with the cultural clashes and hostilities outlined above. Measures would include: the use of mentors, short visits to host countries to learn about attitudes to women managers and how to deal with them, preparing host countries to accept women managers (Caligiuri and Cascio, 1998; Wah, 1998).

International management development: a world tour?

In this section we will embark on a 'world tour' to explore the way managers are being developed in different countries. You will recall the point made earlier, that it is difficult to separate development approaches from the cultural, social and economic context in which they are located. This raises a number of issues, not least the problems associated with transferring Western models to other countries. This will become even clearer as the 'tour' progresses.

● United States/United Kingdom

In respect of management development, both the USA and the UK are very similar in their approach. Management development is often viewed as a separate, discrete and heavily individualised activity, aimed at correcting identified 'weaknesses' in skills and knowledge or 'deviances' in individual attitudes and behaviour (Mumford, 1997). In essence, development approaches are dominated by a powerful rational-functional philosophy, which views the main justification for any development programme as being its direct contribution to business strategy and organisational performance. In other words, the view is that management development must add value to the business and maintain competitiveness in the face of environmental threats (Woodall and Winstanley, 1998; Thomson *et al.*, 2001).

Increasingly, the aim is to develop generalist managerial rather than narrow specialist skills to improve mobility and the ability to take on new assignments and challenges – especially in a global environment (Heisler and Benham, 1992). Development has often been synonymous with management education and/or short, intensive training courses. For example, both countries now focus attention on competence-based approaches. In the UK such approaches are institutionalised and championed through initiatives such as the Management Charter Initiative (see the earlier discussion on competency-based development, found on pages 377–9). However, as we have seen in this chapter, there is now a growing emphasis on more holistic, contextual, work-based forms of development that are experientially based, e.g. action learning projects, coaching and mentoring (Vicere, 1998).

● Europe

In contrast to the Anglo-Saxon model described above, many continental European approaches have in the past been less concerned with management development as a discrete activity. In France, for example, the development of managers is linked more closely to its social and historical context. Rather than management being something that can be explicitly developed in individuals, it is perceived as 'more a state of being' (Lawrence, 1992). Those who become managers form part of a social elite (*cadre*), and much of their development begins within the higher education institutions (*grandes écoles*), where the study of natural sciences and mathematics predominates. However, concerns are now being expressed about the ethnocentrism and insularity that is permeating French business schools (*grandes écoles de commerce*), creating structural and cultural barriers to a wider system of management education that is adapted to global market situations (Kumar and Usunier, 2001).

In Germany, the approach to development is much more functional, with specialist expertise, especially in engineering and science, being closely linked to the vocational system of education built around the concept of 'Technik' and the production of 'Technikers' – technical experts who dominate in management (Randlesome, 2000). As in France, the concept of management is not considered as something to be seen as separate, but more as part of the overall functional system within the organisation. Managers have less mobility than in the USA/UK, tending to stay in their functional role much longer.

In terms of the content of management development activity, there is less perceived need for generalist skills development and generalist business education such as that represented by the MBA, which in the past has been 'regarded with great suspicion' (Randlesome, 2000). Discrete management development activity is seen as less salient, and does not flourish to the same extent (Lawrence, 1992). Where management development is carried out it is mainly in-house (Thomson *et al.*, 2001). For instance, German managers tend to favour 'structured learning situations with precise objectives, detailed assignments and strict timetables' (Hill, 1994).

Despite their relatively weak tradition and the problem of 'cultural insularity' in terms of management development, France, Germany and other European countries are beginning to establish institutions specifically aimed at developing managers. For example, despite past reservations, there has been a growth of MBA activity in both Germany and France (Easterby-Smith, 1992; Randlesome, 2000). In major German companies such as Siemens and BMW there is a greater awareness of the importance of managerial competencies (Randlesome, 2000) and in France there is a belated emergence of US-style business schools (Hill, 1994; Kumar and Usunier, 2001).

Another important influence on management development is the increasing monetary, economic and social convergence and cooperation across the European Union. This has focused attention on the 'Europeanisation' of management and, more recently, on how to develop what might be termed the *Euro-manager*. This is seen by some as an essential requirement if Europe is to be properly equipped to fend off the competitive challenges posed by global markets (Tijmstra and Casler, 1992). However, some take a more cautious view. Hilb (1992) argues that there are major disparities in selection, appraisal and reward systems across Europe, and that management development is neither strategically oriented nor properly evaluated. Additionally, HRD practices in general are too heavily influenced by variations in national labour markets, cultures and legislative frameworks. Kakabadse and Myers (1995), studying 959 chief executives in Europe, found wide variations in terms of management orientation across a number of criteria that are predicted to have implications for management development. For Thornhill (1993), any move towards Europeanisation raises significant issues for management trainers, who have to contend with variations over job content, context, expectations, experiences and work-related values. Hilb (1992) reports the following statistics to illustrate the variation in approaches to development:

- Job rotation is used in 32% of Italian firms but only 8% of French.
- Career high-fliers are identified in 44% of French firms but only 22% of German.
- Assessment centres are used in 22% of UK firms but only 3% of Norwegian.
- In Swiss organisations 66% of promotions are internal but only 31% in Danish.

Thurley and Wirdenhuis (1991) also point to these cultural and other national variations, arguing that the concept of the Euro-manager will be relevant only in certain industrial contexts. Storey (1992) identifies managerial parochialism and the lack of a European 'mindset' as a barrier, concluding that:

> The notion of the Euro-manager may not quite be a myth but the extent to which there is a clear conceptual and practical difference between this species and the international manager is open to question.
>
> (p. 2)

● Far East

In the past, considerable attention was focused on the prowess of Japanese (and more recently, Korean and Taiwanese) management practices in attaining organisational success in a global marketplace. This success may have as much to do with social and cultural factors as the ways in which Japanese managers are developed, since the two are inextricably linked. For Japanese managers, the experience of development is much more likely to be a long-term affair rather than the short-term, 'sink-or-swim' approach that characterises development in Western, Anglo-Saxon countries. In Japan there is a strong foundation of individual loyalty to the organisation, and an emphasis on providing job security for employees. The approach to development is likely to be much more systematic, structured and carefully planned (Neelankavil, 1992). Whereas Anglo-Saxon models stress individualism and development through short, intensive bursts of training to prepare managers for assignments characterised by challenge and risk, Japanese development programmes are longer and more culturally reflective in focusing on collectivism and group/team effort. The influence of role models is also strong. Unlike the USA/UK, where management development is in the hands of specialists, the Japanese view the relationship between the individual and the boss as a significant factor in developing the manager. The aim is to nurture growth, loyalty, commitment and retention (Storey *et al.*, 1991).

In China there is a massive shortage of managers with global management skills. Management training has therefore become a national imperative as the country opens itself up to global markets and Western capitalism: 'There is a pressing need for a class of professional managers in China capable of facing the challenges of a market economy' (Chak-Ming Wo and Pounder, 2000). However, as with other countries, China has experienced the problems of discrepancies between the models of Western management development and Chinese culture and society. For example, many imported Western models of management development are based on techniques such as group discussion and classroom participation, with an emphasis on reflection and abstract reasoning and a free and open critique and challenging of ideas and assumptions. Such techniques are often in conflict with Chinese culture where there is a strong emphasis on collective ideals, conformity, social status, the need to preserve 'face' and self-esteem, an unchallenged acceptance of the 'expert' and associative rather than abstract reasoning. All of these cultural factors, it is argued, tend to militate against the adoption of Western models (Bu and Mitchell, 1992; Cumber *et al.*, 1994). In the past, this has led to a preference for more didactic development methods such as formal management courses. In the past experiential methods were almost unheard of (Kirkbride and Tang, 1992). But more recently there are signs that Chinese managers are becoming more receptive to Western approaches as their own approaches to management education prove too basic and focused on technical skills rather than the softer skills required to manage in complex global enterprises (Chak-Ming Wo and Pounder, 2000).

In Hong Kong, Western management education and know-how have been much in demand as managers in Hong Kong seek the adaptive, flexible skills and knowledge required to handle the challenges of the Confucian, bureaucratic, centralising society of the PRC (Chong *et al.*, 1993). More recently, the economy of Hong Kong has had to cope with an unprecedented economic downturn in the Far East in recent years that has forced them to shed labour and rationalise their organisational structures. This has posed a further challenge for management development, especially in how to develop managers to deal with the human resource issues raised by such events. (See Chapter 17 for more information on HRM in Asia, including China, Japan, Hong Kong, South Korea and Singapore.)

● Central and Eastern Europe

The main force driving the development of managers in countries such as Russia, Poland, Hungary, Bulgaria and Romania is the rapid transition from a centrally planned to a market-based economy and more recently to some of them attaining membership of the EU. However, as Vecsenyi (1992) observes in relation to development in these countries, there are no 'road maps' in respect of management development, and it is often carried out in an atmosphere of crisis. The strategy in the past has been to import ready-made Western models to provide know-how and practical skills. In Russia, for example, management education is booming, and demand massively outstrips supply as the country struggles to adapt to major economic, social and political upheavals. However, in a number of cases Western models have been found wanting as they have failed to adapt to local economic, political and social conditions (Kwiatkowski and Kozminski, 1992). For instance, when faced with the problems of backward technology and hyperinflation, Bulgarian managers said that what they wanted was emergency solutions to pressing problems, not grandiose views about longer-term strategy (Hollingshead and Michailova, 2001).

Western 'recipes for success' may therefore be accused of failing because they do not take into account the context confronting them, they lack strategic credibility, and they have not responded to the variations in learning styles of Eastern European managers (Lee, 1995; Redman *et al.*, 1995a; Hollingshead and Michailova, 2001). Taking a pessimistic outlook, therefore, Western-oriented business schools may be accused of contributing to rampant capitalism and engendering resentment. But if they can adapt they may contribute positively to a more sophisticated economic infrastructure, changing social attitudes, and new forms of political decision-making (Puffer, 1993). This is confirmed by recent research which suggests that Western approaches are more effective if they can be customised to meet local needs. For example, in a recent study of management training in Central and Eastern Europe, Gobell *et al.* (1998) found that when Western trainers took the time to understand their needs, Central and Eastern European managers were as receptive as their US counterparts to open discussion and debate. This was viewed as a welcome change from the 'brute force lectures' they had previously endured as students! (See also Chapter 16 for further information on HRM and Eastern Europe.)

● Africa

Over the whole of Africa, there are considerable variations in approaches to management development and these reflect the different stages of economic, social, cultural and political development across different regions.

South Africa, for example, has undergone massive social and political upheaval in recent years. However, the key issue now currently confronting the country is how to use management development as a tool to overcome major societal gulfs in respect of the disadvantaged black majority and the well-educated white minority (Templer *et al.*, 1992). Recent research indicates that fewer than 5 per cent of blacks occupy managerial posts (McFarlin *et al.*, 1999).

The argument therefore is for the need to 'South Africanise' development through a more holistic, integrative approach that unifies the country by providing and sharing opportunities. Some progress has been made; for instance, the introduction of a strategy of educating black managers, coaching them and then allowing them to practise their management skills in the workplace. But problems can emerge when existing organisational structures and cultures are denying black managers access to the practical opportunities to apply those newly acquired skills. This has led to powerful arguments for a policy of 'aggressive affirmative' action in which the percentage of black managers more closely reflects the population mix (McFarlin *et al.*, 1999).

But is aggressive affirmative action enough? McFarlin *et al.* argue for the need to develop new management styles that are embedded in an African cultural context. They point to the concept of *Ubuntu* as the basis for development. *Ubuntu* is a metaphor for life that stresses support, sharing, community and solidarity that in the past has been essential to survive the harshness of African life. Within this philosophy, management development is premised on the introduction of collective, participative approaches; teaching managers how to build trust, bonding and solidarity with employees and each other while at the same time seeking to mesh with the imperatives of Western material-ism. Such approaches have worked well in organisations such as South African Airways where policies towards customer care are meshed with the notion of managers and employees seeing themselves as part of an extended African family. These arguments made by McFarlin *et al.* and others reinforce the point made earlier in this chapter about the need to manage development as well as doing it – in other words, focusing on those social, structural and cultural barriers that 'interfere with development' (Doyle, 1995, 2000a).

By way of contrast to South Africa, in less developed regions such as Eastern Africa (Ethiopia, Kenya, Uganda, Tanzania) there is a different set of challenges facing manage-ment development. Here, the problem is centred on the economic underdevelopment of the region creating a huge disparity between 'the African reality and the application of imported theories' (Mitiku and Wallace, 1999). Management development approaches are largely geared towards the imperatives of trying to govern or manage donor-aid from institutions such as the World Bank. But this focus, however well intentioned, may be robbing the region of essential wealth-creating skills required to lift the area out of poverty. The need therefore according to Mitiku and Wallace is to refocus management development at a more local level – building on successful examples of enterprise while lowering the costs of training to local entrepreneurs.

To conclude this review of international management development, you have seen that there is a considerable and growing interest in developing the skills and mindsets of the 'global' or 'international' manager. There is also a desire by many countries across the world to import Western (mainly Anglo-Saxon) conceptions and models of management development and to utilise them as powerful tools in their quest for social and economic transformation and renewal. However, you will also have noted that, although Western models are considered by many to be dominant across the world, efforts to import them by different countries have not been entirely successful. This reinforces a point made earlier, that there is growing evidence to suggest that management development cannot easily be removed or separated from the wider cultural, social, political and economic context in which it is embedded (Hansen and Brooks, 1994). It therefore becomes clear that just as in the UK national context, any international development policy, activity or programme is likely to be more effective if it is made *contingent* upon the unique set of circumstances that confront it and proactive efforts are made to manage that context. However, such a perspective of development sets new challenges for those professionals involved in developing international managers.

■ The progression and development of women managers

There is now overwhelming evidence to suggest that women are generally under-repre-sented in UK management, but measuring the extent of this under-representation has not been easy. The problem rests mainly with comparisons between different interpreta-tions of the term 'manager' – defined in terms of work content and scope of responsibility (Davidson and Burke, 1994). In 1989 it was estimated that 44 per cent of the UK labour force were women (this proportion was forecast to rise to some 50 per cent by the year 2000 and has now gone slightly above 50 per cent), and yet only 11 per cent of UK general management were women (Davidson, 1991). At chief executive level the picture was even bleaker, with only 1 per cent of senior management positions occu-pied by women (Davidson and Cooper, 1992).

More recent evidence seems to suggest an improving picture, with the proportion of women 'managers' now approaching some 26 per cent of the managerial workforce (Vinnicombe and Colwill, 1995). However, this figure appears to include all levels of management. Closer examination reveals a less rosy picture. Estimates vary, but it would seem that for middle managers the proportion is still around 8–10 per cent of the managerial workforce (Woodall and Winstanley, 1998). And in respect of senior management positions, the situation has hardly improved at all since the 1980s. For example, a 1995 survey of some 300 enterprises in the UK revealed that only 3 per cent of board directors were women, and in another cited study of 100 major companies it was estimated that only 4 per cent of directors were women (International Labour Organization, 1997). It would seem that the so-called 'glass ceiling' is proving to be stubbornly unbreakable at the higher levels of UK management.

There are a number of explanations cited for the increasing, albeit slowly, proportion of women managers in Western organisations. These include: better educational attainment; better access to training opportunities; and the removal of the more overt forms of gender discrimination in the workplace that have deterred or prevented women from entering management in the past (Larwood and Wood, 1995; Lewis and Fagenson, 1995). But there is less cause for celebration when we examine more closely the type of work that women managers are doing. Traditionally, women have suffered a degree of ghettoising in terms of their managerial roles. For example, women managers are concentrated mainly in the banking, retail and catering industries, at the lower managerial levels, and in the 'softer' areas such as personnel and customer service. It would appear that progress out of the ghetto into more front-line, business-focused roles is a slow process (Ohlott *et al.*, 1994).

Research also suggests a risk that women managers may find themselves caught in a vicious circle. Their very success in these softer roles may serve to stereotype them and encourage organisations to retain them in these roles. Where efforts are made to move them into front-line positions without adequate development there is a risk of creating a self-fulfilling prophecy. For example,

> putting a woman in a highly visible job she is unprepared for could result in visible confirmation of prejudice. The glass ceiling becomes real because in an effort to protect women, hiring managers do not give them the same challenges as men.
>
> (Ohlott *et al.*, 1994: 62)

● What are the factors inhibiting the development of women managers?

Woodall and Winstanley (1998) argue that forging a successful career in management is more difficult for women because it involves them having to jump through a series of 'hoops'. They have to:

- enter management at an early age;
- already have appropriate management qualifications;
- have experience or rapidly gain experience in functions that are seen to be core to the organisation;
- be continuously employed;
- work long hours and conform to the organisation's age-related concept of career;
- be geographically mobile (see the preceding discussion regarding the development of women as international managers);
- conform to promotion criteria (which will invariably be determined in a male-oriented way).

As Woodall and Winstanley remark, 'Thus it should not be surprising that women find career progress more difficult than most of their male counterparts' (p. 224).

Not only do women have to jump through hoops to conform to certain organisational expectations, they have to overcome a number of barriers that inhibit their managerial career progression. Woodall and Winstanley identify three barriers:

- the attitude and behaviour of women managers, e.g. their lack of confidence and perceived low career orientation and lack of competition;
- structural factors such as HR policies and practices which discriminate against women managers, e.g. appraisal and selection criteria that foreclose consideration for certain positions;
- organisational cultural factors such as the attitudes of male managers and informal clubs and networks which serve to exclude women and reinforce gender stereotypes.

Stop and think	Do you detect any barriers to women's development in your organisation?

Any subsequent strategy for developing women managers therefore has to be aware of and prepared to address these barriers if it is to be successful.

● What can be done to remove these barriers?

Davidson (1991) makes the telling point that those organisations that fail to utilise the potential of their women managers will be committing 'economic suicide'. Earlier in the chapter it was pointed out that in the case of international management, the availability of a pool of women with the right qualities for overseas assignments gave organisations a 'tactical advantage'.

The barriers are twofold – barriers to entry and barriers to progression. Hammond (1998) stresses the need for the organisation to conduct a thorough review and diagnosis of the structural and cultural factors that may be acting as barriers at both levels. For example, Hammond advocates a 'Women's experience profile' in which organisations are asked questions such as:

- Are women currently employed as managers?
- What is the proportion at different levels and what jobs do they do?
- Do women apply for managerial jobs in sufficient numbers?
- How do the careers of men and women compare?
- What is the ratio of success in selection between men and women?

In a similar manner, Woodall and Winstanley (1998) suggest that as an *aide-mémoire* to those responsible for promoting women's development the following questions should be investigated:

- What is the pattern of representation in management positions?
- What is the business case?
- Which women want or need development?
- What are the structural or cultural constraints?
- How can politics be used to overcome any barriers?

At a more novel and practical level, Mattis (2001) argues that male middle and senior managers should ask themselves: 'What can one manager do to…

- actively intervene in meetings where the behaviour of others stifles women's contributions;
- assign a proportional representation of women on task forces/projects/committees;
- organise two social events per year in which women can participate comfortably;
- join a committee where he is in the minority;
- have a zero tolerance for overt discrimination, inappropriate behaviour or inappropriate entertainment venues;
- become a diversity thought leader and raise diversity and gender issues for discussion;
- provide feedback, coaching and evaluating the work of their women direct reports?'

Other writers argue that women's development is helped when male and female managers learn to value each other's differences and aim to cooperate in their personal development to increase organisational effectiveness (Fischer and Gleijm, 1992; Whitaker and Megginson, 1992).

● So what practical measures can be taken to develop women managers?

Much of the literature dealing with the development of women managers makes the point that the tasks facing men and women managers are similar but that women managers do face special difficulties. So what practical help/advice can be given? The literature contains many ideas and suggestions. The following list is by no means exhaustive:

- integrating women's development into mainstream HRD;
- mentoring/providing role models;
- reviewing childcare provisions;
- reviewing equal opportunities policies;
- auditing attitudes towards women;
- providing women-only training;
- encouraging women into management education;
- putting equality on the organisational agenda;
- reviewing selection/promotion/appraisal processes;
- promoting the networking of women;
- assertiveness training;
- moving women out of the 'ghetto' into front-line positions;
- career planning strategies for women;
- training before promotion.

ACTIVITY   Looking at this list, identify the initiatives that your organisation is doing to facilitate the entry and progression of women managers. How does it compare with the list above?

It is clear from this extensive list that the progression and development of women managers is complex, and will require a more strategic approach than has hitherto been the case. However, Woodall and Winstanley (1998) sound a cautionary note. They make the point that while these factors are indeed relevant and that a lack of attention to them may help to explain the underachievement of women in management, 'they are by no means universal'. Each factor may apply to different women in different organisational contexts at different times. It is therefore important that organisations carry out a 'prior analysis' before selecting any intervention to improve entry and progression in management. And again echoing a core theme in this chapter, it is also important to ensure that any strategic approach to women's management development takes account of and deals with the wider structural and cultural impediments that continue to give rise to a more covert and often unconscious prejudice.

However, these impediments are deeply ingrained and give grounds for some pessimism. For instance, Veale and Gold (1998), in a study of a UK local authority, conclude that the main cause of the so-called glass ceiling still remains an 'anti-women ethos' permeating the organisation and reflects widely held attitudes that still persist in British society.

Many commentators have in the past advocated special forms of treatment such as positive discrimination and quotas for women or gender-exclusive development programmes. But paradoxically, and somewhat controversially, some commentators are arguing that viewing women managers as requiring 'special' treatment may be exacerbating many of the problems they are experiencing. While organisations should acknowledge the problems to which women managers are exposed, this should be done in a less gender-focused way. Instead, development should seek to integrate women managers both socially and professionally with men in work-related activities (Snyder, 1993; Larwood and Wood, 1995). For Snyder, this means 'systematically and systemically attacking potential sources of segregation' (Snyder, 1993: 104). This suggests less concern with 'special' development arrangements such as women-only training courses – although these remain important. Instead, the focus should be on locating men and women as part of the organisation 'system' and analysing their strengths and weaknesses as individuals in the situational context in which they find themselves, irrespective of their gender, and developing them accordingly (Davidson and Burke, 1994).

In summary, the issue of women's development and career progression remains an area of controversy and debate – not least because of the seeming slow progress that women managers have made in the workplace over the past 15–20 years when compared with the rapid growth in the overall proportion of women in the workforce. Although there are structural issues to address, the root cause of the problem would appear to lie in the attitudes of wider society being carried into and enacted both individually and collectively within work organisations by male managers.

One might draw a rather pessimistic inference from this and argue that the development and progression of women managers will hardly improve (especially at senior level) until work organisations rid themselves of the current generation of male senior and middle managers. The argument is that it these managers who have the power to determine the future of women in management and real progress will only be made when they are replaced by a new generation of men and women in senior positions who do not have the social 'hang-ups' of their predecessors. (See also Chapter 7 for further issues relating to women and women managers.)

The future for management development: the need for new thinking and new practices?

ACTIVITY

- Before you read this section of the chapter, list what you believe to be the way in which management development might evolve over the next 10–15 years. Add a short sentence against each point to explain your reasoning.

- If time and/or circumstances permit, discuss your ideas with a colleague(s). How do your ideas compare with theirs?

In concluding this chapter, we might speculate on the future direction of management development. Perhaps the first thing to note is that the development of managers – like so many aspects of organisational life – is in a state of considerable flux and transformation. This is giving rise to a number of issues and tensions that are continuing to influence the way management development is interpreted, planned, organised and implemented across a wide range of contexts, and these have been touched on in this chapter, e.g. competency-based development. To close the chapter it is useful to pause and, building on the preceding discussion, to speculate about the future shape and direction of management development.

■ Is management development fulfilling its strategic role?

It has been argued throughout this chapter that an open systems perspective offers a valid and useful perspective within which to view management development. In practical terms, management development has to be integrated with organisational development and change in a way that recognises their mutuality and interdependence. As we have seen, for many organisations, management development has now become a strategic imperative for organisational success. But if we are to achieve and maintain the required level of strategic fit, management development has to be managed in a way that accepts and accommodates contextual diversity and organisational complexities. Managing development therefore has to be seen as being just as important as 'doing' development.

So to what extent is management development fulfilling its strategic role in this contextual and contingent manner? The answer has to be a qualified one. There is evidence of success – cited mainly in organisational case studies (Prokopenko, 1998; Syrett and Lammiman, 1999). But there is also evidence that in some situations management development might be considered to be 'failing' in the sense that it is not fully delivering anticipated organisational and individual outcomes (Meldrum and Atkinson, 1998; Currie, 1999; Doyle, 1995, 2000a).

Stop and think	To what extent is management development 'failing' to deliver anticipated outcomes in your organisation?

The notion that management development is somehow 'failing' is not a new one. A number of highly critical reports published in the late 1980s (Handy, 1987, Constable and McCormick, 1987) identified managerial 'underdevelopment' in the UK as undermining UK competitiveness.

Since those critical reports, research has shown that organisations have increased their commitment and investment in management development (Storey *et al.*, 1997; Thomson *et al.*, 2001). But while investment and commitment may have increased, there are still reservations and doubts about the overall *efficacy* of management development and its ability to deliver increased performance and organisational success during times of radical and far-reaching change (Doyle, 1995, 2000a). With a sense of *déjà vu* perhaps, and on a somewhat depressing note, we see that managers are once again being singled out by the government and others as being a key factor in the poor performance of UK companies:

> Recent reports from the consulting firm McKinsey & Company and Proudfoot Consulting identified weak management skills as key in the disappointing performance of UK-owned companies. And last month, the DTI appointed Professor Michael Porter of Harvard University to examine the link between poor management and low UK productivity.
>
> (Dearlove, 2002)

Of course, it is legitimate to point out that management development is only one of a myriad of influencing factors determining UK performance and evaluating the relationship between managerial and organisational performance. Cynics might argue that UK managers are once again a convenient political scapegoat for government ministers to blame.

But there are grounds for critically evaluating the contribution that management development is making. As we have already noted in this chapter, just increasing commitment and investment in management training by itself may not be enough to deliver managerial effectiveness. In complex, diverse and radically changing organisational contexts there may be internal and external factors preventing management development delivering what stakeholders expect and need it to deliver. There may be structural, political, social and cultural barriers that may be 'interfering' with measures to develop managers and contribute to improvements in organisational performance (Hopfl and Dawes, 1995). Another possibility lies in a fundamental lack of awareness amongst key stakeholders as to what constitutes management development, e.g. the dominance of formalised models and practices at the expense of more contextual, work-oriented models (Simpson and Lyddon, 1995).

The future challenge, therefore, for those with responsibilities for developing managers may be to shift from merely 'doing' development (designing and delivering training courses) to managing development in ways that address the wider contextual barriers that inhibit or block effectiveness (Doyle, 2000a; Mole, 2000). But as we have seen throughout this chapter, any shift towards a more systemic perspective to manage development may require a significant reorientation in thinking and practice amongst the professionals involved. For instance, one such reorientation emphasises the greater use of work-based approaches to development (Woodall, 2000).

The need to increase the emphasis on work-based development?

One way to address the issue of contextual diversity and complexity is to place a growing emphasis on developing *managers within the context in which they manage* rather than just in the classroom, the training suite or the hotel conference room.

Of course, work-based development has always occurred in less formalised ways through activities such as coaching and mentoring. However, with cost considerations, time pressures, desire for flexibility and relevance in development activity, the need is for organisations to turn towards the greater use of 'reality-based' tasks, projects and assignments (Vicere, 1998; Paauwe and Williams, 2001). Premised upon an experiential, action learning philosophy, such approaches offer the possibility of overcoming some of the simplistic, generic and contextual problems that have bedevilled management development for so long. However, as Paauwe and Williams note, work-based development does have some disadvantages in terms of the level of cost, commitment and support required. Woodall (2000) cautions that the whole issue of work-based development is not well understood – even amongst those HR professionals who purport to organise and manage development in the workplace (see above).

The evolution of the corporate university

A significant development in recent years has been the growth of corporate universities. In the USA, corporate universities grew from 400 in the late 1980s to some 1000 in the late 1990s (Greco, 1997). A similar pattern is emerging in the UK where there are now an estimated 200 organisations professing to have established a corporate university. Organisations include: Anglian Water, Unipart, Lloyds TSB and British Aerospace (see the Part 3 case study on pages 419–20 which describes Anglian Water's establishment of a corporate university).

What has led to this expansion? There are a number of factors:

- Dissatisfaction with the generic nature of academic programmes which do not always address localised and unique management problems and issues (see above).
- Technological development facilitating new approaches to learning and networking that can be delivered with ease and cost-effectively.
- As organisations grow increasingly more complex and ambiguous, the establishment of a corporate university becomes an important symbol and mechanism for knowledge management.
- It raises the status and prestige of the HRD department.

● It delivers HR benefits, e.g. access to a high standard of development facilities, aiding recruitment by demonstrating commitment to develop.

We can thus see that corporate universities represent a coherent attempt by organisations to plan and organise the whole panoply of training and management development in such a way that it meets the needs of the organisation and the individuals within their workplace reality. In other words, it becomes a way of directly addressing the issue of strategic fit and overcoming the problem of how to meet the needs of contextual diversity and complexity by customising and shaping HRD to suit contingent circumstances. Their aim is 'to align training and development with business strategy while also sending out a clear message to employees that the organisation is prepared to invest in them' (Arkin, 2000: 42).

However, there are a number of issues to address. First, there is a risk that some so-called corporate universities may be nothing more than re-badged training departments where the motive is more political or PR than learning or development (Prince and Beaver (2001). Secondly, at forecasted rates of growth, there is a fear that corporate universities will overtake and become a challenge to traditional universities (Vine, 1999). However, organisations refute this. Rather, what they say they are seeking is a collaboration with Higher Education institutions, e.g. to validate their degree offerings. But there are fears that the values that underpin university education (independence of thought and critical analysis and debate) may not be welcome in some organisational cultures. Thirdly, there are practical concerns too. What happens if students are part-way through their studies and the company decides to close its corporate university as a cost-cutting exercise? Universities too may be chary of linking themselves too closely to a single partner when there is a risk of commercial failure (Arkin, 2000). It remains to be seen how far this ideal will evolve in the years to come.

■ Filling the gaps and meeting the challenges?

A final item for our futuristic 'agenda' is the extent to which the whole notion of management development is seen to fit with the everyday experience and reality of the changing nature of the managerial role. Recent evidence points to some fairly significant shifts in the context and nature of managerial roles, e.g. a greater emphasis on intellectual and influencing capacities (Chapman, 2001). There is also evidence of a growing awareness of how management development should respond – in both theoretical and practical terms (Vicere, 1998; Thomson *et al.*, 2001).

If we look more critically at the current frameworks, approaches and methods still employed in designing and implementing management development, it is not too difficult to identify the gaps, the incompleteness and the sometimes oversimplification that exists when compared with the challenges facing most managers. For example, the development of political skills is often cited as a crucial competence for managerial effectiveness (especially during times of radical change), so why does it not appear in the mainstream course syllabus or competency blueprints and frameworks discussed earlier? Why is there so little apparent attention paid to developing political skills (Baddeley and James, 1990; Buchanan and Badham, 1999)?

The development of change management knowledge and skills is another area that, superficially, receives attention but on closer examination, it becomes clear that the provision for developing change expertise and capability is inadequate (Buchanan *et al.*, 1999; Doyle *et al.*, 2000; Doyle, 2002).

Finally, while the acquisition of functional knowledge and skills dominates individual and organisational development activity, has the time arrived for managers to acknowledge and accept that they are not 'Masters of the Universe' – that they cannot control everything and everyone through the application of rational models of managing? Should development now focus on turning the heads of managers away from generic theories and models of managing that may now have little to offer and instead develop within them the intellectual and personal capacities required to accept, live and cope with diversity and complexity in its myriad forms? The indicators suggest that the answer to both questions is a yes.

Summary

- The terms 'management' and 'manager' have different meanings within different contexts. The role and 'reality' of managing in organisations is often more complex, confusing and chaotic than many management texts would suggest.

- Management development is more than just management education and training. It involves the holistic development of the manager, taking account of such factors as: the needs, goals and expectations of both the organisation and the individual; the political, cultural and economic context; structures, and systems for selection, reward and monitoring performance.

- As part of an overall human resource strategy, management development is now identified by many organisations as a source of competitive advantage and one of the key ingredients for success. However, if management development is to be effective it must link to, and support, the organisation's business strategy. This enables those responsible for development to respond to the question, 'Why are you developing this manager?'

- Development programmes cannot be isolated from other organisational systems and processes in a series of 'piecemeal' approaches. An open systems perspective takes account of the interactions and dependences that exist between the organisation's context and management development programmes. An open systems approach offers a way of constructing a unified, integrated framework within which the organisation can organise and implement development programmes.

- Development is more effective when a stakeholder partnership exists between the individual, their boss and others in the organisation. A wide range of development techniques exist. The selection of the most appropriate techniques will depend upon the learning preferences and needs of managers. To be effective, development must reflect organisational context and the 'reality' of managerial work. An increasing reliance is being placed on the use of experiential techniques.

- A greater emphasis is now required on management development attending to contextual complexity and diversity and meeting the needs of diverse groups of individuals, e.g. public sector and international managers and the specific needs of women and professionals.

- Like many aspects of organisational life, management development cannot be isolated from controversy and debate. Areas of future challenge, conflict, tension and ambiguity remain to be resolved.

Questions

1 What do you understand by the term 'management development'? Distinguish between management development, management education and management training.

2 To what extent does management development influence the human resource strategy in an organisation?

3 Who is responsible for management development? What are their roles and responsibilities?

4 What management skills and knowledge do international managers require? In what way do they differ from those required by UK managers?

5 'To develop managerial effectiveness in today's complex organisations means that the development of social political and emotional skills is just as important as developing functional capabilities'. Discuss.

Exercises

1 List the different methods and techniques used to develop managers. How would you judge and evaluate their effectiveness?

2 Organisations are increasingly turning to self-development as a management technique. Imagine you are the manager responsible for a group of young graduates about to embark upon your organisation's graduate development programme. Working in groups, develop an action plan for achieving a self-learning culture.

Case study

Management development in Mid-County NHS Trust

Introduction

Since the early 1990s, Mid-County NHS Trust has undergone radical and far-reaching change. The aim has been to improve the overall standard of patient care while at the same time increasing efficiency and reducing costs. To this end, the Trust set out to re-engineer its key structures, systems and processes. In 1994, it employed a firm of external change consultants who are acknowledged experts in the field of business process re-engineering (BPR). The firm's BPR methodology was employed to act as a framework for change. It involved the systematic analysis, mapping and reconfiguration of key structures and processes to deliver cost and efficiency benefits.

To assist the consultants, the Trust identified staff from a range of professions across the organisation. These individuals were then seconded to work with the consultants on a full-time basis – acting in the role of internal change agents – and at any one time there were some 30 individuals in the re-engineering team. The team were coached and received extensive training in BPR from the consultants.

The implementation of redesigned processes and structures had a profound impact on the Trust. On a positive front, there were major improvements in the level of service and quality of patient care. But there were negative effects too. For a few individuals, change meant a loss of job. Others found their jobs radically redesigned, involving significant retraining – often for roles far removed from their existing jobs. Some individuals were demoted from their present roles.

Process management

One outcome of BPR was a radical reappraisal of the way the various Directorates were managed. To improve efficiency, the Trust created a new position of Process Manager. Process managers, as their name suggests, were responsible for the patient care process from start to finish. Working alongside their clinical colleagues, their role was primarily to manage the operational and business elements of the process. Many of the newly promoted managers were ex-nursing staff or staff from occupational and support professions. Most had been involved as internal change agents in the BPR change process since its inception in 1994.

Shortly after occupying their new positions, it was clear that a sizeable minority of staff found coming to terms and dealing with managerial issues difficult. While most were competent in their profession, few had any prior managerial

Case study continued

training. Areas such as strategic planning, budgets and finance, dealing with organisational politics and handling conflict were a burden and a strain. Some were also uncomfortable with the philosophy of their new role. They felt it took them away from their previously held 'caring' role.

Their views were communicated to the Trust's senior management who promised to initiate steps to improve the level of managerial capability among this key group.

Management development for process managers

The Trust found the resources and embarked on an urgent management development programme designed to develop the managerial skills required to operate in a more flexible and business-focused culture. It organised a series of in-house management training courses in core subjects delivered by a range of internal and external tutors. Details were circulated to the process managers and they were invited to put their names forward. The number of nominations received was lower than expected given the perceived scale of the 'problem'. When the courses were run, attendance was poor. When individuals were asked why they were not attending, most replied that they did not have the time. However, informally, a number questioned whether – given the changes they and the Trust had gone through – this was the right way to approach their management development. Few changes were made to the programme and eventually it was decided to ter-

minate the programme and channel scarce resources into other training areas.

Recently, a firm of independent management consultants visited the Trust to review and evaluate the organisational change outcomes. They were highly critical of the management capabilities of some process managers. They felt that this lack of skills was severely hampering the anticipated benefits of the overall BPR change programme. They also commented unfavourably on the 'attitudes' of some managers whose view of their new role did not conform to the 'expected professional management behaviours'. They cited a lack of overall organisation and leadership, for example too much time spent concerned with non-managerial problems in a hands-on capacity.

Note: This case study is based on real events. Names have been altered to preserve confidentiality.

Questions

You are a member of the Trust's senior management team and have been asked by the Chief Executive to investigate this problem and design an overall strategy for improving the development of process managers.

1 Adopting a systemic view of the management development 'problem', what do you see as the main issues to be explored in relation to the development of process managers?

2 How should the Trust address them?

Present your findings in the form of a short report/oral presentation to your senior management colleagues.

References and further reading

Those texts marked with an asterisk are particularly recommended for further reading.

Adey, K. (2000) 'Professional development priorities: the views of middle managers in secondary schools', *Educational Management and Administration*, Vol. 28, No. 4, pp. 419–431.

Anderson, V., Graham, S. and Lawrence, P. (1998) 'Learning to internationalise', *Journal of Management Development*, Vol. 17, No. 7, pp. 492–502.

Antonacopoulou, E. and Fitzgerald, L. (1996) 'Reframing competency in management development', *Human Resource Management Journal*, Vol. 6, No. 1, pp. 27–48.

Arkin, A. (2000) 'Combined honours', *People Management*, October, Vol. 6, No. 20, pp. 42–46.

Arnold, J. (1997) *Managing Careers into the 21st Century*. London: Paul Chapman Publishing Ltd.

Baddeley, S. and James, K. (1990) 'Political management: developing the management portfolio', *Journal of Management Development*, Vol. 9, No. 3, pp. 42–59.

Banks, J. (1994) *Outdoor Development for Managers*, 2nd edn. Aldershot: Gower.

Barham, K. and Oates, D. (1991) *The International Manager*. London: Business Books.

Bartlett, C. and Ghoshal, S. (1989) *Managing across Borders: The Transnational Solution*. London: Hutchinson.

Beaver, G. and Lashley, C. (1998) Barriers to development in small hospitality firms', *Strategic Change*, June, Vol. 7, No. 4, pp. 223–235.

Bicker, L. and Cameron, A. (1997) 'From manager to leader: facing up to the challenge of change', *EFMD Forum*, No. 1, pp. 30–32.

Bittel, L. (1998) 'Management development for scientific and engineering personnel', in Prokopenko, J. (ed.) *Management Development: A Guide for the Profession.* Geneva: International Labour Office, pp. 426–445.

Bolam, R. (1997) 'Management development for head teachers: retrospect and prospect', *Educational Management and Administration*, Vol. 25, No. 3, pp. 265–283.

Boydell, T. and Pedler, M. (1981) *Management Self-Development.* Westmead: Gower.

Brewster, C. and Tyson, S. (1992) *International Comparisons in Human Resource Management.* London: Pitman.

Bu, N. and Mitchell, V. (1992) 'Developing the PRC's managers: how can Western Europe become more helpful?', *Journal of Management Development*, Vol. 11, No. 2, pp. 42–53.

*Buchanan, D. and Badham, R. (1999) *Power Politics and Organisational Change: Winning the Turf Game.* London: Sage.

*Buchanan, D. and Boddy, D. (1992) *The Expertise of the Change Agent.* Hemel Hempstead: Prentice Hall.

Buchanan, D., Claydon, T. and Doyle, M. (1999) 'Organisation development and change: the legacy of the nineties', *Human Resource Management Journal*, Vol. 9, No. 2, pp. 20–37.

Burgoyne, J. (1988) 'Management development for the individual and the organisation', *Personnel Management*, June, pp. 40–44.

Burgoyne, J. and Stuart, R. (1991) 'Teaching and learning methods in management development', *Personnel Review*, Vol. 20, No. 3, pp. 27–33.

Burnett, D. and James, K. (1994) 'Using the outdoors to facilitate personal change in managers', *Journal of Management Development*, Vol. 13, No. 9, pp. 14–24.

Caligiuri, P. and Cascio, W. (1998) 'Can we send her there: maximising the success of Western women on global assignments', *Journal of World Business*, Winter, Vol. 33, No. 4, pp. 394–416.

Chak-Ming Wo and Pounder, J. (2000) 'Post-experience management education and training in China', *Journal of General Management*, Vol. 26, No. 2, pp. 52–70.

Chapman, J.A. (2001) 'The work of managers in new organisational contexts', *Journal of Management Development*, Vol. 20, No. 1, pp. 55–68.

Chong, J., Kassener, M.W. and Ta-Lang Shih (1993) 'Management development of Hong Kong managers for 1997', *Journal of Management Development*, Vol. 12, No. 8, pp. 18–26.

Cockerill, T. (1994) 'The kind of competence for rapid change', in Mabey, C. and Iles, P. (eds) *Managing Learning.* London: Routledge.

Constable, J. and McCormick, R. (1987) *The Making of British Managers.* London: BIM/CBI.

Cooper, C. (2002) 'Wanted: leaders to transform public services', *Sunday Times*, 13 January, p. 17.

Cumber, M., Donohoe, P. and Ho Sai Pak (1994) *Making Asian Managers.* Hong Kong: The Management Development Centre of Hong Kong.

Currie, G. (1994) 'Evaluation of management development: a case study', *Journal of Management Development*, Vol. 13, No. 3, pp. 22–26.

*Currie, G. (1999) 'Resistance around a management development programme: negotiated order in an NHS Trust', *Management Learning*, Vol. 30, No. 1, pp. 43–61.

Currie, G. and Darby, R. (1995) 'Competence-based management development: rhetoric and reality', *Journal of European Industrial Training*, Vol. 19, No. 5, pp. 11–18.

Davidson, M. (1991) 'Women managers in Britain: issues for the 1990s', *Women in Management Review*, Vol. 6, No. 1, pp. 5–10.

Davidson, M. and Burke, R. (eds) (1994) *Women in Management: Current Research Issues.* London: Paul Chapman Publishing.

Davidson, M. and Cooper, C. (1992) *Shattering the Glass Ceiling: The Woman Manager.* London: Paul Chapman Publishing.

Davis, T. (1990) 'Whose job is management development: comparing the choices', *Journal of Management Development*, Vol. 9, No. 1, pp. 58–70.

Dearlove, D. (2002) 'Why workers distrust bosses', *The Times*, 31 October, p. 11.

Doyle, M. (1995) 'Organisational transformation and renewal: a case for reframing management development?', *Personnel Review*, Vol. 24, No. 6, pp. 6–18.

*Doyle, M. (2000a) 'Management development in an era of radical change: evolving a relational perspective', *Journal of Management Development*, Vol. 19, No. 7, pp. 579–601.

Doyle, M. (2000b) 'Managing careers in organisations', in Collin, A. and Young, R. (eds) *The Future of Career.* Cambridge: Cambridge University Press, pp. 228–242.

Doyle, M. (2002) 'From change novice to change expert', *Personnel Review*, Vol. 31, No. 2, pp. 465–481.

Doyle, M., Claydon, T. and Buchanan, D. (2000) 'Mixed results, lousy process: contrasts and contradictions in the management experience of change', *British Journal of Management*, Vol. 11, Special Issue, pp. 59–80.

Dulewicz, V. (1991) 'Improving assessment centres', *Personnel Management*, June, pp. 50–55.

Easterby-Smith, M. (1992) 'European management education: the prospects for unification', *Human Resource Management Journal*, Vol. 3, No. 1, pp. 23–36.

*Easterby-Smith, M. (1994) *Evaluation of Management Education, Training and Development.* Aldershot: Gower.

Endres, G. and Kleiner, B. (1990) 'How to measure management training and effectiveness', *Journal of European Industrial Training*, Vol. 14, No. 9, pp. 3–7.

Ferner, A. (1994) 'Multi-national comparisons and HRM: an overview of research issues', *Human Resource Management Journal*, Vol. 4, No. 3, pp. 79–102.

Fischer, M. and Gleijm, H. (1992) 'The gender gap in management', *Industrial and Commercial Training*, Vol. 24, No. 4, pp. 5–11.

Fox, S. (1989) 'The politics of evaluating management development', *Management Education and Development*, Vol. 20, Pt 3, pp. 191–207.

Gobell, D., Przybylowski, K. and Rudlelius, W. (1998) 'Customising management training in Central and Eastern Europe', *Business Horizons*, May/June, Vol. 41, No. 3, pp. 61–72.

Greco, J. (1997) 'Corporate home schooling', *Journal of Business Strategy*, May/June, Vol. 18, No. 3, pp. 48–52.

Hales, C. (1993) *Managing Through Organisation*. London: Routledge.

Hammond, V. (1998) 'Training and developing women for managerial jobs' in Prokopenko, J. (ed.) *Management Development: A Guide for the Profession*. Geneva: International Labour Office, pp. 446–462.

Handy, C. (1987) *The Making of Managers*. London: MSC/ NEDO/BIM.

Handy, L. and Barham, K, (1990) 'International management development in the 1990s', *Journal of European Industrial Training*, Vol. 14, No. 6, pp. 28–31.

Hansen, C.D. and Brooks, A.K. (1994) 'A review of cross-cultural research on human resource development', *Human Resource Development Quarterly*, Vol. 5, No. 1, pp. 55–74.

Harris, H. and Kumra, S. (2000) International manager development: cross-cultural training in highly diverse environments', *Journal of Management Development*, Vol. 19, No. 7, pp. 602–614.

Harrison, R. (1997) *Employee Development*, 2nd edn. London: IPM.

*Harzing, A.-M. and Van Ruysseveldt, J. (1995) *International Human Resource Management*. London: Sage.

Heisler, W.J. and Benham, P. (1992) 'The challenge of management development in North America in the 1990s', *Journal of Management Development*, Vol. 11, No. 2, pp. 16–31.

Hendry, C. (1995) *Human Resource Management: A Strategic Approach to Employment*. Oxford: Butterworth-Heinemann.

Herriot, P. and Pemberton, C. (1995) *New Deals: The Revolution in Managerial Careers*. Chichester: John Wiley.

Hilb, P. (1992) 'The challenge of management development in Western Europe in the 1990s', *International Journal of Human Resource Management*, Vol. 3, No. 3, pp. 575–584.

Hill, R. (1994) *Euro-Managers and Martians*. Brussels: Euro Publications.

Hofstede, G. (1990) 'The cultural relativity of organisational practices and theories', in Rosenfeld, R. and Wilson, D. (eds) *Managing Organisations*. London: McGraw-Hill.

Hollingshead, G. and Michailova, S. (2001) 'Blockbusters or bridge builders? The role of Western trainers in developing new entrepreneurialism in Eastern Europe', *Management Learning*, Vol. 32, No. 4, pp. 419–436.

Honey, P. and Mumford, A. (1986) *Manual of Learning Styles*, 2nd edn. Maidenhead: Peter Honey.

Hopfl, H. and Dawes, F. (1995) 'A whole can of worms! The contested frontiers of management development and learning', *Personnel Review*, Vol. 24, No. 6, pp. 19–28.

Hyland, T. (1994) *Competences, Education and NVQs: Dissenting Perspectives*. London: Cassell Education.

Industrial Society, (1997) 'Senior management development', *Managing Best Practice*, No 80, London.

Industrial Society (1998) 'Graduate recruitment and development', *Managing Best Practice*, No. 53, London.

International Labour Organization (1997) *Breaking Through the Glass Ceiling: Women in Management*. Geneva: ILO Publications.

IRS Employment Review, (1997) 'Developing Managers in Small Firms', April, No. 630, pp. 15–16.

Irvine, D. and Wilson, J.P. (1994) 'Outdoor management development: reality or illusion?', *Journal of Management Development*, Vol. 13, No. 5, pp. 25–37.

Jacobs, R. (1989) 'Getting the measure of management competence', *Personnel Management*, June, pp. 32–37.

Jones, P. and Oswick, C. (1993) 'Outcomes of outdoor management development: articles of faith?', *Journal of European Industrial Training*, Vol. 17, No. 3, pp. 10–18.

Kakabadse, A. and Myers, A. (1995) 'Qualities of top management: comparisons of European manufacturers', *Journal of Management Development*, Vol. 14, No. 1, pp. 5–15.

Kast, F.S. and Rosenweig, J.E. (1985) *Organisation and Management: A Systems Approach*, 4th edn. New York: McGraw-Hill.

Kerr, A. and McDougall, M. (1999) 'The small business of developing people', *International Small Business Journal*, Jan/March, Vol. 17, No. 66, pp. 65–74.

Kilcourse, T. (1994) 'Developing competent managers', *Journal of European Industrial Training*, Vol. 18, No. 2, pp. 12–16.

Kirkbride, P. and Tang, S. (1992) 'Management development in the Nanyang Chinese societies of S.E. Asia', *Journal of Management Development*, Vol. 11, No. 2, pp. 54–66.

Kolb, D. (1984) *Experiential Learning*. New York: Prentice Hall.

Kumar, R. and Usunier, J.C. (2001) 'Management education in a globalising world', *Management Learning*, Vol. 32, No. 3, pp. 363–391.

Kwiatkowski, S. and Kozminski, A. (1992) 'Paradoxical country: management education in Poland', *Journal of Management Development*, Vol. 11, No. 5, pp. 28–33.

Larwood, L. and Wood, M. (1995) 'Training women for changing priorities', *Journal of Management Development*, Vol. 14, No. 2, pp. 54–64.

Lawrence, P. (1992) 'Management development in Europe: a study in cultural contrast', *Human Resource Management Journal*, Vol. 3, No. 1, pp. 11–23.

Lee, G. and Beard, D. (1994) *Development Centres: Realising the Potential of Your Employees through Assessment and Development*. Maidenhead: McGraw-Hill.

Lee, M. (1995) 'Working with choice in Central Europe', *Management Learning*, Vol. 26, No. 2, pp. 215–30.

Lewis, A. and Fagenson, E. (1995) 'Strategies for developing women managers: how well do they fulfil their objectives?', *Journal of Management Development*, Vol. 14, No. 2. pp. 39–53.

Linehan, M. and Walsh, J. (2000) 'Work–family conflict and the senior female international managers', *British Journal of Management*, Vol. 11, special issue, S49–58.

Little, B. (1997) 'I have a plan', *Management Skills and Development*, September, pp. 26–30.

Liu, S. and Vince, R. (1999) 'The cultural context of learning in international joint ventures', *Journal of Management Development*, Vol. 18, No. 8, pp. 666–675.

*Loan-Clarke, J, (1996) 'The Management Charter Initiative: critique of management standards/NVQs', *Journal of Management Development*, Vol. 15, No. 6, pp. 4–17.

Mabey, C. and Salaman, G. (1995) *Strategic Human Resource Management*. Oxford: Blackwell.

Management Charter Initiative (MCI) (1993) *Management Development in the UK*. London: MCI.

Margerison, C. (1991) *Making Management Development Work*. Maidenhead: McGraw-Hill.

Margerison, C. (1994a) 'Managing career choices', in Mumford, A. (ed.) *Gower Handbook of Management Development*. Aldershot: Gower.

Margerison, C. (1994b) 'Action learning and excellence in management development', in Mabey, C. and Iles, P. (eds) *Managing Learning*. London: Routledge.

Mathewman, J. (1995) 'Trends and developments in the use of competency frameworks', *Competency*, Vol. 1, No. 4, whole issue supplement.

Mattis, M. (2001) 'Advancing women in business organisations: key leadership roles and behaviours of senior leaders and middle managers' *Journal of Management Development*, Vol. 20, No. 4, pp. 371–388.

Mavin, S. and Bryans, P. (2000) 'Management development in the public sector: what role can universities play?', *International Journal of Public Sector Management*, Vol. 13, No. 2, pp. 142–152.

McFarlin, D., Coster, E. and Mogale, P. (1999) 'South African management development in the twenty-first century: moving towards a more Africanised model', *Journal of Management Development*, Vol. 18, No. 1, pp. 63–78.

*Meldrum, M. and Atkinson, S. (1998) 'Is management development fulfilling its organisational role?', *Management Decision*, Vol. 36, No. 8, pp. 528–532.

Miller, R. and Cangemi, J. (1993) 'Why TQM fails: perspectives of top management', *Journal of Management Development*, Vol. 12, No. 7, pp. 40–50.

Miroshnik, V. (2002) 'Culture and international management: a review', *Journal of Management Development*, Vol. 21, No. 7, pp. 521–544.

Mitiku, A. and Wallace, J. (1999) 'Preparing East African managers for the twenty-first century', *Journal of Management Development*, Vol. 18, No. 1, pp. 46–62.

Molander, C. and Winterton, J. (1994) *Managing Human Resources*. London: Routledge.

Mole, G. (1996) 'The management training industry in the UK: an HRD director's critique', *Human Resource Management Journal*, Vol. 6, No. 1, pp. 19–26.

*Mole, G. (2000) *Managing Management Development*. Buckingham: Open University Press.

*Morgan, G. (1997) *Images of Organisation*, 2nd edn. Beverley Hills, Calif.: Sage.

Mumford, A. (1988) *Developing Top Managers*. Aldershot: Gower.

*Mumford, A. (1997) *Management Development: Strategies for Action*, 3rd edn. London: IPD.

Munchus, G. and McArthur, B. (1991) 'Revisiting the historical use of assessment centres in management selection and development', *Journal of Management Development*, Vol. 10, No. 1, pp. 5–13.

Neelankavil, J. (1992) 'Management development and training programmes in Japanese firms', *Journal of Management Development*, Vol. 11, No. 3, pp. 12–17.

Odiorne, G.S. (1984) *Strategic Management of Human Resources: A Portfolio Approach*. San Francisco, Calif: Jossey-Bass.

Ohlott, P., Ruderman, M. and McCauley, C. (1994) 'Gender differences in managers' developmental job experiences', *Academy of Management Journal*, Vol. 37, No. 1, pp. 46–67.

Owen, C. and Scherer, R. (2002) 'Doing business in Latin America: managing cultural differences in perceptions of female expatriates', *SAM Advanced Management Journal*, Spring, Vol. 67, No. 2, pp. 37–41, 47.

Paauwe, J. and Williams, R. (2001) 'Seven key issues for management development', *Journal of Management Development*, Vol. 20, No. 2, pp. 90–105.

Pedler, M. (1997) 'Interpreting action learning', in Burgoyne, J. and Reynolds, M. (eds) *Management Learning: Integrating Perspectives in Theory and Practice*. London: Sage, pp. 248–264.

Pedler, M., Burgoyne, J., Boydell, T. and Welshman, G. (1990) *Self-Development in Organisations*. Maidenhead: McGraw-Hill.

Phillips, N. (1992) *Managing International Teams*. London: Pitman.

Prince, C. and Beaver, G. (2001) 'Facilitating organisational change: the role of the corporate university', *Strategic Change*, June/July, Vol. 10, No. 4, pp. 189–199.

*Prokopenko, J. (1998) *Management Development: A Guide for the Profession*. Geneva: International Labour Office.

Puffer, S. (1993) 'The booming business of management education in Russia', *Journal of Management Development*, Vol. 12, No. 5, pp. 46–59.

Rae, L. (1986) *How to Measure Training Effectiveness*. Aldershot: Gower.

Randlesome, C. (2000) 'Changes in management culture and competences: the German experience', *Journal of Management Development*, Vol 19, No. 7, pp. 629–642.

*Ready, D., Vicere, A. and White, A. (1994) 'Towards a systems approach to executive development', *Journal of Management Development*, Vol. 13, No. 5, pp. 3–11.

Redman, T., Keithley, D. and Szalkowski, A. (1995a) 'Management development under adversity: case studies from Poland', *Journal of Management Development*, Vol. 14, No. 10, pp. 4–13.

Redman, T., Snape, E. and Wilkinson, A. (1995b) 'Is quality management working in the UK?', *Journal of General Management*, Vol. 20, No. 3, pp. 44–59.

Reitsma, S.G. (2001) 'Management development in Unilever', *Journal of Management Development*, Vol. 20, No 2, pp. 131–144.

*Revans, R. (1983) *ABC of Action Learning*. Bromley: Chartwell-Bratt.

*Roberts, C. and McDonald, G. (1995) 'Training to fail', *Journal of Management Development*, Vol. 14, No. 4, pp. 1–16.

Roberts, G. (1995) 'Competency management systems: the need for a practical framework', *Competency*, Vol. 3, No. 2, pp. 27–30.

Rosenfeld, R. and Wilson, D. (1999) *Managing Organisations: Texts, Readings and Cases*, 2nd edn. London: McGraw-Hill.

Saee, J. and Mouzytchenko, O. (1999) 'The role of multinational entrepreneurs within the Australian economy: strategic entrepreneurs management training and institutional responses and solutions', *Journal of European Business Education*, December, Vol. 9, No. 1, pp. 62–79.

*Salaman, G. (1995) *Managing*. Buckingham: Open University Press.

Simpson, P. and Lyddon, T. (1995) 'Different roles, different views: exploring the range of stakeholder perceptions on an in-company management development programme', *Industrial and Commercial Training*, Vol. 27, No. 4, pp. 26–32.

Smith, A. (1993) 'Management development evaluation and effectiveness', *Journal of Management Development*, Vol. 12, No. 1, pp. 20–32.

Smith, A. and Porter, J. (1990) 'The tailor-made training maze: a practitioner's guide to evaluation', *Journal of European Industrial Training*, Vol. 14, No. 8, complete issue.

*Snyder, R. (1993) 'The glass ceiling for women: things that don't cause it and things that won't break it', *Human Resource Development Quarterly*, Vol. 4, No. 1, pp. 97–106.

Sparrow, P. and Bognanno, M. (1994) 'Competency forecasting: issues for international selection and assessment', in Mabey, C. and Iles, P. (eds) *Managing Learning*. London: Routledge.

*Stewart, J. and Hamlin, B. (1992a) 'Competence-based qualifications: the case against change', *Journal of European Industrial Training*, Vol. 16, No. 7, pp. 21–32.

*Stewart, J. and Hamlin, B. (1992b) 'Competence-based qualifications: a case for established methodologies', *Journal of European Industrial Training*, Vol. 16, No. 10, pp. 9–16.

Storey, J. (1992) 'Making European managers: an overview', *Human Resource Management Journal*, Vol. 3, No. 1, pp. 1–10.

*Storey, J., Mabey, C. and Thomson, A. (1997) 'What a difference a decade makes', *People Management*, June, pp. 28–30.

Storey, J., Okazaki-Ward, L., Gow, I., Edwards, P.K. and Sisson, K. (1991) 'Managerial careers and management development: a comparative analysis of Britain and Japan', *Human Resource Management Journal*, Vol. 1, No. 3, Spring, pp. 33–57.

Syrett, M. and Lammiman, J. (1999) *Management Development: Making the Investment Count*. London: Profile Books.

Templer, A., Beatty, D. and Hofmeyer, K. (1992) 'The challenge of management development in South Africa: so little time, so much to do', *Journal of Management Development*, Vol. 11, No. 2, pp. 32–41.

Temporal, P. (1990) 'Linking management development to the corporate future: the role of the professional', *Journal of Management Development*, Vol. 9, No. 5, pp. 7–15.

*Thomson, A., Mabey, C., Storey, J., Gray, C. and Iles, P. (2001) *Changing Patterns of Management Development*. Oxford: Blackwell Business.

Thornhill, A. (1993) 'Management training across cultures: the challenge for trainers', *Journal of European Industrial Training*, Vol. 17, No. 10, pp. 43–51.

Thurley, K. and Wirdenhuis, H. (1991) 'Will management become European? Strategic choice for organisations', *European Management Journal*, Vol. 9, No. 2, pp. 127–135.

Tijmstra, S. and Casler, K. (1992) 'Management learning for Europe', *European Management Journal*, Vol. 10, No. 1, pp. 30–38.

Tolentino, A. (1998) 'Training and development of entrepreneur-managers of small enterprises', in Prokopenko, J. (ed.) *Management Development: A Guide for the Profession*, Geneva: International Labour Office, pp. 471–492.

Torrington, D., Weightman, J. and Johns, K. (1994) *Effective Management: People and Organisations*, 2nd edn. Hemel Hempstead: Prentice Hall.

Varma, A., Stroh, L. and Schmitt, L. (2001) 'Women and international assignments: the impact of supervisor–subordinate relationships', *Journal of World Business*, Vol. 36, No. 4, pp. 380–388.

Veale, C. and Gold, J. (1998) 'Smashing into the glass ceiling for women managers', *Journal of Management Development*, Vol. 17, No. 1, pp. 17–26.

Vecsenyi, J. (1992) 'Management education for the Hungarian transition', *Journal of Management Development*, Vol. 11, No. 3, pp. 39–47.

Vicere, A. (1998) 'Changes in practice, changes in perspectives: the 1997 international study of executive development trends', *Journal of Management Development*, Vol. 17, No. 7, pp. 526–543.

Vine, P. (1999) 'Back to school', *British Journal of Administrative Management*, March/April, pp. 18–21.

Vineall, T. (1994) 'Planning management development', in Mumford, A. (ed.) *Gower Handbook of Management Development*, 4th edn. Aldershot: Gower.

Vinnicombe, S. and Colwill, N. (1995) *The Essence of Women in Management*. Hemel Hempstead: Prentice Hall.

Wah, L. (1998) 'Surfing the rough seas', *American Management Association*, September, pp. 25–29.

Warr, P., Bird, M. and Rackham, N. (1970) *Evaluation of Management Training*. London: Gower.

*Watson, T. (1994) *In Search of Management*. London: Routledge.

*Watson, T. (2002) *Organising and Managing Work*. Harlow: Financial Times/Prentice Hall.

*Watson, T and Harris, P. (1999) *The Emergent Manager*. London: Sage.

Whiddett, S. and Branch, J. (1993) 'Development centres in Volvo', *Training and Development UK*, Vol. 11, No. 11, pp. 16–18.

Whitaker, V. and Megginson, D. (1992) 'Women and men working together effectively', *Industrial and Commercial Training*, Vol. 24, No. 4, pp. 16–19.

Winterton, J. and Winterton, R. (1997) 'Does management development matter?', *British Journal of Management*, (June) S65–76.

Wong, C., Marshall, N., Alderman, N. and Thwaites, A. (1997) 'Management training in small and medium-sized enterprises: methodological and conceptual issues', *The International Journal of Human Resource Management*, Vol. 8, No. 1, pp. 44–65.

Woodall, J. (2000) 'Corporate support for work-based management development', *Human Resource Management Journal*, Vol. 10, No. 1, pp. 18–32.

*Woodall, J. and Winstanley, D. (1998) *Management Development: Strategy and Practice*. Oxford: Blackwell.

Woodruffe, C. (1993) *Assessment Centres: Identifying and Developing Competence*. London: IPM.

For multiple choice questions, exercises and annotated weblinks specific to this chapter visit this book's website at www.booksites.net/beardwell

Transforming Anglian Water

The history

Anglian Water is geographically the largest of the ten regional water companies in the UK, delivering clean drinking water and removing sewage and waste-water from the homes and premises of some 5 million customers. Throughout the 1980s there were growing concerns over the standards and level of service delivery afforded by public sector organisations, and in line with the then government ideology and policy Anglian Water was privatised in 1989. Following privatisation, the company introduced a major reorganisation of its business, involving a rationalisation of existing structures and a diversification into new markets – many of them overseas operations. Between 1993 and 1995 the company reduced management layers from eleven to five, and 33 per cent of white-collar jobs were eliminated, bringing a saving of £40 million. However, senior management were conscious that if the organisation was to transform itself into a successful, high-performing international company, a fundamental realignment of its existing culture was required.

Prior to privatisation, the company's culture could be described as 'militaristic' – and with some justification. The risks were high. Any mistake in delivering water to customers could prove disastrous, and the company abided by the principle that 'contaminated water cannot be recalled'. The management solution was to introduce strict rules and procedures that were to be followed to the letter and obeyed without question. Any diversion from routine procedures was alien to an organisation where small risks or mistakes could rapidly and seriously jeopardise health and safety. The result was a culture in which playing by the rules, obeying orders, the acceptance and non-questioning of procedures was (and in the eyes of many had to be) the norm.

Forging a learning organisation

Senior management were under no illusions: the company's future success and survival in an increasingly competitive and aggressive marketplace depended on replacing the company's command-and-control culture with a more outward-looking, entrepreneurial, customer-focused, innovative approach to doing business. But how could this be achieved?

Philosophically, the company's approach was rooted in the need to reorient and prepare its employees for continuing and radical change, and to do this meant creating a more flexible, empowering, learning culture. The need to move in this direction was highlighted by a series of employee attitude surveys carried out after the restructuring of the early 1990s. Among other things, the surveys highlighted a discontent with the existing management style and communication policies. This led the senior management of Anglian Water into a considered debate about the future cultural direction of the business and the decision to create what they termed a *learning organisation*.

As a learning organisation the company would move away from the old public sector, keep your head down, jobs for life, follow the procedure mentality towards an environment in which employee creativity, innovation and challenge would be encouraged and valued. Employees would be empowered to take the lead in change. Individually and in cross-functional teams they would involve themselves in continuous improvement, not only in the area of technological development but – more significantly for a highly rational, technical organisation – in the area of customer service to meet changing needs and demands.

Steps along the way

There were two central, interlocking components designed to transform Anglian Water into a learning organisation. The first was the *Transformation Journey*. The concept of the Journey evolved from a development programme for attitudinal and behavioural change among senior managers. Following its success, a decision was taken to roll it out to all employees. The Journey was not a training programme. Instead it was a holistic strategy designed to prepare and equip employees for the technical and emotional challenges of operating in a turbulent and uncertain environment. The Journey was aimed at changing mindsets and creating self-awareness. It sought to promote teamworking and cooperation, and ultimately to have a direct bearing on operational effectiveness and business performance.

Any employee could 'sign up' for the Journey, and participation was entirely voluntary. However, clear signals were sent to the workforce that individuals were expected to participate, and enrolment on the Journey was regarded as an indication of their commitment to the company and its future.

Employees formed themselves into teams. Sometimes these were work related, but on other occasions individuals from disparate backgrounds came together. The only proviso was that any activity they engaged in was to benefit themselves, their group, and Anglian Water. There were four guiding principles for 'Travellers':

- a willingness to get to know myself;
- a desire to develop myself;
- a desire to realise my full potential with and through others;
- an ability to link my personal development to the development of Anglian Water.

A typical Journey lasted two years and was an essentially self-managed exercise. Each group was expected to acquire its own funding and sponsorship and to arrange its own support and skills development. Regular reviews along the way ensured that there was a basis for learning and reflection.

Journeys included groups who went outside Anglian Water, for example to build a toilet block on top of England's highest mountain, to refurbish a children's hospice, or to dig a well in Africa. Other groups focused on internal projects to improve overall business functioning and 'make things happen'. They involved themselves in more cross-functional teamworking, sought to improve their business knowledge and commercial awareness, became more creative and lateral in their thinking, conducted detailed research into business problems, and explored different options for change.

Between 1995 and 1997, 3000 employees had enrolled on the Journey, with some 300 groups being formed. In a 1996 survey, 88 per cent of respondents felt the Journey had benefited Anglian Water, and 99 per cent said that participation in a Journey had been a 'good learning experience'. Coincident with this survey, it was reported that customer satisfaction ratings had risen from 70 per cent in March 1995 to 90 per cent in March 1996.

The second component in Anglian's strategy to transform itself into a learning organisation was the establishment of the *University of Water* (colloquially known as Aqua Universitas). Knowledge creation and sharing were seen as vital in promoting best-practice networks and better customer service, and in enhancing commercial success. The University was aimed at acknowledging, integrating, supporting and accrediting all forms of learning taking place in the company. Its role was to define and develop the skills and competences – especially management skills – that were required to move Anglian into the twenty-first century and ensure its future as a global player. To this end, considerable resources were made available – for example, a dedicated 'campus' on the shores of Rutland Water and the installation of an intranet to promote information exchange and communication.

Around these two central components throughout the 1990s the company introduced a raft of supporting initiatives, including total quality management, leadership coaching, mass communication strategy development, change agent networks, new HR performance management policies, and vision and values statements designed to inculcate new attitudes and behaviours.

So have efforts to transform Anglian Water into a learning organisation culture been a success? Certainly there are considerable references to the 'old Anglian Water' and the 'new Anglian Water', reflecting a perception of behaviour and attitudinal change. And according to Clive Morton, ex-HR Director of Anglian, there is no doubt that a change in culture has occurred:

> The combination of the Journey and the University of Water with its universal access has created the conditions for a learning business, helping to assure the future for Anglian Water and its stakeholders.
>
> (Morton, 1998: 98)

The future

In 1998 Ofwat (the government's regulatory body for the water industry) recommended a price reduction of at least 17.5 per cent (about £45 on the average bill) in 2000. This one-off cut in charges represented about £130 million loss of revenue, and compares with 1998 profits of £268 million on turnover of £850 million. 'Costs must come down', the company warned. During 1999 the company initiated a major cost-reduction strategy, and this has translated into 400 job losses (10 per cent of the workforce).

References

Morton, C. (1998) *Beyond World Class*. Basingstoke: Macmillan Business Press.

Source: Extracts from *Anglian Water News*

Questions

You are an external consultant(s) advising a company facing similar challenges to those experienced by Anglian Water. It has read an account similar to the one described above, and is interested in exploring the whole concept of the learning organisation as a way of helping it to transform and succeed in the face of radical change. However, the board is cautious, and slightly sceptical of the cultural transformation process that Anglian has undergone. It has asked you to make an assessment. Specifically, they want you to report:

1 on the extent to which Anglian Water's claim to be a learning organisation can be justified. On what grounds should any claims or justifications be made?

2 against the backdrop of recent major job losses, whether or not Anglian can/should sustain the ideals and practices of a learning organisation. Are there any factors that might eventually undermine the concept and call into question the massive investment Anglian has made?

You are to prepare a report for the board of between 1000 and 1500 words, and follow this up with a short presentation (ten minutes).

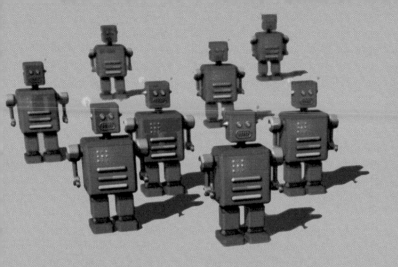

Part 4

THE EMPLOYMENT RELATIONSHIP

Introduction to Part 4

The employment relationship is a key feature in the nature of managing employment. It brings together the sources of power and legitimacy, rights and obligations, that management and employees seek for themselves and apply to others. This Part is concerned with explaining this relationship and examining how it works out through a variety of applications such as the law, collective bargaining, performance and reward, and employee involvement.

Chapter 11 deals with the role and influence of the law in determining the nature of contract. The contract of employment is not simply a document that is presented to employees on appointment, but is a complex set of formal and informal rules which govern the whole basis of the employment relationship. Thus, the way employees and managers conform with, or break, those rules determines how that relationship works out in practice. Moreover, the nature of contract can have an important bearing on whether such newer concepts as human resource management can fundamentally change a relationship that is so dependent upon the interaction of formal and informal legal regulation.

Chapter 12 introduces the concept and practice of collective bargaining. In recent years the collective determination of pay has reduced in coverage and scope in many market economies, but it still remains the most important single method of arriving at broad pay settlement for many employees, and its impact and effect is often felt throughout economies. For these reasons its nature, structure and outcomes form the basis of analysis.

Chapter 13 discusses the processes that go towards settling pay for individuals when criteria which test their own performance are introduced. In recent years there has been an increasing use made of individualised pay, performance-related pay and performance management. This chapter examines some of the problems and issues in operating and evaluating such processes.

Chapter 14 is concerned with the development of employee involvement. This is a topic that has seen great interest recently, but there are contradictory elements within it which this chapter explores, among them whether involvement can genuinely bring employee and managerial interests together and whether involvement is a vehicle for 'empowerment' or simply a further way in which the managerial prerogative is asserted in the employment relationship.

CHAPTER 11

The employment relationship and employee rights at work

Ian Clark

OBJECTIVES

▶ To introduce readers from a variety of backgrounds to the central significance of contract in the employment relationship.

▶ To examine employment contracts and the legal regulation of employee activity within them.

▶ To provide the personnel practitioner or other interested reader with the necessary basic information to enable them to make fair and reasonable decisions within the employment relationship.

▶ To examine the contractual and statutory regulation of employment contracts in a manner that is reader friendly, non-technical but taking as its central focus the manner in which employment rights need to be regulated and proceduralised in the workplace.

▶ To add critical observations on the limitations of employee rights in the UK.

 ## Introduction

This chapter examines the employment relationship and its contractual regulation. In particular, it outlines the central significance of contractual regulation in the employment relationship, and how this legitimises the managerial prerogative. The employment relationship is visualised as a process of socio-economic exchange. That is, unlike other contractual relationships, for example something as mundane as the purchase of a railway ticket, the employment relationship is an open-ended contractual relationship. By this we mean that both parties intend the contract to continue until either party indicates a desire to terminate the relationship. Thus an employment contract is not an immediately closed relationship of exchange. The employment relationship contains an economic component – the exchange of work for payment – but also includes a sociological dimension centred on power and authority. The economic and sociological components of the employment relationship are structured by the contract of employment. In addition to this, the employment relationship is subject to a range of other processes, for example management competence and efficiency, work group control, management and worker motivation and the potential for workplace conflict and disagreement. These factors make the apparently rational process of economic exchange much more complicated and to some extent indeterminate – that is, a relationship in which the specific details are subject to ongoing negotiation and change.

All employees are protected by a series of basic contractual and statutory employment rights which the employment practices of an employer must abide by. In order to provide readers with the necessary basic information on these matters the chapter divides into seven parts:

- Distinguishing contractual and statutory employment rights
- The contract of employment
- Discrimination in employment
- The regulation of working time
- Termination of the employment contract
- Enforcement of contractual and statutory employment rights
- New rights at work?

Throughout the chapter there is a series of Activity boxes and Stop and think boxes that aim to assist the reader apply and digest particular points. Readers should work through these individually or in discussion with their teachers. The material in each part of the chapter, although necessarily legal in nature, is explained as far as possible in terms that are general and straightforward, that is, in a manner that will assist the reader in their application. Some points are repeated as they impact on areas of employment regulation detailed in successive parts of the chapter. Because the aim is to present the material in a 'reader friendly' manner there are few direct references to legal texts or statutes; however, at the end of the chapter a list of law texts is provided for further reading. The reader should view this chapter as a general introduction to the contract of employment and its regulation and readers should be aware that more specialist information may be required in applying the general principles to specific situations.

Distinguishing contractual and statutory employment rights

In a chapter such as this, it is impossible to provide a complete and comprehensive analysis of the employment relationship and its legal regulation – employment contracts and employment statutes are subject to change as practices that were previously 'outwith the law' become subject to legal regulation, for example the recent emergence of paid paternity leave for fathers, hence the law may be further updated after this edition is published. Equally, many areas of contractual and statutory regulation are extremely complicated and disputes between an employer and an employee may require specialist analysis by employment lawyers. Examples of these areas include discrimination claims with respect to pension rights for part-time women employees, disability discrimination claims that relate to the status of an employee as HIV positive and the interpretation of working time regulations for a particular group of employees. Thus, bearing in mind that contractual and statutory regulation of the employment relationship is a 'moving target', our examination of regulation within the employment relationship divides between a discussion of contractual and statutory employment rights.

■ Contractual rights

All employees have a contract of employment that governs the relationship between the employer and an individual employee. As we discuss below, an employment contract has three types of terms and conditions within it – express terms that are usually written down and which govern the specific details of the employee's contract of employment, implied terms that are unlikely to be written down but which nevertheless are considered to be part of an employee's contract of employment. For example, an employer is under a legally enforceable duty to provide a healthy and safe workplace. Equally, employees are likely to find themselves subject to various duties that are derived from custom and practice arrangements in the workplace even though many of them may be unwritten. The third type of term and condition within a contract of employment relates to statutory protection against unfair or unreasonable treatment by an employer and these statutory terms and conditions are incorporated into individual employment contracts. In summary, contractual rights flow from the express, implied and statutory incorporated terms and conditions that create an individual contract of employment. It is important to point out that while employees receive protection via elements of these terms and conditions they are also subject to regulation by them; hence the contract of employment is made up of a balance of rights and obligations between the employer and the employee.

Statutory rights

Statutory employment rights provide a basic floor of rights for all workers. Statutory employment rights are created by legislation in the form of Acts of Parliament and, increasingly, European Union directives that must be incorporated into UK law. A recent example of the latter is the emergence in the UK of the statutory regulation of working time and the introduction, from April 2003, of paid paternity leave for fathers.

In the drafting process, government and European Union civil servants seek to ensure that the legislation covers most eventualities. However, because legislation is necessarily general in its coverage of a particular issue an employer, trade unions and the judiciary must interpret legislation. Interpretation of legislation is a complicated and controversial matter and often turns on the issue of what is 'reasonable'. For an employer's interpretation of a statute to be reasonable the employer must be able to demonstrate to an employee, trade union or, in a matter of dispute, an employment tribunal that another employer faced with the same or a similar situation would have acted in the same way. In a matter of dispute an employee or a trade union must be able to demonstrate that another employer would not have acted in a particular manner. For example, until recently it was common practice for many employers to exclude their part-time workforce from occupational pension schemes on the basis that the salary or wage level of part-timers was too low to generate a sufficient pension fund, particularly as this would reduce the take-home pay of such workers because of the necessary deduction of an employee's contribution to the pension scheme. After a long legal campaign several trade unions, supported by the Equal Opportunities Commission, have established that this practice is unreasonable because many part-time workers are women and their exclusion from company pension schemes amounts to indirect sex discrimination. This is the case because, although the exclusion of part-time workers from pension schemes appears to be sex neutral in its effects, such exclusion has a disproportionate effect on women, so the practice is discriminatory. Common law precedent, that is, judicial decisions of interpretation, guide decisions in disputes where there is no relevant Act of Parliament and thus has the status of an Act of Parliament.

Summary

A central principle of the English legal system operative in contract law, the common law and statute law is that of *reasonableness*. In employment contracts, the common law terms and conditions and statutory interventions both have to be reasonable in their effects on the employer and employee. Thus in many cases judgments in disputes between employer and employee often turn on the question of reasonableness. The notions of reasonable and unreasonable behaviour or instructions are questions of interpretation in the circumstances of particular cases. As explained above, an express, implied or incorporated term in a contract of employment is reasonable if, in a matter of dispute, it is held that a similar employer would have done the same thing, for example discipline or dismiss an employee, in similar circumstances. The discussion of this point is important for the following reasons. As statutory rights are subject to interpretation, challenge and eventual updating either in the form of statutory amendment or a binding precedent created by a court or employment tribunal, personnel practitioners must keep abreast of developments in employment law to ensure that the procedures set in place by their employer reflect the spirit and the letter of the law.

Stop and think	Try to think of five contractual rights and five statutory rights that you have or that your parents or partner have in employment.

The contract of employment

This part of the chapter divides into six subsections. The first distinguishes employment contracts from commercial contracts; this is followed by a brief discussion of contract theory. The third subsection examines the effects of the common law on employment contracts; this is followed by a discussion of different types of employment contracts. The fifth subsection discusses terms and conditions of employment contracts, and finally statutory rights that relate to employment contracts are examined in some detail.

Distinguishing commercial contracts and employment contracts

In order to explain the concept of contract, it is useful to distinguish between commercial contracts and employment contracts, the area of our particular focus. Commercial contracts, for example something as simple as buying a bus ticket or something as complex as a house purchase, contain four elements:

- offer;
- acceptance;
- consideration;
- the intention to create legal relations.

To illustrate these four elements we can draw on the example of a house purchase. An individual may visit a particular house and decide they would like to buy it. As a result of this they decide to make an offer. The current property owner may decide to accept this offer – subject to contract. 'Subject to contract' will necessarily involve the person who wishes to buy the house – the offeror – receiving a satisfactory structural survey and acquiring the necessary purchase price either in cash or (more likely) through a mortgage. If these requirements are satisfactorily fulfilled, a contract can be drawn up. In consideration for the agreed purchase price, the existing property owner – the offeree – agrees to give up their property rights in the house and exchange them through contract to the offeror. Thus consideration is the mechanism that validates the contract: that is, each party gives something to the contract, in this case a house for money by the offeror and money for a house by the offeree. If a contract contains offer, acceptance and consideration, the presence of these factors indicates that the parties to the contract wish to create a legally binding relationship.

A legally binding contract must also satisfy the following factors. First, the contents of the contract, to which the parties have agreed, must be reasonable. Second, the contract in itself must be legal, in terms of the prevailing law. For example, a contract to assassinate a person may contain offer, acceptance and consideration and an intention to create a legally binding relationship between the parties. However, conspiracy to murder is a criminal offence, thus any contractual relationship is void – the legal term for invalid. Third, there must be genuine consent between the parties, and the parties themselves must have the capacity to consent to the agreement. For example, minors and bankrupts have only limited capacities in contract. From this brief introduction we can now proceed to look at employment contracts, which are a very specialised form of contract.

A contract of employment is a *contract of service*, where an employee – the subject of the contract – is in the personal service of their employer. It is necessary to distinguish an employment contract of personal service from a commercial *contract for services*. As Wedderburn (1986: 106) makes clear, the law marks off the employee under a contract of service from independent contractors – self-employed workers – who may provide services to an organisation under a commercial contract. For example, a commercial contract whereby catering or cleaning services are provided to one firm by a second firm is a contract for services, not an employment contract, even though the work is performed by labour. Catering staff may be employees in the offeror firm, but the offeree firm has bought their services under a commercial contract for catering services.

A contract of employment differs from a commercial contract for services in the sense that an employment contract of personal service to an employer is intended to be an open-ended relationship. It is a relationship that continues until either party decides to end it through due notice, whereas a commercial contract is more likely to be a precise exchange of services over a clearly defined period of time. Some employment contracts today are of a temporary or fixed-term nature, but nonetheless an employment relationship is created, whereas in commercial contracts of a long-term duration, for example computer or photocopier servicing, an employment relationship is not created. Equally, such commercial contracts are likely to contain clear and precise contractual duties for each party. Thus commercial contracts are a purely contractual relationship and, unlike employment contracts, are not subject to the *common law duties* of an employer and employee which operate as implied terms and conditions within the contract of employment. The common law refers to areas of law that are not covered by parliamentary or European Union legislation. The common law has been developed by the judiciary: that is, the common law is *judge-made law*. Now that we have defined contract and distinguished between commercial and employment contracts, it is possible to proceed with a discussion of the underlying assumptions behind contract theory.

ACTIVITY   List the differences between commercial and employment contracts. Explain how commercial contracts might create employment. Compare and contrast your views with those of a colleague or the teacher.

Equality and freedom of entry: market individualism

The philosophical basis of contract is derived from the principle of market individualism. Market individualism suggests that the individual is the best judge of his or her own interests. From this suggestion the notion of *freedom of contract* is introduced, which assumes that individuals are self-determining agents, who are primarily self-interested. Thus individuals are able to fulfil their own self-interest most effectively if they are free to enter into contracts between themselves within the market mechanism.

Freedom of contract suggests that individuals act as free agents when they enter into contracts as both parties to a contract have equal status before the law and they jointly determine the terms and conditions of the contract. It follows from this assumption that the component elements of a contract – offer, acceptance and the consideration between the parties – are arrived at through a process of negotiation and then agreement to create legal relations. This may be the situation in the case of a house purchase, but in relation to employment the situation is somewhat different. As Fox (1985: 6) points out, contract theory alone, with all that it entails in terms of equality and references to adjudication by an outside body, cannot be an effective mode of regulation in the case of employment if the parties to the contract are in dispute. In the UK this is the case because the employment relationship remains one of *status*. The notion of status derives from paternalism in the master and servant relationship inherent in 'employment' prior to the rise of industrial economies. Examples of paternal employment include domestic service and tied cottages for estate farmers and general agricultural labourers. In the nineteenth century, domestic servants and agricultural labourers were not employees in the modern sense of the word; rather they were subject to a crude form of commercial contract whereby they provided their labour services to a master in return for board and lodgings. However, once employment became contractually determined in a formal legal sense it did not constitute a clean break with the past. By this we mean that the contractual process incorporates characteristics from pre-industrial 'paternal' employment: for example, the status bias of the master and servant relationship.

Fox (1985: 3–5) identifies paternalism as the basis of status within employment. Paternalism refers to a situation of subordination to legitimate authority. Prior to the contractual determination of employment the process of subordination to legitimate authority was entirely within the master–servant relationship. Within contractually determined employment, the employee subordinates him or herself to the greater legal authority of the employer, the superiority of which is derived from the status-based relationship of master and servant.

So, although employment contracts provide employees with a degree of independence from their employer – for example, employees can terminate their employment through due notice – employees remain subordinate parties to the employment contract. They are subject to the reasonable and legitimate authority of their employer, to whom they provide personal service.

From the above discussion it is clear that equality before the law in employment contracts is a fiction because employer authority is derived from their paternal status which underpins the employment relationship. This is often referred to as the *managerial prerogative*. In most contracts the agreeing parties are assumed to be the best judges of their own interests. However, in employment the status bias of the employer gives them the privilege of determining their self-interest and a partial say in the determination of employee interests. This privilege derives from the concept of *subordination*, which implies that the junior partner to the employment contract cannot perceive all their real interests. Kahn-Freund (1984) described the individually based contract of employment as an act of submission on the part of the employee:

> In its operation it is a condition of subordination, however much the submission and the subordination may be concealed by that indispensable figment of the legal mind known as the contract of employment.

An employer may determine the organisation of work, levels of payment and duration of working time. The employee is bound by such impositions if they are reasonable. Thus the notion of free employment contracts bears little resemblance to the real world (Hyman, 1975: 23). Relatedly, although all employees have an individual contract of employment, the terms and conditions of an individual's contract of employment are likely to be determined and regulated by means of a collective agreement, the details of which are normally incorporated in an individual's contract of employment. These agreements are often negotiated by a trade union through the process of collective bargaining. In the absence of a trade union and collective bargaining 'collective agreements' are unilaterally determined by management on behalf of the employer; they are not the subject of negotiation. This point again illustrates that the notions of individual negotiation and freedom of contract exist at only a superficial level of relations between employer and employee.

> **ACTIVITY**
>
> Summarise what you understand by the terms 'managerial prerogative' and 'subordination' in the employment relationship. Provide two examples of the managerial prerogative and subordination in your employment. Lastly, explain how the notion of 'equality before the law' is not necessarily the same as equality in law within the employment relationship.

■ Common law regulation of employment contracts

There are two features of the English legal system that highlight the contexts within which all aspects of the law operate. First, the English legal system, unlike most other legal systems (for example, those of other European Union states), does not operate in conjunction with a written constitution or a Bill of Rights. In the specific area of employment the absence of a written constitution or a Bill of Rights means that British subjects do not possess any specific inalienable rights as employees: for example, the right to strike. Second, and relatedly, the system is very conservative – some would say obsessed with the past. This conservatism explains why 'precedent' has so prominent a role in the common law. Precedent operates on the basis of decisions previously arrived at in a higher court. It is judge-made law that creates a rule for lower courts and subsequent future cases of a similar nature. Thus a precedent creates an example for subsequent cases or acts as a justification for subsequent decisions.

Advocates of Britain's unwritten constitution argue that its major benefit is adaptability over time, which contrasts with the rigid mechanism of a written constitution around which new developments have to be moulded. In matters of employment many of the rights held by British subjects result from case law and precedent and from trade union activity in collective bargaining. Equally, trade unions have a consultative role in the formulation of statutory protections and provisions such as the national minimum wage or the statutory procedure for trade union recognition under the Employment Relations Act 1999.

● Common law duties of employer and employee

Earlier in this part of the chapter, the concept of 'freedom of contract' was introduced. This concept assumes that individuals are self-determining agents who are primarily self-interested. It follows from this that individuals both freely enter into contractual arrangements and jointly determine the terms and conditions of an employment contract. In the case of employment, the notion of freedom of contract operates in conjunction with the common law duties of employer and employee. That is, although contracts of employment may be entered into freely, the contract of employment itself incorporates the common law duties of employee and employer.

Common law duties of the employer

These are to:

- Provide a reasonable opportunity for the employee to work and pay the agreed wages as consideration for work performed. It is a matter of some debate as to whether the employer has a common law duty to actually provide work; the issue appears to turn on the notion of reasonableness, which will depend on the details of any particular case.
- Take reasonable care to ensure that all employees are safe at the workplace, and indemnify any employee for injury sustained during employment. Employers have a vicarious common law duty to provide a safe working environment for their employees. Vicarious means that a legal duty is delegated to an employer to provide a safe working environment for employees, that is, it is a duty imposed on employers. Aspects of this liability are codified in statute under the Health and Safety at Work Act 1974. In the year 2001–2002 the Health and Safety Commission reported 249 deaths in the workplace, a 15 per cent reduction on the previous year. The most common causes of death in the workplace are falls, moving objects and moving vehicles. Construction with 30 per cent of deaths and agriculture with 16 per cent of deaths are the most dangerous sectors of employment. The average fine for a work-related death is £30 000, with the Health and Safety Commission winning 84 per cent of the cases where it prosecuted employers.
- Treat all employees in a courteous and polite manner. That is, employers should not 'bully' or abuse their employees, or subject them to racist or sexist remarks. Aspects of this liability are codified in the Sex Discrimination Act 1975 (as amended) and the Race Relations Act 1976 (as amended). The common law duties of the employer contrast with those of an employee.

Common law duties of the employee

These are to:

- be ready and willing to work for their employer;
- offer personal service to the employer: that is, not hold a second job without agreement;
- take reasonable care in the conduct of their personal service;
- work in the employer's time, obey reasonable orders during that time, and undertake not to disrupt the employer's business on purpose;
- not disclose any trade secret to their employer's competitors.

The common law duties of the employee and employer are not always detailed in the written particulars of a contract of employment, and may be implied terms in the contract derived from custom and practice or statutes.

In market economies the contract of employment is freely entered into; however, the terms and conditions, whether they are express or implied, are not jointly determined, and in terms of employee and employer obligations they are not equal in terms of their scope and coverage. In most cases the employer is in the dominant bargaining position because they are offering employment. Hence the employer is able unilaterally to determine how the common law duties of the employee are to be fulfilled. The common law duties of the employee, as listed above, are clear and precise but open to considerable interpretation. In contrast to this, the common law obligations of the employer are imbued with the tenet of limited reasonableness: that is, the obligations imposed on the employer should not be unreasonable. Thus the general concept of reasonableness can only be tested in individual cases. As Hyman (1975: 24) argues, the symmetrical equality within the concept of self-determining individuals freely entering into contracts of employment is really asymmetrical because of the form that the notion of equality (before the law) and freedom of entry actually take. Clearly, equality before the law belies the market power held by an employer. Individual equality before the law places firms that have access to necessarily expensive legal advice on the formulation of employment contracts and individuals bereft of such a capability on the same plane. As we pointed out earlier, within the contract of employment freedom and equality are fused with the traditional status bias of employment, and it is this that appears to reduce the equality of the employee and raise the equality of the employer. This dealignment of equality creates the asymmetrical situation described by Hyman.

● Types of employment contract

Every employee has a contract of employment. However, not all workers have a contract of employment. Where an employer provides regular work, defines working hours, the place of work and deducts income tax and National Insurance through the PAYE system, an employment relationship is created and anyone engaged on these terms is likely to be an employee. In contrast to this situation, a worker who is not an employee will pay their own income tax and National Insurance contributions, decide when, where and how they work and make their own holiday and sick pay arrangements. Hence many workers work under a contract for services as described above. However, in addition to self-employed contractors and freelance IT specialists, journalists, consultants etc., some agency workers, casual workers and 'home workers' may be classified as having worker status rather than employee status. A contract of employment is not always written down in one document, and sometimes the contract may not be written down at all.

There are several types of employment contract, as detailed below.

Permanent, ongoing or open-ended contracts

This type of employment contract is assumed to continue until either side gives notice of an intention to terminate the contract.

Temporary contract

This type of contract has a specified duration, but does not contain any restrictive fixed terms or waivers – for example, the requirement that the employee waive their right to statutory protection against a claim for unfair dismissal or redundancy. A temporary contract may be made permanent, and in this case the clause that relates to the specified duration will be removed, and the time served under the temporary contract will constitute continuity of service. Hence in the case of employment rights that are based on an employee's length of service – for example, unfair dismissal, which is currently set at one year's length of service – it is unnecessary for the employee to serve another full year to acquire this protection. However, although the general principle is clear, it is a complex area of law subject to the particular circumstances of individual cases.

Fixed-term contract

This type of contract has a specified duration: that is, a clear start date and a clear and unequivocal termination date. Examples of this might include situations where employment is subject to 'funding arrangements' that are not renewable, a specific one-off project or matters such as maternity and paternity leave. Both parties to a fixed-term contract should be aware that the contract is not renewable. More significant than this, many employees who are subject to fixed-term contracts are required to waive their statutory protections against unfair dismissal and redundancy. The Employment Relations Act 1999 prohibits employers from using waiver clauses against unfair dismissal; however, redundancy waivers continue. Since November 2001, employees under fixed-term contracts have equal rights to those of permanent employees in terms of pay rates and pension provision.

'Casual', 'spot' or zero hours contracts

Under this type of contract the employee must be available for work, but the employer does not have to guarantee work: for example, a retired teacher may be on call to cover for sick colleagues. Equally, banks use call staff to cover busy periods such as lunchtime, whereas the Post Office employs many casual workers at Christmas. In most situations this type of contract is mutually beneficial and not open to abuse; however, if a worker is required to be at work but clock off during slack periods – a practice once common in many fast-food outlets – zero hours contracts are open to abuse. For example, such a worker could remain at the workplace for long periods yet have a very low rate of hourly pay owing to continual clocking off. In an effort to overcome some of the abuses of zero hours contracts a person employed on such a contract is now entitled to the national minimum wage, whereas the Working Time Directive entitles the person to a paid holiday provided they worked during the preceding 13 weeks. The vast majority of individuals who are engaged under a zero hours contract will be classified as an employee; however, some employers have attempted to argue that engagement under a zero hours contract is compatible with worker status. The basis of this argument centres on the 'mutuality of obligation' between the employer and the worker or employee. If someone engaged under a zero hours contract does not have regular hours of work and is able to decline offers of work and/or work elsewhere, there is unlikely to be a mutuality of obligation between the two parties. It is the presence of mutual obligation that creates the employment relationship establishing the employer and employee. This is a controversial area and the distinction between worker status and employee status is persistently criticised by the TUC and other employee groups. Up to 9 million workers in the UK may have worker status, many of whom are arguably *de facto* employees, for example long-term agency workers or temps engaged in one organisation. The TUC is campaigning for all workers to have the status of an employee and therefore receive the basic contractual and statutory protections outlined earlier in the chapter. On the specific issue of agency and temporary workers, the UK's forthcoming adoption of European Union directives may provide the basis of some improvement in employment protection.

We have established that in the vast majority of cases the employer is the dominant party in the employment relationship. This dominance enables the employer to determine many terms and conditions contained within the employment contract.

Stop and think	What types of employment might be offered on the basis of a casual, spot or zero hours contract of employment? What reasons might an employer have to engage an employee on a fixed-term contract of employment?

● Terms and conditions within employment contracts

There are three types of terms and conditions within a contract of employment.

Express terms and conditions

These form an explicit part of an individual contract of employment. They are often referred to as the *written* terms and conditions of the contract that are included in the written *statement of the contract*. Any employee, irrespective of the number of hours they work, must be given a statement of the written terms and conditions of their contract within two months – eight weeks – of starting work. The statement must include the following items:

- Name and address of employer.
- Date employment began.

- Place or places of work.
- Rate of pay or salary point; for lower-paid employees the rate must adhere to the statutory national minimum wage, from 1 October 2002, £4.20 per hour for workers aged 22 or over and £3.60 per hour for those aged 18–21. For more details see www.dti.gov.uk/er/nmw.
- Hours of work; as a result of the Human Rights Act, 1998 it may be necessary for employers to specify the reasons for, frequency of and need to telephone employees at home. This legislation establishes that an employer does not have an automatic right to demand an employee's home phone number unless the express terms of an employment contract state that an employee has a duty to be available outside normal working hours.
- Holiday entitlements; as a result of the working time regulations (see part 4) all employees are now entitled to four weeks' paid holiday, part-time workers on a pro-rata basis. The situation with respect to temporary or agency workers is more complicated. All employees are entitled to a minimum of four weeks' paid holiday but to qualify for this an employee must work for an employer for 13 weeks. Temps employed by an agency are entitled to paid holidays if they work for 13 weeks. This is the case even if they move between different workplaces as long as the employment is continuous. The situation with respect to temporary workers will be further clarified by the EU Agency Workers Directive, see part 7.
- Sick pay arrangements.
- Notice entitlements.
- Pension rights.
- Grievance procedure.
- Discipline procedure.
- Job title.
- Period of employment if job not permanent.
- Name of employee.

Implied terms and conditions

These are terms and conditions that are not explicitly stated in an individual contract of employment but which are assumed to be included in the contract: for example, workplace custom and practice arrangements and the common law duties of the employer and employee.

Incorporated terms and conditions of employment

These are terms and conditions that are incorporated into individual contracts of employment as either express or implied terms. Incorporated terms and conditions of employment include the provisions of collective agreements negotiated between an employer and a recognised trade union and statutory protections passed by Parliament or the European Union. In English law, collective agreements negotiated between employers and trade unions through the process of collective bargaining are not legally binding. However, elements within collective agreements are legally binding if they are incorporated into individual contracts of employment: for example, working hours and pay rates.

■ Changing terms and conditions of employment

Employers are able to change terms and conditions of employment; however, employees have some rights if an employer seeks to change terms and conditions without consultation and agreement. A unilateral change in pay rates represents a serious breach of contract, as does the unilateral removal of a company car, reductions in holiday entitlements and suspension of an employer's pension contribution. Employees can accept unilateral changes and work normally under protest – object to the changes and seek to minimise the effects of the unilateral change and seek representation through a trade union – or leave and claim 'constructive dismissal'.

Stop and think

Ensure that you are clear on the differences between express, implied and statutory incorporated terms and conditions of employment. Check your understanding with a class colleague and the teacher.

ACTIVITY

Examine the points above on express, implied and statutory incorporated terms and conditions of employment against your own job and see if you can state what your express terms are or where details of them can be found.

■ Statutory rights relating to employment contracts

All employees have a contract of employment; equally, all employees receive some level of statutory protection against arbitrary and unreasonable treatment by an employer. Statutory protection can be framed in individual terms, for example protection against sexual and racial discrimination in the workplace; alternatively, rights may be collective, for example the statutory procedure for trade union recognition introduced by the Employment Relations Act 1999.

Since 1995 all workers, either full-time or part-time, have been subject to the same *day one statutory rights* irrespective of how many hours they work. Statutory day one rights provide a minimum level of protection to all workers. Some workers may have additional contractual rights negotiated by their employer and a recognised trade union. In addition to day one rights, other rights depend on an employee's length of service.

● Day one employment rights

Equal pay/equal value

The Equal Pay Act 1970 (EPA) as amended inserts an *equality clause* into contracts of employment that can be enforced by an employment tribunal. Under the EPA clauses within a contract of employment must be equal between the sexes. The equality clause enforces equal terms and conditions in the contracts of men and women employed in the same organisation. The clause covers pay and all other contractual terms of employment. The EPA is applicable in three situations:

- *Like work*. Where men and women are employed to perform like work, that is, the same work or work that is broadly similar, men and women must receive the same rate of pay or be paid on the same salary scale. This is the case even if part-time men and women work fewer hours than full-time men and women, that is, a part-time worker may compare themselves to a full-time employee.
- *Work rated as equivalent under an analytical job evaluation scheme.* Job evaluation describes a set of methods that compare jobs with the view to assessing their relative and comparative worth. The process of job evaluation ranks jobs based on rational and objective assessment of key factors – such as skill, effort and decision-making – from a representative sample of jobs in a particular organisation. The purpose of job evaluation is to produce a reasonable and defensible ranking of jobs. By formalising

and making explicit the basis of payment systems and associated differences in pay levels, employers can expose discriminatory practices and remove them; for more detail on job evaluation see Armstrong and Baron (1995) and Chapter 6.

● Where work is of *equal value*, even though it is not like work or work covered by a non-discriminatory job evaluation scheme in the same employment. Equal value is measured in terms of the demands upon the worker in terms of skill levels, effort and decision-making. If different work is held to be of equal value under these criteria then the two groups of workers must have the same pay levels. Pay is constituted in its widest sense and includes salary scales or pay rates, access to occupational pension schemes, redundancy protection, sick pay, travel concessions and other perks. In the 1980s, USDAW (the shop workers' trade union) and the Equal Opportunities Commission successfully fought equal value cases on behalf of supermarket checkout workers, who are predominantly women, against delivery dock and warehouse workers who were predominantly men. An employer may defend an equal value case on the grounds that differences in pay between men and women are justified on the grounds of a genuine material factor that is both relevant and significant in the particular case. The fact that a particular group of workers who are predominantly women includes a male worker does not constitute a genuine material factor: that is, men who receive lower pay than other men employed in the same organisation are able to claim that their work is of equal value. For example, the presence of a 'token' male checkout worker or school lunch assistant appears insufficient to defeat a claim for equal value. In summary, a claim to equal pay for work of equal value normally involves women in comparison to men; however, the presence of lower-paid men cannot undermine a claim because men are also protected in respect of equal pay for work of equal value.

Sex discrimination/harassment

It is unlawful to discriminate against an employee on grounds of their sex or marital status, or because of pregnancy. Employment protection legislation covers discrimination in respect of pay, whereas the Sex Discrimination Act 1975 as amended (SDA) covers discrimination in respect of selection, training, promotion, termination (e.g. selection for redundancy) or any other detriment in employment (e.g. sexual harassment). The SDA applies equally to men and women except with respect to pregnancy provisions, and defines discrimination in three ways:

● *Direct discrimination.* For example, denying a woman a job or promotion on the grounds that she is a woman, a married woman, a single woman, is pregnant and/or has children.

● *Indirect discrimination.* This category refers to apparently sex-neutral job requirements that have a disproportional effect on men or women, for example height requirements, dress codes or age and length of service requirements for promotion that may preclude married women with children from having sufficient length of service to apply by an upper age limit. Some cases of indirect discrimination appear to be intentional, whereas other cases result from a failure to update personnel procedures in accordance with the law: for example, dress codes that prevent women from wearing trousers. An employer may choose to defend a charge of indirect discrimination on the grounds that the apparently discriminatory provision is a necessary requirement of the job. For example, in selection exercises for the fire service candidates must be able to expand their lung capacity by a certain measurement. Many women applicants are unable to meet this requirement: hence it appears to have a disproportionate effect on women. However, many men are unable to meet the requirement. Lung expansion is a requirement of a firefighter's job because it plays a part in assessing whether or not a candidate would be able to escape from a variety of smoke-filled situations. Claims of direct and indirect sex discrimination are in the majority of cases launched by women; however, the law is equally applicable to men and women, an equality that was recently demonstrated in the decision of an employment tribunal. In this case a male worker in a Stockport job centre won a claim for sexual discrimination because he refused to wear a tie at work. The basis of this claim was that he was told what to wear whereas female colleagues were not and that female colleagues were allowed to wear tee shirts as opposed to more formal blouses. Currently the decision of the tribunal stands, but the Department of Work and Pensions has indicated that it may appeal this decision.

- *Victimisation.* This category covers verbal abuse or suggestive behaviour or harassment. It may also result from an employee's enforcing a statutory right. Certain types of employment are exempt from the provisions of the SDA: for example, employment that is mainly or wholly outside the UK, photographic modelling, and some areas of social work such as child protection from abuse and rape counselling.

Racial discrimination and harassment

The Race Relations Act 1976 (as amended) (RRA) follows the model set by the SDA and defines racial discrimination as direct, indirect and victimisation. Cases of direct racial discrimination in employment on the grounds that a person is black, Asian, or Afro-Caribbean are less in evidence than during the 1960s. However, examples of indirect racial discrimination in employment turn on the relevance of apparently race-neutral job requirements that have a disproportionate effect on ethnic minorities: for example, requirements that preclude candidates on the basis that their grandparents were not British, or English language requirements. If these requirements are unrelated to the job they may well be indirectly discriminatory. Racial victimisation in employment covers matters such as racial abuse, suggestive behaviour or harassment as a result of an employee attempting to enforce a statutory right. Certain types of employment are exempt from the provisions of the RRA: for example, staff in specialised restaurants and community social workers who are required to speak particular ethnic languages.

ACTIVITY   Think of two examples of employer or organisational behaviour that might constitute direct discrimination, indirect discrimination and victimisation in employment in terms of racial and sexual discrimination. Compare your list with one of your class colleagues.

Maternity rights

The rules and regulations in respect of maternity rights are very complicated. It is important that both the employer and the employee follow them carefully. Some employees have better maternity arrangements than the statutory arrangements; this is usually the result of collective bargaining arrangements in the workplace.

All women are entitled to maternity leave, which under the provisions of the ERA was set at 26 weeks and was further extended by the maternity and paternity leave regulations to 52 weeks of which up to 26 weeks are paid maternity leave. The entitlement is unrelated to the number of hours worked or length of service. A pregnant employee must conform to the following requirements:

- provide written notice of pregnancy and due date;
- provide a medical certificate if requested;
- indicate the date the employee intends to begin leave – this cannot be before the 11th week;
- return to work within 26 weeks for paid maternity leave or 52 weeks if the employee is taking a futher 26 weeks unpaid maternity leave.

Maternity leave may be extended if the employee is sick or has an illness related to confinement. The day one employment rights listed above and below establish that employees who are either pregnant or on maternity leave cannot be dismissed or made redundant because of pregnancy or a pregnancy-related illness contracted or diagnosed as commencing before or after the birth of the child.

An employee who fulfils the following criteria is entitled to *statutory maternity pay* when:

● their earnings are equal to £100 per week – the lower earnings limit;
● the employee provides the employer with a maternity certificate giving the due date;
● they were employed up to and including the 15th week before the baby was due;
● they have stopped working;
● they have given the employer 21 days' notice of their intention to stop working;
● at the end of the 15th week of confinement before the baby was due, the employee had worked for this employer for 26 weeks.

Statutory maternity pay is calculated on the basis of 6 weeks at 90 per cent of earnings plus 12 weeks at the basic rate of statutory sick pay. Employees who do not qualify for maternity pay may receive maternity allowance from the Department of Social Security. Awards for maternity allowance depend on an employee's National Insurance contribution.

Disability discrimination

The Disability Discrimination Act 1995 (DDA) makes it unlawful for an employer to discriminate against applicants for employment and employees who have a disability in relation to job applications, promotion, training and contractual terms and benefits. The provisions of the statute cover all employees from permanent to casual. In addition, sub-contract workers are also covered. The DDA is not universal in application. Currently, employers with fewer than 15 workers are exempt from its provisions. Small employers can discriminate against the disabled without the threat of legal sanction.

The DDA defines *disability* as mental or physical impairment that has a long-term and substantial adverse effect on the ability of an individual to perform normal daily activities. The legislation goes on to amplify this definition under several headings. First, the nature of impairment is broadly interpreted to include recognised medical conditions, for example HIV-positive status, schizophrenia and other forms of mental illness. Second, the requirement for a substantial effect rules out minor complaints such as hay fever or colour-blindness. Third, and related, a condition of impairment must last at least a year or the rest of a person's life to qualify as a long-term effect. This requirement rules out impairments such as whiplash resulting from minor motor accidents and other temporary debilitating illnesses. Last, the ability to undertake normal daily activity covers issues such as the ability to hear and learn, comprehend the perception and risk of physical danger, continence, eyesight, hearing, manual dexterity, memory, speech and physical coordination.

The DDA outlines three tests for disability discrimination:

● *Less favourable treatment.* This situation arises when a disabled employee is able to demonstrate less favourable treatment – in comparison with an able-bodied person – that is related to their disability that cannot be justified by the employer. An employer can defend a claim for disability discrimination on the grounds of less favourable treatment if they can demonstrate a relevant or substantial reason for the treatment.
● *A duty to make reasonable adjustments.* A failure to make reasonable adjustments in the workplace may result in disability discrimination. It is likely to be unlawful and unreasonable where a disabled employee is substantially disadvantaged by work arrangements or the layout of the workplace when compared with an able-bodied employee. In this situation the employer is under a legal duty to make reasonable adjustments: for example, the

installation of wheelchair ramps and the provision of ground floor office space for wheelchair users. An employer can justify the discrimination on the grounds that they were unaware that a job applicant or employee was disabled. Alternatively, an employer may justify discrimination with a substantial reason.

- *Victimisation.* It is unlawful under the DDA to victimise a person who alleges disability discrimination, enforces statutory rights under the DDA or gives evidence in a disability case.

Miscellaneous

In addition to the above day one rights, all employees have the following day one rights where relevant:

- time off for trade union duties;
- protection against victimisation due to involvement in trade union duties – for example, unfair selection for redundancy;
- protection against victimisation due to involvement in health and safety activity;
- the right to itemised payslips;
- protection against unlawful deductions from wages;
- written reasons for dismissal during pregnancy or maternity leave;
- time off for antenatal visits;
- basic maternity leave of 26 weeks;
- Sunday working rights, where relevant;
- protection against victimisation for enforcing a day one or length of service statutory right.

● Rights that depend on length of service

Access to the following statutory rights is dependent upon an employee's length of service, but is unrelated to how many hours they work.

- *Written statement of main terms and conditions of employment:* 2 months.
- *Extended maternity leave:* 1 year. Employees who have at least one year's employment service at the beginning of the 11th week before the baby is due are entitled to a longer period of maternity leave, termed extended maternity leave. This leave may extend up to 40 weeks, starting 11 weeks before the birth and lasting up to 29 weeks after birth. As with basic maternity leave, it does not matter how many hours the employee works. An employee who claims extended maternity leave has to follow several procedural rules:
  - work up to the 11th week before the baby is due;
  - give the employer at least 21 days' notice before the start of leave;
  - provide the employer with a statement that she is going on maternity leave and will return afterwards, and state the date the baby is due;
  - provide a certificate of due date signed by a GP or midwife if requested;
  - provide the employer with 21 days' written notice of the date she intends to return to work;
  - return to work within 29 weeks of the start of the week in which the baby is born.
- *Written reasons for dismissal* – 1 year.
- *Protection against unfair dismissal* – 1 year.
- *Protection against unfair dismissal due to 'whistle blowing', i.e. public interest disclosure* – 1 year. Such cases can be expensive for an employer because the public interest disclosure legislation does not impose a cap on tribunal awards. Connex, the train operating company, was recently ordered to pay £55 000 to a train driver who successfully demonstrated his victimisation after he published concerns over safety risks. £18 000 of the award was for aggravated damages and injury to feelings. Connex declined to appeal the tribunal decision.

- *Dismissal due to job redundancy* – 2 years.
- *Guaranteed lay-off pay* – 1 month.
- *Medical suspension pay* – Absence or suspension from work on medical grounds – 1 month.
- *Paid parental leave for fathers* – 1 year, 2 weeks' paid paternity leave at the same rate as statutory maternity pay. This supplements the government decision to introduce the EU minimum 13 weeks' unpaid leave provision.
- *Paid adoption leave* – 1 year, in order to allow one adoptive parent 2 weeks' paid leave at the same rate as statutory maternity pay.

Employers are required to provide employees with the periods of paid notice listed in Table 11.1. Employers must give employees full pay for the notice period even if the worker is off sick or on maternity leave.

Table 11.1 **Minimum notice periods**

Length of service	Notice	Length of service	Notice
4 weeks–2 years	1 week	7–8 years	7 weeks
2–3 years	2 weeks	8–9 years	8 weeks
3–4 years	3 weeks	9–10 years	9 weeks
4–5 years	4 weeks	10–11 years	10 weeks
5–6 years	5 weeks	11–12 years	11 weeks
6–7 years	6 weeks	Over 12 years	12 weeks

ACTIVITY   On the basis of the material on day one and length of service rights, discuss any situation in your employment where such rights may have been infringed. The discussion should test your argument against the law. In areas of disagreement between you and your class colleagues, confer with the teacher.

Discrimination in employment

As the second part of this chapter establishes, employees have statutory protection against discrimination on grounds of sex, race, disability and unequal treatment in terms of pay. However, the presence of discrimination in employment is still evident (see Dickens, 2000 for general discussion of the problem); for example, the Equal Opportunities Commission (2001) reported that women in full-time employment earn 82 per cent of male full-time hourly earnings, a figure that stood at 69 per cent in 1971. Equally, part-time women employees receive only 61 per cent of male full-time hourly earnings against a European Union average of 73 per cent. Further, in some female-dominated occupations, for example nursing, women earn 6 per cent less than average male hourly earnings and survey material continues to demonstrate that female employees argue that pay discrimination remains a persistent problem. For example, a survey of 1500 women managers found that a third of the sample claimed that pay discrimination persists in their organisation (Public Affairs, 2001). More dramatically than this, a recent report by the National Association of Citizens Advice Bureau found that many women are still sacked or threatened with the sack when they become pregnant.

In 2002, in its submission to the Hicks review of non-executive directors, the Equal Opportunities Commission provided evidence that of over 600 senior executive positions of the top 100 firms in the FTSE only 10, or 2 per cent, are filled by women, a proportion that has remained unchanged for the past ten years (EOC, 2002). Only one FTSE 100 company has a woman chief executive – Marjorie Scardino – chief executive of the Pearson Group. Women now account for 30 per cent of managers but earn 24 per cent less than male managers.

The categories of sex and race discrimination – direct discrimination, indirect discrimination and victimisation – are relatively easy to define, and many organisations have taken procedural steps in terms of pay audits, greater transparency over pay, analytical job evaluation schemes and equal opportunities policies to combat such discrimination, yet discriminatory practices remain in evidence. There are four reasons that help to explain the continued presence of discrimination in employment.

Firstly, much discrimination goes unreported and is tolerated by employees, who feel that they have no voice mechanism to complain about such treatment; this is particularly the case in small firms and some non-union employers. However, it is necessary to point out that within workplaces that have collective bargaining and otherwise well-ordered personnel policies, discrimination may occur; for example, recently there was a well-publicised case of racial discrimination at the Ford Dagenham plant. This case was settled by an employment tribunal in 2002 when two former employees were awarded a total of £500 000 in damages for racial discrimination and medical disability. The Ford motor company accepted the decision of the tribunal but added that a policy of zero tolerance of racial abuse had been introduced at the Dagenham plant and further noted that the complaints of both employees had been thoroughly investigated.

A second explanation for the continued presence of discrimination relates to the rather limited nature of employment protection legislation during the 1980s. For much of its period of office the last Conservative government operated differential employment protection legislation for full-time and part-time workers. The results of much of this legislation, for example the lawful exclusion of part-time workers from occupational pension schemes, are now unlawful. However, many claims against this type of discrimination, unequal pay and indirect sex discrimination, lodged on the basis that more part-time workers were women than men, remain in the process of redress and resolution.

In an effort to reduce discrimination between full-time and part-time employees the Part-time Workers' Regulations came into force in July 2000. These regulations state that part-time workers should receive the same pay rates as full-time colleagues and receive the same hourly overtime rate once they exceed normal working hours. In addition to these equal rights, part-time workers must receive the same holiday, maternity and paternity leave entitlements as full-time colleagues on a pro-rata basis. Finally, part-time workers must be included in the provision of workplace training, that is, there must be a single framework for training in the workplace and not separate sets of arrangements for full-time and part-time workers.

The part-time regulations cover 7 million workers working fewer than 30 hours per week, including home workers and those employed on temporary, casual or short-term contracts or by an employment agency. The regulations, although a marked improvement on the previous situation – which forced female part-timers who alleged discrimination to seek redress through the indirect route of the Sex Discrimination Act – are limited. For example, while the regulations call for comparability of pay between full-time and part-time workers, they contain no mechanism to measure or quantify such comparison. Currently a 'comparable worker' – a comparator that a part-time employee uses for comparison – is defined as 'a full-time worker with the same type of employment contract doing the same or similar work'.

A third explanation of the emergence of newly defined forms of discrimination in employment is the UK's further integration within the EU and the adoption by the incoming Labour government of the EU's Social Charter of employment and social rights in 1997. This accession further exposed the limited protection provided for many

British employees; for example, prior to November 2001 individuals employed on fixed-term contracts did not have the same rights as full-and part-time employees in terms of pay, pension entitlement and paid holidays. Further, at the time of writing, agency workers or 'temps' employed directly by employment agencies can be lawfully discriminated against in terms of pay, holiday pay and dismissal. A recently announced EU directive – once approved at EU level – may eventually remedy this source of currently lawful discrimination in the workplace (see part 7).

Lastly, in the UK some areas of discriminatory practice, for example discrimination on the grounds of age, sexual orientation, sexual and racial harassment, remain 'lawful' as they are omitted from specific mention in relevant statutes – racial and sexual harassment are not categorised by Race Relations legislation or Sex Discrimination legislation. Age discrimination is regulated by a voluntary code of practice and is likely to remain so until around 2006 when an EU directive on Equal Rights must be implemented in member states. On a related matter, employees beyond the statutory retirement age have traditionally found themselves beyond employment protection, yet a recent employment tribunal decision that two men over 65 were entitled to claim for redundancy and unfair dismissal may give those who work beyond the statutory retirement age employment rights. However, the situation remains in doubt for two reasons. First, the decision in this particular case is likely to be appealed. Second, the decision in this case turned on the presence of 'disproportionate effects' whereby more men than women remain in employment beyond the normal retirement age. Hence, the 'protection' acquired is indirect in this case as it relates to indirect sex discrimination. The situation for those who work beyond the statutory retirement age may finally be resolved by the EU directive on discrimination that comes into force in 2006.

Protection against discrimination on grounds of sexual orientation and religious belief is beyond specific regulation in the UK and is likely to remain so until the incorporation of an EU directive into English law, banning discrimination on both counts from December 2003. The present government published a discussion document on both issues in October 2002 and in the absence of statutory protection in these areas the Human Rights Act may provide some protection if discrimination in employment contravenes employee rights to the protection of private and family life.

The emergent issue of workplace bullying further demonstrates the limited nature of the UK's discrimination and employment protection laws. A recent survey of 3500 employees found that 20 per cent of the sample had experienced workplace bullying in the past year, with 8 per cent of the sample claiming to have experienced bullying on a regular basis. Bullying is not confined to employees further down the organisational hierarchy; 24 per cent of middle managers and 17 per cent of senior managers reported that they had been bullied at least once over the past year (Mercer Human Resource Consulting, 2002). Currently, workplace bullying is not specifically categorised in employment legislation, and while the practice may constitute disability discrimination or indirect racial or sexual discrimination, in other cases employees may have to resign and claim constructive dismissal, see part 5 of this chapter.

It is important for the personnel practitioner to note that an employer is liable to defend an allegation of discrimination in the workplace and act upon it even if the employer is not directly responsible for it; that is, where another employee is responsible for the discriminatory behaviour. As some recent cases in City of London financial institutions demonstrate, it is not sufficient for an employer to argue that racist and sexist behaviour constitutes workplace 'banter' or that they were unaware that such behaviour occurred or that such behaviour is not discriminatory because all employees are subject to it. Further, other recent cases in financial institutions demonstrate the continued presence of indirect sex discrimination due to unequal pay, such as in the calculation of bonus payments. For example, a female analyst employed by Schroder Securities recently won £1.4 million damages in a sex discrimination case where the applicant to the employment tribunal successfully argued that her results were similar to those of male colleagues but that her bonus payments (£25 000) were significantly lower than those of her colleagues who received 'six-figure' bonuses. The employer, while denying the claim, accepted the tribunal decision and withdrew its application to the Employment Appeal Tribunal. Since April 2003 employees have had the right to require employers to complete equal pay questionnaires on co-workers. The evidence suggests that employers who conduct regular pay reviews and those who are committed to pay transparency are far less likely to have pay systems that discriminate against women workers.

The main themes that emerge from this part of the chapter centre around three issues, each of which is pertinent to the personnel practitioner. First, statutory protection is updated at Parliamentary or EU level and it is essential for personnel practitioners to audit and monitor workplace practices and procedures that are likely to be affected by new legislation. Second, workplaces that have proceduralised systems for personnel management must be vigilant and act quickly to prevent apparently one-off incidents developing into persistent behaviour consistent with emergent bullying or victimisation. Last, much remains to be done in order to remove discriminatory practices in the workplace and it is clear that the discrimination agenda gets not only longer but wider as new areas of activity are drawn into the scope of existing measures; for example, the extension of equal pay legislation to cover pension entitlements and before that, in the 1980s, the introduction of the equal value amendments for different work of equal value to an employer in terms of skill, effort and decision-making.

Stop and think

At the end of the third point on continued sources of discrimination in the workplace the text refers to 'this source of currently lawful discrimination in the workplace'. Is it fair and reasonable to argue that lawful discrimination actually exists?

The regulation of working time

As Chapter 12 demonstrates, historically the UK's industrial relations system exhibits only a few areas of specific regulation. The voluntary nature of the British system witnessed a reliance on the negotiation of voluntary agreements over pay and conditions of employment and working time arrangements in particular (see Clark, 2000 and Edwards, 2003 for a general discussion of voluntarism). The 1999 Working Time Regulations provide one of the first serious attempts to provide for the regulation of hours at work. However, the voluntary and unregulated nature of the British industrial relations system remains significant. Currently, the UK's application of the EU working time directive illustrates the pervasive nature of voluntarism via the inclusion of opt-outs that allow employers – sometimes unilaterally, sometimes in negotiation with trade unions – to regulate working hours as they see fit.

The UK's working time regulations provide the following working time rights for all employees:

● A maximum of 48 hours on the average working week over a 17-week period. 'Working time' includes overtime, workplace training provided by the employer, work time travelling to meet clients or business partners when this is a regular part of a job and hospitality arrangements such as attendance at receptions and working lunches. Working time excludes travelling time to and from work, training at educational institutions, work time breaks and periods 'on call' but not working.

One aim of the working time regulations that remains unfulfilled is a reduction in the effects on employees, of all grades, of the burden of the UK's previously unregulated work culture. The Department of Trade and Industry recently reported that 16 per cent of workers work 60 hours a week in comparison to 12 per cent in 2000 (see *Financial Times*, 30 August 2002) with 4.5 million workers working more than 48 hours per week. Comparatively, British working hours are the longest in Europe and remain so even in face of the provisions contained in the Working Time Directive (see OECD, 2002). The long-hours work culture prevalent in the UK has resulted in the emergence of workplace stress as a major issue for British employers, with work overload often cited as the main cause of stress. The magnitude of the long-hours culture and workplace stress was recently demonstrated by a survey of 5000 employers which found that while 80 per cent of the sample felt vulnerable to possible legal action over workplace stress, 66 per cent of the sample had no stress policies in place. In 2001, over 6000 firms paid an average of £51 000 in damages for workplace stress; this figure represents a twelve-fold increase on the number of employees who successfully sued their employer for stress compared to 2000 (Work Stress Management 2002).

■ The limit of opt-out arrangements

An employer cannot require employees to opt-out of the provisions listed below:

- four weeks' paid holiday;
- a work time break where the working day exceeds 6 hours;
- an 11-hour rest period every working day;
- a 24-hour rest period once every 7 days;
- a maximum of an average of 8 hours' night work in every 24 hours and free health assessments for night workers.

Unlike other EU nations, the British government provides employers with a series of exemptions and also allows employers to seek voluntary opt-outs from the 48-hour working time rule, although not the other provisions within the working time directive. The effect of opt-out provision is that many employers 'ask' their employees to waive this protection against what has become known as 'the long-hours culture'. The opt-out provision allows employers to exclude workers provided for by the regulations, whereas the exemptions negotiated by the British government exclude workers in several sectors of employment and in several job types from the regulations completely. Specific categories of worker exempted from the regulations include:

- bus, lorry and train drivers;
- domestic employees who work in private households, e.g. cleaners, domestic staff and servants;
- members of the police and the armed forces;
- junior doctors;
- employees who have 'unmeasured or undetermined' working time.

The last category represents a catch-all mechanism that covers many white-collar workers who have some measure of autonomy over how and when they perform their work. Junior doctors have voiced strong opposition to their exclusion from the regulations and the British Medical Association has negotiated reductions in the length of their working week. Equally, school teachers in England and Wales are currently campaigning for a 35-hour working week to bring them into line with their colleagues in Scotland.

The EU Commission is reviewing the UK's opt-out provisions in 2003 and it is likely to be made unlawful. If this is the case, it will remain possible to work beyond the 48-hour rule as long as the 17-week average is not greater than 48 hours. In 2002, after a submission by the Amicus trade union, the EU Commission began legal proceedings against the UK in respect of the failure by the British government to implement the

Working Time Directive correctly. The Amicus trade union cited several areas of complaint in their submission to the EU Commission; these included the exclusion of night-time overtime from the calculation of normal working time, failure by employers to measure and record overtime work beyond normal working hours and the failure of some employers to enforce worker entitlement to breaks and holidays (see *Financial Times*, 29 April 2002).

The regulation of working time in the UK demonstrates the partial nature of an apparently inalienable right – the provision of opt-outs creates voluntary exclusion and illustrates the persistence of aspects of Britain's voluntary industrial relations system. In contrast to this, the exclusion via exemptions of many groups of autonomous workers renders working time unregulated in several sectors of employment. Further, low-paid workers who earn only the basic national minimum wage per hour are in effect forced to sign opt-outs to earn a living wage. Lastly, young workers over 16 but younger than 18 are beyond the regulations and covered by the Young Workers' Working Time Directive, which is similar to the regulations for older workers but provides for better rest breaks during working time.

ACTIVITY   In what ways is the exclusion and opt-out provision from the working time regulations fair and reasonable? Is your job included, excluded or opted-out?

If your job is exempt or subject to an opt-out clause in your contract of employment, consider the implications for your employer if, in the future, your job were to be included in the regulations on the 48-hour working week.

Termination of the employment contract

Employment contracts can terminate in a variety of ways, for example job redundancy, voluntary resignation, death in service, non-renewal of a fixed-term contract and summary termination due to conduct – 'the sack'. This part of the chapter examines the issue of termination due to dismissal under the headings of fair dismissal, unfair dismissal, wrongful dismissal and constructive dismissal.

Fair dismissal

In the majority of situations when an employee is dismissed from employment, the reasons for the dismissal are likely to be fair. An employer can fairly dismiss an employee on several grounds; dismissal is likely to be fair if it relates to the following categories:

- Employee conduct – theft or fraud in the workplace, gross insubordination, fighting etc.
- Job redundancy – where a job is no longer needed and the employee is dismissed due to job redundancy through no fault of their own and has been correctly consulted about the situation and fairly selected for redundancy via an agreed process of selection. If an employee has two years of continuous service with the employer, they must be compensated for the redundancy.
- Capability, competence and qualifications. An employer can fairly dismiss an employee on these grounds but must demonstrate that dismissal relates to job capability, not the employee. For example, to obtain dismissal due to capability on the grounds of illness or disability an employer must demonstrate that they have already

made changes to the work situation of an employee and cannot make further changes. Without this evidence the employee may have a claim under the Disability Discrimination Act. If an employee has falsified their qualifications or if they lose a practitioner qualification, for example by being struck off the medical register if they are a doctor, dismissal is likely to be fair. If an employee is deemed to be incompetent it will be necessary to demonstrate this, for example that they have been through an internal disciplinary procedure and been given a reasonable opportunity to improve their performance but failed to do so.

● Statutory bar or other legal requirement that prevents the continuation of employment. For example, if an employee is a driver or needs to be able to drive to perform their job, the loss of a driving licence is likely to be a fair reason for dismissal. Similarly, if there is another legal requirement that the employee can no longer meet, dismissal is likely to be fair; for example, for deep sea divers there are strict age and hours limits due to health and safety considerations. Equally, lorry drivers may have to pass eyesight checks and pilots meet strict health requirements. While dismissals may be fair in some situations, an employer may offer the employee another job. This is more likely if the firm has a collective bargaining agreement with a trade union.

● Some other substantial reason. Here an employer must demonstrate, in a case where a dismissal is disputed, that the dismissal, while it does not relate to the categories listed above, is nonetheless substantive, fair and reasonable.

Unfair dismissal

A dismissal is fair if an employer can demonstrate that the reason for the dismissal fits into one of the five categories listed above. However, as pointed out earlier in the chapter, many aspects of employment law turn on questions of interpretation and the reasonableness of a particular interpretation. So while an employer may deem a dismissal fair, an employee may disagree. For example, they may claim that they were unfairly selected for redundancy, or that they have been victimised for whistle-blowing or that their dismissal on any of the grounds listed above was motivated by discrimination such as disability, race, sex, marital status, pregnancy etc.

In situations where the fairness of a dismissal is disputed and proceeds to an employment tribunal, there are several tests that the tribunal will apply to rule on a dismissal. Dismissals due to conduct, redundancy, statutory bar, competence and qualification and some other substantive reason are termed *potentially fair* reasons for dismissal. A tribunal will examine the dismissal against the facts of a particular case to test whether the dismissal was *fair in the particular circumstances of the case*. If the details of a particular case do not meet the criteria for a potentially fair dismissal then the dismissal is unfair. In some circumstances a reason for dismissal may be fair yet the dismissal may have been conducted in an unfair manner, that is, a dismissal may be *procedurally unfair*. Hence if there are internal procedures that should be followed that relate to grievance and discipline in the workplace it is vital that an employer follows these procedures and is further able to demonstrate to the employee, their representatives and a tribunal that they have done so.

As part 2 of the chapter states, employees need one year of continuous employment service to qualify for protection against unfair dismissal. This extends to unfair dismissals that relate to job redundancy, that is, unfair selection for redundancy, whereas dismissal due to job redundancy requires two years' employment service before an employee qualifies for compensation. Unfair dismissals that relate to race or sex discrimination, including those for unequal pay and those that relate to pregnancy, are automatically unfair and are available to employees as day one rights. For example, a group of part-time women workers employed on a particular pay grade made redundant after six months' service may be able to demonstrate unfair selection for redundancy if no male employees were made redundant and they can establish that they were made redundant because they were the cheapest employees to terminate.

Other situations where no length of service is necessary to claim unfair dismissal include those that relate to trade union membership, participation in lawful industrial action that lasted less than eight weeks, participation as an employee representative for purposes of consultation (where there is no trade union presence), refusal to work on grounds of health and safety or where an employee seeks to assert a statutory right.

Wrongful dismissal

A wrongful dismissal is a dismissal that is in breach of contract, for example dismissal without notice or a failure to pay all due wages and remuneration during the notice period. Many wrongful dismissal cases relate to highly paid business executives who are dismissed but denied some aspect of their remuneration package. Other cases may relate to employees in government service who are dismissed by Ministers. In the early 1990s, Michael Howard, the Conservative government Home Secretary, dismissed Derek Lewis, head of the prison service, without notice in a dispute about who held overall operational responsibility for prisons. Mr Lewis sued for wrongful dismissal and the Home Office later met his claim.

Constructive dismissal

Constructive dismissal refers to a situation where an employee alleges that an employer has acted so contrary to the operation of their contract of employment that the contract is deemed to be unlawfully and immediately terminated. Events that may trigger constructive dismissal include financial loss due to unilateral changes in pay and remuneration, racial or sexual harassment, unilateral relocations to undesirable areas, being unilaterally stripped of authority or persistent victimisation.

Claims for constructive dismissal are risky because an employee has to satisfy a tribunal that they had no alternative but to leave and in the majority of cases it is unlikely that the employee will get their job back. Normally employees who are constructively dismissed pursue a claim for breach of contract where employment tribunals can make an award of up to £25 000. In addition to this, the employee can pursue a statutory award for unfair dismissal.

Redundancy rights

Under current legislation – the Employment Protection Acts and the Employment Rights Act 1996 – employees require two years of continuous service in a particular employment from the age of 18 to qualify for a lump sum compensation award. Further, the employee must have a contract of employment and for each complete year of service between the ages of 18 and 21 they will receive half a week's pay. This increases to one week's pay for employees between the ages of 22 and 40 and rises to one and a half week's pay between the ages of 41 and 65. Redundancy payments are unaffected by the number of hours an employee works but the statutory limit for one week's pay is £250 and redundancy payments up to the value of £30 000 are tax free. An employer must make the payment as soon as the employee is dismissed.

Employers are required to consult the workforce about redundancy and, where collective bargaining is present, a trade union must be consulted. In non-union workplaces employers must establish a representative body of the workforce to consult over redundancy, for example multinational corporations may use an already established European Works Council for this purpose. The employer must notify the consultative body or the trade union of the reasons for redundancy, the numbers involved and the grades of job affected, the method of determining which jobs are redundant and how any payments that supplement the statutory requirements are to be worked out. If an employer has collective bargaining it is likely that there will be an established redundancy procedure negotiated with the trade union.

There is a statutory period for consultation that relates to the number of jobs being made redundant. If over 100 jobs are made redundant the employer must consult over a 90-day period, but only 30 days of consultation are necessary where the number of job redundancies is fewer than 100. Throughout the consultation period an employer must seek alternatives to job redundancy and act in good faith. Both these issues are controversial. Many trade unions argue that it is easier to dismiss British employees than employees in other EU nations because consultation occurs once the decision to make jobs redundant is taken, rather than before the decision is made as is required by law in most other EU nations. In extreme cases some employees, for example those employed at Vauxhall's Luton plant, have first heard of their impending redundancy through the local and national media. The enforcement of a European Union directive on employee consultation may improve this situation, see part 7.

Part 2 of this chapter detailed the contractual and statutory rights of employees, part 3 examined the continued presence of discrimination and part 4 demonstrated the difficulty of establishing employee rights that relate to working time. This part of the chapter illustrated how employers can fairly dismiss employees and how employees can claim unfair, wrongful or constructive dismissal. Part 6 of the chapter examines the issues that relate to the enforcement of employee rights in the employment relationship.

ACTIVITY Provide two potential examples of unfair, wrongful and constructive dismissal. In each case suggest how an employer might avoid the situation.

Enforcement of contractual and statutory employment rights

For the vast majority of employees, enforcement of employment rights is not an issue. Good employers, large and small, ensure that employment contracts reflect existing and new employment rights. Moreover, large employers are likely to have a dedicated personnel function to do this. Furthermore, larger firms are likely to recognise trade unions for the purposes of individual and collective representation and this presence is likely to ensure that terms and conditions of employment and internal procedures reflect employee rights, be they contractual or statutory. In summary, it is not in the interests of employers to 'short change' their employees, particularly in a period of full employment when staff recruitment and retention are recognised personnel problems. Equally, if, as many employers claim, employees are the most valued assets within a firm, demonstrating this through good employment practice and not merely in management rhetoric is one measure of being a good employer. However, some employers do seek to short-change employees by withholding certain rights, such as the minimum wage, or subjecting employees to arbitrary and unreasonable treatment.

If employees feel that a contractual or statutory employment right is either absent or incorrectly proceduralised or not enforced, there are several routes that they can take. Discussion of the situation with a supervisor, line manager or the personnel function may result in corrective action. Alternatively, an employee might raise their grievance with a trade union representative or other employee representative. Lastly, and more often in cases of alleged unfair dismissal, an employee can instigate proceedings against their employer or former employer by making an application to an employment tribunal. In many cases such an application may be sufficient to persuade the employer that they need to take corrective action. However, some cases will go to tribunal either because the dispute cannot be settled in any other way due to employer intransigence or because an employer feels the case must be defended because of its future implications for themselves and other similar employers.

Employment tribunals are now long established and operate as specialist employment 'courts'. Tribunals have a legally qualified chair and two lay members acting as employee and employer nominees. Tribunals are less formal than other courts but over the years they have become more legalistic than was originally intended and more time consuming, particularly in situations where a test case is being heard. Virtually all claims in relation to the employment relationship are heard in tribunals; however some, notably claims for constructive and unfair dismissals that involve a breach of contract, are heard in civil courts.

To begin an application to a tribunal an employee or former employee must complete an application form ET1 within three months of the incident or event they intend to complain about. The ET1 will contain details of the employee's claim and the remedy they are seeking – reinstatement, re-engagement or compensation. The tribunal service will send the ET1 and an ET2 to the employer or former employer; the ET2 summonses the employer to appear before the tribunal. The employer must also complete an ET3, which details their defence.

In 1999 there was a 32 per cent increase in applications to the tribunal service – 164 000, up from 124 000 in 1998; 2000 witnessed a further increase to 167 000, whereas in the year to March 2001 there were 130 408 applications to the tribunal service. However ACAS reported only 94 000 applications to the tribunal service in 2002 (*Financial Times*, 9 September 2003). Employer bodies such as the Engineering Employers Federation argue that only 6 per cent of claims against their members are upheld, with 70 per cent settled or withdrawn. In contrast, the TUC argues that 95 per cent of cases it backs are won. Moreover, employer bodies argue that there are too many applications to tribunals that employers have to defend unnecessarily as many applications are frivolous or vexatious. Even so, the introduction of a fine of up to £10 000 in such cases in July 2001 has failed to stem the large number of applications. Most applications to tribunals relate to claims of unfair dismissal.

The statutory award for unfair dismissal is made up of two components. First, the basic award of up to £375 for each year of completed employment and second the compensatory award of up to a maximum of £52 600. However, in cases that relate to discrimination because of disability, race or gender there is no upper limit on tribunal awards. For example, a City drinks sector analyst employed by Schroder Securities won £1.4 million in a sex discrimination case after successfully claiming that male colleagues were given six-figure bonus payments while she received only £25 000 while delivering similar results in the workplace. While denying the allegation, the employer withdrew an appeal against the decision of an employment tribunal. For details of the case see the *Financial Times* 11 January 2002 and 20 June 2002.

While these compensation awards seem large, the average award is much lower in the majority of cases. Equally, in most cases former employees do not get their job back; for example, in 1999 in only 3 per cent of unfair dismissal cases was the applicant re-employed. Compensation, as opposed to re-employment or re-engagement, is the preferred remedy of most tribunals.

There is, in addition to this argument, evidence that employers, and small employers in particular, lack confidence on the issue of employee rights. The DTI found that only 20 per cent of small employers have confidence in their knowledge of employment legislation, with only 50 per cent aware of the employee right to paid paternity leave (see

Financial Times 13 August 2002). The government has recently taken some steps to allow employees to exercise their rights more effectively by compelling employees to follow internal grievance procedures before taking a case to tribunal. This measure, while sensible and reasonable, rests on the premise that all employers have these procedures in place.

The evidence suggests that employer claims of 'excessive red tape' and the burden of defending unnecessary tribunal applications are not proven. Many employees are denied the opportunity to go through internal grievance procedures. Equally, the growth in employment rights caught some employers – good and bad – off guard, particularly in the area of unfair dismissal. Employer claims of red tape and the cost of defending at a tribunal must be measured against better regulation of the employment relationship and the need for improved best practice. While the majority of applications to tribunals to enforce employee rights are settled on a voluntary basis and withdrawn, the growth in the number of applications demonstrates the absence of best practice in many areas of employment. Lastly, claims that a 'compensation culture' is emerging which is likely to damage the competitiveness of British industry is a very doubtful argument, because if employees win a case at tribunal it demonstrates that their rights were in some way infringed. Alternatively, if an employer settles a claim or takes corrective action in the workplace, this demonstrates that some aspect of employment practice was poorly proceduralised. High-profile compensation awards involving large sums, such as those associated with the 'sexism in the City' cases, are rare if of great interest to the media, but more significantly demonstrate that poor employment practice occurs in all types of employment and that enforcement can be expensive for employers. Furthermore, the actions of some employers in recent cases undermine claims of bureaucracy and red tape and time wasting in the defence of applications to employment tribunals. Applications to tribunals that are withdrawn or settled voluntarily may be settled 'out of court' by employers. For example, Nomura International reached an out of court settlement with an employee made redundant while on maternity leave, who prior to that had been asked to wear short skirts at work and give a male colleague a massage. The former employee dropped her discrimination claim but reached a £70 000 out of court settlement with Nomura, which maintained that the claim was unfounded. In a similar City case, Cru Publishing settled a case of constructive dismissal out of court even though an employment tribunal found that the employee was 75 per cent to blame for her dismissal.

While the growth of out of court settlements does undermine employers' claims of red tape and excessive costs in employment regulation, there are three specific problems with them in respect to the enforcement of employment rights. First, out of court settlements often prevent full disclosure of the facts and while a former employee may be generously compensated, the provisions of a settlement usually remain confidential. Second, withdrawing a claim and settling out of court often enables employers to deny the charges made against them and, more importantly, prevents the creation of what might be a reference point – a precedent for future cases. Third, an employer that settles a case out of court but denies the basis of the claim may fail to improve personnel procedures – a measure often enforced by tribunals, the Equal Opportunities Commission and the Commission for Racial Equality.

In summary, a well-resourced personnel function staffed by CIPD-qualified practitioners is one route to employer best practice in the area of employment rights; trade union recognition is another, and the latter is likely to lead to negotiation and partnership in the management of employee rights. Both routes are likely to become more fruitful for employers, bearing in mind the likelihood of further growth in employee rights and the medium- to longer-term impact of the 1999 Employment Relations Act.

New rights at work?

This final part of the chapter examines the emergence of new rights at work codified within the 1999 Employment Relations Act and briefly discusses the probable emergence of further new rights, several of which are currently at the consultation stage.

■ The Employment Relations Act 1999 (ERA)

The ERA established many new rights, both collective and individual, that represent a significant improvement in workplace rights, bringing many into line with those found in other European Union states. The ERA complements other measures that aim to improve fairness at work, such as the Working Time Directive and the national minimum wage. The legislation aims to achieve decent minimum standards at work that will underpin a flexible labour market and facilitate good industrial relations in the workplace, via trade unions and collective bargaining where desired by employees.

The provisions of the ERA divide into four categories: new and improved individual rights for all employees, new collective rights for all employees, maternity and paternity rights, and rights to representation in the workplace. These areas are briefly reviewed below and where necessary are already incorporated into relevant parts of this chapter, in particular parts two and four.

● New rights for all workers

Improved protection against unfair dismissal

This protection is now available after one year's service rather than two years. Estimates suggest that up to 270 000 workers with between one and two years' employment service are dismissed each year. Some of these employees are 'fairly' unfairly dismissed, hence many will directly benefit from this new right. Moreover, the ERA increased top-level payments in cases of unfair dismissal from £12 000 to £50 000, a figure that has recently been increased further to £53 000. In addition to these improvements, the ERA makes it automatically unfair to dismiss an employee taking part in lawfully organised industrial action for eight weeks. After two months, dismissal will be fair only if the employer can establish that they have taken all reasonable procedural steps to try to resolve the dispute.

Blacklisting

Blacklisting of individual employees for trade union membership or activity is prohibited. This provision relates to blacklists compiled by an employer or by any organisation such as the Economic League or the Freedom Association.

Unpaid parental leave

The ERA established the right of employees with one year's employment service to parental leave (if named as a parent on a birth certificate) for any child born after December 1999 up to the age of 5 years or an adopted child below 18 born after the same date. A parent is entitled to 13 weeks for each eligible child, and this extends to multiple births. The employee remains 'employed' during the leave and on return the employee is entitled to their old job or – if this is unreasonable or impossible – a better job or one of the same standard in terms and conditions. Some employees had paid or unpaid parental leave clauses in their contracts of employment before the provisions of the ERA became effective. These arrangements, many of them arrived at through the process of collective bargaining, remain operative. On return from leave an employee must not have any seniority or pension rights denied as a result of taking leave. If a job is made redundant while an employee is on leave, they must be treated as if they are working normally. In January 2000 the TUC, after taking legal advice, declared an intention to undertake a legal challenge to the December 1999 cut-off date. The TUC was advised that the directive should be retrospective in covering all children under the age of 5 at the date of its implementation, and after the threat and instigation of legal action the government amended the UK's regulations and subsequently introduced paid paternity leave for fathers (details outlined in part 2).

Personal contracts

The ERA makes it unlawful for an employer to dismiss, omit or otherwise act detrimentally towards an employee who refuses to sign a personal contract that excludes the employee from collectively negotiated terms and conditions of employment. This right was recently further strengthened by a ruling in the European court that established that such measures breached the human rights of individual employees. This case concerned a *Daily Mail* journalist and dates from 1989. The journalist was denied a pay increase after he refused to give up the right to have terms and conditions of employment determined through the process of collective bargaining. The Court of Appeal found in favour of the journalist but his employer appealed to Law Lords who held that collective bargaining over terms and conditions of employment fails to represent a defining characteristic of trade union membership. Thus, in this case the use of financial incentives to end collective bargaining and personal contracts that may result in less or more favourable treatment for individual employees does not represent a breach of human rights. However, the European Court of Human Rights held that a state is responsible for ensuring that union members are not restrained from using a union to represent them. As a result of this decision it is now clear that individuals and trade unions can enforce the right to collective representation. Equally, laws that permit British employers to discriminate against, i.e. treat less favourably, workers who seek to retain collective bargaining and collective representation is a breach of human rights.

Prohibition of waiver clauses for unfair dismissal rights in fixed-term contracts

Under the provisions of the ERA it is no longer possible for employers to ask or compel employees on fixed-term contracts to waive the right to complain of unfair dismissal if the contract is not renewed. Waiver clauses in operation before the provisions of the ERA became effective can continue. Equally, the provisions within the ERA make no mention of redundancy rights waivers in fixed-term contracts: hence these waivers remain lawful.

Family emergencies

The ERA provides the right for employees to have reasonable time off work to deal with family emergencies such as accidents or illness to family members, bereavements and severe damage to property. These new rights aim to provide workers with a more effective voice mechanism in the workplace where it was previously restricted or where they had none. Where employers are obstructive over access to new or extended individual employment rights the law will work in favour of employees in imposing trade union recognition where employees desire this.

Maternity and parental leave

The material in part 2 on day one rights and length of service rights established that all employees are entitled to basic maternity leave, whereas those with at least one year's length of service are entitled to extended maternity leave. The ERA increased the period of paid basic maternity leave from 14 to 18 weeks subsequently increased further to 26 weeks and reduced the qualification period for extended maternity leave from two years to one year. The ERA also introduced the provision for parental leave that is discussed above under new individual employment rights.

The right to representation

The ERA establishes that whether a trade union is recognised or not, individual union members and non-union members alike have the right to be accompanied by a trade union official in disciplinary and grievance hearings. If the employer obstructs or denies this, there is a compensatory penalty of up to two weeks' pay.

A lasting effect of the ERA centres on the enforcement of employee rights in the workplace. Trade union recognition and the emergence of collective bargaining in the workplace is one mechanism to monitor the introduction of new employment rights. By negotiating with an employer and seeking partnership in the implementation of new rights, trade unions can ensure that an employer meets their legal obligations. In addition, collective representation may create a workplace 'voice mechanism' that can prevent the emergence of issues that might otherwise lead to conflict, dispute and eventually application to an employment tribunal.

In addition to the contractual and statutory rights examined in part 2 and the collective and individual employment rights associated with the ERA, the following measures either offer new employment rights or will establish them in the near future.

● Collective employment rights: trade union recognition

ERA establishes that a claim for trade union recognition can be made with 10 per cent membership and majority support. To demonstrate support for trade union recognition a union can call upon the findings of a survey or petition. Where a trade union already has over 50 per cent membership within the proposed bargaining group, recognition will be automatic except on two grounds: first, where an employer appeals to the central arbitration committee for a secret ballot on the grounds that a ballot will be good for workplace industrial relations; second, where despite a high level of union membership a significant number of employees express a desire not be union members or to be represented by the union in collective bargaining, or where the central arbitration committee concludes either situation to be the case. The evidence concerning the impact of the legislation leads to two conclusions. First, where there is a majority of union members in a non-unionised workplace employers are likely to offer guarded support for a recognition claim. Second, before the ERA became effective some employers anticipated its provisions and negotiated voluntary recognition before the legislation became operative. Further, where a majority of union members is very high the evidence suggests that employers wish to avoid negative media coverage and so negotiate voluntary recognition agreements. For example, erstwhile anti-union employers such as Dixon's Electrical Stores and Noon's Foods, both of which have very high union membership, have recently negotiated voluntary recognition deals with the AEEU and GMB unions respectively. In addition to this, survey evidence covering the period 1994–98 found that cases of trade union de-recognition fell significantly. In contrast, recognition agreements held constant at an annual level. This evidence demonstrates 44 cases of de-recognition involving 5000 workers and 157 cases of recognition involving 45 000 workers for the years 1997 and 1998 (Gall and McKay, 1999). Further survey evidence for 1999 found 74 recognition agreements covering 21 000 workers. Of more significance, almost 50 per cent of the trade unions in the survey said that recognition deals resulted from an employer approach (TUC, 2000). Equally, in the year to March 2001 trade union membership rose by 46 000 to 7.9 million, the second annual rise in succession after a sustained fall in union membership since the early 1980s (Labour Market Trends, 2001). The data in this report indicate that the period of large-scale decline in union membership has ended and that membership has begun to stabilise since 1997. This suggests that employers are likely to view the issue of trade union recognition more favourably than they did during the 1980s and 1990s when more assertive programmes of trade union de-recognition in the workplace were supported by government policy (see Clark, 1996 and Claydon, 1996). For example, HSBC, formerly Midland Bank, has recently restored union representation for 12 500 junior and middle managers four years after withdrawing recognition for this group of workers.

A recent TUC report, *Focus on Recognition*, found that there were 300 recognition deals in the year up to October 2002, the vast majority of which were concluded on a voluntary basis covering firms such as American Airlines, Boots, Meridian TV, the Church of Scotland, Kwik-Fit, Green Peace and Air New Zealand (TUC, 2000). The overwhelming majority of agreements covered pay, hours and holidays and 91 per cent covered representation at grievance and discipline hearings, 62 per cent covered training, over 50 per cent covered equal rights and information and consultation in the workplace. Lastly, 36 per cent covered pension arrangements. Many of the recognition deals reviewed in the report were concluded in smaller employers, the average size being 260 employees; notwithstanding this, the current Review of the Employment Relations Act excludes any alteration to the rules and procedures on recognition, in particular the exclusion of workplaces employing fewer than 20 workers from the provision of the Act.

In situations where workplace ballots are necessary, a trade union is able to address the workforce directly as well as mail information to employees. When recognition is won, the trade union acquires a legal right to negotiate terms and conditions to include hours, pay, and work allocation and discipline. Equally significant to these collective rights, recognition imposes a duty on the employer to inform and consult about training. In cases where an employer proves to be obstructive in establishing a bargaining procedure, the ERA allows for one to be imposed upon them. In cases where a trade union is unable to prove 50 per cent membership, the statutory procedure for a recognition award will be triggered where there is majority support in a ballot with at least 40 per cent of those eligible to vote taking part. Recently, the Central Arbitration Committee compelled Saudi Arabian Airways at Heathrow airport to introduce collective bargaining after the employer ignored a successful ballot in favour of recognition. Staff employed by the airline voted nine to one in favour of recognition by the MSF technicians' union. Similarly, the Central Arbitration Committee intervened in a dispute between Honda and the AEEU after the firm refused to hold a recognition ballot. As a result of the subsequent ballot the AEEU won recognition for full collective bargaining at Honda's Swindon plant where 1600 of the 4000 workforce were already union members.

■ EU Information and Consultation Directive

The Information and Consultation Directive will compel employers to establish a democratic and collective mechanism in order to consult with a workforce on substantial changes to the terms and conditions of employment such as changes in work organisation, redundancy and the sale of subsidiaries. British workplaces with more than 150 employees will have to introduce this mechanism by 2004; smaller workplaces may get up to a further five years to meet the conditions laid down in the directive.

Employer groups have voiced concern about the effects of this requirement on the competitiveness of British firms, suggesting that the mechanism will add further 'red tape' but no positive business outcomes. However, this is a familiar argument that was voiced previously against the provisions of the national minimum wage, the Working Time Directive and the ERA. None of the projected claims such as growth in unemployment and reduced competitiveness occurred and are unlikely to occur in this case. The persistence of employer opposition to new employment legislation illustrates that a deeply embedded preference for voluntary and unregulated employer 'best practice' remains in the UK. Equally though, the partial failure of voluntary best practice is amply illustrated by the partial enforcement of employment rights and the persistence of discrimination in employment highlighted in earlier parts of this chapter. The information and consultation directive may go some way to improve employee consultation over *proposed* (as opposed to the current situation of *actual*) redundancies, which is a major concern of British trade unions. In January 2003 Alan Johnson, the then employment relations minister, argued that information and consultation committees, when introduced in British firms, would not constitute co-determination or joint decision-making on the continental model and emphasised the consultative nature of the committees (*Financial Times*, 17 January 2003).

■ European Union Agency Workers Directive

The Agency Workers Directive is more controversial and seeks to establish equality between employment rights for workers employed directly by an employment agency as 'temps' and those directly employed in the workplace to which they are assigned by the agency. The directive is likely to have a dramatic impact because the majority of temps employed across the EU work in the UK – over one million workers. The areas covered by the proposed directive include pay, pensions, holiday entitlement and other benefits such as protection against unfair dismissal. The government estimates that the provisions contained within the directive will lead to a rise of approximately £1000 a year in pay levels for temps. Currently, the British government, after lobbying by employer groups, is seeking a six-week exemption to the equal pay rule, provided that an employer demonstrates that 'an adequate level of pay is provided from day one'. In September 2002 the draft directive was complete and ready to be considered by the EU social affairs committee (see *Financial Times*, 3 September 2002).

■ 'Two-tier working' in the provision of public services

'Two-tier' working refers to the situation where a local government service or aspects of health care previously provided by a local authority or the National Health Service is fully or partially contracted out to a private sector provider. The term describes the situation where public sector workers or those transferred to the private sector have terms and conditions of employment that are different from – better than – those of new employees engaged by the private sector provider but working in the provision of the service.

Trade unions such as UNISON and the GMB argue that all workers should have the same terms and conditions of employment guaranteed by statutory guidance written into contracts between local authorities and private sector contractors. In July 2002 the government promised legislation to provide for comparability of terms and conditions of employment. However, in January 2003 the row over the two-tier workforce was reignited because of disagreement over the proposed wording of the government code of practice, which cites a form of wording preferred by the CBI that calls for the terms and conditions of new recruits to be 'broadly comparable' to those of existing employees. A specific area of disagreement relates to the proposed exclusion of pensions from the broadly comparable formula. Some trade unions have expressed guarded support for this, yet experience with previous measures such as paternity leave, the Working Time Directive and the Equal Pay Act suggest that such terms may be broadly reasonable in application and coverage but subject to different interpretation by employers and employees. Differences of interpretation on this issue may result in future legal challenges in particular situations. The situation is Scotland is somewhat different. The Scottish Finance Minister recently signed a protocol agreement with trade unions that represent workers in the public sector. The framework contract guarantees that all workers recruited by private sector contractors under public/private partnership deals will receive fair pay, pension, holiday and sick pay entitlements commensurate with those of existing pubic sector workers. The difference between broadly comparable and commensurate could create problems for contractors who operate in both England and Scotland in respect of the EU Equal Treatment Directive. Further, a key difficulty for trade unions who support the formula and those that do not and the government is that the term 'broadly comparable' in its present constitution appears to allow for the presence of a two-tier workforce and not its elimination as pledged by the Prime Minister in July 2002. The government recognised this as problematic and, following a meeting with prominent trade unions in February 2002, announced that the government will insist that private sector firms taking public services contracts must provide employment contracts that are 'no less favourable' for future employees than contracts enjoyed by public sector workers. This commitment was given an unexpected fillip when the Cleaning and Support Services Association announced its support for the provision, arguing that it would prevent 'cowboy' operators cutting their members out of the market by reducing costs irresponsibly (*Financial Times*, 17 March 2003).

Flexible employment for parents

Since April 2003 all parents of children under six have been entitled to ask their employer to 'seriously consider' requests for flexible work arrangements. Up to four million parents will be eligible to submit such requests. Parents must make written requests and meet with the relevant manager within four weeks to discuss the request and a decision must be made in a further two weeks. Employers are expected to meet the majority of requests and Ministers have included in the guidance an 82 per cent success rate target. If an employer denies a request they must provide the employee with a written explanation of the business reasons for the decision and set out proposals for an internal appeal procedure. In situations where a case remains unresolved, binding mediation and arbitration will be made available. It is important to make clear that the right to flexible working is limited to serious consideration of the request and that this is not the same as a right to flexible working arrangements. The seriousness of this limitation is brought into sharp focus by the results of a survey conducted by the employment law firm Peninsula. Seventy per cent of small firms in the survey asserted that claims for flexible working hours will damage their competitiveness and more than 80 per cent of the companies surveyed said they would attempt to dodge the rules (Peninsula, 2003).

The Human Rights Act, 1998

The Human Rights Act, while wide-ranging in its provisions, fails to create any specific employment rights. To enforce their human rights employees must cite an existing employment right, the infringement of which impacts on their human rights, for example unfair dismissal due to sexual orientation. The latter is not currently covered by the UK's sex discrimination legislation; but a dismissal on these grounds may be unfair if it infringes rights to privacy. However, the basis of the human rights legislation is a balancing of (employer and employee) interests and, where those of an employer and employer conflict, an employment tribunal will have to make a judgment on the balance of these interests.

The probable emergence of many of the proposed employment rights discussed above reinforces the need for good employer practice to be both operational and strategic. The evidence suggests that in relation to the national minimum wage, the ERA and the

Working Time Directive, many employers – large and small – were 'off the pace'. Employers with a personnel function staffed by CIPD-qualified practitioners are more likely to be on the pace, as are those who have a trade union presence that works in partnership or structured negotiation with an employer.

Conclusion

While the employment relationship and within that the employment contract is viewed by many as a private exchange between an employer and an employee, the employment relationship is subject to significant contractual and statutory regulation.

All employees have a contract of employment and some measure of statutory protection against unfair and unreasonable treatment by an employer. However, in the contemporary period since 1997 the contractual and statutory regulation of the employment relationship has tightened. As a result of this, employees have greater protection in the employment relationship than previously; this greater protection creates the need for improved vigilance by employers and reinforces the need in all areas of employment for an effective personnel function. In large and small employers, a personnel function staffed by CIPD-qualified professionals is likely to increase employer confidence in the regulation of employment and may help avoid the infringement of employee rights. Equally, trade unions through the process of collective bargaining – partnership or structured negotiation – have a role to play in the enforcement of employee rights at work. This is the case because although there has been a significant growth in statutory protection for individual employees since 1997, a question remains about its effectiveness. The growth in the number of applications to employment tribunals illustrates that the application of best practice principles in the regulation of the employment relationship is far from universal. Similarly, the continued search for labour market flexibility, as demonstrated by the UK's idiosyncratic application of the working time directive and the weakness in the framework for applications for flexible working, may infringe the employment rights of some workers but go unnoticed. Thus, individual employment rights must be enforced, yet the search for labour market flexibility and the relative weakness of trade unions across the employed labour force (only 29 per cent of the labour force is represented by trade unions) suggests that measures to improve collective representation are more likely to improve the enforcement of individual employment rights than individuals acting alone. This argument is borne out by some of the recent recognition cases where employees in banking, motor manufacturing and civil aviation cited enforcement of employment rights and protection against future consolidation or downsizing in their organisations as two reasons for seeking union recognition. This feature in the trend towards union recognition extends within traditional non-union firms such as Virgin Atlantic and those cited earlier in this chapter. Virgin Atlantic recently signed a recognition agreement with the AEEU for its 2800 cabin crew after previously signing an agreement with BALPA for pilots and flight engineers. Virgin signed these agreements on a voluntary basis after consultation with its employees.

The emergence of employer and employee interest in trade union recognition for purposes of collective bargaining and collective enforcement of individual employment rights flies in the face of recent arguments put forward by Alan Johnson, the then employment relations minister. In an interview with the *Financial Times* (17 September 2002) the minister argued that the expansion of individual employment rights under the current government empowers individual employees and demonstrates that the government is well ahead of trade unions which emphasise rights through union membership rather than individual rights. However, the minister made no points on the issue of enforcement. For a more critical examination of the provisions contained in the Employment Relations Act see Glyn and Wood (2001: 61–63).

If, as many employers assert, employees are the most valued assets within an organisation, fair and reasonable treatment consistent with contractual and statutory rights regulated on an individual or collective basis is one measure of good employment practice. Moreover, the voluntary enforcement of employee rights by employers demonstrates the 'good employer' ethos – best practice in the regulation of the employment relationship. Employees who receive fair and reasonable treatment in the employment relationship are more likely to be retained by an employer, better motivated, more committed and deliver higher productivity than those employees who are not. As this chapter demonstrates, employee rights are extensive but not prohibitive in terms of coverage or the 'red tape' they create. Reasonable treatment requires regulation and enforcement. The evidence suggests that what some employers term 'red tape' is created when unreasonable treatment occurs, that is, when employers deviate from the good employer ethos and fail to follow best-practice procedures.

Summary

This chapter examined the employment relationship and its regulation through the contract of employment under six different headings.

Contractual and statutory employment rights

- All employees have a contract of employment.
- All employees are protected by some statutory rights – day one rights; other rights require some length of service.

Contracts of employment

- Employment contracts are contracts of personal service between an employer and an employee.
- Employment contracts are based on the theory of market individualism, where individuals are seen as rational and self-interested.
- Employment contracts are subject to the common law.
- There are different types of employment contract.
- Employment contracts contain express, implied and statutory incorporated terms and conditions.

Discrimination in employment

- Discrimination remains a persistent feature of the employment relationship.
- Some types of 'discrimination' remain lawful.

Working time

- Traditionally, working time has been unregulated in the UK.
- The Working Time Directive regulates hours of work but contains many exceptions and allows employees to opt out from the provision.
- The Working Time Directive has failed to counter the UK's 'long-hours' culture.
- The UK's application of the directive may soon be challenged.

Termination

● Employees can be fairly, unfairly, wrongfully or constructively dismissed.

● Dismissals may be fair and potentially fair, otherwise they are unfair.

Enforcement of employment rights

● Most employees are treated fairly.

● If employees are treated unreasonably or unfairly they can complain to an employment tribunal.

● Tribunals, personnel departments, the Equal Opportunities Commission, the Commission for Racial Equality and trade unions play a role in enforcing employment rights.

New rights at work

● The Employment Relations Act consolidated some employment rights and introduced other individual and collective rights.

● Further employment rights are in the process of introduction or are at the consultation stage and will be introduced in the near future.

Questions

1 How is a contract formed in the following situations?

   (a) Buying a magazine in a newsagent's.
   (b) An offer of full-time permanent employment.
   (c) The hiring of a subcontractor to perform maintenance work on a firm's computers.

2 How does employment protection legislation actually protect full-time and part-time employees?

3 Do you think that the employment protection legislation provides for effective and reasonable protection of employees?

Case study

The pitfalls that follow a failure of best practice

In June 1996 Jane Smith was engaged by the department of media studies at Cromwell University as a part-time administrative assistant. For non-academic staff and casual employees decisions over recruitment, selection, remuneration and terms and conditions of employment are decentralised to departmental managers who should follow procedures laid down in best-practice manuals supplied by the personnel func-

tion. At the time, Jane was given a 'casual contract' that excluded her from the terms and conditions of employment applied to permanent staff and academic staff employed by the university. Jane was not given a copy of the contract even though she regularly asked for a copy. Two years later, Jane was given a copy of the casual contract. On examining the contract Jane noticed that, although the contract specified that a termination

▶

date must be included, no termination date was included. In addition to this omission, Jane's hours of work were not specified. Jane queried both these omissions but was told by her line manager, Professor Clarke, not to worry about them. On average Jane worked 15 hours per week and was paid at an hourly rate of £10. By June 1999 the hourly rate had risen to £11. In order to receive her pay Jane merely had to include a code on her wage claims and get the signature of Professor Clarke. The code related to funds held and controlled by the department of media studies and as long as this was included on wages claims the wages and salaries section would not query any claims.

In June 1999 Jane became pregnant, and she informed her line manager Professor Clarke, indicating that she would soon seek maternity leave, and asked him what procedures she needed to follow in order to do this. Professor Clarke replied that he didn't know but would find out for her. Since her engagement Jane had worked continuously at the university and had been allowed to take holidays by arrangement with her line manager even though at the time of her engagement this was clearly prohibited within the terms of her casual contract.

Eventually, Jane approached the wages and salaries section of the personnel function to inquire about maternity leave and maternity pay. She was told that as a casual employee she was not entitled to these benefits because she was engaged by the university on a term-by-term basis. Jane countered this argument by stating that she had worked at the university for the past three years, had a staff pigeon-hole and an entry in the university telephone directory. The staff in the wages and salary section, although nominally part of the personnel function, are actually controlled by the university treasury function and are not qualified personnel practitioners. They refused to process her inquiry because as she had no employee reference number she must be an hourly paid casual worker. An argument ensued and Jane was told to stop wasting their time and go away.

Jane went directly to see the head of personnel but found that he was away on holiday; perplexed, Jane sought legal and trade union assistance. Her representatives contacted the pro vice chancellor responsible for staff relations and demanded a meeting. At the meeting, all the above information was presented to the pro vice chancellor, who was unable to deal with it effectively because the head of personnel was on holiday. However, he promised to get this matter sorted out by the middle of the following week and arranged a meeting for the Wednesday.

Activity

Assume you are the personnel manager and a summary of the above lands on your desk when you return from holiday on the Monday morning together with a note from the pro vice chancellor asking you to sort all this out by Wednesday. How would you sort the situation out? And how would you diagnose the situation? The following pointers may help guide you in this task.

- Does the university have to provide Jane with maternity leave and maternity pay? If so, why?
- Is Jane an employee? Does it matter that she is a casual employee?
- Does Jane have continuous service with the university?
- Does Jane's situation suggest that there might be a wider problem in the university? For example, would the apparently less than satisfactory situation concerning Jane's employment go unnoticed if she had not become pregnant or if Jane was a male employee?
- How will you rectify Jane's situation?

Useful websites

Confederation of British Industry	www.cbi.org.uk
Commission for Racial Equality	www.cre.gov.uk
Department of Trade and Industry	www.dti.gov.uk
Equal Opportunities Commission	www.eoc.org.uk
Chartered Institute of Personnel and Development	www.cipd.org.uk
Disability Rights Commission	www.disability.gov.uk
Trade Union Congress	tuc.org.uk
Workplace Bullying: The Andrea Adams Trust	www.andreaadamstrust.org or
UK national workplace bullying advice line	www.bullyonline.org

References and further reading

Those texts marked with an asterisk are particulary recommended as useful legal texts.

*Allen, R. and Crasnow, R. (2002) *Employment Law and Human Rights*. Oxford: Oxford University Press.

*Anderman, S. (2000) *Labour Law, Management Decisions and Worker Rights*. London: Butterworths.

Armstrong, P. and Baron, A. (1995) *The Job Evaluation Handbook*. London: CIPD.

*Barnet, D. and Scrope, H. (2002) *European Employment Law*. London: Butterworths,.

Clark, I. (1996) 'The state and new industrial relations', in Beardwell, I. (ed.) *Contemporary Industrial Relations: A Critical Analysis*. Oxford: Oxford University Press.

Clark, I. (2000) *The State, Regulation and Industrial Relations*. London: Routledge.

Claydon, T. (1996) 'Union derecognition: a re-examination', in Beardwell, I. (ed.) *Contemporary Industrial Relations: A Critical Analysis*. Oxford: Oxford University Press.

*Deakin, S. and Morris, G. (2001) *Labour Law*, 3rd edn. Oxford: Hart Publishing.

Dickens, L. (2000) 'Still wasting resources? Equality in employment' in Bach, S. and Sisson, K. (eds) *Personnel Management in Britain*. Oxford: Blackwell.

Edwards, P. (ed) (2003) *Industrial Relations: Theory and Practice*. Oxford: Blackwell.

Equal Opportunities Commission (2001) Annual Report, Manchester.

Equal Opportunities Commission (2002) – evidence submitted to the Hicks' Inquiry into Non-Executive Directors' Pay. EOC, Manchester.

Financial Times (11/1/02) 'Analyst gets £1.4 million payout for "insulting bonus"'.

Financial Times (29/4/02) 'Brussels starts legal action over working hours'.

Financial Times (20/6/02) 'Sex discrimination appeal dropped'.

Financial Times (13/8/02) 'Employers lack confidence on rights of workers'.

Financial Times (30/8/02) 'More women work even longer hours'.

Financial Times (3/9/02) 'Anger at EU Directive on temporary workers'.

Financial Times (17/9/02) 'Minister blows his own trumpet at the unions'.

Financial Times (17/1/03) 'Managers still rule, unions told'.

Financial Times (17/3/03) 'Support for union demand on equal treatment'.

Financial Times (9/9/03) 'Call for more radical workers' rights'.

Fox, A. (1985) *History and Heritage*. London: Allen & Unwin.

Gall, G. and McKay, S. (1999) 'Developments in union recognition and derecognition in Britain 1994–1998', *British Journal of Industrial Relations*, Vol. 37, No. 4, pp. 601–614.

Glyn, A. and Wood, S. (2001) 'Economic policy under New Labour: how social democratic is the Blair Government?' *Political Quarterly*, Vol. 72, No. 1, pp. 50–66.

*Grant, B. (2002) *Employment Law: A Guide for Human Resource Managers*. London: Thomson Learning.

Health and Safety Commission (2002) Annual Report, London.

Hyman, R. (1975) *Industrial Relations: A Marxist Introduction*. London: Macmillan.

Kahn-Freund, O. (1984) *Labour and the Law*, 2nd edn. London: Stevens.

Labour Market Trends (2001) London: Office of National Statistics

Mercer Human Resource Consulting (2002) *The Prevalence of Bullying in the Workplace*. London: MHRC. Mercer.Pressoffice@mercer.com

National Association of Citizens Advice Bureau (2002) *Report on equal opportunities OECD Economic Outlook*, Paris: OECD.

*Novitz, T. and Skidmore, P. (2001) *Fairness at Work: A Critical Analysis of the Employment Relations Act, 1999 and its Treatment of Collective Rights*. Oxford: Hart Publishing.

Peninsula (2003) *Survey on Flexible Hours*. London: Peninsula.

Public Affairs (2001) *A Women's Place*. public.affairs @imgt.org.uk

TUC (2000) *Trade Union Recognition*. London: TUC.

TUC (2002) *Focus on Recognition*. London, TUC.

Wedderburn, W. (1986) *The Worker and the Law*. London: Penguin.

*Willey, B. (2000) *Employment Law in Context*. Harlow: Prentice Hall.

Work Stress Management (2002) *Survey on Workplace Stress*. www.workstressmanagement.com

For multiple choice questions, exercises and annotated weblinks specific to this chapter visit this book's website at www.booksites.net/beardwell

CHAPTER 12

Establishing the terms and conditions of employment

Sue Marlow and Trevor Colling

OBJECTIVES

▶ To define, examine and discuss the establishment of terms and conditions of employment through collective bargaining processes in the private and public sector where trade unions are recognised for such purposes.

▶ To consider the influence of contemporary government initiatives upon the terms and conditions of employment.

▶ To discuss the manner in which terms and conditions of employment are determined in organisations which do not recognise trade unions or union bargained agreements.

 ## Introduction

Critical to the structure of capitalist economies in the modern era has been the manner in which labour is rewarded for the effort made to produce goods and services – the 'effort–reward bargain'(Burowoy, 1979). As capitalism developed and began to mature, the foundations of a 'wage' economy were formalised. This led to contention regarding how work should be measured and valued. In response to the exploitative nature of early capitalism, trade unions developed as collective forces to protect employment conditions for skilled labour. The state, after some dissension, made union representation legal and laid basic protective rights for labour on statute. Employers, albeit sometimes grudgingly, accepted these constraints upon their freedom, and so the concept of negotiating terms and conditions of employment with labour emerged into modern society (Coates and Topham, 1986). Regarding the establishment of, and improvement to, the terms and conditions of employment, it was determined that the most efficient and equitable manner in which the 'effort–wage bargain' should be negotiated, for the majority of labour in society, was through free collective bargaining (Webb and Webb, 1902; Brown, 1993). Collective bargaining is a process of negotiation undertaken between employers' representatives and trade union representatives to determine the conditions under which labour should be employed. During the latter part of the nineteenth century and for most of the twentieth century, collective bargaining came to be accepted as the most appropriate vehicle for establishing the terms and conditions of employment and to this end, has been tacitly supported by the state and accepted by employers (Brown, 1993).

However, with the election of a Conservative administration in 1979, this supportive stance, from both the state and employers, was actively challenged. With a clear affiliation to a free market philosophy, successive Conservative governments since 1979 have overseen a calculated decline in the influence of trade unions in the UK. Along with the constraint and control of trade union power came a concomitant decline in the coverage of collective bargaining. This decline has been recorded by successive workplace surveys undertaken during this period such that, in 1984, it was found that over 70 per cent of employees were covered by collectively bargained agreements, but this figure had dropped to approximately 45 per cent by 1998 (Cully *et al.*, 1999: 93). However, it was noted that the majority of the largest firms in the economy and a substantial proportion of the public sector still utilise collective bargaining to establish and change the terms and conditions of employment (Cully *et al.*, 1999: 93).

So until recently, in any debate upon how the terms and conditions of employment are agreed, the critical focus would have been upon collective bargaining. However, it is now clear that whilst a substantial minority of employees still enjoy collective bargaining coverage, the majority do not. Bacon and Storey (1996: 43) refer to the 'fracturing of collectivism' by the structural changes in the labour market and the pursuit of individualism by management. This is evident in the increasing number of firms who do not recognise unions as either employee representatives or bargaining agents and contraction of bargaining in traditional bastions of strength such as the public sector (Bach and Winchester, 2002). So, it is recognised that overall, collective determination of the terms and conditions of employment no longer dominates in the UK. Yet, there is little evidence for a credible alternative model of employment relations emerging to replace the collective bargaining approach, leaving what Beaumont (1995) describes as an institutional vacuum. Towers (1997: 64), meanwhile, suggests that there is now a representation gap in the UK, where no formal method of articulation for employee voice has emerged with any coherence to effectively replace collective representation. There may be a role for HRM to fill this vacuum, but there is little indication that there is any wholesale, coherent and strategic adoption of HRM practices and policies by British management. Indeed, rather the opposite would appear to be evident, in that where HRM initiatives are in place they have largely been adopted in an ad hoc, opportunistic fashion and, moreover, are more likely to exist as a coherent policy strategy in unionised firms where collective representation persists (Cully *et al.*, 1999).

It is undeniable that collective representation and bargaining have declined. Towers (1997: 64) raises the pertinent question regarding union and bargaining decline, 'does it matter?' If the modern economy has grown away from collectivity and employees are not overtly resisting this trend, should there be concern over the demise of trade unions and collective bargaining? Based on two main issues, Towers argues that the decline of collectivity is a cause for considerable concern. Briefly, it is argued that employees are denied an independent representative channel within the naturally exploitative capitalist system, and that there are implications for national productivity, given that firms with a strong union presence are more effective at introducing change. Towers notes, 'it is more than arguable that collective bargaining can contribute positively toward the economic performance of individual enterprises and the economy as a whole' (p. 227). Supporting these points, Cully *et al.* (1999) found that investment in high-commitment management practices was more likely where there was a strong union presence whilst only a minority of workplaces without union representation offered employees formally agreed consultation over the organisation of the labour process. Brown (1993) explores the decline in collective bargaining, recorded in the 1992 workplace industrial relations survey (Millward *et al.*, 1992). Based on that evidence, Brown was pessimistic regarding the future of bargaining but noted, 'how much worse off are employees who do not enjoy the protection of collective bargaining. They are, on average, less favoured than their union brothers and sisters in terms of pay, health and safety, labour turnover, . . . consultation, communication and employee representation' (p. 198).

It could be argued that periods of transition, such as that from collective representation to an alternative model, will be turbulent and lead to casualties. Yet, this process of transition has been under way for some time and, to date, the decline in collective representation would appear to have denied labour a democratic channel to articulate their rights and does not appear to have contributed to a sustained productivity growth in the UK (Nolan and O'Donnell, 1995). It would appear, furthermore, that the most innovative firms, in terms of employing new managerial strategies to effect change, are those with a union presence (Cully *et al.*, 1999). Overall, the decline in union representation and collective bargaining would appear to 'matter' and to be a cause for concern regarding the protection of labour rights, the introduction of change and improving productivity levels within the economy.

Stop and think	What do you understand by the term 'the representation gap'?

The extent of collective bargaining coverage in the UK has experienced some change since the election of the Labour government in 1997 and the introduction of a statutory recognition procedure within the Employment Relations Act (1999). Gall and McKay (1999) drew attention to union recognition campaigns aimed at over 300 companies with 235 000 employees where the indications were that many firms were planning to accept such agreements in advance of statutory obligations; and this was supported by the findings from the CBI 1999 Employment Trends Survey which found that from 830 companies currently without union recognition, 60 per cent employing more than 5000 employees, and 50 percent of those employing 500 to 5000, were expecting a recognition claim. While it would appear that substantial increases in membership density have yet to emerge definitively, due to the 'churning' effect of exits and entries into membership, it is probably fair to suggest that union decline has plateaued (Sneade, 2001).

Within this picture of declining trade union affiliation, the public sector appears to be the exception, with union density remaining at just over 60 per cent (Bach, 2002). So, the public sector unions have maintained a presence in the workplace but, even here, there can be little doubt that they have lost influence regarding the determination of the terms of employment. As in the private sector, there has been some constriction of bargaining agendas and shifts in bargaining level. Moreover, since the 1980s successive governments have made greater use of pay review bodies, which, although consulting with unions, effectively bypass the collective bargaining process.

The debate surrounding the contraction and expansion of bargaining coverage in both the private and public sector is set to continue but it is clear that a majority of employees now work in firms that do not recognise trade unions for bargaining purposes. Rather, a range of approaches, from individual negotiation to unilateral management determination, can be identified in this sector. Limited empirical evidence pertaining to such firms has led to descriptors such as 'black holes' (Guest and Hoque, 1994) and 'bleak house' (Sisson, 1993), implying that such firms are steeped in exploitation. This is somewhat simplistic as there is a range of approaches adopted by management in firms without union representation to reward, organise and innovate, and these differing approaches will be explored to illuminate this debate further.

As there are a number of parallel processes regulating terms and conditions of employment in the contemporary economy, it is essential to explore all of these. As such, and in recognition of the growing diversity in establishing terms and conditions of employment, this chapter will:

● offer a comprehensive overview of the collective bargaining process in both the private and public sector;

- discuss recent modernising initiatives and agendas which might impact upon this process;
- consider the manner in which terms and conditions are established in firms which do not recognise trade unions for bargaining purposes.

Collective bargaining – history, definitions, analyses and criticisms

The term 'collective bargaining' was first utilised by Sidney and Beatrice Webb (Webb and Webb, 1902) who believed that this activity was the collective equivalent to individual bargaining, where the prime aim was to achieve economic advantage. So, bargaining had an *economic* function and was undertaken between trade unions and employers or employers' organisations. This 'classical' definition of collective bargaining has been subject to a number of critical analyses. In the late 1960s, Flanders (1968) argued that this view was erroneous; rather, collective bargaining should be understood as a *rule-making process* which established the rules under which the economic purchase of labour could initially take place. By establishing rules, collective bargaining outlines a framework for future negotiations regarding the buying and selling of labour. So, it is not a collective equivalent of individual bargaining, as nothing is actually bought or sold; only the rules under which the commodity of labour can be bought or sold are established. Flanders argued that collective bargaining also entails a power relationship; the imbalance of economic power, status and security between the single employee and that of the management can, to some degree, be addressed by collective pressure such that agreements are compromise settlements of power conflicts. Fox (1975) disputes Flanders' argument that an individual bargain is an economic exchange which always concludes with an agreement, whereas collective bargaining is essentially a process to establish rules for exchange. In fact, Fox argues that there is no assurance that either process will achieve agreement on terms acceptable to the parties involved in negotiation. Moreover, he believes that the economic function of collective bargaining has not been afforded sufficient attention by Flanders in his analysis. Drawing from these arguments, it is useful to recognise that Flanders moves the discussion forward with the emphasis on regulation but the contrast between collective regulation and individual bargaining is debatable, as Fox notes.

Rather than isolating one major function of collective bargaining, Chamberlain and Kuhn (1965) offer an analysis which outlines three distinct activities which interact to form the bargaining process:

- *Market or economic function.* This determines the price of labour to the employer, thus the collective agreement forms the 'contract' for the terms under which employees will work for the employer, i.e. the *substantive terms* (see below) of employment.
- *Decision-making function.* In this role, collective bargaining offers employees the opportunity, if they wish, to 'participate in the determination of the policies which guide and rule their working lives' (Chamberlain and Kuhn, 1965: 130).
- *Governmental function.* Collective bargaining establishes rules by which the employment relationship is governed. Thus, bargaining is a political process as it establishes a 'constitution' (Salamon, 1992).

From the above points it is clear that collective bargaining is concerned with the establishment of:

- *Substantive rules.* These regulate all aspects of pay agreements and hours of work.
- *Procedural rules.* These establish the rules under which negotiation over the terms and conditions of employment can take place and establish grievance and dispute procedures.

Bargaining principles

The aim of collective bargaining is to reach negotiated agreements upon a range of issues pertaining to the employment relationship. From this range of issues, some will hold the potential for a conflict situation where the distribution and division of scarce resources are under negotiation (for example, division of profit as dividends or wages increase). Others, however, will have mutual benefit for employees and management, with the major debate focusing upon the most beneficial manner in which to implement change (for example, introduction of health and safety procedures). These differences were noted by Walton and McKersie (1965) who outlined two approaches to collective bargaining:

- *Distributive bargaining.* One party will seek to achieve gains at the expense of the other; the aim is the division of a limited resource between groups, both of whom wish to maximise their share. Pay bargaining is distributive bargaining as one party's gain is the other's loss.
- *Integrative bargaining.* This approach seeks mutual gains in areas of common interest, with a problem-solving approach from the parties involved. Successful integrative bargaining depends upon a relatively high level of trust between parties and a willingness to share information.

Stop and think

Briefly define the term 'collective bargaining'.

Summary

Collective bargaining remains an important part of the contemporary employment relationship, although since the early 1980s, it has been subject to contraction and decline. Recently however, due to limited political support and new statutory rights, this decline in influence would appear to have halted (Bach, 2002). There has been considerable debate regarding the fundamental nature and purpose of the bargaining process, but any definition of collective bargaining must take account of historical and contemporary influences which impinge upon those involved in bargaining practices.

The collective agreement

At the end of the negotiating and bargaining process, collective agreements are reached. Traditionally, British collective bargaining has been notable for the informality with which agreements are reached but from the early 1970s there has been a growing trend to establish formal written contracts to avoid any potential problems given the possibility of differing interpretations of negotiation outcome. The written agreement also contributes to a rationalisation and codification of employment relations procedures but the existence of formal written agreements will not prevent informal bargaining at local level. Indeed, there are a number of levels, outlined below, at which collective agreements can be reached.

Multi-employer agreements

Such agreements cover specific groups of employees (described within the contract) from a particular industry and are negotiated by employers' associations or federations and full-time national trade union officials. Multi-employer agreements also form guidelines for employers who are not members of the industry association, and for firms that do not recognise unions. There is strong evidence that the incidence of multi-employer bargaining has been in decline for some time, with a growing preference for single employer and more decentralised bargaining (Brown and Walsh, 1991; Cully *et al.*, 1999).

Single-employer bargaining (organisational bargaining)

Organisational bargaining may occur at a number of levels, for example:

- *Corporate* – all those employed by the organisation are covered by agreements bargained by the company and relevant trade union officials.
- *Plant* – the collective agreement is negotiated for a specific site or plant within the corporate structure affecting only the employees of that location. These agreements may be totally independent of national terms or constructed upon an industry agreement.

Determinants of bargaining level within organisations

It is indicated that company-level bargaining is associated with large organisations and the presence of professional HR specialists in corporate-level management (CBI, 1988). Site bargaining is associated with firms where labour costs are a high percentage of total costs and there are substantial numbers of workers on each site. At present, the choice of bargaining level falls within managerial prerogative influenced by a number of variables; for example, corporate-level bargaining may be favoured as one channel to neutralise potentially powerful plant-based union pressure and avoid inter-plant comparisons. Plant-based bargaining, however, will tie down labour costs to local conditions, bargained by negotiators who have a shared awareness of regional conditions which may not always be to management's advantage (Rose, 2001).

The development of collective bargaining in Britain 1945–80

By 1945, 15.5 million employees from a working population of 17.5 million (Palmer, 1983: 157) were covered by some type of national agreement. The influence of corporatism, where joint negotiations between employers and trade unions are encouraged by the state, ensured that industry-level collective bargaining became firmly established. The nationalisation programme and the advent of the welfare system ensured that the state became a major employer and indeed, the postwar Labour government enacted legislation which obliged management in the newly nationalised industries to establish negotiating procedures for all employees. It is incorrect, however, to presume that local or domestic bargaining ceased to be of relevance because of the formal establishment of national bargaining machinery for the majority of British labour by the early 1950s. In fact, the conditions of full employment, coupled with high demand, offered considerable leverage for local bargaining by shop stewards in the less bureaucratic, private manufacturing sector.

Negotiation issues

Such local shopfloor bargaining increased wage drift, growth of short informal disputes and a growing tendency for national agreements to be utilised as a bargaining floor upon which local agreements were based, leading to inflationary pressures. This latter point generated concern from a then Labour government, given the problems of introducing and operating incomes policies in the face of informal, unregulated local bargaining and growing inflation. The growth and economic effect of domestic bargaining was deemed an 'industrial relations problem'.

Batstone *et al.* (1977), however, found that local shop stewards in the car industry were not, in fact, independently bargaining but remained in close contact with full-time officials. In fact, the Commission on Industrial Relations (CIR) found many managers reluctant to move away from the intimate, local channels of negotiation they had established. Given, however, that domestic bargaining was a problem for employers who faced increasing international competition and found wage costs difficult to control and was also a potential threat to government economic policy, a Royal Commission was established to examine industrial relations practices and procedures in both the public and private sector. The Donovan Commission reported in 1968, arguing that Britain had two systems of industrial relations, the formal and informal (Donovan Commission, 1968: 12). In private sector manufacturing, the formal system was based upon national bargaining between employers' organisations and full-time trade union officials. The informal system was based upon local bargaining between management and shop stewards under the influence of full employment and buoyant demand for goods. Overall, the Donovan Commission argued that workplace bargaining had become of greater importance than national bargaining in the private manufacturing sector. This local level of bargaining, it was suggested, was 'largely informal, largely fragmented, and largely autonomous' (Flanders, 1970: 169) as it was based upon verbal agreements backed by custom and practice. Fragmented bargaining was undertaken by individual or small groups of stewards negotiating with individual or small groups of managers who did not consult with employers' organisations or full-time trade union officials, and did not respect national agreements.

The Commission argued that multi-employer bargaining on a national industry level could no longer effectively accommodate differentiated working practices throughout the private sector. The responsibility for introducing reform lay with management; local informal agreements were not dismissed, but it was insisted that local agreements should achieve a level of formality such that they did not totally ignore and undermine national agreements. Moreover, the system of local informal bargaining effectively hampered the development of effective and orderly workplace bargaining: '. . . the objection to the state of plant bargaining at that time, therefore, was its doubtful legitimacy and furtive character' (Clegg, 1979: 237). What was required was a rationalisation of the existing system which would effectively combine the two systems of industrial relations into one coherent, ordered process which did not then undermine the formal rules in multi-employer agreements.

Such reform of the content and structure of existing bargaining arrangements should, it was argued, be undertaken by senior management within their own companies. It was necessary to develop a framework of bargaining issues with extensive procedural agreements where management and trade unions could formally negotiate terms and conditions of employment. Changes in pay should be linked to changes in productivity, establishing a clear connection between formal domestic bargaining and enhanced profitability, with this tactic verified by the National Board for Prices and Incomes.

The reform of local-level bargaining

In consequence, most organisations, encouraged by the Conservative (1970–74) and Labour governments (1974–79), undertook voluntary reform of collective bargaining procedures. Using survey evidence from Brown (1981), it was apparent that by the late

1970s, single-employer bargaining at establishment or corporate level had become the most prevalent level of bargaining for both manual and non-manual employees. The basis of this survey evidence indicated that significant changes had occurred in collective bargaining processes since the recommendations of Donovan. It was found that management had facilitated the formalisation of domestic bargaining by recognising shop stewards, supporting union organisation through closed shop agreements and check-off procedures (whereby union subscriptions are deducted by the company from wages and then paid to the trade union account). It was also noted that industrial sector and size of establishment affected bargaining level where, according to Deaton and Beaumont (1980: 201), single-employer bargaining was associated with larger firms, foreign ownership, multi-site operations and the existence of a professional tier of senior industrial relations management.

The reform of collective bargaining during the 1970s offered clear benefits to trade unions, with increased formal recognition and better facilities (for a critique of the incorporation of shop stewards into formal management/trade union bargaining hierarchy – 'the bureaucratisation thesis' – see Hyman, 1975). It became apparent, however, that rapidly rising inflation, growing international competition and greater foreign ownership, combined with state intervention in industrial relations issues, created a climate favourable for management to press for further reforms. So, for example, there emerged a trend towards decentralisation of bargaining and a growth in formal recognition of domestic bargainers, but there remained considerable variation in collective bargaining processes within British industry during the 1970s.

> **Stop and think**
>
> When Donovan (1968) reported that the UK had two approaches to bargaining, informal and formal, what do you think he meant?

Summary

In the postwar period there was a rapid expansion in domestic bargaining at local level in private sector manufacturing industry despite the existence of national agreements negotiated by multi-employer organisations and full-time trade union officials. The Labour government of 1964–70 was concerned that local bargaining was compromising its incomes policy programme, adding to inflationary pressure and adversely affecting Britain's competitive performance. The Donovan Commission was charged with investigating contemporary industrial relations and concluded that Britain had two systems of industrial relations, informal and formal. The solution was to incorporate the two, establishing formal bargaining processes and procedures at the domestic level with an emphasis upon productivity bargaining. It should be noted that whilst it was recognised that the process of collective bargaining was creating economic and industrial relations problems during this era, there was no suggestion that the practice should be constrained or abandoned, but reformed. Governments throughout the 1960s and 1970s continued to support collective bargaining as the most appropriate and equitable manner in which to establish the terms and conditions of employment.

Changes in collective bargaining since the 1980s

From the late 1970s to the mid-1990s the British economy suffered cyclical economic recession and volatile levels of unemployment. Although unemployment has, according to government figures, been generally falling since the late 1980s (note the increase in

1992 due to recession), the greatest increase in employment has been in part-time labour and low-paid, low-skill private sector work (Clark, 1998). Such structural changes, combined with the election of successive Conservative governments from 1979 to 1997, hostile to the ethos of collective action by trade unions, have prompted substantial change in the nature of collective bargaining in both the public and private sector. It is important to note that such changes have resulted from joint pressures from industry, the government and trade union inability to defend their presence in the workplace. It was a combination of such factors that prompted substantial changes within the scope and influence of the collective bargaining process.

Recent workplace studies (Gregg and Yates, 1991; Cully *et al.*, 1999; Gall and McKay, 1999) found that, while the nature, scope and processes of collective bargaining have changed, collective bargaining remains an important vehicle for fixing pay and conditions in the public sector, and for a substantial minority of employees in private manufacturing. However, it is of little importance for the private service sector. Overall, they agree that the following trends have emerged.

Decentralisation of bargaining

There has been a growing trend towards the decentralisation of collective bargaining, away from multi-employer/industry level to organisation or plant level. This trend continued during the 1980s and 1990s with encouragement from successive Conservative governments during this period who attempted to promote the practice in the public sector. Indeed, the 1990 White Paper *Employment for the 1990s* stated that plant- or company-level negotiations result in more 'realistic pay settlements' and thus, avoid wage inflation. Support from government legislation during this period, constraining industrial action, has also acted to dissipate further any union resistance to plant bargaining. There are no indications that the current Labour administration will take any action to reverse this trend, having declared that they will not be making any substantial adjustments to the labour legislation enacted by their Conservative predecessors (McIlroy, 1998).

From the corporate stance, decentralised bargaining offers the opportunity to link pay and productivity together at local level where regional variations and conditions can be accounted for accurately by local management and trade union officials. The weakened state of contemporary trade unions ensures that they are less able to resist managerial strategy to utilise local bargaining to review labour costs and reform working practices, for example the introduction of new technology, flexible working practices, etc. (Sisson, 1987).

There is a need for a note of caution regarding whether decentralised bargaining is a useful strategy for all corporate structures and also regarding the true extent of the 'decentralisation' process. Considering the issue of decentralisation in more detail, Kinnie (1990) found a false image of local autonomy in bargaining, suggesting that local management are subject to head office directive even when there is an appearance of local autonomy. This is supported in more recent work, with Cully *et al.* (1999) commenting that 'the pay setting process is often handled beyond the workplace and may be opaque to managers at a local level' (p. 106). So, whilst there can be little doubt that there has been a shift in bargaining levels which has complemented contemporary corporate strategies to downsize, focusing upon local profit centres, enabling employers to gain more control in the workplace (Sisson, 1987), the extent to which local management achieve independence and autonomy in the bargaining arena is questionable.

ACTIVITY A corporate enterprise has always undertaken centralised bargaining, with a specialised team of negotiators bargaining annually with full-time trade union officials. However, the corporation is considering a complete restructuring whereby local 'profit centres' would be developed as single business units. As part of this restructuring it has been suggested that collective bargaining should be devolved to local level, with outline directives issued from head office regarding acceptable bargaining agendas and final settlements.

As HRM consultants, outline the presentation you would make to the board to include the following issues:

(a) the origins and extent of local bargaining;
(b) the advantages and potential problems of local bargaining to both management and trade unions;
(c) possible solutions to such problems;
(d) recommendations concerning the move to local bargaining.

◼ Flexibility issues

The introduction of flexible working has been made possible by the deregulation of the labour market, the weakness of trade unions to resist such change, the growth of managerial prerogative and market pressure to cut costs (Pollert, 1988; Legge, 1995). Where changes aimed at the introduction of flexibility within the labour process are being negotiated, the following points have become evident:

● If a company introduces flexible working, not subject to statutory regulation, such changes usually form an overlapping agreement to become part of a complete package which constitutes a flexibility agreement. The terms and conditions of contemporary flexibility agreements evidently will depend on such factors as the state of union–management relations, the bargaining environment and the nature of technology employed.

The implications for collective bargaining of flexibility agreements are as follows:

● Trade unions are no longer bargaining terms and conditions for a specific craft or activity. Flexibility between tasks blurs lines of demarcation such that the possession of a specific skill or talent is no longer exclusive as tasks are spread throughout the workforce. Thus, bargaining leverage is reduced.
● As employees undertake a wider range of tasks throughout the labour process, fewer 'core' workers are required with an increasing dependence upon numerically flexible labour, thus leading to redundancies and a consequent fall in trade union membership and growth in unemployment.
● The growing links between flexibility bargaining and pay increases mean that there is a growing trend to bargain around issues of exchange, for example for wage increases in exchange for changes in work organisation, manning levels and redundancies.

This latter point is of some importance. This notion of exchange between improved pay and acceptance of changes in working methods is reminiscent of productivity bargaining during the 1960s. In return for accepting flexibility agreements, employees have been offered a range of benefits including pay increases, enhanced status and greater job security. Trade unions have been forced to bargain for better conditions on the basis of making concessions allowing significant changes in the labour process. Indeed, a reflection of this stance can clearly be seen in the current government's attitude toward the 2002–3 firefighters' dispute where agreement to changed working practices is deemed essential before meaningful negotiations can occur.

As with many other issues discussed, there is a robust critique of the ideas surrounding the flexible workforce idea. In a succinct, critical review of the flexibility debate, Pollert (1988) and Legge (1995) argue that this is not a new strategic attempt by employers to establish a labour force suitable to meet the needs of changing markets. Rather, employers have always made *ad hoc* attempts to make labour more flexible, but have been hampered by state and union regulation of terms and conditions of employment. Recently, employers have been able to take advantage of a weakened labour movement to introduce greater flexibility, encouraged by governments sympathetic to such changes. Moreover, Legge (1995) argues that flexible working arrangements have largely been introduced in an opportunistic fashion, with the emphasis upon short-term cost savings rather than as any constituent of a longer-term strategic change to working practices.

So, while there is some evidence concerning the development of flexible working and the inclusion of flexibility agreements in the bargaining forum, there is only a limited indication of a link between improved productivity and flexibility initiatives (Edwards, 1987). This, together with the critique of flexibility, suggests that, while flexibility issues are undoubtedly an important HRM initiative to effect change in the labour process, with implications for collective bargaining, caution is required in interpreting the extent of such change. This is particularly pertinent in respect of what degree the utilisation of flexibility represents a strategic or coherent approach to fragmenting the labour force, or to undermining collective coverage.

Successive Labour administrations from 1997 have offered continued support for flexible working, but have claimed to recognise that there is a need to ameliorate the worst effects of such initiatives. It was intended that the statutory protection offered in the Minimum Wage Act (1998), the Employment Relations Act (1999), the Employment Act (2002) and the recognition and adoption of EU Directives would go some way towards offering vulnerable labour greater protection. Moreover, there has been a clear focus upon the development of 'family-friendly policies' which facilitate parents in achieving a so-called 'work–life' balance where work and family commitments can be effectively accommodated. It is recognised that statutory provision obviates the need for collective bargaining (if not for collective representation to ensure that rights are observed: see below) and is indicative that the Labour government has chosen a path which focuses mainly upon individual rights rather than the restoration of collective rights and any ensuing collaboration with trade unions. However, such agreements may be used as a 'floor of rights' in some organisations, whilst scope exists for unions to police the provisions and ensure they are properly represented within the collective bargaining agenda or act to support individual employees pursuing their new rights.

■ Contemporary bargaining initiatives

Since the reform of collective bargaining in the 1980s, a number of discrete initiatives have emerged which have, on the whole, enabled management to reform the bargaining process quite considerably. A number of these are briefly considered:

● Single-union deals are largely associated with Japanese management strategies, given their initiation within Japanese subsidiaries locating on greenfield sites in the UK (Salamon, 1992). The single-union agreement occurs where management grants recognition to only one trade union to represent employees in the bargaining process. The major objection to single-union deals is the promotion of what Salamon describes as a 'beauty contest approach' between trade unions. Management outline the envisaged approach to industrial relations and a personnel strategy, inviting trade unions to state how they might measure up to the managerial view of employment relations – with the reward being a new pool of members during a time when trade unions are experiencing decline. As such, the relationship between management and union becomes one in which unions must offer to fulfil the behavioural expectations of management, in order to be granted recognition, rather than prioritising the needs of the membership. Regarding the collective bargaining process, there will be some employees whose interests will not be best served by a union which has no history of representing them and with which they feel no basis of affiliation. However, it could be argued that, given the labour process of organisations that adopted single-union deals (single-status working, flexibility, fewer separate job titles), the scope for a differentiated approach to bargaining is significantly narrowed. A further constraint upon the bargaining process in single-union firms is the association between single-union deals, no-strike deals and pendulum arbitration.

- A no-strike clause, once accepted by a trade union on behalf of the membership, effectively deprives union negotiators of the threat of strike action should bargaining break down and, moreover, denies employees the option of withdrawing their labour unilaterally.
- No-strike clauses are usually (but not always) accompanied by pendulum arbitration facilities where a third party will arbitrate on behalf of the two principals should they fail to reach agreement. Where both sides are aware that an arbitrator will adopt one side or the other's position and this will represent a cost to the other party, they are more likely to bargain in good faith, making every effort to settle (Singh, 1986; Milner, 1993). The limited use of this practice in Britain makes it difficult to assess the impact upon the bargaining process.
- Single-table bargaining offers employers similar benefits to single-union deals while maintaining a multi-union site. Bargaining takes place between unions to establish a negotiation proposal, which is then articulated by one bargaining unit which negotiates on behalf of all employees. A number of companies within the private manufacturing and service sector have adopted a single bargaining table, although the process is not common. Marginson and Sisson (1990) suggested that such bargaining will become more widespread as the impact of European Union directives and legislation regarding information sharing, communication and collective bargaining encourage management to review bargaining processes. Recent evidence from Cully *et al.* (1999) indicates that this is indeed the case.

ACTIVITY List the major reforms to collective bargaining levels and processes in the 1980s.

HRM and collective bargaining

The early conceptual notion of HRM being focused upon, and only possible in, the unitary firm has not emerged in the modern British economy. In contemporary usage, HRM is employed as a set of strategic initiatives focused upon the employee with the aim of improving competitiveness, where any firm, depending on product and market demands, may utilise any number from a range of initiatives included under the HRM umbrella. Yet, introducing and managing HRM practices in a collective bargaining environment does raise a number of contentious issues, primarily whether a series of initiatives aimed at the individual employee can be compatible within the collective approach.

Overall, there is little evidence for the emergence of a strategic approach to managing labour in the UK economy (Mabey and Salamon, 1995) but it appears that HRM initiatives are more evident in unionised firms. This can be taken as evidence that the two practices, HRM and collective bargaining, are not mutually exclusive (Mishel and Voos, 1992). Guest (1989) argues that the values underpinning HRM – strategic integration and the pursuit of quality – are not incompatible with collective representation where bargaining channels can be effectively utilised to introduce change. Recent evidence from the 1998 Employment Relations Survey found 'high commitment management practices going hand in hand with a union presence' and also found this to be the case for high-productivity firms (Cully *et al.*, 1999: 294). Storey (1989) argues that the two systems can coexist in harmony where HRM initiatives are focused upon areas which do not pose a threat to the scope of collective bargaining, or where they do not attempt to bypass established bargaining channels. Consequently, it is not axiomatic that if HRM initiatives are to be utilised, collective bargaining must be removed from the agenda; the critical issue here is the motivation for the introduction of HRM. If individualised HRM practices are aimed at undermining union effectiveness, there is a real threat to existing procedures. However, if change is deployed after discussion and/or negotiation with existing unions, there is an opportunity for joint regulation of new working practices. This is not to argue that collective bargaining will be unaffected by the adoption of HRM. Storey (1992) found that while collective bargaining had become less of a management priority, new HRM practices and collective bargaining tended to exist as parallel arrangements. The emphasis was upon reducing the union role rather than replacing it. It is apparent that the social partnership agenda will also impact upon the manner in which HRM initiatives are to be integrated into the organisation. It remains to be seen whether the development of partnership agreements in unionised firms will bring more HRM initiatives into the bargaining agenda or facilitate the growth of consultation channels.

Considering the issue of HRM and collective bargaining processes specifically, it appears that the former can coexist with the latter and indeed, HRM initiatives may be introduced through bargaining channels. In established plants, while HRM initiatives are evident, they have not seriously challenged the main focus of collective bargaining upon pay issues, but the scope of bargaining has been narrowed, with consultation being employed as a preferred channel of communication.

Summary

A number of bargaining initiatives emerged during the 1980s which have changed the level and structure of the collective bargaining process. These initiatives have facilitated the exercise of managerial prerogative in the bargaining relationship and further narrowed the scope of bargaining channels. Overall, where it persists, the collective bargaining function has remained intact but has been constrained in scope.

'New Labour' and the contemporary employment relationship

With the election of 'New Labour' in 1997 there has emerged a rather contradictory programme of change and continuity in employment relations. A modernising agenda has been actioned which moves away from the philosophy of state-sponsored wealth redistribution through social ownership to the support of private capital, private enterprise, individualism and a continuation of Conservative expenditure limits. The new administration made it quite clear that the vast majority of the initiatives undertaken by the previous Conservative administration to reform the employment relationship would remain in place. Hence, the anti-union legislation enacted in the past 20 years remains largely untouched such that Britain still has the most restrictive regime of any Western developed nation towards collective representation at work. There has been no noticeable resurgence of the special relationship between Labour and unions evident in previous administrations, while the Labour government has retained an enthusiasm for a deregulated labour market with flexibility as a key factor (Rose, 2001). While retaining some of the frameworks which shaped employment relations over the past 20 years, New Labour has also introduced policies which aimed to redress somewhat the power imbalance between management and labour which have also necessitated the state to develop a model of 'good' employment relations. The key focal points of the administration to date have been the notions of social partnership, fairness at work and recognition of European employment regulation (McIlroy, 1998).

In his commentary, McIlroy emphasises the difficult choices facing the trade union movement in reaching a compromise with the new Labour administration, who were not prepared to abandon the Thatcherite foundation of the contemporary employment relationship. There is some speculation regarding the future of the party–union link – whether it goes further down the path McIlroy (1998: 559) describes as 'arm's-length organisational relationships'. Given the current tension between public sector unions and the government, where Bach (2002: 320) notes, 'public sector trade unions leaders were disappointed by the lack of progress in improving their members' pay and working conditions', plus the bitter Fire Service dispute and the election of more left-leaning trade union officials recently, a distanced toleration would seem, at best, most likely.

However, the notion of social partnerships is one issue where moderate unions have indicated a willingness to comply with political will but, as McIlroy argues, these partnerships do not reflect the robust Rhineland model where consultation, communication and representation are strongly regulated. Hence, suspicion and doubt remain regarding their real utility to employees as the weak UK version clearly underpins the desire to retain flexibility, deregulation and competitiveness, more in accord with the US model (Clark, 1998). In consequence, the current government refers to the mutual responsibilities between employers and employees and is equally encouraging to both unions and management to engage in dialogue to introduce change, improve productivity and resolve disputes.

From trade unions, there has been some support for the social partnership concept (Monks, 1996), although this has been with an element of pragmatism, recognising that the 'New Unionism' agenda must be seen to be moderate and conciliatory to maintain support from employers and the state (McIlroy, 1998). Support for partnerships from unions is, of course, not entirely based on pragmatism. In a number of polls commissioned by the GMB in the late 1980s and early 1990s, it became apparent that employees had concerns relating to issues which were beyond the traditional remit of collective bargaining. These included job fulfilment, worthwhile work, and job security, all of which were ranked above pay in importance. John Edmonds (1997), the GMB General Secretary, argued that the former are most effectively addressed through partnership discussion rather than collective negotiation. This union stance towards social partnerships has fuelled the contemporary debate surrounding the most appropriate strategies for unions to adopt in the workplace to ensure their continued relevance as both employee representatives and bargainers. More recently, there is some indication that the union movement is growing disillusioned with the notion of partnership, particularly as practised by the Labour government. Based on their disappointment with the nature of proposed changes in the public sector, in July 2001 the TUC openly expressed doubts about the government's ability to generate meaningful partnerships. If the union movement feels those who are supposed to be most supportive of the notion of partnerships are not committed to them, this must surely raise questions regarding the whole ethos. Union disillusionment with this process has been further emphasised with Mark Serwotka, the General Secretary of the Public and Commercial Services Union (PCS), openly declaring a clear break with the partnership agenda in his determination to return outsourced employment to the public sector and to use strike action if necessary to achieve this goal (Turner, 2003a).

The radical critique of the concept of social partnerships, however, questions the whole feasibility of such relationships in the first instance. Kelly (1996) argues that it is difficult to form meaningful relationships with a party that wishes you did not exist. Equally, Kelly argues that in an inequitable power arrangement, as exists between capital and labour, the likelihood of meaningful partnerships being established is impossible unless far-reaching coercive measures can be applied. Briefly, Kelly believes that given the current state of management strength and the ambivalence towards unions from the current government, there is little rationale for employers to enter into true partnerships with unions when they can achieve their goals through flexing their prerogative. Critically, Kelly also believes that a partnership stance will undermine the role of collective bargaining and narrow current agendas further. Bacon and Storey (1996: 43), however, describe the 'fracturing of collectivism' and instead argue that unions must find new ways of representing the individual in the workplace and engage with partnership channels. At the same time they recognise that partnership initiatives have been frustrated in a number of firms, owing to the lack of management commitment to the process leading to nothing more than a rhetoric of partnership.

While it is not yet evident how collective bargaining will be affected by the notion of partnership, a number of suppositions are possible. The enactment of the Employment Relations Act (1999) has signalled the current government's intention to tacitly support union recognition, if rather cautiously. There has also been some indication of an emergence of new consultation and partnership agendas (Roche and Geary, 2002). This may be unpalatable to unions but, if they are to be seen to support partnerships, they may have to accept a continued restriction of negotiation, and expansion of consultation. However, management will still have to enter into debate around key issues, and demonstrate progress, if partnerships are to be maintained. What is not in doubt is that partnerships are contentious and their success will depend upon employer and employee representatives being able to demonstrate that they are reaching consensus through cooperation, without one set of interests being consistently subordinated. From limited evidence based upon partnerships in the water industry in the UK and vehicle manufacturing in the USA, Towers (1997: 226) comments that there is 'an essential need for equal partnership reinforced by collective bargaining which accepts the legitimacy of conflict or interests as well as encouraging and institutionalising co-operation'. Further evidence will be required to assess the impact and success of social partnerships. However, recent empirical examinations of partnership in practice found that, while there are mutual gains for both employees and management, the advantage is skewed in the favour of management, who set the partnership agenda and appear to protect their own prerogative (Guest and Peccei, 1998; Roche and Geary, 2002).

ACTIVITY   Briefly outline the major reforms introduced by the Labour government since 1997 which have affected the manner in which the terms and conditions of employment are agreed.

While the changes to national policy regarding the management of employment relations might be viewed as cautious at best and highly conservative at worst, New Labour have actively engaged with recognition of European regulation, which is a notable change from their Conservative predecessors. Whereas the Conservatives had rejected the social aspect of European Union membership, preferring to maintain their autonomy to foster free market individualism, the Blair administrations have recognised this dimension. However, it should be noted that Labour still favours minimal compliance and, in some cases, has not recognised measures in full or met agreed deadlines. So, for example, the Working Time Directive can be applied in such a way that the impact on the working week is minimal. Equally, the initial attempt to use 'employees' rather than 'workers' in the Part Time Workers Directive would have effectively excluded most of the labour that might benefit from the regulation. Even now, the regulation is extremely narrow in its application and, as noted earlier, in the case of new directives such as that on information and consultation, unions are expressing doubts regarding the government's level of commitment to implementation. For unions, the issue of EU regulation is critical as it offers them the opportunity to police the manner in which they are incorporated in the workplace, thus adding value to membership and a more formal role in engaging with management over the terms and processes of implementation.

■ Summary

When the Labour government was elected to power in 1997, it was anticipated that there would be some revival of trade union influence over policy and economic development. However, successive Labour administrations have not demonstrated any enthusiasm to develop a close relationship with the trade union movement. Rather, they have enacted legislation which has strengthened union rights but the overall focus has been upon the individual at work and incorporating weak versions of European regulation rather than supporting collective labour rights. The outcome of this 'distancing' stance has been a growing disillusionment by the union movement with the Labour government. This has been articulated by the election of 'left wing' activists to positions of prominence, and protracted disputes in the public sector such as that in the Fire Service, with the government threatening the union with legislation which would enable them to impose a settlement. There can be little doubt that the ERA (1999) did strengthen unions' ability to influence terms and conditions of employment. However, this fell short of what the trade union movement expected of the Labour government and it appears unlikely that any further government support will be forthcoming.

Establishing the terms and conditions of employment in the public sector

For much of the period following the Second World War, public sector employment relationships were distinctive, and designedly so. Managers were held accountable through political and administrative mechanisms, rather than through the market, and links between management practice and public policy were viewed as obvious and entirely legitimate. Public organisations were required to exemplify 'model employer' practice. Employment procedures were prescribed explicitly, sometimes by statute, and were subject to informal ministerial influence. Collective bargaining and consultation with trade unions were well established, where national bargaining forums sat atop complex local and regional structures setting uniform national pay rates and conditions of service.

Since 1979, there has been some considerable reform of this process, with successive Conservative governments intent on privatisation, cost-cutting and the introduction of market forces into service provision. Contemporary Labour governments have broadly supported many of the Conservative ideas and reforms but within a new framework of a 'modernising' agenda which recognises the need for increasing investment if service provision is to be improved and recruitment and retention problems addressed. While demonstrating more sympathy towards the notion of public sector provision, the current government is determined to continue to foster increasing cooperation with the private sector through the private finance initiative (PFI) and public private partnerships (PPP). To explore these issues in more detail, this section will outline the 'golden era' of public sector development, consider how this has changed in recent years and discuss current government initiatives regarding pay and conditions for public sector employees.

The 'golden era': Morrisonian organisations and model employment

That which until recently was recognised as the public sector developed in the immediate postwar period. Between 1945 and 1950, the Labour government took into public ownership a number of basic industries, including coal, steel and the railways. Together these accounted for approximately 10 per cent of the country's total productive capacity (Dearlove and Saunders, 1984: 268). Services that were to constitute the welfare state, including health and social security, were established under public administration and expanded rapidly. By 1959, almost a quarter (23.9 per cent) of the labour force worked in the public sector (Fairbrother, 1982: 3). Over the next 30 years this diverse range of enterprises, utility industries and services was gradually restructured more or less according to the principles of public corporations established by the Labour politician, Herbert Morrison. During this 'golden era', there was little doubt that employment practice in the public sector was different from that prevailing elsewhere in the economy, and designedly so.

Morrisonian principles were informed by two policy objectives: first, to ensure that the priorities pursued by key industries and services were consistent with macroeconomic, industrial and social policy; and second, to provide within this framework some autonomy for professional managers. These large, integrated organisations were therefore managed through independent industry boards that had responsibility for day-to-day operational matters. But these boards were accountable directly to the relevant ministers, who were also empowered to give 'general direction' (Pendleton and Winterton, 1993). Differing contexts meant that the model could not be implemented uniformly, and some variation was apparent. The principles by which management operated, however, were shared widely. An ethos of public service, founded upon accountability, impartiality and commitment to communitarian values, was fostered deliberately and became a primary motivating factor for employees (Pratchett and Wingfield, 1995). In the interests of equality of treatment, uniform standards of product or service were a priority, and departments would be deployed to ensure consistency across the organisation. Guaranteeing probity in the public interest required complex internal control systems and hierarchies of management and committee structures.

The public sector as a whole was also assigned a particular industrial relations mission: to be a 'model' employer and implement 'a range of practices which today constitute good management' (Priestly Commission, 1955, cited in Farnham and Horton, 1995: 8). The state sector's role in macroeconomic policy was important in this regard. Though the depth of the postwar consensus can be exaggerated, commitments to full employment and the welfare state structured the programmes of both of the key political parties for as long as they could be combined with economic growth (Hills, 1990). The public sector was assigned a key role in job creation, 'mopping up' underemployment created by restructuring in the broader economy. Expanding public sector employment enabled managers to offer meaningful job security. Market notions of efficiency were generally alien to the public sector, and public expenditure planning mechanisms permitted public employers to pass on increasing labour costs to central government (Winchester, 1983).

'Model employer' practices also implied a range of procedures intended to set an example to organisations across the economy, which included promoting collective employment relations. Union growth was consequently stimulated directly (through the promotion of trade union membership) and indirectly (through the involvement of unions with collective bargaining). This growth continued in the 1970s as union membership expanded alongside the growth in public sector employment. Given the strategic importance of public industries in particular, great emphasis was also attached to the collective involvement of employees as a means of identifying and resolving grievances, and thereby avoiding potentially costly disruption. The requirement on public enterprises 'to consult with organisations which appear to them to be representative' was legally specified in their respective nationalisation acts (Kelf-Cohen, cited in Pendleton and Winterton, 1993: 3). Elaborate, formal and bureaucratic systems for negotiation and consultation, often referred to as 'Whitleyism', also developed across the public services. Created with the brief to establish viable industrial relations systems following the end of the First World War, the Whitley Committee advocated centralised bargaining through joint industrial councils with a view to securing 'cooperation in the centre between national organisations' (Whitley Committee, cited in Clegg, 1979: 31).

Consequently, industrial relations were marked by a significant degree of centralisation but there were important variations in this general picture (Fogarty and Brooks, 1986). For example, traditions of local bargaining in some of the nationalised industries (such as coal, docks and steel) remained entrenched long into the 'golden era', and local government employers came to full national bargaining relatively late in the day (Kessler, 1991: 7). Such centralisation was also evident in influencing the determination and negotiation of terms and conditions, and cost constraints, and their ramifications for the management of the public sector, were more prominent features of the 'golden era' than is often acknowledged. Ministerial responsibilities for containing public expenditure generated a compelling interest in the outcome of collective bargaining. As early as the 1950s, government departments intervened to veto agreements in health and public transport that potentially set precedents that were deemed undesirable (Crouch, 1979; Thornley, 1994).

So, model employer principles developed during this period resulted in relatively coherent frameworks for bargaining and consultation and a prominent role for trade unions in the management of change. It is important to maintain an appropriately nuanced perspective, however, and exhortations to 'good management' were laced intermittently with cost pressures backed by ministerial pressure. While public employment was secure, low pay and discriminatory employment procedures remained characteristic of large parts of the public sector (Thornley, 1994). Proclaimed aspirations to industrial harmony were pursued selectively and, increasingly, with only moderate success. As ambivalent as these pressures may have been, both they and their effects rendered public sector employment relationships distinctive throughout the Morrison era.

Summary

The scope and depth of public sector activity grew dramatically during the 'golden era' from the 1940s to the late 1970s. Principles established by Herbert Morrison underpinned management structures and behaviour. A key feature was the need to ensure some degree of congruence between the goals of particular public organisations and espoused public policy. Organisations were highly integrated, characterised by bureaucratic procedures, and managed by professional specialists subject to general direction by the relevant government ministers with a clear emphasis on centralised bargaining and collective industrial relations.

The Conservative era and market reform

From 1979 to 1997 the focus shifted to market-based approaches. Expansion was halted by public expenditure constraints and then reversed, as 'rolling back the frontiers of the state' became a priority. Public enterprises were transferred to the private sector, and market mechanisms and competitive pressures were introduced into the remaining public services. Organisations were fragmented as distinct roles were created for service purchasers and providers. The deliberate diffusion of 'model employer' practice has become a less prominent feature of public policy. Conservative ministers from 1979, and the New Right thinkers who influenced them, were inclined to view trade unions as an impediment to the effective operation of markets. At a more pragmatic level, they also recognised that public sector unions had become a potent source of opposition to government policy, and had contributed in no small measure to the downfall of the 1974–79 Labour government. Therefore, promoting national collective bargaining and trade union organisation became less of a priority. More important perhaps, the very notion of a single set of employment principles was not attractive to policy-makers, who regarded the ability to tailor terms and conditions of employment to specific trading contexts as the hallmark of effective management. During the period of market-based reform, the emphasis shifted from promoting model employment to providing the space in which managers could assume the *right* to manage.

The extent to which this philosophy was reflected in changed management practice is a different matter. As argued in the previous edition of this text (Colling, 1997), government's interest in employment levels and pay remained undiminished and constrained the extent to which decision-making could be left entirely to local actors. Paradoxically, promoting market pressures in these and other areas often required government to intervene more determinedly rather than stand back. Alongside measures promising greater discretion, therefore, initiatives were developed to test performance and to set targets for change and improvement.

Reform of the centralised bargaining and consultation structures, characteristic of the Morrison era, has been one of the most tangible indicators of changing employment practice. After 1979, market orientations fostered an approach to pay determination founded on aligning pay with local labour markets and affordability considerations at the level of service providers. Decentralisation was thus the primary motif of Conservative governments throughout the 1980s and 1990s. It was pursued pragmatically (rather than strategically) however, and was held in tension by a contending desire to maintain central control of the overall pay bill.

The growth of indexation and independent pay review mechanisms played a significant role in reducing the scope of collective bargaining. Where they have been introduced, pay issues are decided through either predetermined formulae, in the case of indexation, or the deliberations of a panel following the submission of evidence from managers, unions and government. While some argue that the latter amounts to 'quasi-bargaining forums' (Winchester, 1996: 10), the removal of formal collective bargaining, and notionally thereby the threat of strike action, was a common element. Although it was reserved initially for judges, doctors and the armed forces, other significant occupational groupings were incorporated gradually. The fire and police services were surprisingly late additions at the end of the 1970s, and schoolteachers, nurses and midwives were added subsequently. One-third of public sector employees were no longer affected by collective pay bargaining by the end of the period of market-based reform (Bailey, 1996: 136).

Throughout the 1980s, centralised bargaining structures came under informal pressure through changes to public sector financial procedures. The switch to cash rather than volume planning required employers to balance increases in pay against levels of service. From the late 1980s, managers in the NHS used the discretion available to them to vary starting salaries and job descriptions for ancillary and administrative staff (Grimshaw, 1999). The creation of market relationships, such as those stemming from competitive tendering, provided additional impetus. Decisions about the allocations of service contracts were based primarily on price, of which labour costs are usually a substantial element. Quests for savings prompted service managers locally to redesign work organisation and terms and conditions of employment (Colling, 1993). *Ad hoc* adjustments to employment packages became common, irrespective of whether or not the work was retained by public sector employers. In local government, for example, reform of bonus payments and working hours disoriented pay and grading structures, increasing pay inequalities, particularly between women and men (Escott and Whitfield, 1995; Colling, 1999).

From the early 1990s attempts were made to extend decentralised bargaining across and up grading structures to include professional and technical staff whose pay and conditions remained subject usually to national negotiations. This required a more direct approach to reform. The 1992 White Paper *People, Jobs and Opportunity* promised to

> encourage employers to move away from traditional, centralised collective bargaining towards methods of pay determination which reward individual skills and performance; respond to the wish of individual employees to negotiate their own terms and conditions, and take full account of business circumstances.   (cited in White, 1994: 7)

For the public sector, which was founded upon the notion of national bargaining, this move to decentralisation was disorienting. Undoubtedly, key aspects such as performance and financial targets remained centralised but devolution of budgets, managerial authority and collective bargaining exposed weaknesses in union effectiveness. This was not the case throughout the sector, however; for example, in local government with some experience of decentralisation, the shock was not as great as elsewhere. Given the general funding constraints, however, bargaining was impeded by the lack of resources and the consequent requirement to balance pay increases against so-called 'efficiency' savings (redundancies, service cuts).

The government's determination in this area is further illustrated by the escalation of pressure on NHS trust managers. Local managers, aware of the considerable opposition of the unions and professional associations, sought initially to innovate through job redesign and to maximise the grading flexibility offered by existing national agreements rather than negotiate locally for professional groups (Bach and Winchester, 1994). Following the 1992 election, however, burgeoning entrepreneurial spirit was galvanised by increasingly explicit exhortations from ministers and the NHS Executive and, after a protracted stand-off with the unions, the 1995 pay settlement eventually permitted some element of local bargaining for health service staff, with the exception of doctors.

ACTIVITY Make a note of the key elements which differentiate the 'golden era' of public sector development from the market reform era of successive Conservative governments 1979–1997.

Decentralisation and market-based reform contributed significantly to changing expectations surrounding public sector pay. Comparability gave way to affordability, and earnings growth considerably fell behind that of the private sector (Elliott and Duffus, 1996: Winchester, 1996). They also generated difficulties of their own, confusion within pay structures, and the inequalities that emerged subsequently (Escott and Whitfield, 1995) arguably did little for morale, and provided the basis for substantial legal challenges. The Acquired Rights Directive and its UK variant, the Transfer of Undertakings (Protection of Employment) Directive (TUPE), provide rights to consultation and prohibit changes to pay and conditions when staff are transferred from one employer to another (e.g. from the public sector to a private contractor). Equal pay legislation makes it illegal to pay different rates to women and men when they carry out similar work, work rated as equivalent by a job evaluation scheme, or work that is of equal value in terms of effort or skill. Though the extent and security of such protections have been far from total (Napier, 1993; Dickens, 2000), unions became adept at selecting test cases to inhibit or reverse market-driven reform of pay systems, and won some notable victories in both domestic and European courts (Colling, 2000). The threat of further proceedings underpinned subsequent bargaining strategies, particularly in health and local government, where potential equal value cases became intertwined with union demands for coordinated reviews of pay and grading.

Summary

The election of successive Conservative governments during the 1980s and 1990s saw the introduction of far-reaching reform into the public sector. There was a marked shift from the centralised, 'model employer' policy to that which focused upon market forces and cost constraints. This stance, combined with the government's evident hostility towards organised labour, substantially reduced the influence of trade unions upon the employment issues. The uneven implementation of Conservative policies, however, led to a degree of confusion and problems in achieving desired outcomes regarding cost savings, productivity and performance. To some extent, these problems are now being addressed by the current Labour administration.

New Labour and the modernising agenda

A 'modernisation agenda', developed and pursued by successive Labour governments since 1997, reveals a 'third way' approach to managing the public sector based on combining elements from planning and market-driven strategies. The denigration of public services has ceased, and their contribution to national economic and social priorities is acknowledged to a greater degree. Some market-driven pressures have been removed, including the internal market in health and CCT in local government, and organisations have been reintegrated. Explicit target-setting has reintroduced elements of planning by ensuring compliance with national policy priorities within and across public services. Although important aspects of policy towards the public sector have changed, current emphases on employment flexibility and performance targets can be clearly identified as key aspects of previous Conservative government policy. So, the 'model employer' model has shifted somewhat from its dominant market focus; the critical notion underpinning current reforms is now that of 'performativity'.

This modernisation agenda of the Labour government articulates a desire to reintroduce coordination into public service employment. Fundamental reviews of pay, grading and bargaining arrangements are in progress for many parts of the sector (Cabinet Office, 1999). For example, in health, comprehensive local reviews have aimed to extend functional flexibility further within and across a broader range of occupational groupings (NHS Executive, 1999). Also, the 'Agenda for Change' proposals outline a simplified pay structure for the NHS with the intention of enabling greater flexibility and addressing persistent equal pay discrepancies. Given the complexity of this new plan, however, full implementation is doubtful before 2005 (Bach, 2002). Regarding the Civil Service, existing performance-related pay (PRP) schemes have been reviewed and reformed and the Makinson Report (2000) has recommended a shift to team bonuses which will also be linked into target attainment. In education, headteachers were assimilated on to new scales incorporating performance elements in 1999 and pay review body recommendations that classroom teachers should be included in this scheme from 2000 have been acted upon. The majority of teachers applying to this scheme (93 per cent) were successful in achieving awards, which, in essence, were pay awards linked to performance and attainment. So, continuities from the previous period of market-based reform are notable, with commitments to link pay with performance sustained and, indeed, intensified:

> A person's pay should reflect their output, results and performance. This means the best performers, both individual and teams, and those who contribute most, should be rewarded. We should challenge systems which give automatic pay increases to poor or inefficient performers.
>
> (Cabinet Office, 1999: para. 20)

As the first Comprehensive Spending Review progressed through 1999, the Chancellor announced higher than expected general settlements for health and for education, but pressure on pay was sustained. New money was tied explicitly to funding new capital projects, such as improved information technology, and meeting previously established service targets, such as hospital waiting lists. Interventions by the Prime Minister made it clear that government did not expect to see pay levels increasing at the same rate as general expenditure unless they were 'linked to results' (Peston and Timmins, 1999: 1).

After re-election in 2001, the second public spending review (2001–2004) committed the government to growth in expenditure of almost 4 per cent per year, with a considerable proportion of this still focused upon health and education. The government's intent is to demonstrate clear improvements in the level of service and also to address recruitment and retention issues through selective improvements in pay and conditions. However, accompanying increasing expenditure is increasing pressure from the Treasury to meet set targets regarding service provisions and performance standards, a task which will present considerable challenges to public sector employers, managers and employees. An apposite example of such pressures is the Fire Service dispute which continues at the time of writing. The Fire Brigades Union (FBU) made an original pay claim of 40 per cent based on the deterioration of firefighters' pay over many years in comparison to such as the police force, where the government had sanctioned considerable investment in an attempt to expand recruitment and encourage retention. This process was not painless, with David Blunkett, the Home Secretary, enduring a number of acrimonious encounters with the Police Federation before reaching agreeable terms in 2001. The government has clearly intervened in the Fire Service dispute, preventing the employers settling in November, 2002 with a 16 per cent pay deal. Rather, in keeping with the modernisation agenda, they are determined that the service should recognise the recommendations of the Bain Report (2002) which linked pay issues to the reform of working practices. The FBU, while articulating support for modernisation, reject the Bain Report which they argue will lead to redundancies and deteriorating conditions of employment – and the government is seemingly determined that any increases in pay above 4 per cent must be linked to productivity and flexibility.

In terms of other areas of public sector pay, Bach (2002: 331) notes, 'For the third year in succession, from 1 April (2002), the government implemented in full recommendations of the pay review bodies for more than one million public-sector workers . . . Headline pay increases clustered around 3.7 per cent'. By agreeing to pay review recommendations, public sector pay is now making some gains in regard to the private sector as the government accepts that if critical recruitment and retention issues (for example, in teaching, health and police services) are to be addressed, comparative pay issues must be addressed.

The current government, while investing substantially in the public sector, has certainly not abandoned its support for private sector involvement in public services. The PFI was first introduced by the Conservative government in 1992 with the aim of securing private sector funding for public sector provision of new hospitals, prisons and schools. Essentially, private contractors construct the buildings or provide the service which the government then 'leases' back over an agreed term.

Such PFI and partnership initiatives have implications for employment conditions. Within the NHS, for example, those transferred to PFI hospitals will be protected through TUPE but unions have argued that new starters should also share the terms and conditions of existing staff to prevent the development of a 'two tier' workforce. In 1999, the then AEEU (now AMICUS) published a report on the PFI where they listed a number of aspects considered essential to protect the rights of those involved in such schemes, namely, protection of existing terms and conditions, protected pensions, union recognition at new sites and employment protection for new and existing staff.

Some concessions have been offered by the government to reassure public sector unions regarding private sector involvement; for example, since April 1998, NHS unions have had the right to interview prospective bidders for PFI projects on their employment practices, equal opportunities and health and safety records. Similar rights were extended to Civil Service unions in October of the same year (Unison, 1998: para. 6.3). Best-value guidelines emphasise repeatedly the need to involve staff in reviews of service provision. This falls short of explicit reference to union representation, but unions have indicated their readiness to use TUPE legislation to secure rights similar to those available in PFI contexts (Unison, 1999: para. 17).

In February 2003, however, in what the *Financial Times* described as a 'U turn', the government made substantial concessions to the unions regarding terms and conditions of employment for private sector workers employed on local government contracts. These concessions require 'all new contractors providing services for local authorities to offer new workers such as cleaners and careworkers terms and conditions "no less favourable" than those already enjoyed by colleagues transferred from the local authority to the new contractor' (Turner, 2003a: 2). This agreement has come as a shock to the CBI who expected a rather more business-'friendly' agreement with a voluntary code of enforcement, whereas new agreements will now have to be written into forthcoming contracts. They believe this policy will make competitiveness within public private partnerships more challenging and so impede what they describe as 'public sector reform' (Turner, 2003a). However, it should be noted that in supporting this reform the government is merely undertaking a commitment which it made in 2001 to address the two-tier workforce (Labour Party, 2001). While the union movement perceive this to be a very positive event, it should be noted that this agreement only applies to local government contracts at the moment. However, unions have already expressed the wish to see this agreement extended to cover all public private partnerships both in the future and those already in existence.

On a final note regarding the PFI schemes which are now well established in the prison service and to a lesser extent in health and education, recent assessments of their efficiency would suggest that the evidence regarding their value for money is by no means certain. Reports from the Institute of Public Policy Research (IPPR, 2001) and the Audit Commission (2003) raised questions about the efficacy of public private partnerships, particularly regarding the provision of value for money. While the IPPR were able to point to success in the Prison Service, the Audit Commission found that in school construction projects, 'traditional funding delivered, on average, better school buildings' (2003: 1). Although both the IPPR and the Audit Commission are supportive of PFI, they drew attention to weaknesses in provision and the need for further monitoring and reform.

Summary

Public sector workforces remain predominantly collectivised despite these substantial challenges, and continued rapid decline in other sectors of the economy means that public sector unions still constitute the core of the labour movement. Data from the

Workplace Employee Relations Survey (WERS) indicates that there is a recognised union in almost all public sector workplaces (95 per cent), but in only a quarter (25 per cent) of private sector ones (Cully *et al.*, 1999: 92). There is some variation in union density – that is, in the proportion of the workforce in union membership. Nearly two-thirds of civil servants are union members, compared with fewer than half (43 per cent) of NHS employees (Cully *et al.*, 1999: 88). Overall density remains markedly higher, at 61 per cent, than elsewhere in the economy, however. However, there is still considerable frustration with the government's determination to keep an 'arm's-length' attitude towards the union movement. As noted, the TUC has expressed criticism and doubt regarding the government's commitment to partnership working and the PCS has overtly expressed its intent to move away from this agenda with the intention of lobbying for the abandonment of the current outsourcing policy and a declared intention to use industrial action, if necessary, to achieve this (Turner, 2003a). Regarding the PFI, this is regarded with suspicion by trade unions in that it is perceived as quasi-privatisation. Unions are intent upon protecting terms and conditions for their members and extending protection to new employees in PFI ventures. The government appears to be supportive of this stance but will also ensure that sufficient employer freedom and flexibility persists to encourage further private sector investment.

Overall, it can be seen that the public sector has changed substantially since 1980. The 'golden era' of centralisation and collectivism was displaced after 1979 with a 'market' model focused upon cost constraint, privatisation and fragmentation. With the election of the Labour government in 1997 came a 'modernising agenda' which certainly maintained many of the market reforms introduced by its predecessors but recognised the need for added investment in both employees and infrastructure and has linked this to performance and target attainments. The planned level of investment in the public sector will ensure some protection for terms and conditions of employment, particularly in areas where recruitment and retention are problematic. There is also a greater role for unions regarding bargaining and influence over review bodies and other pay-fixing initiatives, but this does not signal a new détente between the government and public sector unions, as the current firefighters' dispute would illustrate. Rather, there is a renewed toleration for union engagement to ensure greater fairness but there is a clear government intent that this must not interfere with the effective introduction of change to meet improvements and performance targets promised to the electorate.

So far, this chapter has explored the establishment of the terms and conditions of employment largely in organisations where trade unions still bargain or where they are in a context where they still have considerable influence, such as upon pay review bodies in the public sector. However, it has been established that in the contemporary economy, most employees are no longer covered by collectively bargained agreements, instead working in organisations which do not recognise unions for such purposes. The next section will explore this issue in more detail.

Establishing terms and conditions of employment in non-union organisations

At the beginning of the 1980s, despite the election of a government hostile to collective labour organisation, it was presumed that the domination of collective bargaining, where in 1984, 71 per cent of the workforce were covered by such agreements, would persist into the future (Millward *et al.*, 1992). With hindsight it can be seen that this was to be proved wrong, with a notable decline in both trade union density and consequently, collective bargaining coverage during the 1980s and into the 1990s. Indeed, by

1998, collective bargaining coverage had fallen to 47 per cent (Cully *et al.*, 1999). The reasons underpinning this decline are complex and extensive but can be broadly summarised as:

- constraint and control of the power and influence of trade unions by successive Conservative governments since 1979 hostile to the notion of collective labour organisation;
- active derecognition strategies and support for such from Conservative administrations;
- the enactment of employment legislation to constrain and control the power of trade unions;
- the encouragement and facilitation of the exercise of management prerogative;
- greater focus on the individual at work;
- mass unemployment in the manufacturing sector, an area of traditional strength for trade unions, and an expansion in the service sector, an area of traditional weakness;
- the growth of new managerial strategies such as human resource management, which focused upon the individual at work and managerial prerogative;
- a move away from collective bargaining in the public sector through a shift in 'model employer' policies based on union recognition to a focus on market values and the introduction of competitive tendering whereby private sector firms took over public sector tasks and employment, plus the more extensive use of pay review bodies;
- encouragement of the growth of new small firms, a sector where union presence is negligible;
- the failure of trade unions to develop effective strategies to expand existing membership and to enter growth areas of the economy such as smaller firms and the private sector service.

This list is by no means exhaustive and greater consideration can be found in texts such as Noon and Blyton (2002) and Edwards (2002).

The combination of these issues and wider market shifts has encouraged and facilitated the growth of the non-union sector. Yet it is important to remember that even when collective bargaining coverage was at its peak in the 1970s, nearly a third of the labour force were excluded from such agreements. However, it is evident that this figure has grown quite substantially since the early 1980s. These non-union firms may share their representation status but obviously will differ significantly in other respects given the influence of issues such as sector, markets, location etc. However, to facilitate an overview of the non-union sector, the useful distinction based upon firm size and identified by Rose (2001) will be adopted for the purposes of this brief discussion. Rose argues that it is broadly possible to discriminate between larger and smaller non-union firms when considering the manner in which conditions of employment are established while recognising that there will be areas of commonality and overlap within such divisions. It must be emphasised that such generalisations are sweeping and exceptions to these will be evident. But for the purposes of this discussion these two broad divisions based on size are useful to illustrate the key arguments. However, those wishing to concentrate upon this issue in greater depth are advised to consult further reading and research (McLoughlin and Gourley, 1994; Guest and Conway, 1999; Scase, 2002; Marlow, 2002).

So, it is more usual to find sophisticated *substitutionist* strategies within larger firms where it is essential to ensure that employees will not experience any motivation or desire to seek union recognition. Such an approach must ensure that, for most employees, the terms and conditions of employment offered are at the least as good as, if not better than, those in comparative firms that recognise trade unions for bargaining purposes (McLoughlin and Gourley, 1994). Clearly, the aim is to ensure that employees would not find a union presence or collective bargaining beneficial. Such firms might be described as having a 'soft' HRM style with a focus upon employee involvement, participation, consultation and participation to ensure high performance and individual commitment to the firm. To maintain this situation, the organisation must be able to provide what is perceived as a floor of excellent terms and conditions of employment but also promote an environment which rewards individuality while offering effective channels for employee involvement (Colling, 2002).

This stance has been described as a somewhat 'pyrrhic' or empty victory by Flood and Toner (1997) who argue that if the point of non-unionism is cost containment through the avoidance of collective bargaining and collective leverage, this is unlikely to be achieved through such costly substitution policies. Given the investment required in terms of finance and management time for high reward, consultation, communication etc., the rewards do seem uncertain. However, the key strategic focus must, of course, be upon the retention of prerogative over decision-making, change management, flexibility and the avoidance of disruptive collective resistance. It might be expected that if there has been an expansion in non-union firms developing this type of substitutionist strategies to avoid recognition, there should be some evidence for an expansion in soft HRM practices and policies in the UK. However, drawing on the WERS data, this would not appear to be the case, with such high-commitment practices being relatively rare and indeed, most frequently found in unionised firms (Cully *et al.*, 1999). So, it would appear that this type of 'soft HRM', non-union organisation remains limited in the UK, which suggests that most non-union firms are not pursuing high-commitment strategies.

Many non-union firms have, in the past, actually recognised trade unions, so rather than having a dedicated substitutionist philosophy as described above, they have achieved non-union status by other means such as overt union derecognition. Claydon (1997) notes that this process can occur incidentally, when membership density and employee support for the recognised union is low and falling to the extent that management are able to bypass the bargaining agenda over time until it withers altogether with little union or employee resistance. Alternatively, management develop specific strategies, such as consultation and communication forums, to gradually eliminate union presence over a relatively lengthy period of time with the clear intent of bypassing and undermining the union presence. Overall, derecognition has not been extensively pursued in the UK despite the political hostility towards collective organisation and legislation enacted to facilitate the process (Rose, 2001). This is largely because as unions became weaker in the 1980s and 1990s, management have been able to narrow the bargaining agenda substantially while using union channels to introduce change, secure in the knowledge that collective resistance would be unlikely. Hence, there have been relatively few aggressive derecognition campaigns and those that have occurred have, in fact, encouraged renewed union affiliation while generating poorer employment relations at a time when union influence was minimal.

Firms which have neither derecognised unions nor employed substitutionist strategies are most likely to be found in sectors where unions have been traditionally weak, such as private services or in firms which have grown during the 1980s and 1990s. Such firms are either unlikely ever to have considered union recognition, are unlikely to employ those who might seek such recognition or have been able to ignore any approaches from a relatively weak union movement. In such firms, it would appear that there are a number of initiatives utilised to manage labour and determine the employment conditions. These will range from the unitary application of managerial prerogative to the utilisation of factors such as consultation strategies with elected or appointed employee representatives or communication conduits to share some information (Gennard and Judge, 2002). Hence, within the non-union sector the determination of terms and conditions of employment would appear to be contingent upon a number of issues. These include the organisation's preferred management style regarding the employment relationship and the manner in which management prerogative is exercised; issues which themselves are contingent upon the firm's market position, sector, product and the perceived 'value' of their employees.

It is important to note, however, that in recent years, management prerogative has been somewhat constrained by employment regulation introduced by successive Labour governments and also by recognition and implementation of European regulation by such administrations. So, for example, the Employment Relations Act (1999) legislated for statutory recognition of trade unions where the necessary degree of support could be demonstrated, and the Works Council Directive requires representation and consultation in multinational enterprises. Of particular relevance for this discussion will be the impact of the forthcoming Information and Consultation Directive which will be implemented in 2002 and will require firms with more than 50 employees to consult employee *representatives* on a range of issues. Although the UK will be phasing introduction of the Directive and already has the reputation for diluting the impact of such directives (McKay, 2001), employers are expressing concern regarding compliance. Turner (2003a: 4), writing in the *Financial Times* comments that, 'Business leaders fear the imposition of bodies similar to works councils, which have a say in actual decisions, as opposed to being informed of plans and consulted on implementation'. The increasing raft of regulation which, on the whole, focuses upon individual employee rights will present increasing challenges to the exercise of unfettered managerial prerogative, even if practised benignly, in larger firms.

To summarise this section, generalising cautiously, it would appear that the large non-union firm sector has grown for a number of reasons. Since the 1980s the political environment in the UK has supported a non-union stance, whilst market and sector shifts have made this approach increasingly likely. The manner in which non-unionism has emerged in larger enterprises has taken a number of forms; for some firms, there has been the adoption of clear substitution policies to avoid union recognition in the first instance. Given the level of political encouragement and union weakness, a relatively small number have pursued (either strategically or in an *ad hoc* fashion) derecognition policies with only limited resistance from unions and their members. Those firms falling outside of these categories are those which have grown in sectors where unions have not traditionally had a strong presence and they have not been able to generate an organising agenda to successfully generate a demand for recognition. For employees the consequences differ; for those working in 'high performance' firms, employment conditions will be favourable but on the basis of fulfilling high expectations in terms of productivity, loyalty and commitment. For others, their terms and conditions will depend upon the manner in which management prerogative is exercised within the constraints of the firm's market and sector. However, as noted above, the unrestrained exercise of managerial prerogative in such firms will be subject to the constraints of both national and European employment regulation which has been growing since 1997. Having offered a brief commentary on the manner in which large non-union firms manage their employees, this is now compared and contrasted to the situation within smaller firms.

> ACTIVITY   Make a list of advantages and disadvantages of working in a non-union firm from the perspective of the HR manager and from that of a production worker.

◼ Establishing terms of employment in small non-union firms

There are a number of differing definitions of a 'small' firm. In 1971, the Bolton committee report referred to criteria of independence and a small market share; the Companies Act of 1985 combined turnover and employment criteria, with the EU having the most comprehensive criteria of turnover, employees and independence. In the UK, governments rely on the somewhat simplistic measure of the number of employees within the enterprise such that:

- small firm – 0–49 employees;
- medium firm – 50–249 employees;
- large firm – over 250 employees. (DTI, 1997)

Given the heterogeneity of the sector, it is difficult to find a definition which adequately encompasses all relevant firms. Regardless of how the sector is defined, it is appropriate to consider small firms as a separate entity within the economy. For some time, they have been recognised as being essentially different in their approach to management, markets and business outlook from their larger counterparts; it is no longer presumed that such firms are enterprises which have merely failed to grow to corporate dimensions (Storey *et al.*, 1987). As Cully *et al.* (1999) remark, 'small businesses occupy a distinct part of the lexicon in academic and policy debates' (p. 251); they have their own associations and government representative at Ministerial level. This is not to suggest that small firms can be easily studied as a single entity. A significant challenge in analysing small firm behaviour is identifying common themes and trends in a sector noted for its heterogeneity. So, any conclusions drawn and observations made must always be qualified with the same caution applied to large firms, that there will always be a substantial number of enterprises which refute established trends.

The number of small businesses in the UK economy has grown somewhat since the early 1980s, levelling out in the early 1990s (for more discussion of such growth, see Storey, 1994). The DTI (1998: 2) noted that small firms account for 99 per cent of all businesses, 46 per cent of non-government employment and 42 per cent of turnover (excluding the financial sector). It is apparent that small firms are significant employers in the modern economy and so insight into how labour is managed in such firms is critical. However, the study of employment relations in small firms has been largely neglected (Marlow, 2000). The earliest evidence pertaining to the management of people in small firms initially indicated an environment where the close proximity of owner and worker could overcome the traditional tensions between labour and capital (Goss, 1991). In the late 1960s, a number of studies portrayed employment conditions in small firms as a relative haven of peace and harmony. It was recognised that financial rewards were lower in the sector but this was more than compensated for by low levels of industrial unrest, teamworking with colleagues and low labour turnover (Ingham, 1970; Bolton Report, 1971). This image has since been dispelled by a number of empirical studies undertaken in the 1980s. These studies found that most small firm employees would prefer to work in larger firms, that there were higher levels of job insecurity and labour turnover and owner/manager strategies for labour control were largely authoritarian or based on benevolent autocracy. It was found that the perceptions of owner managers regarding the employment environment in their firms differed significantly from that of their employees (Rainnie, 1989; Scott *et al.*, 1989; Goss, 1991).

Regarding the establishment of terms and conditions in small businesses, the empirical evidence indicates a high degree of informality. Scott *et al.* (1989) found that from initial recruitment and selection to point of dismissal, few formal systems or policies were in evidence. The preferred manner of employee recruitment was through the 'grapevine', i.e. someone known to an existing employee; for many employees, a contract of employment or, indeed, any formal indication of tasks and duties was non-existent. Discipline was relatively *ad hoc*, more dependent on the owner's perception of the problem rather than any objective standard. Only a tiny minority of firms had union recognition or any form of negotiated terms. For the remainder, owners and management teams unilaterally decided upon payment rates and changes to working conditions. Other studies of the period (Rainnie, 1989; Goss, 1991) revealed similar findings, with the emphasis upon owner prerogative and informality; such findings are confirmed by more recent evidence (Ram *et al.* 2001; Marlow, 2002).

When analysing such findings, it is simplistic to suggest that such informality and unitarism arise from a strategic goal to construct authoritarian power structures. Rainnie (1989) develops a somewhat deterministic analysis, arguing that the adverse competitive pressures experienced by many small businesses give the owner or management team little discretion in their approach to managing people. They are forced to minimise labour costs due to external market pressures. Ram (1999) disputes this thesis, suggesting that employees do negotiate around their own employment relationship in small firms but the relatively hidden and individualistic tactics employed somewhat obscure the process. It is also recognised that employers, whether in large or small firms, must have some degree of cooperation and consent from labour so cannot operate on the basis of absolute domination. Owners must be prepared to enter into some form of dialogue with employees. A further explanation for informality and owner prerogative in small firms is the relative absence of professional personnel managers (Wynarczyk *et al.*, 1993). Finally, it is evident that many small firms work almost entirely in the short term due to restricted and uncertain markets, volatile customer bases and uncertain financial strategies with a negotiated employment relationship. So, it is difficult for such businesses to develop structured or strategic approaches to managing their labour and, for many firm owners, there is a belief that they simply do not have the time (Storey, 1994).

Stop and think	How does a firm's size impact upon its propensity to recognise a trade union for bargaining purposes?

To summarise, although there will always be exceptions, it is apparent that establishing terms and conditions of employment in small firms is likely to be conducted on an informal basis, focused on the individual in a framework unilaterally devised by the firm owner. For some employees, there will still be room to construct their own social relations of production and engage in mutual adjustment strategies but, for many, there will be little opportunity to exercise any discretion over the manner in which they work and are rewarded. To some extent, increasing employment regulation should address these issues but this does depend upon employer awareness and observation of the legislation. As Earnshaw *et al.* (1998) found, increasing regulation and legislation is not a problem for many small owners because they simply do not know about it. Given the increasing number of employees within the small firm sector, there is some cause for concern regarding the level of informality and ignorance that persists surrounding the management of labour. However, this overview must again be qualified with the recognition of heterogeneity amongst small firms such that exceptions to these generalisations will be evident throughout the sector.

Summary

- Collective bargaining has customarily been defined in Britain as the process of joint regulation of job control, undertaken by management and trade unions who negotiate to establish the terms and conditions which govern the employment relationship. Human resource management might be viewed as posing a threat to this joint process by its emphasis on the managerial dominance of the relationship which requires that employees accept a managerially derived employment agenda.

- Contemporary developments in collective bargaining in the private sector have seen a narrowing of its coverage as a result of the decline in unionisation and managerial pressure to limit its scope amongst employees. In the public sector, there have been considerable changes regarding the 'model employer' perception during the postwar period. The 'golden era' associated with centralisation, trade union influence and collectivity was replaced in the 1980s with a market approach which focused far more on cost constraints in a context of privatisation and decentralisation. Since 1997, a modernising agenda has been developed to bring greater coherence between cost issues, performance elements and service provision, with implications for pay-setting where emphasis is upon 'performativity' with some evident resistance from public sector employees. While public private partnerships and PFI remain a feature of public sector provision, a recent change in contract conditions to challenge the 'two tier' workforce in local authorities has signalled more sympathy with the union perception of this issue and a greater focus upon quality rather than cost.

● The current Labour government promoted 'social partnerships' based on fairness, equity, information-sharing, employee representation and consultation and a consensual approach to problem-solving. Most trade unions and many employers have embraced the ethos of partnership but recently the failure of these to deliver in regard to improved conditions of employment and clear avenues of information-sharing has led to some discontent and, indeed, disaffection from the notion by the trade union movement. In becoming a full signatory to the Maastricht agreement, the Labour government has committed the UK to the implementation of European Directives on employment but, as McKay (2001) has observed, a rather dilute, weakened form of adoption would seem to be preferred by the present government, adding to union cynicism regarding the desire to establish a new, strong framework of employee rights.

● There has been a significant increase in the number of organisations in the UK which have no form of union representation for employees and it would appear that there are a range of policies and practices employed to establish the terms and conditions of employment for labour in such organisations. Broadly, however, it is possible to examine this sector on the basis of firm size, where larger firms would appear to adopt union substitution approaches, have derecognised unions for bargaining purposes or to have grown in sectors where unions have little presence so have not engaged with recognition. Larger non-union firms have, however, had their degree of prerogative bounded by employment regulation in recent years. This would not appear to be the case in small firms. Until relatively recently, there was a presumption that small businesses enjoyed harmonious industrial relations; this was based on the absence of overt conflict and a perception of greater teamworking due to the owner manager's close working proximity with labour. Recently, this image has been questioned, with evidence suggesting that employees in many small firms have lower rewards, limited benefits and fewer prospects than those of most larger firms. It has also been revealed that agreeing terms and conditions of employment is likely to be undertaken unilaterally by owners or management upon an informal, *ad hoc* basis and, through a combination of ignorance and resistance, has only been marginally affected by new employment regulation.

Questions

1 What have been the major developments in British collective bargaining since 1979?

2 'Collective bargaining processes contradict the basic assumptions of the HRM approach.' Discuss.

3 Discuss the manner in which the Employment Relations Act (1999) impacted upon collective bargaining in the workplace.

4 Critically evaluate the extent to which the partnership approach would appear to be under some stress within the public sector.

5 State and comment upon the underlying reasons for the shifts in the manner in which the terms and conditions of employment have been agreed in the public sector since 1980.

6 Compare and contrast the manner in which the terms and conditons of employment are determined in small and large non-union enterprises.

Exercises

1 Debate the proposition that 'collective bargaining is the most appropriate channel to redress the power imbalance within the employment relationship'.

2 You are the HR director of a private firm wishing to bid for a public sector project as part of the private finance initiative. If the bid were successful, what new challenges would arise in the management of the employment relationship under such circumstances?

3 What are the major challenges facing small firm employees in achieving fair and equitable conditions of employment which observe current regulations?

4 Prepare a workshop presentation which outlines the differing types of non-union firms in the contemporary economy and the labour management strategies employed by such firms.

Case study

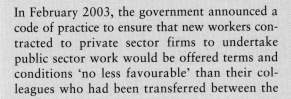

In February 2003, the government announced a code of practice to ensure that new workers contracted to private sector firms to undertake public sector work would be offered terms and conditions 'no less favourable' than their colleagues who had been transferred between the two sectors. This has led to protests from the private sector operators regarding the viability of public private partnerships as competition on the basis of cost will be restricted. This rather surprising move by the government has been reported in the *Financial Times*.

Business views two-tier workforce agreement as dynamite

By David Turner

Yesterday's accord on the 'two-tier' workforce in local government may sound like 'legalese', but as far as business leaders are concerned, it is dynamite. The unions have clinched a code of practice that covers all workers taken on by companies in England that sign new contracts to provide public services for local authorities. They are to enjoy 'fair and reasonable' terms and conditions 'which are, overall, no less favourable' than those of their colleagues who were working for the public sector and were simply transferred.

But until the last minute, the business community had been confidently expecting the considerably vaguer and woollier 'broadly comparable' formula. Under the more watertight deal, employers are allowed to vary the elements within the package but it must be just as good overall. In practice it means that many low-paid workers covered by the new code are likely to enjoy a significant pay increase. The national minimum wage is £4.20 an hour, but from April local authority workers will enjoy a minimum wage of £5.33, following last year's ground-breaking deal, which boosted the earnings of the poorly paid. Employers could pay them less than this, but they would have to offer another benefit as part of the overall package.

Employers' other main gripe is against the enforcement provisions. This is no mere voluntary code of practice, as the Confederation of British Industry wanted, with unions having to wait until the Audit Commission forced a foot-dragging employer into providing better conditions. All new contracts will have to be compatible with the code, and if employers are accused of breaches the ultimate recourse will be to an independent arbitrator. The unions have also won ground on the pensions issue. Pensions are excluded from the overall package of terms and conditions, but joiners under new contracts will have to be offered membership of either the local government pension scheme – an employer pension scheme with matching employer contributions of at least 6 per cent – or a similar stakeholder scheme. This move, the first time private-sector companies have been under a statutory obligation to contribute to a pension, will

Case study continued

be particularly welcome since it bucks the trend towards decreasing corporate pension provision, as stock markets decline and pension obligations become more onerous. Business leaders object to the code on the grounds that giving private-sector workers the same pay and conditions fossilises working practices and artificially bids up wage costs in places where labour is plentiful. A reference to terms and conditions that 'take into account the need to recruit and retain qual-ity employees, and conditions in local labour markets', which featured in last year's draft code, has been removed. They regard the agreement as an unwarranted intrusion by government into their affairs. Union leaders claim that the objections by business expose the fact that exploiting workers has been the main route by which companies have made money out of their private-sector adventures. The government claims that the 'no less favourable formula' allows enough flexibility to transform practices if desired. In practical terms, the code will take a while to have much effect on costs, but has the potential to transform pay throughout the hybrid public-private world. It applies only to public-private partnerships put out for tender after the final details of the code are settled next month. That means that few workers will gain for perhaps nine months after that.

Source: Financial Times, 14 Febuary 2003

Discussion points

1 Why is this new agreement 'dynamite' as far as business leaders are concerned?

2 What do you understand by the expression 'two tier' workforce?

3 How does this agreement challenge the 'two tier' workforce?

4 Why will this agreement mean that the private sector firms bidding for public sector contracts will now have to compete on quality rather than cost?

References and further reading

Those texts marked with an asterix are particularly recommended for further reading.

Amalgamated Engineering and Electricians Union (1999) *The Private Finance Initiative*. London: AEEU Publications.

Audit Commission (2003) 'Early PFI schools not significantly better, says Audit Commission', www.audit-commission. gov.uk/reports, 30 January.

Bach, S. and Winchester, D. (2002) 'Industrial relations in the public sector', in Edwards, P. (ed.) *Industrial Relations: Theory and Practice*. Oxford: Blackwell.

Bach, S. and Winchester, D. (1994) 'Opting out of pay devolution? Prospects for local pay bargaining in the UK public services', *British Journal of Industrial Relations*, Vol. 32, No. 2, pp. 82–96.

*Bach, S. (2002), 'Public sector employment relations reforms under Labour: muddling through on modernization?', *British Journal of Industrial Relations*, Vol. 40, No. 2, pp. 319–341.

*Bacon, N and Storey, J. (1996) 'Individualism and collectivism', in Ackers, P., Smith, C. and Smith, P. (eds) *The New Workplace and Trade Unionism*. London: Routledge.

*Bailey, R. (1996) 'Public sector industrial relations', in Beardwell, I.J. (ed.) *Contemporary Industrial Relations: A Critical Analysis*. Oxford: Oxford University Press, pp. 121–151.

Bain Report (2002) *The Future of the Fire Service: Reducing Risk, Saving Lives*. London: HMSO, 16 December.

Bates Report (1997) *Review of the Private Finance Initiative*, London: HMSO, 30 October.

Batstone, E., Boraston, I. and Frenkel, S. (1977) *Shop Stewards in Action*. Oxford: Blackwell.

Beaumont, P.B. (1995) *The Future of Employment Relations*. London: Sage.

Bolton, J.E. (1971) *Report of the Committee of Inquiry on Small Firms*, Cmnd. 0811. London: HMSO.

Brown, W. (ed.) (1981) *The Changing Contours of British Industrial Relations*. Oxford: Blackwell.

*Brown, W. (1993) 'The contraction of collective bargaining in Britain', *British Journal of Industrial Relations*, Vol. 31, No. 2. pp. 189–200.

Brown, W and Walsh, J. (1991) 'Pay determination in Britain in the 1980s: the anatomy of decentralisation', *Oxford Review of Economic Policy*, Vol. 7, No. 1, pp. 44–59.

Burawoy, M. (1979), *Manufacturing Consent*. Chicago, Ill.: University of Chicago Press.

Cabinet Office (1999) *Modernising Government*, Cmnd. 4310. London: The Stationery Office.

Chamberlain, N.W. and Kuhn, J.W. (1965) *Collective Bargaining*. New York: McGraw-Hill.

Clark, I. (1998), *Stakeholders in Social Partnership*, Occasional Paper No. 26. Leicester: De Montfort University.

Claydon, T. (1997), 'Union derecognition: a re-examination', in Beardwell, I. (ed.), *Contemporary*

Industrial Relations: A Critical Analysis. Oxford, Oxford University Press.

Clegg, H. (1979) *The Changing System of Industrial Relations in Great Britain.* Oxford: Blackwell.

Coates, K. and Topham, T. (1986) *Trade Unions and Politics.* Oxford: Blackwell.

Colling, T. (1993) 'Contracting public services: the management of CCT in two county councils', *Human Resource Management Journal*, Vol. 3, No. 4, pp. 1–15.

Colling, T. (1997) 'Managing human resources in the public sector', in Beardwell, I. and Holden, L. (eds) *Human Resource Management: A Contemporary Perspective.* London: Pitman, pp. 654–679.

Colling, T. (1999) 'Tendering and outsourcing: working in the contract state', in Corby, S. and White, G. (eds) *Employee Relations in the Public Services.* London: Routledge, pp. 136–156.

Colling, T. (2000) 'Personnel management in the extended organisation', in Bach, S. and Sisson, K. (eds) *Personnel Management: A Comprehensive Guide to Theory and Practice.* Oxford: Blackwell, pp. 70–91.

Colling, T. (2002) 'Managing without unions: The sources and limitations of individualism', in Edwards, P. (ed.) *Industrial Relations: Theory and Practice.* Oxford: Blackwell.

Confederation of British Industry (1988) *The Structure and Processes of Pay Determination in the Private Sector: 1979–1986.* London: CBI.

Confederation of British Industry (1999) *The 1999 Employment Trends Survey.* London: CBI.

Crouch, C. (1979) *The Politics of Industrial Relations.* London: Fontana.

*Cully, M., Woodland, S., O'Reilly, A. and Dix, G. (1999) *Britain at Work: As Depicted by the 1998 Workplace Employee Relations Survey.* London: Routledge.

Dearlove, J. and Saunders, P. (1984) *Introduction to British Politics.* Cambridge: Polity Press.

Deaton, D.R. and Beaumont, P.B. (1980) 'The determinants of bargaining structure: some large scale survey results', *British Journal of Industrial Relations*, Vol. 18, No. 4, pp. 201–220.

Department of Trade and Industry (1997) *Small and Medium Enterprise (SME) – Definitions.* London: HMSO, September.

Department of Trade and Industry (1998) *Small Business Action Update.* London: HMSO, June.

Dickens, L. (2000) 'Still wasting resources: equality in employment', in Bach, S. and Sisson, K. (eds) *Personnel Management: A Comprehensive Guide to Theory and Practice.* Oxford: Blackwell, pp. 137–171.

Donovan Commission (1968) *Report of the Royal Commission on Trade Unions and Employers' Associations, 1965–68*, Cmnd. 3623. London: HMSO.

Earnshaw, J., Goodman, J., Harrison, R. and Marchington, M. (1998), *Industrial Tribunals, Workplace Disciplinary Procedures and Employment Practice*, Employment Relations Research Series, 2. London: DTI.

Edmonds, J. (1997), 'Unions and employers, how can partnership work?', in *Creating Social Partnerships.* London: Unions21.

Edwards, P. (1987) *Managing the Factory: A Survey of General Managers.* Oxford: Blackwell.

*Edwards, P. (2003) *Industrial Relations. Theory and Practice.* Oxford: Blackwell.

Elliott, R. and Duffus, K. (1996) 'What has been happening to pay in the public services sector of the economy? Developments over the period 1970–1992', *British Journal of Industrial Relations*, Vol. 34, No. 1, pp. 51–85.

Escott, K. and Whitfield, D. (1995) *The Gender Impact of Compulsory Competitive Tendering in Local Government.* Manchester: Equal Opportunities Commission.

Fairbrother, P. (1982) *Working for the State*, Studies for Trade Unionists, 8.29. London: Workers Educational Association.

Farnham, D. and Horton, S. (1995) 'The new people management in the UK's public services: a silent revolution?', paper presented to the International Colloquium on Contemporary Development in HRM, École Supérieure de Commerce, Montpellier, France, October.

Flanders, A. (1968) 'Collective bargaining: a theoretical analysis', *British Journal of Industrial Relations*, Vol. 6, No. 1, pp. 1–26.

Flanders, A. (1970) 'Collective bargaining: prescription for change', in *Management and Unions: The Theory and Reform of Industrial Relations.* London: Faber.

Flood, P. and Toner, B. (1997) 'Large non-union companies: how do they avoid a catch 22?', *British Journal of Industrial Relations*, Vol. 35, No. 3, pp. 257–277.

Fogarty, M. and Brooks, D. (1986) *Trade Unions and British Industrial Development.* London: Policy Studies Institute.

Fox, A. (1975) 'Collective bargaining, Flanders and the Webbs', *British Journal of Industrial Relations*, Vol. 13, No. 2, pp. 151–174.

*Gall, G. and McKay, S. (1999), 'Developments in union recognition and derecognition in Britain, 1994–1998', *British Journal of Industrial Relations*, Vol. 37, No. 4, pp. 601–614.

Gennard, J. and Judge, G. (2002) *Employee Relations.* London: CIPD.

Goss, D. (1991) *Small Business and Society.* London: Routledge.

Gregg, P. and Yates, A. (1991) 'Changes in wage-setting arrangements and trade union presence in the 1980s', *British Journal of Industrial Relations*, Vol. 29, No. 3, pp. 361–376.

*Grimshaw, D. (1999), 'Changes in skills-mix and pay determination among the nursing workforce in the UK', *Work, Employment and Society*, Vol. 13, No. 2, pp. 295–328.

Guest, D. (1989) 'Personnel and HRM: can you tell the difference?', *Personnel Management*, January.

Guest, D and Conway, N. (1999), 'Peering into the black hole: the downside of the new employment relations in the UK', *British Journal of Industrial Relations*, Vol. 37, No. 3, pp. 369–390.

*Guest, D. and Hoque, K. (1994) 'The good, the bad and the ugly: employment relations in new non-union workplaces', *Human Resource Management*, Vol. 5, No. 1, pp. 1–14.

Guest, D. and Peccei, R. (1998), *The Partnership Company.* London: Involvement and Participation Association.

Hills, J. (1990) *The State of Welfare: The Welfare State in Britain since 1974*. Oxford: Clarendon Press.

Hyman, R. (1975) *Industrial Relations: A Marxist Introduction*. London: Macmillan.

Ingham, G.K. (1970), *The Size of Industrial Organisation and Worker Behaviour*. London: Cambridge University Press.

Institute for Public Policy Research (IPPR) (2001), *Building Better Partnerships*. London: IPPR.

Kelly, J. (1996) 'Union militancy and social partnership', in *Rethinking Industrial Relations*. London: Routledge.

Kessler, I. (1991) 'Workplace industrial relations in local government', *Employee Relations*, special issue, Vol. 13, No. 2, complete issue.

Kinnie, N. (1990) 'The decentralisation of industrial relations? Recent research considered', *Personnel Review*, Vol. 19, No. 3, pp. 33–41.

Labour Party (2001) *Ambitions for Britain: Labour's Manifesto 2001*. London: The Labour Party.

Legge, K. (1995), *Human Resource Management: Rhetoric and Realities*. London: Routledge.

*McIlroy, J. (1998) 'The enduring alliance: trade unions and the making of New Labour, 1994–1997, *British Journal of Industrial Relations*, Vol. 36, No. 4, pp. 537–564.

McLoughlin, I. and Gourlay, S. (1994) *Enterprise Without Unions: Industrial Relations in the Non-Union Firm*. Buckingham: Open University Press.

*McKay, S. (2001), 'Between flexibility and regulation: rights, protection and equality at work', *British Journal of Industrial Relations*, Vol. 39, No. 36, pp. 285–303.

Mabey, C. and Salamon, G. (1995) *Strategic Human Resource Management*. Oxford: Blackwell.

Makinson, J. (2000) *Incentives for Change: Rewarding performance in National Government Networks*. London: The Stationery Office.

Marginson, P. and Sisson, K. (1990) 'Single table talk', *Personnel Management*, May.

Marlow, S., (2000) 'People in the small firm', in *Enterprise and Small Business: Principles, Policy and Practice*. Harlow: Addison-Wesley.

Marlow, S. (2002) 'Managing labour in smaller firms', *Human Resource Management Journal*, Vol. 12, No. 2, pp. 26–47.

Millward, N., Steven, M., Smart, D. and Hawes, W.R. (1992) *Workplace Industrial Relations in Transition*. Aldershot: Dartmouth.

Milner, S. (1993), 'Dispute deterrence: evidence on final offer arbitration', in Metcalf, D. and Milner, S. *New Perspectives on Industrial Disputes*. London: Routledge.

Mishel, L. and Voos, P.B. (eds) (1992) *Unions and Economic Competitiveness*. New York: Sharpe.

Monks, J. (1996) 'Interview: John Monks', *New Statesman*, 6 September.

Napier, B. (1993) *CCT, Market Testing and Employment Rights: The Effects of TUPE and the Acquired Rights Directive*. London: Institute of Employment Rights.

NHS Executive (1999) *Agenda for Change: Modernising the NHS Pay System. Joint Framework of Principles and Agreed Statement on the Way Forward*. Health Service Circular 1999/227.

Nolan, P. and O'Donnell, K. (1995) 'Industrial relations and productivity', in Edwards, P. (ed.) *Industrial Relations: Theory and Practice in Britain*. Oxford: Blackwell.

Noon, M. and Blyton, P. (2002) *The Realities of Work*. London: Palgrave.

Palmer, G. (1983) *British Industrial Relations*. London: Unwin & Hyman.

Pendleton, A. and Winterton, J. (1993) 'Public enterprise industrial relations in context', in Pendleton, A. and Winterton, J. (eds) *Public Enterprise in Transition*. London: Routledge, pp. 1–22.

Peston, R. and Timmins, N. (1999) 'Brown to boost NHS and schools', *Financial Times*, 13 July, p. 1.

Pollert, A. (1988) 'Dismantling flexibility', *Capital and Class*, Vol. 34, Spring, pp. 42–75.

Pratchett, L. and Wingfield, M. (1995) *Reforming the Public Service Ethos in Local Government: A New Institutional Perspective*, Leicester Business School Occasional Paper 27. Leicester: De Montfort University.

Rainnie, A. (1989) *Industrial Relations in Small Firms*. London: Routledge.

Ram, M. (1999) 'Managing autonomy: employment relations in small professional service firms', *International Small Business Journal*, Vol. 17, No. 2, pp. 13–30.

*Ram, M., Edwards, P., Gilman, M. and Arrowsmith, J. (2001) 'The dynamics of informality: employment relations in small firms and the effects of regulatory change', *Work, Employment and Society*, Vol. 15, No. 4, pp. 845–861.

Roche, W. and Geary, J. (2002) 'Advocates, critics and union involvement in workplace partnerships: Irish airports', *British Journal of Industrial Relations*, Vol. 40, No. 4, pp. 659–689.

Rose, E. (2001) *Employment Relations*. Harlow: Prentice Hall.

Salamon, M. (1992) *Industrial Relations: Theory and Practice*. Englewood Cliffs, NJ: Prentice Hall.

Scase, R. (2002), 'Employment relations in small firms', in Edwards, P. (ed), *Industrial Relations: Theory and Practice*. Oxford: Blackwell.

Scott, M., Roberts, I., Holroyd, G. and Sawbridge, D. (1989) *Management and Industrial Relations in Small Firms*, Research Paper no. 70. London: Department of Employment.

Singh, R. (1986) 'Final offer: arbitration in theory and practice', *Industrial Relations Journal*, Winter, pp. 329–330.

Sisson, K. (1987) *The Management of Collective Bargaining: An International Comparison*. Oxford: Blackwell.

Sisson, K. (1993), 'In search of HRM', *British Journal of Industrial Relations*, Vol. 31, No. 2, pp. 201–210.

Sneade, A. (2001) 'Trade union membership 1999–2000: an analysis of data from the Certification Officer and the Labour Force Survey', *Labour Market Trends*, September, pp. 433–443.

Storey, J. (ed.) (1989) *New Perspectives on Human Resource Management*. London: Routledge.

Storey, J. (1992) *Developments in the Management of Human Resources*. Oxford: Blackwell.

Storey, D.J. (1994) *Understanding the Small Business Sector*. London: Routledge.

Storey, D., Keasey, K. and Wynarczyk, P. (1987), *The Performance of Small Firms*. London: Croom Helm.

Thornley, C. (1994) 'Nursing pay policy: chaos in context', paper presented to Employment Research Unit Annual Conference, Cardiff Business School, September.

Towers, B. (1997) *The Representation Gap: Change and Reform in the British and Amercan Workplace*. Oxford: Oxford University Press.

Turner, D. (2003a) 'CBI attacks misguided employment proposals', *Financial Times*, 28 January.

Unison (1998) *A Step by Step Guide to the PFI process*. London: Unison.

Unison (1999) *Unison's Response to Implementing Best Value: A Consultation Paper on Draft Guidance*. London: Unison.

Walton, R.E. and McKersie, R.B. (1965) *A Behavioral Theory of Labor Negotiations*. New York: McGraw-Hill.

Webb, S. and Webb, B. (1902) *Industrial Democracy*. London: Longman.

White, G. (1994) 'Public sector pay: decentralisation versus control', paper to Employment Research Unit Annual Conference, The Contract State: The Future of Public Management, September.

Winchester, D. (1983) 'The public sector', in Bain, G.S. (ed.) *Industrial Relations in Britain*. Oxford: Blackwell, pp. 155–179.

Winchester, D. (1996) 'The regulation of public services pay in the United Kingdom', paper to the Industrial Relations in the European Community (IREC) Network Annual Conference, Industrial Relations in Europe: Convergence or Diversification? University of Copenhagen: FAOS.

Wynarczyk, P., Storey, D., Shot, H., Keasey, K. (1993) *The Managerial Labour Markets in Small Firms*. London: Routledge.

 For multiple choice questions, exercises and annotated weblinks specific to this chapter visit this book's website at www.booksites.net/beardwell

CHAPTER 13

Reward and performance management

Julia Pointon and Alan J. Ryan

OBJECTIVES

▶ To present the historical and theoretical foundations of reward and performance management strategies.

▶ To consider and evaluate the issues concerned in designing performance management and reward systems.

▶ To critically assess the objectives of various reward systems.

▶ To analyse theories of motivation in the context of performance management.

▶ To consider the psychological contract in the context of the employment relationship.

▶ To discuss the interactive links between current trends in human resource management and performance management.

 ## Introduction

This chapter demonstrates the level to which human resource management has developed existing theoretical and practical issues surrounding the management of labour performance within modern organisations. A central element of these debates is the management of reward structures, strategies and systems. In this chapter we introduce the concept of reward(s) as a core function in the development of a strategic role for HR functionaries and offer some explanation of the objectives of current links to performance management.

The often heard comment across many organisations runs along the lines of 'There's only one reason we come here – the money'. Unsurprisingly, these comments reflect the nature of the employment relationship as a reward/effort bargain (Chapters 11 and 12). Whether openly, covertly, personally or collectively, we all become involved in the resolution of this bargain at some time during our working life. This chapter discusses how management have and continue to resolve their problem of converting the labour potential, obtained by their transactions in the labour market, into the labour performance they desire; simply securing the required effort levels without rewarding at levels detrimental to the generation of sufficient profit. In this sense we view reward as a core function for HR managers and rewards as composed of more than the mere 'notes' in the pay packet.

The development of reward systems

As a separate management concern the issue of reward systems is fairly recent, indeed reward management has often been viewed as the 'poor relation' of HRM concerned with 'systems, figures and procedures'. During the development of a 'factory'-based economy, owners found that they were unable to control the 'effort' side of the bargain effectively. Workers, who were previously self-controlled and motivated in many respects by subsistence, worked in small 'cottage' industries within which the product of their labour was owned by the producers (workers themselves; notably in regard to the skilled artisans) and they worked as hard as necessary in order to meet their subsistence needs. As Anthony suggests, 'A great deal of the ideology of work is directed at getting men [sic] to take work seriously when they know that it is a joke' (1977: 5). Owners found that getting workers to keep regular hours and to commit the effort owners considered to constitute 'a fair day's work' was problematic. In response to this dilemma they employed the 'butty' system of reward management. Under this system owners committed a specific level of investment to a selected group of workers (normally skilled artisans) who then hired labour on 'spot contracts' by the day. The major problem for the owners with this system was that these 'subcontractors' had control over the effort/reward bargain and were able to enrich themselves at the expense of the owners. The owners enjoyed little or no control over the process of production so the system was economically inefficient and failed to deliver the returns (rents/profits) required or more importantly that were possible from the process of industrialisation.

From this group of 'favoured' workers, along with the introduction of some university graduates there grew a new management cadre. This was a slow process, as Gospel notes that generally, in UK industry, this group (management, technical and clerical) amounted to only 8.6 per cent of the workforce in most manufacturing organisations (1992: 17), within which development was uneven and patchy. These changes did little to address the problems associated with the effort/reward bargain, meaning productivity was below optimum levels. In part the problem was generated by the fact that 'the managers' brain was still under the workers' cap', more precisely that these managers rarely possessed the skills or knowledge of the production process held by the workers. This led to lower than optimum levels of production and reduced profits, a system F.W. Taylor described as 'Systematic Soldiering'. This activity was engaged in by workers, according to Taylor, 'with the deliberate object of keeping their employers ignorant of how fast work can be done' (Taylor, 1964). From his observations Taylor took the view that workers acting in this manner were merely behaving as 'economically rational actors' desiring their own best interests. It was clear therefore that management needed to take the reins of the production process and reclaim their right to determine the outcome of the wage/effort bargain. Taylor, as the so-called 'father of Scientific Management', developed a system of measuring work which assisted the process of reclaiming managerial rights. Jobs were broken down into specific elements which could then be timed and rated, whilst in the process, returning the determination of the speed of work to management and allowing for the development of pay systems which reflected, however crudely, performance. This scientific system devised by Taylor became the basis of countless pay systems operating effectively alongside the routinisation and deskilling of work which is often associated with Scientific Management within the literature (see, for example, Braverman, 1974; Burawoy, 1985; Hill, 1981; Littler, 1982, 1985; Thompson, 1983; and Wood, 1982). Whilst this allowed management to reassert their control over the level of outputs, to relocate the managers' brain under their own hats and hence the determination of the wage/effort bargain, it did generate problems in relation to managerial attempts to convince workers to take work seriously. In straightforward terms we can suggest that the 'Measured-Work' techniques advocated by adherents of Taylorism further separated conception from execution and led to feelings of alienation. Alienation can be defined as 'various social or psychological evils which are characterized by a harmful separation, disruption or fragmentation which sunders things that properly belong together' (Wood, 2000); in our terms that means the separation of workers from that which they produce. Blauner (1964) argued that such an objective state is created as an offshoot of the subjective feelings of separation which workers experience under modern production systems. These feelings and their outcomes can be briefly outlined in the following manner:

- Powerlessness – the inability to exert control over work processes.
- Meaninglessness – the lack of a sense of purpose as employees only concentrated on a narrowly defined and repetitive task and therefore could not relate their role to the overall production process and end product.
- 'Self-estrangement' – the failure to become involved in work as a mode of self-expression.
- Isolation – the lack of sense of belonging.

Adapted from Blauner (1964)

Although Scientific Management originated at the beginning of the twentieth century, its legacy has lived on in many areas. Similar experiences have been reported in the design of work in service industries and call centres (Ritzer, 1997, and 2000; Taylor and Bain, 1999; Taylor and Bain, 1999; Callaghan and Thompson, 2001). The solution to this problem has been sought, following Taylor's notion of man as an economic actor (see below), by the introduction of various performance and reward systems and mechanisms, the core objectives of which were originally to operationalise effective control over the wage/effort bargain and later with current systems to alleviate the feelings of alienation and generate commitment to organisational goals.

Design and debates

Whilst this section discusses reward systems in a manner which appears to offer a chronological explanation, we should note that the development of 'new' systems does not indicate the total removal of other mechanisms; indeed in many organisations we find that both 'old' and 'new' pay systems operate in tandem, delivering control on different levels for various groups of workers.

In terms of the types of reward mechanism applied we can note the application of a number of different mechanisms based on 'time worked'. Time rates are mechanisms whereby reward is related to the number of hours worked and are often applied to manual workers in the form of hourly rates and non-manual workers by the application of monthly or annual salaries. A criticism of these mechanisms is that they are often related to historic rather than current value, and can result in discrimination, demarcation disputes and a sense of injustice.

Time-related mechanisms are often based on the notion of a pay spine in which groups of skills are banded. Although widely applied in their heyday, basic versions of these instruments are poor in terms of relating wage to current effort; often rewarding effort which has been applied externally (gaining a recognised skill) and are inappropriate to current tasks. The advantages of these systems are that management can control wage costs by limiting the access to various grades on the spine, can limit the range of the grade (say 4 per cent top to bottom) and can demonstrate they are fair in relation to agreed procedures. The problems created are not necessarily with the pay spine system per se but with the manner in which skills relating to specific grades are defined; solutions must then address the structure, strategy and rationale of the reward system rather than the application of such mechanisms.

Conboy (1976) noted that the key advantage of these instruments is that both parties have a clear idea of the 'wage' element of the bargain. For management the problem is that these mechanisms do not give any clear indication of the 'effort' element of the bargain. This led to time rate instruments being complicated by the addition of 'performance' elements, often in the form of 'piece-rates' or other complex 'bonus' calculations in an attempt to determine acceptable effort levels (e.g. Predetermined Motion Time Systems and Measured-Day-Work). The traditional form of such schemes can be demonstrated using the diagram shown in Figure 13.1.

Many schemes give guaranteed basic earnings which are then supplemented in ways which we can class as proportional (wages increase in direct relationship to output), progressive (wages increase more than output) or regressive (wages increase at a slower rate than output).

An important element in this discussion regards the manner in which the 'base' element is decided. We have become familiar with the notion of a National Minimum Wage, which sets the minimum rate for specified groups; outwith this scheme, organisations need some mechanisms by which to assign values to various roles within the organisation. Traditional mechanisms (and in a slightly modified manner 'new pay' systems) have related to job evaluation schemes. A job evaluation scheme operates by allocating values to each of a series of elements (e.g. skill or responsibility) and then measuring each 'job' in order to arrive at an agreed 'score'. The scores are then placed on the pay spine in relation to accepted criteria. These criteria will be formed by the interaction of two sets of relativities. Scores will need to reflect 'external relativities', by which we mean the situation that appears to hold in relation to external markets and environmental conditions, and 'internal relativities', meaning an appearance of fairness in relation to other jobs/roles within the organisation. In the basic form these schemes introduce us to the notion of reward packages under which different elements can be rewarded in various ways. However, these schemes fell out of favour in some respects because they are seen to 'pay-the-job' rather than 'pay-the-worker', and as such were difficult to relate to individual performance.

This is clearly the simplest form of wage payment system, easily understood by both parties; it allows the development of 'overtime' payments for work completed in addition

Figure 13.1   **The traditional form of time rate instruments**

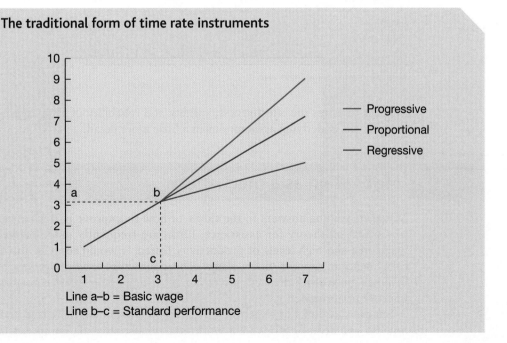

Line a–b = Basic wage
Line b–c = Standard performance

to the contracted hours in any given period and formed the basis of the creation of systems classed as payment by results (PBR).

We can conclude then that such payment by results systems, whilst originally crude, developed alongside the more extensive division of labour achieved by the increasing use and application of technology, ergonomics (pseudo-scientific work measurement) and mechanical production methods. These early techniques can be easily applied to such divided work because of four basic characteristics of such work:

● short job cycles;
● high manual content (which, using sophisticated ergonomic processes, can be measured);
● batch production (with repeated orders/processes);
● no marked fluctuations in required outputs. (Adapted from Conboy, 1976)

The simplistic assumptions underlying these and other PBR systems are twofold. Firstly, workers are motivated to increase performance (work harder) by money, and secondly, any increases in output will result in equivalent increases in wages. The schemes are intended to be self-financing and designed to reduce 'wasteful activity' in that they can be used to redesign the labour process. Whilst such schemes now enjoy less popularity than they have in previous decades, there is still evidence that they are used in relation to specific groups of workers.

Stop and think	To what extent do you think such wage systems reflect management's inability to clearly determine the 'effort' of the bargain?

Table 13.1 shows that while there has been an overall decline in the application of PBR techniques, the decline is not as marked as some proponents of 'new pay' (see below) would argue. The heart of this debate suggests that such schemes can be seen as various techniques designed to act upon worker motivation and as such provide incentives for an individual to reassess the wage/effort bargain.

Table 13.1 **Percentage of employees receiving PBR**

Class of worker	1993	1995	1997
Manual	29.6	28	24
Non-manual	13.9	14.5	12
All	19.4	19.3	16.1

Source: New Earnings Surveys (1993–1997)

In order to assess the effectiveness, validity and reliability of such arguments we need to consider the underlying assumptions in a little more detail.

Motivation as a mechanism

Managers seeking answers to the riddle of how to improve performance will often look to motivation theory for assistance. Links are frequently made between a motivated workforce and high levels of productivity (often, it would seem, with very little empirical evidence to support such a claim). This connection serves to drive managers to strive towards motivating their employees in an attempt to engender positive attitudes and improve performance.

But are such links so clearly defined, and even assuming there is a tenable connection, how do you actually motivate a workforce which, after all, comprises many employees each with their own agenda and 'hot buttons'? Getting it right is not always easy! An independent consulting firm in the USA recently conducted a survey of employees' attitudes which indicated that while most workers were happy with their pay and benefits, fewer than 50 per cent thought their boss was doing a good job of motivating them. This, the research suggested, applies to all levels – shopfloor and boardroom; interestingly, similar results have been found in the UK (Makin *et al.*, 1996: 111).

Stop and think	Writing in *Employee Benefits* (3 July 2002: 3) Carry Cooper, head of organisational psychology and health at the University of Manchester, suggests that '… not all employees are brimming over with motivation', but Cooper believes this is not necessarily a problem: '… as long as they are doing a good job, and that is all they want to do … why not just accept it? 'Why do they have to be high flyers?' 'Not everybody can be a high performing employee … you need some people who can get the job done and do it properly.' *What might be the implications for the organisation if all managers thought this way?*

▪ Defining motivation

A precise definition of motivation is elusive since the concept involves numerous characteristics and perceptions of the employee and the current situation. But it is characterised by a certain level of willingness on the part of the employee to increase effort, to the extent that this exertion also satisfies some need or desire. At a basic level it can be seen that motivation is about 'motives' and 'needs'.

Motives are the internal drives and energies of an employee; they direct behaviour, which results in outcomes. Any single outcome (higher performance levels at work) may be the result of multiple motives (the feeling of achievement, the desire to purchase a new car).

Needs as internal drives are also important and can be physiological (I need sleep, I need warmth), social (I need the company of others) or based on self-esteem needs (I need to gain the respect of my peers for what I do) (Rosenfield and Wilson, 1999: 75).

There are a number of competing definitions, so identifying the one that is just right in relation to reward management is practically impossible. It is better therefore to consider the common underlying assumptions which suggest that motivation is:

● an individual phenomenon – people are unique, and this means that motivation theories usually allow for uniqueness to be reflected in behaviour;
● intentional and results in behaviours that are the result of conscious choices;
● a multifaceted concept, which involves (a) factors that arouse people to action (b) choice of behaviour and (c) choices about the persistency and intensity of behaviour;
● valid as a theory because it helps predict behaviour by explaining what prompts the behaviour of people, which means that it has very little concern with simply describing or categorising behaviour.

An understanding of motivation is important within reward management and the development of reward strategies for a multitude of reasons. Firstly, it enables organisations to 'humanise' work for employees so that work is inherently more satisfying, the assumption being that organisations have a moral obligation to make work as satisfying and enjoyable as possible. Secondly, an appropriate understanding of motivation allows organisations to make the jobs more satisfying for employees within the company. The underlying assumption is clearly that if employees are happier at work then they will be more productive. Finally, we argue that such an understanding enables management to control the behaviour of subordinates more effectively and therefore enables management to 'pull the right strings' in order to secure the ability to set the organisational goals and secure their achievement.

Assuming that you have had some work experience, maybe while on a work placement, through a part-time job – or maybe even a full-time job, write a few lines in response to each of the following questions. This will provide you with an opportunity to reflect on your own motivations.

- Why do I work?
- What motivates me when I'm at work?
- What demotivates me?
- How could my level of motivation be improved?

Content and process theories of motivation

Motivation theory can be classified as representing either a content (needs) or a process approach to motivation. The former helps us to understand what people will and will not value as work rewards; they attempt to identify the specific factors that motivate people. The assumption is that employees have needs which they seek to satisfy inside and outside of work. In this respect we can say that content theories are concerned with the HOW.

Alternatively, process theories offer a more dynamic approach and are more interested in understanding the process of developing motives rather than trying to offer a static analysis of needs. In process theories of motivation there is less emphasis on specific factors (or content) that causes behaviour. For example, a content theory might suggest that 'Increases in pay can improve satisfaction and performance', while a process theory would explain why that might be the case. Thus we can suggest that process theories are concerned with the WHY.

The following section discusses the most well-known content or need theories, and provides an indication of the different needs that employees bring to the working environment. Managers should consider how they can create a working environment in which employees have the opportunity to satisfy their important needs.

The work of Frederick Winslow Taylor (1865–1917)

Taylor believed that the use of money as a motivator linked to various objectives would offer the best motivation for performance. In Taylor's commentary, money was the primary motivator; as such we can suggest that he espoused the rational economic needs concept of motivation. Workers would be motivated by obtaining the highest possible wages through working in the most efficient manner possible – thereby satisfying the

Stop and think   What examples can you identify from your current organisation which are predicated on Tayloristic principles?

How effective are they in motivating employees?

Can you detect any correlation between Taylor's approach to motivation and systems of performance-related pay?

employee and the employer. Taylor's approach to work and motivation has two underlying assumptions: firstly, that all people are rational, and secondly, that they are driven by the need for financial rewards and not interest in the actual work. From this basic proposition he concludes that the natural state of people is one of laziness and hedonism combined with greed.

● The Hawthorne studies

A major revision of 'needs' theory came from work undertaken in the USA in the 1920s and 1930s at the Hawthorne works of the Western Electric Company. This work gave rise to a new school of management thinking (human relations), which suggested that employees have social needs which are as important as economic needs; these studies concluded that social relationships were significant in the satisfaction of the human need for social contact. Thus the key managerial tool for motivation became:

> the emotional, non-rational, and sentimental aspects of human behaviour in organisations, the ties and loyalties that affected workers, the social relations that could not be encompassed by the organisation chart but shaped behaviour regardless.
>
> (Wilson, 1999: 25).

The major contribution of this work in understanding employee motivation at work has been to focus attention on the design of jobs and tasks in an effort to make them attractive and interesting. As O'Doherty notes, these studies 'discovered, like Taylor, that work groups would systematically control and restrict output in order to maintain what they considered to be a fair day's work for a fair day's pay' (2001: 191). While the mechanisms identified in these studies underlie much of the current 'teamworking' culture, their negative findings are lost in the euphoria of controlled participation as an effective instrument for the determination of appropriate reward systems.

● The work of Abraham Maslow

The first comprehensive attempt to classify needs was undertaken by Maslow in the 1940s. In essence Maslow's theory consists of two key parts: the classification of needs and how these classifications are related to each other. The needs, he suggested, are classified in a hierarchy which is normally represented in the form of a pyramid with the more basic physiological needs lying at the base and each higher level consisting of a particular class of needs:

- physiological
- safety
- belongingness
- esteem
- self-actualisation.

According to Maslow, employees work their way up the hierarchy but each level remains dependent on the previous level. Therefore, if you are motivated by the possibility of being able to 'self-actualise' at work but are suddenly made redundant, the whole system collapses as the need to, for example, survive assumes priority.

The theory, especially in relation to reward and performance management, has an uncomplicated appeal because its message is clear – find out what motivates your employees at each of the levels and, more importantly still, at which level each employee is operating, and develop a reward strategy accordingly. However, evaluations have revealed a number of significant flaws which suggest that 'needs' do not always group together in the ways predicted. From this follows the proposition that the theories are unable to predict when a particular need will be manifest because there is no clear relationship between needs and behaviour, so that, for example, the same behaviour could reflect different needs, and different needs the same behaviour. This criticism is further developed as we note that 'needs' are generally imprecisely defined in part due to the notion of need as a biological phenomenon being problematic. These theories ignore the capacity of people and those around them to construct their own perceptions of needs and how they can be met (Arnold *et al.*, 1998: 248/9).

Despite these limitations, Maslow's thinking remains influential and continues to influence management deliberations in respect of job design, pay and reward structures. Huczynski and Buchanan (2001: 242) highlight this by indictaing that 'Many subsequent management fashions, such as job enrichment, total quality management, business process re-engineering, self managing teams, the "new leadership" and employee empowerment incorporated his ideas in the search for practical motivational methods'.

> **Stop and think**
>
> How far do you think it is possible to achieve self-actualisation?
>
> How far do you think the reward system of an organisation may motivate you to achieve self-actualisation?

● The work of Fredrick Herzberg

Herzberg (1966) looked, not at motivation directly, but at the causes of job satisfaction and dissatisfaction in an attempt to more fully understand what motivates people at work and from his research proposed a 'two factor' theory. The two factors were

1 *Motivators.* These were such things as 'a sense of achievement', 'an opportunity for personal growth', 'the sense of having done a job well', 'having responsibility', and 'achieving recognition for your work'.
2 *Hygiene factors.* These included such things as money, working conditions, job security, company policy, and quality of supervision and interpersonal relations.

Motivators and hygiene factors are qualitatively different and have different effects. If the objective is to remove dissatisfaction, then the organisation will need to improve the hygiene factors. However, improving them beyond the level at which dissatisfaction disappears will not result in an increase in satisfaction. The only way satisfaction can be increased further is by giving more of the motivators. The converse also applies in that giving more of the motivators may not, by itself, remove dissatisfaction. For Herzberg, therefore, the opposite of satisfaction is not dissatisfaction, it is merely no satisfaction, and equally, the opposite of dissatisfaction is not necessarily satisfaction, simply no dissatisfaction.

● Job characteristics approach

The job characteristics approach is based on the idea that individual differences are important moderators in the way employees respond to the nature and design of work, irrespective of any performance/reward element. Working from Herzberg's idea that work itself and hence the way in which it is organised are important motivators, Hackman and Lawler (1971) and Hackman and Oldham (1980) set out the first structure of the jobs characteristics model, which is the basis of the job design approach to motivation. They argue that there are five core job dimensions: skill variety, which is concerned with the number and type of different activities the job involves; task identity – the extent to which the employee has some responsibility for the 'whole job'; task significance – essentially how meaningful the job is considered to be by others; autonomy, which refers to the freedom the employee has to determine how to undertake the work; and finally feedback, which refers to the level of information the employee receives about the work and their performance. These five 'core job dimensions' create three 'psychological states' which are founded upon the meaningfulness of work, the extent to which the employees experience responsibility for the outcomes of their work and the knowledge of the results of their actual effort. Where these three 'psychological states' are positively experienced, i.e. there is meaningfulness in the work, the employee does have a sense of responsibility for what they do and they receive appropriate feedback, they are more likely to experience high work motivation, and general work satisfaction.

Working in teams may satisfy some of the criteria for motivating employees, but rewarding teamworking is complicated (see discussion below). Incentive schemes based on the discrete performance of a particular work group attempt to encourage flexibility and cooperation among members of the group, and to some extent provide opportunities for the employees to decide for themselves how to achieve the required results. Such schemes seem to be most effective when the work groups/teams are seen to be stable, mature and naturally forming. In these situations we can argue that such teams will be clearly identifiable as a performing unit with performance outcomes that can be directly measured for each team as they have a significant degree of autonomy and are composed of employees whose work is interdependent. Such interdependence can only really be found where the groups are made up of employees who are flexible, multi-skilled and good team players. (See Armstrong, 2002.)

Roberts (2001: 520) states that 'the introduction of team-based payment schemes may lead to several problems'. Peer pressures to conform and the need to consider others may result in a reduction of effort by the whole group, a sort of 'I'm not working hard if the others aren't going to' attitude. Employees may also resist the transfer out of high-performing into less effective teams because of the potential loss of individual earnings. This may be to the detriment of the organisation as an employee's learning and knowledge are confined to one team and not shared or transferred throughout the organisation. Finally, the move to a team-based reward strategy may require a change in the way employees operate; no longer will their individual efforts be paramount – their pay will not be wholly related to their own efforts, but to the combined efforts of the team.

● The work of Douglas McGregor

McGregor (1957) set out two general sets of extreme propositions about motivation which he labelled Theory X and Theory Y respectively, and which still form an important element of reward management vocabulary today.

In brief we can say that Theory X sets forth the following propositions which can be applied to the development of a reward and performance management strategy. It suggests that the average human being has an inherent dislike of work and will avoid it wherever possible because such behaviour reflects a basic human characteristic, dislike of work. Owing to this characteristic, most people must be coerced, controlled, directed or threatened with punishment to get them to put the necessary effort into work. This offers an explanation for the development of a managerial cadre as most people prefer to be directed by hierarchical superiors, want to avoid responsibility at work, have relatively little ambition and want security more than anything else.

Alternatively, it is suggested, we can say that 'Theory Y' sets forth the following propositions. It argues that the average person does not inherently dislike work. The expenditure of physical and mental effort in work is as natural as play or rest. Employees may appear to be recalcitrant and uncooperative, but this is an outcome of their experience of management's traditional approach (Theory X) to work organisation and control. Therefore external control or threats of punishment are not the only or the most appropriate motivators as employees will exercise self-control and self-direction in the pursuit of objectives to which they are committed. It follows that the most significant rewards are intrinsic to work and relate to the satisfaction of higher-order needs such as the satisfaction of ego and self-actualisation. If conditions are right, it is possible to integrate the achievement of organisational goals with the satisfaction of employees' higher-order needs and improve individual performance. From this perspective it is seen that the average human being learns, under proper conditions, not only to accept, but actively seek responsibility. Avoidance of responsibility, lack of ambition and emphasis on security are generally consequences of their individual experience of management's traditional approach (Theory X) and are not inherent human characteristics. Therefore it can be said that in the right conditions, most people are capable of exercising imagination, ingenuity and creativity in the solution of organisational problems.

ACTIVITY	Complete the following questionnaire by circling the number that best reflects your perception of other people at work.

Most people dislike work	1 2 3 4 5	Work is as natural as rest and play
People need to be directed to work effectively	1 2 3 4 5	Most people will exercise self-control and discretion while at work
Most people prefer not to have any responsibility at work	1 2 3 4 5	People enjoy having responsibility for the work they do
For most, achievement is irrelevant at work	1 2 3 4 5	Achievement is highly valued by people
Most people are dull and uncreative	1 2 3 4 5	Most people have imagination and creativity
For the majority of people the only reason they work is for the money	1 2 3 4 5	Money is only one benefit from work and possibly not the most important
People lack the desire to improve quality of life	1 2 3 4 5	Most people have desires to improve their quality of life
Objectives are a form of control	1 2 3 4 5	Objectives are welcomed as an aid to effectiveness

If you scored 16 or less then you subscribe to Theory X. If you scored 32 or more, you subscribe to Theory Y.

Source: Adapted from Huczynski, A. and Buchanan, D. (2001) *Organisational Behaviour: An Introductory Text*, p. 237

● Criticisms of content theories

A number of points of criticism of content or needs theories is summarised in the following discussion. At the foundation of these theories, it is claimed, lies the suggestion that each school of thought focuses on a single factor to the exclusion of all others – money, social needs or psychological growth. It is assumed within these theoretical frameworks that if reward managers can identify the key motivational factor then an employee will 'naturally' become committed to the goals of the organisation. Hence, as it is assumed that commitment to these goals would be in an employee's best interests, anyone who was not motivated by that factor would be irrational, abnormal or dysfunctional; in other words, these theories take on a unitarist perspective and see conflict as undesirable or illegitimate (see Chapter 12). The theories assume that the task presented to reward and performance management systems is to identify motivational strategies which can, indeed should, be applied in any context for any organisation if management *choose* to do so (e.g. all jobs can be rationalised, redesigned or enriched).

As it is very difficult to predict when certain needs become important, there appearing to be no clear relationship between needs and behaviour, we can argue that the application of 'standardised' solutions is neither possible nor desirable. It is clear that as the different needs are very difficult to isolate, define or describe and further that any suggestion that needs have a biological origin is problematic, performance management involves issues to which there is no 'off the shelf', one-size-fits-all response. However, it can be seen that these theories do tend to assume the application to all people regardless of the historical or social context of a single set of solutions. The theories tend to overestimate the importance of intrinsic factors and work itself. The argument here is that for some people work may not be a central life interest, whilst neo-human relations theory assumes that work is the only site for the realisation of self-actualisation and social needs. Hence content theories tend to assume that all employees have the same type of engagement, or psychological contract, with the organisation. The influence on motivation of an employee's subjective orientation to work and felt 'meaning' of work is insufficiently considered. Thus neo-human relations tends to ignore cognition, the construction of perceptions of needs, how those needs are best met and meaningful action by employees. For example, when we observe ourselves or others behaving in a certain way it is often very difficult to explain it by referring to the desire to satisfy one particular need as people construct their own perception of needs and how they can best meet those needs within a particular situational context.

Ultimately content theories consider *what* things may motivate rather than *why*, which we need to know in order to develop an effective reward and performance management strategy.

Process theories of motivation

The second group of motivation theories, the process theories, focus on how behaviour change occurs, or how an individual comes to act in a different way. Significant in understanding this set of theoretical constructs are the concepts of justice and fairness.

Procedural justice and distributive justice

During the late 1980s and 1990s, equity theory expanded to address theories of organisational justice (see Greenberg, 1987). A distinction is drawn between distributive justice and procedural justice. Distributive justice concerns whether employees believe they have received or will receive fair rewards. Procedural justice reflects whether employees believe the procedures – the actions or measures – used in the organisation to allocate rewards are fair. For example, is the reward system impartial, not favouring one group over another? Does it take into account all the relevant information? Is there a system for detecting and correcting errors? So, if employees believe they are poorly paid relative to others in a similar job in another organisation, they may perceive distributive injustice. However, if at the same time they believe that the employing organisation is actually making available as much reward as is possible and is operating a fair system of distribution, they may perceive procedural justice. It is generally accepted (Arnold *et al.*, 1998: 255; Makin *et al.*, 1996: 139) that distributive justice is associated with individual outcomes, such as satisfaction with pay, while procedural justice is associated with organisational outcomes, such as organisational commitment. Motivation tends to be lowest when injustices in both procedural and distributive procedures are experienced.

Distributive justice

Blau (1994: 1253) refers to five possible pay referent categories against which employees may assess fairness:

- social (e.g. family, friends, relatives);
- financial (i.e. the extent to which one's current income meets one's current financial needs);
- historical (i.e. one's current income in comparison to income received in the past);
- organisation (i.e. pay comparisons within the company);
- market (i.e. pay comparisons outside the organisation).

If the two ratios (i.e. input and output or wage/effort) are not equal then the employee will take action to attempt to restore a sense of equity and maintain motivation. To achieve this, Adams (1963) suggests that employees may change inputs (they can reduce effort) if they feel they are underpaid, or they may try to change their outcomes (ask for a pay rise or promotion). More subtly, they could psychologically distort their own ratios and/or those of others by rationalising differences in the wage/effort bargain (inputs/outcomes) in part by changing the reference group to which they compare themselves in order to restore equity.

Procedural justice

Individual judgements of the fairness of the process of allocating rewards are the second key determinant of an employee's reaction to a pay scheme. Research suggests that an understanding of how pay is determined affects an employee's satisfaction with both the processes and the outcomes of the pay scheme (Dulebohn and Martocchio, 1998; Lee *et al.*, 1999).

Bringing together the work of Leventhal (1976), Lind and Tyler (1988) and Folger *et al.* (1992), we can propose that procedural justice within reward schemes can be enhanced where decisions are transparent to all concerned and based on complete, accurate and timely information. Linked to this, the system should ensure that the procedures are neutral as well as consistent across time and people in the sense that they are free from bias, the pursuit of self-interest and dishonesty. In achieving this aim the procedures will treat all parties with politeness, dignity and respect as decisions are made which will be compatible with prevailing moral and ethical standards. The reward system ought to be based on trust, with procedures that reflect the concerns, values and interests of all parties, as the underlying beliefs are founded on an intention to treat all people in a reasonable and benevolent manner.

Judgements of procedural justice and distributive justice can affect motivation, satisfaction, organisational commitment and judgements of the effectiveness of the reward and performance management scheme (Lind and Tyler, 1988; McFarlin and Sweeney, 1992; Dulebohn and Martocchio, 1998). Essentially, it can be suggested that currently most reward schemes satisfy some the above criteria and hence some employees and not others. Organisations must therefore ensure that although employees may be dissatisfied with the outcomes, they perceive the procedures leading up to the allocation as 'fair'.

Arnold *et al.* (1998: 256) suggests that the role of justice in motivation has become more apparent in recent years due to the downsizing, delayering and restructuring that has occurred within organisations. Over recent years these developments have meant the deal or the 'psychological contract' (see discussion below) employees felt they had with the employing organisation has been broken by that organisation. The psychological outcomes of this process appear to be that some employees experience a strong sense of injustice which may influence their level of commitment to the organisation in terms of actual work performance and 'good citizen' behaviours. Procedural justice appears to play a large part in determining reactions to a broken psychological contract, as does an employee's perception of why the organisation fell short of their expectations.

Equity theory

The equity theory of motivation is based on the principle that since there are no absolute criteria for fairness, individuals generally assess fairness by making comparisons with others in similar situations. Therefore the motivation to put effort into a task will be influenced by the individual's perceptions of whether the rewards are fair in comparison to those received by others. To assess fairness an employee is likely to make a comparison between the level of inputs and outputs they are making compared to the level of input and output they consider the comparator to be making. Inputs are often multiple and consist of things an employee may bring to the task – education, previous experience, effort, while outputs are the rewards for the inputs – salary, performance-related pay incentive, praise. Inputs are essentially costs while the outputs are the benefits. If, following the subjective comparison, a feeling of inequity prevails, this can give rise to tensions and feelings of psychological discomfort. This may result in a desire to 'do something about it' and take action designed to lessen the tension being experienced. Adams (1965) suggests that there are six basic options available to an employee:

- Modify inputs.
- Seek to modify outputs.
- Modify perception of self.
- Modify perception of comparator.
- Change comparator.
- Leave the situation. (Adapted from Rollinson, 2002: 235)

Adams (1963) suggests that adopting one or a combination of the options may result in a feeling of restored balance or equity resulting in the employee accepting the situation.

This theory is straightforward and easy to understand; however, it cannot cover every contingency. For example, some employees are far more sensitive to perceptions of inequity than others. There is some evidence to suggest that even where inequity is perceived to exist, employees have some tolerance providing the reasons for the inequity are explained and justified. This has three major implications for human resource managers when they are designing performance management and reward schemes. Firstly, it is important to be aware that employees will make comparisons; further, because comparisons are subjective, care must be taken to relate similar jobs in terms of the wage/effort bargain; and finally, if managers wish to avoid inaccurate conclusions about equity it is necessary to be open concerning the basis on which the rewards are made.

Generally speaking, it is important for managers to be aware of what employees perceive to be fair and equitable and to recognise that this will vary from group to group. By taking adequate consideration of the employees' perceptions, by providing an adequate explanation of any changes in work process or design and by ensuring that policies etc. are applied consistently and in an unbiased manner, employees are more likely to believe that the organisation is trying to reduce any perceived inequality and that they are being treated fairly in comparison with the treatment received by others.

For the human resource manager, equity theory illustrates how important it is to provide a performance management and reward system in which the outcomes are perceived by individuals to be relevant and to acknowledge the truth that different employees value different things.

Secondly, it is clear that human resource managers need to (re)design current compensations systems in order to avoid the performance-destroying effects of perceived inequities which result from employee perceptions that the wage/effort bargain provides insufficient rewards, and thirdly, that these redesigned systems need to avoid over-rewarding performance as this does not necessarily result in higher productivity or improved performance.

● Expectancy theory

The content theorists (Maslow, Herzberg, Alderfer and McClelland) can lead you to believe that most behaviours are under the voluntary control of a person and are consequently motivators. Because behaviours are voluntary, expectancy theory suggests that employees look at the various alternatives and choose the alternative that they believe is most likely to lead to those rewards that they desire most; simply that individuals are rational actors who, in employment terms, follow a path of economic maximisation.

The fundamental concepts important to expectancy theory are that the anticipation (expectation) of what will occur influences the employee's choice of behaviour. We can therefore suggest that the theory sets out the twin propositions that individuals have the expectation that some outcome will occur, and that this outcome has a value (anticipated satisfaction) to the individual.

These are called expectancies and valences and underlie the argument developed by Vroom (1964). Vroom interpreted motivation as a process in which employees select from a set of alternatives based upon the anticipated levels of satisfaction. He called the individual's perception of this relationship instrumentality.

The first-level outcomes result from behaviour associated with doing the job itself and include productivity, absenteeism, turnover, and the quality of productivity. The second-level outcomes are the events (rewards or punishments) that the first-level outcomes are likely to produce. Commonly accepted second-level outcomes are merit pay increases, group acceptance or rejection, and promotion.

In expectancy theory, valence as well as instrumentality is important. Valence refers to the preferences for outcomes as seen by the employee. Valences can be either positive (preferred) or negative (not preferred or avoided). A potential zero valence can occur when an employee is indifferent to attaining or not attaining the outcome.

The theory considers two types of expectancies important. Effort–performance expectancy is the employee's perception of how hard it will be to achieve a particular behaviour and the probability of achieving that behaviour. Performance–outcome expectancy assumes that in the employee's mind, every behaviour is associated with outcomes.

From a human resource management perspective, it can be argued that expectancy theory proposes that employees ask themselves three questions:

1 What's in it for me?
2 How hard will I have to work to get what's in it for me?
3 What are my real chances of getting the reward if I do what my boss wants?

An employee assigns a value to an expected reward, considers how much effort will be required and works out the probability of success. If the perceived reward is adequate for the effort required, the employee may make the effort. However, when performance accomplishment is reached, resulting in either intrinsic or extrinsic rewards being received, the employee compares the reward to the accomplishment and assesses the extent to which an equitable reward is perceived. Where the assessment of the wage/effort bargain is perceived by the employee to be 'fair', satisfaction results and the process generates positive feedback. If, however, the performance accomplishment does not result in the anticipated rewards or the perception is of inequity and dissatisfaction, the process generates negative feedback.

There are criticisms of expectancy theory which argue that the theory attempts to predict a choice or effort. However, because no clear specification of the meaning of effort exists, the variables cannot be measured adequately. As a process theory it does not specify the outcomes relevant to a particular individual situation and therefore offers little guidance to the human resource manager seeking to design a performance management and reward system as there is an implicit assumption that all motivation is conscious. The employee is assumed to consciously calculate the pleasure or pain that he/she expects to attain or avoid and then a choice is made. The theory says nothing about subconscious motivation.

● Goal-setting theory

This approach to motivation has been demonstrated by Locke and Latham (1984) and is based on a simple premise: performance is caused by a person's intention to perform. Goals are what a person is trying to accomplish or intends to do and, according to this theory, people will do what they are trying to do. What follows is clear:

- A person with higher goals will do better than a person with lower goals.
- If someone knows precisely what they want to do, or is supposed to do, that person will perform better than someone whose goals or intentions are vague.

These two basic ideas underlie the propositions of goal-setting theory which begins by stating that there is a general positive relationship between goal difficulty and performance. This, however, does not hold for extremely difficult goals, which are beyond an employee's ability, only for challenging goals which generally result in improved performance compared to easy goals. Thus, using this prism we can argue that specific goals lead to higher performance than general or vague 'do your best' goals. Specific goals seem to create a precise intention, which in turn aids individual employees to shape their behaviour with the same precision. Further, the theory proposes that knowledge of results (feedback) is essential if the full performance benefits of setting more difficult goals are to be achieved. Hence feedback offered in an appropriate manner can have a motivating effect on the employee. It is suggested that the beneficial effects of goal-setting depend, in part, on the employee's goal commitment; that is, their determination to succeed and unwillingness to abandon or reduce it.

These four principles establish the core of goal-setting theory and make it possibly one of the more consistently supported theories of motivation. Locke *et al.* (1981) suggest that financial incentives can enhance performance by raising the level of the goal or by increasing an employee's commitment to a goal which can be achieved where the employee is involved in establishing the required performance. We can therefore argue that, in the workplace, the value of goal-setting is enhanced by the provision of adequate, timely feedback.

Goal-based theories of motivation emphasise the importance of feedback in order to:

- increase the employee's feeling of achievement;
- increase the sense of personal responsibility for the work;
- reduce uncertainty; and
- refine performance.

However, many systems do not systematically provide for line managers to communicate feedback on performance to those employees for whom they have responsibility. This may be for many reasons such as leadership style, protection of power bases or the information system not providing data for management functions. Often employees are provided with feedback 'by exception', typically when performance has fallen below a certain acceptable level and managers are themselves under pressure to improve performance. However, managers have to maintain a careful balance in providing feedback – too little, too late can be demotivating but too much and too frequently can be 'stifling' and perceived as indicative of a lack of trust or respect.

Austin and Bobko (1985) identified four respects in which goal-setting theory had not been fully tested. First, goals which reflect the quality of work, rather than the quantity, were rarely set in goal theory research, Yet, in many employees' work, quality is as significant as quantity, if not more so. Secondly, jobs often have conflicting goals where achieving one may mean the neglect of another. Equally, it is important to recognise that employees and the organisation may have conflicting goals and this could undermine, or at least complicate, the setting of goals. Thirdly, in research the focus has been on the setting and achievement of individual goals; in organisations the emphasis may be on the achievement of collective or group goals. Two further limitations of goal-setting as a motivational technique are concerned with learning new tasks and organisational culture. Earley *et al.* (1989) suggested that goal-setting may be harmful where a task is new or unfamiliar or where a considerable number of strategies are available to approach it. They suggest that in such situations, the desire to achieve the goal may deter creativity, experimentation and innovation in problem-solving.

● Criticisms of process theories

A key criticism of process theories is that they tend to assume an overly rational view of human decision-making. For example, decision-making is often habitual or unconscious rather than conscious and rational. Furthermore, when making choices people do not have complete knowledge of the possible results of their behavioural options, and are not normally aware of the full range of options available to them.

Another weak assumption of process theories is that individuals have a comprehensive and consistent scale of values with which they might evaluate the value of the various outcomes they are able to identify. Ultimately, process theories do not consider *why* an individual values or does not value particular outcomes, only *how* the motivation develops.

Although there are various problems with each set of motivation theories, surveys of what motivates people show predictable patterns:

● a boss you can respect;
● a job that is worthwhile and of interest to you;
● enough basic pay;
● some degree of personal challenge;
● the opportunity to progress;
● being part of a good team of people;
● being well trained to do the job;
● having sufficient resources to carry the job out;
● having a reasonable degree of stability and security;
● being involved in deciding how to do the job and organise the work.

Like content theories, process theories all have certain similarities and differences. Expectancy theory, equity theory and goal-setting all recognise that motivation and subsequent behaviour are affected by individual differences and features of the organisation environment, its culture, supervisory, mentoring, training, appraisal and development systems. In addition, process theories emphasise the importance of acknowledging that employees make decisions concerning their behaviour and that these decisions are based on previous experiences and evaluation of the rewards obtainable for behaving in a certain manner.

■ Motivation, reward and implications for the management of people

Shamir (1991) proposes that the general motivation of employees is affected by a number of interlinking factors. At a basic level we can identify that motivation is linked to the extent to which job identity is perceived to be important for self-definition relative to other possible alternative social identities in the self-concept. This perception is in part dependent on the extent to which the job offers opportunities to increase self-esteem and self-worth and therefore the extent to which job behaviours are congruent with the self-concept. Looking forward, levels of motivation are affected by the extent to which future job possibilities are congruent with desired possible selves. Any successful performance management and reward system will need to take into account each of these employee-defined elements whilst noting that an employee's general motivation will be lowered by the extent to which the job or environment contains elements that are detrimental to the person's self-esteem or self-worth.

Stop and think

With reference to an organisation with which you are familiar, to what degree do you think the motivational strategies used are based on and reflect the different theories of motivation outlined in this section?

New day, new way, new pay?

This discussion indicates that early PBR mechanisms, discussed above, were in some respects aiming at the wrong target. By concentrating simplistically on the cash nexus they avoided more complex motivators which determine the effort side of the bargain. The realisation amongst managers and academics that the application of greater levels of effort could be achieved more effectively by the application of methods other than money led to the development of a wider discussion.

By the 1980s it had become clear that the traditional (old pay) systems were not effectively delivering in terms of key organisational goals. The developing HRM rhetoric and the more apparent interest in business performance led HR managers to reassess the role of reward management in the delivery of organisational efficiency. As White and Drucker (2000) note, these developments have been escorted by broader economic and social changes which challenged the belief in traditional personnel practices. Within this process of change, reward management underwent a metamorphosis of major proportions in that it was no longer simply about rewarding people for previous attainment but became linked to future performance. According to Armstrong (2002), reward is now 'about how people are rewarded in accordance with their value to the organisation' (2002: 3) and as such can no longer be seen as the mere administration of set procedures and policies. From this perspective the development of HRM has led to an evaluation of reward systems in an attempt to link them more effectively to organisational strategies (fitting in with notions of strategic HRM). Reward strategies, then, are viewed as a key organisational contribution and a central element in the work of HR functionaries.

As we can note from the models and maps of HRM (see Chapter 1), reward systems are seen as one of the four key policy choices (Beer et al., 1984) out of which organisations can aim to develop commitment, competence, congruence and cost-effectiveness, while Storey (1992) indicates reward management as one of the points of difference between personnel and HRM. The old mechanisms, including graded spines based on job evaluation, are considered inappropriate in modern business. Rewards, or more precisely reward strategies, are seen as techniques which organisations can apply in order to secure various behaviours and values. Millward et al. (2000) note that in 1990 the major influence which determined pay settlements in organisations where collective bargaining was not dominant was individual employee performance (2000: 207); by 1998 the focus had shifted, with the main influence in this group of respondents being economic factors and more recognition of limits set by higher authority (2000: 211). These changes have not resulted in reward systems which are any easier for workers to understand or that are less complex than their predecessors. That reward management developed in a manner which encouraged this occupation of a position of central importance has various causes. As we noted above, control of costs is at the heart of managerial responsibilities and, within that, control of the labour costs is fundamental to organisational performance. Further, we have suggested that reward systems form part of the employees' notion of organisational justice and as such underlie a sense of loyalty. This simple statement needs unpacking in terms of the manner in which policy and practice have developed as a result of these changes.

In the 1990s, US writers (Lawler, 1990; Schuster and Zingheim, 1992) offered concepts they labelled 'new pay' as a prism through which we can view these changes. The central idea is intended to signify the realisation that reward strategies have to relate to organisational culture, values, aims and strategies, which in turn must take into account the challenges of a modern economy. As Schuster and Zingheim (1992) note, the rudimentary elements of 'new pay' include an acknowledgement that employees form a core ingredient in the recipe for organisational success. They suggest that the change cannot be one of rhetoric (from reward to compensation) alone but must also be demonstrated in the design of 'total compensation' packages which consistently reward required actions and attitudes. They indicate that a key element in such a total compensation package is variable pay, suggesting that pay remains a crucial mechanism for sending messages to employees in regard to the managerially desired effort levels. In this light, reward strategy needs to be integrated within wider organisational and managerial processes rather than being viewed as a 'bolt-on' optional extra. This whole package approach means that all elements (base, variable and indirect rewards) need to support each rather than compete for supremacy. Base pay remains the foundation of the policy and should be set in line with organisational and societal norms in order to ensure 'felt justice' across the organisation. Alongside this element, however, the organisation may develop variable elements which do not become permanent, remaining subject to criteria related to either individual or organisational performance. These variable elements can therefore go down as well as up, addressing the issue of wage rigidity which adds damaging costs in periods of downturn. There are a number of means by which this variable element can be determined but they are often grouped under the generic term performance-related pay (PRP), indicating that the measurement of such performance may be based on the individual, the team or the organisation.

In this section we begin with consideration of the organisational element commonly called profit-related pay. The underlying idea in the introduction of such a variable element was that employees would identify more readily with organisational goals where part of their compensation package was linked to 'profits'. In simple terms, when the organisation did well they would share in the gain and, therefore, would share the suffering in bad times. This may work where employees can be encouraged to swap a percentage of their base pay for this variable element but many organisations introduced these schemes as additional to existing compensation levels (see Kellaway, 1993). Current research looking at these schemes indicates two main findings:

- They have some positive impact on performance.
- Employees can view the rewards as unrelated to individual performance. (*Source*: Freeman, 2001)

The second point is reason enough to move towards systems which apparently reward individual performance more directly. This has been achieved by the introduction of schemes which are based on modern job evaluation and grading schemes within which the compensation increases the variable element rather than the base as in the past.

Modern organisations focus such grading schemes within notions of competencies. In this world-view competency can be defined as

> an underlying characteristic of an individual which is causally related to effective or superior performance in a job.
> (Mitrani *et al.*, 1993: 5)

> The characteristic set of knowledge, skills, abilities, motivations and procedures that individuals working in specific jobs should possess to allow them to perform their work to minimum standards.
>
> (Cornelius, 2001: 366)

From this we could suggest a list of competencies which would include:

- leadership
- communication skills
- presentation skills
- interpersonal skills
- workflow management
- adaptability
- customer service. (Adapted from Gooch and Cornelius, 2001)

Competence-based payment (CBP) schemes have grown alongside the interest in variable compensation. HR functionaries have expended significant time and energy in the development of 'competence frameworks' which link pay to the achievement of specific behaviours, attitudes and the attainment of required competencies. This differs from traditional 'pay-by-skill' in that it is applied across the organisation to all workers (rather than just the traditional skills) and the required 'competencies' are somewhat broader than the definition of 'skill(s)'. This breadth of definition allows the application and adaptation of traditional job evaluation schemes by taking into account current changes in the organisation of work and the utilisation of new technology. Thus job evaluation techniques were rescued from decline by becoming more flexible, broader in coverage and applicable to modern multi-skilled workers (Pritchard and Murlis, 1992).

Hastings and Dixon (1995) suggest that CBP systems can take three major forms in which the attainment of indicated competencies is:

- the basis for progression within scales;
- the basis upon which the scales are founded; or
- the basis both for progression and for the scale.

Whichever system is applied, a main advantage lies in the versatility available for organisations to set their own 'characteristic set of knowledge, skills, abilities and motivations'.

In recent debates much of the attention has turned to discussion of a contract which is unwritten and yet seen as being equal in relation to influence as any written terms and conditions. The psychological contract is seen to underpin all reward and performance management systems in that it conceptualises the wage/effort bargain for a new generation of workers and owners. In the following section we consider the formation of the contract and identify the 'agreed' terms (if such they can be called) forming the basis from which human resource managers seek to develop performance norms, organisational values and note the psychological contract as a mechanism in the continuing strategy to encourage 'men [sic] to take work seriously when they know that it is a joke' (Anthony, 1977: 5).

The psychological contract

Defining the psychological contract

As with many aspects of human resource management – such as motivation and performance – the psychological contract is somewhat elusive and challenging to define (for a discussion of this, see Guest, 1998a). However, it is generally accepted that it is concerned with an individual's subjective beliefs, shaped by the organisation, regarding the terms of an exchange relationship between the individual employee and the organisation (Rousseau, 1995). As it is subjective, unwritten and often not discussed or negotiated, it goes beyond any formal contract of employment. The psychological contract is promise based, and over time assumes the form of a mental schema or model, which like most schema is relatively stable and durable. (For a more detailed analysis on how the psychological contract is formed see Rousseau, 2001). A major feature of psychological contracts is the concept of mutuality – that there is a common and agreed understanding of promises and obligations the respective parties have made to each other about work, pay, loyalty, commitment, flexibility, security and career advancement.

Research undertaken by Herriot et al., (1997) sought to explore the content of the psychological contract in the UK. They researched the perceived obligations of two parties to the psychological contract by identifying the critical incidents of 184 employees and 184 managers representing the organisation. From the results they inferred seven categories of employee obligation and twelve categories of organisation obligation.

In relation to employee obligations they make reference to both concrete and abstract inputs the organisation hopes/expects the employee will bring to the organisation. At the first level these involve an expectation that the employee will work the hours contracted and consistently do a good job in terms of quality and quantity. The organisation will desire that their employees deal honestly with clients and with the organisation and remain loyal by staying with the organisation, guarding its reputation and putting its interests first, including treating the property which belongs to the organisation in a careful way. Employees will be expected to dress and behave correctly with customers and colleagues and show commitment to the organisation by being willing to go beyond their own job description, especially in emergency. It is possible to suggest that many of these expectations reflect the common law terms implied in the contract of employment and as such it is the 'manifestation' of the required behaviours more than the existence of a psychological contract which is used to manage 'norms' within the organisation.

On the other side of the contract we can note the obligations placed on the organisation in terms of the expectations each employee has of the deal. Most employees would want the organisation to provide adequate induction and training and then ensure fairness of selection, appraisal, promotion and redundancy procedures. While recent legislation has centred on the notion of work–life balance, it is argued that an element of this agreement is an employee expectation that the organisation will allow time off to meet personal and family needs irrespective of legal requirements. It has long been held that workers ought to have the right to participate in the making of the decisions which affect their working lives (see Adams, 1986; Bean, 1994; Freeman and Rogers, 1999); the debate relating to the psychological contract suggests that employees further expect organisations to consult and communicate on the matters which affect them. With the increasingly high levels of 'knowledge' workers it is accepted that organisations ought to engage in a policy of minimum interference with employees in terms of how they do their job and to recognise or reward for special contribution or long service. Organisations are generally depended upon to act in a personally and socially responsible and supportive way towards employees, which includes the provision of a safe and congenial work environment. We have already noted that in relation to reward and performance management systems there is a need to act with fairness and consistency; the expectation goes further in that the application of rules and disciplinary procedures must be seen to be equitable. This perceived justice should extend to market values and be consistently awarded across the organisation, indicating the link therefore to a consistency in the administration of the benefit systems. The final element that many workers expect their employer to provide is security in terms of the organisation trying hard to provide what job security is feasible within the current economic climate.

Stop and think

1 Write down your expectations of your employer and what you consider to be their expectations of you.

2 Reflect on which aspects can be described as formal and which could be considered as unwritten.

3 Consider how you reached this 'psychological contract' – did you, for example, negotiate and agree it or have you assumed aspects?

4 To what extent are both parties, i.e. you and your employer, aware of the existence and the content of the contract; to what extent do you share the same expectations?

5 What might be the issues for you and for the employer if there is a mismatch of expectations?

6 Finally, consider with whom you have the contract – a named individual within the organisation or do you have multiple contracts with different agents within the organisation?

Previous decades have seen many organisations forced, by increased competition and the globalisation of business, to seek to remain competitive by cutting costs and increasing efficiency. This has, in part, given rise to the restructuring endemic in UK and US organisations under the various guises of business process re-engineering, downsizing and rightsizing, all of which apply performance-related pay systems aimed at increasing productivity. The restructuring has also given rise to redundancies, has had the significant impact of reducing job security of those who remained, has removed many of the middle-level management grades and consequently reduced possible promotion opportunities for all employees.

While long-term job security, promotion and career progression were perceived by many employees, whose psychological contract was possibly formed many years earlier, to be the 'key' obligations which were owed by the organisation in return for their loyalty and commitment, modern organisations (and in some respects the 'modern' employee) are learning to live without such elements in the psychological agreement. The consequences have been predictable; employees feel angry at the apparent unilateral breaking of the psychological contract and at the same time insecure, having lost trust in the organisation. Commitment is reduced, with motivation, morale and performance being adversely affected. This is potentially dangerous for the organisation, as lean organisations need effort and commitment in order to get work done and at the same time a willingness to take risks in the pursuit of innovation. It is suggested (Rousseau, 2001; Guest and Conway, 2002) that negative change in the employment relationship may adversely affect the state of the psychological contract.

Sparrow (1996) claims that the psychological contract underpins the work relationship and provides a basis for capturing complex organisational phenomena by acting in a similar manner to that of Herzberg's hygiene factors. Good psychological contracts may not always result in superior performance, or indeed in satisfied employees; but poor psychological contracts tend to act as demotivators, which can be reflected in lower levels of employee commitment, higher levels of absenteeism and turnover, and reduced performance. Herriott and Pemberton (1995: 58) suggest that the captains of industry have set in motion a revolution in the nature of the employment relationship, the like of which they never imagined. For they have shattered the old psychological contract and failed to negotiate a new one.

It has long been accepted that two forms of psychological contract, termed relational and transactional, operate in the employment relationship (Table 13.2). The former refers to 'a long term relationship based on trust and mutual respect. The employee offers loyalty, conformity to requirements, commitment to their employer's goals and

Table 13.2 **Relational and transactional contracts**

	Transactional	**Relational**
Primary focus	Concerned about economic factors	Concerned about people
Time frame	Closed ended and short term	Open ended and indefinite
Stability of the relationship	Static, rarely changing	Dynamic and frequently changing
Scope of relationship	Narrow	Broad and pervasive
Tangibility of terms	Well defined	Highly subjective

trust in their employer not to abuse their goodwill' (Arnold *et al.*, 1998: 388). In return, the organisation supposedly offered security of employment, promotion prospects, training and development and some flexibility about the demands made on the employees if they were in difficulty.

However, as a result of the changes outlined above, it is suggested that some employers have had difficulty in maintaining their side of the bargain. As a result, the old relational contracts have been violated and have been replaced by new, more transactional contracts, which are imposed rather than negotiated and based on a short-term economic exchange. As Arnold *et al.* suggest, 'the employee offers longer hours, broader skills, tolerance of change and ambiguity. . . .In return the employer offers (to some) high pay, rewards for high performance and simply a job' (1998: 388).

Stop and think

If the psychological contract is changing as current research appears to suggest, what are the organisational implications for managing the psychological contract in the future? The psychological contract needs careful management; although it is unwritten it remains a highly influential aspect of the employment relationship. In flatter, delayered organisations with limited opportunities for career progression and the absence of any guarantee of a job for life, attaining and maintaining employee commitment becomes increasingly more challenging for management. To manage the psychological contract in the future, organisations need to offer 'realistic job previews' to new entrants, recognise the impact of change on those remaining and 'invest in the survivors', change the management style to push towards cross-functional teamwork, design tasks and structures to allow employees to feel a sense of accomplishment and develop their skills to increase their own 'employability security', create a new kind of commitment through the creation of meaning and values between employees, not just from a top-down mission statement, be attentive to the need to balance work and other aspects of life and be continuous in communication with employees.

For further reading, see the work of Jean Hiltrop.

Guzzo and Noonan (1994) take the perspective that psychological contracts can have both transactional and relational elements. Employers may have to demonstrate to employees that they can keep to a sound and fair transactional deal before attempting to develop a relational contract based on trust and commitment. Furthermore, as Herriot *et al.* suggest: 'Organisations may be in danger of underestimating the fundamentally transactional nature of the employment relationship for many of their employees' (1997: 161). The essential point is to recognise that all psychological contracts are different. It is important for the organisation to appreciate the complexities of transactional and relational contracts and to recognise that psychological contracts will have elements of all dimensions and that contracts are individual, subjective and dynamic. The significance of the psychological contract in relation to performance management is that it highlights how easy it is for organisations to assume that employees seek primarily monetary rewards; this is not necessarily the case. The evidence suggests that effective performance management and reward structures in organisations must attend to the quality of the relationships employees experience while at work which are an integral aspect of the psychological contract. The message appears simple: improved performance is affected by more than money.

HRM and performance management

We can see that the key issue related to the determination of the wage/effort bargain is not simply a matter of setting a wage relative to the level of effort and letting things 'tick along'. From the dawn of the industrial era managers have sought to control the effort side of the agreement by utilising their power to determine the wage. Performance management (or more accurately forms of performance-related pay) has formed a key activity for managers and management in the quest to increase the benefits gained by the application of labour power. There have been various mechanisms applied in order to secure this advantage which were based on the 'current fad' or understanding of the labour process (for a discussion of the influence of the emergence of SHRM, see Schuler and Jackson, 1999). The choice of which management system to adopt has been driven by the answer proposed to the basic question 'what motivates workers to perform at higher levels?' and more often than not can be located within the various schools of thought outlined above. We can see the development of reward management along the lines suggested by Etzioni (1975) in terms of coercive (work harder or lose your job), remunerative (worker harder and receive more money) and normative (worker harder to achieve organisational goals). Current trends in the management of worker performance fall to be considered in the area of normative managerial practices, but are fraught with difficulty in an era where emotional labour and the knowledge worker hold such a central place in organisational success. These developments need to be considered alongside the evolution of an ambiguous employment relationship (the breakdown of the psychological contract) and the rise of insecurity within modern organisations (reflected in the growth of 'butterfly workers'). As Fisher notes, 'Insecurity is a common phenomenon in organisations' (1999: 167), be it the feelings of insecurity within line managers who have not previously been responsible for the range of issues they now enjoy or that of the HR manager attempting to demonstrate they have put in place all the necessary procedures required to measure performance and show their organisational worth in a modern competitive environment. HR managers, lost in a landscape where memory no longer serves the function of creating security (Schama, 1995), argue that they can apply the techniques presented within expectancy and/or goal-setting theory to the development of procedures which will secure competitive advantage for the organisation. Such procedures are borne within the all-encompassing 'HRM mantra' which declares, for self-assurance as much as public consumption, that the HR function is a strategic player in the organisation network bringing new understanding to the application of personnel practices and organisational changes.

We can suggest from Figure 13.2 that the HRM mantra, which can be considered as the 'self-reassuring' chant of HR managers, indicates the importance of HR procedures in the success of the organisation and note how a number of these link into our discussion of reward systems and performance management. The notions of 'productivity through our people', customer focus, strong(er) leadership, flatter structures and cohesive cultures all suggest a management framework which seeks to improve individual and organisational performance in ways that can be measured, a concentration on competence (inputs) alongside attention to attainment (outcomes).

These elements turn attention to the fact that in modern organisations it is the quality and behaviours of the employees that generate, as much as other inputs, competitive

---

Figure 13.2 The HRM mantra

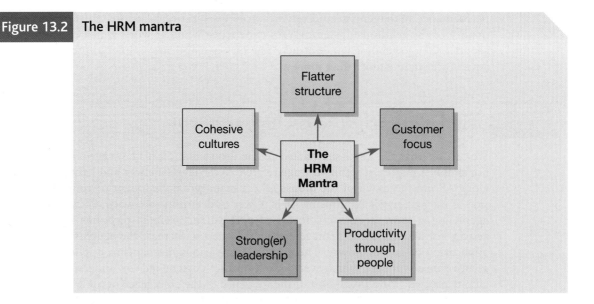

advantage. While much of the business strategy literature since the 1980s has concentrated on the 'setting and achievement' of organisational goals, what has often been lost is the role of human resources in the attainment of competitive advantage (a trend addressed by the application of the ideas associated with the resource-based view of the firm in recent years; see Chapter 2 on strategic HRM in this edition). However, a set of key questions still remain: 'what motivates workers to perform at higher levels?', 'how do we manage this motivation to the best effect?' and 'how do we measure resulting performance levels?'

Some attempt has been made to answer the first of these questions in the preceding sections using the theoretical constructs offered by Maslow, Herzberg, Taylor, Vroom and Locke. These, as our discussion of the psychological contract suggested, leave us with some confusion and inconsistencies which present management with as many questions as answers. The recent developments in this area involve two themes:

- the performance management process, and
- contingency pay.

As Lowry (2002) argues, the management of employee performance is usually seen as a necessary function of the managerial cadre. Centrally, it links a number of themes, including the extent to which the organisation has identified strategic goals reflecting the needs of the business and the degree to which these are communicated to and shared by each employee. We can further note that general definitions suggest that performance management involves a formal and systematic review of the progress towards achieving these goals. In response to the problems this creates, theorists have developed the idea of a performance management cycle within which the elements of the process can be identified, investigated and implemented by HR managers in the attempt to create organisational advantage. The cycle consists of five elements which provide a framework within which we can audit the delivery of strategic objectives with a view to developing continuous improvement. These elements are presented as a common link between organisational and individual performance which underlies the development of a committed, motivated, loyal workforce. In simple terms, it is suggested that the cycle indicates a system within which performance objectives are set, outcomes are then measured, results are fed back, rewards are linked to outcomes and changes are made before new objectives are set for which the outcomes can be measured. We now consider each of these elements individually.

■ Setting objectives

There is any amount of prescriptive advice which indicates that the objectives need to be achievable and linked to organisational objectives. Where the purpose of setting such objectives is to direct, monitor, motivate and audit individual performance they must fulfil both of these criteria, otherwise the process will result in the opposite effects being secured. The application of expectancy and goal-setting theories implies that this is best achieved where the individual has an important role in the determination of the objectives for the period concerned. As suggested in the discussion above, this will encourage the selection of appropriate goals which are specific, attainable and owned by the individual. The process, as a management tool, is established on the basis that organisational objectives can be broken down and translated into individual goals, the attainment of which can then be effectively measured.

In recent debates we find that organisations are said to make frequent use of the acronym SMART to assist in establishing effective objectives:

S – Specific or Stretching
M – Measurable
A – Agreed or Achievable
R – Realistic
T – Time bound

There are, however, difficulties in setting objectives for some jobs, e.g. doctors, lecturers and lower levels in the organisation hierarchy, as they may not have the opportunity to improve their performance or demonstrate merit, and may be unable to identify or relate to organisational goals.

■ Measuring the outcomes

Where the objectives relate to numbers, increased sales or an increased production of widgets, for example, the measurement appears unproblematic. However, not all of us are 'sales' representatives or 'widget'-makers; indeed, in the current economic climate such crude measures may be inappropriate and in some respects a return to 'old pay' notions of piecework. The growth of 'knowledge' workers has been accompanied by a change to competence-based approaches to measurement which centre on the three stages of competence development (know-what, know-why and know-how; see Raub, 2001). Therefore the outcomes can be measured in relation to the individual's success in deploying, integrating and improving their competence in the identified field of activity. This allows the organisation to refocus on the development of competitive advantage through the application of 'core knowledge', including tangible and intangible assets. It allows the application of 'just enough discipline' to establish a relevant 'core knowledge' base which is defined by strategic business drivers and monitored to maintain balance (see Klien, 1998).

The outcomes are often measured by the application of appraisal schemes. The purpose of performance planning, review and appraisal needs to be made clear if employees at all levels in the organisation are to play an active part in the process. It is possible that some employees and line managers may meet performance appraisal schemes with distrust, suspicion and fear, but an integrated and effective process can lead to increased organisational performance and employee motivation. It is important for employees to be genuinely involved in the design of an appraisal scheme, the evaluation of performance, and the objective-setting process. An appraisal scheme should be set up in an atmosphere of openness, with agreement between management, employees and employee representatives on the design of the scheme (Grayson, 1984: 177). Employees need to have a clear understanding of the purpose of the process (evaluative or developmental).

From this we can suggest that the key principles in the design of a performance appraisal scheme are that it should be congruent with the organisation's competitive strategy. It needs to provide direction for continuous improvement activities and identify both tendencies and progress in performance. Manifestly it needs to facilitate the understanding of cause and effect relationships regarding performance while remaining intelligible to those employees to which it applies. It ought to be dynamic, covering all of the company's business processes, and provide real-time information about all aspects of performance. A scheme that does not include employees' attitudes is unlikely to allow performance to be compared against benchmarks because it will not be composed of effective performance measures. Finally, we can note that a performance appraisal system should provide a perspective of past, present and future performance which is visible to both employees and management.

On the basis of seven case studies, IDS produced the following list of factors which were typically appraised:

- job knowledge and abilities (ability to perform all aspects of the job);
- adaptability/flexibility (ability to cope with change; multi-skilling for craft workers);
- productivity (individual work output);
- quality of work (attention to detail; consistent quality);
- attitude to work (commitment; motivation; enthusiasm);
- interaction with others (communication skills; teamworking ability);
- originality of thought/initiative (problem-solving);
- perception (ability to correctly interpret job requirements);
- judgement, use of resources (setting priorities; ability to plan and organise work);
- attendance and time keeping (number of and reasons for absence; punctuality);
- safety awareness (awareness of health and safety standards);
- need for supervision (leadership; ability to develop others);
- performance against targets (extent to which previously set targets have been achieved). (*Source*: IDS, 1992)

From this we can suggest that assessment of these factors is achieved by a mixture of 'subjective' and 'objective' measures, almost always carried out by the employee's immediate superior. The most commonly used measures will therefore relate to the individual's attitude to work as well as the quality of their work and their attendance and time keeping. These will be assessed alongside their knowledge of the job and productivity, while more subjective measures involving a judgement of their ability to interact with others will be included in a good scheme in order to develop an insight into the effectiveness of recruitment procedures. In terms of 'rating' or 'scoring' individual employees, a number of 'target areas' can be identified for assessment.

● Accountabilities

Accountabilities define the responsibilities of a certain job and the results that jobholders are expected to achieve. The employees' actual output in terms of measurable productivity, timeliness and quality may be directly assessed as part of the appraisal scheme. This presupposes the employees' job role is open to such quantitative assessment.

● Skills acquisition

Employees may be assessed on their acquisition of new skills required to further improve their performance in the job or the continued development of essential skills. Jones the Bootmaker, a footwear company in the Midlands, have recently developed a new performance appraisal scheme in which they specifically appraise managers on the job they are currently required to do rather than place undue emphasis on developing skills and competences for future positions. Andrew White, company representative, stated 'We found that the previous scheme was appraising managers on competences beyond their current job role, which in some cases led to demotivation' (White, November 2002).

● Self-assessment

This approach is mainly concerned with the identification of self-development needs by the actual employee. Margerison (1976) has suggested that self-assessment is the only way to give a complete picture of the performance of the employee and to avoid a 'criticise–defend' scenario. It does, however, require the employee to have a detailed and informed understanding of both the current and future needs of the job role and the organisational needs against which they can accurately assess their current performance and so their future development needs.

● Paired comparisons

This is a comparative method of performance assessment in which a superior assesses the performance of pairs of individuals, until each employee has been judged relative to each other employee, or until every possible combination of employees has been considered. A rating scale is then devised to show the number of times an individual employee was judged as 'better' (Roberts, 2001: 542).

● Ranking

This is another comparative measure of assessment in which employees are assessed against pre-set and documented measures of effectiveness and placed in a hierarchy from best to worst. At Cummins Engines the appraisal system is based on a 10:80:10 ranking scheme. Those employees ranked in the top 10 per cent are identified for promotion and special development. Those identified within the next 80 per cent are maintained within the organisation and the remaining 10 per cent are effectively 'managed out' of the organisation. In Cummins the appraisal scheme is very open and there are no 'secrets' over how it operates in practice!

● Rating scale

This is considered to be an 'absolute' method of performance assessment. The method, according to Roberts (2001: 542), lists a number of factors such as job-related qualities or behaviours or can include certain personality traits. Individual employees are then rated on the extent to which they possess these factors. The rating scale can be numerically, alphabetically or graphically represented on a continuum, i.e. from 'very high' to 'very low'. However, when scoring is involved it can get ugly. The attraction of rating systems – the school-report model that ranks you as a team player from one to five, or rates your customer focus from A to E – is that the feedback is easy to gather and produces lots of data that can be aggregated and turned into bar charts. In this respect the HR department is happy because they've made a 'fuzzy' process look scientific, and someone from client services is proud because they got a 4 on knowledge leadership and their colleague only got a 3. But a number may not offer much insight on how to improve. For that you need thoughtful, qualitative comments – harder to gather, but much more helpful.

Behaviourally anchored rating scale (BARS)

This is an attempt to assess actual performance and behaviour, so, for example, it is concerned not with whether an employee has 'initiative', but with specifically identifying what he or she actually does that demonstrates initiative – or the lack of it!
The development of a BARS approach typically involves the following stages:

- Meetings are held with superiors and/or outside consultants to identify several key aspects or categories of performance in particular jobs.
- The same or other sources of information are used to provide examples of good, average and poor performance for each category of performance in an individual's job.
- A number of such categories or anchors are generated (frequently 6–9 per job) and each is ascribed a value, for instance 1–7, or 'average', 'above average', etc. Essentially these define the 'most efficient' through to the 'least efficient' behaviour and performance for the job.
- Appraisers use this format to evaluate the expected behaviour of individual employees holding the jobs concerned.

The underlying job analysis is critical to the success of this approach and many proponents argue that the employee and their superiors should be actively involved in the process to ensure it is relatively realistic.

Development plan approach

In some organisations the link between personal development and the business strategy is weak but is crucial to effective performance management. Effective development plans consider the future skills, knowledge and experiences that will be required by the employee to enable them to do their current job effectively. The identification of needs should also be linked to what the employee may require in the future – needs identification must therefore be closely linked to organisational succession and business plans. The plan may be in the style of an essay or a controlled report which asks for responses to certain headings or sections.

360-degree appraisals

This approach to performance management has grown in popularity and when undertaken correctly is effective, reasonably inexpensive, widely applicable and clearly focused on individual performance.

The idea behind 360-degree feedback is that employees benefit from feedback gathered from a wide range of sources. Characteristically this includes peers, superiors, subordinates and customers; essentially it is designed to obtain comments from 'all directions', above, below and to the side of the employee concerned. It is intended to give a more complete and comprehensive picture of the individual's performance and contribution.

The process typically follows a procedure in which competences have been established and defined and employees are then requested to nominate up to six significant others who cover the range of suitable respondents. Those giving feedback are then asked to use a rating scale or comment on each of the dimensions. For example, Roberts (2001: 543) suggests managers might be assessed by their employees on 'softer' people issues such as communication and support, and their peers on issues such as teamwork. Indicators of both internal and external customer satisfaction may be used, and suppliers and subcontractors may also be asked to give feedback on the individual manager's performance and demonstration of competences.

Possible issues with performance appraisal

Whatever approach to performance appraisal is used, there will inevitably be issues and concerns. In essence, to assess an employee's performance necessarily involves some form of assessment against predetermined standards or behaviours. In both situations there will be an element of human judgement which, as we know, suffers from problems of reliability, validity and bias. Kinnie and Lowe (1990: 47) state that 'appraisers may find it difficult to identify and measure, the distinct contribution of each individual'; this can be because the appraiser doesn't really know the appraisee or because, as suggested by Howell and Cameron (1996: 28), employees are constantly moving from one project to another.

There may also be many external factors beyond the control of the individual employee which affect their performance, such as resources, processes, technology, corporate and HR strategy, working environment, external business context and management. Equally, the appraisal might be skewed because if there is a long time span between appraisals, managers may place greater importance on more recent performance, called the 'recency effect', thereby possibly ignoring incidents that had occurred earlier.

● Role of line manager

Line managers/supervisors may lack the required technical skills and people management skills to be able to conduct an effective appraisal. In addition, a lack of time and resources may hinder line managers in providing comprehensive and effective performance reviews and objective-setting. Managers may perceive the appraisal process as a bureaucratic nuisance and form-filling exercise.

● Demotivation consequences

An appraisal outcome that labels an employee as simply 'average', or determines that he or she is not a 'high flier', may lead to demotivation. To state the general principle: when one person begins to make a judgement on another, unless that judgement is favourable, reaction and resistance begin to set in (Margerison, 1976: 32).

● Interpretation 'spin'

Roberts' (2001: 545) suggestion of the 'cascading' approach, of progressive levels of management setting objectives for the level below and consequently being assessed themselves by the attainment of these objectives can result in the manipulation and 'fudging' of standards. Further, there is a tendency to retain 'understanding' in the language rather than 'cascade' this to lower levels. Managers attempt to maintain their 'hierarchical' authority by using the interpretation of the 'spin' to reinforce relationships of power within the organisation; by so doing they lessen the effectiveness of the communication mechanisms and therefore of the process.

● Conflicting roles

Newton and Findlay (2000: 129) make reference to the writings of McGregor who draws attention to the issues of the conflicting roles of the appraiser as both disciplinary 'judge' and helpful 'counsellor, suggesting the modern emphasis of appraisal is on the manager as a leader who strives to assist employees achieve both their own and the company's objectives – acting as a sort of 'mentor' or 'counsellor' concerned with the personal growth and development of the employee. At the same time the manager is charged with identifying (and hopefully agreeing) strict targets for achievement and performance. This can involve identifying areas where previous performance has been less than satisfactory – leaving the manager in the role of 'judge'. There are obvious tensions between the two roles.

Much of the literature suggests that this tension can, in part, be overcome by the employee taking an active role in the process. But that is assuming the employee wants to be involved and really wants to take responsibility for improving themselves by taking an 'active role' in the process – and they may not. For example, they may see the whole appraisal process as an attempt to control and manipulate them. Newton and Findlay (2000:130) suggest employees may view this as a way of removing the responsibility for their development from the organisation, and placing it on their shoulders. In an era in which the notion of 'employability security' as distinct from 'job security' characterises the employment relationship, it is interesting to consider where the responsibility for investing in development lies – with the organisation, or increasingly as seems likely, directly with the employee. The interesting thing is that even as the appraisal process continues to be utilised as part of a spreading audit culture, some companies are already looking to cast it aside – or if they keep appraisals, making them, as Freeserve does, a process whereby employees solicit feedback rather than having it thrust upon them. It will be interesting to monitor how far this marks a turning of the tide against performance management appraisals.

Current trends

The interest in appraisals and other PBR systems draws on the long-standing tradition to divide reward packages between base and contingent elements. The changes in the mechanisms used to identify and quantify these contingent elements currently focus on the notion of rewarding the person rather than the role and links into the notion of 'new pay' which increases the emphasis on the motivational qualities of PBR systems. By linking pay to achievement, whether such achievement relates to production targets, attainment of competencies or objectives set within an appraisal meeting, organisations are seeking to quantify and reward individual contribution to the attainment of business goals or strategic aims. Individuals, whether pay is determined by position on a spine determined by job evaluation or otherwise, may receive increments based on length of service alongside performance elements; these 'service awards' reward experience and loyalty. However, such awards can be withheld where performance fails to meet the desired targets and are useful once 'poor' performance is identified as signals to other workers. Armstrong (2002) lists 15 features of performance management which were identified as being used by organisations in the 1998 CIPD survey. The results suggest that the most common of these (identified by over 60 per cent of the respondents) were objective-setting and review, annual appraisal and personal development plans (2002; 387). At the bottom of the ladder, despite all the discussion in various HR texts, with under 15 per cent acknowledgement were the balanced scorecard (5 per cent) peer appraisal (9 per cent), 360-degree feedback (11 per cent) and rolling appraisals (12 per cent). The results showed that organisations viewed performance management as integral to the employment relationship, thus an important part of managerial activity despite (as noted by 60 per cent of the respondents) being bureaucratic and time-consuming (2002: 388). In contrasting the results of the 1998 survey to those of the 1991 survey, Armstrong suggests a move from performance management 'systems' to a more holistic performance management 'process'. This process, it is suggested, focuses on inputs/outputs, development, flexibility and a shift of ownership towards the users and away from the HR function. Interestingly, taking the results into account, Armstrong suggests that the process also involves an increase in the application of 360-degree feedback (2002: 389).

The development of a process within which performance is related to both input and output is in part the result of the application of an objective-based approach located in the work of Kaplan and Norton (1992). The so-called balanced scorecard, although acknowledged as a feature by only 5 per cent of the respondents in the CIPD survey, underlies much of the discussion relating to the development of a strategic role for the HR function. In this approach there are four stages which start with a vision of the future, whether in the form of a vision statement *per se* or in terms of an answer to the question 'where do we want to be in x years?' From this we can identify how the organisation will be different if the targets are achieved in terms of four key areas (Financial, Customer, Internal and Innovation/Learning) which will determine the success of the organisation in a competitive environment. Reward strategies will impact on all of these areas to a greater or lesser extent by identifying as performance targets those elements which are critical to the successful acquisition of the vision for the future. The scorecard method can be used to identify specific instruments/measurements which can be used to set interim targets and therefore individual performance objectives. These may be competencies (can do), knowledge indicators (know-what) and/or commitment levels (know-why); critical elements in the attainment of these objectives are a strong psychological contract based on open communication, active participation and high-trust employment relationships. Recent research (The Work Foundation, 2003) indicates that where employers are seeking to promote this type of performance management they will allow their employees to identify their own training needs (86 per cent), run regular team briefings (75 per cent), allow and encourage the development of transferable skills (73 per cent), tie reward to service by offering long-service awards (67 per cent) and operate a system of in-house brainstorming sessions or focus groups (66 per cent). The report suggests that employers are acknowledging that performance management ties broader HR policies into the attainment of the strategic goals of the organisation and that this objective can be achieved by the development of a strong psychological contract. Despite these moves, we can suggest that poor levels of goal attainment within organisations can be the fault of bad management of individual employee performance. A recent study by the consultants Mercer (2003) of 3500 employees concluded that a mere 20 per cent believe that their good performance will be rewarded while some 33 per cent feel their organisation operates in such a way that there is an inadequate link between pay and performance. From these results Gilbert notes that:

> Linking pay to performance requires a robust performance appraisal process and the active support of line managers ... our results indicate that many managers lack either the training or the support to conduct the process.   (Gilbert, P. on mercerhr.com, 2003)

The Mercer survey also noted that while firms may be good at appraising individuals, many are weak on providing effective feedback and offer this as a cause for their finding that performance management systems are rarely effective. We have suggested that in part their effectiveness rests on two foundation stones, high levels of motivation and a strong psychological contract; however, research by the CIPD (2003) notes that while most workers are 'happy in their work', fewer than 30 per cent trust their senior managers to look after their interests, indicating a psychological contract which is far from 'strong'. In order to address these problems and develop high-commitment management (HCM) policies, employers are introducing greater flexibility in terms of the employment relationship. These moves include the introduction of flexible benefits, competency-based pay, merit pay and broadbanding (IRS, 2002). The survey upon which these conclusions are based indicated that more than 60 per cent of the respondents used elements of merit-based pay, while over half operated market-related pay systems, suggesting some confusion and cross-over between internal (individual performance based) and external (market equity based) rationale for the development and implementation of reward strategies. This confusion brings into sharp focus the role of HR as a function in the development and implementation of strategic objectives. HR can measure the contribution it makes and/or impact it has against any number of measures; however, a recent IRS survey found that over half of their sample used business objectives or performance indicators, suggesting a continued link to performance management as a key role for HR practitioners (IRS, 2003). The same survey noted that 64 per cent stated that the HR department maintained sole responsibility for pay determination, with only 4 per cent suggesting this was the sole prerogative of line managers.

> ### Stop and think
>
> The report also notes that the typical week for an HR manager entails one day on strategy, two days on supporting line managers and two days on catching up on paperwork. Linked to the above relating to reward management, do you think the findings of the IRS survey indicate that in the area of reward management HRM is still a case of 'systems, figures and procedures'?
>
> Taking the above results into account, how do you think organisations can convince their staff that performance will be rewarded?
>
> Devise a mechanism by which an organisation you know could effectively get the message that 'performance equals higher rewards' across to their employees. What behaviours would they seek to encourage?

Performance management as a control mechanism

We started by noting that reward management systems can be seen as managerial attempts to gain control over the 'effort' side of the wage/effort bargain which mirrors their unilateral control of the wage side. A fundamental element of performance management is the development of control in relation to employee behaviours, motivation and loyalty. In modern parlance, performance management is a mechanism to control values rather than simply actions. With all the monitoring, discussion, measurement, evaluation and goal-setting, some performance management techniques give the impression that they are effective in controlling actions but often miss the target of securing control over effort levels because they do not develop powerful value systems. It is possible for these systems to have some effect on employee behaviours, to bring them into accord with organisation targets, while never really addressing the problem of underlying values. If, as Grint indicates, the traditional view is that 'good management is really concerned with good boundary management' (1997: 10), then performance management may offer a good traditional style in that it manages the boundary between acceptable and unacceptable performance; whether it moves beyond this to offer higher levels of commitment is debatable – we have suggested above that the process only secures that which it measures. There are more serious questions to be answered with regard to those items it cannot or does not attempt to measure. Without the link to the development and implementation of a system of organisational values it is arguable that performance management, whether seen as a process or a system, lacks the attainment of a self-generated goal. Linking performance, by the use of cafeteria reward systems, to individual choice may actually achieve the opposite by reducing the opportunity to link rewards to organisational values. However, by linking the attainment of performance levels which are sufficient to secure the desired reward the organisation could communicate to the employees that the organisation is changing by moving the goalposts to suit the new desirable set of values. In simple terms, we are suggesting that in order to achieve control over the effort side of the bargain, organisations need to acknowledge and apply management systems to the unarticulated links between

Values – Behaviours – Performance – Growth.

The argument here is that growth and performance are inextricably linked to behaviours which are founded upon personal and organisational values. Performance management is effective, therefore, only to the extent to which it can shape these values, irrespective of the measure to which it can change behaviours, as values are said to set the parameters within which people make decisions. Organisations must define, cascade and supervise their own values as they cannot be effectively imposed or imported; no amount of wall-mounted plaques, posters, credit-card-sized personal reminders or mugs can impose a set of values. Values must be lived and the performance management process should be designed to allow organisations to control the creation of the organisational language upon which values are based if it is to deliver control to the extent required within modern organisations.

 ## Conclusion

In this chapter we have discussed the notion of reward as an integral part of the managerial function which results from the definition of the employment relationship as a wage/effort bargain; as such, it was seen to operate in a contested relationship within which each part sought to determine the level of effort which constituted a 'fair day's work'. We argued that management have adopted various forms of reward system in order to communicate to the employees the required effort levels and to evaluate the levels of effort exerted. These have often been complex, confusing and ultimately failed to deliver the ultimate goal because they often restrict innovation and reward past achievements. It ought to be obvious that motivation occupies a central place in the rationale for the choices made by managers and hence attempts to understand the effectiveness of any particular reward system. In the application of this understanding of motivation, organisational policies have swayed between 'paying for numbers' and 'paying for skills', while always proving ineffective in the longer term because, we can suggest, they failed to convince people to take work seriously.

The issues surrounding the seriousness of work have recently been addressed by the development of the debates linked to the creation and maintenance of a contract in the mind. The psychological contract has been a rich source of ideas for the development of modern reward processes in that it goes beyond mere behaviours to consider the creation of values and understanding. Despite this attention, through which organisations have elaborated the existence of mutual obligations and duties, the psychological contract is seen to be a difficult tool to apply in the development of reward systems. Irrespective of these reservations, organisations have developed a performance management process which relies on the interaction between behaviours and values. These have included cafeteria pay systems, merit-based pay, team-based pay, management by objectives, 360-degree and other appraisal systems, designed to wrestle control of the effort side and return the levels of productivity purchased in the labour market.

HR practitioners have applied themselves to the development of systems of reward which are closely integrated with other organisational aims and reflect the strategic role played by reward in the achievement of these objectives. We argued that recent surveys suggest that all is not as it might appear from a glance at the literature. The employment relationship, and specifically the wage/effort or reward element, is still disputed territory within which neither side secures all their objectives. The Chartered Institute of Personnel and Development (CIPD) has a very useful website to refer to (www.cipd.co.uk).

Summary

● Reward strategies need to be viewed in the light of the employment relationship as an economic exchange. Employers need to exercise control over both sides of the wage/effort bargain to the greatest possible extent and in this light reward management attempts to enlarge the area of managerial control.

● These strategies have developed over the years since the industrial revolution through various phases and periods in response to the changing use and nature of technology. The basic nature of such schemes, however, continues to be that of payment by or for performance, whether such performance be pieces made, hours worked, merit achieved or compliance with organisational norms.

● Reward schemes attempt to generate a motivated workforce which is committed and loyal to the organisation.

● Motivation theory has evolved from a simple assumption based on notions of a rational economic perspective of employees – i.e. being motivated primarily by money – towards a more sophisticated human relations perspective which takes cognisance of the numerous and divergent 'needs' employees have. This more complex, though realistic assessment of what motivates employees requires managers to develop strategies which enable employees to realise an ever-greater sense of personal achievement and satisfaction in exchange for their contribution to the organisation.

● The psychological contract, while often unwritten, seen in terms of transactional and relational elements, is increasingly being acknowledged as a significant aspect of the employment relationship. In the context of delayering, downsizing, limited career progression, the inability to offer a job for life, organisations need to change work patterns to ensure a sense of personal achievement, enhance employability security and engender relationship values in an effort to maintain a healthy psychological contract which will stimulate commitment and loyalty.

● Current debates surround the difficulties inherent in the motivation and management of knowledge workers, the control of emotional labour and the desire to secure additional profits via the application of reward strategies.

● The development of 'new pay' highlights an increased interest in the rules that are applied to the receipt of 'contingent' elements within reward packages.

Questions

1 Does the concept of employment relationships as economic exchange significantly add to our understanding of reward strategies?

2 To what extent is it possible for managers to convince workers 'to take work seriously when they know that it is a joke' (Anthony, 1977: 5) through the application of reward strategies?

3 How would you depict the evaluation of motivation theory?

4 Critically assess the extent to which money is the primary motivator for all employees.

5 In what way does the psychological contract influence the employment relationship?

Exercises

1 Prepare a short report to the HR director in which you make three recommendations for improving performance using modern reward management techniques.

2 Write a short article for an in-house magazine which indicates the effects of poor performance on the attainment of organisational goals and how the use of a performance management system benefits all employees.

3 Prepare a short report to the HR director in which you make three recommendations for improving the morale among the workforce based on sound principles of motivational theory.

4 Debate with colleagues the proposition that 'the psychological contract is a confused and irrelevant concept in the context of the employment relationship'.

Case study

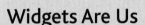

Widgets Are Us

Widgets Are Us is part of a major multinational company which located at a site in the UK in 1990. They manufacture widgets for the electronics industry which are then branded by their various customers. The company is non-union and in order to retain this status operates a 'workers' forum' for consultations; they do not negotiate in relation to reward packages or levels. The main site has three separate units each producing different sizes of widget for various markets.

Units One and Two consist of four production lines each of which runs a continuous assembly process operating seven days a week and 24 hours a day. The bulk of the workforce is female, part-time and/or agency temporary workers, the latter group comprising some 40 per cent of the staff in each Unit. Each line is divided into six 'areas' within which five workers comprise a 'team' with one designated a 'team leader'. They are paid a base rate with additions for each piece produced by the line during each shift; team leaders are paid at a rate which is 5 per cent above the rest of the team to reflect their responsibility for the team. The base rate is in line with the National Minimum Wage and the line is paid an additional 4p for each item passed by quality control as satisfactory. The quality control operatives are placed mid-way along the line to verify quality prior to the widgets being vacuum packed for dispatch and are paid on a monthly basis at a

higher base rate with no incentive element. As staff members they enjoy a choice of additional benefits drawn from the company 'cafeteria' reward system which is not available to other line workers. The widgets are mass produced to agreed specifications for each customer and the line may make widgets with slightly different specifications during each shift (on occasions as many as three different specifications during any one shift). Each line has a line manager who has the responsibility of ensuring that the materials are available for each specification as and when necessary and there are two assistant production managers responsible for two lines each who direct the flow of work to ensure orders are met by priority rather than on a 'first come first served' basis. The team leaders are responsible for ensuring that their teams are up to numbers and report any deficiencies to the line manager. It is the line manager's role to secure authority from the assistant production manager to approach the 'in-house' agency in order to cover any shortfall in the required number of workers.

Each Unit has a goods in/out department which is staffed by a regular crew of 15 workers. These workers are predominately male, semi-skilled, higher earners who are employed on the same basis as the quality control workers. Their main role is to offload materials and transport them to the lines, as and when requested, to collect

▶

completed work and load it for distribution. The Units run a JIT system under which there is little or no storage of materials beyond a single day's requirements and vehicles are loaded during the shift for dispatch that evening; all distribution takes place on an overnight basis. The minimum number of drivers are directly employed, with any shortfall covered by contracts with local distribution organisations.

Each Unit therefore has a total three shift workforce of 200 production and distribution workers split into three shifts over a seven-day rota. No shift allowances are paid and overtime payments are not attracted for any hours below 40 whichever day they are worked; where over 40 hours are worked the overtime rate is time and a half whatever day worked. Production workers, excluding team leaders, are allowed 20 days' holiday a year, attract only statutory sick pay and are excluded from the company staff benefits. Temporary workers are treated as employees of the agency and their payment is left to the agency, which also deducts NI contributions and tax.

The third Unit is somewhat more specialised and produces bespoke widgets on a one-off basis primarily for export. It also includes an R&D section dedicated to advances in both widgets and their production. The Unit employs 20 semi-skilled production workers on the standard staff contracts and 10 specialist engineers paid an annual salary in line with local terms and conditions, which, as the area is depressed, are significantly below national averages.

Staff jobs are rewarded in a different manner in that they receive an annual salary with the additional option of picking benefits from the 'cafeteria' package based on the outcome of their appraisal. Only 'staff' are appraised and the merit element ranges between 1 and 5 per cent of their annual salary; they cannot take this value in cash and must select from the benefits cafeteria. These rules apply to team leaders, quality control operatives, warehouse operatives, line managers, assistant production managers, secretarial and administrative staff and office managers. Higher grades, including the engineers, negotiate their own packages on appointment and are then subject to the appraisal rules.

The organisation has a number of problems which the HR department need to address:

1 Units One and Two have high (up to 10 per cent per day) absence rates amongst the production workers.
2 They have a more serious problem with the weekends when the absence rate can be as high as 20 per cent.
3 Each has a turnover rate above the national average for the industry and they find temporary workers difficult to keep.
4 Unit Three has a higher than average turnover rate amongst the engineers.
5 Staff posts are fairly stable across the units but they find quality control workers are difficult to appoint from existing 'in-house' staff, possibly due to the lack of an incentive scheme which can result in their earnings being lower than those of the line operatives.

Questions

1 As an HR manager, how could you change the reward system to address each of these problems?

2 What measures would you take to strengthen the psychological contract?

References and further reading

Adams, J.S. (1963) 'Toward an understanding of inequality', *Journal of Abnormal and Social Psychology*, Vol. 67, pp. 422–436.

Adams, J. (1965) 'Inequity in social exchange', in Berkowitz, L. (ed.) *Advances in Experimental Social Psychology*, Vol. 2. New York: Academic Press.

Adams, R.J. (1986) 'Two policy approaches to labour-management decision making at the level of the enterprise', in Craig Riddel, W.W. (ed) *Labour–Management Cooperation in Canada*. Toronto: University of Toronto Press.

Anthony, P.D. (1977) *The Ideology of Work*. London: Tavistock Publications.

Armstrong, M. (1996) 'How group efforts can pay dividends', *People Management*, 25 January, pp. 22–27.

Armstrong, M. (2002) *Employee Reward*. London: CIPD.

Arnold, J., Cooper, C. and Robertson, I. (1998) *Work Psychology: Understanding Human Behaviour in the Workplace*, 3rd edn. Harlow: Financial Times.

Austin, J. and Bobko, P. (1985) 'Goal setting theory', *Journal of Occupational Psychology*, Vol. 58, pp. 289–308.

Bean, R. (1994) *Comparative Industrial Relations*. London: Routledge

Beer, M., Walton, R.E. and Spector, B.A. (1984) *Managing Human Assets*. New York: Free Press.

Blau, G. (1994) 'Testing the effect of level and importance of pay referents on pay level satisfaction', *Human Relations*, Vol. 47, No. 10, pp. 1251–1268.

Blauner, R. (1964) *Alienation and Freedom: The Factory Worker and His Industry*. Chicago, Ill.: Chicago Press.

Braverman, H. (1974) *Labour and Monopoly Capital: The Degradation of Work in the Twentieth Century*. London: Monthly Review Press.

Burawoy, M. (1985) *The Politics of Production*. London: Verso.

Callaghan, G. and Thompson, P. (2001) 'Edwards revisited: technical control and call centres', *Economic and Industrial Democracy*, Vol. 22, No. 1, pp. 13–37.

CIPD (2003) *Pressure of Work and the Psychological Contract*. London: CIPD.

Conboy, B. (1976) *Pay at Work*. London: Arrow Books.

Cornelius, N. (2001) *Human Resource Management*, 2nd edn. London: Thomson Learning.

Dulebohn, J.H. and Martocchio, J.J. (1998) 'Employee perceptions of the fairness of work group incentive pay plans', *Journal of Management*, Vol. 24, No. 4 pp. 469–488.

Earley, P., Connolly, T. and Ekergren, G. (1989) 'Goals, strategy development and task performance', *Journal of Applied Psychology*, Vol. 74, pp. 24–33.

Etzioni, A. (1975) *A Comparative Analysis of Complex Organisations*. New York: Free Press.

Fisher, C. (1999) 'Performance management and performing management', in Leopold, J. *et al.* (eds) *Strategic Human Resourcing*. Harlow: FT/Pitman.

Folger, R., Konovsky, M.A. and Cropanzano, R. (1992) 'A due process metaphor for performance appraisal', in Straw, B.M. and Cummings, L.L. (eds) *Research on Organizational Behaviour*, Vol. 13, pp. 129–177.

Freeman, R. (2001) 'Upping the stakes', *People Management*, Vol. 7, No. 3, pp. 25–29.

Freeman, R.B. and Rogers, J. (1999) *What Workers Want*. Cornell, NY: Russell Sage Foundation.

Gooch, L. and Cornelius, N. (2001) 'Perfomance management: strategy, systems and rewards', in Cornelius, N. (ed.) *Human Resource Managment*. London: Thomson Learning.

Gospel, H. (1992) *Markets, Firms, and the Management of Labour in Modern Britain*. Cambridge: Cambridge University Press.

Grayson, D. (1984) 'Shape of payment systems to come', *Employment Gazette*, April, pp. 175–181.

Greenberg, J. (1987) 'A taxonomy of organizational justice theories', *Academy of Management Review*, Vol. 3, No. 3, pp. 61–77.

Grint, K. (1997) *Fuzzy Management: Contemporary Ideas and Practices at Work*. Oxford: Oxford University Press.

Guest, D. (1998a) 'Is the psychological contract worth taking seriously?', *Journal of Organizational Behaviour*, Vol. 19, pp. 649–664.

Guest, D. (1998b) 'On meaning, metaphor and the psychological contract: a response to Rousseau', *Journal of Organizational Behaviour*, Vol. 19, pp. 673–677.

Guest, D. and Conway, N. (2002) 'Communicating the psychological contract: an employer perspective', *Human Resource Management Journal*, Vol. 12 pp. 22–38.

Guzzo, R. and Noonan K.A. (1994) 'Human resources practices as communications and the psychological contract', *Human Resource Management*, Vol. 33, No. 3, pp. 447–462.

Hackman, J. and Lawler, E. (1971) 'Employee reactions to job characteristics', *Journal of Applied Psychology Monograph*, Vol. 55, pp. 259–286.

Hackman, J. and Oldman, G. (1980) *Work Redesign*. Reading, Mass: Addison-Wesley.

Hastings, S. and Dixon, L. (1995) *Competency: An Introduction*. Oxford: Trade Union Research Unit.

Herriot, P., Manning, W. and Kidd, J. (1997) 'The content of the psychological contract', *British Journal of Management*, Vol. 8, No. 2, pp. 151–162.

Herriot, P. and Pemberton, C. (1995) *New Deals*. Chichester: John Willey.

Herzberg, F. (1966) *Work and the Nature of Man*. Cleveland, Ohio: World Publishing.

Hill, S. (1981) *Competition and Control at Work*. London: Heinemann.

Howell, K. and Cameron, E. (1996) 'The benefits of an outsider's opinion', *People Management*, Vol, 8. August, pp. 28–30.

Huczynski, A. and Buchanan, D. (2001) *Organisational Behaviour: An Introductory Text*, 4th edn. Harlow: Prentice Hall.

IDS (1992) 'PRP grows as tax relief doubles', *IDS Study 520*, December.

IRS (2002) *IRS HR Essentials: Employment Facts, Research and Analysis*. Issue 02, December.

IRS (2003) *Employment Review 773*, May.

Kaplan, R.S and Norton, D.P. (1992) 'The balanced scorecard: measures that drive performance', *Harvard Business Review*, January–February, pp. 71–79.

Kellaway, L.G. (1993) 'Nice little earner (profit-related pay), *Financial Times* 23 April 14.

Kinnie, N. and Lowe, D. (1990) 'Performance related pay on the shopfloor', *People Management*, November, pp. 45–49.

Klien, D.A. (1998) *The Strategic Management of Intellectual Capital*. Woburn: Butterworth-Heinemann.

Lawler, E.E. (1990) *Strategic Pay*. San Francisco, Calif.: Jossey Bass.

Lee, C., Law, K.S. and Bobko, P. (1999) 'The importance of justice perceptions on pay effectiveness, *Journal of Management*, Vol. 25, No. 6, pp. 851–873.

Leventhal, G.S. (1976) 'Fairness in social relationships', in Thibaut, J. *et al. Contemporary Topics in Social Psychology*. Morristown, NJ: General Learning Press.

Lind, E.A. and Tyler, T. (1988) *The Social Psychology of Procedural Justice*. New York: Plenum.

Littler, C. (1982) *The Development of the Labour Process in Capitalist Societies*. London: Heinemann.

Littler, C. (ed.) (1985) *The Experience of Work*. Aldershot: Gower.

Locke, E. and Latham, G. (1984) *Goal Setting*. Englewood Cliffs, NJ: Prentice Hall.

Locke, E., Shaw, K., Saari, L. and Latham, G. (1981) 'Goal setting and task performance 1969–1980', *Psychological Bulletin*, Vol. 90, pp. 125–152.

Lowry, D. (2002) 'Performance management', in Leopold, J. (ed.) *Human Resources in Organisations*. Harlow: FT/Prentice Hall.

Makin, J., Cooper, C. and Cox, J. (1996) *Organizations and the Psychological Contract*. Oxford: Blackwell.

Margerison, C. (1976) 'A constructive approach to appraisal', *Personnel Management*, July pp. 30–33.

McFarlin, D.B. and Sweeny, P.D. (1992) 'The psychological contract, organisational commitment and job satisfaction of temporary staff', *Leadership and Organisational Development Journal*, Vol. 21, No. 2, pp. 84–91.

McGregor, D. (1957) 'An uneasy look at performance', *Harvard Business Review*, Vol. 35, pp. 89–94.

Mercer Consultants (2003) 'Mind the productivity gap', in *IRS HR Essentials*, May.

Millward, N., Bryson, A. and Forth, J. (2000) *All Change at Work*. London: Routledge.

Mitrani, A., Dalziel, M. and Fitt, D. (1993) *Competency Based Human Resource Management*. London: Kogan Page.

Newton, T. and Findlay, P. (2000) 'Playing God? The performance appraisal', Chapter 8 in Mabey, C., Salaman, G. and Storey, J. (eds) *Strategic Human Resource Management: A Reader*. London: Sage in association with The Open University.

O'Doherty, D. (2001) 'Job design: signs, symbols and re-signations', in Beardwell, I. and Holden, L. (eds) *Human Resource Management*, 3rd edn. Harlow: FT/Prentice Hall.

Pritchard, D. and Murlis, H. (1992) *Jobs, Roles and People*. London: Nicholas Brealey.

Raub, S.P. (2001) 'Towards a knowledge-based framework of competence development', in Sanchez, R. *Knowledge Management and Organizational Competence*. Oxford: OUP.

Ritzer, G. (1997) *The McDonaldization Thesis*. London: Sage.

Ritzer, G. (2000) *The McDonaldization of Society*. London: Sage.

Roberts, I. (2001) 'Reward and performance management', in Beardwell I. and Holden, L. (eds) *Human Resource Management*, 3rd edn. Harlow: FT/Prentice Hall.

Rollinson, D. (2002) *Organisational Behaviour and Analysis: An Integrated Approach*, 2nd ed. Harlow: Financial Times Prentice Hall.

Rosenfield, R. and Wilson, D. (1999) *Managing Organizational Behaviour: Text, Readings and Cases*, 2nd edn. London: McGraw-Hill.

Rousseau, D. (1995) *Psychological Contracts in Organizations*. Thousand Oaks, Calif.: Sage.

Rousseau, D. (1998) 'The problem of the psychological contract', *Journal of Organisational Behaviour*, Vol. 19, pp. 665–671.

Rousseau, D. (2001) 'Schema, promise and mutuality: the building blocks of the psychological contract', *Journal of Occupational and Organisational Psychology*, Vol. 74, pp. 511–541.

Schama, S. (1995) *Landscape and Memory*. London: HarperCollins.

Schuler, R.S. and Jackson, S.E. (1999) *Strategic Human Resource Management*. Oxford: Blackwell.

Schuster, J.R. and Zingheim, P. (1992) *The New Pay*. New York: Lexington Books.

Shamir, B. (1991) 'Meaning, self and motivation in organizations', *Organizational Studies*, Vol. 12, No. 3, pp. 405–424.

Sparrow, P. (1996) 'Transitions in the psychological contract', *Human Resource Management Journal*, Vol. 6, No. 4, pp. 75–92.

Storey, J. (1992) *Developments in the Management of Human Resources*. Oxford: Blackwell.

Taylor, F.W. (1964) *Scientific Management*. New York: Harper & Row.

Taylor, P. and Bain, P. (1999) 'An assembly line in the head', *Industrial Relations Journal*, Vol. 30, No. 2, pp. 101–117.

Taylor, P. and Bain, P. (2001) 'Trade unions, workers' rights and the frontier of control in UK call centres', *Economic and Industrial Democracy*, Vol. 22, No. 1, pp. 39–66.

The Work Foundation (2003) 'Unwritten rules', in *IRS HR Essentials*. Issue 07, May.

Thompson, P. (1983) *The Nature of Work*. London: Macmillan.

Vroom, V.H. (1964) *Work and Motivation*. New York: John Wiley.

White, A. (2002) Interview with author at Jones the Bootmaker Ltd.

White, G. and Drucker, J. (2000) *Reward Management: A Critical Text*. London: Routledge.

Wilson, F. (1999) *Organisational Behaviour: A Critical Introduction*. Oxford: Oxford University Press.

Wood, A.W. (2000) 'Alienation', in *Concise Routledge Encyclopedia of Philosophy*. London: Routledge.

Wood, S. (ed.) (1982) *The Degradation of Work?* London: Hutchinson.

Wood, S. (1996) 'High commitment management and payment systems', *Journal of Management Studies*, Vol. 3, No. 1, pp. 53–77.

For multiple choice questions, exercises and annotated weblinks specific to this chapter visit this book's website at www.booksites.net/beardwell

CHAPTER 14

Employee involvement and empowerment

Len Holden

OBJECTIVES

▶ To examine the relationship of employee involvement and empowerment.

▶ To examine the relationship of employee involvement and human resource management.

▶ To explore the relationship between employee involvement and issues of control.

▶ To provide a definition of employee involvement and examine its recent historical development, including cycles and waves and other discernible patterns.

▶ To examine the various types of employee involvement schemes practised in organisations.

▶ To critically examine the concept and practice of empowerment.

▶ To examine recent employee involvement trends involving total quality management (TQM) and business process re-engineering (BPR).

▶ To investigate employee involvement practices in Sweden, Germany, Japan and other countries and make a comparative evaluation of them.

▶ To examine recent developments in the European works council issue.

Introduction

In recent years there has been an enormous growth in the popularity of various employee involvement (EI) schemes under the umbrella of *empowerment*. In the light of these developments this chapter could equally have been called 'Empowerment' but, like TQM and quality circles before it, there is no way of telling whether this is a stepping stone on the way to another EI fad or a permanent fixture as a generic term that will supersede EI, just as EI superseded the term 'participation', and 'participation' superseded the term 'industrial democracy'. A starting point in answering this will be to differentiate the terms.

Employee involvement or empowerment?

Employee involvement is a term that has a history, and as Foy (1994: xvii) points out, '*empowering* people is as important today as *involving* them in the 1980s and getting them to *participate* in the 1970s'. But as Lashley (1997) comments:

> Such statements reveal little of the environmental, economic and industrial circumstances which have led to differences in focus and terminology. Nor do they consider the continuity of concerns which they reveal about employing organisations. (p. 10)

It is important to consider not only the economic and industrial context, but also the social and political context and, as Foy suggests, the historical context. In differentiating EI from empowerment it is clear that EI initiatives are support mechanisms for other managerial strategies such as TQM, business process re-engineering, high-performance work systems and the learning organisation. Empowerment is an initiative in its own right, which can be all-pervasive in organisational terms. In addition, both EI and empowerment can be seen to be managerially inspired, with circumscribed powers given to employees. They have also been strongly associated with the introduction of HRM strategies. Participation and, to a greater degree, industrial democracy allow greater autonomy to employees and their representatives, such as trade unions, who decide their own policies in reaction to organisational changes and managerial policy. A generic term is required for all forms of participation and most contemporary writers use the term *employee involvement* (EI). To differentiate the generic term EI from employee involvement associated with HRM schemes, the latter will be labelled *HRM EI* in this chapter.

Human resource management and employee involvement

As we have already noted, employee involvement is not a new concept. It has a rich and varied history, but in recent years many managerial initiatives have sprung up in its name. The best known of these have been quality circles, team-briefing, teamworking and empowerment, which are often connected with organisational culture change schemes such as total quality management, customer service initiatives, business process re-engineering, and the learning organisation. This is the type of employee involvement that we have called HRM EI. It is likely to be part of an overall culture change, which may involve delayering, the creation of flatter organisational structures, and improvements in communication. Nevertheless, the language surrounding these initiatives has generated debates that are central to HRM. To involve employees is to gain their commitment to the organisational goals, and this has often been couched in terms of empowering employees to take responsibility for their roles and function within the organisation.

This resonant rhetoric has been used freely within the more popular managerial literature, often without thought or knowledge of how it translates into day-to-day situations, but in recent years studies have begun to examine these issues more closely.

This chapter will attempt to answer some of these questions. The first part deals with the concept of employee involvement, and the second part examines more closely the concept of empowerment.

HRM and employee involvement

HRM EI began to flourish in the 1980s in the guise of managerial policy initiatives inspired by the new 'excellence' movement and the rise of human resource management. Management gurus such as Tom Peters and Rosabeth Moss Kanter began to preach that people are the most valuable resource of an organisation, and that training and developing them, adequately rewarding their performance and involving them in organisational policy-making, particularly at customer interface level, could only enhance employee motivation and thus performance. In this context there was a need for management to direct employees' efforts 'in pursuit of organisational goals to ensure that tasks are performed in cost-effective and market effective ways' (Hyman and Mason, 1995: 52). Successful companies carrying out such policies were lauded as exemplars of the new managerial approach (Peters and Waterman, 1982; Kanter, 1983).

Much of this rediscovery of the intrinsic worth of the employee was driven by the relative decline in US economic performance, particularly compared with Japan. A considerable literature was generated analysing the key to Japanese success, and one oft-cited element was the involvement of employees in work groups such as quality circles (Lawler, 1986).

Employee involvement was also expounded as a key instrument in the creation of HRM strategies, and the influential Harvard Business School HRM programme proposed by Beer *et al.* (1984) put 'employee influence' firmly in the centre of this approach. The Harvard HRM programme casts employees as one of the main 'stakeholders' in the organisation, and therefore 'it is critical that managers design and administer various mechanisms for employee influence' (Beer *et al.*, 1984: 11). They continue: 'Not only will their [the employees'] interests be heard, but there will be mechanisms to help shape their company's HRM policies' (p. 41).

These questions raise further concerns about the inexactitude of the language of HRM EI. Terms such as 'influence', 'involvement', 'empowerment' and 'commitment' are blithely used by writers on HRM, without any attempt at definition or even clarification. Of the Harvard Business School academics, Walton has had the most to say on the subject. In his view, employee influence is most effective when employees have commitment to the organisation, and this can only be achieved if there is congruence between the HRM and general management policies of the organisation. Walton (1984a) calls this a 'high commitment' work system, and he proposes that 'high commitment is the essential ingredient in the future pattern of HRM' (p. 4). Walton (1984b) sees the HRM conception replacing previous systems 'because the common denomination among systems being replaced is the emphasis on imposing control' (p. 36). In other words, there is a move from 'control to commitment' (Walton, 1985: 36).

Stop and think	What problems face employees in attempting to induce commitment in their employees? Read on for some critical analysis of this concept.

These arguments contain a number of *non sequiturs*. There is no guarantee that mutuality will 'elicit employee commitment', or that it will lead to increased economic effectiveness and human development, although this may be more likely to happen in organisations with positive HRM policies than in those that have negative employee relation policies. In essence, what is happening here is what Keenoy calls a reconstruction of the employment relationship through rhetoric and metaphor (Keenoy, 1990: 371; Keenoy and Anthony, 1992: 235).

As Goss (1994) states, 'the evidence suggests that commitment is a complex phenomenon that operates in different directions and at different levels. It is not something that can easily be generated or sustained, neither does it necessarily lead to improved performance' (p. 101). Noon (1992), in exploring these criticisms further, comments: 'Employees may resent the dissonance created between commitment to the task (encouraged by the individually based performance management mechanisms) and commitment to the company (encouraged through the rhetoric of culture and the rewards of promotion and employment security)' (p. 23).

The economic downturn in the early 1990s led some commentators to ask whether HRM is 'recession proof' (Beardwell and Holden, 1994: 686). Storey (1989: 8) has identified 'hard' and 'soft' types of HRM, which may sit well with different types of organisational culture and, we posit, different economic climates. Legge (1989: 33) has alluded to 'tough love' HRM in such contexts, and this is readily witnessed in the experience of such 'HRM companies' as IBM, with its forced redundancy programme in the early 1990s (Noon, 1992: 24). It is pertinent to ask, therefore, how human resource management changes under such circumstances, and how employee commitment and involvement are affected. Marchington (1995) proposes that EI will be considerably different in nature, or may not exist at all, in organisations that practise forms of hard HRM, compared with those that practise soft HRM. In organisations that practise hard HRM:

> EI may not be seen as important by senior managers, given the emphasis on tight cost control, deskilled jobs, and a lack of investment in training. In others, EI may be little more than one-way communications channels, designed merely to convey the latest news to employees and indicate to them the merits of management's decision. In these cases, if EI is practised, it is likely to take a rather diluted and marginal form.   (p. 28)

HRM can also be affected by changes in the economic climate, and Holden (1996) cites the experience of an organisation in the banking and finance sector. This company was an early convert to HRM, and initiated policies that contained mechanisms to increase employee influence. In the boom economy of the late 1980s 'soft' policies were emphasised, including, for example, training for TQM and other EI measures. In the harsher climate of recessional Britain in the 1990s, downsizing and retrenchment became the order of the day. Survival meant a move to hard HRM policies. In this climate the soft mechanisms of EI tended to be overlooked and even ignored.

Control and employee involvement

One important element in the EI equation is the degree of control given to managers and non-managerial employees. For example, informational, communicational and consultational types of participation tend to come from management initiatives, and are more likely to be controlled by management. However, the term 'control' itself is problematic. For example, a worker can feel in control of his or her work process (the day-to-day operations), but have little control or say in the running of the organisation in terms of influencing overall policy or strategy. Second, various issues at workplace level will allow more control and influence by the workforce than others.

These problems have long been recognised in the vast literature generated around this important subject (Edwards, 1987: 90). Drucker (1961), for example, states that 'control is an ambiguous word. It means the ability to direct oneself and one's work. It can also mean domination of one person by another' (p. 128).

Stop and think Forms of control exist in all organisations. How do teachers control pupils and can these controls be applied to the work situation? Clearly there are differences. What are they?

Positive and negative views of control have spawned a parallel literature rooted in the acceptance and rejection of capitalist values, of which the latter is represented strongly by the *labour process* theory school inspired by the work of Braverman (1974) (see also Chapters 3, 5 and 10).

Control according to the labour process school of thought postulates that technology controls the work process in its drive to help fulfil the requirements of the capitalist organisation (i.e. profits) in response to intensive competition. This obviates the necessity to control the work process in order to extract the maximum output in relation to labour cost and the ability of labour to resist control (Salaman, 1979). According to Braverman (1974), the ability to resist control and exert greater autonomy is higher among workers whose skills are in great demand, and less among workers in unskilled or deskilled situations. Thus deskilling has considerable implications for control and the way it is applied and viewed by participants (employees, managers, employers) and hence for participation schemes, especially in institutions such as banks, which have undergone intensive technological change and reorganisation in the past five years.

Since Braverman's work there have been a number of refinements and challenges to his thesis, many sharing the Marxian perspective. Edwards (1979) focuses on the move away from more coercive methods rooted in new technology, with its associations with Fordist and Taylorist managerial control mechanisms, to bureaucratic control systems aimed at the dual goals of dissolving class solidarity and maximising commitment to, and dependence on, the firm. 'Promotion, pay, security and other benefits go to employees who are good corporate citizens, who are loyal to the company, share its values and integrate themselves and their families into the enterprise community' (Lincoln and Kalleberg, 1990: 9). Such managerial initiatives fit particularly well with HRM conceptualisations.

Friedman (1977) has divided managerial control systems into direct control and responsible autonomy. *Direct control* is associated with rules, regulation, work organisation and technology that directly control the behaviour and work rate of the employee. This is strongly associated with the Fordist–Taylorist approach. *Responsible autonomy* allows the worker and the work team a degree of control over the work process, and

> attempts to harness the adaptability of labour power by giving workers leeway and encouraging them to adapt to changing situations in a manner beneficial to the firm. To do this top managers give workers status, authority and responsibility. Top managers try to win their loyalty, and coopt their organisations to the firm's ideals (that is, the competitive struggle) ideologically.
>
> (Friedman, 1977: 78)

This again has strong resonances with developments in HRM in the 1980s and 1990s, particularly in terms of participation schemes such as TQM, which aim to enhance commitment to the organisation by allowing the workforce a degree of autonomy. Edwards (1992: 390) points out, however, that HRM apologists such as Walton (1985), who speak of a move from control to commitment, partly by means of employee involvement and participation policies, should perceive that commitment 'is still a form of control'.

Burawoy (1979) has also developed a dual perspective of management regimes that rely on coercion or consent. Earlier capitalist systems relied heavily on the former approach, and adopted autocratic methods of workforce control, particularly in response to intensive capitalist competition. Latterly the adoption of more subtle approaches to the employment relationship has emphasised policies designed to induce commitment in the employee. This has been caused to some degree by the softening of overt autocratic systems by state regulation and welfare policy. Burawoy (1983) sees such new approaches as creating a hegemonic regime under which coercive compliance is replaced by normative control, as managers make concessions in order to persuade employees to cooperate in furthering the success of the organisation. Once again we can discern echoes of HRM policy initiatives in such hegemonic systems.

We shall return to some of these questions later in the chapter, but at this point it is appropriate to examine some of the mechanisms and definitions of employee involvement, beginning with communication.

Employee involvement and communication

All organisations need communication systems to function, whether these are overtly recognised or subconsciously taken for granted. In the 1990s it was increasingly recognised by many employers and managers that the creation of effective communication is an extremely important aspect of the efficient running of organisations. Communication is a complex series of processes operating at all levels within organisations, ranging from the 'grapevine', heavily laden with rumour, to formalised systems such as joint consultative committees (JCCs) or works councils. These can operate at the localised level of the shopfloor or office between supervisor and staff and the staff themselves, or at a distance by means of representatives such as union officials or messages from on high from the boardroom or the chief executive, to various branches or subsidiaries of large and complex organisations. They can be one way or two way, top down or bottom up and both top down and bottom up, as well as across the organisation.

It is being increasingly recognised that messages to and, equally important, from the workforce have considerable significance. They are important for conveying the organisation's mission, business aims and objectives, and its general ethos or culture. They are needed to enable the thoughts and feelings of the workforce to be expressed and, of equal significance, heeded and acted upon. Such policies are being heavily influenced and underscored by HRM practices.

Communication systems also carry implicit messages about the mediation of power within organisations. Employee involvement communication systems are processes that enable the workforce to have a greater say in decision-making to varying degrees, with the concomitant loss of managerial prerogatives – an issue that can create conflict, as well as attempting to allay it.

However, even the simplest message can be misunderstood or misconstrued because of the complex influences that act on the communication process. Equally important, and potentially disastrous, is the fact that communication channels can send conflicting messages. An oft-cited case is the company that encouraged employees to take up share options which entitled them to attend the annual shareholders' meeting, where they were told how successfully the company had performed over the previous year. Many of these same employees were also in the union, to which management communicated later that because of the company's poor performance over the previous year, the pay increases requested could not be met!

Stop and think

'Asked by a committee chairman, Mr John Golding, about his views on industrial democracy, Norman Tebitt (Secretary of State for Industry under Mrs Thatcher) said it was "good management" to inform the workers of decisions taken by their employees.'   (*New Statesman*, 1984)

Do you think Norman Tebitt is confusing industrial democracy with communication? Would you say Tebitt approves of industrial democracy? Would his definition be acceptable under present European Union laws on co-determination?

● Communication overload

Many employee relations surveys point to lack of communications or poor communications as an important weakness in organisational operations. This view is not only held by shopfloor workers but also increasingly by middle and even senior managers. However, a recent trend has shown that new technology and e-mail in particular can lead to the reverse – communication overload. Many people speak of the dreaded 'in-box' e-mail problem when one has been away from the office to return only to find their in-box filled with 60 or more new messages. It has reached such proportions that some employees are becoming stressed in trying to keep up with the flow of messages. Up to two hours a day (often more) can be spent in just reading and answering e-mails. A recent survey found that '82 per cent of managers in the UK believe that the volume of information they have to handle has greatly increased over the past three years. And 54 per cent claim to suffer information overload' (Russell, 2001: 38). Some US firms now have an e-mail-free day each week where employees are not encouraged to look at their e-mail in-boxes, and courses are now becoming popular in how to deal with e-mail overload.

The real problem is getting information that is important and relevant to the right person but this can have 'political' implications. Managers as the creators and interpreters of policy have the power to withhold key information. HRM advocates believe that a 'high trust' and open organisational culture can help resolve many of these problems, but it would be naïve to presuppose that the problem would vanish entirely.

Stop and think

Have you ever suffered e-mail overload? How do you think one could solve or alleviate the problem?

▉ Employee involvement: history and development

The idea of involving the workforce may seem self-evident, as employees must be involved in order to do their job. It has long been recognised, however, that doing a job does not necessarily mean being interested in it or doing it well. The school of human relations promoted by thinkers in the field such as Mayo, Vroom, Likert and Maslow, among others, has drawn conclusions from their various studies that positive motivational factors engendered by such methods as employee involvement may develop a more creative, interested and therefore more productive workforce.

Even though employee involvement is just one aspect of organisational communication it is, nevertheless, wide ranging and diverse in its forms. Types of EI also evolve and change with managerial vogues, which are governed by political, economic and social pressures. For example, the First World War witnessed a considerable growth in worker militancy together with an increased popularity of left-wing ideologies, many of which espoused various forms of workers' control, one example being Guild Socialism (Cole, 1917). The Bolshevik revolution in Russia in 1917 also had a significant impact on work relationships, as Marxist ideology is based on an analysis of how capitalism exploits the proletariat in the workplace. These influences had, and still have, a considerable impact on arguments surrounding work-related issues. One attempt to mollify these forces in Britain was to acknowledge legally, in the form of Whitley Councils, that employees and their representatives (trade unions) had some say in negotiations over pay and working conditions. Despite good intentions from some parties on both sides of industry, these arrangements largely fell into disuse once recession hit the British economy after 1921 and the threat of workforce militancy receded.

It was not until the Second World War that a popular revival occurred in EI schemes. The need for huge productivity increases to meet the war effort led workers to demand something in return – a greater say in the operation of the workplace. Works committees or joint consultative committees were set up in many factories. Some continued in existence after the war, but management and unions lost interest in them in the 1950s, and many fell into decline when there was a preference for direct collective bargaining via unions, employer organisations and employers. Nevertheless, there was a considerable revival in the atmosphere of industrial democracy in the 1960s and 1970s, and shop stewards were to be found filling delegational positions (Marchington *et al.*, 1992). Debates concerning the extent to which these committees existed, and the real power they afforded the workforce, still engage social and economic historians.

In the 1970s the Bullock Committee Report (1977) echoed an increased interest in industrial democracy. There was a growing consciousness that, while politics and society were increasingly being 'democratised', the world of work did not reflect this trend. In addition, British membership of the European Community influenced the Bullock Committee to examine forms of industrial democracy among its European partners, such as co-determination in Germany and Sweden, and some societies where more radical forms of employee involvement were being undertaken, such as the worker self-management practised in Yugoslavia and at Mondragon in Spain. These practices attracted considerable interest, as did worker-director schemes and the formation of workers' cooperatives, which often happened in UK companies under threat of liquidation (Broekmeyer, 1970; Brannen *et al.*, 1976; Eccles, 1981; Thomas and Logan, 1982).

The political climate that had engendered industrial democracy swiftly changed under Thatcher's Conservative government, which tarred such policies with the brush of left-wing ideology, and in the economic and political climate of the 1980s managerial EI schemes associated with HRM became popular.

Cycles and waves of participation

It is apparent from even this brief history that numerous influences have a bearing on the type, strength and sustainability of various participation schemes and trends. Unsurprisingly, therefore, commentators have attempted to discover patterns of EI and to place them into a theoretical framework.

For example, the relationship between the introduction of profit-sharing with a high level of employment and industrial unrest down to the First World War has been indicated by Church (1971). Ramsay (1977, 1983) has argued that there are cycles of participation:

> Managements have been attracted to the idea of participation when their control over labour has been perceived to be under pressure in some way. This perception has coincided with experience of a growing challenge from labour to the legitimacy of capital and its agents. In Britain these challenges have coincided with the impact and aftermath of two world wars, and with the rise of shop floor union organisation at the same time as squeezed profit margins in the 1960s and 1970s. In each case mounting pressure, including demands for 'industrial democracy' from sections of the labour movement, helped to precipitate management response.
>
> (Ramsay, 1983: 204)

Marchington *et al.* (1992) have pointed to 'waves' of employee involvement within organisations, which respond to external trends and cause the institution of new schemes and the revamping of old existing ones. For example, a quarter of organisations in their survey sample had introduced their current schemes (survey period 1989–91) between 1980 and 1984, 'and several of these were share ownership schemes which appear to have been stimulated by legislative changes from 1978 onwards' (p. 25). Other schemes such as team briefing were introduced in the early 1980s' recession to communicate 'gloom and doom' messages such as pay freezes and voluntary severance. Over half of the schemes of their survey group had been introduced within the previous five years, and tended to be TQM programmes of various types. The 'wave' concept, they point out,

> is analytically more useful than cycles, in that it does not presuppose any automatic repetition of events in an historical pattern, or any all embracing theory of waxing and waning which applies in the same way across all workplaces. On the contrary waves come in different shapes and sizes and last for different lengths of time in different organisations.
>
> (p. 26)

Thus the importance of EI can be understood only if it is viewed as being central to the organisation, and not necessarily prominent. For example, a joint consultative committee may achieve a central position in an organisation over time, although the most prominent new measure may be team briefings. If the JCC becomes less important or dies out, another scheme may replace it and attain the status of centrality. Whether schemes are retained, reformed or dropped depends on multifarious influences within organisations, for example the values and beliefs of managers, which interact with other influences in complex ways.

Poole has attempted to construct a theoretical framework to explain these influences. He sees workers' participation and control as being understood as a specific manifestation of power. This is linked with 'underlying or latent power resources and a series of values that either buttress particular power distributions or facilitate their successful challenge' (Poole, 1986: 28). The relationship of power sources is illustrated in Figure 14.1.

Figure 14.1	Poole's basic explanatory framework of participation

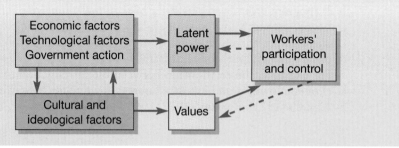

Poole (1986) postulates that:

> Workers' participation and control are reflections of the latent power of particular indus-
> trial classes, parties or groups and the 'value' climate which may or may not be
> favourable to participation experiments. These values thus mediate between certain
> structural factors associated with latent power and their realisation in the form of work-
> ers' participation and control. It will also be seen that the principal structural factors
> associated with the latent power of the main industrial classes, parties or groups are eco-
> nomic factors, such as the levels of employment, the profit margins of particular
> companies, the levels of competition, the degree of industrial concentration and periods
> of economic 'disintegration'; technological factors, such as the approximation of the
> technology of a company to a given point on the 'technical scale', the degree of complex-
> ity and education involved in any given task and the effects of the micro-electronic
> revolution; and finally, various forms of government action such as legislation on labour
> issues, its intervention in the workings of the economic system and so on.   (p. 28)

Finally, 'values about participation and control are shaped by the existing levels of workers' participation and control, latent power, government action and ideologies' (p. 29).

While this framework pinpoints the main factors influencing the types and styles of
employee participation and control, it cannot clearly demonstrate how these factors
interact to produce such systems. Nevertheless, it is a useful model to aid understanding
of these complex processes.

■ Definitions of employee involvement

There is an enormous range of employee involvement schemes, varying from those that
are informational mechanisms to full-blown democratic systems where employees have
as much say in the decision-making processes as does management. This makes an all-
encompassing definition problematic. In addition, different labels have been attached to
these processes, such as employee or worker participation, industrial democracy, organisational communications, co-determination and employee influence, each of which has
its own definitions.

Wall and Lischerson (1977) state that there are three elements central to the concept
of participation: influence, interaction and information sharing. Marchington *et al.*
(1992) divide definitions into three categories: those that refer 'to employees taking part
or having a say or share in decision making, with no attempt to quantify their impact on
the process'; those that 'refer to participation as concerned with the extent to which

employees may influence managerial actions'; and those that 'link together participation and the control over decision making' (pp. 6, 7).

Marchington *et al.* (1992) believe that these definitions also need to take into account:

- the *degree* of involvement (the extent to which employees influence the final decision);
- the *level* of involvement (whether at job, departmental or organisational level);
- the *forms* of involvement (direct, indirect and financial);
- the *range* of the subject matter being considered in the involvement scheme.

For example, quality circles may have a high degree of direct employee involvement and influence on decisions at workplace level, but be limited in range to matters of teamwork and job design. Works councils, on the other hand, will involve employee representatives at organisational level, and may consider a wide range of areas such as business and industrial relations strategies, in joint decision-making with the management.

One problem with this tabular representation (Table 14.1) is that some EI schemes may pervade many or all levels of the organisation, for example financial participation. Others may cascade through many levels, such as team briefings (Ramsay, 1991). Team briefings could also fall into both the 'informational' and 'communicational' categories. Another problem is that the degree of participation with one scheme could differ from one organisation to another. For example, JCCs could vary in power from merely rubber-stamping management decisions to forming joint consultational mechanisms covering a rich variety of organisational topics.

Table 14.1 Some types, levels and degrees of employee involvement

Degree	Levels of involvement		
	Local (workplace level)	Both local and distant	Distant (company or organisational level)
Control (by workers or workers and management together)	Worker self-management		Worker self-management of cooperatives
Co-determinational	Union shop steward representation		JCCs; works councils; worker directors; representation union–management negotiations
Consultational (two-way communication)	Quality circles; job enrichment; suggestion scheme; appraisal	Attitude survey; customer care; TQM, e-mail Internet, intranet	Video conferencing, e-mail, Internet, intranet
Communicational	Team briefings; department or group meetings	E-mail, Internet, intranet	Mass meetings, e-mail, Internet, intranet
Informational (top down)	Noticeboards, e-mail, Internet, intranet	Memos; briefs, e-mail, Internet, intranet	Company newspaper/ magazine; bulletin

Marchington *et al.* (1992: 13) divide EI schemes into four categories:

- *Downward communications* (top down), for example from managers to other employees. This includes forms of EI such as house journals, company newspapers, employee reports and regular briefing sessions, often with videos as well.
- *Upwards, problem-solving forms*, which are designed to tap into employees' knowledge and opinion, either at an individual level or through the mechanism of small

groups. This includes practices such as suggestion schemes, attitude surveys, quality circles and total quality management and customer care programmes.

● *Financial participation* via schemes that attempt to link rewards of individuals to the performance of the unit or the enterprise as a whole. This includes schemes such as profit sharing, employee share ownership, and value-added or establishment-wide bonus arrangements.

● *Representative participation*, in which employees are involved through representatives drawn from among their number, often – though not always – on the basis of union membership, for example JCCs, advisory councils, works councils, co-determination and collective bargaining.

In many organisations a combination of these forms of communication and EI schemes will exist, hopefully supporting and complementing each other.

In a book of this nature it would be impossible to examine all of these approaches, but a closer study of some of the more popular and recent schemes in each category may serve to illustrate current trends.

Downward communications

● The company magazine or newspaper

One of the most common methods of downward communication, which has witnessed a considerable increase over the past 20 years, is the company newspaper or magazine (CBI, 1989). Reviewing methods of communication in six surveys of organisations conducted between 1975 and 1983, Townley (1989) indicates that most put the company newspaper or house journal as either the most popular or the second most popular form of communication. The problem is that they can vary in quality from amateur desktop-published affairs produced by employees in their 'spare' time, to the lavish glossy productions that have been part of the communications systems of many large companies for a number of years.

There is also the question of editorial control, which may restrict the messages conveyed to the workforce. Continual glowing reports of the company successes or anodyne and meaningless information may have negative results in the long run. Genuine expressions of employee feelings via letters pages or forthright quotes from employee representatives, even of a negative nature, may show the management's desire to achieve fairness. Of course, the judgement of the editor will come into play in deciding the content of the newspaper or journal, which in turn will be affected by the organisational culture and management views.

For example, during a dispute a militant shop steward called the managing director a 'fascist', which the personnel director urged the editor to expunge as being insulting. The editor defended the decision to retain the quote on the grounds that he had sought a comment from the shop steward, and not to print it would look like corporate censorship. In addition, such a quote was so patently absurd that it would have a negative effect. In the event the quote was left to stand, and the prediction of the editor proved true when the shop steward was spurned by his fellow employees and the union felt moved to apologise publicly for the comment (Wilkinson, 1989). Unfortunately, many company journal editors are still unable or unwilling to follow such boldly democratic policies, and the workforce often regards publications as a conduit for managerial views. Given their primarily one-way nature and editorial control, this is not surprising.

● Team-briefings

There has been a considerable increase in team-briefings in the past five years, although they have been in existence in some organisations for longer (Marchington *et al.*, 1992).

They are often used to cascade information or managerial messages throughout the organisation. The teams are usually based around a common production or service area, rather than an occupation, and commonly comprise between 4 and 15 people. The leader of the team is normally the manager or supervisor of the section, and should be trained in the principles and skills of how to brief. The meetings last for no more than 30 minutes, and time should be left for questions from employees. Meetings should be held at least monthly or on a regular pre-arranged basis.

Surveys often reveal considerable satisfaction with team-briefings by both employers and management (e.g. CBI, 1989) as they are effective in reinforcing company aims and objectives at the personal, face-to-face level. However, Ramsay (1992a) urges caution in accepting this rosy picture, because success depends on 'context to a significant extent' (p. 223). For example, briefings might be postponed or cancelled at times when business is brisk, which may lessen commitment to holding them at all in the long run. If the intention is to undermine union messages, the success will very much depend on the strength of the union and the conviction of the management. A sceptical and under-trained management and supervisory force can do much to undermine the effectiveness of team-briefings.

Upwards, problem-solving forms of communication

These schemes can also be described as two-way communication, and are most associated with 'new' managerial concepts such as HRM. They are clearly aimed at increasing employee motivation and 'influence' within the organisation, but usually at a localised level – workshop, office or service area. They also aim to improve employee morale, loyalty and commitment, with a view to increasing service and efficiency. Another facet of these types of schemes is that they facilitate acceptance of changes in work practices, functional flexibility and new technology, as well as engendering an atmosphere conducive to cooperation and team-building (Ramsay, 1992a).

Quality circles

One of the first methods identified with the 'new' involved approach to management was the quality circle (QC). This first arrived in Britain via the USA from Japan, although the concept was implanted in Japan in the years after the Second World War by two US consultants, W. Edwards Deming and J.M. Duran (Clutterbuck and Crainer, 1990).

QCs are made up of 6–10 employees, with regular meetings held weekly or fortnightly during working time. Their principal aim is to 'identify problems from their own area and, using data collection methods and statistical techniques acquired during circle training, analyse these problems and devise possible solutions; the proposed solutions are then presented formally to the manager of the section who may decide to implement the circle's proposal' (Brennan, 1991).

Tremendous interest was shown in QCs by British managers in the early 1980s, but within a few years they began to decline in popularity. A number of reasons have been identified for this decline, but principal among these was the attitude of middle managers. For example, it is crucial that a manager or supervisor with the requisite qualities and training leads the circle. Technical competence alone is not enough, and studies began to highlight the need for interpersonal skills. Some managers also felt that their power and authority were undermined by the QC, and others lacked commitment in the initial stages, which had the effect of making the circles difficult to develop effectively. There were also difficulties from overenthusiastic facilitators who deliberately gave an overtly positive but false impression of the circle's operation, possibly for career progression reasons. This made it difficult to identify problems within the circle or improve its effectiveness (Brennan, 1991). Suspicion of circles could be engendered if they were seen as a way of undermining trade union functions. Lack of consultation with the union, particularly when setting up QCs, often bred suspicion that this was another anti-union management ploy, and the initiative was therefore effectively undermined by non-cooperative attitudes.

Other circles failed because suggestions by the workforce were not in fact applied or even considered, thus rendering them a waste of time in the minds of the participants. Finally, many circles simply 'ran out of steam' after the initial burst of enthusiasm. The need for continual reinforcement of their function and purpose was evident (Collard and Dale, 1989; Ramsay, 1992a).

● Teamworking

Teamworking is one of the most recent initiatives in EI; like QCs it was strongly developed in Japan. It emphasises problem solving in a teamworking situation, and in order to function effectively it must be bound up with policies of task flexibility and job rotation (Price, 1989). Teams vary in size from seven to ten, or even more, people and extensive training is necessary to ensure that workers, team leaders, supervisors and managers have the requisite skills to enable the team to function efficiently. A large part of such training is of a managerial or interpersonal skill and communicational nature, as well as of a technical nature.

● Job design and teamworking

Implicit in teamworking developments is its relation to job design. The car industry in particular has experimented with differing types of job design for a variety of reasons, principally to facilitate greater employee motivation by designing jobs that employees could 'own' as a team. This would stimulate a more committed and therefore productive approach to work as jobs are designed to enhance work diversity. In the past the reorganisation of work and job design has been associated with job rotation, job enlargement and job enrichment and is now attached to the more generic form known as 'teamworking.'

In the first half of the twentieth century job design was associated with forms of scientific management. These tended to be Fordist and Taylorite assumptions that jobs and work could be designed on a scientific basis to extract the highest amount of effort from the workforce. Under Fordist principles this was carried out by interfacing employees with machines and mechanised work processes such as the conveyor belt. This had the effect of speeding up production, lowering cost and thus increasing output and sales. Frederick Winslow Taylor and Elton Mayo tended to see the human being as an adjunct to a more efficient process in job design. Trained observers could study the time and motion of a job in order to improve its operating functions, by breaking it down into component parts and redesigning it to be performed more efficiently by the operator.

Later observers such as Blauner (1964) and researchers at the Tavistock Institute noted the alienating effect of concentrating on the job design and not the feelings and perceptions of the employee carrying out the work process. Scientific management tended to leave the human factor out of the equation.

In reality the Fordist type systems were largely confined to the vehicle production industry and some types of large manufacturing. It is not surprising therefore that innovations in job design and work groups tended to appear in these types of industry. In the 1970s various car manufacturers experimented with job rotation, job enlargement and job enrichment.

Job rotation is, as its name suggests, simply rotating jobs between members of a work group to give wider experience and relieve the monotony of job repetition. Job enlargement literally means enlarging the job by increasing other functions to add variety to the work process. Job enrichment is more in line with later teamworking initiatives in that it gives the workforce degrees of autonomy and control over how they achieve targets or even having some input in designing the job. Combinations of these approaches were instituted in the Volvo Kalmar plant in Sweden in the 1970s and the 'Saturn Project' run by General Motors and Toyota in the early 1980s. None survived long, although it has been argued that lessons were learnt and elements of these schemes were incorporated in the development of other forms of teamworking.

By the late 1980s job design in many companies was being integrated with forms of functional flexibility and being combined with HRM and other management initiatives such as total quality management, business process re-engineering, customer service programmes and, in the 1990s, empowerment schemes.

Teamworking took on various forms, depending on the company and its products and services, but essentially the 'team' concept was being perceived as the central operational unit in the work process and more 'progressive' organisations began to concentrate their recruitment, selection, training, development and reward around it.

(For a more detailed discussion of job design see Damian O'Doherty's chapter in the first, second and third editions of this book.)

BOX 14.1 | **Teamworking at Calderdale and Huddersfield NHS Trust**

At Calderdale and Huddersfield NHS Trust teamworking on a multidisciplinary basis has been successfully introduced with excellent results in that patients can be discharged from hospital more quickly. Twenty-three teams are made up of combinations of district nurses, health visitors, practice managers, GPs and practice nurses and administrative staff. The teams are supported with HR, clinical and budgetary systems on a continuing basis. There are weekly support meetings promoting inter-team communication and collaboration.

Feedback through monitoring and evaluation has revealed a number of positive outcomes:

- A climate of cooperation with better communications between the agencies that look after patient health care.
- More integrated care resulting in quicker discharge times, so more hospital beds are available.
- More community care for children with problems such as diabetes and cystic fibrosis.
- Teams can use their budgets in a more effectively targeted way.
- Specialised training requirments have been identified to meet local specific needs.
- General improvement in morale and motivation from feelings of empowerment and involvement by all staff.
- Reduction in sickness and absence of all staff.

Source: West and Johnson (2002)

Stop and think | This box gives a glowing account of successful teamworking in the health sector, but given the problems aired in the media concerning the health sector, what things do you think could possibly disturb this initiative in the future and therefore need to be monitored?

■ Financial participation

The general aim of financial participation schemes is to enhance employee commitment to the organisation by linking the performance of the organisation to that of the employee. Thus, it is argued, employees are more likely to be positively motivated and involved if they have a financial stake in the company through having a share of the profits or through being a company shareholder. Although such schemes are by no means new – early profit-sharing schemes were in operation in the nineteenth century (Church, 1971) – their recent popularity has been partially spawned by the Conservative government's philosophy of creating a property-owning democracy in the 1980s and 1990s in an attempt to individualise work and societal relationships, and also by the rise in human resource management initiatives (Schuller, 1989). The Labour government has continued to encourage financial involvement schemes and in the 2000 budget the all-employee share ownership plan and the enterprise management incentive programme (EMI) were introduced.

In addition, legislation has been introduced to bolster and lay down legal parameters for such schemes in the form of the Finance Acts 1978, 1980, 1984, 1987 and 1989. Evidence suggests that most managers' aims in introducing forms of financial participation are for positive reasons associated with employee motivation, rather than attempts to undermine trade union influence (although this is an objective in some organisations), and schemes were indeed welcomed by most employees in the organisation (Badden *et al.*, 1989; CBI, 1989; Poole and Jenkins, 1990a, 1990b; Marchington *et al.*, 1992; Pendleton *et al.*, 2001).

● Types of financial participation

Schuller (1989: 128) categorises financial participation schemes on a scale that ranges from individualism to collectivism. Towards the individual end there are personal equity plans, profit-related pay, profit-sharing and employee share option schemes; at the collective end there are workers' cooperatives, management buy-outs, pension fund participation and wage earner funds.

Of these categories, individual forms of financial participation are the most common, especially profit-related pay and share option schemes (CBI, 1989; Marchington *et al.*, 1992).

Profit-related pay and employee share options

As already noted, profit-related pay schemes have a long pedigree, and were stimulated by the Finance Act of 1978. In essence, profit-sharing or profit-related pay schemes are those 'where a cash bonus or payment is made to employees based upon the share price, profits or dividend announcement at the end of the financial year' (Marchington *et al.*, 1992: 11).

Employee share options are schemes 'using part of the profits generated or earnings of employees to acquire shares for the employee in the company concerned, or discounted shares on privatisation or public quotation' (Marchington *et al.*, 1992: 11).

There are four main types of scheme (Poole and Jenkins, 1990b):

● profit sharing – with cash rewards;
● profit sharing – through shares in the company (approved deferred share trust, ADST);
● save-as-you-earn share option schemes (SAYE);
● executive share schemes.

There is a degree of overlap in these schemes: for example, ADST and SAYE both concern share options, but the former is often bracketed with profit sharing, where shares are part of the reward, and the latter with employee saving schemes, which lead to the purchase of shares. A considerable amount of financial legislation, and the fact that successive chancellors of the exchequer have made concessions in successive budgets since 1978, bear testimony to the importance that governments have given to such schemes. Between 1978 and 1990 the Inland Revenue approved, for tax purposes, 6349 schemes, which are made up of 909 ADSTs, 919 SAYEs and 4521 executive share option schemes (Dunn *et al.*, 1991: 1).

ACTIVITY   **Financial participation at Vodafone**

More than three-quarters of Vodafone's UK employees own shares in the company. The firm's Sharesave scheme has witnessed the value of their shares grow by an average of 55 per cent a year between 1994 and 2000.

Phil Williams, the company's human resource director, states that every employee has the opportunity to join its various share plans. He states that this 'aggressive reward policy' has contributed to the success of the business and created wealth for employee shareholders (Pendleton and Brewster, 2001, p. 38).

Question

Phil Williams points out the advantages of Sharesave, but what disadvantages could there be for employees owning shares?

How effective are these schemes, given their apparent popularity? In general terms, commentators and researchers divide into two basic camps – the optimists and the more sceptical. The optimists are backed by a plethora of positive literature emanating from consultants and the more popular business journals. The question of success, however, rests on the criteria by which they are judged, and here opinion is much more mixed, but even in-depth studies differ in some of their conclusions (Badden *et al.*, 1989; Poole and Jenkins, 1990b; Dunn *et al.*, 1991; Marchington *et al.*, 1992).

Poole and Jenkins (1990a, 1990b) represent the more optimistic view, but they still distinguish between the effect of such schemes on employee attitudes and the effect on employee behaviour. They believe that employee attitudes are favourably affected in the sense that employees have increased their identity with company goals, feel more involved, and have a more positive attitude towards the company. 'Indeed, the most important impact of profit sharing is almost certainly to improve organisational identification and commitment and hence, indirectly, to enhance industrial relations performance' (Poole and Jenkins, 1990a: 96).

Ramsay *et al.* (1986) are less optimistic in their view, and claim that many surveys play down the negative effects, while Dunn *et al.* (1991: 14), using evidence from their longitudinal survey, claim that there is not even a correlation between improved employee attitudes and the introduction of such schemes. Both studies point to the fact that the 'them and us' attitude that the schemes attempt to break down may well reinforce the status quo, because executives and older workers tend to be the majority of employee shareholders as younger and less senior employees cannot afford shares.

Marchington *et al.* (1992) and Dunn *et al.* (1991) also state that a number of internal and external factors affect employee attitudes and behaviours, and these are difficult to disentangle from perceptions of financial participation schemes. Marchington *et al.* (1992) state that employees viewed the scheme much more negatively in one company that was unable to pay out dividends on shares because of market pressures, than in another company that was relatively financially buoyant.

Whatever the criticisms levelled at financial participation schemes, a recent survey shows that they are on the increase, not only in Britain, but across Europe. Pendleton *et al.* (2001) surveyed 2500 European companies concerning financial participation. The evidence revealed that broad-based schemes (which include all employees) of share ownership and profit sharing were becoming more widespread. More than 20 per cent of UK companies in the survey had share ownership schemes and more than 20 per cent in France and the Netherlands. Of the 14 European Union countries surveyed, all had some companies with share ownership schemes and the authors claim that this seems to be on the increase. Profit-sharing schemes were particularly popular in France and the Netherlands where they are backed by government legislation. The European Union is also supportive and put forward a recommendation for support of financial participation schemes in 1992.

Correlating the findings against other HR and employee relations factors it was found that companies requiring high levels of knowledge are more likely to have these schemes. They also found that those with financial participation schemes tended to spend more on training and have other employee involvement mechanisms. There was no correlation with union membership and many highly unionised companies had these schemes, thus perhaps providing some evidence that not all companies see these schemes as a way of undermining union presence.

■ Representative participation

● Joint consultative committees

Apart from collective bargaining, the most common form of representative participation in the UK is joint consultative committees. As already noted, these received a considerable impetus in the Second World War, declined somewhat in the 1950s and 1960s, and witnessed a revival in the 1970s, which – according to various surveys – has continued. In the late 1990s and early twenty-first century JCCs have been and will continue to be given a considerable boost when the European Union Directive on Works Councils comes into effect in March 2005 (see below for details and Chapter 15).

According to Badden *et al.* (1989), one-third of companies had consultation machinery, and the CBI (1989) survey puts this figure at 47 per cent, though both stress that such mechanisms are more likely to exist in larger organisations. Shop stewards also tend to be employee representatives in unionised firms, indicating a retreat from the view held by many unionists that JCCs were mere talking shops without power, set up to dupe the employees and undermine union presence.

In examining JCCs it soon becomes evident that they operate differently in various organisations and sectors, at different levels within organisations and with different degrees of power (Marchington, 1989b). Thus in one organisation they could be rubber-stamping bodies for management initiatives, discussing at the most 'tea, toilets and trivia', and in other organisations they could be genuine conduits for the expression of employees' views, with some degree of decisional power.

According to Marchington *et al.* (1992) joint consultation is defined as

> a mechanism for managers and employee representatives to meet on a regular basis, in order to exchange views, to utilise members' knowledge and expertise, and to deal with matters of common interest which are not the subject of collective bargaining.   (p. 11)

Organisations with a strong union presence attempt to keep issues such as pay bargaining off the JCC agenda, leaving them to collective bargaining issues. This has led some commentators to the view that management in organisations that encourage employee participation may see JCCs as a less important channel of communication. This relative powerlessness may 'often leave JCCs with a marginal role in labour management relationships' (Ramsay, 1991). Marchington (1989a; Marchington *et al.*, 1992) is, however, more optimistic, and sees their role as often complementing and supporting other channels of communication and EI, such as collective bargaining.

All commentators agree that if JCCs are given only unimportant issues to deal with, then employees themselves will view them as ineffectual, and they will be marginalised.

Ramsay (1992a) recommends that for the joint consultation medium to be effective it needs to be consulted in advance of decision-making, to have a representative range of issues to discuss, to be adequately resourced with proper administrative backup and to have an effective feedback mechanism to employees; management representation should be seen to be of the requisite level (that is, senior managers); action on proposals should be carried out quickly; and unions should be kept officially informed.

This would be very much in line with, and in the spirit of, recent European Union directives on co-determination where JCCs can be perceived as a form of works council. Obviously some JCCs in the UK will have to change procedures and practices to conform with the directive. (See below for more information on EU works councils.)

Empowerment

Empowerment is a concept that gained immense popularity in the 1990s, and looks set to continue as a popular organisational initiative in the twenty-first century. It is a managerial ideology in its own right as well as being used with other initiatives and strategies such as BPR, TQM and the learning organisation. It is strongly associated with culture change initiatives, delayering and restructuring, and usually involves devolving power and responsibilities to teams at workplace or customer level (Arkin, 1995).

ACTIVITY   Before reading the next section, either by yourself or in a group attempt to define empowerment. These words may help you – responsibility, accountability, control, power, influence.

Now read the defintions given below.

■ Defining empowerment

Various one-dimensional definitions of empowerment have emanated from the practitioner literature. Typical of this view is Cook and Macauley's (1997) definition of empowerment as

> a change-management tool which helps organisations create an environment where every individual can use his or her abilities and energies to satisfy the customer.   (p. 54)

Its all-embracing nature skirts over issues of how employees use their abilities, and whether there are boundaries to responsibilities, the degree and type of power employees enjoy, power relations between employee, managers, individuals, teams, customers and the context of empowerment. Both Wilkinson (1998) and Lashley (1997) have commented that empowerment is influenced by historical, economic, social and political factors, and in attempting a definition the context in which it is practised must be considered. Wilkinson (1998) defines empowerment as a managerially led initiative:

> Unlike industrial democracy there is no notion of workers having a right to a say: it is employers who decide whether and how to empower employees. While there is a wide range of programmes and initiatives which are titled empowerment and they vary as to the extent of power which employees actually exercise, most are purposefully designed not to give workers a very significant role in decision making but rather to secure an enhanced employee contribution to the organisation. Empowerment takes place within the context of a strict management agenda.   (p. 40)

Empowerment is thus a managerially controlled phenomenon operating at a work-based rather than a strategic level within the organisation. Honold (1997) implicitly acknowledges this by seeing empowerment as 'control of one's work, autonomy on the job, variations of teamwork, and pay systems that link pay with performance' (p. 202). She further divides empowerment into five groupings: leadership, the individual empowered state, collaborative work, structural or procedural change, and the multidimensional perspective that encompasses the other four categories.

● The leader's role in creating an empowering context

In Honold's first category the leader must set the context and cultural climate for the implementation of empowerment schemes. If by implication power is to be delegated then employees need the requisite training, development and support mechanisms and processes (such as team-building) to enable this to happen. As an initiative this conforms strongly to Wilkinson's (1998) concept of empowerment – that is, being managerially led.

● The individual perspective of empowerment

Honold (1997) reminds us 'that if power is not taken by those it is bestowed upon then, there is no empowerment' (p. 204). In other words, individual employees must feel that it is a worthwhile process for them, for example the satisfaction of gaining influence over events. Menon (1995) surveyed 311 employees in a company and found that greater job autonomy and meaningfulness of the job led to greater perceived control and greater empowerment. He found that the greater the empowerment the greater was the motivation to work among employees. This also led to less job stress and increased employee commitment to organisational goals.

● Collaborative work as empowerment

The individual usually has to work with others, and the element of empowerment combining collaborative efforts has to be acknowledged, such as via quality circles or teamworking measures. This means developing the ability of employees to work together and cooperate, and using this sharing process to empower themselves further (Rothstein, 1995).

● Structural and procedural change as empowerment

This is concerned with the nuts and bolts of the empowerment process, associated for example with TQM systems. Ward (1993: 4) believes that such systems have three crucial components:

- clarity and consistency of the organisation's overall production and development goals, and an alignment of all systems and management and employee levels towards those goals;
- ongoing evaluation and development of the professional needs of the employees, with preparation for a greater sense of process ownership and accountability;
- assurance of congruence between corporate goals, management goals and the goals of the organisation's employees.

Such goals can be achieved only by improving internal and external organisational communications. The use of electronic channels such as e-mail, Internet and intranet systems has important ramifications for the effective operations of such systems.

● Multidimensional perspectives on empowerment

Honold's (1997: 206) final category shows that one approach is insufficient for empowerment to be effective. Others believe that combining education, leading, mentoring and supporting, providing and structuring is more likely to enable empowerment systems to be successful. Human resource systems should also be fully supportive of these components, providing a contextual framework within which empowerment systems are able to operate. This means linking the empowerment process to the vision, goals and aims of the organisation, through HRD, reward systems and employee relations systems combined with adequate feedback measures.

■ The benefits of empowerment to the individual and the organisation

Table 14.2 outlines the proclaimed benefits of empowerment for individual employees and for the organisation. It can be deduced from this table that the benefits to the organisation outweigh those to the staff. However, before embarking on a critique of empowerment it would be apposite to see how it fits into HRM systems as a whole.

Table 14.2 Benefits of empowerment to the individual and the organisation

Benefits for organisations	Benefits for employees
• Greater awareness of business needs among employees	• Increase in job satisfaction
• Cost reduction from delayering and employee ideas	• Increase in day-to-day control over tasks
• Improved quality, profitability and productivity measures	• Ownership of work
• Organisation able to respond more quickly to market changes	• Increase in self-confidence
• Enhanced loyalty and commitment	• Creation of teamwork
• Decrease in staff turnover	• Acquisiton of new knowledge and skills
• More effective communication	

BOX 14.2 | **The 'Service Excellence' scheme and the benefits of empowerment**

Research by Ricardo Peccei and Patricia Rosenthal into an empowerment initiative by a large supermarket chain showed clear benefits to staff, the organisation and the customer. Jobs were redesigned to allow a greater amount of discretion in dealing with customers and this was backed by training and supported by the HR department. The result was that the workforce had real feelings of empowerment and were able to deal with customer issues more effectively and to the benefit of the customer. This had the effect of 'committing' the customer and staff to the organisation. This was all the more impressive as this initiative was for those employees in traditionally routine jobs.

Source: Peccei and Rosenthal, 2001

Empowerment and 'soft' and 'hard' systems of HRM

Claydon and Doyle (1996) distinguish between forms of empowerment in 'soft' and 'hard' HRM systems. The 'soft' aspect can 'provide enhanced opportunities for involvement in decision making' and 'employees will gain those feelings of control, personal efficacy and self-determination which constitute the state of being empowered' (p. 3). They also point out a second but extremely important aspect of the 'soft' system, in that empowerment connects with organisational learning. 'More open communication, shared problem-solving geared to continuous improvement, and a related willingness to expose existing organisational arrangements to critical scrutiny imply more democratic, less authoritarian and bureaucratic work relations' (p. 4). Empowering employees also means that managers lose some control, and must learn to accommodate a more questioning and risk-taking workforce, a problem of which many empowerment schemes fall foul (Arkin, 1995).

The 'hard' aspect of empowerment signifies the exercise of a sense of responsibility, and implies elements of monitoring and accountability: it therefore poses contradictions in its implementation and practice. These elements of 'responsible autonomy' are overseen by forms of surveillance via set objectives, customer reports, the policing by fellow members of autonomous work teams, and other controls. 'Empowerment [like BPR, see below] is also closely linked to organisational restructuring, job cuts and moves towards increasingly fragmented and unstable and contingent employment relationships' (Claydon and Doyle, 1996: 4).

Here we see some of the contradictions inherent in capitalist enterprise and therefore in processes such as empowerment, BPR and TQM, which are related to HRM issues. Is it possible to gain commitment when employees perceive themselves as being merely disposable units of production? These and other controversial questions will continue to exercise the minds of both practitioners and academics in the continual search for congruence between the aims of companies, employees and society.

> **Stop and think**
>
> What disadvantages could empowerment schemes hold for managers and workers?
>
> After you have considered this question, read the section on 'Criticisms of empowerment' below.

Criticisms of empowerment

Writers cited in the preceding text have already implied considerable criticism of the empowerment movement: its imprecise definitions; the fact that it remains, for all its good intentions, a managerial tool to gain employee compliance; and the fact that empowerment as such is restricted to workplace issues, allowing little or no employee voice in strategic organisational concerns.

Most criticism of empowerment can be divided into two categories: reasons for operational failure, and wider ideological critiques.

A number of studies have pointed to practical reasons for the failure of empowerment schemes. These do not tend to take issue with the concept of empowerment as such but are critical of the way in which it has been applied. A study by Rothstein (1995) showed that an empowerment scheme in a US company failed because of management incompetence. Senior management, including the company president, failed to give adequate support, and employees felt they lacked authority to make meaningful decisions. Training in empowerment was cursory, and communication systems were inadequate to deal with the feedback necessary between employees and managers at different levels and across the organisation. Senior management also expected success to be immediate, a situation that would inevitably lead to feelings of thwarted expectations.

Wilkinson (1998) makes the point that empowerment schemes often fail because they are regarded too simplistically in the sense that 'empowerment has different forms and should be analysed in the context of broader organisational practice' (p. 53). Buchanan and Preston's (1992) research into high-performance teams (in which empowerment is central to the operation) showed that management was ever-mindful of how the cell team operations fitted with the broader business strategy. HRM strategy in terms of reward systems, flexitime systems, training and development was also crucial in enabling empowerment to operate effectively. Many schemes fail because senior management has not recognised that the implementation of empowerment schemes usually means a wholesale organisational culture change, which affects all corners of the organisation. Honold (1997) also emphasises that culture change implies a change from a low- to a high-trust culture, including the 'tolerance of risk taking' (p. 208). It is often difficult to prescribe where the limits of risk taking and employee responsibility lie; such issues are not directly confronted in many organisations until a serious problem arises, and then it is often too late. Babson's (1995) research into car plants showed that responsibilities transferred to employees were more symbolic than substantive, relegated to handing out pay cheques on pay day, for example.

Ideological criticisms are often couched in terms that empowerment systems are just another management ruse to exploit the workforce more effectively, and that in reality employee empowerment is limited and ultimately does not 'free' the workforce from the shackles of forms of control, arguments rehearsed earlier in this chapter. This has echoes of Friedman's concept of 'responsible autonomy', in which the perception is given that employees have control over the work process but in reality this is limited and very much contained within the parameters of set performance targets. It is management that usually set the targets, not the employees.

Babson (1995) has raised a recurring concern within the EI literature, that empowerment schemes can undermine and destroy the legitimate and independent voice of the workforce – that is, the trade unions. This may be a deliberate ploy to undermine union presence and power, or to create a climate where the union presence is deemed superfluous as its role in mediating between management and workers is redundant. A European Union-wide study by Wood and Fenton O'Creevy (1999) found that companies which depend on direct employee involvement that bypasses trade unions involved their employees less than those companies that recognised and involved unions. 'This was because they involved workers in fewer issues and, when they did, they were less likely to consult or negotiate rather than simply inform them' (p. 44). Interestingly, they also found that the exclusive use of direct involvement schemes, such as those associated with empowerment, correlated with lower labour productivity.

Another feature of the exploitation argument is that empowerment schemes reduce workforce levels. This follows the logic that as productivity increases fewer staff are needed. In other words, one is empowered out of a job! This is often associated with forms of lean production. Parker and Slaughter (1995) also believe that this creates 'a management by stress approach that pushes people and systems to the breaking point by increasingly forcing workers to do more with less' (Honold, 1997: 209).

Recent analysts have also referred to the ethics of empowerment (Quinn and Davies, 1999) and have attempted to explore the contradictions of the term in this context. Kaler (1999), for example, states that empowerment does not necessarily increase the power of workers and he makes a distinction between personal power and positional power. The former is attributed to in-born characteristics of the individual, the latter to role and function – for example, the promotion of someone to the role of supervisor gives them the powers associated with that position. He argues that organisational power is traditionally associated with positional power and is associated very much with powers of command, acountability and responsibility. Thus just announcing that all employees are 'empowered' does not in Kaler's view mean that they will be.

Business process re-engineering

Business process re-engineering (BPR), a popular initiative in the 1990s, had been hailed as the big solution to the problems facing companies and organisations (Peppard and Rowland, 1995). Its US advocates, such as Michael Hammer, claim that quality in production and service must now be accompanied by efficiency in process – that is, the way that groups and departments function interactively (Hammer and Champy, 1993). BPR has enormous implications for employee involvement as its supporters advocate stripping away unnecessary layers of management and empowering the workforce to seek better process solutions in the drive towards greater efficiency.

There have been studies that relate its successful application in a number of organisations (Buchanan, 1996), but 'emphasis on the ability of re-engineering to reduce employee numbers shows how messages tend to get distorted as they are passed on. Unfortunately, the message wanted and received by most of US industry was not improvement through reorganisation, but reduced costs through staff cuts' (Mumford and Hendricks, 1996: 22). Given such experiences, it is not surprising that these schemes are viewed with an air of cynicism and fear by employees who may well become the next 'victim' in the drive towards efficiency.

Lumb (1996) has defended BPR as being 'about changing the way people think and behave. It means investing employees with the power to make decisions and encouraging them to take risks.' All laudable aims, but the *raison d'être* of companies is to operate profitably; if the confusion of message and intent is responsible for the growing cynicism that sees reduction of costs (BPR's aim) as also incorporating not only efficient processes but reduction of staff levels, then messages of trust, commitment and empowerment could be radically undermined.

Controversy: does employee involvement work? The case of TQM

Whether employee involvement works or not depends on the aims and objectives of the EI scheme. In addition, there are times when certain schemes will work successfully and other times when they will be unsuccessful, and this is why EI, like many other HRM policies, goes through fashion changes. The economic, political and social context influences the type and success of the scheme that organisations adopt (Ramsay, 1992a). Further influencing factors are the type, size and sector of the organisation. What may work in a small firm, for example, may not work so well in a large, bureaucratic organisation. What may work in a democratic organisational culture will probably be unsuccessful in a more authoritarian one (Wilkinson, 1989).

The aims and objectives of an organisation in increasing the number and intensity of communication channels may be specifically 'political'. For example, in times of dispute with the union, the management may feel they need to put their side of the case more effectively to the workforce. In the past many companies found themselves at a comparative disadvantage in disputes, as the unions had a virtual monopoly of the informational channels to the workforce. This was no fault of the unions but more a reflection of the incompetence of management, who were incapable of creating effective communication channels, which they suspected could be used at other times for what might be perceived as more negative purposes (Monks, 1989). In other words, management can themselves suffer from their own ideology of operating 'mushroom systems' (keeping the workforce in the dark and piling 'manure' on them), which maintains a climate of distrust and attitudes of 'us and them'. Fortunately, surveys indicate that in many organisations such ideas are becoming less popular (CBI, 1989; Marchington *et al.*, 1992).

ACTIVITY   Bullet point reasons why you think employee involvement schemes, such as TQM, empowerment and teamworking might fail. Now read the next section.

Even schemes such as TQM, which begin life for the most positive reasons – for example, the enhancement of employee commitment, motivation and empowerment – may become distorted by factors, both internal and external, that turn them into something unworkable and, from the employee point of view, into a sinister attempt to gain more commitment, work and productivity, without the concomitant reward, control or empowerment given to employees.

Total quality management has been increasing in popularity in many organisations in recent years, and is often bound up with culture changes and other HRM and managerial initiatives such as customer service programmes. TQM operates at both a local and an establishment-wide level, and pervades the whole organisation. It is concerned with concepts such as culture change, which in turn engender attitudinal changes in the workforce. At workplace level, emphasis can be placed purely on improving the quality of the product or service and, like customer service schemes, this can also be the implementation of more efficiency between internal departments (which can be seen as internal customers) and external customers themselves. Like quality circles, the idea stems from the writings of Deming, Juran, and more recently Crosby (1979, 1984). It has also been linked to British Standard BS 5750 and ISO 9000 approaches, although many claim that this is more suitable for production-oriented rather than service sector work.

Wilkinson *et al.* (1992: 5) point out clearly the differences between QCs and TQM (and their implications) (Table 14.3). The compulsory nature of TQM, with its top-down overtones, suggests a system in which worker empowerment is very much restricted within the boundaries set by management. In its operation in production companies Sewell and Wilkinson (1992) also propose that it has an air of surveillance, whereby the performance of individual workers is monitored so as to control their work to conform to the group norm – a norm set by management.

Table 14.3 **Ideal types of quality circle and TQM**

	Quality circles	**TQM**
Choice	Voluntary	Compulsory
Structure	Bolt-on	Integrated quality system
Direction	Bottom-up	Top-down
Scope	Within departments or units	Company-wide
Aims	Employee relations improvements	Quality improvements

Source: Wilkinson *et al.* (1992: 5)

They describe how, in an electronic components factory, the teams who make the components, especially the team leader, 'have a great deal of discretion in the way labour resources are deployed across the cell [the unit of manufacture]' (Sewell and Wilkinson, 1992: 104). Multi-skilling is encouraged, and work rotation is allocated by the team and team leader. Within the team, individuals are encouraged to improve personal performance, and innovations should be made to improve productivity and product quality. Team meetings provide the forums where such issues are debated and information shared. Quality is controlled by a visual inspection and electronic tests, which also trace the individual responsible for the fault. This information, together with data on absenteeism, conformity to standard times and production planning targets, is prominently displayed for all the team to see. Naturally, the information forms the basis of much discussion between team members. In turn this creates a situation where the team will 'discipline' those whom they feel are not conforming to the norms. This is a form of what Friedman (1977) called *responsible autonomy*, a situation in which the group acts as the controller of the individual and therefore the team. Thus managers can clearly claim that the workforce is being 'empowered'. This delegation of power, however, has a dual nature, which according to Muetzfeldt (quoted in Sewell and Wilkinson, 1992), 'can actually increase the power of the delegating agency, so long as it can legitimate and retain its authority, and undermine it if the obedience of the delegated agents cannot be assured' (p. 106).

Sewell and Wilkinson see this system of TQM as an analogy of the work of Foucault, who stressed the importance of tracing the loci of power in organisations in order to understand its importance and how it is used, like the panopticon, the hub of the surveillance system in Victorian prisons. The electronic quality-recording mechanisms in the operation of TQM in the electronics factory they dub the *information panopticon*, a device used in the control of team norms set by management.

Wilkinson *et al.* (1992), in their research into EI for the Department of Employment (see also Marchington *et al.*, 1992), visited 25 organisations, of which the majority had TQM programmes in operation. In examining these practices it was evident that TQM operated in a wide variety of forms and, like HRM, was open to a variety of definitions and interpretations. In a close examination of TQM in three typical British companies in engineering, finance and marketing, the researchers discovered several problems in its implementation and operation. All of the schemes were difficult to sustain for four basic reasons.

First, the schemes were narrow in conception and 'bolted-on to rather than integrated in, key management policies' (Wilkinson *et al.*, 1992: 14). As a result, some schemes looked very similar to quality circles and thus had many of their faults. Companies tended to look for immediate gains rather than long-term cultural changes. 'If these are not forthcoming TQM is short lived' (p. 15). In turn this created an obsession with 'the cost of quality and immediacy of return, concepts which are totally different from Japanese thinking' (p. 15).

Second, the role of middle managers became unclear and confused, and was looked upon as one group of managers imposing itself on another. This had the effect of creating conflicts. Because TQM was carried out in a highly centralised framework in most organisations, teams were reliant on the services of other departments, with which they were competing for resources, and each department was often in ignorance of how they were affected by each other. The competition thus militated against mutually cooperative solutions.

Third, industrial relations, while affecting TQM programmes, are rarely considered by employers. Thus there was usually neglect in obtaining union agreement or establishing a positive working climate before implementing TQM schemes, a situation almost guaranteed to create suspicion in either the unions or the workforce. TQM has a strong impact on such issues as job control, working practices and reward, all of which can, if not handled sensitively, create problems, as unions and workers may place obstacles in the way of the system's operation.

Fourth, employee involvement in TQM schemes can have contradictory elements. Similar to the findings of Sewell and Wilkinson, it was discovered that there was a contradiction in the language of employee involvement (empowerment of the workforce, etc.) and the actuality of the work situation, in which power very much rested in the hands of management.

Recent critical studies of the 'quality' movement have drawn attention to its wider implications. Wilkinson and Wilmot (1995) state that it is relevant to place the quality movement 'in the wider context of pressures from shareholders upon managers to organise the work of employees in ways that are more profitable' (p. 13). They continue by stating that 'quality initiatives are often imposed upon an unprepared and hesitant, if not hostile, management by the intensity of (global) competitive pressures'. They also draw attention 'to the strength and depth of the participation promoted by TQM. It is striking that participation does not extend to key decisions relating to the ownership and control of companies' (p. 20). In a recent comparative study of employee involvement in the banking sector in Britain and Sweden, Holden (1996) has concluded that most participation mechanisms, particularly those related to recent HRM initiatives such as TQM, do not encourage participation by the workforce in strategic issues. Most are confined to workplace areas, and therefore tend to be restricted in their sphere of control. This is particularly surprising when much HRM literature advocates the strategic nature of HRM policy in relation to employee influence.

These studies point to a number of problems in the implementation of TQM. Ramsay (1992a) has noted, with some laconic interest, the rise and fall of fads and fashions in employee involvement, and speculates about what might be next on the agenda if TQM does not succeed! What is certain is that easy solutions do not exist, and the implementation of new systems has to be viewed within a long-term framework and reviewed constantly with the full consent and approval of the workforce.

International aspects of employee involvement

In many countries in Europe and the rest of the world, trade unions still act as one of the most important communication channels, despite indications that there has been a decline in membership worldwide over the past ten years (ILO, 1993). Their importance is central in Scandinavian countries, especially Sweden, and they still carry considerable weight in Germany and Britain, though the rise in long-term unemployment and the decline in the old staple industries such as shipbuilding, coal, iron and steel, and engineering, where unionism had a strong traditional base, have tended to erode their power.

Employee involvement rooted in industrial democratic processes has witnessed a surer growth over the past 30 years in legislatively supported systems such as co-determination in Germany and Sweden. The operation of these two contrasting styles of industrial democracy is also reflected by the relative union strength in each country – 85 per cent in Sweden and 35 per cent in Germany in 1988 (OECD, 1991).

Swedish co-determination

In many respects Sweden has the most advanced forms of participation in the world, at both organisational and workplace levels (Wilczynski, 1983). The basis of industrial democracy in the country stretches back to 1948 with the setting up of the National Labour Market Board. This was composed of representatives from labour, employers and government, and participated in economic planning.

In the economic and political climate of the 1970s, demands were made for the extension of industrial democracy, which led to the passage of a body of legislation, most notable of which was the Co-determination at Work Act (MBL) passed in 1977. The aim of the Act was to extend the scope of collective bargaining to areas of management policy, including organisational and technical change. It required all employers to allow consultation with employees and the participation of their representatives in decision-making at both board and shopfloor levels. For example, one of the central provisions of the Act requires that, when employers are contemplating making major changes in their operations or working conditions of employment, they are required to negotiate with employee representatives before the final decisions are taken and changes are introduced (Edlund and Nyström, 1988).

In reality, employee representatives in the co-determination system tend to be union representatives, and it was the unions in Sweden that gave the impetus for much of the drive towards industrial democracy. The union strategy was to focus on issues of health and safety, and 'this created a political climate in which new laws and regulations in support of industrial democracy could be introduced . . . these laws were supplemented by financial support for training and research which to a large extent was channelled through the unions' (Hammarström, 1987). The crucial role of unions, not only in bargaining structures but in the co-determination system, meant that they would always be an important element in Swedish employee relations.

Companies have also enhanced the reputation of Swedish employee involvement. Volvo in particular introduced job enlargement and job enrichment, 'quality of working life' techniques to its Kalmar plant in the 1970s, and became the focus of much attention worldwide as an alternative to the mass-assembly Fordist systems of production (Sell, 1988).

While these systems have been admired, they have also received criticism. The neo-liberalists have seen the corporatist state pay too heavy a price in terms of high wages and high taxes for a regulated labour market that is seen as being heavily influenced by the ability of the workforce to impede management prerogatives in policy creation. Conversely, left-wing critics have attacked the system for not addressing the real needs

| Figure 14.2 | Co-determination: not a drag but a motive force |

Source: Edlund and Nyström, 1988

of the workforce, which have been emasculated by the unions in collusion with the Social Democratic Party in attempts to maintain the corporatist status quo. 'Kalmarism', as one French observer has dubbed the EI initiatives in Volvo (Lipietz, 1992), has also been attacked for being no more than a public relations exercise. Many of the EI initiatives are seen as untypical, and many were dropped as being uneconomic and inappropriate.

A recent trend in Sweden has been seen to be bound up with managerial HRM initiatives, which have shifted from formal to more informal models of participation and decentralised practices. Some observers suggest that these trends might eventually undermine the formal system of participation (Cressey, 1992).

What is certain is that the change in the economic climate in the early 1990s as a result of recession, raising unemployment from 1.5 per cent in 1990 to 8.5 per cent in 1993, had an enormous impact on the Swedish collective psyche, challenging many of the assumptions that were generally acceptable in the agreeable economic environment of the 1980s (Holden, 1996).

The balance of power between state, unions and employers changes continually with each economic phase, but there is no reason to believe that the essence of the system will not survive. Despite the fact that management prerogatives in Sweden still outweigh those of the employee, the culture of involvement is still very well developed compared with most other countries.

German co-determination

Given the embodiment of the concept of consultation and participation in the EU Social Charter and the draft European Works Council Directive, it is not surprising that the German system of co-determination and works councils has been seen by some observers to be a model for the rest of the Union:

> In contrast to other countries, the system of co-determination in Germany is very extensive, and involves the participation of employees and their representatives in nearly all decisions relating to personnel and many aspects of company policy.
>
> (Gaugler and Wiltz, 1992)

Co-determination is legally embodied in the work system by four key Acts: the Montan Co-determination Act 1951, the Workplace Labour Relations Act 1952, the Workplace Labour Relations Act 1972, and the Co-determination law of 1976. Co-determination operates basically at company and plant levels, although there are three methods by which workers can participate: works councils, supervisory boards and management boards. In places of work that have five or more employees the workforce elects a works council, consisting of workers' representatives only. The works council has a right to information concerning:

- health and safety;
- the organisation of work;
- the working environment and jobs;
- the hiring of executives;
- planned changes in the company that could result in considerable disadvantages to employees.

In addition, the works council has the right to make suggestions (Gaugler and Wiltz, 1992):

- during the formulation and implementation of personnel planning;
- regarding vocational training (apprenticeships, etc.);
- about other training and development measures.

The views of the works council must be considered by the employer, although there is no compulsion to accept them. For larger companies (not family owned) employing more than 500 people, representatives elected by the workers sit on the supervisory board, where they make up one-third to a half (depending on size) of the policy-making body. Other board members are elected by the shareholders, and a neutral chairperson is appointed. In companies over 2000 employees in size, trade union representatives are guaranteed places on the board. German workers tend to believe that in general the works councils and co-determination system represent them adequately, and there has been a reluctance to join unions (35 per cent as opposed to Sweden's union density of 85 per cent), although the recession in the early 1990s witnessed a revival of trade union militancy.

The supervisory board meets four times a year, and also appoints members to the management board, a full-time executive body that oversees company policy in its day-to-day operations. (For a fuller explanation of the history and detailed operation of the co-determination system, see Lawrence, 1980; Lane, 1989; Gaugler and Wiltz, 1992.)

Co-determination: an evaluation

In evaluating co-determination one must be aware of the diversity of positions from which views emanate. These are of course influenced by political ideology, position in the organisation (whether management or worker etc.), whether one is a shareholder, and the type of organisation. Lane (1989), in her survey of research analysing the influence of co-determination in Germany, points to the diversity of findings depending on the level (whether workplace or enterprise), company size, sector and managerial style.

Not surprisingly, co-determination at enterprise level has had relatively little impact on the everyday work of employees, but, it can be argued, has had the long-term positive effect of engendering a spirit of cooperation between management and labour. Labour representatives perceive more clearly the reasons for managerial policy initiatives, and conversely the management have more understanding of the concerns of the workforce.

At workplace level there has been a wide variety of research. For example, Wilpert and Rayley (1983) showed that there was a large discrepancy between formal rights and actual rights of participation. They also state that, while participation rights in Germany are high compared with most other European countries, so too is formal and actual managerial control.

Lane (1989) posits the view that 'faced with a strong and control-oriented management and forced to prove themselves *vis-à-vis* their electors by concrete achievements, works councillors may decide to pursue only those issues on which they are confident to get concessions' (p. 232). Thus the degree of participatory influence could also vary with each issue.

Not surprisingly, there are German employers who share the view of past British Conservative governments that the co-determination system undermines the employer's right to manage. Survey evidence suggests, however, that works councils are supported by the overwhelming majority of employers, except in the smallest of firms (Mauritz, 1972, quoted in Lane, 1989: 233).

Works councils bolstered by legislation also exist in Belgium, France, Italy, Luxembourg, Spain and the Netherlands, but the range of issues and decisions submitted for employee approval is smaller than in Germany. The operation of the councils is also affected by employee and management attitudes bound up with the institutions and culture of the country.

For example, the Auroux Laws 1982 extended workers' participation rights in French companies, but research reveals that the consultation process has been ignored or undermined by management accustomed to the hierarchical and often autocratic ways strongly emphasised (although changing) in many French organisations (Lane, 1989: 240). In Sweden there has been much criticism of the relatively weak position of unions in the co-determinational process, particularly in time of recession (Korpi, 1981; Kjellberg, 1992). Unions often do not receive adequate information, and in the recent bank crisis had much less influence than management on the restructuring and downsizing exercises (Holden, 1996).

◼ Works councils and consultation in the European Union

The Works Council Directive was embodied in the Social Charter and was formally adopted by the European Union (EU) in 1994. This requires any company with over 1000 employees in the EU and with at least 150 employees in two different countries to set up a council for the purpose of informing and consulting employees. In December 1999 the UK government embodied this in British legislation. In previous years UK Conservative governments and employer organisations had strongly resisted any attempts by the EU to impose a works council directive, but the Blair Labour government has signed up to the Social Charter and consequently fully subscribes to the principle of works councils.

In December 2001 the EU also passed a directive which requires employers to give proper information to, and allow consultation with, employees. This will come into effect in March 2005 and will apply to all organisations with 150 or more employees. In 2007 it will apply to all businesses of more than 100 employees and in 2008 to those with 50 or more. It will include the following provisions:

- Employees have a right to be informed of a company's economic situation and employment prospects, decisions that may lead to substantial changes in how work is organised and contractual relations.
- Information and consultation must take place at the appropriate time, and at the relevant level of management. This will be done using employee representatives (defined according to national law and practice).
- Employers and employees can meet their obligations through existing agreements in conformance with the directive.
- Employers may withhold information if its disclosure would seriously harm the business. They can also require employee representatives to keep information confidential.

There are also proposals to force companies to consult with employees at national level. This has received continued opposition from the UK government and employer associations, a stand supported by their German counterparts. The European Social Partners failed to agree on this issue in 1998, and Dirk Hudig, secretary-general of the employers' confederation in Europe (UNICE), 'predicts that any definite movement on the proposals, which would force companies to set up works councils at national level, is unlikely' (Rana, 1999: 13). Employers fear that national and pan-European works councils could interfere with their national and international policies, such as downsizing or closing company subsidiaries in other European countries.

Nevertheless, recent evidence shows that the number of works councils (and similar bodies) is on the increase in Britain. More than half are in French and German-owned subsidiaries such as Renault, Crédit Lyonnais, Grundig and Bayer, although increasing numbers are coming from Scandinavia (such as Electrolux and Norsk Hydro). British companies are also creating their own works councils, most notably BP, Coats Viyella and United Biscuits (Carley, 1995). The presence of a works council does not, however, guarantee employee consultation or indeed a voice in managerial policy, as the experience of job losses at Coats Viyella in 1996 clearly displayed. This lack of consultation has outraged unions and employees throughout the company's British and European concerns (Littlefield, 1996). Another British firm, Marks and Spencer, closed stores in France in 2001 with virtually no consultation with the workforce, a decision that led to protests by employees and the media.

Such behaviour is not confined to British-owned companies. In 1998 Renault closed its Vilvoorde plant in Belgium without adequately consulting or informing its employees. Union protests led to a French court ruling that Renault did not act in accordance with the European Works Council (EWC) Directive about the proposed plant closure. Obviously this retrospective censure has not returned those Renault jobs to Belgian workers, and the European trade union movement (ETUC) has demanded amendments tightening the EWC legislation, so far without success.

Such incidents clearly indicate that social dialogue progress remains limited. Nevertheless, research by Marginson *et al.* (1998) shows that companies in France, Germany, the UK and even the USA found a widespread preference for joint employer–employee bodies, be it only at plant level.

■ Japanese employee involvement

Japan is often cited as an exemplar of employee participation practices, particularly giant corporations such as Komatsu, Hitachi, Nissan, Honda, Mitsubishi and Toyota. The most commonly emulated participation technique has been quality circles, which we have already noted were conceived in the USA by Deming and Juran, and were implanted in Japanese organisations in the 1950s. Since then, employee involvement techniques such as QCs and teamworking have been part and parcel of the working practices of Japanese companies in the UK, such as Nissan in Sunderland and Toyota in Derby. Many studies have been made of Japanese organisations in order to discover the secrets of their economic success, and teamworking techniques have received much attention as a perceived key to efficient work practices.

Pascale and Athos (1982) emphasise that the work group is the basic building block of Japanese organisations: 'Owing to the central importance of group efforts in their thinking, the Japanese are extremely sensitive to and concerned about group interactions and relationships' (p. 125). They liken the Japanese worker's view of the group to that of a marriage that rests on commitment, trust, sharing and loyalty, and while power ultimately rests with management, the group leader handles the interaction within the group carefully. This 'participation assumption' is also related to a lifetime employment assumption, which ensures that the worker has a strong stake in the firm and its success. Finally, and perhaps most importantly, participation is backed up by training of both group leaders and workers in the skills of group participation (Dore and Sako, 1989). Employee involvement, like training, is thus embedded in Japanese organisations.

A number of observers (including Klaus and Bass, 1974) have pointed out that employee involvement should not be confused with decision-making, particularly at the higher levels within the organisation: 'The reality is that not all employees wield real power . . . [and] when it comes to making the decision, workers feel under great pressure to agree with supervisors and unpopular decisions are simply ignored' (Naoi and Schooler, 1985, quoted in Briggs, 1991: 40). Briggs sees this paradox of employee involvement and emasculation of power as being explained by the split between opinion and behaviour. In a number of surveys Japanese workers have rated themselves low on job satisfaction and yet they work far more hours for less reward than their US and British counterparts. This cannot be explained by coercive methods alone; Briggs points to the extent of unionisation, albeit organised around large corporations, and finds this view untenable. Her explanation is based on cultural factors in that the Japanese have 'a deep felt desire to keep the realm of duty separate from the realm of personal feeling . . .

duty must come first and must exist totally separate from the domain of personal feelings' (Briggs, 1991: 41).

If this is the case, it has ramifications for the export of such EI practices to other countries, most notably Britain, which has received enormous amounts of Japanese investment. Wickens (1987), in his exposition of how Nissan implanted Japanese practices into its Sunderland factory, strongly believes that people are capable of change and that the institution of Japanese-style working practices was partly effected by a watering-down process to meet British attitudes, combined with a process of education and training to enable newly hired (often novice) workers in car manufacturing to be imbued with Japanese-style practices. This was reinforced by a greenfield culture with workers who had predominantly been recruited from regions where high unemployment meant an eagerness to gain and retain employment.

A number of observers have pointed out that control and the mechanisms of employee involvement in Japanese-owned British organisations still reside firmly in the hands of management. Lewis (1989), in his study of employee participation in a Japanese-owned electronics factory, found that, while a board was set up (a kind of JCC) to represent employee interests, employees were not quite sure what was meant by involvement. Most of the issues raised were not about the overall running of the operation but more parochial shopfloor concerns, and the real aim in setting up the board was to introduce unitarist principles in the company such as single-status terms and conditions, no-strike arrangements and flexible work practices. All were reinforced with powerful symbols of unitarism such as the brightly coloured jackets that everyone wore, replete with the owner's forename. This sent messages of egalitarianism and that the organisation was one happy family. The single-status restaurants and toilets were also part of this symbolic reinforcement of unitarism. Oliver and Lowe (1991) endorse this unitarist view of Japanese-style management. In comparing styles of HRM in Japanese, US and British computer companies based in the UK, they found that the Japanese emphasised consensus and collectivism with 'a thin dividing line between the public and the private and a strong sense of mutual support and awareness'.

In essence, the implementation of EI, even in Japanese organisations that have strong commitments to such systems, is not as a decision-making instrument *per se* or even as a conduit of employee criticism, but as a mechanism that reinforces common aims and goals within the unitarist organisational context.

Ramsay (1992b) has also pointed out that few non-Japanese-owned British organisations have adopted Japanese EI measures in the long term. The use of quality circles, after an initial flurry of interest, dropped from 63 per cent in 1980 to 10 per cent in 1989 in British organisations. He concludes: 'No matter what the degree of genuine autonomy or control Swedish or Japanese work group experiments, the greater constraints on the prospect for worker influence came from the institutional settings and – even more critically – the broader social and cultural contexts' (p. 40).

Stop and think	Why do you think quality circles did not work as well in the UK as in Japan in the 1980s?

Comparative aspects of employee involvement

Comparative research of a statistical and analytical nature into EI is relatively sparse, although there have been numerous international surveys of institutional and legal aspects of employee involvement (Poole, 1986). Studies in the 1980s and 1990s revealed a diversity of trends influenced by a multiplicity of organisational, economic, political and technical factors. The Price Waterhouse Cranfield Survey into International Strategic HRM investigated trends in employee communications in five countries (the UK, Sweden, the then West Germany, Spain and France) in 1990, and ten countries in 1991 (the original five plus the Netherlands, Norway, Denmark, Italy and Switzerland), with subsequent surveys in 1995 and 1999. These surveys reveal a marked increase in attempts at communicating with the workforce, both via staff representative bodies, such as trade unions, and by more direct methods associated with HRM initiatives (Holden, 1990; Price Waterhouse Cranfield, 1990 and 1991). Parallel to overall increases via staff representative bodies were even larger increases in verbal and written communication in all countries. This obviously indicates a greater desire by employers to increase communication, probably inspired by HRM trends, which spread in the 1980s. France and the UK show particularly large increases in both verbal and written communication, which parallel the rise in team briefing and other teamwork methods, as well as increases in the more traditional written forms of communication.

It would seem that communication with and from the workforce is increasing at workplace level, but the more established forms of communication and EI such as unions, works councils and JCCs are still important in those organisations where they are established. The survey conducted by Marchington *et al.* (1992) in UK organisations would seem to confirm this.

Nevertheless, these surveys do not indicate the degree of participation by employees in organisations. Research by Fröhlich and Krieger (1990), Cressey and Williams (1990), Boreham (1992) and Gill (1993) has tried to address this issue in comparative contexts. Fröhlich and Krieger (1990) examined the extent of employee participation in technological change in five EC countries – the UK, France, Germany, Italy and Denmark. They discovered that of the four phases of introducing new technology (planning, selection, implementation and subsequent evaluation) workers were more likely to be involved in the latter stages, and that full participation, particularly in decision-making, remained relatively low for all countries and for all stages. Cressey and Williams (1990), in a similar survey but covering all of the then 12 EC countries, found comparable results and posed a 'paradox of participation'. As the scope for influence by employees over the processes of technological change decreased, so the intensity of participation increased. In other words, there was more scope for participation in the implementation stage (the latter stage) when participative influence concerning fundamental decisions was reduced, and less participation in the crucial earlier planning stages in the introduction of new technology.

Gill (1993), using the same 12-country EC data analysed by Cressey and Williams (1990), perceives differences in attitudes between Northern European and Mediterranean countries, which result in a wide diversity in levels of participation. Denmark, Germany, the Netherlands and Belgium have much greater employee participation than do Portugal, Spain, Italy, Greece, France, Luxembourg and the UK. In France and the UK, however, Gill argues, 'there is a dependence by management on the skills and problem solving abilities of the labour force' (p. 346). Nevertheless, he claims that 'in the United Kingdom there has been a shift away from negotiation towards more consultation during the last decade and management has become increasingly paternalistic in their style' (p. 346). These differences are caused, he argues, by the diverse industrial relations practices in each country, shaped by historical and cultural factors.

In all three studies managers were of the view that increased participation was effective for the efficient implementation of new technology, but this may have the effect of compromising their prerogatives.

Boreham (1992) investigated the degree of employee control over labour processes in seven countries (Australia, Britain, Canada, Germany, Japan, Sweden and the USA). He was particularly interested to know whether employee control was enhanced by the introduction of new practices associated with post-Fordist systems such as flexible working linked to quality improvement and greater response to market conditions. The assumption here was that efficiency was improved by decentralisation and democratised decision-making practices. The findings clearly indicated that 'the nearer one approaches the core of status and power in the enterprise the more likely it is that one be allowed discretion over one's work arrangements' (p. 18). He also found that there was little evidence 'to support the view that management will cede its decision making prerogatives in the interests of more rational production methods' (p. 21). This pattern was generally true of Japanese and Swedish organisations, which are associated with employee involvement styles of management.

These surveys clearly indicate a contradiction in managers' perceptions that employee involvement is an effective way of increasing work efficiency, but is outweighed by the challenge to their prerogatives over decision-making. Thus employee involvement is very limited, and is more likely to take the form of information dissemination to, and consultation with, the workforce, which is not the same as the 'empowerment' to which many HRM textbooks allude.

Boreham (1992) also stresses the significance of flexible employment patterns and involvement. In a world where increases in part-time, fixed-contract and short-term working are becoming more pronounced, he shows that these employees have even less involvement in workplace decisions, and that core groups, particularly in management categories, still hold far greater sway over the organisation and control of work. Such evidence casts huge question marks over growing trends – for example, 'zero hours contracts' alongside involvement schemes aimed at motivating workers.

■ What can we learn from these studies?

The findings of these pieces of research are replicated to some degree by the findings in two studies by the Industrial Democracy in Europe research group (IDE) in 1981 and 1993.

In essence, it seems that there is a contradiction in what employers and managers want from EI and what they are prepared to allow to the workforce in terms of empowerment and control. In ideological terms, the control of the organisation rests in the hands of the upper realms of the hierarchy, either the board or within the senior management teams, and there will be resistance to attempts to extend significant power to workers lower down the organisation. Thus the concept of 'industrial democracy' *per se* is perceived as a power challenge, even in societies that allow considerable autonomy to the workforce and have in place sophisticated structures of co-determination, such as those that exist in Sweden and Germany. This power 'balance' will also shift with changing economic and political climates, and management will allow considerably more concessions in times of labour shortage than in times of recession, when worker power is much weaker.

The ideas of 'empowerment' and 'employee influence' at workplace level have greater justification for management in HRM terms, as the rationale for the introduction of EI policies is ultimately to increase the efficiency of the organisation. The perception of management poses a dilemma in terms of how much power to extend to the workforce while harnessing their creative energies, and at the same time not undermining managerial prerogatives. This conundrum is in many ways a central one to the whole debate concerning HRM and modern organisational practices such as delayering of middle management structures, the introduction of new technology, TQM, the creation of flatter organisations, culture change and empowerment initiatives. Perhaps the working out of these power balances is a continuing part of the managerial process, until, that is, the structure of ownership in society radically changes. Equally important is the relationship between middle management and senior management, which to some extent can be seen as similar to that between workforce and middle management, but overlaid with elements of status and role strain, i.e. squashed between senior management and the workforce.

Another factor at both organisational and workplace levels is the influence of cultural values, to which many commentators on EI ultimately allude. Writers such as Hofstede and Laurent have attempted to examine these influences, and concede that much research has still to be completed before our understanding of these complex issues is clearer. Even then, 'culture' is in a state of permanent flux, and our concept of it is ever-changing, often in subtle ways. Yet observers would have us believe that British adaptations to Japanese work practices are possible despite the different cultural values of British workers. Others have stated that the practices become palatable because of the environment into which they are introduced: greenfield sites with single-union deals and no-strike clauses, and a compliant workforce conscious of the lack of alternative employment in high-unemployment areas.

Several factors emerge that make the proper working of EI mechanisms possible:

- a willingness by management to concede some of their prerogatives;
- the need to train managers in EI initiatives such as teamworking;
- the need for a clear policy regarding the role and prerogatives of line managers in relation to senior management and the workforce under their supervision;
- the need to train workers in group skills such as presentation, leadership, assertiveness and problem-solving;
- the need for providing proper feedback mechanisms that clearly indicate that the workforce is being listened to, and not in a purely lip-service fashion;
- the need for action to implement group decisions, which reinforces the view among the workforce that their contributions are well received;
- the need for conflicting views to have a place in developing initiatives.

Summary

- This chapter began by exploring definitions of employee involvement and empowerment as generic (EI) and specific terms (HRM EI). This was followed by an examination of EI practices in relation to HRM, and EI and forms of control within organisations.

- Employers' increasing recognition of the significance of communications in organisations was acknowledged. Over recent years employee involvement has been recognised as one important communication instrument.

- The history of employee involvement was traced, including forms of industrial democracy, and more recently the fashion for recognition of the centrality that employee involvement has begun to assume in HRM trends. Patterns of EI were investigated, ranging from theories of cycles and waves of participation, proposed by Ramsay and Marchington respectively, to an explanatory framework of participation suggested by Poole.

- Definitions of EI were summarised, with an outline of the types and levels of participation within organisations. These included two broad categories of EI at macro and micro levels: macro level being types of EI at organisational or enterprise level, such as works councils or joint consultative committees (JCCs), and micro level being at the workplace, such as quality circles and team briefings. Types of EI were examined under four basic headings: downward communication from managers to employees, such as company journals, newspapers, videos, briefing sessions; upwards, problem-solving forms, such as quality circles, suggestion schemes, TQM and customer care programmes; financial participation, such as profit-sharing and share ownership schemes; and representative participation, such as JCCs, works councils, co-determination and collective bargaining. The various strengths and weaknesses of the most popular forms of EI were analysed.

● The term 'empowerment' was examined, providing some definitions of the concept. This was followed by some discussion as to how empowerment benefits the individual and the organisation. Empowerment was also examined in relation to HRM initiatives, and this section concluded by proposing some critiques of the concept and practices, revealing its confinement to workplace levels, rather than strategic policy-making levels within the organisation.

● The concept of business process re-engineering (BPR) was briefly examined, and this was followed by an in-depth analysis of total quality management, based on various studies that pointed to common pitfalls in its implementation.

● International aspects of EI were considered, beginning with a review of the Swedish system, noted for its advanced EI practices, particularly the co-determination system and the quality of working life movement. The German co-determination and works council system was also examined in the light of suggestions that it might act as a possible European model. An evaluation of co-determination was then undertaken, followed by an exploration of the European works council issue in the context of the European Union.

● A review of influential Japanese EI methods was undertaken, outlining the difficulties in cross-cultural transfers of work practices. The international section ended by evaluating some comparative surveys of employee involvement, highlighting similar trends as well as common problems in different countries, for example the mediation of power and control in the implementation of EI systems.

● Finally, there was some advice as to which factors should be taken into consideration in implementing EI schemes.

ACTIVITY | **Company newsletter**

The Public Relations and Human Resource Management departments of Flexible Printing Services Ltd oversee 300 workers on 12 different sites, and are conscious of the need to keep their employees aware of new developments within the company. They have therefore decided to produce a small company newsletter for this purpose. There is a relatively small but active number of union members within the company on most of the sites.

1 In groups, role-play the members of the editorial team in the first editorial meeting to discuss the new company newsletter. Decide upon the policies and practices for the newsletter to ensure that it is a genuine communication, reflective of the organisation as a whole.

2 Write a report on the meeting to the Public Relations and Human Resource Management departments describing the issues that were dealt with by the editorial committee.

Questions

1 How is the concept of empowerment different from that of employee involvement and industrial democracy?

2 What forms of managerial control operate in the practice of employee involvement schemes?

3   What forms has employee involvement (EI) taken over the past 50 years? In your answer, give examples from both micro and macro levels in the organisation. What evidence is there to suggest that EI develops in waves according to economic cycles?

4   What are the main issues under discussion at present concerning European works council schemes and participation generally in the European Union?

5   What evidence is there to suggest that schemes of financial participation rarely achieve their goals?

6   Why are empowerment schemes popular at present? What criticisms can be made of such schemes?

7   Why do you think communicational difficulties could be regarded as a 'political' problem in some organisations? (Unions, power struggles in the boardroom and in departments, cliques, knowledge is power syndrome.)

Exercises

1   As editor of a company newspaper, what policies and practices would you follow in order to make it a genuine communication reflective of the organisation as a whole?

2   A prominent British bank is interested in setting up a works council. Write a report recommending the policies in terms of aims, objectives and implementation that should be considered in its foundation.

3   Divide the class into pairs. Ask one group of people to devise reasons why there should be greater participation by employees in the workplace, and ask the other group to put the case against extending participation. Each group should evaluate their reasons from the viewpoint of employers, managers and employees. Then ask the whole group to debate the question of employee participation from each side's viewpoint.

Case study 1

Total quality management

Precision Tool Engineering is a company producing machinery and machine tools and some other related engineering products for specialist production companies. It employs a total workforce of 400, two-thirds of whom work in the production departments.

In late 1993 the company's management decided to introduce a total quality management scheme to increase efficiency and quality control. In 1990 more flexible arrangements had been introduced, accompanied by a breakdown of old work demarcation lines. Machines were now built by flexible teams of workers employing different skills (e.g. fitters, electricians, and hydraulic engineers). In 1994 the first moves towards TQM were made with the introduction of BS 5750. Workers were asked to inspect the quality of their work, with the result that the need for specialist inspectors was greatly reduced, and both time and money were saved. Agreements were negotiated with the union for extra pay as a result of the increase in worker responsibility.

In early 1995 the management decided to introduce a full-blown TQM scheme on the basis of the success of the introduction of BS 5750. Problem-solving groups were formed based on work groups with voluntary participation. Group leaders, who were mainly supervisors, were trained in how to run a group and in prob-

Case study 1 continued

lem-solving techniques. The aims of the groups were to:

- identify problems inside their work area;
- propose solutions;
- identify problems outside their work area;
- refer external problems to a review team.

The review team was made up mainly of managers with one representative from each group, usually the group leader. The unions were lukewarm towards the scheme, and some shop stewards were directly against it.

Within the space of nine months the TQM scheme was reviewed, and senior management came to the conclusion that it had not lived up to expectations, some board members calling it a failure. Some of the areas they identified were that team leaders had felt uncomfortable in their role, and there had been considerable scepticism from some groups of workers.

Questions

1 Why do you think the BS 5750 scheme was successful but the TQM scheme failed in Precision Engineering?

2 What suggestions would you make to a similar company that was thinking of introducing TQM, in order to make it a success?

Case study 2

Empowerment at Semco

Semco, an engineering company in Brazil, caught the attention of the world in the 1990s by the claims of its CEO, Ricardo Semler, that it was a democratic and profitable organisation. On returning from studying for an MBA at Harvard, Semler was convinced that the way to increase the productivity of the workforce was to empower them and involve them in the operation of the business. Since undertaking his empowerment initiatives the company has increased in size 11 times and, in the first half of the 1990s, became one of the fastest-growing companies in Latin America. How did he achieve such impressive results?

According to Semler (1993), 'Democracy is the cornerstone of the Semco system' (p. 249). There is representative democracy through factory committees. All employees, excluding management, elect representatives to serve on these committees. The union is also represented. The committees meet regularly to discuss workplace issues and policy. 'They are empowered to declare strikes, audit the books, and question all aspects of management' (p. 249). Employees have a vote on all important decisions such as plant relocations. There is also a suggestion scheme.

Semler describes Semco as a 'circular organisation'. Bureaucracy has been drastically cut by reducing 12 layers of management down to three. There are only four titles in the company: Counsellors, who are similar to vice-presidents and coordinate general policy and strategy; Partners, who run the business units; Coordinators, senior managers in charge of sales, marketing, production and assembly area foremen; and Associates, who are the rest of Semco employees.

Semco also practises what it calls 'reverse evaluation', which includes what is now generally known as 360-degree appraisal. Every six months managers are evaluated by their employees. This is done anonymously by multiple choice questionnaire, and the grades are publicly displayed. Before anyone is hired or promoted they must be evaluated by all the people who will work with them.

Work is organised in manufacturing cells, with work teams that are given responsibility to create a whole product. This avoids assembly-line-production boredom and alienation, and increases employee control over their work process. This 'makes them happier and our products better' (Semler, 1993: 250). Semco has reduced barriers between departments and encourages 'management by wandering around'. Offices do not have walls, and workplaces are demarcated by plants. Employees can adapt and change their working space as they please.

There is also profit sharing, but with a difference. Management does not decide unilaterally what profit is to be shared; that decision is made after negotiations with the workforce. Semler also allows the workforce to 'self-set pay' – a policy whereby employees decide their own salaries. This is done through negotiations with the unions, comparing local pay rates and consulting with both management and the team. Individuals can also choose how much of their earnings can be basic pay and how much bonus. Employees can also choose when they work, flexitime is encouraged and time punch clocks have been removed. Home working is also encouraged if possible.

There is a high union presence, and Semco encourages union membership as well as carrying out negotiation and discussion with the unions. There are disagreements, and some have led to

strikes, but the strikes are far less than under the old regime.

The ultimate aim is 'transparency': all information within and about the company is available to all employees. Workers are even given training by trade union officials on the company premises and in the company time on issues such as understanding the company balance sheets, to enable more effective participation. All employees are encouraged to have a voice and express their concerns.

Questions

1 Can Semco be rightly regarded as an empowering organisation? Give reasons for your answer.

2 Why can't Semco be a truly democratic organisation?

3 Where is the locus of control in Semco?

4 How could Semco be more democratic in its human resource and managerial policies?

References and further reading

Those texts marked with an asterisk are particularly recommended for further reading.

Arkin, A. (1995) 'The bumpy road to devolution', *People Management*, 30 November, pp. 34–36.

Babson, S. (1995) *Lean Work: Empowerment and Exploitation in the Global Auto Industry*. Detroit, Mich.: Wayne State University Press.

Badden, L., Hunter, L., Hyman, J., Leopold, J. and Ramsay, H. (1989) *People's Capitalism: A Critical Analysis of Profit and Employee Share Ownership*. London: Routledge.

Beardwell, I. and Holden, L. (1994) *Human Resource Management: A Contemporary Perspective*. London: Pitman Publishing.

Beer, M., Spector, B., Lawrence, P., Quinn Mills, D. and Walton, R. (1984) *Managing Human Assets*. New York: Free Press.

Blauner, R. (1964) *Alienation and Freedom*. Chicago, Ill.: Chicago University Press.

Boreham, P. (1992) 'The myth of post-fordist management: work organisation and employee discretion in seven countries', *Employee Relations*, Vol. 14, No. 2, pp. 13–24.

Brannen, P., Batstone, E., Fatchett, D. and White, P. (1976) *The Worker Directors: A Sociology of Participation*. London: Hutchinson.

Braverman, H. (1974) *Labour and Monopoly Capital: The Degradation of Work in the 20th Century*. New York: Monthly Review Press.

Brennan, B. (1991) 'Mismanagement and quality circles: how middle managers influence direct participation', *Employee Relations*, Vol. 13, No. 5, pp. 22–32.

Briggs, P. (1991) 'Organisational commitment: the key to Japanese success?', in Brewster, C. and Tyson, S. (eds) *International Comparisons in Human Resource Management*. London: Pitman, pp. 33–43.

Broekmeyer, M.J. (ed.) (1970) *Yugoslav Workers' Self-Management*. Pordrecht: Reidel.

Buchanan, D. (1996) *The Re-engineering Frame: An Assessment*, Occasional Paper Series. Leicester: Leicester Business School.

Buchanan, D. and Preston, D. (1992) 'Life in the cell: supervision and team in a "manufacturing systems engineering" environment', *Human Resource Management Journal*, Vol. 2, No. 4, pp. 55–76.

Bullock Committee Report (1977) *On Industrial Democracy*. Hendon: HMSO.

Burawoy, M. (1979) *Manufacturing Consent: Changes in the Labour Process Under Monopoly Capitalism*. Chicago, Ill.: University of Chicago Press.

Burawoy, M. (1983) 'Between the labour process and the state: factory regimes under advanced capitalism', *American Sociological Review*, Vol. 48, pp. 587–605.

Carley, M. (1995) 'Talking shops or serious forums: works councils', *People Management*, 13 July, pp. 26–31.

CBI (1989) *Employee Involvement: Shaping the Future Business*. London: Confederation of British Industry.

Church, R. (1971) 'Profit sharing and labour relations in England in the nineteenth century', *International Review of Social History*, No. 14, pp. 2–16.

Claydon, T. and Doyle, M. (1996) 'Trusting me, trusting you? The ethics of employee empowerment', paper presented at the Conference of Ethical Issues in Contemporary Human Resource Management, Imperial College, London, 3 April.

Clutterbuck, D. and Crainer, S. (1990) *Makers of Management: Men and Women who Changed the Business World*. London: Macmillan.

Cole, G.D.H. (1917) *Self Government in Industry*. London: Bell & Sons; 1972 edn, London: Hutchinson.

Collard, R. and Dale, B. (1989) 'Quality circles', in Sisson, K. (ed.) *Personnel Management in Britain*. Oxford: Blackwell, pp. 356–377.

Cook, S. and Macauley, S. (1997) 'Empowered customer service', *Empowerment in Organisations*, Vol. 5, No. 1, pp. 54–60.

Cressey, P. (1992) 'Worker participation: what can we learn from the Swedish experience?', *P+ European Participation Monitor*, Vol. 3, No.1, pp. 3–7.

Cressey, P. and Williams, R. (1990) *Participation in Change: New Technology and the Role of Employee Involvement*. Dublin: European Foundation for the Improvement of Living and Working Conditions.

Crosby, P. (1979) *Quality is Free*. New York: McGraw-Hill.

Crosby, P. (1984) *Quality Without Tears*. New York: McGraw-Hill.

Dore, R. and Sako, M. (1989) *How the Japanese Learn to Work*. London: Routledge.

Drucker, P. (1961) *The Practice of Management*. London: Mercury.

Dunn, S., Richardson, R. and Dewe, P. (1991) 'The impact of employee share ownership on worker attitudes: a longitudinal case study', *Human Resource Management Journal*, Vol. 1, No. 3, pp. 1–17.

Eccles, T. (1981) *Under New Management: The Story of Britain's Largest Cooperative*. London: Pan.

Edlund, S. and Nyström, B. (1988) *Developments in Swedish Labour Law*. Stockholm: The Swedish Institute.

Edwards, P.K. (1987) *Managing the Factory*. Oxford: Blackwell.

Edwards, P.K. (1992) 'Industrial conflict: themes and issues in research', *British Journal of Industrial Relations*, Vol. 30, No. 3, pp. 361–404.

Edwards, R. (1979) *Contested Terrain*. New York: Basic Books.

Friedman, A. (1977) *Industry and Labour: Class Struggle at Work and Monopoly Capitalism*. London: Macmillan.

*Foy, N. (1994) *Empowering People at Work*. Aldershot: Gower.

Fröhlich, D. and Krieger, H. (1990) 'Technological change and worker participation in Europe', *New Technology, Work and Employment*, Vol. 5, No. 2, pp. 94–106.

Gaugler, E. and Wiltz, S. (1992) 'Federal Republic of Germany', in Brewster, C., Hegewisch, A., Holden, L. and Lockhart, T. (eds) *The European Human Resource Management Guide*. London: Academic Press, pp. 163–228.

Gill, C. (1993) 'Technological change and participation in work organisation: recent results from a European survey', *International Journal of Human Resource Management*, Vol. 4, No. 2, pp. 325–348.

Goss, D. (1994) *Principles of Human Resource Management*. London: Routledge.

Hammarström, O.L. (1987) 'Swedish industrial relations', in Bamber, G. and Lansbury, R. (eds) *International and Comparative Industrial Relations*. London: Allen & Unwin, pp. 224–248.

*Hammer, M. and Champy, J. (1993) *Reengineering the Corporation*. London: Nicholas Brealey.

Holden, L. (1990) 'Employee communications in Europe on the increase', *Involvement and Participation*, November, pp. 4–8.

Holden, L. (1996) 'HRM and employee involvement in Britain and Sweden: a comparative study', *International Journal of Human Resource Management*, Vol. 7, No. 1, pp. 59–81.

Honold, L. (1997) 'A review of the literature on employee empowerment', *Empowerment in Organisations*, Vol. 5, No. 4, pp. 202–212.

Hyman, J. and Mason, B. (1995) *Managing Employee Involvement and Participation*. London: Sage.

IDE (1981) *Industrial Democracy in Europe*. International Research Group, Oxford: Clarendon Press.

IDE (1993) *Industrial Democracy in Europe Revisited*. Oxford: Oxford University Press.

ILO (1993) *World Labour Report*. Geneva: International Labour Organization.

Kaler, J. (1999) 'Does empowerment empower?', in Quinn, J. and Davies, P. (eds) *Ethics and Empowerment*. Basingstoke: Macmillan, pp. 90–114.

Kanter, R.M. (1983) *The Change Masters: Innovation and Entrepreneurship in the American Corporation*. New York: Simon & Schuster.

Keenoy, T. (1990) 'Human resource management: rhetoric, reality and contradiction', *International Journal of Human Resource Management*, Vol. 1, No. 2, pp. 363–384.

Keenoy, T. and Anthony, P. (1992) 'HRM: metaphor meaning and morality', in Blyton, P. and Turnbull, P. (eds) *Reassessing Human Resource Management*. London: Sage, pp. 233–255.

Kjellberg, A. (1992) 'Sweden: can the model survive?', in Ferner, A. and Hyman, R. (eds) *Industrial Relations in the New Europe*. Oxford: Blackwell, pp. 88–142.

Klaus, R. and Bass, B. (1974) 'Group influence on individual behaviour across cultures', *Journal of Cross Cultural Psychology*, Vol. 5, pp. 236–246 (quoted in Briggs, 1991).

Korpi, W. (1981) 'Workplace bargaining, the law and unofficial strikes: the case of Sweden', *British Journal of Industrial Relations*, Vol. 16, pp. 355–368.

Lane, C. (1989) *Management and Labour in Europe*. Aldershot: Edward Elgar.

*Lashley, C. (1997) *Empowering Service Excellence: Beyond the Quick Fix*. London: Cassell.

Lawler, E. (1986) *High-Involvement Management*. San Francisco, Calif.: Jossey-Bass.

Lawrence, P. (1980) *Managers and Management in West Germany*. London: Croom Helm.

Legge, K. (1989) 'Human resource management: a critical analysis', in Storey, J. (ed.) *New Perspectives on Human Resource Management*. London: Routledge, pp. 19–40.

Lewis, P. (1989) 'Employee participation in a Japanese owned British electronics factory: reality or symbolism?', *Employee Relations*, Vol. 11, No. 1, pp. 3–9.

Lincoln, J. and Kalleberg, A. (1990) *Culture, Control and Commitment*. Cambridge: Cambridge University Press.

Lipietz, A. (1992) *Towards a New Economic Order: Post Fordism, Ecology and Democracy*. Cambridge: Polity Press.

Littlefield, D. (1996) 'Works council snub infuriates employees', *People Management*, 2 May, p. 5.

Lumb, R. (1996) 'BPR: not a fad, not a failure', *People Management*, 2 May, p. 26.

Marchington, M. (1989a) 'Joint consultation in practice', in Sisson, K. (ed.) *Personnel Management in Britain*. Oxford: Blackwell, pp. 378–402.

Marchington, M. (1989b) 'Employee participation', in Towers, B. (ed.) *Handbook of Industrial Relations Practice*, 2nd edn. London: Kogan Page, pp. 162–182.

Marchington, M. (1995) 'Involvement and participation', in Storey, J. (ed.) *Human Resource Management: A Critical Text*. London: Routledge, pp. 280–305.

Marchington, M., Goodman, J., Wilkinson, A. and Ackers, P. (1992) *New Developments in Employee Involvement*. Employment Department Research Series No. 2. Manchester: Manchester School of Management.

Marginson, P., Gilman, M., Jacobi, O. and Krieger, H. (1998) *Negotiating European Works Councils: An Analysis of Agreements under Article 13*. Dublin: European Foundation for the Improvement of Living and Working Conditions.

Mauritz, W. (1972) '10 Jahre Betriebsverfassungsgesetz aus der Sicht des Eigentümer-Unternehmers', in Lezius, M. (ed.) *10 Jahre Betriebsverfassungsgesetz*. Spardorf: R.F. Wilfer (quoted in Lane, 1989: 233).

Menon, S. (1995) *Employee Empowerment: Definition, Measurement and Construct Validation*. Toronto: McGill-Queen's University Press.

Monks, J. (1989) 'Trade union role in communications', in Wilkinson, T. (ed.) *The Communications Challenge: Personnel and PR Perspectives*. London: IPM, pp. 29–34.

Mumford, E. and Hendricks, R. (1996) 'Business process re-engineering RIP', *People Management*. 2 May, pp. 22–29.

Naoi, A. and Schooler, C. (1985) 'Occupational conditions and psychological functioning in Japan', *American Journal of Sociology*, Vol. 90, No. 4, pp. 729–752 (quoted in Briggs, 1991).

New Statesman (1984) 'This England', 18 March, p. 2.

Noon, M. (1992) 'HRM: a map, model or theory?', in Blyton, P. and Turnbull, P. (eds) *Reassessing Human Resource Management*. London: Sage, pp. 16–32.

OECD (1991) *OECD in Figures: Statistics on the Member Countries*. Paris: Organization for Economic Cooperation and Development.

Oliver, N. and Lowe, J. (1991) 'UK computer industry: American, British and Japanese contrasts in human resource management', *Personnel Review*, Vol. 20, No. 2, pp. 18–23.

Parker, M. and Slaughter, J. (1995) 'Unions and management by stress', in Babson, S. (ed.) *Lean Work: Empowerment and Exploitation in the Global Auto Industry*. Detroit, Mich: Wayne State University Press.

Pascale, R. and Athos, A. (1982) *The Art of Japanese Management*. London: Allen Lane.

Peccei, R. and Rosenthal, P. (2001) 'Delivering customer oriented behaviour through empowerment: an empirical test of HRM assumptions', *Journal of Management Studies*, Vol. 38, No. 6, pp. 831–857.

Pendleton, A and Brewster, C. (2001) 'Portfolio workforce', *People Management*, 12 July, pp. 38–40.

Pendleton, A., Poutsma, E., Van Ommeren, J. and Brewster, C. (2001) *Financial Participation in Europe: An Investigation into Profit Sharing and Employee Share Ownership*, Dublin: European Foundation for Improvement of Living and Working Conditions.

*Peppard, J. and Rowland, P. (1995) *The Essence of Business Process Re-engineering*. Hemel Hempstead: Prentice Hall.

Peters, T. and Waterman, R. (1982) *In Search of Excellence: Lessons from America's Best Run Companies*. New York: Harper & Row.

Poole, M. (1986) *Towards A New Industrial Democracy: Workers' Participation in Industry*. London: Routledge & Kegan Paul.

Poole, M. and Jenkins, G. (1990a) *The Impact of Economic Democracy: Profit Sharing and Employee Shareholding Schemes*. London: Routledge.

Poole, M. and Jenkins, G. (1990b) 'Human resource management and profit sharing: employee attitudes and a national survey', *International Journal of Human Resource Management*, Vol. 1, No. 3, pp. 289–328.

Price, R. (1989) 'The decline and fall of the status divide?', in Sisson, K., (ed.) *Personnel Management in Britain*. Oxford: Blackwell, pp. 271–295.

Price Waterhouse Cranfield Project on International Strategic Human Resource Management (1990) *Report*. London: Price Waterhouse.

Price Waterhouse Cranfield Project on International Strategic Human Resource Management (1991) *Report*. Cranfield: Cranfield School of Management.

Quinn, J. and Davies, P. (eds.) (1999) *Ethics and Empowerment*. Basingstoke: Macmillan.

Ramsay, H. (1977) 'Cycles of control', *Sociology*, Vol. 11, pp. 481–506.

Ramsay, H. (1983) 'Evolution or cycle? Worker participation in the 1970s and 1980s', in Crouch, C. and Heller, F. (eds) *International Yearbook of Organisational Democracy*, Vol. 1. Chichester: John Wiley.

Ramsay, H. (1991) 'Reinventing the wheel? A review of the development and performance of employee involvement', *Human Resource Management Journal*, Vol. 1, No. 1, pp. 1–22.

Ramsay, H. (1992a) 'Commitment and involvement', in Towers, B. (ed.) *The Handbook of Human Resource Management*. Oxford: Blackwell.

Ramsay, H. (1992b) 'Swedish and Japanese work methods: comparisons and contrasts', *P+ European Participation Monitor*, Vol. 3, No. 1, pp. 37–40.

Ramsay, H., Leopold, J. and Hyman, J. (1986) 'Profit sharing and employee share ownership: an initial assessment', *Employee Relations*, Vol. 8, No. 1, pp. 23–26.

Rana, E. (1999) 'Europe split on issue of worker consultation plans', *People Management*, 11 November, p. 13.

Rothstein, L.R. (1995) 'The empowerment effort that came undone', *Harvard Business Review*, January–February, pp. 20–31.

Russell, P. (2001) 'In-box clever,' *People Management*, 5 April, p. 38, 39.

Salaman, G. (1979) *Work Organisations: Resistance and Control*. London: Longman.

Schuller, T. (1989) 'Financial participation', in Storey, J. (ed.) *New Perspectives on Human Resource Management*. London: Routledge, pp. 126–136.

Sell, R. (1988) 'The human face of industry in Sweden', *Industrial Society Magazine*, March, pp. 30–32.

Semler, R. (1993) *Maverick: The Success Story Behind the World's Most Unusual Workplace*. London: Century.

Sewell, G. and Wilkinson, B. (1992) 'Empowerment or emasculation? Shopfloor surveillance in a total quality organisation', in Blyton, P. and Turnbull, P. (eds) *Reassessing Human Resource Management*. London: Sage, pp. 97–115.

Storey, J. (ed.) (1989) *New Perspectives on Human Resource Management*. London: Routledge.

Thomas, H. and Logan, C. (1982) *Mondragon: An Economic Analysis*. London: George Allen & Unwin.

Townley, B. (1989) 'Employee communication programmes', in Sisson, K. (ed.) *Personnel Management in Britain*. Oxford: Blackwell, pp. 329–355.

Wall, T.D. and Lischerson, J.A. (1977) *Worker Participation: A Critique of the Literature and Some Fresh Evidence*. London: McGraw-Hill.

Walton, R.E. (1984a) 'The future of human resource management: an overview', in Walton, R.E. and Lawrence, P.R. (eds) *HRM: Trends and Challenges*. Boston: Harvard Business School Press, pp. 3–11.

Walton, R.E. (1984b) 'Towards a strategy of eliciting employee commitment based on policies of mutuality', in Walton, R.E. and Lawrence, P.R. (eds) *HRM: Trends and Challenges*. Boston, Mass.: Harvard Business School Press, pp. 35–65.

Walton, R.E. (1985) 'From control to commitment in the workplace', *Harvard Business Review*, March/April, pp. 76–84.

Ward, P.J. (1993) 'A study of organisational variables affecting worker empowerment', *Educational and Psychological Studies*, Miami, Fla.: University of Miami.

West, M and Johnson, R. (2002) 'A matter of life and death', *People Management*, 21 February, pp. 30–36.

Wickens, P. (1987) *The Road to Nissan: Flexibility, Quality and Teamwork*. Basingstoke: Macmillan.

Wilczynski, J. (1983) *Comparative Industrial Relations*. London: Macmillan.

Wilkinson, A. (1998) 'Empowerment: theory and practice', *Personnel Review*, Vol. 27, No. 1, pp. 40–56.

Wilkinson, A., Marchington, M., Ackers, P. and Goodman, J. (1992) 'Total quality management and employee involvement', *Human Resource Management Journal*, Vol. 2, No. 4, pp. 1–20.

*Wilkinson, A. and Wilmot, H. (1995) *Making Quality Critical: New Perspectives on Organisational Change*. London: Routledge.

Wilkinson, T. (ed.) (1989) *The Communications Challenge: Personnel and PR Perspectives*. London: IPM.

Wilpert, B. and Rayley, J. (1983) *Anspruch und Wirklichkeit der Mitbestimmung*. Frankfurt: Campus (quoted in Lane, 1989: 232).

Wood, S. and Fenton O'Creevey, M. (1999) 'Employee involvement: channel hopping', *People Management*, 25 November, pp. 42–45.

 For multiple choice questions, exercises and annotated weblinks specific to this chapter visit this book's website at www.booksites.net/beardwell

Malone Superbuy Ltd

Malone Superbuy is a large food retail company that has been established since the beginning of the twentieth century. Over the last 100 years the organisation has built a reputation for quality foods, and so depends on relatively discerning shoppers for its market; most of its outlets are in the South-West and South-East of Britain. The organisation is a large employer (more than 4000 employees); it is highly dependent upon part-time, female labour and casual student workers for shopfloor employees, with full-time management staff consigned to given stores. The firm does experience costly medium-to-high labour turnover, largely because of the unsocial hours to which all employees are rostered, and the transient nature of student labour. Wage rates are average for the sector, and were unaffected by the Minimum Wage Regulation. The organisation has never recognised trade unions, but has had a fairly informal system of local employee representation committees, many of which have fallen into disuse in recent years.

The food retail sector has recently experienced growing competition between the market leaders as attention has been drawn to the differentials between the price of food in the UK and in other European countries. British farmers have also been active in publicly denouncing the profiteering that has been evident in the retail food sector. Consequently, the big firms are engaged in 'price wars' and are actively increasing the quality and variety of goods on offer while also focusing on the level of sevice offered within their stores. Malone Superbuy is not in the top league, but nevertheless has been affected by increasing competition in the sector. To add to its troubles, the TGWU is actively recruiting employees, and it looks as if Malone's will be presented with a recognition claim for bargaining rights in the near future. To remain competitive in the market the firm must:

- improve the quality of service offered to customers throughout the organisation;
- find ways of cutting labour costs.

Further to developing a strategy for change to deal with market pressures, the firm must also decide whether it intends to:

- accept a trade union presence and attempt to build a partnership agreement;
- adopt a substitution or suppressionist approach to union recognition.

Activity

You are a member of an external team of HR consultants employed by the company to outline a strategy which will achieve employee support for increased competitiveness in an environment of change. The Managing Director has already decided that he wants a comprehensive report to indicate how the firm will move forward and this will be presented under the title, 'Superbuy Shapes Up For The Future!'. As a team your remit is to construct that report and your particular responsibility is to write the following sections:

1 Outline and discuss an appropriate HR Strategy (see also Chapter 2) for this organisation which will facilitate the coherent development of the firm within its particular context.

2 Suggest policy initiatives to address the labour turnover problems currently affecting the firm.

3 Develop a training programme which will enhance customer service skills amongst shop floor staff.

4 Address the issue of employee representation with a reasoned consideration of whether to adopt substitution/exclusion approaches or to negotiate a recognition agreement with trade unions.

5 Consider how employee reward policies might be re-evaluated to encourage greater employee motivation and loyalty (without substantially affecting the wages bill!).

Part 5

INTERNATIONAL HUMAN RESOURCE MANAGEMENT

The considerable growth of interest in international human resource management (IHRM) emanates from the rise of globalisation over the past half century, a phenomenon that has considerably accelerated over the past decade. This term describes the proliferation of world trade, foreign direct investment, worldwide mergers and acquisitions and a burgeoning of telecommunications, faster and cheaper transport and rapid technological change. Globalisation has also been considerably enhanced by the integration of markets both worldwide and at regional level, as well as witnessing the rise of new and potentially powerful markets in China and Central and Eastern Europe. The trend towards privatisation and deregulation has led to an increase in cross-border integration in areas such as telecommunications, energy and finance.

The 1990s witnessed rapid economic growth particularly associated with the activities of multinational companies (MNCs), reflected in the considerable increase in foreign direct investment (FDI). There are 53 000 MNCs that control 450 000 subsidiaries, and these MNCs account for approximately a quarter of output in the developed economies (Kozul-Wright and Rowthorn, 1998). More importantly, FDI is of immense importance to world economic growth, and the 1990s witnessed a strong expansion of FDI flows. OECD countries set a new FDI record in 1998 with inward investment reaching $465 billion (a 71 per cent increase over 1997), and outflows reached an unprecedented $566 billion (Miyake and Thomsen, 1999).

As companies and organisations expand their cross-border activities there has been a concomitant increase in business activity together with an increase in cross-border integration of their production and services. This in turn has created an increasing interest in the processes by which international management coordination and control can be exercised.

The United States still remains dominant in the global economy, and over a quarter of the 100 largest MNCs are US owned. Although the considerable expansion of Japanese companies overseas in the 1980s caused the USA to briefly lose its premier position as the world's leading foreign direct investor, by the latter part of the 1990s the USA had regained its former position while the Japanese banking and financial crisis had taken its toll. Such economic hegemonies influence labour market and management trends. As Hyman (1999) states:

> After two decades in which the superior performance of such 'institutionalised economies' as Germany and Japan was widely recognised, the conventional wisdom of the 1990s has been that dense social regulation involves rigidities requiring a shift to market liberalism. (p. 93)

Such shifts in the managerial climate influence approaches to the employment relationship and ultimately to HRM. However, IHRM is still very much in its infancy, and its parameters are still being set. The problem with examining HRM in a global context is that it raises far-reaching and complex questions, and the present state of research and theory is a long way from producing satisfactory explanations.

Globalisation has taken place against a backcloth of social and political turbulence in the twentieth century, and has continued in the wake of the fall of communism in Eastern Europe and the resulting economic and political problems. There has been a huge and continuing growth of the world's population, which has intensified the problems of poverty for many poor nations. Pollution has brought green issues to the forefront of the consciousness of political and business policy-makers. We have witnessed a challenge to Western economic supremacy with the rapid growth of the Asia Pacific states, led by the 'tigers' – Japan, China, South Korea, Taiwan and Hong Kong – as well as Singapore and Malaysia.

The chapters in this section cannot do justice to these massive changes within the narrow context of HRM, and they will serve, therefore, merely to give the reader a flavour of some of the developments in the field and some of the major debates that are now emerging.

The section begins with an examination of the concept of IHRM and the environments within which it operates. In the first half of Chapter 15 the authors have emphasised a comparative and contextual approach to IHRM rooted in an understanding of national institutions and business systems. The second part of the chapter examines HRM in an organisational context as practised particularly in multinational corporations. The authors have not reviewed the cultural context as they feel this has been given extensive coverage in many books and articles relating to IHRM.

This is followed by a chapter reviewing some of the developments of HRM in a European context. This updates developments in the European Union in regard to approaches to harmonisation as reflected in social policy in the wake of the Amsterdam Treaty (1997) and the Lisbon Conference (2000). Also included are recent developments and analysis of aspects of the employment relationship and HRM in Eastern Europe.

The last chapter examines trends in the Asia Pacific rim, especially in Japan, China and the other 'tiger' economies. We have not included a chapter on the United States mainly because much of the ideas and literature on human resource management emanate from there, and thus a general discussion of it is by implication a reference to its US origins and influence.

References and further reading

Hyman, R. (1999) 'National industrial relations systems and transnational challenges: an essay in review', *European Journal of Industrial Relations*, Vol. 5, No. 1, pp. 80–110.

Kozul-Wright, R. and Rowthorn, R. (1998) 'Spoilt for choice? Multinational corporations and the geography of international production', *Oxford Review of Economic Policy*, Vol. 14, No. 2, pp. 74–92.

Miyake, M. and Thomsen, S. (1999) 'Recent trends in foreign direct investment', *Financial Market Trends*, No. 73, June, pp. 109–126.

CHAPTER 15

HRM in multinationals: a comparative international perspective

Phil Almond, Ian Clark and Olga Tregaskis

OBJECTIVES

▶ To demonstrate what is institutionally distinctive and particular about one type of business system and demonstrate how economic and political strategies and those of firms are embedded within a national institutional framework. For example, what is distinctive about the US, British and German business systems?

▶ To demonstrate how national distinctiveness impacts on corporate strategies and how this distinctiveness manifests itself in terms of HRM in multinational firms from different countries of origin; for example, what is distinctive about the international operation of US multinational firms?

▶ To demonstrate how national business and employment systems are likely to affect the overall nature of HRM in different countries.

▶ To examine the demands of international markets on how MNCs manage their international and local workforces. How do the demands for local sensitivity, international integration and global learning influence the role and organisation of the international HR function and its relationship with subsidiaries?

▶ To examine the various external factors which impact on HR strategies within MNCs. Does HR policy in MNCs stem from the country of origin business and employment system, the host country or international patterns of economic and political dominance?

▶ To examine whether contemporary pressures such as globalisation are bringing about processes of convergence (practices becoming more similar across countries), and to examine the role of MNCs within this debate.

▶ To demonstrate what is institutionally distinctive and particular about one type of business system and demonstrate how economic and political strategies and those of firms are embedded within a national institutional framework.

▶ To demonstrate how national distinctiveness impacts on corporate strategies and how this distinctiveness manifests itself in terms of HRM in multinational firms from different countries of origin.

▶ To demonstrate how national business and employment systems are likely to affect the overall nature of HRM in different countries and in MNCs.

▶ To consider the limitations of current work in the field and future directions for research.

▶ To examine the structure, role and activities of international HRM functions in MNCs and how these are influenced by factors such as integration-responsiveness demands, internal and external organisational factors and management mindsets.

▶ To examine the role of expatriates in MNCs, how the transfer process is managed and to consider some of the dilemmas and shortcomings setting the agenda for the future role of the expatriate manager.

▶ To demonstrate the value of combining comparative/institutional and strategic perspectives to gain a more comprehensive and specific understanding of HRM in MNCs.

▶ To outline the convergence/divergence debate and illustrate its relevance to the MNC.

Introduction

This chapter examines HRM from a comparative and international perspective. The comparative and international study of HRM is born out of quite distinct theoretical research traditions, namely institutional and strategic perspectives respectively, and as such are concerned with addressing different questions about the nature of HRM. Despite this, we will illustrate the significance of the institutional approach to further explicating international HRM and addressing questions of convergence and divergence.

Comparative HRM is concerned with understanding in what ways and why HRM differs across countries. The 'national business systems' approach provides a basis for analytical comparison emphasising the institutional structures that have a direct and indirect influence on corporate strategies and in turn on HR practice. The primary analytical focus is the institutional environment – namely the legal and regulatory frameworks, industrial relations traditions and employment systems – in terms of its impact on organisations. This perspective zooms in on the institutional influences that constrain or enable organisational action. This gives rise to questions such as to what extent are the HR policies adopted in one country relevant or feasible for organisations in other countries? This perspective rejects unitarist theoretical perspectives that attempt to prescribe universal models of HRM.

In contrast, international HRM is concerned with identifying and understanding how multinational organisations manage their geographically dispersed workforces in order to leverage their HR resources for both local and global competitive advantage. The focus here is on organisational strategy and structure and its interaction with market competition. Organisations are assumed to have a high degree of strategic choice enabling them to find the best way of organising their resources for competitive advantage, in other words achieving a 'fit' between the organisation's strategy-structure and its external business environment. The types of questions addressed by academics in this field are concerned with what are the 'best' ways of organising the HR function to meet the divergent needs of multidomestic, global and transnational competition; what role can expatriate managers play in achieving strategic integration and control for multinationals? While environmental constraint is recognised, its influence tends to be under-emphasised and under-explored. As a consequence, the approach towards international HRM is prescriptive in nature and directed towards defining universal organisational models, i.e. models of international HR organisation, policy and practice that fit the competitive context. The ways in which this competitive context is affected by, for example, cooperative institutional links or collective tradition and the implications for strategic choice go largely unrecognised.

The study of international and comparative HRM may be considered relatively embryonic up until now. International organisations and the business markets they operate in are notoriously complex and dynamic. Conducting research in the field is often expensive and methodologically difficult (Adler, 1984; Brewster *et al.*, 1996; Tregaskis *et al.*, 2003) owing to the complex interplay of organisational and environmental factors. Despite this, we would argue that it is precisely this dynamic and complex area of interplay between institutional and strategic factors that warrants greater attention and is necessary as one means of taking theory and empirical work in the field of international HRM forward. In this chapter we attempt to address some of the issues of importance here by outlining the current empirical and theoretical contributions in the comparative and international HRM fields and demonstrating the significance of an institutional analysis to the examination of HRM in multinationals.

The chapter begins by introducing the concept of 'national business systems' as a basis from which to understand the emergence of comparative analysis in HRM. Applying this analytical perspective to indigenous organisations, the divergent nature of HRM across countries is illustrated. Moving to an analysis of MNCs, the literature and models of international HRM and their limitations are considered. To conclude, we draw together themes from both the comparative and international HRM fields as a means of considering the state of the current debate regarding the convergence and divergence of HRM practice and the implications this has for the management of HRM in MNCs and ultimately for the future direction of international HRM.

National business systems (NBSs)

Before examining comparative and international HRM in detail, it is necessary to examine the sources of cross-national variety in employment policy and practice. Accordingly, this part of the chapter examines the institutional distinctiveness of NBSs, and provides some historical and contemporary analysis of how global pressures impact on NBSs to create pressures for convergence towards the US business system.

■ The distinctiveness of NBSs

The global economy is an amalgamation of independent national states. While the majority of these states are broadly capitalist – they are based on a system of production that emphasises the market as the main mechanism for exchange, consumption and distribution – each has followed a distinctive and unique pathway to industrial capitalism. The economic, political and social characteristics of individual market economies are shaped by and embedded within a social system that provides them with distinctively national characters.

These national characteristics impact on and inform the manner by which business systems operate. For example, for much of the twentieth century the US economy was characterised by a business system that emphasised very large vertically integrated firms engaged in the mass production and mass marketing of highly standardised products. In contrast to this, the British business system emphasised less standardised craft production by smaller, less integrated specialist firms which produced goods for distinct and more differentiated markets. Other economies, for example the German and Japanese economies, followed different paths that emphasised either high-quality system production or the production of standardised products that were continuously improved through the use of quality programmes. In order to appreciate these different routes that characterise national patterns of competitiveness it is necessary to specify the institutional character of national business systems. These national patterns are likely directly to influence patterns of human resource management and industrial relations; this point is further developed in subsequent parts of this chapter.

● Theoretical specification of NBSs

A key theoretical theme of institutional analysis is the persistence of differences in the organisation and activities of the state, capital, labour and financial systems in different national economies. The economic and political strategies of state actors and those who represent the interests of capital and finance and organised labour are embedded within a social system of class relations, institutional regulation and culture that characterises their national qualities. Hence the US, British, German or Japanese business system exhibits a series of distinctively national characteristics that shape the strategies and structures of US, British, German or Japanese firms, including their particular approaches to the management of human resources. The institutional characteristics of national business systems impact on firms in terms of their corporate strategies, both domestically and in terms of internationalisation. Equally, the role and make-up of financial capital will have some impact on corporate strategies, as will the industrial relations system.

So, institutional analysis suggests that economic, political and social processes and structures particular to one business system are embedded within a national institutional framework. The contemporary make-up and operation of NBSs results from historical developments, in particular the route taken to industrialisation and the role of the state in this process, specifically, whether the state encouraged the development of non-market patterns of coordination or if the state encourages market patterns of regulation. It follows from this that national patterns of industrial organisation in and between the state, industrial and finance capital and labour are embedded within enduring institutional frameworks. These frameworks of national regulation – markets, non-market institutions or some combination of the two – enable and constrain corporate strategies, the strategies of organised labour and those of the national state. Therefore capital, labour and the state within a particular business system operate within a web of relationships characterised by significant differences in terms of the presence or absence of social institutions that regulate activities beyond the confines of market institutions.

As the following subsections further amplify, by demonstrating what is special or particular about one type of business system, it is possible to consider different national features – the comparative analysis – of economic, political and social institutions that regulate economic organisation within distinct NBSs, in particular the management of human resources. To summarise, empirically and historically, national business systems represent distinctive patterns of economic organisation. Theoretically, observable differences and similarities between NBSs stem from the constitution and role of regulatory institutions in and between capital, labour, the state and the financial system.

ACTIVITY   Before reading the following subsections, list any differences that come to mind between the US, British, German and Japanese business systems. Keep your list at hand and then examine its contents against the further specification of differences and similarities between NBSs contained in the following subsections.

● The theoretical literature on NBSs

The literature on business systems is extensive and wide-ranging in coverage and in the context of an introductory chapter such as this it is necessary to confine our discussion and review of this literature to three central sources, Lane (1995), Whitley (2000) and

Hall and Soskice (2001). While these contributions cover much common ground, they provide subtle variations in the description, evaluation and conceptualisation of business systems and the institutional depth and embeddedness of national patterns of regulation. Thus, the bases upon which they compare NBSs differ in formulation, particularly in terms of how these contributions measure the effects of NBSs on labour market regulation, education and training, patterns of corporate governance, innovation and corporate strategy.

Lane – national industrial orders

Lane (1995) examines patterns of stability and change in the British, French and German business systems. Her approach follows the theoretical specification outlined above to argue that national patterns of industrial organisation are embedded in society, but distinguishes between economic and social embeddedness in the creation of national industrial orders. For Lane the degree of social embeddedness, that is, the depth and scope of non-market institutions, defines patterns of divergence in national regimes. For example, Lane contrasts the British system with that of the German system to argue that Britain's industrial order is characterised by the dominant position of finance capital and voluntary market-driven relationships within and between capital and labour. Because the capital-based financial system is largely unregulated by intermediary institutions beyond the immediate market actors, a pattern of arm's-length short-termism ensues, encouraging firms to make low-risk investments in capital and labour. This pattern of self-regulation by economic actors is reproduced in other areas of the British business system: training and development is largely in the hands of employers (see Keep and Rainbird, 2000); equally, many areas of the employment relations system such as the wage–effort bargain and collective bargaining arrangements have traditionally been beyond extensive social regulation by the state, see Hyman (1995). In contrast, Lane argues that the German business system exhibits a production rather than a financial orientation that creates a closer integration between the interests of capital and labour. For example, many aspects of employment relations are regulated by social institutions such as works councils for consultation and information-sharing. Equally, a nationally regulated system of vocational education and training emphasises skill development in accordance with the needs of industry. These factors combine with a credit-based finance system that encourages closer links between financial institutions and industry than found in the UK and fosters longer-term time frames for capital provision and investment returns as distinct from short-term pressures for shareholder value that are more pressing in the UK. The essential difference between the regulation of capital, labour, training and the provision of finance in Britain and Germany is that while the British state has traditionally encouraged market regulation by immediate actors, the German state has encouraged and institutionalised a network of local and national institutions beyond the market. In the contemporary period the British business system is developing some examples of social regulation such as the regulation of working time beyond the confines of collective bargaining. Equally, the German business system is subject to some deregulation of social institutions, for example those controlling hostile takeovers by foreign firms and aspects of the employment relations system. However, the differences between the two business systems remain deeply embedded.

In summary, Lane outlines patterns of divergence that highlight the impact of social institutions beyond the control of immediate market actors to illustrate the different capacities of British and German firms and businesses to respond to external shocks and emergent international developments. Essentially, the absence of social institutions beyond the market for capital, labour, the regulation of corporate governance, training and development etc. create a short-term framework for order and stability in the British business system. In contrast, the presence of social institutions stimulates a longer-term framework in the German business system.

Whitley – divergent capitalisms

Whitley (2000) provides a more wide-ranging examination of national business systems through a comparative framework of analysis that identifies critical variations in coordination and control mechanisms across *divergent* forms of capitalism to identify different forms of business system. While the depth and scope of Whitley's contribution is significant, the limitations of space prevent a comprehensive review of his material. However, the major discerning elements of his approach are examined.

Whitley (2000), who argues that there are persistent differences in capitalist organisation across national business systems that reflect distinctive development pathways pursued by different nations, further consolidates the institutionalist approach developed by Lane (1995). Within particular national business systems institutions persist over time, that is, they are embedded by the interaction of social groups and actors at critical historical junctures within the process of industrialisation. Institutions and patterns of institutional relationships persist until the emergence of significant developments, either internally or externally, creates pressures for institutional restructuring. For example, for European states the emergence of the EU as a centralising agency for economic, political and social policy has created pressures for institutional change; as Chapter 10 discusses, these pressures are particularly manifest in the UK's case in the area of individual and collective employment rights. Equally, the emergence of the euro has created pressures of institutional convergence across EU states that use the euro, for example centralised monetary and fiscal policy, a process that limits the institutional freedom of central banks in member states as well as the taxation policy of national governments.

Whitley visualises national business systems as economic control and coordination mechanisms for firms and work systems where patterns of national institutional distinction create different varieties of capitalism. By this, Whitley suggests that owners and controllers of capital (e.g. shareholders and managers, labour, the state and the national financial system) create divergent capitalisms whereby institutional actors (i.e. capital, labour, the state and the financial system) will cooperate and compete in different ways in different capitalisms. For example, as the following subsection demonstrates in more detail, historically, US firms tend to be large, vertically integrated and employ mass production techniques. In contrast, British firms have tended to be smaller, locally dominant but vertically disintegrated, utilise craft production and skilled labour as opposed to deskilled labour associated with volume mass production. These historical pathways to economic development reflect and reinforce distinct patterns of institutional interrelationship within capital, labour, the state and the financial system. For example, in both the United States and the UK firms tend to grow and finance investment from retained earnings, indicating an arm's-length relationship with financial institutions. Equally, the central state plays only a marginal role. In the USA this mainly consisted of the development of an anti-trust framework to prevent cartels, reinforcing the tendency for firms to grow by acquisition and merger. In the UK, on the other hand, for much of the twentieth century the state was concerned to control access to British and imperial markets – protecting them for British firms. These types of relationship contrast strongly with those found in Germany and Japan where institutional actors operate within a more coordinated framework, particularly in terms of finance, training and development systems and employment relations.

Whitley also identifies that while patterns of national competition and coordination appear functional for the institutional actors, the pattern of relations creates conflicts within and between different fractions of capital, notably finance capital and industrial capital. However, the embeddedness of institutional relations creates a pattern of institutional and organisational routine that is difficult to dislodge. For example, in the UK, despite criticisms that the institutional structure of the British state creates an arm's-length relationship to capital and labour, a series of voluntary arrangements continues to persist. Equally, in Germany the institutional embeddedness of the employment relations system, the quality but comparative slowness of its systems of vocational training and bureaucratic regulations over corporate governance, particularly acquisition and merger by foreign capital, each result in the charge that the German business system is institutionally inflexible and over-regulated. Yet in both the British and the German case the measures that might be required to reform these routine criticisms tend to be resisted by institutional actors. For example, in the face of the failure of the EU to provide pan-European legislation and associated procedures for hostile takeovers by foreign capital, the German parliament legislated on the issue. This arose after lobbying from the auto and chemical sectors whose aim is to prevent another external hostile takeover similar to Vodaphone's acquisition of Mannesmann. The legislation reinforces the defensive role of the *Vorstand* (Board of Directors) in such situations, see Clark *et al.* (2002). In comparison, in the UK 'better' regulation of capital and labour on the EU model of social partnership has met with heavy resistance from interest groups representing capital such as the IoD, CBI and British Chambers of Commerce. Each of these argues that institutional regulation, supported by the force of law, over either capital or the labour it employs, is bureaucratic and creates excessive red tape, preferring instead voluntary or deregulated patterns of control and coordination that promote employer *best practice*.

In summary then, Whitley (2000) conceives business systems as nationally distinctive patterns of economic coordination and control. The institutional make-up of these NBSs varies, to demonstrate divergence of interconnection between institutional actors such as capital owners and providers, managers, customers and suppliers, employees and the financial system. Relationships vary from being organisationally integrated to disintegrated and separate. Ultimately, Whitley (2000) distinguishes between national business systems in terms of, first, institutional pluralism, particularly in relation to the interests of labour in the employment relations system, and second, the role of the state in terms of active or passive coordination of institutional actors, particularly capital. Hall and Soskice (2001), whose contribution is summarised below, further develop this approach.

Hall and Soskice – comparative patterns of institutional advantage

In some respects, Hall and Soskice (2001) cover much the same ground as Whitley (2000) and Lane (1995). However, they develop the institutional approach further by examining how a broadly defined distinction between *liberal* market economies (LMEs) and *coordinated* market economies (CMEs) creates different national patterns of corporate strategy and associated patterns of institutional comparative advantage.

Within national pathways, distinct patterns for the organisation of production develop. A key factor that differentiates LMEs and CMEs is the presence of external institutions beyond the market mechanism for the regulation of the labour market, education and training and corporate governance. Clearly, in a similar vein to Whitley's (2000) arguments, the presence of such institutions depends in large measure on the capacity of the state to develop and maintain regulatory regimes. As a result of differences in national pathways to capitalist development, national-level differences persist. In both types of economy firms necessarily face coordination problems in terms of their relationship to employees – their skill base and vocational training – and other firms in terms of inter-firm cooperation and competition. In LMEs firms tend to face and manage coordination problems on the basis of markets and hierarchies, that is, they make a rational choice as to whether to enter into market relationships for, say, skilled labour or manage the process internally, see Williamson (1975). Coordinating the activities of capital on the basis of markets or hierarchies creates arm's-length – contractually and economically separate – relationships with other institutional actors. For example, in LMEs dominated by market and hierarchy relations the provision of investment funds tends to be capital based whereby the provision of funds operates within an open market. Here capital providers and institutional investors such as pension fund managers and venture capitalists make funds available on a short-term basis that in turn requires firms to secure relatively rapid returns to the investors. By association, ensuring shareholder value for investors creates short-term time horizons for firms. In contrast to this, in CMEs the provision of investment funds tends to operate on a credit basis whereby investors take greater interest in the firms where they invest, often taking up share ownership and participating in the management of the enterprise. Equally, in Germany and Japan for example, there is less of an active free market for equity capital, with many shares in firms being retained by the founders of the firm, the local state, and capital providers in national institutions such as Japan's MITI (*Ministry of International Trade and Investment*). The lesser presence of a free market for equity capital in CMEs and the presence of more credit-based investment funds encourage a pattern of interrelated institutional action. For example, fewer pressures for shareholder value enable firms to concentrate on product market development and R&D over longer time frames than those typical of LMEs.

In summary, the presence or absence of non-market institutions creates or inhibits capacities to exchange information and monitor institutional actors beyond the confines of the market. For Hall and Soskice (2001) the institutional make-up of particular nation-states is distinctive and marked by their historical development in two respects. First, institutions are created and formalised by market action or statutory action to establish their operating procedures – liberal or coordinated. Second, what Whitley (2000) terms institutional routine creates a set of common expectations that legitimises liberal or coordinated action among institutional actors. We can see these differences quite clearly in relation to the reactions of national airlines to the events of 11 September 2001. The reaction of US and British airlines was immediate, announcing redundancies and reductions in operating capacities, measures that were necessary to protect share price and calm institutional investors. In contrast, Air France, Lufthansa and Iberia reacted in a more measured manner. A combination of negotiated reductions in working hours and wages, cancellation of options for new units and the cancellation of some routes maintained employment levels over the short term. The lesser presence of shareholder value pressures combined with more coordinated institutional responses led by the French, German and Spanish states protected employment across the sector, as did more coordinated responses in European works councils, see Clark *et al.* (2002).

As Hall and Soskice (2001) concede and as Broadberry (1997) and Clark (2000) demonstrate, both types of market economy are capable of providing satisfactory levels of long-run economic performance, but with different patterns of distribution in civil society. However, the predominant patterns of distribution and corporate strategy will differ, as will degrees of innovation. For example, LMEs exhibit more radical patterns of innovation, labour market regulation tends to be more flexible, labour markets more mobile and restrictions on redundancies are fewer. Equally, equity markets provide for ready funds for venture capital and patterns of corporate organisation are more fluid whereby firms can be broken down into smaller customer-focused trading units – *re-engineered, downsized etc.* – very rapidly. This pattern of market regulation tends to create radical patterns of innovation, for example the rapid growth and proliferation of low-cost airlines, the dot-com investment revolution and rapid changes of corporate ownership more generally. For example, during the past six years, Go Fly was a subsidiary of British Airways, then an independent operator resulting from a management buyout and is now part of the easyJet group.

In contrast to this, CMEs exhibit more incremental innovation based on longer-term product development and brand building that emphasises quality and continuity, not necessarily short-term improvements in market share based on outperforming the market in order to satisfy institutional investors and provide rapid shareholder value. However, recently pressures have built in CMEs such as Germany, centred around the charge that the business system is inflexible and over-regulated, with institutional inertia preventing rapid innovations. The patterns of corporate strategy and corporate innovation associated with LMEs and CMEs create different patterns of institutional competitive advantage, with the locus of difference represented by the degree of institutional support actively promoted by the state beyond the coordinating mechanism of markets and hierarchies. As Hall and Soskice (2001) argue, if each market type is capable of sustaining satisfactory levels of economic performance it must be the case that the patterns of institutional routine and regulation (market or non-market) in different systems of production create common expectations in the face of criticism of national regimes. For example, the reaction of LMEs and CMEs to globalisation is likely to be radical and incremental respectively. The institutional structure of LMEs supports radical innovation whereas the institutional structure of CMEs is more likely to seek institutional modification to, and institutional regulation of, emergent global pressures. In each case the different type of economy is likely to modify its own systems of institutional regulation in order to sustain respective patterns of competitive advantage. This suggests that the pressures of globalisation are unlikely necessarily to transform national business systems. We can see these divergent pressures within the European context where the British state and capital have reacted violently against EU-wide regulatory measures such as the Information and Consultation Directive and the Agency Workers Directive, see Chapter 10. Hence national business systems and associated approaches to the management of industrial relations and human resources may remain distinctive within the global business system.

Empirical and historical specification of NBSs – the USA, Britain, Germany and Japan

The analysis of national business systems has thus far been theoretical, focusing on the impact of market and non-market patterns of institutional regulation in and between institutional actors such as capital, labour, the state and the finance system, with only passing reference made to the details of particular business systems. In this section the historically embedded features of four business systems are briefly detailed and summarised in terms of the arguments developed by Lane (1995), Whitley (2000) and Hall and Soskice (2001). Subsequent parts of this chapter examine how the institutional characteristics of the four business systems are likely to impact on patterns of HRM within these systems and within multinational corporations that originate in one of these systems.

The empirical and historical specification of the features of capitalist development in the four business systems is presented in summary bullet-point form and in each case draws on substantive works on this issue by Best (1990), Chandler (1977, 1990) and Lazonick (1991). While Best and Chandler concentrate on institutional features that distinguish business systems, Lazonick examines these differences in terms of patterns of industrial dominance and decline within business systems. The bullet-point summaries identify historically embedded institutional features in the four business systems, the effects of which remain significant in the contemporary operation of each business system, and their respective systems for industrial relations and the management of human resources.

● The US business system

Chandler (1977, 1990) and Lazonick (1991) characterise the historical development of the US business system and its subsequent patterns of institutional coordination as a competitive managerial capitalism or a managerial capitalism exhibiting the following features. In some cases we have added qualification to the points if they are subject to recent developments.

- Large firms, with large managerial hierarchies, recently subject to 'downsizing'.
- Complex coordination of production chains, early deployment of scientific management techniques.
- Firms tend to be vertically integrated backwards (e.g. fast food providers) and forwards (oil companies).
- Emphasis on large-scale volume mass production, standardised goods for mass markets – some debate on the extent of mass production and its significance in the contemporary period.
- Separation between owners and professional salaried managers.
- Significant use of retained profits or income for investment.
- Capital-based investment funds available.
- Early movement to use of multidivisional structures for corporate organisation and associated centralisation of financial control and HR strategies.
- Vertically integrated large firms tend to out-compete smaller specialist suppliers by developing specialist purchasing and supply contracts with suppliers to reduce unit costs but retain profitability, e.g. in food retailing – Wal-Mart, books and music retailing – Amazon, Barnes and Noble and Tower Records. Earlier, this process saw the emergence in the automobile sector of three large firms, Chrysler, Ford and General Motors, a process replicated in many other sectors such as railroads, aircraft manufacturing, steel etc.
- Many vertically integrated firms are also horizontally diversified, i.e. operating in several sectors.
- Significant management control over production or emotional labour in the supply of services with systematic mechanisation, deskilling and control procedures.
- Arm's-length market relations dominate within and between capital, labour and the state.

> **Whitley:** Institutional actors coordinate by market relations, organisational capabilities developed and maintained by professional management. Institutional pluralism, beyond the market very limited, contemporary focus of business system short-termism and shareholder value.
>
> **Hall and Soskice:** Liberal market economy, highly developed stock and capital markets reinforce market relations and institutional separation.

● The British business system

Sometimes referred to as personal capitalism, the British system exhibits much individualism within its institutional framework and in the contemporary period is seen as a very flexible, open and deregulated economy dominated by domestic and foreign multinational firms. In addition, the British business system exhibits a thriving small to medium size enterprise sector that reprises many of the historically embedded features summarised below.

- Historically dominated by family owned and family managed firms.
- Firms traditionally undertook low investment in new technology and labour saving technology.
- Investments tend to be short-term and low risk.
- Comparatively low levels of investment in manufacturing sector, comparatively low levels of investment in management training and marketing.
- Firms tend to be specialist, vertically and horizontally separate. Industry traditionally seen as locally and regionally concentrated; significant feature was single plant operations, for example local breweries.

- Adversarial industrial relations system, voluntary agreements, management and labour restrictive practices.
- Traditionally, business system seen as financier dominated.
- Arm's-length relationships between institutional actors – market coordination between actors.
- Since the Second World War, manufacturing industry dominated by defence-related industry and aerospace sector.
- Networks of local cartels, growth of firms locally and nationally by merger and acquisition.
- Privileged access to empire, imperial and Commonwealth markets, subsequently challenged by membership of EU.

Lane: Financier dominated, short-termist individualist business system.

Whitley: Market relations dominant, limited institutional pluralism.

Hall and Soskice: Liberal market economy, capable of radical innovation; however, comparatively low level of institutional regulation in capital and labour markets, education and vocational training often prevents effective implementation and longer-term operation of corporate strategies.

● The German business system

The German system is often referred to as more institutionally coordinated than the US and British business systems. The historically embedded features listed below were challenged by defeat in the First World War and occupation after the Second World War and again by reunification in 1989. However, many of these features remain present.

- Management systems incorporate some aspects of US management systems, notably 'system' approach to construction and manufacturing; retains a comparatively large manufacturing sector in the contemporary period.
- Large managerial hierarchies; however, significant levels of family control and share ownership in manufacturing industry, e.g. BMW and Siemens.
- Integrated production chains, contemporary focus on 'diversified quality production'.
- Significantly higher levels of inter-firm cooperation than found in the UK and USA.
- Paternalism, then codified institutional pluralism towards the workforce.
- Corporate strategies focus on innovation and competitive-based approaches.
- System is production oriented with management and labour integrated around productive tasks.
- Credit-based investment funds, integrated institutional relationships between financial institutions and industry, combined with lesser focus on shareholder value and institutional investors, create longer-term investment and payback horizons.
- Education and vocational training system highly developed and nationally certificated.

Lane: Productivist-based system with collectivist orientation.

Whitley: Significant degree of institutional pluralism, especially in industrial relations system; active institutional regulation by the central and local state acts as a constraint on short-termist inclinations of capital.

Hall and Soskice: Coordinated market economy, sustained competitive advantage in manufacturing sector, exhibits incremental change and innovation.

See also Chapter 9 on aspects of German vocational training.

● The postwar Japanese business system

The Japanese business system is sometimes referred to as a collective form of capitalism, one that reflects particular historical features of Japanese society which in turn are one explanation for the success of *Japanese* approaches to the organisation of capitalist production. Less than a hundred and fifty years ago Japan was a feudal pre-capitalist society; hence, as a late-industrialising nation, its rise by the 1980s to a world-class manufacturing economy feted and emulated by US and British businesses is all the more remarkable.

Japan's feudal system was characterised by two elements each of which has a bearing on the process of successful industrialisation, particularly in the period since 1945. Diligence and self-sacrifice epitomised by the mason-like samurai are embedded features of Japanese society that have been reinvented as cultural and institutional explanations for Japanese economic success. Diligence manifests itself in the hard-working 'live to work' culture of many Japanese workers, a culture that is reinforced by willingness and an ability to identify with common or collective goals in the workplace. The presence of dedicated, diligent and collectively oriented but not oppositional workers has led some observers to argue that the Japanese business system exhibits both mutuality and high-dependency relations within and between institutional actors representing the interests of capital, labour and the state, a pattern of relations clearly absent in the British business system (see Oliver and Wilkinson, 1988).

In addition to the importance of cultural and historical factors that effectively incorporate workers within capitalist production relations, Japanese economic success in the postwar period is also attributable to a method of organising of production, centred on a system of flexible mass production, the *Kanban* system of just-in-time production pioneered by Kiichiro Toyoda (see Wada and Shiba, 2000 and Chapter 16 for more details). Just-in-time systems produce precise, defect-free quantities just in time for the next stage of production. For success, such systems require total commitment by the workforce and suppliers and usually operate in conjunction with TQM that is driven by customer needs and expectations. JIT and TQM represent two parts of a process – if only the precise amount is produced at each stage, any quality defects halt production. As Wada and Shiba (2000) point out, it is remarkable that JIT and TQM were heralded as innovations in production superior to those of mass production techniques when both were developed by Toyoda precisely because low capital levels precluded the luxury high-stock levels and inspection teams. It was Toyoda's inability to compete head-on with US mass production that stimulated what became termed JIT and TQM and in the contemporary period both highlight embedded features of Japanese feudal society – diligence, self-sacrifice and identification with collective goals in situations of mutual dependence – that have come to be seen as features that are embedded within the Japanese business system and which also contribute to its following characteristics.

- Very high levels of organisational integration.
- Long-term collaboration between firms via established business networks.
- Commitment and loyalty between employers and employees.
- Active role undertaken by the state to provide inexpensive finance funds.
- Enterprise group capitalism originally controlled by family, the *Zaibatsu*, later developed into large corporate actors, some built by banks or industrial enterprises such as MITI, e.g. Sony and Toyota.
- 'Core companies', e.g. Fujitsi and Mitsubishi, plan for wider industrial groups and are able to exercise strategic choice in locating labour-intensive manufacturing and assembly work within smaller firms.
- Cooperative investment strategies across enterprises and industrial groups.
- Permanent employment status for some workers operates as a coordinated and planned training system; promotion and rewards based on seniority.
- Significant innovation and organisational capability in manufacturing, e.g. early use of quality circles, TQM, JIT and inventory control and statistical quality control.

> **Whitley:** Collective business system that incorporates workers and managers within corporate strategies of core companies to promote innovation and organisational capability in design, problem-solving and production. However, limited institutional pluralism.
>
> **Hall and Soskice:** Coordinated market economy, significant institutional regulation beyond the market. Active state role in finance provision and promotion of inter-firm cooperation reduces market uncertainty and promotes cooperation within hierarchies and between them.

See also Chapter 17 on the Japanese employment system and HRM.

Section conclusion

This summary of the historically embedded features of different business systems characterises the long-term nature of individual systems. The characteristics and institutional approaches within systems – market, individualist and separate or non-market collectivist and integrated – change only slowly. Significant restructuring necessitates substantial institutional reform that is likely to be challenged and contested by institutional actors. The evidence suggests that business systems retain many institutional characteristics even when subject to dramatic interventions such as those experienced by Germany and Japan following Allied occupation and reconstruction following the Second World War. Equally, British membership of and further integration within the EU has to date had only a marginal impact on the character and institutional operation of the British business system. Further, globalisation, while for some representing the harbinger of convergence between business systems, has yet to undermine the divergent nature of national business systems. As other parts of this chapter demonstrate, the persistence of national characteristics extends to policies and strategies for the management of human resources, underpinning our concern to emphasise the importance of not only the emergence of *international* HRM within multinational firms but the significance of national approaches to HRM that suggest the importance of comparative approaches.

Comparative HRM

This chapter argues that an understanding of international HRM (i.e. the policies and processes of HR management in MNCs) is dependent on an understanding of comparative HRM (i.e. an understanding of the reasons for cross-national differences and similarities in HR practice). This section therefore explores how the differences in national business systems explored in the first part of the chapter create differences in human resource practices between different societies.

Cross-national differences in HR policy and practice

Much research in the field of international and comparative management has followed a unitarist 'one best way' perspective, with cross-national differences either downplayed or simplified into cultural divergences from the dominant US ideology of management. Not only does this contradict the hypotheses of institutionalist researchers into the nationally specific development of capitalism, but it also runs contrary to a wide range of comparative research in HRM, organisational studies and industrial relations, indicating that national rules and understandings are of considerable importance in affecting the nature of the employment relationship. For example, the work of the LEST school

(Maurice *et al.*, 1986) found substantial differences between France and Germany in the relative pay levels and degree of authority of workers at different levels of the corporate hierarchy. Subsequent research has found significant differences, even between European Union countries, in areas as central to the employment relationship as recruitment (Windolf, 1986; Quack *et al.*, 1995), training (Sako, 1990; Felstead *et al.*, 1994) and pay practices (Festing *et al.*, 1999; Black, 2001; Almond, forthcoming), while differences in industrial relations and employee representation systems have been thoroughly analysed (cf. for example, Ferner and Hyman, 1998; Bamber and Lansbury, 1998 etc.). Equally, there is now a substantial body of research examining the degree to which 'Anglo-Saxon' models of HRM are applicable to other cultures and societies (Sparrow and Hiltrop, 1994; Brewster, 1991; Gooderham *et al.*, 1999; Clark, 1996). While such analyses have different emphases, and different interpretations on the degree of commonality or dissimilarity between nations in the means by which firms manage the human resource, it is sensible to conclude that significant differences between countries continue to exist.

The significance of these differences impacting on HR policy and practice can be illustrated by examining the use of part-time employment in the EU (Table 15.1). The issue of part-time employment is of particular interest here for a number of reasons. Firstly, for employers, using part-timers is frequently seen as a method of matching labour supply and demand on a temporal basis. It would thus appear to fit within familiar arguments within the HRM and organisational literatures for – numerical – 'flexibility' (Guest, 1987; Atkinson, 1984; Sparrow and Hiltrop, 1994; Chapter 4 in this volume). Second, since the early 1990s, increasing the level of part-time employment has been promoted by the European Commission as a means of combating unemployment (Commission of the European Communities, 1993). There are thus, at least apparently, strong reasons to imagine that this practice might have become more popular throughout the European Union.

Table 15.1 **Part-time employment as a percentage of total employment, EU countries, 1990 and 2000**

	1990	2000
Austria	–	12.2
Belgium	14.2	19.0
Denmark	19.2	15.7
Finland	7.5	10.4
France	12.2	14.2
Germany	13.4	17.6
Greece	6.7	5.4
Ireland	9.8	18.5
Italy	8.8	12.2
Luxembourg	7.6	13.0
Netherlands	28.2	32.1
Portugal	6.8	9.2
Spain	4.6	7.8
Sweden	14.5	14.0
UK	20.1	23.0

Source: OECD, 2002

This supposition is generally confirmed by the available statistics. Over the decade covered, an increased proportion of employment became part-time in all of the EU countries, with the exceptions of Denmark, Greece and Sweden (in the last case, there was subsequently an increase to 17.8 per cent in 2001).

Notwithstanding these trends, however, there remain very substantial differences between the countries in the extent to which the practice is used. A range of factors join together to explain such differences. It has been suggested, for example, that the high rate of part-time employment in the UK can be explained by a wide range of social and economic factors: the concentration in ownership in services such as retail and catering, enabling employers to plan staffing levels at a very detailed level; long male working hours; a lack of affordable childcare facilities; the increased supply of students for part-time work; and welfare state policies such as the system of National Insurance exemptions, among other factors (cf. Almond and Rubery, 2000: 283).

In Spain, meanwhile, the level of part-time employment, though increasing, remains very low by European Union standards. Alongside the comparatively low degree of female participation in the labour market, which given the gender division of household labour is likely to affect the extent to which there is a large group of workers seeking part-time employment, the most significant factor here is probably the fact that fixed-term (full-time) employment contracts – very widely used in Spain – offer employers a considerable degree of numerical and temporal flexibility without the same need for recourse to part-time employment.

Furthermore, the differences between countries go beyond differences in the extent to which a given practice is used. It is important to bear in mind that the specific form a given policy takes will also differ between countries. For example, the part-time working week is much shorter in the UK (15.4 hours), than in, say, France (23.1 hours), (EIRO, 2002). This is important because it means that the implications for employers of using part-time labour are likely to be different. Again, the reasons for this discrepancy can readily be explained by institutional factors: for example, women returning to the work-place after childbirth in France are much more likely to seek full-time employment than their UK counterparts, a fact explicable in terms of the better childcare provision in the former country, and the lesser degree of wage inequality between women and men, meaning it makes more sense, economically, to share paid work more evenly within couples than in the UK. As a consequence, in France, part-time employment, while popular with employers, is very often entered into only when full-time employment is not available, hence those constrained to work part-time will seek comparatively long working hours in order to maximise their earnings. In the UK, meanwhile, there is a ready supply of labour for short-hours part-time employment (mainly women with caring responsibilities and students), as we have seen.

The point here is that the employer policy of using part-time employees is likely both to be adopted to different extents, and to take different forms, in different countries, and that the explanations for these cross-national differences are to be found in employer calculations as to what is an appropriate policy in a given national institutional and societal setting. The explanations for cross-national differences, therefore, may include such factors as the nature of capitalism in the country, the labour market system, the education and training system, the regulatory system, and the 'system of social reproduction', including the nature of the welfare state (cf. Rubery *et al.*, 1999).

ACTIVITY   Imagine you are the HR Director of a UK food retail chain, expanding into continental Europe. How would some of the factors above be likely to affect you firm's HR strategy in different European countries?

Similar arguments can be applied equally to other substantive elements of the employment relationship (see, for instance, Almond and Rubery (2000: 285) on the UK training system; Gonzalez-Menendez (1998) on the practice of profit sharing in a range of EU countries). They apply all the more strongly to industrial relations systems, i.e. the interaction between employers and trade unions, as well as the legal regulation of the employment relationship. For example, it is perfectly feasible for a large firm operating in the UK or USA to operate unitarist HRM policies and avoid having to negotiate with trade unions. This is not the case in most EU countries, where there is generally some combination of collective bargaining at a level higher than that of the firm, often extended to all relevant employers in a sector, for example. Equally, at the firm or workplace level there are often legal requirements for either co-determination mechanisms such as works councils, a requirement for firms with any union members to engage in company-level collective bargaining, or both (cf. Ferner and Hyman, 1998; Chapter 16 in this volume).

■ National varieties of HRM?

As the above examples make clear, the human resource policy choices made by firms are generally influenced by a complex set of interrelated institutional forms within society. Thus, at least to some extent, national institutional and cultural environments create tendencies towards national 'systems' of human resource management, in parallel with wider national business systems. Keeping this firmly in mind, we now highlight some of the more important features of systemic effects on national patterns of human resource management within those countries examined in part 1.

● USA

Many of the concepts behind recent models of HRM are seen, at least by UK academics, as originating in the United States (cf. Guest, 1990; Sparrow and Hiltrop, 1994). It is certainly the case that the USA is the birthplace of modern management (Chandler, 1977), and that, at least at first glance, firms in the USA have a relative lack of institutional, legal or cultural 'constraints' on the means by which they manage their workforces. As was explained above, the US business and employment systems are seen as market-based (Whitley, 2000), in the sense that the degree of active regulation of firms' activities by the state is relatively low.

This clearly extends to the regulation of the employment relationship. It is well established that the USA has the weakest system of employment protection among major industrialised countries (OECD, 1998). Indeed, the relative ease and cheapness of dismissing employees is likely to have informed some of the early messages of 'hard' HRM (Tichy *et al.*, 1982). The message that people 'have to be obtained cheaply, used sparingly and exploited as fully as possible' (Sparrow and Hiltrop, 1994: 7) is clearly more feasible to put into practice in the USA than in some of the more actively regulated employment systems of continental Europe.

While this lack of regulation reduces the 'constraints' or 'barriers' faced by employers, whether it leads to enhanced business performance is quite another issue. From this regard, it is interesting to note that more recent US HRM models frequently promote the concept of employment security (cf. for example, Pfeffer, 1994), on the grounds that workers with longer-term prospects within the organisation are likely to be more committed to it.

Aside from the relative lack of protective legal regulation of most areas of the employment relationship, collective regulation is also generally weak. Although there are firms and workplaces, particularly in manufacturing sectors, where trade unions have considerable defensive strength, trade union density and, above all, influence are low by any sensible comparative measure. Equally, there is a very low level of collective bargaining coverage. Even to the extent that collective regulation does exist, it is unco-ordinated, with virtually no sectoral regulation, and very little cooperation between rival employers, or indeed active coordination of trade union policies across firms. Thus, to a much greater extent than elsewhere, 'systems' of employment regulation are largely firm-based, with a generally high degree of managerial autonomy in setting human resource policies.

One consequence of these factors is a very wide variety of practice within US firms. However, this does not mean that institutional and social factors are absent. The large size of firms, due partly to the early establishment of mass markets and hence mass pro-duction (see above), led to the widespread diffusion of Taylorist management practices, and formalised management systems (Chandler, 1977). Although the economic efficacy of Taylorism came to be questioned following the rise of competition from Japan, it remains the case that US firms tend to be relatively centralised and formalised in their setting of policy (Ferner *et al.* forthcoming).

Another characteristic of many US employers is an ideological, and sometimes vio-lent, opposition to the concept of trade unionism (Babson, 1999). When, following the crisis of the 1930s Depression, it became necessary for large corporations to accommo-date organised labour, the collective agreements reached in this era were effectively quasi-legal contracts, which represented a constraint on the adaptability of firms' HR practices. This in turn led to further attempts to escape organised labour (Katz, 1985). Equally, a significant group of large employers successfully avoided trade union influ-ence through the use of paternalist, human-relations-style personnel strategies, sometimes referred to as 'welfare capitalism' (Jacoby, 1997).

From the late 1970s onwards, the competitive threat from the Far East, combined with increasing pressures on corporations to maximise shareholder value, led many firms partially to break with the tenets of Taylorism and existing collective bargaining structures. While some firms attempted change through the use of employee involvement programmes (Appelbaum and Batt, 1994), others sought to reimpose management uni-lateralism (Thelen, 2001; Wever, 1995). Aggressive attempts have been made to reduce the inflexibilities caused by collectively negotiated job classification systems, work rules and seniority provisions, and in some cases to reorganise production along more flexible lines, inspired by the Japanese example (Katz and Darbishire, 1999).

In spite of these attempts at change, and the lack of regulatory constraints in the sphere of employment relations, attempts to develop 'soft' or 'best practice' HR policies in the USA have been rendered difficult by the increasingly short-term nature of US capi-talism. Many of the policies favoured by advocates of the more humanistic models of HRM are difficult to square with the lack of employment security inherent in the US labour market, making, for instance, the development of strong internal labour markets difficult to achieve.

● Germany

In marked contrast to the US system, in Germany organisational autonomy in human resource and employment relations policy is limited through three main channels. First, there are relatively strong firm-level institutions of co-determination. Large German firms usually (although not always) have a works council. This body has extensive co-determi-nation and consultation rights, particularly at times of organisational change affecting the workforce. Alongside this, worker representatives are to be found on the supervisory boards of directors of large German enterprises. Second, sectoral collective bargaining is deeply entrenched within the German system as a method of wage determination. Sectoral bargaining covers more than 80 per cent of German employees, creating a high degree of standardisation in pay and working conditions within industries. Thirdly, train-ing and human resource planning policies are greatly affected by strong initial vocational training institutions. These are governed by a tripartite system, with the state and trade unions, as well as employers' associations, governing national and sectoral vocational training policy, hence shaping the labour supply available to firms.

Such institutions have sometimes been seen as 'barriers to HRM' (i.e., as preventing moves towards US models of HRM). This would seem to be supported by findings that although German firms have recently shown increased levels of interest in mechanisms imported from the English-speaking world, such as performance-related pay, attitude surveys and developmental assessment centres, these often meet with considerable resistance by employee representatives (Muller, 1999).

In spite of this, the argument that the German institutional system is incompatible with modern models of HRM can be challenged. Indeed, as Muller (1999) argues, the German system fosters the use of many HRM practices. For example, a strongly embedded system of initial vocational training contributes towards a relatively high emphasis on training within firms, often seen as an important component within softer models of HRM. Co-determination, meanwhile, exerts pressures on German companies to guarantee employment security. This, as Hall and Soskice (2001: 24–5) argue, is likely to encourage firms to invest in firm-specific skills. It also offers a significant mechanism for employee participation and involvement. Finally, industry-level bargaining has, in principle, the effect of equalising wages at equivalent skill levels across the country. This system makes it difficult for firms to poach workers from rival organisations, hence encouraging the development of strong internal labour markets (Hall and Soskice, 2001: 24–5).

Muller (1999) concludes that the effect of the German employment system is to create a form of 'pluralist' HRM. In other words, the system does not prevent the emergence of HRM policies and techniques; indeed, as argued above, it may in fact encourage many of them. However, the unitarist, non-union 'ideal' of HRM is generally unobtainable for medium and large firms in Germany.

It has to be added, though, that this system, while deeply embedded, is not quite as stable as it might appear. The twin influences of globalisation, particularly of capital (cf. Lane, 2000; Beyer and Hassel, 2002), and of reunification with the former German Democratic Republic, have created tensions within the German national system, such that the continued survival of the system outlined above has been brought into question in recent years (for contrasting views on this, see Hassel, 1999; Klikauer, 2002). However, it remains the case that the human resource policy decisions of firms operating in Germany are strongly influenced and regulated by the present system.

● UK

The employment system of the UK, as reflected in Chapter 11 of this volume, is strongly associated with the notion of voluntarism. In other words, the UK state has historically tended to abstain from direct 'interference' in the conduct of employment relations, preferring to encourage trade unions and employers to regulate the employment relationship through collective bargaining. This can largely be explained through the traditional opposition to legal regulation which has been prevalent, albeit for different reasons, among both employers and trade unions (for further explanation, see Hyman, 2003). Until the election of the Thatcher government, therefore, a relative lack of legal regulation of the employment relationship was combined with generally strong collective regulation at the workplace level, at least in manufacturing industry. However, such relations were generally seen as low-trust and defensive in nature, and the system became blamed for the poor performance of British manufacturing industry.

The 'deregulation' of the Thatcher and Major governments consisted primarily, in this sphere, of a legislative assault on the rights of trade unions (Dickens and Hall, 1995). This, along with other social and economic changes, led to sharply declining trade union influence at the firm and workplace level (c.f. Millward *et al.*, 2000), and enabled the 'individualisation' of the employment relationship. The increasingly non-union nature of much of the UK private sector would seem to make the UK employment system more amenable to (US) models of HRM.

However, as is the case in the USA, a lack of institutional constraints can also be interpreted as a lack of institutional supports for (soft) HRM. The lack of coordination in such central areas of the employment relationship as vocational training and pay determination means that, unlike in Germany, firms' attempts to develop strong internal labour markets with extensive provision for training are likely to be hampered by the 'poaching' of employees from rival firms. UK firms have hence placed a very heavy reliance on numerical forms of flexibility, rather than the more qualitative forms of flexibility favoured both by soft HRM models and theories of 'flexible specialisation'. Hence, the increased liberalisation of the UK employment system has not led to the widespread adoption of 'best practice' models of HRM, but rather to a continuance and intensification of the traditional short-termist pragmatism of UK employers. In other words, the UK system creates 'islands' (often foreign-owned) of contemporary 'best practice' in a sea of pragmatism. The lack of any institutional 'lock-in' to soft HRM means that firms, unionised or not, often eventually resort to management unilateralism to deal with immediate, short-term pressures (Almond *et al.*, 2001).

● Japan

The current Japanese system, as established in the postwar years, is based primarily on the institutionalisation of two policies, namely seniority-based wages and 'lifetime' employment.

It is important to understand fully the meaning of 'lifetime' employment. This does not refer to all the employees of a firm, and neither is it a general practice across the Japanese economy. Rather, in larger companies, or groups of companies, there is an entrenched practice of hiring *core employees* from the pool of young talent available. Once recruited, such people will remain within the company group until they are aged between 55 and 60, with a corporate undertaking not to dismiss such workers except in very exceptional circumstances (Japanese Ministry of Labour, 1995). Hence, core employees have had extensive guarantees of career-long employment. However, at the same time, to achieve flexibility in labour costs and to be able to offer employment security to a core group, employers also created a separate group of temporary workers it could lay off easily. Flexibility was also achieved through varying the overtime hours of permanent workers, and through putting intense pressures on firms in the supply chain in order to adjust overall system labour costs (Koshiro, 1994). As Ornatowski (1998) argues, this system was neither created by employers alone, nor was it the simple result of Japanese cultural values. Rather, it was the direct result of union demands for living wages and no lay-offs, followed by management accession to these demands for core employees, incorporating them into a system that maintained overall labour cost flexibility (Koshiro, 1994).

This system, alongside a financial system that favoured growth over short-term profit maximisation (see above), helped to foster many of the well-known work organisation practices of the larger Japanese manufacturing companies, later imitated by Western firms without the support of the accompanying human resource policies. It is, therefore, a combination of these practices, rather than any single policy, which contributed to Japanese economic success.

In recent years, however, faced with wider pressures on the nature of the Japanese business system, and declining economic success, there has been much talk of change in the Japanese human resource management system (see Chapter 17). In particular, the seniority system of determining pay and promotion is seen as being replaced by performance-based pay systems, increasingly labelled as an 'annual salary system'.

However, such speculation may be premature; although it is true that some large firms have begun to replace seniority-based pay and promotion systems (*nenko*), with more Westernised performance-based systems (*nen posei*), such firms remain a minority – around 10 per cent of large firms in 1998 – and even some of this minority guarantee wage levels within a more performance-related system (Ornatowski, 1998). Equally, the performance-related elements tend to apply more to managers than to shopfloor workers.

Equally, although there have been several cases of large Japanese firms making (core) employees redundant for the first time, it would be wrong to conclude that this marks the end of this pillar of the Japanese system. Although the lack of ability to dismiss workers within the system would seem, from an orthodox point of view, to present rigidities, defenders of the Japanese system (cf. Ornatowski, 1998; Imai and Komiya, 1994) argue that offers of long-term employment continue to encourage strong employee loyalty and motivation, internal communication and long-term training, as well as pointing out that the system has always had substantial 'flexibility' owing to the presence of a large non-core workforce.

■ Section conclusion

This part of the chapter has argued that the institutional nature of national business systems, and differences in the regulation of employment relations, join together to create nationally distinct modes of practice of HRM. Such effects on employer practice frequently go beyond the regulation of the workplace, to wider elements of the national business and societal system, including diverse elements such as the nature of the welfare state, the means by which firms obtain finance, etc.

Turning to the regulation of employment, some analyses of HRM in more actively regulated countries have argued that wide-ranging collective or individual rights for employees constrain employees, reduce flexibility and constitute 'barriers to HRM'. However, we have argued that in many ways the institutional form of employment relations in Germany, or in the larger firms in Japan, would appear to support many of the practices found in 'best practice' HRM models. In some ways this is unsurprising, given that the inspiration for many of the original HRM models was the competitive threat that Japanese firms posed to US firms.

The field of comparative HRM (the comparison of personnel practices between firms in different countries) is often neglected, yet is important in establishing the links between personnel policies, institutional systems of regulating businesses, economic success and social cohesion. Furthermore, an understanding of how a given policy (or set of policies) is interpreted across a range of countries is a critical issue for those responsible for human resource strategies in firms that transcend national boundaries. With this in mind, we turn to an examination of HRM within such firms.

Stop and think	Do the differences in national HR systems between the countries examined above imply different overall national 'styles' of HRM? Justify your answer.

International HRM

This part examines the ways in which human resources are managed in the multinational corporation, usually referred to as international HRM. Taylor *et al.* (1996) define international HRM as:

> The set of distinct activities, functions and processes that are directed at attracting, developing and maintaining an MNC's human resources. It is thus the aggregate of the various HRM systems used to manage people in the MNC, both at home and overseas.
>
> (Taylor *et al.*, 1996: 960)

As such the emphasis is on the role and organisation of international HR functions, the policies and practices they adopt and the relationship between the parent and its subsidiary operations in managing HR issues. As indicated in the introduction to this chapter, international HRM adopts a strongly strategic perspective in its examination of HRM. Thus its starting point is not the institutional environment, but rather the competitive environment. A strategic perspective defines local competition in the form of, for example, the nature and degree of product demand or expectation of customer service, and so forth, and the extent to which corporate strategy needs to take these into account, i.e. to be locally sensitive. At the same time the multinational's competitive advantage over national firms is based on its capacity to leverage resources on a global scale. For example, to use the 'know-how' developed in one country to meet a market need in another, or to locate workforce resource-intensive activities in low-wage or less-regulated economies. However, leveraging global capability in these ways requires a degree of integration and/or coordination across the organisation. This is most effectively achieved through some degree of standardisation, frequently referred to as globalisation, in the HR policies and practices of the multinational. The demands for localisation and globalisation do not always sit comfortably together, and in part 3 of this chapter we consider how this dualism is addressed theoretically and the impact it has on HR policy and practice. For example, the types of concerns that dominate this field are: How can such organisations most efficiently structure their geographically dispersed operations? What is the nature of the control relationship between the parent and its subsidiaries? Can and should human resource management policy and practice developed by the parent (headquarters) be transferred to subsidiaries in other countries? What types of human resource management activity should be centralised and what should be decentralised, why and how? How do the international mindsets of senior managers affect strategic orientation? What is the role and function of international managers?

We begin by examining the strategic priorities facing MNCs and considering some of the typologies proposed for understanding these organisations' strategy and structure. Second, specific models of international HRM will be considered. Here the concern of the theorist is with what constitutes key international HRM activity, where it is located, and how it should be implemented to ensure a congruence between the organisation's business strategy and the management of its human resources. Here you may recognise the parallel with debates in the field of domestic strategic HRM (Chapter 2). Third, we look at the role of expatriate managers in international organisations. Expatriates have received considerable attention over the years because of their extensive use by international parent firms to control and coordinate subsidiary activity. A lot of the work in this field focuses on the selection process, training provision and expatriation failure.

■ Strategic priorities in international organisations

● Key concepts: integration, responsiveness and transfer of learning

The strategic priorities of a multinational play a key role in shaping the human resource strategies adopted. For this reason it is important to consider, in brief, three key concepts, integration, responsiveness and transfer of learning. These strategic concepts have their origins in the international business strategy literature, an area of theory that international

HRM draws heavily upon. By gaining an appreciation of these concepts it becomes more transparent why multinationals are attempting to design human resource management systems and processes that attend to some or all of the following:

(a) are sensitive to cultural and institutional variation across countries;
(b) create an integrating global culture and way of managing employees;
(c) coordinate scarce, expensive and critical human resources;
(d) leverage learning across the network of subsidiaries.

International business strategists have attempted to generate theory that makes it easier to interpret the complex world of international business. One of the best known is Prahalad and Doz's (1987) Integration–Responsiveness (IR) grid. They argue that international organisations are faced with pressures to integrate and coordinate their activities on the one hand and on the other to respond to local (national) variations. The pressures driving integration and responsiveness faced by international organisations are summarised in Table 15.2.

These two pressures, namely integration and responsiveness, form the Integration–Responsiveness grid and MNCs adopt different strategies and structures depending on where they sit within this grid (see Harzing, 1999 for an in-depth review). So for example in a multi-domestic industry, such as utilities (e.g. water services), con-

Table 15.2 Summary of the pressures making up the I–R grid

I–R grid	Pressures
Strategic coordination need is high where:	• Multinational customers are a large proportion of the customer base. For example, it is important to coordinate pricing, service and product support worldwide as the multinational customer has the ability to compare prices on this basis.
	• Global competition is likely. If companies operate in multiple markets, global competition is highly likely; as such it is important to monitor and collect information on competitors' activities in the different countries in readiness for an appropriate and timely strategic response.
	• Investment in one or more parts of the business is high. For example, high-tech manufacturing and R&D are common high fixed costs. To maximise the benefits and yield the best return on capital investments, global coordination is necessary.
Operational integration need is high where:	• Technological intensity is high. Technology intensive businesses often require a small number of manufacturing sites that enable quality and costs to be centrally controlled while serving widely geographically dispersed markets.
	• Cost reduction is a priority. This can be achieved through locating in low-cost economies or building plants designed to maximise economies of scale.
	• The product is universal and requires minimal adaptation to local markets. This is typical in consumer electronics.
	• Manufacturing needs to be located close to essential raw materials or energy such as in the petrochemicals business.
Local responsiveness is high where:	• Customer demands vary across nations or regions.
	• Distribution channels need to be tailored to the characteristics of the country or region. For example, marketing of products may need to be nationally specific.
	• There are other similar products or where the product needs to be adapted to local needs.
	• Local competitors rather than multinational competitors define the market competition.
	• The host country places restrictions on the operating subsidiary.

sumer demands and service provision are highly context-specific. Thus the competitive strategy of a multinational's French subsidiary, for example, is largely independent of that of its UK counterpart. This is necessary because regulatory requirements, customer norms or government policy requires a strategy that is responsive to local conditions. As such these subsidiaries compete in domestic markets and frequently with domestic companies. Equally, a decentralised organisational structure where subsidiaries are given a high degree of strategic and operational autonomy from their parent is the most efficient. However, often the parent retains some degree of control through setting performance targets. This type of organisation would be located in the bottom right-hand side of the grid (Figure 15.1). By contrast, in a global industry, such as consumer electronics, standardised product/service demands by customers and economies of scale dominate. The organisation's strategy prioritises efficiencies by producing standardised products, locating in the most cost-effective economies and coordinating expensive resources such as equipment or R&D. These organisations tend to centralise resources and responsibilities to the parent company, while the role of the subsidiaries tends to be sales and services. The strategic responsibility and operational freedom of subsidiaries are usually fairly tightly controlled by the parent. This type of organisation would be located in the top left-hand side of the grid.

There is a considerable degree of empirical evidence supporting the existence of multi-domestic and global organisational forms (Bartlett and Ghoshal, 1989; Harzing, 2000; Leong and Tan, 1993; Moenaert et al., 1994; Roth and Morrison, 1990). And the I–R grid is a simple and effective tool for explaining the key priorities shaping these organisations' strategies and structures. However, it is less effective at capturing the significance of the transfer of learning and innovation, which is an important strategic priority for the third type of international organisation, namely the transnational. This organisational form is located in the top right-hand portion of the grid. In the transnational industry organisations must respond to the simultaneous and often conflicting demands for integration and responsiveness, in addition to learning transfer. Learning transfer refers to the diffusion of learning across the organisation; for example, a technology developed by a subsidiary or parent in one country may be transferred to other parts of the organisation located in other countries. The strategy in these organisations is more 'incremental' or 'emergent' (Mintzberg and Waters, 1989). Equally, the structure is more flexible and frequently referred to as an integrated network (Bartlett and Ghoshal, 1990). There is a growing body of work illustrating that MNCs incorporate features of this ideal type (Bartlett and Ghoshal, 1989; Ghoshal and Westney, 1993; Harzing, 1999, 2000). Equally, it has undeniably 'taken a strong foothold in the world of academics, consultants and MNCs' top executives alike' (Harzing, 1999: 43–4) and

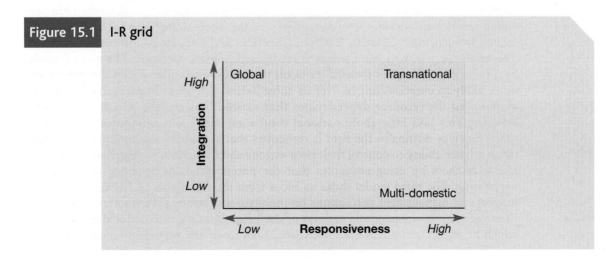

Figure 15.1 **I-R grid**

as such it has contributed to theorising and practice in the management of human resources in contemporary international organisations. However, as Harzing (2000) points out, there is no empirical evidence, as yet, supporting the notion that transnational, nor indeed the multi-domestic or global, organisational forms yield the high-level performance outcomes that warrant their promotion as 'ideal types'.

In sum, MNCs are faced, to differing degrees, with the need to meet demands for local responsiveness, strategic integration and global learning and this in turn defines the international strategy of the organisation as being multi-domestic, global or transnational in character. The difference in strategy explains the difference in the structure of multinationals, as the two are interdependent, although the direction of causal relations is unclear. These strategies also make quite different demands on the HR processes and practices adopted. For example, the extent to which subsidiary HR practices need to be sensitive to local employee values, the need for common management training programmes across the global organisation to facilitate integration and a common organisational culture, and the presence of processes and systems that allow knowledge to be generated collectively and dispersed where necessary are all tied into the strategic priorities of the MNC. It is to these HR issues that the following section turns.

Stop and think	What sources of pressure are likely to demand strategic responsiveness by a multinational? Explain.

What consequences does the pursuit of economic efficiencies have on local economies?

Suggested reading: Ghoshal, S. and Bartlett, C.A. (1998) *Managing Across Borders*. London: Random House: Part 1, pp. 1–81.

Models of international HRM

Here we consider the models of international HRM that have been put forward to explain how the function is configured, the activities and roles undertaken and the factors affecting these. In contrast to the comparative HRM literature, discussed in the previous sections, it is interesting to consider how external and institutional factors are treated within these models. First, we will consider two models of strategic international HRM developed by Schuler *et al.* (1993) and Taylor *et al.* (1996). The first and most comprehensive of these is the Schuler *et al.* model which was developed as an analytical framework that pulled together various conceptual and empirical work in the field providing researchers with a potential roadmap of the internal and external organisational factors influencing the issues, function, practices and impacts of international HRM. The importance of national context is recognised but not specified. The second model by Taylor and colleagues focused more on the conditions under which the parent was more likely to exercise control over its subsidiaries' activities. In particular, the model emphasised the resource dependencies that existed between the parent and its subsidiaries. This says little about national contextual issues, but is important, for unlike much previous writing in the field it recognises that subsidiaries of multinationals have much greater ability to control their own actions and influence the degree of parent control over them by using resources that the parent needs as a means of trading or negotiating. The third model shifts its focus from the international HR function to the influence of management perceptions on multinational strategy. Perlmutter (1969) identifies variation in the mindsets or ways of thinking about the international environment, which he argues can affect the international nature of the organisation's management processes. Schuler *et al.* (1993) have used Perlmutter's model to consider the implications for the role of the international HR function. The fourth and fifth models, by Adler and Ghadar (1990) and Milliman and Von Glinow (1990) respectively, are models of organisational change. They focus more on the relative influence of host and home country factors in shaping the role of the international HR function and in particular the role of expatriate managers in enabling international strategy. Both models adopt a similar perspective in terms of seeing the multinational progress through various stages of internationalisation, with each stage bringing into focus the importance of home and host country priorities. Here we see the potential for overlap between much of the comparative work and international HR theory; however, as will be illustrated, the discussion of home and host contextual issues is scant.

● Schuler *et al.*, (1993): integrative framework of international HRM

The Schuler *et al.* (1993) integrative framework of international HRM was, in essence, a conceptual framework that attempted to map HRM activity to the varying strategic requirements for integration and local responsiveness which define MNC strategy (Figure 15.2). Because of this, it is extremely comprehensive in terms of the breadth of issues addressed, although this is at the expense of depth in the explanation of these issues. This framework built upon the work of strategic HRM theorists researching HRM in domestic companies (Boam and Sparrow, 1992; Schuler, 1992; Lengnick-Hall

Figure 15.2   Integrative framework of strategic international HRM in MNEs

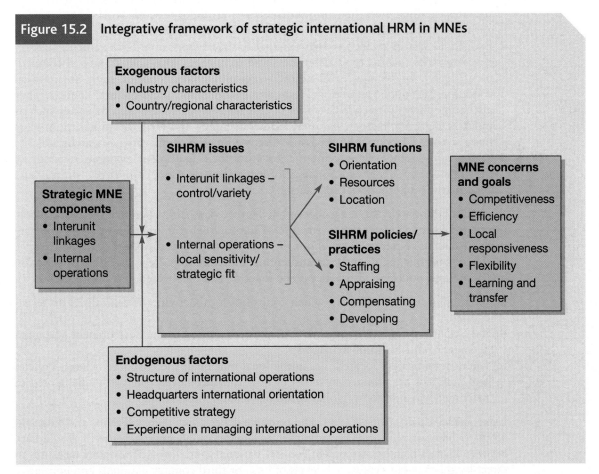

Source: Schuler et al., 1993: 722

and Lengnick-Hall, 1988; Wright and McMahan, 1992). As such, Schuler *et al.* define strategic international HRM as:

> *Human resource management issues, functions, policies and practices that result from the strategic activities of multinational enterprises and that impact the international concerns and goals of those enterprises.*

The overlap between the study of domestic and international HRM is discussed explicitly by Taylor *et al.* (1996: 960):

> *Strategic Human Resource Management (SHRM)..., is used to explicitly link with the strategic management processes of the organisation and to emphasise coordination or congruence among various human resource management practices. Thus, SIHRM is used to explicitly link IHRM with the strategy of the MNC.*

This integrative framework of SIHRM identifies a series of strategic MNE (multinational enterprise) components, endogenous factors and exogenous factors that shape the issues, policy, practices and functions of HRM in international organisations. These determinants are explained, briefly:

1 Strategic MNE components include interunit linkages and internal operations. Interunit linkage is concerned with the need to differentiate or integrate several operations which are geographically dispersed (Ghoshal and Bartlett, 1998; Prahalad and Doz, 1987). Internal operations refer to how each unit operates within its local environment. The restrictions of national institutional or legisative frameworks are recognised, along with the cultural diversity in attitudes towards work, management, authority and so forth (Hofstede, 1980; Laurent, 1983; Schein, 1984).
2 Exogenous factors relate to issues external to the organisation. For example, industry characteristics such as type of business and technology available, nature of competitors, degree of change; and country/regional characteristics such as political conditions, economic conditions, legal requirements and socio-cultural context. They also argue that an extended version of this framework would include issues such as industry maturity, history, national industrial policy and level of unionisation. Here there is a clear overlap with the issues discussed by the comparative researchers.
3 Endogenous factors relate to internal organisational issues. For example, structure of the organisation, experience, or stage of internationalisation, competitive strategy and headquarters' international orientation.

Essentially the above three aspects of the framework bring together the work of the international management theorists and argue for their impingement on the management of human resources throughout the organisation. Specifically they argue that the strategic components, exogenous and endogenous factors affect the SIHRM function and associated policies and practices. The function can be affected in terms of its:

(a) orientation, i.e. the extent to which control of local activities is centralised or decentralised;
(b) the amount of financial and time resources committed to the development and management of international managers;
(c) where activities are located, i.e. in the local unit or at the corporate centre. Policies and practices are affected in terms of how they are developed and implemented to promote local autonomy, global coordination and integration.

Using agency theory (Jones, 1984) and resource dependency theory (Pfeffer and Salancik, 1978), Schuler *et al.* (1993) propose that an organisation's approach to HRM will vary between using a high level of parent country nationals and normative control measures to direct local behaviour versus high levels of local or third country nationals and normative control measures to enable the centre to guide policies while still allowing for local adaptation. HR philosophy will play a key role in providing local sites with general statements to guide their practices so they are in tune with the corporate approach but locally sensitive. There is also a need for local HR policy to fit with corporate policy if personnel are to be able to be selected, transferred and developed as an organisational resource as opposed to a subsidiary resource. As such they argue that in order for multinational companies to be flexible and adaptable to local circumstance, transfer learning and retain strategic integration, HR practices need to match strategic and cultural demands at the local level. A 'modus operandi' needs to be developed to enable HR practices to fit changing circumstances, while global HR policies need to be developed to be flexible enough to be applied to local HR practice. This perspective therefore focuses not only on HR policies and practices for the management of international managers but on HR policies and practices for the management of local employees.

As indicated earlier, the role of national institutional factors is incorporated within the framework. Specifically, they argue that uncertain political environments and high economic risk demand greater monitoring and control from the parent, while high levels of heterogeneity and complexity in legislative conditions affecting labour relations are likely to lead to the greater utilisation of local employees, rather than expatriates, in senior management positions at the subsidiary level. They also recognise that cultural diversity will demand greater attention by HR professionals in contexts where there is a business demand for integration and coordination. Thus the effects of the national institutional context are recognised in terms of the degree of control or autonomy given to the subsidiary by the parent and in terms of the centrality of expatriates.

They also discuss the relationship between organisational structures and strategic international HRM policy and practice. They look at four structures, the international divisional structure, the multinational structure, the global and the transnational. They argue:

> Different structures of international operations create different requirements for autonomy, localisation and co-ordination, thus affecting the nature of and extent of SIHRM policies and practices; and the structures of the international operations of the MNE will impact the need for the units to develop mechanisms to respond to local conditions and to develop a flexible capability.   (p. 446)

Given this, they propose that international divisional structures result in a strategic international HRM orientation that focuses on a single issue, namely the selection of senior managers to head up local operations. The multinational structure focuses on selecting managers from anywhere in the company who can run local operations autonomously and with sensitivity to local conditions. The global structure requires a strategic international HRM orientation that selects managers who can operate under centralised control conditions. The transnational structure requires selecting and developing managers who can balance both local and global perspectives. Here again we see that the focus of the model is on explaining and matching the internal HR resources, via recruitment, selection or development, to meet the strategic needs of the organisations.

Schuler *et al.* (1993: 451) conclude that strategic international HRM is concerned with:

> *Developing a fit between exogenous and endogenous factors and balancing the competing demands of global versus local requirements as well as the needs of coordination, control and autonomy.*

While the model is comprehensive, it has been criticised for failing to explain the micro political processes that underpin parent–subsidiary relations (Quintanilla, 1999) and for being overly descriptive (Holden, 2000). In addition, while the model alludes to the impact of international HRM on both the international and local workforces, in reality the discussion tends to focus on management employees only (Ferner, 1994).

Stop and think

Using Schuler *et al.*'s framework of SIHRM:

(a) Identify the key concerns of the HRM function at the headquarters level.
(b) Identify the key concerns of the HRM function at the subsidiary level.

What is the role of the HR philosophy in MNCs?

Suggested reading: Schuler, R., Dowling, P., and De Cieri, H. (1993) 'An integrative framework of strategic international human resource management', *Journal of Management*, Vol. 19, No. 2, pp. 419–459.

● Taylor *et al.*, (1996): exportive, integrative and adaptive model

Taylor *et al.* (1996) apply the resource-based theory of the firm to explain and predict why international organisations adopt different forms of strategic international HRM. Resource-based theory of the firm (Barney, 1991) applied to HR issues (Lado and Wilson, 1994) argues that HR can facilitate strategic goals by developing competencies within the organisation that are valuable, rare, hard to imitate and non-substitutable. Competencies are:

● *valuable* if they are differentiated and provide the company with something that they lack;
● *rare* if they are scare or in short supply;
● *hard* to imitate where, for example, they are embedded within the firm's culture or history and thus based on collective values;
● *non-substitutable* where they cannot be easily replaced through recruitment, for example in the case of tacit knowledge.

Applying this perspective, Taylor *et al.* suggested that the multinational could leverage resources at the national, firm and subsidiary level that could contribute to competitive advantage. Some of these resources would be context specific while others were context generalisable. This is illustrated by the exportive, integrative and adoptive strategic international HRM orientations towards corporate, subsidiary and employee group-level HR issues, policies and practices. The concepts of these three SIHRM forms are based on previous work in international management and SIHRM (Hedlund, 1986; Perlmutter, 1969; Rosenzweig and Nohria, 1994; Rosenzweig and Singh, 1991). Each of these three orientations is explained below:

● *Adaptive*: HRM reflects subsidiary HRM systems designed to match the local environment. Differentiation is emphasised and HRM is concerned with the appointment of local senior mangers but also with little transfer of HRM philosophies, policies, or practices from the parent to subsidiary or between subsidiaries. This approach focuses on attending to local differentiation needs and is polycentric in nature.
● *Exportive*: HRM focuses on replication of parent HR systems in subsidiaries. Integration is a key priority and all HRM functions are affected, not just the international 'cadre' (managers). This approach focuses on maximising global integration and is ethnocentric in nature.
● *Integrative*: HRM is based on the notion of taking the best HRM systems from anywhere in the company and allowing for both global integration and local differentiation and is geocentric in nature.

At the level of the subsidiary the strategic international HRM orientation determines the level of transfer of parent HRM systems, which is based on the resource-dependency relationship between the parent and subsidiary. For example, exportive HRM leads to high control by the parent attained by the high level of transfer of its HRM systems to achieve global integration. Under these conditions the subsidiary is highly dependent on the parent for HR systems and processes to enable integration. In contrast, the adaptive HRM orientation demands little control and transfer of practices by the parent as differentation is the priority. Under these conditions resource-dependency by both the parent and subsidiary is low. In the middle we have the integrative orientation which demands a balance between the transfer of some systems while maintaining the flexibility in the system to allow the subsidiary to adapt to the local context. Under these conditions, there is a parent–subsidiary inter-dependency. Finally, from the resource-dependence perspective they argue that parent control and standardisation of parent and subsidiary practice will be greater in those areas affecting employees 'most critical to the MNC's performance' (Taylor *et al.*, 1996: 978).

Taylor *et al.* also recognise that there are a number of factors that are likely to constrain the degree of parent control over subsidiary behaviour, namely method of subsidiary establishment, cultural and legal distance of host country from the parent or home country of the multinational. With respect to the first of these points, the evidence suggests that subsidiaries that have been acquired have less in common with their parent HR systems than those that are greenfield sites, although this pattern may change over time. Equally, the greater the dissimilarity between the parent company's national culture and legal context, the less commonality between the parent and subsidiary's HR systems. This would follow from many of the institutional arguments outlined earlier.

Their work raises a number of implications. First, unlike much of the previous work, Taylor *et al.* (1996) are more explicit about the impact of SIHRM on different occupational groups. They recognise that not all employees provide the same level of value to the company or provide the same level of critical resources. Traditionally, broad distinctions have been made between white-collar and blue-collar workers. However, there is a need to further refine this by looking at other occupational groups that may be critical to competitive advantage, such as research staff or product designers. Second, their work raises a key question about the generalisability of HR practice beyond the context in which it was developed. What aspects of HRM practice are generalisable? Why? Third, their work does not acknowledge country of origin effects as important. Fourth and finally, their model lacks specificity with regard to what is transferred and how.

ACTIVITY   Now read the section below on Perlmutter's mindset and consider the following question. Taylor *et al.* (1996) argued that the exportive, adaptive and integrative SIHRM orientations are linked to Perlmutter's ethnocentric, polycentric and geocentric mindsets, respectively. Explain why and what this means for HRM practice in the case of each of the three orientations.

Suggested reading: Taylor, S., Beechler, S. and Napier, N. (1996) 'Toward an integrative model of strategic international human resource management', *Academy of Management Review*, Vol. 21, No. 4, pp. 959–985.

● Perlmutter (1969): mindsets

Perlmutter (1969) is widely recognised as one of the first theorists to propose a network-based model of how international companies organise globally. Perlmutter's classification has been applied primarily in the international human resource management literature rather than the international business field, from where it originated. Kobrin (1994) explains that Perlmutter's adoption by the international HRM theorists is largely because the classification is defined in terms of human resource management issues (e.g. training, recruiting, selecting people and resources). Perlmutter initially defined three organisational types based on senior management's cognitions or mindsets: the ethnocentric, polycentric and geocentric organisation. Later he defined a fourth mindset, namely, the regiocentric. He argues that senior management mindsets reflect the extent to which home, host, global or regional values are perceived as important and in turn influence the international nature of management processes used in the company. These mindsets have been adopted by many in the international HRM field as a way of classifying different HRM approaches, for example:

- *The ethnocentric mindset* reflects a focus on home country values and ways of operating. As a consequence, key positions in subsidiaries are filled by parent country nationals (i.e. expatriates). This gives the parent a high degree of direct control over the subsidiaries' operations.
- *The polycentric mindset* focuses on host country values and ways of operating. As a result, key positions in the subsidiary are more likely to be filled by local employees and the parent company is less interested in controlling and homogenising the organisational culture.
- *The geocentric mindset* focuses on global values and ways of operating. These global values are not nationally specific but instead transcend national boundaries and become almost acultural. This approach looks to use the best people for the job, selecting from all over the global organisation.
- *The regiocentric mindset* focuses on regional values and ways of operating. As a result, the organisation is usually structured along regional geographical lines (e.g. Europe, America and Asia Pacific Rim) and employees move around within these regions. This approach allows some degree of integration, but recognises regional diversity.

Schuler *et al.* incorporate Perlmutter's ideas into their framework, arguing that these attitudes underpin a multinational's strategic international HRM orientation in terms of autonomy and standardisation of local HR practice (e.g. staffing, appraisal, compensation and training). The ethnocentric mindset promotes control and centralisation of HR activity, the polycentric mindset is aligned with local decentralisation, the geocentric mindset does not develop HR activity on the basis of nationality. We also saw how these mindsets were associated with Taylor *et al.*'s integrative, adaptive and exportive orientations. While these relationships are somewhat scant in their detail, they allude to the widening scope of the role of a corporate strategic international HRM function as organisational structures become more complex and network rather than hierarchical in nature. One of the primary problems with Perlmutter's approach is that it provides little explanation of how or why the organisation may move from one type of mindset orientation to another.

● Adler and Ghadar (1990) and Milliman and von Glinnow (1990): organisational change models

Two models based on an organisational change perspective have been put forward, namely the Product Life Cycle model of Adler and Ghadar (1990) and the Organisational Life Cycle model of Milliman and Von Glinnow (1990). These models have been designed to explain how and why the international HRM orientation of a multinational changes over time in line with changes in its corporate strategy. Both approaches also recognise the variable importance of the parent or home country context and the host country context throughout each stage. In doing so they take a largely cultural approach.

The Adler and Ghadar (1990) model is based on the product life cycle (PLC) during internationalisation, first observed and described by Vernon (1966), and is a stage model of organisational change. In Adler and Ghadar's model they describe how the role of culture changes in salience and how HRM activities are modified at each stage in response to product strategic requirements and cultural requirements. These phases are described briefly in Table 15.3.

Table 15.3 Globalisation and human resource management

	Phase I Domestic	Phase II International	Phase III Multinational	Phase IV Global
Primary orientation	Product or service	Market	Price	Strategy
Strategy	Domestic	Multi-domestic	Multinational	Global
Worldwide strategy	Allow foreign clients to buy product/service	Increase market internationally, transfer technology abroad	Source, produce and market internationally	Gain global strategic competitive advantage
Staffing expatriates	None (few)	Many	Some	Many
Why sent	Junket	To sell control or transfer technology	Control	Coordination and integration
Whom sent		'OK' performers, salespeople	Very good performers	High-potential managers and top executives
Purpose	Reward	Project 'To get job done'	Project and career development	Career and organisational development
Career impact	Negative	Bad for domestic career	Important for global career	Essential for executive suite
Professional re-entry	Somewhat difficult	Extremely difficult	Less difficult	Professionally easy
Training and development	None	Limited	Longer	Continuous throughout career
For whom	No one	Expatriates	Expatriates	Managers
Performance appraisal	Corporate bottom line	Subsidiary bottom line	Corporate bottom line	Strategic positioning
Motivation assumption	Money motivates	Money and adventure	Challenge and opportunity	Challenge, opportunity, advancement
Rewarding	Extra money to compensate for foreign hardship		Less generous, global packages	
Career 'fast track'	Domestic	Domestic	Token international	Global
Executive passport	Home country	Home country	Home country, token foreigners	Multinational
Necessary skills	Technical and managerial	Plus cultural adaption	Plus recognising cultural differences	Plus cross-cultural interaction, influence and synergy

Source: Adler and Ghadar, 1990

Phase I: domestic – here the focus is on the home market. The products/services are unique, they have not been available before, therefore the price is high relative to cost and competition minimal. As the products are unique there is no need for cultural sensitivity and if they are exported they are in a significantly strong position not to need adaptation. Indeed, exportation of the product/service is based on the premise that 'foreigners' want the product/service unadapted. The HR needs are therefore not that demanding in international terms, i.e. expatriate assignments, internal business trips, cross-cultural training are not warranted for the export market. The international work is restricted to product or project-specific technical competence (Mendenhall *et al.*,

1987). As domestic sales tend to dominate profits, international aspects of management are not given to the best people nor seen as a valuable career move. International organisational development is not seen as relevant.

Phase II: International – competition increases and international markets become more important for profit. There is a shift in focus from product development (R&D) to manufacturing and plants are set up locally and divisional structures emerge. Cultural sensitivity becomes critical to effective corporate strategies. However, decision-making and control tend to remain with the parent. HR performs a vital role in attaining control of local operations. Home country personnel are used to transfer technology and management systems overseas where replication, rather than innovation, is the prime objective. Training in cultural sensitivity and adaptability is key at this stage.

Phase III: Multinational – the product/service reaches maturity, competition is intense and the price has fallen. Coordination of resources becomes a vital tool in the reduction of costs. The role of culture becomes less important as the issue of reducing costs takes central position. As such the best people are usually chosen for international posts to increase profits and control costs. The management assumption at this phase is that organisational culture is more important than national culture, therefore sensitivity to local cultures is seen to be less important and recruitment of international managers tends to be from those familiar with the parent culture.

Phase IV: Global – the three prior phases were based on hierarchical structures. This phase is based on the assumption that the organisation will need to operate in all three

---

ACTIVITY

Drawing on your understanding of the PLC model, consider the role of expatriates, local employees, host national culture and organisational training during each phase.

	Phase 1	Phase 2	Phase 3	Phase 4
Expatriates	• Expatriates are from the parent company. • Focus on the transfer of technical competence to overseas operations; otherwise input is limited.			
Local employees				
Host national culture				
Organisational training				

Suggested reading: Adler, N. and Ghadar, F. (1990) 'Strategic human resource management: a global perspective', in Pieper, R. (ed.) *Human Resource Management: An International Comparison*. Berlin: Walter de Gruyter.

phases simultaneously and therefore build 'complex networks of joint ventures, wholly owned subsidiaries and organisational and project defined alliances' (Adler and Ghadar, 1990: 240). Under such conditions the role of culture comes again to the fore. These organisations operate at a strategic level to combine responsive design and delivery quickly and cheaply. This negates the development of global R&D, production and marketing and therefore requires the management of culture and relationships external to the organisation. Success is based on international managers being able to communicate effectively in a culturally diverse environment. The delineation between expatriate and local managers disappears and the organisation needs to manage the dual demands of integration and local responsiveness (Doz and Prahalad, 1986).

However, the Adler and Ghadar (1990) model is criticised for its emphasis on the role of the expatriate manager and management expertise, with little reference to other employee groups. Milliman and Von Glinow (1990) also argue that as it focuses on a product life cycle it is too narrow. International organisations often have multiple products and the stage of the cycle may vary across the strategic business units (SBU), changing the parent–SBU relationship. Therefore, in response Milliman and Von Glinow (1990) apply the organisational life cycle (OLC) approach to provide a more general framework to understanding SIHRM at the parent and subsidiary level. This model was further refined in the paper by Milliman *et al.*, (1991). This approach is based on the premise that HRM responses will predictably vary in line with stages of organisational development. Their work highlights the importance of recognising the interrelationships between the parent and subsidiary level in defining the nature of international HRM. They note that:

> The degree to which the corporate business and human resource strategies affect the SBU's strategic choices and practices depends on a number of fundamental characteristics of the MNC, such as its organisational culture, management style, and control systems.
>
> Milliman and Von Glinow (1990: 28)

The Milliman and Von Glinnow (1990) model identifies four international HRM objectives, namely, timing, cost versus development, integration and differentiation:

- *Timing* refers to whether the organisation takes a short-term or long-term perspective in its business and international HRM strategy. The former requires quick responses, the latter allows a longer period for implementation, which can mean longer international assignments and commitment to overseas operations.
- *Cost* refers to whether the organisation needs to focus on lowering costs or can focus on longer-term development issues in its overseas operations and the career paths of its expatriate managers.
- *Integration* relates to the use of expatriate managers in implementing informal control systems.
- *Differentiation* refers to the development of a network of home and host country managers to facilitate communication and control between the parent and subsidiary. These four objectives change over four OLC stages, leading to a different pattern of international HRM. These stages are explained in brief below.

Stage 1. As the firm starts out, most of the international HRM is conducted on an *ad hoc* basis and international assignments focus on technical work skills, with little emphasis on cultural training. The need for integration or differentiation is minimal.

Stage 2. The number and extent of commitments in overseas operation increases. Short-term savings remain a priority and the need for integration is minimal. However, for successive growth of the overseas markets, greater knowledge of the local environment is needed. Thus expatriate training in cultural sensitivity and languages becomes more important.

Stage 3. As the business becomes well established, the organisation can take a longer-term perspective and integration becomes key, particularly for controlling costs. Home country expatriates provide control, along with the transfer of home HRM systems and organisational culture. But as cultural sensitivity is less important, training in this area for expatriates diminishes and career development for this group is not so long-term. Sophisticated control systems such as socialisation, mentoring and succession planning are vital for promoting a unified organisational culture and integration.

Stage 4. The demands for both integration and differentiation are evident. In response, organisations need to invest in training and development to enhance the flexibility of the organisation to meet these demands. They also need to evolve a 'multicentric cultural perspective' (Milliman and Von Glinow, 1990: 32) which ensures awareness of the national cultures and subcultures at the subsidiary level.

The Milliman and Von Glinow (1990) model parallels closely the stages models proposed by Adler and Ghadar (1990). Both models provide prescriptions of international HRM types. While stages 1 to 3 are themselves supported by empirical work, the associated international HRM forms are theoretically extrapolated. Stage 4, like the work of the international management theorists, is largely a theoretical concept. Mayrhofer and Brewster (1996) argue that in practice MNCs, irrespective of their need for integration or diversity, adopt an ethnocentric approach to IHRM, with many relying heavily on the use of expatriate managers to control overseas operations. Another problem with the stages model is that it has become less relevant as MNCs adopt both domestic and international markets simultaneously (Taylor and Beechler, 1993) and with acquisitions, mergers and de-mergers there is less evidence that multinationals have to pass through each of these phases in order to internationalise.

■ Expatriates

Here we turn our attention to one particular group of employees that many of the models of international HRM have been particularly occupied with, namely the expatriate. The expatriate manager is particular to the international organisation. These are employees who transfer from one country to another to undertake assignments that may vary from a few months to a few years (Brewster and Harris, 1999). They are often seen as one of the key mechanisms through which an organisation attends to the demand for integration and are viewed as a critical and significant resource (Adler and Bartholomew, 1992; Dowling *et al.*, 1994; Forester and Johnson, 1996). One of the major criticisms of the field of international HRM until recently has been its over-emphasis on the expatriate manager. Given their central place in the evolution of the study of international HRM, we consider some of the reasons why this group of employees has been singled out as of particular importance.

The importance of the expatriate manager to multinationals' strategy became apparent through the now classic study undertaken by Edström and Galbraith (1977). They explained theoretically why expatriates are used by multinationals. The threefold classification they put forward has changed little over the years and remains one of the most widely cited texts on this issue in the field. The three primary motives for using expatriates are:

● *To fill positions.* The lack of availability of managerial or technical knowledge in some countries means that the parent company will resource this through its own staff (Brewster and Scullion, 1997). In the past, expatriates have often been used for operations in Third World countries; however, the opening up of Eastern Europe also created a demand for expatriates (Hillman and Rudolph, 1996).

- *To provide management development opportunities.* Here international assignments offer the individual and the company the opportunity to develop international management expertise. This seems more common in British than US international organisations (Brewster and Scullion, 1997).
- *To support organisational development.* Here the concern is with altering or maintaining the company's structures and processes. The process of socialisation, whereby expatriate managers build social networks across the parent–subsidiary structure, is seen as critical here. Socialisation is also recognised as a key mechanism of control. There have been many studies on the use of expatriates as a mechanism of control (see Harzing, 1999: 116–127 for a review). These highlight the role of expatriates in transferring the values of the parent to the subsidiary as a means of controlling its activities and achieving integration.

While the Edström and Galbraith (1977) study has been widely accepted and adopted by researchers in the field, Harzing (1999) raises a number of legitimate concerns regarding its disjunction from the empirical evidence. She concludes that there are a number of organisational factors that are likely to affect the importance of each role for each company (i.e. country of origin and destination, international strategy, industry, size and age of subsidiary). These are not accounted for by the classification. In addition, the empirical evidence suggests that many organisations use expatriates for direct control and not only indirect control via socialisation as emphasised in the Edström and Galbraith classification.

● The transfer cycle

Much of the work on expatriates addresses the phases in the transfer cycle (Figure 15.3), namely, selection and training, relocation, adjustment and repatriation. Given their criticality to a multinational, it seems logical that a key concern of companies is how best to select and train such individuals. Research in the field has tended to focus on the criteria used to select expatriates. Interestingly, this suggests that technical expertise and domestic track record dominate over issues of language skills and cultural adaptability (Mendenhall *et al.*, 1987). However, the strategic antecedents of selection decisions are under-researched (Brewster and Scullion, 1997). Where evidence is available it suggests that selection decisions are informal and reactive (Brewster, 1991) rather than strategic in nature.

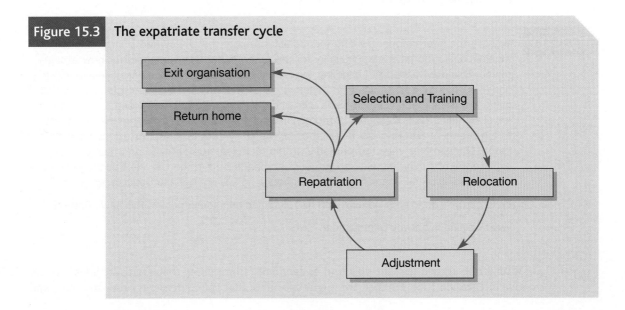

Figure 15.3   The expatriate transfer cycle

In terms of formal training for expatriate assignments, this tends to be geared toward addressing the needs of the expatriate in terms of adjusting to the culture of the host country or the adjustment needs of the expatriate's family (Dowling *et al.*, 1994, 1999). Formal training tends to be limited (Scullion, 1993) and support focuses on practical relocation issues such as information on schools, assistance with moving, sorting visas, medical cover etc. Informal development techniques are more common and tend to take the form of briefings, shadowing and visits (Scullion, 1993). Cross-cultural training has been identified by researchers (e.g. Brislin, 1986; Mendenhall and Oddou, 1986) as key to improving cross-cultural interactions, although a lack of belief in cultural training programmes by top management means that it tends not to be used by companies (Dowling and Schuler, 1991). This is surprising given the strategic importance of culture outlined by Adler and Ghadar (1990). Equally, evidence on the failure of expatriate assignments indicates that poor cross-cultural communications or 'culture clash' (Torbiörn, 1985), alongside unhappiness of family members and language difficulties, are often relevant. For these reasons, training is argued as critical to enhancing the success of an assignment through easing the adjustment process. Equally, the lack of training provision is seen as one explanation of assignment failure.

Returning to the parent on completion of an assignment, repatriation, has proved problematic for many companies and failure to successfully repatriate managers has led many to leave the company. Some of the problems identified (Brewster and Scullion, 1997) include:

- *Loss of status.* This may arise because an expatriate returns to a position they once held prior to the assignment or takes on a new position in the parent company that offers less status than the assignment position.
- *Loss of autonomy.* Assignments may involve the expatriate heading up new operations. In such circumstances they are frequently given a high degree of operational autonomy, often because of the distance between themselves and the parent company, which is withdrawn when the expatriate returns home.
- *Loss of career direction.* In many instances the international experience gained by expatriates is not a prerequisite for career advancement in the parent company. As such, many expatriates feel that their competence in this area is undervalued and not fully utilised by the company in settings outside of the expatriate assignment.

The cost of expatriate turnover due to repatriation failure is high, and is something companies have not addressed.

ACTIVITY

You are the international training manager for Trixon, the UK-owned pharmaceutical multinational. You have responsibility for preparing expatriate managers for new assignments. This may range from handling the logistics of a relocation (e.g. visas, insurance) to providing cultural training. Duncan Jones, an IT expert, has just been selected for his first overseas assignment. Duncan has a wife and 14-month-old baby boy, both of whom will travel with him. He is to spend 12 months in Barcelona at one of the company's manufacturing plants overseeing the installation of the IT system that supports a new product range. Duncan was selected primarily on his technical competence and his successful experience of similar installation projects he headed up in the UK. He has some basic understanding of the Spanish language, although he has not been to Spain in ten years.

What can you do to help Duncan with his relocation and adjustment to this new context?

What training might you offer Duncan? Why?

It might be argued that the cost and assignment failure make the expatriate a less attractive integration tool. Further, we might speculate that the increase in other international

HR forums such as task forces, or HR committees, may in part take over the socialisation and control roles of the expatriate. Furthermore, with the increasing emphasis on global learning, it suggests a need to consider the role of other occupational groups, particularly those more knowledge-intensive workers, in diffusing knowledge, again limiting the importance of the expatriate. However, as yet, there is no empirical work that would support this speculation.

Work in this field has been heavily criticised for its emphasis on description over theoretical explanation (Kochan *et al.*, 1992). Studies have a normative tendency focusing on how expatriates are managed. As this is a relatively embryonic field of study, the need for description has been important. Equally, a functional focus is important and valuable for the practitioner community. However, as in any field of research, there is also a need to move beyond description if the field is to develop. There is a need to develop the theoretical relations that underpin the concepts and issues that abound in the literature and empirical research to test and substantiate many of the concepts used. Brewster and Scullion (1997), in their review of the state of the field, also recognised the need to expand the study of international transfers to non-profit organisational contexts such as the United Nations, ILO, EU, charities, government and non-governmental aid organisations.

The developments in the study of strategic international HRM (discussed above) have widened the definition of the term. This has the potential for integrating expatriate policy with corporate and HR strategy. Some attempts have been made to develop models of international assignment appropriate to different strategic contexts (Welch and Welch, 1994), but work in this area is limited. Bonache and Cerviño (1997: 96) suggest that it is possible to meet many of the needs of globalisation without the use of expatriates, using instead 'temporary foreign assignment for start-up operations; the hiring of competent local managers; socialisation of local managers into the corporate culture; extensive use of international management procedures; audits from headquarters; and formalisation and centralisation procedures'. They argue that it is possible to find MNCs with the same international corporate strategy that each use expatriates in very different ways; equally, MNCs with very different corporate strategies may use expatriates in the same way. These apparent incongruities arise because strategy formulation is not undertaken by rational decision-makers, but by managers who socially construct reality helping to create their managerial vision. This perspective highlights the importance of considering not only the international corporate strategy of the firm in defining the international HR response but wider issues including environmental pressures and managerial vision.

Stop and think

Do you see a place for the expatriate manager in contemporary MNCs? Justify.

Suggested reading: Bonache, J. and Cerviño, J. (1997) 'Global integration without expatriates', *Human Resource Management Journal*, Vol. 7, No. 3, pp. 89–100.

■ Section conclusion

In this part we have looked at the organisational processes, policies and practices adopted by multinationals to address their international strategic goals. This has considered the question of the role of the international HR function, how it is organised and the activities undertaken. Furthermore, complex relationships between the internal configuration of organisational strategies and structures have been considered in terms of how these meet variable external influences. The resource-dependent nature of parent–subsidiary relations as a mechanism of influence highlighted the multiple levels at which international HRM operates, and its differential impact on home and host country employees. Expatriates were identified as one employee group that have received considerable attention in the international HRM literature and their potential limitations as an internationalising force were considered. Throughout, the prescriptive and conceptual nature of much of the work in this field was highlighted as detrimental to the theoretical robustness of the models and their utility in practice. Equally, the under-specification of national institutional factors in combination with strategic issues was evident. We argue that to fully understand and explain HRM in MNCs it is important to consider both strategic and institutionalist/comparative perspectives. However, these issues tend to be considered in relative isolation from each other. Further examination of the interdependency of strategic and institutional factors and their effect on HRM practice warrants greater emphasis. It is to these issues we now turn.

HRM in multinationals

The aim of the final part of this chapter is to consider how and why a closer integration of the institutionalist/comparative and strategic approaches is beneficial to our understanding of HRM in MNCs. The institutionalist/comparative and strategic approaches to international HRM have generally, despite examining similar issues, developed separately and with relatively little cross-reference between the two. However, the two approaches should not be seen as being in opposition to each other; they are appropriate, in effect, for answering different parts of the same basic question as to how firms with employees in more than one country coordinate their human resource management systems. Here, we illustrate how the combination of the two perspectives can help further our understanding of HRM in multinationals, as well as pursuing the question of convergence and divergence.

■ HRM in MNCs: towards a combined institutional and strategic approach

The third part of this chapter concentrated on the strategic context of multinational practice. One weakness of the models available is that national contextual factors, while acknowledged, are not fully explained. In order to resolve this problem, it is necessary to qualify the insights of the strategic model with the implications of institutionalist research into comparative HRM, as reviewed in the second part of the chapter.

One useful starting point here is the 'four influences' model elaborated by Edwards and Ferner (2000). They suggest that HR practice in MNCs is influenced by factors emerging from four sources, namely:

● home country effects;
● dominance effects;
● pressures for international integration;
● host country effects.

● Home country effects

Home country effects cover elements of the human resource practices of MNCs, which can be traced back to the characteristics of the business and employment system from which the MNC originates. In other words, home country effects exist where the human resource policies of an MNC in a foreign country are affected by national institutions or understandings, which can be traced back to the *country of origin* of the firm. For example, research has repeatedly shown that US-owned MNCs are more likely than those from other countries to have relatively centralised and formalised systems of human resource and industrial relations management (cf. Ferner *et al.*, forthcoming). This can be traced back to the nature of the US business system. Effectively, US MNCs investing abroad have tended to export the organisational forms and management methods that had been established in the USA in order to serve mass markets in the USA (Ferner, 2003). As Ferner (2003) argues, they thus introduced to the UK (and other countries) the multidivisional organisational form, with its division of management functions into distinct and highly specialised areas such as production, finance and personnel (Dunning, 1998). Hence, in the sphere of human resource management, the relatively high degree of centralisation of US MNCs can be traced back to some of the embedded features of the US economy reviewed in part one.

Such effects also occur in a number of substantive areas of practice. The effects of the civil rights movement and anti-discrimination legislation in the USA have led US MNCs to adopt relatively strong formal policies on 'diversity', which are often exported overseas, such that the managers of foreign subsidiaries are assessed against diversity targets (Ferner, 2003: 93). Equally, the strongly market-based assumptions behind the employment relationship in the USA have led to US firms being keen to export systems of performance appraisal and performance-related pay (Muller, 1999). Additionally, the entrenched, ideological anti-unionism of many US managers and firms, reviewed in part one, have led many US MNCs to seek to avoid trade unions in their foreign as well as domestic operations (cf. Royle 2000 on the particular case of McDonald's; Almond *et al.*, 2001).

Similarly, Japanese transplants in the UK have transferred a number of practices which are innovative in the British context, such as flexibility of working methods, teamworking, continuous improvement of quality, and attempts to establish strong corporate cultures, on the Japanese model, through 'high commitment management' methods (cf. Oliver and Wilkinson, 1992). Japanese firms have tended to seek either to imitate the Japanese industrial relations system of company unions (Bassett, 1986), or, as in cases such as Honda UK, to avoid trade unions altogether. It should be noted, however, that the twin policies of 'lifetime' employment and seniority-based pay and promotion, seen as cornerstones of the domestic Japanese system, have not been transferred to foreign environments. Hence, the conscious use of domestic policy to inform HR practice overseas is, in this and other cases, selective rather than total.

● Dominance effects

Dominance effects are influences on host country operations, which are seen to flow from the hegemony of one or more countries. These can arise from two main sources. The first, control of the international political economy, can be seen in the case of the USA, in its attempts to internationalise US management methods, and to some extent industrial relations institutions, in postwar Europe (cf. Clark, 2000; Djelic, 1998). Second, economic dominance has been illustrated recently in widespread attempts at the diffusion of 'Japanese' forms of work organisation in the 1980s and 1990s. Dominance effects impinge on the choices of MNCs in several ways. Whatever the source of 'dominance' is, the management methods of that country may become seen as a cross-national 'best way'. This is picked up in the international HRM literature with regard to geocentric approaches to international HRM and geocentric mindsets driving global integration via the diffusion and standardisation of HR practices that are not necessarily parent driven. Hence, for example, an MNC from, say, France, may choose to adopt a combination of 'US' and 'Japanese' methods abroad, rather than home country practices, owing to a widespread belief that such methods are more efficient, either for a particular sector, or more generally. This has particularly been the case with regard to 'Japanisation'. In the 1980s and 1990s, the widespread debate on 'global Japanisation' (Oliver and Wilkinson, 1992) arose not merely because of investment by Japanese firms in the West, but mostly because of the attempts made by Western firms to copy such enterprises.

● **Pressures for international integration**

Multinational corporations also face pressures to integrate their operations between sites in different parts of the world. The demands for integration and the mechanisms adopted have been addressed at length above. Integration applies not only when there is substantial intra-corporate trade, but also where customers themselves are large multinationals which desire commonality of service provision worldwide, as discussed in Prahalad and Doz's I–R grid. Corporations also display a tendency to attempt integration in order to mitigate the inevitable problems of controlling subsidiary behaviour. This may be achieved through attempts to impose uniformity of vision around a 'corporate culture', as well as through formal rules and/or financial controls. Such pressures, the extent of which will depend on product market strategy and the market position of the firm, have been linked with the greater use of mechanisms to control subsidiary action, including the standardisation and diffusion of HR practices.

● **Host country effects**

Finally, the nature of the host country business system is likely to have a distinct effect (discussed at length in part 1). Carrying out production or service provision abroad will involve employing workers and managers from the host country. On the one hand, these might well have different understandings of issues such as appropriate management methods, the collective representation of employees and the wage–effort bargain than those that predominate in the home country of the MNC. On the other, the firm will have to obey the legal and collective employment regulations of the home country, with inevitable effects on the conduct of employment relations and human resource management. Such effects may be more pronounced in some countries than others. For example, the German system, with its strong system of collective regulation of the employment relationship, is likely to move a US MNC further away from home country practices than, say, the less regulated systems of the UK or Ireland might. Meanwhile, it is important to recognise that host country regulations and historically embedded features of business systems can provide 'foreign' firms with resources, as well as the more widely recognised constraints. In other words, an advanced system of vocational education and training might lead foreign MNCs to be more likely to invest in a given host country where particular skills are required.

   In summary, this model provides one way of illustrating the combined effects of institutional and strategic issues on MNCs. It weakness lies in its underspecification of the precise relationship between these factors and how they combine to influence MNC practice. However, it provides an attempt to bring together work from two divergent fields of study, namely institutional and strategic.

■ **The convergence/divergence debate and its relevance to MNCs**

The convergence/divergence debate questions whether national business systems – and, consequently, employment systems and HR practices – are converging cross-nationally, such that the management of personnel is likely to become more similar across different countries. For MNCs, whether the country contexts across which they operate are converging or diverging has important implications for how they manage employees and the effectiveness of processes and structures aimed at global integration and local responsiveness. The MNC has also benefited strategically from the diversity in national business systems by, for example, exploiting knowledge and expertise not easily available elsewhere or by exploiting the lack of employment regulation or low skills to enhance efficiency gains. Equally, the MNC can be seen as a driving force of convergence, by promoting standardised human resource management tools applicable across countries.

These debates are long-standing and the evidence is equivocal. It is clear that national business systems, and elements within them, do not exist independently of global economic dynamics; they must react to global pressures within the international economic system. Does this mean that countries facing similar pressures are likely to react in similar ways, however? Evidence from recent history would tend to show that significant global pressures and structural crises during the past century – such as the Second World War, the collapse of fixed exchange rates and the postwar economic order centred around the dollar, the oil and commodities crises of the 1970s and 1980s, the Kuwait crisis, and the emergence of new economic powers such as Japan and the East Asian 'tiger' economies – were managed in nationally specific ways. The comparative approach to the analysis of business systems and associated institutional characteristics such as the management of human resources examines how global pressures for and processes of economic and political change are filtered, mediated and structured in nationally specific ways. One question frequently posed, however, is whether contemporary international pressures, usually conflated into the notoriously imprecise term '*globalisation*', will bring about new forms of cross-national convergence, or whether national business and HR systems will continue to differ.

● Converging on US HRM?

It is frequently argued that economic 'globalisation', however defined, is a major contributory factor to the pressures being faced in recent years by the more densely institutionalised business and employment systems. Although the examples of CME used in this chapter are Germany and Japan, this argument is often extended to those countries where there is extensive legal, rather than collective, regulation of the employment relationship, such as France, Spain or Portugal. The argument is that the recent increase in global forms of competition is likely to lead to 'convergence' in human resource practices across the world, such that employment policy and practice throughout the (developed?) world will eventually approximate much more closely to the systems found in LMEs, of which the USA is the exemplar.

Such arguments are far from new. Early convergence theorists (cf. Kerr *et al.*, 1960) argued that developments in technology would lead to the development of similar economic, political, social and organisational patterns across industrialised societies, with convergence on the hegemonic US model. More recently, globalisation and international competition have brought about discussion on the possibility of convergence on US models of HRM, sometimes mitigated by talk of 'cultural effects'. In other words, although differences of detail may remain, human resource management systems across the globe will come to be based mainly on a neo-liberal ideology, taking elements of the firm-based systems of the larger (non-union) US employers, such as performance-based pay and promotion and efforts to promote corporate 'culture'. To this will be added policies, such as employee involvement, and company-specific training programmes, believed, from the experience of competition with Japan, to boost productivity and performance.

Clearly, there is some evidence of elements of such a system encroaching into areas where certain 'HRM' practices might previously have been seen as alien. We have seen, for example, that there is evidence of performance-related elements in pay packages becoming a more prominent feature in the German and Japanese systems than previously. However, there remain several grounds on which assumptions of convergence can be challenged.

Firstly, it is often argued, within the 'varieties of capitalism' literature, that different national configurations of business and employment systems might be more appropriate to some industries than others (cf Whitley, 2000; Hall and Soskice, 2001; Sorge, 1991). Hence, firms within a given national system are likely to specialise in those sectors where national institutions offer a form of institutional comparative advantage. There is some evidence that this is the case; for instance, German firms, due in no small part to the vocational training system, tend to specialise in incremental innovation within established industries, while US firms, with greater access to speculative capital, are more likely to specialise in radical innovation. This is reflected in statistics on the sectors in which firms in these two countries have been granted patents in recent years (cf. Hall and Soskice, 2001). Hence CMEs should not, as some have predicted, become uncompetitive because of the globalisation of firms and markets. Instead, their business and employment relations systems might promote competitiveness in different sectors of the 'global' economy, such as sectors reliant on high levels of vocational training rather than labour cost minimisation.

Further, it is important to be careful with regard to how the term 'convergence' is used. Very often, it is taken to imply merely the existence of trends in the same direction, such as, for example, the general increase in the proportion of employment within the countries of the European Union that is part-time. However, if we interpret convergence in its stricter sense, that of 'moving towards uniformity', it is clear that, with regard to the part-time employment example, convergence cannot be said to be occurring. While, as we saw in part two, the use of part-timers increased in 12 of the 15 countries between 1990 and 2000, the figures remain highly different between countries, and there is no overall trend suggesting that countries with previously low rates of part-time employment are generally 'catching up' with countries such as the Netherlands and the UK, which had higher rates of part-time employment at the beginning of the period under consideration.

Much comparative research on human resource management and industrial relations has focused on the question of convergence versus divergence. However, it is not always very clear what the terms mean; very often, trends in a given direction are interpreted as 'convergence', and continued difference as 'divergence'. It is perhaps useful to frame the debate slightly differently. It would appear that there are four different possible outcomes, rather than just two:

- *Strong convergence*, i.e. practices in different countries becoming more similar. This would occur if, for example, firms in countries such as Germany and Japan increasingly applied the individualistic elements of HRM, such as performance-related pay and promotion, such that there was a 'catching up' in this respect with practice in liberal market economies.
- *Weak convergence*, i.e. there are similar trends in different countries, without outcomes becoming more similar. This would occur, for example, if every country in the EU had witnessed growth in the proportion of employment which is part-time, but without an overall tendency towards uniformity. From Table 15.1, this was the case between 1990 and 2000 with regard to this particular HRM practice (if for a moment we ignore the three countries where the proportion of part-time employment in fact diminished).
- *Strong divergence*, i.e. the opposite of strong convergence. This would have occurred if the nature of policies was becoming more different across countries, rather than more similar. This would be likely to occur if the normative message of the 'varieties of capitalism' literature were obeyed, and firms used the comparative advantages offered by their embedded institutional systems to specialise in the appropriate areas.
- *Weak divergence*, i.e. differences remain, and there is no overall trend. One might well argue that this is the case with regard to national industrial relations systems: in recent years there have been cases of centralised systems attempting decentralisation (France), decentralised systems attempting a degree of centralisation (Ireland), and decentralised systems becoming more decentralised (UK).

Overall, it is difficult to conclude in which of these directions human resource systems have moved in recent years, and still more difficult to predict what is likely to happen in even the immediate future. There is some evidence that a number of large firms in CMEs have adopted some of the well-established, individualised practices of US firms; this would appear to offer support to the strong convergence thesis, although it should be noted that these trends are, at least so far, relatively limited in CMEs, and often led, as in Germany, by foreign MNCs. However, support for any form of convergence remains much more limited with regard to other areas of the employment relationship, such as collective labour relations. Even with regard to an issue such as part-time employment, where there would appear to be strong reasons to expect at least weak convergence, it should be remembered that there are EU countries where the practice has in fact diminished. Hence, it is probably more sensible to discuss convergence with regard to specific elements of employment practice, rather than with reference to human resource management as a whole. Finally, it is important not to mistake what may be popular fads among employers and managers for more durable changes in the nature of the employment relationship at a societal level.

The question of convergence versus divergence is of direct significance to a debate on HRM in MNCs. As the most visible manifestations of 'globalisation', they clearly have at least some power to bring about convergence, at least to the extent of developing similar policies across their various national operations. However, as we have seen above, there may be good strategic reasons why a given MNC does not pursue this route. Firms may have different HR policies in their different national subsidiaries for a number of reasons, including market responsiveness, and the nationally variable skills and costs of labour. In other words, nationally specific institutional factors affecting the quality and cost of labour are not simply environmental factors that strategic decision-makers in MNCs have to tolerate; they can also be used strategically by MNCs themselves. A firm may well centre its research facilities in countries with excellent educational facilities, and segment its production strategy in order that elements of production which can be carried out in lower-cost and/or less regulated economies are relocated. Hence, while some highly integrated MNCs may bring about a degree of cross-national convergence, this is not necessarily the case. This, and the fact that home country business systems may affect firms' choices of overall business and HR strategies, underlines our point that the insights of the strategic and institutional schools on international HRM need to be combined, rather than compartmentalised.

Conclusion

This chapter has argued that strategic influences on international HRM need to be considered alongside a range of institutional factors, as considered in Edwards and Ferner's (2000) 'four influences' model. Too often in the past, strategic research has tended to treat institutional influences from the home and host countries in a purely descriptive manner, as a background contingency, rather than as an active variable, or antecedent, in the formulation of strategy. Equally, in examining home or host country effects, the institutional HR literature often fails to consider the MNC as a whole as an institution capable of creating and maintaining rules. It is to be hoped that future students and researchers in this area will attempt to reach a better synthesis between these two literatures.

Summary

- International HRM is examined in terms of the models put forward by Schuler *et al.*, Taylor *et al.*, Perlmutter, Adler and Ghadar, and Milliman and Von Glinow. These perspectives are examined and their shortcomings outlined. The treatment of national contextual/institutional factors is considered.

● The role and importance of expatriate managers to MNCs' international HRM strategy are discussed. The process of managing the expatriate is considered. The descriptive nature of this field is considered alongside the directions of future research and the future role of expatriates.

● The importance and rationale for greater integration between the comparative/institutional HRM literature and strategic international HRM literature is addressed. As a first step in achieving greater integration, the Edwards and Ferner four-forces model is reviewed.

● The nature of the convergence–divergence debate and its importance to the MNC are explored. The evidence to date is reviewed and the tensions between the two perspectives outlined. The MNC is not only affected by trends towards converging and diverging management practice but also players in the process.

● The chapter concludes that there is great value in considering institutional/comparative work alongside the strategic perspective to gain a more comprehensive understanding of the factors influencing HRM in MNCs and the specific nature of this influence.

Questions

1 Explain what is meant by the terms integration and responsiveness in the context of MNCs. What effect can these have on how the MNC is structured, the nature of the parent–subsidiary control relationship, and the flow of knowledge across the MNC?

2 Outline and explain the key internal and external organisational factors that influence an MNC's approach to international strategic human resource management.

3 Explain the role of the expatriate manager in MNCs.

4 What factors can be used to explain why HR practices might differ from one country to another?

5 Explain what is meant by 'convergence' and 'divergence' with regard to comparative HRM. What role do MNCs play in this debate?

Case study

All change at Linkz

Linkz is a German-owned transnational telecommunications company. It was established in 1935 as a domestic company. Since then, the company has expanded internationally. It now operates in 140 countries, employs 104 000 people worldwide, including 22 000 in design centres spread across 25 countries. Approximately 40 per cent of the staff are employed within Germany, but expansion in employee numbers over the past ten years has been greatest outside of Germany.

Linkz began as a wireline telecommunications network supplier. In recent years it moved into wireless software design and it is in this, the area of mobile phones and networks, that the business has expanded rapidly in the past 15 years. Linkz has 30 per cent of the global market share in mobile systems, making it one of the leading mobile communications suppliers worldwide. Sales figures are largest for the Europe, Middle East, Africa regions, followed by the Asia Pacific region, Latin America region and finally the North America region. Sales figures increased in 2001 by 10 per cent on the previous year. Japan is the company's largest market for third-generation mobile phones. However, the European markets have shown some increase during 2000–01. In 1999 Linkz invested 20 per cent of its sales revenue in technical development.

The telecommunications industry has changed significantly in recent years. In the past, Linkz sold telecommunications equipment to large monopolistic operators. Datacom and computer companies are venturing into traditional areas of the telecommunications market, and as these voice and data industries converge a single multimedia industry is emerging. In addition, wireline and wireless phone technology has moved towards increasingly advanced digital technology and Internet technology, giving rise to 'third generation' technology and products, e.g. mobile phones with video and Internet services. Worldwide deregulation has enabled the merging of wireline and wireless operators with global capabilities. As a result, the market is becoming more transnational in nature. The number of global operators is shrinking, while at the regional or local level the number of operators is expanding. This means that there is greater pressure for global standards across the industry that enable compatibility between datacom and telecom systems, while at the local level the advances in technology have led to fierce competition between companies to deliver the latest innovations in products and services to customers. All this leaves Linkz with the demand for increased global efficiency and learning transfer to maximise on its investment in design capability, and the need to be highly sensitive to the demands of local customers given the nature of the competition.

Faced with these many pressures, Linkz restructured in a bid to move away from strong parent hierarchical control over its subsidiary operations, while still building on its global strengths and capability. It established four additional corporate headquarter offices, one for each of its regions (Europe, Middle East and Africa with a corporate office in London; North America with a corporate office in Texas; Asia Pacific with a corporate office in Hong Kong; Latin America with a corporate office in Miami), in addition to the home headquarters in Hamburg. The majority of the senior managers in these offices are German. The corporate offices hold responsibilities for finance,

technology, supply and information technology, human resource management (HRM), marketing and strategic business development, corporate communications, and legal affairs.

The restructuring had notable implications for the design and HRM functions. In terms of design a corporate function was created with responsibility for coordinating R&D across the multinational network, particularly in relation to standardisation, patents and strategic partnerships. In addition, a research centre was established in Hamburg responsible for advanced early 'blue sky' research. The role of design in the subsidiaries was reduced and shifted towards the development of highly specialised products for local customer markets.

The corporate HRM function had the responsibility of creating a global philosophy that enabled best practice and policy from across the network to define the organisational culture. Diversity was seen as a feature of the organisation to be built upon rather than smoothed over. To facilitate this philosophy, annual audits were carried out whereby HR teams from the regional corporate offices would visit subsidiaries to gain evidence of local best practice that they deemed useful for global dissemination. In addition, HR professionals across the network would attend an annual internal HR conference where issues and experiences faced by the HR teams were discussed. The HR intranet bulletin board and chat room provided additional mechanisms for the spread of innovation and networking among the internal HR community. The Linkz Management Academy (LMC) was established in Hamburg, mandated to develop the managerial capability of its worldwide workforce. The LMC designed management development programmes for graduates and junior managers through to its senior managers. These involved academic and practitioner guest speakers from all over the world and usually combined off-site development with on-the-job learning, international transfers or secondments.

This restructuring created many challenges for how the corporate HR functions would achieve their mandate, and the competency requirements of these HR professionals to deliver in this changed context. The changes also created a trade-off between greater autonomy for the subsidiary in some areas versus the loss of control in others. For example, the subsidiary design functions now had almost total control over their activities relating to product design for local customers. However, they were no longer permitted

Case study continued

to engage in long-term strategic R&D as this responsibility now lay with corporate R&D. For the design function the reorganisation also brought new challenges for local managers with regard to how to motivate and develop the necessary technical capability to cope with the changes in the industry and the organisation, while it also changed the career landscape for local senior managers in terms of their opportunity for local and international career advancement.

Questions

Given the reorganisation and changes in the market context faced by Linkz, consider the following:

1 What types of competencies do you feel the HR professionals in the corporate and regional

headquarter offices would need to demonstrate to deliver against the international strategic demands of the organisation?

2 If you were tasked with designing a Linkz management development programme for middle managers, what types of issues would it address and how would it be delivered?

3 Assess the nature of the motivational problems the design function's managers are likely to face, given the organisational changes and changes in the external context. As an HR manager working in partnership with design, what solutions would you suggest?

4 What opportunities and threats might an international career structure bring to local managers?

References and further reading

Adler, N. (1984) 'Understanding the ways of understanding: cross-cultural management methodology reviewed', *Advances in International Comparative Management*, Vol. 1, pp. 31–67.

Adler, N. and Bartholomew, S. (1992) 'Managing globally competent people', *Academy of Management Executive*, Vol. 6, No. 3, pp. 52–64.

Adler, N. and Ghadar, F. (1990) 'Strategic human resource management: a global perspective', in Pieper, R. (ed.) *Human Resource Management: An International Comparison*. Berlin: Walter de Gruyter.

Almond, P. (forthcoming) 'Wage determination and job classification in France', *International Journal of Human Resource Management*.

Almond, P., Carroll, M., Grimshaw, D., Rubery, J. and Ward, K. (2001) 'Strategic employment planning or drifting in the wind? Evidence from case studies of large UK organisations', Paper presented at the 19th International Labour Process Conference, March, Holloway.

Almond, P., Edwards, T. and Muller M. (2001) 'The embeddedness of US multinational companies in the US business system: implications for their employment relations in the UK', Paper presented at the IIRA European Congress, Oslo, June.

Almond, P. and Rubery, J. (2000) 'Deregulation and societal systems', in Maurice, M. and Sorge, A. (eds) *Embedding Organizations*. Amsterdam: John Benjamins.

Appelbaum, E. and Batt, R. (1994) *The New American Workplace: Transforming Work Systems in the United States*. Ithaca, NY: ILR Press.

Atkinson, J. (1984) 'Manpower strategies for flexible organisations', *Personnel Management*, August.

Babson, S. (1999) *The Unfinished Struggle: Turning Points In American Labor*. Lanham, MD: Rowman & Littlefield.

Bamber, G. and Lansbury, R. (eds) (1998) *International and Comparative Employment Relations: A Study of Industrialised Market Economies*, 3rd edn. London: Sage.

Barney, J. (1991) 'Firm resources and sustained competitive advantage', *Journal of Management*, Vol. 17, pp. 99–120.

Bartlett, C.A. and Ghoshal, S. (1989) *Managing Across Borders: The Transnational Solution*. Boston, Mass.: Harvard Business School Press.

Bartlett, C.A. and Ghoshal, S. (1990) 'The multinational corporation as an interorganizational network', *Academy of Management Review*, Vol. 15, No. 4, pp. 603–625.

Bassett, P. (1986) *Strike-free: New Industrial Relations in Britain*. London: Macmillan.

Best, M. (1990) *The New Competition: The Institutions of Industrial Restructuring*. Oxford: Polity.

Beyer, J. and Hassel, A. (2002) 'The effects of convergence: internationalisation and the changing distribution of net value added in large German firms', *Economy and Society*, Vol. 31, No. 3, pp. 309–332.

Black, B. (2001) 'National culture and industrial relations and pay structures', *Labour*, Vol. 15, No. 2, pp. 257–277.

Boam, R. and Sparrow, P. (1992) *Designing and Achieving Competency*. London: McGraw-Hill.

Bonache, J. and Cerviño, J. (1997) 'Global integration without expatriates', *Human Resource Management Journal*, Vol. 7, No. 3, pp. 89–100.

Brewster, C. (1991) *The Management of Expatriates*. London: Kogan Page.

Brewster, C. and Harris, H. (eds) (1999) *International HRM: Contemporary Issues in Europe*. London: Routledge.

Brewster, C. and Scullion, H. (1997) 'A review and an agenda for expatriate HRM', *Human Resource Management Journal*, Vol. 7, No. 3, pp. 32–41.

Brewster, C., Tregaskis, O., Hegewisch, A. and Mayne, L. (1996) 'Comparative research in human resource management: a review and an example', *International Journal of Human Resource Management*, Vol. 7, No. 3, pp. 585–604.

Brislin, R.W. (1986) 'A culture general assimilator: preparation for various types of sojourns', *International Journal of Intercultural Relations*, Vol. 10, No. 2, pp. 215–234.

Broadberry, S. (1997) *The Productivity Race*. Oxford: Clarendon Press.

Chandler, A. (1977) *The Visible Hand*. Boston, Mass: Harvard University Press.

Chandler, A. (1990) *Scale and Scope*. Boston, Mass: Harvard University Press.

Clark, I. (2000) *Governance: The State, Regulation and Industrial Relations*. London: Routledge.

Clark, I., Colling, T., Almond, P., Gunnigle, P., Morley, M., Peters, R. and Portillo, M. (2002) 'Multinationals in Europe 2001–2: home country and sector effects in the context of crisis', *Industrial Relations Journal*, Vol. 33, No. 5, pp. 446–464.

Clark, T. (ed.) (1996) *European Human Resource Management: An Introduction to Comparative Theory and Practice*. Oxford: Blackwell.

Commission of the European Communities (1993) *Growth, Competitiveness, Employment*. White Paper. London: Commission of the European Communities.

Dickens, L. and Hall, M. (1995) 'The state: labour law and industrial relations', in Edwards, P. (ed.) *Industrial Relations: Theory and Practice*. Oxford: Blackwell, pp. 255–303.

Djelic, M.-L. (1998) *Exporting the American Model: The Post-War Transformation of American Business*. Oxford: Oxford University Press.

Dowling, P. and Schuler, R.S. (1991) *International Dimensions of Human Resource Management*. Boston, Mass.: PWS-Kent.

Dowling, P. Schuler, R.S. and Welch, D.E. (1994) *International Dimensions of Human Resource Management*. Belmont, Calif.: Wadsworth.

Dowling, P., Welch, D. and Schuler, R. (1999) *International Human Resource Management: Managing People in a Multinational Context*. Cincinnati, Ohio: South Western College Publishing.

Doz, Y.L. and Prahalad, C.K. (1986) 'Controlled variety: a challenge for human resource management in the MNC', *Human Resource Management*, Vol. 25, No. 1, pp. 55–72.

Dunning, J. (1998) *American Investment In British Manufacturing Industry*. London: Routledge.

Edström, A. and Galbraith, J.R. (1977) 'Transfer of managers as a co-ordination and control strategy in multinational organizations', *Administrative Science Quarterly*, Vol. 22, No. 2, pp. 248–63.

Edwards, T. and Ferner, A. (2000) 'Multinationals, reverse diffusion and national business systems', Presented at Conference on Multinationals and Employment Relations at Douglas Fraser Center for Workplace Issues, Wayne State University, Detroit.

EIRO (2002) 'Working time developments 2002'. European Industrial Relations Observatory, www.eiro.eurofound.ie .

Felstead, A., Ashton, D. and Green, F. (1994) *International Study of Vocational Education and Training in the Federal Republic of Germany, Japan, Singapore and the United States*. Leicester: University of Leicester Centre for Labour Market Studies.

Ferner, A. (1994) 'Multinational companies and human resource management: an overview of research issues', *Human Resource Management Journal*, Vol. 4, No. 2, pp. 79–102.

Ferner, A. (2003) 'Foreign multinationals and industrial relations innovation in Britain', in Edwards, P. (ed.) *Industrial Relations: Theory and Practice*, 2nd edn. Oxford: Blackwell.

Ferner, A., Almond, P., Clark, I., Colling, T., Edwards, T., Holden, L. and Muller-Camen, M. (forthcoming) 'The dynamics of central control and subsidiary autonomy in the management of human resources: case study evidence from US MNCs in the UK', *Organisation Studies* (in press).

Ferner, A. and Hyman, R. (eds) (1998) *Changing Industrial Relations in Europe*. Oxford: Blackwell.

Festing, M., Groening, Y., Kabst, R. and Weber, W. (1999) 'Financial participation in Europe: determinants and outcomes', *Economic and Industrial Democracy*, Vol. 20, No. 2, pp. 295–330.

Forester, N. and Johnson, M. (1996) 'Expatriate management policies in UK companies new to the international scene', *International Journal of Human Resource Management*, Vol. 7, No. 1, pp. 177–205.

Ghoshal, S. and Bartlett, C.A. (1998) *Managing Across Borders*. London: Random House, Part 1, pp. 1–81.

Ghoshal, S. and Westney, D.E. (1993) 'Introduction and overview', in Ghoshal, S. and Westney, D.E., *Organisation Theory and the Multinational Corporation*. London: St Martin's Press, pp. 1–3.

Gonzalez-Menendez, M. (1998) 'Pay flexibility through profit-sharing in Europe: explaining cross-national differences', communication to *International Industrial Relations Association World Congress*, Bologna, 22–26 September.

Gooderham, P. Nordhaug, O. and Ringdal, K. (1999), 'Institutional determinants of organizational practices: human resource management in European firms', *Administrative Science Quarterly*, Vol. 44, No. 3, pp. 507–531.

Guest, D. (1987) 'Human resource management and industrial relations', *Journal of Management Studies*, Vol. 24, No. 5, pp. 503–521.

Guest, D. (1990) 'Human resource management and the American Dream', *Journal of Management Studies*, Vol. 27, No. 4, pp. 377–397.

Hall, P. and Soskice, D. (2001) *Varieties of Capitalism: The Institutional Foundations of Comparative Advantage*. Oxford: Oxford University Press.

Harzing, A.W. (1999) *Managing the Multinationals: An International Study of Control Mechanisms*. Cheltenham: Elgar Publishing.

Harzing, A-W. (2000). 'An empirical analysis and extension of the Bartlett and Ghoshal typology of multinational companies', *Journal of International Business Studies*, Vol. 31, No. 1, pp. 101–119.

Hassel, A. (1999) 'The erosion of industrial relations in Germany', *British Journal of Industrial Relations*, Vol. 37, No. 4, pp. 483–505.

Hedlund, G. (1986) 'The hypermodern MNC – a heterarchy?', *Human Resource Management*, Vol. 25, No. 1, pp. 9–35.

Hillman, F. and Rudolph, H. (1996) *Jenseits des Brain Drain*. WZB Discussion Paper, no. FSI 96-103.

Hofstede, G. (1980) *Culture's Consequences: International Differences in Work-Related Values*. Beverly Hills, Calif.: Sage.

Holden, L. (2000) 'International human resource management', in Beardwell, I. and Holden, L. (eds) *Human Resource Management*. Harlow: Prentice Hall, pp. 633–676.

Hyman, R. (1995) 'The historical evolution of British industrial relations', in Edwards, P. (ed.) *Industrial Relations: Theory and Practice*. Oxford: Blackwell.

Hyman, R. (2003) 'The historical evolution of British industrial relations', in Edwards, P. (ed.), *Industrial Relations: Theory and Practice*, 2nd edn. Oxford: Blackwell.

Imai, K. and Komiya, R. (1994) 'Characteristics of Japanese firms', in Imai, K. and Komiya, R. (eds) *Business Enterprise in Japan*. Cambridge, Mass.: MIT Press.

Jacoby, S. (1997) *Modern Manors: Welfare Capitalism Since the New Deal*. Princeton, NJ: Princeton University Press.

Japanese Ministry of Labour (1995) *The Present Situation and Future Prospects of the Japanese Employment System*. Toyko: JMOL, cited in Ornatowski, G. (1998) 'The end of Japanese-style human resource management?', *Sloan Management Review*, Vol. 39, No. 3, pp. 73–84.

Jones, G. (1984) 'Task visibility, free riding, and shirking: explaining the effect of structure and technology and employee behaviour', *Journal of Financial Economics*, Vol. 3, pp. 305–360.

Katz, H. (1985) *Shifting Gears: Changing Labor Relations in the US Automobile Industry*. Cambridge, Mass.: MIT Press.

Katz, H. and Darbishire, O. (1999) *Converging Divergencies*, New York: ILR Press/Cornell University Press, pp. 263–283.

Keep, E. and Rainbird, H. (2000) 'Towards the learning organization', in Bach, S. and Sisson, K. (eds) *Personnel Management in Britain*. Oxford: Blackwell.

Kerr, C., Dunlop, J., Harbison, F. and Myers, C. (1960) *Industrialism and Industrial Man*. Cambridge, Mass.: Harvard University Press.

Klikauer, T. (2002) 'Stability in Germany's industrial relations: a critique of Hassel's erosion thesis', *British Journal of Industrial Relations*, Vol. 40, No. 2, pp. 295–308.

Kobrin, S.J. (1994) 'Is there a relationship between a geocentric mind-set and multinational strategy?', *Journal of International Business Studies*, third quarter, pp. 493–511.

Kochan, T., Batt, R. and Dyer, L. (1992) 'International human resource management studies: a framework for future research', in Lewin, D., Mitchell, O. and Scheller, P. (eds) *Research Frontiers in Industrial Relations*. Madison, Wis: Industrial Relations Research Association.

Koshiro, K. (1994) 'The employment system and human resource management', in Imai, K. and Komiya, R. (eds) *Business Enterprise in Japan*. Cambridge, Mass.: MIT Press,

Lado, A. and Wilson, M. (1994) 'Human resource systems and sustained competitive advantage: A competency-based perspective', *Academy of Management Review*, Vol. 19, pp. 699–727.

Lane, C. (1995) *Industry and Society in Europe*. Aldershot: Elgar.

Lane, C. (2000) 'Understanding the globalization strategies of German and British multinational companies: is a "societal effects" approach still useful?', in Maurice, M. and Sorge, A. (eds) *Embedding Organizations*. Amsterdam: John Benjamins.

Laurent, A. (1983) 'The cultural diversity of Western conceptions of management', *International Studies of Management and Organization*, Vol. 13, No. 1–2, pp. 75–96.

Lazonick, W. (1991) *Business Organization and the Myth of the Market Economy*. Cambridge: Cambridge University Press.

Lengnick-Hall, C. and Lengnick-Hall, M. (1988) 'Strategic human resource management: a review of the literature and proposed typology', *Academy of Management Review*, Vol. 13, pp. 454–470.

Leong, S.M. and Tan, C.T. (1993) 'Managing across borders: an empirical test of the Bartlett and Ghoshal [1989] organizational typology', *Journal of International Business Studies*, Vol. 24, No. 3, pp. 449–464.

Maurice, M., Sellier, F. and Silvestre, J.J. (1986) *The Social Foundations of Industrial Power*. Cambridge, Mass.: MIT Press.

Mayrhofer, W. and Brewster, C. (1996) 'In praise of ethnocentricity: expatriate policies in European multinationals', *International Executive*, Vol. 38, No. 6, pp. 749–778.

Mendenhall, M., Dunbar, E. and Oddou, G. (1987) 'Expatriate selection, training and career pathing: a review and critique', *Human Resource Management*, Vol. 26, Fall, pp. 331–345.

Mendenhall, M. and Oddou, G. (1986) 'Acculturation profiles of expatriate managers: implications for cross-cultural training programs', *Columbia Journal of World Business*, Vol. 21, No. 4, pp. 34–67.

Milliman, J.F. and Von Glinow, M.A. (1990) 'A life cycle approach to strategic international human resource management in MNCs', *Research in Personnel and Human Resources Management*, Supplement 2, pp. 21–35.

Milliman, J.M., Von Glinow, A. and Nathan, M. (1991) 'Organizational life cycles and strategic international human resource management in multinational companies: implications for congruence theory', *Academy of Management Review*, Vol. 16, No. 2, pp. 318–339.

Millward, N., Bryson, A. and Forth, J. (2000) *All Change At Work?* London: Taylor & Francis.

Mintzberg, H. and Waters, J.A. (1989) 'Of strategies, deliberate and emergent', in Asch, D. and Bowman, C. (eds) *Readings in Strategic Management*. Milton Keynes: Open University and MacMillan.

Moenaert, R.K., Caeldries, F., Commandeur, H.R. and Peelen, E. (1994) 'Managing Technology in the International Firm: An Exploratory Survey on Organisational Strategies'. Paper presented at the 20th Annual Conference of the EIBA (Dec), Warsaw.

Muller, M. (1999) 'Unitarism, pluralism, and human resource management in Germany', *Management International Review*, 15 Oct.

OECD (1998) *OECD Employment Outlook 1998*. Paris: OECD.

OECD (2002) *OECD Employment Outlook 2002*. Paris: OECD.

Oliver, N. and Wilkinson, B. (1992) *The Japanization of British Industry*. Oxford: Blackwell.

Ornatowski, G. (1998) 'The end of Japanese-style human resource management?', *Sloan Management Review*, Vol. 39, No. 3, pp. 73–84.

Perlmutter, H.V. (1969) 'The tortuous evolution of the multinational corporation', *Columbia Journal of World Business*, Vol. 4, pp. 9–18.

Pfeffer, J. (1994) *Competitive Advantage through People: Unleashing the Power of the Workforce*. Boston, Mass.: Harvard Business School Press.

Pfeffer, J. and Salancik, G.R. (1978) *The External Control of Organizations*. New York: Harper & Row.

Prahalad, C.K. and Doz, Y. (1987) *The Multinational Mission: Balancing Local Demands and Global Vision*. New York: The Free Press.

Quack, S., O'Reilly, J. and Hildebrant, S. (1995) 'Structuring change: training and recruitment in retail banking in Germany, Britain and France', *International Journal of Human Resource Management*, Vol. 6, No. 4, pp. 759–794.

Quintanilla, J. (1999) 'The configuration of human resource management policies and practices in multinational subsidiaries: the case of European retail banks in Spain', Unpublished PhD Thesis, University of Warwick.

Rosenzweig, P.M. and Nohria N. (1994) 'Influences on human resource management practices in multinational corporations', *Journal of International Business Studies*, second quarter, pp. 229–251.

Rosenzweig, P.M. and Singh, J.V. (1991) 'Organizational environments and the multinational enterprise', *Academy of Management Review*, Vol. 16, No. 2, pp. 304–316.

Roth, K. and Morrison, A.J. (1990) 'An empirical analysis of the integration–responsiveness framework in global industries', *Journal of International Business Studies*, Vol. 22, No. 4, pp. 541–561.

Royle, T. (2000) *Working For McDonald's in Europe: The Unequal Struggle*. London: Routledge.

Rubery, J., Smith, M. and Fagan, C. (1999) *Women's Employment in Europe: Trends and Prospects*. London: Routledge.

Sako (1990) 'Institutional aspects of youth employment and training policy – a comment on Marsden and Ryan', *British Journal of Industrial Relations*, Vol. 29, No. 1, pp. 485–494.

Schein, E. (1984) 'The role of the founder in creating organizational culture', *Organizational Dynamics*, Summer, pp. 13–28.

Schuler, R. (1992) 'Strategic human resources management: linking the people with the strategic needs of the business', *Organizational Dynamics*, Summer, pp. 18–32.

Schuler, R., Dowling, P. and De Cieri, H. (1993) 'An integrative framework of strategic international human resource management', *Journal of Management*, Vol. 19, No. 2, pp. 419–459.

Schuler, R.S. and Jackson, S. (1987) 'Linking competitive strategy and human resource management practice', *Academy of Management Executive*, Vol. 3, pp. 207–219.

Scullion, H. (1993) 'Creating international managers: recruitment and development issues', in Kirkbride, P. (ed.) *Human Resource Management in Europe*. London: Routledge.

Sorge, A. (1991) 'Strategic fit and the societal effect: interpreting cross-national comparisons of technology, organisation and human resources', *Organisation Studies*, Vol. 12, No. 2, pp. 161–190.

Sparrow, P. and Hiltrop, J.M. (1994) *European Human Resource Management in Transition*. Hemel Hempstead: Prentice Hall.

Taylor, S. and Beechler, S. (1993) 'Human resource management integration and adaptation in multinational firms', in Prasad, S. and Peterson, R. (eds) *Advances in International Comparative Management*, Vol. 8, pp. 155–174.

Taylor, S., Beechler, S. and Napier, N. (1996) 'Toward an integrative model of strategic international human resource management', *Academy of Management Review*, Vol. 21, No. 4, pp. 959–985.

Thelen, K. (2001) 'Varieties of capitalism: labour politics in the developed democracies', in Hall, P. and Soskice, D. (eds) *Varieties of Capitalism: The Institutional Foundations of Comparative Advantage*. Oxford: Oxford University Press.

Tichy, N., Fombrun, C. and Devanna, M. (1982) 'Strategic human resource management', *Sloan Management Review*, Vol. 23, No. 2, pp. 47–61.

Torbiörn, I. (1985) 'The structure of managerial roles in cross cultural settings', *International Studies of Management and Organization*, Vol. 15, No. 1, pp. 52–74.

Tregaskis, O. (2003) 'Learning networks, power and legitimacy in multinational subsidiaries', *International Journal of Human Resource Management*, Vol. 14, No. 3, pp. 431–447.

Tregaskis, O., Atterbury, S. and MaHoney, C (2003) 'International survey methodology', in Brewster, C., Morley, M. and Mayhofer, W. *Comparative HRM Practice*. Oxford: Butterworth Heinemann. Forthcoming.

Vernon, R. (1966) 'International investment and international trade in the product cycle', *Quarterly Journal of Economics*, Vol. 8, No. 2, pp. 190–207.

Wada, K. and Shiba, T. (2000) 'The evolution of "the Japanese production system" indigenous influences and American impact' in Zeitlin, J. and Herrigel, G. (eds) *Americanization and its Limits*. Oxford: Oxford University Press.

Welch, D. and Welch, L. (1994) 'Linking operation mode diversity and IHRM', *The International Journal of Human Resource Management*, Vol. 5, No. 4, pp. 1–16.

Wever, K. (1995) *Negotiating Competitiveness: Employment Relations and Organizational Innovation in Germany and the United States*. Boston, Mass.: Harvard Business School Press.

Whitley, R. (ed.) (2000) *Divergent Capitalisms: The Social Structuring and Change Of Business Systems*. Oxford: Oxford University Press.

Williamson, O. (1975) *Markets and Hierarchies*. New York: The Free Press.

Windolf, P. (1986) 'Recruitment, selection and internal labour markets in Britain and Germany', *Organisation Studies*, Vol. 7, No. 3, pp. 235–254.

Wright, P. and McMahan, G. (1992) 'Theoretical perspectives for strategic human resource management', *Journal of Management*, Vol. 18, No. 3, pp. 295–320.

For multiple choice questions, exercises and annotated weblinks specific to this chapter visit this book's website at www.booksites.net/beardwell

CHAPTER 16

Human resource management and Europe

Len Holden and Tim Claydon

OBJECTIVES

▶ To examine the origins, development and operations of the European Union and the Social Charter.

▶ To highlight the difficulties in framing, interpreting and enforcing social legislation in the European Union.

▶ To examine the controversy over the effects of the implementation and non-implementation of the Social Charter, the Amsterdam Treaty and Lisbon Agreement.

▶ To examine HRM and labour market trends in Western Europe.

▶ To examine the degrees of convergence of HRM practices within Europe.

▶ To survey the recent history of and contemporary developments in Eastern European management and labour relations.

Introduction

Most of the nation states of Europe, as we know them, have emerged over the past 150 years, and many of these have experienced considerable changes in borders and ethnic composition since then. This process has radically continued with the break-up of the former Soviet Union and its satellite states, and the former Yugoslavia.

Thus the concept of a unified Europe begs many questions, which must fundamentally include an answer to 'What is Europe?' and 'How unified can it be?' The latter question has already caused considerable controversy over the ratification of the Maastricht Treaty, and the former over whether Eastern European states, as well as Turkey, should be included in the European Union. Answers to these basic but essential questions have a fundamental influence on the shaping of economic, political and social policy.

This chapter will examine Europe from the perspective of HRM, but as we have noted in the previous chapter on international HRM, the concept itself has a number of interpretations depending on the context in which it is used, which include: exploring the European Union social dimension (Gold, 1993; Wise and Gibb, 1992; Leat, 1998); trends in industrial relations systems and individual European countries (Baglioni and Crouch, 1990; Ferner and Hyman, 1992, 1998; Hyman and Ferner, 1994; van Ruysseveldt and Visser, 1996); labour market trends across Europe (Adnett, 1996; Addison and Siebert, 1997); under the banner of HRM of individual countries (Brewster *et al.*, 1992; Clark, 1996); and in analysis of HRM trends (Lane, 1989; Hegewisch and Brewster, 1993; Brewster and Hegewisch, 1994; Kirkbride, 1994; Sparrow and Hiltrop, 1994). Some of these surveys confine themselves to EU countries only and others to a wider range of European nations, including the former Soviet Union and its satellites. Thus the field is wide, and a chapter on this subject can only hope to give a general picture of the major issues and trends.

There are a number of issues that have been the subject of discussion and debate over the past decade and longer, and some that have emerged more recently. The aim of this chapter is to divide issues into those that are relevant to the European Union and those that have wider significance for all European countries, and concern general trends in HRM and HR-related issues.

European Union issues

Within the European Union (EU) the central platform for HRM issues has been the Social Charter and the Social Action Programme to implement it. The main concerns here have been the debates over the form and content of the Social Charter, how to integrate its provisions within the existing employment relations systems of member states, and how to harmonise aspects of the Charter's provision across the Union. These debates have taken place in the context of ideological positions within and between member states concerning degrees of regulation.

The main issue to the forefront of the European Union social agenda has been unemployment, which increased considerably across the Union in the 1990s. It is particularly high among certain social groups, such as young people, ethnic minorities and women, and in regions undergoing structural change.

Other issues have concerned 'social dumping' (see section on 'The regulationists') and recently the impact of European Monetary Union. Single issues such as the minimum wage in the British context provoked some controversy when adopted by the Labour government in 1998 along with the UK's signing up to the Social Charter. There has also been the long-festering issue of TUPE (the Transfer of Undertakings (Protection of Employment) Directive (see later in this chapter), and more recently the debates over degrees of employee voice that include, most importantly, the issue of the form and powers of works councils.

There has also been considerable work on general labour market trends and a concern with issues such as trends in flexibilisation, decentralisation of bargaining, the role and strength of unions, the changing nature of corporatism and collective bargaining generally, and the growth in size and influence of multinational corporations. We shall deal with these issues later under the heading of HRM and labour market trends. Most of these issues have been debated within the ideological context of deregulation and regulation, which will also be examined in greater depth later in this chapter.

■ The European Union: origins and development

It is neither possible nor appropriate to cover the historical origins of the EU in detail in this book, but a brief outline of the relevant events should help students new to the subject to put into context some of the factors that influence European human resource issues.

The European Union arose out of the wreckage of the Second World War. There was a consensus among most politicians that the devastation wreaked upon Europe should never be repeated, and that cooperation between nations was one important way to prevent conflict. Partly towards this end, and to help war-torn economies to revive, the

European Coal and Steel Community (ECSC) was set up between France, West Germany, Belgium, the Netherlands, Italy and Luxembourg in 1952. The general aim was to dismantle tariff barriers between these nations, affording a single market for iron, steel and coal. Robert Schuman, one of its prime architects, anticipated that one day the ECSC would broaden into a movement towards economic and even political unity.

The success of these early attempts at cooperation led to the forging of stronger links, and after a number of preliminary reports and meetings the six ECSC countries formed the European Economic Community (EEC) under the Treaty of Rome 1957. The aim of the Treaty was to create a 'common market' among its members, although it was accepted at this time that political union was a long way off. The Treaty of Rome also established the European Atomic Energy Community (EURATOM), which still influences many aspects of EU legislation.

The positive progress of the EEC influenced other European states to become members, and Britain, Denmark and the Republic of Ireland joined in 1973. In 1981 Greece joined, and in 1986 Spain and Portugal. In 1995 Sweden, Austria and Finland were granted membership of what by then had become the European Union (EU), although after a referendum Norway decided to stay out of the Union. This makes 15 member states in all, but in April, 2003 another ten countries were accepted for membership at an accession meeting in Athens: Cyprus, Czech Republic, Estonia, Hungary, Latvia, Lithuania, Malta, Poland, Slovakia and Slovenia. This will expand the number of member states to 25 and add a further 75 million people, making a total of 450 million people in the EU by May 2004. This will also have considerable influence on future political, economic and social issues of the EU. Turkey has also been given time to meet the requirements for membership within the next five years. Such an enlargement will constitute a much more representative bloc of European states.

> **Stop and think**
>
> What influences might the expansion of the European Union, to include Eastern European states, have on social and employment issues?
>
> These words might help you: *unemployment, labour markets, cost of labour, wages, migrant labour.*

● A chronology of the EU

1952   European Coal and Steel Community founded (Belgium, France, Italy, Luxembourg, the Netherlands and West Germany)

1957   Treaty of Rome sets up the European Economic Community or 'Common Market' (Belgium, France, Italy, Luxembourg, the Netherlands and West Germany)

1957   Treaty of Paris sets up European Atomic Energy Community (Belgium, France, Italy, Luxembourg, the Netherlands and West Germany)

1958   EEC and EURATOM come into being

1972   Paris Summit gives commitment to action in social field

1973   UK, Denmark and Republic of Ireland join EC

1974   Commission's 'Action Programme' comes into being

1981   Greece joins the EC

1986   Spain and Portugal join the EC

1987   Single European Act passed

1989   Social Charter ratified by 11 states except the UK

1991   Austria, Norway and Sweden apply to join the EC

1992   Hungary, Poland and the former Czechoslovakia express a desire to join

1992   Maastricht Treaty signed but UK insists on separate protocol for the Social Charter (Chapter). The European Community is renamed the European Union

1995   Austria, Finland and Sweden join the EU
1997   Treaty of Amsterdam incorporates the Social Charter into four pillars of employment policy: employability, entrepreneurship, adaptability, equality of opportunity
1997   Agenda 2000 reviews the criteria for membership of aspiring states
1999   European Monetary Union
1999   Treaty of Amsterdam came into force 1 May
2000   Lisbon Special Council – Towards a Europe of Innovation and Knowledge
2001   Stockholm Council
2003   Accession of 10 states at Athens Conference
2004   Cyprus, Czech Republic, Estonia, Hungary, Latvia, Lithuania, Malta, Poland, Slovakia and Slovenia formally admitted to the European Union.

● The institutions of the EU

There are four main institutions that govern the European Union:

- the European Council or the Council of Ministers (based in Brussels);
- the Commission (based in Brussels);
- the Court of Justice (sits in Luxembourg);
- the Parliament (based in Strasbourg).

The European Council

The European Council (or Council of Ministers) consists of the heads of each member state, who usually meet twice a year to give overall direction to the EU's programme.

The European Council is made up of one representative, usually a government minister or highly placed politician, from each member state, and is presided over in turn by each state for a six-month period. The Council is the EU's main decision-making body; it acts on proposals by the Commission. Decisions are taken on a unanimous vote, although majority voting was introduced via the Single European Act for some issues.

The Commission

The Commission is composed of 20 members or commissioners, and is made up of two representatives from each of the larger countries (France, Germany, Italy, Spain, the UK) and one from the rest. Commissioners are appointed for four years, and act only in the interests of the Union. The President serves for a four-year period on a renewable basis. The Commission proposes and executes EU policies, and acts as a mediator between the 15 governments of the Union. It also has the power to bring legal action via the Court of Justice against member states that it deems to have violated EU laws. It is ultimately subservient to the Council of Ministers. Under the Treaty of Nice (December 2000) there will be only one representative or commissioner for each member state. This will come into effect in 2005.

The European Court of Justice

The European Court of Justice comprises one judge from each member state assisted by advocates-general, who rule on questions of community law. Judgments are by majority vote, and directly binding on all parties. This is the final court of appeal for member states, and is often used by individuals, groups and organisations to challenge national laws or rulings that are perceived as being in contravention of EU law. It has become increasingly important in enforcing EU regulations by adjudicating individual, group and company cases brought before it, such as interpretations on the application of TUPE (see below).

The European Parliament

The European Parliament has 626 members: 99 from Germany, 87 each from France, Italy and the UK, 64 from Spain, 31 from the Netherlands, 25 each from Belgium, Greece and Portugal, 22 from Sweden, 21 from Austria, 16 each from Denmark and Finland, 15 from Ireland and 6 from Luxembourg. Under the Treaty of Nice 2000 the number of seats will be restricted to 732 allotted between present and future member states and will come into effect for the 2004 elections.

Members of the European Parliament (MEPs) are directly elected by citizens of their countries for a five-year term. The last election took place in June 1999. The European Parliament does not have the same power as the Council of Ministers or a national parliament, but very few proposals can be adopted without its opinion being sought. It also has the power to dismiss the Commission on a two-thirds majority vote. While its powers are limited, under the Treaties of Amsterdam and Nice its powers of veto were further extended.

● Other institutions concerned with human resource issues

Economic and social committee

This is an advisory body that is consulted by the Commission and Council. It is made up of representatives of employers, trade unions, and other interests including consumers, small firms and professions. It provides detailed information and advice in the following areas:

- agriculture;
- transport and communications;
- energy and nuclear questions;
- economic and financial questions;
- industry;
- commerce, crafts and services;
- social questions;
- external relations;
- regional development;
- protection of the environment, public health and consumer affairs.

European Foundation for the Improvement of Living and Working Conditions

This is a body set up primarily for investigating and disseminating information on living and working conditions in the EU, including health and safety, environmental protection, industrial relations, restructuring working life and assessing new technologies and the future of work. It is based in Dublin.

Employer and employee representative groups (the Social Partners)

EU-wide groups were set up to represent the interests of employers and employees. These included the European Trade Union Confederation (ETUC), the Union of Industrial and Employers Confederations of Europe (UNICE), and the European Centre for Public Enterprise (CEEP), which represents public sector employer interests. In addition, the national 'peak' organisations of employers and employees are regarded as the Social Partners at the level of each member state. Thus for the UK, the Social Partners are the Confederation of British Industry (CBI) and the Trades Union Congress (TUC).

Talks between employer and employee representatives of member countries concentrated on examining macroeconomic policy and employment, and new technology and work. From these talks two committees were formed, which deal with training and labour market issues. In recent years there has been concentration on examining flexibility and adaptability of the workforce.

These meetings also led to the creation of the European Framework Agreement, which proposed that the Commission would consult the Social Partners at European level before putting proposals forward. This could have important ramifications in creating controversy between those states that have relied on negotiations at the workplace (Denmark, Ireland and the UK) and those that rely on centralised regulation in their industrial relations systems (Germany and Sweden) (Lockhart and Brewster, 1992).

■ The legislative process

In simplistic terms, legal proposals emanate from the Commission and are sent for consideration to the Council, which seeks approval from the Parliament and advice and information from the Economic and Social Committee. The Commission then has the right to amend the proposal in the light of these opinions and return it to the Council for acceptance or rejection.

There are four types of EU legislation, as follows:

● *Regulations* are binding on all member states without any further process of confirmation by national parliaments.
● *Directives* are binding on all member states, but leave to national discretion how these laws are to be complied with. Target dates are also set for implementation.
● *Decisions* are binding on those to whom they are addressed (member states, enterprises, individuals).
● *Recommendations and opinions* are not binding. These are not laws as such, but may help to encourage particular responses. 'The Commission places emphasis on using such Recommendations to achieve "convergence", i.e. to move towards harmonisation of policy and practice' (Hughes, 1991).

Regulations are generally used when an identical law is required across the Union, often where none has existed in member states previously. Directives are more appropriate as a mechanism where the method of implementation may vary at national level and has to be related to existing laws. This incorporates the principle of 'subsidiarity', that is, that legislation should be passed by the lowest level of government competent to enact it.

Stop and think

What difficulties could the European Union have in enforcing regulations and directives?

Think about this and read the section on 'Difficulties of implementation and interpretation' later in the chapter.

There are four procedural routes through which EU legislation can be enacted:

● *Consultation Procedure* is the traditional legislative procedure set out in the original Treaty of Rome. Commission proposes legislation and consults with Parliament, Council, the Economic and Social Committee and the Social Partners. Legislation has to be approved unanimously by the Council of Ministers before it can be implemented.
● *Co-operation Procedure* was created by the Single European Act 1987. Under this procedure the Parliament has further consultation rights and legislation can be approved on the basis of a majority vote in the Council of Ministers.
● *Co-decision Procedure* was introduced in 1991 in the Maastricht Treaty. Under this procedure the European Parliament has certain rights to veto legislative proposals on the basis of a majority vote of Members of the European Parliament.
● *Protocol Procedure* was also introduced in the Maastricht Treaty. Its aim is to encourage social dialogue between the Social Partners.

Figure 16.1   EU legislation procedure

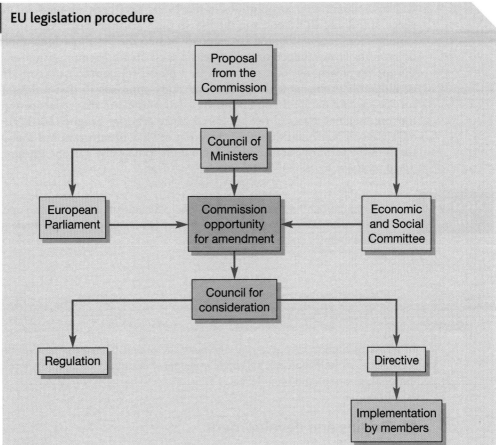

● The open method of coordination and benchmarking

The Amsterdam Treaty 1997 introduced a new procedure for coordinating and monitoring the implementation of the employment policies of member states. This is known as the Open Method of Coordination (OMC). The OMC is an alternative to the legislative forms and procedures described above. In place of substantive legislation on specific issues, strategic objectives and operational guidelines are set for member states and monitoring procedures put in place to assess their performance. Under the provisions of the Amsterdam Treaty, member states are required to draw up National Action Plans for achieving progress under four strategic 'pillars' (see below). The Council of Ministers establishes annual employment guidelines for member states to incorporate into their plans, and is empowered to conduct an annual examination of member states' employment policies.* This annual examination and evaluation provide a way of calling governments to account where they are failing to make sufficient progress towards objectives and an opportunity to learn from each other's experiences of successes and failures of policy. On the basis of this examination the Council may make specific recommendations to member states in areas where policy development or outcomes are seen to be deficient (Sisson *et al.*, 2003).

The OMC can be seen as an application of benchmarking practices. Sisson *et al.* (2003) believe that benchmarking practices first undertaken in a formal and structured

---

* Acting by a Qualified Majority Vote in the Council of Ministers on the basis of a recommendation from the European Commission. See Sisson *et al.* (2003: 21).

way by multinational corporations in the 1980s have been adopted as a tool for convergence of HR and IR practices in the EU. In the 1990s the then President of the European Commission, Jacques Santer, strongly advocated the benchmarking approach as a way of avoiding over-reliance on legal measures to create harmonisation of policies across Europe by presenting 'best practices' as a model for countries to copy. While there are considerable problems with the benchmarking approach in that it does not suit all sectors or specific national conditions, its advocates claim that it has proved successful in moving member states closer to convergence criteria. Teague (2001) believes that the advantage of benchmarking from the point of view of integration is that it helps to keep issues in the forefront of attention, fuelling the process of 'Europe learning from Europe' (cited in Sisson *et al.*, 2003: 26).

Stop and think	In the light of your thoughts concerning the difficulties of implementing and enforcing Regulations and Directives, consider whether benchmarking avoids these problems or replicates them.

The Social Charter

In terms of human resource management the Social Charter is the key indicator of EU legislation, as its proposals will have considerable impact on employee relations at international, national and local levels.

■ Origins and development

Much of the Social Charter is an amalgam and extension of the articles embodied in the various treaties that jointly created the EU: the Treaty of Paris, which set up the ECSC in 1952, and the Treaties of Rome and Paris, which created the EEC and EURATOM respectively in 1957.

At the Paris summit in 1972 it was agreed that much importance should be attached to reducing disparities of living conditions and improving the quality of life within the community. This resulted in the creation of an 'Action Programme' in 1974, which became committed to the promotion of employment, upward harmonisation of living conditions, and the increased involvement of management and labour in the decision-making processes of organisations. This was to be achieved by coordinating provisions in the treaties with new initiatives. A number of economic problems were besetting the community, and the reaction by member states at the time was, at best, mixed. In this period of 'Europessimism', however, it can be argued that incremental agreements, particularly in areas such as equal opportunities, witnessed the foundation of what is still the most effective part of legislation embodied in the Social Charter (Lockhart and Brewster, 1992).

A revival of interest in the 'social dimension' occurred in the 1980s as a result of the debate over, and the subsequent agreement to, the creation of a single European market (SEM) under the Single European Act 1987. The creation of a unified market across 12 European states would have deep implications for the labour market and employment relationships, and therefore under the influence of Jacques Delors, the President of the Commission (1985–95), it was proposed that policies that addressed employment relations issues should be created. In December 1989 the Social Charter was finally adopted by the Council of Ministers (with the exception of the UK), and a Social Action Programme was set up to implement it. The UK eventually signed up to the Social Charter in 1997, when New Labour came to power.

▓ The Social Charter provisions

The Social Charter states that:

> the completion of the internal market must offer improvements in the social field for workers of the European Community, especially in terms of freedom of movement, living and working conditions, health and safety at work, social protection education and training.
>
> Whereas, in order to ensure equal treatment, it is important to combat every form of discrimination, including discrimination on grounds of sex, colour, race, opinions and beliefs, and whereas in a spirit of solidarity it is important to combat social exclusion.

The 12 main provisions are as follows:

- *Free movement.* All workers have the right to free movement within the Union.
- *Employment and remuneration.* All employment should be fairly remunerated. Workers should have an equitable wage – that is, a wage sufficient to enable them to have a decent standard of living (often interpreted as a minimum wage). Workers subject to atypical terms of employment (such as part-time work) should benefit from an equitable reference wage – that is, a wage in line with full-time employee remuneration.
- *Improvement of living and working conditions.* The process must result from an approximation of conditions, as regards, in particular, the duration and organisation of working time and forms of employment. The procedure must cover such aspects of employment as collective redundancies and bankruptcies. Every worker must have a weekly rest period, annual paid leave, and a contract of employment.
- *Social protection.* Every worker in the Union shall have a right to adequate social protection and shall, regardless of status, enjoy an adequate level of social security benefits. Persons outside the labour market (those unable to work, e.g. retired, ill) must receive sufficient resources and social assistance in keeping with their particular situation.
- *Freedom of association and collective bargaining.* Employers and employees have the right of association (that is, employers' associations and trade unions) to protect their social and economic interests. There is also the right not to join. There shall be the right to negotiate and conclude collective agreements, and the right to collective action (such as strikes and lock-outs), subject to national legislation.
- *Vocational training.* Every worker must have access to and receive vocational training, with no discrimination on grounds of nationality.
- *Equal treatment for men and women.* This applies in particular in regard to access to employment, remuneration, working conditions, social protection, educational training and career development.
- *Information, consultation and participation of workers.* These must be developed along appropriate lines, taking account of the practices in force in the various member states. This shall apply especially in companies or groups of companies with establishments in several member states. These processes must be implemented: when technological change occurs that has major implications for the workforce; in connection with restructuring operations or mergers; in cases of collective redundancy; and when trans-frontier workers in particular are affected by the employment policies of the undertaking where they are employed.
- *Health protection and safety in the workplace.* Every worker must enjoy satisfactory health and safety conditions in the workplace. Appropriate measures must be taken to achieve further harmonisation of conditions in this area.
- *Protection of children and adolescents in employment.* The minimum employment age must not be lower than school-leaving age, and neither of these can be lower than

15 years of age. The duration of work must be limited, and night work prohibited under 18 years of age. After compulsory education young people must be entitled to receive initial vocational training of reasonable duration.

- *Elderly persons.* Every worker must, at the time of retirement, be able to enjoy resources affording him or her a decent standard of living, and those not entitled to a pension must be provided for.
- *Disabled persons.* All disabled people must be entitled to additional measures aimed at improving their social and professional integration. These measures must address vocational training, ergonomics, accessibility, mobility, means of transport and housing.

Stop and think	In a workplace where you have been employed, have any of the Social Charter provsions not been observed? If so, which ones and why?

■ Difficulties of implementation and interpretation

The implementation of the Social Charter has proved to be more controversial than the debate over what it should contain, although these processes are inextricably intertwined (Hughes, 1991). Implementation hinges on the influence and interpretations of:

- political parties and groupings;
- national governments;
- employers and employee bodies;
- multinational corporations;
- the economic and political climate;
- the ambiguities and imprecisions of Charter policies.

Deciding on the provisions of the Social Charter was, and still is, a difficult process given the varied opinions within the EU in terms of political and economic ideology.

Margaret Thatcher's Conservative government was the most prominent and vocal opponent. Given her neo-liberalist position she was never happy with the Social Charter *per se*, and raised many objections to proposals, ultimately refusing to ratify it in 1989 – the UK being the only government of the 12 member states not to do so. John Major, her successor, continued this policy and demanded that the Maastricht Treaty should have a separate protocol for the Social Chapter, as the Social Charter is also called, upon which member states vote separately. However, Tony Blair's Labour government has completely reversed this position: it has subscribed to all the provisions of the Social Charter, and finally ratified the treaty on behalf of the UK when elected in 1997. Nevertheless, Mr Blair has continued to advocate many of the deregulatory policies of the previous Conservative administrations.

The process of amendment and change is still continuing, and past and present efforts to please Margaret Thatcher and other critics have meant that the original proposals from the mid-1980s have been watered down, some considerably. The implementation of the Charter under the Social Action Programme has also been significantly revised, and the biting recession of the early 1990s had another slowing effect on its implementation. Thus Jacques Delors, and other parties of the opinion that a strong social dimension is an important part of the Single European Market, have had to revise their views on the timetable for implementation. It is now agreed, even by its strongest advocates, that the full Charter will take a very long time to complete, if at all (Piachaud, 1991; Goodhart, 1992; Milne, 1992b.)

Although a great deal of the Social Action Programme has been accepted, the consultation process has ensured that many of the original proposals have been diluted, and some have been blocked entirely. Even if the Social Charter had been accepted in principle by all member states, interpretation of the directives is problematic. Directives rather than regulations were deliberately used in framing the Charter in order to allow for national differences and the accommodation of existing laws. As one commentator accurately notes, 'responsibilities for such implementation often rest with national governments who have a reputation for giving variable priority both to implementation and enforcement' (Butt Philips, 1988).

In addition, some of the directives are so vague that they are open to wide interpretation. The provision for 'information, consultation and participation of the workforce' has many varied interpretations, ranging from works councils in Germany, Belgium and the Netherlands to multifarious practices in the UK, covering schemes as representative as works councils to organisations that give the workforce the bare minimum of information. Yet the CBI claimed that British organisations already conform adequately to the provisions of this directive.

Another directive, the Transfer of Undertakings (Protection of Employment) or TUPE, has caused considerable controversy over interpretation in the UK. This directive (2001/23/EC) protects employees' pay and conditions when an undertaking is transferred as, for example, when privatisation of government and local government services takes place. 'If the directive applies a successful bidder must take over staff on their existing terms and conditions which will reduce scope for saving through lower pay or staff cuts' (Willman, 1993). This would in effect

> put an end to private contractors depressing their pay and conditions to lower bid costs when competing for contracts against the public sector. Contractors are increasingly jittery about the lack of clarity and are reluctant to bid for contracts without knowing the extent of their liabilities.
>
> (Weston, 1993)

UK governments under Major and Thatcher argued that the directive did not apply to contracting out, but the European Court of Justice has forced the government to amend the existing law that covers this situation, the new wording of which, trade unions believe, extends protection to cover many public sector and former public sector activities.

There is also the problem of enforcement. The EU has no inspectorate, and relies heavily on member states' ability and willingness to enforce directives, which, as we have already noted, can vary widely. The most common way is through legal action by individuals or groups via the Commission. These actions take time to investigate, prepare and process through the Court of Justice. Leaving the enforcement to individuals or groups often means that such contraventions of directives depend on the strength of mind of individuals and groups in bringing the action, who may be subject to pressures not to protest, particularly if it is against their employer. However, as Singh (1999) states: 'there is little doubt that the European Court of Justice continues to give rulings in employment law cases which have a profound impact on national legal systems' (p. 385).

■ Labour market trends in Europe

Along with the difficulties of implementing the social agenda are the problems associated with a constantly changing labour market. As we have seen in the previous chapter on international HRM, there have been numerous influences on the way that economies and organisations are developing, thanks to – among other things – the increasing intensification of world competition for global markets and the impact of new technology.

In addition, demographic changes have witnessed declining birth and falling mortality rates, with the consequent effect that the EU population is ageing and so too therefore is the workforce. This has considerable implications for future labour supply. Will there be enough young people to fill employment positions in the future? This looks not to be a problem at present, given the high percentage of youth unemployment across Europe. Another effect of these changing demographics is that social welfare measures such as pensions and health will take up increasing resources of the member states.

There have also been significant sectoral shifts over the past 20 years, with a continuing decline in agriculture and the old 'smoke stack' industries such as coal, iron and steel, textiles, shipbuilding and traditional engineering. This in turn has caused high unemployment in regions where these industries once thrived. In contrast, new 'high tech' industries (such as computer technology and communications) have arisen, along with a considerable increase in financial services and the service sector generally. The demand for the old traditional skills has thus been in deep decline, while demand for skills relevant to the newly predominant sectors has witnessed a steep rise in this 'new European economy,' as this trend has been recently dubbed. Technology has also reduced the demand for unskilled and semi-skilled workers as many of these jobs become automated.

In attempts to maintain competitiveness, employers have increasingly introduced new work forms and contracts of employment. Flexibility, not only in job functions but in numerical terms and hours of work, has witnessed a considerable increase across Europe. Atypical work has also increased significantly, with more part-time, short- and fixed-term and temporary contracts.

There have also been increasing levels of unemployment among women, the young and ethnic minorities, as well as increases in the long-term unemployed, especially in depressed regions and among workers aged over 50. This general picture is complex and while, for example, there is a rise in female unemployment there has also been a percentage rise in women participating in the labour market. But as some observers have pointed out, women are much more likely to be employed in less well-paid and less secure jobs than men (Rees, 1998). The picture is also complicated by the variations between EU regions. The *La Dorsale* regions (London, Belgium, Frankfurt, Luxembourg and Milan), the *East–West core* regions (Paris, Frankfurt and Berlin) and the *Arc Mediterranean* (Barcelona, Marseilles and Rome) are characterised by high growth and low unemployment. By contrast, low growth and high unemployment zones are on the periphery of the EU: for example, most of the UK excluding the South East, Midlands and East Anglia, Southern Italy, Greece and Southern Spain (Sapsford *et al.*, 1999). The European Social Fund has tried to compensate for these divergences in the past by directing funds to those areas with particularly high unemployment rates, especially among the long-term unemployed.

Stop and think	Why could present and projected demographic changes impact on labour market issues such as equal opportunities, immigration and youth employment?

The regulation–deregulation debate

These problems and how to resolve them are part of a wider debate that emerged strongly in the 1980s, rooted in the differing ideological viewpoints concerning degrees of regulation of labour markets. Essentially, two main opinions predominate: the *deregulationists* or *neo-liberals*, and the *regulationists* or *interventionists*. These two stances are a polarised simplification of varied political positions. There are prominent trade unionists who view some of the provisions as undermining collective bargaining by a greater emphasis on individual rights and consultative arrangements (Gospel, 1992). There are some employers who believe that the full adoption of the Social Charter will bring order and the advantage of homogeneity to a European-wide market. Nevertheless, the argument to date has been based on the regulatory and deregulatory schools and median positions.

● The deregulationists or neo-liberal school

The minimalist or deregulatory school was strongly advocated by Margaret Thatcher in the 1980s and John Major in the 1990s, as well as many employer groups and conservative or right-wing political parties. It posited the view that government and legislative interference prevents the efficient operation of the labour market.

In political terms the minimalists see the Social Charter as a 'socialists' charter' and Delors, its past champion, as an 'old-fashioned bureaucratic socialist'. Deregulationists believe that 'prosperity, progress and liberty presuppose economic freedom' (Marsland, 1991). Economic freedom means freedom from any regulatory influences that might hinder the industrial and commercial competitive process and therefore the operation of the market.

In economic terms, the neo-liberals see the provisions of the Charter as creating the conditions for 'Eurosclerosis', a hardening of the free flow of labour-market arteries. The Eurosclerosis view emanated from the 1970s and 1980s, when the EU states were perceived as doing less well economically than the United States. 'Reaganomics' (the policies of Ronald Reagan, US Republican President 1980–88) argued that abolishing or moderating regulatory restrictions had freed up the labour market and had lowered unemployment by enabling the creation of more jobs. 'Thatcherism' (the policies of British Conservative Prime Minister Margaret Thatcher, 1979–91) had attempted similar deregulatory measures in the UK with comparable success in the 1980s, or so claimed her supporters. Such Social Charter proposals as a minimum wage would create a rigid high-wage economy with small differentials where workers would be priced out of a job. 'Furthermore, legally based labour rights and employment protection schemes have gone too far, leading to high labour costs which in turn cause redundancies and discourage hiring' (Teague, 1991: 4).

The cost to employers of implementing this and other provisions would have the effect of decreasing jobs and slowing the labour market. For example, the UK Conservative government claimed that 100 000 jobs would be lost in Britain in implementing maternity rights for women and safeguards for working hours and part-time working contained in the Charter.

Other critics believe that the imposition of a Europe-wide Social Charter would not benefit those for whom it was intended – the poorer workers (Addison and Siebert, 1991, 1992). They argue that 'it will not succeed in making the desired transfer to disadvantaged groups. Since mandated benefits work at the level of the firm, rather than at the level of the tax transfer system, firms will tend to make countervailing moves which frustrate the redistributive aims of the policy' (Addison and Siebert, 1992: 511). They also claim that the unskilled will lose out as a result of better safety protection because 'they were the ones doing the unsafe jobs for high pay; now the unsafe jobs have been removed, wages have been reduced but the skill gap remains' (p. 511). In addition, the attempts to impose uniformity on nations with diverse systems of social legislation will impede competition (p. 495).

Most minimalists do support some of the measures in the Social Charter to varying degrees, namely:

- freedom of movement of workers;
- provision of training;
- harmonisation of qualifications;
- pensions to become portable;
- help to the less favoured regions through the Social Fund;
- schemes to help the long-term unemployed.

They remain, however, strictly against measures to regulate the labour market, which they believe should be made freer by clipping the power of trade unions, reducing the government role in industrial relations, and increasing forms of flexibility.

Why do you think most neo-liberalists (deregulationists) would, despite their
ideological position, support the above six points of the Social Charter?

Hint: Think about the purity of market forces in terms of a level playing field concept.

● The regulationists

The regulationist or interventionist position is generally held by those who believe that if
the single European market is to create a free market in terms of a competitive 'level
playing field' for goods, industry and services, then the same principle should apply to
the social dimension to prevent the exploitation of various work groups or giving one
organisation or economy an advantage over another in the naked drive towards profit.
Unregulated markets would lead to poorer countries and employers holding down
'wages and social benefits to limit imports from richer member states and at the same
time increase their exports to those countries. Such a strategy would amount to exporting domestic unemployment . . . Such action would inevitably force richer countries to
check real wage growth and streamline existing labour market regulations triggering a
price and cost reducing war inside the community (Teague, 1991: 7). From this would
ensue redundancies and high unemployment. This is one version of what has come to be
called *social dumping*.

A second and concomitant view of social dumping envisages

> a sizable shift in production from Northern to Southern Europe as companies chase after
> low wage investment sites. It is feared the combination of these two processes would
> destabilise European economies by shifting the concern of governments and managers
> away from product and process innovations, towards cost reducing strategies. In this
> scenario of social dumping the main casualties of the competitive regime would be work-
> ers and their families who would experience a lowering of their incomes.
>
> (Teague, 1991: 7)

An example of this was the exposure by a television documentary of the high incidence
of illegal child labour in Portugal, which had the effect of removing manufacturing jobs
from the UK shoe industry as labour costs were so much cheaper in Portugal.
Consequently, many British companies choose to manufacture there rather than in the
UK (Twenty Twenty Television, 1993).

Another example seized on by the regulationists to illustrate their argument was the
decision by the Hoover Company to transfer its production facilities from Dijon, France
to Cambuslang, near Glasgow, Scotland. Hoover president, William Foust, claimed that
the prime motive for moving the company's whole production facilities was that non-
wage labour costs added only 10 per cent to the cost of employing a worker in Scotland
as opposed to 45 per cent in France (Goodhart, 1993). A further example is Bowater,
the UK-based packaging group, which shifted production of some of its cosmetic packaging to the UK from Italy and France. 'The company has calculated national ratios for
average employment costs at its plants, from managing director down to apprentice. If
the UK is 100,' says Michael Hartnell, Bowater's Finance Director, 'Italy is 130, France
140 and Germany 170' (Jackson, 1993).

The regulationists claim that such practices play off one national workforce against
another in an attempt to bid down labour costs. The deregulationists point out that
companies will be attracted by cheap labour costs because they reflect maximum efficiency in terms of productivity. However, despite the examples referred to above, by the
end of the 1990s there was not a great deal of evidence that social dumping is wide-

spread in Europe. There have been more significant shifts globally from Europe and North America to Asian and South American states, thus reinforcing the view that Europe is part of a global economy.

Some also claim that these ideological tensions are reflected in the differences between the Commission, served with the responsibility of implementing the social agenda, and the European Parliament, representative of the national interests of member states (Towers and Terry, 1999).

By the latter part of the 1990s the power balance in many European states and in the European Parliament had shifted to the centre left as conservative and right-wing governments were replaced by parties of a more social democratic orientation. Consequently there was a re-emphasis on the idea of social partnership and what the Blair government in the UK has called the 'Third Way', a 'position between the Old Left and the New Right' (Pierson *et al.*, 1999). Thus while social concerns and welfare measures have been revisited, it is in accordance with the need to create proactive labour markets that do not create barriers to entrepreneurship and job creation. This emphasis on creating a social dialogue between the social partners of the EU (trade unions, employer associations, governments and EU agencies) led, through a series of meetings, to the Amsterdam Treaty.

Stop and think

Why do you think most regulationists want to regulate the European Union labour market?

Hint: Think about which types of worker or employee might suffer and why in an unchecked labour market.

The Amsterdam Treaty, 1997

The Amsterdam Treaty was an attempt to prepare the EU labour force to deal with a world where work design, organisational forms and labour markets are constantly changing and, most importantly, in the process to decrease levels of unemployment. By the mid-1990s the social affairs agenda of the EU was in need of a fresh impetus. As Padraig Flynn (Commissioner for Employment, Industrial Relations and Social Affairs, 1995–99) stated:

> There was a number of moribund proposals and a general lack of interest in the Member States in dynamically pursuing the social agenda. In addition, DGV (Directorate-General V for Employment, Industrial Relations and Social Affairs) badly needed to improve its image. In far too many instances, there was too much emphasis on drawing down budget funds rather than making effective use of them.   (European Commission, 1999a: 3)

White Papers were published, and a number of meetings of member states were held at the instigation of Flynn to hammer out a social affairs strategy in an attempt to move the process forward. Major mistakes were pinpointed in past attempts to implement social policy. First, there was an absence of coordinated economic policies, which have failed to keep pace with European integration. Governments have operated independently of one another and so fiscal and monetary policies were not integrated at EU level. This was sometimes damaging in social and economic terms. Second, there has been an inability to modernise the labour market to keep pace with the changing conditions of modern economies.

The response to the first mistake was to establish European Monetary Union (EMU), establishing convergence and coordination of economic policies, in order to prevent fluctuations in exchange rates and reduce shocks to the European economy. The response to the second problem was to make reduction of unemployment and the generation of new employment opportunities an explicit goal of the EU by giving them the status of an 'issue of common concern'. The Amsterdam Treaty 'constitutionalised' employment issues, that is, brought them within the sphere of EU competence, by including employment as a separate Title within the Consolidated European Treaty, thus allowing the formulation of a European Employment Strategy (EES). The general aims of the EES are:

- to create a realistic strategy for social affairs;
- to make the process of convergence of social policy more effective across the EU;
- to have more effective monitoring based on national action plans with specific objectives and targets;
- to place emphasis on an integrated approach 'across a number of policy fields instead of isolated measures and "quick fixes"' (European Comission, 1999a: 7).

The four pillars upon which this new strategy is based are designed ultimately to provide solutions to the high levels of unemployment among the young, ethnic minorities, women and the long-term unemployed as well as the unemployed in general by preparing people for economic and labour market changes. These pillars are:

- *Employability*. This is concerned with investment in human resources within a new active policy: how to cover the skills gap in Europe and create attachments to the world of work for the young and long-term unemployed and other groups who are less competitive in the labour market so that they do not drift into exclusion. Equally important is the enhancement of the skills and motivation of people in order to deal with the rapidly changing world of work, and to create in turn successful industries and a successful EU economy. Emphasis is placed on active rather than passive support.
- *Adaptability*. This is concerned with how to strengthen the capacity of workers to meet the challenges of change and how to change the organisation of work in such a way that structural adjustment can be managed and competitiveness maintained. This means also investment in lifelong learning, and reforming contractual frameworks to take into account new emerging work forms, but maintain the right balance between flexibility for enterprises and security for workers.
- *Entrepreneurship*. This is concerned with how to create a new entrepreneurial culture and spirit in Europe by encouraging self-employment, cutting red tape, reforming taxation systems, and identifying new sources of jobs, especially at local level and in the social economy. This encapsulates a series of measures to make it easier to start and run a business, to develop new jobs, and tap the employment potential of the information society.
- *Equal opportunities*. This is concerned with how to create conditions where men and women have equal responsibility and opportunities in family and working life, and how to respond to the demographic challenges that require us to maintain conditions of growth through high female participation in the labour market.

Stop and think

In what way are the four pillars moving from a passive to an active labour market approach to solving unemployment?

Hint: Think in terms of employment (i.e. job creation) rather than unemployment.

◼ The Lisbon Summit and the Stockholm Council

The Lisbon Summit in 2000 set a strategic target for the EU to become the world's leading 'knowledge economy' by 2010. It also identified the key conditions for fulfilling this goal as being:

- upgrading of skills;
- participation in lifelong learning;
- gender equality;
- promotion of high-quality jobs.

Underlying all of these was the key goal of increasing the rate of employment across the EU. Raising the employment rate was seen to be crucial to both the EES and the Lisbon Strategy by stimulating more rapid economic growth and enabling the European social model to be maintained by providing a sounder basis for financing pension and other social welfare provisions (Goetschy, 2002). This led to the Lisbon Summit marking a new stage in the development of the EES in that for the first time the Council of Ministers set specific employment targets for member states to achieve by 2010. Among the most important were that 70 per cent of the working-age population of the EU should be in employment by 2010, including 60 per cent of working-age women.

In 2001 the Stockholm Council confirmed the Lisbon employment targets but added intermediate targets to be achieved by 2005 – an overall employment rate of 67 per cent and 57 per cent for women – and a new requirement to raise the employment rate for older workers to 50 per cent by 2010. This reflected the fact that the employment rate among the prime working-age group, i.e. 25–55-year-olds, is already 77 per cent (European Commission, 2002: 173). Therefore it is perceived that there is more scope for increasing the employment rate among women and older people, since on the basis of figures for 2001 this is currently low at 38.5 per cent and 54.9 per cent respectively (European Commission, 2002: 173).

These are ambitious targets. The overall employment rate fell during the recession of the early 1990s and although it recovered from 1995 onwards, it was at the same level in 1999 as it had been in 1991 – just over 62 per cent. The employment rate for people aged 55–64 followed a similar pattern and was only 1.5 percentage points higher in 2001 than it had been in 1991. Employment among women has shown stronger growth, from 50.2 per cent in 1991 to 54.9 per cent in 2001 (European Commission, 2002: 173). In order to achieve these targets, policy has not only to provide incentives for unemployed workers to rejoin the labour market but also to encourage those already in work not to withdraw from it, especially women and older workers who are more likely to do so. According to Goetschy (2002), this has led to a growing focus on the need to improve the quality as well as the quantity of jobs, since '(t)he decision to remain in the labour market depends very much on the quality of work...' (p. 413).

◼ The European employment strategy: key policy issues

● Unemployment and social policy

During the 1990s increasing importance was attached to reducing unemployment and increasing the EU's capacity to create jobs. The Commission produced a White Paper on growth, competitiveness and employment in 1993, which 'focused on training, flexibility in the labour market and work reorganisation'. In 1994 the main business of the Essen summit was how to reduce unemployment and create more jobs. Significantly, its recommendations included reducing the non-wage costs of employment such as social security charges and, implicitly, costs of redundancy (Gill et al., 1999: 315). This thinking subsequently informed the employment chapter of the Amsterdam Treaty of 1997, which defined the current employment strategy of the Union.

The main aim of the treaty was to deal with unemployment not just by advocating welfare support and funding but actively closing the gap between job vacancies and the unemployed. Unemployment in the EU has compared unfavourably with the major economies and the G7 average, as Table 16.1 illustrates.

Table 16.1 **Unemployment in the EU and the major economies (percentages)**

	1996	1997	1998	1999	2000	2001	2002
EU average	10.8	10.4	9.9	9.2	7.8	7.4	7.6
G7 average and OECD*	6.8	6.5	6.4	6.4	6.3	6.5	6.6
Euro zone	–	–	10.9	9.9	8.5	8.0	8.3
USA	5.3	4.7	4.3	4.2	4.0	4.7	5.8
Japan	3.3	3.4	4.1	4.7	4.7	5.0	5.4
UK	7.7	6.4	6.2	6.1	5.4	5.0	5.1
Germany	–	–	9.4	8.6	7.8	7.8	8.2
France	–	–	11.7	11.3	9.3	8.5	8.7

Sources: *Labour Market Trends*, 1998, 1999; OECD Outlook, No. 69, 2000; Bradley, 2002; OECD (2003).

ACTIVITY

- Which countries have had the lowest unemployment rates over the past seven years?

- Which countries have had the highest unemployment rates over the past seven years?

- How would you explain the differences between Japan's, the USA's, the UK's and the EU's unemployment rates?

- How would regulationists and deregulationists explain these national trends?

These figures clearly indicate that the combined EU economies have been less successful in tackling unemployment than the USA, Japan and the G7 nations, and critics of regulationism have pointed to the better performance of economies such as the USA and UK. They strongly advocate deregulationist policies in order to facilitate job creation and bring unemployment down.

The question of what approaches to take to tackle unemployment has divided the social democratic governments that came to power in the EU in the 1990s. The European Employment Strategy represents a significant development in this respect in that, through the open method of coordination, it sets out a common set of strategic goals for member states while allowing for national differences in the policy approaches that are designed to achieve them. In particular, it places considerable emphasis on the need for more flexibility with respect to types of employment contract and the organisation of work and working hours, and on the need to reduce the non-wage costs of employment to employers. Three main issues can be identified in discussions of the wider significance of the employment strategy for the future of the social policy within the EU.

Firstly, the strategy has been seen as a reorientation of the 'social Europe' project since the 1989 Social Charter. This involves moving away from a preoccupation with workers' rights in employment and instead prioritising the need to reduce unemployment (Gill *et al.*, 1999). This shift reflects the influence of those who see certain aspects of the existing framework of employment rights and social protections within the member states as contributing to unemployment and hindering the creation of jobs (see European Commission, 1999b: 20).

The second point concerns how far these changes amount to a long–term programme of labour market deregulation and convergence towards the US model of social policy, based on economic liberalism and individualism and the pursuit of labour market 'flexibility'. Certainly the Commission does not see labour flexibility as being in competition with labour market regulation *per se*. Thus, when discussing the need for member states to create 'the conditions in which the flexible firm can exist', it advocates 'reforming, where necessary, the rules governing contractual relationships' between employer and employee. But it goes on to say, 'This does not mean deregulating labour markets but permitting the existence of various types of work contract, all on an equal footing, with none offering particular advantages over any other' (European Commission, 1999b: 20). This offers the prospect of regulations to ensure that 'flexible workers' share the same rights in employment as 'standard' workers. An example of this is the 2002 Temporary Workers Directive. This requires member states to remove 'unnecessary' political and bureaucratic obstacles to the wider use of temporary agency workers, but also states that agency temps should not be employed on worse terms and conditions than they would be if employed directly by the organisation using their services.

In the light of this, some analysts have suggested that we should not interpret the changes as a simple move towards deregulation of labour markets and society. Rather than a straightforward move to deregulation, analysts have observed an attempt at *re-regulation* of labour markets and society (Gill *et al.*, 1999). This means changing the form of regulation. Indeed, there may be more state intervention in some areas, such as training, to improve economic performance and compensate for market failure. On the other hand, others have argued that pressures for deregulation have been mounting within the EU for some time. Social protection and employment rights are under pressure from European competition law and from the perceived need to reduce costs in order to sustain international competitiveness (Barnard and Deakin, 1998). Such pressures appear to be reflected in the bias of most National Action Plans towards the 'employability' and 'entrepreneurship' pillars, with much less being done to address issues of 'adaptability' and 'gender equality' (Goetschy, 2002: 408).

Thirdly, the strategy has been seen as redefining European social policy increasingly in terms of employment policy. This redefinition has been described as a shift away from the traditional view of the welfare state in which social policy and welfare can be seen as independent of the economy (Pierson *et al.*, 1998; Barnard and Deakin, 1998). In the traditional view, social rights and social protection are seen to be desirable in themselves and tend to be based on a redistributive ethic. That is, taxation of the better off should finance social benefits for the worse off as well as paying for communal services such as health, education and pensions. Social rights and social protection may aid economic performance, but this is not their main justification.

According to a number of analysts (Pierson *et al.*, 1998; Barnard and Deakin, 1998; Standing, 1999), the employment strategy of the EU involves a significant move away from this traditional idea of the welfare state. It replaces it with the concept of the 'workfare state', in which social policy is subsumed within, and subordinated to, the needs of the competitive economy. Rather than emphasising redistribution of income and the provision of tax-financed benefits to support the disadvantaged in society, the workfare state emphasises policies aimed at equipping and encouraging and, if need be, forcing disadvantaged individuals to be active producers, either as employees or as self-employed entrepreneurs.

The effects of such a reorientation of social policy at the EU level are difficult to calculate, since historically the EU has had little impact on welfare state policy at national level. If member states should retain a traditional concept of the welfare state, this will limit the impact of the change in EU policy. However, it seems to be the case that the reorientation of social policy at EU level is, in part at least, a reflection of and a response to similar reorientations within the member states. Since the 1980s there has been a growing tendency among member states to limit their financial obligations to their citizens, especially the less well off. This is reflected in reductions in the relative value of minimum wages, social security benefits and pensions by cutting the link with average earnings (Standing, 1999). Therefore there seems to be a strong case for arguing that EU employment policy reflects the growing pressures for economic liberalisation and labour market flexibility that have been manifesting themselves on a global scale for some time. European Monetary Union may intensify these pressures.

● European Monetary Union

The possible adverse effects of EMU on employment policy have caused these two issues to rise to the top of the EU agenda. In general, two positions have been taken: that of the optimists, and that of the pessimists. The third stage of EMU, leading to full monetary union, was completed in 1998 with 11 of the 15 member countries joining. Convergence criteria required participating member states to preserve price inflation within certain limits, to restrict national debt to 60 per cent of gross domestic product (GDP), and to confine budget deficits to no more than 3 per cent of GDP. Optimists see this as another opportunity for further convergence and harmonisation of economic and social policy in the wake of the single European market of 1992 and in the spirit of the Amsterdam Treaty.

Pessimists believe that, in striving to maintain these criteria, economies will create higher unemployment 'by eliminating exchange rate flexibility as a means of adjustment' (Towers and Terry, 1999):

> The continuing absence of good, secure, reasonably paid work for large segments of the working population could then have major adverse political consequences for the progress or even cohesion of the EU.
> (p. 274)

While there are built-in monitoring processes in the operation of EMU, it also has a deregulatory dimension, and this could clash with EU social aims. Barnard and Deakin (1999) see these developments as

> an attempt to lock member states into a path of economic development based on economic convergence around tight budgetary controls and the maintenance of price stability. Labour flexibility . . . is the corollary of this process. Some of these reforms, it is clear would be deregulatory, in the sense of removing indirect labour costs through reforms to employment protection legislation and the tax benefit system.
> (p. 363)

In other words, such measures could benefit employers more than workers by removing protections. It is not surprising therefore that the EU employers' association UNICE, as one of the Social Partners, has been more cooperative than in the past in participating in the social dialogue. Up to late 2003 the more pessimistic prognostications have not been fulfilled, mainly because the monetary convergence criteria have been maintained without undue stress. However, if economic difficulties were to arise, then there could well be serious implications for European social and employment policy.

● Equal opportunities

As we have noted, equal opportunities (EO) is one of the pillars of the Amsterdam Treaty proposals. It is concerned with eliminating the gender gaps and the development of a social infrastructure to enable better reconciliation between family life and working life. It is also concerned with developing a framework to respond to the demographic changes that shape economic and social life.

BOX 16.1 'Hire and fire, is no recipe for Europe', says EU jobs chief

Employment commissioner insists there are more pressing issues than labour market rigidity, writes George Parker.

Europe has a strong record in creating jobs and does not need a US-style hire and fire labour market, according to the European Union's employment commissioner. In spite of German unemployment above 4m and sclerotic EU growth, Anna Diamantopoulou insisted a rigid labour market was not the main problem facing the European economy.

Ms Diamantopoulou says new employment figures, out tomorrow, show the EU economy produced a net 12m new jobs over the last six years, and that overall employment rates were up. She said that although further labour reforms were needed, the EU economy was being hindered by more important problems, such as a failure to fully open up Europe's internal market.

Ms Diamantopoulou's comments are likely to provoke claims of complacency at the European Commission, which co-ordinates employment policies at EU level.

The European seasonally adjusted unemployment rate currently stands at 8.3 per cent, compared with 5.6 per cent in the US, and the US growth rate has constantly outstripped that of the EU over the last decade...

Ms Diamantopoulou, a Greek socialist, believes it would be wrong to jettison Europe's social model in favour of US-style labour policies, although the Commission itself has largely abandoned attempts to introduce new labour market legislation. In an interview with the *Financial Times*, she said: 'It is a very simplistic approach to say that we are not flexible enough to hire and fire people.'...

Although Ms Diamantopoulou admits more needs to be done, particularly in bringing older workers back, she says the EU labour market functioned well in the second half of the 1990s. She also insists that a 'high level of social protection does not necessarily equate to high unemployment'. The Netherlands, with an unemployment rate of 2.9 per cent, is an example she likes to cite. She concedes Germany's labour market and social net do need reforming, a process which started with the return of Chancellor Gerhard Schroder's new government in September...

Source: Financial Times, 12 November 2002, p. 6

Question

Consider and discuss Ms Diamantopoulou's views in the context of the preceding discussion of unemployment and social policy in the EU. How does the reportage of her views illustrate the debate over labour market regulation within Europe?

Equal opportunities is a complex issue: merely making it a pillar of EU social policy will not necessarily resolve all the questions about gender differences in the labour market. The principle of equal treatment for men and women was embodied in the Treaty of Rome 1957, and is one the 12 provisions of the Social Charter (see above). While some progress has been made on these issues, the situation within the EU varies widely between member states, with the Scandinavian countries having the most progressive legislation and Greece the least.

As Leat (1998) states, there are three types of equality, each of which varies in terms of progress towards implementation:

- *Equality of opportunity* may encompass pre-work experience and circumstance as well as opportunities to compete for work and for advancement within a particular employment organisation.
- *Equality of treatment* may encompass such issues as the allocation of tasks, working conditions, issues of harassment and conditions governing dismissal.
- *Equality of outcome* is likely to encompass issues of pay and other substantive terms and conditions of employment, as well as quotas of the working population.   (p. 172)

Each of these types of equality has had varying degrees of implementation across the EU, and some member states will have to make considerable progress if harmonisation is to be achieved. Recently, emphasis has been placed on the concept of *mainstreaming*, which 'involves the incorporation of EO issues into all action programmes and policies from the outset. It moves beyond equal treatment and positive action approaches to EO' (Rees, 1998: 4).

One of the key actors in the field in forging EO initiatives has been the European Court of Justice (ECJ), which has become involved in resolving individual cases that in turn set precedents for future judgments across the EU. For example, indirect discrimination was demonstrated in the *Bilka-Kaufhaus* judgment. This deemed that the exclusion of part-time workers from a company pension scheme (made up mainly of women workers) was indirect discrimination. The *Hill and Stapleton* judgment concerned women who moved from job sharing to full-time work but were placed on a lower pay scale despite the fact they had worked at the company as long as full-time workers, who were paid more (Barnard and Deakin, 1999: 365).

Women were also helped indirectly by the UK government's recent adoption of the minimum wage, which helped many female workers to raise their salaries. The preponderance of women in atypical and lower-paid work has considerable implications for the satisfactory operation of the EO provisions of the Amsterdam Treaty. If the entrepreneurial agenda is overtly deregulatory, in that it is seeking the removal of social charges and other potential restrictions on business start-ups, this could well clash with attempts to maintain and improve protective legislation.

Rees (1998), however, argues that

> While the legal framework for EO is essential, it is inevitably limited in its effectiveness. Positive action projects, while creating spaces for women and being laboratories for the development of good practice, appear to be precariously funded, provision is *ad hoc*, and there are few linkages to mainstream providers. It is mainstreaming which is likely to have the most significant impact on developing women's skills and the rigidities of gender segregation in the labour market. It also has the potential capacity to move beyond gender into other dimensions of equality, such as race and disability. (p. 4)

● Vocational education and training

In order to fulfil the Amsterdam Treaty's pillars of employability, adaptability and entrepreneurship, considerable reliance has been placed on vocational education and training (VET) as tools to enable the creation of a more skilled and educated workforce, able to respond and adapt to the demands of a rapidly changing and increasingly competitive world. The Social Commission has emphasised the active nature of VET proposals, in contrast to the passive measures associated with the Social Charter. The need to create a more employable workforce and in turn reduce unemployment places a huge emphasis on the ability of VET initiatives to equip people with the requisite skill and knowledge for a world of high technology, increased communication, and growth in the service sector, as well as enabling them to deal with the forms of flexibilisation demanded by neo-Fordist systems.

How this is achieved depends on initiatives to help the individual, the organisation and the economy – a theme running through Part 3 of this book. Such initiatives may come from the EU, from national governments, from organisations or from individuals themselves. The role of the EU and national governments often rests on political positions. Britain has strongly advocated a neo-liberalist position over the past 20 years: successive governments have adopted a voluntarist approach, which encouraged rather than compelled organisations and individuals to train. Germany, Sweden and France, by contrast, have advocated more compulsory initiatives, including legislation to increase levels of training. Neo-liberalists claim that the persistence of high unemployment levels in many European countries testifies to the failure of these compulsory initiatives (Addison and Siebert, 1991; Marsland, 1991).

Success has been mixed in the past, with the much-vaunted German dual system (see Chapter 9) receiving a considerable degree of praise and attention, but Leat (1998) suggests that 'attempts to directly transpose the German arrangements to member states with different traditions, cultures and maybe even different production systems and strategies may not be at all successful' (p. 239).

The dual system in Germany and the reliance on internal markets in French and Italian companies have been successful but only for those who have employment. The core problem of moving the unemployed, and in particular the long-term unemployed, into work has proved more problematic in these economies. Provision of the requisite skills for them to gain employment has been no easy task, and even if the skills are acquired there is no guarantee of work in regions where traditional industries have declined and little new industry has replaced it.

Regini (1995) has drawn attention to the diversity of strategies that companies use to gain competitive advantage, ranging through forms of flexible mass production (or mass customisation) to flexible specialisation, neo-Fordism, diversified quality production and the traditional small firm. Each will require its own mix of skills, and will in turn impose its own particular demands on the labour market, but at the same time will be subject to the characteristics of the existing supply of labour nationally and locally (Leat, 1998: 240). Institutional theorists would add that historical, cultural and institutional forces will also serve to shape the particular nature of a country or region's VET.

All this makes for considerable difficulties in meeting the aim of harmonisation of EU social policy, and given these constraints it is unlikely to see convergence within the near future. The Amsterdam Treaty's proposals imply a mix of approaches, finding a marriage point between EU suggested policy, local prevailing conditions, and responses to a rapidly changing global competitive environment.

● Social partnership and social dialogue

As mentioned earlier in this chapter, the term 'Social Partners' refers to representative organisations of employers and employees at EU level and, more recently, at the level of the member states. 'Social dialogue' refers to processes of consultation and negotiation between the Social Partners on matters of EU policy formulation and implementation. The Protocol procedure (see above) represents the most developed form of social dialogue at EU level. Social dialogue is seen as an example of a neo-corporatist approach to policy-making. This in turn is linked to social democratic principles of state action. Social dialogue does not include negotiation over pay and does not cover the right to strike. Therefore it should not be seen as EU-level collective bargaining. The concept of social dialogue within the European Community goes back to the 1960s and 1970s but was undeveloped at that time.

Obstacles to the development of social partnership and social dialogue during the 1970s and 1980s

- Fundamental disagreements between the Social Partners on the issue of social/employment policy within the EU.
- The Partners' lack of a mandate to bargain on behalf of workers and employers in member states.
- Partners were not fully representative of employers or workers at the sector level.
- The Partners lacked authority over their constituent members.

- Both sides needed to satisfy the national interests of their members.
- The lack of appropriate EU institutions to promote social dialogue and enforce subsequent agreements.

Measures to promote social partnership and social dialogue 1985–2001

Measures to promote social dialogue were developed during the 1980s and 1990s in order to stimulate progress towards an integrated European Social Policy. In addition, there was growing commitment to the principle of subsidiarity, the principle that decisions should only be taken at EU level if it could be shown that the objective cannot be achieved by action by individual member states. Subsidiarity also involves trying to formulate EU policy initiatives in such a way as to give member states as much scope as possible to interpret and implement them in the light of their own national circumstances. The promotion of social dialogue was one effect of the influence of the subsidiarity principle, which required the Social Partners to have increased influence on the formulation of EU policy and its implementation at national level.

- *The 1985 'Val Duchesse' process.* This was introduced by the Commission under Jacques Delors. It provided for Joint Committees consisting of representatives of the social partners to be appointed by the Commission as required, and for Informal Working Parties to be established on a voluntary basis by the Social Partners themselves. These bodies could issue non-binding 'Joint Opinions and Recommendations'.
- *The 1991 protocol procedure.* The protocol procedure aimed to strengthen social dialogue through:
  - A procedure whereby the Commission has to consult the Social Partners formally before presenting legislative proposals to the Council of Ministers.
  - The protocol procedure, which allows the Social Partners to negotiate framework agreements – European Community Agreements – on matters identified by the Commission. These can then be implemented through national collective bargaining procedures or else the Social Partners can ask the Commission to put the agreement as a proposal for decision by the Council of Ministers.
- *Sectoral Dialogue Committees 1998.* The Joint Committees and Informal Working Parties established under the Val Duchesse process were abolished in 1998 and replaced by Sectoral Dialogue Committees. These have the right to be consulted on any EU-level developments that have social policy implications. They are also charged with promoting social dialogue at sectoral level. This is an attempt to encourage the Social Partners to negotiate more binding sectoral framework agreements in place of non-binding joint opinions that required subsequent legislation.
- *2001 Lisbon Summit.* At the Lisbon Summit it was decided that the Social Partners should play a more active role in the development and implementation of the European Employment Strategy. As a result, the Social Partners at EU level have been given responsibility for implementing two of the employment guidelines under the 'adaptability' pillar of the EES. These are modernisation of work organisation, and enhancing the contribution of lifelong training and learning to worker adaptability. The partners are supposed to negotiate agreements on both of these issues. In addition, Lisbon encouraged the Social Partners to contribute more fully to the EES by:
  - developing benchmarking processes for existing employment guidelines;
  - negotiating framework agreements and issuing joint opinions on particular guidelines;
  - proposing some new guidelines of their own;
  - monitoring the participation of the Social Partners at national level in developing and implementing National Action Plans.

Stop and think | Why do you think the EU has encouraged the development of social dialogue as an alternative to formal legislation on social and employment issues?

● The effectiveness of social dialogue mechanisms

The evidence on the effectiveness of mechanisms to promote social dialogue is mixed. Some have argued that the protocol procedure introduced in 1991 has had little effect in strengthening social dialogue. The protocol procedure has a number of limitations:

- National procedures for implementing agreements are weak and EU legislation states that they are to be implemented by collective bargaining according to the rules of each member state. Thus there is no obligation on states to apply the agreements directly or establish rules for their implementation (Hall, 1994).
- Member states' representatives in the Council of Ministers are reluctant to give legislative backing to regulations that they have not been involved in developing (Hall, 1994).
- Social Partners themselves have reservations concerning European Community Agreements. The ETUC is concerned that European Community Agreements do not undermine national collective bargaining arrangements. UNICE is hostile to sectoral-level Community Agreements (Keller and Bansbach, 2001).
- Sectoral Dialogue Committees so far comprise the old Joint Committees and Informal Working Parties in a new guise – old wine in new bottles. There is little likelihood that the new structures will lead to more binding agreements because the Commission has no power to force the Social Partners to negotiate and because UNICE has no proper organisation at the sectoral level (Keller and Bansbach, 2001).
- The outcomes of social dialogue since the 1991 protocol procedure have been limited, with only three successful framework agreements being reached during 1991–9. Also, the regulatory force of these agreements has been weak, with agreements containing many exemptions and opening clauses, allowing member states effectively to opt out of them. Traditional legislation remains the main vehicle of social policy (Keller and Bansbach, 2001). One recent example is the issue of temporary workers, where dialogue broke down in 2001 and the issue became subject to formal legislative procedures in the form of the Temporary Workers Directive (Gilman and Broughton, 2002).
- There is little evidence of negotiation between national governments and Social Partners over National Action Plans for employment, except where there is an existing framework of national negotiations over economic and social policy. Thus, where social partnership and social dialogue have been undeveloped in the past, they continue to remain so (Leonard, 2001).

The pessimists also point out that most of the obstacles of the 1970s and 1980s remain. In particular, UNICE remains opposed to further EU-level social policy initiatives. UNICE is also organisationally fragmented and therefore lacks representativeness and authority at national and sectoral levels. At national and sectoral levels, declining membership of both trade unions and employers' federations threatens to undermine the legitimacy of the social partners and the basis for social dialogue. There is also evidence of a growing political challenge to social dialogue in countries such as France, the Netherlands and Austria (Ebbinghaus, 2002).

On the positive side however, it has been argued that:

- The new arrangements are changing the status of trade unions and employers' organisations from pressure groups to recognised partners in 'an emergent corporatist policy community' (Keller and Bansbach, 2001: 45). For example, in December 2001 the Social Partners issued a joint statement setting out the development of a work programme for developing autonomous Social Dialogue and identifying 'a specific role for the social partners in European governance' (Gilman and Broughton, 2002: 539). In May 2001 the ETUC and the European Federation of Small and Medium Enterprises issued a joint declaration on the development of social dialogue in the SME sector (Gilman and Broughton, 2002: 539).

● This emergent community is encouraged by the experience of engaging in social dialogue as it builds trust between the Social Partners, encouraging further development and cooperation between them (Teague, 2001). There has been development of social dialogue at sectoral level, with 26 Sectoral Dialogue Committees established by 2001. Dialogues have covered a range of issues such as training, health and safety, modernisation of work, teleworking and enlargement (Gilman and Broughton, 2002: 539).

Overall, social dialogue to date has had a mixed record, with those member states that have subscribed to a corporatist approach for some time, Germany and Sweden for example, happy to continue with that system and seemingly performing well in labour market terms (Crouch, 1996; Traxler, 1999).

Stop and think	What conditions do you think are necessary to support effective social dialogue?

● Employee participation and involvement

A significant part of the social dialogue ardently advocated by the European Commission has been the strengthening of employee participation at enterprise level, and the European Works Council (EWC) has been seen to be a major institution to promote it. An important aim behind the social dialogue is that if a forum can help the major partners (Germany, France, the UK, Italy) to agree on proposals then it is more likely that the social agenda will be adopted, leading to a greater harmonisation of social policy across the community.

Experience suggests that this is stretching logic too far. Like many of the social proposals, it is adhered to more in theory than in practice. The question of adopting EWC proposals has been contentious since the framing of the Social Charter, and the Directive was adopted in 1994 in the face of strong opposition from the employers' association UNICE. It was adopted by the Commission by a majority vote, but the closure of the Renault plant at Vilvoorde in Belgium has shown that its application in terms of the spirit intended still has some way to go. Subsequently a French court ruled that management should have informed employees and consulted about the proposed closure in advance.

The ETUC (European Trades Union Confederation) responded by demanding amendments to the EWC Directive that would tighten employees' rights by strengthening the terms on which information is given and consultation takes place. UNICE in its turn made it clear that it would resist such proposals (Gilman and Weber, 1999).

The ETUC has pointed to five major areas of weakness in framing its proposals for amending the EWC Directive:

● a lack of clarity on the type of information and consultation to be provided to employee representatives;
● a lack of recognition of the important role played by trade union representatives;
● insufficient resources for translations and preparatory meetings;
● prevalence of management control of the agenda of meetings;
● the limited competence of the EWCs. (Gilman and Weber, 1999: 424).

The last point has also been emphasised by Miller and Stirling (1998), who have highlighted the specific need for training for participants in transnational meetings of EWCs.

The picture is not entirely pessimistic, however, and research by Marginson *et al.* (1998) shows that multinational companies of French, German, British and US origin operating in the EU have a widespread preference for joint employer–employee bodies. While this points to a more hopeful future for works councils and by implication the social dialogue, it does not really attest to a dialogue between equals.

In addition, works councils received a considerable boost when in February 2002 the consultation directive was finally adopted by member states. This requires all companies with more than 150 employees to establish a works council by 2005. By 2008 all organisations with 50 or more staff will have to set up one as well (EWCB, 2002). However, this may not be totally good news for unions as the directive covers all employees, not just union members. Thus already in the UK and Ireland, where the directive will have the greatest impact, unions are scrabbling to make 'sweetheart' deals with employers in order that they become the main or only voice as employee representatives on the works councils (Younson, 2002).

Certainly, unions hope that the directive will prevent such happenings as the GM closure of Vauxhall car production at their Luton plant which took place without any consultation with unions or employees (Holden, 2003).

◼ Human resource management and the European Union

While speculation on the influence of the Social Charter and the subsequent provisions of the Amsterdam Treaty and the Lisbon Summit on labour markets has fuelled debates, there has been little research into its actual influence on organisations. Research carried out by Wood and Peccei (1990) on the preparation of personnel strategies for the single European market (SEM) in British organisations showed that most firms did not perceive this as a critical issue. The minority of companies that did have some sort of human resource strategy were those already involved in EU trading, with more awareness of the need for policies for the SEM. However, many of these HR initiatives were business led, and 'more often than not are developed downstream from corporate strategy and are treated as "third order" within the strategic planning process' (Wood and Peccei, 1990: 84).

The Price Waterhouse Cranfield Project (1991) surveyed human resource initiatives in organisations across ten countries in Europe. While concern was expressed about the effects of the SEM, few organisations had developed a conscious strategy for the SEM, and even fewer had a human resource strategy for it. Most had positive policies on the Social Charter directives associated with equal opportunities and health and safety, but many of these policies had been established long before by national legislation. It would seem from these studies that most organisations will respond to the influences of the Social Charter and the SEM only when it is necessary to do so. Many HRM policies are still influenced by the attitudes of national governments towards enforcement of directives, which in turn rest on varying interpretations of the subsidiarity process.

However, despite a picture of relative parochialism in terms of organisational responses to the Social Charter and the SEM, the Price Waterhouse Cranfield Survey revealed many similar human resource trends taking place across Europe, despite the varying employee relations systems at both macro and micro levels. There are strong trends towards the decentralisation of human resource functions in terms of the devolvement to line management of recruitment and selection, training and development and other functions. However, in such areas as pay bargaining and industrial relations responsibility still resides very much in the personnel function and is strongly influenced by national bargaining structures, particularly in Germany and Sweden. Nevertheless, 'decentralisation in the level of decisions within the organisation and devolution to line management continues apace. Line management responsibility is increasing in all countries and for all subjects with the single exception of Italian industrial relations' (Price Waterhouse Cranfield Project, 1991: 8). Equally, the surveys (retitled Cranet – E in 1995) have found a considerable spread of forms of flexibility in large and medium sized companies in its 'newer' forms (functional and contractual) and is increasing in its older forms (overtime and part-time working) (Brewster et al., 2000).

This seems to suggest that it is premature for EU initiatives to have had an influence on personnel and HR policies in organisations. It seems that organisations are still influenced more by their own particular markets and global trends in HRM than by regional initiatives. Thus local, national and international organisations have been influenced by many trends in HRM emanating from, in particular, the USA and Japan, but the extent and the ways in which these strategies are adopted depend on the size, sector, geographical distribution of the market, industrial relations and bargaining systems in which organisations are placed.

Eastern Europe

Employee relations in the Central and Eastern European states (CEE) have been undergoing enormous change in the post-communist era since 1989. Most CEE countries have been wedged in a transitional phase between the former Soviet system and a market economy (Blanchard *et al.*, 1991; EBRD, 1999), although there are strong signs that each economy is beginning to exert a distinctive pattern of development peculiar to its own economic, social and political circumstances. In the past three years there have been further developments in CEE countries that do not bode well for systems of industrial relations rooted in tripartism (a system of industrial relations whereby the state, employer associations and trade unions oversee aspects of labour market policies).

■ Changing nature of the CEE economies

In the post-communist collapse there was a widespread assumption that free market capitalism would bring the benefits so transparently obvious in the West: consumer products, full shops, a higher standard of living, and economic and political freedom. This was reinforced by a huge initial interest from Western businesses and governments, which saw the potential for cheap labour and ultimately a large new market to exploit. The immediate repercussion, however, was a steep rise in unemployment, accompanied by inflation and the undermining of currencies. The early 1990s witnessed a fall in standards of living for many people, and the emergence of poverty. Thousands of enterprises went into liquidation, unable to compete in open markets after being confronted with their inefficiencies (Blanchard *et al.*, 1991).

Responses to these changes have varied considerably throughout CEE countries, influenced by cultural and historical factors. The former Czechoslovakia and Hungary, which had developed industries before the advent of communism, have been able to use these pre-communist memories and experiences in the process of adaptation and change. Bulgaria, Romania, Albania and the newly constituted states of Yugoslavia, coming from peasant pre-communist conditions, had and are still having greater difficulties in constructing a modern economy (Smith and Thompson, 1992; Holden, 1993).

Channon and Dakin (1995) believe that the former Soviet states can now be divided into three regions according to geography, responses to and experiences of the post-communist world:

● Central Europe – the Czech Republic, Poland, Slovakia, Hungary and Slovenia, the Baltic States (Latvia, Lithuania and Estonia);
● Russia and the former Soviet Union;
● South-central region (the Balkans) – Romania, Bulgaria, Albania and the former Yugoslavia.

The Central European states have fared the best, partly because they have proved most attractive to foreign capital investment. The South-central region has been less attractive to capital investors, due to the rise of nationalist turbulence in the former Yugoslavia and also the relatively underdeveloped nature of their economies.

Russia has in many ways proved the most difficult for foreign companies to deal with, because of the deep-rooted nature of the old communist system and its greater historical isolation from Western Europe:

> There was autocratic government and a peasant culture, with a strong tradition of collectivism and mutual support or patronage mechanisms in the face of a harsh external climate. This is a far more difficult culture in which to establish an operation, because there are no deep seated traditions of private enterprise or private property.
>
> (Channon and Dakin, 1995: 26)

The economic crisis that hit Russia in the late 1990s has also served to further undermine confidence, and there is a widespread view that privatisation has led to profiteering by the 'Mafiosi', leading to the plundering of state property and the widening of inequalities. Unemployment remains generally high, and is probably higher than the unreliable official statistics indicate, and wage levels, compared with the West, remain relatively low (Martin and Cristescu-Martin, 1999).

Over the past three years these economies have been further hit by the collapse of the new technology boom and the general malaise in Western economies which in turn has led to a reluctance to increase investments generally and particularly in CEE countries. The after-effects of the '9/11' terrorist attacks on New York and Washington have further reinforced this trend. However, these influences have not been even and groups of countries such as the Czech Republic, Estonia, Latvia and Lithuania and Hungary have fared better than Bulgaria, Poland, Slovakia and Slovenia where unemployment remains high (Martin and Cristescu-Martin, 2002: 525).

■ Employee relations in the 'new' economies

Trade union density has been high in many CEE economies but is in decline. Levels initially remained high partly because of the backlash against the hardships wrought by free market policies. As early as 1992 the old 'official' unions had fared the best, 'partly because of organisation, habit and resources, partly because they are the more consistent opponents of the new power' (Milne, 1992a). Subsequent rises in unemployment have, however, caused membership to fall. The efficacy of the unions has not been aided by the attitude of government, which is perceived by union officials to be hostile to the point of wishing them to be non-existent (Brewster, 1992).

This decline in membership and influence of trade unions has been further reinforced by emerging trends. Firstly, a decline in industrial enterprises has witnessed diminishing levels of employment and thus trade union membership in this sector. This has been associated with a rise in the service sector not noted for its encouragement of unionisation. Secondly, and influenced by the first trend, there has been a rise in importance of small to medium sized firms in CEE economies, particularly Hungary, the Czech Republic, Poland and the Baltic states, although this trend is apparent in all economies (Martin and Cristescu-Martin, 2002).

In Poland, OPZZ, the old 'official' union organisation, while experiencing some decline, has been relatively successful in the long term compared with Solidarnost, which has witnessed a fall in membership from 10 million to below 2 million (Milne, 1992a). In Hungary the main union organisation, MSZOSZ, has fared less well, 'and is now less than half of its [communist government-controlled] predecessor SZOT' (Gill, 1990; Brewster, 1992), and this trend has continued. In Bulgaria a large independent trade union, Podkrepa, was created in the aftermath of the fall of the communist regime. Initially born out of the desire to defend workers' rights against communist abuse, it joined forces with a united front of anti-communist groups under the banner of the Union of Democratic Forces (UDF), but in the post-communist Bulgarian state has threatened and initiated strikes in protest at the undermining of its members' living standards (Holden, 1991).

In Russia the old unions remain the most important organisation representative of the workers. The Soviet All Union Council of Trade Unions (AUCTU) had 142 million members in 32 branch unions in 1990, although since then its membership has witnessed some decline (Lloyd, 1990). As one Moscow worker stated, 'most of us belong to the official trade unions, because there is no serious alternative' (Weir, 1992). As with many of the new non-communist governments in Eastern Europe, trade unions are not encouraged. In the initial desire to copy Western government practices many anti-union laws have been passed. For example, the draft law on collective agreements states that groups other than trade unions can participate in collective bargaining. As one Russian trade unionist states, 'Of course it undermines the position of the union. At any workplace or enterprise, the manager can say to the workers "Why do you need to join the union in order to have a collective agreement?"' (Cathcart, 1992).

Nevertheless, the unions have expressed dissatisfaction with government and organisational policies: strikes have occurred in Russia, Poland, Bulgaria and the former East Germany, and there was a particularly bitter coal strike in Romania in 1998–9. However, these disputes were the exception to the rule and the general lack of militancy seems to be more of a characteristic of trade union responses to change in CEE countries and is reflective of their relative decline and the changing nature of their economies and the new political agendas. Government responses have not been encouraging, and the argument is regularly stated that industrial unrest will have the effect of discouraging foreign investment.

The future for trade unionism is not particularly optimistic, although the experience across CEE states has varied. Increased privatisation has helped to undermine union membership, and evolving industrial relations legislation by many governments has curbed trade union powers (Blanchard *et al.*, 1991; Smith and Thompson, 1992; Weir, 1992). Trade union influence at company level remains weak (Mason, 1995; Standing, 1997), and Western companies seek to exclude them, particularly on greenfield sites (Martin and Cristescu-Martin, 1999).

■ The stagnation and decline of tripartitism?

Despite the difficulties that have faced the CEE economies, forms of tripartitism have emerged, with the state continuing to have a major influence on employment relations. This is partly because the state still remains a major employer, and it also sets the agenda for policy reforms. Martin and Cristescu-Martin (1999) define tripartitism as 'the institutional expression of the concept of social partnership' (p. 392). Under a tripartite system the government, employers and trade unions negotiate issues related to employment relations, such as wage bargaining, in order to come to some consensual agreement. Such systems create a forum for discussion, and reduce the potential for conflict and damaging disputes.

While trade union density remains high, its influence at company level is limited. At national level trade unions have had more impact, particularly by the use of strikes to defend employees against redundancy when restructuring has taken place. Employers' associations, by contrast, remain weak, but management prerogative is strong at company level where collective bargaining takes place. This dichotomy is also one cause of the decline in union membership, as employees do not perceive their trade union representatives as being effective in collective bargaining. This is partly because trade unions in CEE countries have emerged from the old communist organisations, and have found difficulties in adapting to the free bargaining system, which requires their officials to have skills in negotiating and employee representation.

While tripartitism does not seem to serve employers and employees very well in the short term, it is a framework within which employment policy can be forged in the long term, and it can help to frame protections for both employees and employers. Sceptics, however, see it as 'a political shell for a neo-liberal economic strategy (Thirkell *et al.*, 1998: 166) – a guise for the introduction of anti-union legislation.

Tripartite institutions are stronger in some countries than in others. East Germany has unsurprisingly adopted it and adapted to it well, whereas in Hungary the industrial relations system is more decentralised and less likely to serve its members' interests (Frege and Tóth, 1999). Other observers are sceptical about the survival of tripartitism owing to the weakness of employer and employee associations and the decentralisation of economic management from the state to the enterprise (Mason,1995). Recently Martin and Cristescu-Martin (2002: 529) have seen tripartitism as being in decline or at best in some states, in stagnation, and they quote a report by Hungarian Trade Unions (2001):

> Tripartite institutions survived in Hungary and Poland, but became increasingly formal. In Hungary social dialogue became empty and reached the lowest point '... the institutional possibility of carrying on negotiations on taxation and contribution issues affecting the purchasing power of wages has ceased to exist. The government appears to have no real intention to reach agreement, it has not accepted a single proposal from the social partners, what is more it pushed through the amendments to the world of work against their will.'

While tripartite systems exist in Bulgaria, Rumania, the former GDR and Poland, their effectiveness is very much reliant on the power of trade unions and the willingness of governments and employers to work within the spirit of the system. Given the changing economic circumstances in CEE economies and in the world generally, this seems increasingly unlikely.

The fragile tripartite system may survive in some countries but not in others. This will depend on the continuing strength of trade unions, the effectiveness of state interventions at macro level in the economy, the continuing weakness of employer organisations, and the way HRM practices are filtered through the back door of foreign companies at micro level.

■ HRM and management in Eastern Europe

One of the main problems facing both economies and organisations is the change not only in organisational structures but also in management attitudes, which in many organisations remain locked in the old bureaucratic ways (Holden and Peck, 1990; Watts, 1991; Elenkov, 1998).

Attempts at reform in management practices were already under way in many Eastern European states before 1989, with patchy results. Management in post-communist society was seen as gaining the right to manage, unfettered by the shackles of the Communist Party, state and trade unions, and hence creating an efficient human resource capable of competing with Western countries (Landa, 1990). Not surprisingly, there has been a considerable emphasis on management development, with many Eastern European managers and academics forging links with Western business schools, universities, companies and organisations to set up business management courses of various kinds. There have been considerable problems, largely because of differences in attitudes and perceptions. Though many senior managers lost their positions after 1989 because of their associations with the communist system, others have thrived in the new atmosphere, holding on to their positions and making full use of their connections and networks built up under the old regimes (Meyer, 1990; Pieper, 1990; Elenkov, 1998; Kelemen, 1999).

Personnel and HRM continue to have a low priority in most CEE organisations; many training and recruitment functions are still entrenched in practices associated with the former regimes, although attempts to bring in payment systems linked to performance have been more successful (Landa, 1990; Koubek and Brewster, 1995; Kelemen, 1999). HRM practices are making headway, however, in foreign-owned subsidiaries that can operate fairly autonomously. In state-owned enterprises, and even in joint ventures, new management approaches remain relatively rare, although changes are beginning to take place.

Recently companies have given much more emphasis to HRM issues since initially having had their 'fingers burnt' by underestimating personnel problems. A survey conducted by the School of Slavonic Studies at London University and a corporate language training company, Communicaid, found that 'almost all HR directors and managers of 30 British companies questioned agreed that Western companies had generally underestimated cultural differences and their impact on the establishment of operations and the nature of the local workforce' (Channon and Dakin, 1995: 24). As a result, a number of recommendations are beginning to emerge for companies setting up and operating in Eastern Europe. Training of staff has become a high priority, and this includes not only training in work skills but also attitudinal training. Another problem is poaching: as some companies train, other companies will attract away workers with desirable skills by offering larger wages and salaries. This means that the compensation package also becomes important in retaining staff.

Another consideration is succession planning and the takeover of operations by host country staff from expatriate staff. Considerations of when and how this should take place are also important. It is vital to have 'connections' (someone who can 'fix' things, and who has contacts to smooth operations), especially in Russia and the South-central region (the Balkans). The system of patronage can cause difficulties in removing staff who may appear no longer to fit the job. In this respect recruitment and selection will prove crucial, but the criteria used in Western companies may not always be appropriate.

Despite the resistance to changing practices there is emerging evidence that multinational corporations are infiltrating their HR practices more effectively into their CEE subsidiaries. The effect, to which we have already alluded, is, according to some commentators, to undermine collective bargaining positions by introducing individualised forms of pay related to performance criteria, to reduce pay bargaining to company and even workplace levels, the introduction of rigorous recruitment and selection (to exclude potential troublemakers and create company-minded employees according to some) and to introduce thoroughgoing training programmes to reinforce not only policy and practice but company culture as well. Martin and Cristescu-Martin (2002) are not sure that this is necessarily a conscious effort to undermine tripartitism or trade union power but just an extension of what these multinational corporations institute throughout their global operations. Nevertheless, the effect is the same.

With the passage of nearly a decade and a half since the fall of the Soviet systems in the CEE countries, a diverse pattern is emerging based much more on the individual strengths of economies and their previous development. This trend will continue, and employment relations institutions and practices will vary increasingly between states.

Stop and think

Why is the tripartite system in CEE countries being undermined?

Is there any possibility that a system of social partnership along these lines might emerge in the future?

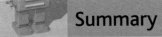

Summary

- Human resource management is a concept that is slowly becoming absorbed into the language of European models of personnel management, but within different institutional structures from those that obtain in the UK, the USA or Japan. Within many Western European countries there is a strong tradition of employee rights incorporated into state provision and the nature of the employment relationship. This explains the move towards social integration that dominated the EU agenda in the early 1990s. The advent of the single European market stimulated a debate about the proper role of a 'social dimension' in the operation of the EU and the Maastricht Treaty, committing the EU to ever-closer monetary and political union.

- By the mid-1990s the debate within the EU concerning the pursuit of regulation or deregulation was set against the backdrop of a moribund Social Charter. The Amsterdam Treaty 1997 is an attempt to rejuvenate the social agenda through the adoption of a 'third way'.

- This has been reinforced by the recognition that the intensification of global competition has created the need for a much more proactive labour market to solve the problems of unemployment and skill shortages. This view has been embodied in the Amsterdam Treaty in terms of the four pillars: employability, adaptability, entrepreneurship, and equal opportunities.

- Nevertheless, there is evidence that some common HRM developments are occurring across Europe within EU members as well as in those economies that are not as yet members. Among the more notable HRM shifts are those connected with the decentralisation of decision-making and the devolution to line managers of decisions relating to the management of employees, as well as increases in forms of flexible working.

- In Eastern and Central Europe the agenda for change has been sudden and large: the replacement of highly centralised state-run economies with the 'shock treatment' of market forces has led to vast upheaval in terms of unemployment. Recent slumps in the world economy have not helped these processes and while they proceed apace there has been a slowing effect on economic growth in some economies.

- A form of tripartitism has emerged in most CEE states but in varying degrees of strength. Despite relatively high union membership, union influence is relatively weak, particularly at company level.

- Management attitudes in CEE economies have equally felt the stress of reform and the difficulty of transition to more market-oriented and less bureaucratic modes of operation. In these circumstances HRM is a concept that has little currency. Most HRM innovations are being implemented in fully foreign-owned subsidiaries, some say to the detriment of trade unions and tripartite systems.

ACTIVITY *Hotel group in Poland*

Kotel is a British-based hotel group that has recently acquired a group of five hotels in Poland. The board of the company is divided over which human resource strategy it should pursue. One board group, represented by the finance director and marketing director, wants to go for a policy whereby labour is recruited from other hotels at the cheapest possible price. The other group, represented by the human resource director and operations manager, desires a full HRM strategy based on careful recruitment and selection, with full training and development policies, and remuneration policies based on performance and quality of service.

▶

1   Divide into three groups, two of these representing the two strategies proposed for the Kotel Group. Role-play a board meeting, with each group putting forward its views, backed by rational argument as to why their strategy should be adopted. A person should be selected to act as managing director to chair the meeting. The third group will act as neutral observers, with the power to question members of each group on their views. At the end of the meeting the third group will decide by vote which is the most convincing strategy to adopt.

2   Draw up a list of problems, particularly related to human resource and employment relationship issues, which would face the Kotel Group setting up its company in Poland.

Questions

1   What difficulties might there be in the operation of the principle of subsidiarity in enforcing the provisions of the Social Charter?

2   What are the main arguments for and against the regulationist and deregulationist views of labour market policy in the European Union?

3   How effective do you think the Amsterdam and Lisbon Treaties will be in producing solutions to unemployment in the European Union?

4   Can a tripartite system of employee relations survive in the former Soviet, Central and Eastern European states?

Case study

A human resource strategy for Europump Ltd

Background

Europump is a UK-based engineering company specialising in hydraulic and pumping equipment. It was founded as a partnership by John Wall, an engineer, who has responsibility for research and development and the production side of the company; Bill Hodges, an accountant with managerial experience; and Paul Marceau, a manager experienced in the engineering business. The company was founded in 1976, saw considerable growth in the earlier years, and although experiencing some difficulties in the 1980s' recession, survived to prosper in the late 1980s.

The board members have cultivated a profile of looking to the future, and with the imminence of the European Single Market in 1992 decided on expansion into continental Europe. A small subsidiary was set up in Lyons, France, in 1987, the founding of which was greatly facilitated by

Paul Marceau, who speaks fluent French as a result of having a French father. The company quickly expanded and, influenced by this success, the UK board decided to set up another subsidiary in the Netherlands. Because of the specialised nature and excellent marketing of its products it was able to establish a successful medium-sized company in Groningen, which, while not enjoying the same degree of success as the UK and French companies, has managed to establish a market niche.

Structure of the company

The UK-based Northampton operation is situated on a greenfield site in a business park on the edge of the town, and employs 340 people, 35 per cent of whom are in unions. Pay is in line with national trends in the engineering and related industries. There is a personnel department with three full-time and two part-time staff. The production department employs 295 people, making up the majority of the workforce.

The research and development department (R&D) employs 5 people, and the finance and marketing department 35 people. Some extra services in these areas are purchased on an agency or consultancy basis.

The French operation in Lyons, Europump (France), employs 200 people, with a composition in a similar ratio to that of the UK company in regard to departmental size and functions, although there is no R&D department. It has a French director, who is ultimately responsible to the UK board. Only 10 per cent of the workforce is unionised, but pay reflects national standards. There is, however, a works council that conforms to French law.

The Dutch operation (Europump AB) employs 175 people with a similar composition to the French organisation in terms of size and function; 25 per cent of the workforce is unionised, and there is a works council in operation.

Developments since 1990

In 1993 Europump opened a subsidiary near Barcelona employing initially 20 workers, and since 1996 the workforce has increased to 50. They are paid in line with local engineering pay rates. While Europump Ltd as a whole enjoyed considerable success in the 1990s, the recession in the early part of the decade affected sales badly, particularly in the UK. As a result, redundancies occurred in all the European operations but particularly so in Northampton. In the post-redundancy period from 1996 on, the UK HQ has increasingly introduced various forms of flexibility. It has pursued functional flexibility backed by considerable training and development for employees. But it has also introduced atypical working in the form of short-time and temporary contracts and the increasing use of agency staff.

While this has brought down production costs and has greatly helped in increasing company profits, it has not pleased the union, which views this as a threat to its membership and, it claims, has had a derogatory effect on its members' conditions.

Performance management has also been introduced, with the result that there are now varied pay packages based much more on individual effort. Again, the unions are not happy with this situation.

The UK board decided to invite the directors and personnel managers to an international board meeting in a London hotel to hammer out an HRM policy for the organisation as a whole. While all the board are 'good' Europeans, John and Bill hold the view that EU social policy can be detrimental to the company's future. Paul, however, believes that following EU social policy will pave the way for more harmonised and harmonious working conditions within the company. At the end of the meeting it was decided to ask Jane Lawson, the UK HRM manager, to prepare a report for the extension of the British HR policy to the European subsidiaries.

Questions

1 What problems might Jane Lawson, the UK HRM manager, envisage in extending the proposals for flexible working practices and performance management to the company's subsidiaries in France, the Netherlands and Spain?

2 What suggestions could she make to overcome these difficulties, given the high union density and existence of works councils in these countries?

References and further reading

Those texts marked with an asterisk are particularly recommended for further reading (but bear in mind that books on the European Union quickly become out of date). The issues covered in this chapter are also addressed in Chapters 3, 8, 13 and 15.

Addison, J.T. and Siebert, W.S. (1991) 'The Social Charter of the European Community: evolution and controversies', *Industrial and Labor Relations Review*, Vol. 44, No. 4, pp. 597–625.

Addison, J.T. and Siebert, W.S. (1992) 'The Social Charter: whatever next?', *British Journal of Industrial Relations*, Vol. 30, No. 4, pp. 495–513.

*Addison, J.T. and Siebert, W.S. (eds) (1997) *Labour Markets in Europe: Issues in Harmonisation and Regulation*. London: Dryden.

*Adnett, N. (1996) *European Labour Markets: Analysis and Policy*. Harlow: Longman.

Baglioni, G. and Crouch, C. (eds) (1990) *European Industrial Relations: The Challenge of Flexibility*. London: Sage.

Barnard, C. and Deakin, S. (1998) 'European Community social law and policy: evolution or regression?', in Towers, B. and Terry, M. (eds), *Industrial Relations Journal European Review 1997*. Oxford: Blackwell.

Barnard, C. and Deakin, S. (1999) 'A year of living dangerously? EC social rights, employment policy and EMU', *Industrial Relations Journal*, Vol. 30, No. 4, pp. 355–372.

Blanchard, O., Dornbusch, R., Krugman, P., Layard, R. and Summers, L. (1991) *Reform in Eastern Europe*. Cambridge, Mass.: MIT Press.

Bradley, S. (2002) 'Unemployment, the "New Economy" and EU economic performance', *Industrial Relations Journal*, Vol. 33, No. 5, pp. 392–404.

Brewster, C. (1992) 'Starting again: industrial relations in Czechoslovakia', *International Journal of Human Resource Management*, Vol. 3, No. 3, pp. 555–574.

Brewster, C. and Hegewisch, A. (1994) *Policy and Practice in European Human Resource Management*. London: Routledge.

Brewster, C., Hegewisch, L., Holden, L. and Lockhart, T. (eds) (1992) *The European Guide to Human Resource Management*. London: Academic Press.

Brewster, C., Mayerhofer, W. and Morley, M. (eds) (2000) *New Challenges for European Human Resource Management*. Basingstoke: Macmillan.

Butt Philips, A. (1988) 'Management and 1992: illusions and reality', *European Management Journal*, Vol. 6, No. 4, pp. 345–350.

Cathcart, R. (1992) 'Struggling to survive in the "free" market', *Morning Star*, 16 May, p. 3.

Channon, J. and Dakin, A. (1995) 'Coming to terms with local people', *People Management*, 15 June, pp. 24–29.

Clark, T. (ed.) (1996) *European Human Resource Management*. Oxford: Blackwell.

Crouch, C. (1996) 'Revised diversity: the neo-liberal decade to beyond Maastricht', in Van Ruysseveldt, J. and Visser, J. (eds) *Industrial Relations in Europe: Traditions and Transitions*. London: Sage, pp. 337–357.

Ebbinghaus, B. (2002) 'Trade unions' changing role: membership erosion, organisational reform, and social partnership in Europe', *Industrial Relations Journal*, Vol. 33, No. 5, pp. 465–482.

EBRD (1999) *Transition Report, 1998*. London: European Bank for Reconstruction and Development.

Elenkov, D. (1998) 'Can American management concepts work in Russia? A cross-country comparative study', *California Management Review*, Vol. 40, No. 4, pp. 133–156.

European Commission (1999a) 'Forum special: 5 years of social policy', *Employment and Social Affairs*. Brussels: European Commission.

European Commission (1999b) *Employment in Europe 1998*. Luxembourg: Office for Official Publications of the European Communities.

European Commission (2002) *Employment in Europe 2002*. Luxembourg: Office for Official Publications of the European Communities.

EWCB (2002) 'Consultation directive adopted but new EU measures in prospect', *European Works Council Bulletin*, Issue 38, March/April, p. 1.

Ferner, A. and Hyman, R. (eds) (1992) *Industrial Relations in the New Europe*. Oxford: Blackwell.

*Ferner, A. and Hyman, R. (eds) (1998) *Changing Industrial Relations in Europe*. Oxford: Blackwell.

Frege, C. and Tóth, A. (1999) 'Institutions matter: union solidarity in Hungary and Eastern Germany', *British Journal of Industrial Relations*, Vol. 37, No. 1, pp. 117–140.

Gill, C. (1990) 'The new independent trade unionism in Hungary', *Industrial Relations Journal*, Vol. 21, No. 3, pp. 14–25.

Gill, C., Gold, M., and Cressey, P. (1999) 'Social Europe: national initiatives and responses', *Industrial Relations Journal* Vol. 30, No. 4, pp. 313–329.

Gilman, M. and Broughton, A. (2002) 'European industrial relations in 2001: a chronicle of events', *Industrial Relations Journal*, Vol. 33, No. 5, pp. 536–558.

Gilman, M. and Weber, T. (1999) 'European industrial relations in 1998: chronicle of events', *Industrial Relations Journal*, Vol. 30, No. 4, pp. 405–429.

Goetschy, J. (2002) 'A transition year for employment in Europe: EU governance and national diversity under scrutiny', *Industrial Relations Journal*, Vol. 33, No. 5, pp. 405–423.

Gold, M. (ed.) (1993) *The Social Dimension: Employment Policy in the European Union*. Basingstoke: Macmillan.

Goodhart, D. (1992) 'Community's social action plans succumb to sabotage and recession', *Financial Times*, 19 November, p. 8.

Goodhart, D. (1993) 'Social dumping: hardly an open and shut case', *Financial Times*, 4 February, p. 9.

Gospel, H. (1992) 'The Single European Market and industrial relations', *British Journal of Industrial Relations*, Vol. 30, No. 4, pp. 483–494.

Hall, M. (1994) 'Industrial relations and the social dimension of European integration: before and after Maastricht', in Hyman, R. and Ferner, A. (eds) *New Frontiers in European Industrial Relations*. Oxford: Blackwell, pp. 281–311.

Hegewisch, A. and Brewster, C. (eds) (1993) *European Developments in Human Resource Management*. London: Kogan Page.

Holden, L. (1991) *Bulgaria, Perestroika, Glasnost and Management*. Cranfield School of Management Working Paper SWP 14/91.

Holden, L. (1993) 'Bulgaria: economic and political change', *Critique: Journal of Socialist Theory*, No. 25, pp. 133–143.

Holden, L. (2003) *Vauxhall Motors and the Luton Economy*, 1900–2002. Woodbridge: Boydell & Brewer.

Holden, L. and Peck, H. (1990) 'Perestroika, glasnost, management and trade', *European Business Review*, Vol. 90, No. 2, pp. 26–31.

Hughes, J. (1991) *The Social Charter and the Single European Market*. Nottingham: Spokesman.

Hungarian Trade Unions Report (2001) Budapest: Hungarian Trade Unions.

Hyman, R. and Ferner, A. (eds) (1994) *New Frontiers in European Industrial Relations*. Oxford: Blackwell.

Jackson, T. (1993) 'Footloose across Europe's frontiers', *Financial Times*, 9 March.

Kelemen, M. (1999) 'The myth of restructuring "competent" managers and the transition to a market economy: a Romanian tale', *British Journal of Management*, Vol. 10, No. 3, pp. 199–208.

Keller, B. and Bansbach, M. (2001) 'Social dialogues: tranquil past, troubled present and uncertain future', *Industrial Relations Journal*, Vol. 32, No. 5, p. 45.

Kirkbride, P. (ed) (1994) *Human Resource Management in Europe*. London: Routledge.

Koubek, J. and Brewster, C. (1995) 'Human resource management in turbulent times: HRM in the Czech Republic', *International Journal of Human Resource Management*, Vol. 6, No. 2, pp. 223–247.

Labour Market Trends (1998) London: The Stationery Office, Vol. 106, No. 2, p. S40.

Labour Market Trends (1999) London: The Stationery Office, Vol. 107, No. 3, p. S46.

Landa, O. (1990) 'Human resource management in Czechoslovakia: management development as the key issue', in Pieper, R. (ed.) *Human Resource Management: An International Comparison*. New York: Walter de Gruyter, pp. 155–176.

Lane, C. (1989) *Management and Labour in Europe*. Aldershot: Edward Elgar.

*Leat, M. (1998) *Human Resource Issues of the European Union*. London: Financial Times/Pitman.

Leonard, E. (2001) 'Industrial relations and the regulation of employment in Europe', *European Journal of Industrial Relations*, Vol. 7, No. 1, pp. 27–44.

Lloyd, J. (1990) 'Trade unions: a tough transition', *Financial Times*, Soviet Union Supplement, 12 March, p. 10.

Lockhart, T. and Brewster, C., (1992) 'Human resource management in the European Community', in Brewster, C., Hegewisch, A., Holden, L. and Lockhart, T. (eds)

The European Human Resource Management Guide. London: Academic Press, pp. 6–41.

Marginson, P., Gilman, M., Jacobi, O. and Krieger, H. (1998) *Negotiating Works Councils: An Analysis of Agreements Under Article 13*. Dublin: European Foundation.

Marsland, D. (1991) 'The Social Charter: rights and wrongs', *The Salisbury Review*, June, pp. 16–18.

Martin, R. and Cristescu-Martin, A. (1999) 'Industrial relations in transformation: Central and Eastern Europe in 1998', *Industrial Relations Journal*, Vol. 30, No. 4, pp. 387–402.

Martin, R. and Cristescu-Martin, A. (2002) 'Employment relations in Central and Eastern Europe in 2001: an emerging capitalist periphery', *Industrial Relations Journal*, Vol. 33, No. 5, pp. 523–535.

Mason, B. (1995) 'Industrial relations in the unstable environment: the case of Central and Eastern Europe', *European Journal of Industrial Relations*, Vol. 1, No. 3, pp. 341–367.

Meyer, H. (1990) 'Human resource management in the German Democratic Republic: problems of availability and the use of manpower potential in the sphere of the high qualification spectrum in a retrospective view', in Pieper, R. (ed.) *Human Resource Management: An International Comparison*. New York: Walter de Gruyter, pp. 177–194.

Miller, D. and Stirling, J. (1998) 'European works council training: an opportunity missed?', *European Journal of Industrial Relations*, Vol. 4, No. 1, pp. 35–56.

Milne, A. (1992a) 'The past with a punch', *Guardian*, 13 March, p. 14.

Milne, A. (1992b) 'Delors' social Europe is workers' paradise lost', *Guardian*, 14 November, p. 13.

OECD (2000) Outlook, No. 69.

OECD (2003) *Standardised Unemployment Rates for OECD Countries*, Paris, www.oecd.org.

Piachaud, D. (1991) 'A Euro-Charter for confusion', *Guardian*, 13 November, p. 12.

Pieper, R. (1990) 'The history of business administration and management education in the two Germanies: a comparative approach', *International Journal of Human Resource Management*, Vol. 1, No. 2, pp. 211–229.

Pierson, C., Forster, A. and Jones, E. (1998) 'The politics of Europe: (un)employment ambivalence', in Towers, B. and Terry, M. (eds) *Industrial Relations Journal European Review 1997*. Oxford: Blackwell.

Pierson, C., Forster, A. and Jones, E. (1999) 'Politics of Europe 1999. Changing the guard in the European Union: in with the new, out with the old?', *Industrial Relations Journal*, Vol. 30, No. 4, pp. 277–290.

Price Waterhouse Cranfield Project (1991) *Report on International Strategic Human Resource Management*. Cranfield: Cranfield School of Management.

Rees, T. (1998) *Mainstreaming Equality in the European Union: Education, Training and Labour Market Policies*. London: Routledge.

Regini, M. (1995) 'Firms and institutions: the demand for skills and their social production in Europe', *European Journal of Industrial Relations*, Vol. 1, No. 2, pp. 191–202.

Sapsford, D., Bradley, S., Elliott, C. and Millington, J. (1999) 'The European economy: labour market efficiency, privatisation and minimum wages', *Industrial Relations Journal*, Vol. 30, No. 4, pp. 291–312.

Singh, R. (1999) 'European Community employment law: key recent cases and their implications for the UK', *Industrial Relations Journal*, Vol. 30, No. 4, pp. 273–386.

Sisson, K., Arrowsmith, J. and Marginson, P. (2003) 'All benchmarkers now? Benchmarking and the "Europeanisation" of industrial relations', *Industrial Relations Journal*, Vol. 34, No. 1 pp. 15–31.

Smith, C. and Thompson, P. (1992) *Labour in Transition: The Labour Process in Eastern Europe and China*. London: Routledge.

Sparrow, P. and Hiltrop, J.M. (1994) *European Human Resource Mangement in Transition*. Hemel Hempstead: Prentice Hall.

Standing, G. (1997) 'Labour market governance in Eastern Europe', *European Journal of Industrial Relations*, Vol. 3, No. 2, pp. 133–159.

Standing, G. (1999) *Global Labour Flexibility*. Basingstoke: Macmillan.

Teague, P. (1991) 'Human resource management, labour market institutions and European integration', *Human Resource Management Journal*, Vol. 2, No. 1, pp. 1–21.

Teague, P. (2001) 'Deliberate governance and EU social policy', *European Journal of Industrial Relations*, Vol. 7, No. 1, pp. 7–26.

*Thirkell, J., Petkov, K. and Vickerstaff, S. (1998) *The Transformation of Labour Relations: Restructuring and Privatization in Eastern Europe and Russia*. Oxford: Oxford University Press.

Towers, B. and Terry, M. (1999) 'Editorial: Unemployment and social dialogue', *Industrial Relations Journal*, Vol. 30, No. 4, pp. 272–275.

Traxler, F. (1999) 'Employers and employer organisations: the case of governability', *Industrial Relations Journal*, Vol. 30, No. 4, pp. 345–354.

Twenty Twenty Television (1993) 'The secret children', in the *Storyline Series* for Carlton Television.

Van Ruysseveldt, J. and Visser, J. (eds) (1996) *Industrial Relations in Europe: Traditions and Transitions*. London: Sage.

Watts, S. (1991) 'Clasping the competitive nettle', *The Times*, 1 August, p. 22.

Weir, F. (1992) 'When thunder roars', *Morning Star*, 9 May, p. 3.

Weston, C. (1993) 'Whitehall farce over EC job directive row', *Guardian*, 23 March, p. 8.

Willman, J. (1993) 'EC laws "will not delay tendering"', *Financial Times*, 12 March, p. 4.

Wise, M. and Gibb, R. (1992) *A Single Market to a Social Europe*. Harlow: Longman.

Wood, S. and Peccei, R. (1990) 'Preparing for 1992? Business-led versus strategic human resource management', *Human Resource Management Journal*, Vol. 1, No. 1, pp. 63–89.

Younson, F. (2002) 'Works councils: power struggles', *People Management*, 12 September, p. 2.

For multiple choice questions, exercises and annotated weblinks specific to this chapter visit this book's website at www.booksites.net/beardwell

CHAPTER 17

Human resource management in Asia

Len Holden and Linda Glover

OBJECTIVES

▶ To explore the extent of convergence of HRM practices in the Asia region.

▶ To examine the origins of and recent developments in Japanese human resource management.

▶ To explore the developments in human resource management in the People's Republic of China and Hong Kong.

▶ To explore developments in human resource management in Singapore and South Korea as examples of the growing 'tiger' economies.

Introduction

This chapter will examine the growth of some of the main Asian economies and in particular explore their human resource practices. Japan has become an exemplar of and model for HRM practices, and is the subject of so many published works that the observation of its organisational working practices has become an industry in itself, despite recent severe setbacks to the Japanese economy. Hong Kong has also witnessed extraordinary growth over the past 20 years, and has become a major centre in Asia for commerce and finance despite its absorption into the communist mainland regime. The People's Republic of China (PRC) has potentially the largest market in the world in terms of population, and foreign investors have been keen to gain a foothold there. Foreign companies have set up manufacturing bases and established joint ventures, and the export of Chinese goods has seen a huge expansion. This is an economy with an enormous potential. Its management processes have not been scrutinised to the same extent as the Japanese systems, but there is a burgeoning literature on management and HRM in China.

In addition, Singapore and South Korea are examined here as examples of other 'tiger' economies in the region, although space limits further investigation of important Asia Pacific economies such as Australia, India, Indonesia, Malaysia, New Zealand, the Philippines, Taiwan and Thailand.

◼ Convergence or divergence in the Asia Pacific Rim?

The assumption in the past was that management and employee relation practices could be transposed to any international context with requisite training and the implementation of proper systems of management, usually American. Another assumption by many Westerners was that Asian cultural influences on management could largely be ignored. This was a perspective strongly informed by imperialist attitudes that assumed that what was good for Western economies could automatically be transplanted into any socio-cultural context. As has already been noted in Chapter 15 on international HRM, these convergence assumptions have been rigorously challenged by divergence theorists from a cultural and institutional perspective, as well as by Whitley (1992) and his followers, who believe that each national context throws up its own unique business system. However, more recently there has been a return to the convergence view, much influenced by the phenomenon of 'globalisation' (a concept still largely ill defined and subject to much misunderstanding) and the relative decline of Japan in relation to the United States in the latter part of the 1990s. Separating and analysing the relative strength of convergent and divergent variables of international HRM has become the main focus of a number of studies in the Asia Pacific region (Warner, 1993; Easterby-Smith *et al.*, 1995; Leggett and Bamber, 1996; Paik *et al.*, 1996; Rowley, 1997; Sparrow and Wu, 1999; Warner, 2000).

Recent studies that have examined the specific question of divergence and convergence in the Asia Pacific region have come to the general conclusion that divergence of HRM practices remains predominant (Leggett and Bamber, 1996; Rowley, 1997; Warner, 2000). This is due to socio-cultural differences, varied investment patterns and financial institutional practices, and political and historical factors that have led to different stages of economic development. Leggett and Bamber (1996) claim that despite enormous growth, high investment from foreign companies and closer cooperation through the Association of South East Asian Nations (ASEAN) and the Asia-Pacific Economic Cooperation (APEC) forum, Asia Pacific economies diverge into three tiers or levels of development. The top tier, led predominantly by Japan, also includes Australia, Hong Kong, New Zealand, Singapore, Taiwan and South Korea. The non-Anglo-Saxon countries are generally known as the *Asian tigers*, and are made up of what has come to be called *newly industrialised economies* (NIEs). These have witnessed impressive growth rates in their economies over the past 20 years, and are moving into a second phase of development where the reliance on cheap labour is being superseded by investment in high technology and service industries.

The second tier is a second generation of tigers, comprising Malaysia, the PRC and Thailand. They reflect the earlier experience of the older tigers, and are at present at the stage of being 'caught in a "sandwich trap" of cheap labour competition from below and exclusion from higher value-added markets from above' (Deyo, 1995: 23).

The third tier, made up of Burma, India, Indonesia, the Philippines and Vietnam, comprises a diverse range of economies that have not reached the overall developmental stages of the first two tiers. Sections of the Indian economy, however, have experienced enormous growth in the past ten years, albeit from a comparatively low base, and some sectors are highly developed. What characterises this tier is the availability and abundance of cheap and unskilled labour. Nevertheless, to put these economies into one all-embracing category does not do justice to the diversity of their cultures, nor the political and social structures that create their unique business systems. As Warner (2000) states: 'There is hardly any evidence to support the classic convergence hypothesis . . . it is hard to argue that Asian HRM is fast converging to a common model' (p. 177). In separating forms of convergence into 'hard' and 'soft' ('hard' being labour market and economic influences exemplified by deregulation and privatisation and institutional structures, and 'soft' being more concerned with sociocultural variables) Warner (2000) concludes that the Asia-Pacific model is far from homogeneous [and that there is] a vast range of geographical and demographic variation. The economic systems range from emerging from a communist planned economy to fully fledged liberalised market-based ones. The political systems also differ greatly, as do the social arrangements. There is probably less cultural variation but more variety than acknowledged by many writers in the field. There is in this sense a fair degree of residual cultural diversity in the Asia-Pacific region that is likely to continue into the new millennium. On the other hand, if there is a common direction in which the HR systems are moving, it is most likely to be towards business restructuring, deregulation and liberalisation vis-à-vis the challenges of globalisation.   (p. 181)

In studying the management practices of the five Asian countries in this chapter we are also studying the uniqueness of each business system – the factors that make Chinese systems in Hong Kong different from those of the PRC and of Japan. We begin by examining the Japanese business system from the perspective of its human resource management practices.

Stop and think	What factors would prevent a true convergence of HRM practices in the Asia Pacific region?

Japan: economic growth and HRM

In the 1970s and 1980s the Japanese economy and its managerial and working practices came under intense investigation, mainly because of the phenomenal growth in its economy led by a number of Japanese multinationals in the vehicle and electronic industries. Incursions were made into previously dominated European and US markets, and by the 1980s, according to Vogel (1980), Japan had become 'number one nation' by outstripping US growth. The Japanese phenomenon generated an entire literature devoted to understanding and explaining this miracle, ranging from prescriptive eulogistic texts such as Ouchi's (1981) *Theory Z* to more critical analyses rooted in careful research (Dore, 1973; Gerlach, 1992). Much of this literature concentrated on the role of human resource management in creating higher Japanese employee productivity, product quality and company expansion. This has usually been encapsulated in the pattern of employee relations in the form of the *three pillars*: lifetime employment, the seniority system (*nenko*) and enterprise unionism. However, this simplistic view of the Japanese system of employee relations has been criticised by numerous observers from various positions, including historical, cultural, economic and labour market perspectives (Berggren and Nomura, 1997; Sako and Sato, 1997).

■ The classical Japanese model: the three pillars

The basis for the three-pillar approach has been described by Abegglen and Stalk (1987) thus:

First, the employee is hired directly from school, rather than from an open job market. Second, he [sic] is hired for his general characteristics and abilities, rather than for a particular skill or a particular job. Third, he is expected to remain with the company for a lifelong career and in turn expects not to be laid off or discharged.   (p. 199)

● The establishment of enterprise unionism

The company is also the basic unit for employee representation through company unionism, which forms the third pillar of the Japanese employee relations system, together with lifetime employment and the seniority wage system. While industrial unions exist in Japan, most large corporations allow only one union based around the enterprise itself.

The origins of enterprise unionism date back to the 1920s (Gordon, 1985), although the system as we recognise it today stems from the period after the Second World War. The American occupation enacted a trade union law allowing trade unions the right to exist with full legal rights, and by 1949 trade union density had risen to 56 per cent, but by the late 1980s had fallen to 27 per cent (Tsuru and Rebitzer, 1995).

There are two major controversial reasons for this growth and decline in trade unions. Growth took place after the Second World War. First, workers wanted to safeguard their rights amid the collapse of the industrial structure and wholesale inflation. Second, for the first time blue-collar and white-collar workers cooperated in controlling production for the sake of their own living standards. It therefore made sense to combine into one enterprise union. Third, the unions demanded a number of conditions:

- removal of the old grades and status;
- job security;
- reform of management organisation;
- the setting up of participation systems;
- recognition of the unions;
- the right to negotiate and conduct labour agreements;
- the democratisation of management;
- expansion of workers' rights.

The best way for the two groups of workers (white and blue collar) to cooperate to gain and maintain these initiatives was at the enterprise level.

Employers also encouraged enterprise unions, primarily because in the 1950s there was high employment and high demand for labour in a rapidly expanding economy. However, employers also saw the advantages of promoting enterprise unionism, and they ensured that labour relations were conducted vertically, thus weakening the horizontal solidarity of the workers. It also emphasised cooperation in the workplace: supporting the desire for consensus made it easier to remove workers who propagated radical ideas and were aggressive towards management. This also had the effect of creating a unitarist style of organisation.

However, the path of industrial relations was not always smooth, and up to the 1960s there were often disputes, sometimes of a violent nature. The cooperative industrial relations that have been identified with Japanese management style only began in, and developed after, the 1960s. Thus the so-called 'traditional model' is really quite a recent phenomenon.

The decline in union density began after 1975, and a number of reasons for this have been put forward by Tsuru and Rebitzer (1995). First, and most important, has been the inability of unions to organise in new firms. Second, unions have had a limited effect on wage levels. This perceived lack of influence limits the attractiveness of union membership. The non-effectiveness of unions, particularly in times of crisis, as in the recessions of the 1970s and the 1990s, has shown the unions to be 'overly accommodating' to the employer's position rather than rigorously protecting their members.

● Community consciousness

Enterprise unionism has thus been seen to be synonymous with unitarist HRM practices, reinforcing company objectives and allowing for only limited independent action on behalf of the workforce. This paternalist nature of large Japanese corporations creates an understanding between employer and employed. Sako (1997) describes this relationship as existing within a community – that is, the corporation:

> For a community to be viable, there has to be a two way process between management and workers. In particular not only should the firm offer employment security and a career to its employees, the employees must also expect employment security and identify with the firm. The boundary of a firm as community, and hence the criterion for full membership in the community, are defined by the matching in mutual expectations between the firms and its employees.
>
> (p. 4)

Sako (1997) believes that this mutual interest between employer and employee cannot be expressed in terms of the psychological contract, which has elements of instrumental bargaining rather than shared values, or even common interest (p. 5). A more apposite description, he believes, is the term *community consciousness*, in that employees identify closely with the organisation, and the 'community' extends beyond the firm into shaping individual identity, and influences life beyond the workplace itself. In return for this employment security the company expects worker commitment and flexibility.

This community consciousness is reinforced by internal labour markets that encourage the development of employees through training and development, mentoring, and teamworking, leading to progression through the organisation, until 55 or 60 years of age when the intensity of work is reduced in preparation for retirement. Promotion is based heavily on seniority, as are wages and salaries and other forms of remuneration. However, *nenko* is not just about seniority; it is also increasingly about merit. Within the first 10 or 15 years of employment each employee cohort will move together, but after that promotion is based on merit. This gives management a long period to screen people for selection to senior positions.

This community consciousness is also reinforced by employee participation at workplace levels. This form of participation (*ringi*) is less about workplace democracy in the Western sense and more about reaching consensus (*nemawashi*) and harmony (*wa*) in the decision-making processes.

Stop and think | What contemporary factors are undermining the traditional three-pillar approach to HRM in Japan?

Perspectives on Japanese HRM

This view of the classical Japanese model of HRM is, of course, simplistic, and critics of the system have challenged the outward appearances of harmony and cooperation, particularly in the light of the economic crisis that began in the 1990s and is continuing into the new millennium. In 1999 unemployment had risen from a consistently low level to 5 per cent and probably double that for young workers, and the percentage of temporary and part-time workers rose to 7 per cent (*Japan Labour Bulletin*, 1999). Before examining some of these criticisms it is appropriate to explain how the Japanese classical model originated and developed.

● Analytical approaches to understanding the Japanese system of HRM

In general, four approaches have been taken in analysing the origins, influences and development of Japanese HRM: history and tradition, the influence of culture on work attitudes, industrialisation as bound up with the 'late developer' thesis, and politico-economic arguments (Stam, 1982). Others might describe these influences as cultural, institutional and politico-economic influences, or attribute developments to the unique business system of Japan which incorporates most of these factors (Whitley, 1992).

The historical view

This view emphasises the unique historical context within which Japanese HRM has emerged, and highlights the pre-industrial influences of the Samurai as an elite group in a feudal society, with its emphasis on fealty (duty and loyalty) and a strict code of conduct, the *Bushido* – the way of the warrior. In a sense the continuity through history lies in the development of large family-owned companies, the *zaibatsu*, which acted as small fiefdoms that emphasised these historical values.

This feudal form of managerial 'familyism' (the organisation perceived as one big family) was a means of integrating employees into the quickly expanding enterprises. After the First World War this was extended to include *welfare corporatism*, in which the enterprise provided protection through welfare measures as befits family duty.

The cultural view

The cultural view incorporates some of the concepts of the historical perspective, and in reality they cannot be separated.

Geographical and commercial isolation until the late nineteenth century, and racial and linguistic homogeneity, have resulted in a unique culture in which the Japanese strongly value the social nexus or social structure in which they function. This can be in either the family, a circle of school friends or the company where one works. Such bonding groups provide certainty and security.

Second, there is a strong emphasis on anti-individualism. In other words, the group has a strong priority over the individual. This can be associated with Hofstede's and Trompenaars' forms of collectivism as the opposite characteristic to individualism. These relations are structured through hierarchy in the enterprise. However, while different grades of status exist, all members of the organisational community are valued.

Third, and as we have already noted, harmony and consensus are significant in Japanese culture. The importance of preserving these values is reflected in the intensive informational and communication networks within and between groups in the organisation. Nothing is acted upon until consensus has been reached (see Chapter 14 on employee involvement for further reference to this). Group orientation and consensus support loyalty to the enterprise and further act to underpin lifetime employment and collective responsibility.

The late developer view

This is often associated with the institutional and business systems perspective of HRM. The work of Dore (1973) proved seminal in developing this perspective in his examination of the origins of national diversity in industrial relations in a comparative analysis of Britain and Japan. In essence this view maintains that countries that start to industrialise late show a number of specific institutional and organisational characteristics caused by the fact that they can benefit from the experiences of their industrial predecessors. The state's role in helping to foment the conditions favourable for enterprise growth is also significant. The Meji governments of the late nineteenth century set up the core of Japanese industry, transferred it to private interests, and provided these enterprises with government contracts. These eventually developed into the zaibatsu, such as Mitsui, Mitsubishi and Sumitomo. Companies formed after the Second World War, such as Matsushita, Sony and Honda, in having to adapt quickly to expansion adopted the models of corporate structure that already existed, and became part of the mutual nurturing growth mechanism between the state and large private corporations.

These large enterprises allow no direct personal relationships to develop, instead of which an extensive administrative apparatus is required. Standardisation and formalisation in the Japanese enterprises have led to precise relations, ranging from a clear-cut career structure based on *nenko* (seniority) to a diversity of benefits such as allowances for housing, family and study. From the 1920s this developed into a form of welfare corporatism in which the company performs many of the welfare functions that in other industrial economies are performed by the state. This has the effect of binding the workforce into the objectives, values and culture of the company. The nurturing relationship of the state and companies is thus important in the late developer's view of how corporate HRM systems develop in Japan.

The politico-economic view

As with the historical and cultural views there is a considerable degree of overlap between the late developer view and the politico-economic view. Both emphasise, for example, the importance of the role of the state in developing privately owned capitalist enterprises. This form of development has often been called *alliance capitalism* (Gerlach, 1992; Berggren and Nomura, 1997). Another feature of alliance capitalism is the weaker control of shareholders over managerial decision and company strategy formulation compared with US and British companies. Whereas US and UK companies are conscious of the requirement to provide high dividends for their shareholders in the short term, Japanese corporations have been less subject to these immediate financial pressures, and can consequently indulge more effectively in long-term strategy-making.

This in turn enables them to take a long-term view in considering HRM policy and practice, and two of the three pillars – lifetime employment and the seniority system – could only exist within such a politico-economic national context.

Stop and think	Which of the above perspectives do you think convincingly explains the origins, influences and development of Japanese HRM?

● Criticisms of the Japanese system

There have been many observers who have been sceptical of the Japanese miracle and its ability to last. These views command a wide breadth of opinion in the politico-economic spectrum.

Left-wing critics tend to the view that the Japanese system has been strongly bolstered by US capital since the Second World War as a bulwark against communism, especially in the wake of the fall of China to Mao Zedong's forces in 1949. US wealth in essence nurtured and sustained the 'miracle' for essentially political reasons.

Other commentators in a similar vein have criticised the three-pillar model as being only partly representative of the workforce of Japan as a whole, as it excludes peripheral workers, many blue-collar workers, women, and those who do not work for large corporations, where the model predominantly operates. Small-firm suppliers, it is claimed, bear the exploitative costs of the system, where workers lack the security of the large corporations, and are often the first to be made redundant in times of restructuring. Chalmers (1989) also found clear divisions between core and peripheral workers. Peripheral workers tended to be segmented by age, gender, education and skill, and they were most likely to exist in small firms. Recent critics have claimed that Japanese companies cannot sustain the expensive three-pillar model in the face of recent financial and economic disasters. Benson (1996) believes that limiting the core of workers in corporations, emphasising the greater number of peripheral workers and operating lean practices with smaller supplier firms is a labour strategy to offload the high costs of lifetime employment and the seniority wage system.

One extreme US critic, Kroll (1993), claims that the 'final, frantic climax of capitalism without cost' ended with the collapse of the 'bubble economy' in 1986–90. He also claims that the low-cost capital that accounted for Japan's unique HRM systems could not be sustained after this period, and that Japanese companies will have to compete on Western terms – another slant on the convergence view.

Other commentators believe that this view is a gross exaggeration. Kawakita (1997) claims that while Japanese companies have been adapting their strategies to changes in the economy, with for example increases in peripheral workers, this must be seen in context. The high cost of the three-pillar system has been recognised by employers for a long time, but there is still a strong belief that companies do not lay off redundant workers as this would destroy the whole psychological basis of the high-trust work system that has been so painstakingly built up. Companies thus proceed with caution even in times of crisis, and resort to large-scale redundancies and restructuring only when no other course can be taken. Berggren and Nomura (1997) also believe that the system with adaptations is still resilient.

Free-market critics emphasise the obstructive forces posed by Japanese governments to free trade: the imposition of barriers on foreign imports, while Western economies accept Japanese goods, and also welcome Japanese investment. This lack of free trade reciprocation came under fire by US critics in the 1980s when Japan overtook the US lead in terms of growth.

Recent trends in Japanese HRM

There has been an awareness for some time of the negative influence of demographic trends and increased globalisation on the Japanese economy and labour market. The population is ageing, and this is having and will continue to have enormous implications for human resource policy and practice in Japanese companies.

As Table 17.1 indicates, there is an older labour force and fewer young people entering the labour market. This is putting, and will continue to put, a strain on the pensions system and the *nenko* system as remuneration rises with age. There is a shortage of senior positions. There has also been a significant increase in female labour participation, and new technology has replaced a considerable number of jobs. The rise of the service sector and relative decline of the older industries have also had an impact on the economy (Sano, 1993). Highly educated younger workers are less likely to stay with one company for long periods, thus creating greater fluidity in the labour markets.

Table 17.1 The Japanese population and labour force

Year	Population			Labour force		
	1980	1990	2000[a]	1980	1990	2000[a]
Age 55 or over (%)	17.7	23.6	28.7	16.1	20.2	23.6
Age 65 or over (%)	9.1	12.0	16.3	4.9	5.6	8.0

[a] Estimates

Source: Sasajima, 1993

Stop and think In what ways could demographic changes affect Japanese HRM?

There is also a significant and growing number of female workers who are seeking senior positions and a career structure. There has been a considerable increase of women in the expanding service sector such as banking, retailing, insurance, especially in the 25–29 age group. Women's rising level of education, the drive for equal opportunities, and female take-up in employment have increased pressures for equal opportunities policies. This was backed by equal opportunities legislation in 1985, and companies are now required to provide equal opportunities in recruitment, employment, work assignments and promotion. The law also forbids sexual discrimination with regard to training and education, employee welfare benefits, retirement age, resignations and dismissals. This is further supported by the provision of childcare leave.

The traditional internal labour markets of large Japanese corporations are at a turning point, and some characteristics that were considered unique to Japanese companies may be disappearing. The hierarchical structure of companies has been considerably flattened, and formerly bureaucratic organisations have become more flexible units, with project teams working with subsidiary and subcontracting companies. The compensation system is also changing to cope with these influences. Shibata (2000) states that 'generally it appears that employees' age and seniority have become less important while their performance has become more influential in Japanese wage determination' (p. 312). As Table 17.2 indicates, Sano (1993) has systematised these changes.

Table 17.2 Changes in HRM patterns in large Japanese firms

Past	Present
Internal labour markets	Enlargement of related internal labour markets (related firms)
Hierarchical pyramid-type organisation	Flat organisation
Lifetime employment	Variety of employment contracts
Job segmentation	Flexible job categories
In-house on-the-job training	Emphasis on out-of-house interaction
Manual skilled oriented	Conceptual skill oriented
Internal human network	External human network
Firm-specific skills	Firm-specific culture
Systematic job rotation	Failure of internal career development plan
Manufacturing factory model	Flexible unit model
Mass production oriented	Value-added oriented
Long-range evaluation of performance	Short-range evaluation of human resource performance
Money value of work for employees	Non-pecuniary value of work for employees
Bureaucratic control	Partnership relations

A solution to the problem of the ageing work force has been raising the pensionable age. In 1985 the retirement age was raised to 60 years, with the possibility of its being raised to 65 years in the future. As we have already noted, there have been modifications to the seniority wage system. Many companies have now set an age where wages start decreasing, or at least increasing at a rate less than average. There have also been revisions to the retirement benefits policy – for example, reducing the proportion of salary that makes up the lump sum received on retirement.

Because there are not enough senior positions for the 'baby boomer' generation (those born after the Second World War and now aged 40 and over), many companies are beginning to emphasise ability and other factors besides age and service for promotion.

Many companies are requiring resignation from a senior position at a certain age to make room for younger managers.

Some observers believe that, as a result of these changes, it will spell the end of the classic Japanese model based on the three pillars. Many authoritative writers (Berggren and Nomura, 1997; Sako and Sato, 1997; Kuwahara, 1998), however, while accepting that change is inevitable, still believe that the ingredients and uniqueness of the Japanese system remain largely intact. As Sako (1997) states: 'The principle of lifetime employment continues to be upheld by management because without it, the motivational basis of workers' and unions' cooperation would falter . . . but in order to maintain the life-time employment principle, pressures are placed elsewhere in the system' (p. 11).

While the employee relations system will evolve and change slowly, there is no sign that it is converging towards the US model.

China: economic growth and HRM

Introduction

The People's Republic of China (PRC) has an area of 9 561 000 square kilometres, and had an estimated population of 1.3 billion people in 2001 (Thornhill, 2002a). Its capital is Beijing, which had a population of 13 800 000 in 2001 (*Financial Times*, 1999a). China has experienced rapid economic, political and social development in the past two decades. The death of Mao Zedong in 1976 heralded the beginning of a period of economic reform led by Deng Xiaoping. During this period China adopted an 'open door' policy for encouraging trade and technology transfer. The management of the economy moved from a centrally planned *command economy* to a *socialist market economy* (CCCC, 1993). Annual economic growth has averaged 9 per cent since 1978. Domestic spending rose by five times in the 1990s. There has been a rapid increase in the number of foreign-invested enterprises in China (Ding and Warner, 1999). Foreign investment in early 1996 was US\$ 7.74 billion. This had risen to record levels of US\$ 46.8 billion by 2001 and is predicted to rise to \$53.8 billion by 2003 (Thornhill, 2002a). China was the largest recipient of foreign investment after the United States. The levels of China's foreign currency reserves were second only to those of Japan in 1999 (Kynge, 1999). China's main trading partners were the United States, Japan and the EU to which it exported goods totalling 20.4, 16.9 and 15.4 per cent of its output respectively in 2001 (Thornhill, 2002a). It was anticipated that the value of merchandise exports would rise from \$266.2 billion in 2001 to \$324.2 billion in 2003 and that these levels could increase significantly in years to come as a result of China's entry into the World Trade Organisation (WTO) in December 2001.

The speed of economic development slowed down slightly after 1998. While China was not severely affected by the economic crisis in Asia during 1997–8, it was exhibiting certain institutional weaknesses. The World Bank highlighted three main problems in its report 'China: weathering the storm and learning the lessons' (1999). These were:

● weaknesses in corporate governance, and a poor definition of ownership and accountability;
● government interference in investment decisions;
● a lack of speed in terms of setting up satisfactory mechanisms by which to regulate the financial sector.

In conjunction with these institutional weaknesses, there were associated problems of corruption within the system. It was estimated that one-fifth (Rmb 117bn) of central government revenues had been misused in the first eight months of 1999 (Kynge, 1999).

The lack of legal regulation meant that foreign businesses often experienced problems when setting up businesses within China (Murray, 1994; Peng, 1994). These included dealing with broken contracts, incurring bad debts, and completing property developments. However, there is evidence that government is beginning to make progress with such issues, spurred by the need to implement rules and regulations in order to comply with its membership of the WTO.

China is now facing a changing climate of export opportunities and foreign investment on the one hand and industrial restructuring, downsizing and unemployment on the other. Some commentators have observed that the massive influx of foreign investment could 'undermine the viability of the country's remaining state-owned enterprises which still employ millions of workers' (Thornhill, 2002b: vi) and that membership of the WTO could accelerate the speed of redundancies in state-owned enterprises (SOEs). The industrial restructuring and related unemployment could be potentially critical given the lack of an adequate social security net at present (Mok *et al.*, 2002).

However, it is anticipated membership of the WTO will lead to soaring export growth as restrictive quotas set by other countries are reduced or scrapped (Lardy, 2002). Other developing countries in Asia fear that foreign direct investment will centre upon China and that they will find it difficult to compete against Chinese exporters (Burton *et al.*, 2001). The question is whether the predicted 'export boom' will be sufficiently able to mediate the predicted levels of unemployment. Later in this section we provide an overview of some of the key business and HR issues that are impacting upon China today.

■ The 'iron rice-bowl' to 'socialism with Chinese characteristics'

An historical overview serves to provide a framework for understanding some of the contemporary human resource issues that are impacting upon China. The historical review begins by focusing upon the period during which Mao Zedong was in power. Child (1994: 36–38) suggests that one can categorise four main phases of industrial governance during this period. These are summarised below.

● Phase 1: Central planning 1953–56

Mao Zedong came to power in 1949. He advocated that China should move to an economy based upon socialist ownership. The *Five Year Plan* was launched in 1953. This included moves towards centralised planning and control from the state. Trade unions did exist, but their role was confined to dealing with welfare issues. Complicated piece-rate systems were used to reward many workers.

● Phase 2: Decentralisation and the Great Leap Forward 1957–61

The system of industrial governance that developed as part of the five-year plan was influenced by the Soviet system. Child argues that this tended to be very hierarchical, and as such was not in sympathy with a Chinese culture in which collectivism was a central feature. The Great Leap Forward was a period within which many of the collectivist values came to the fore. During 1957–61 control for much of industry passed from central to provincial government. However, a great emphasis was placed upon allegiance to the Communist Party, and factory directors had to report to party committees. The system of bonus payments was reduced.

● Phase 3: The period of readjustment 1962–65

The 1959–61 period saw a drop in agricultural output, followed by a famine. This was partly caused by an overemphasis on expanding the manufacturing sector during the Great Leap Forward. The period of readjustment saw moves back towards more centralised planning; however, factory directors were given more control over day-to-day production issues.

● Phase 4: The Cultural Revolution 1966–76

The Cultural Revolution was a distinctive period, during which politics and ideology were the predominant concerns. There was a great emphasis upon allegiance to the Party. Factories moved away from hierarchical control towards using factory revolutionary committees as the management mechanism. In terms of rewards, 'competitive, individual and material incentive was rejected in favour of cooperative, collective and moral incentive' (Child, 1994: 37). Therefore, a context of collectivism and control developed. Child comments that

> The Cultural Revolution was seen to have dissipated incentive and responsibility for economic performance through egalitarianism, the weakening of management, the general devaluation of expertise and the claim that ideological fervour and inspired leadership could substitute for technical knowledge . . . The xenophobia of the period had denied the country opportunities for inward investment and technology transfer.   (p. 39)

Child's summary of the *four phases of industrial governance* gives an insight into the context that developed during the rule of Mao Zedong. The role of the state was central throughout. The state managed the economy, and increasingly enforced its ideology upon the citizens. China was relatively undisturbed by foreign influence during this period. Child notes that social and political discipline was used as an effective force for controlling the Chinese people.

One of the legacies of Mao's rule was the system that became known as the *iron rice-bowl*. This related to the provision of lifetime employment and cradle-to-grave welfare structures (Ding *et al.*, 2000). The enterprise played both an economic and a social role, and would provide its employees with housing, medical support and education provision. Central to the enterprise were work units (*danwei*). The *danweis* formed the core of the community. Ding *et al.* (2000) comment that a number of writers have suggested that the iron rice-bowl encouraged a high degree of 'organisational dependency' (p. 218). They argue that organisational dependency is a deep-seated feature of the Chinese system, and that it has encouraged attitudes and behaviours that are difficult to change. The implications of organisational dependency interlinked with many of the HR issues that are discussed below.

China's industrial production was dominated by state-owned enterprises. These accounted for 80 per cent of industrial production in 1978 (Warner, 1997). Under the full employment system that emerged, the dismissal of workers was allowed only if a worker had committed 'gross negligence', but this term was open to interpretation, and the sanction was rarely used even if the individuals concerned were undisciplined. In order to avoid the problems that are associated with unemployment, a system of 'featherbedding' was used, which resulted in enterprises that were overstaffed, with low levels of productivity (Child, 1994). Wages were based on seniority, and there was no real incentive for employees to strive for promotion. There was no concept of a labour market, and individuals were not allowed to move within China to 'follow work'. Trade unions existed, but had a different role from their Western counterparts:

> The All China Federation of Trade Unions (ACFTU) were assigned two functions: by top-down transmission, mobilisation of workers for labour production on behalf of the State, and by bottom-up transmission, protection of workers' rights and interests.
>
> (Chan, quoted in Warner, 1997: 37)

Therefore the union role centred upon production and welfare issues. They would not be involved in negotiations on pay and conditions, as would be the norm in Western countries.

Stop and think

What are the key characteristics associated with the 'iron rice-bowl'? What behaviours did it encourage?

Identify some of the key HR issues related to this period.

● Post-1976: 'Socialism with Chinese characteristics'

After the death of Mao Zedong in 1976, Deng Xiaoping assumed power in China. Under his leadership China embarked on an economic reform programme. This included the commencement of an 'open door' policy in which international trade and the influx of foreign technology were encouraged. The term 'socialism with Chinese characteristics' was first used by Deng Xiaoping in 1982 to describe the approach to economic reform. China allowed joint ventures to operate from the early 1980s onwards. From this point, foreign invested enterprises (FIEs) became widespread. Foreign companies provided technology and managerial knowledge (Ding et al., 2000).

In 1999 the government amended the constitution to formally recognise the concept of private ownership. Employment in the private sector rose from 150 000 to 32.3 million in the period from 1980 to 1999 (Montagnon, 1999a). FIEs were important in terms of providing employment, technology and modern management techniques.

However, the process of modernisation has not been painless. One of the key problems was that the SOEs were overmanned and underinvested. Reports suggest that the number of bankruptcies in the PRC rose from 98 in 1989 to 8939 in 2001 and approximately 60 per cent of these were in SOEs (Thornhill, 2002a). In the period between 1998 and 2001, 25 million employees lost their jobs in SOEs. In 2002, 150 000 SOEs remained, employing 50 million workers. Workers in the SOEs had been socialised into the iron rice-bowl mentality, in which they expected that the organisation would provide cradle-to-grave employment and welfare. One of the aims of the modernisation programme was to move away from this. In 1992 personnel legislation was introduced that became known as the *three systems reforms*. The three key areas were: the introduction of labour contracts, performance-related rewards, and social insurance reforms. Warner (1996) provides a useful summary of the key differences between the traditional system and the emerging system of labour reforms within China (see Table 17.3).

The 1994 Labour Law provided a further spur to the modernisation. It aimed to provide regulation for 'a labour system compatible with a social market economy' (Warner, 1997: 33). The law covered a variety of issues, including the right for workers to choose jobs, equal opportunities, minimum wage levels, directives on working hours, and provisions for dispute handling and resolution. Warner comments that one of the implications of the 1994 Labour Law was that the distribution of power would be readjusted so that the trade unions could have more autonomy from the state.

The process of modernisation has meant that there is no longer a 'job for life'. Other aspects of the iron rice-bowl are also beginning to wane. From 1998 the *danweis* were no longer allowed to allocate subsidised housing, and allowances for education and medical support were slowly being reduced (Kynge, 1999). The modernisation programme led to

Table 17.3 Summary of the differences in characteristics of the labour-management reforms

System characteristic	Status quo	Experimental
1 Strategy	Hard-line	Reformist
2 Employment	Iron rice-bowl	Labour market
3 Conditions	Job security	Labour contracts
4 Mobility	Job assignment	Job choice
5 Rewards	Egalitarian	Meritocractic
6 Wage system	Grade based	Performance based
7 Promotion	Seniority	Skill-related
8 Union role	Consultative	Coordinative
9 Management	Economic cadres	Professional managers
10 Factory party-role	Central	Ancillary
11 Work organisation	Taylorist	Flexible
12 Efficiency	Technical	Allocative

Source: Warner, 1996: 33

SOEs being restructured and downsized. However, it is estimated that SOEs currently have 20 million employees excess to requirements (Montagnon, 1999a). Mok *et al.*, (2002: 411) found that a 'strong sense of destitution and betrayal [was] experienced by most state workers who used to be the 'labour aristocracy' in China'. They go on to note that the sense of inequity has been fanned by the media attention that has focused upon successful millionaires. There is a concern that unemployed workers from the SOEs may not pass easily into the labour market. Evidence of worker unrest is emerging; for example, 216 750 strikes and demonstrations were recorded in 1998 which included 3.5 million workers. Within this number, there were some instances of violence and 78 deaths occurred (Mok *et al.*, 2002).

The government has set up a system of social security. The cost of the social security bill rose by 23 per cent in 1998, and unemployment rose from 3.1 per cent in 1998 to 5.5 per cent in 1999 (Montagnon, 1999a). Clearly, unemployment will remain as a key concern for some time to come, especially given the huge levels of surplus labour within the SOEs. Chinese officials are predicting that 10 million people may be affected by unemployment in urban areas in the period up to 2006 (Mok *et al.*, 2002). A process of modernisation is taking place, but the size and historical development of China mean that this is a slow process. The legacy of the iron rice-bowl is still apparent, and complete reform is still a long way off.

Stop and think

Identify key strengths and weaknesses in the Chinese economy.

What human resource issues emerge from this context?

HRM with 'Chinese characteristics'?

Economic reforms in China have allowed the influx of foreign interests, and have set a new context in which both indigenous Chinese and foreign invested companies manage the employment relationship. There is a debate as to whether employment systems in the Asian bloc are converging towards common approaches to HRM or, alternatively, whether they are becoming more divergent as time goes by. Some have argued that an Asian model of HRM exists. The Asian model has been characterised by: non-adversarial relationships; low union density, or unions (as in China) that are closely controlled by the state; and low instances of overt industrial conflict. However, as we have already noted, academics are now beginning to appreciate that the Asian bloc is far from homogeneous, and differences in IR/HRM systems reflect different national histories and cultures (Leggett and Bamber, 1996; Rowley, 1997; Warner, 2000). Part of the remit of this section is to explore the extent to which employment systems in China are becoming more 'Westernised'. This seems possible for two main reasons: first, the high levels of foreign investment in the country, and second, the fact that the modernisation programme has increasingly subjected the SOEs in particular to the logic of the market.

The debate regarding the extent to which Chinese enterprises are adopting HRM is a problematic one. Academic perspectives on this issue relate back to the wider debate about the nature of HRM itself. Child (1994) questions the extent to which one can utilise the term 'HRM' as a descriptor for the management of personnel in Chinese enterprises:

> Although definitions of personnel management and human resource management vary considerably, modern Western thinking tends to be predicated upon assumptions such as the primary contribution of competent and motivated people to a firm's success, the compatibility of individual and corporate interests, the importance of developing a corporate culture which is in tune with top management's strategy for the firm, and the responsibility of senior management rather than employees' own representative bodies for determining personnel practices. It attaches importance to systematic recruitment and selection, training and development (including socialisation into corporate culture), close attention to motivation through personal involvement and participation in work and its organisation, appraisal and progression procedures and incentive schemes . . . This concept of human resource management is not found in Chinese enterprises.   (p. 157)

Therefore authors such as Child believe that the term 'HRM' is unsuitable as a model for analysis to be used within the Chinese context. Others, however, are explicitly using mainstream HRM models in order to analyse human resource issues within China. Benson and Zhu (1999) use Storey's model of HRM, which categorises four key elements of HRM (beliefs and assumptions, strategic aspects, management role, and key levers), in order to evaluate the extent to which six SOEs were adopting HRM practices. They refute Child's assertion that the concept of HRM is not found within Chinese enterprises. By reference to the Storey model, they conclude that there were three models of HRM within their sample. The first model was a minimalist approach, in which two of the SOEs had made few attempts to adopt an HRM approach. The second model was one in which two companies had attempted to adopt an HRM paradigm. Part of this was related to the fact that both of these companies were relatively small, and had strong connections with foreign companies via joint ventures or contracting arrangements. The third model represented a transitional stage between the old and the new. Benson and Zhu argue that there is evidence that some enterprises had developed the concept of and practices associated with HRM, and the extent to which this had happened depended upon factors such as market forces and changes in legislation. Their evidence does not, however, suggest that HRM is the dominant paradigm, and they acknowledge that factors such as China's historical development and cultural traditions can act as a barrier to the development of a Western model of HRM.

Clearly, the extent to which China is adopting an 'HRM' approach is a matter of some debate. The evidence seems to suggest that some enterprises may be adopting some of the practices that are associated with Western models of HRM, but it is unlikely that full-blown models are widespread. Some authors have focused upon the linkages between HRM and organisational performance within the Chinese context. Bjorkman and Xiucheng (2002), for example, found some support for the notion that organisational performance appeared to be positively influenced where companies had a strong integration between HRM and strategy. They also suggested positive relationships between performance-based rewards, individual performance appraisal and organisational performance. They do, however, acknowledge the relatively small size of their sample and the relative lack of understanding at present about the intervening variables that 'knit together' HRM and organisational performance. The following sections will review some of the evidence regarding different aspects of contemporary HR/personnel practice within China.

● Employment contracts, surplus labour and social insurance

Part of the modernisation process has included the shift to a more decentralised and flexible labour market. The employment contract system was formally implemented in 1986, and it gave employers the ability to hire employees on contracts that specified the terms of employment. Under this system, enterprises were able to downsize and remove problematic employees (Ding and Warner, 1999). The drive to modernise the labour market was further progressed by the provision of subsequent legislation such as the personnel legislation of 1992 and the 1994 Labour Law. This meant that both individual and collective labour contracts could be set up. The collective contracts would cover employees belonging to an enterprise, and would be arranged via the trade union. Collective contracts would cover areas such as pay and conditions, working hours, holidays and welfare (Ding and Warner, 1999: 249).

As highlighted above, one outcome of the reform programme has been that a substantial number of redundancies have been made. Seventeen million employees of SOEs had been laid off by the end of 1998 (Benson and Zhu, 1999). Prior to the economic reforms, the enterprise took responsibility for welfare issues such as pensions and medical cover. Since the reforms, the government has had to set up a system of social insurance. The funds for social insurance are contributed to by the state, the enterprise and individual employees (Ding and Warner, 1999). Social insurance is designed to act as a safety net, particularly for employees who are made redundant. One of the issues that China will have to deal with is the rising cost of social insurance (Montagnon, 1999a). For example, the cost of moving towards a fully funded pension system by 2030 could reach Rmb 3000 billion (Thornhill, 2002a). In conjunction with this is the fear of further social unrest resulting from mass redundancies (Mok et al., 2002).

● Recruitment, selection and training

One of the impacts of the reforms has been that there is now greater mobility within the labour market. Prior to the reforms, workers were assigned to firms from labour bureaus. This often meant that workers were assigned even when they did not hold the requisite skill and knowledge for the job. While there is the possibility for greater labour mobility now, evidence suggests that mobility remains fairly low, especially in the shopfloor workers category (Tsang, 1994; Ding and Warner, 1999; Benson et al., 2000). Table 17.4 demonstrates the continuing role of external agencies in the recruitment process.

Evidence suggests that mobility is higher within the managerial ranks. There are reports, however, that joint ventures continue to find it difficult to recruit employees of SOEs (Tsang, 1994). This is due to a number of reasons, including SOEs retaining employee files, which means that the employee can be cut off from a range of benefits.

Zhu and Dowling (2002) have suggested that recruitment and selection practices were becoming less influenced by political bureaucracy and more influenced by economic and market concerns. For example, there is more emphasis upon personal competency as a criteria, rather than an individual's political background. This trend was more evident within foreign invested enterprises. Overall, China has a large pool of unskilled and semi-skilled labour from which to draw, but there is a dearth of managerial employees and engineers with the skills and knowledge that modern industry and commerce require (Ding and Warner, 1999).

Table 17.4 **Multiple recruitment methods in state-owned enterprises (SOEs) and joint ventures (JVs)**

	SOEs N = 12	JVs N = 11
Sources for recruiting workers		
Secondary/technical school	11 (92%)	7 (64%)
Allocated by labour bureau	9 (75%)	2 (18%)
Labour market	7 (58%)	9 (82%)
Transferred from Chinese partner firm	NA	3 (27%)
Internal recruitment	2 (17%)	NA
Sources for recruiting managers		
Promoted from within the firm	12 (100%)	11 (100%)
Appointment by superior government body	7 (58%)	11 (100%)
Open recruitment	4 (33%)	7 (64%)
Appointed by parent firm	0	3 (27%)
University graduates	0	1 (9%)

Source: Ding and Warner, 1999: 247

One of the HR problems confronting China is the huge scale of training and development that is needed to ensure that industry and commerce can continue to develop. Warner (1992) suggests that this relates back to two key factors. First, education and development were severely disrupted during the Cultural Revolution; for example, management development and training were banned during this period. The lack of effective training and development meant that there was a lack of educated managers and engineers, and the legacy of this still remains today. Second, the speed of economic development in China has meant that there is a great demand for educated, skilled staff. The state has responded by encouraging the development of an infrastructure for management development and training (Child, 1994). However, there remains a lack of systematic training within companies. Foreign investors in joint ventures (JVs) can find that Chinese partners often request an enormous amount of overseas training for indigenous employees. FIEs can also experience problems in retaining staff they have trained, especially given the tight labour market for skilled managerial and technical employees (Tsang, 1994). Training and development issues are likely to remain as continuing concerns for the future within China (Glover and Siu, 1999).

● Reward systems and employee relations

The review above has highlighted some of the changes in relation to reward systems. The seniority-based flat rate system is now being replaced by systems that often have some link to performance. Wages were determined by legislation and regional agencies until the mid-1980s, and seniority was the most important factor in terms of employee earnings, but other aspects were entering the equation by the mid-1990s. Factors such as responsibility and qualifications have started to be taken into account (Benson *et al.*, 2000). However, the evidence remains that SOEs are often unwilling to increase wage differentials. State enterprises have tended to pay equal bonuses to all employees regardless of the performance of individual employees. They have also retained a great degree of harmonisation of work conditions (Benson *et al.*, 2000). This appears to be an example of the way in which the principle of equality has endured post-Mao.

Ding and Warner (1999) carried out a study that compared the average monthly wages of SOE and JV employees. Their evidence demonstrated that while SOEs and JVs tended to adopt the same basic wage structure – a basic salary plus bonuses and allowances – the

Table 17.5 **Average monthly wages (RMB) 1994–96**

Type of employee	SOEs (*N* = 12)	JVs (*N* = 12)
1994		
Workers	610	763
Section heads	745	933
Middle managers	758	1731
Senior managers	928	2479
1995		
Workers	722	933
Section heads	878	1103
Middle managers	894	1994
Senior managers	1048	2765
1996		
Workers	741	1098
Section heads	867	1294
Middle managers	930	2300
Senior managers	1150	3144

Source: Ding and Warner, 1999: 251

JVs tended to pay much more on average. The results are summarised in Table 17.5.

Therefore, while there have been overall moves to increase flexibility within reward systems and linkages between pay and performance, some aspects of the old system endure, including the reluctance of SOEs to penalise poor performers (Benson *et al.*, 2000).

The discussion will now turn to employee relations. The role of trade unions has been highlighted above. Trade unions have in the past tended to play a different role within Chinese enterprises, tending to concentrate on welfare issues and assist in production issues. This situation remains much the same today. Benson *et al.* (2000) comment that while trade unions currently seem to be 'relegated' to the role of 'watchdog' over issues such as health and safety and workers' rights, they could potentially play a role in securing better conditions for their members in the future. However, they point out that the traditional role of assisting management in achieving optimum performance could eventually create conflicts, and that

> workers can become the victims of reform rather than the vehicle for change. Chinese workers are therefore in a similar situation to workers in most other countries. (p. 193)

The preceding review has given an overview of the current situation in key areas such as employee resourcing, development and relations. It seems that China is beginning to use techniques that are derived from Western and Japanese practices. However, the full-scale adoption of Western-style techniques is unlikely, at least in the short term, as these would be incongruent with Chinese culture and the historical development of their business traditions. The following section will highlight some of the issues that impact upon the management of people in China.

Stop and think

- Why has the number of redundancies increased in China in recent years?
- Why is training and development likely to be a key issue in years to come?
- What are some of the key trends in terms of rewarding employees in China?

Some issues influencing HRM in China

● Culture

This section will provide an overview of some of the issues that influence the management of people in China. These include the impact of culture, the lack of managerial skills, problems of labour discipline, and dealing with low motivation. Warner (2000) has noted that a great deal of divergence remains within the Asian bloc, and that one of the explanatory variables for this is the impact of national cultures upon human resource systems. Culture is a notoriously difficult concept to define, and it is hard to make broad generalisations that would fit all individuals and groups within a particular country. China, for example, comprises a huge land mass, and many argue that one can find differences in culture between people from the North compared with those of the South. For example, Northern Chinese tend to speak Mandarin, while many southerners speak Cantonese. However, it is useful to outline some of the features that are associated with Chinese culture, in order to understand some of the HR issues that are affecting both SOEs and FIEs.

Child (1994: 28–32) provides an overview of some of the key aspects of Chinese culture. He points out that there is a degree of agreement that Confucianism is the basis for many Chinese traditions. An understanding of Confucianism does help one to understand certain values, attitudes and behaviours within the Chinese context. Fan (1995) suggests that Confucian ideologies are relevant to contemporary studies for four main reasons:

- Confucian ideology has become firmly rooted as an 'undeniable' system that governs many aspects of Chinese lives.
- Thousands of years of a feudalistic system have dominated the Chinese view of themselves and the world.
- To gain acceptance in China, new ideas have to be proved to be compatible with classics and tradition.
- The current economic reforms are not necessarily changing Chinese people's fundamental mentality or behaviour.

Kong Fu Ze (551–479 BC) was called Confucius by Jesuit missionaries. His philosophy on life became popular some 300 years later. The fifth Han Emperor, Wu, found that Confucian ideologies fitted well with the need to create a strong, centralised monarchy. Confucianism emphasised a respect for elders and the family, order, hierarchy, and a sense of duty. Confucius believed that individuals had a fixed position in society, and that social harmony could be achieved when individuals behaved according to rank (Jacobs *et al.*, 1995). There was an emphasis upon the 'correct and well-mannered conduct of one's duties, based upon a sound respect for the social conventions of a patrimonial society' (Child, 1994: 29). Age was respected, particularly in the case of male elders.

Child quotes Lockett (1988), who identified four values that are central to Chinese culture, and which are based upon Confucian ideologies:

- respect for age and hierarchy;
- orientation towards groups;
- the preservation of 'face';
- the importance of relationships.

'Face' is an important concept, and it relates to a person's social standing, position and moral character. Child (1994: 30) comments that the Chinese attach great importance to how they are viewed by others. 'Face' means that conflicts within a group would be kept private, as the group would be demeaned in the eyes of the wider community if conflict were overt. The importance of relationships is captured in the concept known as *guanxi*. Luo and Chen (1997) note that '*guanxi* refers to the concept of drawing on connections or networks to secure favours in personal or business relations' (p. 1). *Guanxi* relates to relationships that are outside the person's immediate family (Child, 1994: 30). The concepts of *guanxi* and face are intertwined, and some have argued that they can act as inhibitors to the modernisation programme (Chen, 1995).

The preceding paragraphs have given a short overview of a complex subject. There is much evidence that FIEs often find it difficult to operate within China, and that some of the problems are caused by a lack of appreciation of Chinese culture. The examples quoted have highlighted some of the underlying tensions that have developed between foreign and Chinese partners. Peng (1994) has commented that foreign investors have complained that Chinese managers lack initiative, are unwilling to delegate, and are perceived to be unsystematic. Lockett (1988) argues that such behaviours reflect aspects of Chinese culture: for example, he reminds us that during the Cultural Revolution managers were promoted according to Party allegiance rather than on the basis of merit. He argues that this legacy has hampered the level of management skill in China. The tendency towards collective rather than individual orientation often leads to behaviours that clash with the behaviours expected by foreign counterparts. Chinese managers will often avoid taking individual responsibility, and Child (1994) argues that this is due to a combination of Chinese traditions and the Cultural Revolution.

Jacobs *et al.* (1995) argue, however, that there is too much emphasis upon the negative implications of Chinese culture. They argue that Confucian-based philosophies can lead to positive outcomes in the workplace, because of the emphasis upon 'diligence, responsibility, thrift, promptness, cooperation and learning' (p. 33). More research is needed in order to evaluate the impact of Chinese culture upon business performance.

● Management skills, labour discipline and motivation

One of the issues affecting China today is a dearth of appropriate management skills. Tsang (1994) argues that the lack of skills relates to four main factors. First, the Cultural Revolution severely disrupted education, training and development. Second, central planning meant that managers had little autonomy. For example, all products were sold to the state at a predetermined price. Therefore managers did not have the scope to develop entrepreneurial skills. Third, mistakes were severely penalised, but achievements were not rewarded. Fourth, important decisions were made by collective consensus, managers saw themselves as an 'information conduit' and individuals were unwilling to take risky decisions (relating back to the danger of losing face). Again, these behaviours relate back to a combination of Confucian ideology and the legacy of the Cultural Revolution. The development of adequate levels of managerial skill is likely to remain as a key issue for the future.

Two linked issues are the problems of labour discipline and low motivation. Evidence suggests that Chinese managers are often unwilling to discipline staff, as they prefer to avoid overt conflict and maintain harmony (Tsang, 1994). While Chinese culture emphasises the importance of hard work and diligence, the system of featherbedding in SOEs meant that the enterprises were overstaffed and productivity was low. Tsang quotes from the *China Daily*:

Labour discipline in our enterprises is very lax. Some workers don't work eight hours a day, a few are absent for a long time to engage in speculation and profiteering. Others even turn to street brawling and stealing of state property. There are also technically incompetent people who do not seek improvement, but just drift along, wasting their own and other people's time.

(Tsang, 1994: 5)

This comment reflects the fact that China is going through the equivalent of an industrial revolution, in that many workers are being drawn from agricultural work to factory work. The problems highlighted above are reminiscent of those that faced nations such as the USA, Japan and the United Kingdom as they went through their own industrial revolutions and sought to find ways in which to control and motivate agricultural/migrant workers (Zuboff, 1988; Buchanan and Huczynski, 1997).

Glover and Siu (1999) have pointed out that FIEs based in Southern China often employ migrant workers from the North of China. Their case study evidence suggested that the main aim of the migrant workers was to accumulate money and return home as soon as possible. For this reason, they were not motivated by the prospect of career development. As a result of this, they had a purely instrumental attachment to the company, and no real stake in the long-term prosperity of the firm. It is also important to point out that part of the attraction of the joint venture was that the company could take advantage of the low pay levels in China. In other words, the company itself was operating in an instrumental way in respect of its use of manual labour in China. Glover and Siu identify a range of problems that were being encountered by the company, many of which were related to human resources issues rather than equipment failures. Burrell (1997) describes such workers as the 'peasantariat', and argues that

> they retain much if not all of their deep-seated social and political characteristics. They remain 'peasants who travel'.
> (p. 14)

Burrell argues that although many of the world's workers are in fact peasants, traditional organisational theory has ignored this and has essentially led to a lack of knowledge and understanding about the motivations and aspirations of a numerically significant group of workers. More research is needed in this area.

| Stop and think | How might an understanding of Chinese culture and traditions help FIEs when setting up new businesses in China? |

Hong Kong: economic growth and HRM

It is relevant to refer to Hong Kong here, as it has a different history from that of mainland China. Hong Kong has a relatively small land mass of 1095 square metres. It has an estimated population of 6 687 200. It enjoyed rapid economic growth until the Asian crisis of 1997–98. This section will give a short review of Hong Kong's historical development, and will highlight some of the issues that face the territory after its reunification with China.

Hong Kong became a British colony in 1843. The British wanted to secure a base from which to trade. Initially, one of the key exports to China was opium, which proved to be a lucrative business for the British. Drug taking was illegal, but there was a high demand for opium within China in the mid to late 1800s. The Japanese invaded China and subsequently Hong Kong in the Second World War, and occupied Hong Kong between 1941 and 1945. They surrendered in 1945. The Communist Party came to power in China in 1949, and this provoked a wave of immigration from China to Hong Kong. Many of the immigrants were traders and businessmen. Many had fought against the Communists during the civil wars in China, and tensions remained between the two factions. Hong Kong became wealthy in the period after the Second World War. Central

696 Chapter 17 · Human resource management in Asia

to its success were the Asian 'tycoons', many of whom were immigrants who had left mainland China in 1949–50. The tycoons preferred to work with family members or close contacts, relating back to the Chinese concept of *guanxi*. However, there is an argument that Hong Kong will slowly move away from its patriarchal culture. Four main reasons have been highlighted. First, the first generation of Chinese businessmen are preparing to hand over to their children, many of whom have been educated in the West. Second, the financial crisis of 1997–98 made the businesses more reliant on Western capital. Third, the Internet may pose a threat to more traditional businessmen. Finally, Asia's maturing legal and financial framework may undermine the influence of Chinese networks overseas (Anon, 2000a).

Hong Kong was ruled under British sovereignty until 1997. As a result, it developed a capitalist business system that was influenced by Chinese culture and traditions. Sovereignty was handed back to mainland China in 1997. Hong Kong became a Special Administrative Region (SAR), and the agreement was that it would maintain its legal system and capitalist approach for at least 50 years. There were many concerns that the agreement would not protect the democratic rights of the people of Hong Kong, or that reunification would affect the economic progress of Hong Kong. In the event, the handover appeared to run smoothly. Hong Kong now has an executive-led, non-elected government and a legislative council (elected by universal suffrage). The system has not been without its problems, and Hong Kong must decide in 2008 whether or not it wishes to move to a fully elected government (*Financial Times*, 1999b). The main problem that has faced the government since 1997 is how to respond to the Asian economic crisis.

Hong Kong's economy was badly hit by the Asian economic crisis. GDP growth fell by 5.1 per cent in 1998 and by 1.5 per cent in 1999. Unemployment levels rose from 4.7 per cent in 1998 to 7 per cent in 1999 (*Financial Times*, 1999b). Indeed, when South Korea, Singapore and the Philippines began to emerge from the Asian crisis, Hong Kong's GDP continued to fall. After 1997, Hong Kong began to be regarded as having an uncompetitive cost base. Several factors were cited as contributing to Hong Kong's problems, and four key issues emerged. First, property values were too high. Second, property rentals were too high. Third, service charges levied at ports and airports were too high (Lucas, 1999a). A fourth key problem related to wage levels within the territory. Prior to 1997, wage levels were spiralling without concomitant increases in productivity. After the onset of the Asian crisis, some large companies cut salaries and others moved operations abroad (Lucas, 1999a). Hong Kong had been used as a gateway to China, but China was increasingly shipping direct from its own ports (Lucas, 1999a).

Hong Kong's economy experienced two economic slowdowns in the five-year period from 1997/8 to 2002 (Leahy, 2002). During this period, property prices fell by 65 per cent and this contributed to a four-year period of deflation. In addition, unemployment rose and hit a record level of 7.8 per cent in 2002 (Leahy, 2002). Large companies, including Motorola, the Bank of Asia and Swire Pacific, continued to shed staff (Grammaticas, 2002). Hong Kong's ports continued to lose market share to mainland China by 2002, but air cargo exports rose and tourist arrivals increased in 2002.

Some experts predict that Hong Kong's GDP growth could rebound to 5.5 per cent by 2003 and that GDP could rise by 3.5 per cent a year in the period until 2008 (Jacob, 2002). If China's entry into the WTO leads to the predicted growth of exports, Hong Kong's small and medium sized company sector could benefit in that they currently operate more than 6000 factories in mainland China (Jacob, 2002). Some believe that the future for Hong Kong's economy will lie in high technology. For example, it may be used as a base for developing China-relevant software (Lucas, 1999b). However, there are concerns that it is less advanced in this sphere than countries such as Singapore. In common with Hong Kong, Singapore has also been used as a small open economy that is a springboard to less developed economies. However, Singapore has been more aggressive in terms of offering incentives to attract preferred industries such as banking, technology and the media (Lucas, 1999b). Hong Kong has not offered the same degree of incentives to potential businesses. In terms of technology, in particular, there is also a concern that there could be a lack of skills to service the fast-growing technology sector within the local labour market (Lucas, 1999b). There is also a concern that only 25 per cent of school leavers go on to university within Hong Kong (Jacob, 2002).

Hong Kong has acted in recent years as 'a "half-way" house between a modern Western business society and the mainland China context' (Selmer *et al.*, 2000: 237). However, this role may diminish as the process of modernisation and openness in China continues to develop. Some of the specific HR issues include the fact that Hong Kong has strictly limited the importation of labour. Businesses are allowed to import construction workers and domestic help, but it has been more difficult to import potential managers (Fields *et al.*, 2000). Some studies have suggested that labour turnover of educated workers and managers tends to be high, and can pose a problem for Hong Kong businesses. Some companies are placing more emphasis upon internal development and promotion to try to alleviate this problem. Fields *et al.* (2000) have found that retention rates are higher in these cases. However, an adequate supply of skilled managers will be critical for Hong Kong's future, especially in the information technology sector.

Investment in training is a key issue. Fields *et al.* (2000) have found, for example, that some companies are reluctant to invest in training, and this is possibly linked to the problem of 'job-hopping' in Hong Kong. In addition, evidence suggests that training budgets have been cut in the light of economic slowdowns (Chu and Siu, 2001). The issue of wage rises has been dealt with above. Wage rises prior to 1997 tended to run ahead of productivity, so contributing to the fact that it was expensive to operate from Hong Kong. These were reigned in after 1997, and some employees had their salaries cut. This caused conflict in some industries. For example, Cathay Pacific cut the salaries of its pilots, and this led to 17 days of disruption in 1999, which cost the company between HK$ 400m and HK$ 700m.

This short review has highlighted some of the key differences in the historical and economic context of Hong Kong. It is clear that there are substantial differences between the system in Hong Kong and that of its mainland counterpart. It is also clear that Hong Kong's role of 'middle-man' between the West and the East may be further compromised as China continues to modernise.

| **Stop and think** | What impact did the Asian crisis have on Hong Kong and why has the economy continued to suffer? |

South Korea: economic growth and HRM

South Korea (referred to hereafter as Korea) has an area of 99 313 square kilometres and an estimated population of 46.4 million people (*Financial Times*, 1999c). Its capital is Seoul, which has an estimated population of 10.5 million (*Financial Times*, 1999c). Korea is a relatively new industrialised country, which experienced rapid economic growth from the 1960s to the early 1990s (Anon, 1995). It was badly affected by the Asian crisis in 1997–98. The percentage GDP growth fell by 5.8 per cent in 1998 (*Financial Times*, 1999c). One of the biggest shocks to hit the economy after 1998 was the financial crisis within Daewoo. Daewoo was one of the influential *chaebols*, which are large, family-owned conglomerates that dominate Korea's economy. The five leading *chaebols* prior to the collapse of Daewoo were Hyundai, Samsung, Daewoo, Lucky Goldstar and the SK group.

South Korea received a $58 billion bail-out from the International Monetary Fund in order to prevent economic collapse in 1997 (Ward, 2002a). However, the situation was quickly reversed, and Korea's GDP rose by almost 11 per cent in 1999 (Anon, 2000b). Inflation rose by 7.5 per cent in 1998 and then fell back to 1.3 per cent in 1999. Similarly, industrial production fell by 7.3 per cent in 1998 and then rose by 16 per cent in 1999. The unemployment rate rose to 8.4 per cent in 1999, but fell back to 3.7 per cent by 2000 (Rowley and Bae, 2002).

In the five-year period from 1998 to 2002, Korea went from the brink of economic disaster to one of the region's best economic performers (Thornhill, 2002c). Gross domestic product was recorded at 6.1 per cent growth in the first half of 2002 (Ward, 2002a). Underpinning the turnaround has been the restructuring of activities in the financial and corporate sectors. Since 1998, 25 per cent of financial institutions and 16 of the largest conglomerates have been closed or broken up. Domestic demand has underpinned growth and the construction and service sectors have expanded rapidly (Ward, 2002a). In respect of the *chaebols*, Samsung Electronics has performed particularly well. It was named as the fastest-growing brand in 2002 and has been successful in terms of developing and marketing advanced mobile phones, such as camera phones, that China was not able to imitate (Ward, 2002b). In addition to developing successful products, *chaebols* such as Samsung have been working to improve corporate governance and have had to move away from supporting non-viable companies by internal financing arrangements (Ward, 2002c).

However, some commentators are concerned that despite the turnaround, some economic weaknesses remain (Ward, 2002a). Firstly, more work is required to ensure that South Korea reaches global standards of corporate governance. Secondly, the government (via the banking system) continues to support manufacturing companies who are not generating enough income to pay their debts. Thirdly, the shift from a nation of 'savers' to credit-funded spenders has led to some problems. Some householders unaccustomed to managing credit have fallen into financial difficulties and this has been exacerbated by the lax approach to lending by banks and financial institutions. Fourthly, China's entry into the WTO could potentially increase the competitive pressure on South Korea. Burton (1999a) suggests that Korea risks being 'squeezed economically' as it occupies a middle ground between China's low-wage economy and Japan's high-technology economy. In addition, the threat of a US attack on Iraq in 2002/3 meant that oil prices could rise, thus pushing up operating costs and potentially sparking a decline in export demand (Ward, 2002a).

Some key historical issues

In order to understand some of the contemporary economic and HR issues that are impacting upon Korea, it is useful to give a brief review of its history. This allows an insight into the way in which the business context has developed and the legacy that this has created. In comparison with other Asian countries such as Japan, relatively little has been written about general business and HR issues in Korea. Whitley (1999) provides one of the most useful insights into the business context in Korea, giving an overview of Korea's history that is summarised below. Whitley argues that the dominant institutions in Korea can be understood by reference to pre-industrial society, the period of Japanese colonial rule and the Korean War. He argues that the present structures for governance and business reflect three key aspects from the past. First, there has always been a tendency towards a high degree of political centralisation. Second, there is a continuing Confucian influence in terms of the importance attached to superior authority and moral worth, and these are linked to examination success. Third, there has been a history of factional struggles among the aristocracy, and aristocratic status and ancestry have always been viewed as important (Whitley, 1999: 152). These will now be expanded upon.

Korea was ruled by the Yi or Chosun dynasty between 1392 and 1910. Confucianism was predominant during this period. In particular, political power was highly centralised, and success in examinations was prized. There was a sharp division between the aristocratic elite and others. Within the aristocracy, success in examinations tended to secure senior posts. Although the monarch was revered, the aristocratic bureaucracy that developed ensured that the monarch would never achieve despotic power. There was much competition between different factions, which was encouraged by the monarch, so that local power bases would not develop. Another related aspect was that the

> private accumulation of wealth was officially regarded as an indicator of corruption and Confucian rulers established it as their ethical right to prevent it as part of their duty to preserve harmony and frugality.
>
> (Whitley, 1999: 154)

This meant that there was a relatively small merchant class, and they were regarded with suspicion. While there were factional struggles, the society did not disintegrate owing to the 'finely tuned mechanisms of checks and balances' (p. 154). Collectivism was never a central feature of Korean society, and there was always a great distance between rulers and the ruled.

Japanese colonial rule spanned from 1910 to 1945. While the Japanese made some changes, Whitley argues that many of the aspects of Korea's pre-industrial past were sustained. This included the 'capricious and unpredictable behaviour of the executive' (1999: 155). Korea was awarded its independence again in 1948. Power was centralised among the elite once more. The entrepreneurs of the 1947–57 period were men who were favoured by the president. The president virtually gave away businesses that had been owned by the Japanese. These firms form the basis of the *chaebols* that are central to the Korean economy today. The state continued to play a key role in terms of the development of the *chaebols*. It offered cheap credit to them via the banking system, and as the president controlled access to the credit, he maintained a strong position. The family members that owned the *chaebols* continued to operate on a factional basis. The Korean War raised the power of the military elite. Korean management style is often described as authoritarian, and this reflects the influence of the military after the Korean War.

Whitley argues that the growth and diversification of the *chaebols* was influenced by the requirements of the state. The state offered subsidised credit, and in return the *chaebols* developed in accordance with state priorities. These included a desire to expand rapidly and to 'catch up' with Japan, and as a result the *chaebols* grew and diversified rapidly. Second, the *chaebols* developed heavy engineering and chemical production in the 1970s because of the military threat from North Korea.

Education and qualifications continued to be prized, to the extent that there was a dearth of workers with manufacturing skills in the 1990s. The authoritarian management style was, as we have said, influenced by the military, and subordination was reinforced by Confucian traditions. While trade unions exist in Korea, the state has acted to limit their power – for example, by intervening in disputes. A considerable distance between the business-owning elite and the masses persists, and *chaebol* owners have had little need to harness the support of trade unions or workers. All these themes reflect Korea's historical development, and they continue to impinge upon business relationships in Korea today.

Stop and think   How did the *chaebols* come to be a central feature of the South Korean economy?

◼ The contemporary business and human resource context

This historical overview has offered an insight into some of the contemporary business and HR issues that face Korea as it enters the twenty-first century. The economy continues to be dominated by the *chaebols*. They operate in heavy engineering, car production, electronics, construction, transport, insurance and finance. There is an argument that the economic environment has not supported the development of small, entrepreneurial businesses, but an explanation for this can be found in the historical overview above. The South Korean president Kim Dae-jung (appointed in 1998) began a programme of reform that was spurred by the Asian crisis of 1997–98.

The economic crisis in Korea was at least partly related to the actions of the *chaebols*. The government has recently attempted to put measures into place to stem those practices of the *chaebols* that have had negative consequences for the economy. The *chaebols* had over-invested in production facilities, which had created huge debts (Burton, 1999a). Another related problem has been that stronger businesses within *chaebol* empires have supported weaker ones. When the government eased restrictions on cross-shareholding for the *chaebols* in an attempt to encourage consolidation, many *chaebols* used this as an opportunity to rescue weaker businesses, by using money from the stronger businesses to purchase shares in them (Burton, 1999b). This meant that internal shareholdings often represented as much as 34 per cent in 1998 (Burton, 1999b). The government has moved to counter the power of the *chaebols* and has encouraged outside investors and is considering strengthening shareholder rights (Thornhill, 2002d). The proportion of independent outside directors has risen and this has diluted the power of the founding families (Ward, 2002c).

The economic crisis was closely linked to the debt-ridden banking sector. The government injected Won 64 trillion into the banking sector during the economic crisis. This was equivalent to approximately 16 per cent of the GDP (Montagnon, 1999b). In 1999, of 33 commercial banks, five were closed and four were merged. This led to a wave of redundancies, which many argued was necessary given the fact that the banks were overstaffed. However, the evidence suggested that many employees were rehired on short-term contracts (Montagnon, 1999b). The government encouraged foreign investment after the economic crisis, partly to try to bring more discipline into the banking sector in particular. The economy has recovered in the short term, but many commentators argue that continued reforms are necessary in order to secure its long-term prosperity.

Stop and think	Which factors underpinned the economic crisis in South Korea in 1997–98?

◼ Human resource issues

This section will give a short overview of some of the HR issues that are affecting contemporary Korea. One such issue has been highlighted in the historical review above. Some commentators have argued that the predominantly authoritarian, military-influenced management style is likely to prove unsuitable for the long term (Burton, 1999a). The preferred style tends to be reminiscent of a scientific management approach, within which subordinates are closely controlled by supervisors. The approach encompasses low levels of trust between managers and subordinates. Work is often organised such that surveillance of subordinates is made possible. In common with the principles of scientific management, jobs tend to be broken down into narrowly defined tasks. Workers in manual grades are not promoted, and tend to stay in initial jobs (Whitley, 1999). This is especially the case within smaller *chaebols*. The situation is different for white-collar workers. They tend to be moved around, and are often transferred across subsidiaries either within Korea or abroad. This is reflective of the historical development of Korea, in which educated employees were regarded as superior and those with technical and manual skills as inferior. Finally, roles and responsibilities were often defined more in terms of authority relations than in terms of formally documented job descriptions (Whitley, 1999). Therefore the traditional approach to management tended to be informed more by scientific management than by 'modern management techniques'. Modern management techniques such as quality management and human resource management emphasise worker involvement as a route to quality enhancement and increased performance. Burton (1999a) has argued that the authoritarian management style of the Korean *chaebols* could limit their development as global players in the future. There is also evidence that levels of employee participation dropped sharply between 1996 and 1998 as the economic crisis hit and that this partly reflected their fragility within the Korean business system (Park and Yu, 2000).

Kim and Briscoe (1997) provide an overview of some of the traditional human resource practices used by the *chaebols*. They recruit and select college graduates twice a year. Graduates from the top universities are preferred. The graduate trainees undergo four weeks of training, in order to turn them into 'warrior workers' for the *chaebols* (p. 299). During this period the graduates are socialised into the history, norms and behaviours required by the *chaebols*. Interestingly, there was less emphasis upon technical skills, which again reflects the historical development of Korea. Rewards were traditionally based upon seniority. Posts tended to have a minimum tenure before an employee could be promoted to the next level. *Chaebols* would normally offer a bonus that was linked to the overall performance of the company. Performance appraisals were not widely used, partly because managers preferred not to give critical feedback. Most employees would retire by the age of 55.

Kim and Briscoe (1997) go on to provide some evidence of the modernisation of some of the HR practices. They use the example of Samsung, which is generally regarded as a *chaebol* that has attempted to restructure after the Asian crisis. Kim and Briscoe argue that Samsung had to respond to a new paradigm of domestic and international competition. They outline three key areas of modernisation in terms of HR policy and practice: job hierarchy and promotion, compensation, and performance appraisals. The key differences are summarised in Table 17.6.

Rowley and Bae (2002) confirm that there is continuing evidence of shifts in these areas. They also highlight evidence that suggests increased uses of numerical and functional flexibility. Park and Yu (2000) suggest that there is also a trend towards flattening organisational hierarchies and movement towards team-based structures. Therefore, there is some evidence that *chaebols* are beginning to modernise their human resource practices. Interestingly, Park and Yu (2000) observe that whilst traditionally HRM practices in Korean companies were almost identical, there is now more evidence of divergence, as companies adjust to a changing economic and environmental context. This is interesting in respect of the extent to which HRM may be seen as a source of competitive advantage in the future and in the way in which this may shape managerial choices and employee experiences as time progresses.

Korean trade unions have been weak in the past. Strikes and stoppages do occur, but the state often intervenes to dissipate them. There was a significant increase in strike activity during 1996–97. Morden and Bowles (1998) suggest that this was related to four key factors. First, the government had passed new labour laws, which were aimed at increasing the flexibility of the labour market. This included removing the provisions for lifetime employment and as a result, making workers redundant. Second, the International Labour Organization (ILO) and the OECD had called for a reduction in statutory curbs on trade union activities. Third, the state had recognised the Korean Confederation of Trade Unions (KCTU), which was more vocal than its predecessor, the Federation of Korean Trade Unions (FKTU).

Table 17.6 Samsung's 'new HR policy'

HR practice	Traditional approach	New approach
Job hierarchy and promotion	• Based on seniority • Younger employee could not supervise older employee	• Promotion linked more tightly to performance • Minimum tenure for each position abolished
Compensation	• Compensation had three main elements: basic salary (50%), allowances (10%) and a bonus (40%) • Lack of individual performance measurement/problems of 'free riders'	• Compensation has two main elements: base pay (related to position and seniority) and performance pay (related to individual performance). The percentage of performance pay is highest for senior managers (68%)

Performance appraisal	• No history of performance appraisal	• Performance pay related to performance ratings. Appraisal has four key aspects:
		  – Supervisor keeps a diary recording performance
		  – 360-degree appraisal introduced
		  – Appraisal interview introduced
		  – Forced distribution of performance ratings

Source: Adapted from Kim and Briscoe, 1997

Strikes were sparked by the Daewoo crisis. Workers in both Daewoo and Hyundai walked out in April 2000 to protest against plans to sell Daewoo in an international auction. The police arrested 20 trade unionists during the dispute, and this sparked a further strike within Daewoo (Burton, 1999c). In addition to conventional strike activity, workers at Daewoo Motors blocked attempts by Hyundai officials to carry out due diligence in respect of a possible takeover of the car division. This is an example of continuing factionalism between the rival *chaebols* (Burton, 1999c). More recently, strikes have been reported in Hyandai, Kia Motors and Ssangyong Motors in protest at government plans to shorten the working week and reduce the number of public holidays and in the public sector (including gas and railway workers) as a response to threatened privatisation and in the airline and chemicals industries (Ward, 2002e, 2000f).

ACTIVITY
- Compare and contrast key differences between the 'traditional' and the 'new' approach to human resource management in South Korea.

- What factors might act as a barrier to further modernisation in the future?

Singapore: economic growth and HRM

As we noted earlier in this chapter, Singapore is one of the first-tier economies in South East Asia, along with Japan and others. It has witnessed remarkable growth in the past 35 years, and between 1965 and 1980 its GDP growth rate averaged 10 per cent. Since 1980 the GDP growth rate has fallen slightly below 10 per cent, although the recessions in the mid-1980s and recently have hit the economy hard. Much of this long-term growth has been put down to the economic strategies of the government of Singapore (Aryee, 1994; Teen and Phan, 1999).

Singapore is a small state with a population of 2.8 million, and is located on the southern tip of the Malaysian peninsular. Until 1965 it was a British colony and briefly part of the Malaysian state until it gained independence. As Singapore lacks natural resources, including land, the People's Action Party, which has been in power since 1959, decided that economic survival and prosperity rested on the abilities of its people. In attempting to understand Singapore's economic development, an analysis of human resource development in relation to national strategy is pivotal.

The development of Singapore's economy

Singapore's institutional structures are heavily underpinned by government support, and the role of the state has been crucial in its development. From the 1960s to the present, economic policy and national economic strategy formulation have gone through three stages. In the first stage, in the 1960s, the government decided that economic growth rested on the development of industry, the attraction of foreign capital, and the promotion of Singapore as a centre of trade in the region. This form of alliance capitalism, while underpinned by a socialist (or social democratic) philosophy, also encouraged free enterprise. As the Prime Minister, Lee Kuan Yew, stated concerning Singapore's initial independent state:

> The sole objective was survival. How this was to be achieved by socialism or free enterprise was a secondary matter. The answer turned out to be free enterprise tempered with the socialist philosophy of equal opportunities for education, jobs, health and housing.
>
> (Vickers da Costa, 1983: 14)

In this first phase economic strategy was focused on developing low added value and labour-intensive industries – a mixture of steel mills, shipyards, oil refineries and electronics. This development coincided with a boom in the world economy and MNCs that were seeking competitive advantage through reduced labour and running costs by opening subsidiaries in developing countries such as Singapore.

By the end of the 1970s that advantage was no longer so apparent as other, less developed economies began to offer even lower labour and production costs, and so a second economic strategy was formulated in the 1980s. This concentrated on high-tech industries, and moved away from labour-intensive industries. High-tech industries focus on science, technology, skill and knowledge, and to realise this strategy the government set about attracting foreign high-technology companies through high tax breaks and other inducements, and embarked on a massive, long-term human resource development programme.

The government itself also provided a considerable amount of capital and became a major shareholder in and owner of many of the new industries, though in the 1990s many were subsequently privatised (Teen and Phan, 1999). This approach is similar to the alliance capitalism that created the *zaibatsu* in Japan. Ashton and Sung (1994) describe this model as one where 'the political need to secure long-term survival of the society meant that the short-term interests of the class-based groupings such as landowners or capitalists were subordinated to the wider goal of collective economic growth' (p. 4). Ayree (1994) sees the government's role in human resource terms as an allocator within the labour market and also as a developer of unique human resource capabilities and competences to enable Singapore to have a critical competitive edge.

Considerable money was poured into high-tech research and development and the building of science parks. The success of this strategy is evidenced by Singapore's continuing high economic growth rates in the 1980s and 1990s, by when it had become, for example, the leading world producer of hard disk drives. It had also developed a thriving stocks and securities market and had become a regional leader in this area. There was considerable investment in education, particularly in the tertiary sector, and human resource development became a central focus of the government manpower development programme (Low *et al.*, 1991).

In the 1990s the Singapore government launched a third economic strategy to take the economy well into the twenty-first century. This was precipitated by a sharp downturn in growth in the mid-1990s, caused by the impact of the financial crisis and consequent recession in South East Asia and the slowdown in global electronics demand. The manufacturing sector was further weighed down by excess capacity and keen regional competition in the non-electronics industries. In the light of these developments Singapore's Economic Development Board (SEDB) created a 'blueprint' for the future grounded in a knowledge-based economy. Singapore will become 'a vibrant and robust global hub of knowledge-driven industries. Singapore's manufacturing and service sectors will be further developed with a strong emphasis on technology, innovation and capabilities' (SEDB, 2000). To sustain economic growth Singaporean companies are being strongly encouraged to move out into the Asia Pacific region and form a 'second ring'. Advantage would then be taken of the abundance of cheaper labour in these surrounding economies, and Singapore would become the hub of this ring as a powerful international economic centre (Low, 1993). The main aim of the blueprint is for the people of Singapore to achieve the same living standard as the Swiss by the year 2020 or 2030.

In human resource terms there are two main consequences of these strategic changes in the light of increased global competition: first, the continuing development of the Singaporean education and human resource development systems to high levels; and second, the restructuring of the labour markets between the declining old industries and the rising new ones. The latter development is having and will continue to have negative effects, especially on marginalised elements in the labour force, who lack the skills, knowledge and youth to adapt to these changes.

■ Human resource development in Singapore

Central to Singapore's economic strategies has been the development of the educational and knowledge levels of the population. Ashton and Sung (1994) believe that advanced NIEs such as Singapore are significant examples of a new model of skill formation and economic development in which changes in education policy are linked directly with the current and future demands of the economy. As late-developing countries they have had the advantage of learning from the examples and mistakes of the older, established economies. This can take the form of transferring specific skills and knowledge directly through education and training programmes, through gaining knowledge and skills from and through foreign-based companies, and through sending students to foreign countries to learn. An important factor is that the whole population is encompassed as well as groups within the economy such as unions, companies and employer groups. This will often mean that individual and separate group interests have to be subordinated to the long-term aims of the nation, and that some elements of freedom may be sacrificed. For example, in the first economic phase, dating from the 1960s to the 1980s, the government acted to contain labour costs by repressing labour organisations, and in the recent crisis wage costs have been cut to bring them in line with 1994 levels (SEDB, 2000).

The centrality of human resource development has been emphasised at all stages: in the first phase by developing the basic education level and skills of the population, and in the second phase by raising them to the more sophisticated level required by an advanced, high-tech economy. This required the upgrading of the education system and the creation of a training infrastructure coordinated by the Vocational and Industrial Training Board.

The Ministry of Trade and Industry and the Investment Board define the vision of the national economic strategy and then set the goals. The Ministry gathers information on the future skill and knowledge needs to fulfil the strategy, and these are compared with estimates of present skills. The Economic Development Board then calculates targets to achieve the set goals, which are then given to the Council for Professional and Technical Education to implement. They in turn set targets for schools, colleges, polytechnics, universities and other educational and training establishments.

In the third phase much emphasis has been placed on work-based learning, because the new organisational forms require not only technical skills but also the ability to work flexibly and with a greater degree of group autonomy within a problem-solving context. Studies have been made of the best systems, perceived to be Japanese, German and Australian on-the-job training. The German dual system has been particularly admired, and elements of it were borrowed in developing Singaporean apprenticeship systems in the early 1990s.

The successful growth of the Singapore economy has been ascribed to the role of the state and the institutions it has developed to enhance the knowledge and skills of its people to meet the challenges of the twenty-first century. This has taken place in the context of a mixed economy where foreign investment and subsidiaries of MNCs have been welcomed. However, the need to achieve a balance between state and private capital interests within a unitarist HRM state means that individual and group freedoms have had to be curtailed from time to time in the long-term interests of the economy. Thus at times trade union and individual rights have been side-stepped, as have the short-term profit motives of individual companies, and while the model has been eulogised by some observers there are doubts as to its applicability to economies outside the Asia Pacific region.

Stop and think How has a strategic approach to HRM and HRD aided the Singaporean economy?

Summary

- The chapter began by briefly examining the controversy of whether Asian business systems and practices were converging and conforming more to a US managerial approach. The consensus among observers is that while elements of Western HRM practices are more prevalent, divergences of practices remain marked owing to socio-cultural differences, varied investment patterns and financial institutional practices, and the political and historical factors that have led to different stages of economic development.

- The origins and development of the Japanese employment relations system were examined from four perspectives: the historical view, the cultural view, the late developer view and the politico-economic view. An examination was then made of the 'three pillars' (lifetime employment, seniority system and enterprise unionism) that underpin the employment system in large Japanese corporations. This was followed by a critique of this simplified version of the Japanese employment system, which emphasised its narrow application in organisational and working population terms. The section finished with an examination of recent trends in Japanese HRM, exploring the problems of an ageing population, the effects of increased global competition and changing patterns of HRM in Japanese companies in response to these pressures.

● The section on the People's Republic of China discussed key issues relating to human resource management, and outlined some of the key points in China's historical development under Mao. It illustrated the way the system known as the 'iron rice-bowl' continued to exert some degree of influence over contemporary practices. While China has enjoyed rapid economic growth, it is now confronting a number of problems, including restructuring, downsizing and unemployment. In response to this, it is having to develop a system of social insurance. There is a debate as to the extent to which HR practices within China are converging with Western approaches. This section concluded that while there is some degree of similarity, full-blown Westernised models of HRM are unlikely to take hold because of cultural and institutional differences. There are a number of issues that are impacting upon people management in China, including skills gaps, problems of labour discipline, and low motivation.

● The short review of Hong Kong highlighted the clear and substantial differences from the PRC, its mainland counterpart. It is also clear that Hong Kong's role of 'middleman' between the West and the East may be further compromised as the PRC continues to modernise.

● Four key issues were highlighted in the development of South Korea's HRM systems. First, there has been a historical tendency towards the centralisation of power. Second, Confucian influences were important, particularly in relation to superior authority and moral worth and the importance attached to examination success. Third, there is a history of factional struggles among the elite. Finally, the *chaebols* are central to the Korean economy and have been closely linked to the state via the control of cheap credit. Some key HR issues were highlighted. These included: the continuation of an authoritarian management culture; the predominance of white-collar, educated workers; the role of trade unions; and the moves toward modernisation within some of the *chaebols*. While some convergence towards Western models of HRM is apparent, it is likely that historical traditions will continue to impact upon HRM both within Korea and within the foreign subsidiaries of the *chaebol* empires. However, the decline of Daewoo served to highlight that the *chaebols* cannot ignore domestic and foreign competition.

● The section on Singapore noted the impressive growth of the economy from the 1970s, and the various stages of and adjustments to its national economic strategy in the light of changing external influences. An examination of the vocational and training system was seen as one of the key policies in creating a vibrant economy. Raising the skill and knowledge levels of the population was seen as pivotal in the twenty-first century in order to meet the challenges of a high-growth economy based on high-technology industries and services.

ACTIVITY   ## China

As a member of the human resource development department of a large multinational corporation you have been given responsibility to devise a programme to prepare managers and other parent company employees who will be working in China.

Prepare a presentation that you might give to these employees, including general information on the country, history, culture, language and customs and work-related attitudes. Use anecdotes and solid examples to illustrate your presentation.

ACTIVITY **Japan**

Divide the lecture group into four smaller groups and give each group the task of preparing a presentation on the origins of the Japanese employment system from the perspectives given in the section on Japan:

- the historical view;
- the cultural view;
- the late developer view;
- the politico-economic view.

Emphasise that material in addition to that presented in the Japan section of this chapter will be given extra credit.

Questions

1 To what extent would you agree with the contention that existing models of HRM fail to recognise cultural differences, and that this is a weakness given the rapid rate of globalisation?

2 Outline the similarities and differences in terms of the approaches to the management of people in the Asian countries outlined above.

3 To what extent would you agree with the view that there is an 'Asian model of HRM'?

4 Describe the employment polices in large Japanese companies. How have these changed over the last few years and why?

Case study

Yummee Biscuits: Part 1

Yummee Biscuits is a large UK-based snack manufacturer that was set up in the nineteenth century. It is now one of the largest snack manufacturers in the UK. Over the past two decades it has been internationalising its operations, and has acquired companies in the USA and Australia. In 1995 it became involved in a joint venture in the south of the People's Republic of China (PRC). The Chinese partners were local businessmen who had no prior experience in biscuit-making. Yummee pumped in money and resources, and the Chinese partners set up the land deal. The biscuit factory was built on a greenfield site, and was equipped with state-of-the-art machinery. Work was organised on scientific management (Taylorist) lines, with

strictly demarcated jobs and close supervision. Yummee took the view initially that it would be best to employ local Chinese managers to run the factory. However, in the following two years numerous problems occurred within the factory. These included problems of quality control, stock control, and failing to deliver orders to customers on time.

Yummee sent out a delegation of senior managers to investigate the problem. They found that many of the problems were related to a lack of managerial skill and poor coordination between different departments. They realised that it had been a mistake to assume that the indigenous Chinese managers could run the factory to British standards with little support or training. Yummee put all managers through management development training. This included topics such as leadership skills, communication skills, time management skills, and dealing with conflict. The training programmes were adapted from programmes that were delivered in the UK. Individual training needs were not assessed. The managers said that they had enjoyed the training, but the trainer felt that there could be an element of politeness involved. There was little improvement in the performance of the subsidiary one year later.

A senior executive from Yummee travelled to the subsidiary to inspect the plant. He sent a report outlining the key problems in the factory. These were the main points of his report.

Shopfloor problems

- There were low levels of motivation within the shopfloor ranks. Most of the shopfloor workers were from the north of China.
- Shopfloor workers seemed unwilling or unable to take on any level of responsibility.
- There seemed to be little interest in promotion or development opportunities.
- There was no appreciation of hygiene rules and regulations.

Management problems

- Many managers seemed unwilling to take responsibility.
- Managers would often prefer to hire members of their family rather than the best person for the job.
- Managers were often unwilling to discipline subordinates.
- Interdepartmental communication was poor.
- Managers seemed to spend a lot of time dealing with the personal problems of subordinates.

Questions

1 Does a knowledge of the historical and cultural development of China help you to understand the problems experienced in the PRC subsidiary? Give examples.

2 You have been asked to take over the running of the PRC subsidiary. What managerial initiatives would you implement to help resolve the above problems? What barriers would you face and how would you deal with them?

3 To what extent could a Western model of HRM be applied to the context of this factory? If not, why not? Give specific examples.

Yummee Biscuits: Part 2

Yummee Biscuits is now interested in opening a new biscuit factory in Shanghai. It is predicted that the factory will require 800 employees at all levels from senior management to shopfloor workers. The new factory will contain the following departments: human resource management, finance, sales and marketing, food production and distribution and quality control. Yummee will install new German biscuit-making machines, as it feels that these are the best on the market at the moment. The machines will be shipped in from Germany. The factory will produce a range of savoury and sweet biscuits.

Yummee has already purchased a site and expects the building to be complete by December 2003. It would like to put in place a skeleton staff in November and full staffing in place by the end of December. It is especially keen to ensure that the factory produces quality products from the beginning and that production is

brought on line as smoothly as possible. The new factory will include a fully equipped training centre and the company will supply a learning resource centre as part of this development. It believes that training is crucial to the success of the venture. It is also keen to attract high-calibre staff, particularly at management levels. It expects to utilise some expatriate staff, but is keen to employ a high percentage of indigenous Chinese staff. It is also keen to avoid the problems that it experienced in its factory in the South of China.

Questions

Yummee has asked for guidance on the following issues:

1 How should it go about recruiting workers for the new factory? What recruitment channels would you recommend and why?

2 How would it organise the selection process for managers and shopfloor workers?

Case study continued

3 Provide guidance that focuses upon how it would develop a reward system for managers and shopfloor workers.

4 Produce a plan that focuses upon meeting training and development needs. This should include the following details: timescale, resourcing requirements and staffing needs.

5 Are there any training programmes that would be compulsory for all?

6 What systems should be put in place to ensure that individual training needs were met?

Identify the critical success factors and barriers that would be related to each of these activities.

References and further reading

Those texts marked with an asterisk are particularly recommended for further reading. The issues covered in this chapter are also addressed in Chapters 8, 13 and 15.

There are also regular articles on Asian countries in the *International Journal of Human Resource Management* and the *Asia Pacific Business Review*. These two journals and the *Human Resource Management Journal* have had special editions on HRM in the Asian region in recent years. There are also occasional articles on Asian HRM in the many other journals that cover HRM subjects.

Abegglen, J. and Stalk, G. (1987) *Kaisha: The Japanese Corporation*. Tokyo: Charles F. Tuttle.

Anon (1995), 'The economic growth of Korea', *Asian Wall Street Journal*, 15 September, p. 3.

Anon (2000a) 'The end of tycoons', *The Economist*, 29 April.

Anon (2000b) 'Let the good times roll', *The Economist*, 18 April.

Aryee, S. (1994) 'The social organisation of careers as a source of sustained competitive advantage: the case of Singapore', *International Journal of Human Resource Management*, Vol. 5, No. 1, pp. 67–88.

Ashton, D. and Sung, J. (1994) *The State Economic Development and Skill Formation: A New Asian Model?* Working Paper 3, Centre for Labour Market Studies, Leicester University, May.

Benson, J. (1996) 'Management strategy and labour flexibility in Japanese manufacturing enterprises', *Human Resource Management Journal*, Vol. 6, No. 2, pp. 44–57.

Benson, J., Debroux, P., Yuasa, M. and Zhu, Y. (2000) 'Flexibility and labour management: Chinese manufacturing enterprises in the 1990s', *International Journal of Human Resource Management*, Vol. 11, No. 2, pp. 183–196.

Benson, J. and Zhu, Y. (1999) 'Markets, firms and workers in Chinese state-owned enterprises', *Human Resource Management Journal*, Vol. 9, No. 4, pp. 58–74.

*Berggren, C. and Nomura, M. (1997) *The Resilience of Corporate Japan: New Competitive Strategies and Personnel Practices*. London: Paul Chapman.

Bjorkman, I. and Xiucheng, F. (2002) 'Human resource management and the performance of Western firms in China', *International Journal of Human Resource Management*, Vol. 13, No. 6, pp. 853–864.

Buchanan, D. and Huczynski, A. (1997) *Organisational Behaviour: An Introductory Text*. Hemel Hempstead: Prentice Hall.

Burrell, G. (1997) *Pandemonium: Towards a Retro-Organisation Theory*. London: Sage.

Burton, J. (1999a) 'Economic squeeze calls for change', *Financial Times*, 20 October.

Burton, J. (1999b) 'The chaebol: the empire strikes back', *Financial Times*, 20 October.

Burton, J. (1999c) 'Banking: still reluctant to change', *Financial Times*, 20 October.

Burton, J., Jonquieres, G., Kazmin, A. and Mandel-Campbell, A. (2001) 'Enter the dragon: economic uncertainties raised by China's accession to the WTO are likely to put pressure on international trade relations for years to come', *Financial Times*, 10 December.

CCCC (1993) *The Work Report of the 14th Conference of the Central Communist Party*. Peoples Republic of China.

Chalmers, N. (1989) *Industrial Relations in Japan: The Peripheral Workforce*. London: Routledge.

*Chen, M. (1995) *Asian Management Systems: Chinese, Japanese and Korean Styles of Business*. London: Thunderbird/Routledge Series in International Management.

*Child, J. (1994) *Management in China in the Age of Reform*. Cambridge: Cambridge University Press.

Chu, P. and Siu, W. (2001) 'Coping with the Asian economic crisis: the rightsizing of small and medium sized enterprises', *International Journal of Human Resource Management*, Vol. 12, No. 5, pp. 845–858.

Deyo, F. (1995) 'Human resource strategies in Thailand', in Frenkel, S. and Harrold, J. (eds) *Industrialization and Labor Relations: Contemporary Research in Seven Countries*. Ithaca, NY: ILR Press, pp. 23–36.

Ding, Z., Goodall, K. and Warner, M. (2000) 'The end of the "iron rice-bowl": whither Chinese human resource management?', *International Journal of Human Resource Management*, Vol. 11, No. 2, pp. 217–236.

Ding, Z. and Warner, M. (1999) 'Re-inventing China's industrial relations at enterprise level: an empirical field-study in four major cities', *Industrial Relations Journal*, Vol. 30, No. 3, pp. 243–260.

*Dore, R. (1973) *British Factory: Japanese Factory*. London: Allen & Unwin.

Easterby-Smith, M., Malina, D. and Yuan, L. (1995) 'How culture sensitive is HRM? A comparative analysis of practice in Chinese and UK companies', *International Journal of Human Resource Management*, Vol. 6, No. 1, pp. 31–59.

Fan, X. (1995) 'The Chinese cultural system: implications for cross-cultural management', *SAM Advanced Management Journal*, Vol. 60, No. 1, pp. 14–20.

Fields, D., Chan, A. and Akhtar, S. (2000) 'Organisational context and human resource management strategy: a structural equation analysis of Hong Kong firms', *International Journal of Human Resource Management*, Vol. 11, No. 2, pp. 264–277.

Financial Times (1999a) 'Country survey of China', 1 October.

Financial Times (1999b) 'Country survey of Hong Kong', 30 June.

Financial Times (1999c) 'Country survey of Korea', 20 October.

Gerlach, M. (1992) *Alliance Capitalism: The Social Organisation of Japanese Business*. Berkeley, Calif.: University of California Press.

Glover, L. and Siu, N. (1999) *The Human Resource Barriers to Managing Quality in China*, Leicester Business School Occasional Papers Series, Number 55.

Gordon, A. (1985) *The Evolution of Labor Relations in Japan*. Cambridge, Mass.: Council on East Asian Studies, Harvard University.

Grammaticus, D. (2002) 'Hong Kong unemployment surges', BBC News, 17 January.

Jacob, R. (2002) 'From lavish parties to pessimism: businessmen say they feel "awful" but believe their prospects are good', *Financial Times*, 1 July.

Jacobs, L., Gao, G. and Herbig, P. (1995) 'Confucian roots in China: a force for today's business', *Management Decision*, Vol. 33, No. 9, pp. 29–35.

Japan Labour Bulletin (1999) August.

Kawakita, T. (1997) 'Corporate strategy and human resource management', in Sako, M. and Sato, H. (eds) *Japanese Management and Labour in Transition*. London: Routledge, pp. 79–103.

Kim, S. and Briscoe, D.R. (1997) 'Globalisation and a new human resource policy in Korea: transformation to a performance based HRM', *Employee Relations*, Vol. 19, No. 4, pp. 298–308.

Kroll, J. (1993) 'From capitalism without cost towards competitive capitalism', *Nikkei Weekly*, 25 October, pp. 9–10.

Kuwahara, Y (1998) 'Employment relations in Japan', in Bamber, G. and Lansbury, R. (eds) *International and Comparative Employment Relations*. London: Sage, pp. 249–279.

Kynge, J. (1999) 'Reflections on half a century', *Financial Times*, 1 October.

Lardy, N. (2002) 'Problems on the road to liberalisation: China has joined the WTO on stricter terms than fellow members. If it is to succeed in opening its markets, the world should resist using protectionist provisions', *Financial Times*, 15 March.

Leahy, J. (2002) 'Still waiting for the correction: Hong Kong property prices have fallen 65% in the bubble years, but they remain expensive and could slide further', *Financial Times*, 30 November.

Leggett, C. and Bamber, G. (1996) 'Asia Pacific tiers of change', *Human Resource Management Journal*, special issue: *HRM in the Asia Pacific Region*, Vol. 6, No. 2, pp. 7–19.

Lockett, M. (1988) 'Culture and the problems of Chinese management', *Organisation Studies*, Vol. 9, No. 4, pp. 475–496.

Low, L. (1993) 'From entrepôt to a newly industrialising economy', in Low, L., Heng, T.M.H., Wong, T.W., Yam, T.K. and Hughes, H. (eds) *Challenge and Response: Thirty Years of the Economic Development Board*. Singapore: Times Academic Press.

Low, L., Toh, M.H. and Soon, T.W. (1991) *Economics of Education and Manpower Development: Issues and Policies in Singapore*. Singapore: McGraw-Hill.

Lucas, L. (1999a) 'Still lingering in negative territory', *Financial Times*, 30 June.

Lucas, L. (1999b) 'Tiger rivalry: jury still out on best methods', *Financial Times*, 15 September.

Luo, Y. and Chen, M. (1997) 'Does guanxi affect company performance?', *Asia Pacific Journal of Management*, Vol. 14, No. 1, pp. 1–16.

Mok, K., Wong, L. and Lee, G. (2002) 'The challenges of global capitalism: unemployment and state workers reactions and responses in post-reform China', *International Journal of Human Resource Management*, Vol. 13, No. 3, pp. 399–415.

Montagnon, P. (1999a) 'Agonising choices accompany change', *Financial Times*, 1 October.

Montagnon, P. (1999b) 'Banking: still reluctant to change', *Financial Times*, 20 October.

Morden, T. and Bowles, D. (1998) 'Management in South Korea: a review', *Management Decision*, Vol. 36, No. 5, pp. 316–330.

Murray, G. (1994) *Doing Business in China*. Kent: China Library.

Ouchi, W. (1981) *Theory Z*. New York: Avon.

Paik, Y., Vance, C. and Stage, D. (1996) 'The extent of divergence in human resource practice across three Chinese national cultures: Hong Kong, Taiwan and Singapore', *Human Resource Management Journal*, Vol. 6, No. 2, pp. 7–19.

Park, W. and Yu, G. (2000) 'Transformation and new patterns of HRM in Korea', Conference paper at the International Conference on Transforming Korean Business and Management Culture, Michagan State University, 19–20 September.

Peng, F.C. (1994) 'China: managers can learn from the methods of venture partners', *South China Morning Post*, April, Vol. 13, No. 15.

Rowley, C. (1997) 'Conclusion: reassessing HRM's convergence', *Asia Pacific Business Review*, special issue: *Human Resource Management in the Asia Pacific Region: Convergence Questioned*, Vol. 3, No. 4, pp. 197–210.

Rowley, C. and Bae, J. (2002) 'Globalisation and transformation of human resource management in South Korea', *International Journal of Human Resource Management*, Vol. 13, No. 3, pp. 522–549.

Sako, M. (1997) 'Introduction: forces for homogeneity and diversity in the Japanese industrial relations system', in Sako, M. and Sato, H. (eds) *Japanese Management and Labour in Transition*. London: Routledge, pp. 1–28.

*Sako, M. and Sato, H. (eds) (1997) *Japanese Management and Labour in Transition*. London: Routledge.

Sano, Y. (1993) 'Changes and continued stability in Japanese HRM systems: choice in the share economy', *International Journal of Human Resource Management*, Vol. 4, No. 1, pp. 11–28.

Sasajima, Y. (1993) 'Changes in labour supply and their impacts on human resources management: the case of Japan', *International Journal of Human Resource Management*, Vol. 4, No. 1, pp. 29–44.

SEDB (2000) 'EDB launches economic blueprint for the 21st century', Singapore Economic Development Board, website: www.sedb.com.sg/home.html

Selmer, J., Ebrahimi, P. and Mingtao, L. (2000) 'Personal characteristics and adjustment of Chinese mainland business expatriates in Hong Kong', *International Journal of Human Resource Management*, Vol. 11, No. 2. pp. 237–250.

Shibata, H. (2000) 'The transformation of the wage and performance appraisal system in a Japanese firm', *International Journal of Human Resource Management*, Vol. 11, No. 2, pp. 294–313.

Sparrow, P. and Wu, P.-C. (1999) 'How much do national value orientations really matter? Predicting HRM preferences of Taiwanese employees', in Lähteenmäki, S., Holden, L. and Roberts, I. (eds) *HRM and the Learning Organisation*. Turku, Finland: Turku School of Economics, pp. 239–284.

Stam, J.A. (1982) *Human Resource Management in Japan: Organisational Innovation in Three Medium Sized Companies*. Rotterdam: Erasmus University.

Teen, M.K. and Phan, P.H. (1999) 'Corporate governance in Singapore: current practice and future developments', Paper to OECD conference on Corporate Governance in Asia: A Comparative Perspective, Seoul, South Korea, 3–5 March (unpublished).

Thornhill, J. (2002a) 'Private enterprise seen as way forward', *Financial Times*, 12 December.

Thornhill, J. (2002b) 'Companies rush in with the cash', *Financial Times*, 12 December.

Thornhill, J. (2002c) 'Asia's recovery "exposed to oil price volatility"', *Financial Times*, 10 April.

Thornhill, J. (2002d) 'Rebuilding the tiger: five years after East Asia suffered a devastating financial crisis, John Thornhill finds that the region has gone a long way towards improving corporate governance', *Financial Times*, 5 June.

Tsang, E.W.K. (1994) 'Human resource management problems in Sino-foreign joint ventures', *Employee Relations*, Vol. 15, No. 9, pp. 1–14.

Tsuru, T. and Rebitzer, J. (1995) 'The limits of enterprise unionism: prospects for continuing union decline in Japan', *British Journal of Industrial Relations*, Vol. 33, No. 3, pp. 459–492.

Vickers da Costa (1983) *Singapore's High Technology Future: Singapore*. Vickers da Costa.

Vogel, E. (1980) *Japan as No. 1*. Tokyo: Charles F. Tuttle.

Ward, A. (2002a) 'Hailed as an example to other Asian countries: economic transformation by Andrew Ward: But despite dramatic progress, economic weaknesses remain', *Financial Times*, 29 October.

Ward, A. (2002b) 'Country's largest company shifts upmarket and wins accolade: Samsung Electronics', *Financial Times*, 29 October.

Ward, A. (2002c) 'Benefits of restructuring are starting to filter through', *Financial Times*, 29 October.

Ward, A. (2002e) 'Strike hits Korean car makers', *Financial Times*, 6 November.

Ward, A. (2002f) 'South Korean unions set for privatisation protest', *Financial Times*, 25 February.

Warner, M. (1992) *How Chinese Managers Learn: Management and Industrial Training in China*. London: Macmillan.

Warner, M. (1993) 'Human resource management with Chinese characteristics', *International Journal of Human Resource Management*, Vol. 4, No. 1, pp. 45–65.

Warner, M. (1996) 'Human resources in the People's Republic of China: the "three systems reforms"', *Human Resource Management Journal*, Vol. 6, No. 2, pp. 32–43.

Warner, M. (1997) 'Management–labour relations in the new Chinese economy', *Human Resource Management Journal*, Vol. 7, No. 4, p. 3.

Warner, M. (2000) 'Introduction: the Asia-Pacific HRM model revisited', *International Journal of Human Resource Management*, Vol. 11, No. 2, pp. 171–182.

*Whitley, R. (1992) *Business Systems in East Asia*. London: Sage.

Whitley, R. (1999) *Divergent Capitalisms: The Social Structuring and Change of Business Systems*. Oxford: Oxford University Press.

World Bank (1999) 'China: weathering the storm and learning the lessons', *Country Studies*, 8 January, p. 114.

Zhu, C. and Dowling, P. J. (2002) 'Staffing practices in translation: some empirical evidence from China', *International Journal of Human Resource Management*, Vol. 13, No. 4, pp. 569–597.

Zuboff, S. (1988) *In the Age of the Smart Machine: The Future of Work and Power*. Oxford: Heinemann Publishing.

 For multiple choice questions, exercises and annotated weblinks specific to this chapter visit this book's website at www.booksites.net/beardwell

Global and local: the case of the inoperable HRM strategy

Medical Precision Systems (MPS) is a US-owned company based on the outskirts of Birmingham, Alabama, USA. It has been producing medical precision tools used in surgery since 1972, and has built up a well-respected business in the USA with a turnover of $150 million annually. Its Birmingham plant employs 2000 staff made up of skilled and semi-skilled workers. Most staff are employed in production process work, but a significant number work in research and development and other highly skilled and knowledge-based areas.

There are no unions and the Human Resources Department has consciously followed a policy of best-practice HRM to keep out union influence. There is a an excellent pensions scheme, a successful profit-sharing scheme, and a share options scheme whereby employees can choose to have bonuses in the form of company shares if they have worked at MPS for more than two years. Laying employees off is avoided as much as possible during slack periods in order to retain staff loyalty.

However, a performance management culture is strong at MPS, and there is an astringent appraisal system linked to remuneration and promotion. Target setting for groups and individuals has been strongly implemented for the past 20 years and refined over that time. A total quality management (TQM) programme has been in operation for the past 15 years, and work areas or cells are operated by teams. Under the TQM system groups of ten workers are allowed to elect a leader, who organises feedback sessions and reports to senior production managers. Annual staff opinion surveys are conducted on a range of employment and production issues. Training is taken seriously, and all employees attend sessions to train in teamworking and people skills, as well as sessions and courses of a more technical nature. MPS prides itself on its strong culture, and likes to communicate its values and vision clearly and frequently to the workforce. The mission statement 'MPS – working for the health of America' is printed on all pay packets and slips, and most communication bulletins.

There are excellent canteen and recreational facilities, the employees have a number of sports teams, and social events take place regularly.

Expanding overseas

Since the early 1990s MPS has decided to set up plants overseas, but in doing so is conscious that it needs a fairly educated workforce that can cope with the highly technical nature of the work. In addition, it has recognised that its major markets are in Europe, where it has been exporting since the early 1980s. The MPS board thus decided to open subsidiaries in the UK initially, followed by Sweden and later France.

The UK operation was acquired by taking over a medical engineering company in 1991 near Bath and initially employed 150 people rising to 350 by the end of the decade. The Swedish subsidiary was set up on a greenfield site in a business park on the outskirts of the university city of Uppsala in 1994, employing 50 and then 250 staff by the end of the decade. A new plant was set up in Lyons, France, in 1997 that employs fewer than 200 staff.

In 2001 the MPS HQ in Alabama was revamping its strategy in line with its global developments and commitments. The production and marketing side of the business were doing well, and there had been steady growth in the UK subsidiary in Bath and the Swedish subsidiary at Uppsala. Preliminary reports also indicated that the French subsidiary had enormous potential. However, the Director of Human Resources, Jim Grant, commissioned a full report on the overseas HRM operations as there had been difficulties experienced in HRM. Jim wanted to create an HRM strategy that would complement the new business strategy and at the same time solve the problems in the overseas subsidiaries.

The existing international HRM strategy

Using Perlmutter's typology, MPS's international HRM strategy can only be described as ethnocentric (see Chapter 15). It attempts to exert strong controls over its subsidiaries through the extensive use of expatriate managers in both technical and managerial areas of the business. Its goals in financial and production terms have been set by the parent company, and the local subsidiaries have little say. The feedback mechanisms have been implemented from the USA, backed with training programmes for all employees.

Expatriate managers have been told either to keep the unions out or to ensure that their influence is as minimal as possible. Loyalty schemes such as profit sharing have been introduced, and it is planned that the company share scheme will be introduced in 2002 across all subsidiaries. Annual staff opinion surveys have been implemented, and communication is emphasised as being fluid and as frequent as possible between expatriate managers, host country managers and employees.

TQM programmes have also been introduced, and are run with the teamworking systems and workplace feedback and improvement mechanisms. The strong MPS culture has been effectively reinforced through regular staff bulletins, and local company magazines in the language of the subsidiary company country. The mission statement is widely displayed, and a strong public relations image also supports the company culture.

While many of these initiatives have had success, there has been some reluctance and even opposition to others in the three European subsidiaries. In 2001 Jim Grant carried out a full review, and was able to make the following points in a report to the US HQ board.

HRM overseas in MPS: report by Jim Grant

One of the problems we have faced is the diversity of conditions in the subsidiaries, and the practices we follow in the USA do not always translate well in the local context. These problems concern expatriate managers, industrial relations, management style and the degree of control that subsidiaries believe is being exerted over them. Expatriate managers faced a considerable degree of difficulty when given assignments, particularly in the European subsidiaries. While all the senior managers in France and Sweden spoke excellent English, there were considerable communication barriers between the American expatriates and their subsidiary workforces. Common problems were incomprehension of each other's culture and working practices.

Expatriate manager feedback, Bath, UK

Joe Mendes, who runs the English operation, also commented that, despite the common language, he didn't always understand the British mentality. There was considerable resentment when it was suggested that weekend working be brought in to fulfil some emergency orders.

He also said the plant we inherited was highly unionised, with several technical and other unions operating. When he suggested having one union for negotiating purposes there was nearly a mass walk-out, and union officials became very obstructive. Another problem was the performance management system, which met with considerable initial difficulties in being set up. The unions and many employees felt the targets were too harsh and divisive, and they also felt that they had little control over them.

Expatriate manager feedback, Lyons, France

Andy Smith, who runs the French operation, had no problems in regard to the unions, as it was a green-

field site and it was relatively easy to exclude unions by recruiting new staff, although some of the technical staff had union membership. The major problem concerned management style. While there were some initial difficulties in setting up the performance management system, the main problem was with the feedback mechanisms. The French workforce could not see the point of the cellular feedback mechanisms, and preferred to have a line manager with an authoritative air, technically proficient and capable of directing the workforce towards work tasks.

Andy also had problems in getting the workforce to work extra hours, and he felt there were excessive holidays in France. 'Every time production seemed to be up running perfectly, another saint's day holiday would put out our schedule,' he said.

A works council was set up in accordance with French law, but in the eyes of most of the French workforce did not operate very effectively.

Expatriate manager feedback, Uppsala, Sweden

Gary Alder, head of the Swedish operation, reported that despite the subsidiary being a greenfield site start-up operation the workforce very soon joined unions, and by the end of the first year over 65 per cent of employees were union members. As in France and the UK, the Swedish workforce baulked at the targets set under the performance management scheme. However, there was considerable enthusiasm for the feedback mechanisms in the cellular manufacturing processes, and many interesting ideas and innovations emerged as a result of this.

The Swedes, like the French and the British, were not impressed by the attempts by American management to engender a 'gung ho' culture through culture training and attitudinal orientation sessions. Most employees in all three countries paid lip service to these sessions.

Under Swedish and EU law a works council had to be set up for management and employees, but the Americans, although having to conform to European and national laws, resented these meetings and tended to treat them with less than enthusiasm. They appeared in the eyes of one Swedish union organiser at times to be almost non-cooperative.

The general conclusion that Jim drew was that some HRM policies had been more successful than others.

Questions

1 Given the report, what would you advise Jim to recommend to the board in drawing up a new international HRM strategy?

2 How could this strategy be locally responsive and yet global in its scope?

GLOSSARY OF TERMS AND ABBREVIATIONS

ACFTU The All China Federation of Trade Unions.

Added value Technically the difference between the value of a firm's inputs and its outputs; the additional value is added through the deployment and efforts of the firm's resources. Can be defined as FVA (financial value added), CVA (customer value added) and PVA (people value added).

AEL Accreditation of Experiential Learning.

Alienation Marx suggests it is a condition in which a worker loses power to control the performance, processes and product of his/her labour. Thus the very worker becomes a thing rather than a human being, in which state they experience powerlessness, meaninglessness, isolation and self-estrangement.

Androgogy 'The art and science of helping adults learn' (Knowles, 1984: 60).

Annualised hours contract Relatively novel form of employment contract that offers management, and sometimes workers, a considerable degree of flexibility. The hours that an employee works can be altered within a very short time frame within a day, a week, or even a month. So long as the total hours worked do not exceed the contractually fixed annual amount an employee can be asked and expected to work from 0 up to anything in excess of 80 hours in any one week.

APL Accreditation of Prior Learning.

Appraisal The process through which an assessment is made of an employee by another person using quantitative and/or qualitative assessments.

Appraisal (360 degree) A system of appraisal which seeks feedback from 'all directions' – superiors, subordinates, peers and customers.

Attitude survey Survey, usually conducted by questionnaire, to elicit employees' opinions about issues to do with their work and the organisation.

Balanced scorecard An integrated framework for balancing shareholder and strategic goals, and extending these balanced performance measures down the organisation.

Best-fit Models of HRM that focus on alignment between HRM and business strategy and the external context of the firm. Tend to link or 'fit' generic type business strategies to generic HRM strategies.

Best practice A 'set' or number of human resource practices that have the potential to enhance organisational performance when implemented.

Usually categorised as 'high commitment', high involvement' or 'high performance'.

BMA British Medical Association.

Broadbanding: Pay systems which have a wide range of possible pay levels within them. Unlike traditional narrow systems, there is normally a high degree of overlap across the grades.

BS 5750 British standard of quality, originally applied to the manufacture of products but now also being used to 'measure' quality of service. Often used in EI as a way of getting employees to self-check their quality of work against a standardised norm.

BTEC Business and Technology Education Council.

Bundles A coherent combination of human resource practices that are horizontally integrated.

Bushido Japanese term meaning 'the way of the warrior'.

Business process re-engineering (BPR) System that aims to improve performance by redesigning the processes through which an organisation operates, maximising their value-added content and minimising everything else (Peppard and Rowland, 1995: 20).

Career 'The evolving sequence of a person's work experiences over time' (Arthur *et al.*, 1989: 8); 'the individual's development in learning and work throughout life' (Collin and Watts, 1996: 393).

CATS Credit Accumulation and Transfer Scheme.

Causal ambiguity The cause or source of an organisation's competitive advantage is ambiguous or unclear, particularly to the organisation's competitors.

CBI Confederation of British Industry. Powerful institution set up in 1965 to promote and represent the interests of British industry. Financed by subscription and made up of employers' associations, national business associations and over 10 000 affiliated companies. Works to advise and negotiate with the government and the Trades Union Congress.

CCT Compulsory competitive tendering.

CEE Central and Eastern European states formerly of the Soviet system including Russia, Bulgaria, Czech Republic, East Germany (GDR), Estonia, Hungary, Latvia, Lithuania, Poland, Rumania, Slovakia, Slovenia.

CEEP European Centre of Public Enterprises.

Chaebols The large, family-owned conglomerates that dominate Korea's economy. The five leading *chaebols* prior to the collapse of Daewoo were Hyundai, Samsung, Daewoo, Lucky Goldstar and the SK group.

Chaos and complexity theories In contrast to traditional science, these more recent theories draw attention to the uncertainty, non-linearity and unpredictability that result from the interrelatedness and interdependence of the elements of the universe.

CIPD Chartered Institute of Personnel and Development – the professional organisation for human resource and personnel managers and those in related fields such as training and development. Website: www.cipd.org.uk

Closed system System that does not interact with other subsystems or its environment.

COHSE Confederation of Health Service Employees.

Collective bargaining Process utilised by trade unions, as the representatives of employees, and management, as the representatives of employers, to establish the terms and conditions under which labour will be employed.

Competence 'The ability to perform the activities within an occupational area to the levels of performance expected in employment' (Training Commission, 1988).

Competences Behavioural repertoires that people input to a job, role or organisation context, and which employees need to bring to a role to perform to the required level (see also **Core competences**).

Competency-based pay An approach to reward based on the attainment of skills or talents by individuals in relation to a specific task at a certain standard.

Competitive advantage The ability of an organisation to add more value for its customers than its rivals, and therefore gain a position of advantage in the marketplace.

Configurational approach An approach that identified the benefits of identifying a set of horizontally integrated HR practices that were aligned to the business strategy, thus fitting the internal and external context of the business.

Contingent pay: Elements of the reward package which are contingent on other events (performance, merit, attendance) and are awarded at the discretion of the management.

Cooperatives Organisations and companies that are collectively owned either by their customers or by their employees.

Core competences Distinctive skills and knowledge, related to product, service or technology, that can be used to gain competitive advantage.

CPSA Civil and Public Servants Association.

Culture The prevailing pattern of values, attitudes, beliefs, assumptions, norms and sentiments.

Danwei Central to the state-owned enterprises in China were work units or *danweis*.

DES Department of Education and Science, now renamed the Department for Education and Skills (DfES).

Deskilling The attempt by management to appropriate and monopolise workers' knowledge of production in an effort to control the labour process. To classify, tabulate, and reduce this knowledge to rules, laws and formulae, which are then allocated to workers on a daily basis.

DETR Department of the Environment, Transport and the Regions.

Development The process of becoming increasingly complex, more elaborate and differentiated, by virtue of learning and maturation, resulting in new ways of acting and responding to the environment.

Development centres Normally used for the selection of managers. They utilise a range of intensive psychological tests and simulations to assess management potential.

DfEE Department for Education and Employment, now renamed the Department for Education and Skills (DfES).

Discourse The shared language, metaphors, stories that give members of a group their particular way of interpreting reality.

Downsizing Possibly the simplest explanation is given by Heery and Noon (2001: 90) as 'getting rid of employees'. A modern 'buzzword' used to indicate the reduction of employment within organisations.

Double-loop learning *See* single-loop learning.

Dual system German system of vocational training for apprentices, which combines off-the-job training at vocational colleges with on-the-job training under the tutelage of *meister* (skilled craft) workers.

EC European Community. The term superseded the EEC after the SEM, as describing more than purely economic union. Since 1992 has been renamed European Union (see below).

ECSC European Coal and Steel Community, founded in 1952.

EEC European Economic Community. A term used to describe the Common Market after the Treaty of Rome 1957.

Efficiency The sound management of resources within a business in order to *maximise* the return on investment.

Effectiveness The ability of an organisation to meet the demands and expectations of its various stakeholders, albeit some more than others!

EI Employee involvement; a term to describe the wide variety of schemes in which employees can be involved in their work situation.

e-Learning Use of new technology such as e-mail, the Internet, intranets and computer software packages to facilitate learning for employees.

Emergent Strategies which emerge over time, sometimes with an element of trial and error. Some emergent strategies are incremental changes with embedded learning, others may be adaptive in response to external environmental changes.

Employability The acquisition and updating of skills, experience, reputation – the investment in human capital – to ensure that the individual remains employable, and not dependent upon a particular organisation.

Empowerment Recent term that encompasses EI initiatives to encourage the workforce to have direct individual and collective control over their work processes, taking responsibility for improved customer service to both internal and external customers. Generally confined to workplace-level issues and concerns.

EMU European Monetary Union.

Enterprise unions Japanese concept of employee unions associated with only one enterprise and the only one recognised by the company. One of the 'three pillars' of the Japanese employment system.

Epistemology The assumptions made about the world which form the basis for knowledge.

EPU European political union.

ESOPS Employee share option scheme, whereby employees are allowed to purchase company shares or are given them as part of a bonus.

ET Employment Training.

ETUC European Trade Union Confederation.

EU European Union, so named in 1992 (formerly EC).

EURATOM European Atomic Energy Community.

Factor of production An input into the production process. Factors of production were traditionally classified as *land* (raw materials), *capital* (buildings, equipment, machinery) and *labour*. Labour is usually seen as a variable factor of production because labour inputs can be varied quite easily at short notice, unlike capital, the amount of which cannot be varied easily in the short run. Internalising the employment relationship transforms labour into a *quasi-fixed factor of production* because it restricts the employer's freedom to cut jobs at short notice.

FIEs Foreign invested enterprises.

Firm-specific skills Skills that can be used in only one or a few particular organisations.

Fit The level of integration between an organisation's business strategy and its human resource policies and practices. 'Fit' tends to imply a top-down relationship between the strategy makers and the strategy implementers.

FKTU Federation of Korean Trade Unions.

Forked lightning, the Mae West Language and concepts used by city financiers working on the international currency and commodity markets. Used to describe the patterns formed by fluctuating price movements as they get represented on dealers' screens.

GDP Gross domestic product.

GNVQs General National Vocational Qualifications.

Guanxi Chinese term that refers to the concept of drawing on connections or networks to secure favours in personal or business relations.

Hard HRM A view of HRM that identifies employees as a cost to be minimised, and tends to focus on 'flexibility techniques' and limited investment in learning and development (see also **Soft HRM**).

Hegemony The imposition upon others of a powerful group's interpretation of reality.

High-performance work practices A term that gained currency in the 1990s that sought to link bundles of HR practices with outcomes in terms of increased employee commitment and performance which in turn enhances the firm's sustained competitive advantage, efficiency and profitability.

HMSO Her Majesty's Stationery Office. Publishers of parliamentary proceedings, official government documents and reports.

Holistic Treatment of organisations, situations, problems as totalities or wholes as opposed to a specific, reductionist approach.

Horizontal integration Level of alignment across and within functions, such that all functional policies and practices are integrated and congruent with one another.

HRD Human resource development.

Human capital The knowledge, skill and attitudes, the intangible contributions to high performance, that make employees assets to the organisation.

Human relations Associated with the pioneering work of Roethlisberger and Dickson, Elton Mayo and others, who studied the importance of community and collective values in work organisations. These studies first identified that management needed to attend to the 'social needs' of employees.

Ideology The set of ideas and beliefs that underpins interpretations of reality.

IIP Investors in People.

ILO International Labour Organization.

IMS The Institute of Manpower Studies. Located at the University of Sussex.

Institutional vacuum/representation gap Situation in which collective bargaining is no longer the dominant form of establishing terms and conditions of employment, but no recognisable or regulated channel of employee representation or employee voice has emerged to replace it.

Intellectual capital The hidden value, and capital, tied up in an organisation's people (knowledge, skills and competencies), which can be a key source of competitive advantage and differentiate it from its competitors.

IPD Institute of Personnel and Development; see also **CIPD**.

IRDAC Industrial Research and Development Advisory Committee of the Commission of the European Communities.

IRS Industrial Relations Services. A data gathering and publications bureau that collects and analyses movement in key variables of importance to the study and practice of industrial relations.

ITBs Industrial Training Boards. Set up in 1964 to monitor training in various sectors of the economy. Most were abolished in 1981, but a few still survive.

JCC Joint consultative committee; body made up of employee representatives and management, which meets regularly to discuss issues of common interest.

Job enlargement Related to job rotation, whereby a job is made bigger by the introduction of new tasks. This gives greater variety in job content and thereby helps to relieve monotony in repetitive jobs such as assembly line working.

Job enrichment Adds to a cycle of work not only a variety of tasks but increased responsibility to workers. Most associated with autonomous work groups introduced into Volvo's Kalmar plant in Sweden in the 1970s.

Job rotation Originally introduced in the 1970s for members of a team to exchange jobs to enliven work interest, but also used recently to promote wider skills experience and flexibility among employees.

JV Joint venture.

KCTU Korean Confederation of Trade Unions.

Knowledge-based age Reflects the move to a global environment, where tacit and explicit knowledge becomes a key source of competitive advantage for organisations.

Knowledge-based organisation One that manages the generation of new knowledge through learning, capturing knowledge and experience, sharing, collaborating and communicating, organising information and using and building on what is known.

Labour process The application of human labour to raw materials in the production of goods and services that are later sold on the free market. Labour is paid a wage for its contribution, but capital must ensure that it secures value added over and above what it is paying for. Some call this efficiency. Others prefer the term 'exploitation'.

Learning Complex cognitive, physical, and affective process that results in the capacity for changed performance.

Learning cycle Learning seen as a process having different identifiable phases. Effective learning may be facilitated if methods appropriate to the various phases are used.

Learning style Individuals differ in their approaches to learning, and prefer one mode of learning, or phase of the learning cycle, to others.

Learning organisation (LO) 'A Learning Company is an organisation that facilitates the learning of all its members and consciously transforms itself and its context' (Pedler *et al.*, 1997: 3).

LECs Local Enterprise Companies. Scottish equivalent of TECs. There are 22 in existence. (*See* TECs.)

Leverage The exploitation by an organisation of its resources to their full extent. Often linked to the notion of stretching resources.

Lifetime employment Japanese concept whereby in large corporations employees are guaranteed a job for life in exchange for loyalty to the organisation. One of the 'three pillars' of the Japanese employment system.

LMS Local management of schools.

LSC Learning and Skills Council.

Maastricht Protocol Part of the Maastricht Treaty dealing with the Social Chapter (Social Charter), allowing Britain to sign the treaty without signing the Maastricht Protocol or Social Chapter.

Maastricht Treaty The content was agreed at a meeting at Maastricht in the Netherlands and signed in a watered-down form in Edinburgh in 1992. It was rejected and then accepted by the voters of Denmark in two referendums. It concerns extending aspects of European political union (EPU) and European and Monetary Union (EMU).

Management gurus Phenomenon of the 1980s, when academics, consultants and business practitioners began to enjoy celebrity status as specialists on the diagnosis of management problems and the development of 'business solutions'. Includes people such as Tom Peters, Rosabeth Moss Kanter, John Harvey Jones, and M.C. Robert Beeston.

McDonaldisation The reduction of organisation to simple, repetitive, and predictable work processes that make the labour process more amenable to standardised calculation and control.

MCI (Management Charter Initiative) Employer-led initiative with the aim of developing recognised standards in management practice.

Measured day work: MDW is a system within which pay is fixed against specific levels of performance during the 'day' rather than by the hourly performance or piece-rates.

Mentor More experienced person who guides, encourages and supports a younger or less experienced person.

MSC Manpower Services Commission. Previously had responsibility for training but was abolished in 1988.

Mission statement A statement setting out the main purpose of the business.

NACETT National Advisory Council for Education and Training Targets now incorporated into the Learning and Skills Councils.

NALGO National and Local Government Officers Association.

NASUWT National Association of School Masters/Union of Women Teachers.

National curriculum Obligatory subjects of the UK's school system, introduced via the Education Reform Act 1989.

National minimum wage Introduced by the National Minimum Wage Act 1998, this sets the minimum rate of reward any worker can receive on an hourly basis. The scale is age related and linked to inflation through an annual upgrade.

NATO North Atlantic Treaty Organization. Western defensive alliance set up originally in 1949 to promote economic and military cooperation among its members. The original members were Belgium, Britain, Canada, France, Italy, Norway, Portugal and the Netherlands. Greece and Turkey joined in 1952, and the former West Germany in 1955.

NCU National Communications Union.

NCVQ (National Council for Vocational Qualifications) Government-backed initiative to establish a national system for the recognition of vocational qualifications.

Nemawashi Japanese term for consensus.

NHS National Health Service.

Nenko Japanese term meaning seniority and/or age. One of the 'three pillars' of the Japanese employment system.

Networking Interacting for mutual benefit, usually on an informal basis, with individuals and groups internal and external to the organisation.

New Deal Government initiative that provides training for 18–24-year-olds who have been out of work for more than six months, and 25-year-olds and over who have been unemployed for longer than two years.

Non-union firms Organisations which do not recognise trade unions for collective bargaining purposes; this may be throughout the organisation or at plant or business unit level. So, for example, IBM, frequently quoted as an example of a soft-HRM non-union firm, does, in fact, recognise unions in Germany, as does McDonald's, another organisation strongly associated with an anti-union stance.

NSTF National Skills Task Force.

NUCPS National Union of Civil and Public Servants.

NUPE National Union of Public Employees.

NUT National Union of Teachers.

NVQs National Vocational Qualifications. An attempt to harmonise all VET qualifications within the UK by attributing five levels to all qualifications, from level 1, the lowest, to level 5, the highest.

OMC Open Method of Coordination is an alternative to previous attempts at harmonising legislative forms and procedures within the European Union. In place of substantive legislation on specific issues, strategic objectives and operational guidelines are set for member states and monitoring procedures put in place to assess their performance.

Open system System that is connected to and interacts with other subsystems and its environment.

OSC Occupational Standards Council.

Paired comparisons A system of appraisal which seeks to assess the performance of pairs of individuals, until each employee has been judged in relation to each other.

Paradigm A well-developed, and often widely held, set of associated assumptions that frames the interpretation of reality. When these assumptions are undermined by new knowledge or events, a 'paradigm shift' occurs as the old gives way (often gradually and painfully) to a new paradigm.

Payment by results Reward systems under which worker output or performance determines elements of the package.

Performance-related pay Payment systems which in some way relate reward to either organisational or individual performance. Often used as a way to motivate white-collar workers, usually based on a developed appraisal system.

PFI Private Finance Initiative.

Pluralism Theoretical analysis of the employment relationship that recognises inequality between capital and labour where each of the interest groups has some conflicting and some common aims. To address these issues, pluralists argue that employees should be facilitated to act collectively, usually as a trade union, to redress such imbalances. Management, as the representatives of employers, should engage in collective bargaining with trade unions to establish consensual agreements on issues of conflict and commonality.

Positivism The orthodox approach to the understanding of reality, and the basis for scientific method.

Post-Fordism A claimed epochal shift in manufacturing that sees a move away from mass production assembly lines and the development of flexible systems that empower and reskill line workers. Associated with the move towards niche products and volatile consumer demand.

Postmodernism A term used (often loosely) to denote various disjunctions from, fragmentations in, or challenges to previously common understandings of knowledge and social life.

PRB Pay review body.

Predetermined motion time systems A member of the time-rate pay systems family under which rewards are calculated based on time and piece. As a standard form of incentive bonus scheme, PDMT schemes rewards are set using the pseudo-scientific measurement of activity.

Profit sharing Scheme whereby employees are given a bonus or payment based on a company's profits.

Private Finance Initiative Where the government contracts out projects such as prison management, hospital building, road construction etc. to the private sector, then leases back the service over an extended period of time.

Psychological contract The notion that an individual has a range of expectations about their employing organisation and the organisation has expectations of them.

Psychological (psychometric) testing Specialised tests used for selection or assessing potential. Usually in the form of questionnaires. They construct a personality profile of the candidate.

Quality circle (QC) Group made up of 6–10 employees, with regular meetings held weekly or fortnightly during working time. The principal aim is to identify problems from their own area.

Ranking A method of assessing and ordering individual performance using a predetermined scale.

Rating A determined measure or scale against which an individual's performance is measured.

Reification The conceptualisation and treatment of a person or abstraction as though they were things.

Resource-based view Strategy creation built around the further exploitation of core competencies and strategic capabilities.

RCN Royal College of Nursing.

Rhetoric The often subtle and unacknowledged use of language to 'persuade, influence or manipulate'.

Rightsizing See Downsizing.

Ringi Japanese form of employee involvement.

SCOTVEC Scottish Vocational Education Council.

SEA Single European Act 1987. Proposed the creation of a single European market for trade on 31 December 1992.

SEDB Singapore Economic Development Board.

SEM Single European market, also known as '1992' owing to the date it was set up. See SEA.

Single-loop learning Detection and correction of deviances in performance from established (organ-isational or other) norms. Double-loop learning is the questioning of those very norms that define effective performance. (Compare efficiency and effectiveness.)

Single-table bargaining Arrangement under which unions on a multi-union site develop a mutually agreed bargaining agenda, which is then negotiated jointly with management.

Single-union deal Arrangement under which one trade union operates to represent all employees within an organisation; this is usually a preferred union sponsored by management.

Social Chapter Another name for the Social Charter, which emerged from the Maastricht meeting in 1989.

Social Charter A programme to implement the 'social dimension' of the single market, affording rights and protection to employees.

Social complexity The complex interpersonal relationships that exist within organisations, within and between teams and individuals.

Social constructionism An approach that challenges positivism, arguing that objective reality is not directly knowable: the reality we know is what we construct ourselves through language and in interaction with others.

Social partnership Process whereby employers and employees establish a framework of rights based upon minimum standards in employment, flexibility, security, information sharing and cooperation between management and employees' representatives.

Social relations in production The patterns and dynamics produced and reproduced in action by individuals and collectives employed in the labour process.

Sociotechnical The structuring or integration of human activities and subsystems with technological subsystems.

SOE State-owned enterprise.

Soft HRM A view of HRM that recognises employees as a resource worth investing in, and tends to focus on high-commitment/high-involvement human resource practices. See also **Hard HRM**.

Stakeholders Any individual or group capable of affecting or being affected by the performance and actions of the organisation.

Stakeholder society One in which individuals recognise that only by making a positive contribution to contemporary society can they expect a positive outcome from society.

Stakeholders in social partnership Those groups with an interest in promoting strong social partnerships at work, i.e. the state, employers and their organisations, employees and their organisations.

Strategic management The process by which an organisation establishes its objectives, formulates strategies to meet these objectives, implements actions and measures and monitors performance.

Suggestion scheme (box) Arrangement whereby employees are encouraged to put forward their ideas for improving efficiency, safety or working conditions. Payment or reward is often given related to the value of the suggestion.

Sustainable competitive advantage The ability of an organisation to add more value than its rivals in order to gain advantage and maintain that advantage over time.

SVQs Scottish Vocational Qualifications.

Synergy Added value or additional benefit that accrues from cooperation between team members, or departments, such that the results are greater than the sum of all the individual parts.

System Assembly of parts, objects or attributes interrelating and interacting in an organised way.

Systemic Thinking about and perceiving situations, problems and difficulties as systems.

Tacit knowledge Knowledge that is never explicitly taught, often not verbalised, but is acquired through doing and expressed in know-how.

Team briefing Regular meeting of groups of between 4 and 15 people based round a common production or service area. Meetings are usually led by a manager or supervisor and last for no more than 30 minutes, during which information is imparted, often with time left for questions from employees.

TECs Training and Enterprise Councils. These operated in England and Wales and were made up of local employers and elected local people, to create local training initiatives in response to local skill needs. Their function was taken over in 2002 by Learning and Skills Councils.

Theory 'X' & 'Y' Based on McGregor's thesis on managerial change. Two contrasting views of people and work. Theory X sees people as inherently lazy, unambitious and avoiding of responsibility. Theory Y sees work as natural as rest or play and being capable of providing self-fulfilment and a sense of achievement for those involved.

Thinking performer A set of competencies that should guide CIPD members (Chartered Institute of Personnel and Development) through their careers.

TQM Total quality management, an all-pervasive system of management-controlled EI based on the concept of quality throughout the organisation in terms of product and service, whereby groups of workers are each encouraged to perceive each other (and other departments) as internal customers. This ensures the provision of quality products and services to external customers.

Transferable skills Skills that can be used anywhere in the economy.

Tripartitism Systems of industrial relations whereby the state, employers associations and trade unions oversee and govern labour market initiatives and related policies, e.g. wage levels and increases.

TUC Trades Union Congress.

TUPE Transfer of Undertakings (Protection of Employment) Regulations.

UNICE Union of Industrial and Employers Confederations of Europe.

Unison Public service union formed following merger of COHSE, NALGO and NUPE.

Unitarism Theoretical analysis of the employment relationship based on managerial prerogative, valuing labour individually according to market assessments, and which views organised resistance to management authority as pathological.

Value chain A framework, for identifying where value is added and where costs are incurred.

VDU Visual display unit – a computer screen, for example. That component of a computer that transmits often dangerous levels of radiation.

VET Vocational education and training.

Vertical Integration In terms of SHRM, the level of alignment between an organisation's business strategy and its HR strategy, policies and practices.

Vision (statement) A desired future state, or an attempt by an organisation to articulate that desired future state.

VQs Vocational qualifications.

Wa Japanese term for harmony.

Wage drift A gradual and uneven increase in wages in certain sectors of the economy resulting from variable, informal bargaining activities reflecting areas of localised union strength. Such increases are supplementary to any formally agreed wages formula. If allowed to grow unchecked, this practice can lead to inflationary measures.

Weberian bureaucracy Associated with the research and writing of the sociologist Max Weber (1864–1920), who observed and studied the growth of vast organisational bureaucracies. Notable for the extreme degree of functional specialisation, formal rules and procedures, and long lines of command and authority. Staffed by professional, full-time, salaried employees who do not own the resources and facilities with which they work.

Works councils Committees made up either solely of workers or of joint representatives of workers, management and shareholders, which meet, usually at company level, to discuss a variety of issues relating to workforce matters and sometimes general, wider-ranging organisational issues. Usually supported by legislation, which compels organisations to set them up.

YOP Youth Opportunities Programme. A programme initially set up in 1978 and revived in 1983 to help unemployed youth to gain employment skills.

YT Youth Training (formerly Youth Training Service, YTS).

Zaibatsu Large, diversified Japanese business groups, which rose to prominence in the early twentieth century, such as Mitsubishi, Mitsui and Sumitomo.

References

Arthur, M.B., Hall, D.T. and Lawrence, B.S. (eds) (1989) *Handbook of Career Theory*, Cambridge: Cambridge University Press.

Collin, A. and Watts, A.G. (1996) 'The death and transfiguration of career: and of career guidance?', *British Journal of Guidance and Counselling*, Vol. 24, No. 3, pp. 385–98.

Knowles, M.S. and Associates (1984) *Androgogy in Action*. San Francisco, Calif.: Jossey–Bass.

Pedler, M., Burgoyne, J. and Boydell, T. (1997) *The Learning Company: A Strategy for Sustainable Development*. London: McGraw-Hill.

Peppard, J. and Rowland, P. (1995) *The Essence of Business Process Re-engineering*. Hemel Hempstead: Prentice Hall.

Training Commission (1988) *Classifying the Components of Managing Competencies*, Sheffield: Training Commission.

INDEX